RECORDS OF
NORTH AMERICAN
WHITETAIL DEER

World's Record
Typical Whitetail Deer

World's Record
Non-typical
Whitetail Deer

World's Record
Non-typical Coues'
Whitetail Deer

World's Record
Typical Coues'
Whitetail Deer

WORLD'S RECORD
WHITETAIL DEER

RECORDS OF NORTH AMERICAN WHITETAIL DEER

**A book of the Boone and Crockett Club
containing tabulations of whitetail deer of
North America as compiled from data in the
Club's Big Game Records Archives.**

Edited by Eldon L. "Buck" Buckner and Jack Reneau
Design and Layout by Julie T. Houk

BOONE AND CROCKETT CLUB®

Missoula, Montana
2003

Records of North American Whitetail Deer
Fourth Edition 2003

Library of Congress Catalog Card Number: 2003104871
ISBN Number: 0-940864-43-6
Published September 2003

Published in the United States of America
by the
Boone and Crockett Club
250 Station Drive
Missoula, MT 59801
406/542-1888
406/542-0784 (fax)
www.booneandcrockettclub.com

INTRODUCTION

By Jack Reneau

WHY A RECORDS BOOK DEDICATED TO WHITETAIL DEER?

A Boone and Crockett Club records book about whitetail deer of North America began in the minds of B&C staff more than 10 years before the first edition was published in 1987. Whitetail deer are unquestionably the most popular big-game animal in North America. They are also the first big-game animals sought by the majority of first-time hunters. So, it seemed fitting that B&C should publish a records book solely dedicated to whitetail deer to record the accomplishments of hunters and document the successes of wildlife conservation. Sorting trophies by state and listing the county where the "big ones" were taken makes this book an exceptionally valuable aid for hunters planning their own excursions.

This book is also a useful tool that should help individuals sort out those trophies that are Boone and Crockett trophies and those that are not. Numerous claims appear in the outdoor press and advertisements about "B&C trophies" that have never been entered or accepted by B&C. Unless a trophy has been scored by a qualified B&C Official Measurer and passed B&C's due diligence process and accepted, it is not a B&C trophy.

Whitetail deer are the most ubiquitous big-game animal in North America, which significantly contributes to

TABLE ONE

BOOK	YEAR	ENTRIES
1st Edition	1987	1,292
2nd Edition	1991	2,120
3rd Edition	1995	4,166
4th Edition	2003	7,692

the reason for their popularity. Well-established populations thrive in all states except California, Nevada, and Alaska, as well as all Canadian provinces with the exception of Newfoundland/Labrador and Nunavut. A friend traveling the Alcan Highway earlier this summer reported seeing a whitetail doe alongside the road nine miles west of Watson Lake in the Yukon Territory. Also, there have been reports of whitetails currently occupying habitat in Colorado and Wyoming where they did not exist in the early 1970s when I regularly hunted mule deer in both states.

The whitetail deer's popularity is reflected in the increasing number of trophies entered in the Club's Awards Programs each year. Forty-one percent (1,394) of the 3,420 trophies accepted in the 25th Awards Program from 2001 to August 2003 are whitetail deer. Table 1 illustrates how this whitetail deer book has grown over the last 16 years, proving that wildlife management is alive and working in North America. There are countless rumors floating around about what is or isn't a state and provincial record. This fourth edition of the whitetail records book establishes the number one typical and non-typical B&C deer for each state, Canadian province, and Mexico that were accepted prior to the December 31, 2002 cut-off date for this book. These are current regardless of what you hear or read.

Since publication of the last edition of this book in 1995, we have 17 new typical and 19 new non-typical state/provincial records. Among these are five states or provinces that have a state record listed for their typical and/or non-typical categories for the first time. Delaware, Massachusetts, and North Carolina list non-typical state records for the first time. Both New Jersey and Quebec, which have not been included in any previous editions of this book, have number one records listed in both categories for the first time.

Considering the distribution and number of whitetail deer in North America today, it is hard to believe their continued existence was in doubt in the late 1800s and early 1900s. However, early conservationists were alarmed about the status of all native North American big-game animal populations, including whitetail deer, when their populations were at their lowest numbers in recorded history. This is one of the primary reasons Theodore Roosevelt and a close circle of his friends established the Boone and Crockett Club in 1887.

"Endangered" or "threatened" are concepts hard to imagine today when we're talking about whitetail deer. Whitetails were not common back in the 1950s when I was growing up in rural western Pennsylvania. Back then I spent all my free time exploring the out-of-doors. I observed rabbits, squirrels, ground hogs, pheasants, grouse, and many other animals that excite children exploring their universe. However, I don't ever recall seeing a doe or buck in our area. They were there, but they were rare and elusive. I clearly remember, however, my excitement at finding the shed antler of a small four-point buck that was gnawed by rodents. I lay awake that night imagining what that deer must look like, where it had come from, and where it was going.

When someone saw a deer track or scat back in those days, it was worth mentioning at the dinner table that evening. I remember taking a short drive with my parents in our 1950 Studebaker to see a road-killed deer my uncle told us about. Deer simply were not common in our region of Pennsylvania. Since then, Pennsylvania's game managers have done an excellent job of restoring native wildlife populations where

I grew up. I am pleased to note that I have seen many deer in the area when I return to visit family and friends. I have even seen turkeys that did not exist there when I was a kid. I am especially pleased to report that just this year we accepted the first B&C buck (also the new non-typical state record) ever recorded from Lawrence County, Pennsylvania, my old stomping grounds. It isn't the fact that there wasn't deer habitat back then, as Lawrence County was and basically still is a rural area interspersed with overgrown strip mines. It's simply the fact that there were relatively few deer in Lawrence County back then.

Similar increases can be noted in many other states and provinces as whitetail deer populations have continued to increase and disperse into new areas since the 1950s. This fourth edition of the whitetail records book includes all those trophies that meet the Awards Program records book minimums. I expect the fifth edition to carry on the same tradition when it is published a few years from now. Who knows, there might even be a new World's Record by then. Or, you might have your own trophy listed in the next edition.

OTHER B&C RECORDS BOOKS

The Boone and Crockett Club is the universally recognized source for the records of native North American big game. The Club publishes its all-time records book, **Records of North American Big Game**, an average of once every six years. The first edition of **Records of North American Big Game** was published in 1932 and the most recent edition, the 11th, was published in 1999. Other editions, all considered collector items by big-game hunters, were published by the Boone and Crockett Club in 1939, 1952, 1958, 1964, 1971, 1977, 1981, 1988, and 1993.

A series of popular records books highlighting the accepted entries of three-year entry periods began in 1984 with the release of **Boone and Crockett Club's 18th Big Game Awards, 1980-1982**. Each Big Game Awards book features the finest examples of North American big game entered during that Awards Program Entry Period. Hunting stories, as told by the sportsmen and sportswomen who took the award-winning trophies, are included as well as portrait and field photographs of the trophies. The Club has published Awards Entry books for the 18th through the 24th Awards Programs and will continue to do so for each succeeding Entry Period. The next book in the series, **Boone and Crockett Club's 25th Big Game Awards, 2001-2003**, will be published in September 2004.

In addition to the whitetail book, B&C has published other popular specialty records books, starting with two editions (1991 and 1996) of **Records of North American Elk and Mule Deer**. As with the whitetail deer records books, the elk and mule deer book includes the state and provincial rankings as well as vital statistics related to each accepted elk and mule deer trophy since 1950. A photograph of the top-ranked trophy from each state and province is featured and data for 1,803 typical and non-typical elk and mule deer are listed. This series of specialty books was rounded out with the publication of **Records of North American Sheep, Rocky Mountain Goats and Pronghorn** (1996) and **Records of North American Caribou and Moose** (1997). These specialty books are designed to fit nicely in your hunting backpack or vehicle glove compartment.

SCORING TROPHY WHITETAIL DEER

The current copyrighted scoring system, with few changes, is essentially the same one developed by a committee of Boone and Crockett Club Members and adopted in 1950. Exact reproductions of typical and non-typical whitetail deer score charts are included in this book with the precise measurements of two award-winning bucks, the current World's Record typical whitetail buck (213-5/8 points) taken by Milo N. Hanson near Biggar, Saskatchewan, in 1993 and the new World's Record non-typical Coues' deer (186-1/8 points), taken by Peter M. Chase in 1941, in Hidalgo County, New Mexico.

Should someone question an individual measurement or the entire score chart, the measurements and scores can be repeated to demonstrate correctness, even years after the original measurement. Measurements can be replicated because of the enduring nature of the whitetail deer antler. Had body length or weight or some combination of such factors been used for the Boone and Crockett Club's scoring system, confirming measurements would not be possible. The scoring system for other B&C trophies is also based on the enduring nature of skulls, antlers, horns, and tusks.

Scoring of a whitetail or Coues' deer begins with careful reading of the official score charts reproduced in this book. More detailed scoring instructions are included in B&C's second edition of **Measuring and Scoring North American Big Game Trophies** that was last revised in 2000 or the Club's new **Field Guide to Measuring and Judging Big Game** released in August of 2003. Care must be taken to follow scoring instructions properly to determine the correct measurements. If a rough score is close to the Boone and Crockett Club's minimum scores, the owner should contact the Club's headquarters for a list of measurers in his or her area to officially measure a rack, skull, or set of horns for entry into B&C's records keeping program. Official Measurers have all the necessary materials for trophy entry, including the score charts for recording the measurements taken. B&C Official Measurers donate their time to measure trophies as a public service. A trophy must be taken to the Official Measurer and the measurements must be taken at their convenience, since their time is donated.

An official measurement cannot be made until the trophy has dried at least 60 days, under normal atmospheric conditions, after the date of kill or 60 days after it is removed from a freezer or boiling pot. A drying period is necessary to allow for the normal shrinkage that occurs in all trophies. The standard drying period ensures shrinkage will be relatively the same for all trophies, an impossible condition if "green" scores were allowed.

Trophy owners should be aware that no trophy may be scored by more than one Official Measurer. If someone "shops for a higher score," his or her trophy will receive the lowest score arrived at by any qualified B&C measurer.

To contact a Boone and Crockett Club Official Measurer in your area or to purchase Boone and Crockett Club records books, call the Boone and Crockett Club's national headquarters in Missoula, Montana, at (406) 542-1888.

FAIR CHASE MAGAZINE

Fair Chase magazine is the primary source for current information on big-game trophies, including whitetail deer, which have been entered and accepted between all B&C records books. *Fair Chase* magazine is the premier benefit for being a Boone and Crockett Club Associate. It is published four times a year and includes a variety of articles on conservation and hunting tailored to the hunter with a special interest in trophy hunting, records-book animals, and conservation. Each issue includes a list of all trophies accepted by B&C since the last issue in a section called "Recently Accepted Trophies." You can't obtain more current information on trophies accepted by B&C anywhere else. You can receive *Fair Chase* magazine four times a year for $25 by calling toll-free (888)840-4868.

TYPICAL OR NON-TYPICAL?

This may sound like heresy to some, but there is no difference in scoring a typical or a non-typical buck. In other words, a whitetail buck is scored the same regardless of the configuration of the antlers. One should never say or think, "I will score this projection as an abnormal point because I am scoring this buck as a non-typical." An abnormal point is always an abnormal point just as a normal point is always a normal point.

There is no minimum amount of abnormal points necessary to classify a trophy as a non-typical. The only real difference between the two categories is the treatment of abnormal points. They are recorded in the abnormal point box on both score charts, and the normal points are entered on the lines provided for normal points. To arrive at a typical score for a trophy, the total of the lengths of the abnormal points is deducted to arrive at the final score, but they are added into the measurements to determine the final score for non-typical trophies.

Usually a trophy clearly makes it in one category or the other. However, a trophy will occasionally meet the minimum score of both categories. When this happens, it can only be entered in one category, and the decision is actually left up to the trophy owner. It is suggested, however, to list such a trophy in the category where it has the highest relative rank. For example, there is no reason to list a trophy in the non-typical category where it might rank in the bottom 10 percent when it can be listed in the typical category in the top 50 percent or more.

So, pull up a chair and carefully flip through the pages of this book. There is a wealth of information here that will aid you in your trips afield. For more information about B&C, check out our web site at: www.booneandcrockettclub.com. ∎

ABOUT THE AUTHOR

Jack Reneau is the Director of Big Game Records for the Boone and Crockett Club and co-editor of many Boone and Crockett Club books since 1977, including this one. Reneau is a certified wildlife biologist who earned a M.S. in wildlife management from Eastern Kentucky University (1979) and a B.S. in wildlife management from Colorado State University (1973). He worked for the National Rifle Association from 1976 to 1979 when B&C and NRA co-sponsored the Club's records-keeping activities. He has been the Director of Big Game Records for the Club from January 1983 to the present.

TABLE OF CONTENTS

Tabulations of Recorded Whitetail Deer in the U.S. *continued*

List of Field Photos

LIST OF FIELD PHOTOS continued...

RECORDS OF NORTH AMERICAN WHITETAIL DEER

More Bucks, Bigger Bucks, and Greater Opportunities

By Larry L. Weishuhn

The salt and pepper bearded hunter, still fully camouflaged in the latest and greatest camo clothing, stared momentarily into the glowing embers of the ritual campfire. Slowly he raised his cup, took a deep drink of its contents and then started unfolding the tale of his day spent afield. "Can't believe I passed up that 10-pointer today. Three years ago I would have shot him in a heartbeat. I musta watched him for a good ten minutes as he worked a scrape, then literally tore up a small sapling, and later chased a doe back and forth in front of my stand. Had the crosshairs on him a couple of times, but I looked past his antlers and saw his relatively thin neck, and his straight back and flat belly. He could not have been more than three years old. Can you imagine what he might look like in a couple of years when he's fully mature? He could be an absolute monster, possibly even a B&C records book contender." He set the cup down next to the log he was sitting on, stretched, and poked at the dying embers of the fire with a stick which sent glowing sparks skyward, almost as if like an offering. "Maybe tomorrow will be the day for that monster buck I've been hunting for . . . but right now I really feel good about passing up that young 10-pointer," he concluded, not really to anyone other than to himself.

As a hunter and a wildlife biologist who started his hunting career as a mere youngster back in the 1950s, when whitetail deer were still in their "infancy" compared to today, and as a professional biologist who began working with whitetails back in the late 1960s, it's been extremely interesting to see and experience the "whitetail phenomenon" that has occurred and continues to occur. Beginning about the late 1960s, whitetails were already considered our most important big-game species in North America. But little did anyone realize that over the next 40 years they would be elevated to a class of royalty with almost a cult following of hundreds of thousands of disciples.

Interesting how things change. For many years when asked how big a buck was, in the North body weight in pounds was the benchmark; throughout much of the East and Southeast it referred to the total number of tines or points on a buck's rack; in the Southwest, antler spread seemed to be what mattered most to hunters. But over the years "How big

The number of typical whitetail deer entries from Virginia more than doubled in the last seven years. This buck was taken in 2000 by Clyde E. Eppard, Sr. in Green County, Virginia. Publicity of big deer and the challenge of taking a mature buck with big antlers, as well as general interest by hunters and land managers alike is one of the contributing factors for the increase in whitetail deer entries.

was it?" has changed throughout the whitetail's range to "What did it score?" and "How old was it?"

How and when did the change occur? One cannot discount the fact that the Boone and Crockett Club itself has had a role in the whitetail boom. After all, it was B&C and its members who got the conservation and management ball rolling all the way back in the late 1800s helping bring whitetail numbers back from their all-time low point in the 1920s. Add to this their efforts in raising hunting and our natural resources to a higher plain of public stewardship, plus their records-keeping program, and you have all the ingredients for an overarching change in the perception of whitetail deer.

Another boost in the tremendous interest in whitetail deer can be traced back to a handful of individuals, most notably outdoor writer John Wootters and wildlife photographer Jerry Smith, both Texans by birth. Wootters was the first to start writing about mature bucks and trophy deer. His articles were most often accompanied by photos taken by Jerry Smith, bucks few people dreamed existed. Between the two they stirred tremendous interest in hunting big antlered whitetail bucks throughout North America. Hunters who previously cared little about the size of a buck's rack started paying attention to how many points a buck had, how tall its tines were, the massiveness and length of main beams, the rack's spread, and even his age. Farmers and casual hunters who had simply cut the racks off of the bucks they'd taken in the past and nailed them to their barns or garages retrieved those racks and started taking better care of them than they had in the past.

About the same time as Wootters and Smith, two biologists from Texas, Al Brothers and Murphy Ray wrote a book titled, **Producing Quality Whitetails**, which has gone on to become a classic, as well as the Bible for those interested in quality deer management.

In time, specialty publications aimed directly at the whitetail and whitetail hunter started appearing on the newsstands. Article after article was written about where to find and how to take bigger and better bucks. Very quickly, any magazine with a big whitetail buck on the cover far outsold every other publication. This increased interest in whitetails also lead to the foundation of other organizations following in the footsteps of the Boone and Crockett Club — coalitions of hunters working for wildlife management and conservation. As their memberships grew, so did the necessary programs and funding that brought about more and better deer.

As a natural extension of this phenomenon, outdoor sports shows multiplied drawing huge crowds, as hunters showed off the latest and

STATES WITH DRAMATICALLY INCREASED NUMBER OF ENTRIES

Comparing the number of whitetail deer entries in the third edition to the fourth edition of Records of North American Whitetail Deer.

States	Typical 3rd Ed.	Typical 4th Ed.	Non-typical 3rd Ed.	Non-typical 4th Ed.
Arkansas	45	79	17	39
Colorado	11	17	5	15
Indiana	40	119	18	60
Iowa	119	426	137	266
Kentucky	79	213	47	113
Massachusetts	1	4	0	1
New Hampshire	11	29	3	6
New Jersey	0	2	0	1
North Carolina	6	16	0	4
Ohio	73	175	48	91
Ontario	8	29	2	8
Quebec	0	3	0	2
South Carolina	1	4	1	2
Tennessee	11	20	6	12
Virginia	24	58	16	27

This typical whitetail deer scoring 172 points was taken by Guy Euler in Jennings County, Indiana, in 2001. Indiana has nearly three times the number of entries in this book compared to the third edition that was published just seven years earlier.

biggest bucks of the year and past seasons, while wildlife biologists and researchers presented seminars about what you as an individual could do to improve the quality of the deer habitat and the deer herd in your immediate area.

Interestingly, over the past several years, especially the latter part of the 20th century, there suddenly seemed to be more and better bucks produced by those states and Canadian provinces with a history of big deer, but also in several states which previously had not yet produced even one buck whose antlers met Boone and Crockett minimums. Why has this and is this occurring? Why more big bucks now than ever in memorable history? Part of this question I've already answered. In many years past the whitetail was simply looked upon as a source of food, hides, or as a nuisance because they were eating a farmer's small garden or crops. Little attention was paid to either age or the buck's rack. A deer was simply a deer. Then with the publicity of big deer and the challenge of taking a mature buck with big antlers, as well as genuine interest by hunters and land managers alike, things started changing. Supply and demand also came into play. The supply of mature, big-racked whitetails was low and the demand became high. "Things" regarding whitetail hunting and management began to change . . . and change they did!

In the third edition of this book devoted entirely to whitetails meeting minimum Boone and Crockett Club scores in the typical and non-typical categories, there were 4,166 entries. In this fourth edition there are 7,702. States such as Iowa tended to lead the way in terms of additions to the book. In the third edition, Iowa recorded 191 typicals and 137 non-typicals. In this new edition there are 426 typicals and 266 non-typicals. Pretty substantial increase!

Since the 1995 edition there have been 36 new state or provincial records recorded. State records for both typical and non-typical were recorded from Arkansas, Colorado, Kentucky, Massachusetts, New Jersey, Ontario, and Quebec; typicals were recorded from British Columbia, Georgia, Maryland, New Hampshire, North Dakota, Ohio, Oklahoma, South Dakota, and Virginia; and non-typicals were recorded from Connecticut, Delaware, Illinois, Indiana, Manitoba, Pennsylvania, Tennessee, Washington, West Virginia, Mississippi, North Carolina, and Wisconsin. (See accompanying sidebar regarding current dramatic increased numbers of B&C record book heads from these states.)

Even more interesting is the fact that Delaware, Massachusetts, and North Carolina are listing non-typical whitetail records for the very first time. And, both New Jersey and Quebec are represented for the first

Iowa has the more whitetail deer entries than any other state or province. The third edition of Records of North American Whitetail Deer listed 119 typical whitetails. That number has grown to over 400 entries listed in this edition. The whitetail shown above was taken by Clark A. Corbin in Crawford County, Iowa, in 2000. The buck scores 178-3/8 points.

time in this whitetail book series with entries in both typical and non-typical categories.

I've briefly discussed some of the reasons for these increases, such as the public's awareness and increased interest in quality deer as determined by the size of their antlers. But there are other reasons. One of the reasons for bigger and better bucks can be attributed to weather conditions, which have been conducive to allowing more animals to survive the winters, either because of milder weather and/or as a result of increased food supplies allowing more fawns and mature deer to survive. Increased nutrition through agricultural practices such as more crops and croplands has greatly aided deer survival and as a result produced bigger antlers than before. In Canada what once was "bush" is becoming a scattering of farmland interspersed with pockets of bush and trees.

The increased sense of looking at deer and hunting as a means to maximize income on agricultural lands has also had a definite positive effect on deer and deer herds. Previously often considered "crop predators" farmers and ranchers now sell hunting rights to hunters to help recoup some of the crop damage caused by deer. As a result deer are viewed totally differently by landowners and managers. As a potential "cash crop," the whitetail's needs of habitat and food are taken into consideration.

Farming practices, too, have changed and today often allow for deer food and cover being left in the fields during the winter. From a management perspective, increased awareness of the whitetail deer's nutritional needs have led to the development and planting of forages developed primarily for use by deer and other wildlife. An entire industry has grown around whitetail deer in terms of their nutritional needs.

In many areas where there was previously little other than seasonal food, woods and fields are being turned into edges of cities. And while cities and people bring with them predators (dogs), they also plant a wide variety of ornamental plants which deer equate as "palatable deer browse." This is one of the reasons the suburbs often produce big-antlered bucks—not only do they have a year-round food supply, which has often been fertilized, but they also live to maturity under the security of suburbia.

With changes in agricultural practices and moderate weather conditions throughout much of North America, the whitetail has continued to expand its range to the eastern edge of the Rocky Mountains and in some instances beyond. As whitetails invade new territory they find great food supplies, predators relatively scarce, and as a result grow to maturity and produce larger racks.

As we enter the 21st century we have more whitetails than ever before in North America, thanks again, in part, to ideal weather conditions and the transformation of mature forests and grasslands to the "edge effect" vegetation that whitetails thrive on. With more whitetails and especially more bucks living to maturity, big bucks also become somewhat of a "numbers game." Only a very small percentage of bucks are truly destined for greatness in the antler development department and the difference in more records book bucks may also in part be due to simply a high overall whitetail population. Using one percent as an estimate for the number of bucks that will grow to maturity and produce truly quality antlers; one percent of 10 million is a much greater number than one percent of 500,000.

One of the other factors that has been conducive to more and better bucks is management practices initiated by both private individuals and state-employed biologists. Many states now make it considerably easier to truly manage whitetails for quality. Some states strive to greatly increase the harvest of the doe segment of the population, allowing for more food for the buck segment. Other states have established minimum antler restrictions, which prevent the harvest of younger bucks giving them the opportunity to mature and produce the quality of antlers they are capable of once their bodies are completely developed.

In the same respect, the various state wildlife departments have provided hunters with longer seasons, often allowing hunting early while bachelor groups of bucks are still in their late summer patterns and during the rut when mature animals are more apt to be seen. In many states, archery season begins in September and continues with muzzleloader or shotgun season followed by rifle season, so that the season ends in late November, December or January. Earlier seasons also mean one of the best opportunities, next to the rut, to harvest a mature buck. Summer feeding pattern bucks hunted with archery gear while entering and exiting crop fields has accounted for many of the entries in this book.

With more and bigger deer being taken each year and more emphasis being placed on big antlers by hunters, organizations, publications, television, and consumer shows, it would only seem natural for the Boone and Crockett Club to have increased their number of Official Measurers. This, too, in its own way, may have contributed to the greatly increased number of entries in the whitetail category of the Boone and Crockett records book.

In the end, the whitetail hunter is the ultimate manager because he or she decides which animals are taken and what is done to improve the habitat. Thus they tend to have the greatest effect on whitetail populations. Change has been afoot, when it comes to whitetail deer, and it began and continues through the actions of hunters.

Regardless of the many and varied reasons for the great interest and existence of big-racked whitetails these days, one thing is for certain. Those of us who lived and hunted during the latter part of the 20th century and the early years of the 21st century have truly experienced the "golden age" of whitetail deer!" ■

ABOUT THE AUTHOR

From his many years spent managing, researching, hunting, and promoting whitetail deer, Larry has become one of the most highly respected and sought

after wildlife biologist, outdoor writers, and outdoor television personalities. His expertise in whitetail deer is unequaled. To date, he has been responsible for quality deer management programs on well over 15 million acres.

His features and columns have appeared in nearly every popular outdoor publication and he has authored or provided chapters to numerous books on the subject of whitetail deer hunting and management.

Not Just For Records Books

Applying the Scoring System to Trophy Restitution

By Frederick J. King

During the early formation of the Boone and Crockett Club in 1887, the immediate concern for Theodore Roosevelt and his selected friends was trying to turn the momentum of the all out slaughter of North American wildlife due to uncontrolled market hunting, a disregard for the few existing laws, and the inability of the government to initiate adequate law enforcement.

As time went on, Members of the Boone and Crockett Club did have a positive impact on the direction of the protection and management of North American wildlife. "Fair chase" became a household word for responsible hunters starting in 1893 and that code of conduct, which has been modified and added to because of new technology and machinery, continues to be the norm of what the Boone and Crockett Club represents.

In 1932 the Boone and Crockett Club published the first edition of **Records of North American Big Game**. This publication documented the initial attempt of the Club and the activities associated with measuring, scoring and recording trophies taken by hunters. The first records book also set the tone for the Boone and Crockett Club to deal responsibly with the legality and credibility of trophies that are entered into the records book.

The Boone and Crockett Club put together a committee to fine tune the process for scoring North American big game. As a result of the work, the Boone and Crockett Club's copyrighted scoring system was adopted in 1950. Since then the measuring process for determining a final score for a trophy animal has changed very little. What has not changed, however, is the accountability of the hunter to sign and submit an "Entry Affidavit," which is also known as the "Fair Chase Statement."

The past history of the Boone and Crockett Club's system of measuring and scoring North American big game has established its credibility and value with American sportsmen, scientists, and professional wildlife managers. Now the Boone and Crockett measuring system is positioned to help wildlife law enforcement personnel attach additional penalties, or restitution, for the illegal taking of wild animals for their trophy status.

Bighorn Sheep:	$30,000
Elk:	$ 8,000
Antlered Deer:	$ 8,000
Moose:	$ 6,000
Mountain Goat:	$ 6,000
Pronghorn Antelope:	$ 2,000

license to another.
e or permit of another.
false statement when obtaining

ncourage others to commit

law enforcement authorities.
guide without being licensed to

sed on size of game animals.

nting in Montana, persons may be
the kill site if requested to do so
employee.
he
nimals that comply with the "Evi-
uirements" and that were lawfully
se holder may be transported by an
an the license holder. All shippers of
n-game birds, game animals or
or parts ... are required to
... by parcel post

- The law specifically outlines minimum standards for a trophy under this regulation, but authorizes the Fish, Wildlife and Parks Commission to adopt more specific criteria. The following proposal for specific criteria was brought before the Commission and was accepted for tentative consideration in November 1999, and approved as proposed in February 2000.
- For the purposes of assessing restitution for illegally taken wildlife u... ... 87-1-115, the following are considered ... ... horn equal to or

  Bighorn she ... ... curl as defined in the
  greater ... ... ide spread tip to tip
  annual ...
  Moose ha ... least 30 ...
  Any mo ...

Photograph by Neal and Mary Jane Mishler

Not just for records books – state game and law enforcement agencies are now using aspects of the Boone and Crockett scoring system to access restitutions for game violators caught with "trophy" animals.

Included below is a reprint from the **2003 *Montana Hunting Regulations for Deer–Elk–Antelope*.** This section of the General Regulations For Montana specifically describes additional fines for a person that has illegally taken what the State of Montana considers a trophy animal.

RESTITUTION FOR ILLEGALLY TAKEN WILDLIFE

- Montana law orders that, *"In addition to other penalties provided by law, a person convicted or forfeiting bond or bail on a charge of the purposeful or knowing illegal killing, taking, or possession of a trophy animal listed in this section shall reimburse the state for each trophy animal..."* The law goes on to set the amount for restitution for each animal under Montana Code 87-1-115 as:
    - Bighorn sheep: $30,000
    - Elk: $8,000
    - Antlered Deer: $8,000
    - Moose: $6,000
    - Mountain Goat: $6,000
    - Pronghorn Antelope: $2,000

- *The law specifically outlines minimum standards for a trophy under this regulation, but authorizes the Fish, Wildlife and Parks Commission to adopt more specific criteria. The following proposal for specific criteria was brought before the Commission and was accepted for tentative consideration in November 1999, and approved as proposed in February 2000, and modified in February 2003.*
- For the purposes of assessing restitution for illegally taken wildlife under Montana Code 87-1-115, the following are considered "trophy" animals:
    - Bighorn sheep with at least one horn equal to or greater than three-fourth curl as defined in the annual regulations.
    - Moose having a widest outside spread, tip to tip, of at least 30 inches
    - Any mountain goat
    - Antelope with at least one horn greater than 14 inches in length, as measured along the outside curve from base to tip
    - Elk (must meet all three criteria)
        1. At least six points on one antler, <u>and</u>
        2. A main beam length on each antler of at least 43 inches, <u>and</u>
        3. An inside spread of at least 36 inches
    - Mule Deer (must meet all three criteria)
        1. At least four points on one antler, excluding brow tine, <u>and</u>

Although the word "trophy" has been in the Boone and Crockett vocabulary for over 116 years, some states are now realizing what they really loose to poachers who target mature animals.

2. A main beam length on each side of at least 21 inches, _and_
3. A greatest inside spread across the main beams of at least 20 inches, OR any mule deer with at least one four point antler and having a green Boone and Crockett score of 160 points or greater.

- Whitetail Deer (must meet all three criteria)
    1. At least four points on one antler, excluding brow tine, _and_
    2. A main beam length on each side of at least 20 inches, _and_
    3. A greatest inside spread across the main beams of at least 16 inches, OR any whitetail deer with at least one four point antler and having a green Boone and Crockett score of 140 points or greater.

- A "point" as defined in these regulations is at least four inches long for elk and at least one inch long for deer, measured from base to tip. Boone and Crockett measuring procedures or standards are used for criteria measurement. The official measurements for the purpose of this regulation are those that are taken at the time of confiscation or seizure of the trophy. Any Boone and Crockett measurements will be considered final when taken by an official B&C scorer, regardless of drying time. If the skullcap of antlers or horns is broken in such a manner to render an official Boone and Crockett score invalid, three official B&C scorers will estimate a score. The three scores will be averaged and the average score used to determine trophy status in accordance with Montana Code 87-1-115.

The Montana system of restitution for illegally taken wildlife trophies not only leans heavily on the Boone and Crockett Club's system of measuring North American big game, but the system also depends on the need for the measurements to be completed by a Boone and Crockett Official Measurer to add validity, consistency, and credibility for use of the measurements in a potential case.

It is now time that other wildlife agencies throughout North America to follow Montana's lead. The Boone and Crockett Club's scoring system is the cornerstone on how hunters judge and measure trophy animals. There are over 900 B&C Official Measurers scattered throughout North America. They are thoroughly screened, trained, and updated regularly on scoring procedures. Wildlife agencies wishing to host a B&C Official Measurer Training Workshop can obtain the necessary information by contacting B&C headquarters at the address and telephone number given on page iv of this book.

Much has changed in the hunting world since the time the Boone and Crockett Club was formed in 1887. At hand to the modern day hunter are improved transportation systems, a multitude of vehicles for any type of terrain or conditions, new rifles and new calibers, new archery equipment, a complete new line of muzzle-loading firearms and the availability of all kinds of gadgets to help the hunter to be more comfortable and more successful. What has not changed for wild animals over all these years is the need for adequate habitat for survival, along with the continued respect and support from the hunting community to carry the "fair chase" tradition into the future.

What does need to change in the hunting community is increased support to the wildlife agencies for expanding and increasing the penalties to those criminals that will kill a trophy-class animal for their own personal greed. Another arena of equipment that has dramatically improved for the hunter is optics. The quality and variety of rifle scopes, binoculars, spotting scopes, range finders and night vision optics is unending. In this modern day and age the criminal that will illegally kill an animal of trophy quality knows exactly what they are looking at and should be held accountable to a higher degree of restitution to the public for the loss of that animal. ∎

ABOUT THE AUTHOR

Frederick J. King of Bozeman, Montana, joined the Boone and Crockett Club as a professional member in 1994. He is currently an active member

of the Records Committee. Fred has been an official measurer for the Boone and Crockett Club since 1984, and also measures for the Pope & Young Club and the Longhunter Society. He is a wildlife area manager in southwest Montana for Montana Fish, Wildlife & Parks (MFWP), a position he has held since 1975. He joined MFWP in 1968. He is a life member of the National Rifle Association and has been a Montana hunter education instructor since 1975. Fred is also a member of the Rocky Mountain Elk Foundation, Amateur Trapshooting Association, and The Wildlife Society.

CHRONIC WASTING DISEASE

COURSE, CONTROL, AND CONSEQUENCES

By Wayne van Zwoll

By August 6, 2002, when 453 wildlife biologists, pathologists, and veterinarians met with natural resource administrators in Denver to discuss chronic wasting disease, it had become big news. A quarter century on the back burner, with laboratories unable to find its cause, CWD had not gone away. In fact, it seemed to be on the march.

Chronic wasting disease is a degenerative, ultimately fatal TSE, or transmissible spongiform encepalopathy. To date, CWD in natural form affects only cervids – specifically deer and elk. It has been here since 1967, probably earlier. But chronic wasting disease wasn't identified as such until the 1970s, and little testing ensued until its apparent spread caused alarm 20 years later. Now present on both sides of the Mississippi, into central Canada and as far south as New Mexico, CWD has been found in wild herds of whitetail and mule deer far from infected game farms and the "endemic" area of northeastern Colorado, where it was first discovered in captive deer. Since 1981, it has also been reported in Rocky Mountain elk. CWD has not yet been found in moose or caribou.

"We don't know what causes CWD," says Gary Wolfe, a Boone and Crockett Club Professional Member and wildlife conservationist who completed a Ph.D. on New Mexico's Vermejo Park Ranch and later helped build the Rocky Mountain Elk Foundation. Gary now coordinates information flow for the CWD Alliance. "Nobody's sure whether the deer first diagnosed at Colorado State's research lab had CWD when captured, or whether they contracted it inside." About a decade later, CWD was identified as a form of TSE. That family of diseases includes scrapie in sheep and a TSE that affects mink in captivity. Scrapie has been known for more than 200 years and may have reached North America with the Conquistadors! Perhaps the best-known version of TSE is BSE – bovine spongiform encephalopathy, or mad cow disease. All forms attack central nervous and lymphatic systems. Sponge-like vacuoles or pockets form in the brain – hence, the name.

Getting more information on CWD in wild cervids is difficult because only about 1 percent of the elk and, on average, fewer than 7 percent of the deer tested in the endemic region have been found with the infection. Incubation can take months to years. In the absence of clinical signs, testing is both random and costly. Until recently, the only sure test was immunohistochemistry, or IHC, performed on sectioned brain tissue. Outward signs – emaciation, lethargy, frequent drinking and urination, excessive salivation, staggering and other uncharacteristic behaviors – do not occur until the latter stages.

The causative agent is thought to be a prion. "Prions, a type of protein in normal brain cells, can be changed to a mutant form that appears only in CWD-positive animals," says Glenn Telling, who works at the University of Kentucky's Department of Microbiology. "These proteins don't replicate themselves in the manner of bacteria or viruses; rather, they force the normal prions in the host animal to change. This can take two to eight years." He concedes that the origin and mode of transmission of CWD remain unclear, and that we don't know if it will cross species boundaries. "The human form of TSE is Creutzfeld-Jakob Disease. It has been documented since the 1920s, occurs randomly in one of every million or so people and is usually fatal within six weeks." People past middle age seem most apt to contract it. *Variant* CJD, says Telling, is linked to exposure to BSE and has affected young people as well as old. Still, rates of infection are very low. In the late 1990s, while nearly 178,000 British cattle were diagnosed with BSE, 100 people in Great Britain died from variant CJD. Since variant CJD has commanded the attention of public health officials, roughly 80 million people have consumed products from BSE-infected cattle; 131 people have died as a result.

In 2002, lethal brain disorders in three Wisconsin men who shared venison fueled speculation that CWD also might make the jump to humans. And the discovery of infectious prions in the leg muscle of a laboratory mouse called into question the long-held assumption that CWD confines itself to soft tissues: brain, tonsils, eyes, spleen, pancreas. But thorough investigation of the three human deaths revealed only one attributable to CJD. A similar alarm had been raised three years earlier, when CJD had been diagnosed in three people, ages 20 and 40. All had eaten venison. More than 1,000 samples of deer were then taken from the area where the meat had been obtained. No CWD was found.

Because of human health concerns, federal money has been allocated to states for CWD research and testing. As biologists gathered for the 2002 symposium, 21 states had testing programs in place. Many now restrict importation of captive deer and elk. Facilities where captive animals have tested positive are depopulated and sanitized. Disease-free certification, used to safeguard livestock health, is being urged for privately owned cervids.

Captive herds of deer and elk have come under increased scrutiny as CWD evidently made its way from the U.S. to Canada and then to Korea in captive elk. But while confined animals are assumed to be at greatest risk, wild populations are the hardest to monitor and cleanse. Colorado, then Wisconsin embarked on aggressive culling programs to substantially reduce deer densities where CWD was found. Other states have accelerated random testing of hunter-killed animals. New facilities for testing are needed to meet anticipated demands, even with hunters voluntarily submitting specimens. Currently, there are no practical live tests for CWD.

Elizabeth Williams of the University of Wyoming says the disease may not be more prevalent than before. "But it does seem to be spreading. Finding the transmission pathway is crucial to throttling CWD. It may spread through direct contact or as a result of animals eating waste on infected ground – anything from feces to placentas to carcasses." Animal concentrations and migrations speed both kinds of delivery. A genetic link has yet to be established. Williams says that the disease corridor seems to differ in deer and elk but that in both "infection targets soft tissue: brain, spinal cord, spleen, tonsils, eyes and lymph nodes. Immunohistochemistry is still the best diagnostic tool, but a tonsil test for live deer shows promise."

As with any disease that stumps people in white lab coats, CWD has drawn much media attention. Public perception of CWD and control efforts could profoundly affect hunting, big game management and funding for other conservation programs. The need for accurate, up-to-date CWD information in lay form led to the CWD Alliance and its web site, www.cwd-info.org. Hunters remain not only an integral part of big game management but an important tool in combating CWD. Wildlife agencies are acutely aware that unless they attack CWD with vigor, control programs could fall to animal health professionals. Witness the brucellosis threat in Yellowstone Park bison.

"Public concern about CWD is understandable," says Gary Wolfe. "But research has yet to find a connection between CWD and any human health disorder. The interruption of wildlife management by a sudden widespread aversion to either deer and elk hunting or eating venison could have grave consequences for big game and the many other animal species that share its habitat."

WHERE IT IS AND WHAT'S BEING DONE

The disease was long thought to be limited in the wild to a relatively small endemic area in northeastern Colorado, southeastern Wyoming

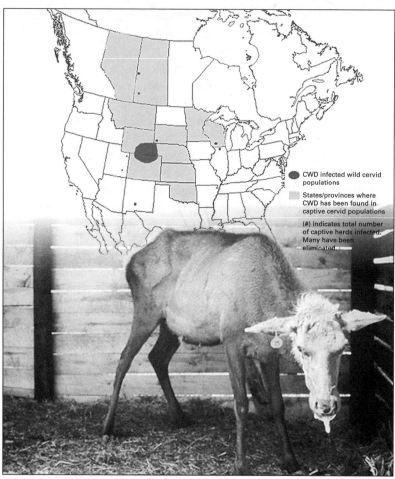

CWD infected wild cervid populations

States/provinces where CWD has been found in captive cervid populations

(#) Indicates total number of captive herds infected. Many have been eliminated.

Elk photograph courtesy of the Wyoming Game and Fish Department.

The map above indicates where CWD has been found in North America as of June 2003. Up to date information can be found on the CWD Alliance web site at www.cwd-info.org. The elk pictured here show clinical signs of Chronic Wasting Disease – emaciation, wide stance, lowered head, droopy ears, and excessive salivation.

and southwestern Nebraska, but it has recently been found in new areas of these states, as well as in wild deer and elk in western South Dakota, and wild deer in northern Illinois, south-central New Mexico, northeastern Utah, south-central Wisconsin and west-central Saskatchewan.

The disease also has been diagnosed in commercial game farms in Colorado, Nebraska, Minnesota, South Dakota, Montana, Oklahoma, Kansas, Wisconsin, Saskatchewan and Alberta. The history of CWD varies from state to state, and wildlife agencies have reacted differently.

Mike Miller of Colorado's Division of Wildlife reports that this agency's targeted surveillance – shooting and testing suspect animals – is obviously biased but helps them track CWD. "In Colorado, we've done that since the 1970s. Random testing of all dead deer and elk is more aggressive and costly, but some states are adopting it to check game farm elk for CWD. Since 1991, testing hunter-killed game has helped Colorado determine prevalence as well as the distribution of cases." Miller identifies 19 game management units in northeastern Colorado as the epicenter of CWD but adds that the disease has been found in Routt County in the state's northwest sector. "By summer, 2002, we'd examined more than 11,500 deer and elk. Prevalence in tested deer approaches 11 percent but averages around 5 percent. It appears to be increasing. Fewer than 1 percent of tested elk come up positive."

Rick Kahn, who also works for Colorado's DOW, points out that the state's management plans for deer and elk emphasize CWD control over recreation in game management units where CWD has been found. When just 1 percent of sampled mule deer tested positive for CWD near Craig, the state authorized helicopter use to kill as many deer and elk as possible in an area 10 miles across. Colorado deer herds may be in for a 50-percent reduction where CWD has been identified. "Those herds will be maintained at reduced levels for five seasons, to see if the disease abates. We're also culling small groups of deer in areas known for CWD. Where culling is impractical, we take tonsil biopsies from live deer, then, if they test positive, find them again by telemetry and kill them. To reduce deer numbers on a large scale, the Division may boost the number of deer tags available.

Wyoming's first recorded case of CWD was a captive deer at the Sybille Wildlife Research and Conservation Education Unit in 1978. It appeared in free-ranging elk eight years later. Tom Thorne, a wildlife veterinarian and former director of the state's Game and Fish Department, reports that CWD surveillance began in 1983. Control measures have included research, transport restrictions on cervids, removal of suspect animals and education. Hunter-shot game has been randomly tested in the endemic area of southeastern Wyoming since 1997. Twelve percent of mule deer, 16 percent of whitetails, and 3 percent of elk have tested positive. In 2001, state legislators established a Wildlife/Livestock Disease Research Partnership and identified CWD as a priority issue. At this writing, Wyoming has tested 2,550 deer and elk. Biologists conclude that the disease has occurred in 23 of the state's 152 deer units, all in the southeast quadrant. "It will cost more than $2 million annually to maintain our current surveillance work," cautions Thorne.

"Nebraska's CWD testing program began in 1997 when we asked hunters to submit deer," says Bruce Morrison of the state's Game and Parks Commission. "Recently our state Department of Agriculture made testing mandatory." He notes that 2,900 deer and 150 elk had been tested by the end of 2001. Just 12 deer tested positive. There's now a restriction against the importation of any cervid from a county where CWD has been found in wild animals, or from any place that has not had a monitoring program for at least five years. There's also a freeze on transport of deer and elk to reestablish or augment herds in Nebraska. "Three Nebraska elk farms have turned up CWD-positive," adds Morrison, who ranks among the most well-informed people on CWD nationwide. "One, in Sioux County, produced 11 positive tests by the time it was depopulated early in 2002. Also, 98 of 191 whitetail deer that happened to get in the pen came down with CWD. We tested about 3,500 hunter-killed deer by the end of the 2002 hunt, focusing on the state's panhandle but including at least 100 animals from each of our other deer units." To keep the public aware of CWD, "we make every effort to provide clear, accurate information through guides, media releases and Commission literature." Hunting is an important part of CWD management, says Morrison. In Nebraska as in Colorado, where disease control is at odds with recreational hunting, disease control is taking priority.

In nearby South Dakota, tests from 1997 through 1999 yielded no signs of CWD in 519 whitetails, 128 mule deer and 368 elk. No tests were done in 2000. The following year a sampling of 241 whitetails, 95 mule deer and 166 elk yielded one positive test: a whitetail in southwestern South Dakota. Since then, a total of 11 deer and one elk have been identified with CWD in South Dakota. Ron Fowler of the state's Department of Game, Fish and Parks reports that, "beginning in 1997, we conducted random surveillance. Then, in 2001, CWD appeared just 15 miles south of the Dakota-Nebraska line. We killed additional deer outside hunting season and reduced deer density targets on our southern border."

Lloyd Fox of the Kansas Department of Wildlife and Parks emphasizes that the biological effects of CWD could pale next to an erosion of public confidence in wildlife management. "Support for agencies depends partly on the continued health of deer and elk herds." Kansas is now one of 13 states bordering a state where CWD has been confirmed, notes Fox. "As yet no new regulatory actions have been taken by KDWP, the Kansas Animal Health Department or the USDA." Targeted surveillance began in 1996, and random testing on hunter-killed game a year later. So far, none of 1,167 animals tested have turned up with CWD – but that testing program is accelerating. "We tested 1,200 animals in 2002 alone," Fox points out. "We've also taken preemptive steps by reducing herd size in northwest counties. Hunters don't like that. At the same time, we're committed to delivering clear, factual updates to the public."

Perhaps the most widely publicized "outbreak" of CWD occurred near Mouth Horeb, Wisconsin during the 2001 hunting season. Three bucks shot near each other were the first wild deer testing positive for CWD east of the Mississippi. "Subsequently, 15 more deer (of 505 shot in the area) were confirmed to be infected; but only seven showed outward symptoms of CWD," reports Julia Langenberg, for the state Department of Natural Resources. The DNR established a 361-square-mile eradication zone, declaring open deer season one week a month for landowners and contract shooters. The aim: kill 25,000 deer in three years. Langenberg adds that, "our plans included testing 500 deer from each of Wisconsin's counties to determine the extent of this disease." Though a testing program began in 1999 (via IHC at the National Veterinary Services Laboratory at Ames, Iowa), it has accelerated sharply to target hunter- and agency-shot deer from high-density whitetail populations throughout Wisconsin. Other places on the hit list: any of the state's 975 game farms that received animals from infected Colorado and Nebraska farms and wherever the DNR introduces wild elk. Tom Hauge, who directs control efforts, is unapologetically aggressive. "We'll do what it takes. Until we know the limits of this disease, we can't take chances. We'll need federal help."

By mid-2003, $5.2 million in grants had been awarded to the University of Wisconsin for CWD research. The DNR has also established a 25-square-mile CWD eradication zone along its border with Illinois to halt any incursion of the disease from the south. In mid-2002, Department officials told 2,000 landowners and hunters of its intent to kill 14,000 to 15,000 animals in Dane, Sauk and Iowa counties. A total of 107 Iowa County deer had tested positive for CWD by mid-2003. Dane County was running close behind with 97 confirmed cases. Of 207 infected deer that had turned up positive in Wisconsin's massive testing program (41,000 deer to June, 2003), 201 had come from the 411-square-mile eradication zone in these three counties. The DNR has committed to a 90-percent herd reduction in the area. Projected to take at least five years, it will be accomplished mainly by landowners and hunters they choose to accommodate. Public response has been predictably diverse. A local dairy farmer fears infected deer could transmit CWD to his cattle. Another citizen argued that the plan is too drastic. A woman who claimed she was speaking "for the animals" has protested the killing on the grounds it's not our solution to the AIDS problem.

Utah reported its second case of CWD in May, 2003, in the La Sal Mountains about 10 miles from Moab. The first deer yielding a positive test was shot during the 2002 hunting season many miles north. In Illinois, 14 whitetails had been documented with CWD by summer, 2003, though neighboring Missouri failed to find any sign of the disease in tests of 5,972 free-ranging deer shot during the 2002 season. That year, the Montana Department of Fish, Wildlife and Parks likewise came up with no CWD in 997 hunter-killed deer and elk tested. Georgia has reported no CWD but tested 436 deer in 2002 and will continue to monitor its whitetails. By mid-2003, Maine's Department of Inland Fisheries and Wildlife had tested 831 deer with no positive results. Florida's Fish and Wildlife Commission detected no CWD in 483 wild deer. Oregon and Washington have tested 670 and 785 free-ranging elk; none have shown signs of the disease.

CWD may have entered Canada in 1974, through an infected mule deer imported to a zoo. Lynn Bates of the Canadian Food Inspection Agency says CWD appeared in game farm elk came two decades later. In 1996 Saskatchewan found CWD in a captive elk, the province's first case. Testing of 283 wild deer and 46 captive animals over three years showed no new cases. In 2000, the Fish and Wildlife Branch of Saskatchewan Environment accelerated surveillance, testing 1,500 animals in the west-central target area and 3,300 animals province-wide. Three wild deer tested positive. "Since February, 2000, CWD has been found in 40 Saskatchewan captive herds and one in Alberta," says Bates. "Thirty-eight of those cases have been traced to the one elk in Saskatchewan, which may have arrived in 1989 from South Dakota." By late 2002, more than 8,400 elk had been killed in a surveillance program that tested 10,278 farmed cervids and 7411 in the wild. Of these, 228 captive and three wild animals tested positive. "Canada made CWD a reportable disease in 2000," concludes Bates, "following up with a certification plan for trade in cervids."

Deer densities in Alberta are much lower than in many Midwest states – "typically below five per square mile," declares Margo Pybus of Alberta's Wildlife Division. "And because the province has fewer than 1,200 imported game farm elk, our exposure to CWD is limited." Surveillance of hunter-killed animals the past three years has showed no CWD. "If CWD appears, we will take strong countermeasures," Pybus says. "Voluntary testing, our rigorous game farm policy and a ban on baiting deer and elk should help keep Alberta's free-roaming animals from contracting this disease." Killing at the farms continues. In the summer of 2003, a herd of 95 whitetail deer was eliminated after laboratory results indicated its potential for disease transmission.

With heightened concern over CWD's effects on wild herds, U.S. game farms have also borne increased scrutiny. "If not the source of CWD, they certainly have the potential to harbor it and move it," says Lynn Creekmore of the U.S. Department of Agriculture's Animal and Plant Health Inspection Service (USDA-APHIS). Since 1997, when South Dakota reported a positive test on an elk, 23 game farms in six states have turned up infected animals. Twenty of these herds were depopulated. Creekmore adds that of 3,600 farmed elk killed between 1997 and 2002, 195 tested positive. Of these, 119 or 61 percent came from two herds. USDA funds have been used to compensate owners of condemned herds. The agency plans a herd certification program similar to that already used by 20 states. It would apply to red deer as well as to elk, mule deer and whitetails.

PROBLEMS AND STRATEGIES

"The spread of Chronic Wasting Disease is of national concern," affirmed U.S. Fish and Wildlife Service Director Steve Williams at the 2002 symposium. But he emphasized that states would take the lead in research and control efforts. Williams co-chairs a CWD task force with Bobby Acord, USDA-APHIS Chief Administrator. The task force, comprising top wildlife biologists and veterinarians from universities and government agencies, has developed recommendations to arrest the spread of CWD. But Congress has yet to appropriate the necessary funds to fully implement the plan.

Some federal money has funded experimental live tests for CWD – a requisite for any certification program. Katherine O'Rourke of the USDA's Agricultural Research Service in Pullman, Washington, says that "live-culture tests on blood, urine and lymph tissue, have been unsuccessful, but a tonsil biopsy shows most promise. It's not for elk because lymphoid accumulation of prions occurs later in elk than in deer."

Dr. Lisa Wolfe, a DVM with Colorado's Division of Wildlife, has used the tonsil test. "It is more costly than IHC analysis of brain stems, and a lot of trouble. You must anesthetize the animal. Accuracy is on par with IHC, but only about 92 percent of tonsil samples are usable, because the operation is done by feel. You can't know if you got the target tissue until afterward." Wolfe agrees with O'Rourke that hunter demands for testing could easily flood lab capacity for either test. The commercial company, BioRad, has developed a rapid screening test, called ELISA, using brain samples and lymph nodes from Colorado deer and elk.

One problem impedes both research into CWD transmission and development of test procedures: the availability of material. Trials with domestic sheep in Europe have been inconclusive in differentiating BSE from scrapie, the most common TSE in sheep. Likewise, distinctions among TSEs in sheep, deer and elk have not been confirmed. Laboratory rodents haven't been ruled out for research. Says Glenn Telling: "Mice are already being used in studies aimed at determining the prevalence of CWD in wild and captive deer and elk. They'll certainly play a part in our work on species barriers." Another small mammal being considered for CWD studies is the ferret. Captive ferrets inoculated (orally or through brain injection) with the saliva, brain homogenates or white blood cells of infected deer soon show signs of the disease.

Efforts to transmit TSEs across species boundaries in the laboratory have met with little success. Gregory Raymond of the U.S. Department of Health and Human Services (USDHHS) indicates that test-tube conversion of protease-sensitive prions to protease-resistant prions is relatively easy. "Conversion in live animals is less efficient, especially from one species to another." Using protein from CWD-positive cervids, it's difficult to produce the conversion in humans, cattle, sheep or rodents. "There seems to be a transmission barrier at the molecular level," says Raymond.

Inoculations of CWD-positive material from mule deer into the brains of living cattle began at the National Animal Disease Center in 1997. Three of 13 cattle showed TSE symptoms. Two others were killed and turned up CWD-negative. One of eight sheep was tested by IHC and declared "clean." Three years into the study, the remaining sheep and cattle, and all the raccoons appeared healthy. Patrick Bosque of the University of Colorado Health Sciences Center notes that prion amino acid sequences play a big part in confining CWD to cervids. "Our experiments show mice to be CWD-resistant, even when inoculated with brain homogenates from infected animals." He warns that findings with mice may not apply to other species, and that repeated passage of CWD prions through a new host might eventually cause a TSE in that species.

Surveillance for TSE in humans began in Colorado five years ago. "At that time the state Board of Health made TSE a reportable disease in people under age 55," said John Pape of the state's Department of Public Health and Environment. "From 1998 through 2001, we found 18 cases of human TSE, plus three in visitors from other states (NE, KS, NC). Ages ranged from 40 to 79. Ten victims were women. In no case could CWD be implicated. Ermais Belay of the Center for Disease Control points out that while the apparent spread of CWD has heightened concern about variant CJD, "there's no compelling evidence of a causal link between CWD and recent CJD in young patients." TSE research findings are collected at the National Prion Disease Pathology Surveillance Center, established at Case Western Reserve University in 1997.

State agencies share a need for money, as CWD control is expensive. While Federal coffers have been opened , that funding typically comes with strings. Among the immediate problems facing states with herd-reduction efforts is carcass disposal. Doris Olander and Joe Brusca of Wisconsin's Department of Natural Resources point out that an estimated 3 percent infection rate in the 20,000 deer the DNR plans to cull would leave 600 tainted carcasses. "Hunters will kill the majority of these whitetails," they say. "And likely few will want the meat." Complicating disposal are questions: Does CWD remain infectious after bodies decompose? How can we best sample air, water and soil for prions? Wisconsin has investigated five disposal options:

1. Landfilling at modern, controlled sites,
2. Burial at uncontrolled sites,
3. Dedicated rendering with controlled disposal,
4. Incineration, and
5. Digestion by high-temperature, high-pressure alkaline hydrolysis.

Olander says that landfill and uncontrolled burial are inexpensive, high-capacity options. "But they have no effect on the infectious agent, other than to localize it." Dedicated rendering is popular for disposing of cattle carcasses in BSE control programs. It deactivates the agent. So can incineration, albeit there's the risk of smoke carrying active agent aloft. Both these options are costly and may be impractical for large numbers of carcasses. "Among incinerators, only ACDs (air curtain destructors) have the needed capacity," notes Olander. "Digestion is a low-volume alternative, and the liquid product requires special

CWD PRECAUTIONS FOR HUNTERS

1. Avoid shooting, handling, or eating any animal with CWD symptoms or that has tested positive.
2. Wear latex gloves when field dressing deer and elk.
3. Bone out meat; avoid touching meat with a knife used on the brain, spleen, eyes, lymph nodes, tonsils, pancreas or spinal cord.
4. Wash your hands and knife thoroughly after field dressing. Use Clorox to sterilize.
5. Insist that meat processor not mix your venison with that of other hunters.

Photo courtesy of George A. Bettas

handling because of its high oxygen demand and pH." Zoning restrictions and public concerns over CWD have eliminated uncontrolled burial as an option in Wisconsin. Others are still being considered.

POLICY CONSEQUENCES
Biological and logistical problems still plague agencies fighting CWD. But Brian Murphy of the Quality Deer Management Association says its effect on hunter perceptions may matter most. "Whitetail deer are the most economically important animals in the U.S. In 2001, nearly 11 million big game hunters spent over 153 million days afield, contributing almost $20 billion to the U.S. economy." Whitetail hunters generated the bulk of this revenue. "While many hunters are still unaware of CWD," says Murphy, "many more are concerned or confused about its effects on venison." Deer managers worry that CWD will turn hunters away from the sport – or against sound management. "If hunters stopped eating venison on a large scale, or became disenchanted with agency herd reduction programs, we'd quickly see a general resistance to doe shooting. Herd manipulation by sportsmen, important for regulating deer densities and age and sex ratios, would have to be replaced by regimented culling. Public opposition to that would be strong. Funding for all state wildlife management would be imperiled."

Stephen Torbit from the National Wildlife Federation echoes Murphy's concerns. "CWD could profoundly affect the traditional model of wildlife management in the U.S. Not only might it affect hunter attitudes and participation, and land access; it could jeopardize state and federal management prerogatives." Torbit pointed to the Animal Health Protection Act, passed in 2002 largely because of the brucellosis found in Yellowstone Park bison. "AHPA has ominous implications for wildlife management because it places diseased animals under control of the USDA. Agricultural interests typically do not favor wildlife. CWD must not be allowed to drain professional biologists and ecologists of their ability to influence policy and to design and implement strategic management plans."

Jack Ward Thomas, former chief of the U.S. Forest Service and Boone and Crockett Professor of Wildlife Conservation, notes that inaccurate and misleading media coverage of CWD can undermine efforts to control the disease. So can wrangling among scientists and wildlife managers over "turf." Thomas says that CWD funding depends on a disciplined, coordinated effort among state and federal agencies and among conservation groups like the Boone and Crockett Club, Rocky Mountain Elk Foundation and Mule Deer Foundation. "We need accelerated research but also more effective communication to the general public. The CWD Alliance, with its web site updates and resources, is a good start."

But public concern over CWD has already resulted in legislation that reaches deep into the lives of people with no such concern. An interim BSE Canadian cervid rule banning the import of meat and other products (published May 29, 2003) did not specifically exclude trophies and meat taken for personal use by hunters returning from Canada to their homes in the U.S. John Jackson, chairman of Conservation Force, a group representing well-heeled hunters in Dallas and Houston Safari Clubs, Grand Slam/OVIS, Foundation for North American Wild Sheep (FNAWS) and similar organizations, pointed out in a memo that Canada's outfitting industry brings in $500 million (U.S.) annually. Most comes from hunters in the lower 48, who bring their Canadian trophies to 78,000 U.S. taxidermists. These businesses, he said, would suffer if wild game was not specifically excluded in a ban. Such wording came through in August, 2003, when Secretary of Agriculture Ann Veneman declared that hunters could bring wild meat into the U.S. clarifying the May ban on ruminant meat imports. She emphasized that documentation regarding origin and method of take would still be required on all imports.

Canada's bout with BSE has already been bruising. In the first half of 2003, testing had resulted in the quarantine of 18 farms in Alberta, Saskatchewan and British Columbia. A BSE-positive cow, found in northern Alberta that spring, is from a herd that contained five bulls from Montana. All were reportedly slaughtered. Beef exports totaling $20 million (mainly to Korea and Japan) may be nixed. Elk antler sales to the far East have been banned since 2000, due to CWD. The Canadian Cervid Council claims it has lost $32 million in sales to South Korea.

Scrapie too has cost Canada dearly. In Quebec alone, nearly 22,000 sheep were slaughtered from 1998 to 2003 in an effort to rid the province of this TSE.

Stateside, places with little or no CWD exposure have shuffled priorities and funding to guard the gate. And they've stiffened policy. Tennessee courts, for example, have upheld a 1991 ban on the private ownership of whitetails. Such caution mirrors that exhibited by the federal government in its first defensive measures against BSE. In August, 1997, the Food and Drug Administration began prohibiting the feeding of ruminant products to other ruminants (suspected cause of the BSE outbreak in Great Britain). It inspects 100 percent of the firms handling animal protein now disallowed in feeds. By international standards, a BSE-free country like the U.S. is required to test only 433 cattle per year. But the USDA tests 46 times that number.

Interstate shipment of live animals and whole carcasses is under more scrutiny now too, especially into and out of endemic areas. "Colorado has already implemented regulations on the removal of carcasses from hunting areas where CWD has been detected," Gary tells me. "Requiring hunters to bone the meat before packing up may help slow the spread." Another option: a requirement that game farms be monitored for five years and declared "CWD-free" before any shipments are allowed out of state. Several other states have also added regulations on the import and/or export of meat from CWD infected areas.

Game farmers won't like that any more than they've taken to the bans and restrictions already in force. Compensation from states has not mollified all of them. Ten Colorado elk ranchers sued Colorado's Department of Agriculture for $10 million over compensation (in the millions) they received for the loss of their elk. They claim the initial payments did not match fair market value.

At this writing, a number of CWD bills have been introduced to Congress and action on them is still pending. While federal money gets support from everyone receiving it, CWD won't likely be spent into submission. Scientist, Boone and Crockett Club Professional Member, and retired University of Calgary Professor Val Geist points out that "if you want progress, assemble experts from diverse fields and perspectives and encourage them to converse freely. What's inconsequential to one may prove a vital link to another. For example, the observation that CWD progresses down waterways has limited value unless you're familiar with female dispersal of mule deer. Then you realize it could advance faster among whitetails, and that it's probably not a disease spread by breeding males." He notes that an understanding CWD may hinge on the study of wild cervid behavior. "We know, for instance, that the spread of BSE is linked to the eating of bone meal. But so far we haven't looked at bones as carriers. Does CWD reside there? How often do wild cervids chew bones?"

Reprimanding scientists and policy-makers who fail to build upon the work of colleagues, Geist says that, "we're also moving from the hugely successful model of North American wildlife management to one emphasizing husbandry of semi-domestic animals. Among inherent dangers is increasing unregulated transport of wild stock, which apparently can spread CWD." Geist suggests replacing wildlife case law with more effective treaty law.

Len Carpenter of the Wildlife Management Institute stresses the need for even-handed and well-articulated reports on CWD. "There is no way to divorce the clinical aspects of CWD from its social and political ramifications. Public perceptions of things biological depend almost entirely on how biologists and their colleagues dispense news. Until we can get a rope around the causes and transmission of CWD, we'll reap great benefits by controlling how hunters and the general public view CWD." He observes that concern for public support need not reduce management options. "The long-term costs of doing nothing may be very high. The only way to further our knowledge of the disease while reducing transmission may be vigorous thinning of herds in affected areas."

PRECAUTIONS FOR HUNTERS
Should hunters be concerned about CWD? Gary Wolfe stresses that even in the endemic areas of Wyoming and Colorado, fewer than six percent of the deer and one percent of resident elk have tested positive for CWD. "Besides, there's no scientific evidence that CWD can spread to humans, either by contact with infected animals or by eating their meat." But he noted the Center for Disease Control's ambiguous caveat: "However, there is not yet strong evidence that such transmissions could not occur." So, to stay safe:

1. Avoid shooting, handling or eating any animal with CWD symptoms or that has tested positive.
2. Wear latex gloves when field dressing deer and elk.
3. Bone out meat; avoid touching meat with a knife used on the brain, spleen, eyes, lymph nodes, tonsils, pancreas or spinal cord.
4. Wash your hands and knife thoroughly after field dressing. Use Clorox to sterilize.
5. Insist that meat processor not mix your venison with that of other hunters.

THE CWD ALLIANCE
Throughout 2001, Boone and Crockett Club Members expressed growing concerns about chronic wasting disease (CWD). Club Members were deeply concerned about the impact CWD was having, and may continue to have, on North America's wild deer and elk populations. They were also concerned about the impact this disease may have upon millions of Americans' opportunity to hunt deer and elk each fall, and upon their confidence to put healthful wild venison on their families' tables. As a result of these concerns, in January 2002 the Club initiated a col-

laborative project called the **Chronic Wasting Disease Alliance.**

Founding partners were the Boone and Crockett Club, Mule Deer Foundation, and Rocky Mountain Elk Foundation. Other organizations soon joined the effort, and the Alliance presently consists of the original three partners plus Pope and Young Club, Quality Deer Management Association, Wildlife Management Institute, National Shooting Sports Foundation, Camp Fire Conservation Fund, Bowhunting Preservation Alliance, Cabela's, and Bio-Rad, Inc. Alliance partners agreed to pool resources, share information, and cooperate on projects and activities to positively impact the CWD issue. These partners collectively contributed more than $100,000 to the project during 2002 and 2003.

The mission of the CWD Alliance is to *promote responsible and accurate communications regarding CWD, and to support strategies that effectively control CWD to minimize its impact on wild, free-ranging deer and elk populations.* The Alliance encourages the development of solutions that do not necessitate the depopulation of wild cervid populations.

The Alliance recognizes that appropriate public information and education are vital to the resolution of the CWD dilemma. In an effort to promote responsible, timely and accurate communications the Alliance has:

- Developed a comprehensive CWD website (www.cwd-info.org) to function as a clearinghouse for timely and accurate information;
- Co-sponsored the National CWD Symposium, August 6 & 7, 2002 in Denver, Colorado;
- Participated in numerous local and regional CWD conferences in the United States and Canada;
- Served on several CWD task forces and committees;
- Worked with state and federal agencies to develop policy recommendations for the management and eradication of CWD;
- Provided testimony before the United States Congress;
- Cooperated on the publication of responsible and accurate CWD articles in their respective organization's member magazines; and
- Served as a credible resource for media sources seeking information about CWD.

The CWD Alliance has been well received by the professional wildlife resource managers, as evidenced by the following comment made by Bruce Morrison, Chair of the National CWD Plan Implementation Team: "The CWD Alliance has brought a much needed resource to the battle against Chronic Wasting Disease. The provision of current, factual information to the media, the general public, and professionals was the missing ingredient in the effort to keep everyone informed on the facts. The web site developed by the Alliance provides this information. Additionally, the ability of the Alliance to act as a central clearing house on information and speaking requests insures that the most qualified professionals are able to present the facts to a variety of audiences that can assist in the fight against CWD. The nonprofit organizations that founded the Alliance have, once again, stepped up to the plate to insure that wildlife management in the United States is a participatory citizen effort while supporting the professionals in their efforts to manage the disease." ∎

ABOUT THE AUTHOR

Full-time journalist and Professional Member of B&C, Wayne van Zwoll lives in northern Washington State. He has authored 8 books and more than 1,000 magazine articles on big game hunting, marksmanship, rifles,

and optics. Once editor of Kansas Wildlife, he's been shooting editor for Bugle since working as one of RMEF's first field directors. With wife Alice, he assembles Shooter's Bible. Wayne is also publications director for the Mule Deer Foundation. For 14 years he has conducted shooting programs for Safari Club International and now coaches at his own High Country Adventures camp for women. He has taught English and Forestry classes at Utah State University, where he earned a doctorate studying effects of post-war hunting motive on wildlife policy. Wayne jogs to stave off old age and has run several marathons, three at Boston.

Why We Score Big Game

History Worth Knowing

By Keith Balfourd

What do these statements have in common?

> He was a big ten-pointer.
> That buck was a clean 5x5, past his ears with mass all the way out.
> All I saw were tines as tall as he was wide.
> I don't know, he just looked massive.
> He's a freezer full, that's for sure.
> Twenty inches inside with G1's over 10 and G2's over 13.
> He would have to go in the mid one-seventies.
> A "Booner," just a "Booner."

In one form or another, they all refer to the size of a whitetail buck. Everyone has a different perspective when it comes to the concept of "what is a trophy" and how we communicate what we may have seen, or put our tag on. These descriptions are usually based on either what a buck weighs or the size of its antlers. When we speak of freezer space, we speak in pounds. When we speak of antlers, we speak in inches. And in inches, we talk "score."

We score big game. We put a tape to their headgear and do the math. Sometimes this is for status, bragging rights, or some form of contest between other hunters. Sometimes it's to paint a mental picture for an eager listener, and sometimes it is for the ultimate—an entry into the records book.

As you can see from the number of new entries in this fourth edition (see introduction), there has been a noticeable increase in the number of entries since the third edition was published in 1995, and not just in whitetail deer. Over the past ten years the Boone and Crockett Club's Big Game Records Department has seen an increasing number of qualifying entries in all categories, as well as a general increased interest in trophy animals, scoring, and records books. There are a number of theories as to "why." One perspective is that the "trophy" concept is everywhere, and along with it, "score."

Hunting product manufacturers market their products with the notion that, "this will help you bag that trophy of a lifetime." We see suc-

Photo from B&C Archives

Circa 1910 — *The Boone and Crockett Club's National Collection of Heads and Horns opened for public display at the Bronx Zoo in New York City in 1922. The inscription over the entrance to the exhibit read "In Memory of the Vanishing Big Game of the World." The display sparked public interest in big-game animals and created the momentum needed to launch a conservation and recovery effort that saved many of these great animals and hunting from extinction.*

cessful hunters posing with their trophies and all the "stuff" that made their success possible. The covers and pages of hunting magazines are graced with the images of the ultimate prize. Hunting expos across the country feature trophy displays as a major attraction. "Score" is everywhere, but what is scoring and where did it come from?

Whatever the motivation for using or talking score, there is something we hunters should understand because it is a big part of the reason why we can still enjoy hunting today. What's important to know are the real reasons why we score big game, what this means to hunting, and how all this scoring business got started.

The Boone and Crockett Club is to blame for this phenomenon, but the more we understand why B&C started scoring and keeping records, the more we can appreciate what this has meant to our hunting heritage and what this means to the future of big-game hunting. To do this, we need to go back to a time when game was overly abundant and then threatened with extinction.

The Boone and Crockett Club came into existence in 1887 when a group of hunters, including Theodore Roosevelt, decided something had to be done before it was too late. The general consensus at the time was that big-game animals, including the bison, elk, pronghorn, sheep, and whitetail deer might become extinct. The lack of game laws, unregulated market hunting, habitat destruction, western expansion, and a whole host of other factors were to blame for the decline. To make matters worse, there were no records of big-game populations, ranges, and distribution. Back then there wasn't any accurate data to work from as a baseline for a recovery effort or to point out problem areas.

By nature, we humans are accounting junkies. We like keeping score, knowing the numbers, and drawing conclusions based on the numbers. Since the Boone and Crockett Club was founded as the first conservation organization in North America and due to the fact that its membership was made up of hunters, it stands to reason that the measuring and scoring system they came up with is based on what hunters like to see—big racks, big horns, big skulls, and big tusks. The Club's system measures the lengths, widths, and circumferences of antlers, horns, and tusks and the length and width of skulls in 38 categories of native North American big game.

When the Boone and Crockett Club's Executive Committee appointed Casper Whitney, Archibald Rogers, and Theodore Roosevelt to the Club's first Records Committee in 1902 it wasn't to develop a scoring system for bragging rights or celebrity endorsements. Their goal was to systematically record biological data on the vanishing big-game animals of North America. Today, extinction seems a bit out of place, but in the early 1900s it was the reality of the times.

The first scoring system used was quite simple, measuring only skull length, or the longer antler or horn, plus one base circumference. Later, in 1950, a more elaborate system was developed, and it is this copyrighted system that is the universally recognized scoring system used in North America today.

In addition to recording data on the size of an animal's antlers, horns, skull, or tusks, the Club collected harvest and location data. With newly formed conservation and recovery efforts underway in the early 1900s, those tasked with bringing our wild game back to viable populations used this data to monitor success and failures in game management practices. The belief that a trophy animal represented a mature animal was the cornerstone of early game management philosophy. Wildlife managers used this information to identify problem areas. Mature animals being taken meant that there was balance in a specific area or herd, and all was well. If the Boone and Crockett data showed that an area historically holding mature animals had suddenly stopped producing, this was a red flag. A closer look into the reasons for the decline was then warranted.

As the success of our game management system began to pay dividends it became apparent that these species were not vanishing. At this point in history (around 1950) the Club was faced with the decision whether to continue keeping data and publishing records books. Thankfully for us accounting junkies they chose to continue, but with different purpose. Game departments and law enforcement agencies still relied on the data, but more important to B&C was the ideal of ethical hunting and the public's interest in hunting and wildlife.

WHY FAIR CHASE?

In a lawless time of abundance, telling free-spirited outdoorsmen and pioneers they had to change their ways was unpopular indeed. As part of the Club's master plan, a set of guidelines needed to be established—an ethical code for all sportsmen to follow to ensure that the last piece of the recovery and conservation puzzle was in place. As a vital element of the foundation supporting our nation's budding conservation system, the Club developed and championed a "fair chase" hunting ethic in the late 1800s. The Club's fair chase statement was part of the Club's by-laws and established a code of ethics for sport hunting, and these philosophies later became the foundation for the hunting and game laws we have today.

The Club's fair chase principles encourage the states and provinces to maintain sport hunting at a high level of sportsmanship and ethics, and provide standards for the individual hunter to enjoy hunting in an ethical fashion. The Club also uses its records program to keep hunters engaged and interested in further conservation to ensure hunting's future.

Today, the Club continues to track and record data on our big game populations. Using its records program to communicate the basics of conservation and fair chase to the hunting public, emphasizing that an understanding of species biology and proper habitat management is necessary to ensure the future of all species.

TROPHY HUNTING IS NOT BAD FOR HUNTING!

With all of the hype, marketing onslaught, big dollar endorsement deals, and exclusive trophy ranches we have today it's no surprise that some members of the hunting community have lost their center of gravity as to what's important. We have lost our roots to the point that some think that trophy hunting is now bad for the future of hunting. Most of this

Photo from B&C Archives

Circa 1950 — Grancel Fitz, one of the original architects of the Club's present-day scoring system, takes a circumference measurement on what was then the World's Record Alaska-Yukon moose, shot in 1900.

thinking is based on the current commercialization of hunting and trophies, along with land being "locked out" to the hunting public. With "trophy" being used to sell everything from soup to nuts, plus the imaginary payday that awaits those lucky enough to bag an exceptional trophy, it's easy to see how some hunters have lost their bearing. While it can be argued that these by-products of trophy hysteria can put a negative spin on big-game hunting, there are benefits we often overlook or have forgotten altogether.

Since we have opened the bank vault in reference to trophy hunting, we should consider the revenue that otherwise wouldn't be there if there wasn't this thirst for a trophy. The allure of a trophy nets our state game departments millions of dollars annually in general operating funds, as well a specific funding for a particular species. The state of Utah alone raised $345,000 additional funding in 2003 through the auction of its 11 special sheep tags, with 90 percent going to fund its bighorn sheep programs. This is the case in almost every western state with the sale and auction of special moose, elk, deer, pronghorn, and mountain goat tags.

Another interesting twist to the concept of "trophy" and the Boone and Crockett Club's records-keeping program is the instant economies that emerge after the recognition of a particular species by the records book. The Club didn't always recognize 38 categories of big game. Over its 70-year history of records keeping it has added classifications of big game as biological and range data warranted a separate category. For example, the Club didn't always have a category for Central Canada barren ground caribou taken in the Northwest Territories. Until 1983 these specimens were classified as barren ground caribou. When the Club declared this as a separate records book category a new industry was born overnight and along with it funding, protection, and management. Between new guiding and outfitting operations, license and tag sales, and a new interest in these animals, the government in Northwest Territories received a vital boost of funds and the need to better manage their herds.

The truth is, trophy hunting is selective hunting and selective hunting is good for hunting. It helps keep an age balance to herd populations; gives immature animals the opportunity to grow and contribute to the herd; gives game managers a viable option to improve herd balance; and with a one tag-one animal approach, it allows for a longer-lasting, more enjoyable hunting season overall. More importantly, it also pays for most modern day management and protection.

It would be safe to say that given the choice between taking a spike or waiting a few seconds longer for a nice 10-point to step into view, the odds are overwhelming that the 10-point is going to get it. Admit it or not, most hunters like "big" and will hunt for "big or bigger" until they're out of time. Then it's the next best buck we can find.

TYPICAL AND NON-TYPICAL

Since this scoring business is all about the animals and recording biological data, the original designers of the Club's scoring system devised a system that records the most common or typical antler configuration found for a given species. For an animal's final score, the most common characteristics are rewarded, while abnormalities are deducted. For whatever reason, Mother Nature plays funny tricks on antlered game. Those specimens that grow enough abnormal points are classified as non-typical, and listed separately.

GROSS AND FINAL SCORE

As interest in trophies increased and since higher scores mean higher recognition for the hunter, the great debate over gross and final score started to build. "Give the animal credit for what it grew" is the most common opinion tossed around hunting camps today. The issue of deductions seems to bother some people, especially when personal status or financial reward comes into play. Some have developed their own scoring system and records book patterned after the B&C system, but with no deductions.

Interest in scoring and records books is a good thing. The fact that others have knocked off the B&C scoring system simply means hunters are interested, engaged, and passionate about their sport, which means more money, and votes for wildlife and hunting. Remember, B&C was founded to raise hunting and our natural resources to a higher level of public stewardship. The Club's scoring system was intended to be biological in nature, yet create interest and support for diminishing wildlife populations. Of course B&C prefers that you enter your qualifying trophy in its records program, however, the mere fact that you care enough about big game and hunting to have your trophy scored at all accomplishes what Club Members set out to do 116 years ago. Hunters do care and are involved. That's why we have wildlife and wild places today. It is also why we have hunting today. We can thank Theodore Roosevelt and the Boone and Crockett Club for that. ▪

ABOUT THE AUTHOR

Keith Balfourd is the Marketing Coordinator for the Boone and Crockett Club, an Official B&C and P&Y Measurer, and a avid whitetail hunter, and outdoor writer. He grew up in big whitetail country (east-central Ohio) and received a degree in marketing and forestry from Oregon State University. Keith has worked in the outdoor industry for the past 15 years in publishing, marketing, and sales.

SPECIAL BONUS SECTION

COLOR PHOTOGRAPHS FROM THE FIELD

HUNTER: Charles W. Via
SCORE: 174-1/8
CATEGORY: typical whitetail deer
LOCATION: Starke County, Indiana
DATE: 2000

HUNTER: Craig R. Belknap
SCORE: 198-5/8
CATEGORY: non-typical whitetail deer
LOCATION: Des Moines County, Iowa
DATE: 1998

LEFT: HUNTER: David K. Wachtel III **SCORE:** 244-3/8 **CATEGORY:** non-typical whitetail deer **LOCATION:** Sumner County, Tennessee **DATE:** 2000

RIGHT: HUNTER: Perry Stanley **SCORE:** 170 **CATEGORY:** typical whitetail deer **LOCATION:** Pike County, Illinois **DATE:** 1996

BOTTOM: HUNTER: Larry D. Napier **SCORE:** 171-6/8 **CATEGORY:** typical whitetail deer **LOCATION:** Adams County, Ohio **DATE:** 2000

HUNTER: Mark Wimpy
SCORE: 226-6/8
CATEGORY: non-typical whitetail deer
LOCATION: Piatt County, Illinois
DATE: 2000

LEFT: HUNTER: Leland N. Dye, Jr. **SCORE:** 195-2/8 **CATEGORY:** non-typical whitetail deer **LOCATION:** Tunica County, Mississippi **DATE:** 2001

RIGHT: HUNTER: Kirk Kelso **SCORE:** 124-7/8 **CATEGORY:** typical Coues' whitetail deer **LOCATION:** Santa Cruz County, Arizona **DATE:** 2001

BOTTOM: HUNTER: J. Brett Evans **SCORE:** 203-2/8 **CATEGORY:** non-typical whitetail deer **LOCATION:** Pike County, Illinois **DATE:** 2001

HUNTER: Jeffrey K. Volk
SCORE: 114
CATEGORY: typical Coues' whitetail deer
LOCATION: Pima County, Arizona
DATE: 2001

LEFT: HUNTER: Jody Tomala **SCORE:** 168-5/8 **CATEGORY:** typical whitetail deer **LOCATION:** Morrison County, Minnesota **DATE:** 2001

RIGHT: HUNTER: B. Tyler Fenley **SCORE:** 198-6/8 **CATEGORY:** non-typical whitetail deer **LOCATION:** Angelina County, Texas **DATE:** 1999

BOTTOM: HUNTER: Karl Oliver **SCORE:** 181-6/8 **CATEGORY:** typical whitetail deer **LOCATION:** Cando, Saskatchewan **DATE:** 1998

HUNTER: Kevin L. Olson
SCORE: 170-1/8
CATEGORY: typical whitetail deer
LOCATION: Lake of the Woods County, Minnesota
DATE: 2000

LEFT: HUNTER: Ronald N. Carpenter **SCORE:** 175 **CATEGORY:** typical whitetail deer **LOCATION:** Lac La Biche, Alberta **DATE:** 1998

RIGHT: HUNTER: Freeman R. Bell **SCORE:** 181-3/8 **CATEGORY:** typical whitetail deer **LOCATION:** Meadow Lake, Saskatchewan **DATE:** 1997

BOTTOM: HUNTER: John Proud **SCORE:** 176-4/8 **CATEGORY:** typical whitetail deer **LOCATION:** Oldman Lake, Alberta **DATE:** 1997

HUNTER: Ronald N. Riche
SCORE: 217-4/8
CATEGORY: non-typical whitetail deer
LOCATION: Bethune, Saskatchewan
DATE: 1998

LEFT: HUNTER: Chuck Adams **SCORE:** 110-5/8 **CATEGORY:** typical Coues' whitetail deer **LOCATION:** Pinal County, Arizona **DATE:** 1989

RIGHT: HUNTER: James D. Vitcenda **SCORE:** 205-3/8 **CATEGORY:** non-typical whitetail deer **LOCATION:** Winona County, Minnesota **DATE:** 1998

BOTTOM: HUNTER: Ronald J. Jilot **SCORE:** 203-5/8 **CATEGORY:** non-typical whitetail deer **LOCATION:** Buffalo County, Wisconsin **DATE:** 1997

HUNTER: Scott R. Busch
SCORE: 197-7/8
CATEGORY: non-typical whitetail deer
LOCATION: Madison County, Iowa
DATE: 1997

LEFT: HUNTER: Shawn R. Keegan **SCORE:** 205-2/8 **CATEGORY:** non-typical whitetail deer **LOCATION:** Morgan County, Illinois **DATE:** 2000

RIGHT: HUNTER: Richard N. Kimball **SCORE:** 205 **CATEGORY:** non-typical whitetail deer **LOCATION:** White Fox, Saskatchewan **DATE:** 1997

BOTTOM: HUNTER: Cullen R. Spitzer **SCORE:** 211-6/8 **CATEGORY:** non-typical whitetail deer **LOCATION:** Clark County, Kansas **DATE:** 2001

HUNTER: Walter L. Baker
SCORE: 216-3/8
CATEGORY: non-typical whitetail deer
LOCATION: Jersey County, Illinois
DATE: 1998

LEFT: HUNTER: Eric Coleman **SCORE:** 184-5/8 **CATEGORY:** typical whitetail deer **LOCATION:** Champaign County, Ohio **DATE:** 2000

RIGHT: HUNTER: Ronald R. George **SCORE:** 170 **CATEGORY:** typical whitetail deer **LOCATION:** Pratt County, Kansas **DATE:** 1999

BOTTOM: HUNTER: David J. Lechel **SCORE:** 111-1/8 **CATEGORY:** typical Coues' whitetail deer **LOCATION:** Sonora, Mexico **DATE:** 2001

North American Whitetail Deer State Listing

TOP TEN WHITETAIL DEER

TYPICAL WHITEAIL DEER

RANK	SCORE	LOCATION – HUNTER – DATE KILLED — PAGE NUMBER
1	$213\frac{5}{8}$	Saskatchewan – Milo N. Hanson – 1993 – 580
2	$206\frac{1}{8}$	Wisconsin – James Jordan – 1914 – 484
3	205	Missouri – Larry W. Gibson – 1971 – 318
4	$204\frac{4}{8}$	Illinois – Mel J. Johnson – 1965 – 114
5†	$204\frac{2}{8}$	Kentucky – Robert W. Smith – 2000 – 220
5	$204\frac{2}{8}$	Alberta – Stephen Jansen – 1967 – 530
7	$202\frac{6}{8}$	Saskatchewan – Bruce Ewen – 1992 – 580
8	202	Minnesota – John A. Breen – 1918 – 276
9	$201\frac{4}{8}$	Iowa – Wayne A. Bills – 1974 – 162
10	201	Minnesota – Wayne G. Stewart – 1961 – 276

NON-TYPICAL WHITEAIL DEER

RANK	SCORE	LOCATION – HUNTER – DATE KILLED — PAGE NUMBER
1	$333\frac{7}{8}$	Missouri – Picked Up – 1981 – 330
2	$328\frac{2}{8}$	Ohio – Picked Up – 1940 – 398
3	$295\frac{6}{8}$	Mississippi – Tony Fulton – 1995 – 314
4†	$291\frac{1}{8}$	Illinois – Jerry D. Bryant – 2001 – 134
5	$284\frac{3}{8}$	Texas – Unknown – 1892 – 454
6	282	Iowa – Larry Raveling – 1973 – 184
7	$281\frac{6}{8}$	Louisianna – James H. McMurray – 1994 – 242
8	$280\frac{4}{8}$	Kansas – Joseph H. Waters – 1987 – 210
9	$279\frac{6}{8}$	Alberta – Neil J. Morin – 1991 – 540
10	$277\frac{5}{8}$	Alberta – Doug Klinger – 1976 – 540

† The scores and ranking for trophies from the 25th Awards Entry Period are not final until the banquet is held on June 19, 2004.

TABULATIONS OF RECORDED WHITETAIL DEER

By Jack Reneau

The trophy data shown on the following pages are taken from score charts in the Records Archives of the Boone and Crockett Club from 1950 through December 31, 2002, the second year of the 25th Awards Program Entry Period. Trophies accepted in the 25th Awards Program are indicated with a cross symbol (†). The score and rank of trophies so designated will not be final until after the 25th Awards Program banquet that takes place on June 19, 2004. The scores of a few of the higher scoring 25th Awards Program entries need to be verified by the 25th Awards Program Judges Panel that will convene in late April 2004.

A comparison of the all-time rankings of this book with those of the current all-time records book (Records of North American Big Game, 11th Edition, 1999) will show some significant differences due to the addition of trophies accepted during the 24th Awards Program (1998 – 2000) and the first two years of the 25th Awards Program (2001 – 2002). The rankings in this book supercede those in the 11th Edition.

Whitetail deer are found over most of the eastern two-thirds of the United States and Canada, as well as portions of Mexico. Geographic boundaries are not described for whitetail deer, as whitetail racks can be easily distinguished from the other deer categories. The geographic boundary for the smaller Coues' whitetail deer, which is described on page 527, is intended to prevent the inclusion of the more common and larger whitetail deer variety into the diminutive Coues' whitetail deer category.

The scores and ranks of trophies shown with an asterisk (*) at the end of a state/provincial listing are not final. The asterisk identifies entry scores subject to verification by an Awards Program Judges Panel. The asterisk can be removed (except in the case of a potential new World's Record) by the submission of two additional, independent scorings by B&C Official Measurers. The Club's Records Committee will then review the three scorings available and determine which, if any, will be accepted in lieu of the Judges Panel measurement. When the score of an asterisked trophy has been accepted as final, the asterisk will be removed and that trophy will take its rightful place in the listings of future editions of the Club's records books. If an asterisk is not removed as outlined above, that trophy will be listed in one Awards book and one All-time book before it is dropped from the trophy listings.

In the case of a potential new World's Record, the trophy *must* come before an Awards Program Judges Panel or a Special Judges Panel, which may convene during an Awards Program to certify the status and score of a potential World's Record. A potential World's Record will be asterisked if its score is not verified by a Judges Panel since only a Boone and Crockett Club Judges Panel can certify a new World's Record.

Dates of kill for years preceded with the abbreviation "PR" in the following trophy listings means the exact date that trophy was taken, found, acquired, etc., is unknown, but that it was known to exist "Prior to" the year listed. Unless stated otherwise, photos are courtesy of the trophy owner.

ALABAMA
RECORD WHITETAILS

12 Typical whitetail deer entries
9 Non-typical whitetail deer entries
7,265 Total whitetail deer entries

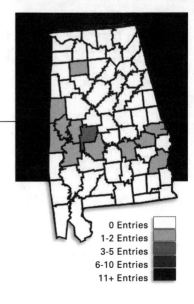

0 Entries	
1-2 Entries	
3-5 Entries	
6-10 Entries	
11+ Entries	

ALABAMA
STATE RECORD
Typical Whitetail Deer
Score: 186 3/8
Location: Lee Co.
Hunter: Picked Up
Owner: George P. Mann
Date: 1986

ALABAMA
STATE RECORD
Non-Typical Whitetail Deer
Score: 259⁷/8
Location: Perry Co.
Hunter and Owner: Jon G. Moss
Date: 1989

ALABAMA

TYPICAL WHITETAIL DEER

Score	Length of Main Beam Right	Left	Inside Spread	Greatest Spread	Circumference at Smallest Place Between Burr and First Point Right	Left	Number of Points Right	Left	Lengths Abnormal Points	All-Time Rank	State Rank
					■ *Location of Kill – Hunter – Owner – Date Killed*						
186³/8	28	28	23¹/8	24⁶/8	4⁶/8	4⁶/8	5	6		210	1
	■ *Lee Co. – Picked Up – George P. Mann – 1986*										
182⁷/8	27⁴/8	28²/8	19³/8	21⁴/8	5⁵/8	5⁵/8	6	5	2²/8	401	2
	■ *Hale Co. – James C. Bailey – James C. Bailey – 1974*										
172¹/8	26³/8	26⁴/8	21⁵/8	23⁷/8	5¹/8	5³/8	5	5		2286	3
	■ *Pickens Co. – Walter Jaynes – Walter Jaynes – 1968*										
171¹/8	25⁷/8	27	18⁴/8	20	5⁴/8	5⁵/8	5	6	1¹/8	2665†	4†
	■ *Lamar Co. – Richard L. Moore – Richard L. Moore – 2001*										
170⁴/8	25⁴/8	25¹/8	16⁷/8	19¹/8	5³/8	5⁵/8	5	6	2¹/8	2933	5
	■ *Marengo Co. – Frank W. Gardner – Frank W. Gardner – 1967*										
170²/8	27¹/8	27²/8	21	22⁶/8	5³/8	5³/8	4	4		3063	6
	■ *Lee Co. – George P. Mann – George P. Mann – 1980*										
168²/8	24³/8	23⁶/8	17⁶/8	20	4⁵/8	4⁶/8	6	6	1⁴/8	3414	7
	■ *Marengo Co. – William L. Wright – William L. Wright – 1979*										
163⁴/8	25¹/8	25	20⁴/8	22⁴/8	5	5	5	5		3984	8
	■ *Macon Co. – George P. Mann – George P. Mann – 1994*										
162⁷/8	26¹/8	24⁴/8	18³/8	20⁴/8	4⁷/8	5¹/8	6	6	2	4067	9
	■ *Perry Co. – Rodney A. Pilot – Rodney A. Pilot – 1987*										
161⁶/8	25⁵/8	25	19²/8	22	4⁶/8	4⁶/8	6	5		4223	10
	■ *Greene Co. – William H. Fincher – William H. Fincher – 1982*										
161⁴/8	24⁵/8	24²/8	17⁴/8	19	5²/8	5⁴/8	5	5		4258	11
	■ *Barbour Co. – Craig Thompson – Craig Thompson – 1979*										
161²/8	25⁶/8	25⁷/8	21⁴/8	23⁵/8	5	5²/8	5	5		4310	12
	■ *Montgomery Co. – Dan McGee – Dan McGee – 1978*										

† The scores and ranking for trophies from the 25th Awards Entry Period are not final until the banquet is held on June 19, 2004.

ALABAMA

NON-TYPICAL WHITETAIL DEER

Score	Length of Main Beam		Inside Spread	Greatest Spread	Circumference at Smallest Place Between Burr and First Point		Number of Points		Lengths Abnormal Points	All-Time Rank	State Rank
	Right	Left			Right	Left	Right	Left			
	■ Location of Kill – Hunter – Owner – Date Killed										
259⁷/₈	27	28⁴/₈	22¹/₈	24³/₈	5	5⁶/₈	27	9	79⁶/₈	23	1
	■ Perry Co. – Jon G. Moss – Jon G. Moss – 1989										
224⁵/₈	24⁶/₈	27¹/₈	25¹/₈	27⁴/₈	5⁷/₈	5⁴/₈	15	7	70	325	2
	■ Perry Co. – Robert E. Royster – Robert E. Royster – 1976										
223¹/₈	23⁷/₈	24⁵/₈	15	19⁵/₈	6	5⁶/₈	21	12	87¹/₈	361	3
	■ Sumter Co. – James L. Spidle, Sr. – Elizabeth McCormick – PR 1942										
217²/₈	24⁵/₈	24²/₈	17⁴/₈	21²/₈	5⁵/₈	6³/₈	5	14	40	519	4
	■ Dallas Co. – Robert Tate – Robert Tate – 1988										
216⁴/₈	18	18	17	21	5⁴/₈	5⁶/₈	14	13	65²/₈	546	5
	■ Macon Co. – George B. Bulls – George B. Bulls – 1995										
205⁷/₈	26⁶/₈	25¹/₈	19⁷/₈	29³/₈	5³/₈	5²/₈	10	11	33²/₈	1080†	6†
	■ Lawrence Co. – Ronald R. Laymon – Ronald R. Laymon – 2000										
200¹/₈	24³/₈	25⁴/₈	18²/₈	23¹/₈	5¹/₈	5²/₈	12	7	34⁵/₈	1577	7
	■ Dallas Co. – H. Lloyd Morris – H. Lloyd Morris – 1989										
199²/₈	28⁷/₈	27³/₈	23⁵/₈	27⁵/₈	5²/₈	5²/₈	7	9	19¹/₈	1649	8
	■ Winston Co. – James W. Huckbay – James W. Huckbay – 1973										
187	27⁴/₈	26¹/₈	21	22⁶/₈	5⁶/₈	5⁶/₈	6	8	17²/₈	2545	9
	■ Greene Co. – William H. Fincher – William H. Fincher – 1976										

† The scores and ranking for trophies from the 25th Awards Entry Period are not final until the banquet is held on June 19, 2004.

ARKANSAS
RECORD WHITETAILS

79 Typical whitetail deer entries
39 Non-typical whitetail deer entries
7,265 Total whitetail deer entries

0 Entries
1-2 Entries
3-5 Entries
6-10 Entries
11+ Entries

ARKANSAS
STATE RECORD
Typical Whitetail Deer
Score: 189
Location: Crawford Co.
Hunter and Owner: Tom Sparks, Jr.
Date: 1975

ARKANSAS
NEW STATE RECORD
Non-Typical Whitetail Deer
Score: 238^3/$_8$
Location: Prairie Co.
Hunter and Owner: William Dooley
Date: 1999

ARKANSAS

TYPICAL WHITETAIL DEER

Score	Length of Main Beam Right	Length of Main Beam Left	Inside Spread	Greatest Spread	Circumference at Smallest Place Between Burr and First Point Right	Circumference at Smallest Place Between Burr and First Point Left	Number of Points Right	Number of Points Left	Lengths Abnormal Points	All-Time Rank	State Rank
189	25 1/8	25 4/8	17 2/8	19 3/8	4 5/8	4 4/8	6	6		131	1
■ Crawford Co. – Tom Sparks, Jr. – Tom Sparks, Jr. – 1975											
187 3/8	24 7/8	25 2/8	23 3/8	26 2/8	5 3/8	5	6	8	5 2/8	178	2
■ St. Francis Co. – Andy Anderson – Andy Anderson – 1998											
186 7/8	25 5/8	25 3/8	20 1/8	21 4/8	4 7/8	5	5	5		194	3
■ Arkansas Co. – Walter Spears – Cabela's, Inc. – 1952											
185 7/8	29 7/8	30 1/8	19 5/8	22 4/8	5	5 1/8	6	6	3 6/8	244	4
■ Prairie Co. – Lonnie W. Copeland – Jack G. Brittingham – 1992											
184 6/8	26 7/8	27	24 4/8		5 3/8	5 3/8	8	9	12 2/8	285	5
■ Desha Co. – Lee Perry – Walter Brock – 1961											
184	25 2/8	25 1/8	16 2/8	18 4/8	4 3/8	4 3/8	6	6		334	6
■ Arkansas Co. – Willard L. Harper – Delwyn E. Harper – 1946											
183 7/8	26 6/8	27 6/8	23 2/8	25 4/8	4 3/8	4 3/8	6	5	1 5/8	343	7
■ White Co. – W.A. Harden & C. Craven – Wilburn A. Harden – 1993											
183 3/8	27 5/8	27 4/8	20 5/8	22 2/8	5 2/8	5 2/8	5	6	3 6/8	365	8
■ Drew Co. – Jimmy Monk – Jimmy Monk – 1978											
183	27 1/8	27 7/8	18 6/8	20 4/8	4 6/8	4 6/8	5	5		392	9
■ Desha Co. – R.J. Diekhoff – Franzen Bros. – 1954											
180 7/8	22 1/8	23 1/8	16 7/8	19 6/8	5 3/8	5 1/8	7	8	8	573	10
■ Chicot Co. – Lee R. Mathews – Henry Mathews – 1963											
180 2/8	26 5/8	27 5/8	21 1/8	22 6/8	5 1/8	5 1/8	6	6	2 5/8	651	11
■ Drew Co. – Terry Tackette – Terry Tackette – 1989											
180	26 6/8	26 5/8	19 6/8	23	4 4/8	4 4/8	7	5	1 4/8	688	12
■ Desha Co. – Turner Neal – Turner Neal – 1962											
179 2/8	27 2/8	27 1/8	23 3/8	28 4/8	5	5 2/8	9	11	11 7/8	763	13
■ Prairie Co. – Charles Newsom – Charles Newsom – 1962											
178 3/8	27 2/8	26	17 1/8	19 1/8	5 2/8	5	7	8	10 2/8	868	14
■ Carroll Co. – Roy F. Bartlett – Roy F. Bartlett – 1975											
178 3/8	27 6/8	27 3/8	22 4/8	24 6/8	5 3/8	5 3/8	7	6	3 5/8	868	14
■ Phillips Co. – Christopher Warren – Christopher Warren – 1993											
178 1/8	29 1/8	28	19 5/8	22	4 3/8	4 3/8	5	7	2 4/8	905	16
■ Arkansas Co. – Roger Hansell – Roger Hansell – 1992											
177 7/8	27	28 4/8	20	24 1/8	4 6/8	5	6	6	3 7/8	936	17
■ Chicot Co. – George Matthews – W.T. Haynes – 1923											
176 5/8	26	26	17 1/8	20	5 2/8	5 3/8	8	7	1 4/8	1134	18
■ White Co. – Dickie P. Duke – Dickie P. Duke – 1996											
175 7/8	26 1/8	25 1/8	20 7/8	25 4/8	4 5/8	4 6/8	5	8	7 4/8	1287	19
■ Pulaski Co. – Charles L. Marcum, Jr. – Charles L. Marcum, Jr. – 1996											

Score	Length of Main Beam Right	Left	Inside Spread	Greatest Spread	Circumference at Smallest Place Between Burr and First Point Right	Left	Number of Points Right	Left	Lengths Abnormal Points	All-Time Rank	State Rank
	■ Location of Kill – Hunter – Owner – Date Killed										
175³/8	22⁴/8	23²/8	16³/8	18⁵/8	4¹/8	4²/8	6	6		1377	20
	■ White Co. – Jerry Parish – Jerry Parish – 1984										
175³/8	28⁴/8	29²/8	20⁵/8	22⁴/8	4⁶/8	4⁶/8	5	5		1377	20
	■ Mississippi Co. – Luther Gifford – Luther Gifford – 1994										
174⁶/8	26³/8	26⁶/8	19	21²/8	5²/8	5³/8	6	6		1534	22
	■ Desha Co. – James F. Finch – James F. Finch – 1999										
174⁵/8	26³/8	25	16⁷/8	19⁵/8	6²/8	6²/8	5	7	5	1561	23
	■ St. Francis Co. – J.S. & J.R. Cook – J.S. & J.R. Cook – 1996										
174²/8	25³/8	24²/8	17²/8	19⁷/8	6¹/8	5⁴/8	8	8	10⁴/8	1652	24
	■ St. Francis Co. – Brice Fletcher II – Brice Fletcher II – 1995										
174	25⁶/8	26	19⁶/8	21⁶/8	4³/8	4³/8	5	5		1717†	25†
	■ Desha Co. – David Wren – Maurice Abowitz – 1962										
173⁷/8	28	28	17³/8	19²/8	4²/8	4	5	6		1743	26
	■ Drew Co. – Ronald E. Pearce – Ronald E. Pearce – 1996										
173³/8	26³/8	26³/8	19¹/8	22¹/8	5³/8	5³/8	7	7	6⁶/8	1883	27
	■ Arkansas Co. – Jimmy Hanson – Jimmy Hanson – 1948										
173²/8	30³/8	29⁶/8	21¹/8	23⁵/8	5	5⁷/8	6	8	3³/8	1914	28
	■ Chicot Co. – Yan Sturdivant – Bruce Sturdivant – 1951										
173²/8	26	26⁶/8	20	21³/8	4	4	5	7	3⁶/8	1914	28
	■ Lincoln Co. – Billy McGriff – Billy McGriff – 1962										
173²/8	26	24⁶/8	19	21	4²/8	4²/8	5	5		1914	28
	■ Chicot Co. – James W. Brown – James W. Brown – 1991										
173¹/8	25⁶/8	25⁶/8	17⁶/8	19⁴/8	5²/8	5³/8	7	7	2⁷/8	1950†	31†
	■ Union Co. – James O. Cox – Arkansas County Seed – 1973										
173¹/8	26²/8	25⁶/8	18	20	4³/8	4⁴/8	6	7	1³/8	1950	31
	■ White Co. – Ricky S. Cantrell – Ricky S. Cantrell – 1996										
172⁵/8	25⁴/8	26³/8	20⁵/8	22¹/8	4⁵/8	4⁴/8	5	6		2113	33
	■ Greene Co. – Unknown – Harry Willcockson – PR 1940										
172	26¹/8	25	24²/8	26²/8	4⁵/8	4⁴/8	5	5		2330	34
	■ Bearden – Buddy Wise – Buddy Wise – 1962										
172	26²/8	26	20	21⁷/8	5³/8	5³/8	5	6		2330	34
	■ Arkansas Co. – Donald R. Sweetin – Donald R. Sweetin – 1996										
171⁷/8	25³/8	25⁷/8	18²/8	21¹/8	4⁷/8	5¹/8	8	5	5¹/8	2382	36
	■ Prairie Co. – C.L. Vanhouten – C.L. Vanhouten – 1964										
171⁷/8	25²/8	25⁷/8	18⁵/8	20¹/8	4⁷/8	4⁷/8	6	6		2382	36
	■ Lafayette Co. – Billy D. Bland, Jr. – Billy D. Bland, Jr. – 1986										
171⁷/8	27⁶/8	27⁷/8	22²/8	24⁷/8	5¹/8	5¹/8	4	6	1¹/8	2382	36
	■ Cross Co. – Mark C. Taylor – Mark C. Taylor – 1992										
171⁷/8	27⁴/8	28²/8	17⁷/8	20¹/8	4⁷/8	4⁶/8	5	5		2382	36
	■ Pulaski Co. – Charles L. Marcum, Jr. – Charles L. Marcum, Jr. – 1994										
171²/8	29²/8	28⁶/8	19²/8	21⁶/8	4⁶/8	4⁴/8	6	5		2621	40
	■ Arkansas Co. – Wilbur Stephens – Wilbur Stephens – 1953										

Score	Length of Main Beam Right	Left	Inside Spread	Greatest Spread	Circumference at Smallest Place Between Burr and First Point Right	Left	Number of Points Right	Left	Lengths Abnormal Points	All-Time Rank	State Rank
	■ Location of Kill – Hunter – Owner – Date Killed										
171 1/8	26 7/8	27	18 7/8	21	5	5 1/8	5	7	2 2/8	2665	41
	■ Lafayette Co. – Picked Up – John Upton – 1975										
171	23 3/8	24 3/8	19	20 6/8	4 3/8	4 4/8	7	8	5 4/8	2707	42
	■ Independence Co. – Frankie Felton – Frankie Felton – 1986										
170 7/8	25 7/8	26 1/8	16 6/8	18 7/8	4 4/8	4 3/8	6	5	1 3/8	2769	43
	■ Monroe Co. – William E. Bartlett – William E. Bartlett – 1990										
170 6/8	27 4/8	26 4/8	18	21	5	5 2/8	6	7	4 2/8	2828	44
	■ Chicot Co. – Mrs. L.M. Hamilton – Mrs. L.M. Hamilton – 1960										
170 6/8	25 7/8	25 3/8	16 2/8	18 5/8	4 6/8	4 4/8	5	5		2828	44
	■ Union Co. – Chester New – Chester New – 1968										
170 4/8	27	27 2/8	20 6/8	22 7/8	5 2/8	5 2/8	6	5		2933	46
	■ Desha Co. – Bob Norris – Bob Norris – 1948										
170 4/8	23 6/8	23 3/8	18 4/8	20 3/8	4 2/8	4 3/8	6	6		2933	46
	■ Bradley Co. – Joe Hairston – Joe Hairston – 1989										
170 3/8	26	26	19 1/8	21 1/8	5 3/8	5 3/8	6	5	1	2992	48
	■ Woodruff Co. – R.L. Taylor – R.L. Taylor – 1960										
170 2/8	25 3/8	26 3/8	19 4/8	21	5 2/8	5 2/8	5	5		3063	49
	■ Calhoun Co. – George M. Gorman – George M. Gorman – 1961										
170 2/8	25 2/8	24 6/8	19 4/8	21 5/8	5 1/8	5 2/8	6	6	4	3063	49
	■ Bradley Co. – Brad J. Davis – Brad J. Davis – 1979										
170 1/8	28 3/8	28 3/8	21 5/8	22 4/8	4 6/8	5	6	6	8 4/8	3143†	51†
	■ White Co. – Ernest W. Stephenson – Ernest W. Stephenson – 1971										
170	27 1/8	27 1/8	21 6/8	23 5/8	5 3/8	5 3/8	5	5		3224	52
	■ Desha Co. – Ben J. Miller – Ben J. Miller – 1994										
170	28 4/8	27 2/8	21 6/8	24	4 1/8	4 1/8	5	5		3224	52
	■ Cross Co. – Clay C. Bassham – Clay C. Bassham – 1996										
169 2/8	24 2/8	23 7/8	20 4/8	22 3/8	5 1/8	5 1/8	6	6		3336	54
	■ Garland Co. – Shane Lambert – Shane Lambert – 1991										
167 7/8	29 4/8	26 7/8	18 5/8	20 6/8	5 4/8	5 7/8	5	8	5	3451	55
	■ Desha Co. – Dick White – Dick White – 1996										
167 3/8	26 1/8	26 3/8	19 4/8	20 2/8	4 4/8	4 2/8	7	6	2 5/8	3500	56
	■ Conway Co. – Chad D. Mallett – Chad D. Mallett – 1995										
167 1/8	26 4/8	25 4/8	16 5/8	18 7/8	4 3/8	4 4/8	5	5		3539	57
	■ Saline Co. – Kris Holiman – Kris Holiman – 1990										
166 6/8	27 2/8	28 4/8	22 4/8	24 3/8	4 5/8	4 5/8	5	5	1 2/8	3582	58
	■ Cross Co. – Paul Latham – Paul Latham – 1993										
166 2/8	25 2/8	26 3/8	17 3/8	19 2/8	4 5/8	4 7/8	7	6	4 1/8	3632	59
	■ Sharp Co. – Picked Up – Doug Masner – 1993										
166 1/8	23 5/8	23 3/8	17 3/8	19 3/8	5 3/8	5 5/8	5	5		3643	60
	■ Arkansas Co. – Bill Bowman – Bill Bowman – 1981										
165 6/8	25 1/8	25 3/8	17	19 3/8	5	5	5	5		3680	61
	■ Arkansas Co. – Lonnie C. Childers – Lonnie C. Childers – 1958										

Score	Length of Main Beam Right	Left	Inside Spread	Greatest Spread	Circumference at Smallest Place Between Burr and First Point Right	Left	Number of Points Right	Left	Lengths Abnormal Points	All-Time Rank	State Rank
165⁵/₈	25³/₈	25	18	22⁷/₈	4²/₈	4²/₈	5	6	1³/₈	3696	62
■ Clay Co. – Richard Catt – Richard Catt – 1999											
165³/₈	25²/₈	25⁵/₈	16⁶/₈	19³/₈	5²/₈	5	6	6	9⁷/₈	3731	63
■ Desha Co. – Calvin Walker – Calvin Walker – 1956											
165³/₈	24²/₈	23²/₈	14⁷/₈	16⁵/₈	5²/₈	5¹/₈	5	5		3731	63
■ Howard Co. – Roy L. Beason – Roy L. Beason – 1991											
165²/₈	24¹/₈	24	19²/₈	21⁴/₈	4⁵/₈	4⁵/₈	5	5		3748	65
■ Columbia Co. – John D. Gosdin – John D. Gosdin – 1978											
164⁷/₈	30	29⁷/₈	20⁵/₈	22⁶/₈	4⁶/₈	4⁷/₈	4	4		3792	66
■ Desha Co. – Alfred Johnston – Alfred Johnston – 1995											
164¹/₈	23⁴/₈	24³/₈	19⁵/₈	21	4¹/₈	4²/₈	5	5		3886	67
■ Prairie Co. – John H. Henderson II – John H. Henderson II – 1995											
164	24⁶/₈	24⁷/₈	19³/₈	21⁷/₈	5³/₈	5⁵/₈	7	6	5⁷/₈	3908	68
■ Arkansas Co. – Picked Up – Tony Vaughn – 1989											
163⁷/₈	25	26	20⁵/₈	22³/₈	4²/₈	4¹/₈	5	4		3928	69
■ Ashley Co. – Picked Up – James Crossley – 1952											
163³/₈	29	27⁷/₈	21³/₈	23⁴/₈	4⁴/₈	4⁴/₈	4	4		4002	70
■ Poinsett Co. – Guy W. Scudder – Guy W. Scudder – 1990											
163²/₈	27¹/₈	26	20⁴/₈	24	5	4⁷/₈	8	11	10⁶/₈	4017	71
■ Union Co. – Johnny Gathright – Johnny Gathright – 1983											
162⁷/₈	26²/₈	28¹/₈	20⁷/₈	22⁶/₈	5²/₈	5²/₈	6	6	6⁴/₈	4067†	72†
■ Ashley Co. – Picked Up – Arkansas Game & Fish Comm. – 1995											
162⁷/₈	25³/₈	26³/₈	18¹/₈	20⁴/₈	4⁴/₈	4⁴/₈	5	5		4067	72
■ Desha Co. – Wesley Murphy – Wesley Murphy – 1962											
162⁶/₈	24³/₈	24¹/₈	21⁶/₈	23⁷/₈	4⁴/₈	4⁴/₈	5	5		4089	74
■ Calhoun Co. – Vernon Evans – Vernon Evans – 1962											
162¹/₈	22²/₈	19⁵/₈	18³/₈	19⁶/₈	3⁷/₈	3⁷/₈	6	7		4174	75
■ Clark Co. – Terry B. Kinser – Terry B. Kinser – 1998											
162	26	26⁴/₈	20⁶/₈	22⁵/₈	4⁵/₈	4⁵/₈	6	5	1⁶/₈	4184	76
■ Fulton Co. – John Brink – John Brink – 1978											
162	27⁵/₈	26¹/₈	18³/₈	20⁷/₈	4⁶/₈	4⁷/₈	6	7	7⁵/₈	4184	76
■ Lonoke Co. – Picked Up – C.J. Fuller – PR 1990											
161⁴/₈	24⁷/₈	24⁴/₈	20³/₈	21³/₈	4¹/₈	4²/₈	6	5	1³/₈	4258	78
■ Sebastian Co. – Gary Coward – Gary Coward – 1989											
161²/₈	24³/₈	24	18⁴/₈	20	5	4⁶/₈	5	5		4310	79
■ Desha Co. – Charles Walker – Warren Walker – 1955											

■ Location of Kill – Hunter – Owner – Date Killed

† The scores and ranking for trophies from the 25th Awards Entry Period are not final until the banquet is held on June 19, 2004.

ARKANSAS

NON-TYPICAL WHITETAIL DEER

Score	Length of Main Beam Right	Left	Inside Spread	Greatest Spread	Circumference at Smallest Place Between Burr and First Point Right	Left	Number of Points Right	Left	Lengths Abnormal Points	All-Time Rank	State Rank
$238\frac{3}{8}$	$24\frac{2}{8}$	$23\frac{2}{8}$	$13\frac{2}{8}$	$21\frac{7}{8}$	6	$5\frac{6}{8}$	12	15	$84\frac{5}{8}$	134	1
■ Prairie Co. – William Dooley – William Dooley – 1999											
$237\frac{5}{8}$	25	$22\frac{7}{8}$	$17\frac{3}{8}$	$24\frac{5}{8}$	$5\frac{2}{8}$	$5\frac{2}{8}$	18	18	$92\frac{4}{8}$	145	2
■ Cross Co. – Picked Up – Kevin Ward – 1994											
232	$17\frac{4}{8}$	$16\frac{6}{8}$	$18\frac{3}{8}$	$23\frac{7}{8}$	$4\frac{4}{8}$	$4\frac{4}{8}$	26	22	$102\frac{6}{8}$	209†	3†
■ Monroe Co. – Picked Up – Kirk Brann – 2000											
$223\frac{5}{8}$	$26\frac{2}{8}$	$26\frac{3}{8}$	$19\frac{6}{8}$	$26\frac{5}{8}$	$5\frac{1}{8}$	$5\frac{1}{8}$	12	11	$47\frac{3}{8}$	345	4
■ St. Francis Co. – Tony Gore – Tony Gore – 1999											
$222\frac{3}{8}$	$24\frac{2}{8}$	$23\frac{3}{8}$	18	$23\frac{7}{8}$	$4\frac{2}{8}$	$4\frac{3}{8}$	15	14	$67\frac{3}{8}$	384	5
■ Ashley Co. – Picked Up – Al Bilgisher – 1959											
220	$26\frac{3}{8}$	$26\frac{2}{8}$	$18\frac{7}{8}$	$23\frac{3}{8}$	$4\frac{4}{8}$	$4\frac{5}{8}$	16	13	$41\frac{3}{8}$	441†	6†
■ Scott Co. – Daniel Boyd – Daniel Boyd – 2001											
$217\frac{3}{8}$	$30\frac{4}{8}$	29	$28\frac{4}{8}$	$30\frac{5}{8}$	5	5	8	8	$26\frac{7}{8}$	514	7
■ Cross Co. – Randal Harris – Randal Harris – 1986											
216	$29\frac{4}{8}$	$29\frac{4}{8}$	$19\frac{1}{8}$	$24\frac{4}{8}$	$5\frac{2}{8}$	$5\frac{2}{8}$	11	10	$23\frac{3}{8}$	565	8
■ Prairie Co. – Cecil M. Miller – Cecil M. Miller – 1973											
$210\frac{3}{8}$	$25\frac{1}{8}$	$25\frac{1}{8}$	$20\frac{6}{8}$	25	$5\frac{2}{8}$	5	10	9	$25\frac{3}{8}$	796	9
■ White Co. – Chester Weathers, Sr. – Chester Weathers, Jr. – 1973											
$209\frac{5}{8}$	$25\frac{1}{8}$	$25\frac{3}{8}$	$16\frac{5}{8}$	$23\frac{3}{8}$	$5\frac{3}{8}$	$5\frac{2}{8}$	13	12	$49\frac{6}{8}$	840	10
■ Jefferson Co. – Kenneth Colson – Kenneth Colson – 1968											
$208\frac{7}{8}$	$24\frac{5}{8}$	$23\frac{3}{8}$	$18\frac{4}{8}$	$22\frac{3}{8}$	$4\frac{2}{8}$	$4\frac{2}{8}$	11	16	$55\frac{5}{8}$	877	11
■ Bradley Co. – Carthel Forte – Carthel Forte – 1971											
$208\frac{5}{8}$	$27\frac{4}{8}$	$26\frac{5}{8}$	$22\frac{4}{8}$	$24\frac{1}{8}$	$4\frac{6}{8}$	5	9	12	$36\frac{7}{8}$	888	12
■ St. Francis Co. – George W. Hobson – George W. Hobson – 1987											
$208\frac{4}{8}$	$23\frac{4}{8}$	$23\frac{1}{8}$	$19\frac{7}{8}$	$27\frac{1}{8}$	$4\frac{2}{8}$	$4\frac{2}{8}$	17	10	$50\frac{7}{8}$	894	13
■ Pope Co. – Danny L. Reed – Danny L. Reed – 1999											
$208\frac{1}{8}$	$23\frac{5}{8}$	$24\frac{2}{8}$	21	$24\frac{2}{8}$	$5\frac{3}{8}$	$6\frac{2}{8}$	10	11	$31\frac{7}{8}$	920†	14†
■ Monroe Co. – Picked Up – Donald Barkley – 2000											
$207\frac{7}{8}$	$28\frac{3}{8}$	$28\frac{3}{8}$	$18\frac{4}{8}$	$25\frac{2}{8}$	$5\frac{3}{8}$	$5\frac{1}{8}$	14	8	$33\frac{1}{8}$	938	15
■ Union Co. – Unknown – Travis Worthington – PR 1952											
$207\frac{6}{8}$	18	$18\frac{1}{8}$	$16\frac{4}{8}$	$21\frac{1}{8}$	5	5	14	13	64	951	16
■ Cross Co. – Picked Up – Aaron Mauldin – PR 1996											
$205\frac{3}{8}$	$19\frac{7}{8}$	$23\frac{4}{8}$	20	24	$5\frac{6}{8}$	$4\frac{7}{8}$	12	7	$74\frac{3}{8}$	1116	17
■ White Co. – Charles L. Marcum, Jr. – Charles L. Marcum, Jr. – 1998											
$205\frac{2}{8}$	$27\frac{5}{8}$	$27\frac{1}{8}$	$19\frac{4}{8}$	$21\frac{3}{8}$	5	5	7	11	$22\frac{4}{8}$	1131	18
■ Cross Co. – Gordon R. Banton – Gordon R. Banton – 1992											
$204\frac{6}{8}$	$24\frac{5}{8}$	$25\frac{1}{8}$	$18\frac{3}{8}$	$20\frac{4}{8}$	$5\frac{2}{8}$	$5\frac{4}{8}$	11	16	$34\frac{5}{8}$	1165	19
■ Clay Co. – Rob W. Boling – Rob W. Boling – 1996											

■ Location of Kill – Hunter – Owner – Date Killed

Score	Length of Main Beam Right Left	Inside Spread	Greatest Spread	Circumference at Smallest Place Between Burr and First Point Right Left	Number of Points Right Left	Lengths Abnormal Points	All-Time Rank	State Rank
	■ Location of Kill – Hunter – Owner – Date Killed							
203 6/8	27 1/8 28	19 7/8	23 1/8	4 7/8 4 7/8	10 9	16 7/8	1237	20
	■ Phillips Co. – Dolph Horton – N.V. Hyde, Jr. – 1948							
201 4/8	22 5/8 23	15 4/8	17 6/8	4 3/8 4 4/8	8 8	27	1443	21
	■ Monroe Co. – Hugh Erwin – Randy Erwin – 1962							
201 1/8	28 2/8 27 3/8	16 5/8	21 6/8	5 1/8 5 2/8	8 9	24 4/8	1489	22
	■ Arkansas Co. – Daniel B. Bullock – Daniel B. Bullock – 1953							
201 1/8	20 3/8 19 3/8	20 3/8	27 4/8	4 4 2/8	10 9	33 2/8	1489	22
	■ Lincoln Co. – H.R. Morgan, Jr. – H.R. Morgan, Jr. – 1977							
200 7/8	22 5/8 28 4/8	18 6/8	22 3/8	4 5/8 4 6/8	10 9	36 5/8	1512	24
	■ Lawrence Co. – E.B. Ivie – Jimmy Huskey – 1928							
200 7/8	26 1/8 26 4/8	18	21	5 2/8 5 1/8	10 11	25 3/8	1512	24
	■ Desha Co. – Edgar Farmer – Harold Farmer – 1963							
200 7/8	23 6/8 19 4/8	20	25 7/8	4 5/8 4 5/8	13 14	58 3/8	1512	24
	■ Pulaski Co. – Lyle K. Sinkey – Lyle K. Sinkey – 1994							
199 4/8	26 2/8 27 2/8	22 4/8	24 6/8	5 1/8 5	9 15	46 2/8	1631	27
	■ Cross Co. – Picked Up – William Loyd, Jr. – 1992							
197 7/8	22 5/8 25 7/8	29 7/8	30 6/8	4 7/8 4 7/8	10 10	30 2/8	1816	28
	■ Cross Co. – Picked Up – Jimmy W. Rhodes – 1993							
197 4/8	26 6/8 26 4/8	19 1/8	22	5 1/8 5 1/8	7 7	19 3/8	1866	29
	■ Independence Co. – Terry L. Pease – Terry L. Pease – 1993							
196 4/8	26 6/8 28 5/8	19	21 6/8	5 4 7/8	8 8	20	1999	30
	■ Desha Co. – Turner Neal – Turner Neal – 1955							
196 4/8	27 27 7/8	23 6/8	27 4/8	5 1/8 5	10 10	20	1999	30
	■ Garland Co. – Eldon G. Sisney – Eldon G. Sisney – 1986							
195 1/8	25 3/8 24 6/8	19 1/8	27 3/8	4 2/8 4 2/8	10 9	32	2208	32
	■ Lonoke Co. – John W. Henderson – John W. Henderson – 1995							
191 7/8	25 2/8 24 3/8	19	25 3/8	4 3/8 4 2/8	11 7	42 3/8	2351	33
	■ Cross Co. – John H. Andrews – John H. Andrews – 1994							
190	24 6/8 24 5/8	14 3/8	17 3/8	6 6	8 9	17 1/8	2418†	34†
	■ Crittenden Co. – Warren H. Barry, Jr. – Warren H. Barry, Jr. – 2000							
189 1/8	24 4/8 24 7/8	16 6/8	18 3/8	4 7/8 5	10 10	45 3/8	2450	35
	■ Garland Co. – John D. Robinson – John D. Robinson – 1993							
188 7/8	24 2/8 24 1/8	15 5/8	16 1/8	6 4/8 6 2/8	10 10	34 6/8	2462	36
	■ Benton Co. – Bill Gregory – C.L. Gunter – PR 1972							
186 6/8	25 6/8 26	21 7/8	26 2/8	4 7/8 4 7/8	8 7	18 5/8	2559	37
	■ Clark Co. – Dwight A. Cupples – Dwight A. Cupples – 1993							
186 1/8	27 7/8 27	17 6/8	19 7/8	5 3/8 5 2/8	6 8	15 3/8	2581	38
	■ Sevier Co. – Tracy Runnels – Tracy Runnels – 1994							
185 6/8	24 5/8 24 3/8	16 3/8	20 1/8	5 5	10 7	9 7/8	2605	39
	■ Washington Co. – Gary D. Powell – Gary D. Powell – 1994							

† The scores and ranking for trophies from the 25th Awards Entry Period are not final until the banquet is held on June 19, 2004.

COLORADO
RECORD WHITETAILS

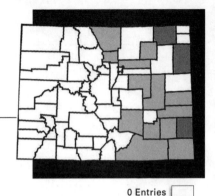

17 Typical whitetail deer entries
15 Non-typical whitetail deer entries
7,265 Total whitetail deer entries

0 Entries
1-2 Entries
3-5 Entries
6-10 Entries
11+ Entries

NEW
STATE
RECORD

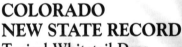

COLORADO
NEW STATE RECORD
Typical Whitetail Deer
Score: 186^3/8
Location: Adams Co.
Hunter and Owner: David A.
        McCracken
Date: 1996

Photograph by Susan C. Reneau,
Colorado's Biggest Bucks and Bulls

COLORADO
NEW STATE RECORD
Non-Typical Whitetail Deer
Score: $239^2/8$
Location: Prowers Co.
Hunter and Owner: Scott M. Tenold
Date: 1997

Photograph courtesy of Gale Sup

COLORADO

TYPICAL WHITETAIL DEER

Score	Length of Main Beam Right	Left	Inside Spread	Greatest Spread	Circumference at Smallest Place Between Burr and First Point Right	Left	Number of Points Right	Left	Lengths Abnormal Points	All-Time Rank	State Rank
	■ Location of Kill – Hunter – Owner – Date Killed										
186³⁄₈	25⁴⁄₈	24⁴⁄₈	18⁴⁄₈	20³⁄₈	5⁶⁄₈	5⁶⁄₈	8	8	6⁵⁄₈	210	1
	■ Adams Co. – David A. McCracken – David A. McCracken – 1996										
183	29⁴⁄₈	28⁵⁄₈	20⁴⁄₈	23³⁄₈	5³⁄₈	5³⁄₈	5	5		392†	2†
	■ Sedgwick Co. – Glenn W. Vinton – Glenn W. Vinton – 2000										
182⁵⁄₈	23⁶⁄₈	24³⁄₈	19⁴⁄₈	22¹⁄₈	5⁵⁄₈	5⁷⁄₈	6	8	4⁵⁄₈	420	3
	■ Yuma Co. – Ivan W. Rhodes – Ivan W. Rhodes – 1978										
180²⁄₈	25¹⁄₈	25³⁄₈	20⁴⁄₈	22⁶⁄₈	4⁴⁄₈	4³⁄₈	5	5		651	4
	■ Yuma Co. – Jeff L. Mekelburg – Jeff L. Mekelburg – 1989 ■ See photo on page 83										
178⁴⁄₈	25¹⁄₈	25³⁄₈	16¹⁄₈	18⁷⁄₈	5²⁄₈	5²⁄₈	6	6	3⁵⁄₈	850	5
	■ Yuma Co. – Terry M. Scheidecker – Terry M. Scheidecker – 1979										
176³⁄₈	27²⁄₈	28	20⁵⁄₈	26⁴⁄₈	5²⁄₈	5²⁄₈	4	4		1182	6
	■ Boulder Co. – Picked Up – Michael J. Scrivner – 1989										
175⁷⁄₈	24⁶⁄₈	25⁵⁄₈	17¹⁄₈	19⁵⁄₈	4⁵⁄₈	4⁴⁄₈	5	5		1287	7
	■ Logan Co. – Picked Up – Marvin Gardner – 1971										
175⁶⁄₈	24¹⁄₈	24²⁄₈	21¹⁄₈	22⁴⁄₈	5⁷⁄₈	5⁷⁄₈	6	7	5¹⁄₈	1310†	8†
	■ Logan Co. – Thomas P. Grainger – Thomas P. Grainger – 2000										
175¹⁄₈	25¹⁄₈	24⁵⁄₈	23⁷⁄₈	25⁶⁄₈	6²⁄₈	6²⁄₈	5	6	2	1440	9
	■ Otero Co. – Kenny D. Mills – Kenny D. Mills – 1992										
174⁵⁄₈	25¹⁄₈	25⁵⁄₈	30⁴⁄₈	31⁴⁄₈	4⁴⁄₈	4⁵⁄₈	5	6	1⁶⁄₈	1561	10
	■ Larimer Co. – George S. Sumter, Jr. – George S. Sumter, Jr. – 1990										
173³⁄₈	26³⁄₈	24⁴⁄₈	16⁵⁄₈	18⁶⁄₈	5⁶⁄₈	5⁶⁄₈	6	5		1883	11
	■ Bent Co. – Rick J. Tokarski – Rick J. Tokarski – 1994										
173³⁄₈	26⁵⁄₈	26⁴⁄₈	20¹⁄₈	23¹⁄₈	5⁶⁄₈	5⁶⁄₈	7	5	1	1883	11
	■ Prowers Co. – Les F. Ohlhauser – Les F. Ohlhauser – 1997										
171²⁄₈	21¹⁄₈	21	16⁷⁄₈	19⁴⁄₈	5	5¹⁄₈	8	7	8¹⁄₈	2621	13
	■ Yuma Co. – John O. Cletcher, Jr. – John O. Cletcher, Jr. – 1985										
170⁵⁄₈	25²⁄₈	26⁶⁄₈	20²⁄₈	22¹⁄₈	6	5⁷⁄₈	7	6	5⁵⁄₈	2876	14
	■ Prowers Co. – Douglas W. Kuhns – Douglas W. Kuhns – 1987										
170²⁄₈	26³⁄₈	27	20⁴⁄₈	23¹⁄₈	5¹⁄₈	5²⁄₈	5	5		3063	15
	■ Lincoln Co. – Joseph C. Fox – Joseph C. Fox – 1992										
164²⁄₈	22⁶⁄₈	21⁶⁄₈	15²⁄₈	17²⁄₈	5²⁄₈	5¹⁄₈	4	4		3876	16
	■ Lincoln Co. – Richard J. Larson – Richard J. Larson – 1995										
162⁷⁄₈	27⁴⁄₈	26⁴⁄₈	19²⁄₈	23¹⁄₈	5²⁄₈	5	7	5	9⁵⁄₈	4067	17
	■ Elbert Co. – Michael A. Franek – Michael A. Franek – 1993										

†The scores and ranking for trophies from the 25th Awards Entry Period are not final until the banquet is held on June 19, 2004.

TROPHIES IN THE FIELD

HUNTER:	Jeff L. Mekelburg
SCORE:	180-2/8
CATEGORY:	typical whitetail deer
LOCATION:	Yuma County, Colorado
DATE:	1989

COLORADO

NON-TYPICAL WHITETAIL DEER

Score	Length of Main Beam		Inside Spread	Greatest Spread	Circumference at Smallest Place Between Burr and First Point		Number of Points		Lengths Abnormal Points	All-Time Rank	State Rank
	Right	Left			Right	Left	Right	Left			

Location of Kill – Hunter – Owner – Date Killed

239^2/8	25^5/8	26^6/8	22^4/8	24^6/8	7^1/8	6^6/8	13	9	59^6/8	124	1

■ *Prowers Co. – Scott M. Tenold – Scott M. Tenold – 1997*

233^3/8	27	26^4/8	18^3/8	25^2/8	5^3/8	5^6/8	13	12	40^4/8	191	2

■ *Pueblo Co. – Raymond A. Vertovec – Raymond A. Vertovec – 1994*

228^2/8	24^5/8	26^1/8	20^4/8	23^5/8	6^4/8	6^4/8	15	12	49^6/8	263†	3†

■ *Weld Co. – Ronald E. Kammerzell – Ronald E. Kammerzell – 2001*

228	23^2/8	23^3/8	18^1/8	24^3/8	5^5/8	5^6/8	13	12	64^7/8	268	4

■ *Las Animas Co. – Brad C. Hardin – Brad C. Hardin – 1998*

209^1/8	25^4/8	26	26	28	6	5^7/8	11	9	43^3/8	863	5

■ *Prowers Co. – Paul D. Mirley – Paul D. Mirley – 1997*

204^2/8	27^3/8	27^7/8	21^4/8	23^4/8	6^2/8	6	9	8	26^2/8	1199	6

■ *Yuma Co. – Jeff L. Mekelburg – Jeff L. Mekelburg – 1986*

203^2/8	26^2/8	25^1/8	24^4/8	26^7/8	4^7/8	5	6	6	18	1287†	7†

■ *Logan Co. – Wade D. Shults – Wade D. Shults – 2000* ■ *See photo on page 85*

202^5/8	29	28^2/8	20^5/8	23^7/8	4^7/8	4^7/8	7	8	19^4/8	1346†	8†

■ *Weld Co. – Picked Up – Matt Yocam – 1999*

201^3/8	26^6/8	26^3/8	20	24^1/8	5^5/8	5^4/8	9	9	14^7/8	1461	9

■ *Kiowa Co. – Dale A. Dilulo – Dale A. Dilulo – 1991*

200^3/8	25^3/8	27^4/8	20^4/8	25^2/8	5^3/8	5^5/8	6	10	19^1/8	1556	10

■ *Logan Co. – Picked Up – Dennis D. Reid – 1994*

200	26^6/8	25^6/8	17^5/8	24^2/8	5^4/8	5^3/8	10	8	34^1/8	1591	11

■ *Baca Co. – David Sanford – David Sanford – 1996*

199^1/8	25^2/8	24^3/8	19^4/8	22^2/8	5	5	8	8	27^7/8	1660	12

■ *Morgan Co. – Michael L. Furcolow – Michael L. Furcolow – 1997*

197^6/8	24^5/8	24^6/8	13^4/8	16^4/8	4^6/8	4^4/8	11	9	25^2/8	1833	13

■ *Prowers Co. – Samuel S. Pattillo – Samuel S. Pattillo – 1988*

186	22	21^2/8	21^2/8	25^6/8	4^6/8	5^1/8	9	10	28^6/8	2586†	14†

■ *Logan Co. – Bucky D. Barber – Bucky D. Barber – 2000*

258^2/8	23	23	16^2/8	25^5/8	6^4/8	6^1/8	14	15	1	*	*

■ *Cheyenne Co. – Michael J. Okray – Bass Pro Shops – 1992*

---

† The scores and ranking for trophies from the 25th Awards Entry Period are not final until the banquet is held on June 19, 2004.

* Final score is subject to revision by additional verifying measurements.

TROPHIES IN THE FIELD

HUNTER: Wade D. Shults
SCORE: 203-2/8
CATEGORY: non-typical whitetail deer
LOCATION: Logan County, Colorado
DATE: 2000

CONNECTICUT
RECORD WHITETAILS

4 Typical whitetail deer entries
4 Non-typical whitetail deer entries
7,265 Total whitetail deer entries

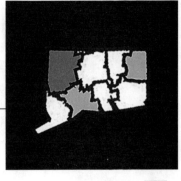

0 Entries
1-2 Entries
3-5 Entries
6-10 Entries
11+ Entries

CONNECTICUT STATE RECORD
Typical Whitetail Deer
Score: 179 $^4/_8$
Location: Litchfield Co.
Hunter and Owner:
    Garry J. Lovrin
Date: 1993

CONNECTICUT
NEW STATE RECORD
Non-Typical Whitetail Deer
Score: 201$^{7}/_{8}$
Location: New London Co.
Hunter and Owner:
  Henry M. Konow, Jr.
Date: 2000

New state record pending approval from the 25th Awards Program Judges Panel.

CONNECTICUT

TYPICAL WHITETAIL DEER

Score	Length of Main Beam Right	Left	Inside Spread	Greatest Spread	Circumference at Smallest Place Between Burr and First Point Right	Left	Number of Points Right	Left	Lengths Abnormal Points	All-Time Rank	State Rank
	■ Location of Kill – Hunter – Owner – Date Killed										
179⁴/8	30¹/8	29²/8	23	25³/8	4⁶/8	5	5	5		733	1
	■ Litchfield Co. – Garry J. Lovrin – Garry J. Lovrin – 1993										
177²/8	27⁵/8	29	21⁷/8	24³/8	6	6	5	6	5⁵/8	1025	2
	■ Litchfield Co. – Picked Up – Rickey A. Vincent – 1984										
176²/8	26²/8	26³/8	20⁴/8	23¹/8	4⁶/8	5	5	7	4	1209	3
	■ Litchfield Co. – Frederick H. Clymer – Frederick H. Clymer – 1987										
167⁶/8	25³/8	24¹/8	17¹/8	19⁶/8	4⁷/8	5	6	6	1¹/8	3461	4
	■ Litchfield Co. – Charles D. Brown – Charles D. Brown – 1981										

CONNECTICUT

NON-TYPICAL WHITETAIL DEER

Score	Length of Main Beam		Inside Spread	Greatest Spread	Circumference at Smallest Place Between Burr and First Point		Number of Points		Lengths Abnormal Points	All-Time Rank	State Rank
	Right	Left			Right	Left	Right	Left			
	■ Location of Kill – Hunter – Owner – Date Killed										
201⁷/8	28²/8	28⁴/8	24	29⁷/8	5¹/8	5²/8	10	9	38¹/8	1410†	1†
	■ New London Co. – Henry M. Konow, Jr. – Henry M. Konow, Jr. – 2000										
195	27²/8	25⁵/8	21⁵/8	27⁶/8	5³/8	5⁴/8	9	7	18⁵/8	2233	2
	■ Windham Co. – Harold Tanner – Warren W. Rogers – 1970										
188³/8	25²/8	26³/8	17¹/8	20²/8	5¹/8	5	7	9	34⁴/8	2478	3
	■ New Haven Co. – Christopher K. Krista – Christopher K. Krista – 1998										
186⁶/8	24⁷/8	23⁷/8	23⁴/8	25	4²/8	4³/8	8	10	38⁴/8	2559†	4†
	■ Windham Co. – Theodore G. Decyk – Theodore G. Decyk – 2000										

† The scores and ranking for trophies from the 25th Awards Entry Period are not final until the banquet is held on June 19, 2004.

DELAWARE
RECORD WHITETAILS

12 Typical whitetail deer entries
2 Non-typical whitetail deer entries
7,265 Total whitetail deer entries

0 Entries	
1-2 Entries	
3-5 Entries	
6-10 Entries	
11+ Entries	

DELAWARE
STATE RECORD
Typical Whitetail Deer
Score: 185⁴/₈
Location: Sussex Co.
Hunter and Owner: Herbert N. Milam
Date: 1978

DELAWARE
STATE RECORD
Non-Typical Whitetail Deer
Score: 190$^4/_8$
Location: Kent Co.
Hunter: Russell C. Bowdle
Owner: William A. Wise
Date: 1960

DELAWARE

TYPICAL WHITETAIL DEER

Score	Length of Main Beam Right	Length of Main Beam Left	Inside Spread	Greatest Spread	Circumference at Smallest Place Between Burr and First Point Right	Circumference at Smallest Place Between Burr and First Point Left	Number of Points Right	Number of Points Left	Lengths Abnormal Points	All-Time Rank	State Rank

■ Location of Kill – Hunter – Owner – Date Killed

Score	Right	Left	Inside	Greatest	Right	Left	Right	Left	Abnormal	All-Time	State
185 4/8	26 2/8	26 3/8	20 2/8	22 4/8	4 6/8	4 6/8	5	5		251	1
				■ *Sussex Co. – Herbert N. Milam – Herbert N. Milam – 1978*							
181 6/8	27 5/8	27 7/8	21 4/8	22 2/8	4 4/8	4 3/8	5	5		492	2
				■ *Sussex Co. – Donald L. Betts – Donald L. Betts – 1989*							
174 2/8	27 3/8	27 2/8	19 4/8	21 4/8	5	4 6/8	5	5		1652	3
				■ *Sussex Co. – J.R. Cropper – J.R. Cropper – 1997*							
173 2/8	24 7/8	26	17 6/8	19 2/8	4 3/8	4 2/8	6	6	2 2/8	1914	4
				■ *Kent Co. – William R. Conner – William R. Conner – 1984*							
172 2/8	26 3/8	25 5/8	19 5/8	21 7/8	5	5 1/8	6	7	1 5/8	2237	5
				■ *Sussex Co. – David T. Murray – David T. Murray – 1992*							
168 6/8	26	27	19 2/8	21 3/8	4	3 7/8	5	5		3367	6
				■ *Sussex Co. – William H. Cropper, Jr. – William H. Cropper, Jr. – 1996*							
168 2/8	27 5/8	27 2/8	18 4/8	22 3/8	4 1/8	4 1/8	7	8	9 4/8	3414†	7†
				■ *Sussex Co. – Edward L. Howell, Jr. – Edward L. Howell, Jr. – 2000*							
164 6/8	27 1/8	27 4/8	19 6/8	21 5/8	5 2/8	5 2/8	5	6	2 6/8	3809†	8†
				■ *New Castle Co. – John H. Doherty – John H. Doherty – 2001*							
163 1/8	23 1/8	24 4/8	18 3/8	20 4/8	5 1/8	5	5	5		4035	9
				■ *Kent Co. – Austin M. Carney – Austin M. Carney – 1989*							
162 7/8	25 2/8	27 4/8	17 6/8	21 1/8	5 4/8	5 6/8	6	7	9 3/8	4067	10
				■ *Kent Co. – Michael J. Biggs – Michael J. Biggs – 1991*							
160 6/8	25 4/8	25 2/8	19 6/8	21 6/8	5	4 6/8	4	5	2	4402†	11†
				■ *Sussex Co. – Harry H. Isaacs III – Harry H. Isaacs III – 2001*							
160 6/8	25 1/8	25 1/8	21 6/8	23 6/8	6 3/8	6 3/8	4	6	3	4402	11
				■ *Sussex Co. – Richard A. Davis – Richard A. Davis – 1999*							

† The scores and ranking for trophies from the 25th Awards Entry Period are not final until the banquet is held on June 19, 2004.

DELAWARE

NON-TYPICAL WHITETAIL DEER

Score	Length of Main Beam Right Left	Inside Spread	Greatest Spread	Circumference at Smallest Place Between Burr and First Point Right Left	Number of Points Right Left	Lengths Abnormal Points	All-Time Rank	State Rank
	■ *Location of Kill – Hunter – Owner – Date Killed*							
190⁴/₈	26⁷/₈ 27⁶/₈	19²/₈	20⁷/₈	4⁴/₈ 4⁴/₈	6 7	16⁴/₈	2401	1
	■ *Kent Co. – Russell C. Bowdle – William A. Wise – 1960*							
189¹/₈	22⁷/₈ 23⁵/₈	16	18⁶/₈	4⁵/₈ 4⁵/₈	9 7	34⁷/₈	2450	2
	■ *Kent Co. – Barry D. Smith – Barry D. Smith – 1996*							

FLORIDA
RECORD WHITETAILS

0 Typical whitetail deer entries
2 Non-typical whitetail deer entries
7,265 Total whitetail deer entries

0 Entries
1-2 Entries
3-5 Entries
6-10 Entries
11+ Entries

FLORIDA
STATE RECORD
Non-Typical Whitetail Deer
Score: 201³/₈
Location: Wakulla Co.
Hunter and Owner: Clark Durrance
Date: 1941

FLORIDA

NON-TYPICAL WHITETAIL DEER

Score	Length of Main Beam Right Left	Inside Spread	Greatest Spread	Circumference at Smallest Place Between Burr and First Point Right Left		Number of Points Right Left		Lengths Abnormal Points	All-Time Rank	State Rank
	■ Location of Kill – Hunter – Owner – Date Killed									
201³/8	24¹/8 23⁵/8	17³/8	27	5³/8	5⁴/8	11	14	40⁶/8	1461	1
	■ Wakulla Co. – Clark Durrance – Clark Durrance – 1941									
186¹/8	23³/8 23⁶/8	18³/8	23⁷/8	4⁶/8	5	17	12	35²/8	2581	2
	■ Jackson Co. – Henry Brinson – T.L. Brinson – 1959									

GEORGIA
RECORD WHITETAILS

118 Typical whitetail deer entries
34 Non-typical whitetail deer entries
7,265 Total whitetail deer entries

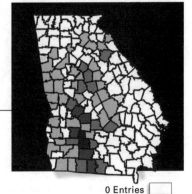

0 Entries
1-2 Entries
3-5 Entries
6-10 Entries
11+ Entries

GEORGIA
NEW STATE RECORD
Typical Whitetail Deer
Score: 191⁴/8
Location: Monroe Co.
Hunter and Owner: Buck Ashe
Date: Prior to 1962

Photograph courtesy of Bill Cooper

NEW STATE RECORD

**GEORGIA
STATE RECORD**
Non-Typical Whitetail Deer
Score: 240³/₈
Location: Monroe Co.
Hunter and Owner: John L. Hatton, Jr.
Date: 1973

GEORGIA

TYPICAL WHITETAIL DEER

Score	Length of Main Beam Right	Left	Inside Spread	Greatest Spread	Circumference at Smallest Place Between Burr and First Point Right	Left	Number of Points Right	Left	Lengths Abnormal Points	All-Time Rank	State Rank
	■ Location of Kill – Hunter – Owner – Date Killed										
191 4/8	30 7/8	30 4/8	22 3/8	24 7/8	5 7/8	5 2/8	9	7	12 5/8	82	1
	■ Monroe Co. – Buck Ashe – Buck Ashe – PR 1962										
184 3/8	26	26 6/8	20 6/8	23 4/8	5 3/8	5 6/8	5	6	2 1/8	313	2
	■ Paulding Co. – Floyd Benson – Floyd Benson – 1962										
184 2/8	25 5/8	24 7/8	17 6/8	19 6/8	5 2/8	5 1/8	6	6		319	3
	■ Dooly Co. – Joe Morgan – Joe Morgan – 1985										
184	27 4/8	29 1/8	18 4/8	20 5/8	5	4 7/8	5	6		334	4
	■ Newton Co. – Gene Almand – Duncan A. Dobie – 1966										
184	25	24 4/8	17 4/8	20 3/8	4 1/8	4	6	6		334	4
	■ Hart Co. – Kenton L. Adams – Kenton L. Adams – 1986										
180 7/8	29	29 6/8	20 4/8	23 1/8	5 2/8	5 2/8	7	6	5 5/8	573	6
	■ Jones Co. – James H.C. Kitchens – James H.C. Kitchens – 1957										
180 2/8	28 1/8	28 4/8	18 4/8	21 4/8	4 6/8	4 6/8	5	5		651	7
	■ Newton Co. – David Moon – David Moon – 1972										
179 2/8	25 4/8	24 6/8	21 3/8	23 2/8	4 5/8	4 6/8	7	7	1 3/8	763	8
	■ Lamar Co. – Gary Littlejohn – Gary Littlejohn – 1968										
179 1/8	28 6/8	27 1/8	18 2/8	20 2/8	4 4/8	4 4/8	6	6	2 1/8	779	9
	■ Twiggs Co. – Cy Smith – Duncan A. Dobie – 1970										
179	26 6/8	26 2/8	21 4/8	23 2/8	4 4/8	4 6/8	5	6		786	10
	■ Jasper Co. – Hubert R. Moody – Hubert R. Moody – 1957										
179	28 4/8	28 5/8	20 6/8	15 2/8	4 5/8	4 7/8	5	5		786	10
	■ Dooly Co. – Shannon Akin – Shannon Akin – 1981										
178 5/8	28 5/8	26 3/8	20	22 4/8	5 2/8	5 1/8	6	5	2 1/8	819	12
	■ Thomas Co. – Clyde E. Anderson – Clyde E. Anderson – 1969										
178 5/8	26 6/8	26 7/8	17 3/8	19 3/8	4 5/8	4 6/8	5	5		819	12
	■ Taylor Co. – W. Michael Layfield – W. Michael Layfield – 1997										
178 5/8	26 2/8	28	19 3/8	21 3/8	4 4/8	5 1/8	6	5	2	819	12
	■ Macon Co. – Brent McCarty – Brent McCarty – 1999										
178 3/8	29 4/8	29 7/8	19 5/8	21 6/8	5 2/8	5 2/8	5	6		868	15
	■ Mitchell Co. – Ricky C. Dowis – Ricky C. Dowis – 1997										
177 7/8	27 6/8	26 1/8	18 5/8	20 5/8	5 3/8	5 1/8	5	5		936	16
	■ Haralson Co. – Picked Up – Alfred Wright – 1982										
177 5/8	25	24 3/8	17 6/8	19 6/8	4 1/8	4 1/8	6	8	2 7/8	972	17
	■ Macon Co. – James W. Athon – Mike's Gun Shop – 1976										
177 5/8	25	25 4/8	17 5/8	19 7/8	5	5 2/8	6	6		972	17
	■ Macon Co. – Dalton H. Cannon – Dalton H. Cannon – 1977										
177 5/8	27 6/8	28 5/8	18	20 3/8	5 5/8	5 4/8	6	6	1 3/8	972	17
	■ Colquitt Co. – Timothy Carter – Timothy Carter – 1990										

Score	Length of Main Beam Right	Left	Inside Spread	Greatest Spread	Circumference at Smallest Place Between Burr and First Point Right	Left	Number of Points Right	Left	Lengths Abnormal Points	All-Time Rank	State Rank

■ *Location of Kill – Hunter – Owner – Date Killed*

Score	R	L	Inside	Greatest	Circ R	Circ L	Pts R	Pts L	Abn	All-Time	State
176²/8	28	26⁴/8	21	23³/8	5⁴/8	5⁴/8	8	7	7²/8	1209	20

■ *Macon Co. – Charles M. Wilson – Charles M. Wilson – 1981*

176²/8	24⁷/8	25⁴/8	20⁶/8	22⁵/8	4⁵/8	4⁷/8	6	6		1209	20

■ *Troup Co. – Claude A. McKibben, Jr. – James E. Lasater – 1984*

176¹/8	28⁴/8	26	23⁶/8	26¹/8	5	4⁷/8	5	5	3¹/8	1243	22

■ *Randolph Co. – Jeff Hill – Jeff Hill – 1991*

175⁷/8	26³/8	26³/8	17¹/8	19⁴/8	4⁶/8	4⁶/8	6	7		1287	23

■ *Brooks Co. – Joseph J. Freeman – Joseph J. Freeman – 1978*

175⁴/8	24⁵/8	25⁶/8	16²/8	18³/8	4⁷/8	5²/8	7	7	5²/8	1352	24

■ *Macon Co. – Charles W. Haynie – Charles W. Haynie – 1987*

175³/8	27¹/8	26⁶/8	18⁴/8	21³/8	5⁵/8	5⁵/8	6	5	2¹/8	1377	25

■ *Worth Co. – Picked Up – L. Edwin Massey – 1962*

174⁶/8	26⁵/8	26¹/8	20¹/8	22¹/8	4⁴/8	4⁶/8	6	5	1³/8	1534	26

■ *Talbot Co. – Harold Cole, Sr. – Harold Cole, Sr. – 1985*

173⁶/8	25²/8	25³/8	18²/8	20³/8	4³/8	4⁴/8	7	7		1766	27

■ *Carroll Co. – Ken Yearta – Ken Yearta – 1983*

173¹/8	24⁷/8	24⁶/8	16²/8	18³/8	5¹/8	5¹/8	5	6	3¹/8	1950	28

■ *Dodge Co. – Paul W. Smith – Paul W. Smith – 1993*

172⁷/8	26¹/8	27	18	20⁴/8	5³/8	5³/8	6	7	5¹/8	2038	29

■ *Newton Co. – L.W. Shirley, Jr. – L.W. Shirley, Jr. – 1967*

172⁷/8	26	27³/8	22⁵/8	24⁶/8	4⁴/8	4⁶/8	7	10	10⁴/8	2038	29

■ *Heard Co. – Keith McCullough – Keith McCullough – 1982*

172⁶/8	27¹/8	27⁷/8	17⁴/8	19³/8	5	5¹/8	5	5		2065	31

■ *Mitchell Co. – Al Collins – Al Collins – 1991*

172⁴/8	27⁵/8	27	23³/8	25¹/8	5³/8	5¹/8	7	5	1¹/8	2156	32

■ *Dougherty Co. – J.P. Flournoy – J.P. Flournoy – 1969*

172⁴/8	26⁷/8	25²/8	19	13¹/8	4⁶/8	4⁵/8	5	5		2156	32

■ *Randolph Co. – Robert D. Bell – Robert D. Bell – 1979*

172⁴/8	26⁵/8	27⁴/8	17²/8	20	4⁴/8	4⁵/8	5	5		2156	32

■ *Colquitt Co. – Alan Whitaker – Alan Whitaker – 1996*

172³/8	25⁶/8	26³/8	17	19⁴/8	6³/8	6²/8	7	9	8¹/8	2200†	35†

■ *Morgan Co. – Jeff L. Banks – Jeff L. Banks – 2001*

172³/8	28¹/8	28⁴/8	22⁵/8	24⁶/8	4³/8	4³/8	5	5		2200	35

■ *Fulton Co. – Michael Gregory – Lee E. Johnson – 1986*

172²/8	24⁷/8	25	18²/8	20⁵/8	4⁷/8	5	6	5	1⁶/8	2237	37

■ *Putnam Co. – Spunky Thornton – Spunky Thornton – 1983*

172¹/8	27⁶/8	27⁴/8	17⁵/8	19³/8	4³/8	4¹/8	6	6		2286	38

■ *Dooly Co. – Marty T. McNulty – Marty T. McNulty – 1990*

172	24¹/8	24¹/8	20²/8	22³/8	6⁵/8	6⁴/8	8	7	8²/8	2330	39

■ *Butts Co. – Jack Hammond – Jack Hammond – 1963*

172	24	25⁷/8	18	19⁷/8	4²/8	4²/8	6	5		2330	39

■ *Tift Co. – Mayo Tucker – Mayo Tucker – 1982*

Score	Length of Main Beam Right	Left	Inside Spread	Greatest Spread	Circumference at Smallest Place Between Burr and First Point Right	Left	Number of Points Right	Left	Lengths Abnormal Points	All-Time Rank	State Rank
					■ Location of Kill – Hunter – Owner – Date Killed						
171 6/8	28 3/8	29 2/8	23 7/8	25 7/8	6	6	8	8	7 7/8	2418	41
	■ Taylor Co. – Picked Up – Charles L. Childree – 1985										
171 6/8	26 6/8	27 3/8	20 2/8	22 4/8	4 3/8	4 4/8	5	6		2418	41
	■ Telfair Co. – Craig Walker – Craig Walker – 1993										
171 5/8	25 1/8	26 1/8	16 7/8	19 2/8	4	4	6	7	6	2470	43
	■ Baldwin Co. – Picked Up – E. Donald Graham – 1977										
171 3/8	26 7/8	26 6/8	17 7/8	21	4 7/8	4 6/8	8	6	5 4/8	2564	44
	■ Turner Co. – Jerry S. Cook – Jerry S. Cook – 1986										
170 6/8	24 4/8	24 1/8	16 4/8	18 4/8	4	4	7	7	2 4/8	2828	45
	■ Harris Co. – Gorman S. Riley – Gorman S. Riley – 1983										
170 6/8	28 5/8	29 1/8	20 4/8	23 1/8	5 2/8	5 2/8	5	6		2828	45
	■ Laurens Co. – Darrell Evans – Darrell Evans – 1992										
170 5/8	27 1/8	26 1/8	19 3/8	21 4/8	4 6/8	4 5/8	6	5		2876	47
	■ Jasper Co. – Gordon W. Cown – Gordon W. Cown – 1961										
170 5/8	28 7/8	28 2/8	19 5/8	21 5/8	4 6/8	4 6/8	7	7	5 4/8	2876	47
	■ Lowndes Co. – Jack L. Garrison – Jack L. Garrison – 1983										
170 5/8	26	25	20 2/8	23	4 7/8	4 7/8	6	6	3 5/8	2876	47
	■ Lee Co. – Stan R. Steiner – Stan R. Steiner – 1991										
170 4/8	25 3/8	25 4/8	18 3/8	19 7/8	5 2/8	5 2/8	6	6	2 7/8	2933	50
	■ Monroe Co. – T.E. Land – Jerry Moseley – 1958										
170 3/8	26 6/8	26 3/8	17 3/8	19 2/8	4 3/8	4 2/8	6	7	4 4/8	2992	51
	■ Coweta Co. – Douglas R. Freeman – Douglas R. Freeman – 1978										
170 3/8	23 6/8	24 3/8	15 7/8	18 2/8	4 4/8	4 4/8	5	6		2992	51
	■ Wilcox Co. – Scott H. Urguhart – Scott H. Urguhart – 1981										
170 3/8	25 2/8	25 4/8	18 6/8	20 4/8	5 2/8	4 7/8	6	6	2 1/8	2992	51
	■ Wilkinson Co. – James W. Whitaker – James W. Whitaker – 1982										
170 2/8	23 6/8	26 4/8	18 2/8	21	5 2/8	5 4/8	5	5		3063	54
	■ Oglethorpe Co. – H.D. Cannon – H.D. Cannon – 1971										
170 1/8	23 7/8	24 7/8	18 3/8	21 1/8	4 7/8	4 6/8	5	5		3143	55
	■ Oglethorpe Co. – Robert C. Thaxton – Robert C. Thaxton – 1978										
170 1/8	28 4/8	28 1/8	17 2/8	20 1/8	4 2/8	4 4/8	6	6	7 5/8	3143	55
	■ Taylor Co. – Joseph J. Ryals – Joseph J. Ryals – 1998										
170	25 6/8	25 4/8	16 1/8	18 4/8	5 4/8	5 3/8	6	7	1 1/8	3224	57
	■ Tift Co. – Alan Parrish – Alan Parrish – 1990										
170	28 3/8	27 4/8	17 4/8	19 6/8	4 1/8	4	6	6		3224	57
	■ Worth Co. – Travis Strenth – Travis Strenth – 1990										
169 7/8	25 1/8	25 4/8	19 4/8	21 4/8	4 2/8	4 3/8	8	5	5 7/8	3302	59
	■ Crawford Co. – Alan R. Williams – Alan R. Williams – 1975										
169	24 3/8	24 6/8	18 4/8	20 3/8	4	4 2/8	5	5		3348	60
	■ Colquitt Co. – Timothy G. Huffman, Sr. – Timothy G. Huffman, Sr. – 1984										
168 7/8	27 4/8	26 6/8	17 3/8	19 5/8	5 3/8	5 2/8	7	5	7 2/8	3361	61
	■ Brooks Co. – Mickey Tillman – Mickey Tillman – 2000										

Score	Length of Main Beam Right	Length of Main Beam Left	Inside Spread	Greatest Spread	Circumference at Smallest Place Between Burr and First Point Right	Circumference at Smallest Place Between Burr and First Point Left	Number of Points Right	Number of Points Left	Lengths Abnormal Points	All-Time Rank	State Rank
$167^7/8$	$25^4/8$	$26^2/8$	$20^5/8$	$22^3/8$	$4^7/8$	$4^6/8$	5	5		3451	62
■ Meriwether Co. – A.C. Heath, Jr. – A.C. Heath, Jr. – 1995
$167^4/8$	$30^2/8$	$30^6/8$	$19^6/8$	22	5	$4^2/8$	8	6	$8^2/8$	3485	63
■ Dougherty Co. – Bobby L. Joiner – Bobby L. Joiner – 1999
$167^3/8$	$25^1/8$	$24^6/8$	18	$20^3/8$	$4^2/8$	$4^3/8$	6	6	$1^5/8$	3500†	64†
■ Crawford Co. – Grant Allen – Grant Allen – 2000
$167^3/8$	$26^3/8$	$26^2/8$	$24^3/8$	$25^7/8$	$4^2/8$	4	6	6		3500	64
■ Telfair Co. – David A. Rawlins – David A. Rawlins – 1997
$167^1/8$	$28^5/8$	$26^7/8$	$19^1/8$	$21^1/8$	$4^4/8$	$4^4/8$	5	6		3539	66
■ Brooks Co. – Roger D. Meeks, Jr. – Roger D. Meeks, Jr. – 1991
167	$24^4/8$	$25^1/8$	$18^4/8$	21	4	4	5	5		3552	67
■ Dougherty Co. – Rhonda J. Smith – Rhonda J. Smith – 1991
167	$25^4/8$	$25^7/8$	$19^2/8$	$22^5/8$	$5^1/8$	$5^1/8$	5	5		3552	67
■ Lee Co. – Charles W. Peek, Jr. – Charles W. Peek, Jr. – 1995
$166^5/8$	$25^1/8$	$25^6/8$	$16^5/8$	$19^2/8$	$4^4/8$	$4^4/8$	6	7	3	3598	69
■ Tift Co. – Thomas W. Johnson – Thomas W. Johnson – 1993
$166^3/8$	$27^1/8$	$26^2/8$	$18^4/8$	$20^1/8$	5	$4^6/8$	8	6	$5^5/8$	3620	70
■ Lowndes Co. – Jack D. Knight – Jack D. Knight – 1981
$165^5/8$	$27^3/8$	$27^6/8$	$23^3/8$	$25^7/8$	5	$4^7/8$	5	4		3696	71
■ Sumter Co. – Heath Bass – Heath Bass – 1989
$165^1/8$	$27^4/8$	26	$18^7/8$	21	$4^4/8$	$4^4/8$	5	5		3767	72
■ Dooly Co. – Billy W. Gilbert – Billy W. Gilbert – 1990
$165^1/8$	25	$23^6/8$	22	$24^3/8$	$4^2/8$	$4^3/8$	6	6	$8^1/8$	3767	72
■ Worth Co. – Leon McDonald – Leon McDonald – 1999
$164^6/8$	$25^7/8$	$27^2/8$	$18^6/8$	$20^4/8$	$4^6/8$	$4^4/8$	5	5		3809	74
■ Hall Co. – Donnie Mitchell, Sr. – Donnie Mitchell, Sr. – 1994
$164^6/8$	$25^5/8$	$24^7/8$	$18^6/8$	$21^6/8$	$4^4/8$	$4^5/8$	5	6	2	3809	74
■ Worth Co. – Alan D. Brightwell – Alan D. Brightwell – 1998
$164^5/8$	$25^2/8$	$25^5/8$	$19^4/8$	$24^1/8$	5	5	7	7	$4^5/8$	3835†	76†
■ Berrien Co. – Tim L. Touchton – Tim L. Touchton – 2000
$164^5/8$	$24^2/8$	$24^2/8$	$17^7/8$	$19^5/8$	$4^3/8$	$4^5/8$	5	5		3835	76
■ Jones Co. – Larry D. Scarborough – Larry D. Scarborough – 1981
$164^2/8$	25	$25^5/8$	18	23	$5^4/8$	$5^6/8$	7	8	$11^2/8$	3876	78
■ Early Co. – Denny D. Morgan – Denny D. Morgan – 1990
$163^6/8$	$27^1/8$	26	$18^4/8$	$20^4/8$	$4^4/8$	$4^3/8$	5	5		3946	79
■ Colquitt Co. – Delbert Brown – Delbert Brown – 1971
$163^5/8$	$26^1/8$	$25^5/8$	$18^5/8$	$20^6/8$	$4^5/8$	$4^5/8$	5	5		3961†	80†
■ Cook Co. – Andrew L. Jaramillo – Andrew L. Jaramillo – 2001
$163^2/8$	$26^4/8$	$27^6/8$	$19^3/8$	$21^3/8$	$4^7/8$	$4^7/8$	5	6	$2^5/8$	4017	81
■ Dooly Co. – David L. Register – David L. Register – 1985
$163^2/8$	$25^2/8$	$25^4/8$	$19^6/8$	$21^6/8$	$4^3/8$	$4^3/8$	6	6		4017	81
■ Wilcox Co. – Danny Luke – Danny Luke – 1987

Score	Length of Main Beam		Inside Spread	Greatest Spread	Circumference at Smallest Place Between Burr and First Point		Number of Points		Lengths Abnormal Points	All-Time Rank	State Rank
	Right	Left			Right	Left	Right	Left			
	■ Location of Kill – Hunter – Owner – Date Killed										
163²/8	22²/8	23⁶/8	15²/8	17⁴/8	5²/8	5⁵/8	5	5		4017	81
	■ Baker Co. – Herman W. Haire – Herman W. Haire – 1995										
163¹/8	24⁷/8	24⁴/8	17⁶/8	20²/8	4⁶/8	4⁶/8	7	5	6⁷/8	4035	84
	■ Haralson Co. – Picked Up – Courtney White – 1980										
163¹/8	24⁷/8	24⁵/8	14⁷/8	17¹/8	4²/8	4²/8	6	7		4035	84
	■ Wilcox Co. – Roy Bloodworth – Roy Bloodworth – 1986										
163¹/8	26	26³/8	19⁵/8	21³/8	4²/8	4¹/8	5	5		4035	84
	■ Macon Co. – Gary E. Campbell – Gary E. Campbell – 1996										
163	23⁵/8	23⁵/8	16²/8	18	3⁷/8	4	6	6		4051†	87†
	■ Terrell Co. – Gary W. Freeman – Gary W. Freeman – 2000										
162⁶/8	25⁷/8	25⁴/8	17⁴/8	19²/8	4⁶/8	5	6	6	3	4089	88
	■ Worth Co. – Ezekiel A. Woodall – Ezekiel A. Woodall – 1974										
162⁵/8	27⁷/8	27³/8	21⁶/8	24	4⁵/8	4⁵/8	6	5	3⁵/8	4109	89
	■ Turner Co. – Paul M. Anderson III – Paul M. Anderson III – 1995										
162⁴/8	24	23¹/8	18⁶/8	20⁶/8	5¹/8	5²/8	7	7		4129	90
	■ Dooly Co. – Andy Colter – Andy Colter – 1990										
162⁴/8	26³/8	26¹/8	20²/8	22²/8	5³/8	5¹/8	6	5	3⁴/8	4129	90
	■ Lee Co. – Wannie C. Brookerd – Wannie C. Brookerd – 1991										
162⁴/8	25⁵/8	25⁵/8	18⁴/8	20²/8	4³/8	4⁴/8	6	5	2⁴/8	4129	90
	■ Thomas Co. – Kenneth E. Harvey – Kenneth E. Harvey – 1995										
162³/8	28⁴/8	29	22¹/8	24¹/8	5¹/8	5	4	5	3²/8	4140	93
	■ Lee Co. – Steven W. Ruckel – Steven W. Ruckel – 1982										
162²/8	25³/8	26⁴/8	16	20¹/8	4²/8	4⁵/8	5	7	4⁶/8	4153†	94†
	■ Worth Co. – J.L. Pritchard – Marcus E. Evans – 1963										
162	23²/8	22⁴/8	17⁴/8	20¹/8	5⁴/8	5¹/8	5	6	2	4184	95
	■ Jackson Co. – Teddy Parker – Teddy Parker – 1984										
162	23⁶/8	22⁷/8	19⁶/8	21⁴/8	4³/8	4²/8	5	5		4184	95
	■ Stewart Co. – Judge W. Lanneau – Judge W. Lanneau – 1986										
161⁷/8	27¹/8	25⁶/8	18⁴/8	20⁶/8	4⁷/8	4⁷/8	6	6	6⁷/8	4212	97
	■ Laurens Co. – Phillip Flanders – Phillip Flanders – 1988										
161⁵/8	26	25³/8	15⁷/8	17⁷/8	5	4⁷/8	5	6	1	4234	98
	■ Lee Co. – Ray Carter – Ray Carter – 1982										
161³/8	23⁷/8	23⁵/8	22¹/8	24²/8	5⁷/8	5⁷/8	8	7	8⁶/8	4285	99
	■ Coweta Co. – Kinney Hudgens – Kinney Hudgens – 1983										
161³/8	25³/8	25	16⁴/8	18³/8	4⁴/8	4⁴/8	5	6	1⁵/8	4285	99
	■ Lowndes Co. – Picked Up – John Reed, Jr. – 1997										
161	26²/8	27³/8	20⁷/8	22⁷/8	4⁴/8	4⁶/8	6	6	1⁷/8	4356†	101†
	■ Mitchell Co. – Jerome J. Tallent – Jerome J. Tallent – 2000										
161	27⁴/8	28	19²/8	21²/8	4²/8	4²/8	5	5		4356	101
	■ Worth Co. – Mike D. Roberts, Jr. – Mike D. Roberts, Jr. – 1989										
161	23²/8	24	15⁵/8	17³/8	5³/8	4⁷/8	6	6	2³/8	4356	101
	■ Crisp Co. – Picked Up – Jimmy Sapp – 1991										

Score	Length of Main Beam Right Left		Inside Spread	Greatest Spread	Circumference at Smallest Place Between Burr and First Point Right Left		Number of Points Right Left		Lengths Abnormal Points	All-Time Rank	State Rank
	■ *Location of Kill – Hunter – Owner – Date Killed*										
161	25 1/8	25 6/8	19 4/8	21 4/8	5 3/8	5 4/8	6	5	4 4/8	4356	101
	■ *Brooks Co. – Elmer E. Bertschy – Elmer E. Bertschy – 1994*										
160 7/8	25	25 1/8	17 7/8	20	4 2/8	4 3/8	5	5		4380†	105†
	■ *Colquitt Co. – W. Neal Hager – W. Neal Hager – 2000*										
160 7/8	25 6/8	25 5/8	17 3/8	20	5 4/8	5 4/8	5	5		4380†	105†
	■ *Hall Co. – Bonnie L. Harrison – Bonnie L. Harrison – 2001*										
160 7/8	24 7/8	25	17 3/8	19 2/8	5 3/8	5 2/8	6	6	2	4380	105
	■ *Brooks Co. – Joseph J. Freeman – Joseph J. Freeman – 1976*										
160 6/8	27 6/8	27 1/8	19 5/8	22 7/8	4 4/8	4 4/8	6	6	2 1/8	4402	108
	■ *Worth Co. – Jerry W. Green – Jerry W. Green – 1991*										
160 6/8	24 2/8	25 2/8	17 5/8	20 6/8	4 6/8	4 6/8	6	6	7 5/8	4402	108
	■ *Dooly Co. – Jarrod Brannen – Jarrod Brannen – 1997*										
160 4/8	25 5/8	26	20 4/8	23 2/8	4 6/8	4 5/8	5	5		4443	110
	■ *Dooly Co. – Joe V. Fraser – Joe V. Fraser – 1997*										
160 3/8	28	27 7/8	19 5/8	21 4/8	4 4/8	4 4/8	4	4		4470	111
	■ *Lee Co. – Robert A. Robinson – Robert A. Robinson – 1994*										
160 2/8	24 1/8	23 4/8	18	20 2/8	4 4/8	4 5/8	6	8	10 6/8	4495	112
	■ *Early Co. – Todd Bell – Todd Bell – 1985*										
160 2/8	25 2/8	25 7/8	21	22 6/8	5 3/8	5	5	5		4495	112
	■ *Telfair Co. – Wendell H. Bullard – Wendell H. Bullard – 1988*										
160 2/8	28 1/8	28	21 3/8	23 4/8	4 6/8	5	5	6	2 3/8	4495	112
	■ *Grady Co. – Picked Up – Brian K. Steele – 1997*										
160 1/8	28 4/8	27 3/8	16 5/8	19	4 6/8	4 5/8	5	5		4534	115
	■ *Calhoun Co. – Alan Lee – Alan Lee – 1979*										
160 1/8	26 7/8	26 1/8	22 6/8	24 7/8	5 2/8	5 2/8	5	6	1 5/8	4534	115
	■ *Colquitt Co. – James L. Malone – James L. Malone – 1989*										
160 1/8	26 1/8	26 7/8	17 3/8	19 2/8	4 2/8	4 2/8	5	5		4534	115
	■ *Brooks Co. – Carl L. Doane, Jr. – Carl L. Doane, Jr. – 1997*										
160	24 7/8	25 1/8	16	17 7/8	5 1/8	5	5	5		4565	118
	■ *Dodge Co. – Jay Mullis – Jay Mullis – 1984*										

† The scores and ranking for trophies from the 25th Awards Entry Period are not final until the banquet is held on June 19, 2004.

GEORGIA

NON-TYPICAL WHITETAIL DEER

Score	Length of Main Beam Right	Left	Inside Spread	Greatest Spread	Circumference at Smallest Place Between Burr and First Point Right	Left	Number of Points Right	Left	Lengths Abnormal Points	All-Time Rank	State Rank
240³/8	24²/8	24⁶/8	18⁵/8	24²/8	7²/8	7²/8	18	20	70⁴/8	115	1
■ Monroe Co. – John L. Hatton, Jr. – John L. Hatton, Jr. – 1973											
231²/8	25	25²/8	17⁵/8	20	8¹/8	5⁷/8	21	12	60¹/8	221	2
■ Muscogee Co. – Blakely H. Voltz – Blakely H. Voltz – 1997											
215⁷/8	29⁶/8	27⁷/8	16⁷/8	22⁵/8	6¹/8	6⁴/8	13	13	46	569	3
■ Putnam Co. – Thomas H. Cooper – Thomas H. Cooper – 1974											
211⁴/8	23³/8	23	18⁶/8	22⁴/8	4⁷/8	5	13	14	33²/8	739	4
■ Worth Co. – Wade Patterson – Wade Patterson – 1988											
210¹/8	26⁷/8	26⁵/8	20	24¹/8	5¹/8	4⁶/8	10	7	20¹/8	808	5
■ Crawford Co. – Walter Keel – Grace Stinson – 1971											
208³/8	27⁵/8	28¹/8	21⁷/8	25	5	4⁷/8	11	7	34²/8	905	6
■ Decatur Co. – James L. Darley – James L. Darley – 1964											
206⁴/8	16⁵/8	18⁷/8	15⁷/8	23¹/8	4⁵/8	5	15	13	82⁷/8	1043	7
■ Madison Co. – Picked Up – GA Dept. of Natl. Resc. – 1993											
206³/8	24⁶/8	24⁷/8	14	18⁶/8	4⁵/8	4⁶/8	9	9	40⁷/8	1051	8
■ Colquitt Co. – Picked Up – GA Dept. of Natl. Resc. – 1990											
204⁴/8	28	27⁵/8	23³/8	25²/8	5²/8	4⁷/8	9	8	21⁵/8	1259	9
■ Jones Co. – Curtis F. Long – Mrs. Curtis F. Long – 1965											
202³/8	26⁴/8	26¹/8	19	21¹/8	4⁵/8	4⁵/8	9	8	22⁷/8	1362	10
■ Thomas Co. – Rolf Kauka – Rolf Kauka – 1991											
202²/8	25⁵/8	25⁶/8	19⁵/8	22³/8	5	5¹/8	11	9	20⁵/8	1377†	11†
■ Mitchell Co. – Tommy S. Burford – Tommy S. Burford – 2001											
202²/8	28⁴/8	28³/8	20¹/8	28⁴/8	6²/8	5⁷/8	8	10	34⁵/8	1377	11
■ Oglethorpe Co. – J. Richard Mocko – J. Richard Mocko – 1983											
201	25⁴/8	26¹/8	22²/8	24⁶/8	5⁷/8	5⁷/8	9	9	28⁴/8	1500	13
■ Wilkinson Co. – E. Dwaine Davis – E. Dwaine Davis – 1990											
199⁶/8	26⁵/8	27²/8	18⁵/8	22³/8	5²/8	4²/8	9	7	20⁵/8	1613	14
■ Harris Co. – Kenneth H. Brown – Kenneth H. Brown – 1974											
198⁴/8	22⁶/8	26	21¹/8	25⁴/8	5²/8	4⁵/8	12	8	51¹/8	1736	15
■ Wheeler Co. – David Frost – David Frost – 1983											
197⁴/8	26³/8	27³/8	18	23	4⁶/8	4⁵/8	10	12	36⁶/8	1866	16
■ Dooly Co. – Wayne Griffin – Wayne Griffin – 1984											
197³/8	24	26⁵/8	16⁴/8	19¹/8	5⁶/8	5⁶/8	9	10	35⁵/8	1884	17
■ Newton Co. – R.H. Bumbalough – R.H. Bumbalough – 1969											
196⁷/8	27¹/8	27²/8	23²/8	23⁴/8	5²/8	5¹/8	10	5	21⁵/8	1950	18
■ Macon Co. – Major Beard – Major Brannon – 1972											
196	25¹/8	25⁵/8	16¹/8	19³/8	4¹/8	4⁴/8	11	11	18³/8	2059	19
■ Jasper Co. – Frank M. Pritchard – Frank M. Pritchard – 1968											

Score	Length of Main Beam Right Left	Inside Spread	Greatest Spread	Circumference at Smallest Place Between Burr and First Point Right Left	Number of Points Right Left	Lengths Abnormal Points	All-Time Rank	State Rank
	■ Location of Kill – Hunter – Owner – Date Killed							
195 4/8	25 3/8 24 3/8	21 6/8	23 5/8	4 3/8 4 4/8	7 10	38	2134	20
	■ Worth Co. – Shane Calhoun – Shane Calhoun – 1985							
195 3/8	27 3/8 29 7/8	20 5/8	23 5/8	6 5 4/8	6 7	14	2163	21
	■ Colquitt Co. – Olen P. Ross – Olen P. Ross – 1976							
195 3/8	21 1/8 21 4/8	19 7/8	24 4/8	4 1/8 4 2/8	9 15	48	2163	21
	■ Johnson Co. – Picked Up – Jackie Bailey – 1999							
195 2/8	31 6/8 31	21 5/8	24 2/8	4 7/8 5	10 9	13 1/8	2186†	23†
	■ Brooks Co. – Donald K. Duren – Latrelle D. Burkholder – 1970							
195 1/8	23 1/8 23 5/8	15 3/8	19 6/8	4 5/8 4 7/8	8 8	26	2208	24
	■ Macon Co. – Wesley E. Jones – Wesley E. Jones – 1986							
193 7/8	28 6/8 28 7/8	19	21 7/8	5 5/8 5 5/8	7 10	20 7/8	2277	25
	■ Lee Co. – John T. Marbury – John T. Marbury – 1990							
193 5/8	27 26 6/8	16 2/8	23 4/8	5 4/8 5 5/8	8 9	21 7/8	2281	26
	■ Henry Co. – Jason J. Patrick – Jason J. Patrick – 1986							
192 4/8	23 5/8 25 3/8	19 5/8	26 2/8	6 1/8 6 3/8	12 10	48 5/8	2325	27
	■ Jones Co. – Fred H. Maxwell – Fred H. Maxwell – 1962							
192 2/8	26 2/8 25 6/8	17 2/8	20 7/8	5 1/8 5 4/8	8 7	38	2335	28
	■ Macon Co. – Emily M. McDaniel – Emily M. McDaniel – 1996							
191 2/8	23 5/8 24 1/8	16	18 3/8	4 3/8 4 3/8	9 8	19	2371	29
	■ Worth Co. – Mike D. Roberts, Sr. – Mike D. Roberts, Sr. – 1963							
190 5/8	27 3/8 27 2/8	20 7/8	23 4/8	5 6/8 5 6/8	12 11	24	2393	30
	■ Worth Co. – George L. Houston – George L. Houston – 1997							
189 1/8	25 6/8 26 2/8	17 7/8	19 2/8	4 5/8 4 5/8	9 9	16 4/8	2450	31
	■ Wilcox Co. – Ronnie Wilcox – Ronnie Wilcox – 1984							
188 1/8	26 5/8 26 3/8	17 6/8	24	4 6/8 4 7/8	8 9	16 1/8	2497	32
	■ Colquitt Co. – Mike T. Hampton – Mike T. Hampton – 1991							
188	25 25 3/8	17	20 1/8	5 1/8 5 1/8	8 7	36 4/8	2504	33
	■ Jones Co. – Abe Northcutt – Abe Northcutt – 1958							
185 2/8	25 4/8 23 4/8	16 1/8	19	6 6 2/8	11 11	23 3/8	2632	34
	■ Lowndes Co. – Ted A. Sauls, Jr. – Ted A. Sauls, Jr. – 1995							

† The scores and ranking for trophies from the 25th Awards Entry Period are not final until the banquet is held on June 19, 2004.

IDAHO
RECORD WHITETAILS

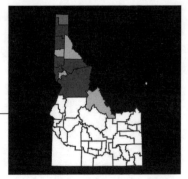

28 Typical whitetail deer entries
31 Non-typical whitetail deer entries
7,265 Total whitetail deer entries

0 Entries
1-2 Entries
3-5 Entries
6-10 Entries
11+ Entries

IDAHO
STATE RECORD
Typical Whitetail Deer
Score: $182^5/8$
Location: Boundary Co.
Hunter and Owner: Aaron M. McNall
Date: 1993

IDAHO
STATE RECORD
Non-Typical Whitetail Deer
Score: 268
Location: Idaho
Hunter: Unknown
Owner: D.J. Hollinger & B. Howard
Date: Prior to 1982

IDAHO

TYPICAL WHITETAIL DEER

Score	Length of Main Beam Right Left	Inside Spread	Greatest Spread	Circumference at Smallest Place Between Burr and First Point Right Left		Number of Points Right Left		Lengths Abnormal Points	All-Time Rank	State Rank
	■ *Location of Kill – Hunter – Owner – Date Killed*									
182⁵/₈	24 23⁷/₈	20¹/₈	24	5⁴/₈ 5³/₈		5 5			420	1
	■ *Boundary Co. – Aaron M. McNall – Aaron M. McNall – 1993*									
181⁷/₈	26⁵/₈ 27³/₈	21⁵/₈	22⁶/₈	4⁴/₈ 4⁴/₈		5 5			478	2
	■ *Clearwater Co. – Richard E. Carver – Richard E. Carver – 1985*									
177⁵/₈	26 25⁶/₈	21³/₈	24²/₈	4⁵/₈ 4⁵/₈		5 5			972	3
	■ *Idaho Co. – Donna M. Knight – Donna M. Knight – 1986*									
176⁶/₈	22³/₈ 23⁶/₈	16²/₈	18²/₈	4¹/₈ 4¹/₈		7 7		3²/₈	1103	4
	■ *Idaho Co. – Edward D. Moore – Edward D. Moore – 1986*									
176⁶/₈	26⁵/₈ 25⁶/₈	17	20¹/₈	5²/₈ 5¹/₈		6 7		3	1103	4
	■ *Idaho Co. – Frank J. Loughran – Frank J. Loughran – 1987*									
175⁷/₈	24⁵/₈ 23¹/₈	18⁷/₈	20⁶/₈	5¹/₈ 5		6 6			1287†	6†
	■ *Nez Perce Co. – Rusty P. Kirtley – Rusty P. Kirtley – 2000*									
175⁵/₈	25⁵/₈ 25	17⁷/₈	23³/₈	4⁵/₈ 4⁵/₈		6 7			1333	7
	■ *Benewah Co. – Carl Groth – Carl Groth – 1982*									
175³/₈	26⁴/₈ 26⁶/₈	22¹/₈	24	5²/₈ 5¹/₈		5 6		2⁴/₈	1377†	8†
	■ *Jefferson Co. – Daniel R. Merrill – Daniel R. Merrill – 2001*									
174²/₈	26¹/₈ 26⁵/₈	22⁶/₈	25²/₈	5 4⁷/₈		7 6		2²/₈	1652	9
	■ *Clearwater Co. – Douglas B. Crockett – Douglas B. Crockett – 1983*									
173⁶/₈	26⁶/₈ 27⁶/₈	20³/₈	22⁷/₈	5⁷/₈ 5⁴/₈		9 6		8¹/₈	1766	10
	■ *Bonner Co. – Robert L. Campbell – Robert L. Campbell – 1967*									
173¹/₈	25¹/₈ 26	18¹/₈	20³/₈	4⁶/₈ 4⁵/₈		5 8		3⁴/₈	1950	11
	■ *Latah Co. – John D. Kauffman – John D. Kauffman – 1991*									
172⁷/₈	25²/₈ 24³/₈	18	20⁷/₈	4²/₈ 4¹/₈		7 7		3⁵/₈	2038	12
	■ *Kootenai Co. – Kevin L. Lundblad – Kevin L. Lundblad – 1992*									
172⁵/₈	26¹/₈ 26	20⁷/₈	25⁵/₈	4⁶/₈ 4⁵/₈		5 5			2113	13
	■ *Kootenai Co. – Shane Moyer – Shane Moyer – 1996*									
172	24⁶/₈ 24⁶/₈	17²/₈	21⁵/₈	4³/₈ 4⁴/₈		6 5			2330	14
	■ *Joseph Plains – Jim Felton – Jim Felton – 1965*									
171⁵/₈	26 26⁷/₈	18⁷/₈	21³/₈	4²/₈ 4²/₈		6 5		1⁴/₈	2470†	15†
	■ *Latah Co. – Glen D. Barnett – Glen D. Barnett – 2000*									
171⁴/₈	24⁷/₈ 25²/₈	19⁴/₈	21⁵/₈	4⁷/₈ 5²/₈		6 6		1⁶/₈	2513	16
	■ *Latah Co. – Darwin L. Baker – Darwin L. Baker – 1986*									
171³/₈	24³/₈ 24²/₈	17⁵/₈	20	5¹/₈ 5¹/₈		6 7		4⁶/₈	2564	17
	■ *Boundary Co. – Donald B. Vickaryous – Donald B. Vickaryous – 1995*									
171	27⁵/₈ 27	19²/₈	21²/₈	4⁶/₈ 4⁶/₈		7 7		3²/₈	2707	18
	■ *Nez Perce Co. – Paul A. Eke – Paul A. Eke – 1993*									
170³/₈	26²/₈ 25³/₈	17⁷/₈	20¹/₈	5 5¹/₈		5 6			2992†	19†
	■ *Idaho – Unknown – Larry Haines – PR 2002*									

Score	Length of Main Beam		Inside Spread	Greatest Spread	Circumference at Smallest Place Between Burr and First Point		Number of Points		Lengths Abnormal Points	All-Time Rank	State Rank
	Right	Left			Right	Left	Right	Left			
	Location of Kill – Hunter – Owner – Date Killed										
170	28 4/8	27 3/8	21 4/8	24 1/8	4 7/8	5	8	7	10 4/8	3224	20
	■ *Latah Co. – Lewis L. Turcott – Lewis L. Turcott – 1974*										
169 4/8	26 4/8	26	19	22 3/8	4 4/8	4 4/8	7	8	5 4/8	3316	21
	■ *Clearwater Co. – Frederick R. Staab – Frederick R. Staab – 1990*										
168 1/8	26 6/8	26	18	21	4 7/8	5	6	6	2 1/8	3426	22
	■ *Clearwater Co. – Emerald J. Hutchins – Emerald J. Hutchins – 1994*										
164	23 6/8	23	18 4/8	20 2/8	4 4/8	4 4/8	6	6	1 2/8	3908	23
	■ *Latah Co. – Gary Esser – Michael J. Stewart – 1979*										
163 3/8	25	26	18 3/8	20 2/8	4 5/8	4 5/8	4	4		4002	24
	■ *Latah Co. – Steven J. Funke – Steven J. Funke – 1997*										
163	26 2/8	26 3/8	19 6/8	22	4 2/8	4 3/8	6	5	1 2/8	4051	25
	■ *Kootenai Co. – David A. Neighbor – David A. Neighbor – 1994*										
162 6/8	24 4/8	24 3/8	22 4/8	24	4 5/8	4 6/8	6	6	2 6/8	4089	26
	■ *Latah Co. – Larry Stohs – Larry Stohs – 1986*										
161 3/8	24 4/8	23 4/8	20 7/8	23	4 5/8	4 3/8	5	5		4285	27
	■ *Idaho Co. – Douglas Lamm – Douglas Lamm – 1978*										
160 4/8	25	25 6/8	18 4/8	22 2/8	4 2/8	4	7	6	3 2/8	4443	28
	■ *Boundary Co. – Christopher E. Collecchi III – Christopher E. Collecchi III – 1992*										

† The scores and ranking for trophies from the 25th Awards Entry Period are not final until the banquet is held on June 19, 2004.

IDAHO

NON-TYPICAL WHITETAIL DEER

Score	Length of Main Beam Right	Left	Inside Spread	Greatest Spread	Circumference at Smallest Place Between Burr and First Point Right	Left	Number of Points Right	Left	Lengths Abnormal Points	All-Time Rank	State Rank
	■ Location of Kill – Hunter – Owner – Date Killed										
268	25 4/8	25	18	24 2/8	4 3/8	4 7/8	15	16	91 4/8	15	1
	■ Idaho – Unknown – D.J. Hollinger & B. Howard – PR 1982										
267 4/8	26 6/8	27 6/8	29 1/8	35 5/8	5 1/8	5 6/8	16	23	94 4/8	17	2
	■ Idaho – Unknown – Jack G. Brittingham – PR 1923										
257 6/8	24 3/8	22 1/8	22 1/8	28 1/8	5	6 3/8	9	17	104 5/8	33	3
	■ Nez Perce Co. – John D. Powers, Jr. – Bass Pro Shops – 1983										
226 3/8	25 7/8	27 3/8	18 2/8	20 2/8	5 5/8	5 3/8	10	8	22 3/8	296	4
	■ Nez Perce Co. – Mrs. Ralph Bond – Mrs. Ralph Bond – 1964										
222 1/8	26 5/8	26 1/8	22 2/8	27 2/8	5 4/8	5 1/8	11	11	47 5/8	392	5
	■ Latah Co. – Randy L. Clemenhagen – Randy L. Clemenhagen – 1995										
220 2/8	26 6/8	27 5/8	20 2/8	26 7/8	4 7/8	4 6/8	9	9	28 6/8	434	6
	■ Lewis Co. – Steavon C. Hornbeck – Steavon C. Hornbeck – 2000										
219 7/8	25 4/8	25 7/8	20 4/8	24 7/8	5 3/8	5 3/8	11	10	30 1/8	444	7
	■ Clearwater Co. – Kipling D. Manfull – Kipling D. Manfull – 1989										
214 4/8	25 4/8	25 4/8	22 2/8	28 5/8	5	5	12	9	27 6/8	617	8
	■ Clearwater Co. – Don L. Twito – Don L. Twito – 1975										
213 7/8	29 1/8	29 2/8	19 3/8	23 6/8	5 3/8	5 5/8	8	9	20 6/8	635†	9†
	■ Bonner Co. – Fred B. Post – Michael R. Damery – 1978										
213 5/8	27 1/8	24 6/8	23 6/8	27 5/8	5 4/8	7	9	9	52 1/8	649	10
	■ Bonner Co. – Rodney Thurlow – Rodney Thurlow – 1968										
208 6/8	24 4/8	25	21 5/8	29 5/8	4 2/8	4 3/8	7	6	32 1/8	883	11
	■ Idaho – Unknown – Richard J. Dorchuck – PR 1975										
206	24 1/8	25 1/8	17 5/8	22	5 3/8	5 3/8	8	11	32 3/8	1075	12
	■ Shoshone Co. – Marion G. Macaluso – Marion G. Macaluso – 1993										
205 1/8	21	22 2/8	14 6/8	25 6/8	5	5	12	13	57 5/8	1138	13
	■ Bonner Co. – Clinton M. Hackney – Clinton M. Hackney – 1990										
205	21	25 1/8	18	25 1/8	4 1/8	4 4/8	14	5	76 6/8	1144	14
	■ Boundary Co. – Lee Mahler – Lee Mahler – 1961										
203 4/8	24 4/8	25 2/8	16 4/8	19 3/8	5 6/8	5 5/8	9	13	54 6/8	1259	15
	■ Kootenai Co. – A.P. Hegge – Kevin L. Lundblad – 1929										
203 1/8	23 7/8	24 3/8	17 6/8	20 5/8	4 4/8	4 6/8	13	9	44 1/8	1305	16
	■ Kootenai Co. – William M. Ziegler – William M. Ziegler – 1965										
202 4/8	22 4/8	25 4/8	19 4/8	23 3/8	6 3/8	5 2/8	11	9	34 2/8	1355	17
	■ Boundary Co. – Picked Up – Steve Crossley – 1990										
201 3/8	21 1/8	21 6/8	21 3/8	23 4/8	5 2/8	4 6/8	16	11	33	1461	18
	■ Bonner Co. – Leroy Coleman – Leroy Coleman – 1960										
200 3/8	25	26 2/8	17 4/8	25 1/8	4 6/8	4 7/8	11	10	21 1/8	1556	19
	■ Nez Perce Co. – Tim C. Baldwin – Tim C. Baldwin – 1987										

Score	Length of Main Beam Right Left	Inside Spread	Greatest Spread	Circumference at Smallest Place Between Burr and First Point Right Left	Number of Points Right Left	Lengths Abnormal Points	All-Time Rank	State Rank
	■ Location of Kill – Hunter – Owner – Date Killed							
198³/8	20⁷/8 22²/8	17⁵/8	19⁵/8	4⁴/8 4⁷/8	10 10	33⁶/8	1762	20
	■ Nez Perce Co. – Milton R. Wilson – G. & J. Reed – 1983							
198¹/8	24⁶/8 24³/8	19⁶/8	23³/8	5⁵/8 5⁴/8	10 9	23¹/8	1785	21
	■ Kootenai Co. – Frank J. Cheney – ID Fish & Game Dept. – 1967							
198¹/8	25¹/8 25²/8	19¹/8	22⁶/8	4²/8 4²/8	11 8	19-8/8	1785	21
	■ Kootenai Co. – Luke D. Finney – Luke D. Finney – 1998							
197⁷/8	22²/8 23	19²/8	24⁵/8	5¹/8 5¹/8	8 12	30⁵/8	1816	23
	■ Latah Co. – Dean C. Weyen – Dean C. Weyen – 1992							
197	24²/8 26⁴/8	25³/8	28⁷/8	5 5¹/8	8 9	18³/8	1939	24
	■ Kootenai Co. – D.L. Whatcott & R.C. Carlson – D.L. Whatcott & R.C. Carlson – 1980							
195⁷/8	23¹/8 23⁴/8	19	21⁴/8	4⁷/8 4⁵/8	9 9	26¹/8	2076	25
	■ Latah Co. – Cecil H. Cameron – Cecil H. Cameron – 1989							
195⁶/8	23 23	17	18⁴/8	4 4¹/8	9 8	28²/8	2094	26
	■ Bonner Co. – Picked Up – Brian T. Farley – PR 1994							
195⁵/8	24⁶/8 24⁷/8	19²/8	22¹/8	5²/8 5	10 9	19³/8	2116	27
	■ Nez Perce Co. – Paul S. Snider – Paul S. Snider – 1989							
195¹/8	25⁵/8 23⁴/8	18	23⁶/8	4³/8 4⁴/8	15 13	34¹/8	2208	28
	■ Bonner Co. – George B. Hatley – George B. Hatley – 1939							
191³/8	26⁵/8 26	22²/8	27¹/8	4⁵/8 4⁷/8	9 9	28¹/8	2364	29
	■ Lemhi Co. – Unknown – Aly M. Bruner – PR 1930							
186⁷/8	24 24³/8	17⁵/8	21	4²/8 4¹/8	8 6	20⁶/8	2550	30
	■ Latah Co. – Tami M. VanNess – Tami M. VanNess – 1990							
185¹/8	24¹/8 24	21¹/8	24¹/8	5²/8 5⁴/8	8 8	15²/8	2641	31
	■ Nez Perce Co. – Nick Roberson – Nick Roberson – 1977							

† The scores and ranking for trophies from the 25th Awards Entry Period are not final until the banquet is held on June 19, 2004.

ILLINOIS
RECORD WHITETAILS

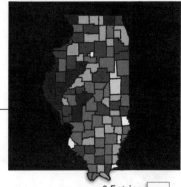

380 Typical whitetail deer entries
264 Non-typical whitetail deer entries
7,265 Total whitetail deer entries

0 Entries	
1-2 Entries	
3-5 Entries	
6-10 Entries	
11+ Entries	

ILLINOIS
STATE RECORD
Typical Whitetail Deer
Score: 204⁴/8
Location: Peoria Co.
Hunter: Mel J. Johnson
Owner: Bass Pro Shops
Date: 1965

Photograph from B&C Archives

ILLINOIS
NEW STATE RECORD
Non-Typical Whitetail Deer
Score: 291$^1/_8$
Location: Fulton Co.
Hunter and Owner: Jerry D. Bryant
Date: 2001

New state record pending approval from the 25th Awards Program Judges Panel.

ILLINOIS

TYPICAL WHITETAIL DEER

Score	Length of Main Beam Right	Left	Inside Spread	Greatest Spread	Circumference at Smallest Place Between Burr and First Point Right	Left	Number of Points Right	Left	Lengths Abnormal Points	All-Time Rank	State Rank
204⁴/8	27⁵/8	26⁶/8	23⁵/8	26¹/8	6¹/8	6²/8	7	6	1¹/8	4	1

■ *Peoria Co. – Mel J. Johnson – Bass Pro Shops – 1965*

| 200²/8 | 32 | 32⁴/8 | 28³/8 | 30⁶/8 | 5⁴/8 | 5³/8 | 9 | 8 | 22⁵/8 | 11 | 2 |

■ *Macon Co. – Brian S. Damery – Bass Pro Shops – 1993*

| 197¹/8 | 31 | 29⁷/8 | 21²/8 | 23⁷/8 | 6¹/8 | 6⁵/8 | 7 | 7 | 12⁷/8 | 28 | 3 |

■ *Macoupin Co. – Kevin L. Naugle – Bass Pro Shops – 1988*

| 196⁶/8 | 29⁶/8 | 29 | 21 | 23⁶/8 | 5²/8 | 5⁶/8 | 6 | 8 | 8⁶/8 | 29† | 4† |

■ *Kane Co. – Ray Schremp – Ray Schremp – 2000*

| 195⁵/8 | 29⁴/8 | 27⁵/8 | 18⁷/8 | 21⁶/8 | 4⁶/8 | 4⁷/8 | 9 | 8 | 3⁶/8 | 35 | 5 |

■ *Rock Island Co. – Kent E. Anderson – Kent E. Anderson – 1999*

| 192⁷/8 | 28²/8 | 28⁵/8 | 22 | 24²/8 | 5²/8 | 5²/8 | 7 | 7 | 5⁷/8 | 58† | 6† |

■ *Mercer Co. – Jerry W. Whitmire – Cabela's, Inc. – 2000*

| 192⁷/8 | 28¹/8 | 28¹/8 | 19⁷/8 | 24 | 5⁷/8 | 6 | 10 | 7 | 11⁶/8 | 58 | 6 |

■ *Williamson Co. – A. & J. Albers – A. & J. Albers – 1991*

| 191⁷/8 | 29⁵/8 | 30¹/8 | 20⁴/8 | 23⁵/8 | 5⁷/8 | 5⁷/8 | 9 | 8 | 13³/8 | 73 | 8 |

■ *Wayne Co. – Leo E. Elliott – Leo E. Elliott – 1990*

| 191⁶/8 | 27⁷/8 | 28 | 21 | 23¹/8 | 5 | 4⁶/8 | 7 | 7 | 8²/8 | 76 | 9 |

■ *Union Co. – Everett F. Ellis – Everett F. Ellis – 1994*

| 191⁴/8 | 28⁵/8 | 28⁵/8 | 21²/8 | 23⁵/8 | 4⁶/8 | 4⁶/8 | 5 | 5 | | 82 | 10 |

■ *Henry Co. – Keith Hamerlinck – Keith Hamerlinck – 1999*

| 190⁵/8 | 27⁶/8 | 29²/8 | 20¹/8 | 23 | 4⁶/8 | 5 | 5 | 5 | | 95† | 11† |

■ *Ogle Co. – Geoff Lester – Geoff Lester – 2000*

| 190⁴/8 | 28²/8 | 29¹/8 | 24³/8 | 27⁷/8 | 5⁵/8 | 5⁵/8 | 8 | 8 | 4⁷/8 | 100 | 12 |

■ *Menard Co. – Dwaine E. Heyen – Dwaine E. Heyen – 1997*

| 190¹/8 | 26⁴/8 | 27 | 18⁴/8 | 21⁷/8 | 6¹/8 | 5⁷/8 | 9 | 7 | 9⁷/8 | 106 | 13 |

■ *Randolph Co. – Kevin Leemon – Kevin Leemon – 1990*

| 189⁷/8 | 26⁶/8 | 26¹/8 | 22¹/8 | 24²/8 | 4⁷/8 | 5¹/8 | 5 | 6 | 1⁴/8 | 113 | 14 |

■ *Henry Co. – Reginald M. Anseeuw – Reginald M. Anseeuw – 1992*

| 189⁷/8 | 25⁵/8 | 26⁴/8 | 23²/8 | 24⁷/8 | 5⁷/8 | 6¹/8 | 6 | 6 | 11⁷/8 | 113 | 14 |

■ *Sangamon Co. – Leo J. Romanotto – Leo J. Romanotto – 1994*

| 189⁵/8 | 26³/8 | 27³/8 | 25¹/8 | 28¹/8 | 6²/8 | 6⁷/8 | 9 | 7 | 15 | 116 | 16 |

■ *Schuyler Co. – Picked Up – Bass Pro Shops – 1990*

| 188⁷/8 | 28²/8 | 27³/8 | 19²/8 | 21⁶/8 | 5¹/8 | 5¹/8 | 6 | 7 | 1⁷/8 | 134 | 17 |

■ *Shelby Co. – James M. Holley – James M. Holley – 1995*

| 188⁷/8 | 28²/8 | 28⁷/8 | 19⁴/8 | 21⁵/8 | 6 | 6¹/8 | 6 | 6 | 4⁵/8 | 134 | 17 |

■ *Clark Co. – Larry Shaw – Larry Shaw – 1998*

| 188⁶/8 | 26⁶/8 | 28⁵/8 | 18⁴/8 | 21 | 5³/8 | 5³/8 | 5 | 5 | | 136 | 19 |

■ *Shelby Co. – Elmer Agney – Elmer Agney – 1992*

Score	Length of Main Beam Right	Left	Inside Spread	Greatest Spread	Circumference at Smallest Place Between Burr and First Point Right	Left	Number of Points Right	Left	Lengths Abnormal Points	All-Time Rank	State Rank
	■ Location of Kill – Hunter – Owner – Date Killed										
188³/8	27⁷/8	27⁶/8	21⁷/8	23⁷/8	5	5¹/8	5	5		147	20
	■ Peoria Co. – Jill M. Adcock – Jill M. Adcock – 1993										
188³/8	28³/8	29¹/8	22⁴/8	25³/8	4⁷/8	5	10	10	13⁵/8	147	20
	■ Montgomery Co. – Travis L. Hartman – Travis L. Hartman – 1999										
187⁷/8	27⁶/8	25⁶/8	20⁷/8	23⁶/8	4⁶/8	4⁴/8	5	5		156†	22†
	■ Schuyler Co. – Donald L. Smith – Donald L. Smith – 2001										
187⁴/8	27	27⁴/8	19⁵/8	21⁷/8	5²/8	4⁷/8	9	8	4¹/8	172	23
	■ Brown Co. – Charles A. Howell – Charles A. Howell – 1988										
187	29⁵/8	29	18	20³/8	4⁴/8	4³/8	7	6	2	191	24
	■ Warren Co. – John K. Poole – John K. Poole – 1994										
186⁴/8	28⁶/8	28	26²/8	28²/8	5⁴/8	5⁵/8	5	5		205	25
	■ Coles Co. – Charles H. McElwee – Charles H. McElwee – 1994										
186³/8	28⁵/8	28⁴/8	20⁷/8	23¹/8	5³/8	5²/8	5	5		210	26
	■ Pike Co. – Merle L. Shull – Merle L. Shull – 1985										
186³/8	27⁷/8	29²/8	19¹/8	21	4⁷/8	5⁶/8	6	7	3²/8	210	26
	■ Greene Co. – Picked Up – Cory L. Walker – 1992										
186¹/8	26²/8	25⁴/8	22	23⁷/8	6	5⁵/8	6	5	1³/8	228	28
	■ Pope Co. – Picked Up – Jim Frailey – 1990										
186	28	27⁷/8	19¹/8	21⁶/8	5⁴/8	5⁴/8	6	6	5⁵/8	238	29
	■ Macoupin Co. – Picked Up – Darrell Baker – 1998										
185²/8	24⁷/8	27	23²/8	25¹/8	5⁷/8	5³/8	6	5	2	263	30
	■ Mercer Co. – Richard L. McCaw – Richard L. McCaw – 1997										
184⁵/8	26	25²/8	21	25	6¹/8	5⁵/8	6	6	4⁷/8	294	31
	■ McDonough Co. – Louise Thompson – Louise Thompson – 1991										
184⁴/8	30¹/8	30⁷/8	19⁶/8	26	5²/8	5³/8	4	7	4²/8	303	32
	■ McHenry Co. – Russell A. Lovins – Russell A. Lovins – 1999										
183³/8	27²/8	25	21⁵/8	23⁶/8	5⁴/8	5³/8	5	5		365	33
	■ La Salle Co. – Bernard Ernat – Bernard Ernat – 1996										
183²/8	29¹/8	29⁶/8	27	29⁴/8	5	4⁷/8	5	6	2⁴/8	378	34
	■ Whiteside Co. – Jacob A. Amesquita – Jacob A. Amesquita – 1995										
183²/8	28⁷/8	27⁶/8	18⁵/8	22¹/8	4⁶/8	4⁶/8	7	7	1¹/8	378	34
	■ Knox Co. – Bradley A. Wunder – Bradley A. Wunder – 1995										
183¹/8	26¹/8	26⁴/8	21¹/8	23⁵/8	5	5²/8	6	6		385	36
	■ Wabash Co. – Dale E. Strockbine – Dale E. Strockbine – 1994										
182⁷/8	22	23¹/8	19⁵/8	23¹/8	5	4⁷/8	8	7		401	37
	■ Rock Island Co. – Clifton L. Webster – Clifton L. Webster – 1986										
182⁵/8	25⁴/8	26⁴/8	20¹/8	22²/8	5⁷/8	5⁷/8	8	6	9²/8	420	38
	■ Jefferson Co. – Jerry R. Simmons – Jerry R. Simmons – 1993										
182⁴/8	27	28⁴/8	19²/8	21	4²/8	4²/8	6	6		431	39
	■ Franklin Co. – Tim Broy – Tim Broy – 1997										
182²/8	30¹/8	30	19²/8	21²/8	4⁵/8	4⁵/8	5	5		450†	40†
	■ Hancock Co. – Jeffrey L. Akers – Jeffrey L. Akers – 2000										

Score	Length of Main Beam		Inside Spread	Greatest Spread	Circumference at Smallest Place Between Burr and First Point		Number of Points		Lengths Abnormal Points	All-Time Rank	State Rank
	Right	Left			Right	Left	Right	Left			
182 2/8	28 1/8	27	20	22 6/8	5 3/8	5 5/8	5	6		450	40
■ Champaign Co. – Tom Babb – Tom Babb – 1985											
182 2/8	27 1/8	25 6/8	23 4/8	26	5 3/8	5 4/8	5	5		450	40
■ Hancock Co. – Robert A. Reed – Robert A. Reed – 1988											
182	24 1/8	23 6/8	22 3/8	24 2/8	5 4/8	5 5/8	6	6	5 3/8	469†	43†
■ Henderson Co. – Jeffrey A. Bloise – Jeffrey A. Bloise – 2000											
182	27 1/8	27 1/8	25	26 6/8	5	5	5	6		469†	43†
■ Peoria Co. – Thomas Missen – Thomas Missen – 2001											
182	25	24 1/8	22 6/8	25 2/8	5 7/8	5 7/8	5	6		469	43
■ Henderson Co. – Nicky J. Clark, Jr. – Nicky J. Clark, Jr. – 1999											
181 5/8	24	26 5/8	19	21 1/8	5 4/8	5 2/8	6	8	5 7/8	500†	46†
■ Edgar Co. – Christopher L. Newhart – Christopher L. Newhart – 2001											
181 5/8	26 4/8	27 6/8	21 5/8	26 5/8	6 1/8	6 3/8	6	6	2 6/8	500	46
■ Wabash Co. – Mike Drone – Mike Drone – 1987											
181 5/8	27	27 2/8	17 5/8	20	4 6/8	4 6/8	5	5		500	46
■ Pike Co. – George R. Metcalf – George R. Metcalf – 1995											
181 5/8	24 1/8	24	17 7/8	20 7/8	5	5 1/8	5	5		500	46
■ Fulton Co. – George S. Hadsall – George S. Hadsall – 1999											
181 4/8	26	28 5/8	18 6/8	26 5/8	5 2/8	5 2/8	9	7	10 4/8	516	50
■ Canton – Arnold C. Hegele – Arnold C. Hegele – 1968											
181 4/8	26 6/8	26	18 2/8	20 3/8	5 3/8	5	7	7	1 2/8	516	50
■ Will Co. – James J.A. O'Keefe – James J.A. O'Keefe – 1989											
181 3/8	24 7/8	24 5/8	18 5/8	20 6/8	6 5/8	6 2/8	6	7	1	528	52
■ Pope Co. – Jack A. Higgs – Jack A. Higgs – 1963											
181 2/8	30	30 1/8	20	22 4/8	4 3/8	4 3/8	6	5	1 4/8	540	53
■ Pike Co. – Stephen J. Smith – Stephen J. Smith – 1973											
181 2/8	28 2/8	27 7/8	23 6/8	26 5/8	4 7/8	4 7/8	6	5	1 6/8	540	53
■ Sangamon Co. – Jack D. Davis – Jack D. Davis – 1995											
181 2/8	26 2/8	25 2/8	22 2/8	26 3/8	4 7/8	4 5/8	5	6	5 2/8	540	53
■ Will Co. – Jozef H. Skubisz – Jozef H. Skubisz – 1996											
181 2/8	28 4/8	28 5/8	18	20 4/8	4 7/8	5	5	5		540	53
■ Sangamon Co. – Sean Shymansky – Sean Shymansky – 1997											
181 1/8	29 5/8	28 5/8	18 4/8	23 5/8	5 7/8	5 7/8	5	6	8 1/8	551	57
■ St. Clair Co. – Dean R. Billhartz – Dean R. Billhartz – 1999											
180 5/8	29 6/8	29 3/8	22 5/8	25	4 4/8	4 4/8	5	5		599	58
■ Adams Co. – Kenneth E. Klauser – Kenneth E. Klauser – 1990											
180 5/8	25 1/8	25 2/8	18 1/8	21 6/8	5 3/8	5 3/8	6	7	1 6/8	599	58
■ Coles Co. – H. Lee Adams – H. Lee Adams – 1999											
180 3/8	28 1/8	28	19 6/8	25 4/8	5 5/8	5 3/8	6	4	3 3/8	630	60
■ Menard Co. – Ronald J. Wadsworth – Ronald J. Wadsworth – 1993											
180	25 2/8	25 6/8	22 7/8	24	5 4/8	4 7/8	7	8	1 3/8	688	61
■ Pulaski Co. – Picked Up – Pat Kearny – 1988											

■ Location of Kill – Hunter – Owner – Date Killed

Score	Length of Main Beam Right / Left		Inside Spread	Greatest Spread	Circumference at Smallest Place Between Burr and First Point Right / Left		Number of Points Right / Left		Lengths Abnormal Points	All-Time Rank	State Rank
	■ Location of Kill – Hunter – Owner – Date Killed										
180	$25\frac{7}{8}$	26	$20\frac{2}{8}$	$23\frac{7}{8}$	$5\frac{1}{8}$	$5\frac{3}{8}$	5	7	$2\frac{2}{8}$	688	61
	■ Brown Co. – Rocco Gibala – Rocco Gibala – 1995										
$179\frac{6}{8}$	$26\frac{5}{8}$	$28\frac{2}{8}$	$22\frac{1}{8}$	$24\frac{1}{8}$	5	5	6	8	$2\frac{7}{8}$	712†	63†
	■ Lawrence Co. – Donald E. Stangle – Donald E. Stangle – 2001										
$179\frac{6}{8}$	27	$26\frac{6}{8}$	$15\frac{6}{8}$	18	$4\frac{5}{8}$	$4\frac{4}{8}$	7	8	2	712	63
	■ Clark Co. – Robert E. Sweitzer – Robert E. Sweitzer – 1994										
$179\frac{4}{8}$	$25\frac{2}{8}$	$25\frac{2}{8}$	$19\frac{4}{8}$	23	$5\frac{2}{8}$	$5\frac{6}{8}$	5	5		733	65
	■ Macoupin Co. – Kurt A. Bohl – Kurt A. Bohl – 1997										
$179\frac{2}{8}$	$28\frac{7}{8}$	$27\frac{1}{8}$	$19\frac{2}{8}$	$23\frac{1}{8}$	$5\frac{3}{8}$	$5\frac{3}{8}$	5	5		763	66
	■ Peoria Co. – Christopher M. McNulty – Christopher M. McNulty – 1994										
$179\frac{1}{8}$	$24\frac{6}{8}$	$25\frac{1}{8}$	$19\frac{3}{8}$	21	$4\frac{4}{8}$	$4\frac{6}{8}$	6	6		779	67
	■ Fulton Co. – Jerry D. Manning – Jerry D. Manning – 1977										
$179\frac{1}{8}$	$25\frac{6}{8}$	$25\frac{6}{8}$	$16\frac{3}{8}$	$18\frac{5}{8}$	$4\frac{4}{8}$	$5\frac{4}{8}$	6	5	$1\frac{2}{8}$	779	67
	■ Macoupin Co. – William T. Wiser, Sr. – William T. Wiser, Sr. – 1994										
179	$27\frac{6}{8}$	$29\frac{1}{8}$	$20\frac{7}{8}$	$23\frac{3}{8}$	$5\frac{6}{8}$	$5\frac{5}{8}$	8	11	$12\frac{3}{8}$	786	69
	■ Perry Co. – Roy A. Smith – Roy A. Smith – 1987										
179	$29\frac{2}{8}$	$29\frac{1}{8}$	$19\frac{6}{8}$	$22\frac{4}{8}$	5	$5\frac{1}{8}$	6	7	3	786	69
	■ McLean Co. – Ryan B. Bottles – Ryan B. Bottles – 1999										
$178\frac{7}{8}$	$28\frac{3}{8}$	$27\frac{6}{8}$	22	$25\frac{2}{8}$	5	$5\frac{1}{8}$	6	5	$1\frac{5}{8}$	801	71
	■ Brown Co. – Joseph V. Barnett – Joseph V. Barnett – 1988										
$178\frac{7}{8}$	30	$29\frac{4}{8}$	$18\frac{1}{8}$	$20\frac{5}{8}$	5	5	5	5		801	71
	■ Whiteside Co. – Bernard J. Higley, Jr. – Bernard J. Higley, Jr. – 1990										
$178\frac{6}{8}$	$29\frac{2}{8}$	$27\frac{6}{8}$	$21\frac{5}{8}$	$24\frac{3}{8}$	$5\frac{3}{8}$	$5\frac{5}{8}$	5	6	$4\frac{3}{8}$	808	73
	■ Hancock Co. – Carl A. Lee – Carl A. Lee – 1996										
$178\frac{5}{8}$	$25\frac{7}{8}$	$23\frac{7}{8}$	$18\frac{7}{8}$	$22\frac{3}{8}$	$5\frac{1}{8}$	$5\frac{1}{8}$	8	7	$8\frac{6}{8}$	819	74
	■ Grundy Co. – Charles H. Frantini – Charles H. Frantini – 1987										
$178\frac{5}{8}$	$26\frac{4}{8}$	$26\frac{1}{8}$	$20\frac{7}{8}$	24	$5\frac{5}{8}$	$5\frac{4}{8}$	7	7	$3\frac{6}{8}$	819	74
	■ La Salle Co. – Larry G. Simmons – Larry G. Simmons – 1995										
$178\frac{5}{8}$	$27\frac{1}{8}$	$27\frac{1}{8}$	$22\frac{7}{8}$	$24\frac{6}{8}$	$5\frac{4}{8}$	$5\frac{3}{8}$	6	5	4	819	74
	■ Peoria Co. – Steven M. DeSmet – Steven M. DeSmet – 1998										
$178\frac{4}{8}$	$28\frac{2}{8}$	29	$21\frac{4}{8}$	$23\frac{7}{8}$	$5\frac{1}{8}$	$5\frac{1}{8}$	5	5		850†	77†
	■ Jo Daviess Co. – Jack R. Herman – Jack R. Herman – 2000										
$178\frac{4}{8}$	$24\frac{2}{8}$	$25\frac{2}{8}$	$18\frac{1}{8}$	$19\frac{7}{8}$	$5\frac{5}{8}$	$5\frac{5}{8}$	5	6	$1\frac{1}{8}$	850	77
	■ St. Clair Co. – Emil W. Kromat – Emil W. Kromat – 1981										
$178\frac{4}{8}$	$25\frac{1}{8}$	25	$18\frac{4}{8}$	21	$4\frac{7}{8}$	$4\frac{6}{8}$	5	5		850	77
	■ Fulton Co. – Locie L. Murphy – Locie L. Murphy – 1985										
$178\frac{3}{8}$	$25\frac{1}{8}$	$26\frac{1}{8}$	$21\frac{1}{8}$	$23\frac{4}{8}$	$4\frac{5}{8}$	$4\frac{7}{8}$	6	6		868	80
	■ Clinton Co. – Richard V. Spihlmann – Richard V. Spihlmann – 1961										
$178\frac{3}{8}$	$26\frac{4}{8}$	25	19	22	$4\frac{7}{8}$	$4\frac{6}{8}$	6	7	$5\frac{7}{8}$	868	80
	■ Jo Daviess Co. – Gary J. Flynn – Gary J. Flynn – 1986										
$178\frac{2}{8}$	28	$25\frac{7}{8}$	$21\frac{2}{8}$	$23\frac{1}{8}$	$5\frac{1}{8}$	$5\frac{3}{8}$	5	5		891	82
	■ Lawrence Co. – Brian M. Dining – Brian M. Dining – 1987										

Score	Length of Main Beam Right	Left	Inside Spread	Greatest Spread	Circumference at Smallest Place Between Burr and First Point Right	Left	Number of Points Right	Left	Lengths Abnormal Points	All-Time Rank	State Rank
178²/₈	27⁶/₈	27¹/₈	21⁵/₈	23⁶/₈	5⁶/₈	5⁴/₈	8	9	8⁷/₈	891	82
■ *Warren Co. – Picked Up – Tory Mills – 1999*											
178¹/₈	25⁵/₈	25⁵/₈	19⁶/₈	22²/₈	5⁵/₈	5⁵/₈	6	6	3⁵/₈	905†	84†
■ *Johnson Co. – Jordan R. Lewis – Jordan R. Lewis – 2000*											
178¹/₈	26⁷/₈	27	21³/₈	24	4²/₈	4²/₈	5	6	5⁴/₈	905	84
■ *Morgan Co. – Clark K. Dirden – Clark K. Dirden – 1999*											
177⁷/₈	26³/₈	26⁶/₈	22¹/₈	24⁶/₈	5²/₈	5²/₈	6	6	3⁴/₈	936	86
■ *Christian Co. – Rodney J. Gorden – Rodney J. Gorden – 1974*											
177⁶/₈	25⁷/₈	26⁴/₈	18	20³/₈	4³/₈	4²/₈	6	7	1	956	87
■ *Kankakee Co. – Robert R. Tolmer, Jr. – Robert R. Tolmer, Jr. – 1987*											
177⁵/₈	26⁴/₈	26⁶/₈	18⁴/₈	20⁷/₈	5¹/₈	5¹/₈	5	6	1¹/₈	972	88
■ *Schuyler Co. – Archie D. Stagner – Archie D. Stagner – 1997*											
177⁴/₈	27⁶/₈	26⁶/₈	20⁵/₈	22⁴/₈	5¹/₈	5	6	5	4³/₈	993†	89†
■ *Pike Co. – Chad S. Lankford – Chad S. Lankford – 2001*											
177³/₈	28³/₈	29⁵/₈	23⁷/₈	25⁶/₈	4⁶/₈	4⁵/₈	5	4		1011†	90†
■ *Madison Co. – Joseph S. Cannon – Joseph S. Cannon – 1998*											
177²/₈	25⁴/₈	24⁶/₈	21⁶/₈	23⁶/₈	4⁶/₈	4⁷/₈	5	5		1025†	91†
■ *Grundy Co. – Brandon Smith – Brandon Smith – 2001*											
177¹/₈	26³/₈	25⁵/₈	21⁶/₈	23³/₈	5²/₈	5³/₈	6	8	6¹/₈	1048	92
■ *Calhoun Co. – Paul V. Stumpf – Paul V. Stumpf – 1979*											
177¹/₈	25²/₈	24⁷/₈	20⁵/₈	22⁶/₈	5	5	7	5	5⁶/₈	1048	92
■ *Ogle Co. – Daniel L. Bouton – Daniel L. Bouton – 1993*											
176⁷/₈	25⁶/₈	25²/₈	18¹/₈	20²/₈	4⁵/₈	4⁷/₈	7	7	4²/₈	1086	94
■ *McDonough Co. – Richard F. Krohe – Richard F. Krohe – 1986*											
176⁷/₈	27¹/₈	27⁶/₈	18⁵/₈	20⁵/₈	4⁴/₈	4⁵/₈	5	5		1086	94
■ *Cass Co. – Mark A. Kluckman – Mark A. Kluckman – 1988*											
176⁷/₈	26⁷/₈	26⁶/₈	21³/₈	24⁵/₈	5⁵/₈	5⁴/₈	5	5		1086	94
■ *Saline Co. – Edward L. Brown – Edward L. Brown – 1991*											
176⁶/₈	26¹/₈	25¹/₈	19⁶/₈	22⁴/₈	4⁴/₈	4⁴/₈	6	7		1103†	97†
■ *Jasper Co. – Marty A. Draves – Marty A. Draves – 2001*											
176⁶/₈	27⁴/₈	26	22⁷/₈	24⁵/₈	4⁵/₈	5¹/₈	7	5	1⁵/₈	1103	97
■ *McHenry Co. – Eugene Melby – Eugene Melby – 1988*											
176⁶/₈	25⁷/₈	25¹/₈	21⁴/₈	24³/₈	4⁵/₈	4⁶/₈	6	6		1103	97
■ *Kane Co. – Mark O. DuLong – Mark O. DuLong – 1991*											
176⁶/₈	25⁴/₈	25⁶/₈	21¹/₈	23	4⁶/₈	4⁶/₈	7	6	1¹/₈	1103	97
■ *Bureau Co. – John Binz – John Binz – 1996*											
176⁶/₈	26⁷/₈	26³/₈	23⁶/₈	26¹/₈	6²/₈	5⁵/₈	6	7	2	1103	97
■ *Jefferson Co. – Steve S. Shields – Steve S. Shields – 1996*											
176⁵/₈	26⁶/₈	25⁵/₈	18⁵/₈	21³/₈	4⁴/₈	4⁶/₈	6	6		1134	102
■ *Henderson Co. – Quinton R. Koch – Quinton R. Koch – 1991*											
176⁵/₈	28	27⁵/₈	20⁵/₈	23⁴/₈	5⁵/₈	5⁶/₈	9	5	9	1134	102
■ *McHenry Co. – David J. Binz – David J. Binz – 1992*											

Score	Length of Main Beam Right	Left	Inside Spread	Greatest Spread	Circumference at Smallest Place Between Burr and First Point Right	Left	Number of Points Right	Left	Lengths Abnormal Points	All-Time Rank	State Rank
176⁴/₈	27²/₈	28²/₈	20⁷/₈	22⁷/₈	4⁷/₈	4⁵/₈	7	8	7⁵/₈	1158	104
■ Saline Co. – John D. Jackson – John D. Jackson – 1999											
176³/₈	27³/₈	26⁵/₈	21⁶/₈	24	5³/₈	5⁴/₈	5	6	1⁵/₈	1182	105
■ Hamilton Co. – Dennis W. Woolard, Jr. – Dennis W. Woolard, Jr. – 1989											
176³/₈	28⁴/₈	28³/₈	22³/₈	24³/₈	4⁷/₈	4⁶/₈	5	5		1182	105
■ Rock Island Co. – Douglas J. Grudzinski – Douglas J. Grudzinski – 1995											
176³/₈	27⁷/₈	28¹/₈	20⁵/₈	23²/₈	5⁴/₈	5³/₈	5	5		1182	105
■ Knox Co. – Jason McCulloch – Jason McCulloch – 1996											
176³/₈	28⁷/₈	27⁵/₈	21²/₈	23⁴/₈	5	5	6	6	12³/₈	1182	105
■ Adams Co. – Lawrence Walton – Lawrence Walton – 1997											
176²/₈	26²/₈	25⁵/₈	18⁴/₈	21	4⁷/₈	4⁷/₈	6	8	8⁴/₈	1209	109
■ Brown Co. – Picked Up – William S. Boyd – PR 1992											
176²/₈	28⁵/₈	30³/₈	20⁴/₈	22⁶/₈	4⁷/₈	4⁵/₈	7	7	3	1209	109
■ Wayne Co. – Kent A. Ochs – Kent A. Ochs – 1997											
176¹/₈	26⁶/₈	26⁵/₈	19⁵/₈	23	5²/₈	5²/₈	6	6	2	1243	111
■ Jackson Co. – Aaron E. Harsy – Aaron E. Harsy – 1994											
176¹/₈	24³/₈	24	17⁷/₈	19⁵/₈	4⁶/₈	4⁷/₈	6	6		1243	111
■ Adams Co. – Thomas M. Foote – Thomas M. Foote – 1998											
175⁷/₈	23⁴/₈	25	17¹/₈	23²/₈	5²/₈	5²/₈	6	5	1⁶/₈	1287	113
■ Johnson Co. – Thomas F. Byrne – Thomas F. Byrne – 1993											
175⁷/₈	26⁷/₈	26³/₈	16⁵/₈	19	5²/₈	4⁷/₈	8	10	9⁴/₈	1287	113
■ Brown Co. – Mark W. West – Mark W. West – 1997											
175⁶/₈	29³/₈	29⁵/₈	28⁴/₈	31	6	6	5	7	14⁴/₈	1310	115
■ Randolph Co. – Picked Up – Bass Pro Shops – 1965											
175⁶/₈	26²/₈	26⁵/₈	22⁴/₈		5¹/₈	5	5	6	4⁶/₈	1310	115
■ Pope Co. – Picked Up – James W. Seets – PR 1982											
175⁶/₈	28⁶/₈	29¹/₈	21⁴/₈	23⁵/₈	5⁷/₈	5⁵/₈	8	8	3⁶/₈	1310	115
■ Williamson Co. – Timothy S. Holmes – Timothy S. Holmes – 1991											
175⁵/₈	26⁵/₈	26³/₈	24⁵/₈	26³/₈	5⁵/₈	5⁶/₈	7	6	6⁶/₈	1333	118
■ Randolph Co. – Larry A. Ruebke – Larry A. Ruebke – 1993											
175⁴/₈	30²/₈	29	22³/₈	25	5⁶/₈	5⁷/₈	8	7	8⁷/₈	1352	119
■ Jo Daviess Co. – J.O. Engebretson – J.O. Engebretson – 1963											
175⁴/₈	27⁵/₈	27³/₈	22⁶/₈	25	5	4⁶/₈	5	5		1352	119
■ Jo Daviess Co. – Richard J. McCartin, Sr. – Richard J. McCartin, Sr. – 1991											
175⁴/₈	30¹/₈	30⁴/₈	23⁴/₈	25²/₈	5⁴/₈	5	9	5	5⁴/₈	1352	119
■ Wayne Co. – Donald L. Sutton – Donald L. Sutton – 1994											
175³/₈	24⁵/₈	25²/₈	20⁴/₈	22⁵/₈	5⁶/₈	5⁵/₈	5	6	2³/₈	1377	122
■ Williamson Co. – Lewis F. Simon – Lewis F. Simon – 1973											
175³/₈	26	25⁴/₈	17⁷/₈	20³/₈	5¹/₈	5³/₈	5	6		1377	122
■ Clark Co. – Gary L. Lovell – Gary L. Lovell – 1986											
175²/₈	28⁷/₈	27⁶/₈	19¹/₈	21⁵/₈	4⁵/₈	4⁵/₈	8	7	6¹/₈	1403†	124†
■ Pike Co. – Lewis W. Henry, Jr. – Lewis W. Henry, Jr. – 2000											

Score	Length of Main Beam		Inside Spread	Greatest Spread	Circumference at Smallest Place Between Burr and First Point		Number of Points		Lengths Abnormal Points	All-Time Rank	State Rank
	Right	Left			Right	Left	Right	Left			
	Location of Kill – Hunter – Owner – Date Killed										
175²/8	26⁷/8	27²/8	21	23¹/8	4⁷/8	5	5	6		1403†	124†
	■ *Jersey Co. – Jacob J. Laramee – Jacob J. Laramee – 1998*										
175²/8	27¹/8	27	19	21³/8	6	6¹/8	5	5		1403	124
	■ *Union Co. – Randy Edmonds – Randy Edmonds – 1984*										
175²/8	30	28³/8	22	24	6¹/8	6¹/8	8	7	11⁴/8	1403	124
	■ *Schuyler Co. – Rodney C. Chute – Rodney C. Chute – 1989*										
175²/8	26⁶/8	27⁴/8	23	25⁴/8	5¹/8	5³/8	5	6		1403	124
	■ *Henry Co. – Bradley DeMay – Bradley DeMay – 1989*										
175²/8	25⁶/8	26²/8	19⁵/8	22⁷/8	4³/8	4⁴/8	5	7	3⁷/8	1403	124
	■ *Jo Daviess Co. – Michael J. Traum – Michael J. Traum – 1989*										
175²/8	27¹/8	27²/8	21¹/8	23⁵/8	5⁴/8	5⁴/8	5	9	8⁵/8	1403	124
	■ *Greene Co. – Picked Up – Mark B. Thompson – 1991*										
175²/8	27⁴/8	26⁷/8	21⁷/8	26	5³/8	5⁴/8	6	6	8⁵/8	1403	124
	■ *Richland Co. – Cory A. Ristvedt – Cory A. Ristvedt – 1997*										
175²/8	25⁴/8	25⁴/8	22⁶/8	25⁷/8	4⁶/8	4⁶/8	6	7	5²/8	1403	124
	■ *Piatt Co. – Jerry Rudisill – Jerry Rudisill – 1999*										
175	26²/8	25⁷/8	20²/8	22²/8	5²/8	5³/8	5	5		1472†	133†
	■ *Knox Co. – Joel P. Catlin – Joel P. Catlin – 2001*										
175	28¹/8	28²/8	21⁴/8	24	5¹/8	5	6	5	1⁶/8	1472†	133†
	■ *Lake Co. – Picked Up – Nancy L. Egbert – 1998*										
175	26³/8	25⁴/8	17	19	4⁷/8	4⁶/8	6	5		1472	133
	■ *Bureau Co. – Paul S. Cobane III – Paul S. Cobane III – 1990*										
175	28³/8	28⁵/8	21	23⁵/8	5⁴/8	5³/8	5	7	4⁶/8	1472	133
	■ *Schuyler Co. – Marc S. Anthony – Marc S. Anthony – 1995*										
174⁷/8	27⁵/8	27⁵/8	20¹/8	22⁴/8	4³/8	4⁴/8	6	6		1513	137
	■ *Clinton Co. – Mark A. Porter – Mark A. Porter – 1991*										
174⁷/8	25⁵/8	25⁶/8	21³/8	23⁶/8	4⁷/8	4⁶/8	5	6		1513	137
	■ *Jo Daviess Co. – W.V. Patrick – Jerry Patrick – 1983*										
174⁶/8	25⁷/8	27¹/8	24⁴/8	26⁷/8	4⁶/8	4⁵/8	6	6		1534†	139†
	■ *Winnebago Co. – Charles P. Lanzendorf – Charles P. Lanzendorf – 1998*										
174⁶/8	27¹/8	25	19²/8	23⁶/8	4⁶/8	4⁷/8	5	5		1534†	139†
	■ *Vermilion Co. – Chris W. Magrini – Chris W. Magrini – 2000*										
174⁶/8	26⁶/8	26	20⁶/8	23²/8	4⁶/8	4⁵/8	6	5		1534	139
	■ *Jo Daviess Co. – Steven C. Rosenthal – Steven C. Rosenthal – 1993*										
174⁶/8	27⁷/8	27⁶/8	18⁶/8	22	4⁵/8	4⁶/8	5	5		1534	139
	■ *Union Co. – Dirk A. Hernandez – Dirk A. Hernandez – 1997*										
174⁵/8	26⁴/8	26⁴/8	18¹/8	20²/8	4⁶/8	4⁶/8	5	5		1561	143
	■ *Jasper Co. – Harold L. Ochs – Harold L. Ochs – 1982*										
174⁵/8	27	27³/8	19³/8	21²/8	5	5	6	6		1561	143
	■ *Jefferson Co. – Brian G. Pierce – Brian G. Pierce – 1992*										
174⁴/8	27²/8	26³/8	18³/8	20⁴/8	5²/8	4⁶/8	8	5	6³/8	1592	145
	■ *Lee Co. – Fred L. Schimel – Fred L. Schimel – 1988*										

Score	Length of Main Beam Right	Left	Inside Spread	Greatest Spread	Circumference at Smallest Place Between Burr and First Point Right	Left	Number of Points Right	Left	Lengths Abnormal Points	All-Time Rank	State Rank
	■ *Location of Kill – Hunter – Owner – Date Killed*										
174⁴/₈	27³/₈	27⁶/₈	18	20	5	5¹/₈	5	5		1592	145
	■ *Calhoun Co. – Michael L. Moore – Michael L. Moore – 1989*										
174⁴/₈	29	28¹/₈	19⁷/₈	22⁴/₈	5¹/₈	5	6	5	1¹/₈	1592	145
	■ *McDonough Co. – Gary Shelley – Gary Shelley – 1991*										
174⁴/₈	27³/₈	28³/₈	23²/₈	25⁴/₈	5²/₈	5¹/₈	8	7	9²/₈	1592	145
	■ *Massac Co. – Josh A. Bowman – Josh A. Bowman – 1997*										
174⁴/₈	30¹/₈	28⁶/₈	22⁵/₈	24⁵/₈	5²/₈	5³/₈	7	6	2¹/₈	1592	145
	■ *Randolph Co. – William S. Simmons – William S. Simmons – 1998*										
174³/₈	26	25¹/₈	20²/₈	23⁶/₈	5²/₈	5⁶/₈	5	7	3¹/₈	1619†	150†
	■ *Fulton Co. – Robert V. Stevenson, Jr. – Robert V. Stevenson, Jr. – 1999*										
174²/₈	25²/₈	24⁵/₈	20⁴/₈	22³/₈	4⁴/₈	4⁴/₈	6	6		1652†	151†
	■ *Brown Co. – David A. Bowen – David A. Bowen – 2001*										
174¹/₈	25⁶/₈	25⁵/₈	19⁶/₈	22⁷/₈	5	4⁷/₈	6	6	2¹/₈	1678	152
	■ *McDonough Co. – Jack C. Icenogle – Jack C. Icenogle – 1986*										
174¹/₈	26²/₈	27	20	22³/₈	4⁷/₈	5¹/₈	7	5	2⁷/₈	1678	152
	■ *Adams Co. – Robert Daly – Robert Daly – 1993*										
174¹/₈	28	27²/₈	25	27	5⁴/₈	5⁶/₈	6	5	1³/₈	1678	152
	■ *Montgomery Co. – Justin K. Arndt – Justin K. Arndt – 1994*										
174	25⁷/₈	26³/₈	23	24⁷/₈	5¹/₈	5¹/₈	8	5	10²/₈	1717	155
	■ *Vermilion Co. – Alex L. Ramm – Alex L. Ramm – 1995*										
174	26⁴/₈	26⁴/₈	18	20	6	6	5	5		1717	155
	■ *La Salle Co. – Michael Armstrong – Michael Armstrong – 1996*										
173⁷/₈	26³/₈	27⁷/₈	21⁴/₈	23⁷/₈	6¹/₈	5⁷/₈	6	6	2¹/₈	1743	157
	■ *Will Co. – Harry D. Hammock – Harry D. Hammock – 1995*										
173⁶/₈	26⁶/₈	27¹/₈	19⁷/₈	22	5⁵/₈	5³/₈	7	5	6¹/₈	1766	158
	■ *Mercer Co. – Floyd A. Clark – Floyd A. Clark – 1961*										
173⁶/₈	25⁶/₈	25⁶/₈	19⁶/₈	21⁴/₈	4¹/₈	4⁴/₈	5	5		1766	158
	■ *Pulaski Co. – Rose M. Blanchard – Rose M. Blanchard – 1973*										
173⁶/₈	26⁴/₈	25²/₈	21⁴/₈	27	5²/₈	5³/₈	6	5	3⁶/₈	1766	158
	■ *Mercer Co. – Clarence R. Howard – Clarence R. Howard – 1990*										
173⁶/₈	27¹/₈	27	24⁴/₈	26	5	5	5	6		1766	158
	■ *McHenry Co. – Richard E. Pope – Richard E. Pope – 1997*										
173⁶/₈	27⁴/₈	26⁴/₈	21²/₈	23	5¹/₈	5²/₈	6	5	5⁴/₈	1766	158
	■ *Brown Co. – Michael P. Postema – Michael P. Postema – 1997*										
173⁵/₈	25⁵/₈	25⁵/₈	19⁷/₈	23	4³/₈	4²/₈	5	5		1819†	163†
	■ *Jo Daviess Co. – William B. Bland – William B. Bland – 2001*										
173⁵/₈	25⁷/₈	25	19²/₈	21⁶/₈	5⁶/₈	5⁷/₈	6	6	7¹/₈	1819†	163†
	■ *Adams Co. – Mike L. Melton – Mike L. Melton – 2000*										
173⁵/₈	27³/₈	27⁷/₈	18⁷/₈	21	6⁴/₈	5⁵/₈	7	5	3⁶/₈	1819	163
	■ *Pike Co. – Jimmy Howard – Jimmy Howard – 1989*										
173⁵/₈	27⁵/₈	26⁶/₈	25¹/₈	27²/₈	4⁴/₈	4⁶/₈	8	8	10⁴/₈	1819	163
	■ *Will Co. – Jeremy L. Johnson – Jeremy L. Johnson – 1994*										

Score	Length of Main Beam Right Left	Inside Spread	Greatest Spread	Circumference at Smallest Place Between Burr and First Point Right Left		Number of Points Right Left		Lengths Abnormal Points	All-Time Rank	State Rank
173 5/8	26 4/8 27 4/8 ■ Location of Kill – Hunter – Owner – Date Killed	20	23 1/8	4 6/8	4 5/8	8	5	3 1/8	1819	163
	■ Kankakee Co. – Tim Lynch – Tim Lynch – 1999									
173 4/8	25 1/8 24 3/8	18 6/8	21	5 3/8	5 4/8	5	5		1847†	168†
	■ Adams Co. – Wayne A. Brinkley – Wayne A. Brinkley – 2000									
173 4/8	26 26 5/8	20 6/8	22 5/8	4 4/8	4 2/8	5	6	3 4/8	1847†	168†
	■ Greene Co. – Ryan M. Swearingin – Ryan M. Swearingin – 2001									
173 4/8	25 7/8 27	23	25 2/8	5	5 1/8	5	5		1847	168
	■ McHenry Co. – Gordon R. Sunderlage – Gordon R. Sunderlage – 1987									
173 3/8	26 5/8 26 1/8	18 7/8	21	4 6/8	4 5/8	7	9	9 4/8	1883	171
	■ Montgomery Co. – Douglas C. Furtwengler – Douglas C. Furtwengler – 1988									
173 3/8	23 3/8 26 7/8	18 6/8	21 2/8	5 3/8	5 4/8	7	5	1 3/8	1883	171
	■ Coles Co. – Thomas D. Simmering – Thomas D. Simmering – 1989									
173 3/8	27 2/8 27	28 7/8	31 2/8	5	5 1/8	5	6	1 5/8	1883	171
	■ Kane Co. – James Meyer – James Meyer – 1995									
173 2/8	24 3/8 24 4/8	24 4/8	25 4/8	5 2/8	5 2/8	6	8	2 6/8	1914†	174†
	■ Henderson Co. – David L. Alberts – David L. Alberts – 2000									
173 2/8	30 1/8 27 5/8	20 6/8	23 3/8	5	5	6	6	13 6/8	1914	174
	■ Calhoun Co. – Picked Up – Dean Diaz – 1990									
173 2/8	27 1/8 28 1/8	19 3/8	21 7/8	5 2/8	5 1/8	6	4	1 1/8	1914	174
	■ Sangamon Co. – Brian Daily – Brian Daily – 1995									
173 2/8	21 3/8 22 4/8	15	18 4/8	5 1/8	5 2/8	5	6		1914	174
	■ Pope Co. – James W. Sanderson – James W. Sanderson – 1997									
173 1/8	27 3/8 27	22 1/8	24 4/8	4 7/8	5	5	6	1 2/8	1950†	178†
	■ Williamson Co. – Jay Johns – Jay Johns – 1997									
173 1/8	27 6/8 28 2/8	20	22 1/8	5 6/8	6	5	6	2 3/8	1950†	178†
	■ Coles Co. – Ron Osborne – Ron Osborne – 2000									
173 1/8	26 3/8 26 2/8	19 5/8	22 3/8	5 3/8	5 4/8	5	5		1950	178
	■ Macon Co. – Stuart A. Wolken – Stuart A. Wolken – 1996									
173	26 25 7/8	21 6/8	24	4 7/8	4 5/8	6	6		1991†	181†
	■ McHenry Co. – Chase M. Ziller – Chase M. Ziller – 2001 ■ See photo on page 133									
173	26 6/8 26 5/8	17 6/8	20 4/8	4 4/8	4 4/8	8	6	7 6/8	1991	181
	■ Macoupin Co. – Dickie A. Spurgeon – Dickie A. Spurgeon – 1995									
172 7/8	28 2/8 27 7/8	21 3/8	23 4/8	5 5/8	5 4/8	5	5		2038†	183†
	■ Scott Co. – Josh L. Roach – Josh L. Roach – 2001									
172 7/8	25 4/8 26 5/8	19 7/8	22 3/8	5 5/8	5 4/8	5	6	1 6/8	2038	183
	■ Williamson Co. – Picked Up – John L. Roseberry – 1975									
172 7/8	25 7/8 26 5/8	20 6/8	22 4/8	4 6/8	4 6/8	6	5	4 7/8	2038	183
	■ Pike Co. – Robert L. Hubbell – Robert L. Hubbell – 1987									
172 7/8	27 6/8 27 1/8	18 5/8	20 4/8	5 3/8	5 2/8	5	6	1	2038	183
	■ Vermilion Co. – Edwin B. Gudgel – Edwin B. Gudgel – 1988									
172 6/8	27 3/8 28 2/8	20 2/8	24	4 6/8	4 7/8	5	5		2065	187
	■ Pope Co. – George Koderhandt, Sr. – David Koderhandt – 1963									

Score	Length of Main Beam Right / Left		Inside Spread	Greatest Spread	Circumference at Smallest Place Between Burr and First Point Right / Left		Number of Points Right / Left		Lengths Abnormal Points	All-Time Rank	State Rank
	■ Location of Kill – Hunter – Owner – Date Killed										
172 6/8	27 4/8	27	24 4/8	26 6/8	4 5/8	4 6/8	6	6	4 4/8	2065	187
■ Henderson Co. – Larry Spiker – William H. Lilienthal – 1988											
172 6/8	29 4/8	26 2/8	22 6/8	24 7/8	6 1/8	6 2/8	7	6	6 2/8	2065	187
■ Richland Co. – Donald L. Ginder – Donald L. Ginder – 1991											
172 6/8	28	28 7/8	19 2/8	21 5/8	5 1/8	5 1/8	6	5		2065	187
■ Moultrie Co. – Joseph D. Nelson – Joseph D. Nelson – 1991											
172 6/8	26 1/8	25 3/8	17 4/8	19 4/8	4 5/8	4 6/8	7	6		2065	187
■ Cass Co. – Tom M. Roberts – Tom M. Roberts – 1995											
172 6/8	25	25 6/8	19 1/8	21 2/8	6 3/8	6 3/8	5	8	7 5/8	2065	187
■ McLean Co. – Picked Up – Matt Cheever – 1998											
172 5/8	27 1/8	26 4/8	21 2/8	23 2/8	4 7/8	5 2/8	5	6	1 7/8	2113	193
■ Marshall Co. – Oscar C. Weber – Oscar C. Weber – 1991											
172 5/8	25 1/8	25 6/8	17	18 5/8	4 7/8	4 7/8	6	5	2 3/8	2113	193
■ Menard Co. – Jeffrey M. Balding – Jeffrey M. Balding – 1996											
172 5/8	27 5/8	26 6/8	19 7/8	22 1/8	5 4/8	5 4/8	4	5	1 4/8	2113	193
■ Coles Co. – Shane D. Duzan – Shane D. Duzan – 1996											
172 5/8	25 4/8	26	20 1/8	22 2/8	5	4 7/8	5	6		2113	193
■ Fayette Co. – Joseph M. Kirk – Joseph M. Kirk – 1996											
172 4/8	23 5/8	25 2/8	20	22 5/8	6 1/8	5 7/8	6	5	7	2156	197
■ Franklin Co. – Joseph S. Smothers – Joseph S. Smothers – 1984											
172 4/8	26 2/8	26 4/8	20 4/8	23 1/8	5 1/8	5	5	5		2156	197
■ Fulton Co. – Marcus E. Christensen – Marcus E. Christensen – 1990											
172 4/8	27 5/8	27 3/8	20 2/8	24 1/8	4 7/8	4 6/8	8	9	9	2156	197
■ Marion Co. – Michele Hanks – Michele Hanks – 1991											
172 4/8	24 5/8	26 2/8	16 6/8	19 4/8	4 2/8	4 3/8	5	5		2156	197
■ Bond Co. – William G. Brown – William G. Brown – 1995											
172 3/8	27	27 3/8	23 5/8	26 6/8	5 3/8	5 3/8	6	6	4 2/8	2200	201
■ McHenry Co. – Kevin Rubow – Kevin Rubow – 1990											
172 3/8	26 5/8	27 5/8	18 7/8	21 1/8	5	5	5	5		2200	201
■ La Salle Co. – William J. Keith – William J. Keith – 1994											
172 2/8	31 4/8	30 7/8	23 5/8	26	4 7/8	5 1/8	6	5	1 3/8	2237	203
■ Perry Co. – Raymond E. Haertling – Raymond E. Haertling – 1968											
172 2/8	25 4/8	22 4/8	23 3/8	24 3/8	4 7/8	5	7	6	1 1/8	2237	203
■ Perry Co. – Ralph J. Przygoda, Jr. – Ralph J. Przygoda, Jr. – 1978											
172 2/8	25 1/8	25	18	20 4/8	5 2/8	5	6	6		2237	203
■ Union Co. – Richard A. Sotiropoulos – Richard A. Sotiropoulos – 1990											
172 2/8	27 4/8	28	20 2/8	22 4/8	4 7/8	5 1/8	6	6	4	2237	203
■ Peoria Co. – Heye H. Peters, Jr. – Heye H. Peters, Jr. – 1999											
172 1/8	25 1/8	25 5/8	19 1/8	22 7/8	4 4/8	4 3/8	6	5	2	2286†	207†
■ Rock Island Co. – Ron Baum – Keith Hogan – 1985											
172 1/8	24 7/8	24	18 6/8	22 1/8	4 6/8	4 6/8	6	7	1 1/8	2286	207
■ Clinton Co. – James D. Rueter – James D. Rueter – 1984											

Score	Length of Main Beam Right Left	Inside Spread	Greatest Spread	Circumference at Smallest Place Between Burr and First Point Right Left	Number of Points Right Left	Lengths Abnormal Points	All-Time Rank	State Rank
172 1/8	25 1/8 24 6/8	22 5/8	25 1/8	5 7/8 5 7/8	8 8	10	2286	207
	▪ Lake Co. – Mark J. Kramer – Mark J. Kramer – 1990							
172 1/8	27 5/8 27 5/8	20	22 2/8	5 2/8 5 1/8	8 7	8 1/8	2286	207
	▪ Kankakee Co. – Darrel L. Duby – Darrel L. Duby – 1999							
172 1/8	26 2/8 25 6/8	22 7/8	26	5 3/8 5 3/8	5 5		2286	207
	▪ Lake Co. – Derrell W. Listhartke – Derrell W. Listhartke – 2000							
172	27 2/8 26 6/8	20 7/8	22 6/8	4 7/8 4 6/8	6 9	6 1/8	2330†	212†
	▪ St. Clair Co. – James R. Smith – James R. Smith – 2001							
172	25 2/8 25 6/8	18 4/8	21 2/8	5 3/8 5 2/8	5 7	6 4/8	2330	212
	▪ Henderson Co. – Harry M. Carner – Harry M. Carner – 1959							
172	29 5/8 29 4/8	22 2/8	24 2/8	5 4/8 5 4/8	4 4		2330	212
	▪ Edwards Co. – Picked Up – George W. Flaim – 1985							
172	27 5/8 28	23 5/8	25 6/8	5 5/8 6	6 6	2 5/8	2330	212
	▪ Greene Co. – B. David McCarthy – B. David McCarthy – 1992							
171 7/8	27 7/8 26 6/8	22 7/8	25	4 3/8 4 5/8	5 5		2382†	216†
	▪ Putnam Co. – Robert D. Koeppel – Robert D. Koeppel – 1985							
171 7/8	27 7/8 27 6/8	20 5/8	22 7/8	5 4 7/8	5 6	1 2/8	2382	216
	▪ Whiteside Co. – Ann M. Ryan – Ann M. Ryan – 1991							
171 7/8	27 4/8 26 7/8	20 7/8	23	4 6/8 4 6/8	6 5		2382	216
	▪ Jo Daviess Co. – Donald W. Hansen, Jr. – Donald W. Hansen, Jr. – 1994							
171 7/8	24 2/8 25 6/8	22 7/8	26 3/8	5 2/8 5 3/8	8 8	8 4/8	2382	216
	▪ Peoria Co. – Richard W. Winship – Richard W. Winship – 1996							
171 6/8	27 3/8 26 2/8	21	23 1/8	4 5/8 4 4/8	6 5	1 4/8	2418	220
	▪ Adams Co. – R.C. Stephens – R.C. Stephens – 1975							
171 6/8	26 6/8 26 3/8	19 7/8	24 4/8	5 3/8 5 3/8	7 10	12 3/8	2418	220
	▪ Perry Co. – Daniel P. Hollenkamp – Daniel P. Hollenkamp – 1982							
171 6/8	27 7/8 29 3/8	22 6/8	24 6/8	5 5/8 5 5/8	7 6	6 4/8	2418	220
	▪ Hancock Co. – Garold E. McConnull – Garold E. McConnull – 1993							
171 5/8	27 26 6/8	18 4/8	21	4 5/8 4 5/8	6 7	1 1/8	2470†	223†
	▪ Vermilion Co. – Jeff Dodd – Jeff Dodd – 2001							
171 5/8	25 6/8 26 2/8	21 5/8	23 4/8	4 6/8 4 7/8	5 5		2470†	223†
	▪ Dewitt Co. – William A. Steward – William A. Steward – 2001							
171 5/8	26 26 5/8	19 5/8	21 5/8	4 6/8 4 6/8	5 5		2470	223
	▪ Grundy Co. – Joseph A. Gray – Joseph A. Gray – 1997							
171 4/8	26 26 7/8	17	20 4/8	5 2/8 5 3/8	6 5	2	2513	226
	▪ Kankakee Co. – Dennis Schneider – Dennis Schneider – 1988							
171 4/8	25 3/8 24 3/8	21	23 3/8	5 4/8 5 2/8	5 5		2513	226
	▪ Rock Island Co. – David Parchert – David Parchert – 1990							
171 4/8	24 1/8 24 5/8	18 4/8	20 6/8	4 6/8 4 5/8	6 6		2513	226
	▪ Sangamon Co. – Michael R. Vincent – Michael R. Vincent – 1991							
171 4/8	26 3/8 26 2/8	21 4/8	23 2/8	5 5 1/8	6 6		2513	226
	▪ Whiteside Co. – William D. Kruse – William D. Kruse – 1992							

Score	Length of Main Beam Right Left	Inside Spread	Greatest Spread	Circumference at Smallest Place Between Burr and First Point Right Left	Number of Points Right Left	Lengths Abnormal Points	All-Time Rank	State Rank
171 4/8	27 26 6/8	22 6/8	24 7/8	4 6/8 4 6/8	5 6	1	2513	226
■ Jasper Co. – Rick N. Strole – Rick N. Strole – 1992								
171 3/8	25 3/8 26 2/8	16 2/8	19 2/8	4 6/8 4 6/8	6 7	4 1/8	2564	231
■ Pike Co. – John C. Shover – John C. Shover – 1979								
171 3/8	24 3/8 24 7/8	21 1/8	23 1/8	5 4 7/8	5 5		2564	231
■ Jersey Co. – Louis E. Johnson – Louis E. Johnson – 1992								
171 3/8	27 2/8 27 4/8	19 2/8	21 6/8	4 5/8 4 6/8	7 8	4 3/8	2564	231
■ Madison Co. – Keith T. Probst – Keith T. Probst – 1993								
171 2/8	27 3/8 27	21	22 3/8	4 5/8 4 5/8	5 5		2621	234
■ Randolph Co. – Steven R. Thompson – Steven R. Thompson – 1986								
171 2/8	27 5/8 27 2/8	19 1/8	20 5/8	5 1/8 5 1/8	5 6	1 1/8	2621	234
■ Henry Co. – Kevin P. Casteel – Kevin P. Casteel – 1992								
171 2/8	26 1/8 26	21	22 7/8	5 5 1/8	6 7	4 4/8	2621	234
■ Warren Co. – R. Craig Akers – R. Craig Akers – 1996								
171 2/8	27 6/8 26 4/8	20 4/8	24 4/8	4 5/8 4 6/8	5 5		2621	234
■ Logan Co. – Brian M. Laubenstein – Brian M. Laubenstein – 1997								
171 1/8	25 5/8 25 6/8	19 2/8	21 3/8	4 4/8 4 5/8	7 7	5 1/8	2665	238
■ Pike Co. – Jarrod Kirk – Jarrod Kirk – 1991								
171 1/8	25 3/8 26	21 4/8	23 4/8	6 5 6/8	7 6	7 1/8	2665	238
■ Jersey Co. – Allen E. Conrad – Allen E. Conrad – 1992								
171	26 2/8 25 4/8	21 6/8	23 6/8	4 4/8 4 7/8	5 5		2707	240
■ Williamson Co. – Ronnie G. Fletcher – Ronnie G. Fletcher – 1988								
171	24 6/8 25	18 6/8	21	4 4/8 4 5/8	6 6		2707	240
■ Peoria Co. – Leslie G. Shipp – Leslie G. Shipp – 1991								
171	24 4/8 24 7/8	20 4/8	22 5/8	5 2/8 5 4/8	5 5		2707	240
■ Livingston Co. – Lloyd D. Kemnetz, Jr. – Lloyd D. Kemnetz, Jr. – 1992								
171	29 4/8 27 7/8	26 4/8	29	6 6	4 6	4	2707	240
■ Alexander Co. – Robert A. Kaufman – Robert A. Kaufman – 1995								
171	26 5/8 25 5/8	19 4/8	22 2/8	5 3/8 5 4/8	7 7	3 2/8	2707	240
■ Lawrence Co. – Picked Up – Michael E. Neikiek – 1996								
170 7/8	29 29 3/8	21 5/8	24 4/8	6 3/8 5 3/8	4 4		2769	245
■ Shelby Co. – Paul C. Marley, Sr. – Paul C. Marley, Sr. – 1985								
170 7/8	30 4/8 30 2/8	24 7/8	26 3/8	4 2/8 4 2/8	5 5		2769	245
■ Alexander Co. – Kenneth L. Karhliker – Kenneth L. Karhliker – 1986								
170 7/8	24 25 2/8	20 1/8	22 3/8	4 7/8 4 7/8	6 6		2769	245
■ Knox Co. – Carl A. Swanson – Carl A. Swanson – 1989								
170 7/8	26 4/8 27 7/8	19 1/8	24 5/8	4 3/8 4 4/8	6 6	7	2769	245
■ St. Clair Co. – Donald F. Mehrtens – Donald F. Mehrtens – 1993								
170 7/8	23 3/8 23 3/8	18 1/8	20	5 5	7 6	4 4/8	2769	245
■ Shelby Co. – Robert A. Howell – Robert A. Howell – 1998								
170 6/8	26 2/8 25 6/8	19	21 1/8	5 2/8 5 1/8	6 6		2828	250
■ Coles Co. – Jeff D. Shrader – Jeff D. Shrader – 1990								

Score	Length of Main Beam Right	Left	Inside Spread	Greatest Spread	Circumference at Smallest Place Between Burr and First Point Right	Left	Number of Points Right	Left	Lengths Abnormal Points	All-Time Rank	State Rank

■ *Location of Kill – Hunter – Owner – Date Killed*

Score	Main Beam R	L	Inside	Greatest	Circ R	Circ L	Pts R	Pts L	Abnormal	All-Time	State
170 6/8	28 4/8	26 7/8	18 7/8	21 3/8	4 3/8	4 4/8	5	6	1 1/8	2828	250
170 6/8	27 1/8	27 3/8	18 6/8	21	5 4/8	5 5/8	5	5		2828	250
170 5/8	26 1/8	26 4/8	19 5/8	21 3/8	4 5/8	4 3/8	7	6	5	2876†	253†
170 5/8	26 1/8	25 4/8	16 7/8	18 6/8	5	4 7/8	6	6		2876†	253†
170 5/8	29	27 4/8	21 1/8	23 5/8	5 1/8	5 1/8	5	5		2876	253
170 4/8	26 3/8	26	19 6/8	22 7/8	4 2/8	4 2/8	5	5		2933	256
170 4/8	26 6/8	26 2/8	21 2/8	23 6/8	5 3/8	5 3/8	7	6	8 2/8	2933	256
170 4/8	25 4/8	24 7/8	22 2/8	23 2/8	5 1/8	5 1/8	5	5		2933	256
170 4/8	26 1/8	26 5/8	21 5/8	23 7/8	4 6/8	4 7/8	6	8	4 7/8	2933	256
170 4/8	24 2/8	23 7/8	19 3/8	21	5 2/8	5 3/8	6	5	1 1/8	2933	256
170 3/8	28 1/8	25 2/8	25 7/8	28 1/8	4 6/8	5	4	4		2992	261
170 3/8	27 5/8	27 5/8	21 5/8	23 7/8	4 6/8	4 7/8	5	5		2992	261
170 3/8	26 5/8	26 4/8	19 6/8	23 2/8	5 1/8	5 1/8	6	7	9 1/8	2992	261
170 3/8	23	23 2/8	17 3/8	19 4/8	5 6/8	5 7/8	6	6		2992	261
170 3/8	26 6/8	27 2/8	22 4/8	26 5/8	6	5 5/8	6	6	2 3/8	2992	261
170 2/8	24 4/8	25 4/8	17	19 4/8	5 3/8	5 3/8	5	5		3063	266
170 2/8	26 2/8	25 7/8	19 2/8	21	4 3/8	4 4/8	5	5		3063	266
170 2/8	28 1/8	27 4/8	22 6/8	25 4/8	5 3/8	4 6/8	7	6	12	3063	266
170 2/8	25 2/8	24 2/8	20 5/8	23 2/8	5 2/8	5 3/8	6	6	5 3/8	3063	266
170 2/8	24 3/8	24 5/8	23	25 5/8	4 6/8	4 7/8	5	6	3 2/8	3063	266
170 2/8	28 1/8	27	21 6/8	24 3/8	5 3/8	5 3/8	7	4	10 2/8	3063	266

■ *Tazewell Co. – Steve R. Larimore – Steve R. Larimore – 1995*
■ *Adams Co. – Steven A. Schwartz – Steven A. Schwartz – 1997*
■ *Mason Co. – Randall E. Ballard – Randall E. Ballard – 2001*
■ *Lawrence Co. – Tim Golden – Tim Golden – 2000*
■ *Adams Co. – Randy J. Kurz – Randy J. Kurz – 1998*
■ *Rock Island Co. – Joseph V. De Schepper – Joseph V. De Schepper – 1991*
■ *Jasper Co. – Joseph W. McIntyre – Joseph W. McIntyre – 1991*
■ *Pike Co. – Donald E. Stefancic, Sr. – Donald E. Stefancic, Sr. – 1991*
■ *Livingston Co. – Alan E. Gray – Alan E. Gray – 1994*
■ *Marion Co. – Louis P. Williams, Jr. – Louis P. Williams, Jr. – 1997*
■ *Saline Co. – Jack Crain – Jack Crain – 1966*
■ *Jasper Co. – Skip Moore – Skip Moore – 1994*
■ *Grundy Co. – Robert Alfonso, Jr. – Robert Alfonso, Jr. – 1996*
■ *McHenry Co. – Donald E. Hoey – Donald E. Hoey – 1996*
■ *Jo Daviess Co. – Cliff Perry – Cliff Perry – 1998*
■ *Ogle Co. – Dick V. Lalowski – Dick V. Lalowski – 1992*
■ *Boone Co. – Matthew L. Schaller – Matthew L. Schaller – 1994*
■ *Edgar Co. – Sharon McDaniel – Sharon McDaniel – 1995*
■ *Clay Co. – Jeremy D. Current – Jeremy D. Current – 1996*
■ *Pike Co. – Michael E. Kennedy – Michael E. Kennedy – 1997*
■ *Hancock Co. – James E. Lenix – James E. Lenix – 1998*

Score	Length of Main Beam Right	Left	Inside Spread	Greatest Spread	Circumference at Smallest Place Between Burr and First Point Right	Left	Number of Points Right	Left	Lengths Abnormal Points	All-Time Rank	State Rank
									■ Location of Kill – Hunter – Owner – Date Killed		
170¹/8	22⁴/8	25⁵/8	20⁵/8	24³/8	4⁶/8	4⁵/8	6	6	1	3143	272
	■ Logan Co. – Gary L. Humbert – Gary L. Humbert – 1979										
170¹/8	26	25⁵/8	20¹/8	21⁷/8	5³/8	5³/8	6	5	1²/8	3143	272
	■ Perry Co. – Stephen E. Brand – Stephen E. Brand – 1991										
170¹/8	28²/8	27⁴/8	22³/8	25⁴/8	4⁶/8	4⁶/8	6	5		3143	272
	■ Lake Co. – John W. Schnider, Jr. – John W. Schnider, Jr. – 1992										
170¹/8	26⁷/8	25	23¹/8	26	5⁵/8	6¹/8	5	5		3143	272
	■ Iroquois Co. – Michael L. Krumweide – Michael L. Krumweide – 1993										
170¹/8	26⁷/8	25³/8	18	21	4²/8	4³/8	6	5	1⁷/8	3143	272
	■ Adams Co. – Jeffrey J. Rakers – Jeffrey J. Rakers – 1994										
170¹/8	26²/8	26⁶/8	16¹/8	20⁶/8	5⁴/8	5⁴/8	6	6	6²/8	3143	272
	■ Brown Co. – Todd D. Carlton – Todd D. Carlton – 1998										
170	27	26²/8	18²/8	20⁵/8	5	4⁴/8	6	5	1⁴/8	3224†	278†
	■ Tazewell Co. – Picked Up – Melissa A. Chirello – 2000										
170	26⁶/8	27	20⁶/8	22⁴/8	5	4⁷/8	5	6	2	3224†	278†
	■ Edgar Co. – K. David Neal – K. David Neal – 2001										
170	23²/8	26	19⁶/8	23	5¹/8	5²/8	7	6	1	3224	278
	■ Henderson Co. – Donald R. Vaughn – Donald R. Vaughn – 1960										
170	28³/8	25⁶/8	21¹/8	23⁵/8	5²/8	5³/8	6	7	4⁷/8	3224	278
	■ Hancock Co. – Henry F. Collins – Henry F. Collins – 1973										
170	28¹/8	27³/8	21³/8	26¹/8	5⁵/8	5⁶/8	9	9	11¹/8	3224	278
	■ Bond Co. – Mark A. Carr – Mark A. Carr – 1991										
170	28⁷/8	27³/8	23¹/8	25²/8	4²/8	4²/8	5	6	1³/8	3224	278
	■ McHenry Co. – Daniel L. Doherty – Daniel L. Doherty – 1992										
170	25⁴/8	25¹/8	20²/8	23⁷/8	5⁶/8	5⁵/8	5	5		3224	278
	■ McHenry Co. – Mike R. Fischer – Mike R. Fischer – 1993										
170	25	24⁶/8	23⁴/8	26²/8	5¹/8	5¹/8	6	6		3224	278
	■ De Witt Co. – Charles A. Leimbach – Charles A. Leimbach – 1994										
170	25⁶/8	27⁵/8	22²/8	24²/8	5	5²/8	4	4		3224	278
	■ Brown Co. – Paul I. Reid – Paul I. Reid – 1994										
170	26⁵/8	25²/8	20⁵/8	22⁶/8	6²/8	6²/8	5	8	4¹/8	3224	278
	■ Pike Co. – Perry Stanley – Perry Stanley – 1996 ■ See photo on page 51										
170	27¹/8	25¹/8	19	22²/8	4⁶/8	4⁷/8	5	5		3224	278
	■ Whiteside Co. – Arlyn D. Hamstra – Arlyn D. Hamstra – 1998										
170	24⁶/8	25⁴/8	19²/8	21²/8	5	4⁷/8	5	5		3224	278
	■ Kane Co. – Bradley J. Lundsteen – Bradley J. Lundsteen – 1998										
169⁴/8	27⁶/8	27⁴/8	22²/8	24²/8	4⁵/8	4⁶/8	5	6		3316†	290†
	■ Cook Co. – Richard P. Bielik, Sr. – Richard P. Bielik, Sr. – 1999										
169²/8	23⁷/8	24⁶/8	18⁶/8	20⁶/8	4³/8	4⁶/8	7	9	11	3336†	291†
	■ Shelby Co. – Scott Reed – Scott Reed – 2001										
168⁷/8	25⁷/8	26	21³/8	25	5⁶/8	5⁶/8	5	6	1²/8	3361†	292†
	■ Greene Co. – David R. Flatt – David R. Flatt – 2001										

Score	Length of Main Beam Right	Length of Main Beam Left	Inside Spread	Greatest Spread	Circumference at Smallest Place Between Burr and First Point Right	Circumference at Smallest Place Between Burr and First Point Left	Number of Points Right	Number of Points Left	Lengths Abnormal Points	All-Time Rank	State Rank

■ Location of Kill – Hunter – Owner – Date Killed

Score	R	L	Inside	Greatest	R	L	R	L	Abnormal	All-Time	State
168⁶/₈	25⁶/₈	26	16²/₈	18⁴/₈	7¹/₈	6⁶/₈	6	5		3367	293
■ McHenry Co. – Charles N. King – Charles N. King – 1995											
168⁵/₈	22⁷/₈	25⁷/₈	19⁵/₈	22¹/₈	4⁷/₈	5²/₈	6	6	2⁶/₈	3376†	294†
■ Pope Co. – Gary A. Roepke – Gary A. Roepke – 2000											
168⁴/₈	26⁴/₈	24⁷/₈	20⁶/₈	22²/₈	4⁶/₈	5	5	5		3385	295
■ Bureau Co. – Jerry M. Nichols – Jerry M. Nichols – 1996											
168⁴/₈	24²/₈	24⁷/₈	19⁶/₈	22	5¹/₈	5¹/₈	5	5		3385	295
■ Clark Co. – Dane E. Thompson – Dane E. Thompson – 1997											
168²/₈	27²/₈	27⁴/₈	22	24⁷/₈	5⁷/₈	5⁷/₈	5	6	1⁶/₈	3414†	297†
■ Macon Co. – Scott Hartman – Scott Hartman – 2001											
167⁷/₈	26²/₈	26⁵/₈	27⁷/₈	28⁶/₈	5⁷/₈	5⁵/₈	5	5		3451	298
■ Mercer Co. – Neil A. Hamerlinck – Neil A. Hamerlinck – 1993											
167⁵/₈	27	26⁵/₈	20	22³/₈	5³/₈	5³/₈	5	6	1¹/₈	3476	299
■ Sangamon Co. – Bruce D. Horne – Bruce D. Horne – 1986											
167³/₈	25	24⁷/₈	19³/₈	21⁶/₈	5³/₈	5⁶/₈	6	5	1²/₈	3500	300
■ Adams Co. – Jay W. Brackensick – Jay W. Brackensick – 1989											
167³/₈	25	26	20⁵/₈	22³/₈	4⁴/₈	4⁶/₈	5	6		3500	300
■ Hancock Co. – Trevor G. Akers – Trevor G. Akers – 1997											
167³/₈	26⁷/₈	25¹/₈	18⁵/₈	20²/₈	4⁶/₈	4⁵/₈	8	7	7⁴/₈	3500	300
■ Alexander Co. – Tom M. Swanson – Tom M. Swanson – 1998											
167²/₈	31²/₈	30³/₈	24²/₈	26⁷/₈	4⁷/₈	4⁵/₈	4	4		3519	303
■ Shelby Co. – Daniel J. Verhasselt – Daniel J. Verhasselt – 1990											
167¹/₈	23⁴/₈	24	18⁵/₈	21	5²/₈	5²/₈	6	5	2⁴/₈	3539	304
■ McHenry Co. – Charlie H. Rand – Charlie H. Rand – 1989											
166⁷/₈	24	23⁶/₈	20⁷/₈	22⁷/₈	5	4⁷/₈	5	5		3568	305
■ McHenry Co. – David A. McGinnis – David A. McGinnis – 1986											
166⁷/₈	24	22⁷/₈	19⁵/₈	21²/₈	6	5⁶/₈	5	6		3568	305
■ Jersey Co. – William P. O'Neal – William P. O'Neal – 1999											
166⁶/₈	23⁶/₈	25²/₈	17²/₈	19⁴/₈	6	6¹/₈	6	5	4²/₈	3582†	307†
■ Calhoun Co. – Mel Eltora – Mel Eltora – 2000											
166⁶/₈	24³/₈	23⁶/₈	18⁶/₈	21⁴/₈	4³/₈	4³/₈	5	5		3582	307
■ De Kalb Co. – Leon Tuestad – Leon Tuestad – 1990											
166³/₈	26⁷/₈	26⁶/₈	19⁵/₈	21⁴/₈	5³/₈	5²/₈	5	5		3620	309
■ Macoupin Co. – Jim D. Hitchings – Jim D. Hitchings – 1995											
166²/₈	29⁴/₈	28¹/₈	28¹/₈	30³/₈	5⁴/₈	5⁴/₈	6	5	7⁵/₈	3632	310
■ La Salle Co. – Jeffrey A. Sampson – Jeffrey A. Sampson – 1990											
166²/₈	24⁵/₈	24⁷/₈	19²/₈	21³/₈	4⁶/₈	5⁵/₈	6	7	3²/₈	3632	310
■ Kane Co. – Roy D. Howard – Roy D. Howard – 1991											
166²/₈	26³/₈	26¹/₈	19²/₈	21⁶/₈	4³/₈	4⁴/₈	6	6	2⁴/₈	3632	310
■ Sangamon Co. – John W. Jacobs – John W. Jacobs – 1994											
166¹/₈	24²/₈	26²/₈	18⁴/₈	20⁵/₈	5	5²/₈	7	6	4⁵/₈	3643	313
■ Clark Co. – Brett A. Higginbotham – Brett A. Higginbotham – 1999											

Score	Length of Main Beam Right	Left	Inside Spread	Greatest Spread	Circumference at Smallest Place Between Burr and First Point Right	Left	Number of Points Right	Left	Lengths Abnormal Points	All-Time Rank	State Rank
	■ Location of Kill – Hunter – Owner – Date Killed										
166	23	22 5/8	20 6/8	24	4 1/8	4 3/8	5	6		3657	314
	■ Jo Daviess Co. – Jaime Marsden – Kyle L. Marsden – 1994										
166	25 2/8	26 1/8	18 6/8	22 4/8	5 1/8	5	5	5		3657	314
	■ McHenry Co. – Brent A. Smith – Brent A. Smith – 1994										
165 6/8	28 4/8	28 4/8	18 1/8	20 2/8	5 3/8	5 2/8	6	5	3 7/8	3680	316
	■ Jersey Co. – David A. Balaco – David A. Balaco – 1999										
165 5/8	25	23 6/8	16 2/8	18 2/8	5 6/8	6	6	7	3 5/8	3696	317
	■ Pike Co. – Gregory S. Guerrieri – Gregory S. Guerrieri – 1994										
165 4/8	25 7/8	25 7/8	20	23 2/8	5 3/8	5 1/8	5	5		3714†	318†
	■ Vermilion Co. – Benjamin J. Self – Benjamin J. Self – 2001										
165 4/8	28	27 7/8	18 4/8	21 6/8	5 5/8	5 5/8	7	6	7 6/8	3714†	318†
	■ Johnson Co. – David M. Uhls – David M. Uhls – 2001										
165 4/8	24	22	21 2/8	23 2/8	5	5	5	5		3714	318
	■ Randolph Co. – Jeffrey C. Biethman – Jeffrey C. Biethman – 1993										
165 4/8	27	26 7/8	23	24 7/8	5 4/8	5 7/8	6	7	4 4/8	3714	318
	■ Ogle Co. – Wayne T. Seymour – Wayne T. Seymour – 1993										
165 4/8	24 1/8	25 2/8	17 6/8	20 1/8	4 4/8	4 4/8	7	6	4	3714	318
	■ Henderson Co. – Jason B. Eland – Jason B. Eland – 1996										
165 3/8	23 6/8	23 5/8	17 3/8	21	5 5/8	5 6/8	5	5		3731	323
	■ McHenry Co. – Jared A. Gratz – Jared A. Gratz – 1998										
165 2/8	25 1/8	24 7/8	18 2/8	20 6/8	4	4 1/8	5	5		3748	324
	■ Jo Daviess Co. – Daniel W. Allen – Daniel W. Allen – 1992										
165 1/8	23 7/8	26 4/8	22 7/8	26 2/8	4 6/8	4 6/8	6	6	2	3767	325
	■ McLean Co. – Kevin A. Miner – Kevin A. Miner – 1988										
165	23 4/8	22 7/8	20 2/8	23 2/8	5 4/8	5 4/8	6	5	1 4/8	3782	326
	■ Adams Co. – Alan R. Garrison – Alan R. Garrison – 1994										
165	26	26 3/8	17 6/8	20 1/8	5 2/8	5 2/8	5	5		3782	326
	■ Pike Co. – George R. Metcalf – George R. Metcalf – 1998										
164 7/8	25 4/8	26	21 3/8	23 3/8	5 1/8	4 7/8	6	7	4 6/8	3792	328
	■ Coles Co. – Ralph Garland – Ralph Garland – 1988										
164 7/8	25 7/8	27 1/8	19 6/8	22	5 3/8	5 3/8	5	4	1 3/8	3792	328
	■ Coles Co. – Walter C. Watson – Walter C. Watson – 1989										
164 7/8	28 2/8	26 3/8	21	24 1/8	5	5	5	8	4 7/8	3792	328
	■ Hancock Co. – John R. Gibbs – John R. Gibbs – 1990										
164 6/8	23 5/8	22 4/8	20 2/8	23	5 2/8	5 2/8	5	5		3809†	331†
	■ Lake Co. – Jerry R. Dobbs – Jerry R. Dobbs – 2001										
164 6/8	25	24 7/8	17 4/8	20 4/8	5 3/8	5 2/8	6	8	8 4/8	3809†	331†
	■ Hardin Co. – Walter Talandis, Jr. – Walter Talandis, Jr. – 2001										
164 6/8	26 7/8	26 2/8	18 5/8	20 5/8	5	4 7/8	5	6	4 3/8	3809†	331†
	■ Brown Co. – Todd A. Wills – Todd A. Wills – 2000										
164 6/8	25 2/8	26 1/8	18 6/8	21	4 5/8	4 6/8	5	5		3809	331
	■ Adams Co. – James H. Gieker – James H. Gieker – 1995										

Score	Length of Main Beam Right	Left	Inside Spread	Greatest Spread	Circumference at Smallest Place Between Burr and First Point Right	Left	Number of Points Right	Left	Lengths Abnormal Points	All-Time Rank	State Rank
	■ Location of Kill – Hunter – Owner – Date Killed										
164 5/8	27 2/8	26 6/8	21 7/8	24 1/8	5 3/8	5 4/8	7	8	12	3835	335
	■ Brown Co. – Larry O. Greene – Larry O. Greene – 1999										
164 4/8	26 7/8	27 2/8	18 2/8	20 6/8	4 4/8	4 2/8	5	5		3855	336
	■ Jo Daviess Co. – Jacob Marsden – Jacob Marsden – 1996										
164 1/8	28 3/8	26 2/8	21 7/8	24	4 7/8	4 7/8	8	7	5 6/8	3886	337
	■ Macoupin Co. – Paul D. Tonsor – Paul D. Tonsor – 1989										
163 7/8	24 6/8	26 1/8	21 5/8	23 3/8	4 4/8	4 3/8	5	5		3928	338
	■ Pulaski Co. – Bobby W. Stricker – Bobby W. Stricker – 1992										
163 7/8	29 5/8	29 2/8	24	27 3/8	4 6/8	4 4/8	5	4	1 3/8	3928	338
	■ Macon Co. – Jerry J. Wilson – Jerry J. Wilson – 1999										
163 6/8	26 4/8	25 7/8	21 4/8	23 5/8	6 1/8	6	6	5		3946	340
	■ McHenry Co. – Matthew W. Grismer – Matthew W. Grismer – 1991										
163 6/8	25 3/8	25 4/8	17 5/8	19 6/8	5	5	5	6	3 1/8	3946	340
	■ Madison Co. – J. Michael Corby – J. Michael Corby – 1995										
163 5/8	26 3/8	29	21	23 1/8	4 6/8	4 4/8	8	6	8 7/8	3961	342
	■ Vermilion Co. – James D. Rueter – James D. Rueter – 1992										
163 2/8	24 7/8	27	22 4/8	24 6/8	5 6/8	5 5/8	5	4	1	4017	343
	■ Adams Co. – Leslie E. Voorhis – Leslie E. Voorhis – 1998										
163	26 4/8	25 7/8	18 7/8	21 1/8	5 3/8	5 5/8	7	8	9 3/8	4051	344
	■ Effingham Co. – Todd J. Bloemer – Todd J. Bloemer – 1995										
163	23 4/8	24 6/8	18 5/8	22 3/8	4 5/8	4 7/8	6	7	5 5/8	4051	344
	■ Jo Daviess Co. – Dennis D. Wurster – Dennis D. Wurster – 1998										
162 7/8	26 6/8	26 5/8	24 3/8	26 4/8	4 5/8	4 7/8	4	4		4067†	346†
	■ Schuyler Co. – Michael Glasby – Michael Glasby – 2000										
162 7/8	27 3/8	27	21 7/8	24 4/8	5 1/8	4 7/8	4	5		4067	346
	■ McHenry Co. – Troy D. Erckfritz – Troy D. Erckfritz – 1996										
162 6/8	23 7/8	22 4/8	16	18 3/8	4 3/8	4 4/8	6	6		4089†	348†
	■ Greene Co. – Larry A. Marks – Larry A. Marks – 2001										
162 6/8	25 4/8	26 6/8	20 6/8	23 4/8	5	5	7	5	2 2/8	4089	348
	■ McHenry Co. – James A. Brazzale – James A. Brazzale – 1994										
162 5/8	24 4/8	24	19 3/8	21 4/8	5 4/8	5 4/8	8	5	10	4109†	350†
	■ Macoupin Co. – Curtis A. Reznicek – Curtis A. Reznicek – 2001										
162 4/8	29 4/8	30 5/8	21	23 6/8	5 6/8	5 6/8	6	9	6 6/8	4129	351
	■ Jackson Co. – Michelle F. Smith – Michelle F. Smith – 1986										
162 1/8	26 2/8	26 1/8	17 6/8	20 3/8	4 4/8	4 4/8	5	6	1 3/8	4174	352
	■ Fulton Co. – C. Wayne Miller – C. Wayne Miller – 1995										
162	24	25	19 2/8	21 2/8	4 4/8	4 3/8	7	6	11 4/8	4184	353
	■ Henderson Co. – Robert G. Hosford – Robert G. Hosford – 1984										
162	23 4/8	23 6/8	16 2/8	18 3/8	4 7/8	5 1/8	5	7	3	4184	353
	■ Madison Co. – David M. Jones – David M. Jones – 1989										
161 7/8	23 7/8	25 3/8	20 5/8	21 6/8	4	4 2/8	5	5		4212	355
	■ Sangamon Co. – Clarence E. Brown, Sr. – Clarence E. Brown, Sr. – 1992										

Score	Length of Main Beam Right	Left	Inside Spread	Greatest Spread	Circumference at Smallest Place Between Burr and First Point Right	Left	Number of Points Right	Left	Lengths Abnormal Points	All-Time Rank	State Rank
	■ Location of Kill – Hunter – Owner – Date Killed										
161⁵/₈	22	22	19⁵/₈	21²/₈	4⁵/₈	4⁶/₈	5	5		4234	356
	■ Jo Daviess Co. – Bradley E. Giertz – Bradley E. Giertz – 1983										
161⁵/₈	25⁵/₈	25¹/₈	20⁶/₈	22⁷/₈	5²/₈	5²/₈	7	6	2⁷/₈	4234	356
	■ McHenry Co. – John S. Nelson – John S. Nelson – 1988										
161⁵/₈	26¹/₈	24⁴/₈	23⁷/₈	26¹/₈	5¹/₈	6	6	7	7⁶/₈	4234	356
	■ Piatt Co. – Robert W. James – Robert W. James – 1993										
161³/₈	25	25	16⁷/₈	19²/₈	5²/₈	5²/₈	6	7	4	4285	359
	■ McHenry Co. – Timothy L. Harkness – Timothy L. Harkness – 1998										
161²/₈	22⁴/₈	21⁶/₈	20²/₈	23	5	4⁶/₈	5	5		4310	360
	■ La Salle Co. – Picked Up – William H. Goodin – 1995										
161²/₈	24⁶/₈	25	18²/₈	20¹/₈	4⁶/₈	4⁵/₈	5	5		4310	360
	■ La Salle Co. – Thomas L. Sroka – Thomas L. Sroka – 1996										
161¹/₈	24³/₈	25⁴/₈	21⁵/₈	24²/₈	4³/₈	4⁵/₈	5	5		4332	362
	■ Lake Co. – John W. Schnider, Jr. – John W. Schnider, Jr. – 1987										
161¹/₈	26	25⁵/₈	17⁷/₈	20⁵/₈	6	6¹/₈	5	7	9²/₈	4332	362
	■ Fulton Co. – Robert L. Chasteen – Robert L. Chasteen – 1988										
161	25¹/₈	24³/₈	20	22⁴/₈	4⁶/₈	4⁶/₈	5	5		4356†	364†
	■ Fayette Co. – Scott L. Hunt – Scott L. Hunt – 2000										
161	23⁴/₈	23⁵/₈	17	19³/₈	4⁴/₈	4³/₈	5	6	1⁴/₈	4356†	364†
	■ Washington Co. – John V. Rickhoff – John V. Rickhoff – 1999										
160⁶/₈	27	27¹/₈	20⁶/₈	23⁴/₈	6	6³/₈	4	6	7	4402	366
	■ Mason Co. – George E. Buck – George E. Buck – 1996										
160⁶/₈	22⁴/₈	24	22²/₈	24¹/₈	5¹/₈	5¹/₈	5	5		4402	366
	■ Marshall Co. – Aron W. Shofner – Aron W. Shofner – 1998										
160⁵/₈	22⁶/₈	22⁴/₈	15¹/₈	17²/₈	5²/₈	5	6	6		4423	368
	■ Schuyler Co. – Edward L. Clack – Edward L. Clack – 1995										
160⁴/₈	27⁶/₈	27³/₈	20⁴/₈	23	5⁶/₈	5⁶/₈	6	5	2⁶/₈	4443	369
	■ McLean Co. – Larry D. Martin – Larry D. Martin – 1989										
160³/₈	26⁴/₈	27¹/₈	19⁷/₈	22¹/₈	5¹/₈	5	5	4	1⁴/₈	4470	370
	■ Shelby Co. – Stephen A. Tripp – Stephen A. Tripp – 1995										
160³/₈	27⁷/₈	28¹/₈	21³/₈	23⁴/₈	5	4⁷/₈	7	5	3²/₈	4470	370
	■ Menard Co. – George E. Hypke – George E. Hypke – 1996										
160³/₈	27⁴/₈	26	19⁶/₈	22²/₈	5	5¹/₈	5	5	2³/₈	4470	370
	■ Vermilion Co. – John E. Hubbard – John E. Hubbard – 1997										
160²/₈	24²/₈	24⁶/₈	22²/₈	26	5	5⁴/₈	5	5		4495†	373†
	■ Ogle Co. – Philip H. Nye, Jr. – Philip H. Nye, Jr. – 2000										
160²/₈	25⁷/₈	25⁶/₈	22	24⁶/₈	5⁷/₈	5⁷/₈	7	5	6⁶/₈	4495	373
	■ Kankakee Co. – Brian Grob – Brian Grob – 1995										
160¹/₈	25⁵/₈	24⁴/₈	20⁷/₈	22⁶/₈	5³/₈	5²/₈	5	6	3⁴/₈	4534†	375†
	■ Jo Daviess Co. – Scott L. Havens – Scott L. Havens – 2000										
160¹/₈	25²/₈	25¹/₈	19²/₈	21⁴/₈	5¹/₈	5⁴/₈	5	6	1¹/₈	4534	375
	■ Adams Co. – Gerald Giesing – Gerald Giesing – 1979										

Score	Length of Main Beam Right	Left	Inside Spread	Greatest Spread	Circumference at Smallest Place Between Burr and First Point Right	Left	Number of Points Right	Left	Lengths Abnormal Points	All-Time Rank	State Rank
■ Location of Kill – Hunter – Owner – Date Killed											
160¹⁄₈	23²⁄₈	23²⁄₈	19³⁄₈	23⁴⁄₈	4⁴⁄₈	4⁶⁄₈	7	7	14	4534	375
■ Williamson Co. – Frank E. Czarnecki – Frank E. Czarnecki – 1991											
160¹⁄₈	25	26²⁄₈	22⁴⁄₈	25	6¹⁄₈	6	7	6	8⁵⁄₈	4534	375
■ Schuyler Co. – Michael S. Helsley, Jr. – Michael S. Helsley, Jr. – 1999											
160¹⁄₈	23²⁄₈	23	18⁶⁄₈	22	5⁴⁄₈	5²⁄₈	7	6	8⁷⁄₈	4534	375
■ Champaign Co. – Matthew M. Pacunas – Matthew M. Pacunas – 1999											
160	24⁴⁄₈	25³⁄₈	18²⁄₈	20¹⁄₈	4⁶⁄₈	4⁷⁄₈	5	6	1²⁄₈	4565	380
■ Pulaski Co. – Paul F. Landewee – Paul F. Landewee – 1996											

† The scores and ranking for trophies from the 25th Awards Entry Period are not final until the banquet is held on June 19, 2004.

TROPHIES IN THE FIELD

HUNTER: Chase M. Ziller
SCORE: 173†
CATEGORY: typical whitetail deer
LOCATION: McHenry County, Illinois
DATE: 2001

† The scores and ranking for trophies from the 25th Awards Entry Period are not final until the banquet is held on June 19, 2004.

ILLINOIS

NON-TYPICAL WHITETAIL DEER

Score	Length of Main Beam Right Left	Inside Spread	Greatest Spread	Circumference at Smallest Place Between Burr and First Point Right Left		Number of Points Right Left		Lengths Abnormal Points	All-Time Rank	State Rank
	■ Location of Kill – Hunter – Owner – Date Killed									
291¹/8	27⁴/8 27⁵/8	23¹/8	26⁵/8	5¹/8 5⁷/8		16 20		106²/8	4†	1†
	■ Fulton Co. – Jerry D. Bryant – Jerry D. Bryant – 2001									
267³/8	25⁴/8 28²/8	20	29¹/8	6⁵/8 6³/8		18 7		88¹/8	18	2
	■ Peoria Co. – Richard A. Pauli – Richard A. Pauli – 1983									
258⁶/8	24³/8 25⁴/8	22⁷/8	26⁴/8	5⁴/8 5⁵/8		15 15		55⁷/8	27	3
	■ Edgar Co. – Ernest R. Hires – Bass Pro Shops – 1994									
256¹/8	30¹/8 29	21⁷/8	24	5³/8 5⁵/8		11 16		65²/8	40	4
	■ McDonough Co. – Brian E. Bice – Bass Pro Shops – 1992									
250⁴/8	29⁶/8 29⁷/8	20⁵/8	23⁴/8	5⁵/8 5⁷/8		13 9		38¹/8	57†	5†
	■ Alexander Co. – Andrew French III – Andrew French III – 2000									
245⁵/8	28²/8 26⁶/8	18⁵/8	22⁴/8	6²/8 6⁴/8		13 15		55⁶/8	80	6
	■ Kankakee Co. – Lawrence G. Ekhoff – Lawrence G. Ekhoff – 1999									
244¹/8	27⁴/8 28	20⁶/8	23	5 4⁶/8		11 11		65³/8	91	7
	■ Sangamon Co. – William E. Hood – William E. Hood – 1991									
243⁷/8	26³/8 26⁵/8	20⁴/8	27⁷/8	6⁵/8 7¹/8		14 13		54⁵/8	94	8
	■ Cook Co. – Picked Up – Jeffrey A. DeVroy – 1995									
242⁷/8	18¹/8 17²/8	15⁷/8	26	4⁷/8 5²/8		21 21		117⁴/8	98	9
	■ Pope Co. – William E. Henderson – William E. Henderson – 1991									
239¹/8	31¹/8 29²/8	22¹/8	27⁴/8	5⁷/8 5⁴/8		9 11		51²/8	125	10
	■ Illinois – William Seidel – D.J. Hollinger & B. Howard – 1987									
238⁶/8	26²/8 25³/8	20⁵/8	24⁶/8	6⁷/8 7²/8		11 12		48¹/8	130	11
	■ Fulton Co. – Neil M. Booth – Cabela's, Inc. – 1988									
238⁶/8	25⁴/8 18⁶/8	21	26²/8	6⁵/8 6³/8		13 15		88⁴/8	130	11
	■ Schuyler Co. – Kenneth B. Robertson – Kenneth B. Robertson – 1997									
238¹/8	26⁴/8 27⁵/8	27	29³/8	5³/8 5⁶/8		12 17		61¹/8	139	13
	■ Madison Co. – Joe Bardill – Patrick Bardill – 1985									
237⁶/8	23⁴/8 22³/8	15	28⁴/8	6 6		15 12		71	143	14
	■ Henderson Co. – Robert E. Todd – Robert E. Todd – 1978									
236⁵/8	27²/8 26¹/8	20¹/8	22²/8	7¹/8 6⁶/8		11 9		47	157	15
	■ Pike Co. – Floyd Pursley – Floyd Pursley – 1987									
234⁵/8	27 28	25	27⁴/8	6²/8 6²/8		8 7		26³/8	172	16
	■ Gallatin Co. – Scott G. Bosaw – Scott G. Bosaw – 1994									
234⁴/8	27¹/8 26³/8	24²/8	26²/8	5⁷/8 5⁷/8		14 11		35⁶/8	175†	17†
	■ Knox Co. – James R. Hensley, Jr. – James R. Hensley, Jr. – 2000									
234¹/8	26¹/8 26⁴/8	21¹/8	25⁵/8	6 6²/8		11 14		45⁶/8	178	18
	■ Hamilton Co. – Mark A. Potts – Mark A. Potts – 1995									
232⁵/8	23⁷/8 24¹/8	18²/8	20⁶/8	7²/8 6		12 13		63⁷/8	200	19
	■ Fulton Co. – Carl B. Brown – Carl B. Brown – 1997									

Score	Length of Main Beam Right Left	Inside Spread	Greatest Spread	Circumference at Smallest Place Between Burr and First Point Right Left	Number of Points Right Left	Lengths Abnormal Points	All-Time Rank	State Rank
	■ Location of Kill – Hunter – Owner – Date Killed							
231⁴/8	29⁴/8 29⁴/8	18⁶/8	24¹/8	6²/8 6¹/8	14 13	41⁶/8	217	20
	■ Perry Co. – Unknown – Bass Pro Shops – 1968							
231⁴/8	25⁷/8 26⁴/8	27³/8	35¹/8	6¹/8 6²/8	11 14	56⁴/8	217	20
	■ Logan Co. – Donald D. Stiner – Donald D. Stiner – 1993							
230⁶/8	22³/8 23³/8	19⁷/8	23³/8	5⁷/8 5⁴/8	13 10	40⁵/8	231†	22†
	■ Peoria Co. – Picked Up – David T. Lockhart – 2000							
229⁴/8	24²/8 24⁵/8	19³/8	28²/8	5 4⁷/8	10 10	40³/8	246	23
	■ Marshall Co. – Daniel R. Ferguson – Daniel R. Ferguson – 1994							
229³/8	26²/8 26³/8	19³/8	24	5⁶/8 5⁵/8	13 9	50⁶/8	249	24
	■ Montgomery Co. – Lee A. Heldebrandt – Lee A. Heldebrandt – 1996							
229	27¹/8 27⁴/8	16²/8	18⁷/8	6⁷/8 6²/8	8 9	28²/8	254	25
	■ Lake Co. – Rodney J. Rasmussen – Rodney J. Rasmussen – 1995							
228³/8	24⁵/8 26⁵/8	15⁴/8	21¹/8	6⁵/8 5⁶/8	13 10	53⁷/8	261†	26†
	■ Randolph Co. – Aaron L. Eggemeyer – Aaron L. Eggemeyer – 2001							
228¹/8	28⁴/8 27	21⁶/8	26³/8	5¹/8 5⁵/8	11 13	49⁷/8	266	27
	■ Bureau Co. – Keith F. VanderMeersch – Keith F. VanderMeersch – 1992							
226⁶/8	27³/8 27²/8	21²/8	24⁵/8	6²/8 6¹/8	10 9	20⁴/8	285†	28†
	■ Piatt Co. – Mark Wimpy – Mark Wimpy – 2000 ■ See photo on page 52							
226²/8	27⁷/8 28³/8	19⁶/8	22⁷/8	5³/8 5²/8	11 13	50⁶/8	298	29
	■ Fulton Co. – Picked Up – David L. Lidwell – 1996							
224⁵/8	25⁷/8 27⁴/8	19³/8	21⁶/8	5²/8 5²/8	10 8	32⁴/8	325	30
	■ Mercer Co. – Roger R. Roy – Roger R. Roy – 1999							
224⁴/8	27⁷/8 27⁷/8	26³/8	28¹/8	5⁴/8 6	8 12	23⁵/8	327†	31†
	■ Marshall Co. – Frank A. McKean – Frank A. McKean – 2000							
224	31 31²/8	19²/8	22⁴/8	5³/8 5²/8	11 11	26⁶/8	337	32
	■ Hancock Co. – Ronald A. Paul – Bass Pro Shops – 1968							
223⁶/8	28 28	25⁵/8	27¹/8	7¹/8 6⁴/8	10 11	43⁷/8	342	33
	■ Greene Co. – Terry L. Walters – Terry L. Walters – 1982							
223⁵/8	24⁶/8 24⁶/8	24²/8	29³/8	6 6²/8	8 14	49³/8	345	34
	■ Wabash Co. – Tim W. Stout – Bass Pro Shops – 1988							
223²/8	29⁶/8 32⁴/8	22¹/8	27	6⁵/8 5⁷/8	7 13	45¹/8	359†	35†
	■ Fulton Co. – Lyle Mason – Lyle Mason – 2000							
222⁷/8	27⁵/8 28¹/8	18⁶/8	23²/8	5 5	9 7	27⁵/8	368	36
	■ Coles Co. – Kim L. Boes – Bass Pro Shops – 1989							
222⁵/8	24⁵/8 24²/8	20⁷/8	23⁵/8	5⁶/8 5⁴/8	10 10	32⁶/8	373	37
	■ Clark Co. – David E. Morris – David E. Morris – 1997							
222⁴/8	25³/8 29³/8	20⁶/8	27⁶/8	4⁷/8 4⁷/8	12 9	61	378†	38†
	■ Richland Co. – Lloyd E. Lemke – Lloyd E. Lemke – 2000							
222³/8	26²/8 25³/8	23⁵/8	28	5⁴/8 5⁴/8	11 12	37⁴/8	384†	39†
	■ Hancock Co. – James E. Bowdish – James E. Bowdish – 2000							
222³/8	27²/8 27⁶/8	18¹/8	21	6⁵/8 6	9 14	51⁶/8	384	39
	■ Macoupin Co. – Paul Luttmann – Lewis F. Smith – 1993							

Score	Length of Main Beam Right	Left	Inside Spread	Greatest Spread	Circumference at Smallest Place Between Burr and First Point Right	Left	Number of Points Right	Left	Lengths Abnormal Points	All-Time Rank	State Rank
	■ Location of Kill – Hunter – Owner – Date Killed										
221 4/8	25	20 7/8	21 2/8	25 4/8	6 3/8	6 1/8	12	21	57	402	41
	■ Hancock Co. – Neal C. Meyer – Neal C. Meyer – 1987										
221	29 1/8	29	23 4/8	26 5/8	4 5/8	4 4/8	9	9	44	416	42
	■ Pike Co. – Frank C. Skelton – Frank C. Skelton – 1987										
220 4/8	30	30 6/8	20 5/8	24 7/8	4 7/8	4 6/8	12	9	26 7/8	427	43
	■ Mercer Co. – Roger D. Hultgren – Roger D. Hultgren – 1970										
220 1/8	23 6/8	23 3/8	18 4/8	24	5 2/8	5 2/8	17	12	53 3/8	439	44
	■ Iroquois Co. – John P. Boshears – John P. Boshears – 1998 ■ See photo on page 147										
219 6/8	25 4/8	26 2/8	23 7/8	28 4/8	5 1/8	5 1/8	9	10	45 1/8	447	45
	■ Christian Co. – Eric D. Garrett – Eric D. Garrett – 1994										
219 3/8	26 2/8	26 5/8	18 4/8	24 7/8	5 2/8	5 3/8	10	10	34 1/8	455†	46†
	■ Schuyler Co. – James R. Lehman – James R. Lehman – 2000										
219 3/8	26 7/8	26 2/8	18	23 1/8	6 2/8	6	9	6	37 1/8	455	46
	■ Fulton Co. – Christopher W. Schweigert – Christopher W. Schweigert – 1998										
218 6/8	29 4/8	29 3/8	23 3/8	25 2/8	6	6	11	9	27 3/8	477	48
	■ Williamson Co. – Carl W. Norris – Carl W. Norris – 1994										
218 6/8	26	27 7/8	21 7/8	24 2/8	7 3/8	7 4/8	10	8	25 3/8	477	48
	■ Cass Co. – Stanley E. Walker – Stanley E. Walker – 1998										
217 6/8	26 2/8	28 5/8	18 6/8	23 5/8	5 1/8	5	12	12	36 2/8	503	50
	■ Macoupin Co. – Albert Grichnik – Albert Grichnik – 1966										
217 6/8	28 4/8	28 7/8	20 5/8	27 5/8	6 1/8	6	11	9	29 5/8	503	50
	■ Clark Co. – David P. Mosley – David P. Mosley – 1995										
217	29	27 4/8	19 4/8	22 1/8	5 4/8	5 4/8	10	9	34	529	52
	■ Fulton Co. – Picked Up – IL Dept. of Natl. Resc. – 1990										
216 7/8	25 4/8	27 1/8	22 3/8	25 3/8	5 5/8	5 4/8	12	7	39 4/8	533†	53†
	■ Wayne Co. – Kenneth L. Tucker – Kenneth L. Tucker – 2000										
216 7/8	25 4/8	25 7/8	21	24 4/8	4 6/8	5	10	11	44 7/8	533	53
	■ Lee Co. – Clifford L. Walter – Clifford L. Walter – 1997										
216 6/8	26 3/8	26 1/8	25 1/8	27	5	5 4/8	7	11	59 5/8	539	55
	■ Brown Co. – David R. Herschelman – David R. Herschelman – 1991										
216 6/8	25	25	18	25 1/8	5 6/8	5 7/8	12	14	45 2/8	539	55
	■ Menard Co. – Randy Boyle – Randy Boyle – 1995										
216 3/8	29 2/8	27 1/8	17 5/8	20 1/8	6 2/8	7 1/8	8	10	49 4/8	549	57
	■ Jersey Co. – Walter L. Baker – Walter L. Baker – 1998 ■ See photo on page 62										
216 3/8	29 1/8	28 3/8	26 3/8	29 1/8	4 4/8	4 4/8	9	8	21 2/8	549	57
	■ Christian Co. – John R. Reese – John R. Reese – 1998										
216 1/8	26	26 6/8	22 2/8	31	6 3/8	6 3/8	9	10	50 1/8	561†	59†
	■ Grundy Co. – Steven E. Claypool – Steven E. Claypool – 2001										
216 1/8	27	27 6/8	17 7/8	19 7/8	5 6/8	5 7/8	10	11	32 2/8	561	59
	■ Stephenson Co. – Steven M. Knopes – Steven M. Knopes – 1999										
215 7/8	27 1/8	26 5/8	27 7/8	30 1/8	6	5 2/8	9	6	28	569	61
	■ Schuyler Co. – Donald E. Ziegenbein – Donald E. Ziegenbein – 1981										

Score	Length of Main Beam		Inside Spread	Greatest Spread	Circumference at Smallest Place Between Burr and First Point		Number of Points		Lengths Abnormal Points	All-Time Rank	State Rank
	Right	Left			Right	Left	Right	Left			
	■ Location of Kill – Hunter – Owner – Date Killed										
215 6/8	26	25 1/8	24 2/8	26 5/8	4 3/8	5 2/8	6	11	31 4/8	575	62
■ Macoupin Co. – Allen E. McKee – Allen E. McKee – 1992											
215 4/8	23	24 3/8	21 7/8	28 4/8	6 3/8	5 1/8	11	8	73 5/8	583	63
■ Schuyler Co. – Raymond Shouse – Raymond Shouse – 1993											
215 4/8	24 3/8	28 2/8	24 5/8	29 7/8	6 4/8	6 3/8	9	11	41 3/8	583	63
■ Fulton Co. – Roger H. Mann – Roger H. Mann – 1994											
215 1/8	26 5/8	25 6/8	21 6/8	26 4/8	6	6	11	9	38 7/8	593	65
■ Cass Co. – David G. Bolletto – David G. Bolletto – 1988											
215 1/8	25 2/8	24	22 1/8	26	6 7/8	6 4/8	11	10	47 4/8	593	65
■ Winnebago Co. – Dennis F. Shipler – Dennis F. Shipler – 1990											
214 5/8	28	28 5/8	23	25 4/8	5	5 1/8	9	8	26 5/8	614	67
■ Pike Co. – David B. Crown – David B. Crown – 1995											
214 4/8	23 4/8	20 7/8	28 6/8	33	5 7/8	5 5/8	15	12	60 4/8	617	68
■ De Witt Co. – Kelly E. Riggs – Kelly E. Riggs – 1996											
214	24 3/8	20 5/8	19 7/8	24 3/8	6	7 3/8	9	12	60 5/8	629†	69†
■ Scott Co. – James K. Garrett – James K. Garrett – 1994											
214	25 2/8	26 1/8	19	22 4/8	5	5 2/8	9	6	26	629	69
■ Hancock Co. – Steven Guedesse – Steven Guedesse – 1999											
213 7/8	25 6/8	27 5/8	20 7/8	28 6/8	6 1/8	6 6/8	7	9	32 6/8	635	71
■ Pope Co. – Jason B. Potts – Jason B. Potts – 1995											
213 7/8	29 7/8	28 6/8	20	25 7/8	6 5/8	6 2/8	11	9	42 5/8	635	71
■ Greene Co. – Adam T. Hoene – Adam T. Hoene – 1999											
213 6/8	30 2/8	30 6/8	26 5/8	29 2/8	4 6/8	4 7/8	10	9	16 7/8	644	73
■ Fayette Co. – Sammy D. Diveley – Sammy D. Diveley – 1990											
213 6/8	26 1/8	26 7/8	19 6/8	23 5/8	5 4/8	5 6/8	14	13	39 4/8	644	73
■ Adams Co. – Michelle L. Hunter – Michelle L. Hunter – 1991											
213 6/8	28 4/8	27 2/8	20	22 2/8	5 6/8	5 4/8	12	14	37 2/8	644	73
■ Cass Co. – Vince C. Brewer – Vince C. Brewer – 1993											
213 5/8	24 7/8	25 6/8	19 7/8	22 4/8	6 2/8	6 2/8	12	13	46 4/8	649	76
■ Ogle Co. – Jerome F. Bruns – Jerome F. Bruns – 1994											
213 5/8	27 4/8	26 2/8	20 1/8	23	5 4/8	5 6/8	11	11	41	649	76
■ Ogle Co. – Jeffrey R. Breen – Jeffrey R. Breen – 1995											
213 4/8	25 4/8	26	22	29 1/8	6 2/8	6 1/8	11	13	34 4/8	657	78
■ Pike Co. – Donald L. Roseberry – Michael R. Roseberry – 1984											
213 1/8	25 4/8	24 7/8	19	22 4/8	7 4/8	8 1/8	10	10	50 7/8	664	79
■ Schuyler Co. – Todd A. Ritchey – Todd A. Ritchey – 1997											
212 6/8	24 3/8	28 3/8	28 3/8	30	5 2/8	5 1/8	11	6	28 7/8	677	80
■ Illinois – Picked Up – John Brewer – 1989											
212 5/8	24 6/8	23 1/8	19 6/8	22 2/8	6 1/8	6 7/8	12	11	39 5/8	683	81
■ Marshall Co. – Picked Up – Carl H. Kimble – 1998											
212 4/8	25	25 4/8	21	24 6/8	6 1/8	6 3/8	10	11	35 6/8	695†	82†
■ Randolph Co. – Mark E. Houba – Mark E. Houba – 2000											

Score	Length of Main Beam Right Left	Inside Spread	Greatest Spread	Circumference at Smallest Place Between Burr and First Point Right Left	Number of Points Right Left	Lengths Abnormal Points	All-Time Rank	State Rank
						■ Location of Kill – Hunter – Owner – Date Killed		
$212\tfrac{3}{8}$	$25\tfrac{2}{8}$ $22\tfrac{7}{8}$	$22\tfrac{2}{8}$	$26\tfrac{3}{8}$	$6\tfrac{2}{8}$ $6\tfrac{1}{8}$	17 14	$56\tfrac{3}{8}$	697†	83†
	■ Brown Co. – Martin L. Brobst – Martin L. Brobst – 2000							
211	$27\tfrac{3}{8}$ $27\tfrac{7}{8}$	25	31	$5\tfrac{1}{8}$ $5\tfrac{1}{8}$	9 8	$39\tfrac{2}{8}$	764	84
	■ Christian Co. – Jeffery Tumiati – Jeffery Tumiati – 1997							
$210\tfrac{7}{8}$	$25\tfrac{3}{8}$ 27	$20\tfrac{1}{8}$	23	$6\tfrac{2}{8}$ $6\tfrac{6}{8}$	11 9	$48\tfrac{6}{8}$	773	85
	■ Peoria Co. – Picked Up – Randy L. Isbell – 1995							
$210\tfrac{5}{8}$	$26\tfrac{6}{8}$ $27\tfrac{2}{8}$	$22\tfrac{1}{8}$	$24\tfrac{5}{8}$	6 6	9 8	25	783	86
	■ Ogle Co. – Daniel M. Pierce – Daniel M. Pierce – 1994							
$210\tfrac{3}{8}$	$24\tfrac{3}{8}$ $24\tfrac{1}{8}$	16	18	$4\tfrac{7}{8}$ 5	9 9	$28\tfrac{3}{8}$	796	87
	■ Adams Co. – Unknown – Chuck House – 1897							
$210\tfrac{3}{8}$	$30\tfrac{4}{8}$ $29\tfrac{2}{8}$	$24\tfrac{4}{8}$	$27\tfrac{5}{8}$	$5\tfrac{4}{8}$ $5\tfrac{2}{8}$	8 9	$16\tfrac{1}{8}$	796	87
	■ Calhoun Co. – Timothy A. Moore – Timothy A. Moore – 1999							
$210\tfrac{3}{8}$	24 $19\tfrac{5}{8}$	$16\tfrac{2}{8}$	$22\tfrac{6}{8}$	6 $8\tfrac{4}{8}$	7 10	$50\tfrac{5}{8}$	796	87
	■ Morgan Co. – Frankie Wildhagen – Frankie Wildhagen – 1999							
$209\tfrac{6}{8}$	$26\tfrac{5}{8}$ $27\tfrac{5}{8}$	$20\tfrac{7}{8}$	$25\tfrac{3}{8}$	$5\tfrac{3}{8}$ $5\tfrac{5}{8}$	9 8	$46\tfrac{5}{8}$	831	90
	■ Sangamon Co. – Mark A. Rademaker – Mark A. Rademaker – 1994							
$209\tfrac{5}{8}$	$23\tfrac{3}{8}$ $23\tfrac{3}{8}$	$18\tfrac{2}{8}$	$23\tfrac{6}{8}$	$4\tfrac{1}{8}$ $4\tfrac{2}{8}$	10 14	$56\tfrac{1}{8}$	840	91
	■ Logan Co. – Clint M. Awe – Clint M. Awe – 1997							
$209\tfrac{4}{8}$	$28\tfrac{3}{8}$ $27\tfrac{5}{8}$	$22\tfrac{5}{8}$	26	$5\tfrac{2}{8}$ 5	11 8	$16\tfrac{5}{8}$	848	92
	■ White Co. – David J. South – David J. South – 1991							
$209\tfrac{2}{8}$	$25\tfrac{6}{8}$ $22\tfrac{2}{8}$	$20\tfrac{4}{8}$	$26\tfrac{2}{8}$	$5\tfrac{2}{8}$ $5\tfrac{3}{8}$	9 11	$26\tfrac{4}{8}$	859	93
	■ De Witt Co. – Ronald L. Willmore – Ronald L. Willmore – 1997							
$208\tfrac{4}{8}$	$25\tfrac{1}{8}$ $25\tfrac{3}{8}$	$17\tfrac{5}{8}$	$19\tfrac{6}{8}$	$5\tfrac{4}{8}$ $5\tfrac{5}{8}$	10 13	$53\tfrac{3}{8}$	894	94
	■ Fulton Co. – Jeffrey C. Warmath – Jeffrey C. Warmath – 1995							
$208\tfrac{4}{8}$	$24\tfrac{3}{8}$ $24\tfrac{7}{8}$	$14\tfrac{7}{8}$	17	$4\tfrac{5}{8}$ $5\tfrac{2}{8}$	12 10	$28\tfrac{5}{8}$	894	94
	■ Pike Co. – Brian M. Rennecker – Brian M. Rennecker – 1999							
$208\tfrac{2}{8}$	$28\tfrac{4}{8}$ $29\tfrac{1}{8}$	$22\tfrac{6}{8}$	$29\tfrac{4}{8}$	$5\tfrac{2}{8}$ $5\tfrac{2}{8}$	10 12	26	910	96
	■ Saline Co. – Mark A. Sheldon – Mark A. Sheldon – 1999							
$208\tfrac{1}{8}$	$26\tfrac{6}{8}$ $26\tfrac{5}{8}$	$18\tfrac{3}{8}$	25	$5\tfrac{3}{8}$ $5\tfrac{4}{8}$	11 9	$34\tfrac{6}{8}$	920	97
	■ Brown Co. – Mark V. Piazza – Mark V. Piazza – 1989							
208	29 $27\tfrac{1}{8}$	$22\tfrac{2}{8}$	$24\tfrac{6}{8}$	$5\tfrac{3}{8}$ $5\tfrac{3}{8}$	11 13	$31\tfrac{2}{8}$	929	98
	■ Sangamon Co. – Daniel R. Lusardi – Daniel R. Lusardi – 1999							
$207\tfrac{6}{8}$	29 $28\tfrac{4}{8}$	$28\tfrac{2}{8}$	31	$6\tfrac{1}{8}$ 6	8 7	$35\tfrac{6}{8}$	951	99
	■ Henry Co. – Richard Vyneman – Richard Vyneman – 1992							
$207\tfrac{5}{8}$	$25\tfrac{6}{8}$ $25\tfrac{2}{8}$	$18\tfrac{5}{8}$	$25\tfrac{3}{8}$	$5\tfrac{7}{8}$ $6\tfrac{2}{8}$	11 11	$44\tfrac{4}{8}$	957	100
	■ Fulton Co. – Jack L. Link – Jack L. Link – 1999							
$207\tfrac{4}{8}$	27 $26\tfrac{3}{8}$	$17\tfrac{7}{8}$	20	$5\tfrac{2}{8}$ $5\tfrac{1}{8}$	8 9	$27\tfrac{7}{8}$	969	101
	■ Macoupin Co. – John D. Carey – John D. Carey – 1991							
$207\tfrac{2}{8}$	$29\tfrac{5}{8}$ $28\tfrac{2}{8}$	$22\tfrac{1}{8}$	$27\tfrac{1}{8}$	$5\tfrac{5}{8}$ $5\tfrac{7}{8}$	9 8	$28\tfrac{1}{8}$	985	102
	■ Clark Co. – Richard D. Ellington – Richard D. Ellington – 1997							
$206\tfrac{7}{8}$	$27\tfrac{1}{8}$ $27\tfrac{7}{8}$	$19\tfrac{5}{8}$	24	$5\tfrac{2}{8}$ $5\tfrac{2}{8}$	10 10	30	1011†	103†
	■ Jo Daveiss Co. – Picked Up – Doug D. Jones – 1998							

Score	Length of Main Beam		Inside Spread	Greatest Spread	Circumference at Smallest Place Between Burr and First Point		Number of Points		Lengths Abnormal Points	All-Time Rank	State Rank
	Right	Left			Right	Left	Right	Left			
	■ Location of Kill – Hunter – Owner – Date Killed										
206⁶/8	23⁷/8	27	23¹/8	25²/8	5⁶/8	5⁴/8	12	11	50⁷/8	1028†	104†
	■ Vermilion Co. – Ronald Weddle – Ronald Weddle – 2001										
206⁴/8	28⁴/8	26⁷/8	20⁵/8	24⁷/8	5¹/8	5³/8	10	9	25³/8	1043	105
	■ Lawrence Co. – Shirley Lewis – Shirley Lewis – 1976										
206³/8	24⁶/8	20⁶/8	18³/8	20²/8	5	5	12	12	54⁶/8	1051	106
	■ Menard Co. – Frank C. Pickett – Frank C. Pickett – 1985										
206²/8	26⁶/8	27⁵/8	23³/8	26⁴/8	5¹/8	5⁴/8	10	12	27⁵/8	1059†	107†
	■ Henry Co. – Jon R. Wolf – Jon R. Wolf – 2000										
205⁷/8	25	25⁶/8	21⁶/8	24²/8	5⁵/8	6	8	9	33¹/8	1080	108
	■ Greene Co. – Ronald R. Okonek – Ronald R. Okonek – 1998										
205⁴/8	25	25⁶/8	19⁴/8	26⁶/8	6¹/8	5⁶/8	11	7	43⁴/8	1107	109
	■ Adams Co. – Eldon K. Dagley – Eldon K. Dagley – 1981										
205²/8	25⁶/8	25¹/8	19⁷/8	22¹/8	6²/8	6²/8	8	8	29³/8	1131†	110†
	■ Morgan Co. – Shawn R. Keegan – Shawn R. Keegan – 2000 ■ See photo on page 61										
205²/8	28⁶/8	29²/8	18⁷/8	22⁴/8	4³/8	4⁴/8	10	11	22¹/8	1131	110
	■ Effingham Co. – Allen K. Bandelow – Allen K. Bandelow – 1991										
205	25⁵/8	24⁵/8	22¹/8	25	6	5⁵/8	7	11	65³/8	1144	112
	■ Jo Daviess Co. – David L. Virtue – David L. Virtue – 1990										
205	25³/8	25	24¹/8	26	5⁴/8	5⁴/8	9	10	37³/8	1144	112
	■ Peoria Co. – Picked Up – Dick Rossum – 1991										
205	24²/8	22⁴/8	18	20⁶/8	5⁵/8	5⁵/8	9	11	27²/8	1144	112
	■ Carroll Co. – Robert D. Guenzler – Robert D. Guenzler – 1994										
205	26³/8	24⁴/8	22⁴/8	25⁵/8	4⁵/8	4⁴/8	8	9	34²/8	1144	112
	■ Warren Co. – Jason A. Schwass – Jason A. Schwass – 1997										
205	27⁴/8	26²/8	21⁶/8	25²/8	5⁷/8	5⁷/8	10	9	25²/8	1144	112
	■ Fulton Co. – Picked Up – Robert E. Burgard – 1998										
204⁷/8	23³/8	24⁶/8	20²/8	25⁴/8	5³/8	5¹/8	12	10	28¹/8	1156†	117†
	■ Ogle Co. – Troy W. O'Brien – Troy W. O'Brien – 2001										
204⁵/8	29⁵/8	30⁴/8	20³/8	22⁶/8	5⁶/8	4⁴/8	7	6	26	1176	118
	■ Calhoun Co. – Chad Strickland – Chad Strickland – 1999										
204³/8	27¹/8	26⁶/8	18⁷/8	22	5³/8	5⁴/8	13	11	43⁶/8	1186	119
	■ Rock Island Co. – Jeff B. Davis – Jeff B. Davis – 1990										
204²/8	30	27⁶/8	21²/8	24	6³/8	6⁴/8	6	11	19⁶/8	1199	120
	■ Cass Co. – J. David Bartels – J. David Bartels – 1989										
204²/8	25⁶/8	25³/8	18²/8	26¹/8	5¹/8	5³/8	10	12	32⁴/8	1199	120
	■ Livingston Co. – Michael T. Schopp – Michael T. Schopp – 1996										
203⁶/8	23	22⁴/8	16¹/8	23⁴/8	5⁷/8	5⁷/8	11	12	62⁷/8	1237	122
	■ Pike Co. – Randall B. Long – Randall B. Long – 1987										
203⁶/8	25¹/8	23⁶/8	24¹/8	26³/8	6¹/8	6⁵/8	6	14	37¹/8	1237	122
	■ Kendall Co. – Brian Carlson – Brian Carlson – 1998										
203⁴/8	28⁴/8	29	22³/8	26⁴/8	4⁷/8	5¹/8	6	7	27⁵/8	1259†	124†
	■ Greene Co. – Greg L. Griswold – Greg L. Griswold – 2001										

Score	Length of Main Beam Right Left	Inside Spread	Greatest Spread	Circumference at Smallest Place Between Burr and First Point Right Left	Number of Points Right Left	Lengths Abnormal Points	All-Time Rank	State Rank
	■ *Location of Kill – Hunter – Owner – Date Killed*							
203 4/8	27 2/8 26 5/8	24	27 6/8	5 5/8 5 6/8	9 9	37	1259	124
■ *Ford Co. – Gary G. Tessdale – Gary G. Tessdale – 1997*								
203 3/8	28 2/8 29	22 2/8	24 3/8	5 5/8 5 6/8	8 7	17 5/8	1272	126
■ *Fulton Co. – Russell G. White – Russell G. White – 1996*								
203 2/8	22 2/8 21 3/8	15 4/8	23	4 7/8 4 7/8	9 10	47 2/8	1287†	127†
■ *Pike Co. – J. Brett Evans – J. Brett Evans – 2001* ■ *See photo on page 53*								
203 2/8	25 7/8 27 2/8	19	21 6/8	6 1/8 5 6/8	8 8	19	1287†	127†
■ *Iroquois Co. – Michael A. Lucht – Michael A. Lucht – 2002*								
203 1/8	24 5/8 26 1/8	24	26 4/8	5 2/8 5 5/8	10 7	35 1/8	1305†	129†
■ *Bureau Co. – Jack E. Davis – Jack E. Davis – 2001*								
203 1/8	24 4/8 23 5/8	19 2/8	24 4/8	4 7/8 4 6/8	9 7	31 5/8	1305	129
■ *St. Clair Co. – Gary W. White – Gary W. White – 1997*								
203	26 2/8 26 1/8	15	17 3/8	5 2/8 5 1/8	9 11	16 4/8	1317	131
■ *Hancock Co. – S.E. Brockschmidt – S.E. Brockschmidt – 1958*								
203	28 6/8 26 4/8	25 2/8	29	6 1/8 6 1/8	7 7	13 2/8	1317	131
■ *Coles Co. – Richard A. Miller – Richard A. Miller – 1991*								
203	25 6/8 26 2/8	21 2/8		4 5/8 4 6/8	7 10	54 2/8	1317	131
■ *Du Page Co. – Kevin J. Moran – Kevin J. Moran – 1995*								
202 7/8	27 7/8 26 2/8	18	20 6/8	5 2/8 5 3/8	12 7	32 7/8	1327	134
■ *Du Page Co. – Picked Up – E. Dolf Pfefferkorn – 1962*								
202 7/8	27 2/8 28 3/8	22 6/8	24 7/8	5 4/8 5 5/8	10 8	17 5/8	1327	134
■ *Brown Co. – Sylvan Purcell, Jr. – Sylvan Purcell, Jr. – 1992*								
202 7/8	25 2/8 24 4/8	18 2/8	22 2/8	6 3/8 6 2/8	10 11	29 3/8	1327	134
■ *Saline Co. – Lindy R. Potts – Lindy R. Potts – 1995*								
202 7/8	25 5/8 27	20 2/8	22	5 1/8 5 2/8	11 12	22 3/8	1327	134
■ *Adams Co. – Ben H. Myers – Ben H. Myers – 1999*								
202 6/8	27 2/8 27 6/8	22	25 6/8	5 5/8 5 5/8	7 6	15 4/8	1339†	138†
■ *McHenry Co. – Jim Kunde – Jim Kunde – 2001*								
202 5/8	25 1/8 25 6/8	18 7/8	22	5 3/8 4 7/8	9 9	21 2/8	1346	139
■ *Pike Co. – Brian M. Hill – Brian M. Hill – 1994*								
202 3/8	26 1/8 26 6/8	26 1/8	29 1/8	5 7/8 6 4/8	13 13	45 2/8	1362	140
■ *Washington Co. – Richard C. Keller – Richard C. Keller – 1986*								
202 3/8	27 5/8 27 2/8	24 1/8	26 6/8	5 5 1/8	8 7	14 4/8	1362	140
■ *Bond Co. – Douglas E. Hays – Douglas E. Hays – 1992*								
202 1/8	27 5/8 27 2/8	15	20	6 1/8 6 2/8	7 11	20 5/8	1386	142
■ *Peoria Co. – Leonard A. Asbell – Leonard A. Asbell – 1993*								
201 5/8	24 2/8 24 6/8	16 6/8	20 4/8	5 6/8 5 5/8	15 9	37 7/8	1427	143
■ *Kane Co. – Keith R. Kampert – Keith R. Kampert – 1991*								
201 4/8	26 7/8 28	20 2/8	24 6/8	5 6/8 5 6/8	13 11	48 6/8	1443†	144†
■ *Jackson Co. – Mark D. Ralph – Mark D. Ralph – 2000*								
201 4/8	25 5/8 24 4/8	19 6/8	24	5 7/8 6	11 13	48 6/8	1443	144
■ *Fulton Co. – John R. Rosas – John R. Rosas – 1994*								

Score	Length of Main Beam Right	Left	Inside Spread	Greatest Spread	Circumference at Smallest Place Between Burr and First Point Right	Left	Number of Points Right	Left	Lengths Abnormal Points	All-Time Rank	State Rank
	■ Location of Kill – Hunter – Owner – Date Killed										
201²⁄₈	25⁷⁄₈	25⁷⁄₈	18⁶⁄₈	22⁶⁄₈	5¹⁄₈	5	8	11	24⁶⁄₈	1478†	146†
	■ Jefferson Co. – Dwight N. Pfeiffer – Dwight N. Pfeiffer – 1999										
201¹⁄₈	28	27²⁄₈	20⁶⁄₈	25	5⁶⁄₈	5⁷⁄₈	8	10	22¹⁄₈	1489	147
	■ Carroll Co. – Mel Landwehr – Mel Landwehr – 1991										
201¹⁄₈	23⁶⁄₈	23²⁄₈	15⁵⁄₈	20⁷⁄₈	6¹⁄₈	6³⁄₈	11	11	46	1489	147
	■ Jackson Co. – Allen S. Casten – Allen S. Casten – 1996										
201	27¹⁄₈	27⁶⁄₈	21⁴⁄₈	24	5⁴⁄₈	5⁵⁄₈	11	8	23⁶⁄₈	1500	149
	■ Mercer Co. – Gerald L. Olson – Gerald L. Olson – 1972										
200⁵⁄₈	25⁵⁄₈	26²⁄₈	17¹⁄₈	23⁶⁄₈	5	5	14	8	26	1532†	150†
	■ Adams Co. – Edward B. Tucker – Edward B. Tucker – 1999										
200⁴⁄₈	25⁶⁄₈	23⁵⁄₈	17⁷⁄₈	20⁵⁄₈	4⁴⁄₈	4⁵⁄₈	7	9	24¹⁄₈	1545†	151†
	■ Allamakee Co. – Bruce L. Schuttemeier – Bruce L. Schuttemeier – 2000										
200²⁄₈	28	28⁵⁄₈	25³⁄₈	27⁴⁄₈	5⁶⁄₈	5⁶⁄₈	7	7	21³⁄₈	1569	152
	■ La Salle Co. – James A. Carr – James A. Carr – 1999										
200¹⁄₈	25	28³⁄₈	23⁵⁄₈	25⁷⁄₈	5³⁄₈	5⁴⁄₈	8	9	18²⁄₈	1577	153
	■ Macoupin Co. – John M. Ragusa – John M. Ragusa – 1992										
200¹⁄₈	28⁵⁄₈	27	19³⁄₈	23⁶⁄₈	5¹⁄₈	5³⁄₈	12	7	37	1577	153
	■ Ogle Co. – Theodore H. Hysell – Theodore H. Hysell – 1993										
199⁷⁄₈	27	26⁵⁄₈	19⁷⁄₈	22	5¹⁄₈	5	8	11	23⁴⁄₈	1607	155
	■ Knox Co. – Rodney G. Eklund – Rodney G. Eklund – 1990										
199⁶⁄₈	24⁶⁄₈	27⁵⁄₈	22⁵⁄₈	24⁵⁄₈	9⁶⁄₈	5³⁄₈	10	6	62³⁄₈	1613	156
	■ Edgar Co. – Brad Davis – Brad Davis – 1996										
199⁴⁄₈	28⁴⁄₈	28³⁄₈	21⁶⁄₈	24⁵⁄₈	5¹⁄₈	5¹⁄₈	10	6	22⁴⁄₈	1631	157
	■ Sangamon Co. – Kenneth J. Barlow – Kenneth J. Barlow – 1991										
199³⁄₈	22⁷⁄₈	22³⁄₈	20¹⁄₈	22¹⁄₈	6	6	11	9	28	1639	158
	■ Morgan Co. – David W. Roehrs – David W. Roehrs – 1979										
199¹⁄₈	28³⁄₈	26⁶⁄₈	21³⁄₈	27¹⁄₈	6	5⁷⁄₈	10	8	24⁴⁄₈	1660	159
	■ Macoupin Co. – Jerry A. Dittmer – Jerry A. Dittmer – 1994										
199	27⁶⁄₈	27¹⁄₈	22³⁄₈	28¹⁄₈	5²⁄₈	5³⁄₈	8	8	40³⁄₈	1668	160
	■ Adams Co. – Jerry Schaller – Jerry Schaller – 1974										
199	29⁶⁄₈	28⁴⁄₈	20	25	7	6⁶⁄₈	8	10	30⁴⁄₈	1668	160
	■ Lake Co. – Steven Hysell – Steven Hysell – 1994										
199	27⁷⁄₈	27²⁄₈	18⁴⁄₈	21	4⁶⁄₈	5	7	7	21²⁄₈	1668	160
	■ Macoupin Co. – Jon D. DeNeef – Jon D. DeNeef – 1995										
199	28⁴⁄₈	26²⁄₈	26³⁄₈	28⁵⁄₈	4⁷⁄₈	4⁷⁄₈	6	9	15⁷⁄₈	1668	160
	■ La Salle Co. – Hank J. Walsh III – Hank J. Walsh III – 1995										
198⁷⁄₈	25⁴⁄₈	28¹⁄₈	18⁴⁄₈	24⁴⁄₈	4⁷⁄₈	5²⁄₈	13	10	45⁷⁄₈	1686	164
	■ Greene Co. – James M. Bowker – James M. Bowker – 1995										
198⁷⁄₈	25²⁄₈	25¹⁄₈	17²⁄₈	19⁴⁄₈	5⁶⁄₈	5⁷⁄₈	7	7	23⁵⁄₈	1686	164
	■ Pike Co. – James Kruczynski – James Kruczynski – 1998										
198⁷⁄₈	25²⁄₈	24⁴⁄₈	19⁶⁄₈	22	5¹⁄₈	6⁷⁄₈	6	13	51¹⁄₈	1686	164
	■ Fulton Co. – Todd L. DeGroot – Todd L. DeGroot – 1999										

Score	Length of Main Beam		Inside Spread	Greatest Spread	Circumference at Smallest Place Between Burr and First Point		Number of Points		Lengths Abnormal Points	All-Time Rank	State Rank
	Right	Left			Right	Left	Right	Left			
	■ Location of Kill – Hunter – Owner – Date Killed										
198⁶/₈	28³/₈	28³/₈	15¹/₈	19³/₈	5³/₈	5³/₈	9	7	33³/₈	1697†	167†
	■ Madison Co. – Eric W. Barach – Eric W. Barach – 2001										
198⁶/₈	22⁵/₈	24⁵/₈	15	18	6⁵/₈	5⁵/₈	11	11	34	1697	167
	■ Peoria Co. – Roger Woodcock – Roger Woodcock – 1989										
198⁶/₈	23⁷/₈	25⁴/₈	19⁶/₈	24	4⁴/₈	4²/₈	10	7	39⁴/₈	1697	167
	■ Randolph Co. – John A. Brown – John A. Brown – 1992										
198⁵/₈	23⁶/₈	22²/₈	17⁷/₈	22	4⁶/₈	5	14	12	58	1716	170
	■ Will Co. – William H. Rutledge – William H. Rutledge – 1977										
198⁵/₈	25⁵/₈	25⁶/₈	21³/₈	25⁶/₈	5⁵/₈	5⁷/₈	12	9	34⁴/₈	1716	170
	■ Hamilton Co. – Thomas D. Flannigan – Thomas D. Flannigan – 1989										
198⁵/₈	28⁵/₈	27²/₈	22¹/₈	25	5⁵/₈	6²/₈	6	8	14⁴/₈	1716	170
	■ Franklin Co. – Freddie Cooper – Freddie Cooper – 1990										
198⁴/₈	23⁷/₈	23⁵/₈	17⁷/₈	23⁵/₈	4⁶/₈	4⁷/₈	8	9	35³/₈	1736	173
	■ Iroquois Co. – Charles E. Crow – Charles E. Crow – 1974										
198⁴/₈	21⁶/₈	25²/₈	15	17¹/₈	7²/₈	7	13	8	50⁶/₈	1736	173
	■ Adams Co. – Rick L. Dormire – Rick L. Dormire – 1993										
198⁴/₈	29⁴/₈	29⁵/₈	24⁶/₈	27⁷/₈	5⁴/₈	5⁶/₈	10	7	18²/₈	1736	173
	■ Macoupin Co. – Brett E. Bridgewater – Brett E. Bridgewater – 1999										
198³/₈	25	24⁵/₈	22⁴/₈	25²/₈	5²/₈	5¹/₈	8	9	32⁷/₈	1762	176
	■ Adams Co. – Eldie J. Miller – Eldie J. Miller – 1980										
198¹/₈	25²/₈	25	16⁴/₈	18⁴/₈	5⁴/₈	5⁴/₈	8	9	26³/₈	1785	177
	■ Pike Co. – Picked Up – Sam Moore – 1998										
198	28⁶/₈	27³/₈	21⁷/₈	24⁵/₈	5²/₈	5⁴/₈	8	10	21¹/₈	1801	178
	■ Christian Co. – Jack B. Hartwig – Jack B. Hartwig – 1987										
198	28³/₈	26²/₈	18³/₈	20⁵/₈	5⁶/₈	5³/₈	9	10	18³/₈	1801	178
	■ Edgar Co. – Aaron C. Bishop – Aaron C. Bishop – 1990										
198	27	27⁴/₈	20⁴/₈	28	5⁶/₈	5⁷/₈	10	9	22²/₈	1801	178
	■ Jo Daviess Co. – Victor W. Rogers – Victor W. Rogers – 1990										
197⁵/₈	28	28²/₈	21	24⁴/₈	5⁷/₈	5⁶/₈	10	7	19¹/₈	1847	181
	■ Jo Daviess Co. – David H. Carpenter – David H. Carpenter – 1962										
197⁵/₈	28	25²/₈	21⁵/₈	25	5⁵/₈	5⁶/₈	9	11	25⁶/₈	1847	181
	■ Adams Co. – Daniel J. Schlosser – Daniel J. Schlosser – 1987										
197⁵/₈	28⁴/₈	29³/₈	22⁵/₈	24⁷/₈	5¹/₈	4⁵/₈	10	8	17	1847	181
	■ Stephenson Co. – Richard M. Keller – Richard M. Keller – 1988										
197⁵/₈	24⁷/₈	25¹/₈	16⁷/₈	19⁶/₈	4⁵/₈	4⁷/₈	7	9	19	1847	181
	■ McDonough Co. – Jeffery W. Foxall – Jeffery W. Foxall – 1990										
197⁵/₈	26⁵/₈	27¹/₈	17¹/₈	21⁴/₈	5²/₈	5¹/₈	9	10	16⁶/₈	1847	181
	■ McDonough Co. – Thad E. Powell – Thad E. Powell – 1998										
197⁴/₈	25⁶/₈	25⁶/₈	25	28⁶/₈	5⁴/₈	5⁴/₈	10	9	26	1866	186
	■ Pope Co. – Joe C. Schwegman – Joe C. Schwegman – 1961										
197⁴/₈	29	29⁵/₈	27²/₈	29	5⁴/₈	5⁴/₈	9	9	19⁴/₈	1866	186
	■ Pike Co. – Donald Reynolds – Donald Reynolds – 1996										

Score	Length of Main Beam Right	Left	Inside Spread	Greatest Spread	Circumference at Smallest Place Between Burr and First Point Right	Left	Number of Points Right	Left	Lengths Abnormal Points	All-Time Rank	State Rank
	■ Location of Kill – Hunter – Owner – Date Killed										
197 4/8	26	27	19 5/8	23 4/8	6 4/8	6 3/8	8	7	16 1/8	1866	186
■ Vermilion Co. – Alan D. Hingson – Alan D. Hingson – 1997											
197 3/8	24 6/8	24 6/8	16	21	6 6/8	7	8	17	38 7/8	1884	189
■ Perry Co. – Dwayne Rogers – Dwayne Rogers – 1996											
197 2/8	27 6/8	29 4/8	19 7/8	22 1/8	5 2/8	5 2/8	9	8	24 5/8	1901†	190†
■ Fayette Co. – Todd L. Hodson – Todd L. Hodson – 2000											
197 2/8	25	23 7/8	19 5/8	22 7/8	5 5/8	5 6/8	7	8	12 1/8	1901†	190†
■ Fulton Co. – Nicholas P. McElroy – Nicholas P. McElroy – 2000											
197 2/8	27 6/8	25 1/8	21	22 6/8	5 4/8	5 3/8	9	8	24	1901	190
■ Sangamon Co. – Robert W. Penwell – Robert W. Penwell – 1996											
197 1/8	25 3/8	25 2/8	21	25 2/8	5 1/8	5 7/8	10	10	27 7/8	1923	193
■ Jefferson Co. – Unknown – Jeff Sartaine – 1983											
196 7/8	27	25	21 5/8	24 3/8	4 7/8	5 4/8	8	10	27 4/8	1950	194
■ Bureau Co. – Steve M. Mazurek – Steve M. Mazurek – 1995											
196 6/8	27 2/8	26 2/8	21 2/8	22 6/8	5 2/8	5	10	9	18	1968†	195†
■ Pike Co. – Larry D. Grant – Larry D. Grant – 2001											
196 6/8	28 2/8	28	21	22 7/8	5 2/8	5 3/8	7	8	13 6/8	1968	195
■ McHenry Co. – Timothy A. Schulze – Timothy A. Schulze – 1989											
196 5/8	26 4/8	27 6/8	20 6/8	23 4/8	4 7/8	4 6/8	8	6	14 5/8	1985	197
■ Scott Co. – Michael G. Schildman – Michael G. Schildman – 1992											
196 3/8	24 3/8	18 6/8	24	26 3/8	5 4/8	5 3/8	9	10	37 7/8	2010	198
■ Clark Co. – Mary K. LeCrone – Mary K. LeCrone – 1982											
196 2/8	27 6/8	24 3/8	18 1/8	20 6/8	3 7/8	4 2/8	11	11	29 5/8	2028	199
■ Edwards Co. – David Broster – David Broster – 1996											
196 1/8	26 4/8	21 7/8	19 3/8	22 1/8	5 5/8	5 5/8	9	7	30	2045	200
■ Henderson Co. – Bruce Keever – Bruce Keever – 1992											
196	26 6/8	23 3/8	15 5/8	18 7/8	7 1/8	7	9	9	58 1/8	2059	201
■ Cumberland Co. – Jeff A. Light – Jeff A. Light – 1997											
195 6/8	25	24 2/8	20 7/8	24	5 2/8	5 1/8	9	10	27 3/8	2094†	202†
■ Madison Co. – James M. Hoefert – James M. Hoefert – 2001											
195 6/8	28 6/8	30 2/8	22	26	5 7/8	6	7	8	16 4/8	2094	202
■ Illinois – Unknown – Ed Feist – 1945											
195 5/8	28 1/8	27 5/8	21 4/8	25 3/8	5 3/8	5 4/8	8	7	31 7/8	2116	204
■ Brown Co. – Brian Matsko – Brian Matsko – 1994											
195 4/8	25 6/8	16 2/8	20 6/8	25 4/8	6	6	7	7	47 4/8	2134	205
■ Bureau Co. – Picked Up – John Cotter – 1976											
195 4/8	28 6/8	27 5/8	18 2/8	21 1/8	4 7/8	5 3/8	10	15	24	2134	205
■ Hamilton Co. – Douglas P. Collins – Douglas P. Collins – 1985											
195 4/8	26 2/8	27 6/8	17 4/8	21	5	5	10	8	27 6/8	2134	205
■ Peoria Co. – Jerry T. Wyatt – Jerry T. Wyatt – 1989											
195 4/8	28	27 3/8	20 3/8	22 4/8	5 2/8	5 2/8	8	8	19 3/8	2134	205
■ Jo Daviess Co. – Glen M. Volk – Glen M. Volk – 1997											

Score	Length of Main Beam Right	Left	Inside Spread	Greatest Spread	Circumference at Smallest Place Between Burr and First Point Right	Left	Number of Points Right	Left	Lengths Abnormal Points	All-Time Rank	State Rank
	■ Location of Kill – Hunter – Owner – Date Killed										
195³/8	26⁵/8	26³/8	22⁷/8	26	4⁴/8	4⁵/8	8	10	26	2163	209
	■ Jackson Co. – Robert L. Koehn – Robert L. Koehn – 1991										
195³/8	26³/8	27⁴/8	18⁵/8	24⁵/8	4⁵/8	4⁶/8	7	8	27⁴/8	2163	209
	■ Pike Co. – Ray Yates – Ray Yates – 1998										
195²/8	28³/8	28⁶/8	20⁵/8	22⁵/8	6	5⁶/8	9	6	24⁷/8	2186†	211†
	■ Jefferson Co. IL – William C. Bell – William C. Bell – 2000										
195²/8	20	19³/8	15⁷/8	18	5⁶/8	5³/8	12	10	55¹/8	2186	211
	■ Adams Co. – Thomas D. Stice – Thomas D. Stice – 1991										
195¹/8	26⁷/8	25⁵/8	20⁵/8	26⁷/8	5²/8	5¹/8	8	7	17	2208	213
	■ Massac Co. – Kent Sommer – Kent Sommer – 1989										
195	22⁴/8	23⁴/8	20³/8	25	5⁴/8	5²/8	8	9	41¹/8	2233	214
	■ Calhoun Co. – Roger F. Becker – Roger F. Becker – 1983										
195	25³/8	22⁶/8	20⁶/8	23	5⁶/8	5³/8	9	8	28⁴/8	2233	214
	■ Henderson Co. – George S. Worley – William H. Lilienthal – 1989										
195	27⁴/8	27⁷/8	20²/8	23²/8	4⁶/8	5²/8	9	10	26²/8	2233	214
	■ Jersey Co. – Glenn A. Wilson – Glenn A. Wilson – 1994										
195	25⁴/8	26¹/8	22	24²/8	5⁴/8	5³/8	8	9	47	2233	214
	■ McLean Co. – Frank G. Bartels – Frank G. Bartels – 1996										
194⁵/8	26²/8	24	23⁷/8	25⁷/8	4⁵/8	4⁴/8	6	7	18²/8	2263	218
	■ Lake Co. – Paul H. Woit – Paul H. Woit – 1991										
194²/8	24⁴/8	25⁵/8	21	23	6	5³/8	11	7	23⁴/8	2267	219
	■ Menard Co. – John D. Grosboll – John D. Grosboll – 1988										
194¹/8	25⁷/8	24⁷/8	20⁵/8	23	5	5	9	7	17⁴/8	2271†	220†
	■ Du Page Co. – Picked Up – Christopher T. Vasey – 2000										
193⁵/8	24⁴/8	24⁵/8	18	21⁶/8	5⁷/8	6¹/8	6	10	25¹/8	2281†	221†
	■ Mercer Co. – David F. Flickinger – David F. Flickinger – 2000										
193⁴/8	26³/8	25²/8	20²/8	22⁷/8	4⁷/8	5¹/8	7	8	28⁶/8	2288	222
	■ Edgar Co. – Jerry R. David – Jerry R. David – 1988										
193³/8	27⁴/8	24	21³/8	26²/8	5⁴/8	5⁷/8	9	9	15²/8	2293	223
	■ McHenry Co. – Michael W. Kaufmann – Michael W. Kaufmann – 1999										
193²/8	25²/8	23⁶/8	18⁵/8	21²/8	7	7⁵/8	7	8	15³/8	2300	224
	■ Fulton Co. – James Crane – James Crane – 1997										
193	27⁴/8	27¹/8	19⁷/8	24⁵/8	6¹/8	5²/8	8	7	20⁷/8	2310	225
	■ Lake Co. – Steven Derkson – Steven Derkson – 1989										
192⁷/8	27⁴/8	27⁴/8	22¹/8	24¹/8	5⁷/8	5⁴/8	9	9	24⁶/8	2312†	226†
	■ Edwards Co. – Ronald D. Pritchett – Ronald D. Pritchett – 2001										
192⁶/8	27³/8	26²/8	17⁷/8	23³/8	6	6⁴/8	9	7	20³/8	2317	227
	■ Vermilion Co. – Edwin B. Gudgel – Edwin B. Gudgel – 1988										
192⁶/8	25³/8	27¹/8	18²/8	23⁴/8	6⁷/8	7²/8	10	9	37	2317	227
	■ Brown Co. – Thomas March – Thomas March – 1990										
192⁶/8	26⁵/8	26⁷/8	20²/8	24²/8	6¹/8	5⁷/8	11	6	31-8/8	2317	227
	■ Stark Co. – John H. Ford – John H. Ford – 1998										

Score	Length of Main Beam Right	Left	Inside Spread	Greatest Spread	Circumference at Smallest Place Between Burr and First Point Right	Left	Number of Points Right	Left	Lengths Abnormal Points	All-Time Rank	State Rank
	■ Location of Kill – Hunter – Owner – Date Killed										
192 4/8	25 6/8	24	19	21 6/8	5 2/8	5 3/8	5	10	39	2325	230
	■ Greene Co. – Billy L. Pembrook – Billy L. Pembrook – 1994										
191 3/8	24 2/8	25 2/8	23 1/8	26 7/8	6	6	9	8	19 6/8	2364	231
	■ Douglas Co. – Jackie L. Norman – Jackie L. Norman – 1990										
191 3/8	25 1/8	26 6/8	19 7/8	22 4/8	4 4/8	4 3/8	7	9	20 2/8	2364	231
	■ McLean Co. – Virginia D. Gaither – Virginia D. Gaither – 1993										
190 5/8	26 5/8	24 6/8	19 4/8	19 4/8	4 6/8	4 7/8	6	11	30 7/8	2393†	233†
	■ Jackson Co. – Heath R. Rushing – Heath R. Rushing – 2001										
190 3/8	29 2/8	30 5/8	25 1/8	27 1/8	5 7/8	5 5/8	10	9	20	2408	234
	■ McLean Co. – Dwight E. Johnson – Dwight E. Johnson – 1998										
190 1/8	26 3/8	25 2/8	22 1/8	24 5/8	5 1/8	5	10	8	20 6/8	2416	235
	■ Livingston Co. – Daniel P. Olson – Daniel P. Olson – 1995										
190	24	24 6/8	18 4/8	21 2/8	5 2/8	5 3/8	10	9	20 4/8	2418	236
	■ Peoria Co. – Michael C. Moon – Michael C. Moon – 1993										
189 6/8	25 4/8	25 4/8	20 3/8	23	5 7/8	5 7/8	7	8	12 7/8	2425†	237†
	■ Woodford Co. – Gunnar R. Darnall – Gunnar R. Darnall – 2001										
189 6/8	27 6/8	28 7/8	20 3/8	22 7/8	4 6/8	5 1/8	6	7	17 5/8	2425	237
	■ Fulton Co. – Richard J. Burdette – Richard J. Burdette – 1995										
189 5/8	20 6/8	21 1/8	16 2/8	20 3/8	5	4 7/8	9	11	33 1/8	2429	239
	■ Carroll Co. – Thomas D. Drish – Thomas D. Drish – 1984										
189 4/8	24 6/8	25 5/8	18 3/8	21 6/8	5 5/8	6 1/8	8	11	24 5/8	2435†	240†
	■ McDonough Co. – Les Twidwell – Les Twidwell – 2001										
189 4/8	23 7/8	23 6/8	17 2/8	20 2/8	5	5	7	9	16 4/8	2435	240
	■ Cass Co. – Ronald L. McClure, Jr. – Ronald L. McClure, Jr. – 1994										
189	27 7/8	28 2/8	22	24 2/8	5 5/8	5 6/8	8	8	11 6/8	2456†	242†
	■ Ogle Co. – Russell A. Young – Russell A. Young – 2000										
189	26 2/8	25 6/8	21 4/8	23 2/8	5 5/8	5 2/8	11	8	24 6/8	2456	242
	■ Whiteside Co. – Melvin Willey – Melvin Willey – 1991										
188 5/8	23 5/8	24	19 2/8	21 6/8	5 2/8	5 2/8	8	8	25 7/8	2471	244
	■ Knox Co. – Marvin L. Baker – Marvin L. Baker – 1973										
188 4/8	23 3/8	19 1/8	23 3/8	25 7/8	5 7/8	5 7/8	8	10	27 7/8	2475	245
	■ Johnson Co. – David A. Econie – David A. Econie – 1994										
188 3/8	24 6/8	25 5/8	17 1/8	20 6/8	5 2/8	5 1/8	9	8	17 2/8	2478	246
	■ Will Co. – James J.A. O'Keefe – James J.A. O'Keefe – 1993										
188 3/8	24 3/8	26 6/8	19 7/8	22 3/8	5 6/8	5 3/8	8	7	28 2/8	2478	246
	■ Cass Co. – Jack O. McKenzie – Jack O. McKenzie – 1997										
188 2/8	23 1/8	21 5/8	17 4/8	20	6 2/8	6 7/8	9	8	33 2/8	2489†	248†
	■ Morgan Co. – Timothy P. Mason – Timothy P. Mason – 2001										
188 2/8	31 6/8	30 6/8	23 5/8	26 3/8	5 1/8	5	9	9	16 3/8	2489	248
	■ Menard Co. – James H. Elliott – James H. Elliott – 1993										
188 1/8	24 6/8	24 3/8	16 6/8	23 1/8	6 1/8	6	10	8	19 7/8	2497	250
	■ Vermilion Co. – Mark E. Whittington – Mark E. Whittington – 1993										

Score	Length of Main Beam Right	Left	Inside Spread	Greatest Spread	Circumference at Smallest Place Between Burr and First Point Right	Left	Number of Points Right	Left	Lengths Abnormal Points	All-Time Rank	State Rank
	■ Location of Kill – Hunter – Owner – Date Killed										
187 6/8	26	27	21 3/8	28 4/8	7 3/8	6 7/8	8	5	25 3/8	2512†	251†
■ Peoria Co. – Stanley D. Hayes – Stanley D. Hayes – 2000											
187 3/8	28	28 2/8	20 3/8	22 6/8	5 6/8	5 5/8	6	10	22 6/8	2528†	252†
■ Adams Co. – Douglas J. Schutte – Douglas J. Schutte – 1996											
187 1/8	24 6/8	25 4/8	17 6/8	20 3/8	5 6/8	5 3/8	8	6	14 5/8	2540†	253†
■ Pike Co. – Joseph Rizzo – Joseph Rizzo – 2001											
187	25 6/8	27	17 7/8	23 5/8	5 1/8	5 3/8	6	7	27 5/8	2545	254
■ Woodford Co. – David K. Jacocks – David K. Jacocks – 1989											
186 6/8	25 2/8	25 6/8	18 7/8	22 2/8	5 3/8	5	7	7	21 3/8	2559	255
■ Adams Co. – Gregory D. Schutte – Gregory D. Schutte – 1996											
186	25 1/8	25 1/8	18 2/8	21 4/8	4 3/8	4 4/8	7	6	14 4/8	2586	256
■ Brown Co. – John D. Leonard – John D. Leonard – 1993											
185 7/8	26 7/8	26 2/8	18 6/8	20 4/8	5 2/8	5 2/8	6	8	11 1/8	2597†	257†
■ Cook Co. – Timothy L. Harkness – Timothy L. Harkness – 2000											
185 7/8	26 7/8	27 5/8	22 7/8	24 5/8	4 6/8	4 7/8	8	10	27	2597	257
■ Hancock Co. – Joshua T. Baird – Joshua T. Baird – 1998											
185 4/8	29 2/8	27 7/8	19 3/8		5 1/8	5 4/8	6	7	10 5/8	2616	259
■ Clark Co. – Walter Garner – Walter Garner – 1989											
185 3/8	27	27 6/8	20	22 1/8	6 3/8	6	10	11	19 3/8	2622	260
■ Winnebago Co. – David J. Schuler – David J. Schuler – 1994											
185 1/8	24	22 2/8	17 4/8	19 2/8	4 3/8	4 6/8	6	7	18 1/8	2641	261
■ Logan Co. – William D. Maske – William D. Maske – 1994											
256 7/8	26 6/8	26 3/8	20	27 7/8	5	5	16	14	91 3/8	*	*
■ Adams Co. – Todd R. Hurley – Todd R. Hurley – 1995											
251 6/8	30 4/8	31 6/8	25 2/8	30 5/8	5 5/8	5 3/8	12	13	71	*	*
■ Fulton Co. – William K. Brown – William K. Brown – 1999											
244 3/8	23 4/8	24 1/8	20	24 3/8	5 5/8	5 7/8	12	14	72 7/8	*	*
■ Knox Co. – Karl R. Jones – Karl R. Jones – 1992											

† The scores and ranking for trophies from the 25th Awards Entry Period are not final until the banquet is held on June 19, 2004.

* Final score is subject to revision by additional verifying measurements.

TROPHIES IN THE FIELD

HUNTER:	John P. Boshears
SCORE:	220-1/8
CATEGORY:	non-typical whitetail deer
LOCATION:	Iroquois County, Illinois
DATE:	1998

INDIANA
RECORD WHITETAILS

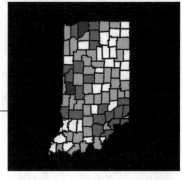

119 Typical whitetail deer entries
60 Non-typical whitetail deer entries
7,265 Total whitetail deer entries

0 Entries	
1-2 Entries	
3-5 Entries	
6-10 Entries	
11+ Entries	

INDIANA
STATE RECORD
Typical Whitetail Deer
Score: 195$^{1}/_{8}$
Location: Parke Co.
Hunter and Owner: B. Dodd Porter
Date: 1985

INDIANA
NEW STATE RECORD
Non-Typical Whitetail Deer
Score: 251^4/$_8$
Location: Hendricks Co.
Hunter: Timothy J. Goode
Owner: Bass Pro Shops
Date: 1980

Photograph courtesy of Bass Pro Shops

INDIANA

TYPICAL WHITETAIL DEER

Score	Length of Main Beam Right	Left	Inside Spread	Greatest Spread	Circumference at Smallest Place Between Burr and First Point Right	Left	Number of Points Right	Left	Lengths Abnormal Points	All-Time Rank	State Rank
	■ Location of Kill – Hunter – Owner – Date Killed										
195¹/8	28⁶/8	28⁴/8	20³/8	22⁵/8	4⁷/8	5	5	5		39	1
	■ Parke Co. – B. Dodd Porter – B. Dodd Porter – 1985										
194²/8	30⁶/8	30³/8	24⁷/8	27¹/8	5³/8	5²/8	9	7	12³/8	45	2
	■ Vigo Co. – D. Bates & S. Winkler – D. Bates & S. Winkler – 1983										
192³/8	24¹/8	23⁶/8	17³/8	19³/8	5	4⁶/8	6	6		64	3
	■ Monroe Co. – Donald L. Fritch – Donald L. Fritch – 1992										
192³/8	26⁷/8	26⁷/8	18⁵/8	21	4⁶/8	5¹/8	5	6	2	64	3
	■ Jennings Co. – Walter M. Johnson – Walter M. Johnson – 1997										
190⁶/8	30	30²/8	20⁶/8	24	5¹/8	5²/8	7	7	6⁶/8	93	5
	■ Union Co. – John R. Ison, Jr. – John R. Ison, Jr. – 1997										
190⁵/8	29	29	19⁴/8	21⁷/8	5⁶/8	5⁶/8	5	7	3⁵/8	95	6
	■ Parke Co. – Tony A. Trotter – Tony A. Trotter – 1992										
190²/8	25⁶/8	26²/8	21³/8	23	5	4⁵/8	13	13	20³/8	104	7
	■ Pike Co. – Vince Brock – Vince Brock – 1993										
187¹/8	27²/8	27⁶/8	17⁷/8	19⁷/8	5	5	8	6	3²/8	185	8
	■ Montgomery Co. – Larry E. Lawson – Larry E. Lawson – 1988										
186²/8	25¹/8	24⁴/8	18	20	5²/8	5²/8	6	6		220	9
	■ White Co. – Samuel T. Young – Samuel T. Young – 1997										
185⁵/8	26	27⁵/8	19⁵/8	22³/8	6	5⁴/8	5	5		248	10
	■ Johnson Co. – Michael J. Arney – Michael J. Arney – 1998										
185¹/8	26²/8	27⁴/8	23¹/8	25⁶/8	4⁵/8	5¹/8	6	7	1⁴/8	266	11
	■ Franklin Co. – Gayle Fritsch – Gayle Fritsch – 1972										
185¹/8	27⁴/8	28	18⁶/8	21²/8	5	4⁶/8	5	8	3⁵/8	266	11
	■ Porter Co. – Mathieu J. Price – Mathieu J. Price – 1990										
185	27⁴/8	27²/8	18⁶/8	21³/8	5³/8	5⁴/8	6	8	9	272	13
	■ Putnam Co. – Earl G. McCammack – Earl G. McCammack – 1985										
183⁶/8	26⁶/8	27⁶/8	19²/8	21⁴/8	4³/8	4⁴/8	6	6		350	14
	■ Clinton Co. – Stuart C. Snodgrass – Stuart C. Snodgrass – 1977										
183⁵/8	30	29³/8	24⁵/8	26⁶/8	4⁷/8	5¹/8	5	5		357†	15†
	■ Clark Co. – Donald B. Minnich – Donald B. Minnich – 1999										
182⁴/8	26³/8	26⁴/8	15⁴/8	19	5	5⁴/8	6	6	1²/8	431	16
	■ Jackson Co. – Rocky Deakin – Rocky Deakin – 1985										
182⁴/8	26³/8	26⁵/8	24⁶/8	26⁵/8	5³/8	5²/8	6	5	2⁴/8	431	16
	■ Wells Co. – Matt Roush – Matt Roush – 1999										
182¹/8	29⁵/8	30⁵/8	24	26³/8	5	5	6	7	5³/8	460	18
	■ Clark Co. – William F. Mills II – William F. Mills II – 1995										
181³/8	27⁴/8	26⁷/8	18⁴/8	21	5¹/8	5¹/8	5	7	1¹/8	528	19
	■ Warren Co. – Todd J. Hemke – Todd J. Hemke – 1987										

Score	Length of Main Beam Right	Left	Inside Spread	Greatest Spread	Circumference at Smallest Place Between Burr and First Point Right	Left	Number of Points Right	Left	Lengths Abnormal Points	All-Time Rank	State Rank
180 7/8	27 2/8	26 6/8	21 5/8	24 2/8	5 2/8	5 4/8	5	5		573	20
	■ Rush Co. – Cain M. Grocox – Cain M. Grocox – 1995										
180 4/8	27	26 6/8	21 1/8	23 1/8	5 4/8	5 6/8	6	7	3 7/8	613	21
	■ Dubois Co. – Kenneth R. Hasenour – Kenneth R. Hasenour – 1995										
180 1/8	25	25 3/8	23 4/8	25 3/8	4 6/8	4 5/8	7	6	2 3/8	669†	22†
	■ Clark Co. – Matthew D. Miller – Matthew D. Miller – 2000										
179 6/8	28 4/8	28	21	23 2/8	4 7/8	4 6/8	5	5		712†	23†
	■ Porter Co. – Herbert R. Smith – Herbert R. Smith – 2001										
179 3/8	25 3/8	27 7/8	21	23 2/8	5 3/8	5 4/8	6	7	12 7/8	749	24
	■ Jennings Co. – Dennis L. Day – Dennis L. Day – 1995										
179 3/8	26 5/8	25 7/8	18 7/8	21	6 1/8	6 2/8	5	8	3	749	24
	■ Warren Co. – Steven B. Childress – Steven B. Childress – 1999										
178 5/8	25	24 7/8	17 1/8	19 3/8	5 5/8	5 5/8	6	6		819†	26†
	■ Noble Co. – William M. Hart, Jr. – William M. Hart, Jr. – 2001										
178 3/8	25 5/8	26	22 1/8	24 3/8	6	6 2/8	7	6	6 2/8	868	27
	■ Tippecanoe Co. – Robert Whitus – Robert Whitus – 1994										
177	26 2/8	27 6/8	18 4/8	21 2/8	4 4/8	4 6/8	5	5		1066	28
	■ Cass Co. – Herbert R. Frushour – Herbert R. Frushour – 1974										
177	28 7/8	28 6/8	22 3/8	25	4 1/8	4	6	5	1 1/8	1066	28
	■ Jasper Co. – Dan Haskins – Douglas R. Plourde – 1975										
176 7/8	25 7/8	25 3/8	17 4/8	20 2/8	4 6/8	5	6	5	1 3/8	1086	30
	■ Sullivan Co. – Larry A. Nash – Larry A. Nash – 1995										
176 5/8	26	25 3/8	23 5/8	25 1/8	4 7/8	4 5/8	7	8	6 2/8	1134	31
	■ La Porte Co. – Alicia Boguslawski – Alicia Boguslawski – 1995										
176 2/8	24 3/8	25 4/8	18 2/8	21	4 3/8	4 2/8	5	9	1 6/8	1209	32
	■ Monroe Co. – Chad A. DeGolyer – Chad A. DeGolyer – 1996										
175 7/8	28 6/8	29 4/8	18 5/8	21 2/8	4 2/8	4 3/8	6	6	2	1287†	33†
	■ Switzerland Co. – Dale A. Dixon, Jr. – Dale A. Dixon, Jr. – 2000										
175 7/8	24 4/8	25 1/8	17 5/8	20 1/8	5 1/8	5 1/8	5	5		1287	33
	■ Putnam Co. – Picked Up – Terry Outcalt – 1993										
175 6/8	27	27 4/8	19 4/8	21 6/8	5 2/8	5 2/8	5	5		1310†	35†
	■ Wayne Co. – Brent E. Ferguson – Brent E. Ferguson – 2000 ■ See photo on page 159										
175 5/8	25 3/8	26 3/8	22	24	4 6/8	4 6/8	5	6	1 7/8	1333	36
	■ Sullivan Co. – Steven L. Hobbs – Steven L. Hobbs – 1991										
175 4/8	26 5/8	26 7/8	21 2/8	23 5/8	5	4 7/8	5	5		1352	37
	■ Wayne Co. – Michael H. Baker – Michael H. Baker – 1993										
175 3/8	25 2/8	26 1/8	20 6/8	22 6/8	6	6 2/8	8	7	7 1/8	1377	38
	■ Shelby Co. – Timothy D. Taggart – Timothy D. Taggart – 1999										
175 2/8	30 3/8	22 6/8	21 2/8	23 4/8	5 2/8	5 1/8	7	5	1 4/8	1403	39
	■ Clinton Co. – William W. Cripe – William W. Cripe – 1974										
175 2/8	28 2/8	28 3/8	19 6/8	22 1/8	5 1/8	5 2/8	7	5	6 4/8	1403	39
	■ Fulton Co. – Larry A. Croxton – Larry A. Croxton – 1984										

■ *Location of Kill – Hunter – Owner – Date Killed*

Score	Length of Main Beam Right	Left	Inside Spread	Greatest Spread	Circumference at Smallest Place Between Burr and First Point Right	Left	Number of Points Right	Left	Lengths Abnormal Points	All-Time Rank	State Rank
175 1/8	28 7/8	29 3/8	19 5/8	22 6/8	4 3/8	4 3/8	5	5		1440	41
Wells Co. – Ryan C. Howard – Ryan C. Howard – 1996											
175	24	24	18 6/8	21 1/8	5 2/8	5 3/8	6	6		1472†	42†
Ohio Co. – Rick T. Henry – Rick T. Henry – 1981											
174 7/8	25 3/8	25 1/8	17 5/8	20 2/8	5 3/8	5 2/8	5	6	1 2/8	1513	43
Scott Co. – Henry E. Reynolds – Henry E. Reynolds – 1994											
174 4/8	28 2/8	29 5/8	16	19 3/8	5 1/8	5 3/8	6	7	3 4/8	1592	44
Washington Co. – Michael L. Bledsoe – Michael L. Bledsoe – 1992											
174 3/8	25 4/8	25 4/8	19 5/8	22	4 2/8	4 3/8	5	5		1619	45
Jackson Co. – Max E. Gambrel – Max E. Gambrel – 1989											
174 1/8	26 3/8	25	19 5/8	21 7/8	5	5	5	6	2 2/8	1678†	46†
Franklin Co. – Clarence G. Hupfer – Clarence G. Hupfer – 2001											
174 1/8	25	25 3/8	21 1/8	23	4 6/8	5	9	7	8	1678†	46†
Starke Co. – Charles W. Via – Charles W. Via – 2000 ■ See photo on page 49											
174	27 7/8	28	23	25 2/8	5 3/8	5 3/8	4	5		1717	48
Allen Co. – James L. Harden – James L. Harden – 1998											
174	25 6/8	26 1/8	20 2/8	22 7/8	5 3/8	5 2/8	6	6	2 2/8	1717	48
Lake Co. – Picked Up – Howard Munson – 1998											
173 6/8	26	25 4/8	20	21 5/8	5	5	5	5		1766†	50†
Montgomery Co. – Andrew A. Horning – Andrew A. Horning – 2001											
173 6/8	26 6/8	26	20 4/8	22 3/8	4 2/8	4 1/8	5	5		1766	50
Vermillion Co. – Brian W. Meeker – Brian W. Meeker – 1992											
173 6/8	25 2/8	24 2/8	19 4/8	26 4/8	5 2/8	5 4/8	6	6	5	1766	50
Owen Co. – Troy C. Denney – Troy C. Denney – 1995											
173 4/8	24 7/8	24 7/8	18	20 2/8	5 1/8	5 2/8	5	5		1847	53
Allen Co. – Douglas R. Hill – Douglas R. Hill – 1993											
173 3/8	26 3/8	26 7/8	20 7/8	23 1/8	6 2/8	6 2/8	5	5		1883†	54†
Clay Co. – Rex A. Treadway – Rex A. Treadway – 2001											
173 1/8	28	28 5/8	23	25 2/8	4 4/8	4 6/8	6	5	1 7/8	1950†	55†
Porter Co. – Joseph J. Marlow – Joseph J. Marlow – 2001											
173 1/8	24 6/8	26 2/8	21 5/8	23 3/8	4 4/8	4 4/8	7	5	2	1950	55
Jackson Co. – Sean C. Ashley – Sean C. Ashley – 1994											
173 1/8	25	24 6/8	17 7/8	20	5	4 7/8	5	5		1950	55
Greene Co. – J.D. Holtsclaw & K.J. Hobson – J.D. Holtsclaw & K.J. Hobson – 1994											
172 7/8	26 6/8	27 3/8	19 6/8	22 7/8	4	4 2/8	6	6	3 3/8	2038	58
Jefferson Co. – Chet A. Nolan – Chet A. Nolan – 1987											
172 4/8	28	27 7/8	20	22 3/8	5 4/8	5 5/8	9	8	9 2/8	2156	59
Putnam Co. – M.R. Abner & C. Yates – M.R. Abner & C. Yates – 1999											
172 3/8	26 4/8	26 1/8	17 3/8	19 6/8	4 5/8	4 5/8	5	5		2200†	60†
Fayette Co. – Lisa A. Tarvin – Lisa A. Tarvin – 2001											
172 3/8	24 6/8	24 6/8	17 5/8	19 5/8	4 3/8	4 3/8	5	5		2200	60
Dearborn Co. – Walter C. Drake – Walter C. Drake – 1990											

Score	Length of Main Beam		Inside Spread	Greatest Spread	Circumference at Smallest Place Between Burr and First Point		Number of Points		Lengths Abnormal Points	All-Time Rank	State Rank
	Right	Left			Right	Left	Right	Left			
	■ Location of Kill – Hunter – Owner – Date Killed										
172 2/8	23 3/8	22 6/8	17	20 2/8	5 3/8	5 3/8	6	6		2237†	62†
■ Bartholomew Co. – Dustin G. Prewitt – Dustin G. Prewitt – 2001											
172 1/8	26 2/8	26 4/8	20 1/8	22 6/8	5 5/8	5 5/8	8	7	10 6/8	2286	63
■ Jennings Co. – Gerald G. Powers – Gerald G. Powers – 1989											
172	27 1/8	26	24 2/8	25 6/8	5 1/8	5 1/8	5	5		2330†	64†
■ Jennings Co. – Guy Euler – Guy Euler – 2001 ■ See photo on page 6											
171 6/8	26 3/8	24 7/8	17 2/8	19 1/8	4 7/8	4 6/8	5	5		2418†	65†
■ Greene Co. – Barry A. Stoner – Barry A. Stoner – 1999											
171 5/8	23 4/8	24	24 4/8	26 2/8	4 4/8	4 5/8	7	5	1 1/8	2470†	66†
■ Putnam Co. – Sharon K. Lepper – Sharon K. Lepper – 2000											
171 4/8	27	26 4/8	21 2/8	24 2/8	4 6/8	4 5/8	5	5		2513	67
■ Greene Co. – Jason B. Anderson – Jason B. Anderson – 1991											
171 3/8	27 2/8	27 2/8	22 5/8	25 4/8	5 1/8	5 1/8	6	6	3 2/8	2564†	68†
■ Parke Co. – Ronald A. Keys – Ronald A. Keys – 1997											
171 3/8	25 7/8	27 2/8	19 3/8	21 1/8	4 3/8	4 4/8	5	5		2564†	68†
■ Dearborn Co. – Nick T. Lobenstein – Nick T. Lobenstein – 2001											
171 2/8	25	25 5/8	20 2/8	22 3/8	5	4 5/8	5	5		2621	70
■ Bartholomew Co. – Gary B. Owsley – Gary B. Owsley – 1995											
171	24 3/8	23 7/8	20 6/8	23 4/8	5	4 4/8	6	6		2707	71
■ Pike Co. – Philip L. Lemond – Philip L. Lemond – 1986											
171	24 2/8	23 4/8	17 4/8	19 4/8	4 1/8	4 1/8	5	7	3 4/8	2707	71
■ Boone Co. – Kevin L. Albert – Kevin L. Albert – 1988											
171	24 5/8	23 7/8	20	22 6/8	4 7/8	4 6/8	5	4		2707	71
■ La Porte Co. – Picked Up – Josh Skalka – 1991											
170 7/8	25 3/8	24 5/8	18 3/8	20 4/8	5 6/8	5 7/8	6	7	5	2769	74
■ Tippecanoe Co. – Harold A. Anthrop – Harold A. Anthrop – 1976											
170 7/8	24	24 3/8	15 5/8	18 3/8	4 4/8	4 5/8	6	5	1	2769	74
■ Spencer Co. – Jamie L. Waninger – Jamie L. Waninger – 1999											
170 6/8	26	28	20 6/8	23	4 6/8	4 5/8	6	6		2828†	76†
■ Greene Co. – Jesse D. Yeryar – Jesse D. Yeryar – 2001											
170 6/8	27 4/8	26 7/8	18 5/8	21	4 7/8	4 7/8	6	6	2 5/8	2828	76
■ Putnam Co. – Mark L. Goodpaster – Mark L. Goodpaster – 1995											
170 4/8	26 5/8	26 4/8	19 4/8	21 5/8	5 7/8	5 6/8	5	6	3 4/8	2933†	78†
■ Posey Co. – Steve Reed, Jr. – Steve Reed, Jr. – 2001											
170 4/8	26 1/8	25 4/8	18	20 4/8	4 4/8	4 4/8	5	5		2933	78
■ Marshall Co. – Alan R. Collins – Alan R. Collins – 1982											
170 3/8	25 2/8	25 3/8	17	19 4/8	4 5/8	4 5/8	5	6	1 1/8	2992	80
■ Madison Co. – George Groff – Larry Shannon – PR 1900											
170 3/8	27 4/8	27 5/8	23 1/8	25 2/8	5	5	5	5		2992	80
■ Orange Co. – John W. Matthew – John W. Matthew – 1989											
170 2/8	25 3/8	25 3/8	20 6/8	22 2/8	4 5/8	4 6/8	6	5	2 4/8	3063	82
■ Tippecanoe Co. – Jimmy M. Crites – Jimmy M. Crites – 1993											

Score	Length of Main Beam Right	Left	Inside Spread	Greatest Spread	Circumference at Smallest Place Between Burr and First Point Right	Left	Number of Points Right	Left	Lengths Abnormal Points	All-Time Rank	State Rank
$170\frac{2}{8}$	$24\frac{7}{8}$	28	$21\frac{4}{8}$	$25\frac{4}{8}$	$4\frac{6}{8}$	$4\frac{6}{8}$	6	6	$2\frac{4}{8}$	3063	82
■ Hamilton Co. – James P. Tomasik – James P. Tomasik – 1997											
$170\frac{1}{8}$	$25\frac{4}{8}$	27	$21\frac{2}{8}$	24	5	$5\frac{4}{8}$	6	9	$8\frac{7}{8}$	3143	84
■ Sullivan Co. – Troy J. Rambis – Troy J. Rambis – 1994											
$170\frac{1}{8}$	$24\frac{2}{8}$	$25\frac{2}{8}$	$19\frac{3}{8}$	$22\frac{5}{8}$	$4\frac{4}{8}$	$4\frac{2}{8}$	5	5		3143	84
■ Clark Co. – Daniel H. Lenfert – Daniel H. Lenfert – 1996											
170	$28\frac{1}{8}$	$28\frac{2}{8}$	$18\frac{2}{8}$	$20\frac{3}{8}$	5	$5\frac{1}{8}$	7	6	$6\frac{2}{8}$	3224	86
■ Ripley Co. – Robert N. Hughes – Robert N. Hughes – 1991											
170	$23\frac{7}{8}$	$24\frac{3}{8}$	$16\frac{6}{8}$	$18\frac{4}{8}$	$4\frac{7}{8}$	5	7	6	$4\frac{2}{8}$	3224	86
■ Harrison Co. – Phillip L. Whiteman – Phillip L. Whiteman – 1994											
169	28	$27\frac{3}{8}$	$16\frac{2}{8}$	$19\frac{2}{8}$	$5\frac{4}{8}$	$5\frac{4}{8}$	9	8	10	3348	88
■ Washington Co. – Harold Mutter – Harold Mutter – 1998											
$168\frac{4}{8}$	$26\frac{6}{8}$	$27\frac{4}{8}$	$24\frac{1}{8}$	$26\frac{3}{8}$	$4\frac{7}{8}$	$4\frac{4}{8}$	7	7	$9\frac{3}{8}$	3385	89
■ Warren Co. – Charles R. Hefley – Charles R. Hefley – 1995											
$168\frac{3}{8}$	$25\frac{2}{8}$	$25\frac{4}{8}$	$17\frac{5}{8}$	$19\frac{4}{8}$	$4\frac{3}{8}$	$4\frac{1}{8}$	5	5		3399†	90†
■ Adams Co. – James M. Everett, Jr. – James M. Everett, Jr. – 1989											
$168\frac{1}{8}$	$23\frac{7}{8}$	24	$17\frac{7}{8}$	20	$5\frac{3}{8}$	$5\frac{2}{8}$	5	5		3426	91
■ La Porte Co. – Roby J. Rogers – Roby J. Rogers – 1996											
$167\frac{4}{8}$	$26\frac{7}{8}$	$26\frac{7}{8}$	$17\frac{7}{8}$	$20\frac{1}{8}$	$5\frac{7}{8}$	6	7	8	$6\frac{1}{8}$	3485	92
■ Morgan Co. – Steve Long II – Steve Long II – 1995											
$167\frac{3}{8}$	$27\frac{6}{8}$	$26\frac{6}{8}$	$20\frac{2}{8}$	$22\frac{1}{8}$	$5\frac{3}{8}$	$4\frac{6}{8}$	5	7	$2\frac{3}{8}$	3500	93
■ St. Joseph Co. – Thomas J. Peterson – Thomas J. Peterson – 1990											
$167\frac{3}{8}$	$27\frac{5}{8}$	$23\frac{2}{8}$	$19\frac{5}{8}$	$22\frac{2}{8}$	6	$6\frac{7}{8}$	4	6	$3\frac{6}{8}$	3500	93
■ Parke Co. – Chester P. Walls – Chester P. Walls – 1990											
$167\frac{2}{8}$	$24\frac{5}{8}$	24	$22\frac{2}{8}$	$24\frac{4}{8}$	$5\frac{4}{8}$	$5\frac{2}{8}$	7	7	7	3519	95
■ Fountain Co. – Joe R. Coffing – Joe R. Coffing – 1999											
$167\frac{1}{8}$	26	$26\frac{2}{8}$	$19\frac{7}{8}$	22	5	5	6	6	$4\frac{4}{8}$	3539	96
■ Jefferson Co. – Pete O. Willingham – Pete O. Willingham – 1995											
$165\frac{6}{8}$	26	$25\frac{7}{8}$	20	$23\frac{4}{8}$	$4\frac{7}{8}$	$4\frac{7}{8}$	5	7	2	3680†	97†
■ Vermillion Co. – Michael A. Still – Michael A. Still – 2000											
$164\frac{5}{8}$	$24\frac{3}{8}$	$24\frac{2}{8}$	$21\frac{3}{8}$	24	$5\frac{3}{8}$	$5\frac{1}{8}$	6	6	$5\frac{4}{8}$	3835	98
■ Marshall Co. – Trent J. Stouder – Trent J. Stouder – 1996											
$164\frac{5}{8}$	$27\frac{2}{8}$	26	$20\frac{1}{8}$	$21\frac{7}{8}$	$4\frac{7}{8}$	$5\frac{1}{8}$	6	5		3835	98
■ St. Joseph Co. – Scott G. Johnson – Scott G. Johnson – 1998											
$164\frac{2}{8}$	$26\frac{4}{8}$	$26\frac{4}{8}$	$20\frac{7}{8}$	$24\frac{4}{8}$	$5\frac{2}{8}$	$5\frac{2}{8}$	6	5	$7\frac{5}{8}$	3876	100
■ Switzerland Co. – Tom A. Andres – Tom A. Andres – 1992											
$164\frac{1}{8}$	$25\frac{7}{8}$	$26\frac{2}{8}$	$19\frac{1}{8}$	$21\frac{7}{8}$	$4\frac{6}{8}$	$4\frac{6}{8}$	6	6	$2\frac{6}{8}$	3886	101
■ Lake Co. – J. Michael Tapper – J. Michael Tapper – 1998											
$163\frac{7}{8}$	$22\frac{3}{8}$	$23\frac{5}{8}$	$20\frac{7}{8}$	23	$5\frac{1}{8}$	$5\frac{1}{8}$	5	5		3928	102
■ Fountain Co. – Jeffrey C. Bane – Jeffrey C. Bane – 1995											
$163\frac{6}{8}$	$27\frac{2}{8}$	$26\frac{7}{8}$	$18\frac{3}{8}$	$20\frac{3}{8}$	$5\frac{3}{8}$	$5\frac{3}{8}$	6	5	$3\frac{3}{8}$	3946	103
■ Lagrange Co. – James J. Fry – James J. Fry – 1993											

Score	Length of Main Beam Right / Left	Inside Spread	Greatest Spread	Circumference at Smallest Place Between Burr and First Point Right / Left	Number of Points Right / Left	Lengths Abnormal Points	All-Time Rank	State Rank
$163\frac{5}{8}$	$24\frac{6}{8}$ $26\frac{5}{8}$	$21\frac{1}{8}$	$23\frac{5}{8}$	$4\frac{2}{8}$ $4\frac{2}{8}$	7 5		3961†	104†
■ Franklin Co. – Glenn E. Willis, Jr. – Glenn E. Willis, Jr. – 1999								
$163\frac{1}{8}$	$24\frac{5}{8}$ $25\frac{2}{8}$	$16\frac{7}{8}$	$19\frac{1}{8}$	5 5	5 5		4035	105
■ Elkhart Co. – Joseph J. Leszczynski – Joseph J. Leszczynski – 1984								
163	$25\frac{5}{8}$ $24\frac{3}{8}$	$19\frac{1}{8}$	$21\frac{4}{8}$	$5\frac{2}{8}$ $5\frac{2}{8}$	8 7	$6\frac{5}{8}$	4051†	106†
■ Morgan Co. – James R. Pritchard – James R. Pritchard – 2000								
$162\frac{7}{8}$	$27\frac{5}{8}$ $27\frac{4}{8}$	$21\frac{2}{8}$	$27\frac{6}{8}$	$4\frac{5}{8}$ $4\frac{2}{8}$	7 7	$12\frac{1}{8}$	4067	107
■ Boone Co. – Richard D. Isenhower – Richard D. Isenhower – 1994								
$162\frac{4}{8}$	24 25	$16\frac{4}{8}$	$18\frac{4}{8}$	$4\frac{2}{8}$ $4\frac{2}{8}$	5 5		4129†	108†
■ La Porte Co. – Gary Leslie – Gary Leslie – 2001								
162	$27\frac{2}{8}$ $26\frac{1}{8}$	$20\frac{4}{8}$	$22\frac{4}{8}$	$5\frac{2}{8}$ $5\frac{2}{8}$	5 5		4184	109
■ Marshall Co. – Leon H. Martin – Leon H. Martin – 1993								
$161\frac{4}{8}$	$25\frac{1}{8}$ $24\frac{1}{8}$	$17\frac{4}{8}$	$20\frac{1}{8}$	$4\frac{4}{8}$ $4\frac{5}{8}$	5 5		4258	110
■ Starke Co. – Roger L. Taulbee – Roger L. Taulbee – 1993								
$161\frac{1}{8}$	$25\frac{1}{8}$ $24\frac{2}{8}$	$17\frac{3}{8}$	$19\frac{3}{8}$	5 5	5 6		4332†	111†
■ Floyd Co. – Earl D. Whitworth III – Earl D. Whitworth III – 2001								
$160\frac{7}{8}$	23 $23\frac{2}{8}$	$17\frac{3}{8}$	$19\frac{1}{8}$	$5\frac{1}{8}$ $5\frac{1}{8}$	5 5		4380	112
■ Porter Co. – Timothy J. Mocabee – Timothy J. Mocabee – 1998								
$160\frac{6}{8}$	$24\frac{3}{8}$ $24\frac{7}{8}$	$17\frac{4}{8}$	$19\frac{4}{8}$	$4\frac{5}{8}$ $4\frac{6}{8}$	6 6		4402	113
■ Orange Co. – Dwight C. Beaty – Dwight C. Beaty – 1995								
$160\frac{5}{8}$	$26\frac{7}{8}$ 27	$16\frac{2}{8}$	$18\frac{4}{8}$	5 $4\frac{7}{8}$	7 6	$3\frac{3}{8}$	4423†	114†
■ Warren Co. – Tim Wadkins – Tim Wadkins – 2001								
$160\frac{5}{8}$	$22\frac{1}{8}$ $22\frac{5}{8}$	19	21	$4\frac{6}{8}$ $4\frac{6}{8}$	6 6	$3\frac{1}{8}$	4423	114
■ Rush Co. – James D. Moffett – James D. Moffett – 1987								
$160\frac{5}{8}$	$26\frac{1}{8}$ $25\frac{4}{8}$	$19\frac{7}{8}$	22	$4\frac{7}{8}$ $4\frac{6}{8}$	7 5	$5\frac{4}{8}$	4423	114
■ Newton Co. – Robert D. Herron – Robert D. Herron – 1994								
$160\frac{4}{8}$	$25\frac{3}{8}$ $23\frac{6}{8}$	$18\frac{5}{8}$	21	$5\frac{1}{8}$ 5	7 5	$7\frac{5}{8}$	4443	117
■ Porter Co. – Donald M. Dolph – Donald M. Dolph – 1997								
$160\frac{2}{8}$	$25\frac{6}{8}$ $25\frac{2}{8}$	$19\frac{4}{8}$	$21\frac{2}{8}$	$4\frac{5}{8}$ $4\frac{5}{8}$	5 5		4495†	118†
■ Franklin Co. – James C. Wilson – James C. Wilson – 2000								
$160\frac{1}{8}$	$24\frac{1}{8}$ $25\frac{3}{8}$	19	21	$4\frac{2}{8}$ $4\frac{2}{8}$	7 5	$4\frac{5}{8}$	4534	119
■ Switzerland Co. – Joseph W. Bacon – Joseph W. Bacon – 1997								

■ *Location of Kill – Hunter – Owner – Date Killed*

† The scores and ranking for trophies from the 25th Awards Entry Period are not final until the banquet is held on June 19, 2004.

INDIANA

NON-TYPICAL WHITETAIL DEER

Score	Length of Main Beam Right	Length of Main Beam Left	Inside Spread	Greatest Spread	Circumference at Smallest Place Between Burr and First Point Right	Circumference at Smallest Place Between Burr and First Point Left	Number of Points Right	Number of Points Left	Lengths Abnormal Points	All-Time Rank	State Rank
	■ Location of Kill – Hunter – Owner – Date Killed										
251 4/8	27 3/8	22 1/8	19 3/8	22 2/8	6 6/8	6 5/8	15	14	59 7/8	50	1
	■ Hendricks Co. – Timothy J. Goode – Bass Pro Shops – 1980										
248 4/8	28	27 4/8	23 5/8	26 2/8	7 7/8	7 4/8	15	13	76 5/8	68	2
	■ Fulton Co. – Robert S. Sears – Bass Pro Shops – 1990										
233 7/8	26	27 2/8	18	22 6/8	5 4/8	5 2/8	14	16	57 1/8	183	3
	■ Carroll Co. – James R. Houston, Jr. – James R. Houston, Jr. – 1995										
233 2/8	27 2/8	25 5/8	18 6/8	23	4 7/8	4 7/8	9	11	30 2/8	193	4
	■ Switzerland Co. – Henry Mitchell – Bass Pro Shops – 1972										
229 7/8	27 4/8	26 7/8	19 7/8	22 5/8	6 4/8	6 2/8	13	11	50 6/8	244	5
	■ Jackson Co. – Larry E. Deaton – Larry E. Deaton – 1990										
226 3/8	27 2/8	26 2/8	22 7/8	25 1/8	5 4/8	5 4/8	8	10	27 2/8	296	6
	■ Clark Co. – Robert L. Bromm, Sr. – Robert L. Bromm, Sr. – 1985										
225 6/8	27 3/8	26 7/8	26 3/8	29 1/8	4 4/8	4 2/8	7	9	29 5/8	306	7
	■ La Porte Co. – David Grundy – Bass Pro Shops – 1987										
223	28 1/8	27 5/8	20 1/8	23 7/8	5 5/8	5 6/8	11	11	47 5/8	365	8
	■ Jefferson Co. – Sam O. Leverett, Jr. – Sam O. Leverett, Jr. – 1997										
219 1/8	26 6/8	26 3/8	19 1/8	22 1/8	5 3/8	5 3/8	13	12	40 6/8	465†	9†
	■ Porter Co. – John S. Biggs, Jr. – John S. Biggs, Jr. – 2000										
217	30 7/8	28 6/8	18 4/8	20 4/8	5 2/8	5	9	10	23 2/8	529	10
	■ Dearborn Co. – Jerry L. Irvine – Jerry L. Irvine – 1990										
216 7/8	25 3/8	28 1/8	19 7/8	24 3/8	6	5 5/8	13	10	26 6/8	533	11
	■ Howard Co. – Jason E. Young – Jason E. Young – 1995										
216 2/8	25	24 3/8	19	21 4/8	6 7/8	7	10	11	38	555	12
	■ Porter Co. – Lester W. Fornshell – Lester W. Fornshell – 1994										
215 4/8	29 1/8	29 4/8	23 2/8	30	6 1/8	6 2/8	11	13	43 6/8	583	13
	■ Wayne Co. – Clyde L. Day – Clyde L. Day – 1986										
212 5/8	29 1/8	28 5/8	19 7/8	24	5 5/8	5 5/8	11	13	34 6/8	683	14
	■ Madison Co. – Michael A. Wallace – Michael A. Wallace – 1993										
211	27 4/8	25 7/8	20 6/8	23	5 6/8	5 3/8	10	10	29	764	15
	■ Dearborn Co. – Chad M. Hornberger – Chad M. Hornberger – 1997										
209 6/8	26 4/8	26 7/8	18 1/8	21 2/8	6	6	12	10	34 3/8	831	16
	■ Union Co. – Billy G. Finch – Billy G. Finch – 1989										
209 3/8	28 3/8	30 3/8	24 4/8	26 3/8	5 3/8	5 4/8	9	7	20 7/8	852	17
	■ Jefferson Co. – Tim L. Brawner – Tim L. Brawner – 1989										
208 6/8	22 3/8	25 3/8	19 1/8	21 6/8	6 7/8	5 3/8	12	7	61 3/8	883	18
	■ Bartholomew Co. – Randy E. Cash – Randy E. Cash – 1997										
207 1/8	27	26 3/8	19 1/8	21 4/8	4 7/8	5 1/8	10	9	32 4/8	995†	19†
	■ Montgomery Co. – Michael R. Davis – Michael R. Davis – 2000										

Score	Length of Main Beam Right	Left	Inside Spread	Greatest Spread	Circumference at Smallest Place Between Burr and First Point Right	Left	Number of Points Right	Left	Lengths Abnormal Points	All-Time Rank	State Rank
$206^6/8$	26	$26^2/8$	$19^2/8$	$21^4/8$	$5^1/8$	5	8	9	38	1028	20
■ Fulton Co. – Lewis Polk – Robert E. VanMeter III – 1960											
$206^3/8$	$26^7/8$	$26^7/8$	19	23	$5^2/8$	$5^3/8$	10	9	$24^7/8$	1051	21
■ Clay Co. – Jason S. Shaw – Jason S. Shaw – 1989											
$205^7/8$	$27^4/8$	$28^6/8$	$19^4/8$	$22^6/8$	5	$5^1/8$	10	8	$29^1/8$	1080	22
■ Switzerland Co. – Paul J. Graf – Paul J. Graf – 1981											
$204^6/8$	$26^3/8$	$26^4/8$	$19^2/8$	23	$5^4/8$	$5^3/8$	11	8	$22^2/8$	1165	23
■ Washington Co. – David Souder – David Souder – 1988											
$203^7/8$	$25^2/8$	$25^5/8$	$24^1/8$	$26^2/8$	$6^7/8$	$6^5/8$	7	10	$23^2/8$	1231†	24†
■ Greene Co. – Robert J. Cornwell – Robert J. Cornwell – 2000											
$202^5/8$	$24^5/8$	$24^7/8$	$17^4/8$	$19^3/8$	$4^1/8$	$4^1/8$	9	10	$46^5/8$	1346	25
■ Ripley Co. – James A. Leveille – James A. Leveille – 1999											
202	$27^4/8$	$27^1/8$	20	$22^6/8$	$5^6/8$	6	8	8	$14^4/8$	1395	26
■ Tippecanoe Co. – Stephen L. Burkhalter – Stephen L. Burkhalter – 1997											
$200^1/8$	$23^5/8$	$24^1/8$	17	$22^6/8$	$5^6/8$	$5^5/8$	10	8	$57^5/8$	1577	27
■ Parke Co. – Chris Ebersole – Chris Ebersole – 1992											
200	27	$25^6/8$	$22^3/8$	$24^5/8$	$5^4/8$	$5^2/8$	11	12	$44^7/8$	1591	28
■ Boone Co. – John E. Wright – John E. Wright – 1989											
$199^2/8$	$28^3/8$	28	$18^5/8$	$22^6/8$	$6^3/8$	$6^3/8$	8	8	$17^1/8$	1649	29
■ Fountain Co. – Ken S. Harmeson – Ken S. Harmeson – 1989											
199	$24^4/8$	26	20	$22^6/8$	5	$5^1/8$	9	9	$18^4/8$	1668	30
■ Harrison Co. – Timothy P. Uhl – Timothy P. Uhl – 1995											
$198^7/8$	$29^2/8$	$28^3/8$	$24^6/8$	$27^4/8$	$4^6/8$	$4^7/8$	8	7	$16^7/8$	1686	31
■ Ripley Co. – William L. Wagner – William L. Wagner – 1982											
$197^6/8$	$25^6/8$	$27^1/8$	$19^4/8$	$22^3/8$	$5^2/8$	$5^5/8$	7	9	23	1833	32
■ Fayette Co. – Boyd L. Lunsford – Boyd L. Lunsford – 1998											
$197^2/8$	$23^4/8$	$24^4/8$	$23^4/8$	$26^2/8$	$4^5/8$	$4^7/8$	10	11	$33^6/8$	1901	33
■ Scott Co. – Wilson D. Barger – Wilson D. Barger – 1991											
$197^1/8$	$25^6/8$	$25^4/8$	18	$21^4/8$	$5^3/8$	6	9	13	$32^7/8$	1923	34
■ Bartholomew Co. – C. Greg Caudill – C. Greg Caudill – 1999											
$196^4/8$	27	$26^4/8$	$19^2/8$	$21^2/8$	$4^4/8$	$4^6/8$	11	8	$20^6/8$	1999	35
■ Franklin Co. – Cory A. Rogers – Cory A. Rogers – 1996											
$196^2/8$	25	$25^7/8$	$18^3/8$	$27^1/8$	$4^7/8$	$5^2/8$	12	8	$41^3/8$	2028†	36†
■ Putnam Co. – Todd G. Barnes – Todd G. Barnes – 2000											
$196^1/8$	$23^4/8$	$23^4/8$	$18^1/8$	$23^2/8$	$5^4/8$	$5^4/8$	9	9	19	2045	37
■ Jefferson Co. – Bill A. Knoblock – Bill A. Knoblock – 1996											
$195^3/8$	$27^1/8$	$26^4/8$	$19^3/8$	$22^3/8$	$4^6/8$	5	10	7	$18^4/8$	2163	38
■ Henry Co. – Donn W. Duncan – Donn W. Duncan – 1994											
$195^1/8$	$25^5/8$	$25^7/8$	$19^1/8$	21	$5^6/8$	$5^6/8$	10	13	$45^6/8$	2208	39
■ Parke Co. – Todd D. Farris – Todd D. Farris – 1998											
$193^4/8$	28	$27^7/8$	$21^2/8$	$24^4/8$	6	$5^3/8$	11	8	$32^6/8$	2288	40
■ Parke Co. – James H. Griggs – James H. Griggs – 1996											

INDIANA NON-TYPICAL WHITETAIL DEER

Score	Length of Main Beam Right	Left	Inside Spread	Greatest Spread	Circumference at Smallest Place Between Burr and First Point Right	Left	Number of Points Right	Left	Lengths Abnormal Points	All-Time Rank	State Rank
193⁴/₈	24⁶/₈	25²/₈	16	20⁵/₈	5⁷/₈	6³/₈	14	12	32	2288	40
■ Warren Co. – Bill D. Wadkins – Bill D. Wadkins – 1999											
192²/₈	26⁵/₈	27²/₈	18⁵/₈	26²/₈	4⁵/₈	4⁴/₈	6	7	27⁷/₈	2335	42
■ Warren Co. – Sam L. Karras – Sam L. Karras – 1998											
191²/₈	22⁴/₈	22⁴/₈	14⁶/₈	20⁷/₈	7⁴/₈	7⁶/₈	8	14	46²/₈	2371	43
■ Delaware Co. – Robert D. McFarland – Robert D. McFarland – 1986											
191¹/₈	25⁷/₈	27¹/₈	20³/₈	22⁴/₈	5⁵/₈	5⁶/₈	8	6	14⁶/₈	2374†	44†
■ Vanderburgh Co. – Rodney J. Schutz – Rodney J. Schutz – 2000											
191	26¹/₈	27⁴/₈	21	23¹/₈	4⁶/₈	4⁵/₈	8	9	18⁴/₈	2380†	45†
■ Warren Co. – Roger A. Parient, Jr. – Roger A. Parient, Jr. – 2000											
190⁷/₈	25⁷/₈	26²/₈	18³/₈	22⁷/₈	5⁷/₈	5⁵/₈	8	10	14⁶/₈	2385†	46†
■ Parke Co. – Burk Collings – Burk Collings – 2000											
188⁷/₈	25³/₈	25¹/₈	17²/₈	19	5³/₈	5¹/₈	8	9	26¹/₈	2462†	47†
■ Elkhart Co. – Kenny H. Cowles – Kenny H. Cowles – 2000											
188⁶/₈	25⁷/₈	27⁵/₈	22⁴/₈	25¹/₈	6²/₈	5⁵/₈	7	7	14⁴/₈	2468	48
■ White Co. – Ronald Sumrak – Ronald Sumrak – 1995											
188⁵/₈	27⁵/₈	27⁷/₈	20⁶/₈	25⁷/₈	4⁷/₈	5	7	6	24³/₈	2471	49
■ La Porte Co. – George J. McCoy – George J. McCoy – 1984											
187⁷/₈	23⁶/₈	25⁷/₈	19¹/₈	21	5²/₈	5¹/₈	9	10	12²/₈	2506†	50†
■ Washington Co. – R. Jeread Abner – R. Jeread Abner – 2000											
187⁷/₈	24²/₈	23²/₈	17⁵/₈	21⁷/₈	5	5²/₈	7	9	12⁶/₈	2506†	50†
■ La Porte Co. – Daniel Hildreth – Daniel Hildreth – 2000											
187⁶/₈	24⁴/₈	24⁷/₈	18	20²/₈	5²/₈	5¹/₈	7	8	20⁶/₈	2512	52
■ St. Joseph Co. – Picked Up – Greg Doms – 1995											
187³/₈	24⁶/₈	25⁵/₈	21	23³/₈	5¹/₈	4⁵/₈	8	10	18¹/₈	2528†	53†
■ Montgomery Co. – Gary W. Harrison – Gary W. Harrison – 2000											
187¹/₈	25¹/₈	25¹/₈	20¹/₈	22³/₈	5²/₈	5	8	8	17⁴/₈	2540†	54†
■ Kosciusko Co. – Edward E. Miller, Jr. – Edward E. Miller, Jr. – 2001											
186⁷/₈	21⁵/₈	22³/₈	20⁵/₈	24⁴/₈	5²/₈	6²/₈	8	9	39⁶/₈	2550	55
■ La Porte Co. – David W. Nelson – David W. Nelson – 1988											
186⁷/₈	25⁴/₈	24⁵/₈	22⁵/₈	24⁶/₈	4⁶/₈	4⁷/₈	8	7	11⁴/₈	2550	55
■ Marshall Co. – Matt J. Meyers – Matt J. Meyers – 1997											
186⁷/₈	28⁵/₈	26⁵/₈	25²/₈	28³/₈	4⁷/₈	4⁵/₈	5	7	23⁵/₈	2550	55
■ Fayette Co. – William C. Powers II – William C. Powers II – 1999											
186	25⁴/₈	25³/₈	18⁷/₈	22⁵/₈	4⁷/₈	4⁷/₈	7	10	22⁷/₈	2586	58
■ St. Joseph Co. – Michael L. Ritter, Jr. – Michael L. Ritter, Jr. – 1992											
185²/₈	28³/₈	28¹/₈	20⁶/₈	23¹/₈	5⁶/₈	5⁶/₈	7	6	16²/₈	2632	59
■ Porter Co. – David A. Bobrowski – David A. Bobrowski – 1997											
185	24⁵/₈	25	22¹/₈	24⁷/₈	5⁵/₈	5⁶/₈	8	7	10¹/₈	2653†	60†
■ Marion Co. – Jason S. Losee – Jason S. Losee – 2001											

†The scores and ranking for trophies from the 25th Awards Entry Period are not final until the banquet is held on June 19, 2004.

TROPHIES IN THE FIELD

HUNTER: Brent E. Ferguson
SCORE: 175-6/8
CATEGORY: typical whitetail deer
LOCATION: Wayne County, Indiana
DATE: 2000

IOWA
RECORD WHITETAILS

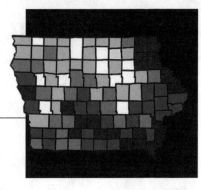

427 Typical whitetail deer entries
266 Non-typical whitetail deer entries
7,265 Total whitetail deer entries

0 Entries
1-2 Entries
3-5 Entries
6-10 Entries
11+ Entries

IOWA
STATE RECORD
Typical Whitetail Deer
Score: 201⁴/₈
Location: Hamilton Co.
Hunter: Wayne A. Bills
Owner: Bass Pro Shops
Date: 1974

Photograph from B&C Archives

IOWA
STATE RECORD
Non-Typical Whitetail Deer
Score: 282
Location: Clay Co.
Hunter: Larry Raveling
Owner: Bass Pro Shops
Date: 1973

Photograph courtesy of Larry L. Huffman, Legendary Whitetails

IOWA

TYPICAL WHITETAIL DEER

Score	Length of Main Beam Right	Left	Inside Spread	Greatest Spread	Circumference at Smallest Place Between Burr and First Point Right	Left	Number of Points Right	Left	Lengths Abnormal Points	All-Time Rank	State Rank
201⁴/8	27⁵/8	29¹/8	23	25²/8	5⁵/8	5²/8	6	6	3²/8	9	1
■ Hamilton Co. – Wayne A. Bills – Bass Pro Shops – 1974											
198¹/8	29⁷/8	29⁴/8	19⁵/8	22¹/8	4⁶/8	4⁷/8	9	8	5⁴/8	20	2
■ Decatur Co. – Kenneth Tilford – Bass Pro Shops – 1985											
196⁴/8	27	26¹/8	22⁴/8	25⁵/8	4⁵/8	4⁵/8	8	7	2	30	3
■ Des Moines Co. – Michael R. Edle – Michael R. Edle – 1989											
196³/8	28⁷/8	30⁵/8	22¹/8	26	6⁵/8	7	7	5	2⁶/8	32	4
■ Plymouth Co. – Picked Up – H. James Reimer – 1952											
194⁴/8	25⁷/8	25⁶/8	18⁶/8	20⁶/8	5¹/8	5²/8	7	7		42	5
■ Monroe Co. – Lloyd Goad – Bass Pro Shops – 1962											
194³/8	29¹/8	28⁶/8	23⁵/8	26	5¹/8	5¹/8	5	5		44	6
■ Warren Co. – Forest H. Richardson – Bass Pro Shops – 1989											
194²/8	26⁵/8	25	21	23²/8	4⁶/8	5	6	6		45	7
■ Jones Co. – Robert Miller – Bass Pro Shops – 1977											
193⁷/8	25²/8	25²/8	21⁵/8	23⁵/8	4⁷/8	4⁷/8	7	6	1²/8	48	8
■ Van Buren Co. – W. Eugene Zieglowsky – W. Eugene Zieglowsky – 1997											
193⁴/8	29	29⁵/8	23⁷/8	26⁴/8	5⁴/8	5³/8	6	6	1⁷/8	51	9
■ Linn Co. – Picked Up – Gary W. Bowen – 1994											
192³/8	28⁴/8	28²/8	19⁴/8	22²/8	5⁷/8	5⁴/8	9	6	10⁷/8	64	10
■ Monroe Co. – Roy E. Allison – Roy E. Allison – 1995											
192²/8	26⁷/8	26⁷/8	18⁴/8	20⁶/8	5⁴/8	5⁴/8	5	5		67	11
■ Mills Co. – John Chase – John Chase – 1997											
191⁷/8	29	27	20⁵/8	23	5¹/8	5¹/8	6	5	3	73	12
■ Monroe Co. – Picked Up – Troy Amoss – 1986											
191	28¹/8	27¹/8	20²/8	22⁴/8	5⁷/8	5⁷/8	5	6	1	87	13
■ Scott Co. – Jeffery L. Whisker – Bass Pro Shops – 1993											
190⁷/8	26⁶/8	26	20⁴/8	22⁵/8	4⁴/8	4³/8	6	5	1¹/8	89†	14†
■ Wayne Co. – Douglas M. Eldridge – Douglas M. Eldridge – 2000											
190⁵/8	28⁶/8	28	17⁶/8	20⁵/8	5⁶/8	6	5	7	10¹/8	95	15
■ Polk Co. – Richard B. Swim – Richard B. Swim – 1981											
190⁴/8	27³/8	27⁶/8	22³/8	24⁶/8	5¹/8	5²/8	6	6	6⁵/8	100	16
■ Monona Co. – Jeffery D. Scott – Jeffery D. Scott – 1996											
190	29¹/8	29	24⁶/8	26⁵/8	5²/8	5²/8	6	6		107	17
■ Fremont Co. – Randall D. Forney – Randall D. Forney – 1971											
190	29²/8	31¹/8	23	26²/8	5¹/8	5	6	6		107	17
■ Cherokee Co. – Dennis R. Vaudt – Dennis R. Vaudt – 1974											
190	27⁵/8	26⁶/8	19⁴/8	23³/8	5	4⁷/8	5	5		107	17
■ Clinton Co. – Merwin E. Koch – Merwin E. Koch – 1994											

Score	Length of Main Beam Right	Left	Inside Spread	Greatest Spread	Circumference at Smallest Place Between Burr and First Point Right	Left	Number of Points Right	Left	Lengths Abnormal Points	All-Time Rank	State Rank
	■ *Location of Kill – Hunter – Owner – Date Killed*										
190	31²/8	31²/8	24⁶/8	27⁴/8	5⁴/8	5²/8	5	5		107	17
	■ *Page Co. – Arlen D. Meyer – Arlen D. Meyer – 1996*										
189³/8	24⁶/8	24⁶/8	23⁶/8	25⁶/8	5	4⁷/8	7	6	5⁵/8	120	21
	■ *Henry Co. – Lamonte A. Stark – Bass Pro Shops – 1984*										
189³/8	29¹/8	29¹/8	19²/8	21⁶/8	5¹/8	5²/8	8	6	4³/8	120	21
	■ *Union Co. – Christopher C. Jimerson – Christopher C. Jimerson – 1995*										
189¹/8	27⁶/8	28³/8	20¹/8	22³/8	5	5¹/8	6	6		127	23
	■ *Allamakee Co. – Randy L. Petersburg – Randy L. Petersburg – 1996*										
187⁶/8	25⁵/8	26⁴/8	19	21²/8	4⁶/8	5¹/8	5	5		160	24
	■ *Johnson Co. – Gregg R. Redlin – Gregg R. Redlin – 1983*										
187⁵/8	28²/8	29	23³/8	26²/8	5⁴/8	5	6	8	7⁴/8	165	25
	■ *Greene Co. – Chris Jones – Chris Jones – 1999*										
187²/8	31⁴/8	30⁶/8	30³/8	32²/8	4⁶/8	4⁵/8	7	8	7⁵/8	180	26
	■ *Warren Co. – Dwight E. Green – Dwight E. Green – 1964*										
187	26⁷/8	27	21⁶/8	24¹/8	5¹/8	5¹/8	6	7		191	27
	■ *Des Moines Co. – Jim Brislawn – Connie Compton – PR 1993*										
186⁷/8	27¹/8	28³/8	17⁴/8	20⁶/8	5²/8	5	7	6	1³/8	194	28
	■ *Adair Co. – Dennis J. Gruss – Dennis J. Gruss – 1995*										
186⁴/8	29	28⁴/8	20²/8	22³/8	4⁵/8	4³/8	5	6	1⁶/8	205	29
	■ *Monroe Co. – Picked Up – H. James Reimer – 1992*										
186⁴/8	28³/8	28⁶/8	24³/8	26⁶/8	5⁴/8	5⁴/8	6	7	4³/8	205	29
	■ *Appanoose Co. – Picked Up – Robert Walker – 1998*										
186³/8	26⁴/8	26	20	22⁵/8	5⁷/8	5⁶/8	5	6	1³/8	210	31
	■ *Monona Co. – Mark Maynard – Mark Maynard – 1992*										
186¹/8	27⁶/8	27³/8	20¹/8	22²/8	5¹/8	5¹/8	5	5		228	32
	■ *Buchanan Co. – Garry W. Rasmussen – Garry W. Rasmussen – 1994*										
186	25⁵/8	25⁶/8	23	25⁵/8	5³/8	5²/8	6	7	1⁶/8	238	33
	■ *Union Co. – Christine A. Weeks – Christine A. Weeks – 1991*										
186	26⁶/8	27⁶/8	16²/8	18⁶/8	6¹/8	6³/8	5	5		238	33
	■ *Monona Co. – David L. Zima – David L. Zima – 1996*										
185¹/8	29⁵/8	29²/8	25⁵/8	28¹/8	5	5¹/8	7	6	5	266	35
	■ *Warren Co. – Joyce McCormick – Joyce McCormick – 1968*										
185¹/8	27⁷/8	27⁴/8	19¹/8	21⁶/8	5²/8	5	6	7	3⁴/8	266	35
	■ *Harrison Co. – Marvin E. Tippery – Marvin E. Tippery – 1971*										
184⁷/8	26⁵/8	26⁶/8	27	29	5⁷/8	5⁶/8	7	7	4³/8	279	37
	■ *Delaware Co. – R.E. Stewart – R.E. Stewart – 1953*										
184³/8	26⁵/8	26	19	21	5¹/8	5	6	6	2⁵/8	313	38
	■ *Keokuk Co. – Randy D. Schmidt – Randy D. Schmidt – 1995*										
184²/8	29¹/8	28²/8	18⁶/8	22¹/8	4⁷/8	5	6	7	8	319	39
	■ *Hardin Co. – Robert D. Imsland – Robert D. Imsland – 1985*										
184²/8	29⁵/8	27³/8	21	23³/8	5⁶/8	5⁶/8	5	6	2²/8	319	39
	■ *Jackson Co. – Unknown – Charles E. Matthiesen – PR 1994*										

Score	Length of Main Beam Right	Left	Inside Spread	Greatest Spread	Circumference at Smallest Place Between Burr and First Point Right	Left	Number of Points Right	Left	Lengths Abnormal Points	All-Time Rank	State Rank
									■ *Location of Kill – Hunter – Owner – Date Killed*		
184¹/₈	28³/₈	27⁵/₈	20³/₈	23³/₈	4⁵/₈	4⁵/₈	6	7		327†	41†
				■ *Wapello Co. – Ryan W. Scott – Ryan W. Scott – 2000* ■ *See photo on page 183*							
184	28⁴/₈	29¹/₈	24⁷/₈	27	5	5¹/₈	7	9	10⁵/₈	334	42
				■ *Allamakee Co. – William P. Mitchell – W.P. Mitchell & J. Bakewell – 1989*							
184	27²/₈	26	20⁴/₈	22⁷/₈	5⁶/₈	5⁴/₈	5	5		334	42
				■ *Wapello Co. – Raymond M. Todey – Raymond M. Todey – 1993*							
183⁷/₈	26⁵/₈	26⁵/₈	18⁵/₈	20⁷/₈	3⁷/₈	3⁷/₈	6	6		343†	44†
				■ *Adams Co. – Gregory L. Andrews – Gregory L. Andrews – 2000*							
183⁷/₈	27⁷/₈	28³/₈	20¹/₈	22⁷/₈	6²/₈	6⁵/₈	6	7	3⁴/₈	343	44
				■ *Taylor Co. – Wayne Swartz – Spanky Greenville – 1953*							
183⁵/₈	27⁶/₈	27¹/₈	20³/₈	22⁷/₈	5⁶/₈	5⁷/₈	5	5		357†	46†
				■ *Guthrie Co. – Charles S. Callaway – Charles S. Callaway – 2001*							
183⁴/₈	26⁵/₈	27⁶/₈	24⁷/₈	27¹/₈	6⁶/₈	6²/₈	5	7	2⁵/₈	361	47
				■ *Madison Co. – Roy P. Mikesell – Roy P. Mikesell – 1995*							
183¹/₈	29⁵/₈	30⁵/₈	22¹/₈	24⁴/₈	5⁶/₈	5⁶/₈	7	6	4⁴/₈	385	48
				■ *Guthrie Co. – Don McCarty – Chad Redfern – 1962*							
183	26³/₈	25³/₈	23	25⁴/₈	4⁶/₈	4⁴/₈	5	5		392	49
				■ *Emmet Co. – Bill Walstead – Bill Walstead – 1974*							
183	28⁴/₈	28¹/₈	20⁴/₈	22⁵/₈	5⁵/₈	5⁵/₈	5	6		392	49
				■ *Union Co. – Randy G. Hall – Randy G. Hall – 1986*							
183	26⁶/₈	28⁴/₈	18⁵/₈	21²/₈	5⁵/₈	5⁵/₈	5	7	2³/₈	392	49
				■ *Van Buren Co. – Picked Up – Timothy J. Wilson – 1990*							
182⁷/₈	28³/₈	27⁷/₈	23⁵/₈	26⁴/₈	5¹/₈	5	6	5	2	401†	52†
				■ *Monroe Co. – Les A. Bateman – Les A. Bateman – 2001*							
182⁶/₈	27⁵/₈	28⁴/₈	19⁴/₈	22⁴/₈	4⁶/₈	4⁴/₈	9	7	4⁴/₈	409	53
				■ *Lee Co. – John L. Kite – John L. Kite – 1990*							
182⁶/₈	29⁷/₈	29⁴/₈	20¹/₈	22⁴/₈	4³/₈	4⁵/₈	7	9	4⁵/₈	409	53
				■ *Wayne Co. – Donald P. Greenlee – Donald P. Greenlee – 1997*							
182⁵/₈	28³/₈	28⁴/₈	24¹/₈	26⁷/₈	5²/₈	5¹/₈	5	6	2⁴/₈	420	55
				■ *Jefferson Co. – William J. Waugh – William J. Waugh – 1985*							
182³/₈	25⁵/₈	25¹/₈	18¹/₈	20⁴/₈	4⁶/₈	4⁶/₈	6	6		438	56
				■ *Marshall Co. – Barbara Daniel – Terry Daniel – 1967*							
182³/₈	27⁷/₈	26⁶/₈	23⁴/₈	26²/₈	5⁵/₈	5⁷/₈	5	5	3³/₈	438	56
				■ *Monroe Co. – Elisha G. Hugen – Elisha G. Hugen – 1996*							
182¹/₈	26⁵/₈	26⁷/₈	18⁶/₈	21⁴/₈	6⁴/₈	6	7	7	2⁵/₈	460	58
				■ *Keokuk Co. – William Musgrove – William H. Lilienthal – 1977*							
182	27⁷/₈	28⁴/₈	21⁴/₈	23⁶/₈	5¹/₈	5¹/₈	6	6		469	59
				■ *Monona Co. – Jerry W. Conover – Jerry W. Conover – 1990*							
181⁷/₈	26³/₈	26³/₈	21¹/₈	24⁶/₈	5	4⁷/₈	6	6	2	478	60
				■ *Jackson Co. – Ambrose Beck – Ambrose Beck – 1963*							
181⁶/₈	27⁷/₈	28⁴/₈	18⁴/₈	21¹/₈	5	5²/₈	7	6	2²/₈	492	61
				■ *Davis Co. – Craig S. Heaverlo – Craig S. Heaverlo – 1994*							

Score	Length of Main Beam Right	Left	Inside Spread	Greatest Spread	Circumference at Smallest Place Between Burr and First Point Right	Left	Number of Points Right	Left	Lengths Abnormal Points	All-Time Rank	State Rank
	■ *Location of Kill – Hunter – Owner – Date Killed*										
181 5/8	28 5/8	28	19 3/8	22	5 4/8	5 2/8	5	5		500	62
	■ *Des Moines Co. – Joseph J. Birkenstock – Joseph J. Birkenstock – 1996*										
181 4/8	26 7/8	26 5/8	21	23	4 5/8	4 4/8	5	5		516	63
	■ *Wayne Co. – Picked Up – Ron King – 1990*										
181 3/8	28	26 6/8	18 5/8	20 5/8	4 5/8	4 6/8	6	5		528	64
	■ *Polk Co. – Bob Boydston – Kevin Freymiller – 1972*										
181 3/8	24 6/8	26 3/8	19 7/8	22 1/8	5 1/8	4 7/8	6	6		528	64
	■ *Adair Co. – Gale D. Johnston – Gale D. Johnston – 1995*										
180 7/8	27 6/8	25 4/8	18 7/8	21	4 5/8	4 4/8	6	7		573†	66†
	■ *Audubon Co. – Michael M. Miller – Keith E. Brock – 1996*										
180 7/8	27 1/8	26	18 1/8	20 6/8	6 4/8	6 1/8	7	5	3 2/8	573†	66†
	■ *Monona Co. – Picked Up – David E. Fender – 1991*										
180 7/8	26 4/8	26 6/8	22	24 4/8	5 2/8	5	7	5	4 1/8	573	66
	■ *Wayne Co. – Richard L. Spencer – Richard L. Spencer – 1990*										
180 7/8	26 7/8	26 5/8	22 1/8	25 1/8	5 3/8	5 3/8	5	5		573	66
	■ *Cedar Co. – Glenn U. Farrington – Glenn U. Farrington – 1994*										
180 7/8	27	25 6/8	19 7/8	21 5/8	5 3/8	5 2/8	5	5		573	66
	■ *Adair Co. – Picked Up – Jerry Funke – 1995*										
180 7/8	25 5/8	26	21 1/8	22 5/8	5 1/8	5	8	7	3 2/8	573	66
	■ *Clayton Co. – Robert M. Hefel – Robert M. Hefel – 1998*										
180 6/8	26 3/8	26 1/8	18 2/8	21	5 5/8	5 5/8	5	6		587	72
	■ *Jefferson Co. – James J. Hoskins – James J. Hoskins – 1982*										
180 5/8	25 6/8	27	19 7/8	23	4 5/8	4 5/8	5	5		599	73
	■ *Cedar Co. – Bobby Smith – William H. Lilienthal – 1998*										
180 4/8	27 1/8	26 6/8	16 6/8	18 6/8	5	4 7/8	6	5	1 2/8	613	74
	■ *Adams Co. – Dale D. Blazek – Dale D. Blazek – 1962*										
180 4/8	24 7/8	26 4/8	21	23 4/8	5 3/8	5 2/8	5	5		613	74
	■ *Henry Co. – Jeff L. Weigert – Jeff L. Weigert – 1991*										
180 3/8	25 1/8	24 7/8	17 2/8	19 2/8	4 7/8	4 5/8	7	6	2 1/8	630	76
	■ *Story Co. – Richard L. Borton – Richard L. Borton – 1987*										
180 2/8	24 1/8	26 6/8	19 1/8	21 5/8	5	4 6/8	6	6	2 3/8	651	77
	■ *Madison Co. – Carl W. Schroder – Carl W. Schroder – 1977*										
180 2/8	28 2/8	26 6/8	21 4/8	23	6 1/8	6 7/8	5	5		651	77
	■ *Cedar Co. – Roger Schoene – Beth Tucker – PR 1981*										
180 2/8	27 1/8	27 1/8	19 4/8	21 5/8	4 4/8	4 4/8	5	5		651	77
	■ *Iowa – Unknown – Tom Williams – PR 1984*										
180 2/8	26 6/8	27 4/8	22 4/8	25	5	4 6/8	6	7	7 4/8	651	77
	■ *Polk Co. – Jeff P. Susic – Jeff P. Susic – 1990*										
180 2/8	25 2/8	25 7/8	20 4/8	22 5/8	4 7/8	4 6/8	5	5		651	77
	■ *Monroe Co. – Michael R. Maddy – Michael R. Maddy – 1992*										
180 2/8	28 4/8	27 6/8	21 1/8	23 3/8	5	5 2/8	6	8	4 3/8	651	77
	■ *Allamakee Co. – David L. Goedert – David L. Goedert – 1995*										

Score	Length of Main Beam Right Left	Inside Spread	Greatest Spread	Circumference at Smallest Place Between Burr and First Point Right Left	Number of Points Right Left	Lengths Abnormal Points	All-Time Rank	State Rank
	▪ Location of Kill – Hunter – Owner – Date Killed							
180	24⁴/₈ 25³/₈	23³/₈	26³/₈	7 7	7 6	9⁷/₈	688	83
	▪ Boone Co. – Loren H. Phipps – Loren H. Phipps – 1993							
179⁶/₈	26⁷/₈ 26⁵/₈	21⁴/₈	23⁵/₈	4⁴/₈ 4⁴/₈	7 7		712	84
	▪ Woodbury Co. – Harlan L. Allison – Harlan L. Allison – 1979							
179⁶/₈	25³/₈ 26	19¹/₈	21²/₈	5³/₈ 5⁴/₈	7 7	4³/₈	712	84
	▪ Decatur Co. – Wayne W. Owens – Wayne W. Owens – 1995							
179⁴/₈	28¹/₈ 28¹/₈	19⁶/₈	22²/₈	6 6¹/₈	6 6		733	86
	▪ Clarke Co. – Rodney D. Hommer – Cabela's, Inc. – 1990							
179³/₈	26³/₈ 25⁷/₈	22¹/₈	24¹/₈	5 5	6 7	2⁴/₈	749	87
	▪ Allamakee Co. – Picked Up – David Gordon – 1994							
179²/₈	26⁵/₈ 25⁵/₈	17⁷/₈	21³/₈	5 4⁶/₈	7 7	3⁷/₈	763	88
	▪ Worth Co. – John Janssen – John Janssen – 1976							
179²/₈	28¹/₈ 28⁴/₈	25²/₈	27⁵/₈	4⁵/₈ 4⁵/₈	6 5	3²/₈	763	88
	▪ Webster Co. – Douglas W. Baedke – Douglas W. Baedke – 1982							
179¹/₈	27 27²/₈	19³/₈	22⁶/₈	5⁶/₈ 5⁶/₈	6 7	7⁴/₈	779†	90†
	▪ Bremer Co. – Blaine A. Davis – Blaine A. Davis – 2000							
179¹/₈	24⁵/₈ 25⁴/₈	15⁷/₈	21	4⁷/₈ 5	7 6		779	90
	▪ Dallas Co. – Steven W. Hick – Steven W. Hick – 1992							
179	27⁷/₈ 29¹/₈	21⁴/₈	24⁴/₈	5⁴/₈ 5²/₈	6 6	5⁶/₈	786	92
	▪ Union Co. – Richard Reed – Richard Reed – 1996							
187⁷/₈	28¹/₈ 26²/₈	19⁵/₈	22	4⁶/₈ 4⁶/₈	6 6		801	93
	▪ Van Buren Co. – Noel E. Harlan – Noel E. Harlan – 1984							
178⁵/₈	26³/₈ 27³/₈	23¹/₈	25³/₈	5⁴/₈ 5⁶/₈	5 7	2	819	94
	▪ Hamilton Co. – Harrison McIntre – William H. Lilienthal – PR 1960							
178⁵/₈	26 26²/₈	19⁵/₈	23¹/₈	5⁴/₈ 5⁶/₈	5 5		819	94
	▪ Jones Co. – Dennis Boots – Dennis Boots – 1988							
178⁵/₈	26 26⁵/₈	20³/₈	22⁷/₈	5¹/₈ 5³/₈	5 6		819	94
	▪ Cedar Co. – Michael M. Hatzky – Michael M. Hatzky – 1999							
178⁴/₈	27⁶/₈ 28⁴/₈	20⁶/₈	23¹/₈	5⁷/₈ 5⁷/₈	7 9	5⁶/₈	850	97
	▪ Cass Co. – Mark A. Funk – Mark A. Funk – 1997							
178³/₈	25²/₈ 24³/₈	19⁵/₈	21⁵/₈	4³/₈ 4⁴/₈	6 6		868†	98†
	▪ Crawford Co. – Clark A. Corbin – Clark A. Corbin – 2000 ▪ See photo on page 8							
178³/₈	25³/₈ 28¹/₈	20	23²/₈	5⁵/₈ 5⁴/₈	7 6	1⁵/₈	868	98
	▪ Allamakee Co. – Stanley L. Jarosh – Stanley L. Jarosh – 1976							
178³/₈	28⁴/₈ 27⁷/₈	17¹/₈	19³/₈	4⁷/₈ 4⁶/₈	6 6		868	98
	▪ Dubuque Co. – Clay W. Gronen – Clay W. Gronen – 1978							
178³/₈	24⁴/₈ 26¹/₈	18⁵/₈	20³/₈	4²/₈ 4²/₈	5 5		868	98
	▪ Fayette Co. – Richard A. Wulfekuhle – Richard A. Wulfekuhle – 1995							
178³/₈	24⁷/₈ 25	19¹/₈	21⁶/₈	5²/₈ 5³/₈	5 6	1	868	98
	▪ Marion Co. – Lyle E. Palmer – Lyle E. Palmer – 1998							
178¹/₈	26⁶/₈ 26⁴/₈	19¹/₈	21⁵/₈	5⁴/₈ 5³/₈	5 5		905	103
	▪ Dallas Co. – Picked Up – William H. Lilienthal – 1995							

Score	Length of Main Beam		Inside Spread	Greatest Spread	Circumference at Smallest Place Between Burr and First Point		Number of Points		Lengths Abnormal Points	All-Time Rank	State Rank
	Right	Left			Right	Left	Right	Left			
	■ Location of Kill – Hunter – Owner – Date Killed										
178	25	24⁶/₈	17²/₈	19⁶/₈	4⁶/₈	4⁵/₈	6	7	3⁴/₈	922	104
	■ Washington Co. – Brad Gardner – Vaughn Wilkins – 1978										
178	29	30²/₈	25	27³/₈	5	5¹/₈	9	7	13	922	104
	■ Appanoose Co. – Steve G. Huff – Steve G. Huff – 1988										
178	25⁷/₈	26²/₈	18¹/₈	20⁴/₈	5²/₈	5¹/₈	6	5	5⁷/₈	922	104
	■ Decatur Co. – Picked Up – Jeffrey R. Danner – 1995										
177⁷/₈	25²/₈	26⁵/₈	18¹/₈	21²/₈	5¹/₈	5³/₈	6	6		936	107
	■ Jefferson Co. – John J. Oberhaus – John J. Oberhaus – 1997										
177⁵/₈	26¹/₈	26¹/₈	22³/₈	24⁴/₈	5⁶/₈	5⁵/₈	5	5		972	108
	■ Winneshiek Co. – Glen J. Gienau – Glen J. Gienau – 1995										
177³/₈	27¹/₈	26³/₈	20³/₈	22⁶/₈	5⁴/₈	5²/₈	6	5	4	1011	109
	■ Greene Co. – Roger V. Carlson – Roger V. Carlson – 1983										
177³/₈	29²/₈	29¹/₈	24²/₈	26¹/₈	5	5¹/₈	6	5	2⁵/₈	1011	109
	■ Clinton Co. – Picked Up – William H. Lilienthal – 1990										
177²/₈	28⁷/₈	29²/₈	22⁶/₈	25	5¹/₈	5¹/₈	5	4		1025†	111†
	■ Page Co. – Darrel L. Vogel – Darrel L. Vogel – 2000										
177²/₈	26⁵/₈	27³/₈	22	24²/₈	4⁶/₈	4⁴/₈	7	5	1	1025	111
	■ Guthrie Co. – Picked Up – Dalton H. Hoover – 1970										
177²/₈	27⁴/₈	28³/₈	18⁶/₈	21	4⁵/₈	4⁷/₈	7	7	3⁶/₈	1025	111
	■ Clarke Co. – Richard Bassett – Richard Bassett – 1989										
177²/₈	26	27	19⁴/₈	22	5⁴/₈	5⁴/₈	5	5		1025	111
	■ Mills Co. – James H. Roberts – James H. Roberts – 1998										
177¹/₈	25⁵/₈	25⁷/₈	23⁵/₈	25⁶/₈	4⁷/₈	4⁷/₈	6	6	9	1048†	115†
	■ Clay Co. – Jeff D. Tiefenthaler – Jeff D. Tiefenthaler – 2001										
177¹/₈	28⁴/₈	26⁶/₈	20²/₈	22⁴/₈	5¹/₈	5	6	7	7⁷/₈	1048	115
	■ Washington Co. – Ernest Aronson – Ernest Aronson – 1985										
177¹/₈	26⁴/₈	27	19⁴/₈	21⁶/₈	4⁶/₈	4⁷/₈	5	6	1¹/₈	1048	115
	■ Cass Co. – Cleve H. Powell – Cleve H. Powell – 1990										
177¹/₈	25⁷/₈	25⁷/₈	18¹/₈	22¹/₈	4⁷/₈	4⁶/₈	5	5		1048	115
	■ Davis Co. – Michael G. White – Michael G. White – 1995										
177	25⁴/₈	25¹/₈	18	20²/₈	4³/₈	4³/₈	6	6		1066†	119†
	■ Union Co. – Michael A. Herrick – Michael A. Herrick – 2000										
177	26²/₈	26¹/₈	20⁴/₈	22³/₈	4³/₈	4⁵/₈	6	6		1066	119
	■ Muscatine Co. – Jack Van Nice – Jack Van Nice – 1986										
177	23⁴/₈	22⁶/₈	16⁴/₈	19¹/₈	4⁶/₈	4⁶/₈	6	5		1066	119
	■ Harrison Co. – Craig D. Mitchell – Craig D. Mitchell – 1988										
176⁷/₈	27³/₈	25⁶/₈	20¹/₈	22⁴/₈	6⁵/₈	6⁷/₈	4	4		1086†	122†
	■ Harrison Co. – Jay D. Jensen – Jay D. Jensen – 2000										
176⁶/₈	26⁴/₈	25⁶/₈	20²/₈	23⁴/₈	4⁶/₈	4⁷/₈	6	6		1103	123
	■ Muscatine Co. – Donald L. McCullough – Donald L. McCullough – 1980										
176⁶/₈	23⁷/₈	26¹/₈	20³/₈	22⁴/₈	5³/₈	5⁴/₈	6	5	1⁵/₈	1103	123
	■ Linn Co. – Douglas D. Kriegel – Douglas D. Kriegel – 1988										

Score	Length of Main Beam Right	Left	Inside Spread	Greatest Spread	Circumference at Smallest Place Between Burr and First Point Right	Left	Number of Points Right	Left	Lengths Abnormal Points	All-Time Rank	State Rank
	■ Location of Kill – Hunter – Owner – Date Killed										
176⁶/8	25²/8	25¹/8	17⁶/8	20²/8	5⁶/8	5³/8	6	6		1103	123
	■ Van Buren Co. – Bruce C. Spiller – Bruce C. Spiller – 1995										
176⁴/8	25⁷/8	25³/8	21⁴/8	24⁶/8	6	5¹/8	10	10	13⁶/8	1158	126
	■ Davis Co. – Jeffrey A. Getz – Jeffrey A. Getz – 1991										
176⁴/8	27²/8	26⁶/8	20³/8	22⁴/8	5	5	6	5	4¹/8	1158	126
	■ Linn Co. – David E. Heck – David E. Heck – 1994										
176⁴/8	28³/8	28	18³/8	20²/8	4⁶/8	5⁶/8	7	10	7⁷/8	1158	126
	■ Muscatine Co. – Tim S. Kroul – Tim S. Kroul – 1997										
176³/8	25²/8	26²/8	17⁷/8	19⁶/8	4⁷/8	5	6	5	2²/8	1182†	129†
	■ Van Buren Co. – Bruce C. Spiller – Bruce C. Spiller – 2000										
176³/8	27⁷/8	26³/8	18⁵/8	20⁷/8	4⁷/8	4⁷/8	6	6		1182	129
	■ Cherokee Co. – Bob Roberts – Bob Roberts – 1963										
176³/8	28	27	20⁵/8	23	4⁷/8	4⁷/8	5	6		1182	129
	■ Montgomery Co. – Stanley D. Means – Stanley D. Means – 1977										
176³/8	26⁶/8	25⁷/8	18⁷/8	20⁷/8	5²/8	5³/8	5	7	3⁶/8	1182	129
	■ Fremont Co. – Scott J. Carnes – Scott J. Carnes – 1987										
176²/8	25²/8	26⁴/8	22²/8	24¹/8	5	5	6	6		1209	133
	■ Des Moines Co. – Virgil Landrum – Virgil Landrum – 1960										
176²/8	25⁶/8	26²/8	20⁶/8	23⁴/8	5⁴/8	5⁶/8	5	5		1209	133
	■ Lucas Co. – Corey E. Gwinn – Corey E. Gwinn – 1992										
176¹/8	27	27⁴/8	21²/8	23²/8	5	5¹/8	6	8	5⁵/8	1243†	135†
	■ Jefferson Co. – Dale E. Manor – Dale E. Manor – 2001										
176¹/8	24¹/8	25⁴/8	19⁵/8	24³/8	4⁷/8	4⁴/8	5	5		1243	135
	■ Jackson Co. – Roy O. Lindemier – Roy O. Lindemier – 1990										
176¹/8	30⁴/8	29⁶/8	20²/8	22⁷/8	5⁵/8	5²/8	6	5	2¹/8	1243	135
	■ Lucas Co. – Justin J. Adams – Justin J. Adams – 1995										
176¹/8	28⁶/8	28¹/8	20²/8	24¹/8	4⁵/8	4⁶/8	6	7	3⁵/8	1243	135
	■ Linn Co. – Rudolph C. Ashbacher – Rudolph C. Ashbacher – 1998										
176	23⁷/8	25²/8	19³/8	21⁶/8	5⁶/8	5⁶/8	8	7	7¹/8	1266	139
	■ Lyon Co. – Duane K. Rohde – Duane K. Rohde – 1964										
175⁷/8	28¹/8	28²/8	21³/8	23	3⁷/8	3⁷/8	5	6		1287†	140†
	■ Iowa Co. – Chris Adams – Chris Adams – 2000										
175⁷/8	26²/8	24⁶/8	19¹/8	21³/8	4⁶/8	5²/8	5	6	2⁴/8	1287	140
	■ Boone Co. – Monte A. Carlson – Monte A. Carlson – 1995										
175⁶/8	30	27⁵/8	18⁵/8	20⁶/8	5⁷/8	6	6	6	3¹/8	1310	142
	■ Montgomery Co. – Randy L. Wienhold – Randy L. Wienhold – 1992										
175⁶/8	26³/8	27³/8	22	23⁷/8	5³/8	5²/8	5	5		1310	142
	■ Davis Co. – Kendall M. Palmer – Kendall M. Palmer – 1997										
175⁵/8	26⁶/8	26	20⁶/8	23¹/8	4⁵/8	4⁴/8	6	6	5⁷/8	1333	144
	■ Warren Co. – Art L. Daniels – Art L. Daniels – 1986										
175⁵/8	24¹/8	23⁴/8	17³/8	20²/8	4⁶/8	4⁷/8	7	7	1	1333	144
	■ Woodbury Co. – Paul Feddersen – Paul Feddersen – 1988										

Score	Length of Main Beam Right Left	Inside Spread	Greatest Spread	Circumference at Smallest Place Between Burr and First Point Right Left	Number of Points Right Left	Lengths Abnormal Points	All-Time Rank	State Rank
	■ Location of Kill – Hunter – Owner – Date Killed							
175⁵/₈	25⁵/₈ 25⁶/₈	19³/₈	20¹/₈	4 4¹/₈	7 7	1⁴/₈	1333	144
	■ Lucas Co. – Dean E. Chandler – Dean E. Chandler – 1991							
175⁵/₈	23⁶/₈ 23²/₈	16³/₈	18⁴/₈	4³/₈ 4⁶/₈	7 7		1333	144
	■ Cedar Co. – Picked Up – Rory Petersen – 1999							
175⁴/₈	26³/₈ 25⁷/₈	21²/₈	23⁴/₈	5¹/₈ 5¹/₈	5 5		1352	148
	■ Winnebago Co. – Joel Kingland – Joel Kingland – 1975							
175⁴/₈	28⁴/₈ 28⁴/₈	22²/₈	24²/₈	4³/₈ 4³/₈	5 5		1352	148
	■ Allamakee Co. – William Moody – William Moody – 1997							
175³/₈	29¹/₈ 28⁷/₈	21⁴/₈	23²/₈	5²/₈ 5²/₈	6 5	1⁷/₈	1377	150
	■ Wright Co. – Picked Up – Ron Schaumburg – 1976							
175³/₈	28³/₈ 28⁵/₈	17⁶/₈	19⁷/₈	4⁶/₈ 4⁴/₈	6 7	5¹/₈	1377	150
	■ Carroll Co. – Edward L. Golay – Edward L. Golay – 1984							
175³/₈	27 26⁶/₈	16⁶/₈	18⁷/₈	4⁷/₈ 4⁷/₈	6 6	2¹/₈	1377	150
	■ Boone Co. – James D. Champion – James D. Champion – 1991							
175³/₈	27⁷/₈ 26⁴/₈	21²/₈	24¹/₈	4⁶/₈ 4⁵/₈	8 9	8⁷/₈	1377	150
	■ Fayette Co. – Donald Massman – Phyllis Massman – 1991							
175³/₈	27³/₈ 26⁵/₈	17⁵/₈	20¹/₈	5⁵/₈ 5⁷/₈	5 6		1377	150
	■ Monona Co. – William Jones – B.A. Tucker – 1991							
175³/₈	26⁶/₈ 26⁶/₈	20¹/₈	22³/₈	6¹/₈ 5⁷/₈	6 6	1²/₈	1377	150
	■ Chickasaw Co. – Dennis P. Troyna – Dennis P. Troyna – 1999							
175²/₈	27²/₈ 27³/₈	15⁴/₈	20²/₈	5²/₈ 6	6 8	11²/₈	1403	156
	■ Cherokee Co. – Unknown – H. James Reimer – 1954							
175²/₈	26⁵/₈ 28³/₈	21⁴/₈	23⁵/₈	5²/₈ 5²/₈	5 5	3	1403	156
	■ Clayton Co. – Thomas J. Shea – Thomas J. Shea – 1995							
175²/₈	25³/₈ 25⁴/₈	20⁴/₈	22⁵/₈	4⁷/₈ 4⁶/₈	5 5		1403	156
	■ Johnson Co. – George J. Hebl – George J. Hebl – 1999							
175¹/₈	25⁶/₈ 25²/₈	16⁷/₈	19⁴/₈	5³/₈ 5⁴/₈	6 7	4⁶/₈	1440	159
	■ Howard Co. – Russell L. Stevenson, Jr. – Russell L. Stevenson, Jr. – 1971							
175¹/₈	25⁷/₈ 26⁵/₈	22⁴/₈	24³/₈	5 5¹/₈	5 6	1¹/₈	1440	159
	■ Sac Co. – Randy J. Bentsen – Randy J. Bentsen – 1973							
175¹/₈	27³/₈ 27⁶/₈	20⁷/₈	23	5⁵/₈ 5⁴/₈	7 7	6⁶/₈	1440	159
	■ Des Moines Co. – Gordon F. Rorebeck – Gordon F. Rorebeck – 1987							
175¹/₈	27⁵/₈ 26⁴/₈	17²/₈	19⁵/₈	4⁶/₈ 4⁴/₈	7 8	7¹/₈	1440	159
	■ Crawford Co. – Kermit Greenstreet – Kermit Greenstreet – 1989							
175¹/₈	27 26⁷/₈	20¹/₈	22	5⁷/₈ 5⁶/₈	6 6	2⁴/₈	1440	159
	■ Scott Co. – Jeffrey R. Coonts – Jeffrey R. Coonts – 1996							
175	28²/₈ 27⁵/₈	18¹/₈	21²/₈	5 4⁷/₈	6 5	4⁷/₈	1472	164
	■ Louisa Co. – Glen D. Brandt – Glen D. Brandt – 1974							
175	28⁵/₈ 29¹/₈	21⁵/₈	24⁵/₈	5¹/₈ 5	7 5	3³/₈	1472	164
	■ Henry Co. – Richard Doggett – Richard Doggett – 1975							
175	27⁶/₈ 28⁶/₈	19	21⁴/₈	4³/₈ 4¹/₈	6 6	2⁶/₈	1472	164
	■ Lee Co. – Stephen D. McKeehan, Jr. – Stephen D. McKeehan, Jr. – 1989							

Score	Length of Main Beam Right	Left	Inside Spread	Greatest Spread	Circumference at Smallest Place Between Burr and First Point Right	Left	Number of Points Right	Left	Lengths Abnormal Points	All-Time Rank	State Rank

■ *Location of Kill – Hunter – Owner – Date Killed*

Score	R	L	Inside	Greatest	Circ R	Circ L	Pts R	Pts L	Abnormal	All-Time	State
175	27	26²/₈	21	23⁵/₈	4⁵/₈	4⁵/₈	6	7	10⁴/₈	1472	164

■ *Dubuque Co. – Lawrence E. Blatz – Lawrence E. Blatz – 1992*

| 175 | 27⁶/₈ | 26⁶/₈ | 21²/₈ | 23³/₈ | 4⁶/₈ | 4⁶/₈ | 6 | 6 | | 1472 | 164 |

■ *Clayton Co. – Clifton L. Kauffman – Clifton L. Kauffman – 1996*

| 175 | 26⁶/₈ | 26¹/₈ | 19 | 21 | 5¹/₈ | 5³/₈ | 8 | 6 | 3²/₈ | 1472 | 164 |

■ *Union Co. – Luke A. Bradley – Luke A. Bradley – 1999*

| 174⁷/₈ | 28⁶/₈ | 27⁵/₈ | 21³/₈ | 24¹/₈ | 5³/₈ | 5³/₈ | 7 | 7 | 5²/₈ | 1513† | 170† |

■ *Clayton Co. – Scott D. Geater – Scott D. Geater – 2001*

| 174⁷/₈ | 24³/₈ | 25⁴/₈ | 20⁷/₈ | 23 | 4⁷/₈ | 4⁷/₈ | 5 | 7 | 1⁴/₈ | 1513† | 170† |

■ *Decatur Co. – Thomas G. Krikke – Thomas G. Krikke – 2001*

| 174⁷/₈ | 28³/₈ | 28⁶/₈ | 18⁷/₈ | 20⁷/₈ | 4³/₈ | 4³/₈ | 7 | 5 | 1²/₈ | 1513 | 170 |

■ *Warren Co. – Picked Up – John I. Kunert – PR 1992*

| 174⁶/₈ | 27²/₈ | 27²/₈ | 21²/₈ | 23⁴/₈ | 5¹/₈ | 5¹/₈ | 8 | 7 | 4⁶/₈ | 1534 | 173 |

■ *Clayton Co. – James Trappe – James Trappe – 1980*

| 174⁶/₈ | 26⁷/₈ | 26⁷/₈ | 20 | 22 | 5 | 5 | 5 | 5 | | 1534 | 173 |

■ *Fayette Co. – Gerald E. Gress – Gerald E. Gress – 1995*

| 174⁶/₈ | 27²/₈ | 26⁷/₈ | 17 | 19²/₈ | 4³/₈ | 4⁴/₈ | 6 | 7 | 1²/₈ | 1534 | 173 |

■ *Allamakee Co. – Dave Moritz, Jr. – Dave Moritz, Jr. – 1996*

| 174⁵/₈ | 25²/₈ | 26¹/₈ | 18³/₈ | 21³/₈ | 5¹/₈ | 4⁷/₈ | 5 | 6 | 2 | 1561 | 176 |

■ *Butler Co. – Vernon Simon – Vernon Simon – 1972*

| 174⁵/₈ | 26 | 25⁴/₈ | 19⁵/₈ | 22¹/₈ | 5¹/₈ | 4⁷/₈ | 8 | 5 | 6⁶/₈ | 1561 | 176 |

■ *Des Moines Co. – Gene L. McAlister – Gene L. McAlister – 1980*

| 174⁵/₈ | 29²/₈ | 26⁶/₈ | 20³/₈ | 23⁴/₈ | 4⁷/₈ | 5¹/₈ | 6 | 6 | | 1561 | 176 |

■ *Jackson Co. – Ronald J. Casel – Ronald J. Casel – 1992*

| 174⁴/₈ | 28²/₈ | 27⁵/₈ | 17 | 19⁴/₈ | 5²/₈ | 5³/₈ | 5 | 7 | 1 | 1592 | 179 |

■ *Boone Co. – Curtis A. Lind – Curtis A. Lind – 1982*

| 174⁴/₈ | 26²/₈ | 25³/₈ | 17⁵/₈ | 21²/₈ | 5⁴/₈ | 5⁵/₈ | 8 | 9 | 10⁷/₈ | 1592 | 179 |

■ *Hamilton Co. – Todd L. Darling – Todd L. Darling – 1994*

| 174⁴/₈ | 27³/₈ | 27⁷/₈ | 22⁴/₈ | 24¹/₈ | 5 | 4⁶/₈ | 5 | 5 | | 1592 | 179 |

■ *Jackson Co. – Ted B. Howell – Ted B. Howell – 1999*

| 174³/₈ | 27⁶/₈ | 27⁶/₈ | 21⁵/₈ | 24⁶/₈ | 5⁵/₈ | 5²/₈ | 7 | 8 | 7²/₈ | 1619 | 182 |

■ *Guthrie Co. – Larry R. Belding – Larry R. Belding – 1965*

| 174³/₈ | 27 | 27⁶/₈ | 22⁷/₈ | 25⁵/₈ | 5²/₈ | 5²/₈ | 8 | 7 | 6²/₈ | 1619 | 182 |

■ *Warren Co. – Craig O. Carpenter – Craig O. Carpenter – 1990*

| 174³/₈ | 26⁵/₈ | 26⁵/₈ | 21⁷/₈ | 24⁴/₈ | 4²/₈ | 4 | 5 | 5 | | 1619 | 182 |

■ *Johnson Co. – Picked Up – Steve Scharf – 1998*

| 174³/₈ | 26 | 26 | 22 | 25 | 5⁵/₈ | 5⁷/₈ | 7 | 5 | 4³/₈ | 1619 | 182 |

■ *Allamakee Co. – Clinton C. Mohn – Clinton C. Mohn – 1999*

| 174²/₈ | 28³/₈ | 28²/₈ | 22²/₈ | 24⁴/₈ | 5⁴/₈ | 5⁴/₈ | 4 | 4 | | 1652 | 186 |

■ *Cass Co. – Cecil Erickson – Cecil Erickson – 1975*

| 174²/₈ | 27⁶/₈ | 25⁷/₈ | 19⁵/₈ | 22¹/₈ | 4⁷/₈ | 4⁶/₈ | 7 | 7 | 8⁵/₈ | 1652 | 186 |

■ *Monona Co. – Larry R. Peterson – Larry R. Peterson – 1990*

Score	Length of Main Beam Right / Left		Inside Spread	Greatest Spread	Circumference at Smallest Place Between Burr and First Point Right / Left		Number of Points Right / Left		Lengths Abnormal Points	All-Time Rank	State Rank
	■ Location of Kill – Hunter – Owner – Date Killed										
174²/8	28¹/8	27⁵/8	23¹/8	25	5	5¹/8	8	5	3⁷/8	1652	186
	■ Jefferson Co. – James W. Ferguson – James W. Ferguson – 1997										
174¹/8	26⁵/8	26³/8	19⁵/8	22²/8	5³/8	5⁴/8	5	5		1678†	189†
	■ Allamakee Co. – Picked Up – IA Dept. of Natl. Resc. – 1998										
174¹/8	25⁶/8	26	18⁵/8	21¹/8	4⁶/8	4⁷/8	6	6		1678	189
	■ Iowa Co. – Ronald L. Brecht – Ronald L. Brecht – 1973										
174¹/8	27³/8	26⁴/8	18¹/8	20¹/8	5⁴/8	5⁴/8	5	6	2	1678	189
	■ Clarke Co. – Lee R. Lundstrom – Lee R. Lundstrom – 1987										
174¹/8	25⁴/8	24⁵/8	21⁵/8	24³/8	5¹/8	5¹/8	6	5		1678	189
	■ Dubuque Co. – James E. Beecher – James E. Beecher – 1998										
174¹/8	26⁴/8	25⁷/8	18¹/8	20⁵/8	5²/8	5³/8	7	7	6	1678	189
	■ Allamakee Co. – Hugh E. Conway – Hugh E. Conway – 1998										
174¹/8	25⁷/8	25²/8	16⁴/8	19	4⁷/8	5	6	8	9¹/8	1678	189
	■ Clayton Co. – Milo Rolfe – Milo Rolfe – 1998										
174	29²/8	28	21²/8	24	5²/8	5	5	5		1717	195
	■ Fayette Co. – Charles Schott – Charles Schott – 1982										
174	27⁵/8	28	24	25⁶/8	5	4⁷/8	5	5		1717	195
	■ Mills Co. – Rick W. Elliott – Rick W. Elliott – 1987										
174	26³/8	26²/8	17⁶/8	19²/8	4²/8	4²/8	6	6	2⁶/8	1717	195
	■ Harrison Co. – Ricky G. Seydel – Ricky G. Seydel – 1989										
173⁷/8	25⁴/8	25⁵/8	18⁷/8	21	4⁷/8	5¹/8	5	5		1743†	198†
	■ Appanoose Co. – Joel V. Ash – Joel V. Ash – 2001										
173⁷/8	25⁷/8	25⁷/8	20⁷/8	23²/8	5¹/8	4⁷/8	5	5		1743	198
	■ Floyd Co. – James R. Lines – James R. Lines – 1968										
173⁷/8	27	26¹/8	19³/8	21³/8	5⁶/8	5⁴/8	6	5	4	1743	198
	■ Henry Co. – Marion L. Shappell – Marion L. Shappell – 1970										
173⁷/8	23⁶/8	24⁴/8	17⁵/8	19⁵/8	4	3⁷/8	6	6		1743	198
	■ Allamakee Co. – Richard Gaunitz – Richard Gaunitz – 1990										
173⁷/8	28	26¹/8	21³/8	21³/8	5³/8	5²/8	5	5		1743	198
	■ Johnson Co. – Unknown – Ruth Waters – 1990										
173⁷/8	29²/8	30¹/8	24³/8	26³/8	4⁵/8	4⁵/8	6	6	2²/8	1743	198
	■ Appanoose Co. – Tim G. Anderson – Tim G. Anderson – 1997										
173⁷/8	29⁵/8	28⁶/8	22³/8	25⁷/8	4⁵/8	4⁷/8	5	7	10²/8	1743	198
	■ Union Co. – David Wetsch – David Wetsch – 1999										
173⁶/8	24³/8	23⁶/8	18²/8	20	4⁶/8	4⁴/8	6	7		1766	205
	■ Lucas Co. – James E. Wolfe – James E. Wolfe – 1964										
173⁶/8	26	25⁷/8	17⁴/8	20⁵/8	4⁷/8	4⁶/8	6	6		1766	205
	■ Johnson Co. – Godfrey Rhyme – William H. Lilienthal – PR 1968										
173⁶/8	25⁵/8	26¹/8	22¹/8	24³/8	4⁷/8	4⁷/8	6	5	3⁵/8	1766	205
	■ Des Moines Co. – Richard R. Hassell – Richard R. Hassell – 1979										
173⁶/8	26¹/8	25	21⁵/8	25⁶/8	4⁴/8	4⁴/8	6	5	1⁵/8	1766	205
	■ Winneshiek Co. – Herbert I. Amundson – Herbert I. Amundson – 1985										

Score	Length of Main Beam		Inside Spread	Greatest Spread	Circumference at Smallest Place Between Burr and First Point		Number of Points		Lengths Abnormal Points	All-Time Rank	State Rank
	Right	Left			Right	Left	Right	Left			
	■ *Location of Kill – Hunter – Owner – Date Killed*										
173⁶/8	29³/8	28⁴/8	20⁶/8	23	5⁵/8	5⁴/8	6	5	2²/8	1766	205
	■ *Mahaska Co. – Gareth P. VandeKieft – Gareth P. VandeKieft – 1988*										
173⁶/8	25³/8	26⁶/8	19³/8	22	4⁵/8	4⁵/8	6	5	6¹/8	1766	205
	■ *Warren Co. – Wayne E. Bueltel – Wayne E. Bueltel – 1989*										
173⁶/8	27¹/8	26⁴/8	20	21	5	5²/8	5	7	2⁶/8	1766	205
	■ *Clinton Co. – Picked Up – Wayne Fowler – 1992*										
173⁶/8	24⁷/8	24⁶/8	18²/8	20²/8	4⁶/8	4⁷/8	6	6		1766	205
	■ *Jasper Co. – Danny E. Keuning – Danny E. Keuning – 1992*										
173⁶/8	28³/8	27⁷/8	20⁷/8	23⁷/8	5¹/8	4⁷/8	6	6	4¹/8	1766	205
	■ *Louisa Co. – Todd J. Parsons – Todd J. Parsons – 1994*										
173⁶/8	25	24⁵/8	24⁴/8	26²/8	5²/8	5	5	5		1766	205
	■ *Clinton Co. – Patrick J. Hall – Patrick J. Hall – 1996*										
173⁶/8	26⁵/8	26⁵/8	20⁷/8	22⁷/8	5	5	7	7	3⁵/8	1766	205
	■ *Allamakee Co. – Joseph Lieb – Joseph Lieb – 1998*										
173⁶/8	26¹/8	26⁵/8	21³/8	24²/8	5⁶/8	5⁶/8	6	7	10-9/8	1766	205
	■ *Cherokee Co. – Robert L. Lundquist – Robert L. Lundquist – 1998*										
173⁵/8	25³/8	26	18⁵/8	20⁷/8	4⁷/8	4⁷/8	5	6	1²/8	1819	217
	■ *Plymouth Co. – Pat Kenaley – Pat Kenaley – 1986*										
173⁴/8	24	25²/8	18⁴/8	20³/8	4⁶/8	4⁶/8	6	6		1847†	218†
	■ *Clinton Co. – Picked Up – Steve Scharf – 1999*										
173⁴/8	26⁶/8	25⁶/8	22	24⁶/8	6¹/8	6²/8	5	5		1847†	218†
	■ *Decatur Co. – Picked Up – Bill J. Timms – 1999*										
173⁴/8	28	27⁴/8	21⁶/8	24⁴/8	4⁷/8	5¹/8	5	5		1847	218
	■ *Union Co. – Danny E. Abbott – Danny E. Abbott – 1966*										
173⁴/8	27⁴/8	29³/8	22	24	4⁵/8	4⁴/8	5	5		1847	218
	■ *Appanoose Co. – Randy Andreini – Randy Andreini – 1999*										
173⁴/8	30	28⁴/8	23²/8	25²/8	4⁷/8	4⁷/8	6	5		1847	218
	■ *Monroe Co. – Glen A. McElroy – Glen A. McElroy – 1999*										
173³/8	28⁷/8	28¹/8	19¹/8	21⁶/8	4⁷/8	5²/8	5	6	1⁴/8	1883	223
	■ *Monona Co. – Steve D. Maher – Steve D. Maher – 1986*										
173³/8	26¹/8	26³/8	21⁵/8	24	5	5²/8	5	5		1883	223
	■ *Jones Co. – Todd J. Rollinger – Todd J. Rollinger – 1997*										
173²/8	26³/8	25¹/8	20¹/8	22³/8	5	5¹/8	6	6	6³/8	1914†	225†
	■ *Harrison Co. – Troy Rath – Troy Rath – 2001*										
173²/8	26³/8	26⁶/8	17⁴/8	20⁴/8	5²/8	5²/8	5	5		1914	225
	■ *Woodbury Co. – Jim C. Jepson – Jim C. Jepson – 1990*										
173²/8	26⁶/8	26⁵/8	18²/8	21¹/8	4⁷/8	5	5	6		1914	225
	■ *Jackson Co. – Pat J. Schilling – Pat J. Schilling – 1996*										
173²/8	25²/8	24³/8	23²/8	25¹/8	5	5	5	5		1914	225
	■ *Marion Co. – Joseph C. Laird – Joseph C. Laird – 1998*										
173¹/8	26⁷/8	26³/8	20³/8	22⁶/8	4⁶/8	4⁵/8	5	5		1950†	229†
	■ *Clayton Co. – Alan E. Troester – Alan E. Troester – 2000*										

Score	Length of Main Beam		Inside Spread	Greatest Spread	Circumference at Smallest Place Between Burr and First Point		Number of Points		Lengths Abnormal Points	All-Time Rank	State Rank
	Right	Left			Right	Left	Right	Left			
	■ Location of Kill – Hunter – Owner – Date Killed										
173 1/8	25 5/8	26 2/8	19 1/8	21 1/8	4 7/8	4 6/8	6	6		1950	229
	■ Mahaska Co. – Ted Smith – Ted Smith – 1991										
173 1/8	24	24 4/8	21 1/8	23 4/8	5 2/8	5	5	5		1950	229
	■ Winneshiek Co. – Kenny J. White – Kenny J. White – 1995										
173	24	25 7/8	18 4/8	20 5/8	4 5/8	4 6/8	5	5		1991†	232†
	■ Crawford Co. – Picked Up – IA Dept. of Natl. Resc. – 1994										
173	27 1/8	27	21 1/8	23 5/8	5 2/8	5 2/8	7	6	1 3/8	1991	232
	■ Monroe Co. – Richard A. Bishop – Richard A. Bishop – 1992										
173	26 5/8	26 6/8	17	19 2/8	5 1/8	5 1/8	6	6		1991	232
	■ Davis Co. – Picked Up – James E. Pierceall – 1992										
173	27	26	20 4/8	23	5 2/8	5 1/8	7	9	8	1991	232
	■ Harrison Co. – Dell C. Wohlers – Dell C. Wohlers – 1996										
173	25 6/8	25 2/8	19 6/8	22 2/8	4 7/8	4 7/8	6	6		1991	232
	■ Allamakee Co. – Thomas E. Peters – Thomas E. Peters – 1997										
172 7/8	22 3/8	23	20	22	4 3/8	4 3/8	6	8	5 3/8	2038	237
	■ Dallas Co. – Gordon Cochran – Gordon Cochran – 1982										
172 7/8	29 3/8	28 4/8	24 7/8	28 2/8	4 7/8	4 7/8	7	4	4 4/8	2038	237
	■ Jackson Co. – Picked Up – Roy Rathje – 1989										
172 6/8	28 2/8	28	20 4/8	22 7/8	5 3/8	5 3/8	5	4		2065	239
	■ Louisa Co. – Merrill Flake – Monna B. Flake – 1974										
172 6/8	24 1/8	24 2/8	20 3/8	23 4/8	6	6	6	5	4 5/8	2065	239
	■ Boone Co. – Lonne L. Tracy – Lonne L. Tracy – 1975										
172 6/8	25 1/8	24 3/8	22 2/8	25 7/8	4 7/8	5 2/8	5	6	1 6/8	2065	239
	■ Allamakee Co. – Picked Up – Tom Kerndt, Sr. – 1976										
172 6/8	27 2/8	26 3/8	17 6/8	19 5/8	3 7/8	3 7/8	5	5		2065	239
	■ Mitchell Co. – Dan A. Block – Dan A. Block – 1981										
172 6/8	27 6/8	27 4/8	20 2/8	23 1/8	5 7/8	6 2/8	6	5	4	2065	239
	■ Fayette Co. – Greg P. Bordignon – Greg P. Bordignon – 1987										
172 6/8	25 4/8	25 4/8	17 4/8	19 5/8	4 6/8	4 5/8	6	7	2 4/8	2065	239
	■ Keokuk Co. – Michael A. Veres – Michael A. Veres – 1995										
172 5/8	26 6/8	27 1/8	22 3/8	24 5/8	5 1/8	5 2/8	4	4		2113	245
	■ Jackson Co. – Robert R. Morehead – Robert R. Morehead – 1990										
172 5/8	25 2/8	25 1/8	20 4/8	24 2/8	6 2/8	6	6	6	14 3/8	2113	245
	■ Crawford Co. – Picked Up – S.L. Reetz & J. Shumate – 1992										
172 5/8	25 7/8	27	18 3/8	20 4/8	4 3/8	4 2/8	5	5		2113	245
	■ Ringgold Co. – Herbert J. Weigel – Herbert J. Weigel – 1994										
172 5/8	30 4/8	28 5/8	18 7/8	20 7/8	4 7/8	5	5	4		2113	245
	■ Jones Co. – Johnny S. Cook – Johnny S. Cook – 1997										
172 4/8	23 5/8	24 3/8	19 6/8	21 5/8	5 1/8	5 1/8	5	5		2156†	249†
	■ Marion Co. – Richard P. Johnson – Richard P. Johnson – 2000										
172 4/8	24 4/8	24 7/8	23 6/8	25 3/8	4 5/8	4 5/8	5	5		2156†	249†
	■ Keokuk Co. – Michael D. Wells – Michael D. Wells – 2000										

Score	Length of Main Beam Right Left ■ Location of Kill – Hunter – Owner – Date Killed	Inside Spread	Greatest Spread	Circumference at Smallest Place Between Burr and First Point Right Left		Number of Points Right Left		Lengths Abnormal Points	All-Time Rank	State Rank
172⁴/8	26²/8 25⁴/8	17⁶/8	20	4⁵/8	4⁵/8	6	8	6²/8	2156	249
	■ Ringgold Co. – Edward D. Miller – Edward D. Miller – 1991									
172⁴/8	26²/8 26⁵/8	21	23⁵/8	4⁶/8	4⁶/8	5	5		2156	249
	■ Lucas Co. – Perry Klages, Jr. – Perry L. Klages, Jr. – 1994									
172⁴/8	27¹/8 27²/8	24	26	4⁶/8	4⁶/8	5	5		2156	249
	■ Muscatine Co. – John D. Russell – John D. Russell – 1997									
172⁴/8	28⁴/8 28²/8	19⁵/8	21⁷/8	4²/8	4¹/8	5	6	2¹/8	2156	249
	■ Fayette Co. – Rick L. Taylor – Rick L. Taylor – 1998									
172⁴/8	24⁵/8 25⁴/8	21¹/8	23⁷/8	5	5	7	5	2³/8	2156	249
	■ Dubuque Co. – Steven W. Berkley – Steven W. Berkley – 1999									
172³/8	27⁶/8 26⁷/8	18	23²/8	5⁶/8	5²/8	7	7	9³/8	2200	256
	■ Boone Co. – Kevin A. Anderson – Kevin A. Anderson – 1989									
172³/8	26³/8 26¹/8	19¹/8	21¹/8	4⁶/8	4⁷/8	6	5	2⁶/8	2200	256
	■ Monona Co. – Larry Hieber – Larry Hieber – 1989									
172³/8	25 25²/8	22⁵/8	24³/8	5	4⁷/8	6	6	8⁴/8	2200	256
	■ Des Moines Co. – Colin J. Gerst – Colin J. Gerst – 1997									
172²/8	27¹/8 27	22	24²/8	5³/8	5	5	5		2237	259
	■ Jefferson Co. – Paul Hagist, Jr. – Paul Hagist, Jr. – 1986									
172²/8	27⁵/8 27⁶/8	19⁴/8	22⁴/8	4	4²/8	5	5		2237	259
	■ Scott Co. – Patrick D. Willhoite – Patrick D. Willhoite – 1994									
172²/8	26²/8 26	22⁴/8	24⁴/8	4⁶/8	4⁷/8	6	5		2237	259
	■ Clayton Co. – Scott L. Doerring – Scott L. Doerring – 1995									
172²/8	26 25⁷/8	19⁷/8	22⁶/8	5	5	7	5	5⁵/8	2237	259
	■ Lee Co. – Chris L. Schiller – Chris L. Schiller – 1995									
172¹/8	25⁶/8 25⁴/8	22³/8	42²/8	5²/8	5⁴/8	5	5		2286†	263†
	■ Van Buren Co. – Picked Up – Bob McWilliams – 2001									
172¹/8	26¹/8 25	18⁵/8	21²/8	5⁵/8	5⁵/8	8	7	4	2286	263
	■ Clinton Co. – R. Dean Grimes – R. Dean Grimes – 1984									
172¹/8	24¹/8 24⁵/8	19⁶/8	22	5³/8	5³/8	7	7	3⁷/8	2286	263
	■ Louisa Co. – John Bloomer – John Bloomer – 1987									
172¹/8	24²/8 23⁷/8	18¹/8	20¹/8	4⁵/8	4⁴/8	6	6		2286	263
	■ Harrison Co. – Picked Up – Chad M. Kuhns – 1994									
172¹/8	27²/8 26⁷/8	21	23	5¹/8	5²/8	7	5	1¹/8	2286	263
	■ Jefferson Co. – Joe F. Arndt – Joe F. Arndt – 1997									
172¹/8	26³/8 26¹/8	20¹/8	23	5	5³/8	6	5	5⁶/8	2286	263
	■ Keokuk Co. – Ric L. Bishop – Ric L. Bishop – 1997									
172¹/8	25⁵/8 24¹/8	22⁵/8	24⁶/8	4⁴/8	4⁴/8	6	6		2286	263
	■ Monroe Co. – Jeffrey A. Butler – Jeffrey A. Butler – 1999									
172	25⁶/8 26⁷/8	24²/8	27¹/8	5²/8	5¹/8	6	6		2330	270
	■ Woodbury Co. – Harold Horsley – Harold Horsley – 1956									
172	26²/8 26²/8	20	23	4⁵/8	4⁴/8	7	5	1⁶/8	2330	270
	■ Fayette Co. – Robert Goad – Robert Goad – 1996									

Score	Length of Main Beam Right	Left	Inside Spread	Greatest Spread	Circumference at Smallest Place Between Burr and First Point Right	Left	Number of Points Right	Left	Lengths Abnormal Points	All-Time Rank	State Rank
	■ Location of Kill – Hunter – Owner – Date Killed										
172	26 2/8	26 2/8	19 2/8	21 4/8	4 6/8	4 6/8	5	5		2330	270
	■ Delaware Co. – Charles E. Fessler – Charles E. Fessler – 1997										
172	25 5/8	25 4/8	20 4/8	22 5/8	5 4/8	5 4/8	7	9	11 2/8	2330	270
	■ Jefferson Co. – Brandon Slaubaugh – Brandon Slaubaugh – 1998										
171 7/8	25 4/8	25 5/8	18 4/8	22 7/8	5	5 3/8	6	7	1 1/8	2382	274
	■ Union Co. – Darrell M. Gutz – Darrell M. Gutz – 1973										
171 7/8	26	26 1/8	20 3/8	23 2/8	5 1/8	5	5	5		2382	274
	■ Clayton Co. – Michael A. Roussel – Michael A. Roussel – 1986										
171 7/8	27 5/8	26 6/8	21 5/8	23 6/8	4 4/8	4 3/8	6	6	1 2/8	2382	274
	■ Lucas Co. – Tim M. Whitlatch – Tim M. Whitlatch – 1989										
171 7/8	25 5/8	24 6/8	16 5/8	18 6/8	5	5 1/8	5	5		2382	274
	■ Winneshiek Co. – Richard A. Bollman – Richard A. Bollman – 1993										
171 7/8	29 6/8	30 3/8	21 3/8	23 7/8	4 6/8	4 5/8	5	6	4 6/8	2382	274
	■ Jones Co. – Michael L. First – Michael L. First – 1993										
171 6/8	27	27	16 2/8		4 3/8	4 5/8	5	5	1	2418†	279†
	■ Linn Co. – Picked Up – IA Dept. of Natl. Resc. – 1996										
171 6/8	28 4/8	29 3/8	21 6/8	24 4/8	4 4/8	4 4/8	4	4		2418†	279†
	■ Linn Co. – Gerald R. Peters – Gerald R. Peters – 2001										
171 6/8	24 4/8	24 3/8	17 1/8	20 2/8	4 1/8	4 1/8	8	8	3 5/8	2418	279
	■ Muscatine Co. – Larry Dipple – Larry Dipple – 1967										
171 6/8	28 1/8	28 1/8	22 1/8	24	5 2/8	5 1/8	6	5	2 7/8	2418	279
	■ Jackson Co. – Rodger L. Johnson – Rodger L. Johnson – 1995										
171 6/8	28 4/8	28 4/8	24 4/8	26 3/8	5	5 1/8	7	9	4 4/8	2418	279
	■ Allamakee Co. – Gregg N. Klein – Gregg N. Klein – 1995										
171 5/8	26 7/8	26 3/8	21 7/8	25 1/8	5 1/8	5	5	5		2470†	284†
	■ Allamakee Co. – John E. Wood – John E. Wood – 2000										
171 5/8	27 1/8	25 7/8	20	22 4/8	4 7/8	5	6	5	3 1/8	2470	284
	■ Pocahontas Co. – Larry G. Almond – Larry G. Almond – 1983										
171 5/8	27 4/8	27 7/8	18 1/8	20 2/8	4 7/8	4 5/8	5	5		2470	284
	■ Lucas Co. – Picked Up – Harry Nicholson – 1995										
171 5/8	25 2/8	26	22 5/8	25	5 5/8	5 4/8	5	5		2470	284
	■ Fremont Co. – Ryan T. Knapp – Ryan T. Knapp – 1996										
171 5/8	26 5/8	24 5/8	18 4/8	21 3/8	5	5 2/8	7	6	1 5/8	2470	284
	■ Clayton Co. – Chris M. Borcherding – Chris M. Borcherding – 1997										
171 4/8	28 6/8	28 7/8	22 7/8	25 4/8	5 1/8	5	5	5	1 1/8	2513	289
	■ Hamilton Co. – Picked Up – Jerry Price – 1972										
171 4/8	27	26	16	18 1/8	4 2/8	4 2/8	6	5		2513	289
	■ Iowa – Unknown – William H. Lilienthal – PR 1991										
171 4/8	25 5/8	26 1/8	21 4/8	24 1/8	4 7/8	5	5	5		2513	289
	■ Scott Co. – William H. Fahrenkrog – William H. Fahrenkrog – 1998										
171 3/8	26	26 3/8	20 1/8	22 1/8	4 4/8	4 6/8	5	5		2564	292
	■ Monroe Co. – Michael L. DeMoss – Michael L. DeMoss – 1997										

Score	Length of Main Beam Right	Left	Inside Spread	Greatest Spread	Circumference at Smallest Place Between Burr and First Point Right	Left	Number of Points Right	Left	Lengths Abnormal Points	All-Time Rank	State Rank
	Location of Kill – Hunter – Owner – Date Killed										
171²/8	27²/8	26⁵/8	22¹/8	24¹/8	5⁵/8	5²/8	6	7	1⁷/8	2621†	293†
	■ Warren Co. – David G.J. Milby – David G.J. Milby – 2000										
171²/8	26⁴/8	26⁶/8	20³/8	24¹/8	4⁵/8	4⁵/8	7	6	6¹/8	2621	293
	■ O'Brien Co. – George Sleeper – William H. Lilienthal – 1959										
171²/8	26	26	18	20¹/8	5	5⁵/8	7	6	4	2621	293
	■ Lucas Co. – James L. Barlow – James L. Barlow – 1985										
171²/8	29⁶/8	27⁴/8	22⁴/8	24⁶/8	4⁶/8	4⁶/8	5	5		2621	293
	■ Ringgold Co. – John H. Good – John H. Good – 1988										
171²/8	26²/8	26¹/8	21²/8	24¹/8	5	5²/8	5	5		2621	293
	■ Marshall Co. – Dale E. Smith – Dale E. Smith – 1988										
171²/8	25¹/8	23²/8	20⁶/8	22⁴/8	6	5⁷/8	5	6		2621	293
	■ Adams Co. – Gary D. Maatsch – Gary D. Maatsch – 1990										
171²/8	25	26³/8	20⁶/8	23⁴/8	4⁴/8	4⁴/8	5	5		2621	293
	■ Union Co. – Trevor Paulus – Trevor Paulus – 1996										
171²/8	25⁶/8	24⁵/8	18²/8	20⁴/8	5¹/8	4⁷/8	5	5		2621	293
	■ Benton Co. – Timothy McLaud – Timothy McLaud – 1997										
171¹/8	28¹/8	28¹/8	23³/8	25³/8	4⁶/8	4⁵/8	5	5		2665†	301†
	■ Fayette Co. – Gerald D. Miller – Gerald D. Miller – 2001										
171¹/8	26¹/8	26²/8	22⁷/8	25¹/8	5⁶/8	6⁴/8	5	5	2	2665	301
	■ Van Buren Co. – Walter S. Church – Walter S. Church – 1988										
171¹/8	23⁷/8	23⁴/8	19³/8	21⁴/8	5¹/8	5¹/8	5	5		2665	301
	■ Ringgold Co. – Darren Martin – Darren Martin – 1998										
171	27	26⁵/8	20²/8	22³/8	4³/8	4³/8	6	6		2707	304
	■ Delaware Co. – G. Covington & A. Schnittjer – Greg Covington – 1986										
171	27²/8	26⁴/8	23⁴/8	25⁵/8	5²/8	5⁴/8	5	5		2707	304
	■ Davis Co. – Picked Up – IA Dept. of Natl. Resc. – 1991										
171	25³/8	24³/8	18⁵/8	21	4⁴/8	4⁴/8	6	6	4³/8	2707	304
	■ Union Co. – Steven A. Wearmouth – Steven A. Wearmouth – 1995										
171	28⁵/8	28	21	24⁷/8	5¹/8	5	7	8	7²/8	2707	304
	■ Palo Alto Co. – Paul R. Demiter – Paul R. Demiter – 1998										
170⁷/8	30	30	20²/8	22⁴/8	5	5	5	8	10³/8	2769	308
	■ Des Moines Co. – Craig A. Field – Craig A. Field – 1967										
170⁷/8	23⁷/8	25⁵/8	22	23⁵/8	5¹/8	5¹/8	7	7	9¹/8	2769	308
	■ Henry Co. – Lewis E. Dallmeyer – Lewis E. Dallmeyer – 1981										
170⁷/8	27²/8	26⁵/8	22²/8	24¹/8	5²/8	5²/8	8	6	7³/8	2769	308
	■ Warren Co. – Gary L. Johnson – Gary L. Johnson – 1981										
170⁷/8	28⁵/8	28⁶/8	26²/8	28⁵/8	5³/8	5²/8	5	5	1³/8	2769	308
	■ Jackson Co. – Clarence E. Gartman – Clarence E. Gartman – 1989										
170⁷/8	26⁴/8	25⁶/8	19²/8	23¹/8	5¹/8	5²/8	7	5	3⁵/8	2769	308
	■ Monona Co. – Byron S. Mesenbrink – Byron S. Mesenbrink – 1989										
170⁷/8	27⁴/8	26⁵/8	21⁵/8	23	5	5	6	8	12	2769	308
	■ Wapello Co. – Ray L. Schafer – Ray L. Schafer – 1990										

Score	Length of Main Beam Right	Length of Main Beam Left	Inside Spread	Greatest Spread	Circumference at Smallest Place Between Burr and First Point Right	Circumference at Smallest Place Between Burr and First Point Left	Number of Points Right	Number of Points Left	Lengths Abnormal Points	All-Time Rank	State Rank
									■ *Location of Kill – Hunter – Owner – Date Killed*		
170 7/8	26 3/8	26 5/8	20 5/8	22 6/8	4 6/8	4 6/8	5	5		2769	308
	■ *Des Moines Co. – Timothy Verhey – Timothy Verhey – 1992*										
170 6/8	25 5/8	25 2/8	18 6/8	21	4 3/8	4 3/8	5	5		2828†	315†
	■ *Monona Co. – James White – George Waters – PR 2000*										
170 6/8	26	25	19 6/8	22 1/8	5 4/8	5 4/8	5	5		2828	315
	■ *Montgomery Co. – Steve Philby – Steve Philby – 1997*										
170 5/8	28 1/8	27 1/8	24 5/8	26 6/8	5 2/8	5 1/8	6	7	6 2/8	2876	317
	■ *Cedar Co. – Robert G. Grunder – Robert G. Grunder – 1974*										
170 5/8	26 2/8	26 6/8	20 5/8	22 5/8	5	5	5	5		2876	317
	■ *Clayton Co. – Todd A. Moon – Todd A. Moon – 1979*										
170 5/8	24 6/8	25 1/8	20 6/8	23 4/8	4 5/8	4 4/8	7	8	9 5/8	2876	317
	■ *Henry Co. – Michael S. Mathews – Michael S. Mathews – 1988*										
170 5/8	28 1/8	27 5/8	21 3/8	23 5/8	5 1/8	4 7/8	5	5		2876	317
	■ *Monona Co. – Unknown – George Waters – 1993*										
170 5/8	26 7/8	25 7/8	18 5/8	23 4/8	5 1/8	5 1/8	6	6	2	2876	317
	■ *Warren Co. – Martin L. Gehringer – Martin L. Gehringer – 1995*										
170 5/8	25 7/8	25 6/8	23 1/8	25	4 7/8	4 5/8	5	5		2876	317
	■ *Clayton Co. – Jerry E. Morris – Jerry E. Morris – 1998*										
170 4/8	25 3/8	25 4/8	18 5/8	21	5 6/8	5 6/8	7	5	5 5/8	2933†	323†
	■ *Warren Co. – George H. Eckstrom II – George H. Eckstrom II – 2000*										
170 4/8	26	25 3/8	19	22 3/8	4 2/8	4 2/8	6	8	6 2/8	2933	323
	■ *Henry Co. – Gerald Bailey – Gerald Bailey – 1970*										
170 4/8	25 6/8	25 2/8	17	19 4/8	4 5/8	4 6/8	6	7	2	2933	323
	■ *Madison Co. – Merle Allen – Merle Allen – 1984*										
170 4/8	25 2/8	24 7/8	17 6/8	20	4 7/8	5	5	5	1 2/8	2933	323
	■ *Taylor Co. – Picked Up – Jim Haas – 1987*										
170 4/8	26 1/8	26 5/8	20 5/8	25 5/8	4 6/8	4 5/8	7	5	3 5/8	2933	323
	■ *Des Moines Co. – Lewis Mehaffy – Lewis Mehaffy – 1987*										
170 4/8	26 4/8	28	18 5/8	22 7/8	4 3/8	4 3/8	6	6	4 1/8	2933	323
	■ *Clinton Co. – Scott Jacobsen – Scott Jacobsen – 1989*										
170 4/8	25 5/8	25 3/8	19 6/8	22 7/8	5 2/8	5 2/8	7	6	10	2933	323
	■ *Appanoose Co. – John M. Aiello – John M. Aiello – 1994*										
170 4/8	28 1/8	28	22 2/8	24 3/8	5 2/8	5 3/8	5	5		2933	323
	■ *Lucas Co. – Rick L. Mitchell – Rick L. Mitchell – 1997*										
170 3/8	25 5/8	26 3/8	17 7/8	20	4 4/8	4 4/8	6	5	1 4/8	2992	331
	■ *Decatur Co. – Julian J. Toney – Julian J. Toney – 1982*										
170 3/8	27 1/8	27 5/8	20 1/8	22 6/8	5 1/8	4 7/8	5	5		2992	331
	■ *Warren Co. – Lanny Caligiuri – Lanny Caligiuri – 1990*										
170 3/8	28 3/8	28 1/8	21 5/8	23 5/8	4 6/8	4 5/8	6	6	4	2992	331
	■ *Dubuque Co. – Richard S. Hillard – Richard S. Hillard – 1990*										
170 3/8	27 3/8	28 4/8	18 5/8	20 6/8	4 5/8	4 6/8	7	6	2 2/8	2992	331
	■ *Howard Co. – Clarence Mincks – Clarence Mincks – 1991*										

Score	Length of Main Beam		Inside Spread	Greatest Spread	Circumference at Smallest Place Between Burr and First Point		Number of Points		Lengths Abnormal Points	All-Time Rank	State Rank
	Right	Left			Right	Left	Right	Left			
	■ Location of Kill – Hunter – Owner – Date Killed										

170³/8	26¹/8	27⁶/8	20⁶/8	22⁶/8	4⁵/8	4⁶/8	5	6	1³/8	2992	331
	■ Warren Co. – Bruce L. Hupke – Bruce L. Hupke – 1994										
170²/8	25⁵/8	25³/8	20¹/8	22⁴/8	4⁶/8	4⁷/8	7	6	6¹/8	3063†	336†
	■ Monroe Co. – Vince L. Feehan – Vince L. Feehan – 2001										
170²/8	28¹/8	29²/8	20⁴/8	24⁵/8	5⁶/8	5⁴/8	9	7	10	3063†	336†
	■ Clinton Co. – Kiner Giddings – Kiner Giddings – 2001										
170²/8	25³/8	25⁵/8	18⁴/8	20⁴/8	4⁵/8	4⁴/8	5	6	4²/8	3063	336
	■ Adair Co. – Gale D. Johnston – Gale D. Johnston – 1984										
170²/8	24⁷/8	24²/8	19⁶/8	22⁷/8	5	4⁷/8	5	5		3063	336
	■ Winneshiek Co. – David Hageman – David Hageman – 1988										
170²/8	25⁴/8	26¹/8	19¹/8	21³/8	5⁴/8	5⁵/8	5	6	2¹/8	3063	336
	■ Clayton Co. – Myles T. Keller – Myles T. Keller – 1989										
170²/8	27⁵/8	27⁴/8	19⁶/8	22⁴/8	4⁷/8	4⁶/8	4	5		3063	336
	■ Page Co. – Arlen D. Meyer – Arlen D. Meyer – 1993										
170²/8	26³/8	26⁴/8	19⁷/8	22¹/8	4³/8	4⁵/8	6	7	7³/8	3063	336
	■ Van Buren Co. – Dennis R. Besick – Dennis R. Besick – 1994										
170²/8	26⁷/8	26²/8	19³/8	22⁵/8	4⁷/8	5²/8	6	6	2¹/8	3063	336
	■ Clayton Co. – Randy D. Reck – Randy D. Reck – 1997										
170²/8	24	24⁶/8	18⁶/8	20⁴/8	4³/8	4⁴/8	6	6		3063	336
	■ Davis Co. – Richard C. Riggenbach – Richard C. Riggenbach – 1997										
170¹/8	29	29¹/8	19⁴/8	21⁶/8	5	4⁷/8	8	6	5¹/8	3143†	345†
	■ Allamakee Co. – Gary W. Anfinson – Gary W. Anfinson – 2000										
170¹/8	24²/8	25⁴/8	15³/8	19	6	5⁷/8	5	5	1⁶/8	3143	345
	■ Iowa Co. – Edward E. Best – Edward E. Best – 1972										
170¹/8	24⁵/8	25⁴/8	19	21⁴/8	5⁵/8	4⁴/8	7	5	1¹/8	3143	345
	■ Warren Co. – Arnold J. Hoch – Arnold J. Hoch – 1975										
170¹/8	22³/8	22³/8	15⁵/8	17⁵/8	5³/8	5²/8	5	5		3143	345
	■ Greene Co. – Charles Gunn – Charles Gunn – 1986										
170¹/8	24⁷/8	26	18⁶/8	21	4⁷/8	4⁶/8	6	7	1¹/8	3143	345
	■ Allamakee Co. – Eric W. Thorstenson – Cabela's, Inc. – 1995										
170¹/8	26⁴/8	26¹/8	19⁵/8	22³/8	4⁶/8	4⁵/8	6	5		3143	345
	■ Clayton Co. – Thomas G. Baumgartner – Thomas G. Baumgartner – 1996										
170	28²/8	27⁴/8	19²/8	21⁴/8	5	5²/8	5	6	2	3224†	351†
	■ Clayton Co. – Kenneth D. Gossman – Darlene Gossman – 1955										
170	27	26¹/8	23⁴/8	25⁴/8	5²/8	5⁴/8	5	5		3224†	351†
	■ Davis Co. – Picked Up – IA Dept. of Natl. Resc. – 1991										
170	25³/8	26⁷/8	19³/8	25¹/8	4⁴/8	4⁵/8	7	6	3⁷/8	3224	351
	■ Des Moines Co. – Dean A. Dravis – Dean A. Dravis – 1983										
170	26²/8	26⁶/8	20²/8	22⁴/8	4⁷/8	4⁵/8	5	7	5⁶/8	3224	351
	■ Wapello Co. – George C. Ellis – George C. Ellis – 1984										
170	25⁶/8	25⁶/8	16⁵/8	18⁵/8	4⁷/8	5	5	8	3³/8	3224	351
	■ Harrison Co. – Rodney P. Stahlnecker – Rodney P. Stahlnecker – 1984										

Score	Length of Main Beam Right Left	Inside Spread	Greatest Spread	Circumference at Smallest Place Between Burr and First Point Right Left	Number of Points Right Left	Lengths Abnormal Points	All-Time Rank	State Rank
	■ Location of Kill – Hunter – Owner – Date Killed							
170	26⁷/₈ 27²/₈	20⁴/₈	23⁶/₈	5⁴/₈ 5⁶/₈	5 5		3224	351
	■ Jones Co. – James L. Coyle – James L. Coyle – 1988							
170	28⁴/₈ 26⁷/₈	20	23³/₈	4⁴/₈ 4⁴/₈	5 5		3224	351
	■ Madison Co. – Terry L. Snyder – Terry L. Snyder – 1989							
170	26 26¹/₈	19²/₈	22²/₈	4²/₈ 4²/₈	7 5	5	3224	351
	■ Webster Co. – Picked Up – Clare E. Bailey – 1990							
170	25²/₈ 26²/₈	20³/₈	23	5¹/₈ 5²/₈	9 7	8⁵/₈	3224	351
	■ Montgomery Co. – Jerry A. Foote – Jerry A. Foote – 1991							
170	23⁷/₈ 23⁷/₈	18²/₈	24	5²/₈ 6	6 7	6²/₈	3224	351
	■ Marion Co. – Helen Hall – Helen Hall – 1991							
170	24⁴/₈ 23⁷/₈	17	20²/₈	4²/₈ 4²/₈	5 5		3224	351
	■ Allamakee Co. – Lloyd O. Griffith – Lloyd O. Griffith – 1998							
170	26⁵/₈ 27³/₈	20⁵/₈	22⁶/₈	4⁶/₈ 4⁴/₈	5 6	1⁷/₈	3224	351
	■ Cherokee Co. – Ben R. Puttmann – Ben R. Puttmann – 1998							
170	25¹/₈ 25¹/₈	20⁷/₈	23³/₈	5³/₈ 5³/₈	7 5	3¹/₈	3224	351
	■ Cedar Co. – Ronald R. Cain – Ronald R. Cain – 1999							
169⁶/₈	27¹/₈ 27	18⁶/₈	21²/₈	4⁷/₈ 4⁷/₈	5 5		3306	364
	■ Allamakee Co. – Kevin McKee – Kevin McKee – 1994							
169³/₈	23⁴/₈ 23⁴/₈	19⁷/₈	21⁶/₈	5⁵/₈ 5⁶/₈	6 7	4⁶/₈	3324†	365†
	■ Marshall Co. – Matthew J. DeSchamp – Matthew J. DeSchamp – 2000							
169	24⁵/₈ 24⁴/₈	20⁶/₈	22⁵/₈	4⁶/₈ 4⁵/₈	6 6	4	3348	366
	■ Dickinson Co. – Ronny Hartwig – Ronny Hartwig – 1973							
168⁶/₈	27¹/₈ 26¹/₈	19⁴/₈	21⁷/₈	5 4⁷/₈	5 6		3367	367
	■ Davis Co. – Brent L. Ludwick – Brent L. Ludwick – 1995							
168⁴/₈	25⁵/₈ 24⁴/₈	18⁴/₈	20⁷/₈	4⁷/₈ 4⁷/₈	5 7	1⁴/₈	3385	368
	■ Van Buren Co. – Alan J. Andrews – Alan J. Andrews – 1995							
168³/₈	26²/₈ 26⁴/₈	22²/₈	24⁷/₈	5²/₈ 5⁴/₈	6 4	1³/₈	3399†	369†
	■ Marion Co. – Randy G. Manuel, Sr. – Randy G. Manuel, Sr. – 1999							
168¹/₈	25⁷/₈ 25⁴/₈	19⁷/₈	22³/₈	5⁴/₈ 5⁴/₈	4 4		3426	370
	■ Mills Co. – Dallas M. Moore – Dallas M. Moore – 1986							
168	24⁶/₈ 23	19	24	5²/₈ 5²/₈	6 8	3⁶/₈	3443	371
	■ Clayton Co. – John F. Miculinich – John F. Miculinich – 1995							
168	26⁴/₈ 26⁶/₈	19⁴/₈	21⁶/₈	4⁴/₈ 4⁴/₈	5 5		3443	371
	■ Monroe Co. – Jason Morgan – Jason Morgan – 1995							
167⁶/₈	24¹/₈ 25¹/₈	20⁴/₈	23¹/₈	5³/₈ 5²/₈	5 5		3461†	373†
	■ Jackson Co. – Dan Oberfoell – Dan Oberfoell – 2001							
166⁶/₈	24³/₈ 24³/₈	19	21¹/₈	3⁷/₈ 3⁷/₈	5 5		3582†	374†
	■ Jefferson Co. – Terry J. Hammes – Terry J. Hammes – 2000							
166⁶/₈	26⁶/₈ 26¹/₈	18⁶/₈	21²/₈	5⁵/₈ 5⁶/₈	9 6	8²/₈	3582	374
	■ Polk Co. – Chris P. Ruggeri – Chris P. Ruggeri – 1994							
166⁶/₈	26⁴/₈ 25²/₈	20⁶/₈	22⁷/₈	4⁶/₈ 5	5 5		3582	374
	■ Lee Co. – John M. Pratt – John M. Pratt – 1995							

Score	Length of Main Beam Right	Left	Inside Spread	Greatest Spread	Circumference at Smallest Place Between Burr and First Point Right	Left	Number of Points Right	Left	Lengths Abnormal Points	All-Time Rank	State Rank
164⁴/₈	26²/₈	25⁵/₈	22³/₈	24²/₈	5¹/₈	5³/₈	4	5	1¹/₈	3609	377
■ Winneshiek Co. – Jeffrey P. Berns – Jeffrey P. Berns – 1996											
166¹/₈	25³/₈	27²/₈	18⁶/₈	21³/₈	4⁵/₈	4⁴/₈	5	6	1⁵/₈	3643	378
■ Boone Co. – O. Scot DeShong – O. Scot DeShong – 1990											
166¹/₈	25⁵/₈	26⁶/₈	19¹/₈	21³/₈	4⁷/₈	5	6	5		3643	378
■ Washington Co. – Allen D. Chapman – Allen D. Chapman – 1995											
165⁶/₈	24⁶/₈	25⁴/₈	20⁴/₈	22⁴/₈	5²/₈	5²/₈	5	5		3680†	380†
■ Appanoose Co. – Melvin T. Digman – Melvin T. Digman – 2000											
165⁵/₈	24³/₈	23³/₈	23²/₈	26¹/₈	5⁶/₈	5⁶/₈	6	5	2¹/₈	3696†	381†
■ Clayton Co. – Michael L. Hertges – Michael L. Hertges – 2000											
165⁵/₈	28²/₈	29²/₈	22⁴/₈	28²/₈	5⁶/₈	5⁶/₈	4	6	5³/₈	3696†	381†
■ Adams Co. – Kenneth D. Toms – Kenneth D. Toms – 2000											
165²/₈	25	25⁶/₈	18	22⁴/₈	5²/₈	5²/₈	6	6	3²/₈	3748	383
■ Van Buren Co. – Richard W. Steinke – Richard W. Steinke – 1978											
165²/₈	25	24⁷/₈	19⁴/₈	20²/₈	4¹/₈	4¹/₈	5	5		3748	383
■ Carroll Co. – Gary Riesselman – Gary Riesselman – 1999											
164⁷/₈	28¹/₈	28¹/₈	19³/₈	22⁶/₈	4⁵/₈	4⁶/₈	8	8	8²/₈	3792	385
■ Fayette Co. – Charley Daisy – Charley Daisy – 1988											
164⁴/₈	25³/₈	25⁵/₈	22⁶/₈	24⁶/₈	4⁶/₈	4⁶/₈	5	5		3855	386
■ Louisa Co. – Jeffrey R. Wilson – Jeffrey R. Wilson – 1987											
164³/₈	24⁷/₈	26²/₈	21⁴/₈	28⁴/₈	5	5¹/₈	7	5	5⁵/₈	3864	387
■ Dubuque Co. – Richard R. Herbst – Richard R. Herbst – 1997											
164¹/₈	26¹/₈	26⁶/₈	21⁵/₈	24⁷/₈	4⁴/₈	4⁴/₈	6	5	1²/₈	3886	388
■ Fayette Co. – Clayton C. Avenson – Clayton C. Avenson – 1989											
164	28⁶/₈	28²/₈	18⁴/₈	20⁶/₈	4⁶/₈	4⁷/₈	4	4		3908†	389†
■ Madison Co. – Raymond Dawson – Raymond Dawson – 2001											
164	26	27⁴/₈	23	25⁷/₈	5⁴/₈	5⁵/₈	6	5	1²/₈	3908†	389†
■ Benton Co. – Brett Pollock – Brett Pollock – 2000											
163⁶/₈	24⁴/₈	25¹/₈	17⁶/₈	19⁷/₈	5¹/₈	5²/₈	5	5		3946	391
■ Lee Co. – Troy Matter – Troy Matter – 1995											
163⁵/₈	24⁷/₈	25⁵/₈	21¹/₈	24⁵/₈	4²/₈	4²/₈	5	5		3961	392
■ Dubuque Co. – Jamey J. Streif – Jamey M. Streif – 1999											
163⁴/₈	24⁷/₈	24¹/₈	16⁷/₈	19¹/₈	4⁶/₈	4⁷/₈	6	6	2⁵/₈	3984	393
■ Wapello Co. – Sean E. Ide – Sean E. Ide – 1989											
163⁴/₈	28⁶/₈	27⁷/₈	21²/₈	23³/₈	4⁵/₈	4⁴/₈	4	5		3984	393
■ Guthrie Co. – Matthew J. Ewing – Matthew J. Ewing – 1996											
163³/₈	23⁴/₈	25⁴/₈	19³/₈	21⁴/₈	5³/₈	5³/₈	5	6	4²/₈	4002†	395†
■ Jefferson Co. – Bryan D. Manor – Bryan D. Manor – 2001											
163³/₈	25⁴/₈	24⁷/₈	17³/₈	19⁵/₈	4²/₈	4³/₈	5	5		4002	395
■ Jones Co. – James D. Hedley – James D. Hedley – 1997											
163³/₈	26⁴/₈	26⁷/₈	21⁴/₈	24	5¹/₈	4⁶/₈	7	6	6³/₈	4002	395
■ Jackson Co. – Doug J. Lange – Doug J. Lange – 1999											

Score	Length of Main Beam Right Left	Inside Spread	Greatest Spread	Circumference at Smallest Place Between Burr and First Point Right Left	Number of Points Right Left	Lengths Abnormal Points	All-Time Rank	State Rank
	■ Location of Kill – Hunter – Owner – Date Killed							
163²/₈	27⁵/₈ 28³/₈	24	27⁴/₈	5¹/₈ 5³/₈	4 4		4017†	398†
	■ Linn Co. – Trent L. Packingham – Trent L. Packingham – 2001							
163²/₈	26³/₈ 24²/₈	17²/₈	19²/₈	4⁵/₈ 4⁷/₈	5 6	2⁶/₈	4017	398
	■ Keokuk Co. – Dennis J. Hammes – Dennis J. Hammes – 1994							
163	26⁴/₈ 25²/₈	19⁷/₈	22²/₈	4⁷/₈ 5	6 5	3³/₈	4051	400
	■ Washington Co. – Joseph Goodell – Joseph Goodell – 1998							
163	27³/₈ 27⁵/₈	19⁶/₈	22⁴/₈	4³/₈ 4⁵/₈	4 6	3²/₈	4051	400
	■ Jones Co. – Ryan F. Frasher – Ryan F. Frasher – 1999							
162⁷/₈	25⁷/₈ 26³/₈	18⁶/₈	21	5 5	7 6	4⁵/₈	4067†	402†
	■ Jasper Co. – Ronald W. Brown – Ronald W. Brown – 2001							
162⁷/₈	23³/₈ 23³/₈	18⁵/₈	21⁴/₈	5¹/₈ 5²/₈	6 5	3²/₈	4067	402
	■ Plymouth Co. – Brandon S. Youngstrom – Brandon S. Youngstrom – 1998							
162⁶/₈	26¹/₈ 25²/₈	17²/₈	19²/₈	4⁴/₈ 4⁷/₈	6 5	7²/₈	4089	404
	■ Muscatine Co. – David W. Howell – David W. Howell – 1987							
162²/₈	23⁵/₈ 22²/₈	20	22	5²/₈ 5¹/₈	6 6		4153	405
	■ Guthrie Co. – James J. Cowan – James J. Cowan – 1999							
162	20 24⁵/₈	21	24²/₈	4³/₈ 4⁴/₈	5 6	5	4184	406
	■ Mahaska Co. – David T. Woodard – David T. Woodard – 1990							
162	24⁷/₈ 23⁶/₈	16⁶/₈	19³/₈	4⁶/₈ 4⁵/₈	5 5		4184	406
	■ Clayton Co. – Michael A. Bries – Michael A. Bries – 1999							
161⁵/₈	23²/₈ 26	21¹/₈	23³/₈	4⁵/₈ 5	5 5		4234†	408†
	■ Sioux Co. – Myron Van Ginkel – Myron Van Ginkel – 2000							
161⁵/₈	23⁵/₈ 23²/₈	18¹/₈	20	5⁵/₈ 5⁶/₈	7 7	6⁴/₈	4234	408
	■ Sioux Co. – William J. Van Maanen – William J. Van Maanen – 1977							
161⁵/₈	24⁴/₈ 25¹/₈	19¹/₈	22⁴/₈	4⁶/₈ 4⁵/₈	5 5		4234	408
	■ Jackson Co. – Robert R. Gross – Robert R. Gross – 1995							
161⁴/₈	25¹/₈ 25	16⁷/₈	19	4⁶/₈ 4⁵/₈	5 6	1¹/₈	4258†	411†
	■ Dallas Co. – David H. Andrews – David H. Andrews – 2001							
161⁴/₈	25⁵/₈ 25²/₈	17	18⁷/₈	5 5	5 5		4258	411
	■ Monona Co. – Randy D. Buschmann – Randy D. Buschmann – 1994							
161²/₈	24⁶/₈ 23⁵/₈	18¹/₈	21²/₈	4³/₈ 4⁴/₈	5 8	7³/₈	4310	413
	■ Louisa Co. – Jeffrey D. McKinney – Jeffrey D. McKinney – 1997							
161¹/₈	27³/₈ 27¹/₈	21²/₈	23³/₈	5¹/₈ 5	6 6	7³/₈	4332	414
	■ Des Moines Co. – Lloyd E. Zink – Lloyd E. Zink – 1969							
161¹/₈	26²/₈ 26⁴/₈	17⁵/₈	20¹/₈	5¹/₈ 5	4 4		4332	414
	■ Monona Co. – Jeffrey L. Spates – Jeffrey L. Spates – 1994							
161	27¹/₈ 26	22²/₈	24³/₈	5⁶/₈ 5⁴/₈	4 4		4356	416
	■ Lucas Co. – Gary Goering – Gary Goering – 1987							
161	26⁴/₈ 25⁶/₈	19⁷/₈	22	4⁷/₈ 5	6 5	1³/₈	4356	416
	■ Louisa Co. – David W. Hotz – David W. Hotz – 1998							
160⁷/₈	24⁶/₈ 25³/₈	20⁶/₈	22²/₈	4 4	5 6	1⁷/₈	4380	418
	■ Taylor Co. – Stanley E. Peterman – Stanley E. Peterman – 1991							

Score	Length of Main Beam Right	Left	Inside Spread	Greatest Spread	Circumference at Smallest Place Between Burr and First Point Right	Left	Number of Points Right	Left	Lengths Abnormal Points	All-Time Rank	State Rank
$160^7/_8$	$30^2/_8$	28	$23^2/_8$	$25^7/_8$	5	5	6	6	$8^5/_8$	4380	418
	■ Warren Co. – Lonnie J. Stringer – Lonnie J. Stringer – 1995										
$160^6/_8$	$25^3/_8$	$24^4/_8$	$16^4/_8$	$18^6/_8$	$4^4/_8$	$4^3/_8$	7	7	$2^2/_8$	4402†	420†
	■ Grundy Co. – Jeff D. Billerbeck – Jeff D. Billerbeck – 1996										
$160^6/_8$	$24^5/_8$	$25^7/_8$	$22^7/_8$	$23^6/_8$	$4^2/_8$	$4^3/_8$	6	5	$1^1/_8$	4402†	420†
	■ Madison Co. – Gale R. Plynesser – Gale R. Plynesser – 2000										
$160^5/_8$	$26^1/_8$	26	$23^3/_8$	25	$4^6/_8$	$4^4/_8$	5	5		4423†	422†
	■ Iowa Co. – Rodney L. Exline – Rodney L. Exline – 2000										
$160^5/_8$	26	$26^6/_8$	$23^3/_8$	$25^6/_8$	$4^5/_8$	$4^6/_8$	6	4	$2^2/_8$	4423	422
	■ Jefferson Co. – Jeffrey J. Parkison – Jeffrey J. Parkison – 1990										
$160^4/_8$	$23^7/_8$	$24^2/_8$	$19^2/_8$	21	$5^3/_8$	$5^4/_8$	6	6	$3^4/_8$	4443	424
	■ Warren Co. – David L. Schaffer – David L. Schaffer – 1999										
$160^1/_8$	$23^6/_8$	$25^4/_8$	$22^7/_8$	$24^7/_8$	$3^7/_8$	4	5	5		4534	425
	■ Allamakee Co. – Chris Schoh – Chris Schoh – 1997										
$160^1/_8$	$23^7/_8$	$23^5/_8$	$18^3/_8$	$21^5/_8$	$5^2/_8$	$5^3/_8$	5	6		4534	425
	■ Dubuque Co. – Stephen M. Seipp – Stephen M. Seipp – 1998										
194	$27^4/_8$	$27^1/_8$	19	21	$4^4/_8$	$4^4/_8$	5	5		*	*
	■ Johnson Co. – Steven E. Tyer – Steven E. Tyer – 1994										

■ Location of Kill – Hunter – Owner – Date Killed

† The scores and ranking for trophies from the 25th Awards Entry Period are not final until the banquet is held on June 19, 2004.

* Final score is subject to revision by additional verifying measurements.

TROPHIES IN THE FIELD

HUNTER: Ryan W. Scott
SCORE: 184-1/8
CATEGORY: typical whitetail deer
LOCATION: Wapello County, Iowa
DATE: 2000

IOWA

NON-TYPICAL WHITETAIL DEER

Score	Length of Main Beam Right Left	Inside Spread	Greatest Spread	Circumference at Smallest Place Between Burr and First Point Right Left		Number of Points Right Left		Lengths Abnormal Points	All-Time Rank	State Rank
	■ Location of Kill – Hunter – Owner – Date Killed									
282	26¹/8 27	24³/8	26⁶/8	6⁵/8	6²/8	15	14	96⁷/8	6	1
	■ Clay Co. – Larry Raveling – Bass Pro Shops – 1973									
258²/8	28⁵/8 28¹/8	24¹/8	26²/8	7	6⁷/8	10	14	55⁷/8	30	2
	■ Louisa Co. – Lyle E. Spitznogle – Bass Pro Shops – 1982									
258¹/8	23¹/8 24⁴/8	18³/8	22²/8	5³/8	5⁴/8	17	12	74	32	3
	■ Cedar Co. – Picked Up – Bass Pro Shops – 1988									
256⁷/8	28³/8 27⁶/8	21	25²/8	5¹/8	5⁴/8	18	17	73¹/8	37	4
	■ Jackson Co. – David B. Manderscheid – Bass Pro Shops – 1977									
256²/8	28⁷/8 28¹/8	20⁴/8	24⁷/8	6⁵/8	6⁴/8	11	16	64	39	5
	■ Monona Co. – Carroll E. Johnson – Carroll E. Johnson – 1968									
252	24³/8 25²/8	19¹/8	30²/8	5⁷/8	5⁴/8	11	16	90⁵/8	49	6
	■ Lee Co. – Carl Wenke – Bass Pro Shops – 1972									
248⁶/8	27⁴/8 28¹/8	20⁵/8	24	6	5⁷/8	18	19	72⁵/8	66	7
	■ Warren Co. – Larry J. Caldwell – Larry J. Caldwell – 1990									
245³/8	28 25⁷/8	18⁴/8	24⁴/8	4⁶/8	4⁷/8	17	16	63¹/8	84	8
	■ Marshall Co. – Don L. Boucher – Don L. Boucher – 1996									
244⁶/8	25⁴/8 28	17⁴/8	22⁵/8	5³/8	5²/8	18	13	65	87	9
	■ Monroe Co. – Robert N. Wonderlich – Bass Pro Shops – 1970									
241⁶/8	25⁷/8 26¹/8	19³/8	21⁶/8	5⁶/8	5³/8	11	10	32⁷/8	105†	10†
	■ Des Moines Co. – Picked Up – IA Dept. of Natl. Resc. – 1999									
240⁶/8	28³/8 28⁶/8	19¹/8	23⁴/8	5²/8	5²/8	10	15	52⁷/8	110	11
	■ Wapello Co. – Picked Up – IA Dept. of Natl. Resc. – 1991									
240⁴/8	27⁷/8 26⁴/8	20⁷/8	24¹/8	5	5¹/8	13	15	40³/8	113†	12†
	■ Allamakee Co. – David Gordon – David Gordon – 2000									
240²/8	28⁴/8 30⁵/8	22⁴/8	25⁷/8	6¹/8	6¹/8	15	12	56	117†	13†
	■ Warren Co. – Rick L. Dye – Rick L. Dye – 2000									
237³/8	27³/8 28³/8	23²/8	29¹/8	6²/8	6³/8	14	11	47¹/8	146	14
	■ Wayne Co. – Picked Up – Cabela's Inc. – 1998									
237³/8	24⁷/8 24⁶/8	16³/8	21⁴/8	5¹/8	5¹/8	13	10	51²/8	146	14
	■ Monroe Co. – Larry V. Zach – Larry V. Zach – 2000									
237	27⁵/8 26³/8	22⁴/8	27	5⁵/8	5⁷/8	14	12	59⁴/8	151	16
	■ Madison Co. – Picked Up – IA Dept. of Natl. Resc. – PR 1989									
236⁷/8	28 27	25³/8	28	5³/8	5⁴/8	11	10	54	154	17
	■ Dallas Co. – Russ A. Clarken – Russ A. Clarken – 1994									
232⁷/8	29¹/8 28¹/8	26⁷/8	28⁴/8	5⁴/8	5⁴/8	10	12	39⁶/8	197	18
	■ Montgomery Co. – Picked Up – Dirk M. Paul – 1988									
231¹/8	25³/8 25⁷/8	21⁴/8	29⁴/8	5⁶/8	5⁶/8	14	12	69¹/8	224	19
	■ Henry Co. – Wendell R. Prottsman – Wendell R. Prottsman – 1988									

Score	Length of Main Beam		Inside Spread	Greatest Spread	Circumference at Smallest Place Between Burr and First Point		Number of Points		Lengths Abnormal Points	All-Time Rank	State Rank
	Right	Left			Right	Left	Right	Left			
	■ *Location of Kill – Hunter – Owner – Date Killed*										
230 1/8	25 6/8	24 7/8	18 5/8	27 3/8	4 6/8	4 7/8	12	11	53 2/8	238	20
■ *Guthrie Co. – Todd A. Hawley – Todd A. Hawley – 1982*											
230	24 5/8	24 2/8	21 7/8	25 5/8	4 7/8	4 6/8	14	13	78 5/8	240	21
■ *Clayton Co. – Fredrick A. Becker – Fredrick A. Becker – 1993*											
229 6/8	26 1/8	26	21 5/8	23 6/8	5 1/8	5 1/8	12	13	57 5/8	245	22
■ *Decatur Co. – Edgar Shields – Edgar Shields – 1986*											
229 4/8	27 5/8	26 2/8	21 3/8	24 2/8	6 7/8	6 6/8	13	9	47 1/8	246	23
■ *Polk Co. – Terry M. Long – Terry M. Long – 1995*											
229 3/8	27 7/8	26 6/8	23 6/8	26 4/8	5 3/8	5 4/8	8	8	21 1/8	249	24
■ *Wapello Co. – Robert D. Harding – Robert D. Harding – 1985*											
228 2/8	28 3/8	28 2/8	19 1/8	22 5/8	6 4/8	6 3/8	7	8	36 1/8	263†	25†
■ *Dubuque Co. – Arthur D. Wille – Arthur D. Wille – 2000* ■ *See photo on page 197*											
227 6/8	21 6/8	25	17	24	6 4/8	6	13	10	51 2/8	269	26
■ *Des Moines Co. – Edgar J. Steward – Edgar J. Steward – 1990*											
227 3/8	27 2/8	26 5/8	17 1/8	19 6/8	5 4/8	5 5/8	7	10	40 6/8	273†	27†
■ *Madison Co. – Jerry L. Wells – Jerry L. Wells – 2001*											
227	26 1/8	25 3/8	18	20 4/8	5 6/8	6	9	12	48 2/8	279	28
■ *Lucas Co. – Picked Up – H. James Reimer – 1992*											
227	29 4/8	30 4/8	23 1/8	26	6 2/8	6 6/8	10	11	27 7/8	279	28
■ *Decatur Co. – Jack J. Schuler, Jr. – Jack J. Schuler, Jr. – 1995*											
226 6/8	24 4/8	22 3/8	19 7/8	26 5/8	5 2/8	5 4/8	13	12	58 7/8	285†	30†
■ *Polk Co. – Picked Up – IA Dept. of Natl. Resc. – 1998*											
226 4/8	27 4/8	27 4/8	20 3/8	24 2/8	4 7/8	4 7/8	11	12	34 7/8	292	31
■ *Plymouth Co. – Ronald H. Junck – Ronald H. Junck – 1995*											
225 2/8	23 2/8	23 5/8	16 7/8	26 4/8	6 3/8	6 1/8	13	10	52 7/8	310	32
■ *Fayette Co. – Duane J. Cahoy – Duane J. Cahoy – 1975*											
225 2/8	24 5/8	21 6/8	24	26 6/8	5 2/8	5 3/8	9	13	44 6/8	310	32
■ *Scott Co. – Rick Porske – Rick Porske – 1996*											
224 6/8	27	26 7/8	27 1/8	28 7/8	5 2/8	5 2/8	11	10	36 6/8	322	34
■ *Mills Co. – James C. Reed – James C. Reed – 1988*											
224 1/8	25 6/8	26 7/8	28 3/8	30 3/8	6 5/8	6 2/8	9	8	45 6/8	334	35
■ *Monona Co. – David Freihage – Bass Pro Shops – 1991*											
223 6/8	24	26 4/8	18 5/8	28	5	5 2/8	11	11	55 7/8	342	36
■ *Jasper Co. – Picked Up – Bruce A. Sanburn – 1997*											
223 3/8	22 5/8	20 5/8	12 5/8	16 7/8	8 1/8	8 7/8	12	12	50 4/8	354	37
■ *Madison Co. – Duane Fick – Duane Fick – 1972*											
223	19 7/8	19 2/8	18 2/8	24 4/8	7 6/8	8 2/8	6	10	83 6/8	365	38
■ *Van Buren Co. – Picked Up – Wade Roberts – 1979*											
222 4/8	25 1/8	24 1/8	18 2/8	22	6 1/8	6 2/8	10	13	63 2/8	378	39
■ *Davis Co. – James L. Fine – James L. Fine – 1987*											
222 3/8	28 1/8	29 3/8	19 7/8	23	5 5/8	5 7/8	9	12	43	384†	40†
■ *Van Buren Co. – Le Roy G. Everhart – Grundy Co. Cons. Center – 1969*											

Score	Length of Main Beam Right Left	Inside Spread	Greatest Spread	Circumference at Smallest Place Between Burr and First Point Right Left		Number of Points Right Left		Lengths Abnormal Points	All-Time Rank	State Rank
	■ Location of Kill – Hunter – Owner – Date Killed									
222³/₈	25 25⁴/₈	17⁴/₈	26	5	5	11	10	38⁷/₈	384	40
	■ Dallas Co. – Chris S. Wilson – Chris S. Wilson – 1996									
222¹/₈	26²/₈ 25⁷/₈	17³/₈	22²/₈	4⁵/₈	4⁴/₈	14	12	50²/₈	392	42
	■ Hancock Co. – Jerry M. Monson – Bass Pro Shops – 1977									
221⁷/₈	26⁶/₈ 26	21³/₈	23³/₈	5	5¹/₈	11	11	49⁶/₈	396	43
	■ Tama Co. – Charles Upah – Richard Upah – 1959									
221⁷/₈	27³/₈ 27¹/₈	21	23³/₈	5⁷/₈	5⁶/₈	10	10	27¹/₈	396	43
	■ Jefferson Co. – Jared L. Rebling – Jared L. Rebling – 2000									
221⁴/₈	30 29²/₈	23³/₈	27²/₈	6²/₈	6²/₈	12	12	36¹/₈	402	45
	■ Humboldt Co. – Donald Crossley – Donald Crossley – 1971									
221¹/₈	27²/₈ 29⁴/₈	22⁶/₈	28	5⁵/₈	5⁴/₈	15	14	50³/₈	415	46
	■ Jefferson Co. – Daniel R. Thurman – Daniel R. Thurman – 1979									
220⁶/₈	27⁴/₈ 22⁶/₈	18	22	5⁴/₈	65-/–9		15	59²/₈	421†	47†
	■ Crawford Co. – Picked Up – Raymond H. Schulte – 2000									
220⁶/₈	26⁴/₈ 27²/₈	27¹/₈	30⁵/₈	5²/₈	5¹/₈	10	9	23⁵/₈	421	47
	■ Dallas Co. – Picked Up – Gale Sup – 1992									
220⁵/₈	28 28	21³/₈	26³/₈	6²/₈	6²/₈	12	8	34²/₈	424	49
	■ Jefferson Co. – Mike Laux – Bass Pro Shops – 1990									
220²/₈	25 26⁴/₈	19¹/₈	24¹/₈	5⁴/₈	5⁴/₈	11	12	31¹/₈	434	50
	■ Union Co. – George L. Foster – George L. Foster – 1968									
220	28¹/₈ 26⁵/₈	18⁵/₈	26⁶/₈	4⁷/₈	4⁵/₈	15	9	47⁷/₈	441	51
	■ Wayne Co. – Dallas Patterson – Dallas Patterson – 1975									
219³/₈	28¹/₈ 27⁵/₈	20⁵/₈	25	4⁵/₈	4⁴/₈	12	17	51²/₈	455	52
	■ Webster Co. – David Propst – David Propst – 1987									
219	24¹/₈ 24⁶/₈	21	23⁶/₈	4⁴/₈	4⁶/₈	11	10	60⁴/₈	470	53
	■ Van Buren Co. – James E. Garrels – Wayne G. Nevar – 1988									
218⁷/₈	25³/₈ 22⁴/₈	18⁷/₈	24⁴/₈	4⁵/₈	4⁷/₈	12	12	51⁴/₈	472	54
	■ Marshall Co. – Picked Up – Charles E. Lewis – 1989									
218⁵/₈	24⁵/₈ 27	18⁵/₈	25⁷/₈	5⁷/₈	5⁶/₈	11	9	39²/₈	480	55
	■ Page Co. – John L. Novy – John L. Novy – 1989									
218²/₈	29³/₈ 29⁷/₈	23⁴/₈	27¹/₈	5³/₈	5³/₈	7	7	28	495	56
	■ Allamakee Co. – Bernard Rank – Bass Pro Shops – 1963									
217⁴/₈	24⁶/₈ 24⁶/₈	19¹/₈	24⁶/₈	4⁶/₈	5	10	13	54³/₈	510	57
	■ Hardin Co. – Picked Up – W.H. Lilienthal & J. Bruce – 1987									
217⁴/₈	24²/₈ 26¹/₈	20³/₈	24⁴/₈	5	5²/₈	8	7	35¹/₈	510	57
	■ Allamakee Co. – George A. Smith – George A. Smith – 1991									
217²/₈	29⁶/₈ 29⁵/₈	25³/₈	26²/₈	5²/₈	5²/₈	8	7	19⁵/₈	519	59
	■ Mills Co. – Rick W. Elliott – Rick W. Elliott – 1976									
216³/₈	26 25⁵/₈	17⁴/₈	24⁵/₈	5⁴/₈	5⁴/₈	10	9	29⁷/₈	549	60
	■ Clay Co. – Blaine Salzkorn – Blaine Salzkorn – 1970									
216³/₈	26³/₈ 27¹/₈	19²/₈	22	6³/₈	6⁴/₈	12	12	28⁵/₈	549	60
	■ Woodbury Co. – Picked Up – Helen Peterson – 1999									

Score	Length of Main Beam Right Left	Inside Spread	Greatest Spread	Circumference at Smallest Place Between Burr and First Point Right Left		Number of Points Right Left		Lengths Abnormal Points	All-Time Rank	State Rank
	■ *Location of Kill – Hunter – Owner – Date Killed*									
216	25³/₈ 25⁶/₈	19²/₈	24⁶/₈	5³/₈	5²/₈	11	9	45²/₈	565	62
	■ *Jackson Co. – Picked Up – Douglas J. Horst – 1992*									
214⁶/₈	26⁶/₈ 28	21⁶/₈	24	5	4⁷/₈	9	8	26²/₈	610	63
	■ *Decatur Co. – Dean D. Grimm – Dean D. Grimm – 1988*									
214²/₈	23⁴/₈ 24⁷/₈	17¹/₈	27¹/₈	6²/₈	5⁶/₈	13	15	67⁵/₈	625	64
	■ *Monona Co. – Brian R. Hebb – Brian R. Hebb – 1996*									
214¹/₈	28 28³/₈	21⁴/₈	25⁷/₈	6¹/₈	6²/₈	7	9	17¹/₈	628†	65†
	■ *Van Buren Co. – Douglas W. Farrell – Douglas W. Farrell – 2001*									
214	26⁷/₈ 26³/₈	21	26³/₈	5⁴/₈	5²/₈	14	9	47	629	66
	■ *Hamilton Co. – Picked Up – Bass Pro Shops – 1987*									
214	24¹/₈ 25³/₈	19	21⁵/₈	6³/₈	6	10	13	38⁶/₈	629	66
	■ *Madison Co. – Merle Allen – Merle Allen – 1998*									
213⁵/₈	29³/₈ 29⁶/₈	21⁴/₈	26⁴/₈	5⁷/₈	5⁷/₈	7	9	17⁵/₈	649	68
	■ *Guthrie Co. – Merle Shirbrown – Sherrill Shirbrown – 1963*									
212⁷/₈	24⁴/₈ 22⁵/₈	17⁶/₈	23²/₈	4⁶/₈	4⁶/₈	12	9	36⁵/₈	674	69
	■ *Boone Co. – Orlin Sorber – Ron Sorber – 1973*									
212⁶/₈	24⁵/₈ 26²/₈	24⁶/₈	31³/₈	4⁷/₈	5¹/₈	8	14	57	677	70
	■ *Fremont Co. – Picked Up – Jeffrey S. Haning – 1989*									
212⁵/₈	23²/₈ 24⁵/₈	29¹/₈	29⁴/₈	5⁴/₈	5⁴/₈	10	9	28²/₈	683	71
	■ *Appanoose Co. – Picked Up – IA Dept. of Natl. Resc. – 1991*									
212⁵/₈	25¹/₈ 24²/₈	21⁶/₈	26¹/₈	5⁴/₈	6¹/₈	6	10	21⁷/₈	683	71
	■ *Page Co. – Kevin L. Reints – Kevin L. Reints – 1995*									
212²/₈	28²/₈ 28⁶/₈	24⁴/₈	27⁷/₈	5³/₈	5	9	8	24⁶/₈	701	73
	■ *Madison Co. – Larry D. Bain – Larry D. Bain – 1984*									
212²/₈	27⁴/₈ 27²/₈	20²/₈	23²/₈	7⁴/₈	6	10	9	35	701	73
	■ *Van Buren Co. – Chris E. Clingan – Chris E. Clingan – 1993*									
212¹/₈	28¹/₈ 28¹/₈	21⁶/₈	28⁶/₈	5³/₈	6	8	10	25⁷/₈	709	75
	■ *Woodbury Co. – Harold M. Leonard – Harold M. Leonard – 1965*									
212	28³/₈ 28³/₈	20⁴/₈	22⁷/₈	5⁶/₈	6	6	9	25⁴/₈	717	76
	■ *Greene Co. – Don Buswell – Don Buswell – 1973*									
211⁷/₈	24¹/₈ 24⁴/₈	19⁵/₈	24⁵/₈	4⁷/₈	4⁷/₈	11	8	26⁶/₈	724	77
	■ *Van Buren Co. – Loras R. Ernzen – Loras R. Ernzen – 1988*									
211⁶/₈	26³/₈ 26	24⁷/₈	25⁷/₈	5³/₈	5²/₈	11	6	25¹/₈	729	78
	■ *Marion Co. – Paul J. Pearson – Paul J. Pearson – 1964*									
211⁵/₈	27³/₈ 26⁶/₈	26²/₈	28	5²/₈	5¹/₈	12	7	29⁵/₈	734	79
	■ *Adair Co. – Bob C. Garside – Bob C. Garside – 1998*									
211³/₈	26²/₈ 26⁶/₈	23⁴/₈	27⁶/₈	5²/₈	5³/₈	12	9	35¹/₈	745	80
	■ *Polk Co. – Picked Up – IA Dept. of Natl. Resc. – 1993*									
211¹/₈	26⁵/₈ 26	22⁴/₈	24⁵/₈	5¹/₈	5	9	9	29⁷/₈	758	81
	■ *Clarke Co. – Randy J. Showers – Randy J. Showers – 1991*									
211	27¹/₈ 26	20¹/₈	23⁶/₈	6⁶/₈	6⁶/₈	9	13	37³/₈	764	82
	■ *Monroe Co. – Picked Up – IA Dept. of Natl. Resc. – 1991*									

Score	Length of Main Beam Right	Left	Inside Spread	Greatest Spread	Circumference at Smallest Place Between Burr and First Point Right	Left	Number of Points Right	Left	Lengths Abnormal Points	All-Time Rank	State Rank
	■ Location of Kill – Hunter – Owner – Date Killed										
210⁷/₈	27⁵/₈	27⁴/₈	20⁶/₈	23⁴/₈	5⁴/₈	5⁷/₈	10	12	21⁷/₈	773†	83†
	■ Wayne Co. – Jack J. Pershy – Jack J. Pershy – 2001										
210⁵/₈	23⁷/₈	23⁷/₈	19³/₈	25²/₈	5⁴/₈	5²/₈	13	14	76²/₈	783†	84†
	■ Wapello Co. – Picked Up – IA Dept. of Natl. Resc. – 1996										
210²/₈	28⁴/₈	27⁶/₈	20⁴/₈	23²/₈	5⁴/₈	5⁶/₈	11	9	26²/₈	803	85
	■ Louisa Co. – Picked Up – William H. Lilienthal – 1959										
210²/₈	25³/₈	26	26⁶/₈	27⁵/₈	8²/₈	5⁴/₈	13	7	27⁶/₈	803	85
	■ Fremont Co. – Mike Moody – Mike Moody – 1990										
210¹/₈	26⁴/₈	23³/₈	20⁶/₈	25⁶/₈	5³/₈	5⁴/₈	15	16	55¹/₈	808	87
	■ Madison Co. – Andy A. Ross – Andy A. Ross – 1994										
210	27⁵/₈	25	24²/₈	26⁷/₈	5²/₈	5²/₈	9	7	19	816	88
	■ Lee Co. – Picked Up – Mike Conger – 1978										
210	26²/₈	25¹/₈	19⁶/₈	25³/₈	4⁵/₈	4⁴/₈	8	7	32⁴/₈	816	88
	■ Dallas Co. – Picked Up – William H. Lilienthal – 1989										
210	22	24	13⁵/₈	21	4⁴/₈	5³/₈	10	8	70³/₈	816	88
	■ Jefferson Co. – Jared L. Rebling – Jared L. Rebling – 1998										
209⁷/₈	25⁷/₈	27	21¹/₈	25²/₈	5⁴/₈	5⁴/₈	12	8	33⁶/₈	825	91
	■ Adams Co. – Gregory L. Andrews – Gregory L. Andrews – 1998										
209⁵/₈	27³/₈	28	21³/₈	24¹/₈	5¹/₈	5	8	10	24⁴/₈	840†	92†
	■ Van Buren Co. – Allen C. Funk – Allen C. Funk – 2000										
209⁵/₈	25²/₈	27⁴/₈	21¹/₈	26	4⁷/₈	5	11	11	39²/₈	840	92
	■ Harrison Co. – James A. Spelman – James A. Spelman – 1991										
209³/₈	27⁶/₈	26⁷/₈	29²/₈	31²/₈	5⁶/₈	5¹/₈	9	8	28⁷/₈	852	94
	■ Keokuk Co. – Michael D. Hoover – Michael D. Hoover – 1991										
209²/₈	23⁷/₈	22	16⁴/₈	27¹/₈	4⁷/₈	6²/₈	8	13	44	859	95
	■ Clarke Co. – James C. Reed – James C. Reed – 1988										
209¹/₈	26	26²/₈	19³/₈	30¹/₈	5	4⁷/₈	8	8	33	863	96
	■ Clinton Co. – Gregory Stewart – Gregory Stewart – 1963										
209¹/₈	26	25⁷/₈	22⁴/₈	24¹/₈	5	5	9	8	29⁷/₈	863	96
	■ Monroe Co. – Kelly J. Willis – Kelly J. Willis – 1988										
209¹/₈	27⁶/₈	30⁵/₈	19⁶/₈	23³/₈	6³/₈	6³/₈	8	10	42¹/₈	863	96
	■ Monona Co. – Vincent P. Jauron – Vincent P. Jauron – 1990										
209	26⁷/₈	28²/₈	23⁶/₈	25⁴/₈	5⁴/₈	5⁴/₈	8	9	17⁶/₈	872	99
	■ Lee Co. – Glenn L. Carter II – Glenn L. Carter II – 1984										
208⁵/₈	26²/₈	24³/₈	20⁴/₈	25¹/₈	6³/₈	7¹/₈	10	12	41⁷/₈	888	100
	■ Woodbury Co. – Ronald J. Eickholt – Ronald J. Eickholt – 1977										
208⁴/₈	24⁴/₈	26³/₈	20²/₈	21³/₈	7⁴/₈	7⁶/₈	12	12	20	894	101
	■ Lee Co. – Dennis L. Case – Dennis L. Case – 1999										
208²/₈	24³/₈	23⁴/₈	19	26⁶/₈	5	5	7	11	30⁴/₈	910	102
	■ Monona Co. – Rob L. Cadwallader – Rob L. Cadwallader – 1984										
208	26³/₈	26	15	21⁵/₈	4¹/₈	4¹/₈	14	10	52⁶/₈	929	103
	■ Buena Vista Co. – Robert L. Vierow – Robert L. Vierow – 1982										

Score	Length of Main Beam Right	Left	Inside Spread	Greatest Spread	Circumference at Smallest Place Between Burr and First Point Right	Left	Number of Points Right	Left	Lengths Abnormal Points	All-Time Rank	State Rank
208	28 1/8	30	22	25 3/8	5 2/8	5 4/8	8	8	14 6/8	929	103
■ Lucas Co. – Mitch W. Hosler – Mitch W. Hosler – 1991											
208	24 4/8	26 2/8	19 1/8	24 3/8	4 7/8	4 6/8	8	10	63 5/8	929	103
■ Wayne Co. – George M. Tonelli – George M. Tonelli – 1993											
207 7/8	23 7/8	24 5/8	22 2/8	24 5/8	5 1/8	5	10	10	27 3/8	938	106
■ Monona Co. – Robert V. Dean – Vernon R. Dean – 1968											
207 7/8	25 3/8	25 7/8	25 2/8	27 1/8	7	6 7/8	8	7	18 5/8	938	106
■ Lee Co. – Timothy A. Miller – Timothy A. Miller – 1994											
207 7/8	29 5/8	29 1/8	21 1/8	23 5/8	5 3/8	5 2/8	7	7	26 4/8	938	106
■ Warren Co. – Michael J. King – Michael J. King – 1995											
207 5/8	30 1/8	29 3/8	20 1/8	22 4/8	5 1/8	5 2/8	10	9	29 2/8	957	109
■ Webster Co. – Larry E. Iles – Larry E. Iles – 1979											
207 3/8	25 7/8	25 6/8	17 6/8	22 4/8	5	5 2/8	8	8	40 5/8	977	110
■ Lee Co. – Donald L. Butler – Donald L. Butler – 1999											
207 1/8	25 5/8	26 7/8	17 3/8	24 4/8	5 5/8	5 1/8	12	9	41 2/8	995	111
■ Clay Co. – Rodney W. Dean – Rodney W. Dean – 1973											
207 1/8	27 5/8	27 5/8	23 2/8	25	5 4/8	5 7/8	10	10	29 7/8	995	111
■ Montgomery Co. – Raymond E. Crouch – Raymond E. Crouch – 1997											
207 1/8	29 3/8	28 4/8	25 4/8	27 2/8	5 5/8	5 4/8	8	7	19 7/8	995	111
■ Page Co. – Jeremy Williams – Jeremy Williams – 1997											
207	22 7/8	23 4/8	18 6/8	21	6 4/8	6 2/8	9	11	32 2/8	1005	114
■ Davis Co. – David L. Johnson – David L. Johnson – 1994											
206 5/8	26	25 5/8	20 1/8	22 4/8	5 5/8	5 4/8	9	7	32 6/8	1036	115
■ Iowa Co. – Picked Up – Ralph McBride – 1990											
206 5/8	26	25 7/8	20 1/8	24	6	6 3/8	11	11	34 6/8	1036	115
■ Guthrie Co. – Terry R. Adams – Terry R. Adams – 1998											
206 3/8	27 4/8	27 7/8	20	24 1/8	4 6/8	4 7/8	7	8	35 1/8	1051	117
■ Cass Co. – Rodney A. Watson – Rodney A. Watson – 1993											
205 6/8	26 2/8	25 5/8	19 2/8	21 7/8	5 6/8	6	8	8	29	1094	118
■ Lucas Co. – William F. Bingaman – William F. Bingaman – 1991											
205 3/8	28 4/8	28	20 2/8	22 4/8	4 7/8	5	7	8	32 3/8	1116†	119†
■ Allamakee Co. – Picked Up – Frank Miller – 1993											
205 3/8	27 1/8	25 7/8	21	24 1/8	6 2/8	6	8	12	27 7/8	1116	119
■ Louisa Co. – Daniel Kaufman – Daniel Kaufman – 1984											
205 3/8	25 5/8	23 6/8	18 4/8	23 7/8	5 6/8	5 4/8	10	8	31 1/8	1116	119
■ Dallas Co. – Picked Up – Jeff Kempf – PR 1996											
205	27 3/8	27 1/8	19 3/8	24	4 7/8	4 5/8	9	11	26 1/8	1144	122
■ Guthrie Co. – James C. Long – James C. Long – 1994											
205	27 3/8	25 6/8	17 6/8	23 5/8	5 3/8	5 1/8	12	13	53 6/8	1144	122
■ Union Co. – Jeff J. Tussey – Jeff J. Tussey – 1995											
204 6/8	24 4/8	23 7/8	17 6/8	22 6/8	4 3/8	4 5/8	10	8	36	1165	124
■ Davis Co. – Unknown – William H. Lilienthal – PR 1994											

Score	Length of Main Beam Right Left	Inside Spread	Greatest Spread	Circumference at Smallest Place Between Burr and First Point Right Left	Number of Points Right Left	Lengths Abnormal Points	All-Time Rank	State Rank
	■ Location of Kill – Hunter – Owner – Date Killed							
204³/8	27³/8 27³/8	20³/8	23¹/8	5⁵/8 5⁴/8	13 8	31²/8	1186	125
	■ Harrison Co. – Raymond McDaniel – Raymond McDaniel – 1970							
204²/8	25⁷/8 25⁴/8	19³/8	24²/8	5⁵/8 5⁷/8	13 12	34³/8	1199	126
	■ Winneshiek Co. – Benjamin Christopher – Benjamin Christopher – 1999							
204¹/8	29¹/8 28⁴/8	22¹/8	24⁴/8	6²/8 6¹/8	10 9	28⁶/8	1210	127
	■ O'Brien Co. – Roy Jalas – Delores Jalas – 1961							
204¹/8	26⁵/8 26²/8	22	23⁴/8	5 4⁷/8	7 9	25⁵/8	1210	127
	■ Dubuque Co. – Joe J. Rettenmeier – Joe J. Rettenmeier – 1987							
204¹/8	25⁴/8 25¹/8	19⁷/8	22	5⁵/8 5⁶/8	12 11	37⁶/8	1210	127
	■ Van Buren Co. – Geoffrey N. Phillips – Geoffrey N. Phillips – 1995							
204	26²/8 26⁴/8	22⁶/8	26²/8	5 5	12 8	42⁶/8	1220	130
	■ Warren Co. – Jack J. Schuler, Jr. – Jack J. Schuler, Jr. – 1997							
203⁵/8	28 27³/8	17⁵/8	24⁷/8	6²/8 5⁷/8	14 9	31⁴/8	1248	131
	■ Page Co. – Picked Up – Rodney S. Brooks – 1981							
203⁵/8	25¹/8 25¹/8	17⁵/8	20	5²/8 5	9 11	30	1248	131
	■ Warren Co. – Ted Miller – Ted Miller – 1986							
203⁵/8	30⁴/8 27⁴/8	21³/8	24²/8	5²/8 5³/8	10 11	17	1248	131
	■ Monona Co. – Robert S. Jensen – Robert S. Jensen – 1991							
203⁴/8	24⁶/8 25³/8	19¹/8	22²/8	5²/8 5⁴/8	9 10	38⁵/8	1259	134
	■ Appanoose Co. – Clem A. Herman – Clem A. Herman – 1990							
203³/8	24⁶/8 20¹/8	18³/8	20⁵/8	6⁴/8 7³/8	9 11	59²/8	1272	135
	■ Van Buren Co. – Robert R. McWilliams – Robert R. McWilliams – 1981							
203³/8	27²/8 27²/8	21⁴/8	26⁷/8	5 5²/8	7 10	22³/8	1272	135
	■ Fayette Co. – Steve M. Loban – Steve M. Loban – 1995							
203²/8	25²/8 25⁵/8	16¹/8	19⁶/8	5¹/8 5¹/8	13 9	49⁷/8	1287	137
	■ Scott Co. – Marv A. Schmidt, Jr. – Marv A. Schmidt, Jr. – 1987							
203²/8	26 27²/8	21⁵/8	27⁶/8	5¹/8 5³/8	12 13	35⁵/8	1287	137
	■ Decatur Co. – Kenneth R. Jones – Kenneth R. Jones – 1995							
203	26³/8 25⁴/8	18⁴/8	23⁵/8	4⁵/8 5	10 8	33⁴/8	1317	139
	■ Madison Co. – Joe Bruns – Tim Bruns – 1967							
203	28⁴/8 27³/8	21⁷/8	25	5⁵/8 5⁵/8	9 8	29¹/8	1317	139
	■ Guthrie Co. – Ronald R. Hoyt – Ronald R. Hoyt – 1974							
203	27 23⁶/8	18¹/8	21²/8	5²/8 5⁴/8	8 9	36⁵/8	1317	139
	■ Lee Co. – Wayne L. McClain – Wayne L. McClain – 1980							
202⁷/8	25³/8 26⁷/8	20¹/8	22⁶/8	5⁵/8 5⁵/8	11 12	31	1327	142
	■ Decatur Co. – Kevin J. Anderson – Kevin J. Anderson – 1992							
202⁷/8	26 26¹/8	17⁶/8	23⁴/8	5¹/8 4⁷/8	8 6	23⁷/8	1327	142
	■ Sioux Co. – Jason W. Davelaar – Jason W. Davelaar – 1999							
202⁶/8	25¹/8 24⁵/8	20⁷/8	22⁴/8	5⁷/8 5⁷/8	9 14	33⁷/8	1339	144
	■ Warren Co. – Leland Cortum – Leland Cortum – 1969							
202⁶/8	25⁶/8 25⁶/8	18⁴/8	25	5³/8 5⁴/8	8 13	25⁴/8	1339	144
	■ Fayette Co. – John M. McMillen – John M. McMillen – 1983							

Score	Length of Main Beam		Inside Spread	Greatest Spread	Circumference at Smallest Place Between Burr and First Point		Number of Points		Lengths Abnormal Points	All-Time Rank	State Rank
	Right	Left			Right	Left	Right	Left			
	▪ *Location of Kill – Hunter – Owner – Date Killed*										
$202^{2}/_{8}$	$27^{6}/_{8}$	$26^{2}/_{8}$	$19^{3}/_{8}$	$28^{6}/_{8}$	$5^{6}/_{8}$	$5^{7}/_{8}$	12	7	$33^{3}/_{8}$	1377	146
	▪ *Louisa Co. – Robert L. McFadden – Robert L. McFadden – 1986*										
202	$25^{3}/_{8}$	$19^{6}/_{8}$	$18^{3}/_{8}$	$21^{7}/_{8}$	$5^{5}/_{8}$	$6^{3}/_{8}$	10	10	$40^{1}/_{8}$	1395	147
	▪ *Monona Co. – Gary W. Anfinson – Gary W. Anfinson – 1988*										
202	$26^{1}/_{8}$	$26^{1}/_{8}$	$22^{7}/_{8}$	$25^{3}/_{8}$	$5^{1}/_{8}$	$5^{2}/_{8}$	9	8	$26^{1}/_{8}$	1395	147
	▪ *Guthrie Co. – Donald E. Jensen – Ronald E. Jensen – 1995*										
$201^{7}/_{8}$	$25^{4}/_{8}$	28	$19^{7}/_{8}$	$26^{4}/_{8}$	$5^{6}/_{8}$	$5^{6}/_{8}$	9	8	45	1410	149
	▪ *Winnebago Co. – Unknown – Peter G. Weiss – PR 1957*										
$201^{7}/_{8}$	$26^{1}/_{8}$	$25^{2}/_{8}$	$17^{4}/_{8}$	$25^{1}/_{8}$	$5^{1}/_{8}$	$5^{1}/_{8}$	8	7	$28^{1}/_{8}$	1410	149
	▪ *Louisa Co. – Jason Gapinski – Jason Gapinski – 1987*										
$201^{6}/_{8}$	$25^{2}/_{8}$	$24^{6}/_{8}$	$18^{7}/_{8}$	21	$5^{7}/_{8}$	$5^{6}/_{8}$	8	7	$25^{7}/_{8}$	1421	151
	▪ *Van Buren Co. – Randy Kramer – Randy Kramer – 1989*										
$201^{5}/_{8}$	$26^{3}/_{8}$	$25^{7}/_{8}$	$16^{2}/_{8}$	$19^{5}/_{8}$	$5^{7}/_{8}$	$5^{7}/_{8}$	9	13	$25^{7}/_{8}$	1427†	152†
	▪ *Tama Co. – Rod L. Waschkat – Rod L. Waschkat – 2001*										
$201^{5}/_{8}$	27	26	$18^{3}/_{8}$	$20^{7}/_{8}$	$5^{5}/_{8}$	$5^{6}/_{8}$	7	10	$17^{2}/_{8}$	1427	152
	▪ *Johnson Co. – Duane E. Papke – Duane E. Papke – 1981*										
$201^{5}/_{8}$	$29^{6}/_{8}$	$28^{2}/_{8}$	22	$24^{5}/_{8}$	$5^{6}/_{8}$	$5^{4}/_{8}$	10	9	$39^{5}/_{8}$	1427	152
	▪ *Madison Co. – Raymond Dawson – Raymond Dawson – 1994*										
$201^{4}/_{8}$	$28^{3}/_{8}$	$27^{6}/_{8}$	$17^{7}/_{8}$	$21^{7}/_{8}$	$4^{6}/_{8}$	$4^{7}/_{8}$	7	8	$17^{3}/_{8}$	1443	155
	▪ *Clayton Co. – Paul C. Crawford – Paul C. Crawford – 1987*										
$201^{4}/_{8}$	$24^{7}/_{8}$	$26^{1}/_{8}$	$20^{2}/_{8}$	$22^{4}/_{8}$	$6^{6}/_{8}$	$6^{3}/_{8}$	8	8	$27^{4}/_{8}$	1443	155
	▪ *Allamakee Co. – Daniel J. Gallagher – Daniel J. Gallagher – 1989*										
$201^{3}/_{8}$	$28^{2}/_{8}$	29	15	18	$4^{6}/_{8}$	$4^{7}/_{8}$	6	11	$27^{7}/_{8}$	1461	157
	▪ *Monona Co. – Thomas R. Flynn – Thomas R. Flynn – 1989*										
201	$24^{7}/_{8}$	$25^{5}/_{8}$	$17^{3}/_{8}$	$21^{7}/_{8}$	$6^{4}/_{8}$	$6^{1}/_{8}$	9	9	$26\text{-}9/_{8}$	1500	158
	▪ *Guthrie Co. – Patrick N. Thompson – Patrick N. Thompson – 1996*										
$200^{7}/_{8}$	24	$22^{5}/_{8}$	$22^{1}/_{8}$	27	$5^{1}/_{8}$	$6^{3}/_{8}$	8	7	$22^{2}/_{8}$	1512	159
	▪ *Davis Co. – R.G. Pettit & W. Van Mersberger – Roger G. Pettit – 1988*										
$200^{7}/_{8}$	$27^{1}/_{8}$	$25^{4}/_{8}$	$23^{6}/_{8}$	$25^{7}/_{8}$	$5^{5}/_{8}$	$5^{4}/_{8}$	7	8	$25^{1}/_{8}$	1512	159
	▪ *Muscatine Co. – William L. Brockert – William L. Brockert – 1998*										
$200^{6}/_{8}$	$24^{7}/_{8}$	$25^{7}/_{8}$	$25^{1}/_{8}$	$26^{7}/_{8}$	$6^{4}/_{8}$	$6^{6}/_{8}$	9	11	$54^{1}/_{8}$	1524	161
	▪ *Wapello Co. – Rod A. McKelvey – Rod A. McKelvey – 1983*										
$200^{6}/_{8}$	$26^{5}/_{8}$	25	$16^{7}/_{8}$	$21^{7}/_{8}$	$4^{7}/_{8}$	$4^{6}/_{8}$	8	8	$25^{5}/_{8}$	1524	161
	▪ *Wapello Co. – Michael W. Garber – Michael W. Garber – 1996*										
$200^{5}/_{8}$	$26^{7}/_{8}$	$26^{7}/_{8}$	$18^{6}/_{8}$	$20^{7}/_{8}$	$5^{7}/_{8}$	$5^{6}/_{8}$	10	7	$29^{3}/_{8}$	1532	163
	▪ *Washington Co. – Bruce Guy – Bruce Guy – 1973*										
$200^{5}/_{8}$	25	$26^{1}/_{8}$	$18^{7}/_{8}$	$21^{4}/_{8}$	$4^{5}/_{8}$	$4^{5}/_{8}$	7	7	25	1532	163
	▪ *Clayton Co. – Dorrance Arnold – Dorrance Arnold – 1977*										
$200^{5}/_{8}$	$26^{5}/_{8}$	$25^{3}/_{8}$	$20^{3}/_{8}$	$23^{1}/_{8}$	$5^{5}/_{8}$	$5^{5}/_{8}$	11	9	$25^{6}/_{8}$	1532	163
	▪ *Mitchell Co. – Dean A. Beyer – Dean A. Beyer – 1991*										
$200^{5}/_{8}$	$26^{2}/_{8}$	$25^{2}/_{8}$	$18^{3}/_{8}$	$20^{3}/_{8}$	$5^{2}/_{8}$	$5^{2}/_{8}$	8	9	$20^{2}/_{8}$	1532	163
	▪ *Madison Co. – Steve A. Marsh – Steve A. Marsh – 1994*										

IOWA NON-TYPICAL WHITETAIL DEER

Score	Length of Main Beam Right	Left	Inside Spread	Greatest Spread	Circumference at Smallest Place Between Burr and First Point Right	Left	Number of Points Right	Left	Lengths Abnormal Points	All-Time Rank	State Rank
	■ Location of Kill – Hunter – Owner – Date Killed										
$200^5/_8$	$27^2/_8$	$25^5/_8$	$20^6/_8$	23	$5^4/_8$	$5^2/_8$	7	8	$20^3/_8$	1532	163
	■ Iowa Co. – Michael L. Ealy – Michael L. Ealy – 1998										
$200^4/_8$	$25^5/_8$	$27^5/_8$	$16^6/_8$	$19^4/_8$	$4^5/_8$	$4^5/_8$	10	7	$32^6/_8$	1545	168
	■ Howard Co. – Victor J. Buresh – Victor J. Buresh – 1990										
$200^3/_8$	$29^1/_8$	$29^6/_8$	$21^3/_8$	$23^5/_8$	$5^4/_8$	$5^6/_8$	7	8	11	1556	169
	■ Marion Co. – Louis L. Floden – Louis L. Floden – 1996										
$200^1/_8$	$29^5/_8$	29	$18^5/_8$	$23^7/_8$	$5^4/_8$	$5^3/_8$	10	7	$18^6/_8$	1577	170
	■ Dallas Co. – Andy J. Lounsbury – Andy J. Lounsbury – 1996										
200	$26^4/_8$	27	$23^4/_8$	$30^2/_8$	$5^5/_8$	$5^6/_8$	8	10	$45^6/_8$	1591†	171†
	■ Clayton Co. – Michael A. Hinzman – Michael A. Hinzman – 2000										
200	$25^3/_8$	26	19	$21^4/_8$	$4^6/_8$	$4^7/_8$	11	10	$27^2/_8$	1591†	171†
	■ Clay Co. – Picked Up – IA Dept. of Natl. Resc. – 1987										
200	$24^6/_8$	25	$20^5/_8$	$26^5/_8$	$5^4/_8$	$5^4/_8$	9	10	$24^5/_8$	1591	171
	■ Monona Co. – Picked Up – Timothy C. Ashley – PR 1990										
$199^5/_8$	$25^2/_8$	22	$18^4/_8$	22	$6^2/_8$	$6^4/_8$	8	12	$44^7/_8$	1621	174
	■ Clinton Co. – Arlo M. Ketelsen – Arlo M. Ketelsen – 1985										
$199^4/_8$	$27^5/_8$	28	$22^2/_8$	$24^5/_8$	$5^4/_8$	$5^3/_8$	8	8	26	1631	175
	■ Linn Co. – Don J. Jilovec – Don J. Jilovec – 1988										
$199^3/_8$	$27^1/_8$	$24^7/_8$	$21^2/_8$	$23^2/_8$	$4^5/_8$	$4^7/_8$	10	7	$26^1/_8$	1639	176
	■ Iowa – Unknown – Charles E. Matthiesen – PR 1995										
$199^2/_8$	$28^1/_8$	$26^4/_8$	$19^4/_8$	$22^7/_8$	$5^3/_8$	$5^2/_8$	7	8	$13^6/_8$	1649	177
	■ Clayton Co. – Shane M. Hass – Shane M. Hass – 1998										
$199^1/_8$	$25^1/_8$	$25^7/_8$	$17^5/_8$	$22^3/_8$	$5^3/_8$	$4^6/_8$	11	7	$27^4/_8$	1660†	178†
	■ Lucas Co. – J.J. Keller & J.R. Keller – J.J. Keller & J.R. Keller – 2000										
199	$23^2/_8$	$22^4/_8$	$15^2/_8$	$20^4/_8$	5	5	10	9	45	1668	179
	■ Harrison Co. – Chester R. Hilton – Chester R. Hilton – 1958										
199	$26^1/_8$	$26^3/_8$	$19^6/_8$	$22^1/_8$	$5^4/_8$	$5^4/_8$	10	8	$27^4/_8$	1668	179
	■ Jackson Co. – John T. Kremer – John T. Kremer – 1983										
199	$25^5/_8$	$24^1/_8$	$18^5/_8$	$28^4/_8$	$5^3/_8$	$5^3/_8$	13	13	$46^1/_8$	1668	179
	■ Harrison Co. – Kody Wohlers – Kody Wohlers – 1998										
$198^6/_8$	26	24	$16^7/_8$	$22^4/_8$	5	$5^1/_8$	9	12	$32^3/_8$	1697†	182†
	■ Story Co. – Jarod J. Pederson – Jarod J. Pederson – 1999										
$198^6/_8$	$26^7/_8$	$26^4/_8$	$17^7/_8$	$24^5/_8$	$4^4/_8$	$4^4/_8$	9	8	$21^1/_8$	1697	182
	■ Butler Co. – Harlan Schmadeke – Harlan Schmadeke – 1999										
$198^5/_8$	$26^6/_8$	$27^6/_8$	$20^4/_8$	$22^4/_8$	$7^2/_8$	6	10	8	$40^5/_8$	1716	184
	■ Des Moines Co. – Craig R. Belknap – Craig R. Belknap – 1998 ■ See photo on page 50										
$198^4/_8$	$26^1/_8$	$25^3/_8$	$19^6/_8$	$21^5/_8$	$5^6/_8$	6	8	7	21	1736†	185†
	■ Pottawattamie Co. – Picked Up – IA Dept. of Natl. Resc. – 2000										
$198^4/_8$	$28^1/_8$	$27^3/_8$	$19^7/_8$	$22^1/_8$	$4^6/_8$	$4^6/_8$	10	9	$15^3/_8$	1736	185
	■ Madison Co. – Elvin H. Dickinson – Elvin H. Dickinson – 1982										
$198^3/_8$	$23^6/_8$	$23^3/_8$	$19^7/_8$	$24^7/_8$	$5^2/_8$	$5^2/_8$	9	7	$33^4/_8$	1762	187
	■ Pottawattamie Co. – Rodney P. Stahlnecker – Rodney P. Stahlnecker – 1991										

Score	Length of Main Beam Right	Left	Inside Spread	Greatest Spread	Circumference at Smallest Place Between Burr and First Point Right	Left	Number of Points Right	Left	Lengths Abnormal Points	All-Time Rank	State Rank
198²/8	26⁴/8	26⁶/8	17⁶/8	19⁶/8	4⁶/8	5¹/8	7	8	14⁶/8	1772	188
■ Madison Co. – Dan L. Bush – Dan L. Bush – 1987											
198²/8	26⁷/8	26⁵/8	19⁷/8	23²/8	5	5²/8	9	8	23¹/8	1772	188
■ Decatur Co. – Julian J. Toney – Julian J. Toney – 1991											
198²/8	25⁴/8	26¹/8	21⁶/8	29²/8	6	6²/8	12	11	44	1772	188
■ Wayne Co. – Dan L. Bishop – Dan L. Bishop – 1993											
198	27¹/8	25⁵/8	17³/8	20⁶/8	5⁵/8	6³/8	10	7	43⁵/8	1801†	191†
■ Jefferson Co. – Jesse Rebling – Jesse Rebling – 2001											
198	25⁵/8	27⁵/8	18⁷/8	21⁷/8	4⁷/8	4⁶/8	8	9	35⁷/8	1801†	191†
■ Jackson Co. – Jesse H. Smith – Jesse H. Smith – 2001											
198	27⁶/8	27⁶/8	21⁴/8	24³/8	5³/8	5³/8	6	9	17	1801	191
■ Louisa Co. – Larry Soteros – William H. Lilienthal – 1981											
197⁷/8	24⁴/8	25	17²/8	21³/8	5	5	9	10	43⁷/8	1816	194
■ Keokuk Co. – Bradley J. Messenger – Bradley J. Messenger – 1988											
197⁷/8	26³/8	27	20⁴/8	23¹/8	4⁶/8	4⁶/8	10	7	31¹/8	1816	194
■ Madison Co. – Scott R. Busch – Scott R. Busch – 1997 ■ See photo on page 60											
197⁵/8	26⁵/8	23¹/8	22⁴/8	26⁷/8	4⁷/8	4⁶/8	9	11	45⁵/8	1847†	196†
■ Appanoose Co. – Bill R. Clark – Bill R. Clark – 2001											
197⁵/8	26⁵/8	27³/8	20⁵/8	23	5	5	8	9	26⁶/8	1847	196
■ Monona Co. – Picked Up – Larry Koch – 1987											
197⁵/8	24	24⁶/8	16⁴/8	18⁶/8	4⁷/8	5¹/8	9	8	25⁷/8	1847	196
■ Monroe Co. – Raymond F. Hinkel – Raymond F. Hinkel – 1995											
197⁴/8	25	23⁷/8	22²/8	24³/8	5³/8	5⁴/8	7	7	15⁴/8	1866	199
■ Johnson Co. – Dennis R. Ballard – Dennis R. Ballard – 1971											
197⁴/8	27¹/8	27	20¹/8	22⁶/8	5²/8	5³/8	9	9	21⁵/8	1866	199
■ Boone Co. – Grant E. Saunders – Grant E. Saunders – 1990											
197⁴/8	23³/8	23	19¹/8	21	4⁶/8	4⁷/8	8	8	23³/8	1866	199
■ Lee Co. – Carl A. Bell – Carl A. Bell – 1995											
197²/8	26³/8	26²/8	22¹/8	25	4⁶/8	4⁴/8	10	11	20¹/8	1901	202
■ Winneshiek Co. – Richard M. Blaess – Richard M. Blaess – 1997											
197²/8	24³/8	26	23⁴/8	29¹/8	5⁴/8	4⁶/8	9	7	40⁶/8	1901	202
■ Marion Co. – Larry J. Lautenbach – Larry J. Lautenbach – 1998											
197	28²/8	26⁵/8	22¹/8	25²/8	5⁵/8	6	6	9	18¹/8	1939	204
■ Fayette Co. – Stanley E. Harrison – Stanley E. Harrison – 1973											
197	22	22⁵/8	14⁵/8	18⁴/8	4³/8	4⁶/8	13	11	52⁷/8	1939	204
■ Montgomery Co. – Picked Up – M. & S. Philby – 1988											
196⁷/8	24¹/8	24²/8	22⁶/8	24⁵/8	4⁵/8	4⁴/8	7	7	29⁵/8	1950	206
■ Wayne Co. – Marshall V. Ruble – Marshall V. Ruble – 1985											
196⁷/8	21⁶/8	25⁵/8	17⁶/8	19⁶/8	5⁶/8	5²/8	8	10	28⁷/8	1950	206
■ Linn Co. – James L. Newman – James L. Newman – 1996											
196⁷/8	28	28²/8	22	24⁶/8	5⁶/8	6¹/8	7	11	21³/8	1950	206
■ Winneshiek Co. – David G. Baumler – David G. Baumler – 1997											

Score	Length of Main Beam		Inside Spread	Greatest Spread	Circumference at Smallest Place Between Burr and First Point		Number of Points		Lengths Abnormal Points	All-Time Rank	State Rank
	Right	Left			Right	Left	Right	Left			
	■ Location of Kill – Hunter – Owner – Date Killed										
196 6/8	21 2/8	20 6/8	18 2/8	21 5/8	4 4/8	4 3/8	10	11	46 4/8	1968†	209†
■ Butler Co. – Edwin T. Blanchard – Edwin T. Blanchard – 2000											
196 6/8	27	28 2/8	18 6/8	22	4 4/8	4 4/8	9	9	24 6/8	1968	209
■ Clinton Co. – Robert W. Franks – Robert W. Franks – 1994											
196 6/8	26 2/8	26 4/8	25 1/8	26 7/8	6 1/8	6 1/8	8	6	16 3/8	1968	209
■ Jackson Co. – James L. Beetem – James L. Beetem – 1996											
196 5/8	25 6/8	25 1/8	20 6/8	23	5 7/8	5 5/8	9	8	37 3/8	1985	212
■ Van Buren Co. – Kenneth R. Barker – Kenneth R. Barker – 1984											
196 5/8	26 7/8	26 3/8	21 7/8	24 3/8	4 4/8	4 5/8	7	7	17 6/8	1985	212
■ Clarke Co. – Picked Up – William H. Lilienthal – PR 1990											
196 5/8	25	25 1/8	17 5/8	19 3/8	5 7/8	5 5/8	12	10	32 4/8	1985	212
■ Henry Co. – Troy M. Matter – Troy M. Matter – 1998											
196 4/8	26 4/8	25 6/8	17 1/8	19 7/8	5 4/8	5 3/8	8	10	19 3/8	1999†	215†
■ Page Co. – Michael L. Hughes – Michael L. Hughes – 1999											
196 4/8	26 4/8	25 6/8	18 5/8	25 4/8	4 7/8	5	8	11	21 3/8	1999	215
■ Lucas Co. – Steve Shanks – Steve Shanks – 1987											
196 3/8	25 6/8	25 3/8	20 3/8	23 7/8	5 6/8	5 6/8	11	11	27 6/8	2010†	217†
■ Clayton Co. – David D. Sadewasser – David D. Sadewasser – 2000											
196 3/8	24 7/8	25 2/8	15 3/8	18 5/8	4 6/8	4 7/8	10	12	20	2010	217
■ Lee Co. – Douglas W. Hopp – Douglas W. Hopp – 1984											
196 3/8	28 4/8	27	21 3/8	23 4/8	4 6/8	5	9	7	15	2010	217
■ Ringgold Co. – Frank J. Scovel – Frank J. Scovel – 1994											
196 2/8	25 4/8	25 7/8	19 6/8	22 3/8	5 3/8	5 5/8	10	11	21 6/8	2028	220
■ Winneshiek Co. – Picked Up – William H. Lilienthal – 1940											
196 2/8	24 7/8	24 6/8	18 4/8	20 4/8	5 2/8	5 4/8	8	7	15 6/8	2028	220
■ Louisa Co. – Tony Thomas – Tony Thomas – 1996											
196 1/8	28	27 1/8	18 7/8	20 5/8	4 1/8	4 4/8	9	7	30 4/8	2045	222
■ Guthrie Co. – Terry D. Danielson – Terry D. Danielson – 1995											
196	26 5/8	24 7/8	17 2/8	20 4/8	5 3/8	5 4/8	10	9	30	2059	223
■ Dubuque Co. – Terry D. Freese – Terry D. Freese – 1990											
196	21 5/8	22	13 2/8	18 6/8	5 6/8	6 2/8	8	9	31	2059	223
■ Muscatine Co. – James D. Evans – James D. Evans – 1995											
195 7/8	25 4/8	25 1/8	18 6/8	25	4 7/8	5 5/8	7	8	18 7/8	2076	225
■ Allamakee Co. – John L. Cahalan – John L. Cahalan – 1953											
195 7/8	28	28 5/8	20 1/8	26 3/8	5	4 7/8	8	9	20 2/8	2076	225
■ Wayne Co. – Michael S. Perkins – Michael S. Perkins – 1995											
195 6/8	24 4/8	25 2/8	19 4/8	25 4/8	5 6/8	5 4/8	8	10	34	2094	227
■ Lee Co. – Jesse W. Logan – Jesse W. Logan – 1996											
195 5/8	26 2/8	26 1/8	21 3/8	27 3/8	5 3/8	5 2/8	8	7	13 6/8	2116	228
■ Story Co. – Jordan L. Larson – Jordan L. Larson – 1983											
195 5/8	27	25 7/8	19 7/8	21 7/8	4 6/8	5 1/8	10	8	26 4/8	2116	228
■ Winneshiek Co. – Picked Up – Milan Kumlin – 1990											

Score	Length of Main Beam Right Left	Inside Spread	Greatest Spread	Circumference at Smallest Place Between Burr and First Point Right Left	Number of Points Right Left	Lengths Abnormal Points	All-Time Rank	State Rank
	■ Location of Kill – Hunter – Owner – Date Killed							
195⅝	24²⁄8 24³⁄8	13⁷⁄8	16⁴⁄8	5³⁄8 5⁶⁄8	8 9	14⁴⁄8	2116	228
	■ Appanoose Co. – Brent Carlson – Brent Carlson – 1994							
195⅝	27³⁄8 27³⁄8	19⁷⁄8	26⁴⁄8	5²⁄8 5²⁄8	9 10	23⁶⁄8	2116	228
	■ Allamakee Co. – Gary L. Mezera – Gary L. Mezera – 1994							
195⁴⁄8	24⁴⁄8 25³⁄8	16⁶⁄8	21⁴⁄8	6³⁄8 6¹⁄8	8 9	24²⁄8	2134†	232†
	■ Boone Co. – Joe R. Busch – Joe R. Busch – 2001							
195⁴⁄8	23³⁄8 23³⁄8	23³⁄8	25	5⁴⁄8 5³⁄8	8 9	32⁵⁄8	2134	232
	■ Winneshiek Co. – Clair R. Malanaphy – Clair R. Malanaphy – 1998							
195³⁄8	26³⁄8 26	20²⁄8	22¹⁄8	6 5⁷⁄8	9 8	29³⁄8	2163	234
	■ Scott Co. – Jeffrey Rasche – Jeffrey Rasche – 1989							
195³⁄8	25⁷⁄8 25⁶⁄8	19³⁄8	21⁶⁄8	5³⁄8 5²⁄8	8 12	25	2163	234
	■ Allamakee Co. – Picked Up – Douglas A. Bartz – 1998							
195²⁄8	25 23⁴⁄8	18⁴⁄8	22	5⁴⁄8 5³⁄8	11 11	30⁶⁄8	2186	236
	■ Pottawattamie Co. – Ted Houser – Ted Houser – 1968							
195¹⁄8	25⁴⁄8 26	17⁶⁄8	19⁶⁄8	4⁴⁄8 4⁴⁄8	7 8	26³⁄8	2208	237
	■ Lucas Co. – Picked Up – Don Jessop – 1993							
195	26⁴⁄8 26¹⁄8	15²⁄8	19³⁄8	5⁵⁄8 5⁶⁄8	7 7	13⁶⁄8	2233†	238†
	■ Dubuque Co. – Adam W. Anglin – Adam W. Anglin – 2001							
195	26⁶⁄8 26⁶⁄8	19³⁄8	21²⁄8	5⁵⁄8 5⁵⁄8	8 7	14⁷⁄8	2233†	238†
	■ Delaware Co. – Joseph D. Hoeger – Joseph D. Hoeger – 2000							
195	25⁶⁄8 27⁵⁄8	20³⁄8	23³⁄8	5⁴⁄8 5³⁄8	11 13	37⁵⁄8	2233	238
	■ Guthrie Co. – Tom C. Klever – Tom C. Klever – 1982							
195	25⁴⁄8 25	18⁶⁄8	19⁶⁄8	4⁵⁄8 4⁵⁄8	10 9	27	2233	238
	■ Clarke Co. – Picked Up – Jeff Jorgenson – 1985							
195	27⁵⁄8 27¹⁄8	20	22²⁄8	5 5	9 8	14	2233	238
	■ Montgomery Co. – Mark L. King – Mark L. King – 1985							
195	25 25	20¹⁄8	25¹⁄8	5¹⁄8 5²⁄8	9 8	22⁷⁄8	2233	238
	■ Allamakee Co. – Joey Richards – Teresa Waters – 1991							
195	27³⁄8 27	18⁵⁄8	24⁴⁄8	5¹⁄8 5¹⁄8	7 8	21⁵⁄8	2233	238
	■ Guthrie Co. – Chad Laabs – Chad Laabs – 1996							
195	25⁷⁄8 25³⁄8	20⁶⁄8	24²⁄8	4⁶⁄8 4⁷⁄8	7 10	25⁶⁄8	2233	238
	■ Jasper Co. – Ronald D. Steenhoek – Ronald D. Steenhoek – 1996							
193¹⁄8	29¹⁄8 28¹⁄8	21	23²⁄8	5 4⁷⁄8	5 7	19¹⁄8	2305	246
	■ Lucas Co. – Picked Up – Cabela's, Inc. – 1992							
193¹⁄8	24⁵⁄8 23²⁄8	16⁵⁄8	20³⁄8	5³⁄8 5⁴⁄8	6 8	20⁶⁄8	2305	246
	■ Appanoose Co. – Brad Moore – Brad Moore – 1995							
192⁷⁄8	25⁴⁄8 26²⁄8	18	20²⁄8	4⁵⁄8 4⁶⁄8	10 14	26⁷⁄8	2312	248
	■ Warren Co. – Joey B. Ballard – Joey B. Ballard – 1994							
192⁴⁄8	26²⁄8 26³⁄8	19⁶⁄8	25⁶⁄8	4⁷⁄8 5²⁄8	7 8	22²⁄8	2325	249
	■ Wapello Co. – Kennard C. Kaplan – Kennard C. Kaplan – 1990							
192⁴⁄8	22 25	20⁶⁄8	25⁵⁄8	4⁶⁄8 4⁴⁄8	8 8	19	2325	249
	■ Lucas Co. – Brad S. Pruismann – Brad S. Pruismann – 1999							

Score	Length of Main Beam Right	Left	Inside Spread	Greatest Spread	Circumference at Smallest Place Between Burr and First Point Right	Left	Number of Points Right	Left	Lengths Abnormal Points	All-Time Rank	State Rank
191 6/8	27 5/8	26 4/8	17 4/8	22 5/8	5	5	9	9	27	2354	251
■ Davis Co. – Harry E. Nicholson, Jr. – Harry E. Nicholson, Jr. – 1988											
191 5/8	24 7/8	24 6/8	17 6/8	19 7/8	5	4 6/8	9	9	21 7/8	2355†	252†
■ Allamakee Co. – Michael J. Manning – Michael J. Manning – 2000											
191 4/8	24 3/8	24 3/8	21 2/8	23	5 2/8	5 4/8	8	9	21 6/8	2357	253
■ Wayne Co. – Dennis J. Pollock – Dennis J. Pollock – 1996											
191	24 5/8	24 6/8	15 3/8	18 4/8	4 5/8	4 5/8	8	8	20 5/8	2380	254
■ Cedar Co. – Chris E. Bergmann – Chris E. Bergmann – 1997											
189 5/8	21 5/8	23 3/8	18 3/8	19	7 2/8	5 2/8	11	6	27 2/8	2429	255
■ Audubon Co. – Kevin Hinners – Kevin Hinners – 1994											
188 6/8	25 6/8	26 5/8	20 7/8	23 3/8	5 4/8	5	8	8	12 7/8	2468	256
■ Fayette Co. – Darin R. Schrader – Darin R. Schrader – 1995											
188 1/8	26 5/8	28 1/8	22 1/8	24 1/8	4 7/8	5 1/8	6	10	11 6/8	2497	257
■ Clay Co. – Bob Syndergarrd – Bob Syndergarrd – 1984											
187 4/8	23 5/8	24 4/8	19 2/8	22 4/8	5	5 2/8	7	10	12 6/8	2522	258
■ Mahaska Co. – Jason W. Fox – Jason W. Fox – 1989											
187 3/8	26 3/8	24 5/8	15 4/8	19 1/8	5 2/8	5	7	10	27 1/8	2528†	259†
■ Linn Co. – Charles E. Ganoe – Charles E. Ganoe – 2000											
186 4/8	21 6/8	24	20 7/8	23 1/8	4 7/8	5 1/8	8	8	46 3/8	2568	260
■ Clayton Co. – Francis C. O'Donnell – Francis C. O'Donnell – 1988											
186	25 3/8	25	17 4/8	19 5/8	5 5/8	6	8	8	13 4/8	2586	261
■ Guthrie Co. – Kendall D. Kipp – Kendall D. Kipp – 1994											
185 4/8	28 2/8	27 2/8	19 2/8	22 2/8	4 3/8	4 4/8	10	6	11 4/8	2616	262
■ Greene Co. – Dennis Matthews – Dennis Matthews – 1994											
185 3/8	25 7/8	24 4/8	15 4/8	18	4 6/8	4 7/8	9	10	35 3/8	2622	263
■ Madison Co. – Dwayne C. Bechtol – Dwayne C. Bechtol – 1999											
185 1/8	26 4/8	24 2/8	19 1/8	21 7/8	5 4/8	5 6/8	7	5	15	2641	264
■ Mills Co. – John R. McElvain – John R. McElvain – 1999											
185 1/8	26 1/8	24 2/8	19 4/8	23 3/8	5 6/8	5 6/8	7	8	19 5/8	2641	264
■ Fayette Co. – Gerald Miller – Gerald Miller – 1999											
185	25 3/8	24 6/8	22 6/8	25	4 6/8	4 7/8	6	7	17 6/8	2653†	266†
■ Winneshiek Co. – Craig M. Eggert – Craig M. Eggert – 2001											

■ Location of Kill – Hunter – Owner – Date Killed

† The scores and ranking for trophies from the 25th Awards Entry Period are not final until the banquet is held on June 19, 2004.

TROPHIES IN THE FIELD

HUNTER: Arthur D. Wille
SCORE: 228-2/8
CATEGORY: non-typical whitetail deer
LOCATION: Dubuque County, Iowa
DATE: 2000

KANSAS
RECORD WHITETAILS

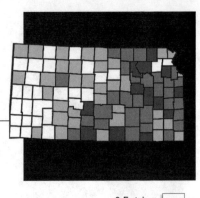

169 Typical whitetail deer entries
126 Non-typical whitetail deer entries
7,265 Total whitetail deer entries

0 Entries
1-2 Entries
3-5 Entries
6-10 Entries
11+ Entries

**KANSAS
STATE RECORD**
Typical Whitetail Deer
Score: $198^2/8$
Location: Nemaha Co.
Hunter and Owner:
    Dennis P. Finger
Date: 1974

Photograph from B&C Archives

KANSAS
STATE RECORD
Non-Typical Whitetail Deer
Score: 280^4/$_8$
Location: Shawnee Co.
Hunter: Joseph H. Waters
Owner: Brad Gsell
Date: 1987

KANSAS

TYPICAL WHITETAIL DEER

Score	Length of Main Beam		Inside Spread	Greatest Spread	Circumference at Smallest Place Between Burr and First Point		Number of Points		Lengths Abnormal Points	All-Time Rank	State Rank
	Right	Left			Right	Left	Right	Left			
	▪ Location of Kill – Hunter – Owner – Date Killed										
198 2/8	27 5/8	26 7/8	20 2/8	22 4/8	5	5	6	8	4 6/8	19	1
	▪ Nemaha Co. – Dennis P. Finger – Dennis P. Finger – 1974										
197 2/8	25 4/8	27 2/8	32	33	5 2/8	5 3/8	6	7		27	2
	▪ Comanche Co. – Picked Up – H. James Reimer – 1991										
194 7/8	26 7/8	27 2/8	23 1/8	25 4/8	6 1/8	5 6/8	7	7	4 6/8	41	3
	▪ Leavenworth Co. – William R. Mikijanis – William R. Mikijanis – 1985										
191 4/8	26 5/8	27 4/8	20	22 2/8	4 7/8	5	6	7	1 4/8	82	4
	▪ Chautauqua Co. – Michael A. Young – Michael A. Young – 1973										
190 7/8	26 3/8	26 1/8	19 5/8	22 2/8	4 4/8	4 6/8	7	6	1 2/8	89	5
	▪ Lyon Co. – Jamie Fowler – Jamie Fowler – 1992										
190 7/8	25 2/8	25 4/8	20 7/8	22 7/8	4 5/8	5	5	5		89	5
	▪ Geary Co. – Gary L. Taylor – Gary L. Taylor – 1994										
190 3/8	29 3/8	28 6/8	22 2/8	24 4/8	5 6/8	5 7/8	10	7	8 1/8	102	7
	▪ Republic Co. – John M. Nylund – John M. Nylund – 1995										
188 4/8	27 2/8	28 7/8	20 1/8	22	5	4 7/8	8	8	9 5/8	141	8
	▪ Riley Co. – Robert E. Luke – Brad Sowter – 1984										
188 2/8	28 1/8	28 6/8	25 7/8	26 7/8	4 4/8	4 5/8	5	7	3 1/8	151	9
	▪ Cowley Co. – Armand L. Hillier – Armand L. Hillier – 1996										
187 5/8	27	27 1/8	17	21	5 3/8	5 2/8	7	6	3 5/8	165	10
	▪ Bourbon Co. – Picked Up – George J. McLiney, Jr. – 1990										
187	29 2/8	28	25 5/8	27 7/8	5 6/8	5 7/8	6	6	3 7/8	191	11
	▪ Geary Co. – Jack Swenson – Brad Sowter – 1997										
186 3/8	27 5/8	27 1/8	20 4/8	22 7/8	6 1/8	5 6/8	7	6	4 1/8	210	12
	▪ Morris Co. – Garold D. Miller – Garold D. Miller – 1969										
186 1/8	29 2/8	28 2/8	20 3/8	23 5/8	4 6/8	4 5/8	7	7	3 4/8	228†	13†
	▪ Franklin Co. – Stephen P. Edwards – Stephen P. Edwards – 2001										
185 3/8	29	28 1/8	23	25 3/8	4 7/8	4 7/8	9	8	6 3/8	256	14
	▪ Riley Co. – Robert L. Tully – Robert L. Tully – 1988										
185 3/8	23 1/8	27 2/8	23 7/8	26	5 1/8	5 5/8	7	9	3 2/8	256	14
	▪ Morris Co. – Gregory A. Glasgow – Gregory A. Glasgow – 1998										
185	28	27 3/8	26 5/8	28 6/8	5 2/8	5 4/8	10	11	20 5/8	272†	16†
	▪ Lyon Co. – Ronald L. Sleisher – Ronald L. Sleisher – 2001										
185	26 7/8	27	17 5/8	20 6/8	5 7/8	6	10	8	17 5/8	272	16
	▪ Seward Co. – Michael D. Gatlin – Michael D. Gatlin – 1987										
184 4/8	30 3/8	30 4/8	20 4/8	25	5	5 1/8	7	7	17 6/8	303	18
	▪ Chase Co. – Thomas D. Mosher – Thomas D. Mosher – 1984										
184 3/8	27 6/8	28	23	26 2/8	5 6/8	5 4/8	8	6	6 1/8	313	19
	▪ Reno Co. – Michael Denney – Michael Denny – 1991										

Score	Length of Main Beam Right	Left	Inside Spread	Greatest Spread	Circumference at Smallest Place Between Burr and First Point Right	Left	Number of Points Right	Left	Lengths Abnormal Points	All-Time Rank	State Rank
	■ Location of Kill − Hunter − Owner − Date Killed										
184	28^1/8	27^6/8	20^5/8	23^4/8	5^2/8	5^1/8	6	6	4^3/8	334	20
	■ Saline Co. − James R. Bell − James R. Bell − 1985										
183^7/8	29^3/8	27^3/8	22^5/8	24^6/8	5^1/8	5^1/8	6	5	1^4/8	343	21
	■ Washington Co. − Rick B. Novak − Rick B. Novak − 1997										
183^6/8	30^7/8	29^7/8	24	26^4/8	5^5/8	5^4/8	5	8	4	350	22
	■ Morris Co. − Craig C. Johnson − Craig C. Johnson − 1991										
183^6/8	27^4/8	27^1/8	22^2/8	25^1/8	5^2/8	5^3/8	6	6	3^2/8	350	22
	■ Franklin Co. − Picked Up − B&C National Collection − 1994										
183^6/8	28^7/8	29^1/8	19^4/8	21^6/8	4^4/8	4^4/8	5	5		350	22
	■ Sumner Co. − Larry D. Bacon − Larry D. Bacon − 1995										
183^3/8	27^4/8	28	19^7/8	22^7/8	5^4/8	5^4/8	5	7	4	365†	25†
	■ Anderson Co. − Brian K. Hanes − Brian K. Hanes − 2001										
183^3/8	26^6/8	26^7/8	21^1/8	23^3/8	4^7/8	5^2/8	6	9	7^4/8	365	25
	■ Nemaha Co. − Roy D. Rissky − Roy D. Rissky − 1998										
183^2/8	29^1/8	28^3/8	20^4/8	22^5/8	4^4/8	4^4/8	5	6		378	27
	■ Shawnee Co. − Mark W. Young − Mark W. Young − 1990										
182^6/8	28^2/8	28^6/8	19	21^2/8	6^3/8	6^2/8	8	6	9	409	28
	■ Labette Co. − David W. Steeby − Cabela's, Inc. − 1989										
182^5/8	27^6/8	28^5/8	19^2/8	21^4/8	5^4/8	5^6/8	7	5	2^5/8	420	29
	■ Republic Co. − Jody Hadachek − Jody Hadachek − 1995										
182^3/8	27	26^5/8	23^1/8	26	5^7/8	5^7/8	6	5	1	438	30
	■ Waubaunsee Co. − Norman Anderson − Norman Anderson − 1966										
181^6/8	23^6/8	23^3/8	20^6/8	23^7/8	5^3/8	5^2/8	5	5		492	31
	■ Lyon Co. − Kenneth C. Haynes − Kenneth C. Haynes − 1969										
181^6/8	27^5/8	28^3/8	21^2/8	23^3/8	4^6/8	5^3/8	6	6		492	31
	■ Bourbon Co. − Larry Daly − Larry Daly − 1990										
181^3/8	28^2/8	29^3/8	21^2/8	24^4/8	5^5/8	5^3/8	8	7	4^3/8	528	33
	■ Stafford Co. − Aaron W. King − Aaron W. King − 1995										
180^2/8	26^1/8	26^1/8	17^4/8	19^6/8	4^6/8	4^7/8	7	8	2^6/8	651	34
	■ Cowley Co. − Thomas W. Jackson − Thomas W. Jackson − 1994										
180	26^4/8	27^1/8	18^2/8	21^3/8	5^3/8	5^5/8	6	5		688	35
	■ Edwards Co. − David R. Cross − David R. Cross − 1985										
179^6/8	25^6/8	26^5/8	21	23^1/8	6^1/8	5^5/8	7	5	3^6/8	712	36
	■ Osage Co. − Ronald D. Fine − Ronald D. Fine − 1999										
179^4/8	26^5/8	25^3/8	22	24^1/8	5^4/8	5^2/8	6	6		733†	37†
	■ Barber Co. − Picked Up − Bill J. Timms − 1999										
179^4/8	27^5/8	27^3/8	19^7/8	23^5/8	5	5	6	6	3^7/8	733	37
	■ Elk Co. − Lowell E. Howell − Lowell E. Howell − 1973										
179^1/8	28^4/8	28^1/8	21^3/8	23^2/8	4^7/8	5	6	7	1^6/8	779	39
	■ Butler Co. − Donald B. Williamson − Donald B. Williamson − 1994										
178^6/8	26	26^5/8	21^2/8	23^6/8	5^2/8	5^2/8	6	8	5^4/8	808	40
	■ McPherson Co. − Larry D. Daniel − Larry D. Daniel − 1967										

Score	Length of Main Beam Right	Left	Inside Spread	Greatest Spread	Circumference at Smallest Place Between Burr and First Point Right	Left	Number of Points Right	Left	Lengths Abnormal Points	All-Time Rank	State Rank
	■ Location of Kill – Hunter – Owner – Date Killed										
$178^5/8$	$27^1/8$	$27^5/8$	$20^3/8$	$22^3/8$	$4^6/8$	$4^6/8$	8	6	$5^6/8$	819	41
	■ Riley Co. – Colt Knutson – Colt Knutson – 1989										
$178^3/8$	$25^2/8$	$23^2/8$	$19^1/8$	$21^4/8$	$4^1/8$	$4^2/8$	7	6		868†	42†
	■ Phillips Co. – Harold Dusin – Robert C. Dusin – 1973										
$178^3/8$	$29^4/8$	$30^2/8$	$18^4/8$	$22^6/8$	$5^5/8$	$5^2/8$	7	6	$4^3/8$	868	42
	■ Bourbon Co. – Ronald D. Pfeiffer – Ronald D. Pfeiffer – 1995										
$177^6/8$	$27^6/8$	$28^1/8$	$19^1/8$	21	$4^3/8$	$4^4/8$	7	8	$12^5/8$	956	44
	■ Anderson Co. – Randall R. West – Randall R. West – 1990										
$177^6/8$	$26^5/8$	$27^4/8$	$19^6/8$	$22^1/8$	$4^6/8$	$4^6/8$	5	5		956	44
	■ Sumner Co. – Alan K. Boyle – Alan K. Boyle – 1995										
$175^5/8$	$27^7/8$	27	$19^2/8$	$21^4/8$	$6^3/8$	$6^5/8$	9	9	$13^7/8$	972	46
	■ Marshall Co. – Terre J. Carter – Terre J. Carter – 1992										
$175^5/8$	$26^5/8$	25	$17^7/8$	$19^7/8$	$5^1/8$	$5^1/8$	5	6		972	46
	■ Nemaha Co. – Stephen C. Damron – Stephen C. Damron – 1995										
$177^3/8$	$25^4/8$	$27^1/8$	$22^3/8$	$24^7/8$	$5^1/8$	$5^4/8$	6	6		1011	48
	■ Chautauqua Co. – Wesley D. Coldren – Wesley D. Coldren – 1991										
$177^3/8$	$26^6/8$	$26^5/8$	$18^7/8$	$20^6/8$	$5^1/8$	$5^2/8$	5	5		1011	48
	■ Gove Co. – Daniel L. Arndt – Daniel L. Arndt – 1997										
$177^3/8$	$27^7/8$	$28^2/8$	$23^1/8$	$25^6/8$	$5^2/8$	$5^3/8$	5	6	$4^6/8$	1011	48
	■ Woodson Co. – Terry S. Wells – Terry S. Wells – 1998										
$177^2/8$	$29^4/8$	$30^2/8$	$18^2/8$	21	$6^5/8$	$6^3/8$	6	6	$4^6/8$	1025	51
	■ Geary Co. – Kelly D. Gulker – Kelly D. Gulker – 1982										
$176^7/8$	$25^2/8$	$25^5/8$	$22^1/8$	$23^5/8$	$4^6/8$	5	5	5		1086	52
	■ Butler Co. – Craig D. Waltman – Craig D. Waltman – 1982										
$176^6/8$	$25^2/8$	25	$23^4/8$	$26^4/8$	$4^4/8$	$4^6/8$	6	6	$2^4/8$	1103	53
	■ Frankfort – Ray A. Mosher – Ray A. Mosher – 1966										
$176^6/8$	$24^4/8$	$24^5/8$	$19^4/8$	$20^7/8$	5	$5^3/8$	6	6		1103	53
	■ Miami Co. – Richard T. Hale – Richard T. Hale – 1985										
$176^6/8$	$28^3/8$	$27^6/8$	$18^4/8$	$20^5/8$	$5^1/8$	$5^2/8$	8	5	6	1103	53
	■ Morris Co. – Nathan D. Muncy – Nathan D. Muncy – 1992										
$176^5/8$	28	$28^6/8$	$19^1/8$	$21^3/8$	$5^2/8$	$5^3/8$	7	6	7	1134	56
	■ Dickinson Co. – Robert L. Aldrich – Robert L. Aldrich – 1986										
$176^3/8$	$28^3/8$	28	$21^4/8$	$23^6/8$	$6^2/8$	$5^7/8$	6	9	$8^7/8$	1182	57
	■ Geary Co. – Donald J. Ereth – Donald J. Ereth – 1994										
$176^2/8$	$27^1/8$	$26^2/8$	24	$25^7/8$	5	5	5	6	$1^2/8$	1209	58
	■ Washington Co. – Roger W. Novak – Roger W. Novak – 1995										
$176^1/8$	$25^7/8$	$25^6/8$	$18^5/8$	$20^6/8$	5	$5^1/8$	6	6	$13^2/8$	1243	59
	■ Brown Co. – Dennis P. Finger – Dennis P. Finger – 1992										
176	$24^5/8$	$25^6/8$	$21^6/8$	24	$4^7/8$	$4^7/8$	5	5		1266	60
	■ Russell Co. – Don Mai – Don Mai – 1981										
176	$26^4/8$	27	$18^4/8$	$21^5/8$	$4^7/8$	$4^6/8$	5	7	$4^2/8$	1266	60
	■ Nemaha Co. – Joseph L. Schmelzle – Joseph L. Schmelzle – 1985										

Score	Length of Main Beam Right	Left	Inside Spread	Greatest Spread	Circumference at Smallest Place Between Burr and First Point Right	Left	Number of Points Right	Left	Lengths Abnormal Points	All-Time Rank	State Rank
175 6/8	26 3/8	24 5/8	19 6/8	22	5 5/8	5 7/8	5	6	1 4/8	1310	62
■ Nemaha Co. – Kevin L. Kramer – Kevin L. Kramer – 1988											
175 5/8	24 6/8	24 6/8	17 5/8	20	4 5/8	4 6/8	5	5		1333	63
■ Pottawatomie Co. – Orten L. Dodds – Orten L. Dodds – 1992											
175 3/8	25 4/8	25	21	23 5/8	4 6/8	4 5/8	6	8	1 1/8	1377	64
■ Linn Co. – Lloyd L. Wilson III – Lloyd L. Wilson III – 1995											
175 1/8	26 3/8	26 2/8	19 7/8	22 1/8	5 2/8	5 1/8	6	7	2 4/8	1440	65
■ Butler Co. – Paul E. Kemp – Paul E. Kemp – 1993											
175	22 7/8	23 5/8	18 6/8	20 3/8	5	5	5	5		1472†	66†
■ Sheridan Co. – Les S. Brown – Les S. Brown – 2001											
175	24 4/8	24 2/8	21 2/8	24 7/8	4 6/8	4 7/8	6	6	3 4/8	1472†	66†
■ Leavenworth Co. – Dennis L. Yarnell – Dennis L. Yarnell – 2001											
174 6/8	25 1/8	24 6/8	18 3/8	20 3/8	4 7/8	4 5/8	7	7	2 7/8	1534	68
■ Leavenworth Co. – Mark R. Wegner – Mark R. Wegner – 1999											
174 5/8	22 4/8	21 4/8	17 1/8	19	5	5	7	6		1561	69
■ Jefferson Co. – Keith D. Hendrix – Keith D. Hendrix – 1973											
174 5/8	25 6/8	25 3/8	18 1/8	22 3/8	5	4 7/8	5	6	4	1561	69
■ Lyon Co. – Joshua W. Koch – Joshua W. Koch – 1997											
174 4/8	26 2/8	27 2/8	16 1/8	18 5/8	5	4 6/8	5	6	1 5/8	1592	71
■ Stafford Co. – Darin J. Brummer – Darin J. Brummer – 1995											
174 3/8	25 4/8	26 3/8	18 3/8	20 4/8	4 6/8	5	9	8	15 4/8	1619	72
■ Marshall Co. – Michael J. Krogman – Michael J. Krogman – 1981											
174 3/8	27 2/8	25 2/8	23 6/8	26	5 1/8	5	7	7	7 1/8	1619	72
■ Geary Co. – James Brethour – James Brethour – 1984											
174 3/8	28 5/8	28 5/8	21 2/8	24 1/8	5 2/8	5 3/8	6	7	3 3/8	1619	72
■ Barber Co. – James B. Talbott – James B. Talbott – 1993											
174 3/8	23 4/8	23 4/8	19 3/8	21 4/8	5 2/8	5 3/8	6	6	4	1619	72
■ Marion Co. – Matt E. Vaughn – Matt E. Vaughn – 1995											
174 3/8	27 6/8	27 3/8	22 3/8	24 7/8	5 1/8	5 1/8	5	5		1619	72
■ Osage Co. – Evans Woehlecke – Evans Woehlecke – 1997											
174 2/8	25 4/8	27 3/8	18 6/8	21 1/8	4 6/8	4 7/8	7	8	4	1652†	77†
■ Saline Co. – Robert L. Darrow – Cabela's, Inc. – 2000											
174 1/8	23 2/8	24 5/8	20 6/8	23	5 1/8	5 2/8	5	5	1 5/8	1678	78
■ Johnson Co. – Ralph E. Schlagel – Ralph E. Schlagel – 1984											
174	29 3/8	29 7/8	19	22 4/8	4 5/8	5	4	4		1717	79
■ Johnson Co. – Kevin M. Hancock – Kevin M. Hancock – 1996											
174	27 6/8	26	18	20	4 6/8	4 6/8	5	5		1717	79
■ Marion Co. – Gerald W. Lock – Gerald W. Lock – 1997											
173 6/8	25 6/8	25 6/8	21 4/8	24	5 2/8	5	6	5	1	1766†	81†
■ Comanche Co. – Kenneth W. Williams – Kenneth W. Williams – 2001											
■ See photo on page 209											
173 6/8	25	23 6/8	22 3/8	24 1/8	6	6	7	5	8 5/8	1766	81
■ Sublette – Neal Heaton – Neal Heaton – 1993											

Score	Length of Main Beam Right	Left	Inside Spread	Greatest Spread	Circumference at Smallest Place Between Burr and First Point Right	Left	Number of Points Right	Left	Lengths Abnormal Points	All-Time Rank	State Rank
$173\frac{6}{8}$	$27\frac{2}{8}$	28	$19\frac{2}{8}$	$21\frac{3}{8}$	$4\frac{4}{8}$	$4\frac{4}{8}$	5	5		1766	81
■ Reno Co. – James E. Dye – James E. Dye – 1997											
$173\frac{6}{8}$	$24\frac{4}{8}$	25	$17\frac{4}{8}$	$19\frac{4}{8}$	$4\frac{3}{8}$	$4\frac{1}{8}$	5	6		1766	81
■ Allen Co. – Dewey L. Lewis – Dewey L. Lewis – 1997											
$173\frac{5}{8}$	24	$22\frac{2}{8}$	$19\frac{1}{8}$	25	5	5	5	6	2	1819	85
■ Morris Co. – Wayne Kasten – Wayne Kasten – 1985											
$173\frac{4}{8}$	$28\frac{4}{8}$	$27\frac{1}{8}$	$22\frac{1}{8}$	$26\frac{7}{8}$	$5\frac{6}{8}$	$5\frac{2}{8}$	5	5	$6\frac{1}{8}$	1847	86
■ Ellsworth Co. – Monte Hudson – Monte Hudson – 1986											
$173\frac{4}{8}$	$25\frac{5}{8}$	$25\frac{3}{8}$	18	$20\frac{3}{8}$	5	5	6	6	$2\frac{6}{8}$	1847	86
■ Barber Co. – James R. Schreiner – James R. Schreiner – 1990											
$173\frac{3}{8}$	$27\frac{4}{8}$	$27\frac{4}{8}$	$17\frac{1}{8}$	$19\frac{6}{8}$	$4\frac{5}{8}$	$4\frac{6}{8}$	7	5	$3\frac{6}{8}$	1883	88
■ Clay Co. – Charles A. Hammons – Charles A. Hammons – 1984											
$173\frac{3}{8}$	$26\frac{3}{8}$	$26\frac{6}{8}$	$25\frac{7}{8}$	$27\frac{5}{8}$	$4\frac{5}{8}$	$4\frac{5}{8}$	6	6	$4\frac{4}{8}$	1883	88
■ Riley Co. – Russell B. Santo – Russell B. Santo – 1989											
$173\frac{3}{8}$	26	$25\frac{4}{8}$	$18\frac{1}{8}$	$21\frac{4}{8}$	$4\frac{1}{8}$	$4\frac{3}{8}$	6	5	$1\frac{4}{8}$	1883	88
■ Chautauqua Co. – Wesley D. Coldren – Wesley D. Coldren – 1992											
$173\frac{3}{8}$	$26\frac{1}{8}$	$26\frac{2}{8}$	23	$25\frac{4}{8}$	$5\frac{1}{8}$	$5\frac{2}{8}$	5	8	$9\frac{7}{8}$	1883	88
■ Linn Co. – Vernon L. Morrell, Jr. – Vernon L. Morrell, Jr. – 1997											
$173\frac{1}{8}$	$28\frac{5}{8}$	$28\frac{6}{8}$	$22\frac{2}{8}$	$25\frac{1}{8}$	$5\frac{4}{8}$	$5\frac{7}{8}$	6	6	$7\frac{5}{8}$	1950	92
■ Wabaunsee Co. – James D. Downey – James D. Downey – 1970											
$173\frac{1}{8}$	$26\frac{4}{8}$	$26\frac{2}{8}$	$20\frac{1}{8}$	$23\frac{2}{8}$	$4\frac{4}{8}$	$4\frac{6}{8}$	5	5		1950	92
■ Pottawatomie Co. – Donald L. Smith – Donald L. Smith – 1990											
$173\frac{1}{8}$	$25\frac{5}{8}$	25	$21\frac{1}{8}$	$22\frac{7}{8}$	$4\frac{2}{8}$	$4\frac{2}{8}$	7	6	2	1950	92
■ Kansas – Unknown – James B. Sisco III – PR 1995											
173	27	$27\frac{2}{8}$	$23\frac{5}{8}$	$25\frac{4}{8}$	$5\frac{7}{8}$	$6\frac{1}{8}$	6	7	$4\frac{7}{8}$	1991	95
■ Doniphan Co. – Charles A. Staudenmier – Charles A. Staudenmier – 1983											
173	$27\frac{1}{8}$	$27\frac{1}{8}$	$21\frac{2}{8}$	$26\frac{7}{8}$	$5\frac{1}{8}$	$5\frac{1}{8}$	5	7	$9\frac{4}{8}$	1991	95
■ Shawnee Co. – Frank R. Murray – Frank R. Murray – 1989											
$172\frac{6}{8}$	$29\frac{3}{8}$	$27\frac{7}{8}$	$18\frac{6}{8}$	21	$4\frac{6}{8}$	5	5	6		2065†	97†
■ Elk Co. – Michael E. Benge – Michael E. Benge – 2000											
$172\frac{6}{8}$	$25\frac{4}{8}$	$25\frac{6}{8}$	22	$23\frac{5}{8}$	$5\frac{4}{8}$	$5\frac{4}{8}$	5	4		2065	97
■ Stafford Co. – Donald G. Fisher – Donald G. Fisher – 1989											
$172\frac{6}{8}$	26	$26\frac{4}{8}$	18	$19\frac{4}{8}$	$5\frac{5}{8}$	$5\frac{5}{8}$	6	6	$4\frac{6}{8}$	2065	97
■ Washington Co. – Todd Jueneman – Todd Jueneman – 1996											
$172\frac{6}{8}$	28	$28\frac{1}{8}$	$24\frac{4}{8}$	27	$4\frac{1}{8}$	$4\frac{2}{8}$	5	5		2065	97
■ Russell Co. – Mark A. Heinz – Mark A. Heinz – 1997											
$172\frac{5}{8}$	$26\frac{1}{8}$	$26\frac{3}{8}$	$17\frac{7}{8}$	$19\frac{5}{8}$	$4\frac{3}{8}$	$4\frac{3}{8}$	6	5	$5\frac{4}{8}$	2113†	101†
■ Stafford Co. – David Carlton – David Carlton – 2000											
$172\frac{5}{8}$	$26\frac{7}{8}$	$27\frac{1}{8}$	$19\frac{2}{8}$	$22\frac{1}{8}$	$4\frac{4}{8}$	$4\frac{4}{8}$	5	6	$3\frac{5}{8}$	2113	101
■ Lyon Co. – Dale L. Hellman – Dale L. Hellman – 1990											
$172\frac{5}{8}$	26	$26\frac{1}{8}$	$22\frac{3}{8}$	$23\frac{6}{8}$	5	$5\frac{1}{8}$	6	6		2113	101
■ Smith Co. – Jonathan D. Weavers – Jonathan D. Weavers – 1998											

Score	Length of Main Beam Right	Left	Inside Spread	Greatest Spread	Circumference at Smallest Place Between Burr and First Point Right	Left	Number of Points Right	Left	Lengths Abnormal Points	All-Time Rank	State Rank
172⁴/8	27⁷/8	28⁴/8	16²/8	18⁴/8	5	5	5	6	7⁶/8	2156	104
■ Stafford Co. – Alan Baldwin – Alan Baldwin – 1995											
172³/8	27	26⁷/8	19¹/8	20⁷/8	5	4⁷/8	5	5		2200	105
■ Johnson Co. – David T. Reed – David T. Reed – 1990											
172²/8	24⁶/8	25³/8	18²/8	20²/8	5²/8	5¹/8	5	5		2237	106
■ Trego Co. – Alan Baldwin – Alan Baldwin – 1982											
172²/8	27³/8	27⁶/8	21³/8	24⁶/8	5⁵/8	5⁶/8	8	8	11³/8	2237	106
■ Norton Co. – Jim Keenan – Jim Keenan – 1993											
172¹/8	24²/8	24⁷/8	19⁵/8	21⁷/8	4³/8	4³/8	5	6	3	2286	108
■ Wyandotte Co. – Earl A. Cooksey – Earl A. Cooksey – 1922											
172¹/8	27²/8	26⁷/8	21¹/8	23²/8	5⁶/8	5⁶/8	4	4		2286	108
■ Chase Co. – Picked Up – Darwin Bailey – 1989											
172	24⁶/8	25⁶/8	22⁶/8	25⁶/8	5³/8	5³/8	5	6	2²/8	2330	110
■ Miami Co. – Dan R. Moore – Dan R. Moore – 1982											
171⁶/8	27⁵/8	25³/8	18	21	5¹/8	5²/8	9	8	7²/8	2418	111
■ Miami Co. – Garth S. Davis – Garth S. Davis – 1992											
171⁶/8	26⁶/8	26⁵/8	18⁶/8	20⁶/8	3⁶/8	3⁶/8	7	6	5⁴/8	2418	111
■ Anderson Co. – Gary Shields – Gary Shields – 1996											
171⁵/8	27³/8	27⁴/8	18³/8	21²/8	5	4⁶/8	6	5		2470	113
■ Riley Co. – Mick McCallister – Mick McCallister – 1980											
171⁵/8	21⁷/8	25⁷/8	18³/8	20⁶/8	5²/8	5²/8	5	5		2470	113
■ Douglas Co. – Jerry S. Pippen – Jerry S. Pippen – 1995											
171⁵/8	27⁶/8	27⁶/8	20⁴/8	25	6¹/8	6²/8	6	6	11¹/8	2470	113
■ Pottawatomie Co. – Kevin P. Devader – Kevin P. Devader – 1997											
171⁴/8	26³/8	26³/8	17⁵/8	19⁵/8	4⁴/8	4⁴/8	5	6	1³/8	2513	116
■ Clay Co. – Eldyn W. Peck – Eldyn W. Peck – 1989											
171³/8	27²/8	28²/8	18¹/8	20¹/8	4⁴/8	4⁴/8	5	5		2564	117
■ Sumner Co. – Jeff D. Ehlers – Jeff D. Ehlers – 1984											
171³/8	27²/8	27⁴/8	20⁷/8		4⁴/8	4⁶/8	7	5	3	2564	117
■ Labette Co. – Dorothea L. Ludwig – Dorothea L. Ludwig – 1994											
171³/8	27⁷/8	26²/8	18²/8	20⁵/8	4	4¹/8	5	6	1⁷/8	2564	117
■ Nemaha Co. – Paul L. Steinlage – Paul L. Steinlage – 1997											
171¹/8	26⁴/8	26³/8	20⁷/8	23	5⁷/8	5⁶/8	6	9	8⁴/8	2665	120
■ Coffey Co. – Gerald L. Garrett – Gerald L. Garrett – 1992											
171¹/8	26²/8	27²/8	20⁵/8	22⁶/8	5³/8	5⁴/8	5	5		2665	120
■ Stafford Co. – Michael E. Read – Michael E. Read – 2000											
171	25⁷/8	26²/8	20²/8	22	5	5¹/8	7	7	6⁶/8	2707	122
■ Comanche Co. – C. Robert Jensen – C. Robert Jensen – 1986											
171	29	29¹/8	23⁵/8	26⁴/8	4⁷/8	5	5	6	1⁷/8	2707	122
■ Sedgwick Co. – John E. McMurry – John E. McMurry – 1995											
170⁷/8	27⁴/8	28⁴/8	21⁴/8	24⁷/8	4⁷/8	5	7	8	7³/8	2769	124
■ Leavenworth Co. – Jacob W. Dragieff – Jacob W. Dragieff – 1987											

Score	Length of Main Beam		Inside Spread	Greatest Spread	Circumference at Smallest Place Between Burr and First Point		Number of Points		Lengths Abnormal Points	All-Time Rank	State Rank
	Right	Left			Right	Left	Right	Left			
	■ Location of Kill – Hunter – Owner – Date Killed										
170$7/8$	26$1/8$	25$6/8$	20$7/8$	22$6/8$	4$5/8$	4$5/8$	7	5	1$2/8$	2769	124
	■ Sumner Co. – Hiram Tucker, Jr. – Hiram Tucker, Jr. – 1992										
170$6/8$	26$5/8$	25$3/8$	20$2/8$	21$5/8$	5	5	5	6	1$4/8$	2828†	126†
	■ Labette Co. – Stefan S. Smith – Stefan S. Smith – 2001										
170$5/8$	25$7/8$	25$2/8$	17$4/8$	21$2/8$	5$1/8$	5$1/8$	7	9	5$5/8$	2876†	127†
	■ Decatur Co. – H. Robert Foster – H. Robert Foster – 2000										
170$5/8$	26$5/8$	27$2/8$	21	23$6/8$	6	5$3/8$	6	7	9$3/8$	2876	127
	■ Lyon Co. – Bill D. Hollond – Bill D. Hollond – 1984										
170$4/8$	25$7/8$	26	19$2/8$	21$1/8$	4$5/8$	4$7/8$	7	6	2$2/8$	2933	129
	■ Rooks Co. – Shawn Sammons – Shawn Sammons – 1998										
170$3/8$	27$4/8$	25$4/8$	21$1/8$	23$6/8$	6$7/8$	6$4/8$	4	4		2992	130
	■ Franklin Co. – Judy E. Wiederholt – Fran E. Wiederholt – 1981										
170$3/8$	25	22$6/8$	18$1/8$	21	4$5/8$	4$5/8$	6	5	1$2/8$	2992	130
	■ Pottawatomie Co. – Larry C. Schroeder – Larry C. Schroeder – 1988										
170$3/8$	26	25$5/8$	18$7/8$	21$1/8$	5$6/8$	5$4/8$	7	5	3$2/8$	2992	130
	■ Coffey Co. – Glen R. Freeman – Glen R. Freeman – 1991										
170$3/8$	27$4/8$	27$6/8$	22$2/8$	26$4/8$	5$2/8$	5	6	7	9$3/8$	2992	130
	■ Crawford Co. – David E. Onelio – David E. Onelio – 1994										
170$2/8$	26$6/8$	26$7/8$	22$2/8$	25$2/8$	5$6/8$	5$6/8$	5	6	2	3063	134
	■ Riley Co. – Paul K. Byarlay – Paul K. Byarlay – 1983										
170$2/8$	24	25	21	22$6/8$	4$4/8$	4$5/8$	5	5		3063	134
	■ Clark Co. – Ray Morais – Ray Morais – 1999										
170$1/8$	28$1/8$	29$4/8$	23$7/8$	27	5$1/8$	4$6/8$	7	5	5$2/8$	3143	136
	■ Douglas Co. – Picked Up – Frank Virchow – 1988										
170$1/8$	30	29	21$5/8$	25$2/8$	5$5/8$	5$5/8$	5	4	2$4/8$	3143	136
	■ Elk Co. – Terry L. Tindle – Terry L. Tindle – 1993										
170$1/8$	24$6/8$	24$4/8$	18$4/8$	22$4/8$	5$2/8$	5$2/8$	6	6	4$1/8$	3143	136
	■ Cowley Co. – Mitchell D. Payne – Mitchell D. Payne – 1996										
170	26$2/8$	26$6/8$	20$2/8$	22$6/8$	4$7/8$	4$7/8$	7	5	6$2/8$	3224	139
	■ Pratt Co. – Ronald R. George – Ronald R. George – 1999 ■ See photo on page 63										
170	29$3/8$	28$6/8$	18	20$2/8$	4$6/8$	4$7/8$	6	6		3224	139
	■ Neosho Co. – Frank L. Pechacek – Frank L. Pechacek – 1999										
169$3/8$	24$3/8$	24	19$5/8$	22$5/8$	5$2/8$	5$4/8$	6	8	6	3324	141
	■ Clark Co. – Kevin E. Shafer – Kevin E. Shafer – 1999										
168$1/8$	26$4/8$	25$4/8$	17$4/8$	20$2/8$	5$5/8$	6$2/8$	6	7	6$1/8$	3426	142
	■ Norton Co. – Scott C. Marlo – Scott C. Marlo – 1994										
168$1/8$	25	22$4/8$	19$1/8$	21$7/8$	5	5	6	5	3$4/8$	3426	142
	■ Harvey Co. – Derrick W. Dollar – Derrick W. Dollar – 1998										
167$7/8$	28$3/8$	27$2/8$	16$5/8$	19	5	4$7/8$	6	9	10	3451	144
	■ Chautauqua Co. – Dan E. Hadley – Dan E. Hadley – 1984										
167$6/8$	27$1/8$	25$7/8$	20$2/8$	22	4$7/8$	4$7/8$	6	6	4$4/8$	3461	145
	■ Allen Co. – Thomas L. Campbell – Thomas L. Campbell – 1992										

Score	Length of Main Beam Right	Left	Inside Spread	Greatest Spread	Circumference at Smallest Place Between Burr and First Point Right	Left	Number of Points Right	Left	Lengths Abnormal Points	All-Time Rank	State Rank
$167^6/_8$	$22^6/_8$	$23^1/_8$	$18^2/_8$	$20^3/_8$	$4^5/_8$	$4^5/_8$	5	5		3461	145
Graham Co. – Daryl J. Popp – Daryl J. Popp – 1992											
$167^3/_8$	$26^4/_8$	$24^4/_8$	$20^5/_8$	$23^2/_8$	$5^4/_8$	$5^5/_8$	6	7	5	3500†	147†
Reno Co. – J. LaVon Bontrager – J. LaVon Bontrager – 2000											
$167^3/_8$	$23^7/_8$	$22^3/_8$	$18^7/_8$	$20^4/_8$	$4^5/_8$	$4^3/_8$	7	7		3500	147
Miami Co. – Curtis W. Hrabe – Curtis W. Hrabe – 1998											
167	$24^1/_8$	$24^4/_8$	$19^4/_8$	$21^3/_8$	$4^7/_8$	$5^1/_8$	6	6		3552	149
Greenwood Co. – William R. Browning – William R. Browning – 1993											
$166^7/_8$	$26^6/_8$	$26^3/_8$	$21^7/_8$	24	$5^3/_8$	$5^2/_8$	7	7	$5^6/_8$	3568	150
Kingman Co. – Ted Z. Stryhas – Ted Z. Stryhas – 1998											
$165^2/_8$	$27^2/_8$	$25^7/_8$	$21^1/_8$	$23^7/_8$	5	5	5	6	$1^1/_8$	3748†	151†
Sumner Co. – Corbin E. Turpin – Corbin E. Turpin – 2001											
$164^5/_8$	$26^3/_8$	$25^2/_8$	$17^3/_8$	$19^3/_8$	$5^2/_8$	$5^2/_8$	5	6	$1^4/_8$	3835	152
Miami Co. – David A. Haake – David A. Haake – 1996											
$164^4/_8$	$28^6/_8$	$28^4/_8$	$22^6/_8$	25	$5^1/_8$	$5^1/_8$	8	4	$8^4/_8$	3855	153
Nemaha Co. – Gerald R. Uphaus – Gerald R. Uphaus – 1999											
$163^7/_8$	$26^5/_8$	$26^3/_8$	$17^1/_8$	$19^7/_8$	$6^1/_8$	$5^4/_8$	5	6	$3^4/_8$	3928†	154†
Barber Co. – Richard M. Young – Richard M. Young – 2001											
$163^7/_8$	26	$25^1/_8$	$15^7/_8$	18	$4^6/_8$	$4^6/_8$	7	6		3928	154
Crawford Co. – Tom L. Glick – Tom L. Glick – 1996											
$163^5/_8$	$24^4/_8$	$24^6/_8$	20	$22^1/_8$	$4^3/_8$	$4^2/_8$	7	8	$5^3/_8$	3961†	156†
Bourbon Co. – Kevin R. Kraatz – Kevin R. Kraatz – 2001											
$163^5/_8$	$24^5/_8$	$24^3/_8$	$19^5/_8$	$21^6/_8$	$5^6/_8$	6	6	6	$1^4/_8$	3961	156
Coffey Co. – James C. Gilliam – James C. Gilliam – 2000											
$163^3/_8$	$25^3/_8$	$27^2/_8$	21	$23^4/_8$	$5^1/_8$	5	6	4	$1^1/_8$	4002†	158†
Harvey Co. – Tim S. Ross – Tim S. Ross – 2001											
$163^2/_8$	$27^3/_8$	$26^1/_8$	20	$22^1/_8$	$5^1/_8$	$5^1/_8$	7	6	$5^4/_8$	4017	159
Reno Co. – Larry D. Kerschner – Larry D. Kerschner – 1990											
$163^1/_8$	$26^1/_8$	$25^1/_8$	$17^1/_8$	20	$4^5/_8$	$4^6/_8$	5	6		4035†	160†
Kingman Co. – Cody B. Purviance – Cody B. Purviance – 2000											
163	$25^3/_8$	$24^1/_8$	$18^2/_8$	$20^2/_8$	$4^6/_8$	$4^6/_8$	6	6	$10^2/_8$	4051	161
Stafford Co. – Robert G. Williams, Jr. – Robert G. Williams, Jr. – 1997											
$162^7/_8$	27	$26^4/_8$	$20^6/_8$	$23^7/_8$	$4^7/_8$	$5^4/_8$	6	6	$8^3/_8$	4067	162
Crawford Co. – Joe E. Aquino – Joe E. Aquino – 1994											
$162^5/_8$	$25^4/_8$	$26^3/_8$	$19^6/_8$	$21^6/_8$	$4^6/_8$	$4^5/_8$	6	5	$1^5/_8$	4109	163
Rice Co. – James R. Henderson – James R. Henderson – 1997											
162	24	$24^1/_8$	$18^4/_8$	$20^4/_8$	$4^4/_8$	$4^5/_8$	5	5		4184	164
Brown Co. – Ronnie W. Gossett – Ronnie W. Gossett – 1998											
$161^2/_8$	$23^3/_8$	$23^3/_8$	16	$18^2/_8$	$4^6/_8$	$4^6/_8$	5	6		4310	165
Ellis Co. – Craig S. Brown – Craig S. Brown – 1990											
$161^2/_8$	$25^7/_8$	$27^5/_8$	$22^6/_8$	25	$5^3/_8$	$5^2/_8$	4	4		4310	165
Comanche Co. – Marvin R. Schwein – Marvin R. Schwein – 1999											

KANSAS TYPICAL WHITETAIL DEER

Score	Length of Main Beam Right Left	Inside Spread	Greatest Spread	Circumference at Smallest Place Between Burr and First Point Right Left		Number of Points Right Left		Lengths Abnormal Points	All-Time Rank	State Rank
	■ *Location of Kill – Hunter – Owner – Date Killed*									
160⁶/8	26⁷/8 27⁴/8	21²/8	23⁵/8	5	5²/8	6	6	11⁴/8	4402†	167†
	■ *Sumner Co. – David W. Troutman – David W. Troutman – 2001*									
160²/8	26¹/8 23⁵/8	19	23⁵/8	4⁷/8	4⁶/8	6	7	1⁴/8	4495	168
	■ *Rice Co. – Mark B. Steffen – Mark B. Steffen – 1996*									
160¹/8	25⁵/8 24³/8	20³/8	22²/8	4⁴/8	4⁶/8	5	5		4534	169
	■ *Rawlins Co. – James Brennan – James Brennan – 1999*									

† The scores and ranking for trophies from the 25th Awards Entry Period are not final until the banquet is held on June 19, 2004.

TROPHIES IN THE FIELD

HUNTER: Kenneth W. Williams
SCORE: 173-6/8
CATEGORY: typical whitetail deer
LOCATION: Comanche County, Kansas
DATE: 2001

KANSAS

NON-TYPICAL WHITETAIL DEER

Score	Length of Main Beam Right	Left	Inside Spread	Greatest Spread	Circumference at Smallest Place Between Burr and First Point Right	Left	Number of Points Right	Left	Lengths Abnormal Points	All-Time Rank	State Rank
■ Location of Kill – Hunter – Owner – Date Killed											
280 $\frac{4}{8}$	25 $\frac{3}{8}$	25 $\frac{2}{8}$	19 $\frac{6}{8}$	26 $\frac{6}{8}$	6 $\frac{1}{8}$	6 $\frac{4}{8}$	16	13	1	8	1
■ Shawnee Co. – Joseph H. Waters – Brad Gsell – 1987											
258 $\frac{6}{8}$	22 $\frac{4}{8}$	26 $\frac{2}{8}$	23 $\frac{6}{8}$	28	6 $\frac{4}{8}$	6	17	15	106 $\frac{4}{8}$	27	2
■ Republic Co. – John O. Band – Bass Pro Shops – 1965											
257 $\frac{1}{8}$	29 $\frac{4}{8}$	27 $\frac{4}{8}$	23 $\frac{2}{8}$	28 $\frac{3}{8}$	6 $\frac{2}{8}$	5 $\frac{6}{8}$	20	14	63 $\frac{1}{8}$	36	3
■ Marion Co. – Jamie L. Remmers – Bass Pro Shops – 1997											
253	29 $\frac{7}{8}$	27 $\frac{2}{8}$	24	28 $\frac{3}{8}$	5 $\frac{3}{8}$	5 $\frac{4}{8}$	12	12	42 $\frac{4}{8}$	45	4
■ Miami Co. – Kenneth R. Cartwright – Bass Pro Shops – 1994											
251 $\frac{1}{8}$	28 $\frac{2}{8}$	28	19	22 $\frac{7}{8}$	5 $\frac{5}{8}$	5 $\frac{6}{8}$	12	13	59 $\frac{1}{8}$	54	5
■ Mitchell Co. – Theron E. Wilson – Theron E. Wilson – 1974											
250 $\frac{2}{8}$	24 $\frac{5}{8}$	28	16 $\frac{1}{8}$	21 $\frac{5}{8}$	7 $\frac{1}{8}$	7	16	12	61 $\frac{1}{8}$	58	6
■ Washington Co. – Picked Up – Gale Sup – 1988											
248 $\frac{7}{8}$	27 $\frac{6}{8}$	27 $\frac{2}{8}$	20 $\frac{1}{8}$	22 $\frac{4}{8}$	5 $\frac{7}{8}$	5 $\frac{7}{8}$	8	10	61 $\frac{2}{8}$	65	7
■ Greenwood Co. – Clifford G. Pickell – Bass Pro Shops – 1968											
248 $\frac{1}{8}$	27 $\frac{5}{8}$	28 $\frac{3}{8}$	20 $\frac{2}{8}$	24 $\frac{5}{8}$	7 $\frac{7}{8}$	7 $\frac{2}{8}$	14	12	69 $\frac{5}{8}$	72	8
■ Crawford Co. – Bruce Jameson – Bass Pro Shops – 1989											
246 $\frac{3}{8}$	27 $\frac{7}{8}$	26 $\frac{1}{8}$	29 $\frac{3}{8}$	30 $\frac{6}{8}$	5 $\frac{1}{8}$	6 $\frac{6}{8}$	9	14	62 $\frac{6}{8}$	77	9
■ Anderson Co. – Richard T. Stahl – Bass Pro Shops – 1992											
244	28 $\frac{7}{8}$	28 $\frac{3}{8}$	20 $\frac{1}{8}$	24	7	6 $\frac{4}{8}$	15	11	38 $\frac{5}{8}$	92	10
■ Morris Co. – Burt Nichols – Cabela's Inc. – 1997											
241 $\frac{7}{8}$	22 $\frac{2}{8}$	28 $\frac{3}{8}$	19	24 $\frac{1}{8}$	5 $\frac{3}{8}$	5	15	11	105 $\frac{3}{8}$	103	11
■ Lyon Co. – Picked Up – D.J. Hollinger & B. Howard – 1996											
240 $\frac{6}{8}$	26 $\frac{2}{8}$	25 $\frac{7}{8}$	20 $\frac{7}{8}$	22 $\frac{2}{8}$	7 $\frac{4}{8}$	7 $\frac{2}{8}$	13	13	34 $\frac{5}{8}$	110	12
■ Clay Co. – Picked Up – H. James Reimer – 1989											
240	28 $\frac{5}{8}$	27 $\frac{5}{8}$	17	24 $\frac{3}{8}$	5 $\frac{1}{8}$	5 $\frac{2}{8}$	10	11	42 $\frac{6}{8}$	119	13
■ Allen Co. – Doug Whitcomb – John L. Stein – 1987											
239	28	29 $\frac{2}{8}$	22 $\frac{3}{8}$	26	5 $\frac{7}{8}$	5 $\frac{5}{8}$	13	13	50 $\frac{5}{8}$	126	14
■ Lyon Co. – Don E. Roberts – Bass Pro Shops – 1987											
239	26 $\frac{2}{8}$	27 $\frac{1}{8}$	16 $\frac{3}{8}$	18 $\frac{6}{8}$	5 $\frac{3}{8}$	5 $\frac{3}{8}$	11	8	38 $\frac{7}{8}$	126	14
■ Montgomery Co. – Picked Up – Cabela's, Inc. – 1992											
237	26 $\frac{6}{8}$	25 $\frac{6}{8}$	21 $\frac{1}{8}$	26 $\frac{3}{8}$	6 $\frac{7}{8}$	6 $\frac{7}{8}$	10	16	44 $\frac{3}{8}$	151	16
■ Barber Co. – Ronald D. Wilt – Cleon Almond – 1986											
237	24 $\frac{4}{8}$	25 $\frac{4}{8}$	23	24 $\frac{4}{8}$	6 $\frac{3}{8}$	5 $\frac{7}{8}$	16	9	74 $\frac{4}{8}$	151	16
■ Douglas Co. – Terry D. Mayle – Terry D. Mayle – 1994											
235 $\frac{5}{8}$	30 $\frac{7}{8}$	29 $\frac{7}{8}$	21 $\frac{4}{8}$	23 $\frac{3}{8}$	5 $\frac{4}{8}$	5 $\frac{7}{8}$	17	13	59 $\frac{3}{8}$	165	18
■ Nemaha Co. – Picked Up – James R. Matlock – PR 1998											
234 $\frac{7}{8}$	27 $\frac{3}{8}$	22 $\frac{3}{8}$	20 $\frac{7}{8}$	22 $\frac{5}{8}$	5 $\frac{3}{8}$	5 $\frac{7}{8}$	8	13	94	171	19
■ Coffey Co. – Danny L. Hawkins – Cabela's, Inc. – 1999											

Score	Length of Main Beam Right	Left	Inside Spread	Greatest Spread	Circumference at Smallest Place Between Burr and First Point Right	Left	Number of Points Right	Left	Lengths Abnormal Points	All-Time Rank	State Rank

■ Location of Kill – Hunter – Owner – Date Killed

Score	Length of Main Beam Right	Left	Inside Spread	Greatest Spread	Circ. R	Circ. L	Points R	Points L	Lengths Abnormal Points	All-Time Rank	State Rank
229²/₈	27	28⁵/₈	21¹/₈	25⁷/₈	6²/₈	7	8	15	55⁷/₈	251	20
	■ Linn Co. – Merle C. Beckman – Merle C. Beckman – 1984										
228³/₈	26⁶/₈	26⁴/₈	23	27²/₈	5³/₈	5⁴/₈	13	11	35³/₈	261	21
	■ Kiowa Co. – Lance P. Ringler – Lance P. Ringler – 1993										
227	25⁷/₈	26⁶/₈	24¹/₈	28⁵/₈	7²/₈	7⁴/₈	12	10	62¹/₈	279	22
	■ Miami Co. – Gary A. Smith – Bass Pro Shops – 1970										
226⁴/₈	26¹/₈	24³/₈	22	25²/₈	6⁷/₈	6⁵/₈	12	10	26⁴/₈	292	23
	■ Linn Co. – Jerry O. Hampton – Bass Pro Shops – 1988										
225⁷/₈	24⁵/₈	24³/₈	18	23⁴/₈	5²/₈	5²/₈	10	8	50¹/₈	304†	24†
	■ Linn Co. – Douglas L. Below – Douglas L. Below – 2001										
225	28⁷/₈	26⁶/₈	20²/₈	23⁷/₈	5⁷/₈	5⁷/₈	10	13	53⁴/₈	318	25
	■ Barber Co. – Picked Up – Bass Pro Shops – 1979										
223³/₈	24⁷/₈	26¹/₈	20²/₈	25¹/₈	5⁵/₈	5⁵/₈	11	15	59¹/₈	354	26
	■ Jefferson Co. – David P. Haeusler – David P. Haeusler – 1990										
223¹/₈	29⁷/₈	29⁵/₈	21¹/₈	22⁷/₈	4³/₈	4³/₈	12	8	23⁶/₈	361	27
	■ Wyandotte Co. – Randy W. Tillery – Randy W. Tillery – 1988										
223¹/₈	26⁴/₈	25⁵/₈	25¹/₈	29	5²/₈	5⁴/₈	10	9	33⁴/₈	361	27
	■ Republic Co. – Roy C. Wilson – Roy C. Wilson – 1995										
222⁴/₈	25	24²/₈	25²/₈	27⁵/₈	6⁴/₈	6³/₈	12	12	52⁶/₈	378	29
	■ Barber Co. – Michel M. Letourneau – Michel M. Letourneau – 1999										
221²/₈	28⁵/₈	28⁷/₈	22³/₈	25	5⁵/₈	5⁴/₈	10	11	28¹/₈	410	30
	■ Franklin Co. – Marvin R. Smith – Brad Sowter – 1988										
220⁷/₈	26⁴/₈	26⁴/₈	22⁴/₈	25⁴/₈	5⁶/₈	5⁶/₈	10	9	25³/₈	417	31
	■ Trego Co. – John M. Benewiat – John M. Benewiat – 1999										
220	30³/₈	28⁶/₈	17⁴/₈	22⁴/₈	6⁶/₈	6⁴/₈	8	15	23⁴/₈	441	32
	■ Allen Co. – Merril R. Lamb – Merril R. Lamb – 1999										
219⁴/₈	26⁵/₈	26¹/₈	21²/₈	24⁵/₈	5	5	11	8	24	453	33
	■ Sumner Co. – Picked Up – Greg L. Hill – 1987										
218⁵/₈	29⁵/₈	30	21⁵/₈	24	5	5	11	7	40	480	34
	■ Kansas – Unknown – Larry D. Bollier – PR 1997										
217⁷/₈	24⁴/₈	26⁵/₈	20	24⁶/₈	6¹/₈	5⁴/₈	18	14	60¹/₈	499	35
	■ Cherokee Co. – Craig E. Ruddick – Craig E. Ruddick – 1983										
216⁷/₈	27³/₈	28⁷/₈	21⁶/₈	27⁴/₈	5²/₈	5¹/₈	12	12	28⁷/₈	533	36
	■ Wilson Co. – Gilbert J. McGee – Gilbert J. McGee – 1988										
216⁶/₈	25¹/₈	25⁴/₈	18²/₈	25¹/₈	6³/₈	6⁴/₈	10	13	38²/₈	539	37
	■ Barber Co. – Robert L. Rose – Robert L. Rose – 1972										
216²/₈	26⁶/₈	26³/₈	20	23⁵/₈	4⁶/₈	5⁵/₈	8	11	54⁴/₈	555†	38†
	■ Lyon Co. – Rodney D. Watson – Rodney D. Watson – 2000										
216	24⁶/₈	22¹/₈	16²/₈	26⁵/₈	4	4⁴/₈	13	12	104⁴/₈	565†	39†
	■ Kiowa Co. – Ray L. Magby – Ray L. Magby – 2001										
215⁷/₈	28	25¹/₈	21²/₈	23³/₈	5⁵/₈	5⁶/₈	9	11	22⁵/₈	569†	40†
	■ Trego Co. – Stephen G. Chaffee – Stephen G. Chaffee – 2000										

Score	Length of Main Beam Right	Left	Inside Spread	Greatest Spread	Circumference at Smallest Place Between Burr and First Point Right	Left	Number of Points Right	Left	Lengths Abnormal Points	All-Time Rank	State Rank
	■ *Location of Kill – Hunter – Owner – Date Killed*										
215	30³/₈	30	22⁷/₈	25⁶/₈	5⁷/₈	5⁷/₈	10	8	19⁷/₈	598	41
	■ *Allen Co. – James W. Baker – James W. Baker – 1992*										
213⁷/₈	28⁵/₈	28⁵/₈	19³/₈	22³/₈	5¹/₈	4⁷/₈	9	10	18⁴/₈	635	42
	■ *Pottawatomie Co. – Picked Up – Tim Wanklyn – 1974*										
212⁵/₈	27³/₈	27⁶/₈	19⁵/₈	22⁴/₈	5⁵/₈	5⁵/₈	9	6	32⁶/₈	683	43
	■ *Greenwood Co. – Picked Up – B&C National Collection – 1998*										
212²/₈	29⁷/₈	27⁷/₈	21⁴/₈	23⁵/₈	5²/₈	5	13	8	39⁶/₈	701	44
	■ *Lane Co. – Picked Up – R. & A. Johnson – 1994*										
211⁶/₈	27¹/₈	26⁴/₈	23⁵/₈	26	6⁴/₈	6²/₈	10	9	33¹/₈	729†	45†
	■ *Clark Co. – Cullen R. Spitzer – Cullen R. Spitzer – 2001* ■ *See photo on page 61*										
211³/₈	29²/₈	27⁶/₈	20⁵/₈	27¹/₈	5⁷/₈	6	10	9	40⁴/₈	745†	46†
	■ *Chase Co. – Picked Up – Tom Crump – 1998*										
210⁴/₈	25⁶/₈	26³/₈	19⁶/₈	23²/₈	6¹/₈	6¹/₈	10	12	27	791	47
	■ *Wabaunsee Co. – Ron E. Pletcher – Ron E. Pletcher – 1994*										
210³/₈	27⁷/₈	26⁷/₈	19²/₈	22¹/₈	6⁴/₈	6⁴/₈	9	8	23¹/₈	796†	48†
	■ *Linn Co. – Randall W. Hinde – Randall W. Hinde – 2001* ■ *See photo on page 217*										
210	29⁴/₈	27⁵/₈	31	33⁴/₈	5⁷/₈	5⁶/₈	10	12	24⁶/₈	816	49
	■ *Kingman Co. – Picked Up – Odie Sudbeck – 1998*										
209⁶/₈	23²/₈	24¹/₈	22⁶/₈	24⁵/₈	4⁴/₈	4⁶/₈	8	10	18	831	50
	■ *Edwards Co. – Tim C. Schaller – Tim C. Schaller – 1984*										
209²/₈	26³/₈	27¹/₈	18⁷/₈	22	5⁷/₈	5⁵/₈	7	12	45¹/₈	859†	51†
	■ *Crawford Co. – Jason C. Ball – Jason C. Ball – 2000*										
209¹/₈	23⁴/₈	22⁷/₈	17³/₈	23⁴/₈	5⁶/₈	5⁴/₈	10	12	51	863	52
	■ *Riley Co. – Jerry P. McIntyre – Jerry P. McIntyre – 1994*										
209	28⁷/₈	29⁵/₈	17⁴/₈	22³/₈	6¹/₈	6³/₈	12	10	32⁴/₈	872	53
	■ *Crawford Co. – Steven R. Burt – Steven R. Burt – 1999*										
208⁴/₈	30⁵/₈	30²/₈	20⁶/₈	23¹/₈	5⁵/₈	5⁴/₈	7	8	19	894	54
	■ *Ford Co. – Picked Up – Bass Pro Shops – 1985*										
207⁴/₈	26⁵/₈	25⁵/₈	18⁷/₈	25²/₈	5²/₈	5²/₈	8	14	42¹/₈	969	55
	■ *Comanche Co. – Picked Up – Bass Pro Shops – 1984*										
207¹/₈	24⁴/₈	23³/₈	16¹/₈	20	6	5⁷/₈	12	12	50	995†	56†
	■ *Linn Co. – Charles E. Jasper – Charles E. Jasper – 2000*										
207	26⁶/₈	26	19¹/₈	21⁶/₈	5⁶/₈	5⁷/₈	9	13	26¹/₈	1005	57
	■ *Cowley Co. – Joyce Williams – Joyce Williams – 1983*										
206⁷/₈	30⁵/₈	29³/₈	21⁶/₈	24⁴/₈	5¹/₈	5¹/₈	8	9	16⁵/₈	1011	58
	■ *McPherson Co. – Dennis G. Bordner – Dennis G. Bordner – 1994*										
206⁵/₈	26	24²/₈	19⁶/₈	22⁶/₈	5³/₈	5²/₈	7	12	23⁷/₈	1036	59
	■ *Chase Co. – Jay A. Talkington – Jay A. Talkington – 1983*										
206²/₈	24⁶/₈	25⁵/₈	24¹/₈	26⁴/₈	5¹/₈	6²/₈	8	13	34¹/₈	1059†	60†
	■ *Jefferson Co. – Michael J. Navrat, Jr. – Michael J. Navrat, Jr. – 2001*										
205⁷/₈	31³/₈	31⁴/₈	22⁵/₈	26²/₈	6¹/₈	6³/₈	10	7	19²/₈	1080	61
	■ *McPherson Co. – Chad Doughman – Chad Doughman – 1999*										

Score	Length of Main Beam Right	Left	Inside Spread	Greatest Spread	Circumference at Smallest Place Between Burr and First Point Right	Left	Number of Points Right	Left	Lengths Abnormal Points	All-Time Rank	State Rank
				■ *Location of Kill – Hunter – Owner – Date Killed*							
205 6/8	23 5/8	23	20 3/8	27 3/8	5 4/8	5 3/8	8	10	39 3/8	1094	62
	■ *Cloud Co. – Gary G. Pingel – Gary G. Pingel – 1982*										
205 5/8	29 1/8	27 7/8	21 4/8	23 5/8	5 3/8	5 1/8	11	8	23 3/8	1102†	63†
	■ *Doniphan Co. – Fran E. Wiederholt – Fran E. Wiederholt – 1996*										
205 3/8	24 4/8	26 2/8	21	22 7/8	8 4/8	8	12	11	50 5/8	1116	64
	■ *Kansas – Picked Up – Keith A. Baird – 2000*										
204 5/8	23 4/8	26 1/8	16 1/8	20 5/8	6 4/8	6 1/8	11	10	25 4/8	1176	65
	■ *Cloud Co. – Darrell L. Zimmerman – Darrell L. Zimmerman – 1994*										
204 3/8	25 4/8	25 2/8	16 7/8	23 1/8	5 4/8	5 7/8	9	9	28 2/8	1186	66
	■ *Jefferson Co. – Michael D. Wright – Michael D. Wright – 1995*										
204 3/8	27	24 3/8	16 2/8	21 5/8	5 1/8	4 7/8	11	12	52 5/8	1186	66
	■ *Doniphan Co. – Robby L. Buford – Robby L. Buford – 1998*										
203 6/8	25 4/8	26 5/8	23 2/8	28 2/8	5 3/8	5 6/8	10	12	33	1237	68
	■ *Neosho Co. – Michael J. Hentzen – Michael J. Hentzen – 1999*										
203 1/8	24 6/8	24 3/8	21 4/8	23	6 5/8	6 6/8	8	12	47 5/8	1305	69
	■ *Greenwood Co. – Paul E. Bunyard – Paul E. Bunyard – 1994*										
203	26 1/8	27 6/8	17 4/8	23 2/8	4 5/8	4 5/8	9	8	12 4/8	1317	70
	■ *Jefferson Co. – Dale Heston – Dale Heston – 1982*										
202 7/8	24 4/8	24 2/8	19	21 3/8	6	5 7/8	10	10	20 1/8	1327	71
	■ *Kingman Co. – Picked Up – Michael L. Piaskowski – 1966*										
202 6/8	25	25 1/8	17 2/8	21	5 4/8	5 3/8	9	10	51	1339	72
	■ *Chautauqua Co. – John L. Brown – John L. Brown – 1990*										
202 3/8	25 2/8	24 2/8	19 5/8	29	4 6/8	4 7/8	13	12	37	1362	73
	■ *Allen Co. – John F. Pfeiffer – John F. Pfeiffer – 1998*										
202 1/8	26 7/8	26 7/8	24 4/8	25 6/8	6 5/8	6 4/8	8	11	14 5/8	1386	74
	■ *Jewell Co. – Rex A. Morgan – Rex A. Morgan – 1998*										
201 7/8	27 4/8	27 2/8	20 1/8	22 4/8	5 3/8	5 5/8	8	7	30 6/8	1410	75
	■ *Anderson Co. – Arthur O. Bell – Arthur O. Bell – 1990*										
201 7/8	25 7/8	25 3/8	20 2/8	22 4/8	5	4 6/8	7	8	28 5/8	1410	75
	■ *Kiowa Co. – Jimmie L. Spencer – Jimmie L. Spencer – 1991*										
201 5/8	28 6/8	28 4/8	19 1/8	21 2/8	4 7/8	4 7/8	10	10	17 6/8	1427	77
	■ *Sumner Co. – Jeremy A. Schroeder – Jeremy A. Schroeder – 1996*										
201 4/8	22	29 2/8	23 6/8		6 7/8	6	9	8	23 2/8	1443	78
	■ *Barber Co. – Joe Ash – Joe Ash – 1975*										
201 4/8	25 1/8	25 7/8	18 7/8	20 5/8	5 7/8	6 4/8	7	9	28 5/8	1443	78
	■ *Sumner Co. – Bradley A. Smith – Bradley A. Smith – 1994*										
201 4/8	28 7/8	29 7/8	22	25	7	6 2/8	12	10	38	1443	78
	■ *Shawnee Co. – J.S. Smith – J.S. Smith – 1999*										
201 3/8	25 7/8	26 1/8	20 7/8	22 5/8	5 2/8	5 3/8	6	9	14 2/8	1461	81
	■ *Mitchell Co. – Terry L. Fiala – Terry L. Fiala – 1998*										
201 1/8	27 5/8	25 5/8	21 5/8	24 4/8	5 2/8	5 2/8	7	9	11 4/8	1489†	82†
	■ *Coffey Co. – Lance W. Jacob – Cabela's, Inc. – 2000*										

Score	Length of Main Beam Right	Left	Inside Spread	Greatest Spread	Circumference at Smallest Place Between Burr and First Point Right	Left	Number of Points Right	Left	Lengths Abnormal Points	All-Time Rank	State Rank
■ Location of Kill – Hunter – Owner – Date Killed											
201	24²/8	24	16⁵/8	20¹/8	6	5⁶/8	12	9	32³/8	1500†	83†
■ Republic Co. – Bucky D. Barber – Bucky D. Barber – 2000											
200⁵/8	24⁶/8	24⁶/8	22²/8	24⁶/8	5⁴/8	5⁵/8	10	9	32⁷/8	1532	84
■ Harper Co. – Robert A. Thomas – Robert A. Thomas – 1990											
199⁷/8	29⁴/8	28⁴/8	18²/8	27⁶/8	5³/8	5¹/8	10	9	24¹/8	1607	85
■ Cheyenne Co. – Picked Up – William H. Lilienthal – 1986											
199⁵/8	27⁷/8	27³/8	23²/8	27⁵/8	5²/8	5⁴/8	8	9	26¹/8	1621	86
■ Labette Co. – John L. Bryant – John L. Bryant – 1987											
198⁴/8	26⁷/8	28¹/8	19²/8	22²/8	5²/8	5¹/8	8	10	12⁴/8	1736	87
■ Wallace Co. – Kent E. Rains – Kent E. Rains – 1993											
198⁴/8	25⁵/8	25²/8	17	20	5³/8	5²/8	11	8	28⁴/8	1736	87
■ Chautauqua Co. – Mark A. Shull – Mark A. Shull – 1998											
198²/8	25²/8	25	16⁵/8	19⁶/8	5¹/8	5²/8	12	9	27¹/8	1772	89
■ Osage Co. – Jerry L. Sand – Jerry L. Sand – 1992											
198¹/8	27³/8	25¹/8	22¹/8	27⁵/8	5	5	12	5	24	1785	90
■ Kingman Co. – Harold W. Hellman – Harold W. Hellman – 1997											
198	25⁵/8	25²/8	17⁵/8	20³/8	6²/8	6⁴/8	9	10	19⁷/8	1801	91
■ Osage Co. – Joe A. Rose, Jr. – Joe A. Rose, Jr. – 1977											
197⁷/8	24⁷/8	24⁶/8	19⁶/8	22³/8	5⁴/8	5	10	9	17¹/8	1816	92
■ Riley Co. – Gary L. Schroller – Gary L. Schroller – 1990											
197⁵/8	26	25⁵/8	21⁵/8	24	5⁶/8	5⁴/8	10	8	28²/8	1847	93
■ Morris Co. – John H. Payne – John H. Payne – 1992											
197⁴/8	25³/8	26³/8	16⁷/8	19	5¹/8	5³/8	6	8	19⁵/8	1866	94
■ Lyon Co. – John R. Clifton – John R. Clifton – 1984											
197⁴/8	27	24²/8	17⁴/8	19³/8	5⁷/8	5⁷/8	8	7	32⁶/8	1866	94
■ Comanche Co. – Allan Prasser – Brant J. Mueller – 1989											
197³/8	22²/8	23⁷/8	21⁶/8	27¹/8	5⁶/8	5¹/8	14	10	42¹/8	1884	96
■ Marshall Co. – Lloyd Wenzl – Lloyd Wenzl – 1983											
197¹/8	26⁶/8	26³/8	19³/8	22²/8	5	5	11	11	20⁶/8	1923	97
■ Franklin Co. – Ron R. Rumford – Ron R. Rumford – 1992											
197	23⁶/8	23⁴/8	20⁴/8	27¹/8	6²/8	6	9	14	32	1939	98
■ Barber Co. – Lewis M. Mull – Lewis M. Mull – 1986											
196³/8	25⁶/8	24²/8	19¹/8	21¹/8	5⁶/8	5⁴/8	10	9	19⁴/8	2010	99
■ Ellis Co. – Douglas W. Carmichael – Douglas W. Carmichael – 1996											
196²/8	29³/8	27	19³/8	23²/8	6¹/8	6²/8	11	12	32³/8	2028	100
■ Pratt Co. – Travis D. Kolm – Travis D. Kolm – 1997											
196²/8	27⁵/8	25²/8	17⁷/8	24	5⁵/8	6⁶/8	11	16	56³/8	2028	100
■ Bourbon Co. – Picked Up – Odie Sudbeck – 1999											
196¹/8	25²/8	24⁴/8	17³/8	21	5⁷/8	5²/8	8	7	18²/8	2045†	102†
■ Lyon Co. – A. Scott Ritchie – A. Scott Ritchie – 2000											
196	27⁶/8	28³/8	23⁶/8	26⁶/8	5³/8	5⁴/8	7	7	25²/8	2059	103
■ Washington Co. – Jeff W. Novak – Jeff W. Novak – 1998											

Score	Length of Main Beam		Inside Spread	Greatest Spread	Circumference at Smallest Place Between Burr and First Point		Number of Points		Lengths Abnormal Points	All-Time Rank	State Rank
	Right	Left			Right	Left	Right	Left			
	■ Location of Kill – Hunter – Owner – Date Killed										
195⁵/₈	20⁶/₈	21⁴/₈	17³/₈	21	5⁷/₈	5³/₈	12	9	17⁶/₈	2116	104
	■ Stafford Co. – Kenneth R. Van Winkle – Kenneth R. Van Winkle – 1994										
194⁴/₈	25²/₈	25⁵/₈	18⁴/₈	20³/₈	6⁶/₈	6³/₈	13	7	27⁶/₈	2134	105
	■ Anderson Co. – H.C. Stokes – H.C. Stokes – 1999										
193³/₈	27⁴/₈	28⁴/₈	19⁵/₈	22¹/₈	4⁵/₈	4⁶/₈	9	7	29⁴/₈	2163	106
	■ Pottawatomie Co. – Thomas G. Holthaus – Thomas G. Holthaus – 1994										
195	22⁶/₈	26⁶/₈	19⁶/₈	22¹/₈	5³/₈	5⁷/₈	10	8	36	2233†	107†
	■ Shawnee Co. – Mark E. Conaway – Mark E. Conaway – 1999										
194⁵/₈	26³/₈	25⁷/₈	20⁴/₈	22⁴/₈	4⁷/₈	4⁷/₈	7	7	24⁵/₈	2263	108
	■ Reno Co. – Sam E. Bontrager – Sam E. Bontrager – 1999										
192⁵/₈	26	24³/₈	22	27	6	5⁵/₈	12	10	40¹/₈	2322	109
	■ Pratt Co. – John V. Black – John V. Black – 1996										
192¹/₈	26²/₈	27	23	27¹/₈	5²/₈	5²/₈	7	7	13⁵/₈	2341†	110†
	■ Kansas – Picked Up – Dusty Van Dorn – 1970										
190⁴/₈	26⁴/₈	27¹/₈	20	21⁷/₈	5	5²/₈	13	14	24⁶/₈	2401	111
	■ Osage Co. – Philip E. Spencer – Philip E. Spencer – 1990										
190³/₈	24³/₈	24³/₈	20²/₈	23²/₈	4⁷/₈	4⁵/₈	6	8	18³/₈	2408	112
	■ Lyon Co. – Wayne F. Redeker – Wayne F. Redeker – 1987										
189⁵/₈	25⁴/₈	26³/₈	17⁶/₈	20	5⁴/₈	5⁶/₈	6	13	34⁷/₈	2429	113
	■ Montgomery Co. – Debbie Blaness – Debbie Blaness – 1991										
189⁴/₈	22³/₈	21¹/₈	18	20⁷/₈	5²/₈	5²/₈	9	10	34	2435	114
	■ Jefferson Co. – Donald R. Evans – Donald R. Evans – 1993										
189¹/₈	24⁴/₈	22¹/₈	16⁶/₈	23⁶/₈	5²/₈	5	11	8	61³/₈	2450	115
	■ Hodgeman Co. – Gary Tenbrink – Gary Tenbrink – 1997										
188⁵/₈	24⁷/₈	25³/₈	18³/₈	20³/₈	4⁷/₈	4⁶/₈	7	7	15²/₈	2471	116
	■ Leavenworth Co. – Kelvin M. Cobb – Kelvin M. Cobb – 1995										
188³/₈	23	23¹/₈	17⁶/₈	20	7¹/₈	6³/₈	9	9	18⁷/₈	2478	117
	■ Clay Co. – Gail W. Steenbock – Gail W. Steenbock – 1999										
187⁷/₈	24²/₈	23⁶/₈	17⁴/₈	21	4⁷/₈	4⁷/₈	10	11	28³/₈	2506†	118†
	■ Cowley Co. – Hal S. Atkinson, Jr. – Hal S. Atkinson, Jr. – 2001										
187²/₈	25⁶/₈	24³/₈	20¹/₈	24⁵/₈	6¹/₈	6¹/₈	7	6	21⁷/₈	2534	119
	■ Coffey Co. – Dennis E. Tougaw – Dennis E. Tougaw – 1991										
187	23²/₈	24⁷/₈	18	20¹/₈	7	6	12	10	24²/₈	2545	120
	■ Coffey Co. – Ty A. Pyle – Ty A. Pyle – 1989										
186⁷/₈	26¹/₈	27	19	22⁴/₈	5⁴/₈	5³/₈	10	7	18⁷/₈	2550†	121†
	■ Pawnee Co. – Gary J. Dechant – Gary J. Dechant – 2000										
186²/₈	24⁵/₈	26	19⁴/₈	23	5³/₈	5⁵/₈	9	7	29	2575	122
	■ Dickinson Co. – Orren L. Holt – Orren L. Holt – 1999										
185⁶/₈	23⁶/₈	25²/₈	18	20⁴/₈	5¹/₈	5⁴/₈	9	10	30	2605†	123†
	■ Sharp Co. – Witt Stephens, Jr. – Witt Stephens, Jr. – 2001										
185³/₈	26⁷/₈	23	15⁶/₈	21⁴/₈	7²/₈	8	8	10	52⁷/₈	2622†	124†
	■ McPherson Co. – Harvey D. Hagen – Harvey D. Hagen – 2000										

Score	Length of Main Beam		Inside Spread	Greatest Spread	Circumference at Smallest Place Between Burr and First Point		Number of Points		Lengths Abnormal Points	All-Time Rank	State Rank
	Right	Left			Right	Left	Right	Left			
	■ Location of Kill – Hunter – Owner – Date Killed										
185³/₈	25⁵/₈	25	19⁶/₈	22	4⁷/₈	5	8	8	15⁵/₈	2622	124
	■ Kingman Co. – Robert L. Ciravolo – Robert L. Ciravolo – 1998										
185	25⁵/₈	25	17⁷/₈	20³/₈	5⁶/₈	6¹/₈	8	17	35³/₈	2653	126
	■ Elk Co. – Darrel E. Schultz – Darrel E. Schultz – 1993										

† The scores and ranking for trophies from the 25th Awards Entry Period are not final until the banquet is held on June 19, 2004.

TROPHIES IN THE FIELD

HUNTER: Randall W. Hinde
SCORE: 210-3/8
CATEGORY: non-typical whitetail deer
LOCATION: Linn County, Kansas
DATE: 2001

KENTUCKY
RECORD WHITETAILS

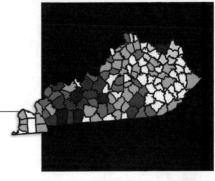

213 Typical whitetail deer entries
113 Non-typical whitetail deer entries
7,265 Total whitetail deer entries

0 Entries
1-2 Entries
3-5 Entries
6-10 Entries
11+ Entries

NEW
STATE
RECORD

KENTUCKY
NEW STATE RECORD
Typical Whitetail Deer
Score: $204^2/8$
Location: Pendleton Co.
Hunter and Owner: Robert W. Smith
Date: 2000

New state record pending approval from the 25th Awards Program Judges Panel.

KENTUCKY
NEW STATE RECORD
Non-Typical Whitetail Deer
Score: 240$^7/_8$
Location: Lewis Co.
Hunter: Anthony D. Mefford
Owner: Cabela's, Inc.
Date: 1996

KENTUCKY

TYPICAL WHITETAIL DEER

Score	Length of Main Beam Right Left	Inside Spread	Greatest Spread	Circumference at Smallest Place Between Burr and First Point Right Left	Number of Points Right Left	Lengths Abnormal Points	All-Time Rank	State Rank
	■ Location of Kill – Hunter – Owner – Date Killed							
204²/₈	30²/₈ 29⁶/₈	20⁴/₈	22⁶/₈	4⁵/₈ 4⁵/₈	6 5	3⁴/₈	5†	1†
	■ Pendleton Co. – Robert W. Smith – Robert W. Smith – 2000							
191³/₈	24⁶/₈ 25¹/₈	25⁵/₈	27³/₈	4⁷/₈ 5¹/₈	5 5		85	2
	■ Meade Co. – Picked Up – William N. Burrell – 1977							
189³/₈	25⁵/₈ 26	18¹/₈	20³/₈	5³/₈ 5²/₈	7 7	2⁴/₈	120	3
	■ Lewis Co. – Jim Cooper – Jim Cooper – 1999							
189	26⁶/₈ 25⁶/₈	20²/₈	22⁷/₈	5⁵/₈ 5³/₈	6 6		131	4
	■ Shelby Co. – Frank W. Kendall – Frank W. Kendall – 1971							
188⁵/₈	27⁴/₈ 29¹/₈	20⁵/₈	22⁴/₈	5²/₈ 5	6 7	3²/₈	139	5
	■ Lewis Co. – Ben C. Johnson – Ben C. Johnson – 1993							
187⁶/₈	27⁴/₈ 27⁷/₈	25²/₈	28³/₈	5²/₈ 5³/₈	6 6		160	6
	■ Union Co. – Charles Meuth – Larry S. Melton – 1964							
187¹/₈	26⁶/₈ 26⁴/₈	18⁷/₈	21	4⁶/₈ 4⁷/₈	6 6		185	7
	■ Pulaski Co. – Scott Abbott – Scott Abbott – 1982							
186⁷/₈	28⁴/₈ 27⁵/₈	20⁴/₈	24⁵/₈	5³/₈ 5³/₈	7 7	2⁷/₈	194	8
	■ Lewis Co. – W. David Mains – W. David Mains – 1996							
186²/₈	29¹/₈ 29	22	24⁵/₈	4⁷/₈ 4⁶/₈	5 6	4⁴/₈	220	9
	■ Carter Co. – Herman G. Holbrooks – Herman G. Holbrooks – 1989							
186	30 29⁴/₈	22	24³/₈	6 5⁴/₈	6 5	2⁴/₈	238	10
	■ Warren Co. – Arnold M. Bush – Arnold M. Bush – 1986							
185²/₈	30 29²/₈	30²/₈	34⁴/₈	5²/₈ 5²/₈	8 8	10⁶/₈	263	11
	■ Todd Co. – C.W. Shelton – Bass Pro Shops – 1964							
184¹/₈	26³/₈ 26⁶/₈	17³/₈	20¹/₈	5 5¹/₈	6 7		327	12
	■ Muhlenberg Co. – Chad Mathis – Chad Mathis – 1995							
184	28⁶/₈ 27⁶/₈	20⁴/₈	23	4⁵/₈ 4⁵/₈	6 6		334	13
	■ Grayson Co. – Floyd Stone – Floyd Stone – 1987							
183⁷/₈	27⁷/₈ 27⁵/₈	20²/₈	22²/₈	5²/₈ 5¹/₈	5 6	1⁵/₈	343	14
	■ Muhlenberg Co. – James E. Brewer – James E. Brewer – 1997							
183³/₈	28 27³/₈	19¹/₈	20⁶/₈	4⁵/₈ 4⁶/₈	6 6		365†	15†
	■ Pulaski Co. – Billy M. Haynes – Billy M. Haynes – 2000							
183³/₈	26⁷/₈ 26¹/₈	18⁷/₈	20⁷/₈	4⁶/₈ 4⁷/₈	5 5	1²/₈	365	15
	■ McLean Co. – Lawrence G. Porter – Lawrence G. Porter – 1980							
181²/₈	25²/₈ 25⁷/₈	25⁷/₈	27³/₈	5¹/₈ 5⁴/₈	5 6	3⁵/₈	540	17
	■ Hardin Co. – Thomas L. House – Thomas L. House – 1963							
181	27⁷/₈ 27	20³/₈	22²/₈	5²/₈ 5¹/₈	8 7	13¹/₈	563	18
	■ Gallatin Co. – Kenneth D. Hoffman – Kenneth D. Hoffman – 1979							
180²/₈	26⁷/₈ 26⁶/₈	18⁷/₈	21	4⁷/₈ 4⁷/₈	6 6	2¹/₈	651	19
	■ Wayne Co. – Green Hamlin – Green Hamlin – 1966							

Score	Length of Main Beam Right	Left	Inside Spread	Greatest Spread	Circumference at Smallest Place Between Burr and First Point Right	Left	Number of Points Right	Left	Lengths Abnormal Points	All-Time Rank	State Rank
	■ *Location of Kill – Hunter – Owner – Date Killed*										
180¹/8	28⁷/8	28⁵/8	20²/8	22²/8	4⁵/8	4⁵/8	6	5	1¹/8	669†	20†
	■ *Ohio Co. – Anthony Goff – Anthony Goff – 2000*										
178⁵/8	23²/8	23²/8	21⁷/8	23³/8	4²/8	4²/8	6	7	1²/8	819	21
	■ *Crittenden Co. – Mendel Davidson – Mendel Davidson – 1994*										
178⁴/8	26¹/8	27³/8	22⁶/8	26⁴/8	4³/8	4⁴/8	6	5		850	22
	■ *Edmonson Co. – Picked Up – Joseph G. Saling – 1984*										
178³/8	27³/8	27⁴/8	18⁶/8	21³/8	5¹/8	5¹/8	7	7	11¹/8	868†	23†
	■ *Perry Co. – Henry Sizemore – Henry Sizemore – 2001*										
178²/8	26⁶/8	28¹/8	19⁶/8	22¹/8	5⁴/8	5⁴/8	7	7	5	891	24
	■ *Ohio Co. – Earl R. Trogden – Earl R. Trogden – 1986*										
178	25¹/8	26²/8	22⁶/8	24⁶/8	6	6	5	5	4	922	25
	■ *Union Co. – Gary L. Gibson – Gary L. Gibson – 1983*										
177⁶/8	25⁴/8	26³/8	20	22	5¹/8	5¹/8	6	7	9	956	26
	■ *Pendleton Co. – Daniel Michalski – Daniel Michalski – 1988*										
177⁴/8	29⁷/8	28⁶/8	21⁶/8	24	4⁶/8	4⁷/8	5	6		993	27
	■ *Grayson Co. – David W. Mercer – David W. Mercer – 1986*										
177²/8	28⁷/8	28²/8	18⁷/8	20⁷/8	5⁴/8	5⁴/8	6	5	1⁵/8	1025†	28†
	■ *Pendleton Co. – John C. Bowers – John C. Bowers – 2000*										
177²/8	27⁵/8	26³/8	17³/8	21¹/8	4⁶/8	4⁴/8	8	7	5⁵/8	1025	28
	■ *Montgomery Co. – Bobby M. Dale – Bobby M. Dale – 1986*										
177¹/8	26⁷/8	27¹/8	22¹/8	24⁴/8	5	4⁷/8	5	6	1⁴/8	1048	30
	■ *Harrison Co. – Picked Up – George Simpson – 1978*										
177	28³/8	26⁶/8	17⁶/8	19⁷/8	4⁷/8	4⁶/8	5	5		1066†	31†
	■ *Casey Co. – Jeff Bastin – Jeff Bastin – 2001*										
177	26	27³/8	21⁶/8	23⁷/8	5³/8	5	10	6	4⁴/8	1066	31
	■ *Lewis Co. – David E. Henderson – David E. Henderson – 1994*										
177	29²/8	27⁶/8	19²/8	21⁴/8	5²/8	5²/8	6	6	2²/8	1066	31
	■ *Nicholas Co. – Jim D. Whisman – Jim D. Whisman – 1998*										
175⁶/8	25²/8	25³/8	18³/8	20⁶/8	5²/8	5³/8	6	8	7¹/8	1310†	34†
	■ *Hart Co. – Patrick Devore – Patrick Devore – 2000*										
175⁴/8	29	27¹/8	21³/8	23²/8	5²/8	5³/8	5	6	8¹/8	1352	35
	■ *Trigg Co. – Picked Up – L.J. Hendon – 1967*										
175⁴/8	26	26⁴/8	22³/8	24³/8	5²/8	5²/8	6	7	5¹/8	1352	35
	■ *Logan Co. – Mark H. Hall – Mark H. Hall – 1992*										
175⁴/8	28³/8	27⁴/8	21²/8	23⁵/8	5³/8	5¹/8	6	5	1²/8	1352	35
	■ *Hart Co. – Randy Ray – Randy Ray – 1998*										
175³/8	29⁶/8	28	22³/8	24⁷/8	4⁶/8	4⁴/8	6	5	3⁶/8	1377	38
	■ *Todd Co. – Gary W. Crafton – Gary W. Crafton – 1981*										
175²/8	28³/8	27⁴/8	21²/8	23⁶/8	4⁶/8	4³/8	5	6	3	1403	39
	■ *Henderson Co. – Donald K. White – Donald K. White – 1987*										
175²/8	25²/8	26¹/8	20²/8	22⁴/8	5²/8	5²/8	5	5		1403	39
	■ *Ohio Co. – James B. Wettstain – James B. Wettstain – 1989*										

Score	Length of Main Beam Right	Left	Inside Spread	Greatest Spread	Circumference at Smallest Place Between Burr and First Point Right	Left	Number of Points Right	Left	Lengths Abnormal Points	All-Time Rank	State Rank
175²/₈	27⁷/₈	28⁴/₈	18⁴/₈	20⁶/₈	4⁶/₈	5²/₈	5	7	1	1403	39
	■ Meade Co. – David M. Jupin – David M. Jupin – 1995										
175	26²/₈	26	23²/₈	25²/₈	5	4⁷/₈	5	5		1472	42
	■ Crittenden Co. – Steve L. Clark – Steve L. Clark – 1997										
175	26⁵/₈	27³/₈	18³/₈	20⁴/₈	5¹/₈	5	6	6	1³/₈	1472	42
	■ Butler Co. – Stevie Henderson – Stevie Henderson – 1998										
174⁴/₈	27³/₈	27⁷/₈	20⁴/₈	23⁶/₈	5²/₈	5¹/₈	6	5		1592	44
	■ Butler Co. – Lonnie D. Hardin – Lonnie D. Hardin – 1966										
174⁴/₈	25⁶/₈	24¹/₈	17⁶/₈	20¹/₈	4¹/₈	4¹/₈	5	5		1592	44
	■ Wolfe Co. – Toy E. Hazenfield – Toy E. Hazenfield – 1993										
174³/₈	26²/₈	25²/₈	20⁵/₈	22¹/₈	4⁴/₈	4²/₈	5	5		1619	46
	■ McCreary Co. – Richmond Keeton – Ruby Keeton – 1982										
174²/₈	26⁶/₈	26¹/₈	23⁵/₈	25⁴/₈	4⁵/₈	4⁴/₈	7	8	2⁷/₈	1652	47
	■ Pulaski Co. – Ishmael R. Helton – Ishmael R. Helton – 1998										
174¹/₈	25	25⁴/₈	18¹/₈	20³/₈	5	5	5	5		1678	48
	■ Mason Co. – Rocky L. Hamm – Rocky L. Hamm – 1989										
174	25⁵/₈	24⁶/₈	17²/₈	19¹/₈	4¹/₈	4¹/₈	5	6	3	1717†	49†
	■ Christian Co. – Christopher Cundiff – Christopher Cundiff – 1985										
174	27⁶/₈	28⁴/₈	19⁶/₈	21⁶/₈	4³/₈	4⁴/₈	5	5	1²/₈	1717	49
	■ Whitley Co. – Edward S. Pittman – Edward S. Pittman – 1988										
173⁷/₈	25⁶/₈	24²/₈	20¹/₈	22¹/₈	5¹/₈	5²/₈	7	6	8	1743	51
	■ Ohio Co. – Rolly Tichenor – Rolly Tichenor – 1982										
173⁷/₈	26¹/₈	26¹/₈	21⁷/₈	23⁷/₈	4²/₈	4⁶/₈	6	8	6⁴/₈	1743	51
	■ Webster Co. – Glenn R. Cummings – Glenn R. Cummings – 1997										
173⁶/₈	27	26⁶/₈	21⁴/₈	23⁴/₈	5	5	7	9	9²/₈	1766	53
	■ Bullitt Co. – George W. Owens – George W. Owens – 1965										
173⁶/₈	30⁶/₈	31²/₈	19⁶/₈	21⁶/₈	5²/₈	5³/₈	7	7	8²/₈	1766	53
	■ Union Co. – Robert C. Caudill – Robert C. Caudill – 1995										
173⁴/₈	30⁵/₈	29⁶/₈	20⁷/₈	23²/₈	5²/₈	5³/₈	7	5	1⁷/₈	1847	55
	■ Todd Co. – Troy L. Harris – Troy L. Harris – 1965										
173⁴/₈	27⁶/₈	27⁶/₈	15²/₈	17	4⁶/₈	4⁵/₈	6	7	4	1847	55
	■ Logan Co. – Jesse Wolf – Jesse Wolf – 1998										
173³/₈	27	27²/₈	21⁴/₈	24	5²/₈	5⁴/₈	5	5	2⁵/₈	1883	57
	■ Lewis Co. – Darrell Tully – Darrell Tully – 1968										
173³/₈	26⁶/₈	26⁵/₈	24²/₈	26⁴/₈	4⁴/₈	4⁵/₈	5	6	1¹/₈	1883	57
	■ Bullitt Co. – Leon R. Allen – Leon R. Allen – 1988										
173²/₈	28	28⁴/₈	20⁵/₈	24⁵/₈	5²/₈	5²/₈	9	8	9¹/₈	1914	59
	■ Allen Co. – Terry W. Sims – Terry W. Sims – 1979										
173	26⁵/₈	25³/₈	19⁴/₈	21⁶/₈	4⁷/₈	5¹/₈	6	8	5	1991	60
	■ Owen Co. – Roger Breeden – Roger Breeden – 1978										
173	26²/₈	26⁶/₈	17⁶/₈	20	5²/₈	5¹/₈	6	6	4⁴/₈	1991	60
	■ Muhlenberg Co. – Larry Vincent – Larry Vincent – 1993										

Score	Length of Main Beam Right	Left	Inside Spread	Greatest Spread	Circumference at Smallest Place Between Burr and First Point Right	Left	Number of Points Right	Left	Lengths Abnormal Points	All-Time Rank	State Rank
	■ Location of Kill – Hunter – Owner – Date Killed										
173	27¹/8	26⁵/8	23⁴/8	25⁵/8	5	5¹/8	6	8	6⁶/8	1991	60
	■ Christian Co. – Mark C. Morris – Mark C. Morris – 1997										
172⁵/8	24⁷/8	25⁷/8	25¹/8	28¹/8	4⁷/8	4⁷/8	5	5		2113	63
	■ Barren Co. – Billy N. Short – Billy N. Short – 1984										
172⁵/8	26⁴/8	26¹/8	17¹/8	18⁶/8	4²/8	4¹/8	5	5		2113	63
	■ Wayne Co. – Ronald G. Sexton – Ronald G. Sexton – 1990										
172⁴/8	26⁴/8	27²/8	24	26¹/8	4³/8	5³/8	5	5		2156	65
	■ Fort Knox – E.G. Christian – E.G. Christian – 1966										
172⁴/8	24³/8	25²/8	23⁴/8	30	5⁶/8	5⁴/8	8	7	12	2156	65
	■ Muhlenberg Co. – Dennis Nolen – Dennis Nolen – 1982										
172³/8	23⁴/8	23³/8	18⁵/8	20	5²/8	5²/8	6	5	1²/8	2200†	67†
	■ Washington Co. – Gordon S. Adam – Gordon S. Adam – 2000										
172³/8	26³/8	26⁶/8	22¹/8	24	4⁷/8	4⁷/8	5	6		2200	67
	■ Harrison Co. – Charles B. Burgess – Charles B. Burgess – 1993										
172³/8	26⁷/8	25⁷/8	17⁷/8	20	4⁷/8	4⁶/8	5	5		2200	67
	■ Hart Co. – Terry Avery – Terry Avery – 1999										
172²/8	26	26⁶/8	19²/8	21¹/8	5¹/8	5²/8	5	6	2⁴/8	2237†	70†
	■ Martin Co. – Julius Jude – Julius Jude – 2001										
172²/8	26²/8	25¹/8	22	23⁴/8	5	5	7	5		2237	70
	■ Pendleton Co. – Kevin L. Galloway – Kevin L. Galloway – 1983										
172²/8	27⁴/8	27³/8	20	22⁴/8	4⁶/8	5	6	5		2237	70
	■ Christian Co. – Randall G. Joiner – Randall G. Joiner – 1992										
172¹/8	27¹/8	26⁵/8	20⁶/8	22⁷/8	6	5⁷/8	6	6	2⁷/8	2286	73
	■ Butler Co. – Bradley D. Cardwell – Bradley D. Cardwell – 1995										
172	25⁶/8	26⁴/8	21⁶/8	25	4⁴/8	4⁴/8	6	6	1	2330	74
	■ Henderson Co. – Gary Hancock – Gary Hancock – 1990										
171⁷/8	27⁷/8	27⁴/8	21¹/8	23⁴/8	4	4¹/8	5	6	1⁶/8	2382†	75†
	■ Larue Co. KY – Gary Polly – Gary Polly – 2001										
171⁷/8	26³/8	25⁴/8	21³/8	23⁵/8	5	5¹/8	5	5		2382	75
	■ Henderson Co. – Aaron D. Parrish – Aaron D. Parrish – 1995										
171⁷/8	26⁶/8	26⁷/8	19⁷/8	21⁶/8	5	4⁷/8	7	5	4⁴/8	2382	75
	■ Muhlenberg Co. – Creighton Spurlock – Creighton Spurlock – 1995										
171⁶/8	27¹/8	27³/8	18⁷/8	21³/8	5³/8	5⁴/8	6	5	2³/8	2418†	78†
	■ Kenton Co. – Mike White – Mike White – 2000										
171⁶/8	26³/8	25⁷/8	14⁶/8	17	4³/8	4³/8	5	6	1	2418	78
	■ Grayson Co. – Jurl Huffman – Jurl Huffman – 1994										
171⁶/8	25⁷/8	26²/8	19⁴/8	21⁴/8	5⁶/8	5⁶/8	5	5		2418	78
	■ Hart Co. – Paul A. Miller – Paul A. Miller – 1998										
171⁵/8	24⁷/8	24⁷/8	20⁴/8	24⁶/8	5³/8	5³/8	7	7	8⁷/8	2470†	81†
	■ Todd Co. – Roger Cherry – Roger Cherry – 2001										
171⁵/8	26³/8	25⁵/8	19³/8	23	5²/8	5²/8	5	5		2470	81
	■ Logan Co. – Alan M. Scott – Alan M. Scott – 1987										

KENTUCKY TYPICAL WHITETAIL DEER

Score	Length of Main Beam Right	Left	Inside Spread	Greatest Spread	Circumference at Smallest Place Between Burr and First Point Right	Left	Number of Points Right	Left	Lengths Abnormal Points	All-Time Rank	State Rank
									■ Location of Kill – Hunter – Owner – Date Killed		
$171\frac{5}{8}$	$26\frac{3}{8}$	$26\frac{4}{8}$	$18\frac{3}{8}$	$22\frac{2}{8}$	$5\frac{4}{8}$	$5\frac{5}{8}$	8	9	$8\frac{2}{8}$	2470	81
■ Anderson Co. – Blaine K. Price – Blaine K. Price – 1990											
$171\frac{5}{8}$	$25\frac{5}{8}$	$27\frac{1}{8}$	$18\frac{5}{8}$	$21\frac{1}{8}$	5	5	5	5		2470	81
■ Marion Co. – Francis M. Hutchins – Francis M. Hutchins – 1999											
$171\frac{4}{8}$	$30\frac{1}{8}$	$30\frac{3}{8}$	$27\frac{2}{8}$	$31\frac{3}{8}$	$5\frac{3}{8}$	$5\frac{2}{8}$	4	4		2513	85
■ Union Co. – Wayne Gibson – Wayne Gibson – 1982											
$171\frac{4}{8}$	$28\frac{2}{8}$	$27\frac{7}{8}$	21	$23\frac{6}{8}$	$4\frac{6}{8}$	$4\frac{5}{8}$	6	5	$4\frac{6}{8}$	2513	85
■ Ballard Co. – Howard P. Gardner – Howard P. Gardner – 1989											
$171\frac{4}{8}$	$26\frac{7}{8}$	$26\frac{6}{8}$	21	$23\frac{4}{8}$	$5\frac{1}{8}$	$5\frac{1}{8}$	5	6	$2\frac{6}{8}$	2513	85
■ Harrison Co. – Ronald Daugherty – Ronald Daugherty – 1994											
$171\frac{3}{8}$	$25\frac{1}{8}$	$25\frac{2}{8}$	$18\frac{7}{8}$	$21\frac{1}{8}$	$4\frac{6}{8}$	$4\frac{6}{8}$	5	5		2564	88
■ Washington Co. – Robert F. Medley – Robert F. Medley – 1988											
$171\frac{3}{8}$	27	$26\frac{7}{8}$	$21\frac{5}{8}$	23	6	$5\frac{7}{8}$	5	6	$4\frac{4}{8}$	2564	88
■ Breathitt Co. – Kenneth J. Minks – Kenneth J. Minks – 1998											
$171\frac{1}{8}$	$30\frac{5}{8}$	$28\frac{3}{8}$	$20\frac{4}{8}$	24	$4\frac{6}{8}$	$4\frac{6}{8}$	8	7	$6\frac{7}{8}$	2665†	90†
■ Kenton Co. – Mike White – Mike White – 2001											
171	$25\frac{2}{8}$	24	$17\frac{2}{8}$	$19\frac{4}{8}$	$5\frac{3}{8}$	$5\frac{2}{8}$	6	6		2707	91
■ Lincoln Co. – Clell T. Gooch, Jr. – Clell T. Gooch, Jr. – 1992											
171	$24\frac{6}{8}$	$25\frac{2}{8}$	$18\frac{2}{8}$	20	$6\frac{2}{8}$	$6\frac{3}{8}$	6	5	$1\frac{6}{8}$	2707	91
■ Crittenden Co. – Marshall Tennison – Marshall Tennison – 1995											
$170\frac{7}{8}$	$26\frac{5}{8}$	$27\frac{4}{8}$	$22\frac{3}{8}$	25	$6\frac{3}{8}$	$6\frac{5}{8}$	5	4		2769†	93†
■ Lewis Co. – Phillip R. Hall – Phillip R. Hall – 2001											
$170\frac{7}{8}$	$27\frac{4}{8}$	$26\frac{4}{8}$	$22\frac{5}{8}$	25	5	5	5	7	4	2769†	93†
■ Boyle Co. – Wilburn Turner – Wilburn Turner – 2000											
$170\frac{7}{8}$	$24\frac{5}{8}$	$24\frac{7}{8}$	$19\frac{1}{8}$	$22\frac{3}{8}$	5	$4\frac{7}{8}$	6	6	$3\frac{2}{8}$	2769	93
■ Christian Co. – Nicholas J. Gresham – Nicholas J. Gresham – 1993											
$170\frac{6}{8}$	$29\frac{4}{8}$	$29\frac{7}{8}$	$27\frac{2}{8}$	$29\frac{2}{8}$	$4\frac{5}{8}$	$4\frac{7}{8}$	5	5		2828†	96†
■ Hart Co. – Darryl L. Shelby – Darryl L. Shelby – 2000											
$170\frac{5}{8}$	$29\frac{3}{8}$	$29\frac{4}{8}$	21	$25\frac{6}{8}$	$4\frac{6}{8}$	$4\frac{6}{8}$	5	6	$4\frac{7}{8}$	2876	97
■ Christian Co. – Henry J. Oliver – Henry J. Oliver – 1978											
$170\frac{4}{8}$	$24\frac{6}{8}$	$24\frac{4}{8}$	21	$22\frac{6}{8}$	$4\frac{6}{8}$	$4\frac{6}{8}$	5	5	$5\frac{6}{8}$	2933	98
■ Carroll Co. – Tracey D. Kelley – Tracey D. Kelley – 1994											
$170\frac{4}{8}$	$28\frac{7}{8}$	$27\frac{7}{8}$	19	$21\frac{4}{8}$	$5\frac{6}{8}$	$5\frac{5}{8}$	7	6	$2\frac{4}{8}$	2933	98
■ Hopkins Co. – Luther T. Mincy, Jr. – Luther T. Mincy, Jr. – 1997											
$170\frac{3}{8}$	$25\frac{2}{8}$	25	$20\frac{2}{8}$	$22\frac{1}{8}$	$4\frac{7}{8}$	$5\frac{2}{8}$	8	6	$6\frac{1}{8}$	2992	100
■ Wayne Co. – Kelvin Casada – Kelvin Casada – 1998											
$170\frac{2}{8}$	$23\frac{7}{8}$	$22\frac{4}{8}$	$17\frac{4}{8}$	$20\frac{2}{8}$	$4\frac{4}{8}$	$4\frac{6}{8}$	5	5		3063	101
■ Hopkins Co. – Michael E. Dillingham – Michael E. Dillingham – 1977											
$170\frac{2}{8}$	$26\frac{3}{8}$	$26\frac{1}{8}$	$19\frac{6}{8}$	$22\frac{4}{8}$	$4\frac{7}{8}$	$4\frac{7}{8}$	5	5		3063	101
■ Whitley Co. – Shevelery C. Sturgill – Shevelery C. Sturgill – 1988											
$170\frac{2}{8}$	$25\frac{4}{8}$	$25\frac{6}{8}$	18	$19\frac{4}{8}$	$4\frac{2}{8}$	$4\frac{1}{8}$	5	5		3063	101
■ Meade Co. – Paul E. Ice – Paul E. Ice – 1991											

Score	Length of Main Beam Right Left	Inside Spread	Greatest Spread	Circumference at Smallest Place Between Burr and First Point Right Left	Number of Points Right Left	Lengths Abnormal Points	All-Time Rank	State Rank
170²/₈	25²/₈ 25¹/₈	17¹/₈	19⁴/₈	4⁷/₈ 4⁶/₈	8 11	7³/₈	3063	101

■ Logan Co. – Jim F. Sweeney – Jim F. Sweeney – 1994

170²/₈	26 25⁵/₈	16⁴/₈	18⁶/₈	5⁵/₈ 5¹/₈	7 5	1²/₈	3063	101

■ Christian Co. – Brian K. Oatts – Brian K. Oatts – 1999

170¹/₈	26⁷/₈ 27	19⁵/₈	21⁵/₈	5¹/₈ 5⁴/₈	7 7	5⁴/₈	3143	106

■ Breckinridge Co. – Thomas F. Dean – Thomas F. Dean – 1982

170¹/₈	25²/₈ 25⁶/₈	17¹/₈	19²/₈	5⁶/₈ 5⁶/₈	5 5		3143	106

■ Butler Co. – David W. Alford – David W. Alford – 1993

170¹/₈	28⁴/₈ 30¹/₈	21⁶/₈	24	5 4⁷/₈	4 6	1³/₈	3143	106

■ Muhlenberg Co. – Jamie G. Noble – Jamie G. Noble – 1994

170¹/₈	28⁵/₈ 29¹/₈	22³/₈	24⁷/₈	5¹/₈ 5³/₈	4 5		3143	106

■ Hart Co. – Paul B. Wilson – Paul B. Wilson – 1997

170¹/₈	28¹/₈ 28³/₈	20⁵/₈	22⁴/₈	4⁴/₈ 4⁴/₈	5 6		3143	106

■ Hart Co. – Doug Fields – Doug Fields – 1998

170	25³/₈ 25²/₈	18	20	4⁵/₈ 4⁵/₈	7 6	1²/₈	3224	111

■ Ballard Co. – Rudolf Koranchan, Jr. – Rudolf Koranchan, Jr. – 1977

170	27⁵/₈ 26³/₈	19⁶/₈	21⁷/₈	4⁶/₈ 4⁶/₈	5 5		3224	111

■ Wayne Co. – Danny Phillips – Danny Phillips – 1995

169⁷/₈	26 25³/₈	18²/₈	22⁴/₈	4⁵/₈ 4⁶/₈	6 7	4¹/₈	3302	113

■ Hart Co. – Nathan A. Piper – Nathan A. Piper – 1993

169⁴/₈	23²/₈ 23¹/₈	17⁴/₈	19⁶/₈	5³/₈ 5²/₈	7 6		3316†	114†

■ Spencer Co. – Keith King – Keith King – 2001

169⁴/₈	28²/₈ 28⁶/₈	14³/₈	16³/₈	4⁷/₈ 5²/₈	6 5	1¹/₈	3316	114

■ Boone Co. – Tim Adams – Tim Adams – 1998

169³/₈	25⁶/₈ 25⁶/₈	18⁴/₈	20²/₈	5 5¹/₈	6 7	3⁵/₈	3324	116

■ Christian Co. – Kelly Slone – Kelly Slone – 1999

169²/₈	24¹/₈ 27³/₈	23⁴/₈	25⁴/₈	4⁶/₈ 5	5 5		3336	117

■ Webster Co. – Wayne Daugherty – Wayne Daugherty – 1990

169	27²/₈ 27³/₈	20³/₈	22⁴/₈	5⁵/₈ 5⁵/₈	6 6	3³/₈	3348	118

■ Breckinridge Co. – Denny Barr – Denny Barr – 1990

168⁷/₈	27⁷/₈ 27⁵/₈	21⁵/₈	24	4⁷/₈ 4⁷/₈	6 6	1²/₈	3361	119

■ Pulaski Co. – Picked Up – Joby Gossett – 1995

168⁵/₈	20³/₈ 19⁶/₈	19	21¹/₈	7 6⁷/₈	6 8	7³/₈	3376†	120†

■ Lyon Co. – Derek West – Derek West – 2000

168⁵/₈	28⁶/₈ 28⁵/₈	17⁵/₈	20²/₈	4⁷/₈ 4⁷/₈	5 5		3376	120

■ Trigg Co. – Robert M. Adams – Robert M. Adams – 1992

168⁴/₈	25⁶/₈ 25²/₈	17²/₈	20	4⁷/₈ 4⁷/₈	6 6		3385†	122†

■ Pulaski Co. – Kevin Hewitt – Kevin Hewitt – 2000

168⁴/₈	23⁷/₈ 23⁴/₈	16⁶/₈	18⁷/₈	5²/₈ 5¹/₈	6 5	1	3385	122

■ Grayson Co. – John D. Johnson – John D. Johnson – 1989

168³/₈	23³/₈ 23⁶/₈	19¹/₈	21³/₈	4³/₈ 4⁴/₈	6 6		3399	124

■ Marion Co. – Terry Allen – Terry Allen – 1993

Score	Length of Main Beam		Inside Spread	Greatest Spread	Circumference at Smallest Place Between Burr and First Point		Number of Points		Lengths Abnormal Points	All-Time Rank	State Rank
	Right	Left			Right	Left	Right	Left			
	■ Location of Kill – Hunter – Owner – Date Killed										
168³/₈	25⁷/₈	26	19¹/₈	21³/₈	4⁴/₈	4⁶/₈	5	5		3399	124
	■ Rockcastle Co. – Brent Boone – Brent Boone – 1998										
168²/₈	25	25	20⁶/₈	23¹/₈	4²/₈	4⁴/₈	6	6		3414†	126†
	■ Scott Co. – Jennifer M. Jacobs – Jennifer M. Jacobs – 2000										
168²/₈	26⁵/₈	26⁶/₈	21⁵/₈	23³/₈	5⁵/₈	5⁴/₈	8	5	7⁵/₈	3414	126
	■ Crittenden Co. – Donald W. Greenwell – Donald W. Greenwell – 1988										
168²/₈	22⁶/₈	24	18⁴/₈	21⁷/₈	4⁴/₈	4⁴/₈	9	6	5	3414	126
	■ Casey Co. – Andrew Weddle – Andrew Weddle – 1998										
168¹/₈	27⁷/₈	28⁷/₈	20⁵/₈	23²/₈	5¹/₈	5¹/₈	6	5	2⁴/₈	3426	129
	■ Ohio Co. – Ray Jenkins – Ray Jenkins – 1994										
168¹/₈	27²/₈	26⁶/₈	18⁷/₈	21¹/₈	4⁴/₈	4³/₈	5	6	1⁴/₈	3426	129
	■ Boyle Co. – Chris Douglas – Chris Douglas – 1997										
168	26¹/₈	29	18²/₈	20²/₈	4⁵/₈	5	6	7	3²/₈	3443†	131†
	■ Perry Co. – Ernie McIntosh – Ernie McIntosh – 2000										
167⁷/₈	28⁷/₈	28²/₈	24⁷/₈	26⁶/₈	4⁶/₈	4⁶/₈	5	5		3451	132
	■ Henderson Co. – Larry W. Floyd – Larry W. Floyd – 1994										
167⁷/₈	28	28¹/₈	20³/₈	21⁷/₈	4⁷/₈	4⁷/₈	5	6		3451	132
	■ Kenton Co. – Harold D. Bowman – Harold D. Bowman – 1995										
167⁵/₈	26⁴/₈	25⁵/₈	26	28	4⁷/₈	5¹/₈	7	7	7¹/₈	3476	134
	■ Muhlenberg Co. – Johnny R. Bethel – Johnny R. Bethel – 1991										
167⁴/₈	26¹/₈	26²/₈	19⁴/₈	22	4³/₈	4³/₈	5	5		3485	135
	■ Ohio Co. – Charles R. Rush – Charles R. Rush – 1990										
167⁴/₈	26⁷/₈	26¹/₈	19⁴/₈	24	5	5¹/₈	6	6	4	3485	135
	■ Trigg Co. – Terry Mitcheson – Terry Mitcheson – 1998										
167⁴/₈	24³/₈	25⁷/₈	18⁵/₈	21⁴/₈	5¹/₈	5¹/₈	5	4	1¹/₈	3485	135
	■ Metcalfe Co. – Tony E. Shockley – Tony E. Shockley – 1998										
167³/₈	28	27²/₈	19⁵/₈	21⁵/₈	4⁵/₈	5⁴/₈	5	8	4⁴/₈	3500	138
	■ Adair Co. – Greg Roy – Greg Roy – 1994										
167³/₈	26	26²/₈	17⁵/₈	20³/₈	4⁷/₈	4⁷/₈	5	5		3500	138
	■ Breckinridge Co. – Ronald D. Keen – Ronald D. Keen – 1996										
167²/₈	26	27⁵/₈	19⁶/₈	23²/₈	4	4	7	7	4	3519	140
	■ Meade Co. – William V. Gilbert – William V. Gilbert – 1969										
167²/₈	24⁶/₈	24⁷/₈	19	21³/₈	5⁷/₈	5⁷/₈	5	5		3519	140
	■ Bath Co. – Phillip S. Welch – Phillip S. Welch – 1972										
167¹/₈	24⁴/₈	23⁷/₈	19⁷/₈	22	4⁴/₈	4⁷/₈	6	7	1⁴/₈	3539	142
	■ Franklin Co. – Jeffrey S. Meece – Jeffrey S. Meece – 1995										
167¹/₈	27⁷/₈	28³/₈	21³/₈	23	4⁵/₈	4⁴/₈	5	7	6²/₈	3539	142
	■ Breckinridge Co. – Ben Whitfill – Ben Whitfill – 1998										
167	26⁶/₈	27	17¹/₈	20⁴/₈	5⁷/₈	6⁴/₈	7	7	7³/₈	3552†	144†
	■ Calloway Co. – Barry B. Caneroy – Barry B. Caneroy – 2000										
166⁶/₈	27³/₈	27⁶/₈	22	24⁴/₈	5	5⁴/₈	5	5	2	3582	145
	■ Green Co. – Orville H. Fancher – J.R. Rock – 1986										

Score	Length of Main Beam		Inside Spread	Greatest Spread	Circumference at Smallest Place Between Burr and First Point		Number of Points		Lengths Abnormal Points	All-Time Rank	State Rank
	Right	Left			Right	Left	Right	Left			
	Location of Kill – Hunter – Owner – Date Killed										
166⁶/₈	25⁴/₈	25⁴/₈	16⁶/₈	18⁶/₈	4⁷/₈	4⁶/₈	6	6		3582	145
	▪ *Hardin Co. – Charles D. Claggett – Charles D. Claggett – 1996*										
166⁵/₈	25¹/₈	24³/₈	18⁶/₈	20⁵/₈	4⁷/₈	4⁶/₈	6	6	2⁵/₈	3598	147
	▪ *Elliott Co. – George Stafford – George Stafford – 1987*										
166⁵/₈	23¹/₈	22¹/₈	21¹/₈	24¹/₈	4²/₈	4²/₈	5	5		3598	147
	▪ *Oldham Co. – Todd E. Lewis – Todd E. Lewis – 1994*										
166⁴/₈	25⁵/₈	25⁵/₈	17	19¹/₈	4⁶/₈	4⁶/₈	6	6		3609	149
	▪ *Todd Co. – Douglas Gibson – Douglas Gibson – 1998*										
166³/₈	26⁴/₈	27³/₈	20⁷/₈	22⁷/₈	4²/₈	4²/₈	5	6	1⁴/₈	3620†	150†
	▪ *Hart Co. – Cheryl Wilson – Cheryl Wilson – 2001*										
166²/₈	25²/₈	25⁷/₈	21	22⁴/₈	4⁷/₈	4⁵/₈	5	5		3632†	151†
	▪ *Bell Co. – Timothy D. Elliott – Timothy D. Elliott – 2000*										
166¹/₈	25	25	22²/₈	24¹/₈	5⁴/₈	5²/₈	8	6	10³/₈	3643	152
	▪ *Christian Co. – Steve R. Walker – Steve R. Walker – 1994*										
166¹/₈	24	23⁶/₈	21	22¹/₈	6	6	7	6	7³/₈	3643	152
	▪ *Wayne Co. – Douglas Watson – Douglas Watson – 1998*										
166¹/₈	27²/₈	27¹/₈	21⁵/₈	23⁵/₈	5²/₈	5	4	5		3643	152
	▪ *Hardin Co. – Ella M. Moore – Ella M. Moore – 1999*										
166	25²/₈	25⁴/₈	18¹/₈	20⁶/₈	5²/₈	5⁴/₈	6	7	2⁵/₈	3657	155
	▪ *Russell Co. – John D. Wilson – John D. Wilson – 1996*										
165⁶/₈	27⁵/₈	26³/₈	21	23⁵/₈	4⁵/₈	4⁴/₈	5	7	2	3680	156
	▪ *Pulaski Co. – Kenny Hyden – Kenny Hyden – 1992*										
165⁶/₈	28	28	24⁴/₈	26⁴/₈	4⁶/₈	4⁶/₈	7	7	6⁴/₈	3680	156
	▪ *Harlan Co. – Rodney D. Howard – Rodney D. Howard – 1996*										
165⁴/₈	26¹/₈	25²/₈	20	22¹/₈	5	5	5	5		3714	158
	▪ *Ohio Co. – Dwight Keith – Dwight Keith – 1994*										
165⁴/₈	26	26³/₈	20	23³/₈	5¹/₈	5¹/₈	5	5		3714	158
	▪ *Hart Co. – Clarence K. Merideth – Clarence K. Merideth – 1997*										
165³/₈	25⁴/₈	25⁵/₈	28	29⁴/₈	5⁴/₈	5⁵/₈	6	5	2	3731	160
	▪ *Ohio Co. – Jimmy W. Rice – Jimmy W. Rice – 1992*										
165²/₈	26²/₈	26²/₈	19⁴/₈	22	4⁷/₈	4⁵/₈	5	6		3748†	161†
	▪ *Christian Co. – Kenny Brown – Kenny Brown – 2000*										
165²/₈	24⁴/₈	25⁴/₈	20	21⁶/₈	5	4⁷/₈	5	5		3748	161
	▪ *Lyon Co. – James Chambers – James Chambers – 1974*										
164⁷/₈	26⁷/₈	26⁷/₈	18⁷/₈	21	5¹/₈	5²/₈	5	5		3792	163
	▪ *Spencer Co. – Mitchell McMichael – Mitchell McMichael – 1990*										
164⁵/₈	24⁶/₈	26²/₈	18⁵/₈	21¹/₈	5⁴/₈	5⁴/₈	6	6		3835	164
	▪ *Christian Co. – Stephen Martin – Stephen Martin – 1996*										
164³/₈	25⁶/₈	24⁷/₈	18	20¹/₈	4⁶/₈	4⁷/₈	5	8	3⁵/₈	3864	165
	▪ *Breckinridge Co. – Richard P. Bagley – Richard P. Bagley – 1994*										
164³/₈	26¹/₈	26¹/₈	21⁶/₈	23⁶/₈	4⁶/₈	4⁷/₈	6	6	1¹/₈	3864	165
	▪ *Hopkins Co. – David L. Roberts – David L. Roberts – 1995*										

Score	Length of Main Beam Right	Left	Inside Spread	Greatest Spread	Circumference at Smallest Place Between Burr and First Point Right	Left	Number of Points Right	Left	Lengths Abnormal Points	All-Time Rank	State Rank
	■ Location of Kill – Hunter – Owner – Date Killed										
164²/₈	23⁴/₈	24¹/₈	18²/₈	20²/₈	5	5	4	4		3876	167
■ Logan Co. – Anthony D. Shoemake – Anthony D. Shoemake – 1998											
164¹/₈	27⁴/₈	27³/₈	19²/₈	21¹/₈	4⁴/₈	4⁴/₈	6	5	1³/₈	3886†	168†
■ Adair Co. – Shane Stonecypher – Shane Stonecypher – 2001											
164¹/₈	26⁴/₈	26²/₈	20³/₈	22⁴/₈	4⁶/₈	4⁷/₈	6	6		3886	168
■ Garrard Co. – Freddie Orange – Freddie Orange – 1994											
164	28⁴/₈	27	22	25	5³/₈	5³/₈	4	4		3908	170
■ Hopkins Co. – Oennis D. Tapp – Dennis D. Tapp – 1984											
163⁷/₈	25²/₈	24⁴/₈	16²/₈	18¹/₈	4⁷/₈	4⁷/₈	6	5	1¹/₈	3928†	171†
■ Taylor Co. – Douglas M. Graham – Douglas M. Graham – 2001											
163⁷/₈	25⁷/₈	26⁵/₈	19⁴/₈	22	5⁵/₈	5⁵/₈	6	6	3¹/₈	3928†	171†
■ Wayne Co. – James J. Worley – James J. Worley – 2000											
163⁶/₈	23⁵/₈	24²/₈	18²/₈	20¹/₈	4¹/₈	4²/₈	6	6		3946	173
■ Henry Co. – Richard Nadicksbernd – Richard Nadicksbernd – 1999											
163⁴/₈	23³/₈	23³/₈	23²/₈	25¹/₈	4⁴/₈	4⁴/₈	6	6		3984	174
■ Daviess Co. – Gregory J. Young – Gregory J. Young – 1995											
163³/₈	25⁶/₈	26⁴/₈	18⁷/₈	20	4⁶/₈	4⁵/₈	5	6	1	4002	175
■ Rowan Co. – Teresa Caudill – Teresa Caudill – 1995											
163³/₈	25	24⁷/₈	17¹/₈	19⁴/₈	5¹/₈	5¹/₈	5	5		4002	175
■ Boone Co. – John R. Stephenson – John R. Stephenson – 1997											
163²/₈	25	24⁴/₈	17²/₈	19³/₈	3⁵/₈	3⁴/₈	6	6		4017	177
■ Edmonson Co. – Melissa Culbreth – Melissa Culbreth – 1994											
163¹/₈	25⁴/₈	26⁴/₈	19⁵/₈	21⁷/₈	5¹/₈	5¹/₈	5	5		4035†	178†
■ Jessamine Co. – Rocky D. Johnson – Rocky D. Johnson – 2001											
163¹/₈	26¹/₈	26³/₈	17⁷/₈	20³/₈	4⁵/₈	4⁵/₈	5	5		4035	178
■ Grayson Co. – Greg A. Oldham – Greg A. Oldham – 1995											
163	24⁵/₈	25⁴/₈	20	22	4⁴/₈	4⁴/₈	5	5		4051†	180†
■ McLean Co. – Patrick Guynn – Patrick Guynn – 2000											
163	28¹/₈	28	19²/₈	21¹/₈	4⁴/₈	4⁴/₈	8	7	4⁶/₈	4051	180
■ Rockcastle Co. – George Bishop, Jr. – George Bishop, Jr. – 1994											
163	22⁷/₈	22⁶/₈	18³/₈	20	5⁵/₈	5⁵/₈	5	6	1¹/₈	4051	180
■ Butler Co. – Gregory J. Hillard – Gregory J. Hillard – 1995											
162⁶/₈	25²/₈	25⁶/₈	22⁴/₈	24	4⁴/₈	4³/₈	5	5		4089	183
■ Christian Co. – Greg Abner – Greg Abner – 1997											
162⁵/₈	24³/₈	24⁷/₈	18⁵/₈	21³/₈	4	4	5	5		4109	184
■ McLean Co. – Jeff Wilkerson – Jeff Wilkerson – 1993											
162⁵/₈	26⁴/₈	26	19⁵/₈	22²/₈	6²/₈	6⁵/₈	4	4		4109	184
■ Marion Co. – Jody E. Yates – Jody E. Yates – 1998											
162⁴/₈	26⁶/₈	27¹/₈	23⁷/₈	25	4⁴/₈	4⁴/₈	5	6	5⁷/₈	4129	186
■ Spencer Co. – John S. Crafton – John S. Crafton – 1995											
162³/₈	24⁷/₈	23⁵/₈	21¹/₈	22⁶/₈	5²/₈	5²/₈	6	6	3⁶/₈	4140	187
■ Christian Co. – John W. Blankenship – John W. Blankenship – 1999											

Score	Length of Main Beam Right	Left	Inside Spread	Greatest Spread	Circumference at Smallest Place Between Burr and First Point Right	Left	Number of Points Right	Left	Lengths Abnormal Points	All-Time Rank	State Rank
162²/₈	25³/₈	25⁶/₈	22⁴/₈	24¹/₈	4²/₈	4³/₈	5	5		4153	188
■ Fayette Co. – Steven R. Wright – Steven R. Wright – 1992											
162²/₈	25⁴/₈	24⁷/₈	18⁴/₈	20⁷/₈	4⁴/₈	4⁴/₈	5	5		4153	188
■ Ohio Co. – Dale Sexton – Dale Sexton – 1994											
162	25²/₈	24⁷/₈	17²/₈	20	4³/₈	4²/₈	6	6	6²/₈	4184	190
■ Henderson Co. – Alan C. Taylor – Alan C. Taylor – 1998											
161⁶/₈	24⁵/₈	24⁴/₈	19²/₈	21⁶/₈	4⁷/₈	4⁶/₈	5	5		4223	191
■ Henderson Co. – Woodrow Bugg, Jr. – Woodrow Bugg, Jr. – 1993											
161⁶/₈	26²/₈	25⁵/₈	17⁴/₈	19⁵/₈	4⁵/₈	4⁴/₈	5	5		4223	191
■ Harrison Co. – Kenneth R. Leach – Kenneth R. Leach – 1994											
161⁵/₈	24¹/₈	23⁴/₈	21¹/₈	23¹/₈	4³/₈	4³/₈	6	6		4234†	193†
■ Garrard Co. – Timothy L. Poynter – Timothy L. Poynter – 2000											
161⁵/₈	26²/₈	26⁵/₈	21	22⁶/₈	5²/₈	5²/₈	7	5	4⁵/₈	4234	193
■ Todd Co. – Brian P. Stratton – Brian P. Stratton – 1996											
161³/₈	25	24⁵/₈	16⁷/₈	19²/₈	5²/₈	5²/₈	6	5		4285	195
■ Marion Co. – Robert G. Buckman – Robert G. Buckman – 1992											
161³/₈	27²/₈	26⁶/₈	17⁵/₈	19⁴/₈	4⁴/₈	4⁵/₈	5	5		4285	195
■ Hart Co. – Michael O. Dennison – Michael O. Dennison – 1994											
161³/₈	26⁴/₈	26	18⁷/₈	21	4⁷/₈	4⁵/₈	4	5		4285	195
■ Ohio Co. – Bruce A. Russell – Bruce A. Russell – 1999											
161³/₈	25²/₈	25⁴/₈	17⁷/₈	19⁶/₈	5	4⁷/₈	5	5		4285	195
■ Marion Co. – Delayne Smothers – Delayne Smothers – 1999											
161¹/₈	24¹/₈	24³/₈	18⁷/₈	21¹/₈	4²/₈	4²/₈	5	5		4332†	199†
■ Barren Co. – James G. Haynes – James G. Haynes – 2000											
161	27¹/₈	27⁶/₈	23²/₈	24⁶/₈	4⁶/₈	4⁷/₈	5	5		4356†	200†
■ Henderson Co. – Picked Up – John Beckham – 2002											
161	24¹/₈	23⁵/₈	18⁴/₈	21	5⁵/₈	6	6	5	2⁴/₈	4356	200
■ Hopkins Co. – Kevin Webb – Kevin Webb – 1995											
160⁷/₈	23⁷/₈	25²/₈	21⁷/₈	23⁶/₈	4³/₈	4⁵/₈	5	5		4380†	202†
■ Graves Co. – Stephen C. Lyell – Stephen C. Lyell – 2000											
160⁷/₈	25¹/₈	24⁴/₈	19³/₈	21	5	5	5	5		4380	202
■ Logan Co. – Thomas E. Rogers – Thomas E. Rogers – 1994											
160⁴/₈	26	25⁶/₈	18⁶/₈	21	5³/₈	5³/₈	5	9	8	4443	204
■ Rockcastle Co. – Danny Bustle – Danny Bustle – 1996											
160⁴/₈	25¹/₈	24¹/₈	18³/₈	20³/₈	4	4	6	5	1¹/₈	4443	204
■ Rockcastle Co. – Lonnie G. Brumett – Lonnie G. Brumett – 1998											
160³/₈	24³/₈	25¹/₈	18¹/₈	20	4⁵/₈	4⁶/₈	7	7	3⁶/₈	4470	206
■ Christian Co. – Johnny Hale – Johnny Hale – 1994											
160²/₈	24⁵/₈	22⁷/₈	19	21	4⁵/₈	4⁵/₈	6	6		4495†	207†
■ Whitley Co. – Chris Tompkins – Chris Tompkins – 2001											
160²/₈	24⁷/₈	25	16⁴/₈	19³/₈	4²/₈	4¹/₈	7	6	3	4495	207
■ Bullitt Co. – Kenneth W. Doan – Kenneth W. Doan – 1966											

Score	Length of Main Beam Right	Left	Inside Spread	Greatest Spread	Circumference at Smallest Place Between Burr and First Point Right	Left	Number of Points Right	Left	Lengths Abnormal Points	All-Time Rank	State Rank

■ Location of Kill – Hunter – Owner – Date Killed

Score	R	L	Inside	Greatest	C-R	C-L	P-R	P-L	Abn	Rank	State
160²/8	24⁴/8	25⁷/8	20⁴/8	22²/8	4⁴/8	4³/8	7	6	4²/8	4495	207
160²/8	25²/8	25³/8	18	19⁷/8	4³/8	4²/8	5	5		4495	207
160²/8	27³/8	27⁶/8	19⁷/8	22³/8	4⁷/8	5	5	6	1³/8	4495	207
160¹/8	27³/8	27³/8	18⁷/8	21⁶/8	5⁷/8	5⁶/8	7	6	6⁶/8	4534†	212†
160	25³/8	24⁷/8	16⁴/8	18⁵/8	5	5	5	5		4565	213
160	26²/8	25⁴/8	22	24	4⁷/8	5²/8	9	8	7⁴/8	4565	213
160	21²/8	22¹/8	19⁶/8	22¹/8	4⁴/8	4⁴/8	7	10	3⁶/8	4565	213
160	24⁴/8	25²/8	15⁴/8	17⁶/8	6⁴/8	6⁴/8	6	7	4²/8	4565	213

- 160²/8 ■ Christian Co. – Ronald R. Morris – Ronald R. Morris – 1991
- 160²/8 ■ Jessamine Co. – Roger Drury – Roger Drury – 1992
- 160²/8 ■ Ohio Co. – Joe Bratcher – Joe Bratcher – 1993
- 160¹/8 ■ Metcalfe Co. – Mark Shirley – Mark Shirley – 2000
- 160 ■ Jefferson Co. – Andrea L. Miles – Andrea L. Miles – 1992
- 160 ■ Jefferson Co. – William S. Finney, Jr. – William S. Finney, Jr. – 1993
- 160 ■ Oldham Co. – James W. Lunsford – James W. Lunsford – 1997
- 160 ■ Oldham Co. – Richard D. Mangum – Richard D. Mangum – 1998

† The scores and ranking for trophies from the 25th Awards Entry Period are not final until the banquet is held on June 19, 2004.

OLD-TIME FIELD PHOTOS

HUNTER: Lawrence E. Vandal
SCORE: 178-1/8
CATEGORY: typical whitetail deer
LOCATION: Concrete, North Dakota
DATE: 1947

KENTUCKY

NON-TYPICAL WHITETAIL DEER

Score	Length of Main Beam		Inside Spread	Greatest Spread	Circumference at Smallest Place Between Burr and First Point		Number of Points		Lengths Abnormal Points	All-Time Rank	State Rank
	Right	Left			Right	Left	Right	Left			
	■ Location of Kill – Hunter – Owner – Date Killed										
240⁷/8	28	28⁶/8	20²/8	26²/8	6³/8	6²/8	13	10	57¹/8	109	1
	■ Lewis Co. – Anthony D. Mefford – Cabela's, Inc. – 1996										
238²/8	27⁶/8	28¹/8	19⁶/8	25⁷/8	6³/8	6²/8	15	17	63⁶/8	136	2
	■ Barren Co. – Picked Up – Ed Rigdon – 1995										
238¹/8	31	28⁴/8	21	25⁶/8	6¹/8	5⁷/8	10	17	61⁵/8	139	3
	■ Lewis Co. – Tom D. Fetters, Sr. – Cabela's, Inc. – 1998										
237¹/8	28³/8	28¹/8	17¹/8	19²/8	6¹/8	6	13	11	38	150†	4†
	■ Wayne Co. – Jessie D. Fulton – Cabela's, Inc. – 2000										
236³/8	25⁷/8	23⁶/8	20³/8	27²/8	5⁴/8	5⁴/8	14	16	93⁶/8	161	5
	■ Union Co. – Wilbur E. Buchanan – Wilbur E. Buchanan – 1970										
234¹/8	29⁶/8	29²/8	19⁷/8	24⁵/8	4⁷/8	4⁶/8	13	10	30	178	6
	■ Lewis Co. – Joey Smith – Cabela's, Inc. – 1997										
232³/8	26³/8	19⁶/8	23²/8	24⁶/8	4⁴/8	6⁷/8	11	12	83⁵/8	204	7
	■ Breathitt Co. – Delmar R. Hounshell – Delmar R. Hounshell – 1990										
226⁵/8	26⁶/8	26	18⁷/8	21⁴/8	6	5⁶/8	7	9	32	289	8
	■ Pulaski Co. – H.C. Sumpter – H.C. Sumpter – 1984										
223¹/8	23⁶/8	24¹/8	18³/8	21⁷/8	5³/8	5⁴/8	21	14	46⁴/8	361	9
	■ McCreary Co. – James H. Sanders – James H. Sanders – 1957										
222⁷/8	29⁷/8	30¹/8	21⁴/8	24¹/8	5	5	15	9	19⁷/8	368	10
	■ Morgan Co. – Denzil C. Potter – Denzil C. Potter – 1999										
222⁵/8	25⁴/8	26⁶/8	22¹/8	26¹/8	6	6⁵/8	11	11	36	373	11
	■ Henderson Co. – Ronnie D. Stacy – Ronnie D. Stacy – 1992										
221⁷/8	25⁴/8	26⁴/8	16⁴/8	23⁶/8	5⁶/8	5⁴/8	12	14	37³/8	396	12
	■ Trigg Co. – Bill McWhirter – Bill McWhirter – 1982										
221²/8	25⁵/8	25⁶/8	19¹/8	25¹/8	5¹/8	5²/8	11	11	38³/8	410	13
	■ Muhlenberg Co. – Mark A. Smith – Mark A. Smith – 1998										
220²/8	27⁴/8	27¹/8	19	23²/8	5¹/8	4⁷/8	13	13	37⁶/8	434	14
	■ Caldwell Co. – Loyd Holt – Loyd Holt – 1984										
219¹/8	27⁶/8	27⁶/8	18⁷/8	24⁵/8	5²/8	5³/8	15	9	47	465	15
	■ Bell Co. – Jeff D. Jackson – Jeff D. Jackson – 1999										
218⁴/8	23¹/8	22⁷/8	20⁵/8	22	7⁵/8	7¹/8	9	12	31⁵/8	487	16
	■ Logan Co. – Robert L. Schrader, Jr. – Robert L. Schrader, Jr. – 1987										
217⁵/8	28⁶/8	27²/8	14⁶/8	24⁷/8	6	6	13	15	55³/8	506	17
	■ Hardin Co. – Michael F. Meredith – Michael F. Meredith – 1980										
217¹/8	27³/8	27⁵/8	21¹/8	27¹/8	6²/8	5⁵/8	13	13	34²/8	527	18
	■ Butler Co. – Merle Raymer – Merle Raymer – 1999										
215²/8	23²/8	23¹/8	17⁷/8	20⁴/8	7¹/8	7²/8	12	12	89⁷/8	589†	19†
	■ Henderson Co. – Gary E. Boucherie – Gary E. Boucherie – 1991										

Score	Length of Main Beam Right	Left	Inside Spread	Greatest Spread	Circumference at Smallest Place Between Burr and First Point Right	Left	Number of Points Right	Left	Lengths Abnormal Points	All-Time Rank	State Rank
215	$24\frac{2}{8}$	$23\frac{3}{8}$	$22\frac{2}{8}$	$25\frac{2}{8}$	$5\frac{3}{8}$	$5\frac{2}{8}$	8	10	60	598	20
	Caldwell Co. – C.J. Brummett – C.J. Brummett – 1998										
$211\frac{2}{8}$	25	$26\frac{2}{8}$	$18\frac{4}{8}$	$20\frac{5}{8}$	$5\frac{7}{8}$	$5\frac{4}{8}$	7	9	$26\frac{2}{8}$	750†	21†
	Breathitt Co. – Michael D. Johnson – Michael D. Johnson – 2000										
211	$29\frac{1}{8}$	30	$19\frac{1}{8}$	$23\frac{4}{8}$	$5\frac{2}{8}$	$5\frac{4}{8}$	13	6	$57\frac{3}{8}$	764	22
	Allen Co. – Danny R. Towe – Ben & Seth Towe – 1987										
$210\frac{3}{8}$	$24\frac{3}{8}$	25	$19\frac{2}{8}$	$21\frac{2}{8}$	5	5	13	12	$43\frac{1}{8}$	796	23
	Lyon Co. – Roy D. Lee – Roy D. Lee – 1975										
$210\frac{2}{8}$	29	27	$19\frac{1}{8}$	$28\frac{7}{8}$	$5\frac{1}{8}$	5	10	11	$31\frac{3}{8}$	803	24
	Grayson Co. – Adam Pence – Adam Pence – 1994										
$209\frac{7}{8}$	29	$28\frac{2}{8}$	$18\frac{4}{8}$	$23\frac{5}{8}$	$5\frac{4}{8}$	$5\frac{3}{8}$	10	8	$25\frac{1}{8}$	825	25
	Todd Co. – Kenny V. Wilson – Kenny V. Wilson – 1990										
$209\frac{6}{8}$	$25\frac{6}{8}$	25	$19\frac{5}{8}$	$24\frac{7}{8}$	$4\frac{5}{8}$	$5\frac{6}{8}$	14	18	$49\frac{5}{8}$	831	26
	Pulaski Co. – Alan Sidwell – Alan Sidwell – 1988										
$209\frac{5}{8}$	$24\frac{4}{8}$	$25\frac{3}{8}$	$22\frac{4}{8}$	24	$4\frac{6}{8}$	5	10	11	$26\frac{5}{8}$	840	27
	Butler Co. – Dean A. Hannold – Dean A. Hannold – 1979										
$209\frac{5}{8}$	$26\frac{4}{8}$	$26\frac{4}{8}$	$16\frac{7}{8}$	$21\frac{2}{8}$	$5\frac{3}{8}$	$5\frac{1}{8}$	13	12	$26\frac{2}{8}$	840	27
	McCreary Co. – Picked Up – Johnny Farmer – 1983										
$208\frac{6}{8}$	24	$24\frac{2}{8}$	$19\frac{2}{8}$	27	5	$5\frac{1}{8}$	13	12	$56\frac{4}{8}$	883	29
	McCreary Co. – Richard G. Lohre – Richard G. Lohre – 1968										
208	$21\frac{2}{8}$	$24\frac{5}{8}$	$17\frac{4}{8}$	$22\frac{2}{8}$	$9\frac{2}{8}$	5	15	6	76	929	30
	Bath Co. – William Shields – William Shields – 1993										
$207\frac{7}{8}$	$23\frac{6}{8}$	$24\frac{4}{8}$	$15\frac{6}{8}$	$21\frac{2}{8}$	5	5	9	9	$42\frac{1}{8}$	938	31
	Breckinridge Co. – Joseph T. Smith – Joseph T. Smith – 1993										
$207\frac{2}{8}$	$27\frac{3}{8}$	$26\frac{2}{8}$	$18\frac{2}{8}$	$20\frac{2}{8}$	$5\frac{3}{8}$	$5\frac{5}{8}$	12	10	$40\frac{2}{8}$	985	32
	Pulaski Co. – Mark Jones – Mark Jones – 1998										
$207\frac{1}{8}$	$27\frac{4}{8}$	$27\frac{7}{8}$	$16\frac{6}{8}$	$23\frac{1}{8}$	$4\frac{6}{8}$	5	9	11	$27\frac{3}{8}$	995	33
	Ohio Co. – Rick Daugherty – Rick Daugherty – 1997										
$206\frac{6}{8}$	$30\frac{2}{8}$	$29\frac{5}{8}$	$20\frac{6}{8}$	$26\frac{7}{8}$	$5\frac{5}{8}$	$5\frac{3}{8}$	8	13	$28\frac{6}{8}$	1028	34
	Hart Co. – Daniel Behr – Daniel Behr – 1998										
$206\frac{5}{8}$	24	$23\frac{3}{8}$	23	$24\frac{7}{8}$	$4\frac{5}{8}$	$4\frac{4}{8}$	9	12	$38\frac{7}{8}$	1036	35
	Marshall Co. – Perry Beyer, Jr. – Perry Beyer, Jr. – 1996										
$205\frac{7}{8}$	$28\frac{2}{8}$	$27\frac{4}{8}$	$23\frac{2}{8}$	$25\frac{2}{8}$	$5\frac{2}{8}$	$5\frac{6}{8}$	5	11	$36\frac{1}{8}$	1080	36
	Breckinridge Co. – Bruce Parris – Bruce Parris – 1991										
$205\frac{6}{8}$	$26\frac{2}{8}$	$25\frac{7}{8}$	$16\frac{6}{8}$	$18\frac{7}{8}$	$5\frac{3}{8}$	$5\frac{3}{8}$	9	11	$36\frac{4}{8}$	1094†	37†
	Trimble Co. – Billy A. Riddell, Jr. – Billy A. Riddell, Jr. – 2001										
$205\frac{6}{8}$	$23\frac{7}{8}$	$26\frac{1}{8}$	20	$27\frac{5}{8}$	$5\frac{3}{8}$	$5\frac{2}{8}$	10	8	$53\frac{6}{8}$	1094	37
	Hickman Co. – Jerry M. Evans – Jerry M. Evans – 1998										
$205\frac{5}{8}$	28	$27\frac{4}{8}$	$18\frac{6}{8}$	$25\frac{1}{8}$	$6\frac{4}{8}$	$6\frac{3}{8}$	10	13	$31\frac{5}{8}$	1102	39
	Spencer Co. – Phillip W. Lawson – Phillip W. Lawson – 1989										
$205\frac{3}{8}$	$26\frac{3}{8}$	$23\frac{2}{8}$	$23\frac{1}{8}$	$29\frac{7}{8}$	$4\frac{7}{8}$	$4\frac{6}{8}$	14	9	$56\frac{2}{8}$	1116†	40†
	Henderson Co. – Stephen L. Arend – Stephen L. Arend – 2000										

Score	Length of Main Beam Right	Left	Inside Spread	Greatest Spread	Circumference at Smallest Place Between Burr and First Point Right	Left	Number of Points Right	Left	Lengths Abnormal Points	All-Time Rank	State Rank
	■ Location of Kill – Hunter – Owner – Date Killed										
204	26⁶/8	27¹/8	21⁷/8	24⁴/8	5¹/8	5⁴/8	9	11	28⁷/8	1220	41
	■ Webster Co. – Jeff Robinson – Jeff Robinson – 1982										
203⁶/8	25⁶/8	27³/8	19⁶/8	26	5⁴/8	5⁵/8	16	7	32	1237	42
	■ Hart Co. – Picked Up – Terry Melvin – 1992										
203⁶/8	23²/8	23⁷/8	17⁷/8	22	5⁷/8	5⁴/8	15	14	45⁷/8	1237	42
	■ Calloway Co. – John D. Morgan – John D. Morgan – 1999										
203⁴/8	22³/8	21³/8	22⁶/8	28⁵/8	4⁶/8	4⁶/8	12	15	45³/8	1259	44
	■ Hardin Co. – Odell Chambers – Odell Chambers – 1999										
203	24	23⁶/8	15	20⁶/8	4⁶/8	4⁷/8	9	12	29	1317	45
	■ Wayne Co. – Jack L. Keith – Jack L. Keith – 1990										
202	26⁷/8	27	23⁴/8	28¹/8	5²/8	5²/8	13	10	41	1395	46
	■ Powell Co. – Hershel Ingram – Hershel Ingram – 1980										
201⁷/8	29⁴/8	28⁴/8	22	24⁷/8	5⁶/8	5⁴/8	9	8	22¹/8	1410	47
	■ Todd Co. – Russell E. Carver – Russell E. Carver – 1966										
201²/8	30⁶/8	28	17⁵/8	20¹/8	4⁷/8	4⁶/8	8	7	20³/8	1478	48
	■ Cumberland Co. – Ewing Groce – Ewing Groce – 1968										
200⁷/8	25³/8	25¹/8	20	22⁴/8	5¹/8	5²/8	10	12	53³/8	1512	49
	■ Morgan Co. – Gregory Powers – Gregory Powers – 1989										
200²/8	26⁶/8	26⁷/8	21⁶/8	25³/8	4⁵/8	4⁵/8	8	7	22⁴/8	1569†	50†
	■ Greenup Co. – Eric E. Sparks – Eric E. Sparks – 2000										
200	30²/8	28⁶/8	19⁵/8	22⁴/8	5⁴/8	5⁴/8	9	8	16⁵/8	1591†	51†
	■ Breckenridge Co. – James Bowles – James Bowles – 2000										
199⁵/8	27⁴/8	27⁵/8	20⁷/8	23	4⁵/8	4⁶/8	9	11	27⁴/8	1621	52
	■ Hopkins Co. – Dwight L. Mason – Dwight L. Mason – 1979										
199⁵/8	30¹/8	29⁶/8	20⁴/8	25	5	4⁷/8	10	7	17⁵/8	1621	52
	■ Hopkins Co. – Picked Up – James D. Spurlock – 1988										
199³/8	24⁶/8	24³/8	16	18³/8	5	5	11	8	16³/8	1639	54
	■ Logan Co. – Michael D. Forrest – Michael D. Forrest – 1998										
199²/8	23⁴/8	22³/8	15⁵/8	21⁶/8	4⁶/8	4⁴/8	14	13	42¹/8	1649†	55†
	■ Johnson Co. – Gary L. Music – Gary L. Music – 2001										
199²/8	26³/8	25⁵/8	19⁷/8	30³/8	5	4⁷/8	8	10	28¹/8	1649	55
	■ Trigg Co. – Picked Up – Michael Shelton – 1990										
198⁷/8	27	26⁷/8	17⁷/8	21⁷/8	4⁶/8	4⁶/8	11	13	35⁴/8	1686	57
	■ Logan Co. – Oscar Howard – Oscar Howard – 1989										
198⁶/8	28⁶/8	28⁴/8	23²/8	27⁷/8	5⁷/8	5⁶/8	9	5	26⁴/8	1697	58
	■ Gallatin Co. – Thomas K. Ernst – Thomas K. Ernst – 1978										
197⁷/8	28⁷/8	27	21²/8	23⁵/8	5²/8	4⁵/8	8	6	23⁵/8	1816†	59†
	■ Hardin Co. – Ellis E. Givens – Ellis E. Givens – 2001										
197⁶/8	26⁷/8	27⁷/8	16⁶/8	24¹/8	4⁵/8	4⁶/8	8	12	26⁴/8	1833	60
	■ Edmonson Co. – Picked Up – Rex Hurt – 1992										
197³/8	22	21⁴/8	17⁶/8	24⁴/8	3⁶/8	3⁶/8	11	10	69¹/8	1884	61
	■ Hopkins Co. – Tim Capps – Brian Capps – 1998										

Score	Length of Main Beam Right	Left	Inside Spread	Greatest Spread	Circ. Right	Left	Points Right	Left	Lengths Abnormal Points	All-Time Rank	State Rank
197^2/$_8$	27	27^2/$_8$	17^1/$_8$	23	4^1/$_8$	4^3/$_8$	11	8	19^1/$_8$	1901	62

■ McCreary Co. – Curtis Morrow – Curtis Morrow – 1996

197^2/$_8$	25^6/$_8$	23^3/$_8$	15	21	5^6/$_8$	5^6/$_8$	9	12	34^2/$_8$	1901	62

■ Casey Co. – Ryan Elmore – Ryan Elmore – 1998

197^1/$_8$	24^3/$_8$	24^1/$_8$	18^3/$_8$	20^5/$_8$	5^6/$_8$	5^3/$_8$	17	14	31^2/$_8$	1923	64

■ Edmonson Co. – Leroy Wilson – Leroy Wilson – 1963

196^7/$_8$	23^6/$_8$	23	22^4/$_8$	25^4/$_8$	5^3/$_8$	5^3/$_8$	12	11	30^5/$_8$	1950†	65†

■ Hart Co. – John L. Seymour – John L. Seymour – 2000

196^7/$_8$	22^6/$_8$	22^1/$_8$	17^1/$_8$	22^6/$_8$	4^2/$_8$	4^4/$_8$	11	9	35	1950	65

■ Trigg Co. – Homer Stevens, Jr. – Homer Stevens, Jr. – 1986

196^7/$_8$	27^1/$_8$	26	18	23^3/$_8$	4^2/$_8$	4^2/$_8$	8	9	21^5/$_8$	1950	65

■ McLean Co. – John D. Greenfield – John D. Greenfield – 1996

196^4/$_8$	24^1/$_8$	23^3/$_8$	18^2/$_8$	26^4/$_8$	5^1/$_8$	5^2/$_8$	9	8	31^2/$_8$	1999	68

■ Trigg Co. – Jeffery Taylor – Jeffery Taylor – 1983

196^2/$_8$	25^4/$_8$	25	24	26^4/$_8$	5^2/$_8$	6^3/$_8$	5	14	35	2028†	69†

■ Henderson Co. – Nathan A. Peak – Nathan A. Peak – 2000

196^2/$_8$	28^4/$_8$	27^5/$_8$	22	24^5/$_8$	4^7/$_8$	4^7/$_8$	6	6	16^6/$_8$	2028	69

■ Henry Co. – Picked Up – Michael L. Roberts – 1965

196^2/$_8$	25^6/$_8$	23^2/$_8$	22^3/$_8$	24^5/$_8$	5^5/$_8$	6	11	9	41^5/$_8$	2028	69

■ Webster Co. – Timothy J. Shelton – Timothy J. Shelton – 1987

196^2/$_8$	26^6/$_8$	26^7/$_8$	22^4/$_8$	25^7/$_8$	5^3/$_8$	5^4/$_8$	6	8	18	2028	69

■ Butler Co. – Bradley S. Pharris – Bradley S. Pharris – 1993

196^1/$_8$	26^1/$_8$	25^7/$_8$	13^6/$_8$	16^6/$_8$	6^1/$_8$	5^7/$_8$	9	9	25^7/$_8$	2045†	73†

■ Whitley Co. – Douglas Angel – Douglas Angel – 2001

196^1/$_8$	24^4/$_8$	26	17^2/$_8$	19^6/$_8$	5^7/$_8$	5^6/$_8$	11	10	23^5/$_8$	2045	73

■ McCreary Co. – Jack W. Bailey – Jack W. Bailey – 1976

196	28^1/$_8$	28^3/$_8$	22^2/$_8$	24	5^2/$_8$	5^4/$_8$	5	9	12^4/$_8$	2059	75

■ Harlan Co. – Lester S. Whitehead – Lester S. Whitehead – 1996

195^7/$_8$	28	27^6/$_8$	21^2/$_8$	26^6/$_8$	5^5/$_8$	5^4/$_8$	6	10	26^3/$_8$	2076	76

■ Meade Co. – J. Mark Stull – J. Mark Stull – 1984

195^4/$_8$	21^3/$_8$	22^4/$_8$	17^2/$_8$	19^6/$_8$	5	5	10	8	29^4/$_8$	2134	77

■ Carlisle Co. – William H. Deane IV – William H. Deane IV – 1979

195^4/$_8$	21^4/$_8$	23^4/$_8$	15^2/$_8$	17	6^1/$_8$	4^2/$_8$	11	8	76	2134	77

■ Jessamine Co. – Tony W. Drury – Tony W. Drury – 1991

195^3/$_8$	25^5/$_8$	26^1/$_8$	19^3/$_8$	22	5^1/$_8$	5^2/$_8$	7	9	24	2163†	79†

■ Hopkins Co. – Picked Up – Brad Nelson – 2000

195^3/$_8$	25^6/$_8$	26^1/$_8$	14^6/$_8$	19^7/$_8$	6^4/$_8$	6^3/$_8$	11	10	25^3/$_8$	2163	79

■ Hart Co. – Robbie Toms – Robbie Toms – 1991

195^3/$_8$	25^3/$_8$	25^6/$_8$	19^7/$_8$	27	4^1/$_8$	4^2/$_8$	7	8	25^2/$_8$	2163	79

■ Lewis Co. – Chris McCane – Chris McCane – 1996

195^2/$_8$	24^4/$_8$	23^5/$_8$	16^6/$_8$	20^6/$_8$	5^6/$_8$	5^7/$_8$	8	9	57^2/$_8$	2186	82

■ Christian Co. – George Hilton, Jr. – George Hilton, Jr. – 1997

KENTUCKY NON-TYPICAL WHITETAIL DEER

Score	Length of Main Beam Right	Left	Inside Spread	Greatest Spread	Circumference at Smallest Place Between Burr and First Point Right	Left	Number of Points Right	Left	Lengths Abnormal Points	All-Time Rank	State Rank
									■ Location of Kill – Hunter – Owner – Date Killed		
$193\frac{6}{8}$	$23\frac{1}{8}$	$27\frac{3}{8}$	18	$20\frac{7}{8}$	$6\frac{4}{8}$	$6\frac{2}{8}$	9	17	$40\frac{6}{8}$	2279	83
	■ Metcalfe Co. – David Dick – David Dick – 1998										
$193\frac{5}{8}$	$24\frac{7}{8}$	$26\frac{5}{8}$	$20\frac{4}{8}$	$23\frac{5}{8}$	5	$5\frac{1}{8}$	9	9	$14\frac{5}{8}$	2281	84
	■ Webster Co. – Picked Up – Kevin R. Townsend – 1992										
$193\frac{3}{8}$	$27\frac{2}{8}$	$27\frac{3}{8}$	$17\frac{7}{8}$	$20\frac{2}{8}$	5	5	8	7	$23\frac{2}{8}$	2293	85
	■ Fayette Co. – Barry L. Patrick – Barry L. Patrick – 1994										
$193\frac{2}{8}$	$27\frac{4}{8}$	$26\frac{3}{8}$	$25\frac{6}{8}$	29	6	$6\frac{2}{8}$	9	7	30	2300	86
	■ Whitley Co. – Henry Barton – Gary Barton – 1967										
$193\frac{2}{8}$	$24\frac{7}{8}$	$24\frac{4}{8}$	$18\frac{2}{8}$	$20\frac{2}{8}$	$4\frac{3}{8}$	$4\frac{3}{8}$	10	10	$17\frac{6}{8}$	2300	86
	■ Hardin Co. – Picked Up – Jeffrey M. Kjelsen – 1993										
$193\frac{1}{8}$	$26\frac{5}{8}$	$26\frac{5}{8}$	$15\frac{6}{8}$	$20\frac{3}{8}$	$5\frac{4}{8}$	$5\frac{2}{8}$	11	10	$31\frac{7}{8}$	2305	88
	■ Breckinridge Co. – David W. Carey, Sr. – David W. Carey, Sr. – 1994										
$192\frac{3}{8}$	$28\frac{6}{8}$	$27\frac{6}{8}$	$19\frac{5}{8}$	$22\frac{1}{8}$	$5\frac{2}{8}$	5	8	10	15	2331†	89†
	■ Knox Co. – Barry F. Yancosek – Barry F. Yancosek – 2001										
$192\frac{2}{8}$	$26\frac{7}{8}$	$26\frac{3}{8}$	$21\frac{5}{8}$	$27\frac{6}{8}$	5	5	8	9	$19\frac{3}{8}$	2335	90
	■ Washington Co. – Randall Burns – Randall Burns – 1973										
$192\frac{1}{8}$	$25\frac{5}{8}$	$26\frac{4}{8}$	$21\frac{6}{8}$	$25\frac{4}{8}$	6	$5\frac{5}{8}$	11	8	$30\frac{3}{8}$	2341	91
	■ Livingston Co. – John W. Layne – John W. Layne – 1969										
192	$26\frac{7}{8}$	$26\frac{6}{8}$	$18\frac{2}{8}$	$24\frac{6}{8}$	$4\frac{6}{8}$	$4\frac{6}{8}$	8	6	15	2344	92
	■ Todd Co. – Brian P. Stratton – Brian P. Stratton – 1997										
$191\frac{5}{8}$	$26\frac{4}{8}$	$28\frac{2}{8}$	$19\frac{1}{8}$	$22\frac{2}{8}$	$5\frac{1}{8}$	$5\frac{2}{8}$	9	9	$25\frac{2}{8}$	2355	93
	■ Barren Co. – Gary Minor – Gary Minor – 1995										
$191\frac{4}{8}$	25	$24\frac{4}{8}$	$17\frac{6}{8}$	$22\frac{3}{8}$	$4\frac{3}{8}$	$4\frac{2}{8}$	9	10	28	2357	94
	■ Breckinridge Co. – Melvin S. Wilcox – Melvin S. Wilcox – 1996										
$191\frac{3}{8}$	$25\frac{5}{8}$	$25\frac{4}{8}$	$18\frac{5}{8}$	$20\frac{4}{8}$	$5\frac{2}{8}$	$5\frac{1}{8}$	7	7	$23\frac{2}{8}$	2364	95
	■ Hopkins Co. – Daniel Young – Daniel Young – 1992										
$190\frac{7}{8}$	$24\frac{6}{8}$	$25\frac{4}{8}$	17	$18\frac{5}{8}$	$4\frac{6}{8}$	$4\frac{6}{8}$	9	10	$21\frac{5}{8}$	2385	96
	■ Logan Co. – Farmer Brown – Farmer Brown – 1995										
$190\frac{7}{8}$	$24\frac{2}{8}$	$27\frac{2}{8}$	$20\frac{5}{8}$	$26\frac{6}{8}$	$5\frac{6}{8}$	$5\frac{6}{8}$	12	9	$37\frac{2}{8}$	2385	96
	■ Christian Co. – Joseph R. Tanner – Joseph R. Tanner – 1999										
$190\frac{3}{8}$	$25\frac{2}{8}$	25	$21\frac{2}{8}$	$23\frac{4}{8}$	$4\frac{3}{8}$	$4\frac{3}{8}$	9	11	$19\frac{1}{8}$	2408	98
	■ Lewis Co. – Bobby J. Whitaker – Bobby J. Whitaker – 1999										
$190\frac{1}{8}$	25	$23\frac{5}{8}$	20	$22\frac{1}{8}$	5	$5\frac{1}{8}$	6	6	$20\frac{7}{8}$	2416	99
	■ Pike Co. – Vernon M. Porter – Vernon M. Porter – 1995										
190	$23\frac{5}{8}$	$26\frac{7}{8}$	$19\frac{6}{8}$	$21\frac{4}{8}$	$5\frac{6}{8}$	$4\frac{7}{8}$	11	6	41	2418	100
	■ Breckinridge Co. – John M. Pollock – John M. Pollock – 1987										
$189\frac{3}{8}$	$24\frac{6}{8}$	$25\frac{3}{8}$	$19\frac{4}{8}$	$21\frac{7}{8}$	$5\frac{3}{8}$	5	8	7	$12\frac{7}{8}$	2443†	101†
	■ Marion Co. – Picked Up – Dan Thompson – 2000										
189	$23\frac{3}{8}$	$22\frac{2}{8}$	20	$22\frac{4}{8}$	$4\frac{5}{8}$	$4\frac{6}{8}$	5	5	$34\frac{6}{8}$	2456	102
	■ Logan Co. – Earl W. Bond – Earl W. Bond – 1994										
$188\frac{3}{8}$	$22\frac{6}{8}$	$23\frac{5}{8}$	$15\frac{6}{8}$	$18\frac{5}{8}$	$5\frac{5}{8}$	$5\frac{1}{8}$	11	9	$43\frac{7}{8}$	2478†	103†
	■ Muhlenburg Co. – Kelly B. Richey – Kelly B. Richey – 2000										

Score	Length of Main Beam Right	Left	Inside Spread	Greatest Spread	Circumference at Smallest Place Between Burr and First Point Right	Left	Number of Points Right	Left	Lengths Abnormal Points	All-Time Rank	State Rank
187⁵/8	29¹/8	29⁶/8	16¹/8	18¹/8	4³/8	4⁵/8	6	12	17⁶/8	2518†	104†
■ Grayson Co. – James E. Crick – James E. Crick – 2000											
187⁴/8	24⁵/8	24³/8	18⁵/8	20⁶/8	5⁵/8	5⁴/8	15	10	30¹/8	2522	105
■ Grant Co. – Jon B. Good – Jon B. Good – 1998											
187²/8	26⁵/8	26¹/8	17⁴/8	21²/8	5⁵/8	5¹/8	10	8	19²/8	2534	106
■ Grayson Co. – Tim Purcell – Tim Purcell – 1995											
187¹/8	26³/8	27⁷/8	22⁴/8	24⁷/8	5⁴/8	5⁴/8	9	8	34⁷/8	2540	107
■ Garrard Co. – Thomas Ballard – Thomas Ballard – 1996											
186⁶/8	25²/8	26⁶/8	18	20⁴/8	6	6¹/8	11	13	43²/8	2559†	108†
■ Carter Co. – Alva R. King – Alva R. King – 2000											
185⁷/8	26³/8	28	18³/8	21⁵/8	5³/8	5³/8	8	6	15⁶/8	2597	109
■ Todd Co. – Alan Mansfield – Alan Mansfield – 1998											
185⁶/8	30³/8	26²/8	21³/8	26⁶/8	4⁶/8	4⁵/8	6	7	30³/8	2605†	110†
■ Grayson Co. – Kermit W. Ayer – Kermit W. Ayer – 2000											
185³/8	23⁶/8	23⁷/8	17⁷/8	19⁶/8	5	5	7	7	29⁴/8	2622	111
■ Metcalfe Co. – Picked Up – David Dick – 1998											
185¹/8	27³/8	26⁷/8	18	19⁶/8	4⁵/8	4⁴/8	9	9	19⁷/8	2641	112
■ Lewis Co. – Jeremie L. Bretz – Jeremie L. Bretz – 1992											
185	25¹/8	25⁵/8	17¹/8	18⁷/8	4⁷/8	4⁷/8	9	12	17⁵/8	2653†	113†
■ Christian Co. – John Blakeley – John Blakeley – 2001											

† The scores and ranking for trophies from the 25th Awards Entry Period are not final until the banquet is held on June 19, 2004.

LOUISIANA
RECORD WHITETAILS

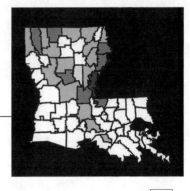

38 Typical whitetail deer entries
21 Non-typical whitetail deer entries
7,265 Total whitetail deer entries

0 Entries
1-2 Entries
3-5 Entries
6-10 Entries
11+ Entries

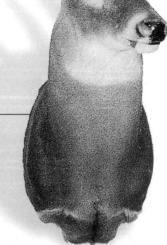

LOUISIANA
STATE RECORD
Typical Whitetail Deer
Score: 184^6/$_8$
Location: Madison Parish
Hunter: John Lee
Owner: Donald R. Broadway
Date: 1943

LOUISIANA
STATE RECORD
Non-Typical Whitetail Deer
Score: 281⁶/₈
Location: Tensas Parish
Hunter and Owner: James H. McMurray
Date: 1994

Photograph from B&C Archives

LOUISIANA

TYPICAL WHITETAIL DEER

Score	Length of Main Beam Right	Length of Main Beam Left	Inside Spread	Greatest Spread	Circumference at Smallest Place Between Burr and First Point Right	Left	Number of Points Right	Left	Lengths Abnormal Points	All-Time Rank	State Rank
					■ Location of Kill – Hunter – Owner – Date Killed						
184⁶/8	28⁵/8	28⁶/8	21⁶/8	24⁶/8	5⁶/8	5⁴/8	6	6	2⁴/8	285	1
	■ Madison Parish – John Lee – Donald R. Broadway – 1943										
184⁴/8	26⁵/8	28³/8	22⁴/8	26⁶/8	5³/8	5¹/8	6	5		303	2
	■ Bossier Parish – Earnest O. McCoy – Lucille McCoy – 1961										
184²/8	28²/8	27⁶/8	24	26⁴/8	5	5¹/8	5	6	1²/8	319	3
	■ Franklin Parish – H.B. Womble – Carey B. McCoy – 1914										
181¹/8	26⁴/8	27¹/8	19³/8	21⁶/8	5⁴/8	5³/8	6	5	5⁶/8	551	4
	■ Avoyelles Parish – Donald A. Riviere – Donald A. Riviere – 1998										
180⁵/8	25	28³/8	18⁷/8	21⁵/8	4⁷/8	5	8	5	11	599	5
	■ St. Landry Parish – Shawn P. Ortego – Shawn P. Ortego – 1975										
180⁴/8	27⁶/8	26²/8	20	22²/8	4⁶/8	4⁶/8	6	7	4²/8	613	6
	■ Madison Parish – Buford Perry – Buford Perry – 1961										
179⁷/8	26²/8	26³/8	19⁵/8	22	5¹/8	5¹/8	6	5		705	7
	■ Tensas Parish – Anthony Guice – Anthony Guice – 1995										
179²/8	25¹/8	25	19⁴/8	21⁵/8	5⁴/8	5⁵/8	7	7		763†	8†
	■ St. Landry Parish – Shannon R. Deville – Shannon R. Deville – 2001										
177⁵/8	28	28²/8	21³/8	23⁴/8	5¹/8	5¹/8	5	5		972	9
	■ Concordia Parish – John W. King – John W. King – 1996										
177³/8	27³/8	28	16⁵/8	18⁴/8	5	5¹/8	5	5		1011	10
	■ Claiborne Parish – Steven L. Morton – Steven L. Morton – 1986										
177	25⁵/8	26²/8	18⁴/8	19⁶/8	4³/8	4⁵/8	5	5		1066	11
	■ Rapides Parish – H. Glenn Feazell – H. Glenn Feazell – 1997										
176²/8	28⁴/8	29²/8	20⁶/8	23	5⁴/8	5⁴/8	5	5		1209	12
	■ Richland Parish – Willard Roberson – Willard Roberson – 1968										
173⁷/8	28³/8	28⁶/8	24⁵/8	26	4³/8	4	7	7	4⁶/8	1743	13
	■ Grant Parish – Dwayne H. Robertson – Dwayne H. Robertson – 1999										
173³/8	26⁶/8	26⁵/8	17⁵/8	20	5⁴/8	5³/8	5	5		1883	14
	■ Grant Parish – Michael G. Hicks – Michael G. Hicks – 1997										
172	24⁴/8	26	18⁴/8	20²/8	5	4⁷/8	5	5		2330	15
	■ Avoyelles Parish – Richard J. Dupuy, Jr. – Richard J. Dupuy, Jr. – 1998										
171⁷/8	27⁶/8	27²/8	20¹/8	23⁵/8	5	5	5	5		2382	16
	■ Madison Parish – M.L. Arnold – David D. Arnold – 1941										
171⁵/8	22¹/8	23	19	21¹/8	5²/8	5⁴/8	5	6	2³/8	2470	17
	■ Tensas Parish – Jim Keahey – Gerald P. Begnaud, Jr. – 1960										
170⁶/8	26⁴/8	26¹/8	21⁴/8	23²/8	4⁴/8	4³/8	5	6		2828†	18†
	■ Natchitoches Parish – Randy K. Ward – Randy K. Ward – 1993										
170⁶/8	23⁷/8	23⁴/8	19²/8	21³/8	4⁶/8	4⁶/8	5	5		2828	18
	■ Winn Parish – William C. Erwin – William C. Erwin – 1980										

Score	Length of Main Beam Right	Left	Inside Spread	Greatest Spread	Circumference at Smallest Place Between Burr and First Point Right	Left	Number of Points Right	Left	Lengths Abnormal Points	All-Time Rank	State Rank
	■ Location of Kill – Hunter – Owner – Date Killed										
170 5/8	22 4/8	24 6/8	16 6/8	21	4 6/8	4 6/8	7	7	3 7/8	2876	20
	■ Webster Parish – Henry G. Gregory – Henry G. Gregory – 1985										
170 3/8	25 7/8	25 4/8	22 3/8	24 3/8	4 6/8	4 7/8	6	5		2992†	21†
	■ Concordia Parish – Ronnie L. Wilkinson – Ronnie L. Wilkinson – 2002										
170 3/8	24 2/8	25	24 4/8	24 2/8	6	6	6	6	4 1/8	2992	21
	■ Madison Parish – Stephens M. White, Sr. – Stephens M. White, Jr. – 1945										
170 3/8	26	25 6/8	18 7/8	20 6/8	5 5/8	5 6/8	6	6		2992	21
	■ E. Carroll Parish – David L. Roselle – David L. Roselle – 1998										
170 1/8	22 3/8	24 3/8	16 1/8	18 2/8	4 7/8	4 7/8	7	6	3 6/8	3143	24
	■ Morehouse Parish – Johnnie Kovac, Jr. – Johnnie Kovac, Jr. – 1979										
170	26 2/8	25 2/8	21	22 7/8	5 4/8	5 4/8	5	5		3224	25
	■ W. Feliciana Parish – Jerry Loper – Jerry Loper – 1960										
168 5/8	23 7/8	23 5/8	20 3/8	21 7/8	5 2/8	5 3/8	7	7	4	3376	26
	■ Avoyelles Parish – Michael G. Willis – Michael G. Willis – 1997										
167 6/8	26	26	19 4/8	21 3/8	5 6/8	5 5/8	5	6		3461	27
	■ Concordia Parish – Gary L. Kinsland – Gary L. Kinsland – 1978										
165 3/8	24 4/8	23 1/8	23 3/8	25 7/8	6 2/8	6 4/8	5	5		3731	28
	■ Avoyelles Parish – Ronald J. Bonnette – Ronald J. Bonnette – 1992										
164 6/8	26 1/8	26 1/8	18 6/8	21	4 2/8	4 3/8	6	5		3809	29
	■ Concordia Parish – Joseph L. Landry – Joseph L. Landry – 1969										
164	25 6/8	25 1/8	16 4/8	18 5/8	4 7/8	5 1/8	5	5		3908	30
	■ Bienville Parish – Charles R. Carr – Charles R. Carr – 1983										
161 5/8	24 5/8	25 7/8	19 6/8	22	6 2/8	6 4/8	4	4	1 3/8	4234	31
	■ Avoyelles Parish – M.J. Hartley – M.J. Hartley – 1980										
161 1/8	25 5/8	26 1/8	18 5/8	20 4/8	4 7/8	4 7/8	5	5		4332†	32†
	■ Natchitoches Parish – Coy Birdwell – Coy Birdwell – 2001										
160 7/8	24 2/8	24 2/8	17 5/8	19 4/8	4 6/8	4 5/8	5	5		4380	33
	■ Tensas Parish – Wilfred J. Dufrene, Jr. – Wilfred J. Dufrene, Jr. – 1994										
160 7/8	25 4/8	24 4/8	17 1/8	18 6/8	4 4/8	4 5/8	5	6	1 4/8	4380	33
	■ Natchitoches Parish – Amos R. Bradley – Amos R. Bradley – 1998										
160 5/8	25	24 7/8	19	22 2/8	5	5	7	5	4 5/8	4423	35
	■ Bienville Parish – William J. Mooney – William J. Mooney – 1998										
160 3/8	24 5/8	24 4/8	18 3/8	20 1/8	5	5 1/8	5	5		4470	36
	■ Catahoula Parish – Julius L. Lovasz – Julius L. Lovasz – 1998										
160 2/8	22 6/8	23 4/8	18 2/8	20 6/8	5 4/8	5 1/8	8	8	9 6/8	4495	37
	■ Bossier Parish – Ralph M. Taylor – Ralph M. Taylor – 1986										
160 1/8	24 6/8	24 1/8	17 7/8	19 6/8	5	5 1/8	5	5		4534†	38†
	■ Claiborne Parish – Kenneth B. Harrison – Kenneth B. Harrison – 2000										

† The scores and ranking for trophies from the 25th Awards Entry Period are not final until the banquet is held on June 19, 2004.

LOUISIANA

NON-TYPICAL WHITETAIL DEER

Score	Length of Main Beam Right Left		Inside Spread	Greatest Spread	Circumference at Smallest Place Between Burr and First Point Right Left		Number of Points Right Left		Lengths Abnormal Points	All-Time Rank	State Rank
	■ Location of Kill – Hunter – Owner – Date Killed										
281⁶/₈	22¹/₈ 20⁶/₈		17⁶/₈	23²/₈	5²/₈ 5		14 16		84⁴/₈	7	1
	■ Tensas Parish – James H. McMurray – James H. McMurray – 1994										
252²/₈	23⁴/₈ 25		21³/₈		4⁷/₈ 5¹/₈		17 18		122⁷/₈	47	2
	■ Concordia Parish – J.D. Shields – J. Logan Sewell – 1948										
228⁷/₈	28¹/₈ 27⁴/₈		22⁵/₈	26	5⁷/₈ 5⁶/₈		13 11		45²/₈	255	3
	■ W. Feliciana Parish – Tommy Rice – Tommy Rice – 1998										
227	26 26²/₈		21⁴/₈	23⁴/₈	6¹/₈ 6²/₈		19 14		53	279	4
	■ Concordia Parish – Picked Up – Sandra Leger – 1969										
219⁶/₈	19¹/₈ 23¹/₈		18⁴/₈	21	4⁴/₈ 4⁶/₈		15 8		61⁶/₈	447	5
	■ Caddo Parish – William D. Ethredge, Jr. – William D. Ethredge, Jr. – 1988										
218⁴/₈	26²/₈ 26³/₈		17²/₈	22³/₈	5⁵/₈ 5³/₈		8 8		33²/₈	487	6
	■ St. Martin Parish – Drew Ware – Gary S. Crnko – 1941										
216⁷/₈	26⁷/₈ 24⁷/₈		17²/₈	21³/₈	6 5⁷/₈		12 17		52⁷/₈	533	7
	■ Concordia Parish – Richard Dale – J. Logan Sewell – 1956										
214⁷/₈	27⁶/₈ 27		20¹/₈	22³/₈	6⁷/₈ 7		7 11		38⁶/₈	605†	8†
	■ Concordia Parish – W.E. Beazley – Mike Harper – 1938										
206⁷/₈	28⁶/₈ 30³/₈		23⁴/₈	32¹/₈	6¹/₈ 5⁶/₈		11 10		26¹/₈	1011	9
	■ Claiborne Parish – J.H. Thurmon – J.H. Thurmon – 1970										
206⁶/₈	25⁴/₈ 26⁴/₈		17²/₈	22	5⁴/₈ 5⁴/₈		8 10		43⁴/₈	1028	10
	■ Grant Parish – Richard D. Ellison, Jr. – Richard D. Ellison, Jr. – 1969										
203²/₈	29 28⁴/₈		23	29⁷/₈	5⁷/₈ 5⁶/₈		10 13		51	1287	11
	■ W. Feliciana Parish – Estus S. Sykes – Estus S. Sykes – 1994										
201³/₈	26⁴/₈ 27		18⁵/₈	23⁵/₈	4⁶/₈ 4⁷/₈		9 10		37²/₈	1461	12
	■ Concordia Parish – G.O. McGuffee – G.O. McGuffee – 1963										
199⁶/₈	26⁷/₈ 27⁵/₈		24	25⁴/₈	5 5²/₈		8 11		19⁶/₈	1613†	13†
	■ Red River Parish – Jason I. Dupree – Jason I. Dupree – 2001										
198⁵/₈	26⁴/₈ 27⁵/₈		22²/₈	25	6⁷/₈ 5⁵/₈		6 11		24¹/₈	1716	14
	■ Concordia Parish – Raymond Cowan – Raymond Cowan – 1961										
198⁴/₈	21⁵/₈ 23		17⁵/₈	23	4⁴/₈ 4³/₈		7 9		60⁵/₈	1736†	15†
	■ Rapides Parish – William A. Jordan, Jr. – William A. Jordan, Jr. – 2001										
196⁷/₈	22⁶/₈ 23⁴/₈		18⁵/₈	24⁴/₈	4⁷/₈ 5²/₈		12 13		44⁶/₈	1950	16
	■ Caddo Parish – Robert W. Anderson – Robert W. Anderson – 1983										
195⁷/₈	25⁶/₈ 25⁴/₈		15¹/₈	17¹/₈	5 5		9 11		31	2076	17
	■ Webster Parish – Shannon Stanley – Shannon Stanley – 1991										
192	21²/₈ 21⁴/₈		17	22⁴/₈	5²/₈ 5⁴/₈		6 6		26⁶/₈	2344	18
	■ W. Feliciana Parish – Robert R. LaVille, Sr. – Robert R. LaVille, Sr. – 1993										
190²/₈	26 27¹/₈		16³/₈	21	7 7		10 6		20⁵/₈	2415	19
	■ Concordia Parish – John T. Lincecum – John T. Lincecum – 1986										

Score	Length of Main Beam Right Left	Inside Spread	Greatest Spread	Circumference at Smallest Place Between Burr and First Point Right Left		Number of Points Right Left		Lengths Abnormal Points	All-Time Rank	State Rank
	■ Location of Kill – Hunter – Owner – Date Killed									
186⁶/8	26²/8 26⁵/8	23²/8	29	5⁷/8	5⁷/8	9	6	24⁴/8	2559	20
	■ Concordia Parish – T.B. Jones – William T. Beasley – PR 1950									
185⁷/8	24⁵/8 24	17⁵/8	20	5⁵/8	5²/8	11	6	25⁴/8	2597	21
	■ Bossier Parish – Larry L. Cook – Larry L. Cook – 1995									

† The scores and ranking for trophies from the 25th Awards Entry Period are not final until the banquet is held on June 19, 2004.

MAINE
RECORD WHITETAILS

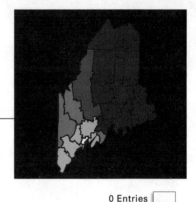

78 Typical whitetail deer entries
35 Non-typical whitetail deer entries
7,265 Total whitetail deer entries

0 Entries
1-2 Entries
3-5 Entries
6-10 Entries
11+ Entries

MAINE
STATE RECORD
Typical Whitetail Deer
Score: 193²/₈
Location: Aroostook Co.
Hunter: Ronnie Cox
Owner: Bass Pro Shops
Date: 1965

Photograph courtesy of Gale Sup

MAINE
STATE RECORD
Non-Typical Whitetail Deer
Score: 259
Location: Washington Co.
Hunter: Hill Gould
Owner: Bass Pro Shops
Date: 1910

Photograph courtesy of Gale Sup

MAINE

TYPICAL WHITETAIL DEER

Score	Length of Main Beam Right	Left	Inside Spread	Greatest Spread	Circumference at Smallest Place Between Burr and First Point Right	Left	Number of Points Right	Left	Lengths Abnormal Points	All-Time Rank	State Rank
	■ Location of Kill – Hunter – Owner – Date Killed										
193²/₈	26	25⁶/₈	22²/₈	25³/₈	5⁶/₈	5⁶/₈	5	6	1⁴/₈	53	1
	■ Aroostook Co. – Ronnie Cox – Bass Pro Shops – 1965										
192⁷/₈	27⁴/₈	27²/₈	19³/₈	21⁴/₈	4³/₈	4⁵/₈	8	9		58	2
	■ York Co. – Alphonse Chase – Earl Taylor – 1920										
186²/₈	28⁶/₈	29¹/₈	19	22²/₈	5²/₈	5¹/₈	8	5	7²/₈	220	3
	■ Hancock Co. – Gerald C. Murray – Gerald C. Murray – 1984										
184⁵/₈	28⁶/₈	28²/₈	22	23²/₈	4⁵/₈	4⁴/₈	6	7	2⁵/₈	294	4
	■ Washington Co. – Unknown – Chuck P. Vose – 1944										
184¹/₈	31³/₈	29	24	28	6	6	8	8	11⁵/₈	327	5
	■ Waldo Co. – Christopher Ramsey – Bass Pro Shops – 1983										
183³/₈	28⁵/₈	29⁵/₈	18⁵/₈	21⁴/₈	5⁴/₈	5³/₈	5	5		365	6
	■ Franklin Co. – Real Boulanger – Real Boulanger – 1990										
181⁴/₈	29	28⁵/₈	23⁵/₈	25⁶/₈	4⁶/₈	4⁵/₈	7	5	3⁵/₈	516	7
	■ Oxford Co. – Dean W. Peaco – Dean W. Peaco – 1953										
181¹/₈	27⁶/₈	26²/₈	17³/₈	20⁷/₈	5⁴/₈	5⁴/₈	5	5		551	8
	■ Waldo Co. – Clarendon Pomeroy – Larry C. Pomeroy – 1946										
180⁶/₈	30	29⁴/₈	23⁴/₈	27	5⁶/₈	5⁶/₈	5	6	2⁴/₈	587	9
	■ Hancock Co. – Cyrus H. Whitaker – Orrin W. Whitaker – 1912										
179⁷/₈	25³/₈	27¹/₈	19	21⁴/₈	5	5¹/₈	9	6	3⁵/₈	705	10
	■ Hancock Co. – Butler B. Dunn – Butler B. Dunn – 1930										
179⁶/₈	28⁵/₈	28³/₈	20⁴/₈	22⁷/₈	4⁶/₈	4⁶/₈	5	6	1	712	11
	■ Hancock Co. – M. Don Betts – Larry Snell – 1884										
179⁶/₈	25⁶/₈	26⁶/₈	21⁵/₈	25	5²/₈	5³/₈	6	5	1⁵/₈	712	11
	■ Penobscot Co. – Dale Rustin – Dale Rustin – 1984										
178⁶/₈	26²/₈	27²/₈	20⁶/₈	23	5	5	6	6		808	13
	■ Aroostook Co. – John R. Hardy – John R. Hardy – 1983										
178⁴/₈	27³/₈	27³/₈	18⁶/₈	21¹/₈	4⁷/₈	4⁵/₈	6	6		850	14
	■ Cumberland Co. – Patrick D. Wescott – Patrick D. Wescott – 1980										
178¹/₈	28⁵/₈	29	21⁷/₈	24⁷/₈	5⁵/₈	5⁵/₈	5	5		905	15
	■ Aroostook Co. – Gary G. Saucier – Gary G. Saucier – 1987										
177⁷/₈	26⁶/₈	26⁶/₈	18²/₈	21⁶/₈	4³/₈	4³/₈	6	6	1³/₈	936	16
	■ Penobscot Co. – Andrew B. Alexander – Andrew B. Alexander – 1985										
177⁶/₈	31	29	23	27²/₈	5	5	5	7	3	956	17
	■ Washington Co. – Edward S. Welsh, Jr. – Edward S. Welsh, Jr. – 1992										
177²/₈	27	25⁶/₈	19⁴/₈	22¹/₈	5⁴/₈	5⁴/₈	6	6		1025	18
	■ Somerset Co. – Richard D. Hagerty – Richard D. Hagerty – 1993										
176²/₈	28³/₈	29⁴/₈	23²/₈	26⁵/₈	5²/₈	5¹/₈	6	6	5⁶/₈	1209	19
	■ Aroostook Co. – Daniel T. Geary – Daniel T. Geary – 1989										

Score	Length of Main Beam Right Left	Inside Spread	Greatest Spread	Circumference at Smallest Place Between Burr and First Point Right Left	Number of Points Right Left	Lengths Abnormal Points	All-Time Rank	State Rank
	■ Location of Kill – Hunter – Owner – Date Killed							
176	27⁶/8 27²/8	26⁴/8	27⁶/8	5 5	4 5		1266†	20†
	■ Penobscot Co. – David R. Morrison – David R. Morrison – 2001							
175⁴/8	22⁴/8 26⁴/8	21⁶/8	24²/8	5¹/8 5¹/8	5 6		1352	21
	■ Maine – Unknown – Richard P. Arsenault – PR 1989							
175¹/8	28 27⁶/8	25	27⁵/8	4⁷/8 4⁶/8	8 7	7¹/8	1440	22
	■ Waldo Co. – Unknown – Kenneth T. Winters – 1924							
175¹/8	27¹/8 28²/8	24³/8	26⁶/8	4³/8 4²/8	9 5	6	1440	22
	■ Penobscot Co. – Peter A. Duncombe – Peter A. Duncombe – 1994							
174⁶/8	28³/8 27⁶/8	21	24	4⁶/8 4⁵/8	5 6		1534	24
	■ Maine – Unknown – Warren H. Delaware – PR 1977							
174⁴/8	27⁴/8 27³/8	21	23¹/8	4²/8 4	6 6		1592	25
	■ Knox Co. – Robert E. Young – Robert E. Young – 1979							
174¹/8	27 26¹/8	21¹/8	23²/8	5²/8 5⁵/8	7 6	4⁴/8	1678	26
	■ Aroostook Co. – Unknown – Vern Black – 1930							
137⁷/8	28⁶/8 27⁵/8	18⁵/8	22⁴/8	5³/8 5³/8	6 7	10	1743	27
	■ Penobscot Co. – Gregory A. York – Gregory A. York – 1986							
173	26 26	21	23²/8	4⁵/8 4⁶/8	6 6		1991	28
	■ Somerset Co. – Charles A. Moulton – Charles A. Moulton – 1981							
172⁶/8	27³/8 27⁵/8	24	25⁷/8	5 5	5 5		2065	29
	■ Waldo Co. – Wallace Humphrey – Arthur Humphrey – 1963							
172⁶/8	27²/8 28²/8	23⁴/8	25¹/8	4⁶/8 4⁵/8	5 5		2065	29
	■ Franklin Co. – Michael W. Auger – Michael W. Auger – 1998							
172⁵/8	26⁶/8 25	17²/8	21³/8	4⁵/8 4⁷/8	9 6	4⁷/8	2113	31
	■ Knox Co. – Willis A. Moody, Jr. – Willis A. Moody, Jr. – 1974							
172⁴/8	28 26³/8	19³/8	23¹/8	4⁷/8 4⁷/8	6 9	10³/8	2156	32
	■ Piscataquis Co. – James A. Nicols – James A. Nicols – 1998							
171⁷/8	26¹/8 25⁶/8	20¹/8	25	5¹/8 5²/8	7 6	5⁶/8	2382	33
	■ Aroostook Co. – Julian B. Perry – Julian B. Perry – 1962							
171⁷/8	25²/8 26¹/8	21¹/8	24	4²/8 4⁴/8	5 5		2382	33
	■ Oxford Co. – Picked Up – Francis Ontengco – 1980							
171⁵/8	26⁵/8 26⁷/8	18¹/8	20³/8	4²/8 4²/8	6 5	1⁴/8	2470	35
	■ Penobscot Co. – David Nadeau – David Nadeau – 1995							
171²/8	27 26⁴/8	21⁴/8	23⁷/8	5³/8 5²/8	6 6	1	2621	36
	■ Waldo Co. – Paul K. Nickerson – Paul K. Nickerson – 1957							
171¹/8	24⁷/8 25	20⁶/8	23⁴/8	6 6	5 5	1¹/8	2665	37
	■ Penobscot Co. – Kenneth Scott – Kenneth W. Bennett – 1960							
171¹/8	28⁴/8 28	18⁶/8	21⁵/8	4⁶/8 4⁶/8	6 8	8⁵/8	2665	37
	■ Franklin Co. – Michael J. Zubiate – Michael J. Zubiate – 1994							
171	26 26	20	22⁴/8	5 4⁶/8	5 5		2707	39
	■ Aroostook Co. – Roland L. Demers – Roland L. Demers – 1983							
171	28⁵/8 30⁴/8	22⁵/8	25	5²/8 5¹/8	7 4	3⁵/8	2707	39
	■ Penobscot Co. – Samuel C. Hands – Samuel C. Hands – 1985							

Score	Length of Main Beam Right	Left	Inside Spread	Greatest Spread	Circumference at Smallest Place Between Burr and First Point Right	Left	Number of Points Right	Left	Lengths Abnormal Points	All-Time Rank	State Rank
	■ *Location of Kill – Hunter – Owner – Date Killed*										
171	25⁵/₈	26	20⁴/₈	22⁴/₈	4⁴/₈	4⁵/₈	6	6		2707	39
	■ *Washington Co. – William S. Lawrence – William S. Lawrence – 1998*										
170⁷/₈	25⁷/₈	25⁵/₈	17⁵/₈	19⁵/₈	5⁴/₈	5⁴/₈	5	5		2769	42
	■ *Washington Co. – Merle G. Michaud – Merle G. Michaud – 1979*										
170⁶/₈	28	28	21³/₈	22³/₈	5³/₈	5³/₈	5	5	3³/₈	2828	43
	■ *Penobscot Co. – William Stratton – William Stratton – 1974*										
170⁵/₈	24⁶/₈	25³/₈	19⁴/₈	21⁶/₈	5⁵/₈	5⁵/₈	6	7	1⁵/₈	2876	44
	■ *Aroostook Co. – Douglas P. Legasse – Douglas P. Legasse – 1993*										
170⁵/₈	24²/₈	25³/₈	17³/₈	19⁵/₈	4⁵/₈	4⁵/₈	6	6	3	2876	44
	■ *Washington Co. – David Shaffner – David Shaffner – 1997*										
170³/₈	27⁷/₈	26⁴/₈	17⁵/₈	14⁶/₈	4⁶/₈	4⁶/₈	5	5		2992†	46†
	■ *Penobscot Co. – Lawrence L. Lord – Lawrence L. Lord – 2000*										
170²/₈	26	25⁶/₈	26⁶/₈	28	4⁴/₈	4⁴/₈	4	5	2⁶/₈	3063	47
	■ *Washington Co. – Phillip R. Dobbins – Phillip R. Dobbins – 1990*										
170²/₈	27²/₈	26	18⁶/₈	20⁴/₈	5²/₈	5¹/₈	6	7		3063	47
	■ *Aroostook Co. – Peter C. Pedro – Peter C. Pedro – 1992*										
170	26⁶/₈	27⁶/₈	21⁶/₈	24	4⁶/₈	4⁷/₈	5	5		3224†	49†
	■ *Oxford Co. – Kenneth A. Zerbst – Kenneth A. Zerbst – 2000*										
170	26⁴/₈	25⁵/₈	19⁵/₈	23²/₈	4⁵/₈	4⁴/₈	6	6	3¹/₈	3224	49
	■ *York Co. – Aubin Huertas – Aubin Huertas – 1973*										
170	28³/₈	27⁴/₈	21	22⁶/₈	4⁶/₈	5	4	6	5⁴/₈	3224	49
	■ *Androscoggin Co. – Ricky D. Cavers – Ricky D. Cavers – 1981*										
170	29¹/₈	27⁷/₈	23⁴/₈	27	5⁴/₈	5⁴/₈	6	6	5	3224	49
	■ *Penobscot Co. – Picked Up – Tad D. Proudlove – 1985*										
168⁷/₈	24⁴/₈	25⁴/₈	18¹/₈	20⁴/₈	5	5¹/₈	5	6		3361	53
	■ *Piscataquis Co. – Daniel E. Swigart – Daniel E. Swigart – 1991*										
168³/₈	27⁴/₈	27	19²/₈	22	5¹/₈	5	5	7	6³/₈	3399	54
	■ *Penobscot Co. – John R. Hollobaugh – John R. Hollobaugh – 1987*										
167⁷/₈	26⁶/₈	26⁵/₈	21⁷/₈	23⁷/₈	5²/₈	5²/₈	5	7	2⁶/₈	3451	55
	■ *Aroostook Co. – Gilbert J. Bois – Gilbert J. Bois – 1990*										
167⁶/₈	26³/₈	26⁶/₈	21²/₈	23¹/₈	4⁵/₈	4⁵/₈	5	5		3461	56
	■ *Piscataquis Co. – Robert L. Collura – Robert L. Collura – 1981*										
166⁵/₈	25⁷/₈	27³/₈	17³/₈	19⁶/₈	5	5	6	5		3598	57
	■ *Somerset Co. – Walter B. Rusak – Walter B. Rusak – 1986*										
166²/₈	24	23⁷/₈	17²/₈	19⁶/₈	4²/₈	4³/₈	6	6		3632	58
	■ *Piscataquis Co. – Kelly D. Easler – Kelly D. Easler – 1996*										
164⁷/₈	26	25⁷/₈	22⁴/₈	24⁵/₈	5³/₈	5²/₈	6	5	2⁷/₈	3792	59
	■ *Piscataquis Co. – Robert J. Fortunati – Robert J. Fortunati – 1987*										
164⁵/₈	27⁴/₈	27⁶/₈	22⁷/₈	25⁷/₈	5	4⁷/₈	5	5		3835	60
	■ *Waldo Co. – Timothy A. Reilly – Timothy A. Reilly – 1985*										
164²/₈	26	27⁴/₈	22¹/₈	26²/₈	4⁶/₈	5	8	6	1⁷/₈	3876	61
	■ *Somerset Co. – James A. Stevens – James A. Stevens – 1983*										

Score	Length of Main Beam Right	Left	Inside Spread	Greatest Spread	Circumference at Smallest Place Between Burr and First Point Right	Left	Number of Points Right	Left	Lengths Abnormal Points	All-Time Rank	State Rank
164	$28^6/_8$	28	$22^7/_8$	$25^2/_8$	$5^2/_8$	$5^2/_8$	7	6	$8^3/_8$	3908	62
■ Penobscot Co. – Henry P. McGhee – Henry P. McGhee – 1994										
$163^4/_8$	$27^4/_8$	$26^3/_8$	$21^2/_8$		$4^6/_8$	$4^6/_8$	5	5		3984	63
■ Hancock Co. – Robert L. Wright – Robert L. Wright – 1998										
$163^1/_8$	$27^3/_8$	$27^5/_8$	$21^7/_8$	24	$5^4/_8$	$5^2/_8$	7	6	$5^4/_8$	4035	64
■ Piscataquis Co. – Irwin A. Ridley – Irwin A. Ridley – 1985										
$162^6/_8$	$25^1/_8$	$25^5/_8$	$16^4/_8$	$18^7/_8$	$4^5/_8$	$4^4/_8$	8	7	$1^4/_8$	4089	65
■ Penobscot Co. – Phil McTigue – Phil McTigue – 1999										
$162^5/_8$	$30^7/_8$	$26^5/_8$	23	$27^2/_8$	$5^5/_8$	$5^2/_8$	5	6	$3^1/_8$	4109	66
■ Oxford Co. – Chester A. Coolidge – Chester A. Coolidge – 1930										
$162^5/_8$	$28^7/_8$	$25^7/_8$	$23^7/_8$	$26^5/_8$	$5^1/_8$	$5^1/_8$	4	4		4109	66
■ Kennebec Co. – James E. Greene – James E. Greene – 1985										
$162^2/_8$	$27^2/_8$	$27^6/_8$	$18^6/_8$	$21^3/_8$	$5^4/_8$	$5^4/_8$	6	6	$5^6/_8$	4153	68
■ Penobscot Co. – David Willey – David Willey – 1998										
$161^6/_8$	$26^2/_8$	$26^3/_8$	$21^6/_8$	$24^2/_8$	$5^1/_8$	$5^2/_8$	5	4	$1^4/_8$	4223	69
■ Waldo Co. – Leon E. Croteau – Leon E. Croteau – 1995										
$161^6/_8$	$25^6/_8$	$23^2/_8$	$22^1/_8$	$24^1/_8$	5	5	5	6	$1^1/_8$	4223	69
■ Hancock Co. – Daniel D. Pert – Daniel D. Pert – 1999										
$161^5/_8$	$22^4/_8$	$22^4/_8$	$20^5/_8$	$22^5/_8$	5	5	7	6	$2^6/_8$	4234	71
■ Penobscot Co. – John D. Hughes – John D. Hughes – 1987										
$161^1/_8$	$25^7/_8$	$27^1/_8$	$17^3/_8$	$19^4/_8$	$4^7/_8$	$5^1/_8$	5	7	$3^4/_8$	4332	72
■ Franklin Co. – James L. Harding – James L. Harding – 1983										
161	$23^4/_8$	$24^4/_8$	$20^6/_8$	$22^6/_8$	$4^5/_8$	$4^7/_8$	5	5		4356	73
■ Waldo Co. – Kenneth E. Bailey – Kenneth E. Bailey – 1999										
161	$21^4/_8$	$22^2/_8$	$17^5/_8$	$20^4/_8$	$4^7/_8$	5	6	5	$1^1/_8$	4356	73
■ Piscataquis Co. – Randy J. Butterfield – Randy J. Butterfield – 1999										
$160^7/_8$	$27^2/_8$	27	$19^6/_8$	23	$4^6/_8$	$4^6/_8$	5	5	$2^7/_8$	4380†	75†
■ Oxford Co. – Stephen A. Marston – Stephen A. Marston – 2000										
$160^4/_8$	$28^4/_8$	$28^4/_8$	$21^4/_8$	$24^2/_8$	$4^6/_8$	$4^6/_8$	6	6	$3^4/_8$	4443	76
■ Penobscot Co. – David P. Chinn – David P. Chinn – 1986										
$160^3/_8$	$24^5/_8$	$27^5/_8$	$17^3/_8$	$19^6/_8$	$4^2/_8$	$4^2/_8$	5	6	$1^2/_8$	4470	77
■ Lincoln Co. – Picked Up – David Teele – 1999										
$160^2/_8$	$24^5/_8$	$25^5/_8$	$18^4/_8$	$21^5/_8$	$5^6/_8$	$5^5/_8$	4	4		4495	78
■ Penobscot Co. – Peter K. Smith – Peter K. Smith – 1997										

† The scores and ranking for trophies from the 25th Awards Entry Period are not final until the banquet is held on June 19, 2004.

MAINE

NON-TYPICAL WHITETAIL DEER

Score	Length of Main Beam Right	Left	Inside Spread	Greatest Spread	Circumference at Smallest Place Between Burr and First Point Right	Left	Number of Points Right	Left	Lengths Abnormal Points	All-Time Rank	State Rank
259	25⁴/₈	26⁷/₈	19⁵/₈	28¹/₈	6¹/₈	5⁷/₈	15	16	66¹/₈	25	1
■ Washington Co. – Hill Gould – Bass Pro Shops – 1910
248¹/₈	31¹/₈	32¹/₈	22⁶/₈	25²/₈	5²/₈	5⁴/₈	15	15	42⁵/₈	72	2
■ Penobscot Co. – Unknown – James L. Mason, Sr. – 1945
238⁴/₈	28³/₈	28⁶/₈	15⁶/₈	23⁴/₈	5³/₈	5²/₈	9	9	49⁶/₈	133	3
■ Piscataquis Co. – Christian B. Oberholser, Jr. – Christian B. Oberholser, Jr. – 1996
228⁷/₈	28²/₈	27²/₈	18⁵/₈	25³/₈	5⁷/₈	6	11	10	54⁴/₈	255	4
■ Cherryfield – Flora Campbell – Dick Idol – 1953
228¹/₈	28⁷/₈	29	20¹/₈	28²/₈	5⁶/₈	6	13	14	49⁴/₈	266	5
■ Maine – Henry A. Caesar – Unknown – PR 1911
224	29²/₈	29²/₈	27	34⁴/₈	5²/₈	5³/₈	7	14	34	337	6
■ Hancock Co. – Picked Up – Wesley B. Starn – PR 1975
223³/₈	28²/₈	27⁵/₈	24¹/₈	26¹/₈	5⁴/₈	5²/₈	10	11	37²/₈	354	7
■ Maine – Frank Maxwell – David G. Cordray – 1900
219³/₈	25²/₈	24	17⁴/₈	28¹/₈	5⁴/₈	5⁵/₈	12	15	59⁷/₈	455	8
■ Maine – Unknown – Gale Sup – PR 1988
219²/₈	24⁶/₈	24⁶/₈	21⁶/₈	27	5⁴/₈	5⁴/₈	9	11	55²/₈	460	9
■ Aroostook Co. – Harold C. Kitchin – Harold C. Kitchin – 1973
218⁷/₈	29²/₈	28⁶/₈	21	23⁴/₈	5⁴/₈	5⁴/₈	6	8	21⁷/₈	472	10
■ Waldo Co. – Roy C. Guse – J. Bruce Probert – 1957
214³/₈	30²/₈	29	22⁷/₈	28³/₈	5	5¹/₈	11	12	46²/₈	620	11
■ Washington Co. – E. Colson Fales – E. Colson Fales – 1999
208⁷/₈	29⁴/₈	27⁵/₈	18⁴/₈	22⁶/₈	4⁶/₈	4⁶/₈	14	10	33¹/₈	877	12
■ Washington Co. – Robert E. Cooke – Robert E. Cooke – 1972
208¹/₈	30	31²/₈	23⁶/₈	26¹/₈	5³/₈	5⁴/₈	8	8	25⁵/₈	920	13
■ Hancock Co. – Hollis Staples – Doug Scott – 1922
207⁶/₈	27	27⁵/₈	25⁴/₈	30	6⁶/₈	6⁴/₈	9	9	17⁴/₈	951	14
■ Aroostook Co. – Alfred Wardwell – Alfred Wardwell – 1945
207⁵/₈	27²/₈	28³/₈	23²/₈	28	6¹/₈	5⁶/₈	12	11	49¹/₈	957	15
■ Penobscot Co. – Picked Up – Randall Madden – 1995
206⁶/₈	25⁶/₈	23³/₈	23⁷/₈	30²/₈	5⁴/₈	5⁵/₈	12	9	49¹/₈	1028	16
■ Somerset Co. – Mark T. Lary – Mark T. Lary – 1979
206²/₈	31¹/₈	31	22⁷/₈	25⁶/₈	6	5³/₈	9	7	18⁵/₈	1059	17
■ Piscataquis Co. – Ralph E. Dow – Ralph E. Dow – 1964
202²/₈	26¹/₈	23¹/₈	26⁶/₈	28⁷/₈	5²/₈	5²/₈	8	9	38¹/₈	1377	18
■ Waldo Co. – James A. Tripp, Sr. – James A. Tripp, Sr. – 1959
202	26⁶/₈	28⁶/₈	26⁶/₈	28⁵/₈	5	5	8	7	15⁶/₈	1395	19
■ Knox Co. – Skip Black – Skip Black – 1981

Score	Length of Main Beam Right	Left	Inside Spread	Greatest Spread	Circumference at Smallest Place Between Burr and First Point Right	Left	Number of Points Right	Left	Lengths Abnormal Points	All-Time Rank	State Rank
									■ Location of Kill – Hunter – Owner – Date Killed		
$199\frac{3}{8}$	$25\frac{6}{8}$	$25\frac{4}{8}$	$19\frac{1}{8}$	$21\frac{4}{8}$	$5\frac{2}{8}$	$5\frac{1}{8}$	9	11	$18\frac{6}{8}$	1639	20
				■ Penobscot Co. – Robert Raymond – Robert Raymond – 1997							
199	$24\frac{2}{8}$	$24\frac{7}{8}$	$19\frac{4}{8}$	$24\frac{1}{8}$	5	$5\frac{1}{8}$	13	8	$24\frac{2}{8}$	1668	21
				■ Penobscot Co. – Picked Up – Todd Affricano – 1971							
199	$25\frac{2}{8}$	$24\frac{5}{8}$	$21\frac{2}{8}$	25	6	$5\frac{6}{8}$	9	10	$25\frac{6}{8}$	1668	21
				■ Hancock Co. – Dale Henderson – Dale Henderson – 1998							
$197\frac{5}{8}$	$25\frac{2}{8}$	$26\frac{2}{8}$	$22\frac{6}{8}$	$24\frac{7}{8}$	$5\frac{2}{8}$	5	9	10	$37\frac{3}{8}$	1847	23
				■ Waldo Co. – Ronald A. Edwards – Ronald A. Edwards – 1998							
$197\frac{2}{8}$	$27\frac{4}{8}$	$26\frac{5}{8}$	21	24	5	5	8	9	$18\frac{4}{8}$	1901	24
				■ Hancock Co. – Hollis Patterson – Reginald R. Clark – PR 1950							
$197\frac{2}{8}$	$28\frac{2}{8}$	$28\frac{6}{8}$	$20\frac{6}{8}$	$23\frac{3}{8}$	$5\frac{7}{8}$	$5\frac{7}{8}$	8	6	$16\frac{6}{8}$	1901	24
				■ Piscataquis Co. – Penny Demar – Penny Demar – 1998							
$195\frac{6}{8}$	$25\frac{4}{8}$	25	$17\frac{4}{8}$	$21\frac{5}{8}$	$5\frac{1}{8}$	$5\frac{1}{8}$	6	9	14	2094	26
				■ Washington Co. – James H. Guertin – James H. Guertin – 1995							
$195\frac{2}{8}$	$28\frac{3}{8}$	$28\frac{3}{8}$	21	$24\frac{1}{8}$	6	$5\frac{4}{8}$	9	8	16	2186	27
				■ Somerset Co. – David A. McAllister – David A. McAllister – 1985							
$195\frac{1}{8}$	$23\frac{2}{8}$	$28\frac{6}{8}$	15	$19\frac{2}{8}$	5	$5\frac{1}{8}$	15	14	$51\frac{3}{8}$	2208	28
				■ Washington Co. – M. Chandler Stith – M. Chandler Stith – 1963							
$193\frac{3}{8}$	25	25	$17\frac{6}{8}$	$23\frac{4}{8}$	6	$5\frac{6}{8}$	10	9	$22\frac{7}{8}$	2293	29
				■ Piscataquis Co. – Paul J. Amos – Paul J. Amos – 1998							
$192\frac{2}{8}$	28	$26\frac{5}{8}$	$32\frac{6}{8}$	$34\frac{3}{8}$	$5\frac{4}{8}$	$5\frac{4}{8}$	9	9	$30\frac{6}{8}$	2335	30
				■ Somerset Co. – Ryan J. Snell – Ryan J. Snell – 1990							
$191\frac{4}{8}$	$24\frac{7}{8}$	$25\frac{1}{8}$	$23\frac{3}{8}$	$26\frac{3}{8}$	5	$4\frac{6}{8}$	9	9	$22\frac{5}{8}$	2357	31
				■ Hancock Co. – Douglas D. Adamson – Douglas D. Adamson – 1988							
$190\frac{5}{8}$	$26\frac{3}{8}$	$25\frac{6}{8}$	19	$21\frac{2}{8}$	$5\frac{2}{8}$	$5\frac{3}{8}$	7	8	$21\frac{3}{8}$	2393	32
				■ Somerset Co. – Richard W. Duffy – Richard W. Duffy – 1993							
$190\frac{4}{8}$	$26\frac{6}{8}$	$28\frac{4}{8}$	19	23	6	$5\frac{7}{8}$	8	9	$22\frac{2}{8}$	2401	33
				■ Piscataquis Co. – Robert J. Pelletier – Robert J. Pelletier – 1988							
$188\frac{1}{8}$	$24\frac{7}{8}$	$25\frac{1}{8}$	$21\frac{3}{8}$	$25\frac{7}{8}$	$5\frac{2}{8}$	$5\frac{3}{8}$	9	7	$16\frac{2}{8}$	2497	34
				■ Aroostook Co. – Fritjof Jacobson – Fritjof Jacobson – 1939							
$185\frac{2}{8}$	$26\frac{1}{8}$	26	$17\frac{4}{8}$	$19\frac{4}{8}$	4	$4\frac{3}{8}$	8	7	48	2632	35
				■ Oxford Co. – Michael R. Morris – Michael R. Morris – 1999							

† The scores and ranking for trophies from the 25th Awards Entry Period are not final until the banquet is held on June 19, 2004.

MARYLAND
RECORD WHITETAILS

35 Typical whitetail deer entries
20 Non-typical whitetail deer entries
7,265 Total whitetail deer entries

MARYLAND
NEW STATE RECORD
Typical Whitetail Deer
Score: 185$^7/_8$
Location: Queen Annes Co.
Hunter and Owner:
  Walter J. Lachewitz, Jr.
Date: 1998

NEW
STATE
RECORD

MARYLAND
STATE RECORD
Non-Typical Whitetail Deer
Score: 228⁴/₈
Location: Montgomery Co.
Hunter and Owner: John W. Poole
Date: 1987

MARYLAND

TYPICAL WHITETAIL DEER

Score	Length of Main Beam Right Left	Inside Spread	Greatest Spread	Circumference at Smallest Place Between Burr and First Point Right Left		Number of Points Right Left		Lengths Abnormal Points	All-Time Rank	State Rank
	■ Location of Kill – Hunter – Owner – Date Killed									
185⁷/8	28²/8 27⁷/8	23⁷/8	26¹/8	4⁴/8 4⁵/8		5 5			244	1
	■ Queen Annes Co. – Walter J. Lachewitz, Jr. – Walter J. Lachewitz, Jr. – 1998									
183³/8	27¹/8 26⁴/8	18⁵/8	21¹/8	4³/8 4⁴/8		8 9		6²/8	365	2
	■ Dorchester Co. – John R. Seifert, Jr. – John R. Seifert, Jr. – 1973									
183³/8	27⁵/8 27¹/8	20¹/8	23²/8	5²/8 5³/8		5 5			365	2
	■ Talbot Co. – Petey L. Councell – Petey L. Councell – 1994									
181⁶/8	25⁵/8 26⁶/8	23⁶/8	26	5 4⁷/8		6 7		1²/8	492	4
	■ Montgomery Co. – Gary F. Menso – Gary F. Menso – 1985									
180⁶/8	27²/8 26⁵/8	17⁶/8	20¹/8	4⁷/8 4⁴/8		5 5			587	5
	■ Anne Arundel Co. – Paul H. Anderson, Jr. – Paul H. Anderson, Jr. – 1995									
180¹/8	29⁷/8 28⁶/8	25¹/8	26⁷/8	5¹/8 5³/8		5 5			669	6
	■ Caroline Co. – Unknown – Charles D. Anderson – 1987									
178¹/8	24⁶/8 25⁵/8	25⁶/8	26⁷/8	4³/8 4³/8		6 6			905	7
	■ Kent Co. – Herman Gravatt – Donald P. Travis – 1955									
177⁷/8	28⁶/8 26⁵/8	23⁷/8	26¹/8	5⁴/8 5³/8		7 10		11	936	8
	■ St. Marys Co. – Timothy B. Moore – Timothy B. Moore – 1990									
177	28²/8 28¹/8	18³/8	20³/8	5 5		8 6		14³/8	1066	9
	■ Baltimore Co. – Richard B. Traband – Richard B. Traband – 1990									
173	28⁶/8 29³/8	21⁶/8	23⁶/8	5⁴/8 5⁶/8		4 4			1991	10
	■ Caroline Co. – Jay Downes, Jr. – Jay Downes, Jr. – 1993									
172⁶/8	26³/8 26⁴/8	20	21⁷/8	4²/8 4²/8		5 5			2065†	11†
	■ Anne Arundel Co. – Gus Andujar – Gus Andujar – 2000									
172³/8	29⁶/8 30²/8	21²/8	24⁷/8	4⁵/8 5		4 6		8¹/8	2200	12
	■ Prince Georges Co. – Lance D. Canter – Lance D. Canter – 1993									
172³/8	24⁵/8 26¹/8	16⁶/8	19⁴/8	5³/8 5		6 5		2³/8	2200	12
	■ Queen Annes Co. – Paul A. Pletzer – Paul A. Pletzer – 1995									
172²/8	28⁴/8 28⁷/8	18⁶/8	21	4⁵/8 4⁷/8		7 5		4⁴/8	2237	14
	■ Talbot Co. – Jack W. Jones – Jack W. Jones – 1998									
172¹/8	27²/8 26⁵/8	18⁶/8	20⁷/8	4⁶/8 4⁶/8		6 5		1⁵/8	2286	15
	■ Queen Annes Co. – James R. Spies, Jr. – James R. Spies, Jr. – 1976									
172	27 27	17¹/8	19²/8	4⁶/8 5²/8		6 5		3¹/8	2330	16
	■ Caroline Co. – Garey N. Brown – Garey N. Brown – 1986									
171⁴/8	25³/8 26	19¹/8	21³/8	5⁵/8 5⁶/8		6 6		5⁷/8	2513	17
	■ Talbot Co. – William D. Collison – William D. Collison – 1998									
171³/8	26⁶/8 26⁷/8	22⁵/8	29	4⁵/8 4⁵/8		5 7		3⁴/8	2564	18
	■ Dorchester Co. – Mark S. Bronder – Mark S. Bronder – 1995									
171³/8	27²/8 27	17⁷/8	20	4⁷/8 4⁷/8		5 5			2564	18
	■ Charles Co. – Patrick E. Langley – Patrick E. Langley – 1997									

Score	Length of Main Beam Right	Left	Inside Spread	Greatest Spread	Circumference at Smallest Place Between Burr and First Point Right	Left	Number of Points Right	Left	Lengths Abnormal Points	All-Time Rank	State Rank
	■ Location of Kill – Hunter – Owner – Date Killed										
171	$27^5/_8$	$26^6/_8$	$20^4/_8$	$22^7/_8$	$5^1/_8$	$5^1/_8$	6	5	$1^6/_8$	2707	20
	■ Somerset Co. – Lloyd B. Bloodsworth – Lloyd B. Bloodsworth – 1995										
$170^7/_8$	$28^7/_8$	$27^4/_8$	$25^1/_8$	$29^3/_8$	$4^7/_8$	$4^5/_8$	5	5		2769	21
	■ Charles Co. – Richard L. Albright – Richard L. Albright – 1997										
$170^6/_8$	$25^7/_8$	$25^6/_8$	20	$22^1/_8$	$4^6/_8$	$4^6/_8$	5	5		2828	22
	■ Carroll Co. – Wes McKenzie – Wes McKenzie – 1971										
$170^6/_8$	$27^2/_8$	$27^1/_8$	$18^4/_8$	$20^3/_8$	$4^2/_8$	$4^4/_8$	6	5	3	2828	22
	■ Kent Co. – Thomas C. Duff, Jr. – Thomas C. Duff, Jr. – 1973										
$170^5/_8$	$24^3/_8$	$26^4/_8$	$17^3/_8$		$5^1/_8$	$4^7/_8$	5	5		2876	24
	■ St. Marys Co. – Brian M. Boteler – Brian M. Boteler – 1980										
$170^1/_8$	$26^7/_8$	26	$20^7/_8$	$22^4/_8$	$4^6/_8$	$4^6/_8$	5	6	$2^6/_8$	3143	25
	■ Harford Co. – Edward C. Garrison – Edward C. Garrison – 1987										
$167^2/_8$	$27^7/_8$	$27^6/_8$	$18^7/_8$	$20^6/_8$	$5^3/_8$	$5^2/_8$	6	5	$1^5/_8$	3519	26
	■ Kent Co. – F. David Black – F. David Black – 1999										
167	$24^7/_8$	$24^2/_8$	$17^7/_8$	$19^4/_8$	$4^4/_8$	$4^4/_8$	8	7	$6^3/_8$	3552	27
	■ St. Mary's Co. – Bryan R. Thrush – Bryan R. Thrush – 1999										
$165^2/_8$	$23^6/_8$	$26^2/_8$	$18^2/_8$	$20^5/_8$	$4^1/_8$	$4^2/_8$	5	5		3748	28
	■ Prince Georges Co. – Anthony B. Long – Anthony B. Long – 1996										
$164^6/_8$	$24^7/_8$	$25^6/_8$	$19^5/_8$	$21^5/_8$	$5^4/_8$	$5^7/_8$	7	7	$4^5/_8$	3809†	29†
	■ Wicomico Co. – C.L. Dutch Workman – C.L. Dutch Workman – 2000										
$164^3/_8$	30	$29^7/_8$	$26^1/_8$	$30^2/_8$	5	$4^7/_8$	6	6	$7^6/_8$	3864	30
	■ Anne Arundel Co. – Douglas M. Christensen – Douglas M. Christensen – 1999										
$163^3/_8$	$27^6/_8$	$26^1/_8$	$22^2/_8$	$25^4/_8$	$4^6/_8$	$4^7/_8$	6	7	$4^5/_8$	4002	31
	■ Baltimore Co. – Christian M. Phillips – Christian M. Phillips – 1995										
$161^2/_8$	$24^4/_8$	$25^1/_8$	$19^6/_8$	22	$4^2/_8$	$4^2/_8$	5	5		4310†	32†
	■ Charles Co. – Jeremy L. Pugh – Jeremy L. Pugh – 2000										
161	$24^4/_8$	$25^4/_8$	$17^2/_8$	$21^5/_8$	$4^7/_8$	$4^6/_8$	6	6	$6^6/_8$	4356†	33†
	■ Caroline Co. – Laura L. Kreis – Laura L. Kreis – 2001										
$160^2/_8$	$27^1/_8$	27	$18^4/_8$	$20^5/_8$	$4^4/_8$	$4^6/_8$	4	4		4495	34
	■ Queen Annes Co. – Michael Chirico – Michael Chirico – 1994										
160	28	$27^2/_8$	$20^3/_8$	23	$4^4/_8$	$4^4/_8$	6	4	$1^5/_8$	4565	35
	■ Charles Co. – David A. Anderson – David A. Anderson – 1997										

† The scores and ranking for trophies from the 25th Awards Entry Period are not final until the banquet is held on June 19, 2004.

MARYLAND

NON-TYPICAL WHITETAIL DEER

Score	Length of Main Beam Right	Left	Inside Spread	Greatest Spread	Circumference at Smallest Place Between Burr and First Point Right	Left	Number of Points Right	Left	Lengths Abnormal Points	All-Time Rank	State Rank
228 4/8	24	26	20 6/8	30 4/8	5 2/8	5 2/8	10	13	64	258	1
■ Montgomery Co. – John W. Poole – John W. Poole – 1987											
221 3/8	21 6/8	19 4/8	17 1/8	20 4/8	10- / –	10- / –	12	13	68	407	2
■ Anne Arundel Co. – Unknown – Frederick H. Horn – 1979											
220 2/8	29 4/8	31 2/8	22 4/8	26 6/8	5 7/8	5 6/8	14	8	50	434	3
■ Prince Georges Co. – Robert Y. Clagett, Jr. – Robert Y. Clagett, Jr. – 1995											
217 2/8	22	20	20	29 6/8	4 5/8	4 5/8	13	12	51 4/8	519	4
■ Talbot Co. – Vincent L. Jordan, Sr. – Vincent L. Jordan, Sr. – 1974											
216 6/8	29	27 3/8	22 7/8	27 4/8	6 2/8	6 4/8	13	13	43 7/8	539	5
■ Charles Co. – Brian G. Klaas – Brian G. Klaas – 1993											
210	28 3/8	26	26 5/8	31 4/8	4 7/8	4 7/8	7	13	35 1/8	816	6
■ Calvert Co. – Robert E. Barnett – Robert E. Barnett – 1984											
208 7/8	26 7/8	26 7/8	26 6/8	30 2/8	5 3/8	5 3/8	10	8	52 7/8	877	7
■ Charles Co. – Robert A. Boarman – Robert A. Boarman – 1984											
206	25	24 3/8	24 3/8	27 1/8	5 1/8	5	8	7	28 1/8	1075	8
■ Queen Annes Co. – Kenneth J. Houtz – Kenneth J. Houtz – 1992											
203 4/8	28	28 3/8	23 5/8	27	6 4/8	6	9	7	42 3/8	1259	9
■ Prince Georges Co. – Charles C. Blankenship, Jr. – Charles C. Blankenship, Jr. – 1995											
201 3/8	24 7/8	25 1/8	19		5 2/8	5 3/8	12	10	49 3/8	1461	10
■ Queen Annes Co. – Franklin E. Jewell – Franklin E. Jewell – 1978											
199 3/8	20 6/8	22 2/8	15	19 2/8	6 6/8	6	13	9	41 5/8	1639†	11†
■ Talbot Co. – William H. Shields – William H. Shields – 2001											
196 3/8	24 5/8	20 7/8	14 3/8	21 1/8	6 4/8	7 3/8	7	12	43 2/8	2010†	12†
■ St. Mary's Co. – Terry L. Starr – Terry L. Starr – 2001											
196 2/8	27	25 1/8	27	31	6	6	7	14	21 2/8	2028	13
■ Dorchester Co. – Kevin R. Coulbourne – Kevin R. Coulbourne – 1979											
195 4/8	27	26	20 3/8	21 1/8	5 6/8	5 6/8	7	9	15 1/8	2134	14
■ Dorchester Co. – Charles D. Anderson – Charles D. Anderson – 1978											
195 1/8	27	26	18 6/8	21	5 2/8	5 2/8	6	8	20 5/8	2208	15
■ Dorchester Co. – Carroll R. Seegard – Charles D. Anderson – 1974											
195 1/8	27	25 7/8	15 5/8	18 2/8	4 6/8	7 2/8	9	9	30 2/8	2208	15
■ Cecil Co. – Charles M. Crouse – Charles M. Crouse – 1995											
193 3/8	29 1/8	28 2/8	19	21 5/8	4 1/8	4 1/8	9	7	24 1/8	2293	17
■ St. Mary's Co. – Ronald D. Cullember – Ronald D. Cullember – 1993											
185 7/8	25 6/8	24 2/8	22 3/8	31 5/8	4 2/8	4 1/8	10	8	27 6/8	2597	18
■ Charles Co. – Robert Sparks – Robert Sparks – 1980											
185 6/8	27 1/8	22 4/8	22 6/8	26 1/8	4 5/8	5	7	9	30 4/8	2605	19
■ Charles Co. – Thomas M. Maddox – Thomas M. Maddox – 1999											

■ Location of Kill – Hunter – Owner – Date Killed

Score	Length of Main Beam		Inside Spread	Greatest Spread	Circumference at Smallest Place Between Burr and First Point		Number of Points		Lengths Abnormal Points	All-Time Rank	State Rank
	Right	Left			Right	Left	Right	Left			
	■ Location of Kill – Hunter – Owner – Date Killed										
185 1/8	22 5/8	22 3/8	18 7/8	23 7/8	4 5/8	4 4/8	8	8	26 6/8	2641†	20†
	■ Kent Co. – Ralph Fleegle – Ralph Fleegle – 2001										

† The scores and ranking for trophies from the 25th Awards Entry Period are not final until the banquet is held on June 19, 2004.

MASSACHUSETTS
RECORD WHITETAILS

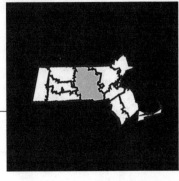

4 Typical whitetail deer entries
1 Non-typical whitetail deer entries
7,265 Total whitetail deer entries

0 Entries
1-2 Entries
3-5 Entries
6-10 Entries
11+ Entries

NEW
STATE
RECORD

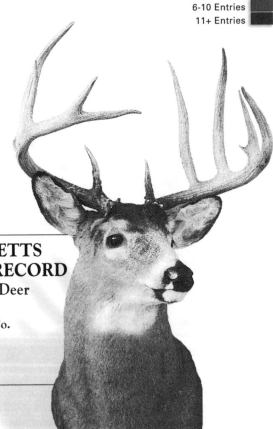

MASSACHUSETTS
NEW STATE RECORD
Typical Whitetail Deer
Score: 177^5/$_8$
Location: Berkshire Co.
Hunter and Owner:
    William E. Tatro
Date: 1995

MASSACHUSETTS
NEW STATE RECORD
Non-Typical Whitetail Deer
Score: 188²/₈
Location: Hampden Co.
Hunter and Owner: Joseph F. Giordano
Date: 1995

MASSACHUSETTS

TYPICAL WHITETAIL DEER

Score	Length of Main Beam Right	Left	Inside Spread	Greatest Spread	Circumference at Smallest Place Between Burr and First Point Right	Left	Number of Points Right	Left	Lengths Abnormal Points	All-Time Rank	State Rank
	■ Location of Kill – Hunter – Owner – Date Killed										
177⁵/₈	28⁵/₈	28²/₈	20¹/₈	22	4⁴/₈	4⁴/₈	6	5		972	1
	■ Berkshire Co. – William E. Tatro – William E. Tatro – 1995										
175³/₈	27²/₈	27²/₈	19³/₈	21⁴/₈	5	4⁷/₈	6	6		1377	2
	■ Worcester Co. – Thomas W. Bombard – Thomas W. Bombard – 1992										
171⁷/₈	27⁴/₈	26⁷/₈	19⁶/₈	22²/₈	5⁴/₈	5⁵/₈	5	6	1³/₈	2382	3
	■ Essex Co. – Michael G. Prescott – Michael G. Prescott – 1999										
160⁵/₈	24⁶/₈	24⁷/₈	18¹/₈	20²/₈	4³/₈	4³/₈	5	5		4423	4
	■ Middlesex Co. – Robert J. Antobenedetto – Robert J. Antobenedetto – 1995										

MASSACHUSETTS

NON-TYPICAL WHITETAIL DEER

Score	Length of Main Beam Right	Length of Main Beam Left	Inside Spread	Greatest Spread	Circumference at Smallest Place Between Burr and First Point Right	Circumference at Smallest Place Between Burr and First Point Left	Number of Points Right	Number of Points Left	Lengths Abnormal Points	All-Time Rank	State Rank
	■ Location of Kill – Hunter – Owner – Date Killed										
188²/8	30¹/8	29⁵/8	19	21²/8	5⁶/8	6¹/8	7	8	11⁶/8	2489	1
	■ Hampden Co. – Joseph F. Giordano – Joseph F. Giordano – 1995										

MICHIGAN
RECORD WHITETAILS

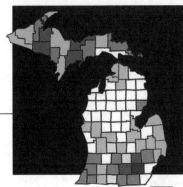

98 Typical whitetail deer entries
66 Non-typical whitetail deer entries
7,265 Total whitetail deer entries

0 Entries
1-2 Entries
3-5 Entries
6-10 Entries
11+ Entries

NEW
STATE
RECORD

MICHIGAN
STATE RECORD
Typical Whitetail Deer
Score: 198
Location: Jackson Co.
Hunter: Troy A. Stephens
Owner: Bass Pro Shops
Date: 1996

MICHIGAN
STATE RECORD
Non-Typical Whitetail Deer
Score: 238²/₈
Location: Bay Co.
Hunter and Owner: Paul M. Mickey
Date: 1976

MICHIGAN

TYPICAL WHITETAIL DEER

Score	Length of Main Beam Right	Left	Inside Spread	Greatest Spread	Circumference at Smallest Place Between Burr and First Point Right	Left	Number of Points Right	Left	Lengths Abnormal Points	All-Time Rank	State Rank
	■ Location of Kill – Hunter – Owner – Date Killed										
198	29²/8	29⁴/8	20²/8	23	5²/8	5¹/8	9	7	6⁶/8	21	1
	■ Jackson Co. – Troy A. Stephens – Bass Pro Shops – 1996										
193²/8	28³/8	27⁷/8	22²/8	24	5²/8	5⁴/8	8	6	1⁶/8	53	2
	■ Jackson Co. – Craig Calderone – Bass Pro Shops – 1986										
190⁵/8	26³/8	26⁵/8	18⁵/8	20⁶/8	4⁵/8	4⁶/8	8	7	1⁴/8	95†	3†
	■ Hillsdale Co. – Gregory D. McCuiston – Gregory D. McCuiston – 2001										
186³/8	26²/8	27²/8	20⁴/8	23¹/8	5²/8	5²/8	8	7	5⁷/8	210	4
	■ Ontonagon Co. – Unknown – Mac's Taxidermy – 1980										
184⁷/8	26³/8	26³/8	21	23⁷/8	6	5⁷/8	6	6	2¹/8	279	5
	■ Baraga Co. – Louis J. Roy – Louis J. Roy – 1987										
182⁷/8	27⁷/8	28¹/8	21¹/8	23¹/8	4⁷/8	4⁷/8	5	5		401	6
	■ Iosco Co. – Harvey H. Keast – Harvey H. Keast – 1938										
181⁵/8	26⁷/8	27⁷/8	22³/8	24¹/8	5²/8	5¹/8	5	5		500†	7†
	■ Berrien Co. – Steven E. Coleman – Steven E. Coleman – 2000										
181⁵/8	27⁶/8	27⁶/8	21⁵/8	23⁵/8	5²/8	5²/8	6	6	8	500	7
	■ Ionia Co. – Lester Bowen – Richard Bowen – 1947										
180⁶/8	27⁴/8	27	20	22²/8	4⁴/8	4⁴/8	5	5		587†	9†
	■ Iosco Co. – Zack T. Shellenbarger – Zack T. Shellenbarger – 2000										
180⁴/8	29²/8	28⁴/8	20⁶/8	23⁴/8	4⁷/8	4⁶/8	6	5	1⁴/8	613	10
	■ Iron Co. – John Schmidt – Robert E. Schmidt – 1927										
180³/8	32⁶/8	32⁴/8	22³/8	25⁴/8	5²/8	5³/8	4	4		630†	11†
	■ Hillsdale Co. – Victor L. Bulliner – Victor L. Bulliner – 2001 ■ See photo on page 269										
180³/8	27	28¹/8	17⁶/8	22⁴/8	4⁵/8	4⁵/8	9	6	8¹/8	630	11
	■ Huron Co. – Picked Up – Raymond W. Hatfield – 1985										
179⁵/8	29⁶/8	29	21³/8	24⁴/8	4⁶/8	4⁷/8	5	5		729	13
	■ Houghton Co. – Matthew R. Usitalo – Matthew R. Usitalo – 1992										
179²/8	27⁵/8	26¹/8	20²/8	22⁵/8	4⁵/8	4⁵/8	8	8	8²/8	763†	14†
	■ Kalamazoo Co. – Steve J. Williams – Steve J. Williams – 2000										
178⁴/8	29⁴/8	28⁶/8	22⁴/8	24⁷/8	4⁷/8	5¹/8	6	5	4⁴/8	850	15
	■ Iosco Co. – Frederic J. Latta – Frederic J. Latta – 1991										
178¹/8	28¹/8	28¹/8	18¹/8	20³/8	4⁶/8	4⁶/8	5	5		905	16
	■ Iron Co. – James Locke – Cabela's, Inc. – 1960										
178	24¹/8	25³/8	16⁶/8	19	4⁶/8	4⁷/8	6	6		922	17
	■ Hillsdale Co. – Dudley N. Spade – Dudley N. Spade – 1972										
177⁷/8	28	27⁴/8	20³/8	22⁷/8	5⁶/8	5⁶/8	5	5		936	18
	■ Iron Co. – Felix Brzoznowski – Joseph Brzoznowski – 1939										
176⁷/8	24¹/8	25⁷/8	20⁷/8	22⁵/8	5¹/8	5	6	6		1086	19
	■ Jackson Co. – David M. Lindeman – David M. Lindeman – 1991										

Score	Length of Main Beam Right Left	Inside Spread	Greatest Spread	Circumference at Smallest Place Between Burr and First Point Right Left	Number of Points Right Left	Lengths Abnormal Points	All-Time Rank	State Rank
176 6/8	25 5/8 27 3/8	20 6/8	23 6/8	5 7/8 5 1/8	12 11	17	1103	20
■ Clinton Co. – Ray Sadler – Ray Sadler – 1963								
176 3/8	26 26 5/8	20 5/8	23	5 4/8 5 6/8	7 5		1182	21
■ Baraga Co. – Paul Korhonen – Paul Korhonen – 1945								
175 6/8	29 5/8 28 6/8	21	23	5 3/8 5 3/8	5 5		1310	22
■ Kent Co. – Ronald L. Visser – Ronald L. Visser – 1992								
175 2/8	28 6/8 30 7/8	19 2/8	21 6/8	4 7/8 4 7/8	5 5		1403	23
■ Van Buren Co. – Daryl D. Kovach – Daryl D. Kovach – 1989								
175 1/8	26 2/8 27 2/8	19 5/8	22	4 4/8 4 7/8	5 5		1440	24
■ Alger Co. – Warren Beebe – Donald J. Docking – 1936								
175 1/8	27 5/8 27 1/8	19 6/8	22 2/8	5 3/8 5 5/8	7 6	4 1/8	1440	24
■ Marquette Co. – Andrew E. Cook II – Andrew E. Cook II – 1987								
174 7/8	24 3/8 24 2/8	23 6/8	24 6/8	4 7/8 4 7/8	7 7	2 3/8	1513	26
■ Delta Co. – Will Wellman – Delor J. Wellman – 1930								
174 7/8	25 7/8 26 4/8	19 2/8	21 1/8	5 1/8 4 7/8	5 6	2 7/8	1513	26
■ Washtenaw Co. – Michael F. Burger – Michael F. Burger – 1993								
174 5/8	25 1/8 25	16 5/8	21	5 3/8 5 1/8	5 5		1561	28
■ Livingston Co. – Nicholas S. Converse – Nicholas S. Converse – 1987								
174 5/8	24 24 3/8	21 5/8	24	5 6/8 5 6/8	5 5		1561	28
■ Jackson Co. – Louise S. Klarr – Louise S. Klarr – 1990								
174 4/8	24 7/8 24 3/8	16 6/8	19 6/8	4 5/8 4 5/8	6 6		1592	30
■ Marquette Co. – Henry L. Terres – Bass Pro Shops – 1944								
174 3/8	27 7/8 28	28	29 3/8	5 3/8 5 3/8	5 5	1 3/8	1619	31
■ Washtenaw Co. – Picked Up – Comm. Bucks of Mich. – 1991								
174 1/8	27 4/8 26	16 1/8	18 4/8	4 5/8 4 6/8	5 7	1 2/8	1678	32
■ Livingston Co. – Dolores E. Kassuba – Dolores E. Kassuba – 1995								
174	25 4/8 25 4/8	20 2/8	22 4/8	4 4/8 4 3/8	5 6		1717†	33†
■ Saginaw Co. – Orrin R. Nothelfer – Orrin R. Nothelfer – 2000								
174	26 4/8 25 6/8	18 2/8	20 5/8	5 7/8 5 4/8	8 5	3 6/8	1717	33
■ Eaton Co. – Rodney S. Brown – Connie Brown – 1984								
173 6/8	25 6/8 25 6/8	18 4/8	20 6/8	4 3/8 4 3/8	6 6		1766	35
■ Livingston Co. – Terry J. Kemp – Terry J. Kemp – 1979								
173 6/8	26 1/8 26 2/8	18 7/8	21 7/8	5 3/8 5 3/8	6 8	2 3/8	1766	35
■ Schoolcraft Co. – Thomas J. Haas – Thomas J. Haas – 1987								
173 4/8	28 3/8 29 7/8	18	20 4/8	4 4/8 4 3/8	5 6	4	1847	37
■ Livingston Co. – Paul M. Peckens – Paul M. Peckens – 1959								
173 1/8	27 7/8 27 3/8	20 3/8	22 2/8	4 2/8 4 4/8	5 5		1950	38
■ Allegan Co. – Charles O. Hooper – Charles O. Hooper – 1990								
172 7/8	27 4/8 28 2/8	18 3/8	21	5 5/8 5 7/8	8 8	8 2/8	2038	39
■ Schoolcraft Co. – Lanny D. Higley – Lanny D. Higley – 1994								
172 5/8	26 7/8 25 5/8	18 4/8	20 7/8	5 4/8 5 3/8	6 5	1 1/8	2113	40
■ Cass Co. – Ben R. Williams – Ben R. Williams – 1971								

■ Location of Kill – Hunter – Owner – Date Killed

Score	Length of Main Beam		Inside Spread	Greatest Spread	Circumference at Smallest Place Between Burr and First Point		Number of Points		Lengths Abnormal Points	All-Time Rank	State Rank
	Right	Left			Right	Left	Right	Left			
	■ Location of Kill – Hunter – Owner – Date Killed										
172⁴/₈	25⁴/₈	25²/₈	18	24	5⁵/₈	6	6	6	2²/₈	2156	41
	■ Hillsdale Co. – Turley G. Crisp – Turley G. Crisp – 1991										
172⁴/₈	26²/₈	25	17⁶/₈	20²/₈	5²/₈	5⁴/₈	6	6		2156	41
	■ St. Clair Co. – Djura Drazic – Djura Drazic – 1998										
172²/₈	25⁷/₈	26	18	20⁵/₈	4⁷/₈	5	5	5		2237†	43†
	■ Berrien Co. – Mike C. Payne – Mike C. Payne – 2000										
172²/₈	26	26	22	24⁶/₈	5⁴/₈	5	5	5		2237	43
	■ Washtenaw Co. – Guy A. Miller – Guy A. Miller – 1989										
172¹/₈	26	25⁵/₈	18	20³/₈	4³/₈	4⁶/₈	6	5	2³/₈	2286	45
	■ Baraga Co. – Gust Varlen – Bass Pro Shops – 1945										
172¹/₈	25⁴/₈	25⁶/₈	19³/₈	22	4⁶/₈	4⁶/₈	5	5		2286	45
	■ Genesee Co. – David C. Bastion – David C. Bastion – 1992										
172	25⁷/₈	26³/₈	20⁴/₈	22⁷/₈	5⁴/₈	6¹/₈	6	7	3²/₈	2330	47
	■ Hillsdale Co. – Art P. Toney – Art P. Toney – 1994										
171⁷/₈	26⁴/₈	25⁶/₈	17⁴/₈	19²/₈	5⁷/₈	6	6	6	4⁷/₈	2382	48
	■ Menominee Co. – Karl Schwartz – Bass Pro Shops – 1974										
171⁶/₈	26³/₈	26³/₈	20⁴/₈	22⁵/₈	4⁵/₈	4⁶/₈	4	5		2418	49
	■ Van Buren Co. – Ronald E. Eldred – Ronald E. Eldred – 1983										
171⁶/₈	28⁵/₈	27¹/₈	19²/₈	21³/₈	4⁵/₈	4⁶/₈	5	7	1²/₈	2418	49
	■ Washtenaw Co. – Richard J. Degrand – Richard J. Degrand – 1995										
171⁴/₈	25¹/₈	25⁶/₈	20⁴/₈	22²/₈	4⁵/₈	4⁷/₈	6	6		2513	51
	■ Delta Co. – Lawrence Charles – Bass Pro Shops – PR 1941										
171⁴/₈	25¹/₈	25⁵/₈	23⁶/₈	25⁵/₈	4⁶/₈	4⁵/₈	5	5		2513	51
	■ Washtenaw Co. – Michael C. Lamirand – Michael C. Lamirand – 1988										
171⁴/₈	26⁷/₈	27⁵/₈	17⁶/₈	20²/₈	5⁴/₈	5³/₈	5	5		2513	51
	■ Lenawee Co. – Robert E. Knight – Robert E. Knight – 1989										
171³/₈	25²/₈	25²/₈	19³/₈	23³/₈	4²/₈	4³/₈	6	7	4⁴/₈	2564	54
	■ Oceana Co. – Delos Highland – Delos Highland – 1967										
171³/₈	28	27¹/₈	18⁴/₈	20⁴/₈	4⁴/₈	4⁷/₈	5	6	1¹/₈	2564	54
	■ Kalamazoo Co. – Harvey B. Braden – Harvey B. Braden – 1984										
171²/₈	26⁶/₈	27	21¹/₈	23³/₈	5¹/₈	5⁴/₈	8	6	5¹/₈	2621	56
	■ Alger Co. – John Peterson – Bass Pro Shops – 1948										
171¹/₈	27⁴/₈	27⁴/₈	21¹/₈	23²/₈	4²/₈	4²/₈	5	5		2665	57
	Charlevoix Co. – Noel Thomson – Ivan Thomson – 1957										
171¹/₈	27²/₈	27¹/₈	18	20³/₈	4⁴/₈	4⁴/₈	8	7	3⁵/₈	2665	57
	■ Alger Co. – Shirley L. Robare – Shirley L. Robare – 1963										
171	26⁴/₈	27¹/₈	22⁴/₈	24⁶/₈	5¹/₈	5¹/₈	6	5		2707	59
	■ St. Clair Co. – John Pierce – John Pierce – 1995										
171	25⁷/₈	26²/₈	19	21⁷/₈	4⁶/₈	4⁶/₈	7	6	3²/₈	2707	59
	■ St. Clair Co. – James R. Hurd, Jr. – James R. Hurd, Jr. – 1998										
170⁷/₈	24⁵/₈	24³/₈	16⁶/₈	18⁶/₈	5⁴/₈	5⁴/₈	5	7	2³/₈	2769	61
	■ Delta Co. – Jim Lawson – Mary J. Wellman – 1939										

Score	Length of Main Beam Right	Left	Inside Spread	Greatest Spread	Circumference at Smallest Place Between Burr and First Point Right	Left	Number of Points Right	Left	Lengths Abnormal Points	All-Time Rank	State Rank
	Location of Kill – Hunter – Owner – Date Killed										
170 7/8	26 1/8	23 5/8	21 1/8	23 1/8	5 4/8	5 1/8	5	5		2769	61
	Van Buren Co. – Donald J. Hamilton, Jr. – Donald J. Hamilton, Jr. – 1994										
170 6/8	24 5/8	23 5/8	14 6/8	17 3/8	4 3/8	4 3/8	6	7		2828	63
	Jackson Co. – Richard J. Galicki – Richard J. Galicki – 1991										
170 5/8	21 5/8	21 7/8	15 3/8	17 3/8	4 5/8	4 5/8	6	6		2876	64
	Allegan Co. – William Caywood – William Caywood – 1948										
170 5/8	25 5/8	26	20 3/8	22 4/8	4 4/8	4 5/8	5	6	5 4/8	2876	64
	Berrien Co. – G. Steven Abdoe – G. Steven Abdoe – 1982										
170 4/8	24 7/8	24 1/8	21	22 7/8	4 7/8	5	5	5		2933	66
	Chippewa Co. – Paul Slawski – Paul Slawski – 1984										
170 3/8	25 6/8	26 1/8	18 5/8	21	4 7/8	5	5	5		2992	67
	Newaygo Co. – Dennis A. Carlson – Dennis A. Carlson – 1978										
170 3/8	23 7/8	23 7/8	19 7/8	23 1/8	4 6/8	4 6/8	5	5		2992	67
	Emmet Co. – Jeffery A. Phillips – Jeffery A. Phillips – 1985										
170 3/8	25 6/8	25 3/8	15 7/8	18 4/8	4 6/8	4 5/8	5	5		2992	67
	Baraga Co. – Howard D. Musick – Howard D. Musick – 1987										
170 3/8	27 5/8	27 3/8	17 7/8	20 2/8	5	5	5	5		2992	67
	Montcalm Co. – Michael R. Nelson – Michael R. Nelson – 1989										
170 2/8	24 4/8	25 6/8	26	27 5/8	5 2/8	5 2/8	8	6	2 4/8	3063	71
	Washtenaw Co. – Tod G. Jaggi – Tod G. Jaggi – 1991										
170 1/8	25 2/8	26 5/8	17 6/8	22 1/8	5 6/8	5 6/8	6	6	2 7/8	3143	72
	Saginaw Co. – Scott M. Hutchins – Scott M. Hutchins – 1990										
170 1/8	28 7/8	29 4/8	26 1/8	28 3/8	5 5/8	5 5/8	5	5		3143	72
	Branch Co. – Jeffrey M. Stauffer – Jeffrey M. Stauffer – 1995										
170 1/8	28 5/8	28 2/8	19 1/8	22	5 5/8	5 6/8	6	6	3	3143	72
	Saginaw Co. – Mario VanderMeulen – Mario VanderMeulen – 1999										
170	26 2/8	26 1/8	18 6/8	20 6/8	4 6/8	4 6/8	7	7	3 6/8	3224†	75†
	Ostego Co. – Robert M. Cannon – Robert M. Cannon – 2000										
170	26	26 6/8	17 5/8	20 4/8	4 1/8	4 1/8	7	6	9 1/8	3224	75
	Schoolcraft Co. – Harold P. Dixner – J. Kenneth Dixner – PR 1918										
170	26	27	19 4/8	21 5/8	4 6/8	4 7/8	6	5	1 4/8	3224	75
	Jackson Co. – Michael D. Fitzgerald – Michael D. Fitzgerald – 1990										
169	26 5/8	27 4/8	18 6/8	20 4/8	4 5/8	4 6/8	5	5		3348	78
	Alger Co. – Mark Whitmarsh – Mark Whitmarsh – 1991										
167 1/8	25 7/8	26	17 7/8	19 5/8	4 2/8	4 2/8	5	5		3539	79
	Oakland Co. – Chris C. Goodwin – Chris C. Goodwin – 1997										
166 1/8	24 7/8	25 4/8	20 5/8	23	4	4 1/8	5	5		3643	80
	Lenawee Co. – Gerb Portenga – Gerb Portenga – 1969										
165 6/8	28 4/8	28 3/8	20 7/8	23 5/8	5 1/8	5 1/8	9	9	13 5/8	3680	81
	Delta Co. – Herbert Lundin – Herbert Lundin – 1946										
165 1/8	25 5/8	24 5/8	17 7/8	20 2/8	5 4/8	5 3/8	5	5		3767	82
	Bay Co. – Terry L. Horner – Terry L. Horner – 1998										

Score	Length of Main Beam		Inside Spread	Greatest Spread	Circumference at Smallest Place Between Burr and First Point		Number of Points		Lengths Abnormal Points	All-Time Rank	State Rank
	Right	Left			Right	Left	Right	Left			
	■ *Location of Kill – Hunter – Owner – Date Killed*										
164³/8	25³/8	24⁷/8	19⁷/8	21⁶/8	4¹/8	4	5	6		3864	83
	■ *Hillsdale Co. – Allan J. Clendening – Allan J. Clendening – 1988*										
163⁷/8	27	26⁶/8	18⁷/8	20⁷/8	5⁴/8	5³/8	5	7	5	3928	84
	■ *Gogebic Co. – Humbert A. Landretti – Jerry D. Prosek – 1958*										
163⁷/8	24⁷/8	25⁷/8	19²/8	21⁶/8	5	5	6	7	1¹/8	3928	84
	■ *Oakland Co. – Michael L. Senia – Michael L. Senia – 1999*										
163⁵/8	25¹/8	26¹/8	24¹/8	25¹/8	4⁷/8	4⁷/8	5	5		3961	86
	■ *Cass Co. – Thomas M. Boynton – Thomas M. Boynton – 1997*										
163¹/8	28⁵/8	28	19³/8	23	5³/8	5⁶/8	5	4		4035	87
	■ *Jackson Co. – Robert A. Lusk – Robert A. Lusk – 1988*										
162⁴/8	26¹/8	25³/8	19³/8	21⁴/8	5	4⁷/8	5	8	4⁵/8	4129†	88†
	■ *Oakland Co. – Keith W. Headley – Keith W. Headley – 2000*										
162³/8	24	24⁷/8	17²/8	19³/8	4²/8	4²/8	5	6	1⁵/8	4140	89
	■ *Oakland Co. – Matthew A. Jameson – Matthew A. Jameson – 1997*										
162	27⁵/8	26⁴/8	22²/8	24⁴/8	5³/8	5⁴/8	4	4		4184	90
	■ *Calhoun Co. – George Satterfield – George Satterfield – 1995*										
161⁴/8	24⁵/8	25	20²/8	22³/8	4⁴/8	4⁵/8	5	5		4258	91
	■ *Washtenaw Co. – Gordon E. Berenson – Gordon E. Berenson – 1999*										
161²/8	25¹/8	25²/8	19⁶/8	21⁷/8	4²/8	4⁴/8	5	5		4310	92
	■ *Ingham Co. – Kent W. Kurtz – Kent W. Kurtz – 1989*										
161¹/8	24⁵/8	25⁵/8	19³/8	21⁶/8	4⁵/8	4⁵/8	5	5		4332	93
	■ *Washtenaw Co. – Daryl G. Zemke – Daryl G. Zemke – 1990*										
161	25⁴/8	23³/8	17²/8	19²/8	4⁶/8	4⁶/8	5	5		4356†	94†
	■ *Missaukee Co. – Jeffrey S. Orr – Jeffrey S. Orr – 2001*										
160⁵/8	24⁷/8	24⁵/8	17³/8	19³/8	5	5²/8	7	7	6⁴/8	4423	95
	■ *Berrien Co. – Dale Gardell – Dale Gardell – 1995*										
160²/8	27¹/8	26⁵/8	19	21⁵/8	5	5	5	5		4495	96
	■ *Hillsdale Co. – Jeffrey D. Gier – Jeffrey D. Gier – 1999*										
160¹/8	25²/8	25¹/8	22³/8	24²/8	4³/8	4⁵/8	5	5		4534	97
	■ *Washtenaw Co. – Duane Scherbarth – Duane Scherbarth – 1993*										
160	24⁵/8	24⁴/8	16²/8	18¹/8	4	4	6	6		4565	98
	■ *Iosco Co. – Randall M. Marich – Randall M. Marich – 1993*										

† The scores and ranking for trophies from the 25th Awards Entry Period are not final until the banquet is held on June 19, 2004.

TROPHIES IN THE FIELD

HUNTER: Victor L. Bulliner
SCORE: 180-3/8
CATEGORY: typical whitetail deer
LOCATION: Hillsdale County, Michigan
DATE: 2001

MICHIGAN

NON-TYPICAL WHITETAIL DEER

Score	Length of Main Beam Right	Left	Inside Spread	Greatest Spread	Circumference at Smallest Place Between Burr and First Point Right	Left	Number of Points Right	Left	Lengths Abnormal Points	All-Time Rank	State Rank

■ *Location of Kill – Hunter – Owner – Date Killed*

238²/8	27¹/8	26²/8	21⁴/8		5⁵/8	5⁷/8	12	17	65²/8	136	1

■ *Bay Co. – Paul M. Mickey – Paul M. Mickey – 1976*

| 236¹/8 | 27 | 27²/8 | 20⁴/8 | 28⁴/8 | 4³/8 | 4²/8 | 15 | 15 | 64¹/8 | 163 | 2 |

■ *St. Joseph Co. – Picked Up – Kenneth L. Moore, Jr. – 1995*

| 230⁵/8 | 25¹/8 | 26⁴/8 | 28⁴/8 | 29³/8 | 6¹/8 | 6³/8 | 13 | 11 | 36⁷/8 | 233 | 3 |

■ *Iron Co. – Carl Runyan – Bass Pro Shops – 1942*

| 230 | 26⁶/8 | 26 | 22²/8 | 25³/8 | 6³/8 | 6¹/8 | 13 | 12 | 57²/8 | 240 | 4 |

■ *Schoolcraft Co. – Bill Ogle – MI Whitetail Hall of Fame Mus. – 1943*

| 221⁴/8 | 27⁴/8 | 27⁵/8 | 15⁵/8 | 20⁴/8 | 5⁴/8 | 5⁴/8 | 12 | 12 | 39¹/8 | 402 | 5 |

■ *Michigan – Unknown – MI Whitetail Hall of Fame Mus. – PR 1964*

| 221²/8 | 25⁷/8 | 26²/8 | 18¹/8 | 25⁷/8 | 4⁵/8 | 4⁵/8 | 15 | 11 | 41¹/8 | 410 | 6 |

■ *Lapeer Co. – Picked Up – William Schmidt, Jr. – 1993*

| 219⁶/8 | 24⁶/8 | 26 | 21²/8 | 23⁴/8 | 5³/8 | 5⁵/8 | 12 | 11 | 41⁶/8 | 447† | 7† |

■ *Cass Co. – Bruce C. Heslet II – Bruce C. Heslet II – 2000*

| 218⁷/8 | 26⁶/8 | 25⁵/8 | 20³/8 | 23¹/8 | 6 | 6 | 8 | 12 | 34⁶/8 | 472 | 8 |

■ *St. Joseph Co. – Picked Up – Rex A. Mayer – PR 1989*

| 218³/8 | 24⁷/8 | 25⁵/8 | 23²/8 | 28¹/8 | 5²/8 | 5²/8 | 10 | 11 | 48¹/8 | 490 | 9 |

■ *Keweenaw Co. – Bernard J. Murn – Bernard J. Murn – 1980*

| 218¹/8 | 27²/8 | 27¹/8 | 15 | 19³/8 | 5⁷/8 | 5⁷/8 | 13 | 8 | 30⁷/8 | 497† | 10† |

■ *Iron Co. – Carl Mattson – Mary J. Wellman – 1945*

| 216⁵/8 | 24⁴/8 | 23⁵/8 | 17²/8 | 23⁷/8 | 5²/8 | 5³/8 | 12 | 13 | 38³/8 | 545 | 11 |

■ *Dickinson Co. – Earl Wilt – Richard H. Wilt – 1943*

| 215⁵/8 | 26 | 25⁶/8 | 20 | 23³/8 | 5⁵/8 | 5⁶/8 | 16 | 12 | 34¹/8 | 578 | 12 |

■ *Iron Co. – C. & R. Lester – C. & R. Lester – 1970*

| 215⁵/8 | 24⁴/8 | 21³/8 | 17⁶/8 | 22⁵/8 | 5³/8 | 6 | 11 | 13 | 56³/8 | 578 | 12 |

■ *Huron Co. – Patrick L. Flanagan, Jr. – Patrick L. Flanagan, Jr. – 1990*

| 213¹/8 | 28⁷/8 | 28⁶/8 | 19 | 21¹/8 | 4⁷/8 | 4⁷/8 | 10 | 10 | 34³/8 | 664 | 14 |

■ *Michigan – Unknown – Keith H. Lundberg – PR 1941*

| 212³/8 | 24⁶/8 | 23⁶/8 | 18²/8 | 22¹/8 | 5²/8 | 5 | 10 | 12 | 40⁷/8 | 697 | 15 |

■ *Alger Co. – Karl Beck – Rick Johnson – 1934*

| 212¹/8 | 26 | 25⁷/8 | 21⁴/8 | 24³/8 | 6¹/8 | 5⁷/8 | 12 | 11 | 30⁷/8 | 709 | 16 |

■ *Clinton Co. – Kenneth V. Montgomery – Kenneth V. Montgomery – 1997*

| 212 | 29 | 27⁴/8 | 23⁶/8 | 26⁵/8 | 6⁷/8 | 6⁵/8 | 8 | 9 | 22⁶/8 | 717 | 17 |

■ *Iron Co. – Ben Komblevicz – Duane K. Wenzel – 1942*

| 211 | 27 | 26⁴/8 | 19³/8 | 22¹/8 | 4⁴/8 | 4⁴/8 | 9 | 10 | 16³/8 | 764 | 18 |

■ *Lenawee Co. – Paul T. Kintner – Paul T. Kintner – 1996*

| 210⁴/8 | 31 | 29²/8 | 21 | 23³/8 | 6 | 5⁵/8 | 10 | 11 | 21 | 791 | 19 |

■ *Allegan Co. – Bruce A. Maurer – Bruce A. Maurer – 1997*

Score	Length of Main Beam Right / Left ■ Location of Kill – Hunter – Owner – Date Killed	Inside Spread	Greatest Spread	Circumference at Smallest Place Between Burr and First Point Right / Left		Number of Points Right / Left		Lengths Abnormal Points	All-Time Rank	State Rank
210¹/₈	23⁶/₈ 24¹/₈	20²/₈	22⁵/₈	5⁴/₈	5¹/₈	9	10	36⁷/₈	808	20
	■ Macomb Co. – Bob H. Dismuke – Bob H. Dismuke – 1992									
209⁵/₈	24⁴/₈ 25³/₈	21	24⁵/₈	5²/₈	5¹/₈	10	10	44⁷/₈	840	21
	■ Livingston Co. – Michel A. LaFountain – Michel A. LaFountain – 2000									
209¹/₈	26³/₈ 26³/₈	19¹/₈	21³/₈	5⁴/₈	5⁴/₈	10	8	23⁶/₈	863	22
	■ Keweenaw Co. – Nathan E. Ruonavaara – Nathan E. Ruonavaara – 1946									
206⁴/₈	21¹/₈ 21¹/₈	16⁶/₈	22⁶/₈	5⁷/₈	5⁷/₈	10	12	36⁶/₈	1043	23
	■ Chippewa Co. – John Nevins – Bass Pro Shops – PR 1904									
203⁷/₈	23 18⁷/₈	16²/₈	21⁷/₈	4³/₈	4⁴/₈	11	14	60¹/₈	1231	24
	■ Eaton Co. – Mark R. Janousek – Mark R. Janousek – 1991									
203⁶/₈	23⁵/₈ 24⁶/₈	14⁵/₈	18²/₈	5¹/₈	4⁷/₈	11	8	37¹/₈	1237	25
	■ Dickinson Co. – Harold Eskil – Bass Pro Shops – 1929									
203⁶/₈	23⁶/₈ 24⁶/₈	19⁶/₈	22⁴/₈	5⁴/₈	5⁴/₈	10	8	18⁶/₈	1237	25
	■ Washtenaw Co. – Ronald R. Chabot – Ronald R. Chabot – 1996									
202³/₈	27²/₈ 27⁵/₈	22⁴/₈	25⁵/₈	5	5²/₈	11	15	21¹/₈	1362†	27†
	■ Keweenaw Co. – Bernard J. Jackovich – Bernard J. Jackovich – 2000									
202²/₈	25⁴/₈ 24³/₈	17⁵/₈	21²/₈	5	5¹/₈	9	9	17⁵/₈	1377	28
	■ Lenawee Co. – Fredrick M. Hood, Jr. – Fredrick M. Hood, Jr. – 1988									
201⁷/₈	27 26⁵/₈	21	26	4⁴/₈	4⁴/₈	12	8	25⁷/₈	1410†	29†
	■ Michigan – Unknown – Steve Crossley – 1945									
201⁵/₈	27 26⁶/₈	18	23⁷/₈	5⁶/₈	5⁶/₈	15	16	40⁷/₈	1427	30
	■ Charlevoix Co. – Robert V. Doerr – Robert V. Doerr – 1973									
201⁵/₈	25¹/₈ 24⁷/₈	19⁷/₈	22⁶/₈	6³/₈	6¹/₈	7	8	23⁴/₈	1427	30
	■ Baraga Co. – Dennis D. Bess – Dennis D. Bess – 1981									
201³/₈	24⁶/₈ 26⁵/₈	18¹/₈	22⁶/₈	4⁶/₈	4⁵/₈	12	10	28²/₈	1461†	32†
	■ Dickinson Co. – Ludvic Riihimaki – Mary J. Wellman – 1948									
201²/₈	24⁶/₈ 26⁵/₈	18¹/₈	22⁶/₈	4⁶/₈	4⁵/₈	12	10	28¹/₈	1478	33
	■ Dickinson Co. – Unknown – Gene R. Barlament – 1948									
201¹/₈	25²/₈ 26¹/₈	20¹/₈	27⁷/₈	5⁴/₈	5¹/₈	9	9	40⁴/₈	1489	34
	■ Jackson Co. – Steven G. Crocker – Steven G. Crocker – 1989									
201	22⁴/₈ 22⁷/₈	15²/₈	20¹/₈	5³/₈	5³/₈	14	12	43	1500	35
	■ Delta Co. – Ernest B. Fosterling – Ernest B. Fosterling – 1953									
200³/₈	25⁶/₈ 25⁷/₈	20³/₈	24³/₈	4⁴/₈	4⁵/₈	8	8	25⁴/₈	1556	36
	■ Branch Co. – Mitchell S. Brock – Mitchell S. Brock – 1995									
195⁵/₈	24⁷/₈ 23⁵/₈	21²/₈	25¹/₈	5⁷/₈	5⁷/₈	8	7	23¹/₈	1621	37
	■ Baraga Co. – William Simula – Kenneth J. Harjala – 1925									
193³/₈	20 17¹/₈	18⁵/₈	21⁷/₈	4⁷/₈	4⁵/₈	17	12	76⁶/₈	1639	38
	■ Van Buren Co. – Michael A. DeRosa – Michael A. DeRosa – 1989									
192²/₈	27⁷/₈ 26⁷/₈	24⁷/₈	27⁴/₈	5⁴/₈	5⁵/₈	9	9	29⁷/₈	1649	39
	■ Delta Co. – Derwood Moore – Michael Waldvogel – 1977									
192²/₈	26¹/₈ 26³/₈	18¹/₈	22³/₈	5²/₈	5³/₈	11	11	45⁷/₈	1649	39
	■ Washtenaw Co. – Donald W. Bollinger – Donald W. Bollinger – 1998									

Score	Length of Main Beam Right	Left	Inside Spread	Greatest Spread	Circumference at Smallest Place Between Burr and First Point Right	Left	Number of Points Right	Left	Lengths Abnormal Points	All-Time Rank	State Rank
	■ Location of Kill – Hunter – Owner – Date Killed										
$198^5/_8$	$26^7/_8$	$26^1/_8$	$18^3/_8$	$22^2/_8$	$5^4/_8$	$5^5/_8$	11	13	$19^2/_8$	1716	41
	■ Iron Co. – Eino Macki – Bass Pro Shops – 1930										
$198^4/_8$	$25^2/_8$	$25^6/_8$	$19^2/_8$	$25^4/_8$	$4^5/_8$	$4^6/_8$	10	11	$29^2/_8$	1736	42
	■ Cheboygan Co. – Maurice G. Fullerton – Robert G. Fullerton – 1943										
$198^1/_8$	$22^3/_8$	$21^6/_8$	18	$25^7/_8$	5	$4^6/_8$	9	12	$34^7/_8$	1785	43
	■ Calhoun Co. – William D. Vickers – William D. Vickers – 1994										
$198^1/_8$	$28^3/_8$	$26^5/_8$	$20^5/_8$	$26^5/_8$	$5^4/_8$	$5^5/_8$	10	14	$34^4/_8$	1785	43
	■ Chippewa Co. – Timothy Spence – Timothy Spence – 1995										
$197^5/_8$	20	24	18	$24^2/_8$	$8^4/_8$	$4^7/_8$	12	8	$68^5/_8$	1847	45
	■ Luce Co. – Sid Jones – Jim Deavereaux – 1917										
$197^2/_8$	$23^1/_8$	$22^7/_8$	$20^3/_8$	$23^5/_8$	$5^5/_8$	$5^3/_8$	10	10	$18^3/_8$	1901†	46†
	■ Van Buren Co. – John Pierson – John Pierson – 2000										
$197^2/_8$	$27^7/_8$	$26^5/_8$	$19^2/_8$	$22^6/_8$	$5^6/_8$	$5^6/_8$	11	9	$25^2/_8$	1901	46
	■ Sanilac Co. – Charles E. Goodfellow – Charles E. Goodfellow – 1998										
197	$27^5/_8$	$27^6/_8$	$22^7/_8$	$25^1/_8$	$5^1/_8$	$5^3/_8$	8	8	$22^5/_8$	1939	48
	■ Houghton Co. – Edward Heinonen – Bass Pro Shops – 1970										
$196^7/_8$	$25^1/_8$	$25^1/_8$	$18^5/_8$	$20^7/_8$	$4^6/_8$	$4^4/_8$	11	11	$30^6/_8$	1950	49
	■ Jackson Co. – Herb C. Miller, Jr. – Herb C. Miller, Jr. – 1993										
$196^5/_8$	$26^3/_8$	$27^3/_8$	$15^5/_8$	$22^2/_8$	$5^6/_8$	$5^6/_8$	11	11	40	1985	50
	■ Delta Co. – Frans Kuula – Bass Pro Shops – 1967										
$196^3/_8$	27	$26^1/_8$	$17^7/_8$	$20^4/_8$	$5^7/_8$	$5^6/_8$	8	7	$15^2/_8$	2010	51
	■ Houghton Co. – Robert L. Marr – Robert L. Marr – 1990										
$196^2/_8$	$22^4/_8$	$22^4/_8$	$20^4/_8$	$21^4/_8$	$4^6/_8$	$4^6/_8$	14	12	$38^4/_8$	2028	52
	■ Delta Co. – William H. Johnson – Bass Pro Shops – PR 1951										
196	$22^3/_8$	$24^5/_8$	$16^5/_8$	$17^3/_8$	$5^1/_8$	$5^2/_8$	13	10	$28^7/_8$	2059	53
	■ Luce Co. – Herbert Miller, Sr. – Bass Pro Shops – 1945										
$195^7/_8$	30	$30^1/_8$	$21^4/_8$	$23^6/_8$	$4^7/_8$	5	7	8	$17^1/_8$	2076	54
	■ Jackson Co. – Picked Up – Ronald D. Murphy – 1984										
$195^6/_8$	$24^1/_8$	$24^4/_8$	$15^6/_8$	$13^4/_8$	$6^1/_8$	$5^6/_8$	7	11	$21^4/_8$	2094	55
	■ Ontonagon Co. – Andrew Pietila – Bass Pro Shops – PR 1920										
$195^5/_8$	$24^1/_8$	$23^5/_8$	$21^7/_8$	$26^2/_8$	$4^4/_8$	$4^2/_8$	12	11	$47^4/_8$	2116	56
	■ Livingston Co. – Patrick M. Harris – Patrick M. Harris – 1995										
$195^4/_8$	$25^6/_8$	24	$15^3/_8$	$21^3/_8$	$4^3/_8$	$4^3/_8$	11	9	$31^7/_8$	2134	57
	■ Allegan Co. – Jason A. Newman – Jason A. Newman – 1994										
195	$26^3/_8$	$25^3/_8$	$20^2/_8$	$24^7/_8$	5	5	7	8	$35^2/_8$	2233	58
	■ Dickinson Co. – Ed Hogberg – Michael Waldvogel – PR 1921										
195	$27^1/_8$	$27^6/_8$	$19^3/_8$	$22^6/_8$	$5^3/_8$	$5^4/_8$	7	7	$21^5/_8$	2233	58
	■ Lenawee Co. – Craig Rodosalewicz – Craig Rodosalewicz – 1998										
192	$24^7/_8$	$27^4/_8$	$13^3/_8$	$18^3/_8$	$5^5/_8$	$5^4/_8$	9	9	$23^3/_8$	2344	60
	■ Menominee Co. – Walter W.E. Lange – William H. Lange – 1949										
$191^2/_8$	$23^6/_8$	$23^2/_8$	$17^1/_8$	$22^4/_8$	$4^5/_8$	5	9	10	$33^7/_8$	2371	61
	■ Alger Co. – David Walther – David Walther – 1990										

Score	Length of Main Beam		Inside Spread	Greatest Spread	Circumference at Smallest Place Between Burr and First Point		Number of Points		Lengths Abnormal Points	All-Time Rank	State Rank
	Right	Left			Right	Left	Right	Left			
	■ *Location of Kill – Hunter – Owner – Date Killed*										
188²/8	25	24¹/8	18²/8	20¹/8	4⁷/8	4⁷/8	7	8	25	2489	62
	■ *Cass Co. – Robert H. Watson – Robert H. Watson – 1983*										
187³/8	26⁵/8	27⁶/8	22	25	5⁶/8	5⁶/8	7	7	12³/8	2528	63
	■ *Gogebic Co. – James W. Ansami – James W. Ansami – 1998*										
186⁴/8	23⁴/8	26³/8	18³/8	21⁶/8	5	5	8	6	46⁵/8	2568	64
	■ *Calhoun Co. – Robert G. Day – Robert G. Day – 1988*										
186¹/8	26²/8	24⁷/8	20⁶/8	21⁴/8	5⁴/8	5⁵/8	8	8	15⁷/8	2581	65
	■ *Eaton Co. – John A. Serniak, Jr. – John A. Serniak, Jr. – 1985*										
186	24⁷/8	24	21³/8	24	5³/8	5³/8	7	7	24³/8	2586	66
	■ *Calhoun Co. – Leland D. Putnam – Leland D. Putnam – 1997*										

† The scores and ranking for trophies from the 25th Awards Entry Period are not final until the banquet is held on June 19, 2004.

MINNESOTA
RECORD WHITETAILS

380 Typical whitetail deer entries
285 Non-typical whitetail deer entries
7,265 Total whitetail deer entries

MINNESOTA
STATE RECORD
Typical Whitetail Deer
Score: 202
Location: Beltrami Co.
Hunter: John A. Breen
Owner: Bass Pro Shops
Date: 1918

Photograph courtesy of Larry L. Huffman,
Legendary Whitetails

0 Entries
1-2 Entries
3-5 Entries
6-10 Entries
11+ Entries

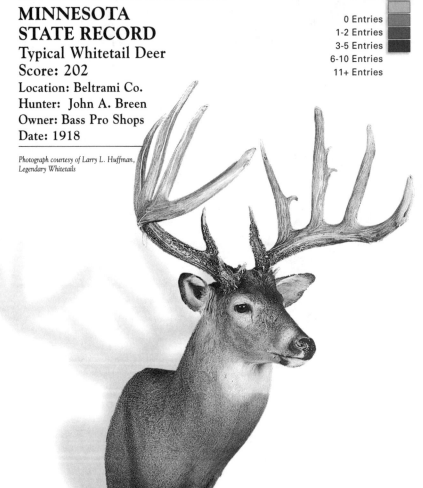

**MINNESOTA
STATE RECORD**
Non-Typical Whitetail Deer
Score: 268⁵/₈
Location: Norman Co.
Hunter: Mitchell A. Vakoch
Owner: Bass Pro Shops
Date: 1974

Photograph courtesy of Gale Sup

MINNESOTA

TYPICAL WHITETAIL DEER

Score	Length of Main Beam Right Left	Inside Spread	Greatest Spread	Circumference at Smallest Place Between Burr and First Point Right Left		Number of Points Right Left		Lengths Abnormal Points	All-Time Rank	State Rank
	■ *Location of Kill – Hunter – Owner – Date Killed*									
202	31²/8 31	23⁵/8	26⁷/8	5⁷/8 6		8 8		8³/8	8	1
	■ *Beltrami Co. – John A. Breen – Bass Pro Shops – 1918*									
201	26²/8 26²/8	15⁵/8	18¹/8	4⁵/8 4⁷/8		8 6		1³/8	10	2
	■ *Kittson Co. – Wayne G. Stewart – Wayne G. Stewart – 1961*									
199²/8	28⁷/8 29	25⁶/8	29⁴/8	5 5¹/8		6 6			16	3
	■ *Lake of the Woods Co. – Vernon Jensen – Vernon Jensen – 1954*									
197⁶/8	29²/8 30	20⁴/8	23	5⁶/8 5⁷/8		6 5		1⁴/8	23	4
	■ *Wright Co. – Curtis F. Van Lith – Bass Pro Shops – 1986*									
195⁷/8	26⁴/8 27¹/8	21¹/8	24⁵/8	4¹/8 4¹/8		6 6			34	5
	■ *Anoka Co. – Barry Peterson – Barry Peterson – 1995*									
195⁵/8	28⁴/8 27⁶/8	22¹/8	24⁵/8	5⁶/8 5⁷/8		6 7		2	35	6
	■ *Marshall Co. – Robert Sands – Robert Sands – 1960*									
193²/8	28⁶/8 28⁶/8	21²/8	23⁶/8	4⁴/8 4⁴/8		5 7		2⁴/8	53	7
	■ *Itasca Co. – Picked Up – Paul M. Shaw – 1935*									
192²/8	28²/8 28⁷/8	23⁵/8	25⁷/8	5³/8 5⁴/8		6 5		1⁷/8	67	8
	■ *Pope Co. – Roger D. Syrstad – B&C National Collection – 1989*									
192	27¹/8 27²/8	19	22⁴/8	4⁵/8 4⁵/8		6 6			70	9
	■ *Pine Co. – Frank Worlickey – Robert Worlickey – 1952*									
192	24³/8 23⁵/8	17	20⁷/8	4⁷/8 4⁶/8		7 7			70	9
	■ *Clay Co. – Mark L. Peterson – Mark L. Peterson – 1984*									
191⁵/8	26 26¹/8	21⁷/8	24⁵/8	5 5¹/8		5 7		3⁴/8	78	11
	■ *Goodhue Co. – David C. Klatt – Bass Pro Shops – 1985*									
189³/8	25⁷/8 24¹/8	23¹/8	26⁴/8	6²/8 6²/8		6 7		1²/8	120	12
	■ *Fillmore Co. – Tom Norby – Tom Norby – 1975*									
189²/8	29⁷/8 29	22³/8	26⁶/8	4⁴/8 4⁵/8		7 6		5⁵/8	125	13
	■ *Hubbard Co. – Hans Lorentzen – Danny L. Cole – PR 1944*									
188	27¹/8 28⁶/8	19	24²/8	5¹/8 5²/8		6 7		2²/8	152	14
	■ *Marshall Co. – Paul J. Wolf – Paul J. Wolf – 1991*									
188	27⁶/8 28⁴/8	21²/8	24⁴/8	5⁶/8 6		7 7		6⁶/8	152	14
	■ *Chisago Co. – John B. Nelson – John B. Nelson – 1992*									
187⁶/8	28 28⁴/8	20⁶/8	24⁴/8	5⁶/8 6¹/8		6 5		3⁴/8	160	16
	■ *Houston Co. – Donald M. Grant – Donald M. Grant – 1978*									
187⁵/8	25²/8 25⁵/8	19²/8	22³/8	5²/8 5³/8		6 8		3³/8	165	17
	■ *Winona Co. – Ken W. Koenig – Ken W. Koenig – 1976*									
187⁴/8	28³/8 27	24⁶/8	28⁶/8	5³/8 5³/8		8 5		6²/8	172	18
	■ *Winona Co. – Dan Groebner – Dan Groebner – 1974*									
187²/8	29 28⁵/8	26⁴/8	28⁴/8	5²/8 5³/8		5 5			180	19
	■ *Lyon Co. – Lynn Jackson – Dick Rossum – 1967*									

Score	Length of Main Beam Right	Left	Inside Spread	Greatest Spread	Circumference at Smallest Place Between Burr and First Point Right	Left	Number of Points Right	Left	Lengths Abnormal Points	All-Time Rank	State Rank
									■ Location of Kill – Hunter – Owner – Date Killed		
$186\frac{6}{8}$	$26\frac{7}{8}$	$26\frac{2}{8}$	19	$22\frac{5}{8}$	$5\frac{5}{8}$	$5\frac{5}{8}$	8	7		200	20
		■ St. Louis Co. – Unknown – George W. Flaim – PR 1983									
$186\frac{4}{8}$	$27\frac{6}{8}$	26	22	$24\frac{4}{8}$	$5\frac{1}{8}$	$5\frac{2}{8}$	6	7	$1\frac{4}{8}$	205	21
		■ Becker Co. – Ilo Dugger – Jeff Dugger – 1930									
$186\frac{4}{8}$	$26\frac{3}{8}$	$26\frac{5}{8}$	$19\frac{6}{8}$	$21\frac{7}{8}$	$4\frac{4}{8}$	$4\frac{4}{8}$	7	7	$2\frac{6}{8}$	205	21
		■ Pine Co. – Unknown – Ralph Blessum – PR 1970									
$186\frac{3}{8}$	$26\frac{1}{8}$	$26\frac{3}{8}$	$18\frac{6}{8}$	$21\frac{5}{8}$	$4\frac{7}{8}$	$4\frac{7}{8}$	7	5	$1\frac{7}{8}$	210	23
		■ Otter Tail Co. – Robert Ames – David R. Brigan – 1977									
$186\frac{1}{8}$	$28\frac{4}{8}$	$27\frac{6}{8}$	$18\frac{5}{8}$	$21\frac{1}{8}$	$5\frac{6}{8}$	6	5	5		228	24
		■ St. Louis Co. – Unknown – George W. Flaim – 1980									
$186\frac{1}{8}$	$27\frac{4}{8}$	$26\frac{5}{8}$	$20\frac{7}{8}$	$23\frac{1}{8}$	5	$5\frac{6}{8}$	5	6		228	24
		■ St. Louis Co. – Mark O. DuLong – Mark O. DuLong – 1988									
186	$30\frac{5}{8}$	$31\frac{3}{8}$	$26\frac{3}{8}$	$30\frac{6}{8}$	$5\frac{1}{8}$	5	5	9	$10\frac{1}{8}$	238	26
		■ Itasca Co. – Knud W. Jensen – Bass Pro Shops – 1955									
$185\frac{7}{8}$	$28\frac{5}{8}$	$28\frac{3}{8}$	$20\frac{5}{8}$	$22\frac{7}{8}$	$5\frac{2}{8}$	$5\frac{2}{8}$	5	5		244	27
		■ Beltrami Co. – Picked Up – Jerome D. Erdahl – 1987									
$185\frac{4}{8}$	$26\frac{6}{8}$	$27\frac{1}{8}$	22	$24\frac{3}{8}$	$4\frac{5}{8}$	$4\frac{5}{8}$	6	6		251	28
		■ Otter Tail Co. – Orris T. Neirby – Orris T. Neirby – 1942									
$185\frac{4}{8}$	29	$28\frac{1}{8}$	$24\frac{6}{8}$	$26\frac{6}{8}$	$5\frac{2}{8}$	$5\frac{3}{8}$	5	6	$2\frac{6}{8}$	251	28
		■ Benton Co. – Clifford G. Knier – Clifford G. Knier – 1992									
$185\frac{3}{8}$	$26\frac{4}{8}$	27	$19\frac{4}{8}$	$22\frac{4}{8}$	$5\frac{1}{8}$	$5\frac{2}{8}$	7	10	$1\frac{1}{8}$	256	30
		■ Marshall Co. – Donald W. Wilkens – Donald W. Wilkens – 1973									
185	$25\frac{7}{8}$	$25\frac{7}{8}$	19	21	$4\frac{7}{8}$	$4\frac{7}{8}$	7	7	$1\frac{2}{8}$	272	31
		■ Winona Co. – Ronald Bunke – B., S., & B. Bunke – 1973									
$184\frac{6}{8}$	$25\frac{4}{8}$	$25\frac{2}{8}$	$19\frac{4}{8}$	$21\frac{4}{8}$	$5\frac{1}{8}$	$5\frac{2}{8}$	7	7	$3\frac{2}{8}$	285	32
		■ Morrison Co. – Mr. Holt – Michael J. Kampa – PR 1960									
$184\frac{3}{8}$	27	26	$17\frac{7}{8}$	20	$4\frac{6}{8}$	$4\frac{6}{8}$	5	5		313	33
		■ St. Louis Co. – Unknown – Dick Rossum – 1935									
$184\frac{1}{8}$	$26\frac{7}{8}$	$27\frac{6}{8}$	21	$23\frac{6}{8}$	5	5	8	7	$4\frac{5}{8}$	327	34
		■ Marshall Co. – Alvin C. Westerlund – Alvin C. Westerlund – 1953									
$183\frac{6}{8}$	$26\frac{7}{8}$	$26\frac{4}{8}$	$21\frac{2}{8}$	24	$5\frac{7}{8}$	$5\frac{5}{8}$	5	6	$2\frac{4}{8}$	350†	35†
		■ Winona Co. – Picked Up – Kevin J. Nelsen – 1967									
$183\frac{3}{8}$	$26\frac{7}{8}$	$27\frac{2}{8}$	$19\frac{7}{8}$	$22\frac{5}{8}$	$5\frac{3}{8}$	$5\frac{2}{8}$	6	6		365	36
		■ St. Louis Co. – Unknown – George W. Flaim – 1982									
$183\frac{2}{8}$	$25\frac{5}{8}$	26	19	$21\frac{2}{8}$	$4\frac{1}{8}$	$4\frac{4}{8}$	6	6		378	37
		■ St. Louis Co. – Unknown – Kenneth Wilson – PR 1917									
$183\frac{1}{8}$	$26\frac{2}{8}$	$26\frac{5}{8}$	$20\frac{3}{8}$	$22\frac{5}{8}$	$5\frac{4}{8}$	$5\frac{4}{8}$	6	6	$3\frac{4}{8}$	385†	38†
		■ Chisago Co. – Timothy L. Ryan – Timothy L. Ryan – 2000									
$182\frac{7}{8}$	$26\frac{4}{8}$	$25\frac{6}{8}$	$19\frac{2}{8}$	$22\frac{1}{8}$	$5\frac{3}{8}$	$5\frac{3}{8}$	6	7	$12\frac{1}{8}$	401	39
		■ Lyon Co. – Jim Anderson – LuAnn Anderson – 1975									
$182\frac{4}{8}$	$28\frac{3}{8}$	$27\frac{1}{8}$	$23\frac{4}{8}$	$26\frac{3}{8}$	$5\frac{5}{8}$	$5\frac{5}{8}$	7	7	10	431	40
		■ Kanabec Co. – Steven R. Berg – Steven R. Berg – 1973									

Score	Length of Main Beam Right Left	Inside Spread	Greatest Spread	Circumference at Smallest Place Between Burr and First Point Right Left	Number of Points Right Left	Lengths Abnormal Points	All-Time Rank	State Rank
	■ Location of Kill – Hunter – Owner – Date Killed							
182³/₈	29⁶/₈ 27⁶/₈	18³/₈	20⁷/₈	5¹/₈ 5¹/₈	5 5		438†	41†
	■ Polk Co. – Benjamin D. Faldet – Benjamin D. Faldet – 2000							
182³/₈	28¹/₈ 27³/₈	20⁵/₈	24	5⁴/₈ 5⁴/₈	5 5		438	41
	■ Itasca Co. – Harry Haug – Harry Haug – 1959							
182³/₈	28²/₈ 27²/₈	17¹/₈	19³/₈	5²/₈ 5⁴/₈	6 6		438	41
	■ St. Louis Co. – Unknown – John R. Steffes, Sr. – PR 1960							
182³/₈	25⁴/₈ 25⁶/₈	21³/₈	24¹/₈	6 5⁶/₈	5 6	2⁴/₈	438	41
	■ Freeborn Co. – Robert H. Dowd – Robert H. Dowd – 1969							
182²/₈	27¹/₈ 26⁶/₈	19³/₈	21²/₈	4⁷/₈ 5¹/₈	6 6	2³/₈	450	45
	■ Nicollet Co. – T.J. Merkley – T.J. Merkley – 1966							
182²/₈	24⁴/₈ 25⁴/₈	17²/₈	20	5⁴/₈ 6	6 6		450	45
	■ Stearns Co. – Michael G. Maki – Michael G. Maki – 1988							
182	28¹/₈ 28⁴/₈	22⁶/₈	25¹/₈	4⁴/₈ 4⁵/₈	5 5		469	47
	■ St. Louis Co. – Unknown – George W. Flaim – 1975							
182	24⁷/₈ 24⁵/₈	18⁴/₈	21⁴/₈	5⁶/₈ 5⁴/₈	5 5		469	47
	■ Polk Co. – E. Norgaard, M. Sorenson, D. Sorenson & K. Oraskovich – E. Norgaard, M. Sorenson & D. Sorenson – 1986							
181⁷/₈	26⁵/₈ 26⁵/₈	20⁴/₈	22²/₈	5²/₈ 5²/₈	7 7	6⁷/₈	478†	49†
	■ Washington Co. – Daniel F. Gallagher – Daniel F. Gallagher – 2001							
181⁷/₈	26⁷/₈ 27¹/₈	23³/₈	25⁵/₈	5⁴/₈ 5³/₈	8 7	10⁶/₈	478	49
	■ Cottonwood Co. – Picked Up – MN Div. of Fish & Wildl. – 1963							
181⁷/₈	24⁵/₈ 25¹/₈	26²/₈	28	5⁷/₈ 5³/₈	7 7	5²/₈	478	49
	■ Todd Co. – Alvin Tvrdik – Alvin Tvrdik – 1965							
181⁷/₈	27 24⁷/₈	22¹/₈	24⁴/₈	4⁷/₈ 5	6 7	2	478	49
	■ Wright Co. – Craig S. Hansen – Craig S. Hansen – 1992							
181⁶/₈	26¹/₈ 26⁴/₈	17⁶/₈	19⁶/₈	6 6¹/₈	5 5		492	53
	■ Wabasha Co. – Lee G. Partington – Lee G. Partington – 1971							
181⁴/₈	28⁴/₈ 27⁷/₈	22	24⁵/₈	5¹/₈ 5³/₈	5 5		516	54
	■ Wadena Co. – Lester Zentner, Jr. – E.E. Patson – 1962							
181³/₈	26²/₈ 27⁶/₈	19³/₈	21⁶/₈	5 5	5 5		528	55
	■ Houston Co. – Picked Up – Robert A. Morken – 1980							
181³/₈	26 25	17⁵/₈	19⁶/₈	4⁵/₈ 4⁵/₈	6 6		528	55
	■ Winona Co. – Kenneth W. Schreiber – Kenneth W. Schreiber – 1980							
181²/₈	26⁵/₈ 26³/₈	23²/₈	25³/₈	6¹/₈ 6³/₈	5 5		540†	57†
	■ Morrison Co. – Scott A. Shonka – Scott A. Shonka – 2000							
181¹/₈	27¹/₈ 27¹/₈	21⁶/₈	23⁶/₈	5²/₈ 5⁴/₈	7 7	9⁵/₈	551	58
	■ Elk River – John E. Bush – Bass Pro Shops – 1870							
181¹/₈	27³/₈ 28	20⁷/₈	25⁷/₈	5²/₈ 5³/₈	6 7		551	58
	■ Polk Co. – Henry Cook – Steven D. Cook – 1938							
181	25⁷/₈ 24⁶/₈	22³/₈	24³/₈	4⁷/₈ 5³/₈	6 8	7³/₈	563	60
	■ Beltrami Co. – Robert C. Shaw – Robert C. Shaw – 1910							
181	26⁵/₈ 26²/₈	21²/₈	26	6²/₈ 6³/₈	7 8	5⁶/₈	563	60
	■ Lac qui Parle Co. – Mary A. Barvels – Mary A. Barvels – 1978							

Score	Length of Main Beam Right	Left	Inside Spread	Greatest Spread	Circumference at Smallest Place Between Burr and First Point Right	Left	Number of Points Right	Left	Lengths Abnormal Points	All-Time Rank	State Rank
	■ Location of Kill – Hunter – Owner – Date Killed										
180⁷/8	28⁵/8	27⁷/8	22¹/8	25¹/8	5²/8	5³/8	5	6	6	573	62
	■ Polk Co. – Daniel Omdahl – Daniel Omdahl – 1987										
180⁶/8	25⁴/8	25⁷/8	19	21³/8	5²/8	5¹/8	5	5		587	63
	■ Marshall Co. – Scott T. Rabehl – Scott T. Rabehl – 1987										
180⁵/8	27³/8	27⁴/8	17⁵/8	20⁶/8	4³/8	4⁴/8	5	5		599†	64†
	■ Wabasha Co. – Bradley S. Kreofsky – Bradley S. Kreofsky – 2000										
180⁴/8	25⁶/8	26²/8	17⁴/8	19³/8	4³/8	4³/8	7	6	1	613	65
	■ Carver Co. – Stephen M. Polston – Stephen M. Polston – 1985										
180⁴/8	25⁵/8	25⁵/8	22⁵/8	25⁷/8	5	5	6	7	5⁷/8	613	65
	■ Olmsted Co. – Thomas C. Kroening – Thomas C. Kroening – 1998										
180³/8	26⁵/8	26⁴/8	16³/8	19	5⁴/8	5⁴/8	7	6	1²/8	630†	67†
	■ Minnesota – Unknown – Isaak Walton League – PR 1901										
180³/8	26⁶/8	25⁵/8	20¹/8	22⁴/8	6³/8	6²/8	6	7	6⁶/8	630	67
	■ Aitkin Co. – Donald J. Sorenson – Donald J. Sorenson – 1963										
180³/8	30	29⁵/8	22³/8	24⁵/8	4⁵/8	4⁵/8	6	8	5	630	67
	■ Meeker Co. – Stanley M. Messner – Stanley M. Messner – 1981										
180³/8	25¹/8	24⁴/8	20¹/8	22⁴/8	5	5	6	6		630	67
	■ St. Louis Co. – Unknown – George W. Flaim – PR 1992										
180³/8	27⁴/8	27¹/8	19⁵/8	21²/8	4⁴/8	4³/8	7	8	2⁶/8	630	67
	■ Dakota Co. – William E. Urbaniak – William E. Urbaniak – 1996										
180²/8	26⁶/8	26³/8	20²/8	22³/8	4⁷/8	4⁵/8	6	6		651	72
	■ Meeker Co. – Harold Nistler – William H. Lilienthal – PR 1975										
180¹/8	25¹/8	25¹/8	19¹/8	21⁶/8	5²/8	5²/8	6	6		669	73
	■ Cottonwood Co. – Charles C. Burnham – Charles C. Burnham – 1983										
180¹/8	24	24⁷/8	19⁴/8	24¹/8	5¹/8	5	7	5	1⁵/8	669	73
	■ Hubbard Co. – Larry D. Dierks – Larry D. Dierks – 1984										
180¹/8	26⁷/8	25⁵/8	18⁴/8	20⁷/8	4³/8	4⁵/8	6	5	1¹/8	669	73
	■ Rice Co. – Picked Up – Stephen L. Albers – 1998										
180	26⁵/8	26⁵/8	18²/8	20⁵/8	4⁷/8	5¹/8	6	6		688†	76†
	■ Winona Co. – James R. Walkes – James R. Walkes – 2001										
179⁷/8	26⁷/8	26⁶/8	21³/8	26	4³/8	4⁶/8	6	7	2⁴/8	705†	77†
	■ Beltrami Co. – Richard L. Dickinson – Richard L. Dickinson – 2001										
179⁷/8	26¹/8	26³/8	19⁴/8	21⁴/8	5³/8	5³/8	6	6	3⁷/8	705	77
	■ Nicollet Co. – Joe Welter – Joe Welter – 1987										
179⁶/8	27¹/8	29³/8	21²/8	23²/8	4⁷/8	5	7	7	2⁴/8	712	79
	■ Steele Co. – Elmer Janning – Elmer Janning – 1972										
179⁶/8	28¹/8	26⁴/8	22²/8	25²/8	4⁶/8	4⁶/8	6	5		712	79
	■ Aitkin Co. – Harland A. Kern – Harland A. Kern – 1973										
179³/8	26¹/8	26⁶/8	22	23²/8	4⁶/8	4⁶/8	8	6	5³/8	749	81
	■ Anoka Co. – Thomas M. Evertz – Thomas M. Evertz – 1996										
179²/8	28⁵/8	28⁵/8	20⁶/8	23⁴/8	5²/8	5³/8	6	5	2²/8	763	82
	■ Koochiching Co. – Ted Davis – Marc M. Jackson – 1963										

Score	Length of Main Beam Right Left		Inside Spread	Greatest Spread	Circumference at Smallest Place Between Burr and First Point Right Left		Number of Points Right Left		Lengths Abnormal Points	All-Time Rank	State Rank
					■ Location of Kill – Hunter – Owner – Date Killed						
179 1/8	27 3/8	27 7/8	21 3/8	23 7/8	5 7/8	5 7/8	5	6	3	779	83
	■ Renville Co. – Todd Swartz – Todd Swartz – 1984										
179	27 1/8	25 5/8	19 4/8	22 3/8	5 5/8	5 4/8	6	7	10 4/8	786	84
	■ Sherburne Co. – Victor Nagel – Victor Nagel – 1956										
179	27 6/8	27 6/8	17 4/8	22 2/8	4 4/8	4 3/8	6	6	6 6/8	786	84
	■ Benton Co. – Michael A. Gapinski – Michael A. Gapinski – 1991										
178 5/8	28 4/8	28 1/8	16 7/8	19 4/8	5 4/8	5 3/8	6	6		819	86
	■ St. Louis Co. – Picked Up – Jerome L. Schaller – 1962										
178 5/8	27 2/8	26 4/8	21 5/8	24 1/8	4 7/8	5	6	6		819	86
	■ St. Louis Co. – John Nordenstam – George W. Flaim – 1977										
178 5/8	25 4/8	25 5/8	22 7/8	25 4/8	4 4/8	4 4/8	5	5		819	86
	■ Itasca Co. – Gino P. Maccario – Gino P. Maccario – 1980										
178 5/8	25 5/8	26 1/8	20 1/8	22 1/8	4 5/8	4 5/8	8	8		819	86
	■ Roseau Co. – Jeffrey Benson – Jeffrey Benson – 1991										
178 4/8	26 6/8	26 1/8	28 2/8	29 7/8	5	4 7/8	5	5		850	90
	■ Beltrami Co. – Arthur I. Hill – Arthur A. Hill – 1954										
178 4/8	27 4/8	27 2/8	19 6/8	23 2/8	5 3/8	5 3/8	6	8	6	850	90
	■ Blue Earth Co. – Harry J. Baker – Harry J. Baker – 1991										
178 3/8	26 7/8	26 5/8	24 3/8	26 7/8	5 4/8	5 2/8	6	5	2	868	92
	■ Aitkin Co. – George E. Jenks – George E. Jenks – 1969										
178 3/8	26 5/8	26 3/8	19 7/8	25 2/8	5 3/8	4 3/8	5	5		868	92
	■ Fillmore Co. – Alanson W. Hamernik, Jr. – Alanson W. Hamernik, Jr. – 1970										
178 3/8	28 4/8	28 7/8	23 7/8	25 7/8	5 1/8	5 2/8	7	8	7 2/8	868	92
	■ Lincoln Co. – Larry Lustfield – Larry Lustfield – 1976										
178 2/8	25 7/8	25	23	24 6/8	5 5/8	5 5/8	7	5	2	891	95
	■ Pope Co. – Greg Kobbermann – Greg Kobbermann – 1976										
178 2/8	26 7/8	25 7/8	21 6/8	25 6/8	4 5/8	4 5/8	7	6	1 4/8	891	95
	■ Clay Co. – Darrin D. Tonsfeldt – Darrin D. Tonsfeldt – 1993										
178 2/8	28 3/8	28 7/8	19 4/8	22 4/8	5 3/8	5 4/8	8	7	7 4/8	891	95
	■ Kanabec Co. – Lennie L. Henning – Lennie L. Henning – 1999										
177 7/8	26 4/8	25 4/8	22 5/8	25 3/8	5	5	6	6	1 4/8	936†	98†
	■ Houston Co. – Oscar W. Bernsdorf – Roger Bernsdorf – 1959										
177 6/8	26 5/8	27 4/8	23 4/8	27	4 5/8	4 4/8	6	5	1 2/8	956	99
	■ Stearns Co. – Robert G. Schwarz – Robert G. Schwarz – 1975										
177 6/8	29	27 7/8	20	22 1/8	5 2/8	5 2/8	6	5		956	99
	■ St. Louis Co. – Ronald R. Anderson – Ronald R. Anderson – 1994										
177 5/8	26 5/8	25 5/8	19 7/8	22 4/8	5 1/8	5	6	5		972	101
	■ Crow Wing Co. – Gil Atwater – Donald McNevin – 1926										
177 5/8	26 2/8	26 6/8	22 6/8	24 4/8	4 7/8	4 7/8	7	6	1 3/8	972	101
	■ Wabasha Co. – Bruce J. Hall – Bruce J. Hall – 1972										
177 5/8	23 4/8	25 7/8	20 7/8	22 3/8	5 1/8	5 4/8	7	9	11	972	101
	■ Morrison Co. – Jeanne Backowski-Jensen – Jeanne Backowski-Jensen – 1991										
177 5/8	25 7/8	25 3/8	18 1/8	20 3/8	4 6/8	4 6/8	7	6		972	101

Score	Length of Main Beam Right	Left	Inside Spread	Greatest Spread	Circumference at Smallest Place Between Burr and First Point Right	Left	Number of Points Right	Left	Lengths Abnormal Points	All-Time Rank	State Rank
	■ *Location of Kill – Hunter – Owner – Date Killed*										
	■ *Kittson Co. – Picked Up – Cabela's, Inc. – 1993*										
177⁴/₈	28⁵/₈	29²/₈	18³/₈	22⁶/₈	5⁵/₈	5⁵/₈	6	9	10⁷/₈	993	105
	■ *Cass Co. – Larry K. Sherman – Larry K. Sherman – 1964*										
177⁴/₈	28²/₈	28³/₈	22⁴/₈	27⁵/₈	5⁶/₈	5⁶/₈	5	6	1	993	105
	■ *Beltrami Co. – Sheldon M. Stockdale – Sheldon M. Stockdale – 1968*										
177⁴/₈	28³/₈	28⁴/₈	23⁵/₈	26⁶/₈	4⁴/₈	4³/₈	8	5	4⁵/₈	993	105
	■ *Otter Tail Co. – Robert J. Perszyk – Robert J. Perszyk – 1985*										
177²/₈	27⁵/₈	28³/₈	19⁴/₈	21²/₈	4⁶/₈	4⁶/₈	7	7	4⁶/₈	1025	108
	■ *Pine Co. – C. Foster & E. Kepler – Lois Youngbauer – 1930*										
177¹/₈	25²/₈	25⁴/₈	21¹/₈	24³/₈	4⁵/₈	4³/₈	7	7		1048	109
	■ *Marshall Co. – Dennis W. Severson – Dennis W. Severson – 1954*										
177¹/₈	28	26⁷/₈	21¹/₈	23⁶/₈	5⁷/₈	5⁷/₈	5	5		1048	109
	■ *Kittson Co. – Unknown – George W. Flaim – 1987*										
177	26²/₈	25⁶/₈	19⁷/₈	23⁷/₈	5	5¹/₈	8	10	10³/₈	1066	111
	■ *Kandiyohi Co. – Dale E. Nelson – Scott Nelson – 1949*										
177	23⁴/₈	24²/₈	16⁶/₈	18⁷/₈	4⁷/₈	5	6	7		1066	111
	■ *St. Louis Co. – Chuck Perkins – Chuck Perkins – 1964*										
176⁶/₈	26³/₈	26	19²/₈	23²/₈	4⁴/₈	4⁴/₈	6	6		1103	113
	■ *Winona Co. – Harry M. Timm – Harry M. Timm – 1964*										
176⁶/₈	26⁵/₈	26⁴/₈	21⁴/₈	25²/₈	5²/₈	5³/₈	5	5		1103	113
	■ *Pine Co. – Kim Shira – Kim Shira – 1977*										
176⁶/₈	28⁶/₈	28	19⁶/₈	22⁴/₈	5²/₈	5¹/₈	5	5		1103	113
	■ *Cottonwood Co. – Cory S. Paplow – Cory S. Paplow – 1999*										
176⁵/₈	27⁴/₈	27²/₈	20⁵/₈	22⁷/₈	5¹/₈	5¹/₈	5	5		1134	116
	■ *Winona Co. – Robert J. Haessig – Robert J. Haessig – 1961*										
176⁵/₈	26¹/₈	25⁷/₈	18⁷/₈	20⁷/₈	4⁶/₈	4⁶/₈	6	6	5⁶/₈	1134	116
	■ *St. Louis Co. – Unknown – Allen Valley – PR 1970*										
176⁵/₈	25²/₈	25²/₈	18³/₈	20⁵/₈	5⁶/₈	5⁵/₈	5	5		1134	116
	■ *Grant Co. – W.R. Freeburg & C. Adams – William R. Freeburg – 1993*										
176⁴/₈	26⁶/₈	26³/₈	18⁴/₈	20⁶/₈	5¹/₈	5¹/₈	6	6		1158	119
	■ *Itasca Co. – Jim Soukup – Jim Soukup – 1960*										
176⁴/₈	23⁵/₈	23⁵/₈	17⁴/₈	20⁴/₈	5⁴/₈	5³/₈	5	5		1158	119
	■ *St. Louis Co. – Michael J. Nielsen – Michael J. Nielsen – 1962*										
176⁴/₈	26⁶/₈	27	26⁶/₈	29³/₈	4²/₈	4⁴/₈	6	6		1158	119
	■ *Houston Co. – James L. Reinhart – James L. Reinhart – 1971*										
176⁴/₈	26¹/₈	25⁵/₈	23⁶/₈	25⁶/₈	5⁴/₈	5³/₈	5	6	1⁴/₈	1158	119
	■ *Todd Co. – Walter Zastrow – Walter Zastrow – 1991*										
176³/₈	24³/₈	23³/₈	17³/₈	20²/₈	5²/₈	5²/₈	6	5		1182†	123†
	■ *Pope Co. – Richard M. Thompson – Richard M. Thompson – 1976*										
176³/₈	26¹/₈	25⁵/₈	22⁴/₈	25	5⁷/₈	5⁶/₈	5	6	2⁷/₈	1182	123
	■ *Koochiching Co. – Picked Up – James R. Smith – 1957*										

Score	Length of Main Beam		Inside Spread	Greatest Spread	Circumference at Smallest Place Between Burr and First Point		Number of Points		Lengths Abnormal Points	All-Time Rank	State Rank
	Right	Left			Right	Left	Right	Left			
	■ Location of Kill – Hunter – Owner – Date Killed										
176³/₈	28¹/₈	28	19⁶/₈	22²/₈	5¹/₈	4⁷/₈	7	7	2⁷/₈	1182	123
	■ St. Louis Co. – Howard Maki – Howard Maki – 1958										
176³/₈	27²/₈	26³/₈	21¹/₈	24⁷/₈	4⁶/₈	4⁵/₈	8	7	12	1182	123
	■ Otter Tail Co. – Steven C. Stinar – Steven C. Stinar – 1968										
176²/₈	26¹/₈	28⁵/₈	23²/₈	25¹/₈	4³/₈	4³/₈	5	5		1209	127
	■ Houston Co. – Harold Kruse – Cabela's, Inc. – 1975										
176²/₈	26⁷/₈	27⁴/₈	21⁶/₈	23³/₈	4⁴/₈	4⁵/₈	5	5		1209	127
	■ St. Louis Co. – Picked Up – George W. Flaim – 1978										
176²/₈	28²/₈	27⁵/₈	21	23⁷/₈	4⁷/₈	4⁶/₈	7	5		1209	127
	■ Houston Co. – John W. Zahrte – John W. Zahrte – 1981										
176²/₈	24⁷/₈	24¹/₈	15⁶/₈	17⁶/₈	4⁵/₈	4⁵/₈	6	7	1²/₈	1209	127
	■ St. Louis Co. – Brian J. Keating – Brian J. Keating – 1995										
176¹/₈	25³/₈	24⁵/₈	19⁷/₈	22⁷/₈	6⁶/₈	6⁷/₈	7	7	7⁴/₈	1243	131
	■ Goodhue Co. – David Anderson – David Anderson – 1960										
176	28³/₈	29	17⁶/₈	20²/₈	4⁴/₈	4⁴/₈	5	5		1266	132
	■ Koochiching Co. – John A. Lind – John M. Lind – 1956										
176	26³/₈	26²/₈	20	23¹/₈	5¹/₈	5¹/₈	5	6	1⁴/₈	1266	132
	■ Goodhue Co. – Martin H. Bollum – Martin H. Bollum – 1986										
175⁷/₈	26⁵/₈	27	21⁷/₈	23⁷/₈	4³/₈	4³/₈	5	6		1287	134
	■ Swift Co. – Kim Manska – Kim Manska – 1982										
175⁶/₈	24⁶/₈	24⁵/₈	17⁷/₈	21	6²/₈	6³/₈	8	10	10¹/₈	1310	135
	■ Marshall Co. – Ell-Kay B. Foss – Ell-Kay B. Foss – 1974										
175⁶/₈	26	25⁴/₈	21	22⁶/₈	4⁴/₈	4⁴/₈	6	6	4⁴/₈	1310	135
	■ Faribault Co. – Lyle D. Ihle – Lyle D. Ihle – 1995										
175⁵/₈	26¹/₈	26⁴/₈	24¹/₈	25⁶/₈	5⁵/₈	5⁵/₈	5	5		1333	137
	■ Itasca Co. – Art R. Swanson – LeRoy R. Swanson – 1945										
175⁵/₈	27⁶/₈	27³/₈	19⁵/₈	21⁶/₈	4⁶/₈	4⁷/₈	5	6	1²/₈	1333	137
	■ Goodhue Co. – Ellsworth Ramseier – Chuck Ramseier – 1972										
175⁴/₈	26⁵/₈	28	20²/₈	22³/₈	5	5¹/₈	6	6		1352	139
	■ Mille Lacs Co. – John Krol – Ronald D. Evensen – 1973										
175⁴/₈	26⁷/₈	27⁷/₈	21	23²/₈	5¹/₈	5¹/₈	5	5		1352	139
	■ Renville Co. – Larry D. Youngs – Larry D. Youngs – 1973										
175⁴/₈	25⁷/₈	26³/₈	19⁶/₈	21⁶/₈	5¹/₈	5²/₈	6	10	4⁶/₈	1352	139
	■ Wabasha Co. – Ronald V. Hurlburt – Ronald V. Hurlburt – 1987										
175⁴/₈	25¹/₈	25²/₈	23⁴/₈	27¹/₈	4⁵/₈	4⁴/₈	5	5	1⁴/₈	1352	139
	■ Houston Co. – Wesley Lapham – Wesley Lapham – 1993										
175²/₈	26⁴/₈	26³/₈	21⁶/₈	24	4⁵/₈	4⁵/₈	6	6		1403	143
	■ Lake Co. – John Brassill – Lorraine Brassill – 1951										
175²/₈	24²/₈	24⁶/₈	20	22²/₈	4²/₈	4²/₈	6	6		1403	143
	■ Aitkin Co. – Terry Kullhem – Terry Kullhem – 1958										
175²/₈	27³/₈	27⁷/₈	22⁴/₈	24⁵/₈	5¹/₈	5	6	7	7	1403	143
	■ Kittson Co. – Fred Bloomquist – Gordon Johnson – 1962										

Score	Length of Main Beam Right	Left	Inside Spread	Greatest Spread	Circumference at Smallest Place Between Burr and First Point Right	Left	Number of Points Right	Left	Lengths Abnormal Points	All-Time Rank	State Rank
	■ Location of Kill – Hunter – Owner – Date Killed										
175 2/8	25	25 1/8	18 6/8	20 7/8	5	5	5	5		1403	143
■ Aitkin Co. – Picked Up – Steven M. Landrus – 1988											
175 1/8	25 5/8	25 1/8	24 2/8	26	4 7/8	4 7/8	6	6	6 7/8	1440	147
■ Lincoln Co. – Robert R. Bushman – Robert R. Bushman – 1973											
175 1/8	27 1/8	25 5/8	18 3/8	20 7/8	5	5	5	5		1440	147
■ Houston Co. – Craig F. Swenson – Craig F. Swenson – 1973											
175 1/8	24 7/8	26 1/8	20 7/8	23	4 4/8	4 4/8	6	7	2	1440	147
■ Lac qui Parle Co. – Harold Kittelson – Harold Kittelson – 1976											
175	28	27 1/8	18 6/8	21 2/8	5	4 6/8	7	7	6 4/8	1472	150
■ Minnesota – Floyd Baade – Maverick Russell – 1944											
175	28 6/8	29 3/8	22 2/8	24 7/8	5 2/8	5 1/8	6	5	4	1472	150
■ Pope Co. – Picked Up – R. Benson & K. Wick – 1957											
175	25 3/8	25 4/8	19 2/8	22	5 4/8	5 4/8	5	5		1472	150
■ Itasca Co. – David A. Frandsen – David A. Frandsen – 1982											
175	31 3/8	31	23 2/8	25 6/8	4 7/8	5	6	8	7 6/8	1472	150
■ Mower Co. – Scott R. Lau – Scott R. Lau – 1983											
175	27 4/8	27 7/8	21	22 6/8	5 1/8	5	7	9	7 2/8	1472	150
■ Stearns Co. – Gregory M.J. Gunnerson – Gregory M.J. Gunnerson – 1992											
174 7/8	27 6/8	27 3/8	20 2/8	22 5/8	5 5/8	5 4/8	6	4	1 3/8	1513†	155†
■ St. Louis Co. – Randy Fredlund – Randy Fredlund – 1999											
174 7/8	25 2/8	25 5/8	16 5/8	19 2/8	4 4/8	5	6	6	1 4/8	1513	155
■ Fillmore Co. – Daniel M. Hansen – Daniel M. Hansen – 1979											
174 6/8	24 6/8	24 2/8	18 2/8	21 6/8	4 4/8	4 4/8	6	6		1534	157
■ Isanti Co. – Larry Roos – Larry Roos – 1971											
174 5/8	27 1/8	27 2/8	20 3/8	22 6/8	4 5/8	4 5/8	5	7	1 2/8	1561	158
■ Isanti Co. – Unknown – Pete Thiry – PR 1940											
174 5/8	24	22 5/8	18 3/8	20 4/8	4 5/8	4 4/8	5	5		1561	158
■ Meeker Co. – James L. Mattson – James L. Mattson – 1973											
174 5/8	29 4/8	28 1/8	21 7/8	25 4/8	6	6	6	9	10 4/8	1561	158
■ Otter Tail Co. – James C. Vorderbruggen – James C. Vorderbruggen – 1976											
174 5/8	27 1/8	26 4/8	20 7/8	23 3/8	4 6/8	4 6/8	5	5		1561	158
■ St. Louis Co. – Unknown – George W. Flaim – PR 1993											
174 4/8	26 5/8	25 1/8	20 6/8	23 3/8	4 7/8	4 6/8	6	6		1592†	162†
■ Polk Co. – Steven R. Cornell – Steven R. Cornell – 2000											
174 4/8	25 6/8	26	16 7/8	19	4 5/8	4 6/8	6	7	1 1/8	1592	162
■ Koochiching Co. – Unknown – Michael Murphy – PR 1950											
174 4/8	27 3/8	27 5/8	24 7/8	26 5/8	5 4/8	5 2/8	5	6	1 5/8	1592	162
■ Nicollet Co. – Ambrose R. McCabe – Ambrose R. McCabe – 1992											
174 4/8	25 5/8	26 2/8	19 7/8	23	5 2/8	5 4/8	6	5	2 3/8	1592	162
■ Wright Co. – Michael J. Buennich – Michael J. Buennich – 1995											
174 3/8	28 6/8	27 2/8	20 5/8	22 6/8	5 1/8	5	5	5		1619†	166†
■ Otter Tail Co. – Picked Up – Frank Virchow – 1999											

Score	Length of Main Beam Right	Left	Inside Spread	Greatest Spread	Circumference at Smallest Place Between Burr and First Point Right	Left	Number of Points Right	Left	Lengths Abnormal Points	All-Time Rank	State Rank
	■ Location of Kill – Hunter – Owner – Date Killed										
174³/₈	24⁷/₈	23⁶/₈	17⁷/₈	20	5⁵/₈	5¹/₈	5	5		1619	166
	■ Aitkin Co. – Christopher W. Steinke – Christopher W. Steinke – 1969										
174³/₈	27¹/₈	27¹/₈	21³/₈	24¹/₈	6²/₈	5²/₈	5	5		1619	166
	■ Itasca Co. – Mark O. DuLong – Mark O. DuLong – 1987										
174¹/₈	27¹/₈	28¹/₈	24⁷/₈	26	5¹/₈	5	5	6	1²/₈	1678	169
	■ Mahnomen Co. – Rolland Agnew – James Frazee – 1941										
174¹/₈	25	25²/₈	23³/₈	25⁴/₈	5¹/₈	5	6	5	2⁶/₈	1678	169
	■ Renville Co. – Galen Kodet – Galen Kodet – 1970										
174¹/₈	23⁷/₈	23⁵/₈	19⁷/₈	22	5	5	5	5		1678	169
	■ Goodhue Co. – Tom Nesseth – Tom Nesseth – 1988										
174¹/₈	28⁴/₈	28³/₈	22³/₈	24¹/₈	5¹/₈	5⁶/₈	5	6		1678	169
	■ Wright Co. – William J. Stuhr – William J. Stuhr – 1990										
174¹/₈	27²/₈	25⁴/₈	20⁶/₈	23³/₈	5³/₈	5⁴/₈	5	6	2¹/₈	1678	169
	■ Freeborn Co. – Charles D. Stadheim – Charles D. Stadheim – 1991										
174¹/₈	25²/₈	27	21³/₈	24²/₈	5	5	5	6	2	1678	169
	■ Chisago Co. – Richard A. Townsend – Richard A. Townsend – 1991										
174	27²/₈	27³/₈	20⁵/₈	23	4⁴/₈	4⁴/₈	5	4	1¹/₈	1717†	175†
	■ Otter Tail Co. – John D. Thorson – John D. Thorson – 2000										
173⁷/₈	25⁷/₈	25	19¹/₈	21⁶/₈	4⁶/₈	4⁶/₈	5	5		1743†	176†
	■ Wadena Co. – Picked Up – Kelly C. Marshall – 1987										
173⁷/₈	25³/₈	26²/₈	20²/₈	23²/₈	4⁷/₈	4⁷/₈	7	6	9³/₈	1743	176
	■ Blue Earth Co. – Jeffery L. Zimmerman – Jeffery L. Zimmerman – 1995										
173⁶/₈	24	24⁴/₈	18	20³/₈	4⁴/₈	4⁴/₈	6	6		1766	178
	■ Marshall Co. – Neil Jacobson – Neil Jacobson – 1984										
173⁵/₈	26²/₈	26⁷/₈	21⁵/₈	23⁴/₈	5	5	5	6		1819†	179†
	■ Hubbard Co. – Justin Sandmeyer – Justin Sandmeyer – 2001										
173⁵/₈	27⁴/₈	27	19⁷/₈	21⁵/₈	4²/₈	4²/₈	6	5		1819	179
	■ Winona Co. – John W. Brand – John W. Brand – 1969										
173⁵/₈	28	26⁴/₈	20³/₈	22²/₈	4⁴/₈	4⁴/₈	5	5		1819	179
	■ Fillmore Co. – Kelly J. McQuay – Kelly J. McQuay – 1986										
173⁵/₈	25⁵/₈	27²/₈	18¹/₈	20³/₈	4⁵/₈	4⁶/₈	6	6		1819	179
	■ Roseau Co. – David A. Harmon – David A. Harmon – 1987										
173⁵/₈	24²/₈	23⁵/₈	17⁶/₈	20⁴/₈	5³/₈	5¹/₈	9	8	12¹/₈	1819	179
	■ Otter Tail Co. – Terry D. Krumwiede – Terry D. Krumwiede – 1995										
173⁴/₈	28	27⁶/₈	18²/₈	20⁵/₈	5	5	5	5		1847	184
	■ Winona Co. – Raymond A. Manion – Raymond A. Manion – 1950										
173⁴/₈	28⁴/₈	28³/₈	20⁵/₈	23¹/₈	5	5	7	5	1³/₈	1847	184
	■ St. Louis Co. – Clarence Lindstrom – Donald A. Fondrick – 1960										
173⁴/₈	25²/₈	25⁵/₈	17⁷/₈	20¹/₈	5	5	7	7	5³/₈	1847	184
	■ St. Louis Co. – Gerald R. Fousone – Gerald R. Fousone – 1999										
173⁴/₈	28¹/₈	27⁴/₈	21	23³/₈	4²/₈	4¹/₈	5	6		1847	184
	■ Chisago Co. – Robert C. Palmer – Robert C. Palmer – 1999										

Score	Length of Main Beam Right Left	Inside Spread	Greatest Spread	Circumference at Smallest Place Between Burr and First Point Right Left	Number of Points Right Left	Lengths Abnormal Points	All-Time Rank	State Rank
	■ Location of Kill – Hunter – Owner – Date Killed							
$173^3/8$	$25^6/8$ $25^7/8$	$19^2/8$	$22^3/8$	$4^7/8$ $\quad$ 5	8 $\quad$ 7	$3^7/8$	1883†	188†
	■ St. Louis Co. – Picked Up – William E. Clink – 1960							
$173^2/8$	$26^4/8$ $26^5/8$	19	$21^1/8$	$4^1/8$ $\quad$ 4	5 $\quad$ 5		1914	189
	■ Chisago Co. – Roger A. Peterson – Roger A. Peterson – 1984							
$173^2/8$	$25^7/8$ $25^6/8$	$20^3/8$	$22^2/8$	$5^2/8$ $5^4/8$	8 $\quad$ 9	$3^5/8$	1914	189
	■ Cass Co. – Picked Up – Robert Johnson – 1993							
$173^1/8$	$26^5/8$ $25^6/8$	20	$23^2/8$	$5^2/8$ $5^4/8$	5 $\quad$ 7	$9^1/8$	1950†	191†
	■ Becker Co. – Cliff C. Wessels – Cliff C. Wessels – 2000							
$173^1/8$	$27^4/8$ $26^3/8$	$21^7/8$	$25^6/8$	$5^5/8$ $5^3/8$	5 $\quad$ 5		1950	191
	■ St. Louis Co. – Unknown – George W. Flaim – 1934							
$173^1/8$	$29^3/8$ $28^7/8$	$25^1/8$	$27^3/8$	$5^2/8$ $5^1/8$	4 $\quad$ 4		1950	191
	■ Fillmore Co. – Gerry D. Arnold – Gerry D. Arnold – 1973							
173	$25^7/8$ $25^6/8$	22	$25^2/8$	$4^7/8$ $4^7/8$	8 $\quad$ 8	$5^6/8$	1991	194
	■ Pope Co. – Unknown – Tom Hammer – PR 1960							
173	$28^3/8$ $27^4/8$	21	$24^7/8$	$4^6/8$ $4^6/8$	7 $\quad$ 6	3	1991	194
	■ Koochiching Co. – Unknown – Marc M. Jackson – PR 1974							
173	$27^1/8$ $27^2/8$	$21^6/8$	$24^2/8$	$4^5/8$ $4^5/8$	5 $\quad$ 6	5	1991	194
	■ Cook Co. – Wesley A. Nelson – Wesley A. Nelson – 1980							
173	$26^4/8$ $25^7/8$	$18^4/8$	$20^4/8$	$4^6/8$ $4^6/8$	5 $\quad$ 6		1991	194
	■ Becker Co. – Albert E. Jahnke – Albert E. Jahnke – 1985							
173	$28^6/8$ $29^3/8$	$16^5/8$	$19^3/8$	$5^7/8$ $5^6/8$	5 $\quad$ 7	$3^3/8$	1991	194
	■ Itasca Co. – Robert W. Bourman – Robert W. Bourman – 1999							
$172^7/8$	$26^4/8$ $26^1/8$	$16^7/8$	19	$4^2/8$ $4^1/8$	6 $\quad$ 6		2038	199
	■ Olmsted Co. – Wesley W. Holtz – Wesley W. Holtz – 1966							
$172^7/8$	$26^7/8$ 27	19	$21^4/8$	5 $\quad$ $4^7/8$	7 $\quad$ 6	$6^7/8$	2038	199
	■ Fillmore Co. – Susan M. LeGare-Gulden – Susan M. LeGare-Gulden – 1996							
$172^6/8$	$27^1/8$ $27^1/8$	$21^1/8$	$23^1/8$	$4^4/8$ $4^3/8$	6 $\quad$ 7	$2^3/8$	2065	201
	■ Renville Co. – Elroy E. Kuglin – Elroy E. Kuglin – 1990							
$172^6/8$	$27^5/8$ $28^3/8$	$22^2/8$	24	$5^6/8$ $5^6/8$	7 $\quad$ 6	$3^2/8$	2065	201
	■ Morrison Co. – Leroy R. Zimmerman – Leroy R. Zimmerman – 1998							
$172^5/8$	$27^6/8$ $28^1/8$	$22^3/8$	$25^3/8$	$4^7/8$ $4^6/8$	5 $\quad$ 5		2113	203
	■ Koochiching Co. – Unknown – Marc M. Jackson – PR 1977							
$172^4/8$	$26^5/8$ $26^5/8$	19	24	$5^5/8$ $5^3/8$	5 $\quad$ 6	$6^2/8$	2156	204
	■ Fillmore Co. – Picked Up – William H. Lilienthal – 1965							
$172^3/8$	$26^5/8$ $27^6/8$	$17^1/8$	$19^2/8$	$4^3/8$ $4^4/8$	8 $\quad$ 5	$2^6/8$	2200	205
	■ Kanabec Co. – Gregory L. Schultz – Gregory L. Schultz – 1976							
$172^2/8$	$26^7/8$ 27	$20^6/8$	$23^1/8$	$4^5/8$ $4^5/8$	5 $\quad$ 5		2237	206
	■ St. Louis Co. – Everett Larson – George W. Flaim – 1942							
$172^2/8$	$24^2/8$ 25	$18^1/8$	$20^1/8$	$4^2/8$ $4^3/8$	8 $\quad$ 5	$2^7/8$	2237	206
	■ Minnesota – Unknown – Jeff A. Puhl – PR 1987							
$172^2/8$	$26^2/8$ $25^5/8$	$23^4/8$	$25^4/8$	$4^4/8$ $4^4/8$	6 $\quad$ 6		2237	206
	■ Scott Co. – Kenneth J. Scherer – Kenneth J. Scherer – 1987							

Score	Length of Main Beam Right Left	Inside Spread	Greatest Spread	Circumference at Smallest Place Between Burr and First Point Right Left		Number of Points Right Left		Lengths Abnormal Points	All-Time Rank	State Rank
	■ Location of Kill – Hunter – Owner – Date Killed									
172²/₈	26¹/₈ 26⁶/₈	21	24⁵/₈	5²/₈ 5²/₈		8 8		10⁶/₈	2237	206
	■ Norman Co. – Corey Hoseth – Corey Hoseth – 1989									
172²/₈	29²/₈ 28⁶/₈	17⁶/₈	19⁷/₈	4⁷/₈ 4⁷/₈		5 5			2237	206
	■ St. Louis Co. – Picked Up – Jerome L. Schaller – 1996									
172²/₈	27²/₈ 27⁴/₈	22⁶/₈	24⁷/₈	4⁷/₈ 4⁶/₈		7 6		4⁶/₈	2237	206
	■ Wabasha Co. – John K. Gusa – John K. Gusa – 1998									
172¹/₈	26¹/₈ 26²/₈	19³/₈	21⁵/₈	4⁴/₈ 4⁴/₈		5 6		5⁴/₈	2286	212
	■ St. Louis Co. – Luke Schoeppner – Ted Schoeppner – 1955									
172¹/₈	30²/₈ 30¹/₈	20⁷/₈	24²/₈	5 4⁷/₈		6 5		1⁴/₈	2286	212
	■ Fillmore Co. – C.J. Semmen & G. Lea – Charles J. Semmen – 1961									
172¹/₈	24 24⁴/₈	20⁶/₈	22⁶/₈	5¹/₈ 5¹/₈		8 7		8³/₈	2286	212
	■ Fillmore Co. – Murrel Mathison – Murrel Mathison – 1977									
172¹/₈	25³/₈ 24²/₈	17⁵/₈	19³/₈	4³/₈ 4²/₈		6 6			2286	212
	■ Wabasha Co. – Timothy R. Pries – Timothy R. Pries – 1977									
172¹/₈	25¹/₈ 25⁵/₈	16⁴/₈	19²/₈	4⁷/₈ 4⁷/₈		6 6		1¹/₈	2286	212
	■ Winona Co. – Robert J. Cordie – Robert J. Cordie – 1979									
172¹/₈	25²/₈ 25²/₈	17²/₈	20⁵/₈	4¹/₈ 4²/₈		5 6		1¹/₈	2286	212
	■ Wabasha Co. – Michael R. Klagge – Michael R. Klagge – 1997									
172¹/₈	27²/₈ 27	18⁴/₈	21⁶/₈	5 5		6 6		2³/₈	2286	212
	■ Todd Co. – Kenneth J. Ostendorf – Kenneth J. Ostendorf – 1998									
172	28⁴/₈ 28	19⁴/₈	22³/₈	5⁷/₈ 5⁶/₈		5 5			2330	219
	■ Carlton Co. – Picked Up – John R. Steffes, Sr. – 1937									
172	27³/₈ 27¹/₈	19³/₈	21³/₈	4⁴/₈ 4⁴/₈		5 6		2⁷/₈	2330	219
	■ Marshall Co. – Keith D. Anderson – Keith D. Anderson – 1982									
172	28 28²/₈	19⁵/₈	23²/₈	4⁷/₈ 4⁷/₈		9 10		12¹/₈	2330	219
	■ Otter Tail Co. – Paul W. Wagner – Paul W. Wagner – 1987									
171⁷/₈	27 27¹/₈	21⁴/₈	23⁵/₈	6³/₈ 6⁵/₈		6 6		2³/₈	2382	222
	■ Fillmore Co. – Maynard Howe – Maynard Howe – 1957									
171⁷/₈	26¹/₈ 27	20⁵/₈	22⁵/₈	4⁶/₈ 4⁵/₈		5 5			2382	222
	■ Houston Co. – Donald R. Sobolik – Donald R. Sobolik – 1958									
171⁷/₈	24⁷/₈ 25⁶/₈	21⁷/₈	24²/₈	5¹/₈ 5¹/₈		5 5			2382	222
	■ Todd Co. – Picked Up – Del Halverson – 1991									
171⁶/₈	26 27	18⁴/₈	21	6²/₈ 6²/₈		5 5			2418	225
	■ St. Louis Co. – Paul S. Paulson – Paul S. Paulson – 1946									
171⁶/₈	26³/₈ 26¹/₈	20⁵/₈	22⁴/₈	5⁶/₈ 5⁵/₈		6 6		8³/₈	2418	225
	■ St. Louis Co. – Unknown – David G. Gagnon – PR 1970									
171⁶/₈	25³/₈ 25²/₈	17⁶/₈	20¹/₈	5²/₈ 5²/₈		7 7		4⁶/₈	2418	225
	■ Winona Co. – James J. Heberlein – James J. Heberlein – 1998									
171⁶/₈	26 25	16³/₈	19⁷/₈	5²/₈ 5³/₈		6 8		9⁵/₈	2418	225
	■ Dakota Co. – Vincent A. LaCroix – Vincent A. LaCroix – 1998 ■ See photo on page 295									
171⁵/₈	26³/₈ 27³/₈	19¹/₈	21³/₈	4³/₈ 4³/₈		5 5			2470†	229†
	■ Sherburne Co. – Jeffrey C. Cox – Jeffrey C. Cox – 2000									

Score	Length of Main Beam Right	Left	Inside Spread	Greatest Spread	Circumference at Smallest Place Between Burr and First Point Right	Left	Number of Points Right	Left	Lengths Abnormal Points	All-Time Rank	State Rank
	■ *Location of Kill – Hunter – Owner – Date Killed*										
171 5/8	25	25 5/8	16 2/8	18 1/8	4 3/8	4 3/8	6	5	1 1/8	2470	229
	■ *Koochiching Co. – Ray W. Bastin – Ray W. Bastin – 1930*										
171 5/8	26 4/8	28 4/8	20 1/8	22 2/8	4 6/8	5	5	6	3 2/8	2470	229
	■ *Meeker Co. – Ronald E. Lampi – Ronald E. Meeker – 1973*										
171 5/8	27	25 5/8	18 2/8	20 7/8	5 2/8	5 2/8	6	6	3 1/8	2470	229
	■ *Otter Tail Co. – Carl D. Hill – Carl D. Hill – 1977*										
171 5/8	25 3/8	24 7/8	18 3/8	20 6/8	4 6/8	4 5/8	5	5		2470	229
	■ *Grant Co. – Gary P. Kollman – Gary P. Kollman – 1980*										
171 5/8	24 2/8	23 2/8	16 1/8	18 4/8	4 6/8	4 6/8	6	6		2470	229
	■ *Carlton Co. – Charles T. Ditmarsen – Charles T. Ditmarsen – 1985*										
171 4/8	26 3/8	27 2/8	23 6/8	27	5 6/8	5 7/8	7	9	9	2513	235
	■ *Clay Co. – Clint Foslien – Clint Foslien – 1965*										
171 4/8	25 3/8	26 6/8	22	25 4/8	5 2/8	5 1/8	8	8	8 6/8	2513	235
	■ *Lac qui Parle Co. – Wayne A. Hegland – Wayne A. Hegland – 1977*										
171 4/8	25	25	18 2/8	20 2/8	4 6/8	4 7/8	6	6		2513	235
	■ *Steele Co. – Craig Evans – Craig Evans – 1978*										
171 4/8	25 6/8	24 5/8	19 6/8	22	4 4/8	4 3/8	5	5		2513	235
	■ *Clearwater Co. – Peter Tranby – Peter Tranby – 1978*										
171 4/8	27 1/8	26 7/8	18 6/8	20 5/8	4 5/8	4 5/8	5	6		2513	235
	■ *Becker Co. – Kraig J. Ketter – Kraig J. Ketter – 1983*										
171 4/8	28 2/8	27 4/8	20	22 2/8	4 5/8	4 6/8	6	6	3 2/8	2513	235
	■ *Carlton Co. – Vincent A. Mullen, Sr. – Vincent A. Mullen, Sr. – 1996*										
171 3/8	23 4/8	24 2/8	23 1/8	25 2/8	4 7/8	4 7/8	5	5		2564	241
	■ *Kandiyohi Co. – Werner B. Reining – Werner B. Reining – 1974*										
171 3/8	25 2/8	24 5/8	22 5/8	25	5	5	7	6	3	2564	241
	■ *Pope Co. – Corbin G. Corson – Corbin G. Corson – 1975*										
171 3/8	25 7/8	26 3/8	21 3/8	26	5 1/8	5 1/8	8	10	12	2564	241
	■ *Douglas Co. – Gregory A. Dropik – Gregory A. Dropik – 1984*										
171 2/8	26 7/8	25 6/8	18 2/8	20 4/8	5 2/8	5 1/8	5	5		2621	244
	■ *Beltrami Co. – Mickey Ewing – Mickey Ewing – 1981*										
171 1/8	26	26 7/8	16 7/8	19 5/8	5 6/8	5 6/8	5	5		2665	245
	■ *Douglas Co. – James M. Bircher – James M. Bircher – 1962*										
171 1/8	26	24 7/8	16 5/8	18 7/8	4 2/8	4 2/8	5	5		2665	245
	■ *Koochiching Co. – Picked Up – Marc M. Jackson – 1977*										
171 1/8	23 7/8	23 5/8	17 1/8	19	5 2/8	5 1/8	8	8	3 4/8	2665	245
	■ *Otter Tail Co. – Thomas E. Berger – Thomas E. Berger – 1985*										
171 1/8	25 2/8	25	17 6/8	20 1/8	4 7/8	5	6	8	7 7/8	2665	245
	■ *Hubbard Co. – Merald D. Folkestad – Merald D. Folkestad – 1987*										
171	26	24 4/8	19 6/8	22	5 2/8	6	5	5		2707	249
	■ *Wabasha Co. – John W. Mussell – John W. Mussell – 1966*										
171	27	26 5/8	26 2/8	28 4/8	5 3/8	5 2/8	7	8	8	2707	249
	■ *Otter Tail Co. – Lawrence J. Anderson – Lawrence J. Anderson – 1974*										

Score	Length of Main Beam Right Left ■ Location of Kill – Hunter – Owner – Date Killed	Inside Spread	Greatest Spread	Circumference at Smallest Place Between Burr and First Point Right Left		Number of Points Right Left		Lengths Abnormal Points	All-Time Rank	State Rank
171	25⁷/₈ 26²/₈	19³/₈	22⁵/₈	5¹/₈	5	6	5	2¹/₈	2707	249
	■ Wabasha Co. – Thomas J. Mullenbach – Thomas J. Mullenbach – 1989									
171	24 24	23³/₈	25	4³/₈	4³/₈	7	6	1¹/₈	2707	249
	■ Pipestone Co. – Scott A. Crawford – Scott A. Crawford – 1995									
171	25⁶/₈ 26	18	20²/₈	5¹/₈	5¹/₈	5	5		2707	249
	■ Blue Earth Co. – Robert E. Richards – Robert E. Richards – 1995									
171	27⁷/₈ 27⁵/₈	18⁵/₈	22²/₈	6¹/₈	6²/₈	8	6	7⁵/₈	2707	249
	■ Wadena Co. – Terry L. Thurstin – Terry L. Thurstin – 1996									
171	26⁴/₈ 27	19	21²/₈	4⁵/₈	4⁶/₈	6	7	2⁴/₈	2707	249
	■ Becker Co. – Jeff D. Holmer – Jeff D. Holmer – 1998									
170⁷/₈	26³/₈ 26	21⁵/₈	23⁴/₈	5³/₈	5²/₈	5	5		2769	256
	■ Cass Co. – Orland Weekley – George W. Flaim – 1929									
170⁷/₈	26³/₈ 27¹/₈	20⁴/₈	23³/₈	5¹/₈	5	6	7	1³/₈	2769	256
	■ Beltrami Co. – Kenneth Slechta – Kenneth Slechta – 1965									
170⁷/₈	26³/₈ 26⁵/₈	17⁷/₈	20²/₈	4²/₈	4¹/₈	5	6		2769	256
	■ Sherburne Co. – Merlin F. Kittelson – Merlin F. Kittelson – 1977									
170⁷/₈	26⁴/₈ 25⁷/₈	17¹/₈	19³/₈	5²/₈	5²/₈	5	5		2769	256
	■ Houston Co. – Tony S. Rostad – Tony S. Rostad – 1988									
170⁷/₈	25⁵/₈ 25⁷/₈	21⁵/₈	23⁷/₈	5²/₈	5¹/₈	5	5		2769	256
	■ Wabasha Co. – Terry P. Ryan – Terry P. Ryan – 1993									
170⁶/₈	24⁶/₈ 23⁴/₈	19²/₈	22⁴/₈	5⁶/₈	6⁵/₈	5	5		2828	261
	■ Aitkin Co. – Unknown – George W. Flaim – PR 1947									
170⁶/₈	23³/₈ 23³/₈	18	19⁷/₈	4¹/₈	4¹/₈	7	6	1	2828	261
	■ Chisago Co. – Gary Thomas – Gary Thomas – 1990									
170⁵/₈	25⁶/₈ 25⁵/₈	18³/₈	20⁴/₈	4⁵/₈	4⁶/₈	6	6		2876	263
	■ Lake Co. – Unknown – George W. Flaim – 1960									
170⁵/₈	27²/₈ 27²/₈	21⁶/₈	23⁶/₈	5⁴/₈	5²/₈	5	7	2⁵/₈	2876	263
	■ Sherburne Co. – Sylvester Zormeier – Sylvester Zormeier – 1967									
170⁵/₈	27 26⁷/₈	19⁵/₈	21⁶/₈	5	5¹/₈	5	5		2876	263
	■ St. Louis Co. – Unknown – George W. Flaim – PR 1979									
170⁵/₈	25²/₈ 27¹/₈	16	19	4⁷/₈	4⁷/₈	7	6	2⁵/₈	2876	263
	■ Big Stone Co. – Jeffrey A. Thielke – Jeffrey A. Thielke – 1985									
170⁵/₈	28¹/₈ 28⁴/₈	23³/₈	26⁶/₈	5⁶/₈	5⁵/₈	4	5		2876	263
	■ Polk Co. – D. Keith Thunem, Jr. – D. Keith Thunem, Jr. – 1990									
170⁴/₈	26¹/₈ 25⁴/₈	20⁴/₈	23	4⁶/₈	4⁵/₈	6	6		2933	268
	■ Beltrami Co. – Hank Sandland – Hank Sandland – 1931									
170⁴/₈	25²/₈ 24⁵/₈	18	20	4⁴/₈	4⁴/₈	6	6		2933	268
	■ Douglas Co. – August P.J. Nelson – Roger M. Holmes – 1946									
170⁴/₈	23⁵/₈ 26¹/₈	22⁴/₈	23⁷/₈	5⁶/₈	5⁷/₈	5	5		2933	268
	■ Kittson Co. – Unknown – George W. Flaim – PR 1950									
170⁴/₈	27⁴/₈ 27²/₈	20²/₈	22⁴/₈	5⁴/₈	5³/₈	5	5		2933	268
	■ St. Louis Co. – Unknown – Cabela's, Inc. – 1974									

Score	Length of Main Beam Right / Left	Inside Spread	Greatest Spread	Circumference at Smallest Place Between Burr and First Point Right / Left	Number of Points Right / Left	Lengths Abnormal Points	All-Time Rank	State Rank
	■ Location of Kill – Hunter – Owner – Date Killed							
170 4/8	26 4/8 25	17 7/8	20 2/8	5 1/8 5 1/8	6 6	5 3/8	2933	268
	■ Winona Co. – Sam Nottleman – Sam Nottleman – 1977							
170 4/8	29 6/8 29 2/8	21 2/8	23 3/8	4 6/8 4 4/8	7 8	6	2933	268
	■ Sherburne Co. – Curtis G. Nelson – Curtis G. Nelson – 1981							
170 4/8	28 5/8 28	20	23	5 5	8 8	6	2933	268
	■ Todd Co. – Freddie H. Peterson – Freddie H. Peterson – 1982							
170 4/8	26 6/8 26 3/8	17 3/8	19 4/8	4 4	5 6	1 1/8	2933	268
	■ Houston Co. – Kenneth Carlson – Kenneth Carlson – 1983							
170 4/8	27 1/8 26 7/8	21 6/8	23 5/8	4 5/8 4 5/8	5 5		2933	268
	■ Washington Co. – Peter J. Mogren – Peter J. Mogren – 1988							
170 3/8	24 2/8 24 1/8	21 2/8	23 1/8	4 6/8 4 6/8	5 6	2 5/8	2992†	277†
	■ Scott Co. – Joe Shotliff – Joe Shotliff – 2000							
170 3/8	25 5/8 25 2/8	22 6/8	25 2/8	5 2/8 5 4/8	7 8	6 1/8	2992	277
	■ Lac qui Parle Co. – Paul W. Hill – Paul W. Hill – 1974							
170 3/8	25 7/8 25 6/8	18 7/8	21 5/8	5 1/8 5 2/8	6 6		2992	277
	■ Beltrami Co. – Floyd Hlucny – Floyd Hlucny – 1985							
170 3/8	23 2/8 24 2/8	17	20 4/8	4 1/8 4 2/8	7 7	2 7/8	2992	277
	■ Marshall Co. – John R. O'Donnell – John R. O'Donnell – 1988							
170 3/8	27 1/8 27 1/8	19 2/8	21 2/8	5 1/8 5	6 6	10 7/8	2992	277
	■ Le Sueur Co. – Roy H. Krohn – Roy H. Krohn – 1994							
170 3/8	28 6/8 27 6/8	19 7/8	22 2/8	4 7/8 4 7/8	7 6	8	2992	277
	■ Houston Co. – Picked Up – MN Dept. of Natl. Resc. – 1999							
170 2/8	24 3/8 25 2/8	16 6/8	19 6/8	5 2/8 5 3/8	5 5		3063	283
	■ Carlton Co. – Unknown – George W. Flaim – 1950							
170 2/8	28 6/8 29 1/8	19 5/8	23 1/8	4 5/8 4 4/8	9 5	11 1/8	3063	283
	■ Blue Earth Co. – Roland Bode – Roland Bode – 1967							
170 2/8	27 4/8 25 5/8	18	20 4/8	4 6/8 4 6/8	6 5		3063	283
	■ Houston Co. – Randy J. Benson – Randy J. Benson – 1972							
170 2/8	25 6/8 25	16 6/8	19 5/8	4 3/8 4 4/8	5 6	1 4/8	3063	283
	■ Olmsted Co. – James L. Miller – James L. Miller – 1981							
170 2/8	26 1/8 28 3/8	25 2/8	28	4 2/8 4 3/8	7 7	9 6/8	3063	283
	■ Houston Co. – Omer M. Wangen – Omer M. Wangen – 1988							
170 2/8	25 5/8 25 7/8	19 1/8	21 4/8	4 5/8 4 5/8	6 6	2 3/8	3063	283
	■ Fillmore Co. – Terry L. Rasmussen – Terry L. Rasmussen – 1991							
170 2/8	27 1/8 26 2/8	22 2/8	24 3/8	5 2/8 5	5 5		3063	283
	■ Chisago Co. – John B. Nelson – John B. Nelson – 1993							
170 2/8	30 2/8 29 2/8	21 1/8	23 3/8	4 7/8 4 7/8	4 6	2 3/8	3063	283
	■ St. Louis Co. – Charles R. Wagaman – Charles R. Wagaman – 1993							
170 2/8	26 6/8 25 7/8	20	21 4/8	5 2/8 5 2/8	6 6	3 4/8	3063	283
	■ Hennepin Co. – Picked Up – Charles G. Nordstrom – 1994							
170 2/8	26 3/8 26 1/8	18 4/8	21 4/8	5 1/8 5 3/8	8 8	6 2/8	3063	283
	■ Hubbard Co. – Michael E. Greetan – Michael E. Greetan – 1998							

Score	Length of Main Beam Right	Left	Inside Spread	Greatest Spread	Circumference at Smallest Place Between Burr and First Point Right	Left	Number of Points Right	Left	Lengths Abnormal Points	All-Time Rank	State Rank
	■ Location of Kill – Hunter – Owner – Date Killed										
$170\frac{1}{8}$	$25\frac{7}{8}$	$26\frac{4}{8}$	$16\frac{7}{8}$	$19\frac{1}{8}$	$4\frac{2}{8}$	$4\frac{2}{8}$	6	7	$4\frac{2}{8}$	3143†	293†
	■ Lake of the Woods Co. – Kevin L. Olson – Kevin L. Olson – 2000 ■ See photo on page 56										
$170\frac{1}{8}$	$25\frac{7}{8}$	$27\frac{6}{8}$	19	$21\frac{6}{8}$	$5\frac{2}{8}$	$5\frac{2}{8}$	5	6	$1\frac{3}{8}$	3143	293
	■ Minnesota – Unknown – Cabela's, Inc. – PR 1950										
$170\frac{1}{8}$	$28\frac{5}{8}$	29	$23\frac{3}{8}$	$25\frac{7}{8}$	$4\frac{2}{8}$	$4\frac{3}{8}$	4	5		3143	293
	■ Faribault Co. – Harlan Francis – Harlan Francis – 1956										
$170\frac{1}{8}$	$25\frac{3}{8}$	$24\frac{6}{8}$	$16\frac{5}{8}$	$19\frac{4}{8}$	$4\frac{7}{8}$	5	6	7	$5\frac{2}{8}$	3143	293
	■ St. Louis Co. – Allan Ramstad – Allan Ramstad – 1959										
$170\frac{1}{8}$	$26\frac{1}{8}$	26	$21\frac{1}{8}$	$23\frac{2}{8}$	$4\frac{6}{8}$	$4\frac{6}{8}$	6	6		3143	293
	■ Lake Co. – Ed Gregorich – George W. Flaim – 1969										
$170\frac{1}{8}$	$25\frac{4}{8}$	$25\frac{7}{8}$	$22\frac{2}{8}$	$24\frac{1}{8}$	$4\frac{5}{8}$	$4\frac{3}{8}$	6	7	$2\frac{3}{8}$	3143	293
	■ Winona Co. – Roger J. Traxler – Roger J. Traxler – 1980										
$170\frac{1}{8}$	27	$27\frac{1}{8}$	19	$22\frac{2}{8}$	$4\frac{6}{8}$	$4\frac{6}{8}$	7	6	$2\frac{3}{8}$	3143	293
	■ Cook Co. – William Bohnen – William Bohnen – 1984										
$170\frac{1}{8}$	$25\frac{6}{8}$	$25\frac{2}{8}$	$21\frac{3}{8}$	$24\frac{3}{8}$	$4\frac{4}{8}$	$4\frac{5}{8}$	5	5		3143	293
	■ Mower Co. – Robert D. Plumb – Robert D. Plumb – 1984										
$170\frac{1}{8}$	$28\frac{6}{8}$	$28\frac{1}{8}$	23	$25\frac{1}{8}$	5	5	6	7	$5\frac{1}{8}$	3143	293
	■ Winona Co. – Picked Up – Gary L. Bornfleth – 1987										
$170\frac{1}{8}$	$24\frac{6}{8}$	$24\frac{2}{8}$	$21\frac{3}{8}$	$23\frac{4}{8}$	$4\frac{6}{8}$	$4\frac{6}{8}$	6	7	$2\frac{2}{8}$	3143	293
	■ Otter Tail Co. – Randle R. Litke – Randle R. Litke – 1995										
$170\frac{1}{8}$	$25\frac{6}{8}$	$25\frac{6}{8}$	$20\frac{1}{8}$	23	$5\frac{6}{8}$	6	6	8	$6\frac{2}{8}$	3143	293
	■ Roseau Co. – R.E. Putney & F. Walker – Rodney E. Putney – 1996										
170	$26\frac{1}{8}$	$25\frac{2}{8}$	$17\frac{4}{8}$	$19\frac{6}{8}$	$4\frac{6}{8}$	$4\frac{6}{8}$	5	6		3224	304
	■ Crow Wing Co. – Unknown – Calvin L. Seguin – PR 1992										
170	$25\frac{2}{8}$	$25\frac{2}{8}$	$18\frac{2}{8}$	$20\frac{6}{8}$	$4\frac{4}{8}$	$4\frac{5}{8}$	7	7	$4\frac{2}{8}$	3224	304
	■ Wabasha Co. – Chad R. Collins – Chad R. Collins – 1999										
$169\frac{6}{8}$	$25\frac{4}{8}$	$26\frac{5}{8}$	$17\frac{3}{8}$	$19\frac{6}{8}$	5	5	6	6	$2\frac{5}{8}$	3306	306
	■ Wadena Co. – Keith Van Orsdel – Keith Van Orsdel – 1984										
$169\frac{6}{8}$	$26\frac{4}{8}$	$26\frac{3}{8}$	18	$20\frac{1}{8}$	5	5	5	6		3306	306
	■ Wright Co. – Michael D. Arnold – Michael D. Arnold – 1989										
$169\frac{2}{8}$	23	$24\frac{2}{8}$	$19\frac{2}{8}$	22	$5\frac{2}{8}$	$5\frac{1}{8}$	5	5		3336	308
	■ Kittson Co. – Frederick G. Johnson – Frederick G. Johnson – 1991										
169	$25\frac{1}{8}$	$25\frac{4}{8}$	$20\frac{2}{8}$	$22\frac{3}{8}$	$4\frac{2}{8}$	$4\frac{6}{8}$	7	7	6	3348	309
	■ Cass Co. – Darrell L. Shaw – Darrell L. Shaw – 1968										
169	$26\frac{3}{8}$	$25\frac{4}{8}$	$22\frac{4}{8}$	25	$4\frac{6}{8}$	$4\frac{5}{8}$	5	5		3348	309
	■ St. Louis Co. – Steven A. Meyer – Steven A. Meyer – 1995										
$168\frac{6}{8}$	$26\frac{4}{8}$	$26\frac{3}{8}$	17	$19\frac{4}{8}$	$4\frac{3}{8}$	$4\frac{5}{8}$	6	7	2	3367†	311†
	■ Todd Co. – Gretchen K. Kircher – G.K. & R. Kircher – 2000										
$168\frac{5}{8}$	$25\frac{2}{8}$	23	$22\frac{6}{8}$	$25\frac{1}{8}$	$5\frac{1}{8}$	$5\frac{1}{8}$	7	6	$6\frac{1}{8}$	3376†	312†
	■ Morrison Co. – Jody Tomala – Jody Tomala – 2001 ■ See photo on page 55										
$168\frac{3}{8}$	$26\frac{6}{8}$	26	$17\frac{2}{8}$	$19\frac{3}{8}$	4	4	7	5	$1\frac{1}{8}$	3399	313
	■ Houston Co. – Robert J. Nontelle – Robert J. Nontelle – 1984										

Score	Length of Main Beam		Inside Spread	Greatest Spread	Circumference at Smallest Place Between Burr and First Point		Number of Points		Lengths Abnormal Points	All-Time Rank	State Rank
	Right	Left			Right	Left	Right	Left			
	■ *Location of Kill – Hunter – Owner – Date Killed*										
168³/₈	26¹/₈	25⁶/₈	22⁶/₈	24⁷/₈	5⁵/₈	5³/₈	6	5	3¹/₈	3399	313
■ *Houston Co. – Bruce C. Norton – Bruce C. Norton – 1995*											
168¹/₈	24⁶/₈	24⁶/₈	19¹/₈	21⁷/₈	5²/₈	5	5	5		3426	315
■ *Wadena Co. – Don Carter – Don Carter – 1984*											
167²/₈	23	22²/₈	18⁶/₈	19²/₈	5³/₈	5⁵/₈	5	5		3519	316
■ *Otter Tail Co. – Gene Allen – Gene Allen – 1958*											
167²/₈	26	25⁷/₈	19⁷/₈	22³/₈	5	5	5	6	3⁵/₈	3519	316
■ *Pope Co. – Hans Engebretson – Hans Engebretson – 1977*											
167¹/₈	27	27²/₈	16³/₈	18⁶/₈	5³/₈	5³/₈	5	6	1⁴/₈	3539	318
■ *Cass Co. – Neil G. Anderson – Neil G. Anderson – 1990*											
166⁷/₈	25²/₈	24⁴/₈	20⁵/₈	22⁶/₈	4⁷/₈	4⁷/₈	5	5		3568	319
■ *Wabasha Co. – Chalmer Boyd – Fred W. King – 1947*											
166⁷/₈	23³/₈	23²/₈	22⁷/₈	24⁷/₈	4⁷/₈	4⁷/₈	5	5		3568	319
■ *Otter Tail Co. – DeWayne Brever – DeWayne Brever – 1965*											
166⁶/₈	25¹/₈	27	20⁶/₈	23²/₈	5²/₈	5³/₈	5	7		3582	321
■ *Blue Earth Co. – Jesse L. Cornish – Jesse L. Cornish – 1983*											
166²/₈	27⁷/₈	28	21	24²/₈	4⁷/₈	4⁵/₈	7	6	9⁴/₈	3632	322
■ *Fillmore Co. – Richard C. Bjortomt – Richard C. Bjortomt – 1972*											
166¹/₈	24	24	18³/₈	20²/₈	4⁷/₈	4⁶/₈	5	5		3643†	323†
■ *Chisago Co. – Jerry A. Smith – Jerry A. Smith – 2000*											
166	25⁶/₈	26³/₈	17⁵/₈	20¹/₈	5	4⁷/₈	6	8	7¹/₈	3657†	324†
■ *Beltrami Co. – Kenneth A. Hovland – Kenneth A. Hovland – 2000*											
166	26¹/₈	25⁴/₈	20⁴/₈	23¹/₈	4⁷/₈	5²/₈	7	7	11²/₈	3657	324
■ *Todd Co. – Thomas Hinrichs – Thomas Hinrichs – 1987*											
166	26²/₈	26⁷/₈	20²/₈	22²/₈	5¹/₈	5	5	5		3657	324
■ *Scott Co. – John E. Mesenbrink – John E. Mesenbrink – 1991*											
165⁷/₈	25	26¹/₈	21¹/₈	21⁷/₈	4⁴/₈	4⁵/₈	5	5		3672	327
■ *Wilkin Co. – Brian Arnhalt – Brian Arnhalt – 1982*											
165⁶/₈	25⁵/₈	27¹/₈	19⁴/₈	22⁷/₈	5¹/₈	5	5	5		3680	328
■ *Cass Co. – Brent M. Beimert – Brent M. Beimert – 1998*											
165⁵/₈	27	26¹/₈	19⁷/₈	21³/₈	4⁴/₈	4³/₈	5	6	1²/₈	3696	329
■ *Cass Co. – Ronald A. Peterson – Ronald A. Peterson – 1987*											
165⁴/₈	23⁴/₈	24⁴/₈	18²/₈	20²/₈	5	5⁵/₈	6	6		3714	330
■ *Winona Co. – John I. Kunert – John I. Kunert – 1990*											
165³/₈	24⁴/₈	24¹/₈	22³/₈	24⁵/₈	4⁴/₈	4³/₈	5	6		3731	331
■ *St. Louis Co. – Joseph D. Thompson – Joseph D. Thompson – 1991*											
165²/₈	28⁶/₈	28⁶/₈	21	22⁴/₈	5⁶/₈	6	7	9	11⁶/₈	3748	332
■ *St. Louis Co. – Harold Wilkins – James P. Wilkerson – 1974*											
165²/₈	27	27²/₈	22²/₈	24¹/₈	4⁴/₈	4⁴/₈	5	5		3748	332
■ *Winona Co. – Gary G. Dumdei – Gary G. Dumdei – 1977*											
165²/₈	24⁷/₈	24⁶/₈	16⁴/₈	18⁷/₈	5⁵/₈	5⁵/₈	6	8	5²/₈	3748	332
■ *Cass Co. – Richard D. Dabill – Richard D. Dabill – 1989*											

Score	Length of Main Beam Right	Left	Inside Spread	Greatest Spread	Circumference at Smallest Place Between Burr and First Point Right	Left	Number of Points Right	Left	Lengths Abnormal Points	All-Time Rank	State Rank
	Location of Kill – Hunter – Owner – Date Killed										
165	22²/8	22⁵/8	17⁶/8	19⁵/8	5	5	5	5		3782	335
	Crow Wing Co. – Michael J. Dullinger – Michael J. Dullinger – 1999										
164⁷/8	25	24⁶/8	22⁶/8	24⁷/8	5²/8	5²/8	5	6	1¹/8	3792	336
	St. Louis Co. – Gerald A. Larson – Gerald A. Larson – 1992										
164⁷/8	26⁵/8	27⁶/8	19	21¹/8	4⁶/8	4⁶/8	8	6	5³/8	3792	336
	Beltrami Co. – Kenneth L. Schmidt – Kenneth L. Schmidt – 1994										
164⁶/8	27³/8	26³/8	22	24¹/8	4⁷/8	4⁶/8	5	5		3809	338
	Fillmore Co. – Russell Ristau – Russell Ristau – 1973										
164⁵/8	24⁶/8	25²/8	16³/8	18⁴/8	4⁵/8	4³/8	6	6		3835	339
	Koochiching Co. – George E. Nelson – George E. Nelson – 1965										
164⁵/8	25⁵/8	25⁵/8	23⁴/8	25⁵/8	4⁵/8	4⁵/8	5	7	2¹/8	3835	339
	Morrison Co. – Bruce D. Edberg – Bruce D. Edberg – 1977										
164⁴/8	27⁷/8	27⁴/8	22	24⁴/8	4³/8	4³/8	7	7	6⁴/8	3855†	341†
	St. Louis Co. – David Willeck – Dan Willeck – 1984										
164⁴/8	27³/8	26³/8	24²/8	26⁶/8	4⁵/8	4⁵/8	6	7	4⁶/8	3855	341
	Pope Co. – Myron A. Forbord – Myron A. Forbord – 1972										
164¹/8	24²/8	25⁴/8	19⁵/8	21⁷/8	4⁶/8	4⁶/8	5	5		3886†	343†
	Beltrami Co. – Jerry D. Hamilton – Jerry D. Hamilton – 2000										
164	24²/8	23⁵/8	16	18⁴/8	4²/8	4²/8	5	5		3908†	344†
	Rice Co. – Thad A. Sunsdahl – Thad A. Sunsdahl – 2000										
164	27¹/8	26³/8	22⁵/8	25⁷/8	5	5	7	8	8⁷/8	3908	344
	Roseau Co. – George Rinde – George Rinde – 1972										
163⁷/8	25³/8	24⁶/8	18¹/8	20⁷/8	4⁴/8	4⁴/8	7	6	2²/8	3928	346
	Polk Co. – Matthew S. Werness – Matthew S. Werness – 1991										
163⁶/8	28⁴/8	27	19	21	4⁷/8	4⁷/8	4	4		3946	347
	Todd Co. – Jacob J. Slabaugh – Jacob J. Slabaugh – 1999										
163⁵/8	23⁴/8	23¹/8	19³/8	21⁴/8	6	6	5	6		3961	348
	Carver Co. – Ryan Jopp – Ryan Jopp – 1991										
163⁴/8	26⁷/8	26⁷/8	19⁶/8	22¹/8	5¹/8	5¹/8	7	9	7⁶/8	3984†	349†
	Lake Co. – Edward M. Plemel – Edward M. Plemel – 2001										
163⁴/8	26²/8	25⁴/8	18²/8	20⁵/8	5⁶/8	5⁶/8	5	5		3984	349
	Goodhue Co. – James N. Reuter – James N. Reuter – 1986										
163⁴/8	23	24¹/8	16⁶/8	19⁴/8	5²/8	5²/8	6	5		3984	349
	Otter Tail Co. – Spencer J. Vaa – Spencer J. Vaa – 1993										
163²/8	26⁵/8	26⁶/8	23	25³/8	4⁷/8	4⁷/8	5	5		4017	352
	Aitkin Co. – John P. Falteisek – David A. Vomela – 1945										
163²/8	25²/8	24¹/8	21²/8	23	3⁷/8	4⁷/8	7	6	4	4017	352
	Douglas Co. – Maynard D. Hoppe – Maynard D. Hoppe – 1990										
163¹/8	24⁷/8	25⁷/8	19¹/8	21	4³/8	4²/8	5	5		4035	354
	Marshall Co. – Robert W. Bidwell – Robert W. Bidwell – 1991										
162⁷/8	24³/8	23⁵/8	17⁶/8	20⁴/8	4³/8	4¹/8	7	6	1³/8	4067†	355†
	Crow Wing Co. – Jake Oravetz – Jake Oravetz – 2000										
162⁶/8	25²/8	25¹/8	21²/8	23¹/8	4⁷/8	5	5	5		4089	356

Score	Length of Main Beam Right Left		Inside Spread	Greatest Spread	Circumference at Smallest Place Between Burr and First Point Right Left		Number of Points Right Left		Lengths Abnormal Points	All-Time Rank	State Rank
	■ *Location of Kill – Hunter – Owner – Date Killed*										
	■ *St. Louis Co. – Eugene Bergman – Jay Bergman – 1956*										
162 6/8	26 1/8	26 1/8	21 3/8	23 2/8	6	6	6	7	8 1/8	4089	356
	■ *Otter Tail Co. – Mark M. Gontarek – Mark M. Gontarek – 1983*										
162 6/8	25 7/8	28 1/8	20 4/8	21 6/8	5 2/8	5 2/8	5	5		4089	356
	■ *Kandiyohi Co. – Eric R. Strand – Eric R. Strand – 1998*										
162 5/8	26 5/8	26 6/8	19 1/8	22	5	5 2/8	6	6	4 2/8	4109†	359†
	■ *Beltrami Co. – Wallace Lamon – Wallace Lamon – 1970*										
162 5/8	25 4/8	25 3/8	16 3/8	18 6/8	4 3/8	4 3/8	7	6	2 2/8	4109	359
	■ *Hubbard Co. – Nick J. Thill, Jr. – Nick J. Thill, Jr. – 1987*										
162 4/8	27	26 4/8	18	19 6/8	4 1/8	4 1/8	6	5	1 4/8	4129	361
	■ *Fillmore Co. – Todd R. Johnson – Todd R. Johnson – 1999*										
162 2/8	25 1/8	25 7/8	19 5/8	21 5/8	4 6/8	4 6/8	7	5	1 5/8	4153	362
	■ *Beltrami Co. – Bendik B. Vik – Bendik B. Vik – 1963*										
162 2/8	26 7/8	25 5/8	18 3/8	19 4/8	4 3/8	4 3/8	6	5	2 1/8	4153	362
	■ *Mahnomen Co. – Robert P. Krenz – Robert P. Krenz – 1994*										
162 2/8	25	24 4/8	18 1/8	20 7/8	4 7/8	4 7/8	6	6	1 7/8	4153	362
	■ *Wadena Co. – James K. Mell – James K. Mell – 1997*										
162	24 7/8	24 2/8	21	23 1/8	4 5/8	4 5/8	7	5	1 6/8	4184	365
	■ *Winona Co. – Jeffrey B. Bunke – Jeffrey B. Bunke – 1986*										
161 4/8	27 1/8	27 4/8	17 4/8	19 6/8	4 6/8	4 7/8	6	5		4258	366
	■ *St. Louis Co. – Mike Gunsolus – Mike Gunsolus – 1987*										
161 3/8	26 6/8	27 5/8	20 5/8	23 4/8	5 5/8	5 5/8	6	5	4 4/8	4285†	367†
	■ *Norman Co. – Kevin C. Bitker – Kevin C. Bitker – 1978*										
161 3/8	27 2/8	28 2/8	17 7/8	24 1/8	5 2/8	5	7	7	10 6/8	4285	367
	■ *Lake Co. – Jacob Ahonen – Jacob Ahonen – 1997*										
161 2/8	24 7/8	25 5/8	21 4/8	23 5/8	5	4 7/8	5	4		4310	369
	■ *Lake Co. – Terry Thewis – Ronald J. Studier – 1991*										
161 1/8	26 7/8	26	21	23	4 6/8	4 6/8	6	7	5 1/8	4332	370
	■ *Pennington Co. – Eric Hoven – Eric Hoven – 1991*										
161	25 3/8	26 1/8	15	17 3/8	4 7/8	4 7/8	7	7	3 2/8	4356	371
	■ *Koochiching Co. – Bradlee Karan – Bradlee Karan – 1987*										
160 7/8	25 1/8	27 7/8	18 1/8	25 1/8	5	5 1/8	5	6	5 4/8	4380	372
	■ *Clearwater Co. – John Veit – Thomas R. Forbes – PR 1905*										
160 5/8	27 1/8	28 3/8	21 6/8	24 1/8	4 6/8	5	6	7	6 5/8	4423†	373†
	■ *Hubbard Co. – Jerry Potratz – James C. Treat – 1974*										
160 5/8	25	24 6/8	20 5/8	22 6/8	5	5	6	6		4423	373
	■ *Redwood Co. – John C. Dunn – John C. Dunn – 1987*										
160 5/8	27 3/8	24 4/8	18 5/8	20 7/8	4 4/8	4 5/8	5	5		4423	373
	■ *Scott Co. – Kris Huber – Kris Huber – 1988*										
160 4/8	25 6/8	25 5/8	20 4/8	23 1/8	5	5	6	8	8	4443	376
	■ *Washington Co. – James A. Thurmes – James A. Thurmes – 1973*										
160 3/8	22	21 2/8	18 1/8	20 1/8	3 7/8	4 2/8	6	8	3 4/8	4470	377

Score	Length of Main Beam		Inside Spread	Greatest Spread	Circumference at Smallest Place Between Burr and First Point		Number of Points		Lengths Abnormal Points	All-Time Rank	State Rank
	Right	Left			Right	Left	Right	Left			

■ *Location of Kill – Hunter – Owner – Date Killed*

■ *Mille Lacs Co. – Scott J. Schmit – Scott J. Schmit – 1997*

| 160²/8 | 26⁴/8 | 24⁶/8 | 18²/8 | 20⁵/8 | 4⁴/8 | 4⁴/8 | 4 | 5 | | 4495 | 378 |

■ *Otter Tail Co. – Jon S. Walker – Jon S. Walker – 1990*

| 160¹/8 | 22¹/8 | 22⁵/8 | 17²/8 | 19²/8 | 5¹/8 | 5³/8 | 5 | 7 | 3³/8 | 4534† | 379† |

■ *Chisago Co. – Steven F. Zupon – Steven F. Zupon – 2000*

| 160¹/8 | 23⁴/8 | 23⁴/8 | 16⁷/8 | 19¹/8 | 4³/8 | 4³/8 | 6 | 6 | | 4534 | 379 |

■ *Koochiching Co. – Robert W. Barnes – Robert W. Barnes – 1999*

† The scores and ranking for trophies from the 25th Awards Entry Period are not final until the banquet is held on June 19, 2004.

294   RECORDS OF NORTH AMERICAN WHITETAIL DEER ■ FOURTH EDITION

TROPHIES IN THE FIELD

HUNTER: Vincent A. LaCroix
SCORE: 171-6/8
CATEGORY: typical whitetail deer
LOCATION: Dakota County, Minnesota
DATE: 1998

MINNESOTA

NON-TYPICAL WHITETAIL DEER

Score	Length of Main Beam Right	Left	Inside Spread	Greatest Spread	Circumference at Smallest Place Between Burr and First Point Right	Left	Number of Points Right	Left	Lengths Abnormal Points	All-Time Rank	State Rank
	■ Location of Kill – Hunter – Owner – Date Killed										
268 5/8	20 6/8	24 6/8	14 2/8		6 4/8	5 3/8	20	21	118 3/8	14	1
	■ Norman Co. – Mitchell A. Vakoch – Bass Pro Shops – 1974										
258 2/8	27	26 6/8	19 5/8	26 3/8	4 7/8	4 6/8	17	17	73 5/8	30	2
	■ Becker Co. – J.J. Matter – J.J. Matter – 1973										
251 4/8	26 3/8	27 5/8	22 7/8	27	5 4/8	5 3/8	17	14	70 1/8	50	3
	■ Beltrami Co. – Rodney Rhineberger – Bass Pro Shops – 1976										
250	29 5/8	30 1/8	23 4/8	27	6 2/8	6 1/8	15	13	58	60	4
	■ Clearwater Co. – Ernest Sauer – Duane O. Bagley Wildl. Mus. – 1931										
249 2/8	29 6/8	28 7/8	21 3/8	23 5/8	5 2/8	5 2/8	10	14	60 5/8	63	5
	■ Fillmore Co. – Dallas R. Henn – Bass Pro Shops – 1961										
245 5/8	25 5/8	25 2/8	24 2/8	30 5/8	5 2/8	5 3/8	12	12	64 7/8	80	6
	■ Itasca Co. – Peter Rutkowski – Bass Pro Shops – 1942										
245 4/8	27 7/8	27 5/8	18 6/8	26 3/8	6 1/8	6 2/8	16	15	65	82	7
	■ Kittson Co. – Lyndon K. Westerberg – Lyndon K. Westerberg – 1990										
245 3/8	24	24 4/8	17 4/8	26 4/8	5 7/8	6 1/8	14	14	75 3/8	84	8
	■ Itasca Co. – Mike Hammer – Bass Pro Shops – 1956										
244	25 4/8	30 3/8	20 2/8	24 7/8	5 5/8	5 4/8	8	10	98	92	9
	■ Becker Co. – James Saurdoff – Bass Pro Shops – 1985										
240 6/8	25 5/8	26 2/8	17 2/8	24 3/8	5 2/8	5 1/8	17	20	62	110	10
	■ St. Louis Co. – John Cesarek – John Cesarek – 1964										
239 4/8	25 7/8	25 6/8	17 2/8	19 3/8	4 4/8	4 4/8	10	12	65	121	11
	■ Meeker Co. – Michael D. Dick – Michael D. Dick – 1994										
236 7/8	24 7/8	24 7/8	18 2/8	26	5 1/8	4 6/8	18	7	66 5/8	154	12
	■ Beltrami Co. – Edwin C. Moe – Edwin C. Moe – 1995										
236 5/8	26	26 3/8	21 4/8	26	6	6 1/8	12	14	64 1/8	157	13
	■ Pope Co. – Douglas D. Vesledahl – Douglas D. Vesledahl – 1961										
236	22 3/8	24 6/8	19 5/8	23 2/8	5 4/8	5 1/8	11	12	71 3/8	164	14
	■ Winona Co. – Francis A. Pries – Bass Pro Shops – 1964										
234 1/8	26 7/8	26 3/8	20 2/8	22 1/8	5 5/8	6 2/8	16	14	50 1/8	178	15
	■ Minnesota – Unknown – Gale Sup – PR 1985										
234	26 7/8	26 2/8	18 5/8	26	6 6/8	6 6/8	14	12	48 7/8	182	16
	■ Lac qui Parle Co. – Clifford A. Estlie – Clifford A. Estlie – 1991										
233 3/8	25 3/8	29 7/8	19 4/8	23 1/8	5 6/8	5 3/8	12	8	80 7/8	191	17
	■ Carlton Co. – Peter Antonson – Roy Ober – PR 1938										
232 5/8	28 3/8	29	23 6/8	26 1/8	5 2/8	5 3/8	9	9	33 7/8	200	18
	■ Wabasha Co. – Robert R. Friese – Robert R. Friese – 1948										
231 2/8	26 1/8	30 1/8	20 6/8	25 6/8	5 2/8	5 1/8	10	9	31 4/8	221	19
	■ Renville Co. – James L. Rath – Bass Pro Shops – 1977										

Score	Length of Main Beam Right Left	Inside Spread	Greatest Spread	Circumference at Smallest Place Between Burr and First Point Right Left		Number of Points Right Left		Lengths Abnormal Points	All-Time Rank	State Rank
	■ *Location of Kill – Hunter – Owner – Date Killed*									
231 1/8	19 5/8 22 3/8	20 4/8	23 6/8	6	5 7/8	12	12	76 5/8	224	20
	■ *Lac qui Parle Co. – Willard Evans – Paul Evans – 1951*									
231 1/8	28 3/8 28 4/8	24 2/8	28	5 1/8	5 3/8	12	9	31 5/8	224	20
	■ *Winona Co. – Robert E. Bains – Robert E. Bains – 1973*									
231	27 5/8 28	21 2/8	25 2/8	5 2/8	5 1/8	8	7	27 4/8	227	22
	■ *Cass Co. – L.S. Hanson – Joel H. Karvonen – 1970*									
230 2/8	26 1/8 26	19 1/8	22 4/8	5	5 1/8	11	11	27 1/8	235	23
	■ *Todd Co. – John Berscheit – John Berscheit – 1976*									
230 1/8	27 2/8 27 1/8	18	23 2/8	5 3/8	5 3/8	15	11	50 3/8	238	24
	■ *Pope Co. – Harvey J. Erickson – Harvey J. Erickson – 1974*									
230	27 1/8 28 1/8	19 7/8	23 1/8	5	5	11	8	47 3/8	240	25
	■ *Houston Co. – Winnie Papenfuss – Winnie Papenfuss – 1973*									
228 4/8	28 6/8 28 3/8	19 5/8	25 2/8	6 2/8	6	14	11	47 5/8	258	26
	■ *Lake Co. – Lisa A. Baxter – Lisa A. Baxter – 1991*									
226	23 4/8 25 2/8	26 2/8	30 3/8	5 2/8	5	11	11	52	303	27
	■ *Winona Co. – Terry D. Masso – Terry D. Masso – 1991*									
225 6/8	26 7/8 24 5/8	21 5/8	25 1/8	5 2/8	5 2/8	9	8	27 5/8	306	28
	■ *Yellow Medicine Co. – Glen Bullick – Glen Bullick – 1989*									
225 2/8	29 1/8 29 2/8	23 4/8	28 6/8	6 2/8	6 1/8	9	8	29 2/8	310	29
	■ *St. Louis Co. – Elmer H. Sellin – Bass Pro Shops – 1938*									
225 1/8	28 3/8 28 1/8	20 2/8	25 7/8	6	6	8	9	35 5/8	314	30
	■ *Winona Co. – Jeffrey S. Wilder – Jeffrey S. Wilder – 1977*									
224 4/8	25 3/8 27 6/8	20 2/8	23 2/8	5 5/8	5 4/8	9	8	27 2/8	327	31
	■ *Cass Co. – Roy K. Blowers, Sr. – Roy K. Blowers, Sr. – 1947*									
224 3/8	30 5/8 30 1/8	21 2/8	24	4 7/8	4 5/8	11	8	36 1/8	330†	32†
	■ *Chisago Co. – Nathan Stimson – Nathan Stimson – 2001*									
224 3/8	26 7/8 27	21 2/8	25 7/8	5 1/8	5 2/8	8	7	31 5/8	330	32
	■ *Lac qui Parle Co. – Mike Unzen – Mike Unzen – 1969*									
224 2/8	23 2/8 23 2/8	22	26 7/8	5 3/8	5 2/8	18	15	54	332	34
	■ *Pine Co. – Greg S. Blom – Greg S. Blom – 1980*									
224	29 4/8 29 2/8	20	22 4/8	6 2/8	5 4/8	15	13	29 4/8	337	35
	■ *Minnesota – Unknown – Harvard Univ. Mus. – 1890*									
222 7/8	26 6/8 27 6/8	19 7/8	23 4/8	5 7/8	5 7/8	12	12	46	368	36
	■ *Murray Co. – Clyde Robbins – David C. Robbins – 1964*									
222 6/8	21 4/8 22 7/8	16 1/8	20 6/8	5 7/8	5 3/8	11	10	45 1/8	371	37
	■ *Itasca Co. – Picked Up – James R. Smith – 1936*									
222 3/8	25 2/8 25 6/8	19 1/8	26 6/8	5 6/8	5 6/8	14	12	45 2/8	384	38
	■ *Itasca Co. – Lumie Jackson – Rick Ferguson – 1942*									
222 3/8	27 3/8 27 5/8	22 3/8	25 2/8	6 5/8	6 7/8	9	7	39 6/8	384	38
	■ *Stearns Co. – Richard E. Sand – Richard E. Sand – 1988*									
222 1/8	27 1/8 28 1/8	22 3/8	28 3/8	4 6/8	4 7/8	12	10	43 4/8	392	40
	■ *Cass Co. – Marvel R. Utke – Marvel R. Utke – 1977*									

Score	Length of Main Beam		Inside Spread	Greatest Spread	Circumference at Smallest Place Between Burr and First Point		Number of Points		Lengths Abnormal Points	All-Time Rank	State Rank
	Right	Left			Right	Left	Right	Left			
	■ Location of Kill – Hunter – Owner – Date Killed										
221⁵/8	25²/8	24⁶/8	23⁷/8	26⁷/8	5	5	10	11	36	401	41
	■ Clearwater Co. – Kevin Crane – Kevin Crane – 1994										
221²/8	22⁵/8	23⁶/8	17¹/8	26⁴/8	4⁵/8	4⁴/8	16	11	63⁵/8	410	42
	■ Itasca Co. – Richard I. Goble – Richard I. Goble – 1955										
220⁶/8	26²/8	25⁶/8	19⁶/8	25²/8	6¹/8	6³/8	12	15	47⁴/8	421	43
	■ Anoka Co. – Donald Torgerson – Bass Pro Shops – 1946										
220⁵/8	29¹/8	28²/8	20⁶/8	23⁵/8	5⁴/8	5⁶/8	13	12	26³/8	424	44
	■ Kittson Co. – Todd J. Porter – Dick Rossum – 1986										
220³/8	25¹/8	25⁶/8	18⁶/8	22⁶/8	5	5	14	13	53¹/8	431	45
	■ Olmsted Co. – E.E. Comartin III – E.E. Comartin, Jr. – 1963										
220³/8	27¹/8	27	19⁷/8	23²/8	5⁶/8	5⁵/8	10	12	40⁶/8	431	45
	■ Todd Co. – Gary V. Martin – Gary V. Martin – 1992										
219⁴/8	27	27²/8	24²/8	26⁶/8	5⁶/8	6¹/8	11	11	36	453	47
	■ Lake of the Woods Co. – Thomas Barden – Robert V. Ellenson – PR 1951										
219	27³/8	27	17⁶/8	22³/8	5⁶/8	5⁷/8	8	11	37	470	48
	■ Morrison Co. – Michael R. Langin – Michael R. Langin – 1992										
218⁶/8	23⁵/8	24⁷/8	19²/8	22²/8	6²/8	5⁴/8	14	7	48	477	49
	■ Morrison Co. – Wilfred LeBlanc – George W. Flaim – 1938										
218⁵/8	25	25²/8	14⁴/8	24	5¹/8	5¹/8	13	15	46¹/8	480	50
	■ Itasca Co. – John W. Pierson, Sr. – John W. Pierson, Sr. – 1945										
218⁵/8	28⁶/8	27⁴/8	20	25⁷/8	6¹/8	6	14	11	42⁵/8	480	50
	■ St. Louis Co. – Unknown – George W. Flaim – PR 1983										
218⁵/8	25³/8	24⁶/8	18	24¹/8	6⁷/8	6³/8	17	13	46⁵/8	480	50
	■ Otter Tail Co. – Gerald P. Lucas – Gerald P. Lucas – 1985										
218³/8	23	26	16⁷/8	23²/8	5⁴/8	5⁴/8	15	11	50²/8	490	53
	■ Itasca Co. – Unknown – George W. Flaim – 1983										
218³/8	29²/8	29⁵/8	19⁵/8	24³/8	5¹/8	4⁷/8	12	10	28⁶/8	490	53
	■ Fillmore Co. – Darrel R. Highum – Darrel R. Highum – 1989										
218	25⁴/8	25³/8	19	23⁵/8	5⁴/8	5³/8	11	15	48⁶/8	498	55
	■ Otter Tail Co. – Dennis A. Pearson – Dennis A. Pearson – 1977										
217⁴/8	25⁵/8	25	19⁴/8	23²/8	6²/8	6³/8	11	12	31⁴/8	510	56
	■ Aitkin Co. – Fred C. Melichar – Fred C. Melichar – 1973										
217³/8	27	28⁵/8	18³/8	24⁵/8	5²/8	5⁴/8	12	15	38⁶/8	514	57
	■ Meeker Co. – Steven R. Turck – Steven R. Turck – 1982										
217²/8	29²/8	29⁴/8	20	23⁷/8	5⁶/8	5⁶/8	12	9	35⁴/8	519	58
	■ St. Louis Co. – Unknown – George W. Flaim – 1957										
217²/8	30	29²/8	21²/8	24²/8	4⁶/8	5	6	12	35⁶/8	519	58
	■ Kandiyohi Co. – Picked Up – Dean Salzl – 1988										
216⁶/8	24⁴/8	24¹/8	17	23¹/8	7	7¹/8	11	11	43²/8	539	60
	■ Lake of the Woods Co. – Andy Streiff – Andy Streiff – 1974										
216²/8	30	28²/8	23	26	5⁷/8	5⁵/8	7	9	36⁴/8	555	61
	■ Blue Earth Co. – Marion Abbas – Harold Abbas – 1961										

Score	Length of Main Beam		Inside Spread	Greatest Spread	Circumference at Smallest Place Between Burr and First Point		Number of Points		Lengths Abnormal Points	All-Time Rank	State Rank
	Right	Left			Right	Left	Right	Left			
	■ Location of Kill – Hunter – Owner – Date Killed										
216 1/8	23 1/8	19 4/8	15 2/8	26	5 3/8	6 1/8	15	16	48 7/8	561	62
	■ Itasca Co. – Thomas Thurstin – Thomas Thurstin – 1977										
215 7/8	27 1/8	27 5/8	22 2/8	24 6/8	5 5/8	5 6/8	9	13	34 1/8	569	63
	■ Wabasha Co. – Leroy Goranson – Leroy Goranson – 1990										
215 6/8	24 4/8	24 4/8	23 3/8	25 3/8	6 2/8	7 4/8	10	12	45 3/8	575	64
	■ Chippewa Co. – Micheal Allickson – Micheal Allickson – 1974										
215 4/8	26 7/8	26 6/8	19 3/8	21 4/8	5 3/8	5 3/8	10	9	30 5/8	583	65
	■ Morrison Co. – James P. Poser – James P. Poser – 1978										
215 2/8	24 3/8	27 1/8	18 2/8	21 6/8	5 3/8	5 3/8	9	9	33 2/8	589	66
	■ Fillmore Co. – George E. Holets – George E. Holets – 1960										
215	28 1/8	27 5/8	19 5/8	23 2/8	6 7/8	7 2/8	8	10	36 1/8	598†	67†
	■ Todd Co. – Picked Up – Tom Kendall – 2000										
215	26 3/8	25 6/8	15 6/8	25	5 2/8	5 2/8	13	13	42	598	67
	■ Fillmore Co. – Picked Up – Jeffrey S. Mackey – 1968										
214 7/8	26 3/8	24 6/8	21 1/8	28 4/8	5 1/8	6 4/8	9	13	54 4/8	605	69
	■ Cass Co. – Glen W. Slagle, Sr. – Glen W. Slagle, Sr. – 1959										
214 5/8	25 5/8	25 7/8	16 5/8	25 5/8	5	4 7/8	15	14	54	614	70
	■ Koochiching Co. – Unknown – Wilbur Tilander – 1956										
214 4/8	26 6/8	26 4/8	20 1/8	25 2/8	5 2/8	5	11	9	30 7/8	617	71
	■ Swift Co. – Leonard N. Kanuit – Leonard N. Kanuit – 1972										
214 3/8	24 1/8	26 2/8	18 3/8	21	5 1/8	5 2/8	14	13	27 2/8	620	72
	■ Roseau Co. – Warren Tveit – Warren Tveit – 1976										
214	28 7/8	28 6/8	23 1/8	28 2/8	4 5/8	4 4/8	10	9	19 1/8	629	73
	■ Clay Co. – Dean Klemetson – Dean Klemetson – 1984										
213 5/8	24 2/8	24 2/8	17 1/8	20 5/8	5 6/8	5 5/8	12	6	35 4/8	649	74
	■ Beltrami Co. – Unknown – Jim Smith – 1924										
213 2/8	27 2/8	27 1/8	18 5/8	21	5	5 1/8	7	8	39 5/8	662	75
	■ Fillmore Co. – Steven A. Johnson – Steven A. Johnson – 1988										
213	27	27 7/8	15 5/8	24	4 5/8	4 6/8	14	12	31 3/8	671	76
	■ St. Louis Co. – Walfred Olson – Erling H. Olson – 1935										
212 7/8	25 5/8	29 1/8	20 6/8	22 3/8	5 3/8	5 2/8	10	13	44 3/8	674	77
	■ Otter Tail Co. – Harold L. Collins – Harold L. Collins – 1985										
212 2/8	26 6/8	26 1/8	23 6/8	25 4/8	5 4/8	5 3/8	9	7	18 4/8	701	78
	■ Houston Co. – Alfred C. Pieper – Alfred C. Pieper – 1977										
212 1/8	27	28 5/8	18 5/8	25 4/8	5 6/8	6 2/8	11	1	51 4/8	709†	79†
	■ Koochiching Co. – Tom Sutch – Tom Sutch – 2000										
212 1/8	24	24 3/8	20 1/8	25 6/8	5 1/8	5	16	13	37	709	79
	■ Minnesota – Unknown – John R. Steffes, Sr. – PR 1960										
212 1/8	26 5/8	25 6/8	20	23 1/8	4 7/8	5	9	8	28 7/8	709	79
	■ Stevens Co. – Ronald J. Mohr – Ronald J. Mohr – 1963										
212 1/8	27	27 2/8	19 6/8	25 7/8	5 2/8	5 3/8	14	16	41 3/8	709	79
	■ St. Louis Co. – Robert J. LaPine – Robert J. LaPine – 1968										

Score	Length of Main Beam Right	Left	Inside Spread	Greatest Spread	Circumference at Smallest Place Between Burr and First Point Right	Left	Number of Points Right	Left	Lengths Abnormal Points	All-Time Rank	State Rank
									■ *Location of Kill – Hunter – Owner – Date Killed*		
212 1/8	28 1/8	28	18 1/8	22 3/8	5 4/8	5 4/8	9	8	26 2/8	709	79
	■ *Winona Co. – Donald J. Mehren – Donald J. Mehren – 1985*										
212	26 7/8	25	16 7/8	21	4 7/8	5 1/8	14	13	35 7/8	717	84
	■ *Becker Co. – Unknown – John R. Steffes, Sr. – 1922*										
212	28 4/8	27 7/8	24 5/8	26 5/8	6	6 1/8	7	8	18 5/8	717	84
	■ *Big Stone Co. – Picked Up – Danny L. Cole – 1993*										
211 6/8	22 3/8	25 5/8	21	26 3/8	5	5	10	11	24 4/8	729	86
	■ *Cottonwood Co. – James A. Sykora – James A. Sykora – 1981*										
211 6/8	26 5/8	27 7/8	18 4/8	22 3/8	5 1/8	4 6/8	12	12	34 4/8	729	86
	■ *Roseau Co. – Edward L. Quiring – Edward L. Quiring – 1988*										
211 4/8	27 2/8	25 6/8	20 2/8	23 6/8	5 3/8	5 3/8	10	9	30 6/8	739	88
	■ *Minnesota – Picked Up – David Cater – 1960*										
211 4/8	25 3/8	25	18 3/8	25 4/8	5 1/8	4 7/8	14	17	43 5/8	739	88
	■ *St. Louis Co. – John E. Peterson, Jr. – John E. Peterson, Jr. – 1963*										
211 2/8	24 5/8	26 6/8	14 7/8	17 6/8	6	6 2/8	9	8	15 7/8	750	90
	■ *Kittson Co. – Picked Up – Floyd R. Nelson – 1942*										
211 2/8	27 7/8	27	19 2/8	23 1/8	6 2/8	6 1/8	8	9	33 4/8	750	90
	■ *Marshall Co. – Picked Up – Robert Sands – 1959*										
211 2/8	26 1/8	25 5/8	19 4/8	21 5/8	4 2/8	4 2/8	9	7	30 2/8	750	90
	■ *Stearns Co. – Ronald Steil – Ronald Steil – 1983*										
211 1/8	27 5/8	28	18 6/8	21	5 6/8	5 6/8	9	10	30 7/8	758	93
	■ *Itasca Co. – Glen V. Jones – Mark W. Jones – PR 1948*										
211 1/8	24 2/8	24 6/8	17 2/8	20 2/8	5 4/8	5 1/8	15	11	35 5/8	758	93
	■ *Houston Co. – Daniel P. Gade – Daniel P. Gade – 1998*										
210 7/8	23 4/8	19 4/8	15 5/8	18 7/8	5 3/8	7 2/8	12	11	67 2/8	773	95
	■ *Winona Co. – Donald D. Zenk – Donald D. Zenk – 1998*										
210 6/8	26 2/8	26 7/8	21 1/8	23 7/8	5 5/8	5 4/8	12	9	30 3/8	779	96
	■ *Todd Co. – Paul E. Berscheit – Paul E. Berscheit – 1990*										
210 4/8	26 1/8	26	21 7/8	26 1/8	5 1/8	5 2/8	14	11	42 3/8	791	97
	■ *Stearns Co. – Kim C. Kirckof – Kim C. Kirckof – 1992*										
210 4/8	27 2/8	27 5/8	23 5/8	30 2/8	4 3/8	4 3/8	10	8	31 3/8	791	97
	■ *Pope Co. – Scott G. Finn – Scott G. Finn – 1993*										
210	23 1/8	23 5/8	17 3/8	19 7/8	5 4/8	5 4/8	12	10	38 3/8	816†	99†
	■ *Wright Co. – Picked Up – John R. Thole – 1998*										
209 7/8	25 6/8	25 4/8	18 1/8	20 6/8	4 5/8	4 5/8	10	15	34 6/8	825	100
	■ *Pine Co. – Scott A. Miller – Scott A. Miller – 1980*										
209 6/8	27	27 2/8	17 1/8	19 6/8	5 2/8	5 1/8	11	10	29 3/8	831	101
	■ *Koochiching Co. – Harry Van Keuren – Louis E. Muench – 1929*										
208 7/8	24 1/8	25 3/8	19 2/8	21 7/8	5	4 7/8	8	7	44 3/8	877	102
	■ *Anoka Co. – Picked Up – Becky Wozney – 1998*										
208 4/8	25 4/8	25 6/8	19 1/8	27 2/8	5 6/8	5 5/8	13	10	38 5/8	894†	103†
	■ *Mille Lacs Co. – Picked Up – Louis J. Los – 2002*										

Score	Length of Main Beam Right	Left	Inside Spread	Greatest Spread	Circumference at Smallest Place Between Burr and First Point Right	Left	Number of Points Right	Left	Lengths Abnormal Points	All-Time Rank	State Rank
	■ Location of Kill – Hunter – Owner – Date Killed										
208⁴/₈	26⁶/₈	27³/₈	21⁶/₈	27¹/₈	6	6¹/₈	9	8	24	894	103
	■ Itasca Co. – Unknown – William L. Achman – 1945										
208³/₈	25²/₈	28²/₈	18⁷/₈	21¹/₈	5¹/₈	4⁷/₈	13	13	46	905	105
	■ St. Louis Co. – Unknown – George W. Flaim – PR 1940										
208³/₈	24⁴/₈	24⁴/₈	17⁷/₈	23⁴/₈	4³/₈	4⁵/₈	13	10	26²/₈	905	105
	■ Isanti Co. – Richard C. Hansen – Richard C. Hansen – 1995										
208²/₈	27	26¹/₈	20⁴/₈	23²/₈	4⁷/₈	4⁶/₈	11	11	37²/₈	910	107
	■ St. Louis Co. – Walter H. Enzenauer – Walter H. Enzenauer – 1961										
208²/₈	27	26	22²/₈	27²/₈	5⁴/₈	5³/₈	10	7	21⁶/₈	910	107
	■ St. Louis Co. – Ed Mikulich – Terry Mikulich – 1964										
208	22	22²/₈	25²/₈	28⁶/₈	6¹/₈	6³/₈	11	11	45	929	109
	■ Olmsted Co. – Glen E. Leighton – Glen E. Leighton – 1991										
207⁵/₈	27¹/₈	26⁵/₈	22²/₈	27⁵/₈	6⁶/₈	7	11	9	30¹/₈	957	110
	■ Lincoln Co. – Joe Ness – Joe Ness – 1961										
207⁴/₈	27⁷/₈	27⁷/₈	17³/₈	21²/₈	5⁴/₈	5⁴/₈	12	8	17⁷/₈	969†	111†
	■ Winona Co. – Picked Up – Ray T. Charles – 2001										
207³/₈	25³/₈	26	26³/₈	30¹/₈	5²/₈	5³/₈	8	11	43⁷/₈	977	112
	■ Aitkin Co. – Viola Scott – Viola S. Weimer – 1954										
207²/₈	27⁷/₈	27	20⁶/₈	24⁶/₈	5⁵/₈	5⁵/₈	11	9	23⁴/₈	985	113
	■ Wilkin Co. – Richard K. Christopher – Richard K. Christopher – 1999										
207¹/₈	23⁴/₈	23⁴/₈	15⁶/₈	21¹/₈	4⁷/₈	4⁶/₈	11	8	40⁵/₈	995	114
	■ Traverse Co. – Joel E. Kuschel – Joel E. Kuschel – 1996										
206⁷/₈	26²/₈	29⁵/₈	27⁷/₈	30⁴/₈	5²/₈	5⁴/₈	11	10	21	1011	115
	■ Wright Co. – Richard A. Erickson – Richard A. Erickson – 1983										
206⁷/₈	28³/₈	27⁷/₈	20¹/₈	24⁴/₈	5²/₈	5¹/₈	9	6	21⁶/₈	1011	115
	■ Stearns Co. – Steven J. Sperl – Steven J. Sperl – 1987										
206⁴/₈	23²/₈	23¹/₈	16⁴/₈	26	5⁴/₈	5⁴/₈	14	8	44	1043	117
	■ Norman Co. – Unknown – Tom Williams – 1950										
206⁴/₈	26	26¹/₈	19²/₈	24²/₈	6³/₈	6¹/₈	11	6	13²/₈	1043	117
	■ Lac qui Parle Co. – Steven J. Karels – Steven J. Karels – 1974										
206³/₈	26⁶/₈	26⁵/₈	21⁶/₈	26⁶/₈	5⁷/₈	5⁴/₈	9	8	14⁷/₈	1051†	119†
	■ St. Louis Co. – Picked Up – Paul Coughlin – 2002										
206²/₈	31⁵/₈	29³/₈	23⁴/₈	26⁴/₈	4⁶/₈	4⁴/₈	8	9	27²/₈	1059	120
	■ Benton Co. – Kenneth R. Nodo – Kenneth R. Nodo – 1987										
206¹/₈	25¹/₈	26¹/₈	19⁷/₈	25⁷/₈	5⁴/₈	5⁵/₈	10	12	38²/₈	1068	121
	■ Lake of the Woods Co. – Keith D. Yahnke – Keith D. Yahnke – 1987										
206	25⁶/₈	24⁵/₈	15⁶/₈	19	4⁷/₈	4⁷/₈	10	14	40	1075	122
	■ St. Louis Co. – Earl Skarp – George W. Flaim – 1938										
205⁷/₈	27³/₈	26²/₈	18¹/₈	21⁴/₈	5⁶/₈	5⁷/₈	10	10	23⁶/₈	1080†	123†
	■ Todd Co. – Ben Sadlovsky – Matthew K. Sadlovsky – 1973										
205⁷/₈	23⁴/₈	23⁴/₈	19³/₈	23⁴/₈	6¹/₈	5⁷/₈	7	8	21⁴/₈	1080	123
	■ Swift Co. – A.P. Vander Weyst – A.P. Vander Weyst – 1954										

Score	Length of Main Beam		Inside Spread	Greatest Spread	Circumference at Smallest Place Between Burr and First Point		Number of Points		Lengths Abnormal Points	All-Time Rank	State Rank
	Right	Left			Right	Left	Right	Left			
	■ *Location of Kill – Hunter – Owner – Date Killed*										
205⁶/8	25³/8	26⁴/8	18¹/8	21³/8	4⁵/8	4⁴/8	11	9	19³/8	1094	125
	■ *Minnesota – Unknown – Greg Jensen – 1965*										
205⁶/8	26²/8	25²/8	15⁶/8	19³/8	5⁷/8	6	14	10	25²/8	1094	125
	■ *Koochiching Co. – Unknown – Marc M. Jackson – PR 1979*										
205⁵/8	26	25²/8	21²/8	23²/8	5⁴/8	5⁷/8	14	9	32³/8	1102	127
	■ *Cottonwood Co. – Larry G. Gravley – Larry G. Gravley – 1975*										
205⁴/8	27²/8	25⁴/8	22⁴/8	26¹/8	5⁵/8	5⁶/8	9	9	29⁶/8	1107	128
	■ *Roseau Co. – Erwin Klaassen – Erwin Klaassen – 1955*										
205⁴/8	23⁵/8	23	19⁶/8	23²/8	5⁵/8	5⁶/8	12	16	49²/8	1107	128
	■ *St. Louis Co. – Picked Up – George W. Flaim – 1985*										
205⁴/8	26	25⁷/8	20²/8	22⁴/8	5⁴/8	5⁶/8	8	8	22⁴/8	1107	128
	■ *Washington Co. – Lonnie J. Diethert – Lonnie J. Diethert – 1987*										
205³/8	22⁴/8	23²/8	17	26	6	6	10	12	46¹/8	1116	131
	■ *Todd Co. – Mark A. Miksche – Mark A. Miksche – 1979*										
205³/8	24⁷/8	24¹/8	17⁴/8	19⁵/8	4⁵/8	4⁶/8	10	9	28⁵/8	1116	131
	■ *Wadena Co. – Donald R. Brockob – Donald R. Brockob – 1990*										
205³/8	25¹/8	24	15	20²/8	6	7³/8	8	12	40⁷/8	1116	131
	■ *Beltrami Co. – Matt E. Stone – Matt E. Stone – 1990*										
205³/8	26	26¹/8	19¹/8	23⁷/8	5³/8	5⁴/8	10	10	24²/8	1116	131
	■ *Freeborn Co. – Picked Up – Kevin J. Nelson – 1997*										
205³/8	25	25³/8	19²/8	24	4⁷/8	5²/8	7	13	55⁷/8	1116	131
	■ *Winona Co. – James D. Vitcenda – James D. Vitcenda – 1998* ■ *See photo on page 59*										
205	26³/8	26⁴/8	16⁷/8	19⁴/8	6¹/8	5⁷/8	12	9	25⁵/8	1144	136
	■ *St. Louis Co. – Ed Nelson – George W. Flaim – 1964*										
204⁷/8	23³/8	23¹/8	22⁷/8	25⁴/8	4⁷/8	4⁵/8	10	11	60⁴/8	1156†	137†
	■ *Minnesota – William Egli – Steve Scholl – 1941*										
204⁷/8	25²/8	25²/8	21⁷/8	25¹/8	5	5³/8	13	12	29²/8	1156	137
	■ *Roseau Co. – Andy Streiff – Andy Streiff – 1967*										
204⁷/8	26	24⁵/8	18⁵/8	24¹/8	4⁵/8	4⁶/8	9	12	32⁴/8	1156	137
	■ *Winona Co. – Picked Up – Gary L. Bornfleth – 1979*										
204⁶/8	22⁷/8	24¹/8	21²/8	25³/8	5	4⁷/8	7	14	54⁴/8	1165	140
	■ *Koochiching Co. – H.T. Hanson – Kevin Blomer – 1920*										
204⁶/8	28⁴/8	27⁶/8	26¹/8	29⁵/8	4⁴/8	4⁵/8	8	7	22⁷/8	1165	140
	■ *Stearns Co. – Curt Fettig – Curt Fettig – 1975*										
204³/8	26²/8	26²/8	17²/8	22	5²/8	4⁵/8	12	7	20⁷/8	1186†	142†
	■ *Otter Tail Co. – John L. Sabbin – John L. Sabbin – 2001*										
204³/8	25	25⁶/8	14⁷/8	19⁴/8	5¹/8	5²/8	10	10	38⁴/8	1186	142
	■ *Clearwater Co. – Gilbert Oien – Vance R. Norgaard – 1976*										
204²/8	25²/8	25⁵/8	23²/8	26⁷/8	6⁵/8	6⁴/8	9	10	32⁴/8	1199	144
	■ *Meeker Co. – Walter J. Tintes – Walter J. Tintes – 1975*										
204¹/8	28¹/8	27²/8	22³/8	25⁷/8	6	5⁴/8	10	12	32²/8	1210	145
	■ *Lyon Co. – Ray Evans – David C. Johnson – 1940*										

Score	Length of Main Beam Right Left	Inside Spread	Greatest Spread	Circumference at Smallest Place Between Burr and First Point Right Left		Number of Points Right Left		Lengths Abnormal Points	All-Time Rank	State Rank
	■ *Location of Kill – Hunter – Owner – Date Killed*									
204¹/₈	28 27³/₈	24⁵/₈	30⁵/₈	5²/₈	5²/₈	8	11	28⁶/₈	1210	145
	■ *Pope Co. – LeRoy D. Hausmann – LeRoy D. Hausmann – 1967*									
204¹/₈	25²/₈ 26¹/₈	18³/₈	22⁷/₈	5⁵/₈	5⁵/₈	14	11	38²/₈	1210	145
	■ *Douglas Co. – Samuel Knapp – Samuel Knapp – 1993*									
204	26¹/₈ 27³/₈	16²/₈	18⁵/₈	5¹/₈	5³/₈	10	11	16²/₈	1220	148
	■ *Carlton Co. – Erick Zack – Glen Van Guilder – 1964*									
204	26¹/₈ 25⁵/₈	18⁶/₈	25³/₈	5³/₈	5²/₈	13	10	38²/₈	1220	148
	■ *Grant Co. – Douglas S. Olson – Douglas S. Olson – 1977*									
204	26³/₈ 26⁷/₈	17⁴/₈	24⁴/₈	5¹/₈	5	8	9	29	1220	148
	■ *Beltrami Co. – Terence C. Derosier – Terence C. Derosier – 1991*									
203⁷/₈	22 22⁵/₈	19	22⁵/₈	5¹/₈	5¹/₈	10	10	40¹/₈	1231	151
	■ *Pope Co. – Irwin E. Stangeland – Irwin E. Stangeland – 1980*									
203⁵/₈	24³/₈ 26³/₈	21⁷/₈	25⁵/₈	5⁵/₈	5⁷/₈	12	11	25⁶/₈	1248	152
	■ *St. Louis Co. – Picked Up – Phillip A. Roalstad – 1981*									
203⁴/₈	25³/₈ 23¹/₈	18⁶/₈	21¹/₈	5⁶/₈	6	12	12	49	1259	153
	■ *Clearwater Co. – Craig Maxwell – Craig Maxwell – 1998*									
203³/₈	27⁴/₈ 26⁴/₈	16	22⁴/₈	5⁴/₈	5⁵/₈	8	9	32⁷/₈	1272	154
	■ *St. Louis Co. – Eino W. Nurmi – Eino W. Nurmi – 1934*									
203³/₈	25¹/₈ 24¹/₈	21	23¹/₈	5⁴/₈	5³/₈	8	10	46⁵/₈	1272	154
	■ *Olmsted Co. – Logan Behrens – Logan Behrens – 1961*									
203³/₈	26²/₈ 26¹/₈	17⁶/₈	22	5⁴/₈	5⁴/₈	8	10	24⁵/₈	1272	154
	■ *Olmsted Co. – Daniel J. Bernard – Daniel J. Bernard – 1967*									
203²/₈	25²/₈ 25¹/₈	21⁶/₈	24²/₈	4¹/₈	4²/₈	7	8	19⁴/₈	1287	157
	■ *Marshall Co. – Andrew Anderson – Elmer Anderson – 1947*									
203²/₈	25⁶/₈ 26²/₈	18⁴/₈	22¹/₈	5⁷/₈	5⁶/₈	9	11	16	1287	157
	■ *McLeod Co. – William Sandman – William Sandman – 1994*									
203¹/₈	23⁵/₈ 25⁵/₈	16	22²/₈	4⁷/₈	4⁶/₈	11	10	56¹/₈	1305	159
	■ *Koochiching Co. – Unknown – George W. Flaim – 1934*									
202⁷/₈	30¹/₈ 29⁶/₈	21	23²/₈	5³/₈	5³/₈	8	7	15³/₈	1327	160
	■ *Houston Co. – John B. Broers – John B. Broers – 1991*									
202⁷/₈	26 26	19¹/₈	26²/₈	5²/₈	5²/₈	10	10	22²/₈	1327	160
	■ *Clearwater Co. – Donald E. Holm – Donald E. Holm – 1993*									
202⁵/₈	21 23	17⁴/₈	21⁶/₈	5¹/₈	4⁷/₈	13	11	50³/₈	1346	162
	■ *St. Louis Co. – Timothy Rosendahl – Timothy Rosendahl – 1995*									
202⁴/₈	27⁵/₈ 29⁷/₈	22⁴/₈	24⁷/₈	5⁷/₈	6¹/₈	7	6	16	1355	163
	■ *St. Louis Co. – Jeff P. Marczak – Jeff P. Marczak – 1991*									
202³/₈	26 24⁵/₈	21²/₈	24⁶/₈	5⁴/₈	5⁴/₈	11	12	30⁷/₈	1362	164
	■ *Koochiching Co. – George A. Balaski – George A. Balaski – 1955*									
202³/₈	26⁴/₈ 26¹/₈	17⁵/₈	21⁶/₈	4⁷/₈	5²/₈	8	9	34⁴/₈	1362	164
	■ *Lac qui Parle Co. – Donald M. Nygaard – Donald M. Nygaard – 1958*									
202³/₈	26¹/₈ 27	20⁷/₈	23⁴/₈	5	5¹/₈	10	10	23	1362	164
	■ *Aitkin Co. – Joe Clarke – Joe Clarke – 1960*									

Score	Length of Main Beam Right Left	Inside Spread	Greatest Spread	Circumference at Smallest Place Between Burr and First Point Right Left		Number of Points Right Left		Lengths Abnormal Points	All-Time Rank	State Rank
	■ Location of Kill – Hunter – Owner – Date Killed									
202³/8	26²/8 25⁴/8	18¹/8	21	4⁷/8	4⁶/8	10	7	32⁴/8	1362	164
	■ Cass Co. – Hollace Brockoff – Hollace Brockoff – 1976									
202³/8	23¹/8 26³/8	20¹/8		6	5⁷/8	11	6	27	1362	164
	■ Lake Co. – Lawrence J. Simonich – Lawrence J. Simonich – 1987									
202³/8	26⁷/8 28²/8	22⁷/8	26¹/8	6¹/8	6²/8	10	9	43⁴/8	1362	164
	■ Douglas Co. – Timothy C. Sukke – Timothy C. Sukke – 1988									
202³/8	26⁷/8 26³/8	25²/8	28	4³/8	4⁷/8	9	9	34¹/8	1362	164
	■ Chisago Co. – John W. Holmblad – John W. Holmblad – 1992									
202²/8	22⁵/8 22²/8	13⁶/8	16	5⁷/8	5⁵/8	9	8	42⁶/8	1377†	171†
	■ Crow Wing Co. – Michael L. Daly – Michael L. Daly – 2000									
202¹/8	25⁴/8 25⁴/8	19¹/8	21³/8	4⁵/8	4⁶/8	10	7	22²/8	1386	172
	■ Pennington Co. – R. Scott Sorvig – R. Scott Sorvig – 1980									
202¹/8	23⁷/8 24⁴/8	19³/8	25⁶/8	6⁵/8	6⁴/8	9	11	45	1386	172
	■ Wright Co. – Picked Up – Jacob Burley – 1999									
202	28⁴/8 28³/8	20⁵/8	22⁵/8	4⁵/8	4⁴/8	8	9	13¹/8	1395	174
	■ Roseau Co. – Picked Up – Phillip C. Larson – 1999									
201⁷/8	25 24¹/8	14⁵/8	17⁴/8	5⁷/8	5⁷/8	8	7	29	1410	175
	■ Itasca Co. – Lewis Rocco, Sr. – Lewis R. Rocco, Jr. – 1944									
201⁷/8	28²/8 27	17²/8	19⁶/8	6	6	11	11	29⁷/8	1410	175
	■ Itasca Co. – Picked Up – J. Gorden & G. Dopp – 1981									
201⁶/8	25¹/8 25	19⁴/8	23⁶/8	5²/8	5⁴/8	7	8	24⁴/8	1421†	177†
	■ Minnesota – Unknown – Larry D. Bollier – 1969									
201⁵/8	25⁵/8 24³/8	17²/8	19⁷/8	4³/8	4⁴/8	9	9	34¹/8	1427	178
	■ Cass Co. – Guy Chisholm – Charles F. Green – 1945									
201⁴/8	29⁷/8 28⁵/8	19⁷/8	23²/8	5²/8	5⁴/8	10	10	23¹/8	1443	179
	■ Hubbard Co. – Duane G. Lorsung – Duane G. Lorsung – 1973									
201⁴/8	25⁶/8 25	21⁴/8	24	5⁵/8	5⁵/8	10	9	20⁶/8	1443	179
	■ Douglas Co. – Gerald F. Hoppe – Gerald F. Hoppe – 1992									
201³/8	26³/8 25⁷/8	18⁴/8	21¹/8	5²/8	5¹/8	10	8	28⁷/8	1461	181
	■ St. Louis Co. – Andrew G. Groen – Andrew G. Groen – 1958									
201³/8	26⁶/8 26⁶/8	19³/8	22⁵/8	5⁵/8	5³/8	13	9	30⁶/8	1461	181
	■ Swift Co. – Joel T. Schmidt – Joel T. Schmidt – 1973									
201²/8	26⁷/8 26⁴/8	16	21²/8	5³/8	5⁵/8	17	14	48⁶/8	1478	183
	■ Pennington Co. – Glenn Tasa – Glenn Tasa – 1940									
201²/8	26³/8 27³/8	16⁵/8	18⁶/8	5⁶/8	5⁴/8	10	7	17⁵/8	1478	183
	■ Itasca Co. – Cecil L. Johnson – Cecil L. Johnson – 1976									
201¹/8	25 25¹/8	20⁴/8	23⁷/8	6¹/8	6⁴/8	10	8	29¹/8	1489	185
	■ Freeborn Co. – Jim Palmer – Jim Palmer – 1972									
201	28⁵/8 26⁴/8	18⁴/8	21⁶/8	4⁷/8	5	11	10	38²/8	1500	186
	■ Becker Co. – Gill S. Gigstead, Jr. – Gill S. Gigstead, Jr. – 1964									
200⁶/8	24⁴/8 24	18²/8	21⁶/8	5¹/8	5	10	8	32²/8	1524	187
	■ Morrison Co. – Elmer J. Hollenkamp – Elmer J. Hollenkamp – 1977									

Score	Length of Main Beam Right	Left	Inside Spread	Greatest Spread	Circumference at Smallest Place Between Burr and First Point Right	Left	Number of Points Right	Left	Lengths Abnormal Points	All-Time Rank	State Rank
		Location of Kill – Hunter – Owner – Date Killed									
200 4/8	27	26 2/8	22	24 6/8	5 5/8	5 7/8	8	8	22	1545	188
	Clearwater Co. – Ronald O. Halvorson – Ronald O. Halvorson – 1987										
200 3/8	23 5/8	24	18 6/8	21 3/8	4 6/8	4 6/8	8	8	21 5/8	1556	189
	Lake of the Woods Co. – Mark H. Hagen – Mark H. Hagen – 1974										
200 2/8	26 1/8	26 3/8	18 1/8	23 4/8	5 5/8	5 4/8	7	10	26 1/8	1569†	190†
	Isanti Co. – Michael W. Shattuck – Michael W. Shattuck – 2001										
200 2/8	24 7/8	25	21 5/8	25	5 3/8	4 7/8	11	10	28 5/8	1569	190
	Swift Co. – George Piotter – George Piotter – 1983										
200 2/8	24 4/8	24 5/8	19 5/8	21 4/8	4 5/8	4 4/8	12	11	37 5/8	1569	190
	Koochiching Co. – Jack Karsnia – Jack Karsnia – 1994										
200 1/8	27	26 4/8	21 7/8	24 2/8	5 6/8	5 5/8	9	9	22	1577	193
	Itasca Co. – Clyde Sucher – James Davidson – 1926										
200 1/8	27 3/8	26 6/8	21 2/8	26 1/8	4 7/8	5 1/8	12	12	38 3/8	1577	193
	Kandiyohi Co. – Robert J. Custer – Robert J. Custer – 1966										
200 1/8	26 3/8	26 7/8	20 7/8	27 2/8	5 2/8	5 1/8	11	9	25 4/8	1577	193
	St. Louis Co. – Picked Up – John R. Steffes, Sr. – 1992										
200	26 2/8	25 2/8	21 7/8	27 6/8	5 4/8	5 7/8	12	12	37 7/8	1591	196
	Todd Co. – James J. Carr – James J. Carr – 1978										
200	25 5/8	26 1/8	18 2/8	24 2/8	4 6/8	4 6/8	8	7	29	1591	196
	Stearns Co. – David L. LaVoi – David L. LaVoi – 1990										
200	26 3/8	26 3/8	20 3/8	24	5 7/8	6	6	8	12 1/8	1591	196
	Otter Tail Co. – Timothy J. Kapphahn – Timothy J. Kapphahn – 1998										
199 4/8	25 2/8	25 2/8	20 6/8	24 3/8	5 1/8	5 4/8	8	8	30 2/8	1631	199
	Aitkin Co. – Sanford Patrick – Sanford Patrick – 1963										
199 3/8	27 2/8	28	20 4/8	22 5/8	6 1/8	5 4/8	8	9	21 1/8	1639	200
	Chisago Co. – Helmer Benson – Jeff Benson – 1965										
199 3/8	24 2/8	23 4/8	17 2/8	21 5/8	5 3/8	5 3/8	10	8	26 5/8	1639	200
	Houston Co. – Picked Up – MN Dept. of Natl. Resc. – 1997										
199 2/8	29 1/8	28 1/8	21 3/8	25	5	5	7	8	13 7/8	1649	202
	Todd Co. – Wayne V. Jensen – Wayne V. Jensen – 1965										
199 1/8	25 2/8	25 7/8	17 4/8	21 1/8	5 1/8	5 2/8	10	13	30 7/8	1660	203
	St. Louis Co. – Orville Schultz – Orville Schultz – 1978										
199	25	24 6/8	16 3/8	25 3/8	5 3/8	5 6/8	9	8	44 5/8	1668	204
	Cottonwood Co. – Lane L. Horn – Lane L. Horn – 1972										
199	26 3/8	25	19 1/8	24	5 1/8	5	10	8	26 1/8	1668	204
	Yellow Medicine Co. – William A. Botten – William A. Botten – 1976										
198 7/8	26 7/8	25 6/8	21 4/8	31 1/8	5 4/8	5 2/8	10	7	23 5/8	1686	206
	Chippewa Co. – Ray N. Strand – Ray N. Strand – 1976										
198 6/8	25 6/8	25 4/8	18 4/8	26 2/8	5 4/8	5 2/8	9	11	31 2/8	1697	207
	Aitkin Co. – John Baker – Don Anderson – 1910										
198 6/8	28 4/8	28 4/8	21 4/8	24	4 3/8	4 3/8	8	9	21 6/8	1697	207
	Crow Wing Co. – Unknown – George W. Flaim – 1965										

Score	Length of Main Beam Right	Left	Inside Spread	Greatest Spread	Circumference at Smallest Place Between Burr and First Point Right	Left	Number of Points Right	Left	Lengths Abnormal Points	All-Time Rank	State Rank
	■ Location of Kill – Hunter – Owner – Date Killed										
198 6/8	29 7/8	27 1/8	15 7/8	19 1/8	5 3/8	5 3/8	11	7	25 5/8	1697	207
	■ Fillmore Co. – Phillip S. Hansen – Phillip S. Hansen – 1973										
198 6/8	24 6/8	25 3/8	24	26 4/8	5 7/8	6 2/8	5	9	39 6/8	1697	207
	■ Lake of the Woods Co. – Gerald K. Sorenson – Gerald K. Sorenson – 1977										
198 5/8	24 3/8	22 5/8	21 3/8	23	5 7/8	6 2/8	12	11	36 4/8	1716	211
	■ Otter Tail Co. – Roger A. LeBrun – Roger A. LeBrun – 1992										
198 4/8	27 2/8	27	22 2/8	25 4/8	5 3/8	5 1/8	6	9	18 2/8	1736	212
	■ Kanabec Co. – Unknown – David G. Gagnon – 1927										
198 4/8	26 4/8	22 5/8	18 7/8	22	5 6/8	5 5/8	9	10	44 3/8	1736	212
	■ Clay Co. – F.W. Kolle – Kolle Farms, Inc. – 1946										
198 4/8	24	23 5/8	19	20	5 5/8	5 6/8	11	11	29 6/8	1736	212
	■ Itasca Co. – Wayne W. Blesi, Jr. – Wayne W. Blesi, Jr. – 1968										
198 4/8	26 2/8	24 2/8	21 5/8	24 2/8	4 7/8	4 6/8	7	8	17 3/8	1736	212
	■ Lincoln Co. – Dennis G. Geiken – Dennis G. Geiken – 1980										
198 3/8	24 4/8	24 4/8	20 5/8	24 3/8	6 6/8	6 4/8	9	6	15 6/8	1762	216
	■ Sherburne Co. – David J. Valerius – David J. Valerius – 1997										
198 2/8	23 3/8	22 5/8	21 6/8	24 2/8	5	5	9	12	33	1772	217
	■ Crow Wing Co. – Harold B. Stotts – Harold B. Stotts – 1941										
198 2/8	27	26 2/8	21	26	4 7/8	4 5/8	8	9	33 4/8	1772	217
	■ Cass Co. – Timothy L. Anderson – Timothy L. Anderson – 1987										
198 1/8	25 3/8	25	23	25 1/8	5 1/8	5 2/8	10	10	25 7/8	1785	219
	■ Koochiching Co. – Maris Stolcers – Maris Stolcers – 1963										
198 1/8	29	28 5/8	18 5/8	25 2/8	5	5 2/8	12	13	32 4/8	1785	219
	■ Itasca Co. – Dennis C. Campbell – Dennis C. Campbell – 1995										
198	26	26 2/8	20	27	5	4 6/8	7	11	37 6/8	1801	221
	■ McLeod Co. – Owen L. Knacke – Owen L. Knacke – 1990										
197 7/8	25 4/8	25	18 1/8	20 5/8	5	5	10	9	23 6/8	1816	222
	■ Clearwater Co. – Unknown – Danny L. Cole – PR 1975										
197 7/8	25	24 7/8	18 6/8	24 6/8	5 2/8	5 2/8	10	8	24 5/8	1816	222
	■ Aitkin Co. – Thomas N. Sauro – Thomas N. Sauro – 1998										
197 5/8	25 1/8	24 6/8	22 4/8	25 6/8	5 4/8	5 4/8	10	8	26 3/8	1847	224
	■ Blue Earth Co. – Daniel R. Nelson – Daniel R. Nelson – 1981										
197 4/8	24 4/8	24 6/8	21 6/8	25 2/8	7	6 7/8	8	10	18	1866	225
	■ Chippewa Co. – Dean D. Anspach – Dean D. Anspach – 1973										
197 3/8	27 3/8	26 3/8	20 4/8	26 1/8	5 2/8	5 2/8	8	9	22 1/8	1884	226
	■ Faribault Co. – Randy L. Sandt – Randy L. Sandt – 1982										
197 3/8	26 5/8	27 2/8	16 5/8	22 5/8	5 1/8	5 1/8	8	14	24 6/8	1884	226
	■ Kittson Co. – Unknown – George W. Flaim – PR 1988										
197 3/8	29 1/8	27 2/8	18	22	4 7/8	5 3/8	8	11	26 7/8	1884	226
	■ Anoka Co. – Dale M. Zimmerman – Dale M. Zimmerman – 1990										
197 2/8	22 6/8	23 1/8	20	28 4/8	6 2/8	5 6/8	13	10	45 2/8	1901	229
	■ Koochiching Co. – John Erickson – Marc M. Jackson – 1951										

Score	Length of Main Beam Right Left	Inside Spread	Greatest Spread	Circumference at Smallest Place Between Burr and First Point Right Left	Number of Points Right Left	Lengths Abnormal Points	All-Time Rank	State Rank
	■ Location of Kill – Hunter – Owner – Date Killed							
197²/8	29⁷/8 30	21¹/8	28²/8	5⁵/8 5⁴/8	6 8	14⁵/8	1901	229
	■ Douglas Co. – David S. Paulson – David S. Paulson – 1966							
197¹/8	27⁵/8 27²/8	21⁴/8	24⁴/8	4⁵/8 4⁷/8	9 9	32⁷/8	1923	231
	■ Becker Co. – Unknown – George W. Flaim – 1924							
197	27²/8 26³/8	20⁴/8	26³/8	4⁴/8 4⁵/8	7 13	19⁴/8	1939	232
	■ Cook Co. – Edwin F. Niemeyer – Helen Niemeyer – 1947							
196⁷/8	26²/8 27¹/8	20⁶/8	23²/8	4⁷/8 5¹/8	11 12	29⁵/8	1950	233
	■ St. Louis Co. – James A. Guist – James A. Guist – 1963							
196⁷/8	25⁶/8 25⁶/8	20⁶/8	23²/8	7 6⁵/8	7 8	13³/8	1950	233
	■ Becker Co. – James A. Henderson – James A. Henderson – 1998							
196⁶/8	26⁷/8 27⁶/8	21⁴/8	23⁵/8	5²/8 5³/8	13 10	32	1968	235
	■ Lake Co. – Unknown – George W. Flaim – PR 1984							
196²/8	23²/8 23¹/8	17⁵/8	22²/8	5²/8 4⁷/8	11 7	34¹/8	2028	236
	■ Lake of the Woods Co. – Ralph Rehder – Ralph Rehder – 1951							
196²/8	29³/8 29²/8	22⁴/8	24⁷/8	5 5¹/8	10 10	13⁴/8	2028	236
	■ Crow Wing Co. – LeRoy E. Pelarski – LeRoy E. Pelarski – 1975							
196²/8	23⁷/8 25⁶/8	17³/8	20	6³/8 6¹/8	10 8	26⁷/8	2028	236
	■ Otter Tail Co. – William J. Klyve – William J. Klyve – 1987							
195⁷/8	25²/8 27⁶/8	20⁶/8	25⁶/8	4⁶/8 5	11 7	20⁷/8	2076†	239†
	■ Marshall Co. – Picked Up – Vernon Blazejewski – 1997							
195⁷/8	26³/8 26⁵/8	19²/8	21⁵/8	6 6	10 7	14³/8	2076	239
	■ Beltrami Co. – Ollie Jamtaas – James Gorden – 1938							
195⁶/8	25⁶/8 25	20²/8	25	5³/8 5²/8	10 7	13	2094	241
	■ St. Louis Co. – Mike Desanto – Mike Desanto – 1963							
195⁶/8	25⁴/8 26⁵/8	19⁵/8	23⁴/8	6⁵/8 7	11 12	27¹/8	2094	241
	■ Roseau Co. – George H. Tepley – George H. Tepley – 1984							
195⁶/8	24⁴/8 23⁵/8	21³/8	23⁶/8	4⁴/8 4⁵/8	8 7	48³/8	2094	241
	■ Lake Co. – Corey A. Swartout – Corey A. Swartout – 1998							
195⁵/8	25⁵/8 24²/8	19¹/8	24⁷/8	5⁴/8 5⁵/8	8 16	44⁴/8	2116	244
	■ Carlton Co. – Nick Rukovina – George W. Flaim – 1960							
195⁵/8	24⁶/8 25³/8	21³/8	23³/8	5⁵/8 5⁴/8	11 9	30⁶/8	2116	244
	■ Jackson Co. – Allan Amundson – Allan Amundson – 1973							
195⁴/8	28⁵/8 27³/8	21²/8	27⁵/8	4 4	8 7	21	2134	246
	■ Fillmore Co. – Jim Sletten – Mrs. Jim Sletten – 1974							
195⁴/8	26 25³/8	16⁶/8	21⁷/8	4⁷/8 4⁶/8	10 7	20⁴/8	2134	246
	■ Winona Co. – Patrick Bartholomew – Patrick Bartholomew – 1976							
195⁴/8	26³/8 27²/8	20²/8	22⁵/8	5¹/8 4⁷/8	11 9	28	2134	246
	■ Kanabec Co. – Kenneth L. Smith – Kenneth L. Smith – 1976							
195⁴/8	21⁶/8 23⁷/8	22¹/8	24³/8	4⁷/8 5²/8	9 13	30¹/8	2134	246
	■ St. Louis Co. – LeRoy N. Nelson – LeRoy N. Nelson – 1987							
195³/8	23⁷/8 24²/8	18³/8	20³/8	4³/8 4³/8	11 11	20⁴/8	2163	250
	■ Pope Co. – Kenneth M. Besonen – Kenneth M. Besonen – 1975							

Score	Length of Main Beam Right Left	Inside Spread	Greatest Spread	Circumference at Smallest Place Between Burr and First Point Right Left		Number of Points Right Left		Lengths Abnormal Points	All-Time Rank	State Rank
	■ Location of Kill – Hunter – Owner – Date Killed									
195³/8	20¹/8 22⁴/8	16²/8	19⁵/8	7³/8	7⁵/8	10	12	40³/8	2163	250
	■ Beltrami Co. – John G. Binsfeld – John G. Binsfeld – 1980									
195²/8	25¹/8 25⁵/8	19⁴/8	23⁵/8	5²/8	5³/8	8	9	30⁴/8	2186	252
	■ Dakota Co. – Mark A. LeMay – Mark A. LeMay – 1993									
195¹/8	20³/8 20	15³/8	19⁵/8	4³/8	5⁴/8	6	17	91²/8	2208	253
	■ Carlton Co. – Unknown – George W. Flaim – 1910									
195¹/8	25³/8 25⁵/8	19²/8	22	6	6¹/8	9	9	20³/8	2208	253
	■ Otter Tail Co. – Thomas E. Joseph, Jr. – Thomas E. Joseph, Jr. – 1992									
195¹/8	25¹/8 26⁴/8	17¹/8	19³/8	5²/8	5⁴/8	7	9	22⁶/8	2208	253
	■ Otter Tail Co. – Allen Antonsen – Allen Antonsen – 1995									
195	25⁶/8 26¹/8	17	19⁷/8	4³/8	4³/8	11	7	26⁶/8	2233	256
	■ Goodhue Co. – Darrin L. Goplen – Darrin L. Goplen – 1990									
194⁴/8	28²/8 28²/8	19¹/8	21⁶/8	5¹/8	5²/8	9	7	14⁷/8	2266	257
	■ Marshall Co. – Timothy F. Johnson – Timothy F. Johnson – 1988									
193¹/8	26⁵/8 25³/8	20³/8	24⁷/8	5³/8	5⁶/8	8	8	26²/8	2305	258
	■ Koochiching Co. – Unknown – Marc M. Jackson – 1974									
192⁷/8	26 26⁵/8	18²/8	21¹/8	6²/8	5⁷/8	7	8	13⁷/8	2312†	259†
	■ Morrison Co. – Brent M. Beimert – Brent M. Beimert – 2001									
192⁷/8	26²/8 26⁷/8	19⁶/8	24	5³/8	5¹/8	7	7	15⁵/8	2312	259
	■ Minnesota – Picked Up – Gary W. Haeckel – PR 1991									
192	23³/8 23⁴/8	18⁶/8	20⁷/8	5³/8	5⁴/8	9	8	22²/8	2344	261
	■ McLeod Co. – Leonard V. Krulikosky, Jr. – Leonard V. Krulikosky, Jr. – 1982									
191⁴/8	25⁴/8 26	19³/8	21⁴/8	5²/8	5¹/8	6	6	15¹/8	2357†	262†
	■ Todd Co. – Picked Up – MN Dept of Natl. Resources – 1994									
191¹/8	26⁶/8 27³/8	19³/8	23⁵/8	6	6	7	7	23⁶/8	2374	263
	■ Douglas Co. – Cory D. Mikkelson – Cory D. Mikkelson – 1993									
190⁷/8	26¹/8 27²/8	21	22⁷/8	6³/8	6¹/8	9	11	17¹/8	2385	264
	■ Wright Co. – Keith A. Rudolph – Keith A. Rudolph – 1989									
189⁴/8	21⁶/8 23¹/8	18⁶/8	24	3⁷/8	3⁷/8	7	8	14	2435	265
	■ Clearwater Co. – H.G. Meyer – H.G. Meyer – 1970									
189²/8	28³/8 27¹/8	17⁴/8	19⁴/8	5²/8	5	9	11	26⁶/8	2447	266
	■ Itasca Co. – James S. Bischoff – James S. Bischoff – 1973									
189	25²/8 25⁶/8	17⁴/8	21¹/8	4⁷/8	4⁷/8	7	8	18²/8	2456	267
	■ Pennington Co. – Myles Olsen – Myles Olsen – 1991									
188⁷/8	26⁷/8 26¹/8	21⁴/8	27³/8	5⁵/8	5⁶/8	6	7	14³/8	2462	268
	■ Stevens Co. – Edward Wilson – Edward Wilson – 1965									
188⁷/8	26¹/8 25⁷/8	20³/8	22⁷/8	5	5²/8	10	12	27	2462	268
	■ Pine Co. – Peter J. Feider – Peter J. Feider – 1974									
188²/8	25⁷/8 27⁴/8	23	27⁶/8	5⁵/8	5⁶/8	8	8	21	2489	270
	■ Becker Co. – Kenneth R. Ringstad – Kenneth R. Ringstad – 1987									
188²/8	26 25⁷/8	21³/8	23	5	5⁴/8	6	8	17⁷/8	2489	270
	■ Morrison Co. – Roland Schallberg – Roland Schallberg – 1987									

Score	Length of Main Beam Right	Left	Inside Spread	Greatest Spread	Circumference at Smallest Place Between Burr and First Point Right	Left	Number of Points Right	Left	Lengths Abnormal Points	All-Time Rank	State Rank
	■ Location of Kill – Hunter – Owner – Date Killed										
188⅛	23⁶⁄8	23³⁄8	16⁵⁄8	19⁶⁄8	4⁶⁄8	4⁴⁄8	12	10	33⁴⁄8	2497†	272†
	■ St. Louis Co. – Leslie J. Soular – Leslie J. Soular – 1999										
187⅞	28²⁄8	27⁴⁄8	22	24⁴⁄8	5²⁄8	5⁷⁄8	8	9	20⁵⁄8	2506	273
	■ Chisago Co. – Christopher L. Johnson – Christopher L. Johnson – 1998										
187⅝	26¹⁄8	25⁶⁄8	28⁵⁄8	30	6³⁄8	5⁶⁄8	9	9	44⁶⁄8	2518	274
	■ Blue Earth Co. – Galen Paul – Galen Paul – 1964										
186⅞	25¹⁄8	25	18²⁄8	21¹⁄8	4⁴⁄8	4⁴⁄8	8	9	16¹⁄8	2550	275
	■ Roseau Co. – John R. Franke – John R. Franke – 1990										
186⅝	26¹⁄8	27³⁄8	19³⁄8	22³⁄8	5⁴⁄8	5¹⁄8	9	9	22⁴⁄8	2565	276
	■ Brown Co. – Gerald W. Griebel – Gerald W. Griebel – 1978										
186²⁄8	23¹⁄8	22⁵⁄8	17⁶⁄8	19⁵⁄8	5⁷⁄8	5⁷⁄8	8	10	22⁶⁄8	2575	277
	■ Traverse Co. – Terry L. Miller – Terry L. Miller – 1987										
186	24²⁄8	24¹⁄8	18¹⁄8	23⁶⁄8	4⁷⁄8	5	5	10	15³⁄8	2586	278
	■ St. Louis Co. – Richard Nevalainen – Terry J. Nevalainen – 1961										
185⅞	27⁵⁄8	27⁷⁄8	21²⁄8	23⁷⁄8	5²⁄8	5²⁄8	8	7	24¹⁄8	2597	279
	■ Fillmore Co. – Calvin Anderson – Calvin Anderson – 1986										
185⅞	25¹⁄8	24⁴⁄8	18³⁄8	20²⁄8	5³⁄8	5³⁄8	9	8	16⁶⁄8	2597	279
	■ Becker Co. – Anthony J. Donner – Anthony J. Donner – 1998										
185⅝	22⁷⁄8	23	22⁴⁄8	24⁵⁄8	4⁴⁄8	4⁶⁄8	7	8	22³⁄8	2610	281
	■ Polk Co. – Delphus H. Hanson – Delphus H. Hanson – 1988										
185³⁄8	23⁷⁄8	24⁴⁄8	18	20	5	5	7	8	13³⁄8	2622	282
	■ Clay Co. – Todd M. Landa – Todd M. Landa – 1999										
185²⁄8	27⁴⁄8	28	21⁴⁄8	23⁵⁄8	4⁶⁄8	4⁵⁄8	9	10	15²⁄8	2632	283
	■ Beltrami Co. – John A. Dick – John A. Dick – 1991										
185	24⁶⁄8	25⁷⁄8	18²⁄8	23³⁄8	4²⁄8	4²⁄8	9	8	18²⁄8	2653	284
	■ Itasca Co. – Fred Sandness – E.F. Anderson & H. Westrom – 1912										
185	26⁶⁄8	26	20¹⁄8	22⁴⁄8	4⁷⁄8	4⁵⁄8	11	8	19⁷⁄8	2653	284
	■ St. Louis Co. – David A. Wuorinen – David A. Wuorinen – 1999										

† The scores and ranking for trophies from the 25th Awards Entry Period are not final until the banquet is held on June 19, 2004.

MISSISSIPPI
RECORD WHITETAILS

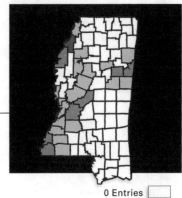

40 Typical whitetail deer entries
29 Non-typical whitetail deer entries
7,265 Total whitetail deer entries

MISSISSIPPI STATE RECORD
Typical Whitetail Deer
Score: $182^7/8$
Location: Noxubee Co.
Hunter and Owner:
  Glen D. Jourdon
Date: 1986

MISSISSIPPI
NEW STATE RECORD
Non-Typical Whitetail Deer
Score: 295^6/8
Location: Winston Co.
Hunter and Owner: Tony Fulton
Date: 1995

Photograph from B&C Archives

MISSISSIPPI

TYPICAL WHITETAIL DEER

Score	Length of Main Beam Right	Left	Inside Spread	Greatest Spread	Circumference at Smallest Place Between Burr and First Point Right	Left	Number of Points Right	Left	Lengths Abnormal Points	All-Time Rank	State Rank

Location of Kill – Hunter – Owner – Date Killed

Score	R	L	Inside	Greatest	Circ R	Circ L	Pts R	Pts L	Abn	Rank	State
$182^7/8$	$27^2/8$	$27^3/8$	$19^2/8$	$21^4/8$	5	$5^3/8$	7	7	$6^5/8$	401	1

■ *Noxubee Co. – Glen D. Jourdon – Glen D. Jourdon – 1986*

$182^2/8$	$27^1/8$	$26^4/8$	$19^6/8$	$21^6/8$	$5^1/8$	$5^2/8$	5	5		450	2

■ *Claiborne Co. – R.L. Bobo – R.L. Bobo – 1955*

$181^5/8$	$25^6/8$	$25^7/8$	$19^7/8$	$21^6/8$	$5^4/8$	$5^4/8$	6	7	$2^4/8$	500	3

■ *Wilkinson Co. – Ronnie P. Whitaker – Ronnie P. Whitaker – 1981*

$180^4/8$	28	27	$22^7/8$	$25^3/8$	$5^3/8$	$5^1/8$	6	6	$1^5/8$	613	4

■ *Leflore Co. – W.F. Smith – W.F. Smith – 1968*

$180^2/8$	$26^7/8$	$28^5/8$	$19^4/8$	22	$5^2/8$	$5^1/8$	5	6		651	5

■ *Madison Co. – Stephen C. Greer – Stephen C. Greer – 1996*

$179^2/8$	$25^4/8$	$25^6/8$	$20^6/8$	$22^3/8$	$4^7/8$	5	6	7	$1^4/8$	763	6

■ *Hinds Co. – Marlon Stokes – Marlon Stokes – 1988*

$178^5/8$	$25^6/8$	$27^2/8$	$20^2/8$	23	$5^4/8$	$5^4/8$	6	5	$3^3/8$	819	7

■ *Bolivar Co. – Grady Robertson – Merigold Hunting Club – 1951*

$176^5/8$	$25^4/8$	$25^4/8$	$21^7/8$	$17^4/8$	$4^5/8$	$4^7/8$	5	5		1134	8

■ *Bolivar Co. – Sidney D. Sessions – Sidney D. Sessions – 1952*

$176^1/8$	$26^4/8$	$27^3/8$	$24^3/8$	$26^4/8$	$5^1/8$	5	5	5		1243	9

■ *Monroe Co. – J.D. Hood – Michael D. Steadman – 1972*

$175^2/8$	$28^6/8$	$28^5/8$	19	21	$5^6/8$	$5^3/8$	6	4	$1^2/8$	1403†	10†

■ *Neshoba Co. – Charlie G. Wilson II – Charlie G. Wilson II – 2001*

$175^2/8$	$26^1/8$	$25^6/8$	$21^1/8$	$25^4/8$	$5^1/8$	$5^2/8$	8	6	$3^5/8$	1403	10

■ *Wilkinson Co. – Johnnie J. Leake, Jr. – Johnnie J. Leake, Jr. – 1978*

$174^6/8$	$27^2/8$	$29^1/8$	$21^2/8$	$24^2/8$	$5^1/8$	5	5	5		1534	12

■ *Coahoma Co. – O.P. Gilbert – O.P. Gilbert – 1960*

$174^6/8$	$28^2/8$	28	$18^6/8$	21	6	$5^6/8$	5	5		1534	12

■ *Adams Co. – Jeremy E. Boelte – Jeremy E. Boelte – 1997*

$174^1/8$	$25^7/8$	$26^5/8$	$22^1/8$	$26^5/8$	$5^2/8$	$5^1/8$	5	7	$6^2/8$	1678	14

■ *Coahoma Co. – William L. Walters – William L. Walters – 1995*

$173^5/8$	25	$25^6/8$	$22^5/8$	$24^5/8$	$4^2/8$	$4^4/8$	6	6		1819	15

■ *Lowndes Co. – Geraline Holliman – Geraline Holliman – 1982*

$173^3/8$	$25^2/8$	25	$17^5/8$	$19^7/8$	$5^1/8$	5	7	6	$2^6/8$	1883	16

■ *Coahoma Co. – Richard D. Powell – Richard D. Powell – 1994*

$172^5/8$	$28^4/8$	28	22	$25^2/8$	$6^2/8$	$6^3/8$	8	8	$4^3/8$	2113	17

■ *Adams Co. – Adrian L. Stallone – Adrian L. Stallone – 1983*

172	25	$25^2/8$	$18^6/8$	$20^7/8$	$5^2/8$	$5^2/8$	6	5		2330	18

■ *Adams Co. – Nan F. New – Nan F. New – 1977*

$171^6/8$	$24^5/8$	$24^7/8$	$19^7/8$	$21^2/8$	$4^7/8$	$5^1/8$	6	6	$1^5/8$	2418	19

■ *Tunica Co. – Delton D. Davis – Delton D. Davis – 1990*

Score	Length of Main Beam Right Left	Inside Spread	Greatest Spread	Circumference at Smallest Place Between Burr and First Point Right Left	Number of Points Right Left	Lengths Abnormal Points	All-Time Rank	State Rank
	■ Location of Kill – Hunter – Owner – Date Killed							
171 4/8	24 6/8 24 5/8	17 6/8	20 6/8	6 3/8 6 3/8	9 7	8	2513	20
	■ Tallahatchie Co. – Ricky Lee – Ricky Lee – 1999							
170 7/8	28 1/8 27 1/8	19 2/8	23	5 5	5 4	2 1/8	2769	21
	■ Issaquena Co. – Warren A. Miller – Alford M. Cooley – 1920							
170 2/8	27 5/8 26 6/8	23 6/8	26 2/8	5 5 3/8	6 7	3 4/8	3063	22
	■ Madison Co. – David G. McAdory – David G. McAdory – 1994							
169 6/8	27 2/8 28 1/8	22 6/8	25	5 4/8 5 1/8	7 5	9 2/8	3306	23
	■ Coahoma Co. – Steven R. Williams – Steven R. Williams – 1998							
168	25 2/8 25	18 4/8	21	5 4/8 5 6/8	6 5	1	3443	24
	■ Warren Co. – Frank Dorroh – Martha Dorroh – 1952							
167 1/8	30 1/8 28 6/8	21 7/8	23 6/8	5 2/8 5 2/8	4 4		3539	25
	■ Yazoo Co. – Howard T. Hayman – Howard T. Hayman – 1995							
166 7/8	24 7/8 25 4/8	19 1/8	21 3/8	4 5/8 4 5/8	5 5		3568	26
	■ Hinds Co. – Edwin F. Schmidt IV – Edwin F. Schmidt IV – 1997							
166 5/8	28 1/8 28 1/8	20 1/8	23 6/8	4 7/8 4 7/8	5 5		3598†	27†
	■ Marshall Co. – Michael W. Janes – Michael W. Janes – 2000							
165	26 7/8 25 7/8	17 6/8	19 4/8	4 7/8 5	6 5	1 2/8	3782	28
	■ Copiah Co. – William M. Campbell – William M. Campbell – 1997							
163 5/8	23 4/8 24 2/8	21 1/8	22 4/8	4 4/8 4 4/8	5 5		3961†	29†
	■ Wilkinson Co. – Lynwood Williams III – Lynwood Williams III – 2000							
162 5/8	24 1/8 24	17 3/8	18	4 3/8 4 4/8	5 6	1	4109	30
	■ Bolivar Co. – Michael W. Sanders – Michael W. Sanders – 1996							
162 1/8	25 6/8 25 7/8	18 3/8	20 2/8	5 4 7/8	5 5		4174	31
	■ Jefferson Co. – Jason B. Brown – Jason B. Brown – 1995							
162	26 7/8 27	20 6/8	23 3/8	5 3/8 5 2/8	5 5		4184	32
	■ Coahoma Co. – Duncan F. Williams – Duncan F. Williams – 1997							
161 4/8	24 7/8 23 6/8	21 2/8	23 4/8	5 3/8 5 3/8	5 6	2 6/8	4258	33
	■ Claiborne Co. – Steve Amos – Steve Amos – 1984							
161 2/8	24 6/8 26	18 4/8	20 6/8	5 4/8 5 4/8	5 5	2 6/8	4310	34
	■ Franklin Co. – Robert L. Wattigny – Robert L. Wattigny – 1985							
161 1/8	23 2/8 23 2/8	16 5/8	19	4 7/8 4 6/8	9 7	5	4332	35
	■ Coahoma Co. – Terry L. Dulaney – Terry L. Dulaney – 1984							
161 1/8	26 1/8 26 4/8	17 5/8	19 4/8	4 4/8 4 4/8	8 5	2 4/8	4332	35
	■ Amite Co. – Preston Jones – Preston Jones – 1995							
160 4/8	23 23	15 6/8	17 2/8	4 7/8 5	5 5		4443	37
	■ Noxubee Co. – Doug Borries – Doug Borries – 1988							
160 3/8	25 2/8 24 7/8	20 4/8	22 1/8	5 5/8 5 3/8	6 5	2 7/8	4470†	38†
	■ Wilkinson Co. – Danny W. Frazier – Danny W. Frazier – 2000							
160 3/8	23 7/8 24 2/8	17 3/8	19 7/8	5 2/8 5	6 5	1 2/8	4470	38
	■ Tunica Co. – Neil Robbins – Neil Robbins – 1994							
160 1/8	23 1/8 23 2/8	16 3/8	18 2/8	4 2/8 4 2/8	5 5		4534†	40†
	■ Hinds Co. – Roger A. Hudson – Roger A. Hudson – 2000							

MISSISSIPPI

NON-TYPICAL WHITETAIL DEER

Score	Length of Main Beam Right	Left	Inside Spread	Greatest Spread	Circumference at Smallest Place Between Burr and First Point Right	Left	Number of Points Right	Left	Lengths Abnormal Points	All-Time Rank	State Rank
295 6/8	21 2/8	18 2/8	22 3/8	29	5 5/8	5 3/8	21	24	133 4/8	3	1
■ Winston Co. – Tony Fulton – Tony Fulton – 1995											
225	24 1/8	24 7/8	24 7/8	29 2/8	4 7/8	5	11	9	45 3/8	318	2
■ Lowndes Co. – Richard Herring – Richard Herring – 1988											
221 2/8	20 5/8	23 6/8	19 2/8	25 4/8	4 7/8	5	13	19	81	410	3
■ Holmes Co. – Milton Parrish – Milton Parrish – 1970											
220 3/8	26 2/8	26 7/8	21	23 3/8	5 5/8	5 4/8	10	10	33 1/8	431	4
■ Oktibbeha Co. – Dean E. Jones – Dean E. Jones – 1976											
219 2/8	27 3/8	27 3/8	17	21 6/8	5 1/8	5 1/8	8	10	42 2/8	460	5
■ Hinds Co. – Matt M. Woods – Matt M. Woods – 1998											
217 5/8	27 3/8	24 6/8	23	28	4 6/8	5 3/8	14	14	55 7/8	506	6
■ Carroll Co. – Mark T. Hathcock – Mark T. Hathcock – 1978											
212	23 5/8	23	14 5/8	20 7/8	6 3/8	5 6/8	11	14	78 3/8	717	7
■ Madison Co – Richard W. Parker – Richard W. Parker – 1999											
209 6/8	24 6/8	24 2/8	20 7/8	25 7/8	5 6/8	5 3/8	10	11	48 5/8	831	8
■ Franklin Co. – Ronnie Strickland – Ronnie Strickland – 1981											
205 6/8	23 1/8	21 4/8	21	25 7/8	4 7/8	4 4/8	12	12	56	1094	9
■ Lowndes Co. – Joe W. Shurden – Joe W. Shurden – 1976											
204 6/8	25 4/8	22 6/8	19 6/8	23 4/8	5 2/8	5 4/8	10	9	56 2/8	1165	10
■ Lowndes Co. – Picked Up – Thomas B. Yeatman – 1959											
204	27 1/8	25 2/8	16 6/8	20 4/8	5 4/8	5 6/8	14	12	44 4/8	1220	11
■ Webster Co. – William D. Eshee III – William D. Eshee III – 1996											
202 5/8	22 5/8	23 4/8	18 4/8	24 1/8	4 6/8	4 6/8	16	9	66 1/8	1346	12
■ Carroll Co. – George Galey – Terry Galey – 1960											
202 4/8	23 3/8	24 2/8	19 5/8	23 4/8	5 6/8	5 3/8	10	8	59 3/8	1355†	13†
■ Pontotoc Co. – William H. Westmoreland – William H. Westmoreland – 2001											
202 1/8	28 7/8	28 1/8	16 7/8	26 7/8	5 6/8	5 4/8	15	11	44	1386	14
■ Oktibbeha Co. – Oliver H. Lindig – Oliver H. Lindig – 1983											
201 6/8	24	24	17 6/8	19 7/8	6	6	17	15	42	1421	15
■ Wilkinson Co. – Jimmy Ashley – Jimmy Ashley – 1985											
198 5/8	25 4/8	24 4/8	20 5/8	24 7/8	4 5/8	4 7/8	12	15	57 4/8	1716	16
■ Oktibbeha Co. – Timothy P. Watson – Timothy P. Watson – 1997											
198 4/8	28 2/8	27 4/8	19 4/8	26 2/8	6 7/8	6 4/8	11	10	42	1736†	17†
■ Issaquena Co. – John T. Campbell – John T. Campbell – 2001											
196 7/8	23	23 1/8	23 1/8	24 2/8	6	5 6/8	8	9	32	1950	18
■ Yazoo Co. – Eddie J. Alias, Jr. – Eddie J. Alias, Jr. – 1989											
196 5/8	21 2/8	20 5/8	19 4/8	23 5/8	4 7/8	4 7/8	10	12	74 5/8	1985	19
■ Wilkinson Co. – Robert D. Sullivan – Robert D. Sullivan – 1982											

■ Location of Kill – Hunter – Owner – Date Killed

Score	Length of Main Beam		Inside Spread	Greatest Spread	Circumference at Smallest Place Between Burr and First Point		Number of Points		Lengths Abnormal Points	All-Time Rank	State Rank
	Right	Left			Right	Left	Right	Left			
	■ Location of Kill – Hunter – Owner – Date Killed										
195 7/8	24 5/8	23 7/8	18 2/8	20 2/8	6	5 5/8	7	7	27 1/8	2076	20
	■ Monroe Co. – Kenneth A. Dye – Kenneth A. Dye – 1986										
195 5/8	24 3/8	24	18 3/8	20 3/8	4 2/8	4	7	7	24 6/8	2116†	21†
	■ Madison Co. – Damon C. Saik – Damon C. Saik – 2001										
195 5/8	23 7/8	24 2/8	13	23 7/8	5	5 2/8	14	10	71 1/8	2116	21
	■ Adams Co. – Kathleen McGehee – Kathleen McGehee – 1981										
195 2/8	24 6/8	23	20 4/8	25 4/8	5 3/8	5 4/8	8	11	34	2186†	23†
	■ Tunica Co. – Leland N. Dye, Jr. – Leland N. Dye, Jr. – 2001 ■ See photo on page 53										
195 2/8	22 2/8	23 1/8	17 3/8	23	4 6/8	4 6/8	11	11	20 7/8	2186	23
	■ Copiah Co. – Bill Kimble – Bill Kimble – 1995										
192	24	23 4/8	17 6/8	21	5 5/8	5 6/8	8	10	26 2/8	2344	25
	■ Tallahatchie Co. – Willie L. Carvan – Willie L. Carvan – 1999										
188 4/8	23 6/8	22 2/8	16	21 1/8	5 1/8	5 7/8	10	10	42 6/8	2475†	26†
	■ Pontotoc Co. – William T. Roberts – William T. Roberts – 2001										
187 6/8	23	24 2/8	18 1/8	20 4/8	5 6/8	5 6/8	8	9	20 5/8	2512†	27†
	■ Holmes Co. – Laurence H. Walker – Frank A. Eakin – 1950										
187 6/8	25 2/8	25 6/8	20 6/8	24 5/8	6 1/8	6 3/8	10	6	13	2512	27
	■ Warren Co. – Ira A. Ervin – Ira A. Ervin – 1993										
185 2/8	23 6/8	24 1/8	17 6/8	21	5	5	7	7	21 6/8	2632	29
	■ Jefferson Co. – Jeff D. Ingram, Jr. – Jeff D. Ingram, Jr. – 1998										

† The scores and ranking for trophies from the 25th Awards Entry Period are not final until the banquet is held on June 19, 2004.

MISSOURI
RECORD WHITETAILS

219 Typical whitetail deer entries
97 Non-typical whitetail deer entries
7,265 Total whitetail deer entries

0 Entries	
1-2 Entries	
3-5 Entries	
6-10 Entries	
11+ Entries	

MISSOURI
STATE RECORD
Typical Whitetail Deer
Score: 205
Location: Randolph Co.
Hunter: Larry W. Gibson
Owner: MO Show-Me
  Big Bucks Club
Date: 1971

Photograph from B&C Archivess

MISSOURI
STATE RECORD
WORLD'S RECORD
Non-Typical Whitetail Deer
Score: 333⁷/₈
Location: St. Louis Co.
Hunter: Picked Up
Owner: MO Dept. of Conservation
Date: 1981

Photograph from B&C Archives

MISSOURI

TYPICAL WHITETAIL DEER

Score	Length of Main Beam Right Left	Inside Spread	Greatest Spread	Circumference at Smallest Place Between Burr and First Point Right Left	Number of Points Right Left	Lengths Abnormal Points	All-Time Rank	State Rank
	■ Location of Kill – Hunter – Owner – Date Killed							
205	26 6/8 25 4/8	24 2/8	25 2/8	4 6/8 4 6/8	6 6		3	1
	■ Randolph Co. – Larry W. Gibson – MO Show-Me Big Bucks Club – 1971							
199 4/8	27 2/8 26 2/8	20	22 4/8	5 4/8 5 1/8	8 5	1 4/8	14	2
	■ Clark Co. – Jeffrey A. Brunk – Jeffrey A. Brunk – 1969							
191	27 6/8 28 3/8	19	21 4/8	5 5 3/8	5 5		87†	3†
	■ Cass Co. – John D. Meyer – John D. Meyer – 2001							
190 3/8	27 26 7/8	20 4/8	23 6/8	4 5/8 4 5/8	6 7	1 3/8	102	4
	■ Pettis Co. – Jesse A. Perry – Jesse A. Perry – 1986							
190	25 24 7/8	23 4/8	25	4 7/8 5	7 7		107	5
	■ Callaway Co. – Ben Barks – Ben Barks – 1995							
188 4/8	30 3/8 30 6/8	21 3/8	23 4/8	5 3/8 5 1/8	8 7	10 3/8	141†	6†
	■ Macon Co. – Eugene J. Bausch – Eugene J. Bausch – 2001							
187 6/8	29 7/8 29 6/8	21	23 2/8	5 5 1/8	5 6	1 4/8	160	7
	■ Clinton Co. – Scott E. Looney – Scott E. Looney – 1994							
187 5/8	27 2/8 28 1/8	22 2/8	24 1/8	4 5/8 4 6/8	7 7	4 7/8	165†	8†
	■ Franklin Co. – Mickey R. Montee – Mickey R. Montee – 2001							
187 4/8	25 4/8 27 4/8	25 4/8	27 3/8	4 2/8 4 4/8	7 6	4	172	9
	■ Warren Co. – Gary D. Schuster – Gary D. Schuster – 1998							
187 2/8	26 26 2/8	19 4/8	21 6/8	4 6/8 4 6/8	6 8	4 6/8	180	10
	■ Scotland Co. – Robin Berhorst – Robin Berhorst – 1971							
187 1/8	26 4/8 26 5/8	19 4/8	21 1/8	4 4/8 4 5/8	6 7	2 5/8	185	11
	■ Cooper Co. – Joe Ditto – Joe Ditto – 1974							
187 1/8	27 7/8 28 3/8	18 7/8	21	5 6/8 5 7/8	5 5		185	11
	■ Mercer Co. – Picked Up – Bob Summers – 1986							
186 7/8	27 7/8 27 2/8	19 1/8	21 2/8	5 5 2/8	7 8	5 2/8	194	13
	■ Atchison Co. – Mike Moody – Mike Moody – 1968							
186 7/8	26 3/8 26 7/8	20 5/8	24 1/8	5 4/8 5 3/8	5 5		194	13
	■ Andrew Co. – Kenneth Till – Kenneth Till – 1989							
186 2/8	25 25 4/8	22 4/8	22	5 5 2/8	6 7	1 4/8	220	15
	■ Laclede Co. – Larry Ogle – Larry Ogle – 1972							
185 5/8	25 2/8 25 4/8	19 2/8	20 6/8	4 5/8 4 3/8	6 7	2 5/8	248	16
	■ Dallas Co. – James E. Headings – James E. Headings – 1986							
185 3/8	26 3/8 27	19 5/8	22	4 2/8 4 3/8	6 6		256	17
	■ Harrison Co. – John W. Rhea II – John W. Rhea II – 1995							
185 2/8	26 4/8 24 3/8	17 2/8	19 6/8	4 5/8 4 6/8	6 7		263†	18†
	■ Adair Co. – Ronald Lene – Bobby D. Lene – 1976							
185	26 6/8 26 7/8	18 6/8	20 5/8	5 1/8 5 1/8	6 6		272	19
	■ Carter Co. – Richard N. Goggin – Richard N. Goggin – 1963							

Score	Length of Main Beam Right Left	Inside Spread	Greatest Spread	Circumference at Smallest Place Between Burr and First Point Right Left		Number of Points Right Left		Lengths Abnormal Points	All-Time Rank	State Rank
	■ Location of Kill – Hunter – Owner – Date Killed									
184⁷/8	25²/8 25	18	20⁷/8	4⁷/8 5		5	7	1⁵/8	279	20
	■ Dallas Co. – Lynn Garner – Lynn Garner – 1992									
184⁵/8	27²/8 27	15⁷/8	18²/8	5³/8 5⁴/8		5	5		294	21
	■ Phelps Co. – Picked Up – Donald E. Davidson – 1988									
183⁴/8	26⁶/8 26⁶/8	18²/8	20²/8	5³/8 5⁴/8		5	6		361	22
	■ Sumner – Marvin F. Lentz – Marvin F. Lentz – 1968									
183¹/8	26³/8 25⁶/8	22¹/8	25⁴/8	4⁶/8 4⁶/8		7	7	2	385	23
	■ Cass Co. – Gerald E. Lemmer – Gerald E. Lemmer – 1997									
182⁶/8	28⁴/8 28⁷/8	19³/8	21	4³/8 4¹/8		6	6	4¹/8	409	24
	■ Osage Co. – Picked Up – Ralph Reynolds – 1972									
182⁴/8	27 26⁶/8	18⁴/8	21⁵/8	5³/8 5³/8		7	5	1⁶/8	431	25
	■ Warren Co. – Donald L. Tanner – Donald L. Tanner – 1968									
182¹/8	27 26⁷/8	22¹/8	24⁴/8	5¹/8 5²/8		5	5		460	26
	■ Lincoln Co. – David L. Mudd – David L. Mudd – 1988									
182¹/8	28²/8 27⁴/8	23¹/8	26⁴/8	4⁷/8 4⁶/8		7	8	7	460	26
	■ Adair Co. – Selby Lusher – Selby Lusher – 1996									
181⁴/8	27⁵/8 28⁴/8	20¹/8	22⁶/8	5⁴/8 4⁷/8		9	9	10³/8	516†	28†
	■ Cole Co. – Douglas S. Middleton – Douglas S. Middleton – 2000									
181²/8	27⁷/8 28²/8	20⁶/8	23⁶/8	5²/8 5³/8		5	6	2²/8	540	29
	■ Scotland Co. – Jerry Kennedy – Jerry Kennedy – 1989									
181¹/8	27⁴/8 27¹/8	19	20⁷/8	5⁷/8 6		7	6	6³/8	551	30
	■ Henry Co. – William C. Buckner – William C. Buckner – 1997									
181	27⁶/8 26⁶/8	20⁶/8	26⁶/8	5³/8 5⁴/8		9	7	7²/8	563	31
	■ Adair Co. – Michael D. Hill – Michael D. Hill – 1992									
180⁶/8	28³/8 28⁵/8	16⁴/8	18⁶/8	5⁴/8 5⁴/8		8	6	4	587	32
	■ Linn Co. – Picked Up – Doug D. Davis – 1998									
180⁴/8	23⁵/8 24⁴/8	17²/8	19	5²/8 5		6	5	1	613	33
	■ Andrew Co. – Virgil M. Ashley – Virgil M. Ashley – 1967									
180⁴/8	25⁶/8 25⁷/8	22²/8	24⁴/8	5³/8 5¹/8		5	5		613	33
	■ Livingston Co. – Jack Hampton – Jack Hampton – 1991									
180¹/8	26⁴/8 26⁵/8	20¹/8	22	4⁴/8 4⁵/8		6	6		669	35
	■ Phelps Co. – William A. Hagenhoff – William A. Hagenhoff – 1973									
180¹/8	27 26	15⁷/8	18	4⁷/8 4⁶/8		5	5		669	35
	■ Chariton Co. – Ricky Pearman – Ricky Pearman – 1982									
180¹/8	27²/8 24⁴/8	15³/8	17⁴/8	4⁶/8 4⁷/8		5	6		669	35
	■ Macon Co. – M.F. Rickwa & S.M. Rickwa – M.F. Rickwa & S.M. Rickwa – 1995									
180¹/8	28²/8 27¹/8	19⁶/8	22⁶/8	4⁵/8 4⁵/8		7	7	6⁷/8	669	35
	■ Boone Co. – Benjamin K. Betz – Benjamin K. Betz – 1999									
179⁵/8	28⁶/8 27⁶/8	21	23	4⁶/8 5		6	5	2¹/8	729	39
	■ Putnam Co. – Wes A. Seaton – Wes A. Seaton – 1992									
179³/8	25 24⁴/8	18³/8	21⁶/8	5²/8 5³/8		5	6	1⁶/8	749	40
	■ Lincoln Co. – Alfred W. Masterson – Alfred W. Masterson – 1995									

Score	Length of Main Beam Right	Left	Inside Spread	Greatest Spread	Circumference at Smallest Place Between Burr and First Point Right	Left	Number of Points Right	Left	Lengths Abnormal Points	All-Time Rank	State Rank
179	$26^2/8$	$26^5/8$	21	$23^2/8$	$4^7/8$	5	5	5		786	41
	■ Monroe Co. – Tommy Garnett – Tommy Garnett – 1988										
$178^5/8$	$25^4/8$	$26^1/8$	$20^1/8$	22	$5^4/8$	$5^3/8$	7	7	4	819	42
	■ Caldwell Co. – Jack L. Murray – Jack L. Murray – 1986										
$178^4/8$	$26^2/8$	$25^3/8$	21	$22^6/8$	$5^3/8$	$5^3/8$	5	5		850	43
	■ Scotland Co. – Picked Up – Roland E. Meyer – 1984										
$178^3/8$	$29^1/8$	$28^2/8$	$17^4/8$	$19^5/8$	$4^3/8$	$4^3/8$	7	7	$7^3/8$	868	44
	■ De Kalb Co. – Merrill Hall – Merrill Hall – 1997										
$178^1/8$	$25^5/8$	$25^3/8$	$19^5/8$	$21^7/8$	$6^1/8$	$5^6/8$	6	6	$6^4/8$	905	45
	■ De Kalb Co. – Kendall J. Weigand – Kendall J. Weigand – 1998										
178	$28^1/8$	$28^2/8$	$21^6/8$	$24^5/8$	$5^2/8$	$5^1/8$	5	5		922†	46†
	■ Chariton Co. – G. Duane Gunn – G. Duane Gunn – 2001										
178	$26^7/8$	$27^2/8$	$21^6/8$	$24^2/8$	$4^3/8$	$4^3/8$	6	6		922	46
	■ Clark Co. – Allen L. Courtney – Allen L. Courtney – 1966										
178	$29^5/8$	$28^2/8$	21	$23^5/8$	$5^2/8$	$5^3/8$	6	5		922	46
	■ Macon Co. – Charles L. Harrington – Charles L. Harrington – 1992										
$177^7/8$	$27^4/8$	$27^2/8$	$18^7/8$	22	$5^4/8$	$5^3/8$	7	6	$6^6/8$	936	49
	■ Bates Co. – Daniel P. White – Daniel P. White – 1995										
$177^7/8$	$25^1/8$	$25^3/8$	$18^5/8$	21	5	5	5	5		936	49
	■ Pettis Co. – Michael J. Macafree – Michael J. Macafree – 1997										
$177^6/8$	$24^3/8$	$23^5/8$	19	22	$4^6/8$	$4^6/8$	5	5		956	51
	■ Clark Co. – Billie G. Noble – Billie G. Noble – 1985										
$177^6/8$	$25^3/8$	$25^2/8$	$20^2/8$	$22^4/8$	$5^1/8$	5	5	5		956	51
	■ Vernon Co. – Darrell Chapman – Darrell Chapman – 1997										
177	$26^1/8$	$25^1/8$	$19^6/8$	22	$4^3/8$	$4^3/8$	6	6		1066	53
	■ Macon Co. – Wilbert R. Freeman – Wilbert R. Freeman – 1991										
$176^6/8$	$29^1/8$	$28^5/8$	20	22	$4^6/8$	$4^7/8$	6	5		1103	54
	■ Jackson Co. – Charles H. Williams – Charles H. Williams – 1996										
$176^3/8$	$25^1/8$	$25^3/8$	$20^2/8$	$22^2/8$	$5^1/8$	$5^2/8$	5	7	$4^1/8$	1182	55
	■ Wright Co. – Mike Napier – Mike Napier – 1986										
$176^2/8$	$26^2/8$	$25^7/8$	20	$22^5/8$	5	5	5	5		1209	56
	■ Worth Co. – David Shipman – David Shipman – 1999										
$176^1/8$	$27^1/8$	$27^4/8$	$23^5/8$	$25^6/8$	$4^7/8$	$5^4/8$	6	5	$3^2/8$	1243	57
	■ Johnson Co. – James A. Stephens – James A. Stephens – 1990										
$176^1/8$	$25^1/8$	$24^5/8$	$16^7/8$	$19^3/8$	5	$5^1/8$	7	8	$4^4/8$	1243	57
	■ Gentry Co. – Frank L. Thomas – Frank L. Thomas – 1998										
$176^1/8$	$24^3/8$	$26^3/8$	$20^3/8$	$22^1/8$	$5^1/8$	$4^7/8$	6	6		1243	57
	■ Pike Co. – Christopher C. Clamors – Christopher C. Clamors – 1999										
176	$25^5/8$	$25^5/8$	$17^6/8$	$19^1/8$	$4^2/8$	$4^1/8$	6	7	$2^2/8$	1266†	60†
	■ Monroe Co. – David J. Godat – David J. Godat – 2000										
176	27	27	19	$20^6/8$	$5^3/8$	$4^6/8$	7	8	$7^6/8$	1266	60
	■ Montgomery Co. – Dave Knoepflein – Dave Knoepflein – 1996										

Score	Length of Main Beam Right Left	Inside Spread	Greatest Spread	Circumference at Smallest Place Between Burr and First Point Right Left	Number of Points Right Left	Lengths Abnormal Points	All-Time Rank	State Rank
	■ *Location of Kill – Hunter – Owner – Date Killed*							
175 4/8	25 6/8 25 4/8	21 2/8	23 1/8	5 5/8 6 1/8	5 5		1352	62
■ *Corning – Orrie L. Schaeffer – Orrie L. Schaeffer – 1962*								
175 1/8	26 6/8 29	19 7/8	22 6/8	5 5	6 7	6 2/8	1440	63
■ *Cole Co. – Brian L. Bruemmer – Brian L. Bruemmer – 1995*								
175	27 26 6/8	18 3/8	20 4/8	4 3/8 4 7/8	5 6	2 3/8	1472†	64†
■ *Cooper Co. – Bradley M. Baker – Bradley M. Baker – 2000*								
175	23 2/8 24	19 6/8	22 4/8	5 1/8 5 2/8	5 5		1472	64
■ *Harrison Co. – Carl J. Graham – Carl J. Graham – 1973*								
174 7/8	23 3/8 23 5/8	16 7/8	18 7/8	4 3/8 4 4/8	5 5		1513	66
■ *Dent Co. – Thomas P. Wylie – Thomas P. Wylie – 1990*								
174 6/8	24 6/8 26 3/8	21 3/8	22 5/8	5 2/8 5 2/8	5 6	3 1/8	1534	67
■ *Shannon Co. – Picked Up – Scott D. Lindsey – 1992*								
174 6/8	27 27	20 2/8	22 2/8	4 1/8 4 2/8	5 5		1534	67
■ *Ray Co. – Douglas Kirk – Douglas Kirk – 1997*								
174 5/8	23 23 2/8	17 7/8	19 7/8	4 7/8 5	8 7	1 2/8	1561	69
■ *Lincoln Co. – William Ziegelmeyer – Ronald Ziegelmeyer, Sr. – 1968*								
174 5/8	28 2/8 28	22 5/8	25 4/8	5 3/8 5 3/8	5 6	2 2/8	1561	69
■ *Johnson Co. – Thomas E. White – Thomas E. White – 1987*								
174 5/8	28 6/8 28	20 4/8	22 1/8	5 4/8 5 5/8	6 9	7 1/8	1561	69
■ *Ray Co. – Dennis B. Bales – Dennis B. Bales – 1990*								
174 3/8	27 27 2/8	20 1/8	3	5 6/8 5 3/8	8 9	11	1619†	72†
■ *Jackson Co. – Mark A. Trowbridge – Mark A. Trowbridge – 2000*								
174 3/8	28 1/8 26 7/8	23 5/8	25 7/8	5 3/8 5 4/8	6 5	3 2/8	1619	72
■ *Knox Co. – Jon Simmons – Jon Simmons – 1972*								
174 3/8	26 1/8 25 5/8	16 3/8	19 2/8	4 5/8 4 4/8	6 6	1	1619	72
■ *Newton Co. – Scott Wolfe – Scott Wolfe – 1994*								
174 2/8	23 3/8 23 5/8	18	18 4/8	5 6/8 5 4/8	7 7	4 2/8	1652	75
■ *Montgomery Co. – S. Douglas Lensing – S. Douglas Lensing – 1999*								
174 1/8	25 25	16 6/8	18 6/8	4 7/8 4 6/8	8 7	4 1/8	1678	76
■ *Callaway Co. – Jac LaFon – Jac LaFon – 1968*								
174 1/8	24 1/8 23 4/8	19 1/8	21 3/8	5 5 2/8	7 5	3	1678	76
■ *Dallas Co. – Otis Villines – Otis Villines – 1999*								
173 7/8	24 24 1/8	22 3/8	24 6/8	6 4/8 6 2/8	5 6		1743	78
■ *Ralls Co. – Nicholas D. Mudd – Nicholas D. Mudd – 1992*								
173 6/8	28 2/8 27 7/8	20 6/8	23	5 5	5 4		1766	79
■ *Atchison Co. – Robert B. Tussing – Robert B. Tussing – 1995*								
173 5/8	25 2/8 25 4/8	18 3/8	20 5/8	5 5	5 8	1 6/8	1819	80
■ *Gentry Co. – William F. Oberbeck – William F. Oberbeck – 1969*								
173 5/8	30 1/8 30	25 3/8	27 3/8	5 5 2/8	6 5	1 2/8	1819	80
■ *Jackson Co. – Michael J. Sytkowski – Michael J. Sytkowski – 1995*								
173 2/8	26 7/8 28 5/8	23 5/8	25 6/8	4 4/8 4 4/8	6 6	4 3/8	1914	82
■ *Warren Co. – Jerome E. Ley – Jerome E. Ley – 1980*								

Score	Length of Main Beam Right	Left	Inside Spread	Greatest Spread	Circumference at Smallest Place Between Burr and First Point Right	Left	Number of Points Right	Left	Lengths Abnormal Points	All-Time Rank	State Rank
$173^{2}/8$	$24^{2}/8$	25	19	$20^{7}/8$	5	$5^{2}/8$	5	5		1914	82
■ Butler Co. – Marcus O. Milligan – Marcus O. Milligan – 1997											
$173^{1}/8$	$26^{4}/8$	26	$17^{7}/8$	19	$4^{5}/8$	$4^{5}/8$	5	5		1950†	84†
■ Saline Co. – Jesse H. Little – Jesse H. Little – 2000											
$173^{1}/8$	$26^{5}/8$	$27^{6}/8$	$19^{5}/8$	$23^{6}/8$	$4^{4}/8$	$4^{5}/8$	7	6	$3^{6}/8$	1950	84
■ Shelby Co. – William A. Light, Jr. – William A. Light, Jr. – 1981											
$173^{1}/8$	$27^{4}/8$	$27^{1}/8$	$20^{2}/8$	$23^{3}/8$	$4^{5}/8$	$4^{6}/8$	5	4	$2^{5}/8$	1950	84
■ Ralls Co. – Picked Up – Les James – 1988											
$173^{1}/8$	26	$25^{6}/8$	17	19	$4^{6}/8$	$4^{5}/8$	7	6	$3^{7}/8$	1950	84
■ Lincoln Co. – Daniel A. Narup – Daniel A. Narup – 1992											
173	28	$28^{2}/8$	$21^{7}/8$	$23^{7}/8$	$5^{3}/8$	$5^{3}/8$	7	6	$1^{1}/8$	1991	88
■ Howard Co. – Thomas R. Banning – Thomas R. Banning – 1978											
173	$25^{4}/8$	$27^{1}/8$	$19^{4}/8$	$22^{1}/8$	$5^{2}/8$	5	9	8	$7^{2}/8$	1991	88
■ Clay Co. – Neal B. Breshears – Neal B. Breshears – 1996											
$172^{5}/8$	$26^{2}/8$	$25^{6}/8$	$18^{6}/8$	$20^{7}/8$	$5^{3}/8$	$5^{5}/8$	5	7	$3^{1}/8$	2113	90
■ Douglas Co. – Virgil Churchill – Virgil Churchill – 1990											
$172^{4}/8$	26	$27^{6}/8$	21	$24^{1}/8$	5	$5^{1}/8$	5	5		2156†	91†
■ Harrison Co. – Bill Cook – Bill Cook – 2001											
$172^{4}/8$	$27^{2}/8$	26	19	$21^{2}/8$	$4^{7}/8$	$4^{7}/8$	6	7	$8^{6}/8$	2156	91
■ Adair Co. – Eldon L. Grissom, Sr. – Eldon L. Grissom, Sr. – 1999											
$172^{3}/8$	$25^{6}/8$	$25^{7}/8$	$16^{2}/8$	$18^{4}/8$	5	5	6	7	$3^{5}/8$	2200†	93†
■ Grundy Co. – Wayne A. Moore, Jr. – Wayne A. Moore, Jr. – 2001											
$172^{3}/8$	26	$26^{2}/8$	$19^{5}/8$	$21^{2}/8$	$4^{6}/8$	$4^{6}/8$	6	5	$1^{6}/8$	2200	93
■ Monroe Co. – Clark E. Bray – Clark E. Bray – 1967											
$172^{3}/8$	$26^{4}/8$	$26^{7}/8$	$16^{2}/8$	$18^{2}/8$	5	$4^{6}/8$	5	7	$1^{1}/8$	2200	93
■ Mercer Co. – Jarin J. Simpson – Jarin J. Simpson – 1988											
$172^{2}/8$	$24^{2}/8$	$25^{4}/8$	18	$19^{4}/8$	4	$4^{3}/8$	6	6		2237	96
■ Mercer Co. – Brad Holt – Brad Holt – 1993											
$172^{2}/8$	27	$27^{2}/8$	$19^{6}/8$	22	$4^{5}/8$	$4^{6}/8$	5	5		2237	96
■ Randolph Co. – Edward L. Sneed – Edward L. Sneed – 1997											
$172^{1}/8$	$25^{2}/8$	$26^{3}/8$	$19^{3}/8$	$21^{6}/8$	$4^{6}/8$	$4^{7}/8$	6	6	$4^{2}/8$	2286	98
■ Miller Co. – Jim L. Bell – Jim L. Bell – 1992											
172	$26^{5}/8$	$28^{3}/8$	$17^{7}/8$	$21^{6}/8$	$4^{6}/8$	$4^{7}/8$	6	7	$7^{1}/8$	2330†	99†
■ Pettis Co. – James R. Ellison – James R. Ellison – 2001											
172	$25^{3}/8$	$24^{6}/8$	$17^{4}/8$	$19^{4}/8$	$4^{5}/8$	$4^{5}/8$	7	6	$1^{2}/8$	2330†	99†
■ Pike Co. – Randall E. Pilliard – Randall E. Pilliard – 2000											
172	$23^{7}/8$	$23^{5}/8$	$15^{6}/8$	$17^{5}/8$	$4^{2}/8$	4	5	5		2330	99
■ Callaway Co. – Picked Up – Larry W. Quick – 1990											
172	$24^{4}/8$	$25^{3}/8$	18	20	$4^{6}/8$	$4^{6}/8$	6	7	$2^{2}/8$	2330	99
■ Harrison Co. – Timothy E. Black – Timothy E. Black – 1991											
172	$24^{2}/8$	$24^{7}/8$	$19^{3}/8$	$23^{3}/8$	$4^{7}/8$	$4^{7}/8$	10	5	$8^{1}/8$	2330	99
■ De Kalb Co. – Dean Davis – Dean Davis – 1991											

Score	Length of Main Beam		Inside Spread	Greatest Spread	Circumference at Smallest Place Between Burr and First Point		Number of Points		Lengths Abnormal Points	All-Time Rank	State Rank
	Right	Left			Right	Left	Right	Left			
	■ Location of Kill – Hunter – Owner – Date Killed										
172	24⁵/₈	22⁷/₈	18⁶/₈	21²/₈	4⁶/₈	4⁴/₈	6	5	2⁶/₈	2330	99
	■ Daviess Co. – David K. DeWeese – David K. DeWeese – 1992										
171⁷/₈	26²/₈	26⁴/₈	24¹/₈	27⁷/₈	4⁴/₈	4⁴/₈	5	5		2382	105
	■ Scotland Co. – David R. Smith – David R. Smith – 1984										
171⁷/₈	26⁷/₈	25⁵/₈	19⁵/₈	22	5³/₈	5⁴/₈	5	6	1⁴/₈	2382	105
	■ Moniteau Co. – Randy Wilson – Randy Wilson – 1999										
171⁵/₈	26	25⁶/₈	17³/₈	19³/₈	4³/₈	4³/₈	5	5		2470	107
	■ Crawford Co. – Chris Glaser – Fred Glaser – 1982										
171⁵/₈	29²/₈	28	22¹/₈	23⁶/₈	5⁴/₈	5²/₈	7	6		2470	107
	■ Warren Co. – Scott Parker – Scott Parker – 1994										
171⁵/₈	28⁷/₈	28	20¹/₈	22⁴/₈	5²/₈	5⁴/₈	5	5		2470	107
	■ Atchison Co. – Frank Hackworth – Frank Hackworth – 1999										
171⁴/₈	25⁵/₈	25⁷/₈	18	20	4⁷/₈	4⁷/₈	6	8	2⁴/₈	2513	110
	■ Bollinger Co. – Darrell L. Bostic – Darrell L. Bostic – 1989										
171⁴/₈	26⁴/₈	25²/₈	18⁶/₈	21	4⁵/₈	5¹/₈	6	6	3	2513	110
	■ Scotland Co. – Harry Robeson – Harry Robeson – 1989										
171³/₈	26²/₈	26⁴/₈	20	21⁶/₈	4³/₈	4⁴/₈	5	6	1¹/₈	2564†	112†
	■ Adair Co. – Karen White – Karen White – 2000										
171³/₈	23¹/₈	23	18	20¹/₈	5	5	6	5	3⁵/₈	2564	112
	■ Washington Co. – Jerry D. Bouse – Jerry D. Bouse – 1987										
171³/₈	26⁴/₈	26⁶/₈	18⁵/₈	22²/₈	5³/₈	5²/₈	7	7	5	2564	112
	■ Howard Co. – Derrick Powell – Derrick Powell – 1992										
171³/₈	28⁵/₈	27²/₈	21³/₈	23⁶/₈	5¹/₈	5³/₈	4	4		2564	112
	■ Oregon Co. – Dale Conner – Scott D. Lindsey – 1996										
171³/₈	27⁴/₈	27⁵/₈	17⁷/₈	20¹/₈	5¹/₈	5¹/₈	6	5		2564	112
	■ Monroe Co. – Shelton Wheelan – Shelton Wheelan – 1999										
171²/₈	24⁷/₈	27	19⁶/₈	21²/₈	4²/₈	4⁴/₈	6	6		2621†	117†
	■ Warren Co. – Billy DeCoster – Billy DeCoster – 2000										
171²/₈	25	25⁴/₈	19⁶/₈	21⁴/₈	4⁶/₈	4⁶/₈	5	6	2²/₈	2621	117
	■ Linn Co. – Bryan H. Mueller – Bryan H. Mueller – 1992										
171²/₈	24	23⁵/₈	17²/₈	18⁷/₈	4³/₈	4²/₈	6	6		2621	117
	■ Lincoln Co. – F. Neil Norton – F. Neil Norton – 1992										
171²/₈	25⁷/₈	26⁷/₈	18⁴/₈	20⁴/₈	5	5	5	5		2621	117
	■ Saline Co. – Jeffrey E. Edwards – Jeffrey E. Edwards – 1995										
171¹/₈	28⁵/₈	26⁶/₈	20¹/₈	21⁵/₈	5	5	6	6	1⁶/₈	2665	121
	■ Livingston Co. – Richard L. West – Richard L. West – 1986										
171¹/₈	25⁴/₈	26⁴/₈	17³/₈	20	4⁴/₈	4⁴/₈	5	6	1⁴/₈	2665	121
	■ Scotland Co. – Joseph Frye – Joseph Frye – 1997										
171	24⁴/₈	25²/₈	17²/₈	21	4²/₈	4¹/₈	6	5	3⁶/₈	2707	123
	■ Ray Co. – Darle R. Siegel – Darle R. Siegel – 1966										
171	25²/₈	24	15⁶/₈	18¹/₈	5¹/₈	5²/₈	5	5		2707	123
	■ Christian Co. – Melba J. Herndon – Melba J. Herndon – 1983										

Score	Length of Main Beam Right	Left	Inside Spread	Greatest Spread	Circumference at Smallest Place Between Burr and First Point Right	Left	Number of Points Right	Left	Lengths Abnormal Points	All-Time Rank	State Rank
	■ Location of Kill – Hunter – Owner – Date Killed										
171	25 5/8	26 1/8	21 2/8	23 5/8	5 3/8	5 2/8	8	7	7 6/8	2707	123
	■ Knox Co. – Herbert J. Wedemeier – Herbert J. Wedemeier – 1997										
171	26 2/8	26 6/8	16 5/8	19 5/8	4 5/8	4 6/8	7	7	3 3/8	2707	123
	■ Callaway Co. – Jeff M. Sumpter – Jeff M. Sumpter – 1999										
170 7/8	26	26 7/8	16 3/8	18 4/8	4 5/8	4 5/8	5	5		2769	127
	■ Grundy Co. – Bill Zang – Bill Zang – 1986										
170 7/8	25 5/8	26	22 5/8	24 5/8	4 6/8	4 6/8	6	5		2769	127
	■ Worth Co. – Duane Hostikka – Duane Hostikka – 1998										
170 6/8	27 2/8	26 4/8	20	23	4 4/8	4 4/8	6	6	2 2/8	2828	129
	■ Howell Co. – Roy W. Woodson – Roy W. Woodson – 1974										
170 6/8	28 6/8	28 2/8	19 2/8	21 5/8	4 5/8	4 6/8	6	6	5 6/8	2828	129
	■ Phelps Co. – Dave Gabel – Dave Gabel – 1996										
170 6/8	26 4/8	25 7/8	20 7/8	23 2/8	4 7/8	4 6/8	6	6	3 5/8	2828	129
	■ Sullivan Co. – Rodney A. Raley – Rodney A. Raley – 1997										
170 5/8	22 5/8	23 2/8	17 7/8	20	4 7/8	5	5	5		2876	132
	■ St. Charles Co. – Oscar Mallinckrodt – Oscar Mallinckrodt – 1962										
170 5/8	26 2/8	26 2/8	18 1/8	20 2/8	4 3/8	4 3/8	6	6	2 2/8	2876	132
	■ Shannon Co. – Garry Bland – Garry Bland – 1971										
170 5/8	26 7/8	25 4/8	18 2/8	20 5/8	5 4/8	5 2/8	5	7	1 5/8	2876	132
	■ Atchison Co. – Roy E. Munsey – Roy E. Munsey – 1980										
170 5/8	27 3/8	27 7/8	18 5/8	20 5/8	5 4/8	5 4/8	5	6	3 2/8	2876	132
	■ Grundy Co. – Michael C. Weathers – Michael C. Weathers – 1988										
170 4/8	25 1/8	25 1/8	19	21 6/8	3 7/8	4 1/8	6	5	3 6/8	2933	136
	■ Sullivan Co. – Randy Tucker – Randy Tucker – 1981										
170 3/8	25 2/8	25 2/8	18 7/8	20 4/8	5 4/8	5 4/8	7	7	4 2/8	2992	137
	■ Mercer Co. – Robert W. Vasey – Robert W. Vasey – 1990										
170 3/8	26 1/8	26 1/8	17 3/8	20 1/8	5	4 5/8	5	5		2992	137
	■ Harrison Co. – Glen D. Gentry – Glen D. Gentry – 1991										
170 2/8	25 6/8	25	17 2/8	19	4 6/8	4 6/8	5	5		3063†	139†
	■ Washington Co. – William M. Hazer – William M. Hazer – 1998										
170 2/8	27	27 2/8	17	19 2/8	4 5/8	4 5/8	5	5		3063	139
	■ Macon Co. – Renee L. DeWeese – Renee L. DeWeese – 1991										
170 2/8	27	26 3/8	21 4/8	24 2/8	5	5 1/8	8	7	6	3063	139
	■ St. Charles Co. – Leroy H. Vehige – Leroy H. Vehige – 1994										
170 1/8	25 3/8	24 5/8	17 1/8	19 2/8	4 4/8	4 5/8	6	6		3143	142
	■ Putnam Co. – Ralph J. Shoultz – Otteline Shoultz – 1973										
170 1/8	25 7/8	25 7/8	21 5/8	23 4/8	4 4/8	4 5/8	6	6		3143	142
	■ Pulaski Co. – Chuck Adkins – Chuck Adkins – 1986										
170 1/8	27 7/8	26 4/8	18 7/8	21 1/8	5 4/8	5 1/8	5	6	1	3143	142
	■ Montgomery Co. – Kenneth B. Maskey – Kenneth B. Maskey – 1988										
170	26 4/8	26 5/8	17 4/8	20 1/8	4 6/8	4 7/8	7	5	2 4/8	3224	145
	■ Bates Co. – Gary Rosier – Gary Rosier – 1969										

Score	Length of Main Beam Right Left	Inside Spread	Greatest Spread	Circumference at Smallest Place Between Burr and First Point Right Left		Number of Points Right Left		Lengths Abnormal Points	All-Time Rank	State Rank
	■ Location of Kill – Hunter – Owner – Date Killed									
170	26³/8 24⁵/8	19⁶/8	23	5²/8	5¹/8	5	5		3224	145
	■ Shelby Co. – Rusty D. Gander – Rusty D. Gander – 1973									
170	24³/8 23²/8	20⁶/8	22⁵/8	4⁷/8	4⁶/8	5	5		3224	145
	■ Scotland Co. – Chester J. Young – Chester J. Young – 1974									
170	27⁷/8 27⁶/8	18⁶/8	20³/8	4⁶/8	4⁶/8	7	7	7²/8	3224	145
	■ Putnam Co. – Unknown – Terry L. Gates – PR 1986									
170	25⁷/8 26¹/8	16³/8	19³/8	4⁴/8	4⁴/8	7	5	2⁷/8	3224	145
	■ Boone Co. – Norman M. Barrows – Norman M. Barrows – 1991									
169³/8	25³/8 23³/8	18⁵/8	20⁵/8	5³/8	5⁴/8	6	6	2	3324	150
	■ Caldwell Co. – Michael D. Robeson – Michael D. Robeson – 1991									
169³/8	27⁶/8 28	16⁷/8	19⁵/8	4²/8	4²/8	7	9	6⁶/8	3324	150
	■ Cooper Co. – Gerald V. Sell – Gerald V. Sell – 1992									
169¹/8	25²/8 25⁶/8	19¹/8	21²/8	4⁶/8	4⁷/8	6	7	2⁴/8	3342	152
	■ Henry Co. – Donald K. Wheeler – Donald K. Wheeler – 1995									
169¹/8	23⁵/8 23²/8	19³/8	21³/8	4⁷/8	4⁷/8	9	7	6⁶/8	3342	152
	■ Holt Co. – Bruce A. Medsker – Bruce A. Medsker – 1997									
168⁷/8	24³/8 25⁶/8	21⁵/8	23⁴/8	6	6	5	5		3361	154
	■ Pike Co. – Terry L. Weier – Terry L. Weier – 1996									
168³/8	25⁷/8 27⁷/8	21³/8	23	4⁶/8	4⁵/8	5	5		3399	155
	■ Reynolds Co. – Rex Mehrhoff – Rex Mehrhoff – 1990									
168¹/8	26⁶/8 27⁶/8	19³/8	22³/8	4⁷/8	4⁷/8	7	6	3⁴/8	3426	156
	■ Harrison Co. – Michael C. Garrett – Michael C. Garrett – 1993									
168	28³/8 28⁷/8	21⁴/8	23²/8	4⁵/8	4⁶/8	6	5	1⁴/8	3443	157
	■ Sullivan Co. – James E. Hines – James E. Hines – 1990									
167⁷/8	25⁴/8 24³/8	18⁷/8	20⁷/8	5³/8	5⁵/8	5	6		3451	158
	■ Ozark Co. – Rex E. Jenkins – Rex E. Jenkins – 1982									
167⁵/8	26 26²/8	18²/8	20⁷/8	5⁷/8	5⁴/8	6	6	2⁷/8	3476	159
	■ Platte Co. – Michael J. Brown – Michael J. Brown – 1987									
167⁵/8	24²/8 24⁶/8	17⁵/8	19⁴/8	4⁷/8	5¹/8	5	5		3476	159
	■ Pike Co. – Guy H. Richardson – Guy H. Richardson – 1995									
167³/8	23³/8 23⁶/8	14⁴/8	17²/8	4⁶/8	4⁴/8	5	6	1¹/8	3500	161
	■ Osage Co. – Scott Morfeld – Scott Morfeld – 1995									
167²/8	27²/8 27⁴/8	21⁶/8	24⁴/8	4⁷/8	4⁷/8	7	10	11	3519	162
	■ Laclede Co. – Eldar R. Krueger – Eldar R. Krueger – 1989									
167²/8	24¹/8 24⁵/8	18⁴/8	20	4³/8	4²/8	5	5		3519	162
	■ Macon Co. – Spencer A. Barron – Spencer A. Barron – 1997									
166⁷/8	25⁵/8 27²/8	17²/8	20⁷/8	4⁴/8	4⁶/8	6	5	1⁵/8	3568	164
	■ Clark Co. – Mary F. Thomson – Mary F. Thomson – 1995									
166⁷/8	23 23⁴/8	17⁵/8	20	4⁶/8	4⁷/8	5	5		3568	164
	■ Randolph Co. – Art J. Crutchfield, Jr. – Art J. Crutchfield, Jr. – 1996									
166⁵/8	26²/8 26¹/8	19⁷/8	22³/8	5	4⁷/8	4	4		3598	166
	■ Adair Co. – Daniel C. Elfrink – Daniel C. Elfrink – 1987									

Score	Length of Main Beam		Inside Spread	Greatest Spread	Circumference at Smallest Place Between Burr and First Point		Number of Points		Lengths Abnormal Points	All-Time Rank	State Rank
	Right	Left			Right	Left	Right	Left			
	■ *Location of Kill – Hunter – Owner – Date Killed*										
165⁵/8	25	24⁶/8	16	18	5¹/8	5	6	5	1³/8	3598	166
	■ *Jefferson Co. – Eli Parkhurst – Eli Parkhurst – 1997*										
166⁴/8	25⁶/8	25⁴/8	18²/8	20	4⁴/8	4⁴/8	5	5		3609	168
	■ *Ripley Co. – Jack R. McGowan – Jack R. McGowan – 1991*										
166³/8	28²/8	27²/8	18⁵/8	19⁶/8	4⁶/8	4⁵/8	7	7	7⁶/8	3620	169
	■ *Montgomery Co. – Thomas W. Ham – Thomas W. Ham – 1990*										
166²/8	25²/8	26¹/8	19²/8	21³/8	4⁶/8	4⁶/8	4	4		3632	170
	■ *Atchison Co. – Vernie A. Rhoades – Vernon F. Rhoades – 1989*										
165⁶/8	27²/8	26⁷/8	19⁵/8	21⁶/8	4⁴/8	4⁷/8	6	8	5¹/8	3680	171
	■ *St. Charles Co. – Gary L. Vails – Gary L. Vails – 1989*										
165⁶/8	26³/8	26³/8	20	22¹/8	4²/8	4²/8	5	5		3680	171
	■ *Harrison Co. – Clark Ferree – Clark Ferree – 1994*										
165⁵/8	26⁴/8	24⁵/8	17	20	5²/8	5¹/8	6	6	2⁵/8	3696	173
	■ *Cooper Co. – Daniel L. Twenter – Daniel L. Twenter – 1997*										
165²/8	25⁵/8	25⁵/8	22⁴/8	24¹/8	4⁵/8	4⁶/8	6	6		3748†	174†
	■ *Ray Co. – Jerry M. Williams – Jerry M. Williams – 2000*										
165²/8	25⁷/8	25¹/8	16²/8	18⁶/8	5¹/8	5²/8	4	4		3748	174
	■ *Vernon Co. – George Brannan – George Brannan – 1990*										
165²/8	23	25⁴/8	21	23¹/8	4⁴/8	4⁵/8	5	5		3748	174
	■ *Lincoln Co. – Ronald D. Olson – Ronald D. Olson – 1996*										
165¹/8	26⁶/8	26	19⁵/8	22	4⁷/8	4⁷/8	7	6	3⁶/8	3767	177
	■ *Harrison Co. – Roger L. Maxwell – Roger L. Maxwell – 1974*										
164⁷/8	25⁵/8	25⁵/8	21¹/8	23	5⁴/8	5²/8	7	5	2⁴/8	3792	178
	■ *Pike Co. – William R. Kimbro – William R. Kimbro – 1995*										
164⁷/8	24⁵/8	24⁶/8	16⁵/8	21²/8	4⁵/8	4⁵/8	7	5	6	3792	178
	■ *St. Charles Co. – Adam C. Bethmann – Adam C. Bethmann – 1999*										
164⁵/8	24⁶/8	23⁷/8	19⁵/8	21⁷/8	4⁷/8	4⁷/8	5	5		3835	180
	■ *Platte Co. – Chris B. Hiatt – Chris B. Hiatt – 1995*										
164⁴/8	25¹/8	24⁷/8	17²/8	19⁷/8	4¹/8	4	5	5		3855	181
	■ *Osage Co. – Derrick J. Roeslein – Derrick J. Roeslein – 1994*										
164³/8	23⁶/8	24²/8	18¹/8	20²/8	4³/8	4⁴/8	5	6		3864	182
	■ *Audrain Co. – Dave Qualls – Dave Qualls – 1995*										
164²/8	24³/8	24⁴/8	17	19²/8	4³/8	4³/8	5	5		3876	183
	■ *Camden Co. – Douglas G. Pruitt – Douglas G. Pruitt – 1995*										
164¹/8	24⁶/8	24⁵/8	17⁶/8	19⁶/8	5	5³/8	5	6	1¹/8	3886	184
	■ *Adair Co. – Rodney E. Baumgartner – Rodney E. Baumgartner – 1993*										
164	26⁶/8	27¹/8	18	20⁵/8	4⁷/8	5	7	7	7²/8	3908	185
	■ *Saline Co. – David L. Cramer – David L. Cramer – 1978*										
163⁵/8	24⁵/8	24⁵/8	17⁵/8	19⁵/8	4⁴/8	4⁵/8	6	6		3961	186
	■ *Shelby Co. – Suzanne S. von Thun – Suzanne S. von Thun – 1996*										
163³/8	25⁷/8	26⁴/8	22⁵/8	24⁵/8	4⁴/8	4⁴/8	5	5		4002	187
	■ *Ray Co. – Kerry R. Hayes – Kerry R. Hayes – 1994*										

Score	Length of Main Beam Right Left	Inside Spread	Greatest Spread	Circumference at Smallest Place Between Burr and First Point Right Left	Number of Points Right Left	Lengths Abnormal Points	All-Time Rank	State Rank
	■ Location of Kill – Hunter – Owner – Date Killed							
163³/8	25³/8 24⁴/8	21⁵/8	22⁵/8	4³/8 4⁶/8	8 9	8²/8	4002	187
	■ Montgomery Co. – Roy L. Smith – Roy L. Smith – 1999							
163¹/8	25⁴/8 25³/8	18⁴/8	20⁶/8	5²/8 5²/8	6 6	9¹/8	4035	189
	■ Jackson Co. – Carl E. Bogue – Carl E. Bogue – 1995							
162⁷/8	27⁷/8 27⁷/8	17⁵/8	19⁵/8	5³/8 5¹/8	5 6	2²/8	4067	190
	■ Camden Co. – Picked Up – Lester Capps – 1984							
162⁷/8	27⁶/8 28⁴/8	18⁴/8	22²/8	5⁷/8 4³/8	8 6	11¹/8	4067	190
	■ Cass Co. – Rick W. Goosey – Rick W. Goosey – 1993							
162⁵/8	25⁶/8 25⁵/8	18⁵/8	22⁴/8	5³/8 6	5 7	10	4109	192
	■ Knox Co. – Doug Perrigo – Doug Perrigo – 1996							
162⁴/8	26⁴/8 26⁵/8	21⁶/8	24³/8	4⁶/8 4⁶/8	5 5		4129	193
	■ Howard Co. – Keith W. Nichols – Keith W. Nichols – 1991							
162¹/8	24 24⁶/8	17⁴/8	19	3⁷/8 3⁷/8	7 6	1¹/8	4174	194
	■ Cole Co. – Carl A. Rackers – Carl A. Rackers – 1996							
162¹/8	25 24	18¹/8	20⁴/8	4⁴/8 4³/8	8 7	6²/8	4174	194
	■ Callaway Co. – Thomas L. Wekenborg – Thomas L. Wekenborg – 1999							
161⁷/8	27⁴/8 27¹/8	19¹/8	21³/8	4²/8 4²/8	5 5		4212	196
	■ Webster Co. – Jack J. Hubbell – Jack J. Hubbell – 1997							
161⁵/8	23⁴/8 23⁴/8	23¹/8	25⁵/8	5 5	6 6	8⁶/8	4234†	197†
	■ Adair Co. – Timothy J. Schepers – Timothy J. Schepers – 2001							
161⁵/8	27¹/8 24⁷/8	16⁷/8	19²/8	4³/8 4⁶/8	8 5	3	4234	197
	■ Warren Co. – Nathan T. Maune – Nathan T. Maune – 1997							
161⁵/8	26⁴/8 28²/8	19⁴/8	21⁷/8	5²/8 5	4 6	2¹/8	4234	197
	■ Platte Co. – Kelly C. Thompson – Kelly C. Thompson – 1997							
161⁵/8	25²/8 25³/8	19¹/8	21¹/8	4⁵/8 4⁴/8	5 5		4234	197
	■ Randolph Co. – Dennis M. Hodgson – Dennis M. Hodgson – 1998							
161⁴/8	26⁶/8 26	18⁵/8	22⁴/8	4¹/8 4	5 6	3³/8	4258	201
	■ Callaway Co. – Michael J. Bernskoetter – Michael J. Bernskoetter – 1996							
161⁴/8	26²/8 26¹/8	19	21³/8	5 4⁷/8	5 5		4258	201
	■ Callaway Co. – Tad R. Smith – Tad R. Smith – 1997							
161⁴/8	26³/8 27¹/8	21³/8	23⁷/8	4⁴/8 4⁴/8	6 7	5⁵/8	4258	201
	■ Worth Co. – Paul D. Watson – Paul D. Watson – 1997							
161³/8	27 25⁵/8	17⁷/8	20¹/8	4⁷/8 4⁶/8	4 5		4285	204
	■ Morgan Co. – Margaret E. Trueblood – Margaret E. Trueblood – 1991							
161³/8	26⁴/8 27⁶/8	18⁵/8	20⁷/8	5²/8 5⁴/8	6 4	4²/8	4285	204
	■ Knox Co. – Bradley P. McArthur – Bradley P. McArthur – 1995							
161²/8	24 24	18⁶/8	20¹/8	5 5¹/8	5 5		4310	206
	■ Carroll Co. – James E. Parker – James E. Parker – 1993							
161	27 25³/8	20⁴/8	23⁵/8	4¹/8 4¹/8	5 5		4356	207
	■ Stoddard Co. – Paul F. Landewee – Paul F. Landewee – 1996							
161	25⁷/8 25	15⁶/8	18²/8	5 5³/8	5 5		4356	207
	■ Sullivan Co. – Monty W. Gordon – Monty W. Gordon – 1998							

Score	Length of Main Beam		Inside Spread	Greatest Spread	Circumference at Smallest Place Between Burr and First Point		Number of Points		Lengths Abnormal Points	All-Time Rank	State Rank
	Right	Left			Right	Left	Right	Left			
	■ Location of Kill – Hunter – Owner – Date Killed										
160⁷/₈	24²/₈	23⁷/₈	18²/₈	20⁷/₈	5	5¹/₈	5	7	1⁵/₈	4380†	209†
	■ Adair Co. – Bruce May – Bruce May – 2001										
160⁶/₈	24⁶/₈	24⁶/₈	21²/₈	23³/₈	5	5	5	5		4402	210
	■ Knox Co. – James A. Baker – James A. Baker – 1997										
160⁵/₈	27⁵/₈	26⁴/₈	15⁵/₈	17⁷/₈	4³/₈	4⁶/₈	5	6	1	4423	211
	■ Montgomery Co. – Dennis E. Alvarez – Dennis E. Alvarez – 1987										
160⁴/₈	25	25⁴/₈	19³/₈	21	4³/₈	4⁴/₈	6	8	2⁷/₈	4443	212
	■ Chariton Co. – Rodney J. Gladbach – Rodney J. Gladbach – 1997										
160³/₈	26¹/₈	25	19¹/₈	23⁷/₈	5	5²/₈	6	7	4²/₈	4470	213
	■ Audrain Co. – William E. Hendrix – William E. Hendrix – 1989										
160³/₈	25	24⁴/₈	15	16⁴/₈	4⁴/₈	4²/₈	6	5	1⁷/₈	4470	213
	■ Lincoln Co. – Scott M. Creech – Scott M. Creech – 1995										
160³/₈	23⁵/₈	23⁷/₈	17⁵/₈	19³/₈	4²/₈	4²/₈	5	5		4470	213
	■ Ralls Co. – John E. Robinson – John E. Robinson – 1998										
160²/₈	26²/₈	25¹/₈	19	21	5	4⁶/₈	5	5		4495	216
	■ Cass Co. – Donald P. Garrett – Donald P. Garrett – 1994										
160²/₈	24	25⁴/₈	16⁶/₈	19	5²/₈	5³/₈	6	7	1⁴/₈	4495	216
	■ Daviess Co. – Larry J. Pagel – Larry J. Pagel – 1999										
160¹/₈	24⁷/₈	25⁶/₈	18⁵/₈	20⁴/₈	4⁵/₈	4⁶/₈	5	5		4534†	218†
	■ Clark Co. – Thomas F. Casey – Thomas F. Casey – 2001										
160	24⁴/₈	24⁵/₈	19³/₈	22²/₈	4⁴/₈	4⁵/₈	5	6	2⁵/₈	4565	219
	■ Knox Co. – Michael D. Harsell – Michael D. Harsell – 1993										

† The scores and ranking for trophies from the 25th Awards Entry Period are not final until the banquet is held on June 19, 2004.

TROPHIES IN THE FIELD

HUNTER:	Gary F. Hoeper
SCORE:	202-1/8
CATEGORY:	non-typical whitetail deer
LOCATION:	Holt County, Missouri
DATE:	1997

MISSOURI

NON-TYPICAL WHITETAIL DEER

Score	Length of Main Beam Right	Left	Inside Spread	Greatest Spread	Circumference at Smallest Place Between Burr and First Point Right	Left	Number of Points Right	Left	Lengths Abnormal Points	All-Time Rank	State Rank
					■ Location of Kill – Hunter – Owner – Date Killed						
333⁷/₈	24¹/₈	23³/₈	23³/₈	33³/₈	5¹/₈	5¹/₈	19	25	184	1	1
	■ St. Louis Co. – Picked Up – MO Dept. of Cons. – 1981										
266¹/₈	26⁶/₈	27	20⁴/₈	27⁵/₈	6⁴/₈	7¹/₈	17	16	90³/₈	19	2
	■ Pike Co. – Randy J. Simonitch – Randy J. Simonitch – 2000										
259⁵/₈	26⁷/₈	26⁷/₈	20³/₈	25⁶/₈	6	5⁴/₈	14	13	58⁴/₈	24	3
	■ Chariton Co. – Duane R. Linscott – Bass Pro Shops – 1985										
235	25⁵/₈	24³/₈	22²/₈	28¹/₈	4⁷/₈	4⁷/₈	13	14	60	170	4
	■ Daviess Co. – Justin K. Moore – Justin K. Moore – 1997										
227	26⁵/₈	26⁶/₈	17²/₈	24³/₈	5¹/₈	5	13	11	52²/₈	279	5
	■ Jackson Co. – Picked Up – H. James Reimer – 1989										
225⁵/₈	25³/₈	25⁴/₈	16⁴/₈	24⁵/₈	5⁶/₈	5⁶/₈	11	14	49⁵/₈	308	6
	■ Laclede Co. – Picked Up – Brad Sowter – PR 1993										
223	24⁵/₈	22⁶/₈	14³/₈	22⁵/₈	6⁶/₈	6⁵/₈	14	17	70⁵/₈	365†	7†
	■ Callaway Co. – Herman D. Stiefferman, Jr. – Herman D. Stiefferman, Jr. – 2000										
222⁵/₈	31⁷/₈	31²/₈	23⁴/₈	29³/₈	5⁵/₈	5⁴/₈	8	10	20⁷/₈	373	8
	■ Nodaway Co. – Kenneth Barcus – Bass Pro Shops – 1982										
221⁴/₈	27⁴/₈	27⁵/₈	20³/₈	23	5⁴/₈	5⁴/₈	10	12	27⁷/₈	402	9
	■ Pike Co. – Billy J. Schanks – Billy J. Schanks – 1991										
219⁵/₈	24⁵/₈	25¹/₈	21¹/₈	25⁴/₈	5⁷/₈	6³/₈	13	12	34⁴/₈	451	10
	■ Warren Co. – James E. Williams – James E. Williams – 1959										
218⁵/₈	26²/₈	25⁶/₈	18⁴/₈	23²/₈	4⁴/₈	4⁴/₈	9	11	36⁷/₈	480	11
	■ Chariton Co. – Stanley McSparren – Stanley McSparren – 1979										
217⁷/₈	27⁷/₈	28²/₈	21³/₈	23⁶/₈	5⁴/₈	5⁷/₈	10	16	30	499	12
	■ Maries Co. – Gerald R. Dake – Gerald R. Dake – 1974										
217²/₈	28⁶/₈	28⁵/₈	21⁶/₈	24⁶/₈	4⁷/₈	5²/₈	11	8	38⁶/₈	519	13
	■ Clark Co. – Lawrence L. Paul – Lawrence L. Paul – 1977										
216⁴/₈	27⁶/₈	26¹/₈	19²/₈	23⁴/₈	5	5⁴/₈	9	10	51	546	14
	■ Jefferson Co. – Picked Up – Jeff L. Vaughan – 1995										
215⁵/₈	28	28	20²/₈	23³/₈	5²/₈	5¹/₈	10	9	21¹/₈	578	15
	■ Worth Co. – B.Miller & R. Nonneman – B.Miller & R. Nonneman – 1974										
214	23⁶/₈	24⁵/₈	17³/₈	22³/₈	5⁴/₈	5⁶/₈	13	14	48¹/₈	629	16
	■ Atchison Co. – Warren E. Davis – Warren E. Davis – 1983										
211³/₈	27³/₈	27⁵/₈	22²/₈	25⁵/₈	5⁴/₈	5⁶/₈	10	9	17-9/₈	745	17
	■ Scotland Co. – Gary L. Childress – Gary L. Childress – 1998										
211	21⁴/₈	21⁶/₈	15³/₈	20⁵/₈	4	4	8	11	53¹/₈	764	18
	■ Mercer Co. – Treve A. Gray – Treve A. Gray – 1995										
209⁶/₈	25⁶/₈	25⁶/₈	17⁷/₈	21¹/₈	5¹/₈	5¹/₈	8	7	37⁵/₈	831	19
	■ Sullivan Co. – Curt E. Richardson – Curt E. Richardson – 1997										

Score	Length of Main Beam Right / Left	Inside Spread	Greatest Spread	Circumference at Smallest Place Between Burr and First Point Right / Left	Number of Points Right / Left	Lengths Abnormal Points	All-Time Rank	State Rank
	■ Location of Kill – Hunter – Owner – Date Killed							
208⁷/₈	25¹/₈ 26	21⁶/₈	24⁶/₈	5 4⁷/₈	8 11	20¹/₈	877	20
	■ Atchison Co. – Kenneth W. Lee – Kenneth W. Lee – 1964							
207⁵/₈	25³/₈ 25	20³/₈	23³/₈	4⁷/₈ 4⁶/₈	8 14	45²/₈	957	21
	■ Gentry Co. – Eric D. Sybert – Eric D. Sybert – 1990							
207⁴/₈	26⁷/₈ 26⁴/₈	19	29⁴/₈	5²/₈ 5²/₈	10 8	30⁶/₈	969	22
	■ Lewis Co. – Leonard G. Grant – Leonard G. Grant – 1999							
207³/₈	28⁷/₈ 29¹/₈	18⁵/₈	16³/₈	6⁵/₈ 6²/₈	10 10	44	977	23
	■ Lincoln Co. – Melvin Zumwalt – Melvin Zumwalt – 1955							
207²/₈	30¹/₈ 29⁵/₈	21	23	5⁵/₈ 5⁴/₈	8 7	18⁶/₈	985	24
	■ Andrew Co. – Frank Kelso – Delores C. Kelso – 1981							
207²/₈	26²/₈ 25⁵/₈	18⁷/₈	21³/₈	5³/₈ 5³/₈	7 7	16¹/₈	985	24
	■ Adair Co. – Kevin Elsea – Kevin Elsea – 1988							
207¹/₈	28⁵/₈ 28⁴/₈	18⁴/₈	21²/₈	6 5⁵/₈	10 10	43¹/₈	995	26
	■ St. Louis Co. – Unknown – Bass Pro Shops – 1958							
206²/₈	29³/₈ 28⁶/₈	20⁵/₈	23³/₈	6 5⁷/₈	6 8	20⁷/₈	1059	27
	■ Adair Co. – Charles M. Zeman – Charles M. Zeman – 1997							
205⁷/₈	25⁵/₈ 25⁵/₈	20⁶/₈	23⁵/₈	4⁶/₈ 5²/₈	9 16	39³/₈	1080†	28†
	■ Franklin Co. – Alfred Osborn – Jack E. Osborn – 1957							
205⁷/₈	23²/₈ 23³/₈	17⁵/₈	24⁴/₈	5⁴/₈ 5⁴/₈	9 13	33⁴/₈	1080	28
	■ Clark Co. – Allen L. Courtney – Allen L. Courtney – 1983							
205⁷/₈	28¹/₈ 28	25⁴/₈	28²/₈	7 6⁶/₈	11 9	36³/₈	1080	28
	■ Atchison Co. – Larry Poppa – Larry Poppa – 1990							
205²/₈	26⁶/₈ 27²/₈	22¹/₈	25¹/₈	4⁶/₈ 4⁷/₈	9 9	31⁷/₈	1131	31
	■ Bollinger Co. – Linda K. Peters – Linda K. Peters – 1998							
204⁴/₈	28⁶/₈ 29	20⁴/₈	23⁶/₈	4⁶/₈ 5¹/₈	10 7	31⁴/₈	1182	32
	■ Monroe Co. – Rogelio L. Bautista – Rogelio L. Bautista – 1996							
204²/₈	26²/₈ 26⁴/₈	22²/₈	26⁶/₈	4⁶/₈ 4⁶/₈	5 8	15⁶/₈	1199	33
	■ Boone Co. – Calvin E. Brown – Calvin E. Brown – 1985							
204¹/₈	25⁴/₈ 26³/₈	19⁵/₈	21⁶/₈	5²/₈ 5²/₈	11 10	17	1210	34
	■ Pike Co. – Robert J. Jeffries – Robert J. Jeffries – 1995							
203⁵/₈	26⁶/₈ 28	15⁵/₈	19⁴/₈	6⁶/₈ 6	18 13	56	1248	35
	■ Chariton Co. – Vernon Sower – Vernon Sower – 1953							
203⁵/₈	23⁶/₈ 24⁷/₈	15²/₈	25	5¹/₈ 6	10 10	56¹/₈	1248	35
	■ Chariton Co. – Kevin R. Stroup – Ann Walton – 1995							
203⁴/₈	22⁵/₈ 24	16⁵/₈	20⁶/₈	6⁴/₈ 6	14 12	32¹/₈	1259	37
	■ Putnam Co. – Casey R. Hartlip – Casey R. Hartlip – 1993							
203²/₈	26⁷/₈ 26⁷/₈	22²/₈	24⁴/₈	7¹/₈ 5	13 7	24²/₈	1287	38
	■ Andrew Co. – James C. Schweizer – James C. Schweizer – 1995							
203	26³/₈ 26⁵/₈	16²/₈	23²/₈	5²/₈ 5¹/₈	6 11	25⁴/₈	1317†	39†
	■ Cooper Co. – Tim Folmer – Tim Folmer – 2000							
202²/₈	25 25⁴/₈	18⁶/₈	21	5³/₈ 5²/₈	8 6	16	1377†	40†
	■ Audrain Co. – Barbara L. Blackmore – Barbara L. Blackmore – 2001							

Score	Length of Main Beam Right	Left	Inside Spread	Greatest Spread	Circumference at Smallest Place Between Burr and First Point Right	Left	Number of Points Right	Left	Lengths Abnormal Points	All-Time Rank	State Rank
	■ Location of Kill – Hunter – Owner – Date Killed										
202 1/8	27 7/8	28 6/8	21 6/8	24	4 7/8	4 7/8	9	8	13 1/8	1386	41
	■ Holt Co. – Gary F. Hoeper – Gary F. Hoeper – 1997 ■ See photo on page 329										
202	28 6/8	27 3/8	15 5/8	21 2/8	5 6/8	6	12	11	26 1/8	1395	42
	■ Nodaway Co. – Richard L. Stewart – Richard L. Stewart – 1972										
202	25	24 6/8	14 7/8	17 5/8	6 6/8	7 2/8	8	9	19 1/8	1395	42
	■ Platte Co. – Steven Richardson – Steven Richardson – 1991										
202	20 4/8	22 4/8	17 4/8	21 3/8	6	6 1/8	12	15	54	1395	42
	■ Macon Co. – Larry Allen – Bill J. Timms – 1994										
202	26 4/8	26 1/8	18 5/8	23 6/8	4 4/8	5	8	10	17 7/8	1395	42
	■ Callaway Co. – Marc E. Meng – Marc E. Meng – 1995										
201 5/8	25 2/8	26 6/8	21 6/8	23 7/8	4 7/8	5	10	10	29 7/8	1427	46
	■ Howard Co. – Gregory A. O'Brian – Gregory A. O'Brian – 1983										
201 5/8	26 4/8	26 2/8	24 7/8	26 7/8	5 1/8	5	8	8	19 2/8	1427	46
	■ Clinton Co. – David E. Eads – David E. Eads – 1989										
201 4/8	22 4/8	21 2/8	14	17 4/8	5 2/8	5 6/8	13	13	45 4/8	1443	48
	■ Wayne Co. – David L. Hays – David L. Hays – 1992										
201 3/8	25 4/8	25 6/8	18 4/8	21	6 2/8	6 4/8	9	9	26 7/8	1461†	49†
	■ De Kalb Co. – Charles F. Christensen – Charles F. Christensen – 1998										
201	22 1/8	25 6/8	15 4/8	22 2/8	5 1/8	7 2/8	6	13	76 4/8	1500	50
	■ Jasper Co. – Picked Up – Richard Morris – 1991										
200 5/8	22 1/8	23 5/8	16 1/8	19 4/8	5 3/8	5 1/8	16	10	38 2/8	1532†	51†
	■ Lewis Co. – Bennett E. Nation – Bennett E. Nation – 2000										
200 4/8	23 1/8	23 2/8	19 2/8	21 5/8	5 3/8	4 7/8	11	9	32 2/8	1545	52
	■ Clinton Co. – R. Rea Norton – R. Rea Norton – 1991										
200 3/8	24 7/8	25 1/8	15 3/8	19 2/8	4 7/8	4 7/8	9	9	35	1556	53
	■ Boone Co. – Kevin B. Sample – Kevin B. Sample – 1999										
200 1/8	26 2/8	24 4/8	19 3/8	22 1/8	4 6/8	4 6/8	10	13	25 2/8	1577	54
	■ Holt Co. – Bruce Copsey – Bruce Copsey – 1994										
199 7/8	20 1/8	20 7/8	14	27 6/8	5 1/8	5	7	14	66 1/8	1607	55
	■ Hickory Co. – Darwin L. Stogsdill – Darwin L. Stogsdill – 1971										
199 4/8	26 2/8	25 4/8	17 5/8	25 2/8	5	5 1/8	13	11	36 1/8	1631	56
	■ St. Francois Co. – Henry A. Hull – Henry A. Hull – 1984										
199 3/8	28	26 4/8	21 6/8	24 5/8	5 6/8	5 6/8	10	8	24 7/8	1639	57
	■ Clark Co. – Bob Arnold – Bob Arnold – 1973										
199 2/8	25 3/8	25 1/8	23 4/8	25	5 7/8	7 1/8	7	8	24	1649	58
	■ Shannon Co. – Charles Martin – Doug Masner – 1996										
198 7/8	28 5/8	28 4/8	21 1/8	23 3/8	6 2/8	6 2/8	5	5	12 6/8	1686	59
	■ Bollinger Co. – Picked Up – Michael W. Welker – 1992										
198 5/8	28 7/8	29 2/8	19 4/8	23 2/8	6 2/8	5 6/8	7	7	23 1/8	1716	60
	■ Ray Co. – Stephen D. Kirk – Stephen D. Kirk – 1997										
198 5/8	23 7/8	24 6/8	20 2/8	22 5/8	4 6/8	4 6/8	10	10	23 1/8	1716	60
	■ Pulaski Co. – Donald R. McGraw – Donald R. McGraw – 1999										

Score	Length of Main Beam Right Left	Inside Spread	Greatest Spread	Circumference at Smallest Place Between Burr and First Point Right Left	Number of Points Right Left	Lengths Abnormal Points	All-Time Rank	State Rank
	Location of Kill – Hunter – Owner – Date Killed							
197 6/8	27 2/8 26 3/8	18 2/8	19 4/8	5 4 6/8	6 8	20	1833	62
	■ *Harrison Co. – Rod L. Shain – Rod L. Shain – 1985*							
197 1/8	28 2/8 26 6/8	18 7/8	21 4/8	5 5 1/8	9 11	32	1923	63
	■ *Worth Co. – Gary G. Kinder – Gary G. Kinder – 1982*							
197 1/8	26 1/8 26 3/8	17 3/8	24 2/8	5 2/8 4 6/8	8 7	27	1923	63
	■ *Jackson Co. – Jim Martin – Jim Martin – 1984*							
197 1/8	22 6/8 24 4/8	17 3/8	19 2/8	6 3/8 4 5/8	8 6	46	1923	63
	■ *Caldwell Co. – James B. Nickels – James B. Nickels – 1990*							
196 6/8	25 7/8 26	21 2/8	23 2/8	5 4 5/8	10 8	15 6/8	1968†	66†
	■ *Lewis Co. – Kenneth W. Brocksmith – Kenneth W. Brocksmith – 2000*							
196	24 6/8 26 2/8	20 4/8	26	5 3/8 5 4/8	9 12	40	2059†	67†
	■ *Mercer Co. – James W. Berryman – James W. Berryman – 2001*							
195 6/8	25 7/8 25 6/8	20 5/8	23 5/8	4 5/8 4 7/8	10 8	27 5/8	2094	68
	■ *Howard Co. – Daniel A. Larkin – Daniel A. Larkin – 1993*							
195 6/8	24 5/8 24 3/8	16 7/8	20 5/8	5 4/8 5 3/8	16 10	27 1/8	2094	68
	■ *Putnam Co. – Douglas E. Gadberry – Douglas E. Gadberry – 1998*							
195 5/8	26 3/8 26	18 1/8	24 7/8	4 7/8 5 1/8	7 8	29	2116	70
	■ *Platte Co. – Lincoln A. Godfrey – Lincoln A. Godfrey – 1999*							
195 5/8	28 21	21	24 3/8	4 4/8 4 6/8	9 10	29 5/8	2116	70
	■ *Schuyler Co. – Jason McCartney – Jason McCartney – 1999*							
195 4/8	24 22	18 1/8	20 1/8	4 6/8 4 6/8	6 9	38 3/8	2134	72
	■ *Lincoln Co. – David M. Thiemet – David M. Thiemet – 1996*							
195 1/8	22 7/8 22 2/8	12 4/8	19 4/8	5 2/8 5 4/8	8 10	28 1/8	2208	73
	■ *Newton Co. – W.P. & J.R. Pritchard – W.P. & J.R. Pritchard – 1993*							
194 2/8	28 7/8 28 7/8	24 1/8	26 1/8	5 5	5 6	19 1/8	2267	74
	■ *Mercer Co. – Dennis D. Schmidt – Dennis D. Schmidt – 1989*							
193 1/8	24 7/8 24 7/8	22 1/8	24 6/8	5 4 7/8	7 8	17	2305†	75†
	■ *Marion Co. – David E. Moss – David E. Moss – 2001 ■ See photo on page 335*							
192 5/8	27 5/8 27 5/8	20 7/8	23	4 5/8 4 4/8	9 8	19	2322	76
	■ *Putnam Co. – Timothy W. Murchison – Timothy W. Murchison – 1995*							
192 3/8	22 5/8 22 3/8	20 5/8	23 1/8	4 7/8 5 1/8	8 8	28 2/8	2331†	77†
	■ *Clark Co. – Larry D. Foust – Larry D. Foust – 2000*							
191 7/8	26 6/8 26 1/8	18 6/8	20 6/8	4 7/8 4 7/8	8 7	22 7/8	2351	78
	■ *St. Louis Co. – David F. Dauster – David F. Dauster – 1996*							
191 4/8	25 3/8 25 6/8	19 5/8	24 4/8	4 6/8 5 3/8	10 9	37 1/8	2357	79
	■ *Holt Co. – Richard D. Wilson – Richard D. Wilson – 1999*							
191 3/8	25 2/8 25 3/8	19	24 1/8	5 6/8 5 5/8	7 9	17 7/8	2364	80
	■ *Bollinger Co. – David L. DeRousse – David L. DeRousse – 1994*							
191 1/8	21 5/8 21 5/8	15 2/8	17 5/8	6 1/8 6	10 11	41 3/8	2374	81
	■ *St. Louis Co. – Eugene M. Werges – Eugene M. Werges – 1996*							
191	23 2/8 23	19 4/8	23 4/8	4 6/8 4 6/8	8 9	32	2380	82
	■ *Macon Co. – Gerald D. Bojarsky – Gerald D. Bojarsky – 1997*							

Score	Length of Main Beam Right	Left	Inside Spread	Greatest Spread	Circumference at Smallest Place Between Burr and First Point Right	Left	Number of Points Right	Left	Lengths Abnormal Points	All-Time Rank	State Rank
190 6/8	26 1/8	27	22 3/8	24	5 4/8	5 5/8	8	11	18 5/8	2390	83
■ *Howard Co. – Curtis Thornhill – Curtis Thornhill – 1998*											
190 5/8	26 1/8	25 6/8	21 6/8	23 6/8	5 2/8	5 3/8	9	8	29 7/8	2393	84
■ *Monroe Co. – Michael F. Strunk – Michael F. Strunk – 1989*											
189 6/8	24 7/8	23 7/8	15	18 3/8	4 5/8	4 5/8	7	8	21 2/8	2425†	85†
■ *Macon Co. – Greg P. Bruno – Greg P. Bruno – 2001*											
189 4/8	27 2/8	26 5/8	19 5/8	22	5 1/8	5 3/8	10	10	20 7/8	2435	86
■ *Morgan Co. – Edward M. James – Edward M. James – 1996*											
188 5/8	25 2/8	24 5/8	14 5/8	17 1/8	4 7/8	4 5/8	10	12	14 4/8	2471	87
■ *Cooper Co. – Steven G. Deuschle – Steven G. Deuschle – 1994*											
187 4/8	21 1/8	21 3/8	15 3/8	18	6	6	9	14	47 7/8	2522	88
■ *McDonald Co. – William J. Mustain – William J. Mustain – 1989*											
187 1/8	26 2/8	27 7/8	16 7/8	20 3/8	5 2/8	6 4/8	8	16	19	2540	89
■ *St. Charles Co. – Mark G. Strauss – Mark G. Strauss – 1994*											
187	27 2/8	28 1/8	23 6/8	26 2/8	6 3/8	6 2/8	6	9	14	2545	90
■ *Putnam Co. – Josh Rennells – Josh Rennells – 1987*											
186 3/8	23 7/8	24 6/8	17	19 6/8	4 2/8	4 3/8	10	8	25 5/8	2570	91
■ *Daviess Co. – Michael E. Cross – Michael E. Cross – 1998*											
186	23 3/8	23 4/8	16 7/8	22 1/8	4 6/8	4 6/8	7	7	17 5/8	2586	92
■ *Pike Co. – Billy Boston – Billy Boston – 1990*											
185 7/8	24	24 4/8	16 2/8	17 1/8	5 1/8	5 4/8	8	10	56-9/8	2597	93
■ *Dent Co. – Brent W. Young – Brent W. Young – 1998*											
185 3/8	24 2/8	24 5/8	22	26 4/8	5 2/8	5 2/8	6	7	17 5/8	2622	94
■ *Putnam Co. – Christina M. Milburn – Christina M. Milburn – 1990*											
185 1/8	26 1/8	26 4/8	17 3/8	19 2/8	4 6/8	4 6/8	8	9	12 4/8	2641†	95†
■ *St. Francois Co. – Timothy R. Williams – Timothy R. Williams – 1996*											
185 1/8	24 5/8	24 1/8	17 4/8	20 3/8	5 4/8	5 1/8	12	8	20 3/8	2641	95
■ *Crawford Co. – Eugene P. Young – Eugene P. Young – 1995*											
185	26 4/8	26 3/8	18 6/8	21 6/8	5 3/8	5 2/8	8	11	20 6/8	2653	97
■ *St. Francois Co. – Bruce L. Jones – Bruce L. Jones – 1995*											

† The scores and ranking for trophies from the 25th Awards Entry Period are not final until the banquet is held on June 19, 2004.

TROPHIES IN THE FIELD

HUNTER: David E. Moss
SCORE: 193-1/8
CATEGORY: non-typical whitetail deer
LOCATION: Marion County, Missouri
DATE: 2001

MONTANA
RECORD WHITETAILS

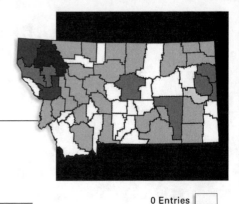

70 Typical whitetail deer entries
49 Non-typical whitetail deer entries
7,265 Total whitetail deer entries

MONTANA
STATE RECORD
Typical Whitetail Deer
Score: $199^3/8$
Location: Missoula Co.
Hunter: Thomas H.
  Dellwo
Owner: Bass Pro Shops
Date: 1974

*Photograph courtesy of Roger Selner,
Trophy Show Productions*

MONTANA
STATE RECORD
Non-Typical Whitetail Deer
Score: 252$^1/_8$
Location: Hill Co.
Hunter: Frank A. Pleskac
Owner: Dick Idol
Date: 1968

Photograph courtesy of Duncan Dobie

MONTANA

TYPICAL WHITETAIL DEER

Score	Length of Main Beam Right	Left	Inside Spread	Greatest Spread	Circumference at Smallest Place Between Burr and First Point Right	Left	Number of Points Right	Left	Lengths Abnormal Points	All-Time Rank	State Rank
					■ Location of Kill – Hunter – Owner – Date Killed						
199³/8	27³/8	27⁴/8	22³/8	24³/8	4⁴/8	4⁶/8	6	7	1	15	1
	■ Missoula Co. – Thomas H. Dellwo – Bass Pro Shops – 1974										
199²/8	27	27¹/8	21⁴/8	24³/8	5²/8	5	5	5		16	2
	■ Flathead Co. – Kent Petry – Bass Pro Shops – 1966										
191⁵/8	26⁵/8	26²/8	19	21⁵/8	5¹/8	5	6	7	1⁵/8	78	3
	■ Flathead Co. – Earl McMaster – Bass Pro Shops – 1963										
189¹/8	28	28¹/8	23⁵/8	30¹/8	4⁴/8	4⁵/8	5	7	3⁶/8	127	4
	■ Blaine Co. – Kenneth Morehouse – Cabela's, Inc. – 1959										
188⁵/8	25⁵/8	27³/8	19⁷/8	24	4³/8	4⁴/8	7	5	1	139	5
	■ Flathead Co. – Len E. Patterson – Len E. Patterson – 1992										
186³/8	30²/8	29	22⁵/8	25⁴/8	4⁴/8	4⁵/8	5	5		210	6
	■ Flathead Co. – Unknown – Wayne D. Williamson – 1973										
186	25¹/8	25³/8	19	22⁴/8	4³/8	4³/8	6	6		238	7
	■ Flathead Co. – Douglas G. Mefford – Douglas G. Mefford – 1966										
184⁷/8	25¹/8	24⁴/8	17⁷/8	19⁵/8	5¹/8	5¹/8	6	7		279	8
	■ Yellowstone Co. – Picked Up – Dennis Helmey – 1984										
184⁴/8	28	27⁶/8	20²/8	23	5⁶/8	5⁶/8	5	6		303	9
	■ Ravalli Co. – Picked Up – Walter R. Willey – 1978										
184⁴/8	26⁷/8	26³/8	19⁷/8	22²/8	4⁴/8	4⁴/8	7	7	3⁷/8	303	9
	■ Missoula Co. – Jack Greenwood – Jack Greenwood – 1985										
183³/8	21⁵/8	23³/8	19³/8	22⁷/8	5⁴/8	5²/8	7	9	2²/8	365	11
	■ Flathead Co. – Unknown – Edwin M. Sager – 1957										
183²/8	26⁵/8	26⁵/8	20⁴/8	22³/8	4⁴/8	4⁴/8	6	5		378	12
	■ Custer Co. – Dennis Young – Dennis Young – 1994										
182²/8	26	26⁴/8	18¹/8	20⁴/8	5²/8	5¹/8	5	5	1¹/8	450	13
	■ Park Co. – Jim Whitt – Jim Whitt – 1983										
181⁵/8	28	27⁵/8	25³/8	28⁶/8	4⁵/8	4⁶/8	5	5		500	14
	■ Blaine Co. – David A. Sprinkle – David A. Sprinkle – 1989										
181²/8	26⁵/8	26	21²/8	23⁷/8	5³/8	5³/8	7	7	3⁶/8	540	15
	■ Sheridan Co. – Arthur M. Hagan, Sr. – Ken Hagan – 1957										
180⁵/8	24⁷/8	25¹/8	18³/8	20⁷/8	4⁷/8	4⁶/8	6	7	1⁶/8	599	16
	■ Treasure Co. – Jack Welch – Jack Welch – 1958										
180³/8	24⁵/8	24⁴/8	19¹/8	21¹/8	5⁴/8	5⁶/8	8	6	4⁴/8	630	17
	■ Ovando – Clinton Berry – Clinton Berry – 1957										
180	25⁷/8	25⁵/8	19⁴/8	22⁷/8	6¹/8	6¹/8	6	8	7	688	18
	■ Big Horn Co. – Clair W. Jensen – Clair W. Jensen – 1967										
179⁴/8	24¹/8	25³/8	19⁵/8	21⁵/8	5	4⁷/8	7	8	8³/8	733	19
	■ Chouteau Co. – Richard L. Charlson – Richard L. Charlson – 1977										

Score	Length of Main Beam Right	Left	Inside Spread	Greatest Spread	Circumference at Smallest Place Between Burr and First Point Right	Left	Number of Points Right	Left	Lengths Abnormal Points	All-Time Rank	State Rank
									■ Location of Kill – Hunter – Owner – Date Killed		
$178\frac{1}{8}$	24	$23\frac{3}{8}$	$16\frac{3}{8}$	$19\frac{5}{8}$	$4\frac{4}{8}$	$4\frac{4}{8}$	7	6	3	905	20
			■ Teton Co. – Ivan F. Holland – Ivan F. Holland – 1991								
$177\frac{7}{8}$	$25\frac{7}{8}$	$25\frac{1}{8}$	$24\frac{3}{8}$	$24\frac{3}{8}$	5	$5\frac{1}{8}$	5	6		936	21
			■ Wibaux Co. – Dan Amunrud – David Welliever – 1967								
$177\frac{7}{8}$	$26\frac{4}{8}$	$27\frac{4}{8}$	23	$26\frac{3}{8}$	$5\frac{5}{8}$	5	7	9	$11\frac{1}{8}$	936	21
			■ Jefferson Co. – Tracy Forcella – Tracy Forcella – 1983								
$177\frac{6}{8}$	$26\frac{4}{8}$	$26\frac{5}{8}$	$20\frac{7}{8}$	$25\frac{2}{8}$	$4\frac{6}{8}$	$4\frac{6}{8}$	5	6	$1\frac{1}{8}$	956	23
			■ Lincoln Co. – Bernard B. White – Bernard B. White – 1990								
$177\frac{4}{8}$	26	$26\frac{4}{8}$	24	26	5	5	6	6	$1\frac{2}{8}$	993	24
			■ Montana – Unknown – Unknown – 1983								
$177\frac{1}{8}$	$26\frac{6}{8}$	$27\frac{1}{8}$	$20\frac{7}{8}$	$23\frac{4}{8}$	$5\frac{1}{8}$	$5\frac{2}{8}$	6	5	$3\frac{2}{8}$	1048	25
			■ **Toole Co. – Anthony W. Enos – Anthony W. Enos – 1994**								
$176\frac{4}{8}$	$27\frac{3}{8}$	28	$21\frac{2}{8}$	24	$4\frac{3}{8}$	$4\frac{4}{8}$	5	5	6	1158	26
			■ Sanders Co. – Dallas J.C. Nelson – Dallas J.C. Nelson – 1983								
$175\frac{5}{8}$	$24\frac{7}{8}$	$25\frac{2}{8}$	$25\frac{1}{8}$	$28\frac{2}{8}$	$4\frac{6}{8}$	$4\frac{4}{8}$	7	7	4	1333	27
			■ Lake Co. – Kenneth D. Johnson – Kenneth D. Johnson – 1974								
$175\frac{5}{8}$	$26\frac{4}{8}$	26	$20\frac{5}{8}$	$24\frac{7}{8}$	$4\frac{6}{8}$	$4\frac{6}{8}$	7	7	7	1333	27
			■ Big Horn Co. – Darell R. Webber – Darell R. Webber – 1991								
$174\frac{6}{8}$	$23\frac{3}{8}$	$24\frac{4}{8}$	23	$24\frac{6}{8}$	$5\frac{3}{8}$	$5\frac{2}{8}$	5	5		1534	29
			■ Lincoln Co. – Daniel P. Murray – Daniel P. Murray – 1993								
$174\frac{4}{8}$	$22\frac{2}{8}$	$23\frac{2}{8}$	$19\frac{5}{8}$	$21\frac{5}{8}$	$4\frac{3}{8}$	$4\frac{6}{8}$	7	7	$5\frac{3}{8}$	1592	30
			■ Powell Co. – Dave Rittenhouse – Dave Rittenhouse – 1973								
$174\frac{3}{8}$	$24\frac{1}{8}$	$24\frac{4}{8}$	$16\frac{1}{8}$	$18\frac{1}{8}$	$4\frac{4}{8}$	$4\frac{5}{8}$	7	6	2	1619†	31†
			■ Mineral Co. – Dan Woodson – Dan Woodson – 2000								
174	$21\frac{6}{8}$	$21\frac{3}{8}$	$15\frac{4}{8}$	18	$4\frac{3}{8}$	$4\frac{4}{8}$	6	7	3	1717	32
			■ Dawson Co. – Clayton L. Verke – Clayton L. Verke – 1991								
$173\frac{5}{8}$	$22\frac{6}{8}$	$21\frac{7}{8}$	$20\frac{5}{8}$	$23\frac{3}{8}$	$4\frac{7}{8}$	$4\frac{7}{8}$	6	6		1819	33
			■ Valley Co. – Scott Fossum – Scott Fossum – 1978								
$173\frac{5}{8}$	$28\frac{3}{8}$	$28\frac{5}{8}$	$20\frac{7}{8}$	$25\frac{4}{8}$	$5\frac{2}{8}$	$5\frac{4}{8}$	6	7	$8\frac{4}{8}$	1819	33
			■ Flathead Co. – Mike J. Beaty – Mike J. Beaty – 1984								
$173\frac{4}{8}$	$27\frac{2}{8}$	28	$19\frac{2}{8}$	$20\frac{5}{8}$	$4\frac{2}{8}$	$4\frac{3}{8}$	5	5		1847	35
			■ Flathead Co. – Ed M. Peter, Jr. – Ed M. Peter, Jr. – 1994								
$173\frac{3}{8}$	$23\frac{3}{8}$	$23\frac{3}{8}$	$23\frac{3}{8}$	$25\frac{6}{8}$	$5\frac{1}{8}$	$5\frac{1}{8}$	5	5		1883	36
			■ Rosebud Co. – Ted Millhollin – Ted Millhollin – 1975								
$173\frac{3}{8}$	$24\frac{4}{8}$	25	$16\frac{7}{8}$	19	$5\frac{1}{8}$	$5\frac{1}{8}$	5	5		1883	36
			■ Valley Co. – Steve K. Sukut – Steve K. Sukut – 1978								
$173\frac{1}{8}$	$26\frac{1}{8}$	$24\frac{6}{8}$	$21\frac{1}{8}$	$23\frac{5}{8}$	$4\frac{7}{8}$	$4\frac{6}{8}$	5	5		1950	38
			■ Lake Co. – Darrell Brist – Darrell Brist – 1971								
173	$27\frac{5}{8}$	28	19	21	$4\frac{3}{8}$	$4\frac{1}{8}$	7	6	$2\frac{2}{8}$	1991	39
			■ Flathead Co. – Derek Schulz – Derek Schulz – 1992								
$172\frac{7}{8}$	$24\frac{3}{8}$	$25\frac{1}{8}$	$21\frac{1}{8}$	24	$4\frac{5}{8}$	$4\frac{4}{8}$	6	8	$9\frac{2}{8}$	2038	40
			■ Cascade Co. – Skip Halmes – Skip Halmes – 1976								

Score	Length of Main Beam		Inside Spread	Greatest Spread	Circumference at Smallest Place Between Burr and First Point		Number of Points		Lengths Abnormal Points	All-Time Rank	State Rank
	Right	Left			Right	Left	Right	Left			
	■ *Location of Kill – Hunter – Owner – Date Killed*										
172⁶/8	27	27¹/8	23⁷/8	26⁵/8	6⁴/8	6⁴/8	5	7	5⁵/8	2065	41
	■ *Custer Co. – Picked Up – George A. Bettas – 1974*										
172⁵/8	26⁷/8	27¹/8	18⁷/8	21⁴/8	5²/8	5⁴/8	5	5		2113	42
	■ *Rosebud Co. – Michael E. Gayheart – Michael E. Gayheart – 1989*										
172⁵/8	24³/8	22⁵/8	18³/8	20⁵/8	5¹/8	4⁷/8	7	7	3²/8	2113	42
	■ *Treasure Co. – Picked Up – Ted K. Welchlin – 1998*										
172³/8	23⁵/8	24	16²/8	18⁶/8	4⁷/8	4⁷/8	8	8	3¹/8	2200	44
	■ *Sheridan Co. – Kent G. Unhjem – Kent G. Unhjem – 1994*										
172²/8	25⁴/8	25²/8	23⁵/8	26⁷/8	5¹/8	5¹/8	5	7	1¹/8	2237	45
	■ *Flathead Co. – Lonny Hanson – Lonny Hanson – 1963*										
172	23⁷/8	23⁴/8	18⁶/8	21	4⁴/8	4⁴/8	5	5		2330	46
	■ *Fergus Co. – Bill Scott – Martin J. Killham, Jr. – 1973*										
171²/8	23¹/8	24	16⁶/8	19²/8	4²/8	4²/8	5	5		2621	47
	■ *Lake Co. – Del A. Niemeyer – Del A. Niemeyer – 1986*										
171²/8	26⁶/8	27³/8	20⁴/8	23¹/8	4²/8	4¹/8	5	5		2621	47
	■ *Missoula Co. – James R. Zullo – James R. Zullo – 1990*										
171¹/8	24⁷/8	25³/8	21¹/8	24⁶/8	4⁶/8	4⁴/8	5	7	1²/8	2665	49
	■ *Sanders Co. – William Brox – Henry C. Bennett – 1948*										
171¹/8	24⁶/8	25¹/8	17⁴/8	19⁴/8	4⁴/8	4⁴/8	7	5	1³/8	2665	49
	■ *Flathead Co. – Gary Packer – Gary Packer – 1992*										
170⁵/8	26²/8	25⁵/8	20⁶/8	23¹/8	5	5	5	5	2¹/8	2876	51
	■ *Toole Co. – Cody P. Voermans – Cody P. Voermans – 1999* ■ *See photo on page 345*										
170³/8	23⁶/8	24³/8	18⁵/8	20⁴/8	4⁴/8	4⁵/8	5	5		2992	52
	■ *Meagher Co. – Randy L. Kunkle – Randy L. Kunkle – 1995*										
170¹/8	24³/8	22⁶/8	18³/8	21⁶/8	5	5¹/8	8	6	9	3143	53
	■ *Sanders Co. – Richard Lukes – Richard Lukes – 1984*										
170	26¹/8	24⁵/8	17⁷/8	20²/8	4⁴/8	4⁴/8	6	6	8⁵/8	3224	54
	■ *Flathead Co. – Dave Delap – Dave Delap – 1966*										
169²/8	24⁵/8	24	18²/8	20	4⁴/8	4⁴/8	5	5		3336	55
	■ *Lincoln Co. – William R. Rowberry – William R. Rowberry – 1995*										
168⁵/8	23¹/8	23	20¹/8	22¹/8	4⁶/8	4⁷/8	5	5		3376	56
	■ *Sanders Co. – Rex Indra – Rex Indra – 1988*										
168¹/8	21³/8	21⁴/8	19⁶/8	21⁴/8	4⁵/8	4⁶/8	7	7	2¹/8	3426	57
	■ *Flathead Co. – Peter Neumann – Peter Neumann – 1989*										
167	24⁵/8	24²/8	19³/8	21⁴/8	4⁷/8	4⁶/8	7	10	9¹/8	3552	58
	■ *Dawson Co. – John R. Arthur – John R. Arthur – 1991*										
165³/8	23	22⁷/8	17⁷/8	20¹/8	4¹/8	4¹/8	6	6		3731	59
	■ *Flathead Co. – Raymond J. Buck – Raymond J. Buck – 1995*										
165¹/8	26	26⁶/8	22¹/8	24¹/8	4⁶/8	4²/8	5	5		3767	60
	■ *Flathead Co. – D. Travis Lang – D. Travis Lang – 1990*										
164⁶/8	24⁵/8	23⁴/8	18²/8	21⁵/8	3⁷/8	4	5	5		3809	61
	■ *Flathead Co. – Stephen Holladay – Stephen Holladay – 1990*										

Score	Length of Main Beam Right	Left	Inside Spread	Greatest Spread	Circumference at Smallest Place Between Burr and First Point Right	Left	Number of Points Right	Left	Lengths Abnormal Points	All-Time Rank	State Rank
	■ *Location of Kill – Hunter – Owner – Date Killed*										
163 5/8	25 4/8	26 2/8	19 5/8	22	4 7/8	4 5/8	6	5	3	3961	62
	■ *Madison Co. – Lia S. Ballou – Lia S. Ballou – 1999*										
163 3/8	21 4/8	23 3/8	15 7/8	17 5/8	4 1/8	4 2/8	5	5		4002	63
	■ *Flathead Co. – C. Gary Cowden – C. Gary Cowden – 1983*										
163 1/8	20 1/8	21	15 3/8	17 6/8	4 2/8	4 2/8	6	7	2	4035†	64†
	■ *Madison Co. – Paul S. Bowles – Paul S. Bowles – 2000*										
162	26 1/8	26 3/8	18 2/8	20 2/8	4	4 2/8	5	5		4184	65
	■ *Daniels Co. – John F. Hrimnak, Jr. – John F. Hrimnak, Jr. – 1985*										
162	22 3/8	22 6/8	18 6/8	20 5/8	6	5 7/8	6	5		4184	65
	■ *Rosebud Co. – Frederick M. Brien – Frederick M. Brien – 1996*										
161 7/8	22 1/8	22 7/8	18 7/8	21	4 1/8	4 1/8	6	6		4212	67
	■ *Powell Co. – Neil Midtlyng – N. Midtlyng & P. Haviland – 1984*										
161 4/8	25	24 6/8	17 4/8	19 7/8	4 7/8	4 7/8	5	7		4258	68
	■ *Dawson Co. – Picked Up – Gregory R. Stroh – 2000*										
160 7/8	21 4/8	21 7/8	20 3/8	22 2/8	4 3/8	4 4/8	5	5		4380	69
	■ *Granite Co. – Billie F. Bechtel – Billie F. Bechtel – 1987*										
160	24 6/8	24 3/8	19 6/8	23 6/8	4 3/8	4 4/8	6	6	8	4565	70
	■ *Roosevelt Co. – Kurt D. Rued – Kurt D. Rued – 1983*										

† The scores and ranking for trophies from the 25th Awards Entry Period are not final until the banquet is held on June 19, 2004.

MONTANA

NON-TYPICAL WHITETAIL DEER

Score	Length of Main Beam Right Left	Inside Spread	Greatest Spread	Circumference at Smallest Place Between Burr and First Point Right Left		Number of Points Right Left		Lengths Abnormal Points	All-Time Rank	State Rank
	■ Location of Kill – Hunter – Owner – Date Killed									
252¹/8	256/8 283/8	195/8	251/8	53/8	56/8	9	9	606/8	48	1
	■ Hill Co. – Frank A. Pleskac – Dick Idol – 1968									
248⁵/8	25 24	205/8	244/8	51/8	52/8	16	12	796/8	67	2
	■ Snowy Mts. – Unknown – McLean Bowman – PR 1980									
241⁷/8	261/8 252/8	201/8	25	45/8	5	14	19	616/8	103	3
	■ Flathead Co. – George Woldstad – George Woldstad – 1960									
234¹/8	257/8 274/8	172/8	22	45/8	42/8	6	10	415/8	178	4
	■ Glacier Co. – Unknown – Larry W. Lander – PR 1968									
232⁷/8	257/8 26	187/8	305/8	51/8	5	13	11	632/8	197	5
	■ Montana – Unknown – Raymond R. Cross – PR 1950									
229²/8	214/8 214/8	163/8	246/8	55/8	54/8	15	13	645/8	251	6
	■ Flathead Co. – Carl E. Goetsch – Carl E. Goetsch – 1992									
229²/8	264/8 263/8	222/8	283/8	42/8	43/8	11	12	454/8	251	6
	■ Lincoln Co. – Picked Up – Steve Crossley – 1994									
224	231/8 24	176/8	32	46/8	5	16	12	516/8	337	8
	■ Lincoln Co. – Ray Baenen – Ed Boyes – 1935									
223⁴/8	237/8 211/8	17	265/8	51/8	53/8	18	13	912/8	350	9
	■ Richland Co. – Verner King – Verner King – 1960									
219¹/8	27 27	182/8	21	54/8	56/8	9	15	341/8	465	10
	■ Flathead Co. – R.C. Garrett – R.C. Garrett – 1962									
216²/8	265/8 275/8	203/8	265/8	56/8	57/8	10	14	403/8	555	11
	■ Richland Co. – Joseph P. Culbertson – Joseph P. Culbertson – 1972									
215	232/8 254/8	155/8	213/8	56/8	54/8	17	13	665/8	598	12
	■ Fergus Co. – Robert D. Fleherty – Robert D. Fleherty – 1958									
214³/8	232/8 24	142/8	182/8	51/8	52/8	14	10	425/8	620	13
	■ Missoula Co. – Lyle Pettit – Lyle Pettit – 1962									
213¹/8	22 22	17	222/8	51/8	51/8	12	10	187/8	664	14
	■ Havre – Unknown – Frank English – 1950									
212⁶/8	271/8 267/8	181/8	203/8	52/8	52/8	14	16	423/8	677	15
	■ Lewis & Clark Co. – Mr. LeFleur – L.S. Kuter – 1952									
212⁵/8	253/8 254/8	236/8	274/8	42/8	44/8	11	11	401/8	683	16
	■ Lincoln Co. – Charles F. Woods, Jr. – Charles F. Woods, Jr. – 1973									
212⁵/8	296/8 282/8	237/8	27	57/8	57/8	10	9	236/8	683	16
	■ Lake Co. – Dennis Courville – Dennis Courville – 1975									
212³/8	232/8 234/8	184/8	223/8	5	47/8	10	10	255/8	697	18
	■ Rosebud Co. – Picked Up – Art F. Hayes III – 1979									
212	205/8 207/8	165/8	185/8	62/8	63/8	11	12	633/8	717	19
	■ Wibaux Co. – Roy Berg – Daniel Burnosky – PR 1963									

Score	Length of Main Beam Right	Left	Inside Spread	Greatest Spread	Circumference at Smallest Place Between Burr and First Point Right	Left	Number of Points Right	Left	Lengths Abnormal Points	All-Time Rank	State Rank
	■ Location of Kill – Hunter – Owner – Date Killed										
210⁵/₈	26²/₈	28³/₈	23⁶/₈	25⁴/₈	5	5	8	9	35¹/₈	783	20
	■ Lincoln Co. – Glen Savage – Patrick W. Savage – 1934										
208³/₈	21⁶/₈	23⁷/₈	24¹/₈	25⁵/₈	5	4⁷/₈	8	8	41²/₈	905	21
	■ Prairie Co. – Charles Danielson – Charles Danielson – 1969										
206²/₈	24⁴/₈	24¹/₈	19	22²/₈	6	5³/₈	10	13	30⁴/₈	1059	22
	■ Lincoln Co. – Larry H. Beller – Larry H. Beller – 1985										
205⁷/₈	25	23²/₈	20²/₈	22²/₈	6	6	13	12	30³/₈	1080	23
	■ Missoula Co. – Unknown – Unknown – 1973										
205²/₈	25⁶/₈	27	21²/₈	27¹/₈	5	5	9	9	31⁴/₈	1131	24
	■ Richland Co. – Loyd Salsbury – Marlo Salsbury – PR 1958										
204⁵/₈	26	27²/₈	17⁴/₈	22⁴/₈	5⁴/₈	5⁶/₈	11	10	37⁷/₈	1176†	25†
	■ Richland Co. – Harold R. Moran – Harold R. Moran – 1956										
203⁴/₈	24	22¹/₈	18⁶/₈	21	5¹/₈	5²/₈	9	9	24⁶/₈	1259	26
	■ Lincoln Co. – Sean M. Blackley – Sean M. Blackley – 1990										
203²/₈	24⁴/₈	25²/₈	21⁷/₈	23⁶/₈	4⁵/₈	5¹/₈	10	12	37³/₈	1287	27
	■ Sanders Co. – Donald W. Heerdt – Donald W. Heerdt – 1992										
203¹/₈	23⁵/₈	23²/₈	16⁶/₈	21²/₈	5²/₈	5²/₈	10	12	35⁵/₈	1305	28
	■ Roosevelt Co. – Jerry L. Altland – Jerry L. Altland – 1991										
202⁷/₈	21⁵/₈	21⁷/₈	16³/₈	23¹/₈	4	4	10	13	42	1327	29
	■ Fergus Co. – Daniel N. Balster – Daniel N. Balster – 1998										
202⁴/₈	24⁴/₈	24⁶/₈	16⁴/₈	19	5	4⁷/₈	13	12	19	1355	30
	■ Missoula Co. – Unknown – Robert A. Bracken – 1962										
202²/₈	21⁶/₈	22⁴/₈	22	23⁷/₈	5	5¹/₈	12	9	20⁶/₈	1377	31
	■ Fergus Co. – Harold K. Stewart – Harold K. Stewart – 1948										
201⁴/₈	28⁵/₈	25⁶/₈	18³/₈	21	6⁷/₈	6⁷/₈	7	7	14³/₈	1443	32
	■ Flathead Co. – Barry L. Wensel – Barry L. Wensel – 1976										
200³/₈	20¹/₈	21⁴/₈	13⁴/₈	22	4⁶/₈	4⁴/₈	13	11	46⁷/₈	1556	33
	■ Powder River Co. – Levi Mitchell – Levi Mitchell – 1996										
199⁵/₈	27³/₈	26⁴/₈	21	24⁴/₈	5⁵/₈	5⁶/₈	11	9	32¹/₈	1621†	34†
	■ Douglas Co. – Timothy J. Hoel – Timothy J. Hoel – 1999										
199⁴/₈	23⁶/₈	23⁵/₈	17⁶/₈	20⁵/₈	5⁴/₈	5⁴/₈	10	10	24⁴/₈	1631	35
	■ Flathead Co. – Unknown – Tom Williams – PR 1980										
199²/₈	24⁶/₈	25⁴/₈	14	21¹/₈	5²/₈	5¹/₈	13	9	39⁴/₈	1649	36
	■ Richland Co. – Aron Schmierer – Raymond Schmierer – 1952										
198⁴/₈	24	23⁷/₈	21²/₈	24⁴/₈	4⁵/₈	4³/₈	8	7	26⁶/₈	1736	37
	■ Lake Co. – Mike Gouge – Jim G. Ferguson III – 1990										
197⁶/₈	25⁶/₈	26⁴/₈	17	20	5³/₈	5	9	11	29	1833	38
	■ Riceville – James R. Eastman – James R. Eastman – 1965										
197²/₈	23	24	20	23¹/₈	6²/₈	5⁶/₈	10	8	28⁶/₈	1901	39
	■ Chouteau Co. – J. Burton Long – J. Burton Long – 1975										
197	21⁴/₈	22¹/₈	15⁴/₈	21²/₈	5⁴/₈	5	11	11	47²/₈	1939	40
	■ Rosebud Co. – Mark D. Holmes – Mark D. Holmes – 1983										

Score	Length of Main Beam Right	Left	Inside Spread	Greatest Spread	Circumference at Smallest Place Between Burr and First Point Right	Left	Number of Points Right	Left	Lengths Abnormal Points	All-Time Rank	State Rank
	■ Location of Kill – Hunter – Owner – Date Killed										
196	25 2/8	25 4/8	19 6/8	21 7/8	4 6/8	4 6/8	13	9	23 2/8	2059	41
	■ Missoula Co. – James D. Pladson – James D. Pladson – 1987										
195 6/8	21	19 6/8	15	19	4 5/8	4 6/8	8	12	44 2/8	2094†	42†
	■ Park Co. – Larry R. Faust – Larry R. Faust – 2001										
195 6/8	24	24	20	22	4 5/8	4 5/8	8	9	29 6/8	2094	42
	■ Missoula Co. – Eugene L. Tripp, Sr. – Eugene L. Tripp, Sr. – 1994										
194 2/8	22 6/8	22 1/8	16 3/8	20 4/8	5	4 7/8	9	7	31 1/8	2267	44
	■ Flathead Co. – Douglas M. DesJarlais – Douglas M. DesJarlais – 1995										
194	25 1/8	27 2/8	19 4/8	22 7/8	4 4/8	4 5/8	8	9	19 4/8	2275	45
	■ Lincoln Co. – Stephen Holladay – Stephen Holladay – 1988										
192 2/8	25 5/8	25 4/8	20 4/8	24 7/8	4 7/8	5	8	8	22 2/8	2335	46
	■ Missoula Co. – Max G. Bauer, Jr. – Max G. Bauer, Jr. – 1977										
189 2/8	25 1/8	24 1/8	18 5/8	20 5/8	4 2/8	4 1/8	8	8	21 1/8	2447	47
	■ Wibaux Co. – Nolan Verke – Nolan Verke – 1992										
186	23 5/8	23 4/8	17 1/8	24 4/8	4 4/8	4 4/8	9	10	28 3/8	2586	48
	■ Flathead Co. – Bruce H. Louden – Bruce H. Louden – 1988										
185 1/8	24 5/8	24 1/8	17 3/8	20 4/8	4 4/8	4 5/8	6	8	16 6/8	2641†	49†
	■ Phillips Co. – Kipp Sjostrom – Kipp Sjostrom – 2000										

† The scores and ranking for trophies from the 25th Awards Entry Period are not final until the banquet is held on June 19, 2004.

TROPHIES IN THE FIELD

HUNTER: Cody P. Voermans
SCORE: 170-5/8
CATEGORY: typical whitetail deer
LOCATION: Toole County, Montana
DATE: 1999

NEBRASKA
RECORD WHITETAILS

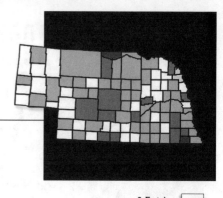

100 Typical whitetail deer entries
53 Non-typical whitetail deer entries
7,265 Total whitetail deer entries

0 Entries
1-2 Entries
3-5 Entries
6-10 Entries
11+ Entries

NEBRASKA
STATE RECORD
Typical Whitetail Deer
Score: $194^1/8$
Location: Dakota Co.
Hunter and Owner: E. Keith Fahrenholz
Date: 1966

NEBRASKA
STATE RECORD
Non-Typical Whitetail Deer
Score: $277^3/8$
Location: Hall Co.
Hunter: Del Austin
Owner: Bass Pro Shops
Date: 1962

Photograph courtesy of Larry L. Huffman, Legendary Whitetails

NEBRASKA

TYPICAL WHITETAIL DEER

Score	Length of Main Beam Right Left ■ Location of Kill – Hunter – Owner – Date Killed		Inside Spread	Greatest Spread	Circumference at Smallest Place Between Burr and First Point Right Left		Number of Points Right Left		Lengths Abnormal Points	All-Time Rank	State Rank
194¹/₈	30	30¹/₈	19⁴/₈	21⁶/₈	4⁶/₈	5	6	7	2⁷/₈	47	1
	■ Dakota Co. – E. Keith Fahrenholz – E. Keith Fahrenholz – 1966										
192⁶/₈	26	27	19²/₈	22¹/₈	5⁶/₈	5⁶/₈	6	6		63	2
	■ Washington Co. – Robert E. Wackel – Robert E. Wackel – 1961										
189¹/₈	27⁵/₈	26⁶/₈	25⁷/₈	27⁵/₈	5¹/₈	5²/₈	6	6		127	3
	■ Nuckolls Co. – Van Shotzman – Van Shotzman – 1968										
185⁵/₈	24³/₈	25	19⁵/₈	21⁴/₈	4⁶/₈	4⁵/₈	6	8	3²/₈	248	4
	■ Nenzel – Richard Kehr – Richard Kehr – 1965										
184⁵/₈	26	25¹/₈	21⁷/₈	24²/₈	5³/₈	5³/₈	5	5		294	5
	■ Polk Co. – Keith Houdersheldt – Keith Houdersheldt – 1985										
183	26	24⁷/₈	18²/₈	20⁶/₈	5⁶/₈	5⁶/₈	5	5		392	6
	■ Lincoln Co. – Kevin L. Wood – Kevin L. Wood – 1999										
182³/₈	26²/₈	26⁵/₈	17⁷/₈	21¹/₈	5	5	7	7		438†	7†
	■ McPherson Co. – Leonard Bergantzel – Leonard Bergantzel – 1999										
182¹/₈	27⁴/₈	26⁶/₈	24	26¹/₈	5¹/₈	5	5	6	1¹/₈	460	8
	■ Frontier Co. – Robert G. Bortner – Robert G. Bortner – 1985										
181⁵/₈	25⁷/₈	25⁵/₈	19⁷/₈	22⁵/₈	7	7	5	9	7⁴/₈	500	9
	■ Dixon Co. – Kirk C. Kneifl – Kirk C. Kneifl – 1999										
180⁷/₈	29⁶/₈	29²/₈	24¹/₈	26⁴/₈	5²/₈	5	6	5	3⁶/₈	573	10
	■ Keya Paha Co. – Steve R. Pecsenye – Steve R. Pecsenye – 1966										
180⁴/₈	26⁵/₈	26³/₈	18⁶/₈	21⁵/₈	5⁴/₈	5³/₈	5	5		613†	11†
	■ Dawson Co. – Jerry Lauby – Jerry Lauby – 1983										
180⁴/₈	27⁷/₈	27⁵/₈	22⁴/₈	25¹/₈	5²/₈	5⁴/₈	9	10	11²/₈	613	11
	■ Holt Co. – Fred L. Kubik – Fred L. Kubik – 1994										
179⁷/₈	28⁴/₈	27⁷/₈	23⁷/₈	25⁶/₈	4⁶/₈	4⁷/₈	6	6	4⁶/₈	705	13
	■ Valley Co. – Leonard L. Krason – Leonard L. Krason – 1998										
179⁴/₈	27³/₈	28⁴/₈	20¹/₈	23²/₈	5³/₈	5⁵/₈	6	5	4⁷/₈	733	14
	■ Pawnee Co. – Kenneth C. Mort – Kenneth C. Mort – 1975										
179³/₈	27⁶/₈	26⁴/₈	18³/₈	21	5⁵/₈	5⁵/₈	6	6	4⁶/₈	749	15
	■ Sherman Co. – Richard McCauley, Jr. – Richard McCauley, Jr. – 1994										
178⁵/₈	25⁵/₈	25⁵/₈	22¹/₈	23¹/₈	5²/₈	5¹/₈	5	5		819†	16†
	■ Franklin Co. – Robert L. Lennemann – Robert L. Lennemann – 2000										
178⁵/₈	27	26⁴/₈	20⁴/₈	22⁶/₈	4³/₈	4³/₈	6	6	3³/₈	819	16
	■ Harlan Co. – Don Tripe – Don Tripe – 1961										
178⁴/₈	30⁴/₈	30³/₈	18²/₈	20⁵/₈	6²/₈	5⁶/₈	10	8	14⁴/₈	850	18
	■ Nance Co. – Robert J. Ziemba – Robert J. Ziemba – 1988										
178³/₈	24³/₈	24²/₈	25³/₈	27¹/₈	5⁴/₈	5³/₈	5	6	1	868†	19†
	■ Fillmore Co. – Jan Rischling – Jan Rischling – 2000										

RECORDS OF NORTH AMERICAN WHITETAIL DEER ■ FOURTH EDITION

Score	Length of Main Beam Right Left	Inside Spread	Greatest Spread	Circumference at Smallest Place Between Burr and First Point Right Left	Number of Points Right Left	Lengths Abnormal Points	All-Time Rank	State Rank
	■ *Location of Kill – Hunter – Owner – Date Killed*							
178³/₈	26⁷/₈ 26⁵/₈	16⁷/₈	19⁴/₈	5¹/₈ 5²/₈	5 6	1	868	19
	■ *Keya Paha Co. – Joseph V. Bauer – Joseph V. Bauer – 1994*							
178²/₈	26⁵/₈ 26¹/₈	20⁶/₈	25⁴/₈	4⁶/₈ 4⁶/₈	5 5		891	21
	■ *Pawnee Co. – Picked Up – Gale Sup – 1960*							
178¹/₈	24¹/₈ 23⁵/₈	19¹/₈	23⁷/₈	4⁴/₈ 4⁵/₈	8 8	6⁶/₈	905	22
	■ *Dismal River – Gift of G.B. Grinnell to NCHH – Unknown – PR 1909*							
178¹/₈	29¹/₈ 28⁴/₈	18⁴/₈	23¹/₈	4⁷/₈ 4⁷/₈	7 7	8⁵/₈	905	22
	■ *Harlan Co. – Duane E. Johnson – Duane E. Johnson – 1967*							
178¹/₈	28²/₈ 28⁶/₈	22³/₈	25	5²/₈ 5²/₈	7 7	6⁶/₈	905	22
	■ *Wheeler Co. – Raymond M. Gay – Raymond M. Gay – 1999* ■ *See photo on page 353*							
177⁶/₈	24⁵/₈ 24⁷/₈	19	24²/₈	4⁵/₈ 4⁶/₈	6 6		956	25
	■ *Paxton – Ole Herstedt – Ole Herstedt – 1956*							
177³/₈	25⁴/₈ 25⁴/₈	18	20⁵/₈	6 6²/₈	5 6	3⁵/₈	1011	26
	■ *Hall Co. – Charles R. Babel – C.P. Medore – 1969*							
177	25 26	19¹/₈	23⁴/₈	6 5⁷/₈	6 5	5¹/₈	1066	27
	■ *Gage Co. – Art Wallman – Art Wallman – 1968*							
176⁶/₈	26³/₈ 26²/₈	18⁴/₈	21⁶/₈	5 5³/₈	5 5		1103	28
	■ *Knox Co. – Alvin Zimmerman – Spanky Greenville – 1966*							
176⁵/₈	23 22⁶/₈	20¹/₈	22⁴/₈	4⁷/₈ 5	6 6		1134†	29†
	■ *Saunders Co. – John I. Kunert – John I. Kunert – 2000*							
176²/₈	28⁴/₈ 27⁴/₈	25	27⁶/₈	5⁴/₈ 5⁴/₈	5 4	3⁶/₈	1209	30
	■ *Washington Co. – Albert Ohrt – Spanky Greenville – 1962*							
176²/₈	28 26	24²/₈	29²/₈	5⁶/₈ 5⁶/₈	6 5	4	1209	30
	■ *Nuckolls Co. – Tim Brewster – Tim Brewster – 1993*							
176	27 25²/₈	20⁴/₈	23³/₈	5²/₈ 5⁶/₈	5 5		1266	32
	■ *Dawson Co. – Unknown – Spanky Greenville – 1957*							
175⁶/₈	26⁴/₈ 25³/₈	16⁷/₈	21²/₈	5⁴/₈ 5⁴/₈	8 6	8¹/₈	1310	33
	■ *Cuming Co. – Herman Blankenau – Herman Blankenau – 1963*							
175⁴/₈	25⁵/₈ 27	20⁴/₈	23	4⁴/₈ 4⁴/₈	5 5		1352	34
	■ *Dodge Co. – Leroy W. Ahrndt – Leroy W. Ahrndt – 1963*							
175	27²/₈ 26⁵/₈	22⁴/₈	24⁴/₈	4⁶/₈ 4⁵/₈	7 6		1472	35
	■ *Washington Co. – Allan K. Wical – Allan K. Wical – 1999* ■ *See photo on page 357*							
174⁶/₈	23⁶/₈ 24⁴/₈	17⁵/₈	20³/₈	6 5⁶/₈	6 7	2⁵/₈	1534	36
	■ *Lancaster Co. – Vaughn Wright – Phillip Wright – 1960*							
174¹/₈	25³/₈ 25²/₈	18⁴/₈	20⁵/₈	4⁵/₈ 4⁶/₈	6 6	1¹/₈	1678	37
	■ *Brown Co. – Marvin D. Hart – Marvin D. Hart – 1993*							
174¹/₈	25⁵/₈ 25	18⁴/₈	21	4⁷/₈ 4⁷/₈	7 5	3⁵/₈	1678	37
	■ *Johnson Co. – Fred Leuenberger – Fred Leuenberger – 1998*							
174	24¹/₈ 24²/₈	18	20²/₈	5¹/₈ 4⁷/₈	6 6	4⁶/₈	1717	39
	■ *Chase Co. – Kent E. Wasieleski – Kent E. Wasieleski – 1993*							
173⁶/₈	26 26	18⁶/₈	21⁴/₈	5⁷/₈ 6¹/₈	6 5	1²/₈	1766	40
	■ *Colfax Co. – Leonard Bowman – Leonard Bowman – 1962*							

Score	Length of Main Beam Right	Left	Inside Spread	Greatest Spread	Circumference at Smallest Place Between Burr and First Point Right	Left	Number of Points Right	Left	Lengths Abnormal Points	All-Time Rank	State Rank
$173^6/8$	$25^1/8$	$25^5/8$	$18^6/8$	21	$5^3/8$	$5^4/8$	7	6	$1^2/8$	1766	40
■ Knox Co. – Paul H. Klawitter – Paul H. Klawitter – 1970											
$173^6/8$	$25^5/8$	$25^1/8$	$18^4/8$	$20^4/8$	$5^6/8$	$5^6/8$	5	5		1766	40
■ Lincoln Co. – Raymond E. Blede – Raymond E. Blede – 1988											
$173^6/8$	$25^6/8$	$26^6/8$	20	$22^7/8$	$4^5/8$	$4^3/8$	5	5		1766	40
■ Dawson Co. – Michael L. Seaman – Michael L. Seaman – 1989											
$173^6/8$	$23^6/8$	$24^5/8$	22	$25^7/8$	$4^3/8$	$4^2/8$	7	7	$5^4/8$	1766	40
■ Grant Co. – Barry Leach – Barry Leach – 1991											
$173^3/8$	$26^1/8$	$25^5/8$	$18^6/8$	$21^4/8$	5	5	5	5	$1^3/8$	1883	45
■ Keya Paha Co. – Gene F. Pool – Gene F. Pool – 1980											
$173^3/8$	$27^4/8$	$26^4/8$	$19^7/8$	$22^1/8$	$5^1/8$	$5^1/8$	6	6		1883	45
■ Gage Co. – Harold G. McPheron – Harold G. McPheron – 1998											
$173^2/8$	29	$29^4/8$	20	$22^4/8$	$5^1/8$	$5^2/8$	6	5	3	1914	47
■ Furnas Co. – Marvin F. Wieland – Marvin F. Wieland – 1969											
$173^1/8$	$22^4/8$	$22^4/8$	$16^1/8$	$18^7/8$	$4^5/8$	$4^6/8$	7	9	$3^2/8$	1950†	48†
■ Custer Co. – Mitch W. Hickey – Mitch W. Hickey – 1999											
173	$25^5/8$	$27^2/8$	$25^3/8$	$27^7/8$	$5^7/8$	$5^6/8$	6	5	$7^7/8$	1991	49
■ Pawnee Co. – Gary G. Habegger – Gary G. Habegger – 1967											
173	27	$27^6/8$	$18^2/8$	$20^4/8$	$4^4/8$	$4^3/8$	8	7	$4^4/8$	1991	49
■ Johnson Co. – Kent Hippen – Kent Hippen – 1994											
$172^6/8$	$25^3/8$	$24^7/8$	$18^2/8$	$20^4/8$	$4^1/8$	$4^2/8$	6	6		2065	51
■ Johnson Co. – Dan Hollatz – Dan Hollatz – 1992											
$172^4/8$	$22^2/8$	$22^3/8$	$18^1/8$	$20^2/8$	$4^4/8$	$4^3/8$	7	6	$5^1/8$	2156	52
■ Dawson Co. – Kim L. Farnstrom – Kim L. Farnstrom – 1992											
$172^3/8$	$26^7/8$	$27^4/8$	$18^3/8$	$21^4/8$	$4^6/8$	$4^5/8$	6	5	$1^4/8$	2200	53
■ Greeley Co. – Alan D. Vanosdall – Alan D. Vanosdall – 1995											
$172^2/8$	$25^6/8$	$25^2/8$	$25^2/8$	$29^6/8$	$4^4/8$	$4^4/8$	5	5		2237†	54†
■ Perkins Co. – G. Michael Martin – G. Michael Martin – 2001											
$172^2/8$	$26^7/8$	$27^6/8$	$26^2/8$	$27^6/8$	$4^2/8$	$4^3/8$	6	5		2237	54
■ Saunders Co. – John I. Kunert – John I. Kunert – 1986											
$172^1/8$	$26^7/8$	$25^3/8$	16	$19^7/8$	$4^1/8$	4	5	6	$2^5/8$	2286†	56†
■ Price Co. – Picked Up – Greg K. Young – 1981											
172	$25^1/8$	26	$19^3/8$	$21^1/8$	$5^2/8$	$4^7/8$	7	5	$2^7/8$	2330	57
■ Furnas Co. – Marvin A. Briegel – Marvin A. Briegel – 1980											
$171^6/8$	$25^1/8$	$24^6/8$	$18^4/8$	$20^4/8$	$4^7/8$	$4^7/8$	5	5		2418	58
■ Dawes Co. – Tim Morava – Tim Morava – 1974											
$171^6/8$	$26^2/8$	26	$21^6/8$	24	$4^6/8$	$4^7/8$	5	5		2418	58
■ Garden Co. – Doreen R. Lawrence – Doreen R. Lawrence – 1989											
$171^4/8$	$24^7/8$	$25^2/8$	$22^3/8$	$24^3/8$	$4^7/8$	5	5	6	$7^3/8$	2513	60
■ Cass Co. – Alvin H. Baller – Alvin H. Baller – 1971											
$171^4/8$	25	$25^4/8$	$19^2/8$	$21^3/8$	$4^6/8$	$4^5/8$	5	5		2513	60
■ Cherry Co. – Jim R. Monnier – Jim R. Monnier – 1981											

Score	Length of Main Beam Right	Left	Inside Spread	Greatest Spread	Circumference at Smallest Place Between Burr and First Point Right	Left	Number of Points Right	Left	Lengths Abnormal Points	All-Time Rank	State Rank
171³/₈	27²/₈	27²/₈	21²/₈	23⁶/₈	5	4⁷/₈	7	6	4³/₈	2564	62
	■ Boyd Co. – Scott A. Sperling – Scott A. Sperling – 1982										
171³/₈	27	26⁶/₈	21²/₈	23¹/₈	4³/₈	4³/₈	6	7	6¹/₈	2564	62
	■ Custer Co. – Larry C. Beitel – Larry C. Beitel – 1990										
171	22⁶/₈	20⁴/₈	19⁵/₈	22⁴/₈	5⁷/₈	5⁶/₈	7	8	4³/₈	2707	64
	■ Antelope Co. – Leo M. Beelart – Leo M. Beelart – 1964										
170⁷/₈	25¹/₈	25³/₈	21¹/₈	23³/₈	5¹/₈	5²/₈	5	5		2769	65
	■ Hamilton Co. – Clint J. Ochsner – Clint J. Ochsner – 1997										
170⁵/₈	26¹/₈	25⁴/₈	19³/₈	23	4²/₈	4²/₈	5	6	1⁶/₈	2876	66
	■ Boyd Co. – Leonard Reiser – Leonard Reiser – 1973										
170⁴/₈	26²/₈	25⁴/₈	18⁴/₈	21	5³/₈	5³/₈	9	7	9	2933	67
	■ Keya Paha Co. – Michael L. LeZotte – Michael L. LeZotte – 1986										
170⁴/₈	24⁷/₈	25⁴/₈	20⁶/₈	24⁵/₈	4²/₈	4²/₈	5	5		2933	67
	■ Clay Co. – James R. Vaughn – James R. Vaughn – 1988										
170⁴/₈	24⁶/₈	24⁵/₈	18	20³/₈	4⁷/₈	4⁷/₈	7	7		2933	67
	■ Pawnee Co. – Kenneth C. Mort – Kenneth C. Mort – 1991										
170³/₈	28⁵/₈	28²/₈	21⁶/₈	25²/₈	4⁶/₈	4⁶/₈	6	4	1¹/₈	2992	70
	■ Hall Co. – Gust Bergman – Gust Bergman – 1965										
170²/₈	26⁶/₈	26²/₈	19⁴/₈	21⁴/₈	4⁵/₈	4⁷/₈	5	5		3063	71
	■ Scotts Bluff Co. – Russel C. McKeehan II – Russel C. McKeehan II – 1996										
170¹/₈	25⁴/₈	23⁷/₈	18⁵/₈	20⁵/₈	4³/₈	4²/₈	5	5		3143	72
	■ Hooker Co. – Jan J. Finley – Jan J. Finley – 1995										
170¹/₈	27	27¹/₈	22⁷/₈	24⁷/₈	5	5	5	5		3143	72
	■ Keya Paha Co. – Picked Up – Teresa A. Bammerlin – 1999										
170	27⁴/₈	27⁶/₈	23¹/₈	25⁴/₈	6⁵/₈	6⁷/₈	6	6	5³/₈	3224	74
	■ Fullerton – Truman Lauterback – Truman Lauterback – 1959										
169⁴/₈	26¹/₈	26	21⁶/₈	24	5³/₈	5²/₈	6	5	3	3316†	75†
	■ Webster Co. – Matthew Cederburg – Matthew Cederburg – 1999										
169⁴/₈	27²/₈	28⁴/₈	19	21¹/₈	4⁵/₈	4⁵/₈	5	5		3316	75
	■ Johnson Co. – Picked Up – NE Game & Parks Comm. – 1995										
169²/₈	26¹/₈	18⁷/₈	24²/₈	26	4⁶/₈	4⁶/₈	6	7	9	3336	77
	■ Thayer Co. – Leonard Prellwitz – Leonard Prellwitz – 1982										
168⁴/₈	26¹/₈	26⁴/₈	21²/₈	23³/₈	5³/₈	5⁴/₈	5	7	2⁶/₈	3385	78
	■ Furnas Co. – Charles C. Mohr – Charles C. Mohr – 1992										
167	27²/₈	26	16	18²/₈	4⁶/₈	4⁶/₈	5	5		3552†	79†
	■ Saline Co. – Randy J. Adams – Randy J. Adams – 1999										
167	24²/₈	24²/₈	18⁴/₈	21¹/₈	4⁶/₈	4⁵/₈	5	5		3552	79
	■ Sarpy Co. – William B. Dillon III – William B. Dillon III – 1970										
166²/₈	24³/₈	24⁵/₈	19²/₈	21⁶/₈	5¹/₈	5³/₈	5	5		3632	81
	■ Keya Paha Co. – Aaron A. Gruber – Aaron A. Gruber – 1999										
165⁷/₈	25⁴/₈	24⁶/₈	23²/₈	25³/₈	4⁷/₈	4⁶/₈	6	5	1³/₈	3672†	82†
	■ Logan Co. – Steve S. Lippitt – Steve S. Lippitt – 2001										

Score	Length of Main Beam Right	Left	Inside Spread	Greatest Spread	Circumference at Smallest Place Between Burr and First Point Right	Left	Number of Points Right	Left	Lengths Abnormal Points	All-Time Rank	State Rank
								■ *Location of Kill – Hunter – Owner – Date Killed*			
165 1/8	22 1/8	23 6/8	19 1/8	21 1/8	4 3/8	4 6/8	6	6		3767†	83†
	■ *Sanders Co. – Brian M. Fosse – Brian M. Fosse – 2000*										
165 1/8	24 3/8	25	16 7/8	18 6/8	4 4/8	4 2/8	5	5		3767	83
	■ *Adams Co. – Michael T. Roth – Michael T. Roth – 1999*										
164 6/8	25 4/8	25 6/8	19 4/8	23	5 3/8	5 2/8	8	5	3 2/8	3809	85
	■ *Lincoln Co. – Gerry T. Palmer – Gerry T. Palmer – 1991*										
164 6/8	23	23	17 4/8	20 1/8	4 3/8	4 2/8	6	6		3809	85
	■ *Dodge Co. – Douglas W. Hoffman – Douglas W. Hoffman – 1998*										
163 6/8	25 5/8	25 2/8	19 2/8	21 4/8	5	5 1/8	5	6	1	3946	87
	■ *Gage Co. – Robert S. Ulmer – Robert S. Ulmer – 1998*										
162 7/8	22 6/8	24 1/8	17 7/8	19 6/8	5 7/8	5 3/8	5	5		4067	88
	■ *Keya Paha Co. – Thomas E. Watkins – Thomas E. Watkins – 1999*										
162 6/8	24 7/8	25 3/8	19 2/8	21 1/8	5 2/8	5 2/8	6	6	1	4089	89
	■ *Otoe Co. – Keith R. Schreiter – Keith R. Schreiter – 1995*										
161 5/8	23 4/8	22 5/8	19 1/8	21 4/8	5 1/8	5 2/8	5	7	4 4/8	4234	90
	■ *Washington Co. – Aaron T. Rosholm – Aaron T. Rosholm – 1998*										
161 4/8	24 2/8	24 1/8	18 4/8	20 4/8	4 2/8	4 3/8	5	6		4258	91
	■ *Brown Co. – Steve K. Kramer – Steve K. Kramer – 1996*										
161 3/8	24 7/8	24 5/8	20 7/8	22 6/8	5 3/8	5 1/8	6	5	1	4285†	92†
	■ *Otoe Co. – Keith G. Merkel – Keith G. Merkel – 2000*										
161 3/8	24 5/8	25 1/8	17 5/8	19 6/8	4 6/8	4 7/8	7	6	1	4285	92
	■ *Lancaster Co. – Fred P. Matulka – Fred P. Matulka – 1998*										
161 2/8	23 3/8	24 1/8	16 5/8	19 6/8	5 2/8	5 1/8	5	6	2 5/8	4310†	94†
	■ *Cherry Co. – Chris A. Benson – Chris A. Benson – 2001*										
160 7/8	24 2/8	23 3/8	16 7/8	18 6/8	4 1/8	4 1/8	6	6		4380	95
	■ *Custer Co. – David A. Doremus – David A. Doremus – 1996*										
160 6/8	23 7/8	23 7/8	17 7/8	19 7/8	4 6/8	4 5/8	5	6	1 7/8	4402†	96†
	■ *Jefferson Co. – Larry Stafford – Larry Stafford – 2001*										
160 5/8	23 5/8	22 2/8	23 1/8	24 4/8	3 6/8	4	5	5		4423	97
	■ *Harlan Co. – Wesley K. Mason – Wesley K. Mason – 1997*										
160 2/8	25 4/8	25 5/8	22	24 1/8	4 7/8	4 5/8	6	5	1 6/8	4495	98
	■ *Lancaster Co. – Daniel L. Weber – Daniel L. Weber – 1994*										
160 1/8	25 6/8	25 5/8	17 2/8	20 2/8	4 4/8	4 4/8	6	5	1 1/8	4534†	99†
	■ *Keya Paha Co. – Robert W. Schmidt – Robert W. Schmidt – 2000*										
160 1/8	25	24 3/8	18 1/8	20	4 5/8	4 6/8	4	4		4534	99
	■ *Cherry Co. – John T. Woloszyn – John T. Woloszyn – 1994*										

† The scores and ranking for trophies from the 25th Awards Entry Period are not final until the banquet is held on June 19, 2004.

TROPHIES IN THE FIELD

HUNTER: Raymond M. Gay
SCORE: 178-1/8
CATEGORY: typical whitetail deer
LOCATION: Wheeler County, Nebraska
DATE: 1999

NEBRASKA

NON-TYPICAL WHITETAIL DEER

Score	Length of Main Beam Right Left	Inside Spread	Greatest Spread	Circumference at Smallest Place Between Burr and First Point Right Left		Number of Points Right Left		Lengths Abnormal Points	All-Time Rank	State Rank
	■ Location of Kill – Hunter – Owner – Date Killed									
277³/8	28¹/8 28³/8	21¹/8	29⁵/8	6⁵/8	6⁷/8	19	18	91⁴/8	11	1
	■ Hall Co. – Del Austin – Bass Pro Shops – 1962 ■ See photo on page 375									
242⁵/8	27²/8 26¹/8	17²/8	23	6	5⁴/8	13	16	56¹/8	100	2
	■ Nance Co. – Robert E. Snyder – Bass Pro Shops – 1961									
239	25³/8 25¹/8	17	21⁴/8	5³/8	5⁶/8	16	12	55²/8	126	3
	■ Pawnee Co. – Danny C. Boliver – Danny C. Boliver – 1996									
238	26⁴/8 27⁶/8	23⁶/8	26⁴/8	5⁶/8	5⁷/8	12	8	42⁴/8	142	4
	■ Keya Paha Co. – Donald B. Phipps – Donald B. Phipps – 1969									
234⁵/8	23⁵/8 24	19⁴/8	22	5⁷/8	6¹/8	15	12	67³/8	172	5
	■ Nebraska – Picked Up – L.B. Philips – PR 1972									
233⁶/8	28²/8 27	21¹/8	24²/8	5	5⁴/8	13	13	33¹/8	187	6
	■ Custer Co. – Lonnie E. Poland – Lonnie E. Poland – 1986									
220⁴/8	28⁶/8 28⁷/8	20²/8	27⁴/8	5⁵/8	5⁶/8	9	8	29	427	7
	■ Dixon Co. – Otto D. Kneifl – Otto D. Kneifl – 1964									
217⁶/8	27⁶/8 24	20³/8	25	4⁷/8	6	8	11	45¹/8	503	8
	■ Otoe Co. – Douglas E. Gregg – Douglas E. Gregg – 1994									
215⁷/8	25 24⁴/8	24³/8	27⁴/8	6⁶/8	6	11	12	48⁴/8	569	9
	■ Long Pine – Picked Up – Duane Lotspeich – 1964									
215¹/8	25⁵/8 25³/8	23⁴/8	25¹/8	5²/8	5²/8	11	11	35⁷/8	593	10
	■ Jefferson Co. – Gary A. Hellbusch – Gary A. Hellbusch – 1994									
214⁶/8	25⁶/8 27⁶/8	22²/8	25²/8	7²/8	6	13	7	36	610	11
	■ Hitchcock Co. – David W. Oates – David W. Oates – 1985									
212³/8	29 28⁴/8	24³/8	27⁶/8	5⁵/8	5⁶/8	11	10	18	697	12
	■ Hershey – Ray Liles – Spanky Greenville – 1959									
211⁵/8	23¹/8 22⁵/8	13⁴/8	20	7	5⁴/8	18	11	78⁵/8	734	13
	■ Alda – Donald Knuth – Donald Knuth – 1964									
208⁴/8	28 27¹/8	23⁵/8	26³/8	6²/8	6¹/8	11	10	35¹/8	894	14
	■ Dixon Co. – Dan Greeny – Dan Greeny – 1969									
208¹/8	24¹/8 25²/8	20²/8	23⁴/8	4⁷/8	4⁷/8	13	8	33¹/8	920	15
	■ Antelope Co. – Leon McCoy – Leon McCoy – 1965									
208¹/8	28¹/8 30¹/8	24²/8	28⁴/8	6²/8	5	10	8	43³/8	920	15
	■ Atkinson Hwy. – Russell Angus – Russell Angus – 1966									
207⁵/8	25 20⁵/8	19⁶/8	25⁴/8	6	6	10	17	47¹/8	957	17
	■ Seward Co. – Ladislav Dolezal – Ladislav Dolezal – 1964									
207²/8	26²/8 22⁷/8	18²/8	24⁷/8	6	6⁵/8	9	11	31²/8	985	18
	■ Brown Co. – Terry J. Graff – Terry J. Graff – 1987									
207¹/8	22 23⁷/8	19²/8	21	8	8⁵/8	14	13	50⁷/8	995	19
	■ Buffalo Co. – Unknown – Unknown – 1978									

Score	Length of Main Beam Right	Left	Inside Spread	Greatest Spread	Circumference at Smallest Place Between Burr and First Point Right	Left	Number of Points Right	Left	Lengths Abnormal Points	All-Time Rank	State Rank
$206\frac{7}{8}$	25	$24\frac{1}{8}$	18	$22\frac{2}{8}$	$5\frac{2}{8}$	$5\frac{3}{8}$	10	12	$27\frac{1}{8}$	1011	20

Loup Co. – T.A. Brandenburg – Dick Rossum – 1963

| 205 | $23\frac{1}{8}$ | 25 | $17\frac{7}{8}$ | 20 | $6\frac{1}{8}$ | $5\frac{2}{8}$ | 9 | 6 | $19\frac{1}{8}$ | 1144† | 21† |

Lincoln Co. – Clyde L. Albers – Clyde L. Albers – 2000

| $204\frac{4}{8}$ | $24\frac{6}{8}$ | $24\frac{2}{8}$ | 16 | $25\frac{4}{8}$ | $5\frac{6}{8}$ | 6 | 7 | 11 | $24\frac{4}{8}$ | 1259 | 22 |

Lincoln Co. – Truman A. Burch III – Truman A. Burch III – 1996

| $203\frac{2}{8}$ | $23\frac{7}{8}$ | $24\frac{1}{8}$ | $20\frac{4}{8}$ | $22\frac{6}{8}$ | $5\frac{4}{8}$ | $5\frac{7}{8}$ | 9 | 9 | $21\frac{6}{8}$ | 1287 | 23 |

Jefferson Co. – Greg D. Hansmire – Greg D. Hansmire – 1996

| $203\frac{1}{8}$ | $28\frac{1}{8}$ | $27\frac{5}{8}$ | 21 | $29\frac{4}{8}$ | $4\frac{7}{8}$ | $4\frac{6}{8}$ | 9 | 7 | $21\frac{5}{8}$ | 1305 | 24 |

Pawnee Co. – Virgil J. Fisher – Virgil J. Fisher – 1970

| $201\frac{4}{8}$ | $28\frac{5}{8}$ | $28\frac{1}{8}$ | $22\frac{1}{8}$ | 26 | $5\frac{3}{8}$ | $5\frac{1}{8}$ | 8 | 9 | $14\frac{5}{8}$ | 1443 | 25 |

Brown Co. – R.L. Tinkham – R.L. Tinkham – 1965

| $201\frac{2}{8}$ | $24\frac{1}{8}$ | $24\frac{6}{8}$ | $18\frac{6}{8}$ | $20\frac{4}{8}$ | 5 | 5 | 8 | 8 | $22\frac{6}{8}$ | 1478 | 26 |

Dawes Co. – Cole Emmett – Cole Emmett – 1998

| $201\frac{1}{8}$ | $25\frac{3}{8}$ | $25\frac{4}{8}$ | $18\frac{2}{8}$ | $21\frac{6}{8}$ | 5 | $4\frac{7}{8}$ | 8 | 7 | $22\frac{7}{8}$ | 1489 | 27 |

Butler Co. – James L. Sklenar – James L. Sklenar – 1973

| $200\frac{6}{8}$ | 28 | $26\frac{2}{8}$ | $19\frac{3}{8}$ | $21\frac{7}{8}$ | 6 | 6 | 9 | 10 | $30\frac{7}{8}$ | 1524† | 28† |

Sarpy Co. – Mark A. Dillon – Mark A. Dillon – 2001

| $200\frac{3}{8}$ | $24\frac{4}{8}$ | $24\frac{2}{8}$ | $20\frac{7}{8}$ | $23\frac{4}{8}$ | $5\frac{6}{8}$ | $5\frac{6}{8}$ | 10 | 11 | $35\frac{4}{8}$ | 1556† | 29† |

Lancaster Co. – Tyler Fountain – Tyler Fountain – 2000

| $200\frac{3}{8}$ | $23\frac{7}{8}$ | $22\frac{1}{8}$ | $21\frac{5}{8}$ | $22\frac{6}{8}$ | 5 | $6\frac{6}{8}$ | 6 | 10 | $59\frac{4}{8}$ | 1556 | 29 |

Keya Paha Co. – Charles V. Stroud – Charles V. Stroud – 1998

| $200\frac{1}{8}$ | $24\frac{3}{8}$ | $24\frac{5}{8}$ | $20\frac{4}{8}$ | $23\frac{1}{8}$ | 5 | 5 | 9 | 8 | $22\frac{3}{8}$ | 1577 | 31 |

Blaine Co. – Pauline C. Sander – Pauline C. Sander – 1983

| 200 | $26\frac{3}{8}$ | $26\frac{3}{8}$ | $21\frac{2}{8}$ | 24 | $4\frac{7}{8}$ | $4\frac{7}{8}$ | 10 | 8 | 19 | 1591 | 32 |

Nance Co. – Gale Sup – Gale Sup – 1998

| $198\frac{7}{8}$ | $25\frac{6}{8}$ | $25\frac{1}{8}$ | $20\frac{3}{8}$ | $22\frac{7}{8}$ | $5\frac{6}{8}$ | $5\frac{6}{8}$ | 10 | 8 | $33\frac{4}{8}$ | 1686 | 33 |

Richardson Co. – Kenneth L. Harmon – Kenneth L. Harmon – 1995

| $198\frac{2}{8}$ | $23\frac{5}{8}$ | $23\frac{1}{8}$ | $19\frac{4}{8}$ | $23\frac{4}{8}$ | $5\frac{7}{8}$ | $5\frac{7}{8}$ | 8 | 8 | $22\frac{6}{8}$ | 1772 | 34 |

Rock Co. – Gerald M. Lewis – Gerald M. Lewis – 1966

| $198\frac{2}{8}$ | $24\frac{6}{8}$ | $24\frac{6}{8}$ | $16\frac{3}{8}$ | $19\frac{4}{8}$ | $5\frac{4}{8}$ | $5\frac{7}{8}$ | 10 | 15 | $44\frac{5}{8}$ | 1772 | 34 |

Rock Co. – Picked Up – Dan L. Sandall – 1987

| 198 | $27\frac{5}{8}$ | $26\frac{7}{8}$ | $22\frac{4}{8}$ | $25\frac{4}{8}$ | 5 | $4\frac{7}{8}$ | 7 | 9 | 19 | 1801† | 36† |

Holt Co. – Randy D. Sell – Randy D. Sell – 2000

| 198 | $26\frac{1}{8}$ | $24\frac{4}{8}$ | 23 | $25\frac{6}{8}$ | $7\frac{4}{8}$ | $6\frac{2}{8}$ | 9 | 7 | $21\frac{6}{8}$ | 1801 | 36 |

Valley – Ivan Masher – Ivan Masher – 1961

| $197\frac{7}{8}$ | $27\frac{4}{8}$ | $28\frac{1}{8}$ | 25 | $27\frac{1}{8}$ | $5\frac{4}{8}$ | $5\frac{2}{8}$ | 9 | 8 | $22\frac{1}{8}$ | 1816 | 38 |

Cheyenne Co. – Reid Block – Reid Block – 1984

| $197\frac{5}{8}$ | $28\frac{2}{8}$ | $27\frac{1}{8}$ | 19 | $23\frac{6}{8}$ | $5\frac{3}{8}$ | $5\frac{4}{8}$ | 7 | 7 | $12\frac{5}{8}$ | 1847 | 39 |

Thurston Co. – Picked Up – Rudy Reichelt – 1989

| $197\frac{2}{8}$ | $23\frac{2}{8}$ | $26\frac{1}{8}$ | $17\frac{1}{8}$ | $22\frac{1}{8}$ | $5\frac{4}{8}$ | $6\frac{1}{8}$ | 10 | 9 | $28\frac{7}{8}$ | 1901 | 40 |

Stanton – Peter Bartman III – Peter Bartman III – 1963

Score	Length of Main Beam Right	Left	Inside Spread	Greatest Spread	Circumference at Smallest Place Between Burr and First Point Right	Left	Number of Points Right	Left	Lengths Abnormal Points	All-Time Rank	State Rank
	■ Location of Kill – Hunter – Owner – Date Killed										
196 1/8	24 3/8	24 1/8	19 3/8	25 4/8	5 4/8	5 6/8	8	11	26 6/8	2045	41
	■ Nemaha Co. – Picked Up – Gale Sup – 1975										
195 1/8	24 7/8	24 3/8	17 5/8	20 3/8	5 5/8	5 4/8	8	8	21 2/8	2208	42
	■ Merrick Co. – Robert K. Betts – Robert K. Betts – 1962										
193 6/8	26	26 2/8	27 4/8	29 6/8	5 6/8	6	8	8	17 2/8	2279	43
	■ Logan Co. – Timothy J. Keidel – Timothy J. Keidel – 1993										
192 4/8	27 6/8	26 3/8	19 7/8	23 4/8	5 4/8	6	7	9	27 1/8	2325†	44†
	■ Garfield Co. – Jerry B. Horwart – Jerry B. Horwart – 2000										
191 3/8	25 3/8	24 7/8	21 7/8	23 7/8	4 6/8	5	6	9	15	2364†	45†
	■ Red Willow Co. – Bud Max – Cody L. Ervin – PR 1994										
191 1/8	24 3/8	26	17	19 1/8	5	4 6/8	9	9	17 5/8	2374	46
	■ Custer Co. – Robert D. Brestel – Robert D. Brestel – 1989										
191	23 4/8	22 4/8	16 2/8	19 6/8	5	4 7/8	8	9	21 2/8	2380†	47†
	■ Holt Co. – Bruce E. Coburn – Bruce E. Coburn – 2001										
187 3/8	26	26 3/8	17 1/8	20 1/8	5	4 4/8	6	7	9 6/8	2528†	48†
	■ Custer Co. – Jerry D. Snitker – Jerry D. Snitker – 1963										
186 2/8	24 2/8	25 3/8	19 2/8	22	5 2/8	5 1/8	8	11	21	2575†	49†
	■ Burt Co. – Leroy G. Townsend – Leroy G. Townsend – 2001										
186 1/8	25 2/8	27	17 4/8	19 6/8	6 2/8	6	10	7	11 3/8	2581	50
	■ Keya Paha Co. – Michael L. Lezotte – Michael L. Lezotte – 1997										
186	23 3/8	22 7/8	17 7/8	21 3/8	4 4/8	4 7/8	9	7	30 5/8	2586	51
	■ Washington Co. – Stephen W. Blankenship – Stephen W. Blankenship – 1988										
185 4/8	23 5/8	23 4/8	17 5/8	20 2/8	5 1/8	5 2/8	9	9	31 7/8	2616	52
	■ Cass Co. – Joseph E. Woitzel – Joseph E. Woitzel – 1998										
185	24 6/8	23 1/8	16	20 7/8	5 3/8	5 3/8	6	13	43 2/8	2653†	53†
	■ Webster Co. – Leonard D. Delka – Leonard D. Delka – 2000										

† The scores and ranking for trophies from the 25th Awards Entry Period are not final until the banquet is held on June 19, 2004.

TROPHIES IN THE FIELD

HUNTER: Allan K. Wical
SCORE: 175
CATEGORY: typical whitetail deer
LOCATION: Washington County, Nebraska
DATE: 1999

NEW HAMPSHIRE
RECORD WHITETAILS

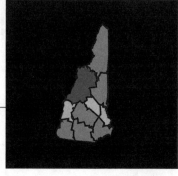

30 Typical whitetail deer entries
6 Non-typical whitetail deer entries
7,265 Total whitetail deer entries

0 Entries
1-2 Entries
3-5 Entries
6-10 Entries
11+ Entries

NEW HAMPSHIRE
NEW STATE RECORD
Typical Whitetail Deer
Score: $183^3/8$
Location: Coos Co.
Hunter and Owner: Frank Thurston
Date: 1997

NEW
STATE
RECORD

NEW HAMPSHIRE
STATE RECORD
Non-Typical Whitetail Deer
Score: 211⁴/₈
Location: Hillsborough Co.
Hunter: Curtiss Whipple
Owner: Herman Whipple
Date: 1947

NEW HAMPSHIRE

TYPICAL WHITETAIL DEER

Score	Length of Main Beam Right / Left	Inside Spread	Greatest Spread	Circumference at Smallest Place Between Burr and First Point Right / Left	Number of Points Right / Left	Lengths Abnormal Points	All-Time Rank	State Rank
						■ Location of Kill – Hunter – Owner – Date Killed		
183 3/8	29 1/8 29 6/8	20 4/8	22 7/8	5 5	6 6	1 1/8	365	1
	■ Coos Co. – Frank Thurston – Frank Thurston – 1997							
172 7/8	29 27 5/8	20 5/8	23 2/8	5 1/8 5 1/8	5 5		2038	2
	■ Sullivan Co. – Gordon E. Adams – Gordon E. Adams – 1992							
172 6/8	26 5/8 27	22 3/8	24 4/8	5 3/8 5 2/8	6 8	13 3/8	2065	3
	■ Cheshire Co. – Peter J. Krochunas – Peter J. Krochunas – 1991							
170 3/8	27 1/8 27 3/8	22 1/8	24 1/8	4 3/8 4 4/8	5 5		2992	4
	■ Grafton Co. – William M. Gordon – William M. Gordon – 1993							
169 5/8	24 6/8 26 5/8	24 3/8	26 3/8	4 4/8 4 5/8	5 5	2 2/8	3314	5
	■ Merrimack Co. – Wallace B. Currier – Wallace B. Currier – 1995							
168 6/8	27 3/8 27 1/8	18 2/8	21 5/8	4 5/8 4 5/8	6 6	4 6/8	3367	6
	■ Grafton Co. – Warren F. Parker – Warren F. Parker – 1959							
168 6/8	26 5/8 26 3/8	18 6/8	21 3/8	4 7/8 4 6/8	6 6		3367	6
	■ Coos Co. – Bernard Petrie – Bernard Petrie – 1998							
168 3/8	23 7/8 23 7/8	23 7/8	26 4/8	4 6/8 4 7/8	6 6		3399	8
	■ Cheshire Co. – Richard J. Jarvis – Richard J. Jarvis – 1988							
167 7/8	27 26 6/8	20 4/8	23	4 2/8 4 2/8	5 6	1 5/8	3451	9
	■ Merrimack Co. – Picked Up – NH Fish and Game Dept. – 1998							
165 3/8	29 1/8 28 6/8	21 3/8	23 5/8	4 7/8 4 7/8	5 6	2	3731†	10†
	■ Grafton Co. – Charles L. Coffin – Charles L. Coffin – 2000							
165 3/8	28 4/8 28 3/8	19 5/8	21 5/8	4 5/8 4 5/8	8 6	6 2/8	3731	10
	■ Hillsborough Co. – John P. Coulter – John P. Coulter – 1998							
165 1/8	25 2/8 25 2/8	16 3/8	18 6/8	4 4/8 4 4/8	5 5		3767	12
	■ Hillsborough Co. – Leon W. Nelson – Leon W. Nelson – 1998							
164 6/8	29 4/8 31 2/8	26 6/8	29 2/8	5 4 6/8	9 6	6 4/8	3809	13
	■ Belknap Co. – Picked Up – NH Fish & Game Dept. – 1981							
163 5/8	27 4/8 26 4/8	20 3/8	22 7/8	4 6/8 4 7/8	5 7	6	3961	14
	■ Carroll Co. – Howard Hawkins – Howard Hawkins – 1966							
163 5/8	24 7/8 23 7/8	17 1/8	19 2/8	4 4/8 4 4/8	5 5		3961	14
	■ Grafton Co. – Lester J. Downing – Lester J. Downing – 1989							
162 7/8	26 5/8 27	22 5/8	24 6/8	5 2/8 5 1/8	4 4		4067	16
	■ Belknap Co. – Lawrence L. Lee, Sr. – Lawrence L. Lee, Sr. – 1958							
	■ See photo on page 363							
162 6/8	25 7/8 28 6/8	18 2/8	20 2/8	5 1/8 5 1/8	4 4		4089	17
	■ Cheshire Co. – David A. Manley – David A. Manley – 1992							
162 3/8	26 6/8 27 2/8	19	22 3/8	4 1/8 4 2/8	6 5	3 3/8	4140	18
	■ Hillsborough Co. – Gary A. Sullivan – Gary A. Sullivan – 1973							
162 3/8	29 1/8 28 6/8	20 1/8	21 7/8	4 5/8 4 6/8	5 5		4140	18
	■ Coos Co. – Richard A. Machia – Richard A. Machia – 1995							

Score	Length of Main Beam Right	Left	Inside Spread	Greatest Spread	Circumference at Smallest Place Between Burr and First Point Right	Left	Number of Points Right	Left	Lengths Abnormal Points	All-Time Rank	State Rank
	■ Location of Kill – Hunter – Owner – Date Killed										
$162\frac{2}{8}$	$27\frac{4}{8}$	$26\frac{1}{8}$	$20\frac{4}{8}$	$22\frac{1}{8}$	$4\frac{1}{8}$	$4\frac{2}{8}$	5	5		4153	20
	■ Merrimack Co. – Dan Thompson – Dan Thompson – 1990										
$162\frac{2}{8}$	$24\frac{5}{8}$	$25\frac{2}{8}$	$18\frac{3}{8}$	21	$5\frac{2}{8}$	$6\frac{1}{8}$	5	6	$1\frac{3}{8}$	4153	20
	■ Hillsborough Co. – David S. Wilson – David S. Wilson – 1992										
162	$26\frac{3}{8}$	$27\frac{4}{8}$	$21\frac{2}{8}$	$23\frac{2}{8}$	$4\frac{3}{8}$	$4\frac{4}{8}$	5	5		4184	22
	■ Grafton Co. – Randy E. Montague – Randy E. Montague – 1989										
$161\frac{5}{8}$	$25\frac{6}{8}$	$24\frac{4}{8}$	$18\frac{3}{8}$	$20\frac{3}{8}$	$4\frac{6}{8}$	$4\frac{5}{8}$	5	5		4234	23
	■ Carroll Co. – Arthur G. Lianos – Arthur G. Lianos – 1991										
$161\frac{5}{8}$	28	$27\frac{7}{8}$	$21\frac{7}{8}$	$24\frac{2}{8}$	$4\frac{5}{8}$	$4\frac{6}{8}$	5	6		4234	23
	■ Strafford Co. – Picked Up – John Puchlopek – 1995										
$161\frac{4}{8}$	$25\frac{5}{8}$	$24\frac{7}{8}$	18	20	$4\frac{6}{8}$	$4\frac{5}{8}$	5	5		4258†	25†
	■ Merrimack Co. – Harry Heath – Harry Heath – 1949										
$161\frac{1}{8}$	$26\frac{6}{8}$	$26\frac{4}{8}$	$20\frac{2}{8}$	$22\frac{3}{8}$	$4\frac{7}{8}$	5	7	7	$10\frac{7}{8}$	4332	26
	■ Merrimack Co. – Robert McDonald – Robert McDonald – 1959										
$160\frac{2}{8}$	$27\frac{1}{8}$	$27\frac{2}{8}$	$20\frac{6}{8}$	$23\frac{2}{8}$	$4\frac{6}{8}$	$4\frac{7}{8}$	6	5	$4\frac{4}{8}$	4495	27
	■ Merrimack Co. – Thomas J. Goonan – Thomas J. Goonan – 1995										
$160\frac{1}{8}$	$27\frac{3}{8}$	$28\frac{6}{8}$	$20\frac{3}{8}$	$22\frac{5}{8}$	$5\frac{3}{8}$	$5\frac{3}{8}$	4	5	$1\frac{4}{8}$	4534	28
	■ Rockingham Co. – Picked Up – Tod Rinfret – 1999										
160	$26\frac{2}{8}$	$25\frac{5}{8}$	$17\frac{3}{8}$	$19\frac{5}{8}$	$4\frac{2}{8}$	$4\frac{4}{8}$	5	6	$1\frac{5}{8}$	4565	29
	■ Grafton Co. – Joseph A. Wigget – Joseph A. Wigget – 1991										
160	$25\frac{3}{8}$	$26\frac{2}{8}$	21	$23\frac{1}{8}$	$5\frac{2}{8}$	$5\frac{2}{8}$	6	5	1	4565	29
	■ Carroll Co. – Joe Nye – Joe Nye – 1999										

† The scores and ranking for trophies from the 25th Awards Entry Period are not final until the banquet is held on June 19, 2004.

NEW HAMPSHIRE

NON-TYPICAL WHITETAIL DEER

Score	Length of Main Beam		Inside Spread	Greatest Spread	Circumference at Smallest Place Between Burr and First Point		Number of Points		Lengths Abnormal Points	All-Time Rank	State Rank
	Right	Left			Right	Left	Right	Left			
	■ Location of Kill – Hunter – Owner – Date Killed										
211⁴/8	26⁴/8	27	20³/8	24⁶/8	6¹/8	6²/8	13	11	54⁵/8	739	1
	■ Hillsborough Co. – Curtiss Whipple – Herman Whipple – 1947										
210⁶/8	27⁶/8	25	20⁴/8	26	5³/8	5⁵/8	10	13	37	779	2
	■ Grafton Co. – David C. Braley – David C. Braley – 1991										
208²/8	27¹/8	25⁴/8	23⁴/8	26³/8	5⁶/8	6	7	13	42⁴/8	910	3
	■ Rockingham Co. – Glenn R. Townsend – Glenn R. Townsend – 2000										
202⁵/8	26³/8	23⁶/8	18⁶/8	24³/8	4⁷/8	5	9	11	46³/8	1346	4
	■ Grafton Co. – Picked Up – Robert Hoffman – PR 1945										
193²/8	27⁶/8	25⁶/8	23¹/8	27⁴/8	4⁶/8	4⁶/8	5	10	39⁵/8	2300	5
	■ Rockingham Co. – A.E. Field – A.E. Field – 1991										
191¹/8	26³/8	27³/8	17⁶/8	21	4⁵/8	4⁵/8	10	9	18¹/8	2374	6
	■ Rockingham Co. – Theron G. Young, Sr. – Theron G. Young, Sr. – 1945										

OLD-TIME FIELD PHOTOS

HUNTER: Lawrence L. Lee, Sr.
SCORE: 162-7/8
CATEGORY: typical whitetail deer
LOCATION: Belknap County, New Hampshire
DATE: 1958

NEW JERSEY
RECORD WHITETAILS

2 Typical whitetail deer entries
1 Non-typical whitetail deer entries
7,265 Total whitetail deer entries

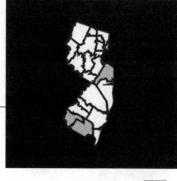

0 Entries
1-2 Entries
3-5 Entries
6-10 Entries
11+ Entries

NEW JERSEY
NEW STATE RECORD
Typical Whitetail Deer
Score: 189 $^4/_8$
Location: Monmouth Co.
Hunter and Owner: Scott W. Borden
Date: 1995

NEW
STATE
RECORD

NEW JERSEY
NEW STATE RECORD
Non-Typical Whitetail Deer
Score: 203³/₈
Location: Cumberland Co.
Hunter and Owner: Darrell T. Capps
Date: 2000

*New state record pending approval from the 25th Awards Program
Judges Panel.*

NEW JERSEY

TYPICAL WHITETAIL DEER

Score	Length of Main Beam Right	Left	Inside Spread	Greatest Spread	Circumference at Smallest Place Between Burr and First Point Right	Left	Number of Points Right	Left	Lengths Abnormal Points	All-Time Rank	State Rank
	■ Location of Kill – Hunter – Owner – Date Killed										
189 4/8	25 4/8	24 7/8	20	23 6/8	5	4 6/8	6	7	1	119	1
	■ Monmouth Co. – Scott W. Borden – Scott W. Borden – 1995										
161 7/8	23 2/8	22 2/8	20 1/8	21 4/8	4 4/8	4 4/8	5	6		4212	2
	■ Salem Co. – Don R. D'Antonio – Don R. D'Antonio – 1998										

NEW JERSEY

NON-TYPICAL WHITETAIL DEER

Score	Length of Main Beam Right Left	Inside Spread	Greatest Spread	Circumference at Smallest Place Between Burr and First Point Right Left		Number of Points Right Left		Lengths Abnormal Points	All-Time Rank	State Rank
				■ *Location of Kill – Hunter – Owner – Date Killed*						
203³/₈	22³/₈ 21²/₈	18²/₈	27¹/₈	4⁴/₈	4³/₈	10	13	68⁵/₈	1272†	1†
	■ *Cumberland Co. – Darrell T. Capps – Darrell T. Capps – 2000*									

† The scores and ranking for trophies from the 25th Awards Entry Period are not final until the banquet is held on June 19, 2004.

U.S. WHITETAIL DEER LISTING BY STATE

367

NEW YORK
RECORD WHITETAILS

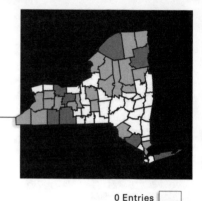

44 Typical whitetail deer entries
17 Non-typical whitetail deer entries
7,265 Total whitetail deer entries

0 Entries	
1-2 Entries	
3-5 Entries	
6-10 Entries	
11+ Entries	

NEW YORK
STATE RECORD
Typical Whitetail Deer
Score: $198^3/8$
Location: Allegany Co.
Hunter: Roosevelt Luckey
Owner: NY Dept. of
   Env. Cons.
Date: 1939

Photograph from B&C Archives

NEW YORK
STATE RECORD
Non-Typical Whitetail Deer
Score: 244^2/$_8$
Location: Allegany Co.
Hunter: Homer Boylan
Owner: Harry J. Boylan
Date: 1939

Photograph courtesy of NY Dept. of Environmental Conservation

NEW YORK

TYPICAL WHITETAIL DEER

Score	Length of Main Beam Right	Left	Inside Spread	Greatest Spread	Circumference at Smallest Place Between Burr and First Point Right	Left	Number of Points Right	Left	Lengths Abnormal Points	All-Time Rank	State Rank

Location of Kill – Hunter – Owner – Date Killed

198³/₈	29⁵/₈	29⁴/₈	18¹/₈	21	4⁶/₈	4⁶/₈	6	8	8⁴/₈	18	1

■ *Allegany Co. – Roosevelt Luckey – NY Dept. of Env. Cons. – 1939* ■ *See photo on page 373*

| 181³/₈ | 24⁷/₈ | 27⁴/₈ | 18¹/₈ | 20 | 5 | 5 | 6 | 7 | 4⁴/₈ | 528 | 2 |

■ *Orange Co. – Roy Vail – Roy Vail – 1960*

| 180³/₈ | 30²/₈ | 30 | 23¹/₈ | 26²/₈ | 5¹/₈ | 5²/₈ | 8 | 6 | 2⁴/₈ | 630 | 3 |

■ *Livingston Co. – Edward Beare – Edward Beare – 1943*

| 180³/₈ | 30⁷/₈ | 28⁵/₈ | 21⁴/₈ | 23⁶/₈ | 4⁶/₈ | 4⁷/₈ | 6 | 8 | 8¹/₈ | 630 | 3 |

■ *Westchester Co. – Richard L. Johnson – Richard L. Johnson – 1998*

| 179³/₈ | 29 | 29²/₈ | 19⁷/₈ | 23 | 4⁶/₈ | 4⁵/₈ | 10 | 8 | 12⁶/₈ | 749 | 5 |

■ *Essex Co. – Herbert Jaquish – Herbert Jaquish – 1953*

| 179³/₈ | 26⁷/₈ | 27⁵/₈ | 19⁵/₈ | 21⁷/₈ | 4²/₈ | 4²/₈ | 5 | 5 | | 749 | 5 |

■ *St. Lawrence Co. – Craig A. Morrill – Craig A. Morrill – 1995*

| 178⁵/₈ | 25⁷/₈ | 25³/₈ | 17⁷/₈ | 20³/₈ | 4⁵/₈ | 4⁵/₈ | 6 | 7 | 2⁴/₈ | 819 | 7 |

■ *Monroe Co. – David P. Ives – David P. Ives – 1993*

| 177⁷/₈ | 25⁵/₈ | 22 | 19⁵/₈ | 22²/₈ | 4²/₈ | 4⁴/₈ | 8 | 7 | 4⁴/₈ | 936 | 8 |

■ *Ontario Co. – Stephen E. McAllister – Stephen E. McAllister – 1996*

| 177⁴/₈ | 28⁶/₈ | 28⁵/₈ | 19²/₈ | 22 | 4⁵/₈ | 4⁵/₈ | 6 | 6 | | 993 | 9 |

■ *St. Lawrence Co. – Timothy B. Lucas – Timothy B. Lucas – 1997*

| 176²/₈ | 25⁶/₈ | 28⁶/₈ | 25⁴/₈ | 28 | 4⁷/₈ | 5 | 5 | 5 | | 1209 | 10 |

■ *Erie Co. – Wesley H. Iulg – Wesley H. Iulg – 1944*

| 176²/₈ | 24⁴/₈ | 26⁴/₈ | 17¹/₈ | 22³/₈ | 5⁴/₈ | 5⁴/₈ | 8 | 7 | 6³/₈ | 1209 | 10 |

■ *Warren Co. – Frank Dagles – Frank Dagles – 1961*

| 175⁷/₈ | 26¹/₈ | 26⁴/₈ | 20³/₈ | 22⁵/₈ | 4³/₈ | 4³/₈ | 7 | 7 | 3²/₈ | 1287 | 12 |

■ *Lewis Co. – Andrew Lustyik – Andrew F. Lustyik – 1942*

| 175⁵/₈ | 26 | 27⁴/₈ | 18¹/₈ | 20²/₈ | 4⁴/₈ | 4⁴/₈ | 5 | 6 | | 1333 | 13 |

■ *Allegany Co. – William L. Damon – William L. Damon – 1981*

| 174⁶/₈ | 28⁴/₈ | 29 | 18⁶/₈ | 22⁵/₈ | 5²/₈ | 5²/₈ | 7 | 7 | 6⁶/₈ | 1534 | 14 |

■ *Essex Co. – Richard Olcott – Richard Olcott – 1967*

| 174³/₈ | 26⁷/₈ | 26⁷/₈ | 18⁵/₈ | 20⁷/₈ | 4⁷/₈ | 5 | 6 | 7 | 2⁴/₈ | 1619 | 15 |

■ *Sullivan Co. – Domenick A. DeMaria – Domenick A. DeMaria – 1998*

| 174²/₈ | 25³/₈ | 26³/₈ | 22 | 24⁴/₈ | 4⁵/₈ | 4⁴/₈ | 5 | 5 | | 1652 | 16 |

■ *Livingston Co. – Kenneth Bowen – Kenneth Bowen – 1941*

| 174¹/₈ | 26³/₈ | 27³/₈ | 16⁷/₈ | 19³/₈ | 4³/₈ | 4²/₈ | 6 | 7 | | 1678 | 17 |

■ *Essex Co. – Denny Mitchell – Lewis P. Evans – 1933*

| 174 | 29¹/₈ | 28³/₈ | 17 | 19³/₈ | 5²/₈ | 5¹/₈ | 5 | 5 | | 1717 | 18 |

■ *Jefferson Co. – James S. Hoar – James S. Hoar – 1988*

| 173³/₈ | 28⁵/₈ | 29³/₈ | 23²/₈ | 25⁴/₈ | 6³/₈ | 6²/₈ | 7 | 8 | 10⁷/₈ | 1883 | 19 |

■ *Ontario Co. – Martin Solway – NY Dept. of Env. Cons. – 1946*

Score	Length of Main Beam Right	Left	Inside Spread	Greatest Spread	Circumference at Smallest Place Between Burr and First Point Right	Left	Number of Points Right	Left	Lengths Abnormal Points	All-Time Rank	State Rank
	■ Location of Kill – Hunter – Owner – Date Killed										
173 2/8	24 2/8	24 1/8	17 2/8	19 1/8	4 4/8	4 4/8	6	6		1914	20
	■ Chautauqua Co. – Brian Whalen – Brian Whalen – 1998										
172 7/8	27 1/8	26 2/8	21 7/8	25	4 6/8	4 7/8	6	5	1 6/8	2038	21
	■ Seneca Co. – Martin J. Way – Martin J. Way – 1968										
172 3/8	27	26	21	27 6/8	5 2/8	5 3/8	7	5	2 3/8	2200	22
	■ Hamilton Co. – Unknown – Donald K. Hamilton – 1956										
172 3/8	25 6/8	27 4/8	19 3/8	21 6/8	5 6/8	5 6/8	7	6	5 2/8	2200	22
	■ Monroe Co. – Picked Up – Joseph Masci – 1997										
172 2/8	25 7/8	25 6/8	20 2/8	22 5/8	4 4/8	4 4/8	5	5		2237	24
	■ Cattaraugus Co. – Thomas J. Hinchey – Thomas J. Hinchey – 1982										
171 6/8	25 5/8	25 6/8	24 1/8	26 1/8	5 6/8	5 6/8	6	6	3 1/8	2418	25
	■ Clinton Co. – William J. Branch – William J. Branch – 1982										
171 4/8	26	26	23 2/8	25 2/8	4 7/8	4 3/8	5	7	1 4/8	2513	26
	■ Essex Co. – Richard E. Johndrow – Richard E. Johndrow – 1968										
171 3/8	26	26 3/8	17 6/8	20 3/8	4 4/8	4 3/8	6	7	4 1/8	2564	27
	■ Herkimer Co. – John Christie – John Christie – 1957										
171 2/8	25 4/8	25 4/8	16 6/8	18 7/8	4 3/8	4 3/8	6	6		2621†	28†
	■ Onondaga Co. – Kenneth L. Lamb – Kenneth L. Lamb – 2000										
171 1/8	27 2/8	27 3/8	21 5/8	24 1/8	5 6/8	5 4/8	5	4		2665	29
	■ Fulton Co. – Kenneth R. Mowrey, Jr. – Kenneth R. Mowrey, Jr. – 1985										
170 7/8	27	26 5/8	23 1/8		4 7/8	5	8	6	5 2/8	2769	30
	■ Steuben Co. – Duane L. Horton – Duane L. Horton – 1976										
168 1/8	26 6/8	26 6/8	19 2/8	23 3/8	5	5	6	5	1 3/8	3426	31
	■ Franklin Co. – James W. Demers – James W. Demers – 1997										
167 4/8	27 2/8	27 4/8	20 2/8	23 6/8	4 5/8	4 4/8	6	5	1 6/8	3485	32
	■ Ontario Co. – Jeremy Thomas – Jeremy Thomas – 1997										
166	25 6/8	28	20	21 4/8	5 3/8	5 4/8	6	5	2 4/8	3657	33
	■ Steuben Co. – Justin Schwabe – Justin Schwabe – 1998										
163 7/8	26 4/8	25 2/8	18 5/8	20 4/8	4 4/8	4 2/8	6	5	1 2/8	3928	34
	■ Orange Co. – Eric W. Johnson – Eric W. Johnson – 1994										
163 3/8	23 6/8	23 1/8	18 2/8	21 4/8	4 4/8	4 5/8	6	7	1 7/8	4002†	35†
	■ Onondaga Co. – Anthony A. Denison – Anthony A. Denison – 2000										
162 5/8	23 6/8	24 7/8	20	21 7/8	4 6/8	4 5/8	6	5	1 3/8	4109	36
	■ Suffolk Co. – Robert A. Catalano – Robert A. Catalano – 1997										
162 2/8	27	25 5/8	19 2/8	21 4/8	5	4 6/8	5	5		4153†	37†
	■ Yates Co. – Robert A. Bradley – Robert A. Bradley – 2000										
162	24 2/8	24 1/8	18	20	5	5	6	7	1 4/8	4184	38
	■ Steuben Co. – Joseph S. Stavalone – Joseph S. Stavalone – 1988										
161 7/8	21 5/8	24 4/8	17 5/8	20	5 4/8	5 5/8	7	6	2	4212	39
	■ Ontario Co. – Adam T. Kupis – Adam T. Kupis – 1989										
161 6/8	25	26 3/8	19 5/8	21 7/8	5	4 6/8	5	5	3 5/8	4223†	40†
	■ Orleans Co. – Duane H. Phillips – Duane H. Phillips – 2001										

Score	Length of Main Beam		Inside Spread	Greatest Spread	Circumference at Smallest Place Between Burr and First Point		Number of Points		Lengths Abnormal Points	All-Time Rank	State Rank
	Right	Left			Right	Left	Right	Left			
	■ Location of Kill – Hunter – Owner – Date Killed										
161⁴/₈	27	26	19⁴/₈	22²/₈	5¹/₈	5³/₈	5	6	2²/₈	4258†	41†
	■ Warren Co. – Paul J. Tubbs – Paul J. Tubbs – 2001										
161³/₈	26²/₈	26²/₈	18⁵/₈	21	5¹/₈	5	6	5	1⁴/₈	4285	42
	■ Herkimer Co. – Jerry Selbach – Jerry Selbach – 1999										
161¹/₈	24⁶/₈	24⁶/₈	18³/₈	20⁵/₈	4⁷/₈	4⁶/₈	6	5		4332	43
	■ Monroe Co. – Dane R. Edwards – Dane R. Edwards – 1999										
160³/₈	27²/₈	27⁴/₈	20⁵/₈	22⁶/₈	4⁷/₈	4⁷/₈	5	5		4470	44
	■ Oneida Co. – Charles E. Roberts – Charles E. Roberts – 1999										

† The scores and ranking for trophies from the 25th Awards Entry Period are not final until the banquet is held on June 19, 2004.

OLD-TIME FIELD PHOTOS

HUNTER: Roosevelt Luckey
SCORE: 198-3/8
CATEGORY: typical whitetail deer
LOCATION: Allegany County, New York
DATE: 1939

NEW YORK

NON-TYPICAL WHITETAIL DEER

Score	Length of Main Beam Right	Left	Inside Spread	Greatest Spread	Circumference at Smallest Place Between Burr and First Point Right	Left	Number of Points Right	Left	Lengths Abnormal Points	All-Time Rank	State Rank
	■ Location of Kill – Hunter – Owner – Date Killed										
244²/8	27	27²/8	16⁵/8	23⁶/8	5⁶/8	5⁵/8	13	13	55³/8	89	1
	■ Allegany Co. – Homer Boylan – Harry J. Boylan – 1939										
225²/8	24⁷/8	26²/8	24³/8	28⁷/8	5²/8	5	12	13	41⁷/8	310	2
	■ St. Lawrence Co. – Kenneth M. Locy – Kenneth M. Locy – 1992										
219⁷/8	27²/8	27⁶/8	19⁷/8	26⁵/8	6	6	10	10	38	444	3
	■ Genesee Co. – Robert Wood – Robert Wood – 1944										
207⁷/8	23⁷/8	23⁵/8	21³/8	23⁶/8	4⁵/8	4⁷/8	13	19	40	938	4
	■ Suffolk Co. – George Hackal – Gary C. Boyer – 1950										
207⁴/8	26⁴/8	26⁴/8	29¹/8	31	6	6	7	10	22	969	5
	■ Portageville – Howard W. Smith – Howard W. Smith – 1959										
206²/8	28⁴/8	28⁵/8	25	32	5⁵/8	5⁶/8	9	11	22⁶/8	1059	6
	■ Cortland Co. – Hank Hayes – Interlaken Sportsmans Club – 1947										
205⁷/8	28⁶/8	27⁴/8	17¹/8	19⁴/8	5	5⁴/8	8	17	28	1080	7
	■ Steuben Co. – Fred J. Kelley – Fred J. Kelley – 1938										
205⁵/8	23³/8	24²/8	20⁶/8	24³/8	5⁶/8	5⁶/8	15	10	46¹/8	1102	8
	■ Orange Co. – Unknown – Victor T. Zarnock – PR 1944										
205¹/8	28⁷/8	29	24¹/8	26⁶/8	5	4⁶/8	9	8	35⁴/8	1138	9
	■ Erie Co. – Mark C. Surdi – Mark C. Surdi – 1996										
199¹/8	21⁷/8	24⁶/8	20	22¹/8	4⁶/8	4⁷/8	12	10	28³/8	1660	10
	■ Clinton Co. – Unknown – William F. Mathieson – PR 1971										
197³/8	28⁵/8	27⁶/8	21⁶/8	23⁶/8	6⁴/8	5²/8	16	14	54⁵/8	1884†	11†
	■ Suffolk Co. – John E. Hansen – John E. Hansen – 2001										
196⁵/8	28⁷/8	25⁴/8	22	25⁴/8	5⁴/8	4⁶/8	10	12	47¹/8	1985	12
	■ Westchester Co. – Picked Up – John J. Vitale – 1968										
196⁴/8	24¹/8	25¹/8	19⁶/8	22¹/8	5¹/8	5	12	10	41²/8	1999†	13†
	■ Wayne Co. – Jonathan S. Countryman – Jonathan S. Countryman – 2001										
196¹/8	25⁵/8	24⁴/8	16⁷/8	20⁵/8	5	4⁷/8	11	10	18⁴/8	2045	14
	■ Wyoming Co. – Eric D. Baney – Eric D. Baney – 1985										
195⁴/8	25⁵/8	24⁶/8	23⁴/8	29	5	5¹/8	11	8	24	2134	15
	■ Suffolk Co. – Eric Kowalski – Eric Kowalski – 1999										
188⁶/8	23¹/8	23²/8	17⁶/8	20⁷/8	4³/8	4³/8	10	10	26⁶/8	2468	16
	■ St. Lawrence Co. – Timothy C. Besaw – Timothy C. Besaw – 1999										
187²/8	24⁴/8	24⁶/8	17³/8	20	5	5	8	8	17⁷/8	2534†	17†
	■ Monroe Co. – William J. Lerkins – William J. Lerkins – 2000										

† The scores and ranking for trophies from the 25th Awards Entry Period are not final until the banquet is held on June 19, 2004.

OLD-TIME FIELD PHOTOS

HUNTER: Del Austin
SCORE: 277-3/8
CATEGORY: non-typical whitetail deer
LOCATION: Hall County, Nebraska
DATE: 1962

NORTH CAROLINA
RECORD WHITETAILS

15 Typical whitetail deer entries
4 Non-typical whitetail deer entries
7,265 Total whitetail deer entries

0 Entries
1-2 Entries
3-5 Entries
6-10 Entries
11+ Entries

NORTH CAROLINA STATE RECORD
Typical Whitetail Deer
Score: $181^7/_8$
Location: Guilford Co.
Hunter and Owner: Terry E. Daffron
Date: 1987

NORTH CAROLINA
NEW STATE RECORD
Non-Typical Whitetail Deer
Score: 228⁴/₈
Location: Person Co.
Hunter and Owner: Don C. Rockett
Date: 1998

NORTH CAROLINA

TYPICAL WHITETAIL DEER

Score	Length of Main Beam Right	Left	Inside Spread	Greatest Spread	Circumference at Smallest Place Between Burr and First Point Right	Left	Number of Points Right	Left	Lengths Abnormal Points	All-Time Rank	State Rank
	■ Location of Kill – Hunter – Owner – Date Killed										
181⁷/8	25³/8	25⁴/8	23⁵/8	25⁵/8	5³/8	5	5	5		478	1
	■ Guilford Co. – Terry E. Daffron – Terry E. Daffron – 1987										
180⁵/8	28³/8	28³/8	17³/8	19⁶/8	4⁵/8	4⁵/8	5	5		599	2
	■ Ashe Co. – William Price – William Price – 1999										
178	25⁴/8	25¹/8	18⁵/8	20⁵/8	4¹/8	4¹/8	7	7	4³/8	922	3
	■ Caswell Co. – Picked Up – Jimmy Koger – 1988										
172⁷/8	28⁷/8	28²/8	18⁷/8	20⁶/8	5²/8	5¹/8	5	6	1²/8	2038	4
	■ Granville Co. – James M. Wilkerson – James M. Wilkerson – 1981										
172⁶/8	24⁷/8	25⁷/8	18⁴/8	20⁴/8	5⁴/8	5²/8	7	7	2²/8	2065	5
	■ Northampton Co. – L. Thomas Baird – L. Thomas Baird – 1999										
172⁴/8	29¹/8	27⁵/8	19²/8	21⁶/8	5	5	5	5		2156	6
	■ Guilford Co. – Rodney D. Summers – Rodney D. Summers – 1993										
172¹/8	27⁶/8	27¹/8	19⁴/8	24²/8	4⁵/8	4⁶/8	7	6	5³/8	2286	7
	■ Granville Co. – Dudley Barnes – Dudley Barnes – 1985										
171⁴/8	26¹/8	25⁵/8	18⁶/8	20⁶/8	4¹/8	4¹/8	8	7	1²/8	2513†	8†
	■ Cumberland Co. – Lucas J. Hinerman – Lucas J. Hinerman – 2001										
170⁶/8	26¹/8	26	18²/8	20²/8	4⁷/8	4⁴/8	5	5		2828†	9†
	■ Moore Co. – Jason A. Cole – Jason A. Cole – 2000										
170⁴/8	28¹/8	29	21⁴/8	23¹/8	5	4⁵/8	5	6	1²/8	2933	10
	■ Rockingham Co. – Lindsey H. Watkins – Lindsey H. Watkins – 1987										
170¹/8	26¹/8	26⁴/8	17¹/8	19	4²/8	4²/8	7	6		3143	11
	■ Gates Co. – William W. Parker – William W. Parker – 1997										
166⁷/8	25³/8	25	17⁷/8	20⁵/8	5²/8	5²/8	5	6	1²/8	3568	12
	■ Yancey Co. – Harvey F. Johnson – Harvey F. Johnson – 1993										
163⁶/8	24¹/8	24⁵/8	18²/8	20⁴/8	4³/8	4⁴/8	5	5		3946	13
	■ Durham Co. – Harvey Garrett – Harvey Garrett – 1984										
161⁴/8	27	27	20⁴/8	22¹/8	5²/8	5²/8	4	4		4258†	14†
	■ Sampson Co. – C. Brady Freeman – C. Brady Freeman – 2000										
160⁶/8	26⁵/8	26⁶/8	21⁶/8	23³/8	5	5²/8	6	8	11⁶/8	4402†	15†
	■ Forsyth Co. – Ronald W. James – Ronald W. James – 2001										

† The scores and ranking for trophies from the 25th Awards Entry Period are not final until the banquet is held on June 19, 2004.

NORTH CAROLINA

NON-TYPICAL WHITETAIL DEER

Score	Length of Main Beam Right Left ■ Location of Kill – Hunter – Owner – Date Killed	Inside Spread	Greatest Spread	Circumference at Smallest Place Between Burr and First Point Right Left		Number of Points Right Left		Lengths Abnormal Points	All-Time Rank	State Rank
228⁴/8	26⁷/8 26²/8	19¹/8	25⁵/8	6	5³/8	12	11	45⁵/8	258	1
	■ Person Co. – Don C. Rockett – Don C. Rockett – 1998									
209²/8	25¹/8 26	19¹/8	21	5	5	15	13	39⁵/8	859	2
	■ Person Co. – Stuart E. Gentry – Stuart E. Gentry – 1996									
204⁷/8	21²/8 22²/8	23⁶/8	25	4⁵/8	4⁵/8	11	8	47⁷/8	1156	3
	■ Anson Co. – Keith M. Reese – Keith M. Reese – 1994									
196¹/8	21⁶/8 19⁵/8	21	27⁴/8	4⁵/8	4⁵/8	20	13	66⁵/8	2045†	4†
	■ Montgomery Co. – Roger D. Hunt – Roger D. Hunt – 2001									

† The scores and ranking for trophies from the 25th Awards Entry Period are not final until the banquet is held on June 19, 2004.

NORTH DAKOTA
RECORD WHITETAILS

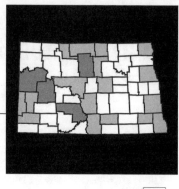

31 Typical whitetail deer entries
19 Non-typical whitetail deer entries
7,265 Total whitetail deer entries

0 Entries	
1-2 Entries	
3-5 Entries	
6-10 Entries	
11+ Entries	

NEW STATE RECORD

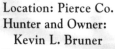

NORTH DAKOTA
NEW STATE RECORD
Typical Whitetail Deer
Score: $195^2/8$
Location: Pierce Co.
Hunter and Owner:
    Kevin L. Bruner
Date: 1994

NORTH DAKOTA STATE RECORD
Non-Typical Whitetail Deer
Score: 254⁶/8
Location: Stanley
Hunter and Owner: Roger Ritchie
Date: 1968

NORTH DAKOTA

TYPICAL WHITETAIL DEER

Score	Length of Main Beam Right	Left	Inside Spread	Greatest Spread	Circumference at Smallest Place Between Burr and First Point Right	Left	Number of Points Right	Left	Lengths Abnormal Points	All-Time Rank	State Rank
	■ Location of Kill – Hunter – Owner – Date Killed										
195²/8	28⁶/8	28²/8	20⁶/8	23¹/8	5¹/8	5	6	6		38	1
	■ Pierce Co. – Kevin L. Bruner – Kevin L. Bruner – 1994										
189³/8	28²/8	27²/8	20¹/8	22⁴/8	4¹/8	4¹/8	5	5		120	2
	■ McKenzie Co. – Gene Veeder – Legendary Whitetails – 1972										
187⁵/8	25	25²/8	20¹/8	23²/8	5²/8	5²/8	6	6	4	165	3
	■ Emmons Co. – Joseph F. Bosch – Joseph F. Bosch – 1959										
187²/8	26³/8	25	18⁶/8	21³/8	5¹/8	5¹/8	7	7		180	4
	■ McLean Co. – Frank O. Bauman – Donald Bauman – 1986										
182	24⁴/8	25	23	25²/8	4³/8	4	7	7		469	5
	■ Zap – Wally Duckwitz – Sioux Sporting Goods – 1962										
181	26³/8	26²/8	20²/8	23⁶/8	4⁷/8	5	5	6	3⁶/8	563	6
	■ Ransom Co. – Gerald V. Sweet – Gerald V. Sweet – 1959										
178²/8	28⁵/8	27⁵/8	21	25¹/8	4⁴/8	4⁴/8	7	6	2⁶/8	891	7
	■ Richland Co. – Jeffrey D. Krabbenhoft – Jeffrey D. Krabbenhoft – 1993										
178¹/8	28²/8	26⁷/8	18⁷/8	21²/8	4⁷/8	5	5	7	1²/8	905	8
	■ Concrete – Lawrence E. Vandal – Lawrence E. Vandal – 1947 ■ See photo on page 231										
177⁷/8	22⁴/8	23²/8	17⁴/8	19⁷/8	5²/8	5²/8	7	8	3⁵/8	936	9
	■ Cass Co. – Joe D. Chesley – Joe D. Chesley – 1987										
177²/8	25³/8	24³/8	21⁵/8	23²/8	4¹/8	4¹/8	8	9	11⁷/8	1025	10
	■ Golden Valley Co. – Allen Goltz – Allen Goltz – 1964										
175⁶/8	22⁶/8	24⁵/8	20	23¹/8	5	5	6	6		1310	11
	■ Burleigh Co. – Earl Haakenson – Earl Haakenson – 1963										
175	25⁶/8	25¹/8	21	23	4⁴/8	3⁷/8	5	5		1472	12
	■ New Salem – John T. Cartwright – John T. Cartwright – 1957										
175	25²/8	25²/8	18²/8	20²/8	5⁴/8	5³/8	7	7	4⁴/8	1472	12
	■ McKenzie Co. – Larry D. Schultz – Larry D. Schultz – 1992										
174⁴/8	22⁶/8	23³/8	18	21	5	5²/8	6	6		1592	14
	■ McKenzie Co. – Ben Dekker – Ben Dekker – 1976										
173⁵/8	27⁴/8	26⁵/8	18⁶/8	21	4⁶/8	4⁶/8	8	5	4³/8	1819	15
	■ Bottineau Co. – Alvin A. Hall – Alvin A. Hall – 1993										
173⁵/8	23¹/8	22⁶/8	22³/8	24²/8	5¹/8	5¹/8	6	6		1819	15
	■ Renville Co. – Shawna R. Atwood – Shawna R. Atwood – 1995										
173¹/8	23³/8	23⁶/8	18³/8	20⁴/8	4	4	6	6		1950	17
	■ Slope Co. – Robert L. Stroup – Robert L. Stroup – 1967										
172⁷/8	25³/8	25	20²/8	22⁶/8	4³/8	4²/8	7	7	2¹/8	2038	18
	■ McHenry Co. – David Medalen – David Medalen – 1959										
171⁷/8	24³/8	23⁴/8	18²/8	21⁵/8	5¹/8	5²/8	5	6	2³/8	2382	19
	■ Dunn Co. – Doug L. Martin – Doug L. Martin – 1991										

Score	Length of Main Beam		Inside Spread	Greatest Spread	Circumference at Smallest Place Between Burr and First Point		Number of Points		Lengths Abnormal Points	All-Time Rank	State Rank
	Right	Left			Right	Left	Right	Left			
	■ Location of Kill – Hunter – Owner – Date Killed										
171 5/8	24 4/8	24 6/8	19 4/8	23 4/8	5	5	9	10	9 3/8	2470	20
	■ Morton Co. – Dick Eastman – Sioux Sporting Goods – 1955										
171 2/8	24	23 7/8	19 4/8	22	5 4/8	5 4/8	5	5		2621	21
	■ Pembina Co. – Lee A. Einarson – Lee A. Einarson – 1985										
171	26 4/8	26 4/8	19 1/8	22	4 7/8	5	7	6	2 3/8	2707	22
	■ Sherwood – Roy Foss – Roy Foss – 1947										
170 7/8	25 5/8	24 6/8	22 5/8	25	5	5 7/8	6	7	8 6/8	2769	23
	■ Burleigh Co. – Ronald C. Wagner – Ronald C. Wagner – 1982										
170 4/8	23 4/8	24 1/8	18 4/8	20 2/8	4 4/8	4 5/8	5	6	1 2/8	2933	24
	■ Logan Co. – Jon M. Midthun – Jon M. Midthun – 1986										
170	27 1/8	27 2/8	18 2/8	20 4/8	4 6/8	4 7/8	7	6	1	3224	25
	■ Bottineau Co. – Ryan M. Bernstein – Ryan M. Bernstein – 1993										
168	25	25	20	23 3/8	4 5/8	4 4/8	5	6		3443	26
	■ Golden Valley Co. – Allen L. Unruh – Allen L. Unruh – 1989										
167 5/8	24 3/8	24 2/8	17 3/8	19 6/8	4 7/8	5 1/8	5	6	1 6/8	3476†	27†
	■ Dunn Co. – Kyle R. Steffan – Kyle R. Steffan – 2001										
165 3/8	25 1/8	25 5/8	17 5/8	20	4 3/8	4 3/8	4	4		3731	28
	■ Rolette Co. – Scott G. Moen – Scott G. Moen – 1999										
163 4/8	23 4/8	23 4/8	18 3/8	20 1/8	5 2/8	5 2/8	6	5	1 1/8	3984	29
	■ Billings Co. – Charles F. Iten – Charles F. Iten – 1990										
163 4/8	24	24 3/8	18 3/8	20 4/8	4 7/8	4 7/8	5	7	1 1/8	3984	29
	■ Dunn Co. – Curtis D. Decker – Curtis D. Decker – 1996										
160 2/8	25 4/8	25 2/8	16	18	4 3/8	4 4/8	5	5		4495†	31†
	■ Logan Co. – Denise R. Groce – Denise R. Groce – 2000										

† The scores and ranking for trophies from the 25th Awards Entry Period are not final until the banquet is held on June 19, 2004.

NORTH DAKOTA

NON-TYPICAL WHITETAIL DEER

Score	Length of Main Beam		Inside Spread	Greatest Spread	Circumference at Smallest Place Between Burr and First Point		Number of Points		Lengths Abnormal Points	All-Time Rank	State Rank
	Right	Left			Right	Left	Right	Left			
	■ Location of Kill – Hunter – Owner – Date Killed										
254 6/8	28 3/8	27	20 2/8	26	5 2/8	5	14	17	77 6/8	43	1
■ Stanley – Roger Ritchie – Roger Ritchie – 1968											
254 3/8	23 3/8	24 2/8	20	23	4 3/8	4 4/8	13	13	69 1/8	44	2
■ McHenry Co. – Austin Dugan – James K. Dugan – 1940											
232 1/8	24 5/8	24 5/8	16 4/8	24 5/8	4 7/8	4 6/8	11	11	41 7/8	208	3
■ McLean Co. – Olaf P. Anderson – Bass Pro Shops – 1886											
220 7/8	23 1/8	23 7/8	14 4/8	21 1/8	6 7/8	6 6/8	17	12	56 1/8	417	4
■ Pembina Co. – Gary F. Bourbanis – Gary F. Bourbanis – 1985											
216 6/8	26	24 4/8	22 3/8	26 1/8	5 2/8	5 1/8	11	13	43 1/8	539	5
■ Kathryn – Gerald R. Elsner – Gerald R. Elsner – 1963											
211 1/8	24 5/8	24 2/8	23	29 1/8	4 7/8	4 6/8	8	9	34 5/8	758	6
■ Wells Co. – Robert Newman – Robert Newman – 1961											
210 5/8	24 7/8	25 7/8	18 6/8	25 4/8	5 6/8	5 5/8	14	10	28 3/8	783	7
■ Renville Co. – Glen Southam – Glen Southam – 1978											
206 1/8	25 4/8	25 3/8	18 1/8	24 7/8	5 2/8	5 1/8	8	9	31 2/8	1068	8
■ Dunn Co. – Kenneth E. DeLap – Kenneth E. DeLap – 1982											
204 3/8	26 7/8	26 4/8	21 2/8	24 1/8	5 2/8	5 5/8	7	12	28 5/8	1186	9
■ Valley City – William F. Cruff – George W. Flaim – 1955 ■ See photo on page 385											
203 5/8	23 2/8	25 2/8	17 3/8	25 5/8	6	5 6/8	10	9	32 2/8	1248	10
■ Grand Forks Co. – Thomas G. Bernotas – Thomas G. Bernotas – 1975											
203 2/8	24 6/8	25 1/8	18 7/8	22	5 3/8	5 1/8	12	11	30 1/8	1287	11
■ McHenry Co. – Garry L. Heizelman – Garry L. Heizelman – 1987											
202 6/8	22 3/8	22	18	20 5/8	5 6/8	5 1/8	7	8	21 2/8	1339	12
■ Garrison – Clarence Hummel – Clarence Hummel – 1961											
201 3/8	24 6/8	23	16 7/8	19 2/8	5 4/8	5 5/8	9	8	26 6/8	1461	13
■ Morton Co. – Paul R. Shannon – Paul R. Shannon – 1995											
201 1/8	21 6/8	22 3/8	16 3/8	21 2/8	5 2/8	5 2/8	9	11	52 2/8	1489	14
■ Slope Co. – Arthur Hegge – J.D. Andrews – 1961											
200 7/8	23 4/8	24 5/8	20 1/8	23 4/8	5 3/8	5 2/8	9	8	24 4/8	1512	15
■ Mandan – Virgil Chadwick – Peter Voigt – 1957											
199 1/8	23 5/8	24 1/8	24 4/8	26 4/8	4 6/8	4 7/8	11	10	39 4/8	1660	16
■ Billings Co. – Jake Braun – Jake Braun – 1949											
198 5/8	27 2/8	26 5/8	22 4/8	25 5/8	5 6/8	5 7/8	8	10	24 5/8	1716	17
■ Morton Co. – Grant C. Starck – Grant C. Starck – 1952											
190 3/8	22 1/8	23 5/8	18 1/8	20 1/8	4 6/8	4 5/8	11	11	18 2/8	2408†	18†
■ Foster Co. – Brad A. Schulz – Brad A. Schulz – 2001											
188 3/8	22 7/8	23 5/8	19	21 4/8	4 7/8	4 6/8	7	8	14 5/8	2478†	19†
■ Benson Co. – Gerald J. Jaeger – Gerald J. Jaeger – 2001											

† The scores and ranking for trophies from the 25th Awards Entry Period are not final until the banquet is held on June 19, 2004.

OLD-TIME FIELD PHOTOS

HUNTER: William F. Cruff
SCORE: 204-3/8
CATEGORY: non-typical whitetail deer
LOCATION: Valley City, North Dakota
DATE: 1955

OHIO
RECORD WHITETAILS

179 Typical whitetail deer entries
91 Non-typical whitetail deer entries
7,265 Total whitetail deer entries

0 Entries
1-2 Entries
3-5 Entries
6-10 Entries
11+ Entries

NEW
STATE
RECORD

OHIO
STATE RECORD
Typical Whitetail Deer
Score: 191$^5/_8$
Location: Scioto Co.
Hunter and Owner:
  Lowell E. Kinney
Date: 2000

New state record pending approval from the 25th Awards Program Judges Panel.

OHIO
STATE RECORD
Non-Typical Whitetail Deer
Score: 328²/8
Location: Portage Co.
Hunter: Picked Up
Owner: Bass Pro Shops
Date: 1940

Photograph from B&C Archives

OHIO

TYPICAL WHITETAIL DEER

Score	Length of Main Beam Right	Left	Inside Spread	Greatest Spread	Circumference at Smallest Place Between Burr and First Point Right	Left	Number of Points Right	Left	Lengths Abnormal Points	All-Time Rank	State Rank
191 5/8	31 1/8	29 4/8	21	32 4/8	5 2/8	4 6/8	8	8	2 5/8	78†	1†
	■ Scioto Co. – Lowell E. Kinney – Lowell E. Kinney – 2000										
188	28 4/8	27 2/8	17 1/8	19 7/8	5 2/8	5 2/8	7	6	1 1/8	152†	2†
	■ Williams Co. – Brad A. McNalley – Brad A. McNalley – 2000										
187 5/8	27 1/8	27 2/8	20 5/8	23 3/8	5 5/8	5 4/8	5	5		165	3
	■ Pickaway Co. – Jeffrey M. Bragg – Jeffrey M. Bragg – 1999										
187 4/8	28	28 1/8	21	24 3/8	4 7/8	5 3/8	5	5		172	4
	■ Miami Co. – Dale L. Bevington – Dale L. Bevington – 1996										
187 1/8	28	28 3/8	22 3/8	24 5/8	4 7/8	4 5/8	7	7	3 2/8	185	5
	■ Hocking Co. – Stephen C. Corley – Stephen C. Corley – 1995										
186 7/8	30 4/8	29 2/8	20 7/8	23 4/8	4 7/8	4 7/8	7	5	4 4/8	194†	6†
	■ Greene Co. – Dale A. Heathcook – Dale A. Heathcook – 2001										
186 6/8	29 1/8	29 7/8	23	24 4/8	4 6/8	4 6/8	5	5		200	7
	■ Logan Co. – Bernard R. Hines – Bernard R. Hines – 1990										
186 2/8	25 6/8	26 6/8	18	21 4/8	5 4/8	5 4/8	7	7	5 2/8	220†	8†
	■ Adams Co. – Larry D. Napier – Larry D. Napier – 2001										
186 1/8	24 7/8	26 2/8	19 1/8	22 3/8	4 7/8	5	6	8	2 4/8	228†	9†
	■ Columbia Co. – Jared T. MacNees – Jared T. MacNees – 2000										
184 6/8	27	26	27 4/8	29	6	6 1/8	6	5	1 4/8	285	10
	■ Muskingum Co. – Dale Hartberger – Dale Hartberger – 1981										
184 5/8	27	27	19 1/8	21 6/8	5 1/8	5 1/8	7	6	2	294†	11†
	■ Champaign Co. – Eric Coleman – Eric Coleman – 2000 ■ See photo on page 63										
184 1/8	29	31	20 5/8	23	5 5/8	4 4/8	6	5	2 2/8	327	12
	■ Vinton Co. – Dan F. Allison – Dan F. Allison – 1965										
184 1/8	25 3/8	25 4/8	18 1/8	21 5/8	4 4/8	4 5/8	6	6		327	12
	■ Carroll Co. – Timothy F. Treadway – Timothy F. Treadway – 1989										
184 1/8	31	30 2/8	22	24 6/8	5 6/8	5 7/8	7	7	6 5/8	327	12
	■ Montgomery Co. – Glenn Parks – Glenn Parks – 1999										
183 3/8	27 4/8	27 2/8	17	19	5	5 2/8	5	6	1 3/8	365†	15†
	■ Wayne Co. – Lloyd K. Eshler – Lloyd K. Eshler – 2000										
183	26 2/8	25	19 6/8	22 6/8	5	5	8	9	9 6/8	392	16
	■ Piedmont Lake – J. Rumbaugh & J. Ruyan – J. Rumbaugh & J. Ruyan – 1958										
182 7/8	28 5/8	28 5/8	19	24 1/8	5 6/8	6	6	6	4 3/8	401	17
	■ Wayne Co. – Gary E. Landry – Gary E. Landry – 1975										
182 5/8	21 5/8	21 2/8	14 2/8	17	5 5/8	5 4/8	8	7	1 1/8	420	18
	■ Noble Co. – William J. Estadt – William J. Estadt – 1993										
182 1/8	27 4/8	28 5/8	20 3/8	22 6/8	5 1/8	5 1/8	6	7	4 2/8	460†	19†
	■ Richland Co. – Bruce L. King – Bruce L. King – 2000										

Score	Length of Main Beam Right	Left	Inside Spread	Greatest Spread	Circumference at Smallest Place Between Burr and First Point Right	Left	Number of Points Right	Left	Lengths Abnormal Points	All-Time Rank	State Rank
182 1/8	28	28 1/8	22	24 2/8	5	5	5	6	1 5/8	460	19
■ Hardin Co. – Tim Campbell – Tim Campbell – 1991											
182	27 7/8	28 1/8	23 7/8	25 6/8	4 5/8	5 1/8	7	7	2 3/8	469†	21†
■ Hancock Co. – Larry G. Rader – Larry G. Rader – 2000											
181 4/8	25 2/8	25 6/8	22 7/8	24 4/8	5 6/8	5 7/8	7	7	2 5/8	516	22
■ Licking Co. – Arlee McCullough – Arlee McCullough – 1962											
181 3/8	27 4/8	27 5/8	20 6/8	23 4/8	4 4/8	4 4/8	7	6	4 5/8	528	23
■ Portage Co. – Robert M. Smith – Robert M. Smith – 1953 ■ See photo on page 397											
180 5/8	26	26 3/8	21 3/8	24 7/8	6 2/8	6 4/8	6	6	4 4/8	599	24
■ Tuscarawas Co. – Thomas K. Winters – Thomas K. Winters – 1991											
180 4/8	27 3/8	27 5/8	20	22 1/8	4 5/8	4 4/8	6	6		613	25
■ Portage Co. – Michael J. Simons – Michael J. Simons – 1990											
180 1/8	27 3/8	28	22 7/8	25 3/8	4 2/8	4	5	5		669	26
■ Medina Co. – Stephen F. DeMeulenaere – Stephen F. DeMeulenaere – 1998											
179 6/8	26 4/8	25 4/8	21 2/8	23	5	4 7/8	6	6		712	27
■ Warren Co. – Rex A. Gill – Rex A. Gill – 1998											
179 6/8	26 7/8	27 7/8	19 6/8	23 6/8	4 6/8	5 2/8	8	6	3 2/8	712	27
■ Madison Co. – Robert E. Hunter II – Robert E. Hunter II – 1999											
179	27 4/8	29 4/8	20 2/8	23 7/8	4 6/8	4 6/8	6	7	5	786	29
■ Logan Co. – Gregory K. Snyder – Greta J. Snyder – 1982											
178 7/8	24 3/8	28	21 7/8	24 3/8	5 3/8	5 3/8	6	6	2 4/8	801	30
■ Monroe Co. – Roger E. Schumacher – Roger E. Schumacher – 1958											
178 7/8	30	28 5/8	21 1/8	22 6/8	5	5 4/8	5	5		801	30
■ Scioto Co. – Craig D. Smith – Craig D. Smith – 1991											
178 2/8	27 4/8	27	19 6/8	21 7/8	4 3/8	4 4/8	5	5		891	32
■ Tuscarawas Co. – Raymond D. Gerber, Jr. – Raymond D. Gerber, Jr. – 1983											
177 5/8	29	28 2/8	22	23 1/8	4 4/8	4 4/8	7	8	4 7/8	972	33
■ Harrison Co. – Mark Dulkoski – Mark Dulkoski – 1984											
177 2/8	27	26 7/8	20 6/8	22 6/8	5	5	5	5		1025	34
■ Belmont Co. – Kevin A. Grimes – Kevin A. Grimes – 1987											
177	27 7/8	28 1/8	26 2/8	28 4/8	4 5/8	4 7/8	8	8	8	1066†	35†
■ Lake Co. – Thomas A. Lasko – Thomas A. Lasko – 2000											
176 7/8	29 2/8	28 3/8	23	26 1/8	5 7/8	5 4/8	5	6	1 7/8	1086	36
■ Logan Co. – David Sutherly – David Sutherly – 1975											
176 7/8	27 4/8	28	25 3/8	28 1/8	5 6/8	5 6/8	5	5		1086	36
■ Marion Co. – Thomas A. Bridenstine – Thomas A. Bridenstine – 1987											
176 7/8	27 4/8	27 5/8	21 1/8	23 4/8	4 5/8	4 4/8	5	5		1086	36
■ Warren Co. – Richard M. Barhorst – Richard M. Barhorst – 1990											
176 7/8	27 1/8	27 1/8	21 6/8	23 5/8	5 5/8	5 4/8	6	5	1 7/8	1086	36
■ Medina Co. – Bradley K. Shafer – Bradley K. Shafer – 1994											
176 5/8	27	27 5/8	22 6/8	25 5/8	5 1/8	5 3/8	7	6	1 1/8	1134	40
■ Fairfield Co. – Harold R. McCafferty – Harold R. McCafferty – 1996											

■ Location of Kill – Hunter – Owner – Date Killed

Score	Length of Main Beam Right	Left	Inside Spread	Greatest Spread	Circumference at Smallest Place Between Burr and First Point Right	Left	Number of Points Right	Left	Lengths Abnormal Points	All-Time Rank	State Rank

■ Location of Kill – Hunter – Owner – Date Killed

Score	R	L	Inside	Greatest	Circ R	Circ L	Pts R	Pts L	Abn	All-Time	State
176 4/8	28 7/8	28 4/8	18 5/8	22 6/8	5 3/8	5 3/8	6	6	3 7/8	1158	41

■ Columbiana Co. – Blane A. Wade – Blane A. Wade – 1997

| 176 3/8 | 25 6/8 | 25 4/8 | 20 1/8 | 22 4/8 | 4 4/8 | 4 4/8 | 6 | 6 | | 1182 | 42 |

■ Logan Co. – Larry D. Hyzer – Larry D. Hyzer – 1987

| 176 3/8 | 22 3/8 | 24 5/8 | 21 7/8 | 24 4/8 | 5 2/8 | 5 1/8 | 6 | 6 | | 1182 | 42 |

■ Champaign Co. – David A. Owen – David A. Owen – 1988

| 176 3/8 | 27 4/8 | 29 3/8 | 21 3/8 | 23 5/8 | 5 2/8 | 5 1/8 | 5 | 6 | 2 | 1182 | 42 |

■ Marion Co. – David B. Lafferty – David B. Lafferty – 1994

| 176 2/8 | 30 | 28 2/8 | 23 | 26 6/8 | 6 1/8 | 6 1/8 | 7 | 6 | 8 2/8 | 1209 | 45 |

■ Coshocton Co. – James R. Gardner – James R. Gardner – 1976

| 176 | 30 | 29 5/8 | 20 7/8 | 24 2/8 | 5 | 5 1/8 | 4 | 6 | 1 1/8 | 1266 | 46 |

■ Butler Co. – Chris Allen – Chris Allen – 1994

| 176 | 27 2/8 | 28 5/8 | 19 | 21 3/8 | 5 6/8 | 5 3/8 | 7 | 6 | 4 6/8 | 1266 | 46 |

■ Butler Co. – Rick Sizemore – Rick Sizemore – 1995

| 175 7/8 | 25 6/8 | 25 5/8 | 21 2/8 | 23 3/8 | 6 | 5 6/8 | 6 | 6 | 3 3/8 | 1287 | 48 |

■ Hardin Co. – Royal R. Chisholm – Royal R. Chisholm – 1988

| 175 7/8 | 26 1/8 | 26 4/8 | 19 5/8 | 21 6/8 | 5 2/8 | 5 3/8 | 5 | 5 | | 1287 | 48 |

■ Huron Co. – Donald W. Howard – Donald W. Howard – 1992

| 175 6/8 | 29 2/8 | 28 6/8 | 21 3/8 | 23 6/8 | 4 6/8 | 5 1/8 | 6 | 5 | 3 1/8 | 1310† | 50† |

■ Brown Co. – Robert W. Young – Mrs. Robert W. Young – 1991

| 175 5/8 | 28 | 28 2/8 | 21 4/8 | 26 | 5 1/8 | 5 | 9 | 6 | 9 5/8 | 1333 | 51 |

■ Morgan Co. – John E. Hite – John E. Hite – 1991

| 175 4/8 | 27 1/8 | 26 3/8 | 19 3/8 | 23 4/8 | 4 6/8 | 4 6/8 | 7 | 6 | 7 1/8 | 1352 | 52 |

■ Preble Co. – Jerry W. Jones – Jerry W. Jones – 2000

| 175 3/8 | 25 2/8 | 25 4/8 | 20 1/8 | 22 6/8 | 5 2/8 | 5 2/8 | 5 | 5 | | 1377 | 53 |

■ Gallia Co. – Jack Auxier – Jack Auxier – 1969

| 175 3/8 | 24 | 22 2/8 | 19 4/8 | 21 2/8 | 4 7/8 | 4 7/8 | 6 | 8 | 1 5/8 | 1377 | 53 |

■ Monroe Co. – David Mancano – David Mancano – 1976

| 175 2/8 | 26 | 28 3/8 | 21 3/8 | 23 4/8 | 5 | 5 | 7 | 5 | 2 3/8 | 1403† | 55† |

■ Logan Co. – Larry E. Pooler – Larry E. Pooler – 2000

| 175 2/8 | 30 1/8 | 30 4/8 | 22 5/8 | 25 5/8 | 4 7/8 | 5 1/8 | 5 | 6 | 2 3/8 | 1403 | 55 |

■ Hardin Co. – Tracey H. Seiler – Tracey H. Seiler – 1999

| 175 1/8 | 29 | 27 7/8 | 19 1/8 | 22 | 5 | 5 | 5 | 5 | | 1440 | 57 |

■ Hardin Co. – Donald O. Braun – Donald O. Braun – 1997

| 175 1/8 | 26 2/8 | 28 4/8 | 23 6/8 | 25 5/8 | 5 1/8 | 5 | 6 | 6 | 1 1 7/8 | 1440 | 57 |

■ Huron Co. – Keith B. Keysor – Keith B. Keysor – 1999

| 175 | 25 3/8 | 24 3/8 | 17 5/8 | 20 1/8 | 5 4/8 | 5 7/8 | 7 | 7 | 8 3/8 | 1472 | 59 |

■ Hardin Co. – Roger E. Titus – Roger E. Titus – 1988

| 174 6/8 | 28 7/8 | 26 3/8 | 20 3/8 | 22 2/8 | 4 6/8 | 4 7/8 | 6 | 7 | 8 1/8 | 1534 | 60 |

■ Medina Co. – Charles M. Hummel – Charles M. Hummel – 1996

| 174 5/8 | 28 2/8 | 28 1/8 | 19 1/8 | 22 2/8 | 5 4/8 | 5 3/8 | 5 | 5 | | 1561 | 61 |

■ Delaware Co. – Robert J. Miller – Robert J. Miller – 1990

Score	Length of Main Beam Right	Left	Inside Spread	Greatest Spread	Circumference at Smallest Place Between Burr and First Point Right	Left	Number of Points Right	Left	Lengths Abnormal Points	All-Time Rank	State Rank
174⁵/₈	27⁵/₈	27⁵/₈	20¹/₈	22³/₈	4⁴/₈	4⁴/₈	5	5		1561	61

■ *Jefferson Co. – Walter R. Sutton – Walter R. Sutton – 1991*

| 174³/₈ | 26 | 26⁶/₈ | 21⁷/₈ | 24 | 5⁴/₈ | 5⁴/₈ | 5 | 5 | | 1619 | 63 |

■ *Hardin Co. – Ron Hamilton – Ron Hamilton – 1989*

| 174²/₈ | 27⁵/₈ | 27⁴/₈ | 20³/₈ | 23³/₈ | 5²/₈ | 5²/₈ | 5 | 6 | 1³/₈ | 1652 | 64 |

■ *Highland Co. – Jeffrey A. Cooper – Jeffrey A. Cooper – 1996*

| 174¹/₈ | 26 | 25⁶/₈ | 22⁷/₈ | 25³/₈ | 5¹/₈ | 5 | 6 | 8 | 2⁶/₈ | 1678† | 65† |

■ *Summit Co. – Robert E. Faber – Robert E. Faber – 2000*

| 174¹/₈ | 27 | 26¹/₈ | 20⁷/₈ | 22¹/₈ | 6⁴/₈ | 6⁷/₈ | 6 | 7 | | 1678 | 65 |

■ *Tuscarawas Co. – Dennis J. May, Jr. – Dennis J. May, Jr. – 1985*

| 174¹/₈ | 25⁵/₈ | 25⁶/₈ | 20⁷/₈ | 23 | 4²/₈ | 4²/₈ | 6 | 6 | | 1678 | 65 |

■ *Seneca Co. – Patrick J. Gillig – Patrick J. Gillig – 1990*

| 173⁵/₈ | 26⁶/₈ | 26²/₈ | 17⁴/₈ | 18⁶/₈ | 5 | 4⁶/₈ | 7 | 5 | 2¹/₈ | 1819 | 68 |

■ *Morgan Co. – Daniel Clemens – Daniel Clemens – 1997*

| 173⁴/₈ | 25³/₈ | 25²/₈ | 20 | 22⁴/₈ | 4¹/₈ | 4⁵/₈ | 5 | 5 | | 1847 | 69 |

■ *Seneca Co. – Peter Lammers – Peter Lammers – 1993*

| 173³/₈ | 30⁴/₈ | 30⁶/₈ | 21⁴/₈ | 23⁶/₈ | 4⁷/₈ | 4⁶/₈ | 6 | 6 | 8³/₈ | 1883 | 70 |

■ *Miami Co. – Mike Newman – Mike Newman – 1996*

| 173³/₈ | 25⁷/₈ | 27²/₈ | 20³/₈ | 22⁶/₈ | 5 | 4⁷/₈ | 7 | 6 | 2 | 1883 | 70 |

■ *Noble Co. – David W. Heeter – David W. Heeter – 1998*

| 173²/₈ | 28³/₈ | 27³/₈ | 21²/₈ | 23⁴/₈ | 5³/₈ | 5²/₈ | 5 | 5 | 4²/₈ | 1914† | 72† |

■ *Pike Co. – Kathleen E. Kellough – Kathleen E. Kellough – 1999*

| 173²/₈ | 25⁷/₈ | 25⁵/₈ | 18 | 12¹/₈ | 4⁵/₈ | 4⁶/₈ | 5 | 5 | | 1914 | 72 |

■ *Delaware Co. – John W. Hill, Jr. – John W. Hill, Jr. – 1996*

| 173²/₈ | 26⁵/₈ | 26⁵/₈ | 24⁶/₈ | 26⁴/₈ | 4¹/₈ | 4³/₈ | 5 | 5 | | 1914 | 72 |

■ *Pickaway Co. – Timothy S. Ritchie – Timothy S. Ritchie – 1997*

| 173²/₈ | 26²/₈ | 26⁶/₈ | 22 | 24²/₈ | 5 | 5 | 7 | 7 | 7⁴/₈ | 1914 | 72 |

■ *Preble Co. – Gary H. Vest – Gary H. Vest – 1999*

| 173¹/₈ | 26²/₈ | 26⁶/₈ | 20⁵/₈ | 23²/₈ | 4²/₈ | 4³/₈ | 5 | 5 | | 1950 | 76 |

■ *Adams Co. – Mark N. Barnes – Mark N. Barnes – 1986*

| 173¹/₈ | 24⁴/₈ | 25⁶/₈ | 20³/₈ | 22²/₈ | 4⁷/₈ | 4⁷/₈ | 5 | 5 | | 1950 | 76 |

■ *Crawford Co. – Roger C. Rothhaar – Roger C. Rothhaar – 1992*

| 173¹/₈ | 30 | 30⁵/₈ | 23 | 25³/₈ | 5²/₈ | 5¹/₈ | 7 | 7 | 9¹/₈ | 1950 | 76 |

■ *Brown Co. – Michael P. Nunnelley – Michael P. Nunnelley – 1995*

| 173¹/₈ | 25 | 25³/₈ | 19¹/₈ | 21¹/₈ | 4⁷/₈ | 5 | 5 | 5 | | 1950 | 76 |

■ *Clermont Co. – Alton L. Cornett – Alton L. Cornett – 2000*

| 173 | 28 | 28⁷/₈ | 20⁴/₈ | 22⁶/₈ | 4⁶/₈ | 4⁵/₈ | 5 | 5 | | 1991 | 80 |

■ *Sandusky Co. – Harold M. Chalfin – Harold M. Chalfin – 1975*

| 173 | 28¹/₈ | 29⁴/₈ | 24⁴/₈ | 26⁶/₈ | 4⁶/₈ | 4⁶/₈ | 5 | 6 | | 1991 | 80 |

■ *Jefferson Co. – Adam Firm – Adam Firm – 1987*

| 173 | 25¹/₈ | 24⁷/₈ | 18⁶/₈ | 20⁷/₈ | 5¹/₈ | 4⁷/₈ | 6 | 5 | 4²/₈ | 1991 | 80 |

■ *Fairfield Co. – James Carmichael – James Carmichael – 1988*

Score	Length of Main Beam Right	Left	Inside Spread	Greatest Spread	Circumference at Smallest Place Between Burr and First Point Right	Left	Number of Points Right	Left	Lengths Abnormal Points	All-Time Rank	State Rank

Location of Kill – Hunter – Owner – Date Killed

Score	R	L	Inside	Greatest	Circ R	Circ L	Pts R	Pts L	Abn	All-Time	State
173	27⁷/₈	28²/₈	19⁶/₈	22³/₈	4⁶/₈	4⁶/₈	7	5	3⁶/₈	1991	80
172⁷/₈	27	27	21⁷/₈	24	4⁷/₈	4⁷/₈	7	7	3	2038	84
172⁶/₈	26²/₈	27⁷/₈	18⁴/₈	21¹/₈	4³/₈	4²/₈	4	5		2065	85
172⁵/₈	24¹/₈	23	18¹/₈	20²/₈	4³/₈	4³/₈	5	6		2113	86
172⁵/₈	26³/₈	26⁴/₈	21³/₈	23⁴/₈	4⁷/₈	4⁷/₈	5	7	4²/₈	2113	86
172⁵/₈	25⁶/₈	25⁶/₈	20⁷/₈	23⁵/₈	5	4⁷/₈	5	5		2113	86
172⁴/₈	26⁴/₈	26²/₈	21⁷/₈	24⁵/₈	5²/₈	5²/₈	6	6	9¹/₈	2156	89
172²/₈	27²/₈	26	20	22⁵/₈	5³/₈	5³/₈	5	5		2237	90
172²/₈	26¹/₈	25	20	22¹/₈	5	5	6	6	3	2237	90
172¹/₈	28⁵/₈	28³/₈	19²/₈	21⁶/₈	4⁶/₈	5	6	7	5⁷/₈	2286	92
172	26³/₈	28¹/₈	27⁴/₈	29²/₈	4⁷/₈	5¹/₈	6	7	4⁴/₈	2330†	93†
172	25⁵/₈	24⁵/₈	25⁶/₈	27⁶/₈	5¹/₈	5⁴/₈	5	6	1¹/₈	2330	93
172	26	25⁶/₈	22³/₈	24	4⁴/₈	4³/₈	6	7	1⁵/₈	2330	93
171⁷/₈	25³/₈	25¹/₈	20⁵/₈	22³/₈	4⁶/₈	4⁵/₈	6	5		2382†	96†
171⁷/₈	25	24⁴/₈	20	22	5	5	5	6	1³/₈	2382	96
171⁶/₈	25⁷/₈	24⁷/₈	20¹/₈	24	5⁶/₈	6³/₈	6	10	10¹/₈	2418†	98†
171⁶/₈	27³/₈	28	21⁷/₈	23²/₈	5⁷/₈	6²/₈	5	4	2³/₈	2418	98
171⁵/₈	25⁶/₈	24⁶/₈	21⁶/₈	23⁷/₈	4⁶/₈	4⁶/₈	7	5	2³/₈	2470	100
171⁴/₈	27²/₈	26⁶/₈	19	21³/₈	5	5	9	7	9	2513†	101†
171⁴/₈	26⁶/₈	25²/₈	19⁶/₈	21⁶/₈	4⁶/₈	4⁶/₈	5	5		2513	101
171³/₈	29²/₈	27⁴/₈	21²/₈	23²/₈	4⁶/₈	4⁷/₈	6	5	2³/₈	2564	103

- Preble Co. – Jeffery T. Haeseker – Jeffery T. Haeseker – 1999
- Huron Co. – James A. McMorrow – James A. McMorrow – 1994
- Pike Co. – James W. Howard – James W. Howard – 1990
- Tuscarawas Co. – Charles Kerns – Charles Kerns – 1972
- Highland Co. – Wilbur D. Rhoads – Wilbur D. Rhoads – 1979
- Holmes Co. – Sam Anderson – Sam Anderson – 1994
- Muskingum Co. – Michael Wilson – Michael Wilson – 1982
- Miami Co. – Donald J. Boehmer, Jr. – Donald J. Boehmer, Jr. – 1992
- Knox Co. – David K. Palmer – David K. Palmer – 1998
- Coshocton Co. – Virgil E. Carpenter – Virgil E. Carpenter – 1972
- Crawford Co. – William E. Crall – William E. Crall – 2000
- Perry Co. – William J. Pargeon – William J. Pargeon – 1976
- Muskingum Co. – David R. Hatfield – David R. Hatfield – 1980
- Meigs Co. – Raymond G. Golden – Raymond G. Golden – 1997
- Washington Co. – Thomas E. Burnette – Thomas E. Burnette – 1982
- Adams Co. – Larry D. Napier – Larry D. Napier – 2000 ■ See photo on page 51
- Hamilton Co. – Donald R. Johnson – Donald R. Johnson – 1997
- Mercer Co. – Daniel J. Garman – Daniel J. Garman – 1988
- Pike Co. – Terry L. Waits – Terry L. Waits – 2001
- Licking Co. – Michael E. Fleitz – Michael E. Fleitz – 1988
- Clark Co. – David A. Arrington – David A. Arrington – 1994

Score	Length of Main Beam Right	Left	Inside Spread	Greatest Spread	Circumference at Smallest Place Between Burr and First Point Right	Left	Number of Points Right	Left	Lengths Abnormal Points	All-Time Rank	State Rank
$171^3/_8$	$24^6/_8$	$26^2/_8$	$25^5/_8$	$27^3/_8$	$5^4/_8$	$5^2/_8$	5	5		2564	103

■ *Wayne Co. – Ivan R. Schlabach – Ivan R. Schlabach – 1997*

$171^2/_8$	$27^1/_8$	$28^7/_8$	22	$24^3/_8$	$5^1/_8$	$5^5/_8$	7	7	4	2621†	105†

■ *Madison Co. – Bartly D. Howerton – Bartly D. Howerton – 2000*

$171^2/_8$	$27^1/_8$	$27^3/_8$	$20^2/_8$	$25^1/_8$	$5^4/_8$	$5^2/_8$	6	5	$3^6/_8$	2621	105

■ *Coshocton Co. – Michael H. Wills – Michael H. Wills – 1996*

$171^2/_8$	$24^6/_8$	$25^4/_8$	18	$20^7/_8$	$4^3/_8$	$4^3/_8$	5	5		2621	105

■ *Ashtabula Co. – Gene E. Clemens – Gene E. Clemens – 1999*

$171^1/_8$	$25^3/_8$	$25^2/_8$	$20^1/_8$	23	$5^2/_8$	$5^3/_8$	5	5		2665	108

■ *Clark Co. – Lafayette Boggs III – Lafayette Boggs III – 1991*

171	$28^2/_8$	$28^7/_8$	$22^4/_8$	$24^4/_8$	$4^6/_8$	$4^7/_8$	6	4	1	2707	109

■ *Clark Co. – Louis J. Graham – Louis J. Graham – 1999*

$170^7/_8$	$26^7/_8$	$27^1/_8$	$21^2/_8$	$25^3/_8$	$5^2/_8$	$5^2/_8$	7	7	$11^7/_8$	2769	110

■ *Holmes Co. – Ken Taylor – Ken Taylor – 1975*

$170^7/_8$	26	26	$17^3/_8$	$19^6/_8$	$5^2/_8$	5	6	6	$2^4/_8$	2769	110

■ *Vinton Co. – Mark Nusbaum – Mark Nusbaum – 1994*

$170^7/_8$	$27^3/_8$	$27^6/_8$	$19^5/_8$	22	$4^4/_8$	$4^3/_8$	6	7		2769	110

■ *Montgomery Co. – Lee H. White – Lee H. White – 1995*

$170^6/_8$	26	$26^1/_8$	$19^2/_8$	$21^6/_8$	$4^7/_8$	5	5	5		2828	113

■ *Seneca Co. – Cheyenne Bloom – Cheyenne Bloom – 1980*

$170^6/_8$	$25^1/_8$	$25^1/_8$	20	22	$4^7/_8$	$4^7/_8$	5	5		2828	113

■ *Richland Co. – Curt McBride – Curt McBride – 1991*

$170^5/_8$	$26^1/_8$	$26^2/_8$	$21^2/_8$	$21^2/_8$	$4^4/_8$	$4^4/_8$	8	7	$6^7/_8$	2876†	115†

■ *Pike Co. – Jesse H. Brubacher – Jesse H. Brubacher – 2000*

$170^5/_8$	$27^7/_8$	$26^4/_8$	$19^3/_8$	$21^1/_8$	5	$5^5/_8$	5	5		2876	115

■ *Highland Co. – Harold D. Jewett – Harold D. Jewett – 1998*

$170^4/_8$	$26^3/_8$	$23^1/_8$	$20^6/_8$	$23^2/_8$	$4^6/_8$	$4^5/_8$	5	6	3	2933	117

■ *Muskingum Co. – Kevin A. Berton – Kevin A. Berton – 1992*

$170^3/_8$	$29^4/_8$	$28^7/_8$	$17^7/_8$	$20^6/_8$	$4^2/_8$	$4^4/_8$	8	8	$6^2/_8$	2992	118

■ *Muskingum Co. – John H. O'Flaherty – John H. O'Flaherty – 1976*

$170^3/_8$	$25^3/_8$	$27^6/_8$	$23^5/_8$	$25^4/_8$	$5^4/_8$	$5^4/_8$	5	5		2992	118

■ *Shelby Co. – Buck Siler – Buck Siler – 1994*

$170^3/_8$	$28^4/_8$	$27^1/_8$	$23^2/_8$	$25^2/_8$	$5^6/_8$	$5^6/_8$	5	8	$3^1/_8$	2992	118

■ *Carroll Co. – Myron L. Miller – Myron L. Miller – 1995*

$170^2/_8$	$27^4/_8$	$27^5/_8$	$19^7/_8$	$22^2/_8$	$4^6/_8$	$4^4/_8$	7	6	$2^7/_8$	3063	121

■ *Jefferson Co. – James S. Pratt – James S. Pratt – 1976*

$170^2/_8$	$24^4/_8$	$24^6/_8$	$19^2/_8$	$21^3/_8$	$4^1/_8$	$4^1/_8$	5	5		3063	121

■ *Jackson Co. – Roger K. Saltsman – Roger K. Saltsman – 1989*

$170^2/_8$	$28^4/_8$	26	$20^2/_8$	$22^4/_8$	$4^7/_8$	$4^7/_8$	5	7	$4^4/_8$	3063	121

■ *Adams Co. – R. Scott Boschert – R. Scott Boschert – 1990*

$170^2/_8$	$27^6/_8$	$26^2/_8$	$19^3/_8$	22	$5^6/_8$	6	7	6	$8^1/_8$	3063	121

■ *Knox Co. – Ralph D. Wiley – Ralph D. Wiley – 1990*

Score	Length of Main Beam Right / Left	Inside Spread	Greatest Spread	Circumference at Smallest Place Between Burr and First Point Right / Left	Number of Points Right / Left	Lengths Abnormal Points	All-Time Rank	State Rank
170¹/₈	27⁶/₈ 24⁷/₈	20⁷/₈	23²/₈	4⁷/₈ 4⁷/₈	6 6		3143	125
■ Jackson Co. – Theodore R. Yates – Theodore R. Yates – 1967								
170¹/₈	25⁴/₈ 24³/₈	19⁵/₈	21³/₈	4¹/₈ 4⁵/₈	6 6		3143	125
■ Ashland Co. – Steven J. Orchard – Steven J. Orchard – 1996								
170	26 24⁵/₈	20	21⁷/₈	5 5	5 6		3224†	127†
■ Logan Co. – Randy D. Longshore – Randy D. Longshore – 2001								
170	29 27¹/₈	21⁴/₈	26	4⁷/₈ 4⁷/₈	5 5		3224†	127†
■ Erie Co. – John A. Smith – John A. Smith – 2001								
170	24¹/₈ 25⁴/₈	18	19⁷/₈	4³/₈ 4³/₈	6 5	1⁶/₈	3224	127
■ Washington Co. – Robert L. Clark, Jr. – Robert L. Clark, Jr. – 1996								
169³/₈	26²/₈ 25⁴/₈	19¹/₈	20⁶/₈	4⁵/₈ 5¹/₈	6 5		3324	130
■ Summit Co. – Bill J. Wright – Bill J. Wright – 1996								
169	28⁶/₈ 29³/₈	20¹/₈	23¹/₈	4⁶/₈ 4⁷/₈	5 6	3¹/₈	3348	131
■ Muskingum Co. – Walter C. Gibson, Jr. – Walter C. Gibson, Jr. – 1995								
168⁵/₈	24⁷/₈ 25⁴/₈	21⁶/₈	23⁷/₈	5³/₈ 5¹/₈	6 7	3³/₈	3376	132
■ Delaware Co. – Steve Downey – Steve Downey – 1994								
168²/₈	26⁷/₈ 26	19	21⁵/₈	5⁴/₈ 5⁵/₈	4 4		3414	133
■ Licking Co. – David J. Alexander – David J. Alexander – 1984								
168¹/₈	26²/₈ 25	19¹/₈	22²/₈	5 5	5 6	3	3426†	134†
■ Muskingum Co. – Chad Fracker – Chad Fracker – 2001								
168¹/₈	24⁵/₈ 23²/₈	24⁴/₈	28²/₈	4⁶/₈ 5	6 6	3¹/₈	3426	134
■ Medina Co. – John P. Kruggel – John P. Kruggel – 1994								
168¹/₈	24⁵/₈ 25¹/₈	17⁷/₈	20⁶/₈	4⁴/₈ 4⁵/₈	6 6		3426	134
■ Monroe Co. – Dan Rush – Dan Rush – 1997								
167⁶/₈	27⁶/₈ 28³/₈	23²/₈	24⁶/₈	5⁶/₈ 5⁷/₈	6 6	5	3461	137
■ Clermont Co. – James W. Neubacher – James W. Neubacher – 1996								
167⁵/₈	25 24⁷/₈	20¹/₈	22²/₈	4⁴/₈ 4⁴/₈	5 6	1	3476	138
■ Preble Co. – Robert D. Ballinger – Robert D. Ballinger – 1999								
167⁴/₈	28 27¹/₈	19	21¹/₈	5 4⁷/₈	5 5		3485†	139†
■ Coshocton Co. – John Mucu – John Mucu – 2000								
167²/₈	25⁴/₈ 25²/₈	17⁴/₈	20	4⁶/₈ 4⁶/₈	6 5	1²/₈	3519	140
■ Belmont Co. – Richard M. Nicholson – Richard M. Nicholson – 1993								
167¹/₈	26¹/₈ 26⁷/₈	23⁷/₈	26¹/₈	5²/₈ 5	6 6	2²/₈	3539	141
■ Clermont Co. – Johnie R. Wardrup – Johnie R. Wardrup – 1999								
166⁶/₈	28⁶/₈ 28⁵/₈	20⁶/₈	23³/₈	5¹/₈ 5³/₈	5 5		3582	142
■ Gallia Co. – Rodger Kern – Rodger Kern – 1982								
166⁴/₈	27²/₈ 26¹/₈	20⁴/₈	22³/₈	4⁶/₈ 4⁴/₈	5 5		3609†	143†
■ Portage Co. – Daniel S. Behm – Daniel S. Behm – 2000								
166³/₈	26⁵/₈ 29⁵/₈	21⁴/₈	26³/₈	5⁷/₈ 6	6 7	1⁵/₈	3620	144
■ Adams Co. – Mitchell Baker – Mitchell Baker – 1997								
166¹/₈	24⁴/₈ 24⁴/₈	17³/₈	19⁴/₈	4⁶/₈ 4⁶/₈	6 6	1⁴/₈	3643†	145†
■ Paulding Co. – Timothy G. Copsey – Timothy G. Copsey – 2000								

Score	Length of Main Beam Right Left	Inside Spread	Greatest Spread	Circumference at Smallest Place Between Burr and First Point Right Left	Number of Points Right Left	Lengths Abnormal Points	All-Time Rank	State Rank
	■ Location of Kill – Hunter – Owner – Date Killed							
166	26¹/8 24⁶/8	18⁴/8	20⁴/8	5 5¹/8	5 6	1⁴/8	3657	146
	■ Coshocton Co. – William R. Warther – William R. Warther – 1999							
165⁵/8	26⁵/8 27³/8	18⁷/8	21¹/8	4⁴/8 4³/8	6 5		3696	147
	■ Richland Co. – Erwin Merkli – Erwin Merkli – 1988							
165⁵/8	27⁴/8 27⁴/8	19³/8	22	5⁴/8 5⁴/8	4 4		3696	147
	■ Lawrence Co. – Melvin A. Baumgardner – Melvin A. Baumgardner – 1991							
165³/8	25²/8 26⁴/8	20⁶/8	23¹/8	4⁴/8 4³/8	6 6	2¹/8	3731	149
	■ Preble Co. – Robert L. Mason – Robert L. Mason – 1988							
164⁶/8	29⁷/8 26	23	25⁶/8	4⁴/8 5	7 9	5⁴/8	3809	150
	■ Portage Co. – Mark T. Long – Mark T. Long – 1995							
164³/8	24⁴/8 24¹/8	18³/8	20⁷/8	5 4⁷/8	6 6		3864	151
	■ Coshocton Co. – Thomas J. Daniels – Thomas J. Daniels – 1994							
164¹/8	26¹/8 25⁴/8	18⁷/8	21	4⁶/8 4⁷/8	6 5		3886	152
	■ Licking Co. – Richard Allen – Richard Allen – 1989							
164	27 27⁴/8	17⁴/8	19⁷/8	5³/8 5²/8	8 6	11⁴/8	3908†	153†
	■ Clermont Co. – David L. Shouse, Jr. – David L. Shouse, Jr. – 2001							
164	25²/8 25⁷/8	17	21	5¹/8 5²/8	5 5		3908	153
	■ Guernsey Co. – Robert R. Crawford – Robert R. Crawford – 1999							
163⁶/8	24 24³/8	18⁴/8	20⁶/8	5 5²/8	5 5		3946	155
	■ Cuyahoga Co. – Ronald C. Seppeler – Ronald C. Seppeler – 1993							
163⁵/8	25 25	16⁵/8	18⁴/8	4⁶/8 4⁴/8	6 9	5⁶/8	3961	156
	■ Tuscarawas Co. – Gordon C. Bohon – Gordon C. Bohon – 1995							
163²/8	27³/8 28²/8	20⁶/8	24⁶/8	5 5²/8	7 7	7⁶/8	4017	157
	■ Geauga Co. – Bruce A. Powell – Bruce A. Powell – 1997							
162⁷/8	23¹/8 24²/8	16⁵/8	19²/8	4¹/8 4¹/8	5 5		4067	158
	■ Cuyahoga Co. – Brett A. Hahner – Brett A. Hahner – 1994							
162⁵/8	28 26⁷/8	18⁶/8	21⁵/8	4²/8 4²/8	7 8	8⁷/8	4109†	159†
	■ Cuyahoga Co. – Jeffery C. Perry – Jeffery C. Perry – 2000							
162²/8	30 28⁷/8	23⁵/8	25⁴/8	4³/8 4⁶/8	5 7	5⁵/8	4153	160
	■ Geauga Co. – Anthony J. Misseri – Anthony J. Misseri – 1997							
161⁷/8	27⁵/8 27⁷/8	16⁵/8	18⁷/8	4¹/8 4²/8	6 6		4212†	161†
	■ Belmont Co. – Sampson Michael III – Sampson Michael III – 2000							
161⁵/8	24¹/8 23⁵/8	19²/8	21	4³/8 4⁴/8	7 6	4³/8	4234†	162†
	■ Butler Co. – Gregory W. Davis – Gregory W. Davis – 2001							
161⁴/8	24⁴/8 25	17²/8	21²/8	4³/8 4⁶/8	5 5		4258†	163†
	■ Athens Co. – Michael V. Schaffer – Michael V. Schaffer – 2000							
161⁴/8	27⁷/8 27³/8	20⁶/8	24¹/8	5 5	6 5	10	4258	163
	■ Vinton Co. – Bradley Houdasheldt – Bradley Houdasheldt – 1990							
161³/8	27⁴/8 27⁶/8	17⁶/8	20¹/8	5⁴/8 5²/8	6 6	2³/8	4285†	165†
	■ Definace Co. – Gerald A. Snyder, Jr. – Gerald A. Snyder, Jr. – 1998							
161³/8	28⁶/8 30⁶/8	20⁵/8	22⁶/8	5 5	4 4		4285	165
	■ Ross Co. – John P. Blesedell III – John P. Blesedell III – 1998							

Score	Length of Main Beam		Inside Spread	Greatest Spread	Circumference at Smallest Place Between Burr and First Point		Number of Points		Lengths Abnormal Points	All-Time Rank	State Rank
	Right	Left			Right	Left	Right	Left			
	■ Location of Kill – Hunter – Owner – Date Killed										
161	24 1/8	23 4/8	18 5/8	22 6/8	5	5	7	6	4 3/8	4356	167
	■ Butler Co. – Fred S. Spurlin – Fred S. Spurlin – 1987										
160 6/8	25 2/8	26 3/8	17	19 3/8	5	4 7/8	6	6	1 2/8	4402	168
	■ Monroe Co. – Greg L. Wise – Greg L. Wise – 1994										
160 6/8	26 1/8	27 2/8	21 4/8	24 1/8	6	6	6	9	11	4402	168
	■ Coshocton Co. – Mario Costanzo – Mario Costanzo – 1995										
160 4/8	24 2/8	25	20 3/8	23 6/8	4 5/8	4 4/8	6	5	1 1/8	4443	170
	■ Athens Co. – T. Jeff Daugherty – T. Jeff Daugherty – 1997										
160 3/8	25	25 5/8	21 7/8	24 1/8	5 1/8	5	5	5		4470†	171†
	■ Geauga Co. – Andrew F. Ule – Andrew F. Ule – 2001										
160 3/8	25 4/8	26	18 7/8	24 4/8	4 4/8	4 6/8	5	7	10 2/8	4470	171
	■ Harrison Co. – Joshua Rinkes – Joshua Rinkes – 1995										
160 3/8	26 2/8	25 5/8	22 7/8	24 6/8	5 2/8	5 2/8	4	4		4470	171
	■ Fayette Co. – Matthew S. Buell – Matthew S. Buell – 1998										
160 1/8	25 6/8	26 3/8	16 5/8	19	4 1/8	4 2/8	6	8	8 6/8	4534	174
	■ Hocking Co. – Jeffery W. Hill – Jeffery W. Hill – 1995										
160	24 4/8	25	15	18	4 5/8	4 6/8	7	7	4 6/8	4565	175
	■ Wyandot Co. – John A. Oleska – John A. Oleska – 1992										
160	27 1/8	27	21 1/8	23 1/8	5	5	6	8	6 7/8	4565	175
	■ Belmont Co. – C. Zack Snider – C. Zack Snider – 1995										
160	25 6/8	24 6/8	21 6/8	24	4 2/8	4 3/8	5	5		4565	175
	■ Geauga Co. – Monte H. Curtis – Monte H. Curtis – 1997										
160	26 3/8	26 3/8	18 2/8	20 4/8	4 7/8	5	7	7	5 6/8	4565	175
	■ Noble Co. – Mark A. Hudak – Mark A. Hudak – 1997										
160	25 1/8	25 2/8	20 2/8	22	5	5 1/8	5	6	3	4565	175
	■ Defiance Co. – Ellis M. Reynolds – Ellis M. Reynolds – 1999										

† The scores and ranking for trophies from the 25th Awards Entry Period are not final until the banquet is held on June 19, 2004.

HUNTER: Robert M. Smith
SCORE: 181-3/8
CATEGORY: typical whitetail deer
LOCATION: Portage County, Ohio
DATE: 1953

OHIO

NON-TYPICAL WHITETAIL DEER

Score	Length of Main Beam Right	Left	Inside Spread	Greatest Spread	Circumference at Smallest Place Between Burr and First Point Right	Left	Number of Points Right	Left	Lengths Abnormal Points	All-Time Rank	State Rank
	■ Location of Kill – Hunter – Owner – Date Killed										
328 2/8	25 5/8	24 4/8	24 3/8	33	6 2/8	5 6/8	23	22	192 7/8	2	1
■ Portage Co. – Picked Up – Bass Pro Shops – 1940											
262 1/8	24 1/8	25 2/8	20	26 3/8	6 2/8	6 4/8	14	13	98 1/8	22	2
■ Ross Co. – Jay Pfankuch – Brad Gsell – 1995											
256 5/8	29 1/8	27 7/8	24 6/8	33 7/8	6 5/8	6 1/8	14	17	69 7/8	38	3
■ Holmes Co. – Picked Up – OH Dept. of Natl. Resc. – 1975											
251 2/8	27 2/8	27 5/8	22 1/8	26 3/8	6 3/8	6 5/8	10	13	59 7/8	53†	4†
■ Lorain Co. – Kirk W. Gott – Kirk W. Gott – 2000											
250 6/8	27 2/8	25 2/8	23 4/8	33	5 4/8	5 2/8	12	12	96	55	5
■ Richland Co. – David D. Dull – David D. Dull – 1987											
243 3/8	27 7/8	29 7/8	17 7/8	26 1/8	4 5/8	4 6/8	11	9	40 4/8	97	6
■ Mahoning Co. – David L. Klemm – Bass Pro Shops – 1980											
238 6/8	22 6/8	22 2/8	18 3/8	30	5 2/8	5	18	15	1	130	7
■ Mahoning Co. – Ronald K. Osborne – Bass Pro Shops – 1986											
236 7/8	24 2/8	26 4/8	18 6/8		5 7/8	5 7/8	13	12	85 5/8	154	8
■ Preble Co. – Bruce A. Turner – Bruce A. Turner – 1994											
235 4/8	29 2/8	27 1/8	22 7/8	38 1/8	5 7/8	5 6/8	11	13	55 7/8	166	9
■ Ashtabula Co. – James L. Clark – Bass Pro Shops – 1957											
233 6/8	30 5/8	30 6/8	21 2/8	28 3/8	5	5	11	13	40 4/8	187	10
■ Morrow Co. – Religh D. Martin – Religh D. Martin – 1995											
231 3/8	29 3/8	27 4/8	23 1/8	28 3/8	4 3/8	4 3/8	9	10	44 6/8	219	11
■ Licking Co. – Norman L. Myers – Norman L. Myers – 1964											
228 6/8	24 3/8	24 5/8	18 1/8	27	6	5 6/8	18	14	73 7/8	257	12
■ Fulton Co. – Bernard Williamson III – Bernard Williamson III – 1989											
226 5/8	29	28 4/8	18 1/8	22	5 3/8	5 2/8	13	13	22	289	13
■ Licking Co. – John S. Blythe – John S. Blythe – 1999											
226 4/8	21 3/8	22 2/8	19 2/8	24	4 6/8	4 5/8	13	11	51 2/8	292	14
■ Muskingum Co. – Rex A. Thompson – Rex A. Thompson – 1981											
226 2/8	26 6/8	25 3/8	24 5/8	26 7/8	6 2/8	6	10	11	40 1/8	298	15
■ Warren Co. – Daniel H. Detrick – Daniel H. Detrick – 1989											
226 1/8	25 5/8	26 3/8	20 3/8	24 6/8	4 7/8	4 7/8	10	10	33 2/8	301	16
■ Trumbull Co. – Paul E. Lehman – Paul E. Lehman – 1948											
225 4/8	23 7/8	26 5/8	19 4/8	24 4/8	6 5/8	7	10	18	48 2/8	309	17
■ Greene Co. – Alan J. Meade – Alan J. Meade – 1999											
225 1/8	27	26 1/8	18 4/8	22 4/8	5 2/8	5 6/8	11	14	42 3/8	314	18
■ Holmes Co. – Chris G. Hider – Chris G. Hider – 1998											
224 6/8	28 2/8	28 2/8	20 4/8	25	5 5/8	5 7/8	9	9	37 2/8	322	19
■ Ross Co. – Richard F. Barnett – Richard F. Barnett – 1995											

Score	Length of Main Beam		Inside Spread	Greatest Spread	Circumference at Smallest Place Between Burr and First Point		Number of Points		Lengths Abnormal Points	All-Time Rank	State Rank
	Right	Left			Right	Left	Right	Left			
	■ *Location of Kill – Hunter – Owner – Date Killed*										
222 4/8	26	26 1/8	18 5/8	21 4/8	6 3/8	5 5/8	11	11	51 1/8	378†	20†
■ *Clinton Co. – Jonathan K. Hale – Jonathan K. Hale – 2001*											
222 3/8	28 1/8	27	18 4/8	21 7/8	6 6/8	6 3/8	12	11	29 7/8	384	21
■ *Pickaway Co. – C. Joseph Schneider – C. Joseph Schneider – 1998*											
220 7/8	26 1/8	27 1/8	19 4/8	26 4/8	5 2/8	5 3/8	11	8	54 7/8	417	22
■ *Ross Co. – Tommy E. Dailey – Tommy E. Dailey – 1993*											
220 4/8	29 2/8	29 2/8	20 2/8	22 5/8	5 1/8	5 6/8	8	8	30	427	23
■ *Knox Co. – Richard E. Boyd – Richard E. Boyd – 1995*											
212 5/8	27 2/8	27 4/8	20 3/8	22 6/8	5	4 4/8	12	8	37 6/8	683†	24†
■ *Licking Co. – J. Chris Lepley – J. Chris Lepley – 2001*											
211 5/8	26 3/8	23 3/8	20 2/8	22 6/8	5 1/8	6 1/8	9	12	52 5/8	734	25
■ *Adams Co. – William J. DeCamp – William J. DeCamp – 1987*											
211	29	29 6/8	22	26 4/8	5 6/8	5 6/8	7	8	22 2/8	764	26
■ *Gallia Co. – Robert D. Wallis – Robert D. Wallis – 1992*											
210 2/8	26 4/8	25 2/8	21 4/8	24	5 3/8	5 3/8	8	9	38 4/8	803	27
■ *Columbiana Co. – Harold L. Hawkins – Harold L. Hawkins – 1981*											
209	23 3/8	22 2/8	17 3/8	22 7/8	5 6/8	6 2/8	9	14	46 3/8	872†	28†
■ *Highland Co. – Eddie Hunter, Sr. – Eddie Hunter, Sr. – 2000*											
208 2/8	25 7/8	22 4/8	17 3/8	23	6 1/8	6	10	13	55 5/8	910	29
■ *Washington Co. – Robert R. Zimmerman – Robert R. Zimmerman – 1995*											
207	26 4/8	27 1/8	25	27 4/8	5 4/8	5 2/8	10	8	18 2/8	1005	30
■ *Stark Co. – Tad E. Crawford – Tad E. Crawford – 1987*											
206 7/8	26 3/8	25	17 2/8	23	5 6/8	5 7/8	11	8	43 1/8	1011	31
■ *Hamilton Co. – Mickey E. Lotz – Mickey E. Lotz – 1995*											
206 3/8	29 6/8	28 5/8	22 2/8	27 5/8	5 4/8	5 5/8	12	10	25 3/8	1051	32
■ *Adams Co. – James M. Wilson – James M. Wilson – 1989*											
206 1/8	23 5/8	23	21	26 3/8	5 2/8	5 1/8	7	9	47 1/8	1068	33
■ *Union Co. – Henry W. Leistritz – Henry W. Leistritz – 1989*											
204 4/8	30	28 6/8	21 1/8	26 3/8	4 7/8	5 2/8	10	12	41 3/8	1182	34
■ *Jackson Co. – Bernard Tennant – Bernard Tennant – 1960*											
204 2/8	29 1/8	27 7/8	23 3/8	27 2/8	6 2/8	6	4	4	25 1/8	1199	35
■ *Ashland Co. – Keith A. Beringo – Keith A. Beringo – 1991*											
203 7/8	24 4/8	25 5/8	22 6/8	26 6/8	4 7/8	5 1/8	6	9	21 1/8	1231	36
■ *Portage Co. – Lee C. Morris – Lee C. Morris – 1994*											
203 5/8	23	30 6/8	15	26 1/8	6 6/8	6 6/8	8	14	70 5/8	1248	37
■ *Meigs Co. – Wesley Gilkey – Wesley Gilkey – 1970*											
203 3/8	29 3/8	28 4/8	21 3/8	23 5/8	6 3/8	6 3/8	10	7	32 4/8	1272	38
■ *Gallia Co. – Hoyle S. Foy, Sr. – Hoyle S. Foy, Sr. – 1998*											
203 2/8	24	23 2/8	19 6/8	22 6/8	6 1/8	7 6/8	7	14	32 2/8	1287	39
■ *Ross Co. – Scott Zurmehly – Scott Zurmehly – 1987*											
202 6/8	24 6/8	22	20	25	5 4/8	5 1/8	10	8	41 2/8	1339	40
■ *Hamilton Co. – Vernon Smith – Vernon Smith – 1993*											

Score	Length of Main Beam Right	Left	Inside Spread	Greatest Spread	Circumference at Smallest Place Between Burr and First Point Right	Left	Number of Points Right	Left	Lengths Abnormal Points	All-Time Rank	State Rank
202³/8	25⁷/8	24⁶/8	22⁷/8	25	5⁶/8	6	9	13	44²/8	1362	41
■ Delaware Co. – Duane E. Robinson – Duane E. Robinson – 1980											
201³/8	30⁴/8	29²/8	21⁶/8	24⁵/8	5³/8	5⁷/8	10	7	37³/8	1461	42
■ Greene Co. – Richard D. Steen – Richard D. Steen – 1996											
201²/8	28³/8	28⁵/8	23¹/8	25²/8	4⁶/8	4⁷/8	11	10	28⁷/8	1478	43
■ Coshocton Co. – Lou L. Rogers – Lou L. Rogers – 1979											
201²/8	23⁶/8	25⁷/8	21⁴/8	24⁴/8	5⁴/8	5³/8	12	5	31⁶/8	1478	43
■ Lorain Co. – D. Cody Kelch – D. Cody Kelch – 1999											
201	22⁶/8	27⁴/8	20⁵/8	25	5³/8	5⁶/8	16	13	39³/8	1500	45
■ Delaware Co. – Charles W. Henderson – Charles W. Henderson – 1997											
200⁵/8	28	27⁶/8	22¹/8	28	5³/8	5²/8	8	7	27⁶/8	1532	46
■ Jackson Co. – Glenn McCall – Glenn McCall – 1970											
200⁴/8	24⁵/8	24⁷/8	19⁷/8	24³/8	5⁴/8	5⁴/8	12	10	26⁷/8	1545	47
■ Geauga Co. – Rudy C. Grecar – Rudy C. Grecar – 1969											
200³/8	25⁴/8	27	19¹/8	22	6⁴/8	5⁴/8	10	10	19	1556	48
■ Tuscarawas Co. – Michael D. Korns, Sr. – Michael D. Korns, Sr. – 1978											
200³/8	27	23¹/8	24⁵/8	27⁷/8	5²/8	5	8	7	16⁶/8	1556	48
■ Knox Co. – Albert Hall – Albert Hall – 1983											
200²/8	26²/8	26	19	24¹/8	5	5²/8	13	14	61⁴/8	1569	50
■ Delaware Co. – Franklin D. Ronk – Franklin D. Ronk – 1990											
200²/8	26⁷/8	27⁴/8	20⁴/8	23³/8	5⁵/8	5⁵/8	8	8	21⁶/8	1569	50
■ Wyandot Co. – Anthony Gentile – Anthony Gentile – 1991											
200¹/8	31	30	22²/8	24⁵/8	4⁶/8	4⁵/8	8	9	16⁷/8	1577	52
■ Coshocton Co. – Edward J. Page – Edward J. Page – 1993											
199⁶/8	28⁶/8	29⁶/8	19²/8	22⁵/8	6⁴/8	6	7	8	16⁴/8	1613	53
■ Meigs Co. – Cody R. Boothe – Cody R. Boothe – 1970											
199⁵/8	29¹/8	29³/8	19³/8	21⁶/8	5³/8	5⁶/8	7	9	17⁴/8	1621	54
■ Jackson Co. – Jerry W. Butcher – Jerry W. Butcher – 1992											
198⁵/8	26²/8	26⁶/8	17⁴/8	22⁴/8	5²/8	5⁴/8	9	6	16³/8	1716	55
■ Jackson Co. – Stanley Elam – Stanley Elam – 1962											
198⁴/8	26¹/8	26²/8	22⁵/8	26	6	5⁴/8	8	8	26³/8	1736	56
■ Perry Co. – Donald J. Griggs – Donald J. Griggs – 1988											
198²/8	27²/8	28⁷/8	21³/8	25⁶/8	5⁶/8	5⁷/8	8	9	42¹/8	1772	57
■ Geauga Co. – Greg Raudenbush – Greg Raudenbush – 1997											
198¹/8	27⁶/8	28²/8	22⁴/8	26³/8	4⁶/8	4⁶/8	7	9	12³/8	1785	58
■ Harrison Co. – Roy Hines – Roy Hines – 1959											
198¹/8	27	26³/8	20²/8	28⁶/8	5	5¹/8	10	7	26¹/8	1785	58
■ Hocking Co. – Hugh Cox – Hugh Cox – 1964											
198¹/8	26³/8	28⁶/8	22⁵/8	25¹/8	5⁴/8	5⁶/8	8	10	21²/8	1785	58
■ Lawrence Co. – Eugene Baisden – Eugene Baisden – 1991											
198¹/8	30¹/8	29⁵/8	22⁴/8	25	4⁶/8	4³/8	8	8	22³/8	1785	58
■ Jefferson Co. – William H. Ferguson III – William H. Ferguson III – 1992											

Score	Length of Main Beam		Inside Spread	Greatest Spread	Circumference at Smallest Place Between Burr and First Point		Number of Points		Lengths Abnormal Points	All-Time Rank	State Rank
	Right	Left			Right	Left	Right	Left			
	Location of Kill – Hunter – Owner – Date Killed										
198	26 5/8	26 5/8	19 4/8	24 6/8	5 3/8	5 1/8	12	8	22 4/8	1801†	62†
	■ *Meigs Co. – Jack Satterfield, Jr. – Jack Satterfield, Jr. – 2000*										
198	25 6/8	25 3/8	20 6/8	23 3/8	5 2/8	5 2/8	8	9	15 6/8	1801	62
	■ *Mercer Co. – Werner H. Schmiesing – Werner H. Schmiesing – 1979*										
197 7/8	26 7/8	25 3/8	22	25 3/8	4 1/8	4 5/8	6	14	34 1/8	1816†	64†
	■ *Richland Co. – James C. Carpenter – James C. Carpenter – 2001*										
197 6/8	31 4/8	30 4/8	23	28	5 3/8	5 4/8	11	9	18 2/8	1833	65
	■ *Fairfield Co. – Bob Sink – Bob Sink – 1997*										
197 6/8	27 3/8	28	20 4/8	23 3/8	5 5/8	5 7/8	6	10	22 6/8	1833	65
	■ *Preble Co. – Larry E. Hickman – Larry E. Hickman – 1999*										
197 5/8	31 5/8	32 3/8	25 2/8	28	5 1/8	5 1/8	5	6	15 1/8	1847	67
	■ *Geauga Co. – Edward Dooner – Edward Dooner – 1956*										
197 4/8	25 3/8	26 3/8	22 6/8	25 6/8	5 2/8	5 2/8	11	8	39 2/8	1866	68
	■ *Tuscarawas Co. – Michael W. McKenzie – Michael W. McKenzie – 1995*										
197 3/8	23 7/8	21 7/8	24	26 1/8	5 2/8	6	7	10	25	1884	69
	■ *Gallia Co. – Jimmy W. Brumfield – Jimmy W. Brumfield – 1992*										
196 6/8	25 4/8	27 5/8	20	22 4/8	6	5 6/8	9	6	14 4/8	1968	70
	■ *Licking Co. – Michael E. Evans, Sr. – Michael E. Evans, Sr. – 1994*										
196 4/8	25 6/8	26 4/8	25 3/8	27	4 6/8	4 6/8	9	8	11 3/8	1999	71
	■ *Jackson Co. – Francis L. Ray – Francis L. Ray – 1988*										
196 3/8	28 3/8	25 6/8	21 1/8	23 3/8	6	6	8	7	17 4/8	2010	72
	■ *Belmont Co. – Brian R. Elston – Brian R. Elston – 1999*										
196	27 5/8	26 3/8	19 1/8	22 6/8	6	6 1/8	6	9	28 7/8	2059	73
	■ *Fayette Co. – Sean C. Huff – Sean C. Huff – 1999*										
195 7/8	29 1/8	21 7/8	21 6/8	30	4 7/8	5	8	8	25 3/8	2076	74
	■ *Perry Co. – Pearl R. Wiseman – Pearl R. Wiseman – 1976*										
195 6/8	21 6/8	24 6/8	20 7/8	25 4/8	4 4/8	4 2/8	15	12	61 7/8	2094	75
	■ *Ashland Co. – Michael R. Dull – Michael R. Dull – 1992*										
195 2/8	26 2/8	24 6/8	18 1/8	22	5 7/8	5 4/8	6	9	19 1/8	2186	76
	■ *Warren Co. – Ronald E. Lay – Ronald E. Lay – 1995*										
195 1/8	26 7/8	27 4/8	19 4/8	22 1/8	5	5	8	10	13 5/8	2208	77
	■ *Holmes Co. – Randy Strohminger – Randy Strohminger – 1987*										
195	25 4/8	26 1/8	22	26 4/8	5 6/8	5 6/8	7	11	32 4/8	2233	78
	■ *Darke Co. – Bob Spitler – Bob Spitler – 1995*										
194 1/8	29 1/8	30 1/8	19	21 2/8	5 2/8	5 2/8	9	10	16 7/8	2271†	79†
	■ *Licking Co. – Roger J. Holbrook – Roger J. Holbrook – 2000*										
192 6/8	25 7/8	25 4/8	18 7/8	20 7/8	5	4 7/8	8	12	24 1/8	2317	80
	■ *Clermont Co. – Robin E. Hazenfield – Robin E. Hazenfield – 1995*										
192 1/8	25 7/8	26 7/8	20	22 2/8	4 4/8	4 3/8	9	8	38 7/8	2341†	81†
	■ *Fayette Co. – Scott A. Boyer – Scott A. Boyer – 2000*										
191 4/8	24 5/8	24 1/8	19 4/8	23	5 5/8	5 1/8	15	10	45 4/8	2357	82
	■ *Wayne Co. – Steve Cherry – Steve Cherry – 1994*										

Score	Length of Main Beam		Inside Spread	Greatest Spread	Circumference at Smallest Place Between Burr and First Point		Number of Points		Lengths Abnormal Points	All-Time Rank	State Rank
	Right	Left			Right	Left	Right	Left			
	■ Location of Kill – Hunter – Owner – Date Killed										
187⁷/₈	27²/₈	27	27	29²/₈	5⁴/₈	5³/₈	7	8	14³/₈	2506	83
	■ Highland Co. – Larry M. Black – Larry M. Black – 1995										
187⁵/₈	27²/₈	27³/₈	20³/₈	23⁴/₈	5⁴/₈	5⁶/₈	7	7	17⁴/₈	2518	84
	■ Geauga Co. – Robert W. Green – Robert W. Green – 1994										
187⁴/₈	28¹/₈	31³/₈	23⁶/₈	28⁶/₈	5²/₈	5³/₈	12	9	18⁶/₈	2522	85
	■ Huron Co. – Rodney L. Cook – Rodney L. Cook – 1999										
186⁷/₈	28⁴/₈	27⁵/₈	21⁶/₈	27³/₈	5³/₈	5⁴/₈	5	11	19¹/₈	2550	86
	■ Fairfield Co. – Stephen E. Boyer – Stephen E. Boyer – 1993										
186⁵/₈	23²/₈	22⁵/₈	17⁴/₈	19⁶/₈	4⁶/₈	4⁶/₈	9	8	17¹/₈	2565	87
	■ Ashtabula Co. – Wesley J. Gaul, Sr. – Wesley J. Gaul, Sr. – 1992										
186³/₈	26	26⁴/₈	18²/₈	23²/₈	4	4¹/₈	6	7	16¹/₈	2570	88
	■ Tuscarawas Co. – Andrew T. Shaw – Andrew T. Shaw – 1995										
186¹/₈	24¹/₈	24⁵/₈	21⁴/₈	30⁵/₈	4³/₈	4¹/₈	8	10	45¹/₈	2581	89
	■ Mahoning Co. – Robert A. Schiele – Robert A. Schiele – 1999										
186	24⁷/₈	24⁷/₈	21	23¹/₈	4⁶/₈	4⁶/₈	10	8	38	2586	90
	■ Lorain Co. – Brian Douglas – Brian Douglas – 1994										
185⁵/₈	27⁵/₈	28⁶/₈	18⁶/₈	23²/₈	4⁷/₈	5¹/₈	8	11	17⁵/₈	2610	91
	■ Meigs Co. – George J. Korn – George J. Korn – 1996										

† The scores and ranking for trophies from the 25th Awards Entry Period are not final until the banquet is held on June 19, 2004.

HUNTER: Mrs. Thelma Martens
SCORE: 198-4/8
CATEGORY: non-typical whitetail deer
LOCATION: Cow Creek, Wyoming
DATE: 1951

OKLAHOMA
RECORD WHITETAILS

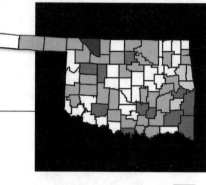

45 Typical whitetail deer entries
55 Non-typical whitetail deer entries
7,265 Total whitetail deer entries

0 Entries
1-2 Entries
3-5 Entries
6-10 Entries
11+ Entries

OKLAHOMA
NEW STATE RECORD
Typical Whitetail Deer
Score: 185$^6/_8$
Location: Bryan Co.
Hunter and Owner: Larry D. Luman
Date: 1997

NEW
STATE
RECORD

OKLAHOMA
STATE RECORD
Non-Typical Whitetail Deer
Score: 247²/₈
Location: Johnston Co.
Hunter and Owner: Bill M. Foster
Date: 1970

Photograph from B&C Archives

OKLAHOMA

TYPICAL WHITETAIL DEER

Score	Length of Main Beam Right	Left	Inside Spread	Greatest Spread	Circumference at Smallest Place Between Burr and First Point Right	Left	Number of Points Right	Left	Lengths Abnormal Points	All-Time Rank	State Rank
185⁶/₈	26³/₈	26²/₈	20⁷/₈	26⁷/₈	5	5²/₈	8	8	5⁷/₈	247	1
▪ Bryan Co. – Larry D. Luman – Larry D. Luman – 1997											
179²/₈	28	27⁷/₈	19⁴/₈	21⁴/₈	5²/₈	5¹/₈	6	6		763	2
▪ Blaine Co. – Matt Parker – Matt Parker – 1999											
177⁷/₈	24³/₈	24	18⁵/₈	20⁷/₈	4⁶/₈	4⁵/₈	5	6	3²/₈	936	3
▪ Harper Co. – Scott Davis – Scott Davis – 1993											
177⁶/₈	26⁶/₈	25⁴/₈	22⁶/₈	25	5	5	5	5		956	4
▪ Atoka Co. – Skip Rowell – Skip Rowell – 1972											
177²/₈	25⁴/₈	25	16⁷/₈	21	5	4⁷/₈	6	6	2¹/₈	1025	5
▪ Pushmataha Co. – Herbert W. Savage – Herbert W. Savage – 1994											
174⁷/₈	26¹/₈	25⁷/₈	19⁵/₈	22⁴/₈	5¹/₈	5²/₈	5	5		1513	6
▪ Woods Co. – Eddie Mustard – Eddie Mustard – 1995											
174⁵/₈	26	25³/₈	22³/₈	24⁵/₈	6⁵/₈	6⁷/₈	8	8	12⁴/₈	1561	7
▪ Beaver Co. – Tanner Alexander – Tanner Alexander – 1990											
173⁵/₈	27⁵/₈	28¹/₈	22⁶/₈	26⁶/₈	5³/₈	5³/₈	4	7	6³/₈	1819	8
▪ Woods Co. – Jack Clover – Jack Clover – 1983											
173⁴/₈	24⁵/₈	25⁵/₈	21⁴/₈	24²/₈	4⁶/₈	4⁶/₈	7	9	6⁴/₈	1847	9
▪ Rogers Co. – Marc Thompson – Marc Thompson – 1991											
173	25⁷/₈	25³/₈	16⁷/₈	18⁷/₈	5	5⁴/₈	6	8	5⁵/₈	1991	10
▪ Adair Co. – Louis C. Mattler – Louis C. Mattler – 1995											
172⁶/₈	26	24¹/₈	22⁷/₈	25²/₈	4⁵/₈	4⁵/₈	6	6	3⁷/₈	2065	11
▪ Seminole Co. – Lester H. Reich – Lester H. Reich – 1994											
171⁶/₈	26⁴/₈	26⁵/₈	19	21⁴/₈	5²/₈	5⁵/₈	5	5		2418	12
▪ Osage Co. – Don Gaddis – Don Gaddis – 1995											
170³/₈	26¹/₈	26⁴/₈	19⁵/₈	24⁵/₈	4⁴/₈	4²/₈	6	7	8⁴/₈	2992	13
▪ Haskell Co. – Loyd Long – Loyd Long – 1985											
169³/₈	26⁷/₈	26⁶/₈	19³/₈	21⁵/₈	5⁴/₈	5³/₈	6	6	2⁶/₈	3324	14
▪ Woods Co. – Paul L. McElveen – Paul L. McElveen – 1995											
168⁶/₈	24¹/₈	24⁶/₈	20⁴/₈	21⁶/₈	5³/₈	5³/₈	5	5		3367	15
▪ Sequoyah Co. – Roger Fargo – Roger Fargo – 1994											
168⁴/₈	24⁵/₈	25²/₈	18³/₈	12⁴/₈	5⁷/₈	5⁷/₈	5	8	3³/₈	3385	16
▪ Marshall Co. – David P. Naeher – David P. Naeher – 1990											
168³/₈	27⁴/₈	27⁴/₈	26	28¹/₈	5⁴/₈	5⁴/₈	4	5	1⁵/₈	3399	17
▪ Pushmataha Co. – Bradley S. Burtch – Bradley S. Burtch – 1992											
168²/₈	28⁵/₈	27⁶/₈	21²/₈	23²/₈	5²/₈	5¹/₈	6	6	4²/₈	3414	18
▪ Dewey Co. – Chad E. Kisinger – Chad E. Kisinger – 1996											
167⁵/₈	22⁴/₈	23	18⁷/₈	21	5⁷/₈	5⁵/₈	6	5		3476	19
▪ Washita Co. – Charles A. Cooper – Charles A. Cooper – 1991											

Score	Length of Main Beam Right	Left	Inside Spread	Greatest Spread	Circumference at Smallest Place Between Burr and First Point Right	Left	Number of Points Right	Left	Lengths Abnormal Points	All-Time Rank	State Rank
	■ Location of Kill – Hunter – Owner – Date Killed										
167 3/8	25 4/8	24 2/8	19 1/8	21 6/8	4 7/8	4 6/8	6	7	1 6/8	3500	20
	■ Blaine Co. – Roger K. Pattinson – Roger K. Pattinson – 1994										
167 2/8	25 5/8	25 4/8	22 3/8	24 6/8	5	5 2/8	8	8	7 5/8	3519	21
	■ Logan Co. – Paul W. Newsom – Paul W. Newsom – 1990										
167 2/8	24 5/8	24 2/8	19 4/8	22 3/8	5	5 2/8	5	6		3519	21
	■ Noble Co. – Monte A. Spears – Monte A. Spears – 1996										
166 6/8	26	26 7/8	19 2/8	21 6/8	4 1/8	4 1/8	6	6	3 6/8	3582†	23†
	■ Pittsburg Co. – Dale Atwood – Dale Atwood – 2001										
166 6/8	24 4/8	24 7/8	16 5/8	18 5/8	5 3/8	5 3/8	6	6	2 5/8	3582†	23†
	■ Rogers Co. – Jesse L. Newton – Jesse L. Newton – 2001										
165 5/8	23 3/8	24 3/8	19 1/8	23 5/8	4 3/8	4 3/8	6	6		3696	25
	■ Haskell Co. – John H. Aldridge – John H. Aldridge – 1994										
165 5/8	24 1/8	25 6/8	17 5/8	19 2/8	4 3/8	4 4/8	7	6	4	3696	25
	■ Coal Co. – Gary D. Bruhwiler – Gary D. Bruhwiler – 1999										
164 1/8	23 2/8	23	19 7/8	23	4 4/8	4 4/8	7	6	2 2/8	3886	27
	■ Love Co. – DeWayne Erwin – DeWayne Erwin – 1964										
164 1/8	23 6/8	23 2/8	22 1/8	23 6/8	4 3/8	4 4/8	5	7	5 2/8	3886	27
	■ Woods Co. – Michael D. Hartwig – Michael D. Hartwig – 1987										
164 1/8	23 1/8	22 4/8	17 5/8	20 5/8	5 1/8	4 4/8	8	7	2 6/8	3886	27
	■ Noble Co. – Patrick O. Pollman – Patrick O. Pollman – 1997										
164 1/8	24 7/8	24 3/8	17 7/8	18 1/8	5	5 3/8	5	5		3886	27
	■ Woodward Co. – Ricky Lamascus – Ricky Lamascus – 1998										
162 7/8	24 3/8	25 6/8	18 7/8	22 1/8	4 7/8	4 5/8	6	7	2 4/8	4067	31
	■ Washita Co. – Bruce D. Sears – Bruce D. Sears – 1988										
162 5/8	23 1/8	23	18 1/8	19 6/8	4 3/8	4 4/8	5	5		4109	32
	■ Harper Co. – Larry A. Beatty – Larry A. Beatty – 1998										
162 2/8	23 3/8	23 6/8	16	18 2/8	4 3/8	4 4/8	6	6		4153	33
	■ Pontotoc Co. – R. Lynn Timberlake – S.R. Noble Foundation – 1988										
162 2/8	25	24 6/8	18 5/8	20 4/8	5	5	9	6	5 5/8	4153	33
	■ Blaine Co. – Kirt E. Curell – Kirt E. Curell – 1994										
162 1/8	25 1/8	25 5/8	17 7/8	20 3/8	4 6/8	5	5	6		4174	35
	■ Dewey Co. – Ronald B. Hall – Ronald B. Hall – 1982										
162	23	21 7/8	17 2/8	19 2/8	4 4/8	5 1/8	5	5		4184	36
	■ Coal Co. – James D. Holder – James D. Holder – 1987										
162	26 1/8	26 1/8	23 5/8	25 6/8	5 2/8	5 3/8	7	7	9 5/8	4184	36
	■ Beckham Co. – John B. Bullard – John B. Bullard – 1997										
161 5/8	26 5/8	26 7/8	20 1/8	23 4/8	4 5/8	4 6/8	6	8	8	4234	38
	■ Woodward Co. – Gregory K. Crouse – Gregory K. Crouse – 1997										
161 3/8	27 2/8	26 1/8	19 2/8	23 3/8	4 5/8	5	8	9	12 7/8	4285	39
	■ Love Co. – Greg French – Greg French – 1994										
161	25 6/8	25 7/8	17 7/8	22 1/8	4 1/8	4	5	5	2 5/8	4356	40
	■ Kay Co. – Frank E. Willard – Frank E. Willard – 1992										

Score	Length of Main Beam		Inside Spread	Greatest Spread	Circumference at Smallest Place Between Burr and First Point		Number of Points		Lengths Abnormal Points	All-Time Rank	State Rank
	Right	Left			Right	Left	Right	Left			
	■ Location of Kill – Hunter – Owner – Date Killed										
160⁵/₈	23¹/₈	23²/₈	20³/₈	22¹/₈	4³/₈	4⁵/₈	9	6	9⁶/₈	4423	41
	■ Pittsburg Co. – William A. Johnson – William A. Johnson – 1988										
160⁴/₈	24⁴/₈	23⁷/₈	18³/₈	20³/₈	4⁶/₈	4⁴/₈	5	7	2⁵/₈	4443	42
	■ Le Flore Co. – Burrus F. Martin – Burrus F. Martin – 1990										
160³/₈	25²/₈	25³/₈	17⁷/₈	19⁷/₈	5	5¹/₈	4	5		4470	43
	■ McCurtain Co. – Clifford A. Citty – Clifford A. Citty – 1988										
160¹/₈	22⁷/₈	23⁵/₈	18	20³/₈	4⁴/₈	4⁴/₈	6	5	1³/₈	4534	44
	■ Latimer Co. – Johnny M. Freeman – Johnny M. Freeman – 1997										
160	25⁴/₈	23⁷/₈	18⁶/₈	20⁷/₈	4¹/₈	4	5	5		4565	45
	■ Le Flore Co. – Carl E. Hale – Carl E. Hale – 1978										

† The scores and ranking for trophies from the 25th Awards Entry Period are not final until the banquet is held on June 19, 2004.

TROPHIES IN THE FIELD

HUNTER: Stephen C. Elias
SCORE: 195-1/8†
CATEGORY: non-typical whitetail deer
LOCATION: Woods County, Oklahoma
DATE: 2000

† The scores and ranking for trophies from the 25th Awards Entry Period are not final until the banquet is held on June 19, 2004.

OKLAHOMA

NON-TYPICAL WHITETAIL DEER

Score	Length of Main Beam Right	Left	Inside Spread	Greatest Spread	Circumference at Smallest Place Between Burr and First Point Right	Left	Number of Points Right	Left	Lengths Abnormal Points	All-Time Rank	State Rank
	■ Location of Kill – Hunter – Owner – Date Killed										
247²/₈	25⁴/₈	25³/₈	24⁶/₈	27	5⁵/₈	6¹/₈	16	14	64	76	1
	■ Johnston Co. – Bill M. Foster – Bill M. Foster – 1970										
237³/₈	25	24⁷/₈	17⁶/₈	22³/₈	5⁶/₈	5¹/₈	17	15	58³/₈	146	2
	■ Delaware Co. – Charles A. Tullis – Charles A. Tullis – 1998										
234²/₈	27³/₈	26⁵/₈	20¹/₈	25	7	7¹/₈	10	12	39⁵/₈	177	3
	■ Alfalfa Co. – Loren Tarrant – Loren Tarrant – 1984										
230⁵/₈	24⁷/₈	24⁶/₈	17⁴/₈	22⁴/₈	5²/₈	5	14	11	64³/₈	233†	4†
	■ Okfuskee Co. – Joe A. Green – Johnny J. Green – 1971										
229⁴/₈	28⁵/₈	28⁴/₈	20⁴/₈	24⁴/₈	5³/₈	5³/₈	9	8	25²/₈	246	5
	■ Dewey Co. – Ricky C. Watt – Ricky C. Watt – 1987										
225¹/₈	27⁷/₈	27⁴/₈	22⁶/₈	24⁶/₈	5²/₈	5	8	9	35¹/₈	314	6
	■ Comanche Co. – Michael C. Apoka – Michael C. Apoka – 1993										
223⁵/₈	28	28³/₈	18⁷/₈	29	4⁷/₈	4⁷/₈	10	12	39⁴/₈	345	7
	■ Woods Co. – Monty E. Pfleider – Monty E. Pfleider – 1987										
221⁴/₈	26²/₈	24²/₈	22	21⁴/₈	5	5²/₈	11	16	44⁴/₈	402†	8†
	■ Comanche Co. – Ted M. Evans – Ted M. Evans – 2001										
219¹/₈	22⁵/₈	22⁵/₈	18⁴/₈	27⁷/₈	5¹/₈	5	17	13	65³/₈	465	9
	■ Pontotoc Co. – Timothy F. Harris – Timothy F. Harris – 1996										
217	23²/₈	22¹/₈	20²/₈	27⁵/₈	4⁷/₈	4⁶/₈	15	10	50⁴/₈	529	10
	■ Love Co. – Greg French – Greg French – 1996										
216³/₈	26	24⁴/₈	18⁶/₈	26³/₈	5³/₈	5⁶/₈	14	17	68⁵/₈	549	11
	■ Comanche Co. – Dwight O. Allen – Dwight O. Allen – 1962										
212⁶/₈	24²/₈	23²/₈	19⁵/₈	26⁴/₈	4²/₈	4⁴/₈	14	9	56¹/₈	677	12
	■ McCurtain Co. – Robert H. Crenshaw – Robert H. Crenshaw – 1988										
211¹/₈	27¹/₈	28⁵/₈	20⁴/₈	29⁶/₈	6¹/₈	6²/₈	11	9	29⁷/₈	758	13
	■ Grady Co. – Bon D. Lentz – Bon D. Lentz – 1999										
209³/₈	26⁴/₈	26⁷/₈	22⁷/₈	25	6⁴/₈	5⁶/₈	9	11	37⁴/₈	852	14
	■ Pittsburg Co. – Unknown – William R. Starry – PR 1994										
209	26⁴/₈	25⁶/₈	20⁵/₈	29	4⁷/₈	5	11	10	55³/₈	872	15
	■ Hughes Co. – Lane Grimes – Lane Grimes – 1987										
208⁶/₈	25²/₈	22²/₈	15⁷/₈	18	4¹/₈	4¹/₈	10	14	43⁵/₈	883	16
	■ Haskell Co. – Michael B. Vail – Michael B. Vail – 1999										
208⁵/₈	22²/₈	22²/₈	13⁴/₈	21⁵/₈	4⁵/₈	4⁵/₈	16	13	62³/₈	888	17
	■ Pontotoc Co. – S. Chris Snell – S. Chris Snell – 1997										
206¹/₈	26³/₈	26²/₈	17⁴/₈	20	6	6	12	12	26³/₈	1068	18
	■ Osage Co. – Wesley D. Coldren – Wesley D. Coldren – 1986										
204⁴/₈	22²/₈	21⁶/₈	16³/₈	19⁴/₈	5¹/₈	5	10	11	41³/₈	1182	19
	■ Love Co. – William B. Heller – William B. Heller – 1970										

Score	Length of Main Beam Right Left	Inside Spread	Greatest Spread	Circumference at Smallest Place Between Burr and First Point Right Left	Number of Points Right Left	Lengths Abnormal Points	All-Time Rank	State Rank
	■ Location of Kill – Hunter – Owner – Date Killed							
203⁶/₈	25 26²/₈	17⁶/₈		4⁴/₈ 4⁴/₈	9 8	30	1237	20
■ McCurtain Co. – Gary L. Birge – Gary L. Birge – 1981								
202	24¹/₈ 23⁵/₈	18	24⁴/₈	5⁷/₈ 4⁷/₈	16 10	40⁴/₈	1395	21
■ Pushmataha Co. – Lucas Young – Lucas Young – 1993								
201³/₈	24⁵/₈ 26⁵/₈	18⁶/₈	24²/₈	4¹/₈ 4²/₈	9 10	19⁷/₈	1461†	22†
■ Le Flore Co. – William M. Russell – William M. Russell – 2001								
201³/₈	24⁵/₈ 25²/₈	15⁷/₈	24	5³/₈ 5⁶/₈	15 17	62	1461	22
■ Pushmataha Co. – Maurice Jackson – Maurice Jackson – 1975								
200⁵/₈	26²/₈ 26²/₈	14	18²/₈	4⁵/₈ 4⁷/₈	6 9	19³/₈	1532	24
■ Texas Co. – Jeffery T. Wright – Jeffery T. Wright – 1987								
200⁵/₈	25⁵/₈ 25³/₈	19⁶/₈	22⁷/₈	4⁷/₈ 5	10 10	20¹/₈	1532	24
■ Woods Co. – Aaron R. Sheik – Aaron R. Sheik – 1998								
197⁷/₈	26²/₈ 27²/₈	19⁶/₈	24⁷/₈	7¹/₈ 6¹/₈	10 7	20⁵/₈	1816	26
■ Woods Co. – Steve Purviance – Steve Purviance – 1997								
197⁴/₈	25⁷/₈ 25⁶/₈	20¹/₈	22⁴/₈	6¹/₈ 6¹/₈	11 10	19³/₈	1866	27
■ Garfield Co. – Derald D. Crissup – Derald D. Crissup – 1980								
197²/₈	24⁵/₈ 25	17⁵/₈	22¹/₈	5 4⁷/₈	12 10	28³/₈	1901	28
■ Stephens Co. – Bryan C. Walker – Bryan C. Walker – 1997								
197¹/₈	26 25⁵/₈	24¹/₈	27⁴/₈	5⁶/₈ 5⁵/₈	8 9	27²/₈	1923†	29†
■ Caddo Co. – Jerid C. Avery – Jerid C. Avery – 2000								
197¹/₈	23 22⁷/₈	17⁷/₈		5¹/₈ 4⁶/₈	10 9	18	1923	29
■ Noble Co. – Kenneth R. Bright – Kenneth R. Bright – 1982								
196⁶/₈	25²/₈ 25²/₈	18²/₈	20²/₈	4⁷/₈ 5¹/₈	8 12	21⁴/₈	1968	31
■ Latimer Co. – Brian K. Paul – Brian K. Paul – 1998								
196⁵/₈	19²/₈ 18	18⁴/₈	21⁵/₈	5¹/₈ 5¹/₈	15 13	69³/₈	1985	32
■ Comanche Co. – R. Dewayne High – R. Dewayne High – 1998								
196¹/₈	23⁵/₈ 25⁴/₈	18¹/₈	25⁴/₈	6 5⁶/₈	11 9	39⁶/₈	2045	33
■ Pontotoc Co. – Bruce A. Hall – Bruce A. Hall – 1999								
195⁶/₈	26²/₈ 24⁴/₈	17⁶/₈	21¹/₈	4³/₈ 4⁴/₈	9 10	25⁴/₈	2094	34
■ Coal Co. – Todd Tobey – Todd Tobey – 1988								
195⁴/₈	22³/₈ 22⁴/₈	17⁶/₈	25⁴/₈	4⁷/₈ 4⁶/₈	12 10	47⁶/₈	2134†	35†
■ Comanche Co. – Jerry L. Timmons – Jerry L. Timmons – 2000								
195⁴/₈	23 22⁶/₈	26⁵/₈	28¹/₈	4²/₈ 4¹/₈	8 11	48⁶/₈	2134	35
■ Hughes Co. – Mike K. Williams – Mike K. Williams – 1998								
195³/₈	23 24⁷/₈	20⁷/₈	24³/₈	6⁶/₈ 6⁶/₈	10 9	20	2163†	37†
■ Stephens Co. – David J. Vassella – David J. Vassella – 2001								
195²/₈	24³/₈ 23⁷/₈	15⁷/₈	22²/₈	5¹/₈ 5¹/₈	7 11	34⁷/₈	2186	38
■ Grady Co. – Robert J. Rempe – Robert J. Rempe – 1994								
195²/₈	24²/₈ 24⁴/₈	19⁶/₈	24⁴/₈	4²/₈ 4³/₈	7 8	30⁶/₈	2186	38
■ Major Co. – Hoot M. Patterson – Hoot M. Patterson – 1997								
195¹/₈	23⁶/₈ 23²/₈	16⁶/₈	21	5¹/₈ 5¹/₈	10 8	14³/₈	2208†	40†
■ Woods Co. – Stephen C. Elias – Stephen C. Elias – 2000 ■ See photo on page 409								

Score	Length of Main Beam Right	Left	Inside Spread	Greatest Spread	Circumference at Smallest Place Between Burr and First Point Right	Left	Number of Points Right	Left	Lengths Abnormal Points	All-Time Rank	State Rank
■ Location of Kill – Hunter – Owner – Date Killed											
195	22 6/8	21 7/8	20	25 4/8	5 4/8	5 4/8	12	14	36 6/8	2233†	41†
■ Carter Co. – William A. Crosby – William A. Crosby – 2000											
193 3/8	22 2/8	23 3/8	19 2/8	22 2/8	4 7/8	4 6/8	10	9	25 7/8	2293	42
■ Cherokee Co. – Douglas P. Montgomery – Douglas P. Montgomery – 1992											
192	25 2/8	25 5/8	19 2/8	21	3 7/8	4 1/8	6	7	32	2344	43
■ Muskogee Co. – Rayna A. Wilson – Rayna A. Wilson – 1992											
190 5/8	21 2/8	21 1/8	14 2/8	20 3/8	4 4/8	4 4/8	11	11	35 3/8	2393	44
■ Johnston Co. – Kevin Lovett – Kevin Lovett – 1993											
190 5/8	23 6/8	25 2/8	18 6/8	22 6/8	4 6/8	5	11	12	35 7/8	2393	44
■ Pawnee Co. – Rick McCracken – Rick McCracken – 1994											
190 4/8	19 2/8	22	14 2/8	22 1/8	5 1/8	5 2/8	18	13	67 6/8	2401†	46†
■ Carter Co. – Walt Spradling – Walt Spradling – 2001											
189 4/8	25 4/8	26 1/8	16 5/8	24 7/8	4 6/8	4 6/8	10	9	20 5/8	2435	47
■ Greer Co. – Ronald D. Meeks – Ronald D. Meeks – 1992											
188 3/8	23 1/8	23 2/8	17	23	4 6/8	4 7/8	7	11	25 3/8	2478†	48†
■ Comanche Co. – John P. Sklaney, Jr. – John P. Sklaney, Jr. – 2000											
188 3/8	25 2/8	24 1/8	16 4/8	18 6/8	6	6	12	8	28 1/8	2478	48
■ Payne Co. – Robert L. Lochmiller – Robert L. Lochmiller – 1995											
187 6/8	24 4/8	26	18 1/8	20 5/8	4 7/8	5	8	9	13 1/8	2512	50
■ Custer Co. – Ricky E. Johnson – Ricky E. Johnson – 1987											
187 4/8	24 2/8	24 1/8	21 2/8	22 4/8	4 6/8	5 2/8	9	9	20 6/8	2522	51
■ Pushmataha Co. – Clyde W. Gibbons – Clyde W. Gibbons – 1999											
186 3/8	25 1/8	23	16 2/8	18 7/8	4 2/8	4 2/8	9	9	33 5/8	2570	52
■ Seminole Co. – Terry W. Northrip – Terry W. Northrip – 1991											
186 3/8	22 7/8	22 7/8	16 1/8	20 3/8	4 4/8	4 2/8	6	10	27	2570	52
■ Le Flore Co. – Tommy Wade – Tommy Wade – 1992											
185 4/8	20 4/8	22 6/8	17 2/8	22 4/8	6 2/8	5 7/8	11	10	28 6/8	2616	54
■ Love Co. – Barry L. Bowker – Barry L. Bowker – 1999											
185 2/8	21 1/8	20 3/8	18 1/8	20 7/8	4 7/8	4 6/8	7	10	32 3/8	2632	55
■ McIntosh Co. – Larry L. Burchfield – Larry L. Burchfield – 1998											

† The scores and ranking for trophies from the 25th Awards Entry Period are not final until the banquet is held on June 19, 2004.

HUNTER: Sam Henry
SCORE: 197
CATEGORY: non-typical whitetail deer
LOCATION: Oak River, Manitoba
DATE: 1946

OREGON
RECORD WHITETAILS

7 Typical whitetail deer entries
0 Non-typical whitetail deer entries
7,265 Total whitetail deer entries

0 Entries ⬜
1-2 Entries
3-5 Entries
6-10 Entries
11+ Entries ⬛

OREGON
STATE RECORD
Typical Whitetail Deer
Score: 178²/₈
Location: Wallowa Co.
Hunter and Owner:
　Sterling K. Shaver
Date: 1982

Photograph courtesy of Northwest Big Game, Inc.

OREGON

TYPICAL WHITETAIL DEER

Score	Length of Main Beam Right	Left	Inside Spread	Greatest Spread	Circumference at Smallest Place Between Burr and First Point Right	Left	Number of Points Right	Left	Lengths Abnormal Points	All-Time Rank	State Rank
	■ Location of Kill – Hunter – Owner – Date Killed										
178²/8	27⁶/8	27³/8	24⁶/8	26²/8	4³/8	4³/8	6	6	2²/8	891	1
	■ Wallowa Co. – Sterling K. Shaver – Sterling K. Shaver – 1982										
167⁴/8	26⁴/8	27²/8	20⁶/8	22	5	4⁵/8	4	3		3485†	2†
	■ Oregon – Cayetano Houk – Cayetano Houk – 1975										
166⁶/8	26	28²/8	20²/8	22⁷/8	4⁷/8	4⁷/8	6	5	10⁶/8	3582	3
	■ Umatilla Co. – Doug Coverdale – Doug Coverdale – 1966										
165⁵/8	24³/8	24	21⁵/8	24⁵/8	4⁵/8	4⁷/8	5	5		3696	4
	■ Wallowa Co. – James H. Hambleton – James H. Hambleton – 1992										
163⁵/8	24	24	19⁶/8	27⁶/8	4⁷/8	4⁶/8	5	6	4¹/8	3961	5
	■ Union Co. – Larry K. Bennett – Larry K. Bennett – 1982										
163¹/8	25	26²/8	22²/8	24¹/8	5	5	6	5	3⁷/8	4035	6
	■ Umatilla Co. – Jeffrey A. Koorenny – Jeffrey A. Koorenny – 1987										
161¹/8	25⁴/8	25⁶/8	20⁷/8	22⁷/8	4⁶/8	4⁶/8	6	5	1²/8	4332	7
	■ Wallowa Co. – Larry V. Haney – Larry V. Haney – 1992										

PENNSYLVANIA
RECORD WHITETAILS

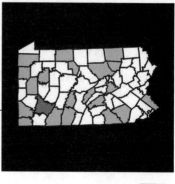

22 Typical whitetail deer entries
12 Non-typical whitetail deer entries
7,265 Total whitetail deer entries

0 Entries
1-2 Entries
3-5 Entries
6-10 Entries
11+ Entries

PENNSYLVANIA STATE RECORD
Typical Whitetail Deer
Score: 184$^6/_8$
Location: Greene Co.
Hunter and Owner: Ivan Parry
Date: 1974

PENNSYLVANIA
NEW STATE RECORD
Non-Typical Whitetail Deer
Score: 230²/₈
Location: Lawrence Co.
Hunter and Owner: Michael D. Ambrosia
Date: 2001

New state record pending approval from the 25th Awards Program Judges Panel.

PENNSYLVANIA

TYPICAL WHITETAIL DEER

Score	Length of Main Beam Right	Left	Inside Spread	Greatest Spread	Circumference at Smallest Place Between Burr and First Point Right	Left	Number of Points Right	Left	Lengths Abnormal Points	All-Time Rank	State Rank
Location of Kill – Hunter – Owner – Date Killed											
184⁶/8	26⁷/8	26⁴/8	20⁶/8	23³/8	4⁵/8	4⁴/8	5	6	3²/8	285	1
■ *Greene Co. – Ivan Parry – Ivan Parry – 1974*											
182²/8	27³/8	27	20⁴/8	23	4⁷/8	5	7	5	1²/8	450	2
■ *Sullivan Co. – Floyd Reibson – Maynard Reibson – 1930*											
177⁴/8	26¹/8	26	21	23⁵/8	4	4¹/8	5	5		993	3
■ *Bedford Co. – Raymond Miller – Raymond Miller – 1957*											
176⁵/8	30	28	21⁵/8	24⁴/8	4⁶/8	4⁴/8	6	7	7⁴/8	1134	4
■ *Mifflin Co. – John Zerba – Kenneth Zerba – 1936*											
176	24⁴/8	24⁷/8	17⁴/8	20¹/8	3⁷/8	4	8	6		1266	5
■ *Bradford Co. – Clyde H. Rinehuls – Clyde H. Rinehuls – 1944*											
175⁵/8	30⁵/8	28⁶/8	23³/8	25⁶/8	6¹/8	5⁵/8	5	5		1333	6
■ *Bucks Co. – Albert J. Muntz – Albert J. Muntz – 1995*											
175⁴/8	25⁵/8	25	21²/8	23¹/8	5	5²/8	6	6		1352	7
■ *McKean Co. – Arthur Young – C.R. Studholme – 1830*											
174²/8	27⁶/8	26⁵/8	19⁴/8	22	5²/8	6¹/8	5	5		1652	8
■ *Butler Co. – Ralph Stoltenberg, Jr. – Ralph Stoltenberg, Jr. – 1986*											
173³/8	27⁶/8	28¹/8	20¹/8	23¹/8	4⁵/8	4⁵/8	5	6		1883	9
■ *Clarion Co. – Mead R. Kiefer – Mead R. Kiefer – 1947*											
173³/8	25⁶/8	26²/8	17⁵/8	20¹/8	4⁴/8	4⁴/8	5	5		1883	9
■ *Clarion Co. – Picked Up – Fred Gallagher – 1954*											
172⁶/8	25⁶/8	24⁶/8	18	20⁴/8	4⁶/8	4⁶/8	5	6	1⁴/8	2065†	11†
■ *Mercer Co. – Michael D. Heckathorn – Michael D. Heckathorn – 2000*											
172⁶/8	26¹/8	23⁶/8	19	22	4⁶/8	4⁶/8	6	7		2065	11
■ *Somerset Co. – Edward B. Stutzman – Edward B. Stutzman, Jr. – 1945*											
172⁶/8	27²/8	27⁷/8	20³/8	22⁶/8	4⁵/8	5¹/8	6	9	5⁵/8	2065	11
■ *Washington Co. – Ronald J. LaBrosse, Jr. – Ronald J. LaBrosse, Jr. – 1996*											
172²/8	28⁶/8	26⁴/8	21⁵/8	24³/8	4¹/8	4³/8	6	6	3¹/8	2237	14
■ *Bedford Co. – John F. Sharpe – John F. Sharpe – 1942*											
171²/8	28²/8	28³/8	28	29⁵/8	5²/8	5⁷/8	6	9	6²/8	2621	15
■ *Somerset Co. – Paul E. Walker – Paul E. Walker – 1941*											
170¹/8	25⁴/8	25³/8	23¹/8	23¹/8	5	5	5	6	2⁴/8	3143	16
■ *Lycoming Co. – Richard C. Tebbs, Jr. – Richard C. Tebbs, Jr. – 1987*											
170	25⁵/8	24¹/8	21⁶/8	23²/8	4⁴/8	4⁶/8	10	10	15	3224	17
■ *Blair Co. – Claude Feathers – Claude Feathers – 1943*											
165⁴/8	24⁴/8	23⁷/8	19³/8	22	4³/8	4³/8	8	5	2⁵/8	3714†	18†
■ *Lehigh Co. – Raymond Nechetsky, Sr. – Raymond Nechetsky, Sr. – 2000*											
165	25	25	18	20¹/8	4²/8	4²/8	5	5		3782	19
■ *Westmoreland Co. – Robert E. Duff, Jr. – Robert E. Duff, Jr. – 1999*											

Score	Length of Main Beam		Inside Spread	Greatest Spread	Circumference at Smallest Place Between Burr and First Point		Number of Points		Lengths Abnormal Points	All-Time Rank	State Rank
	Right	Left			Right	Left	Right	Left			
	■ Location of Kill – Hunter – Owner – Date Killed										
164	25⁷/₈	27¹/₈	20⁷/₈	23¹/₈	4⁷/₈	4⁷/₈	5	6	1⁷/₈	3908	20
	■ Lancaster Co. – Wade A. Conrad – Wade A. Conrad – 1997										
163¹/₈	25⁷/₈	25²/₈	17⁴/₈	19⁶/₈	5	5²/₈	9	8	6⁵/₈	4035	21
	■ Crawford Co. – William N. Novicky – William N. Novicky – 1995										
162⁵/₈	24¹/₈	24⁷/₈	16⁷/₈	21³/₈	4	4¹/₈	7	5	4⁴/₈	4109†	22†
	■ Indiana Co. – Joseph E. Hess – Joseph E. Hess – 2000										

† The scores and ranking for trophies from the 25th Awards Entry Period are not final until the banquet is held on June 19, 2004.

PENNSYLVANIA

NON-TYPICAL WHITETAIL DEER

Score	Length of Main Beam Right	Left	Inside Spread	Greatest Spread	Circumference at Smallest Place Between Burr and First Point Right	Left	Number of Points Right	Left	Lengths Abnormal Points	All-Time Rank	State Rank
	■ Location of Kill – Hunter – Owner – Date Killed										
230²/8	24⁴/8	25¹/8	15⁵/8	21⁶/8	5⁷/8	5⁶/8	17	20	76⁷/8	235†	1†
	■ Lawrence Co. – Michael D. Ambrosia – Michael D. Ambrosia – 2001										
213⁶/8	26⁵/8	26³/8	26⁵/8	32²/8	5³/8	5⁴/8	10	10	21⁵/8	644	2
	■ Lycoming Co. – Al Prouty – Al Prouty – 1949										
207⁷/8	29⁵/8	31¹/8	24⁴/8	28	5⁵/8	5⁵/8	11	7	26⁵/8	938	3
	■ Port Royal – C. Ralph Landis – Ruth V. Landis – 1951										
206	26⁵/8	25⁴/8	18⁶/8	22⁶/8	4⁶/8	4⁶/8	11	11	71⁴/8	1075	4
	■ Cameron Co. – William P. Rhines – David Rhines – 1910										
201¹/8	23	22⁵/8	14⁵/8	20¹/8	4⁶/8	5¹/8	13	16	60⁶/8	1489	5
	■ Westmoreland Co. – Richard K. Mellon – Richard K. Mellon – 1966										
197⁶/8	24³/8	26⁷/8	16	19⁶/8	5²/8	4⁷/8	12	10	39⁶/8	1833	6
	■ York Co. – Kevin R. Brumgard – Kevin R. Brumgard – 1992										
197³/8	22¹/8	21	17⁵/8	19⁵/8	4⁴/8	4⁴/8	16	14	55²/8	1884†	7†
	■ Mifflin Co. – Garry L. Forgy – Garry L. Forgy – 2000										
196⁷/8	24⁶/8	24⁵/8	16	17⁶/8	4³/8	4⁵/8	13	14	33⁵/8	1950†	8†
	■ Allegheny Co. – Charles E. Main – Charles E. Main – 2000 ■ See photo on page 421										
196⁶/8	26²/8	25⁵/8	18²/8	20³/8	5⁶/8	5⁵/8	9	8	39⁶/8	1968	9
	■ Perry Co. – Kenneth Reisinger – Kenneth Reisinger – 1949										
196	25⁵/8	25¹/8	16¹/8	19³/8	5¹/8	5⁴/8	7	12	19³/8	2059	10
	■ Westmoreland Co. – Edward G. Ligus – Edward G. Ligus – 1956										
195	25⁶/8	27²/8	20¹/8	23	5¹/8	5	11	9	26⁵/8	2233	11
	■ Westmoreland Co. – Eugene W. Livingston – Eugene W. Livingston – 1995										
189²/8	26²/8	24⁵/8	20²/8	26	4⁷/8	5⁴/8	7	10	10²/8	2447	12
	■ Northumberland Co. – Thomas E. Messinger – Thomas E. Messinger – 1998										

† The scores and ranking for trophies from the 25th Awards Entry Period are not final until the banquet is held on June 19, 2004.

TROPHIES IN THE FIELD

HUNTER: Charles E. Main
SCORE: 196-7/8
CATEGORY: non-typical whitetail deer
LOCATION: Allegheny County, Pennsylvania
DATE: 2000

SOUTH CAROLINA
RECORD WHITETAILS

4 Typical whitetail deer entries
2 Non-typical whitetail deer entries
7,265 Total whitetail deer entries

0 Entries
1-2 Entries
3-5 Entries
6-10 Entries
11+ Entries

SOUTH CAROLINA
NEW STATE RECORD
Typical Whitetail Deer
Score: 176
Location: Pickens Co.
Hunter and Owner: William C. Wyatt
Date: 1994

NEW
STATE
RECORD

SOUTH CAROLINA
STATE RECORD
Non-Typical Whitetail Deer
Score: 208⁵/₈
Location: Beaufort Co.
Hunter and Owner: John M. Wood
Date: 1971

SOUTH CAROLINA

TYPICAL WHITETAIL DEER

Score	Length of Main Beam Right	Left	Inside Spread	Greatest Spread	Circumference at Smallest Place Between Burr and First Point Right	Left	Number of Points Right	Left	Lengths Abnormal Points	All-Time Rank	State Rank
	■ Location of Kill – Hunter – Owner – Date Killed										
176	27²/8	27²/8	21²/8	23²/8	4⁷/8	4⁶/8	5	5		1266	1
	■ Pickens Co. – William C. Wyatt – William C. Wyatt – 1994										
170⁵/8	26⁶/8	27⁵/8	20¹/8	22⁵/8	5³/8	5³/8	6	5		2876	2
	■ Williamsburg Co. – A. Hugh Gaskins – A. Hugh Gaskins – 1998										
169⁷/8	26³/8	26⁵/8	14⁷/8	17⁵/8	4⁵/8	4⁴/8	6	5	1⁶/8	3302	3
	■ Marion Co. – Richard K. Dover – Richard K. Dover – 1996										
167³/8	26²/8	26³/8	17⁷/8	20²/8	5	4⁶/8	5	5		3500	4
	■ Saluda Co. – Tristan A. DuBose – Tristan A. DuBose – 1993										

SOUTH CAROLINA

NON-TYPICAL WHITETAIL DEER

Score	Length of Main Beam Right	Length of Main Beam Left	Inside Spread	Greatest Spread	Circumference at Smallest Place Between Burr and First Point Right	Circumference at Smallest Place Between Burr and First Point Left	Number of Points Right	Number of Points Left	Lengths Abnormal Points	All-Time Rank	State Rank
■ *Location of Kill – Hunter – Owner – Date Killed*											
208 5/8	19 6/8	23 4/8	18 4/8	21 7/8	5	5	11	10	54 1/8	888	1
■ *Beaufort Co. – John M. Wood – John M. Wood – 1971*											
205 4/8	21	21 3/8	17 3/8	22 6/8	5 1/8	5 1/8	18	16	60 5/8	1107	2
■ *Edgefield Co. – Bradley E. Means – Bradley E. Means – 1994*											

SOUTH DAKOTA
RECORD WHITETAILS

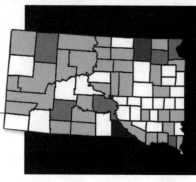

66 Typical whitetail deer entries
35 Non-typical whitetail deer entries
7,265 Total whitetail deer entries

0 Entries	
1-2 Entries	
3-5 Entries	
6-10 Entries	
11+ Entries	

SOUTH DAKOTA
STATE RECORD
Typical Whitetail Deer
Score: 193
Location: South Dakota
Hunter: Unknown
Owner: Eugene J. Lodermeier
Date: 1964

SOUTH DAKOTA
STATE RECORD
Non-Typical Whitetail Deer
Score: 256$^1/_8$
Location: Marshall Co.
Hunter: Francis Fink
Owner: Cabela's, Inc.
Date: 1948

SOUTH DAKOTA

TYPICAL WHITETAIL DEER

Score	Length of Main Beam Right	Left	Inside Spread	Greatest Spread	Circumference at Smallest Place Between Burr and First Point Right	Left	Number of Points Right	Left	Lengths Abnormal Points	All-Time Rank	State Rank
193	25⁶/8	26	25	27⁵/8	5³/8	5⁵/8	6	6		57	1

■ South Dakota – Unknown – Eugene J. Lodermeier – 1964

| 192 | 27⁴/8 | 28 | 19²/8 | 21²/8 | 4⁶/8 | 4⁶/8 | 8 | 9 | 9⁶/8 | 70 | 2 |

■ Lyman Co. – Bob Weidner – E.N. Eichler – 1957

| 191⁷/8 | 30⁵/8 | 30⁷/8 | 19²/8 | 24 | 5⁴/8 | 5 | 6 | 5 | 1³/8 | 73 | 3 |

■ Charles Mix Co. – John Simon – John Simon – PR 1970

| 189⁵/8 | 29²/8 | 29²/8 | 21⁴/8 | 24³/8 | 4⁷/8 | 4⁶/8 | 5 | 6 | 2³/8 | 116 | 4 |

■ Tabor – Duane Graber – Sam Peterson – 1954

| 184³/8 | 28⁴/8 | 29 | 25⁵/8 | 31²/8 | 5⁶/8 | 5⁷/8 | 5 | 7 | 8⁴/8 | 313 | 5 |

■ Kingsbury Co. – Rudy F. Weigel – Rudy F. Weigel – 1960

| 182⁵/8 | 24⁶/8 | 26³/8 | 18¹/8 | 21¹/8 | 5 | 5¹/8 | 5 | 5 | | 420 | 6 |

■ Jones Co. – Richard A. Gordon – Richard A. Gordon – 1989

| 181³/8 | 24¹/8 | 24 | 20⁴/8 | 22⁴/8 | 5¹/8 | 5³/8 | 6 | 8 | 8⁵/8 | 528 | 7 |

■ Harding Co. – Cregg Else – Cregg Else – 1985

| 180⁵/8 | 26³/8 | 26²/8 | 18³/8 | 20⁶/8 | 5¹/8 | 5 | 5 | 6 | | 599 | 8 |

■ Turner Co. – Nicklaus J. Schrag – Nicklaus J. Schrag – 1996

| 180⁴/8 | 26⁷/8 | 25⁵/8 | 19 | 22 | 5¹/8 | 5¹/8 | 6 | 6 | 4 | 613 | 9 |

■ Clay Co. – James E. Olson – James E. Olson – 1975

| 180³/8 | 30⁴/8 | 29²/8 | 22³/8 | 25 | 5⁷/8 | 5⁷/8 | 4 | 4 | | 630 | 10 |

■ Hand Co. – Vernon Winter – J.D. Andrews – 1965

| 180¹/8 | 26¹/8 | 25⁶/8 | 20¹/8 | 23 | 5²/8 | 5²/8 | 5 | 5 | | 669 | 11 |

■ Jackson Co. – Timothy J. Kelley – Timothy J. Kelley – 1988

| 178⁶/8 | 28¹/8 | 27³/8 | 21³/8 | 23³/8 | 4²/8 | 4⁴/8 | 6 | 5 | 1⁵/8 | 808 | 12 |

■ Corson Co. – Dean Little Dog – Dick Rossum – 1984

| 178³/8 | 23¹/8 | 24²/8 | 25 | 25⁵/8 | 5⁶/8 | 6 | 6 | 7 | 2⁷/8 | 868 | 13 |

■ Gregory Co. – Ronald L. Larson – Ronald L. Larson – 1980

| 177¹/8 | 27 | 27 | 18¹/8 | 20³/8 | 4⁶/8 | 4⁷/8 | 6 | 5 | | 1048 | 14 |

■ Gregory Co. – Harold Deering – Harold Deering – 1969

| 176⁷/8 | 28 | 26⁷/8 | 16²/8 | 18¹/8 | 3⁷/8 | 3⁶/8 | 5 | 7 | 1¹/8 | 1086 | 15 |

■ Day Co. – William B. Davis – William B. Davis – 1959

| 176⁵/8 | 25 | 25 | 23²/8 | 24⁷/8 | 5 | 5 | 6 | 5 | 1⁵/8 | 1134 | 16 |

■ Roberts Co. – Fred Kuehl – J.D. Andrews – 1964

| 176⁵/8 | 26⁵/8 | 25⁶/8 | 17³/8 | 19⁴/8 | 4²/8 | 4²/8 | 5 | 5 | | 1134 | 16 |

■ Meade Co. – Jerry Humble – Jerry Humble – 1970

| 176⁴/8 | 26 | 26⁴/8 | 23¹/8 | 26⁴/8 | 4²/8 | 4¹/8 | 6 | 7 | 1¹/8 | 1158† | 18† |

■ Todd Co. – Richard B. Carlson – Richard B. Carlson – 2000

| 176²/8 | 25⁵/8 | 27⁴/8 | 18 | 20⁵/8 | 5²/8 | 5⁴/8 | 7 | 7 | 6²/8 | 1209 | 19 |

■ Bon Homme Co. – Lonnie L. Huber – Lonnie L. Huber – 1991

Score	Length of Main Beam Right	Left	Inside Spread	Greatest Spread	Circumference at Smallest Place Between Burr and First Point Right	Left	Number of Points Right	Left	Lengths Abnormal Points	All-Time Rank	State Rank
	■ Location of Kill – Hunter – Owner – Date Killed										
176	26	26³/8	20	22²/8	5³/8	5⁴/8	5	5		1266	20
	■ Veblen – John W. Cimburek – John W. Cimburek – 1966										
175⁶/8	21⁶/8	23²/8	18	19³/8	4⁴/8	4⁵/8	6	6		1310	21
	■ St. Onge – Don Ridley – Don Ridley – 1957										
175⁵/8	26⁵/8	25⁶/8	17⁵/8	19⁷/8	5¹/8	5¹/8	5	5		1333	22
	■ Mellette Co. – Ben Krogman – Ben Krogman – 1969										
175¹/8	27⁴/8	28⁵/8	22³/8	25⁵/8	4⁷/8	4⁶/8	5	7	2⁶/8	1440	23
	■ Roberts Co. – Rudy Duwenhoegger, Jr. – Rudy Duwenhoegger, Jr. – 1966										
175	27⁷/8	27⁴/8	19³/8	21³/8	4⁶/8	4⁷/8	6	7	3⁷/8	1472	24
	■ Gregory Co. – Ken Dooley – Ken Dooley – 1996										
174¹/8	24³/8	25⁴/8	19²/8	21²/8	5³/8	5⁴/8	7	6	5⁷/8	1678	25
	■ Day Co. – Vernon L. Skoba – Vernon L. Skoba – 1989										
174	27	28¹/8	21	23¹/8	4⁷/8	5¹/8	6	6		1717	26
	■ Brown Co. – John F. Culp – John F. Culp – 1995										
173²/8	26²/8	26²/8	19³/8	22²/8	4⁵/8	4⁵/8	7	6	2³/8	1914†	27†
	■ Hyde Co. – Dillon K. Baloun – Dillon K. Baloun – 2001										
173²/8	25³/8	25³/8	21⁶/8	25¹/8	4³/8	4⁴/8	5	5		1914	27
	■ Lyman Co. – William G. Psychos – William G. Psychos – 1972										
173	28⁷/8	28⁴/8	17²/8	19²/8	4⁶/8	4⁵/8	6	7	8	1991	29
	■ Mellette Co. – Calvin R. Joy – Calvin R. Joy – 1963										
172⁷/8	25⁵/8	26⁵/8	21⁵/8	23³/8	4⁶/8	4⁷/8	6	5	1²/8	2038†	30†
	■ Minnehaha Co. – Daniel D. Anderson – Daniel D. Anderson – 2001										
172³/8	27⁴/8	27²/8	20⁴/8	23²/8	6	6¹/8	5	6	2⁷/8	2200	31
	■ Brookings – Paul W. Back – Paul W. Back – 1967										
172²/8	25⁶/8	26³/8	20	22²/8	5¹/8	5¹/8	5	5		2237	32
	■ Jones Co. – Walter Prahl – J.D. Andrews – 1960										
172²/8	25⁶/8	24²/8	20	23⁵/8	4⁵/8	4⁵/8	6	8	2⁴/8	2237	32
	■ Perkins Co. – Randy G. Swenson – Randy G. Swenson – 1979										
172¹/8	27	27³/8	23²/8	26	4⁶/8	4⁴/8	8	7	8³/8	2286	34
	■ Hughes Co. – Mark Lilevjen – Mark Lilevjen – 1971										
171³/8	25²/8	25³/8	25²/8	27³/8	4³/8	4⁴/8	7	6	5¹/8	2564	35
	■ Bennett Co. – David Risse – David Risse – 1975										
171²/8	25⁶/8	25⁷/8	21³/8	24⁵/8	5	5	6	5	1¹/8	2621	36
	■ Gregory Co. – Leonard L. Nespor – Leonard L. Nespor – 1956										
171²/8	27³/8	27⁶/8	19⁶/8	22⁴/8	4⁵/8	4⁴/8	5	5		2621	36
	■ Todd Co. – Timothy E. Guerue – Timothy E. Guerue – 1994										
171¹/8	23⁶/8	24⁷/8	15⁷/8	18⁶/8	4	4	7	7	3⁶/8	2665	38
	■ Jackson Co. – Dale Jarman – Dale Jarman – 1966										
171	28²/8	25⁶/8	24²/8	27¹/8	5⁴/8	5⁴/8	5	4		2707	39
	■ Brown Co. – Anthony B. Goldade – Anthony B. Goldade – 1960										
171	28⁵/8	27⁷/8	20⁴/8	24²/8	5²/8	5¹/8	7	7	3⁴/8	2707	39
	■ Perkins Co. – Ethel Schrader – Ethel Schrader – 1963										

SOUTH DAKOTA TYPICAL WHITETAIL DEER

Score	Length of Main Beam Right	Left	Inside Spread	Greatest Spread	Circumference at Smallest Place Between Burr and First Point Right	Left	Number of Points Right	Left	Lengths Abnormal Points	All-Time Rank	State Rank
171	26²/8	24⁴/8	18³/8	20⁷/8	4⁵/8	4⁶/8	8	8	9⁷/8	2707	39
	■ Lyman Co. – Art Zimbelmann – Art Zimbelmann – 1973										
171	26⁵/8	26⁵/8	18⁴/8	21	3⁷/8	3⁷/8	5	5		2707	39
	■ Minnehaha Co. – Carl L. Murra – Carl L. Murra – 1996										
170⁵/8	25³/8	24³/8	20⁵/8	23⁵/8	5¹/8	5¹/8	10	6	6	2876	43
	■ Pennington Co. – Glen Wilson – Dick Rossum – 1946										
170⁴/8	24	24²/8	19²/8	21¹/8	4⁵/8	4⁶/8	5	5		2933	44
	■ Day Co. – Credan Ewalt – Credan Ewalt – 1982										
170³/8	25²/8	25⁴/8	23³/8	25¹/8	5²/8	5²/8	6	5	1⁴/8	2992	45
	■ Grant Co. – James Boerger – James Boerger – 1965										
170³/8	28⁵/8	28⁴/8	23⁴/8	26⁴/8	5¹/8	5	8	8	14⁵/8	2992	45
	■ Kingsbury Co. – Jerry Ellingson – Jerry Ellingson – 1969										
170³/8	26⁶/8	26²/8	17⁷/8	20¹/8	4⁶/8	4⁶/8	5	5		2992	45
	■ McCook Co. – Unknown – Sam A. Wilson – PR 1990										
170³/8	26⁶/8	26⁵/8	18	19⁶/8	5¹/8	5¹/8	6	5	4¹/8	2992	45
	■ Ziebach Co. – James S. Nelson IV – James S. Nelson IV – 1992										
170²/8	26²/8	25⁵/8	19⁴/8	21⁵/8	5	5	5	6	1⁴/8	3063	49
	■ Jackson Co. – Jean Amiotte – Jean Amiotte – 1995										
170	24²/8	24²/8	18²/8	20²/8	3⁷/8	3⁷/8	8	8	4⁴/8	3224	50
	■ Hyde Co. – Matthew Kusser – Matthew Kusser – 1990										
169⁶/8	23⁴/8	24⁴/8	20³/8	25²/8	5²/8	5²/8	8	8	14⁷/8	3306	51
	■ Day Co. – Gerald Bartwell – Gerald Bartwell – 1960										
169	22²/8	22⁶/8	13⁷/8	16	5	5¹/8	6	7	1³/8	3348	52
	■ Hand Co. – Dale Simpson – Dale Simpson – 1996										
168⁶/8	25²/8	25⁷/8	20²/8	22⁴/8	4⁶/8	4⁶/8	7	7	4	3367	53
	■ Charles Mix Co. – Gary D. DeJong – Gary D. DeJong – 1985										
167²/8	24⁷/8	24²/8	19⁴/8	21⁷/8	4⁷/8	5²/8	5	5		3519†	54†
	■ Fall River Co. – Donald L. Massa – Donald L. Massa – 2000										
167¹/8	24⁶/8	23⁴/8	20⁴/8	23	4⁵/8	4⁷/8	6	6	3¹/8	3539†	55†
	■ Hutchinson Co. – Bryan Maas – Bryan Maas – 2001										
166³/8	24⁵/8	24⁵/8	19¹/8	23²/8	4¹/8	4¹/8	5	5		3620	56
	■ Dewey Co. – Jeffrey A. Zinter – Jeffrey A. Zinter – 1992										
165⁴/8	27³/8	26²/8	25⁵/8	27³/8	5⁴/8	5⁴/8	7	6	3³/8	3714	57
	■ Clay Co. – Howard W. Bresaw – Howard W. Bresaw – 1970										
165³/8	25	24⁴/8	15⁵/8	18³/8	4⁵/8	4⁵/8	7	7		3731	58
	■ Union Co. – Milton Ustad – Milton Ustad – 1988										
164⁷/8	23³/8	24⁵/8	18³/8	21⁶/8	4⁷/8	4⁶/8	6	6	1²/8	3792	59
	■ Gregory Co. – Grant E. Wild – Grant E. Wild – 1991										
164⁶/8	28⁵/8	28⁶/8	22⁷/8	24⁷/8	6	5⁷/8	5	6	6⁷/8	3809	60
	■ Bonesteel – Clifford L. Johnson – Clifford L. Johnson – 1968										
163⁷/8	24⁴/8	24⁶/8	19³/8	22¹/8	4⁴/8	4⁶/8	5	5		3928†	61†
	■ Yankton Co. – Jeff A. Sayler – Jeff A. Sayler – 2000										

Score	Length of Main Beam Right	Left	Inside Spread	Greatest Spread	Circumference at Smallest Place Between Burr and First Point Right	Left	Number of Points Right	Left	Lengths Abnormal Points	All-Time Rank	State Rank
					Right	**Left**	**Right**	**Left**			
■ Location of Kill – Hunter – Owner – Date Killed											
161²/8	24⁷/8	25	19	22⁷/8	3⁷/8	4	6	6		4310	62
■ Faulk Co. – Robert Knadle – Robert Knadle – 1986											
160⁴/8	25³/8	26¹/8	22	23⁷/8	4²/8	4²/8	5	5		4443	63
■ Hyde Co. – Brandon P. Baloun – Brandon P. Baloun – 1993											
160⁴/8	25⁶/8	25	18¹/8	21²/8	4⁶/8	4⁷/8	5	6	1⁷/8	4443	63
■ Gregory Co. – Kelly J. Wells – Kelly J. Wells – 1996											
160³/8	24	24⁴/8	19⁶/8	21⁶/8	5¹/8	5	6	7	2⁷/8	4470	65
■ Brown Co. – Richard N. Gubler – Richard N. Gubler – 1993											
160³/8	24²/8	25¹/8	22³/8	24⁷/8	4⁷/8	4⁵/8	7	5	1⁶/8	4470	65
■ Gregory Co. – Jerry D. Ostean – Jerry D. Ostean – 1993											

† The scores and ranking for trophies from the 25th Awards Entry Period are not final until the banquet is held on June 19, 2004.

SOUTH DAKOTA

NON-TYPICAL WHITETAIL DEER

Score	Length of Main Beam		Inside Spread	Greatest Spread	Circumference at Smallest Place Between Burr and First Point		Number of Points		Lengths Abnormal Points	All-Time Rank	State Rank
	Right	Left			Right	Left	Right	Left			
	■ Location of Kill – Hunter – Owner – Date Killed										
256¹/8	28⁷/8	26⁵/8	23³/8	30	7⁵/8	7²/8	18	13	69	40	1
	■ Marshall Co. – Francis Fink – Cabela's, Inc. – 1948										
250⁶/8	25³/8	25⁴/8	15¹/8	18⁵/8	5	5³/8	19	13	75¹/8	55	2
	■ South Dakota – Howard Eaton – Jack G. Brittingham – 1870										
249¹/8	26²/8	26⁷/8	19²/8	28²/8	6⁴/8	6²/8	12	20	47⁷/8	64	3
	■ Lily – Jerry Roitsch – J.D. Andrews – 1965										
238²/8	24³/8	25²/8	22⁶/8	26²/8	6²/8	7⁴/8	10	11	54	136	4
	■ Potter Co. – Larry Nylander – Donna Nylander – 1963										
235³/8	21⁷/8	22⁶/8	21⁶/8	23⁵/8	6²/8	6	13	10	71³/8	168	5
	■ Harding Co. – J.H. Krueger & R. Keeton – Bass Pro Shops – 1965										
221³/8	29³/8	29⁵/8	19	21⁵/8	5⁵/8	5⁴/8	11	10	32⁵/8	407	6
	■ Dewey Co. – Leo Fischer – Leo Fischer – 1958										
216⁷/8	19¹/8	21¹/8	13⁷/8	25¹/8	7	6⁵/8	12	15	78²/8	533	7
	■ Brown Co. – Francis Shattuck – D.J. Hollinger & B. Howard – 1960										
212²/8	23¹/8	25¹/8	20³/8	30⁵/8	5¹/8	5	11	10	63⁷/8	701	8
	■ Gregory Co. – Picked Up – J.D. Andrews – 1983										
210⁵/8	28⁵/8	26	24⁶/8	28	6	6⁴/8	8	8	35³/8	783	9
	■ Walworth Co. – H.F. McClellan, Sr. – H.F. McClellan, Sr. – 1952										
210	23⁴/8	23⁶/8	20³/8	28³/8	5⁷/8	6²/8	9	8	26¹/8	816	10
	■ Gregory Co. – Richard C. Berte – Richard C. Berte – 1982										
208⁴/8	30⁵/8	29²/8	17³/8	23	5¹/8	5¹/8	7	9	16⁷/8	894	11
	■ Day Co. – Unknown – J.D. Andrews – PR 1950										
207⁷/8	24⁴/8	25²/8	19	27	5⁷/8	5⁶/8	11	14	34⁷/8	938	12
	■ Perkins Co. – W.E. Brown – Dick Rossum – 1957										
207⁴/8	23⁴/8	22¹/8	18⁵/8	21⁷/8	5³/8	5²/8	9	10	24¹/8	969	13
	■ Lawrence Co. – Ernest C. Larive – J.D. Andrews – 1957										
207³/8	28³/8	27⁶/8	21²/8	24²/8	5⁶/8	5⁷/8	10	11	28¹/8	977	14
	■ Roberts Co. – Delbert Lackey – Delbert Lackey – 1975										
206⁴/8	25⁴/8	24⁷/8	17⁷/8	23⁵/8	6⁶/8	6⁴/8	12	9	42⁵/8	1043	15
	■ Yankton Co. – William Sees – William Sees – 1973										
204⁷/8	26³/8	26⁴/8	18⁵/8	23²/8	5²/8	5²/8	9	12	38²/8	1156	16
	■ Yankton Co. – Daniel M. Rederick – Daniel M. Rederick – 1998										
202¹/8	26¹/8	26⁴/8	19³/8	24⁴/8	6¹/8	6²/8	8	9	26⁴/8	1386	17
	■ Gary – Dennis Cole – Dennis Cole – 1960										
202	24	24³/8	19²/8	21⁵/8	5⁴/8	5⁴/8	12	10	36⁴/8	1395	18
	■ Roberts Co. – Ronnie A. Bucklin – Ronnie A. Bucklin – 1988										
201⁶/8	23³/8	23⁴/8	19⁷/8	25	4⁶/8	4⁴/8	10	10	37¹/8	1421	19
	■ Custer Co. – Unknown – Kenny Spring – PR 1940										

Score	Length of Main Beam		Inside Spread	Greatest Spread	Circumference at Smallest Place Between Burr and First Point		Number of Points		Lengths Abnormal Points	All-Time Rank	State Rank
	Right	Left			Right	Left	Right	Left			
	■ Location of Kill – Hunter – Owner – Date Killed										
201 5/8	24 2/8	24 7/8	21	26 7/8	5	5	8	8	43 7/8	1427	20
	■ Brown Co. – Wallace Labisky – D.J. Hollinger & B. Howard – 1962										
201 5/8	27 6/8	22 2/8	20 5/8	24 1/8	5 6/8	5 5/8	8	12	32 2/8	1427	20
	■ Sisseton – Truman M. Nelson – Truman M. Nelson – 1967										
201 4/8	22 3/8	23 3/8	16 5/8	21	4 1/8	4 2/8	9	8	28 3/8	1443	22
	■ Campbell Co. – Edward J. Torigian – J.D. Andrews – 1957										
200 7/8	26 1/8	22 7/8	18 3/8	21 3/8	4 7/8	5 1/8	8	13	39	1512	23
	■ Davison Co. – Louis W. Cooper – Louis W. Cooper – 1990										
200 4/8	25 2/8	25 2/8	23	25 4/8	6 1/8	6 1/8	9	6	20	1545	24
	■ Brentford – S.C. Mitchell – S.C. Mitchell – 1948										
199 4/8	25 7/8	26 1/8	19 7/8	22 3/8	6 4/8	7 2/8	10	20	46 3/8	1631	25
	■ Gregory Co. – Fred Gnirk – Adeline Gnirk – 1958										
199 1/8	26 3/8	26	24 1/8	26 4/8	5 4/8	5 2/8	11	11	27 2/8	1660	26
	■ Meade Co. – Donald Trohkimoinen – Donald Trohkimoinen – 1966										
198	24 3/8	24 1/8	13 5/8	18 4/8	5 4/8	6 2/8	11	12	32 5/8	1801	27
	■ Brown Co. – Paul J. Hill – Paul J. Hill – 1994										
197 5/8	24	24	17 5/8	22 4/8	5 2/8	4 6/8	11	9	32 4/8	1847	28
	■ Pennington Co. – Lynn Williams – Dick Rossum – 1958										
197 4/8	27 6/8	26 3/8	19 6/8	24 1/8	5 1/8	5 3/8	7	7	13 4/8	1866	29
	■ Clay Co. – Curtis Gregg – Curtis Gregg – 1988										
197 3/8	24 3/8	24 4/8	20 1/8	22 1/8	5 2/8	5 3/8	8	7	16 2/8	1884	30
	■ Clark Co. – Steven R. Frank – Steven R. Frank – 1995										
197 1/8	23 6/8	23 4/8	20 2/8	25 1/8	5 7/8	5 7/8	11	11	27 1/8	1923	31
	■ Clark Co. – Marlin Maynard – Marlin Maynard – 1999										
196 7/8	24 6/8	24 6/8	19	22 4/8	5	5	10	8	25 3/8	1950	32
	■ Edmunds Co. – Melvin Borkirchert – Melvin Borkirchert – 1983										
196 3/8	22 5/8	23 7/8	18 5/8	20 4/8	5 2/8	5 2/8	11	7	26 6/8	2010	33
	■ Gregory Co. – Michael O. Jacobsen – Michael O. Jacobsen – 1999										
194 1/8	26 4/8	25 4/8	16 5/8	19 3/8	5 7/8	5 4/8	7	7	32 6/8	2271	34
	■ Centerville – Ronald Merritt – Ronald Merritt – 1964										
186 3/8	24 2/8	24 6/8	20 1/8	25 2/8	4 6/8	4 6/8	10	9	41 2/8	2570	35
	■ Custer Co. – Unknown – Brad F. Pfeffer – 1977										

TENNESSEE
RECORD WHITETAILS

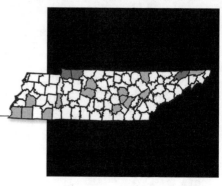

20 Typical whitetail deer entries
12 Non-typical whitetail deer entries
7,265 Total whitetail deer entries

0 Entries
1-2 Entries
3-5 Entries
6-10 Entries
11+ Entries

TENNESSEE
STATE RECORD
Typical Whitetail Deer
Score: $186^1/_8$
Location: Roane Co.
Hunter and Owner: W.A. Foster
Date: 1959

Photograph by Duncan Dobie

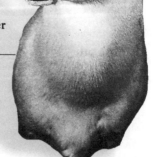

TENNESSEE
NEW STATE RECORD
Non-Typical Whitetail Deer
Score: 244³/8
Location: Sumner Co.
Hunter and Owner: David K. Wachtel III
Date: 2000

New state record pending approval from the 25th Awards Program Judges Panel.

TENNESSEE

TYPICAL WHITETAIL DEER

Score	Length of Main Beam Right Left	Inside Spread	Greatest Spread	Circumference at Smallest Place Between Burr and First Point Right Left	Number of Points Right Left	Lengths Abnormal Points	All-Time Rank	State Rank
	▪ Location of Kill – Hunter – Owner – Date Killed							
186 1/8	25 1/8 26 2/8	20 1/8	22 1/8	4 6/8 4 7/8	6 5	3	228	1
	▪ Roane Co. – W.A. Foster – W.A. Foster – 1959							
184 4/8	23 4/8 23 4/8	17	19 2/8	4 6/8 4 6/8	6 6		303	2
	▪ Fayette Co. – Benny M. Johnson – Benny M. Johnson – 1979							
184 2/8	27 27 4/8	20 6/8	23	4 6/8 4 6/8	5 5		319†	3†
	▪ Shelby Co. – Picked Up – Sammy Beesinger – 2001							
180 1/8	26 4/8 26 1/8	20	22 6/8	4 7/8 4 6/8	6 6	3 5/8	669	4
	▪ Montgomery Co. – Lonnie Hulse – Lonnie Hulse – 1995							
178 5/8	27 26 4/8	21 1/8	23	5 3/8 5 3/8	5 5		819	5
	▪ Scott Co. – Charles H. Smith – Charles H. Smith – 1978							
173 4/8	23 6/8 23 7/8	18 6/8	21 4/8	4 6/8 4 6/8	6 6		1847	6
	▪ Shelby Co. – John J. Heirigs – John J. Heirigs – 1962							
173 2/8	27 3/8 25 3/8	18 4/8	20 6/8	4 4 1/8	6 6		1914	7
	▪ Decatur Co. – Glen D. Odle – Glen D. Odle – 1972							
173 1/8	26 26 6/8	18 5/8	22	4 1/8 3 7/8	6 6	10	1950	8
	▪ White Co. – Sam H. Langford – Sam H. Langford – 1980							
173	25 4/8 25 1/8	19 4/8	21 1/8	4 5/8 4 5/8	5 5		1991	9
	▪ Sullivan Co. – C. Alan Altizer – C. Alan Altizer – 1984							
172 5/8	25 1/8 25 2/8	16 5/8	19	4 4/8 4 4/8	5 6	1 2/8	2113	10
	▪ Stewart Co. – Thomas M. Bowers – Thomas M. Bowers – 1992							
172 4/8	27 5/8 28 6/8	21 5/8	24	4 3/8 4 2/8	6 6	2 7/8	2156	11
	▪ Haywood Co. – Mark S. Powell – Mark S. Powell – 1999							
172 3/8	27 6/8 28 2/8	17 2/8	19 6/8	4 6/8 4 5/8	6 5	2 1/8	2200	12
	▪ Decatur Co. – Danny Pope – Danny Pope – 1982							
172 2/8	26 2/8 25	18 7/8	20 6/8	5 5	6 6	2 1/8	2237	13
	▪ Stewart Co. – Joe K. Sanders – Joe K. Sanders – 1984							
171 7/8	26 5/8 27	19	22	4 7/8 4 6/8	6 5	2 3/8	2382	14
	▪ Grundy Co. – Wilson W. Weaver – Wilson W. Weaver – 1987							
171 2/8	25 26 4/8	18 2/8	21 2/8	5 6/8 5 7/8	6 6	3	2621†	15†
	▪ Meigs Co. – James E. Rose – James E. Rose – 2000							
168 1/8	26 1/8 25 6/8	22 1/8	24 3/8	4 3/8 4 2/8	5 5		3426	16
	▪ Bledsoe Co. – Richard W. Edmons – Richard W. Edmons – 1996							
166 7/8	23 4/8 24 4/8	19 1/8		4 2/8 4 2/8	6 6		3568	17
	▪ Davidson Co. – A. Wade Daugherty – A. Wade Daugherty – 1997							
161 2/8	25 26 5/8	17 4/8	20	5 1/8 4 7/8	7 5	1 4/8	4310	18
	▪ Williamson Co. – James R. Brown – James R. Brown – 2000							
160 4/8	25 6/8 26	18 2/8	20 5/8	5 4 6/8	7 6	5 4/8	4443	19
	▪ Shelby Co. – Ben L. Daniel – Ben L. Daniel – 1998							

Score	Length of Main Beam Right	Length of Main Beam Left	Inside Spread	Greatest Spread	Circumference at Smallest Place Between Burr and First Point Right	Circumference at Smallest Place Between Burr and First Point Left	Number of Points Right	Number of Points Left	Lengths Abnormal Points	All-Time Rank	State Rank
					■ *Location of Kill – Hunter – Owner – Date Killed*						
160²/₈	27⁷/₈	26⁷/₈	20⁴/₈	22¹/₈	4⁶/₈	4⁵/₈	8	5	7	4495	20
	■ *Stewart Co. – Mickey Lehman – Mickey Lehman – 1995*										

† The scores and ranking for trophies from the 25th Awards Entry Period are not final until the banquet is held on June 19, 2004.

U.S. WHITETAIL DEER LISTING BY STATE   437

TENNESSEE

NON-TYPICAL WHITETAIL DEER

Score	Length of Main Beam Right	Left	Inside Spread	Greatest Spread	Circumference at Smallest Place Between Burr and First Point Right	Left	Number of Points Right	Left	Lengths Abnormal Points	All-Time Rank	State Rank

Location of Kill – Hunter – Owner – Date Killed

244 3/8	22 1/8	23 1/8	17 4/8	22 4/8	5 4/8	4 7/8	25	24	89 7/8	88†	1†

■ *Sumner Co. – David K. Wachtel III – David K. Wachtel III – 2000* ■ *See photo on page 51*

| 232 7/8 | 21 2/8 | 20 3/8 | 15 6/8 | 23 3/8 | 4 | 4 | 18 | 19 | 114 3/8 | 197† | 2† |

■ *Haywood Co. – Justin K. Samples – Justin K. Samples – 2001*

| 223 4/8 | 21 3/8 | 23 | 23 4/8 | 27 2/8 | 4 1/8 | 4 2/8 | 19 | 11 | 61 | 350 | 3 |

■ *Hawkins Co. – Luther E. Fuller – Luther E. Fuller – 1984*

| 214 2/8 | 23 3/8 | 22 3/8 | 15 6/8 | 20 4/8 | 4 4/8 | 4 2/8 | 12 | 16 | 44 | 625† | 4† |

■ *Pickett Co. – Ronnie D. Perry, Jr. – Ronnie D. Perry, Jr. – 2001*

| 209 7/8 | 20 6/8 | 19 7/8 | 19 6/8 | 26 3/8 | 4 7/8 | 4 6/8 | 13 | 11 | 66 1/8 | 825 | 5 |

■ *Hawkins Co. – Johnny W. Byington – Johnny W. Byington – 1982*

| 208 2/8 | 25 | 25 5/8 | 17 | 22 | 4 5/8 | 4 4/8 | 11 | 12 | 40 | 910 | 6 |

■ *Van Buren Co. – A. Duane Hodges – A. Duane Hodges – 1994*

| 198 3/8 | 26 2/8 | 26 1/8 | 17 5/8 | 21 4/8 | 4 2/8 | 4 2/8 | 8 | 10 | 30 2/8 | 1762 | 7 |

■ *Montgomery Co. – Clarence McElhaney – Clarence McElhaney – 1978*

| 196 6/8 | 25 | 25 | 19 1/8 | 24 | 4 6/8 | 5 | 9 | 10 | 29 1/8 | 1968 | 8 |

■ *Unicoi Co. – Elmer Payne – Elmer Payne – 1972*

| 196 | 20 6/8 | 24 6/8 | 16 2/8 | 19 | 4 | 4 | 8 | 12 | 63 6/8 | 2059 | 9 |

■ *McNairy Co. – Bradley S. Koeppel – Bradley S. Koeppel – 1993*

| 195 1/8 | 26 2/8 | 26 3/8 | 23 | 26 4/8 | 5 1/8 | 5 | 10 | 8 | 18 5/8 | 2208† | 10† |

■ *Maury Co. – Chris Hagan – Chris Hagan – 2002* ■ *See photo on page 439*

| 192 | 26 | 26 1/8 | 19 1/8 | 25 | 4 4/8 | 4 6/8 | 6 | 7 | 21 7/8 | 2344 | 11 |

■ *Montgomery Co. – John J. Teeter – John J. Teeter – 1998*

| 185 3/8 | 25 2/8 | 28 6/8 | 24 | 26 4/8 | 5 | 5 1/8 | 8 | 6 | 35 5/8 | 2622 | 12 |

■ *Hawkins Co. – Terry H. Burns – Terry H. Burns – 1983*

† The scores and ranking for trophies from the 25th Awards Entry Period are not final until the banquet is held on June 19, 2004.

TROPHIES IN THE FIELD

HUNTER: Chris Hagan
SCORE: 195-1/8
CATEGORY: non-typical whitetail deer
LOCATION: Maury County, Tennessee
DATE: 2002

TEXAS
RECORD WHITETAILS

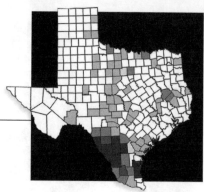

231 Typical whitetail deer entries
128 Non-typical whitetail deer entries
7,265 Total whitetail deer entries

0 Entries
1-2 Entries
3-5 Entries
6-10 Entries
11+ Entries

TEXAS
STATE RECORD
Typical Whitetail Deer
Score: 196⁴/₈
Location: Maverick Co.
Hunter: Tom McCulloch
Owner: McLean Bowman
Date: 1963

Photograph from B&C Archives

**TEXAS
STATE RECORD**
Non-Typical Whitetail Deer
Score: 284³/₈
Location: McCulloch Co.
Hunter: Unknown
Owner: Buckhorn Mus. & Saloon, Ltd.
Date: 1892

Photograph from B&C Archives

TEXAS

TYPICAL WHITETAIL DEER

Score	Length of Main Beam Right Left	Inside Spread	Greatest Spread	Circumference at Smallest Place Between Burr and First Point Right Left		Number of Points Right Left		Lengths Abnormal Points	All-Time Rank	State Rank
	■ Location of Kill – Hunter – Owner – Date Killed									
196⁴/8	28⁶/8 27⁵/8	24²/8	25⁵/8	4⁶/8 4⁶/8		8	6	1⁴/8	30	1
	■ Maverick Co. – Tom McCulloch – McLean Bowman – 1963									
196¹/8	27¹/8 26⁴/8	24⁵/8	26⁶/8	4⁶/8 4⁶/8		8	9	5⁴/8	33	2
	■ McMullen Co. – Milton P. George – John L. Stein – 1906									
192²/8	27²/8 27³/8	22⁶/8	27¹/8	4²/8 4⁴/8		6	7	7⁴/8	67	3
	■ Frio Co. – Basil Dailey – John L. Stein – 1903									
190²/8	26¹/8 23¹/8	25⁷/8	28	4³/8 4²/8		6	7	4⁵/8	104	4
	■ Shackelford Co. – Steven W. O'Carroll – John L. Stein – 1991									
190	24²/8 25²/8	20⁶/8	23	5 5		7	6		107	5
	■ Dimmit Co. – C.P. Howard – C.P. Howard – 1950									
187⁷/8	25⁵/8 26¹/8	21³/8	24	4⁶/8 4⁶/8		7	7		156	6
	■ Zavala Co. – Donald Rutledge – Frank Rutledge – 1946									
187⁵/8	28²/8 27⁶/8	19⁶/8	23⁴/8	5 5		6	8	5⁷/8	165	7
	■ Starr Co. – Picked Up – Jack F. Quist – 1945									
187⁴/8	26⁷/8 27²/8	26²/8	28¹/8	4⁷/8 4⁵/8		8	8	6²/8	172	8
	■ Zapata Co. – Phillip T. Stringer – Phillip T. Stringer – 1992									
186²/8	25²/8 25⁶/8	21	23	4⁶/8 4⁶/8		6	6		220	9
	■ La Salle Co. – Herman C. Schliesing – Herman C. Schliesing – 1967									
186²/8	27⁴/8 27⁴/8	18	20³/8	4⁶/8 4⁶/8		8	10	5⁶/8	220	9
	■ Kenedy Co. – Jack Van Cleve III – McGill Estate – 1972									
186¹/8	29⁴/8 29²/8	21	23³/8	4⁶/8 4⁵/8		8	9	6⁵/8	228	11
	■ Zavala Co. – Picked Up – Paul W. Sanders, Jr. – 1965									
185⁴/8	27⁷/8 25⁶/8	18⁷/8	20⁷/8	5³/8 5⁵/8		8	7	6³/8	251	12
	■ Zapata Co. – Jesus Lopez – John L. Stein – 1969									
185¹/8	25⁶/8 25³/8	27	30²/8	5 4⁶/8		7	6	1³/8	266	13
	■ Webb Co. – Henderson Coquat – Henderson Coquat – 1949									
185	25²/8 25	19²/8	21	4⁶/8 4⁶/8		6	6		272	14
	■ Frio Co. – Loyd Nail – Steven L. Smith – 1941									
184⁶/8	26³/8 26²/8	24²/8	26	4⁶/8 4⁶/8		7	6	3⁶/8	285	15
	■ Starr Co. – Harry Richardson, Jr. – Harry Richardson, Jr. – 1973									
184⁴/8	26¹/8 28⁴/8	22⁵/8	24⁴/8	4⁴/8 4⁴/8		10	8	7⁷/8	303	16
	■ Bandera Co. – Picked Up – Wyatt Birkner – 1949									
183⁷/8	26 26²/8	18³/8	21⁶/8	4²/8 4²/8		5	5		343†	17†
	■ Angelina Co. – Jeffery T. Capps – Jeffery T. Capps – 2000									
183¹/8	27⁷/8 28⁶/8	20⁵/8	22⁴/8	5 5		6	6		385	18
	■ Duval Co. – Charles Drennan – Bill Carter – 1973									
182⁶/8	26 25⁴/8	18	20⁵/8	4⁷/8 5		8	6	1	409	19
	■ Webb Co. – George Strait – George Strait – 1988									

Score	Length of Main Beam Right Left	Inside Spread	Greatest Spread	Circumference at Smallest Place Between Burr and First Point Right Left		Number of Points Right Left		Lengths Abnormal Points	All-Time Rank	State Rank
	■ Location of Kill – Hunter – Owner – Date Killed									
182 6/8	28 6/8 28 3/8	22 6/8	24 6/8	5	4 7/8	5	5		409	19
	■ La Salle Co. – Daniel A. Herson – Daniel A. Herson – 1995									
182 4/8	25 5/8 25 7/8	18 4/8	20 4/8	4 5/8	4 6/8	6	6		431	21
	■ Maverick Co. – Christopher J. Roswell – Christopher J. Roswell – 1997									
181 7/8	24 4/8 24 4/8	15 5/8	17 6/8	4 3/8	4 4/8	6	6		478	22
	■ McMullen Co. – Oscar Hassette – Bill Carter – 1971									
181 5/8	24 1/8 25	21 3/8	22 7/8	4 4/8	4 6/8	6	6		500	23
	■ La Salle Co. – Buck Turman – Lawson W. Walden – 1947									
181 1/8	26 1/8 25 3/8	18 5/8	20 4/8	5	5	6	5	1 6/8	551	24
	■ Frio Co. – Warren Smith – Roy Hindes – PR 1950									
180 6/8	26 6/8 26	25	26 6/8	5	4 4/8	6	9	5 6/8	587	25
	■ Dimmit Co. – Edward Gardner – Edward Gardner – 1937									
180 5/8	25 23 4/8	19 2/8	20 4/8	4 4/8	4 4/8	7	7	1 1/8	599	26
	■ Maverick Co. – Jim Webb – Richard H. Bennett – 1912									
180 5/8	25 6/8 24 7/8	19 3/8	21 3/8	4 5/8	4 3/8	6	6		599	26
	■ Jim Hogg Co. – Michael L. Vickers – Michael L. Vickers – 1991									
180 4/8	28 26 2/8	26 6/8	26 6/8	4 6/8	5 2/8	7	7	3 4/8	613	28
	■ Jim Hogg Co. – Roy L. Henry – Roy L. Henry – 1958									
180 2/8	28 2/8 27 7/8	20 2/8	22 3/8	4 7/8	4 7/8	6	6	4 6/8	651	29
	■ Texas – Alfred Schroeder – John E. Hamilton – PR 1926									
180	26 25 7/8	19	24 1/8	4 7/8	4 7/8	10	7	12 2/8	688	30
	■ Zavala Co. – Mrs. Richard King III – Mrs. Richard King III – 1966									
179 6/8	26 3/8 26 2/8	19 6/8	22	4 6/8	4 5/8	6	6		712	31
	■ Jim Hogg Co. – William B. Van Fleet – William B. Van Fleet – 1979									
179 4/8	28 3/8 28 5/8	21	25 2/8	4 4/8	4 4/8	5	6		733	32
	■ Collingsworth Co. – Picked Up – F. Gus Reinarz – 1987									
179 4/8	25 24 7/8	21	23	4 7/8	5	7	6	4	733	32
	■ Maverick Co. – Lee M. Bass – Lee M. Bass – 1998									
179 2/8	24 2/8 24 2/8	19 4/8	23 7/8	4 4/8	4 5/8	6	6		763	34
	■ Dimmit Co. – William M. Knolle – William M. Knolle – 1982									
179	23 23 7/8	16 5/8	20 5/8	3 5/8	3 5/8	8	9	10 1/8	786	35
	■ La Salle Co. – Charles Duffy – Emory C. Thompson – PR 1941									
178 6/8	27 3/8 27 5/8	20 7/8	22 4/8	4	4 1/8	9	8	11 3/8	808	36
	■ Texas – Unknown – Buckhorn Mus. & Saloon, Ltd. – PR 1920									
178 6/8	27 27	19 2/8	21 3/8	4 6/8	4 5/8	6	6		808	36
	■ Webb Co. – M.J. Satcher – M.J. Satcher – 1987									
178 5/8	26 4/8 25 2/8	18 2/8	20 6/8	5	5	6	5	3 5/8	819	38
	■ Hemphill Co. – Cliff Norris – Cliff Norris – 1999									
178 4/8	25 2/8 25	23 2/8	25	5 4/8	5 4/8	5	5		850	39
	■ McMullen Co. – D.H. Waldron – D.H. Waldron – 1964									
177 6/8	24 24	22	24	4 4/8	4 4/8	6	6	3 6/8	956	40
	■ Kleberg Co. – Elaine A. O'Brien – Patrick O'Brien – 1972									

Score	Length of Main Beam Right	Left	Inside Spread	Greatest Spread	Circumference at Smallest Place Between Burr and First Point Right	Left	Number of Points Right	Left	Lengths Abnormal Points	All-Time Rank	State Rank
177⁶/₈	23⁴/₈	24	24	26	4⁶/₈	4⁶/₈	6	6		956	40

■ Duval Co. – Harry Heimer – Harry Heimer – 1974

| 177⁵/₈ | 25⁵/₈ | 27¹/₈ | 21⁵/₈ | 24 | 4³/₈ | 4³/₈ | 5 | 6 | | 972† | 42† |

■ Frio Co. – Guy S. Perkins – Guy S. Perkins – 2001

| 177⁵/₈ | 24⁶/₈ | 23³/₈ | 24⁷/₈ | 26⁴/₈ | 5¹/₈ | 5²/₈ | 7 | 6 | 3⁷/₈ | 972 | 42 |

■ Dimmit Co. – Carter Younts – Carter Younts – 1963

| 177⁵/₈ | 24⁴/₈ | 25³/₈ | 18³/₈ | 20⁵/₈ | 5¹/₈ | 5¹/₈ | 6 | 7 | | 972 | 42 |

■ Jim Hogg Co. – Howard Sturgess – Lawson W. Walden – PR 1982

| 177⁴/₈ | 27⁶/₈ | 27⁴/₈ | 23⁴/₈ | 27²/₈ | 5 | 5 | 6 | 5 | | 993 | 45 |

■ Dimmit Co. – Tom Brady – McLean Bowman – 1926

| 177²/₈ | 26⁶/₈ | 25³/₈ | 26²/₈ | 28¹/₈ | 5¹/₈ | 5¹/₈ | 7 | 7 | 2⁶/₈ | 1025 | 46 |

■ Webb Co. – Unknown – Eugene Roberts – 1924

| 177²/₈ | 24¹/₈ | 24⁵/₈ | 22²/₈ | 23⁷/₈ | 4²/₈ | 4¹/₈ | 5 | 5 | | 1025 | 46 |

■ La Salle Co. – T.H. Barker – Michael R. Barker – 1939

| 177²/₈ | 25⁶/₈ | 24⁴/₈ | 20²/₈ | 23 | 4⁷/₈ | 4⁷/₈ | 6 | 5 | 1²/₈ | 1025 | 46 |

■ Webb Co. – Gordon Still – Gordon Still – 1999

| 176⁵/₈ | 24⁶/₈ | 26²/₈ | 27²/₈ | 29 | 4⁶/₈ | 5 | 5 | 6 | 2¹/₈ | 1134 | 49 |

■ Hays Co. – Bill Kuykendall – Bill Kuykendall – 1925

| 176⁵/₈ | 24²/₈ | 23³/₈ | 16⁷/₈ | 18⁷/₈ | 4³/₈ | 4³/₈ | 9 | 9 | 10⁶/₈ | 1134 | 49 |

■ Webb Co. – Antonio Gonzalez – Edmundo R. Gonzalez, Jr. – 1929

| 176⁵/₈ | 26³/₈ | 25⁷/₈ | 22³/₈ | 25 | 5³/₈ | 5³/₈ | 7 | 9 | 8 | 1134 | 49 |

■ Kleberg Co. – Donald M. Brock, Jr. – Donald M. Brock, Jr. – 1993

| 176⁵/₈ | 25⁷/₈ | 26³/₈ | 20⁵/₈ | 22¹/₈ | 5⁵/₈ | 5⁴/₈ | 6 | 5 | | 1134 | 49 |

■ Wilbarger Co. – Owen P. Carpenter III – Owen P. Carpenter III – 1999

| 176⁴/₈ | 25²/₈ | 24²/₈ | 19 | 21⁴/₈ | 3⁷/₈ | 4¹/₈ | 6 | 6 | | 1158 | 53 |

■ Shackelford Co. – H.V. Stroud – H.V. Stroud – 1964

| 176⁴/₈ | 23 | 23 | 16⁴/₈ | 19²/₈ | 4²/₈ | 4²/₈ | 9 | 7 | 5⁴/₈ | 1158 | 53 |

■ Carrizo Springs – Lin F. Nowotny – Lin F. Nowotny – 1966

| 176⁴/₈ | 25¹/₈ | 24¹/₈ | 19²/₈ | 21²/₈ | 4⁶/₈ | 4⁶/₈ | 7 | 8 | 1 | 1158 | 53 |

■ Jim Hogg Co. – Picked Up – Eduardo M. Garza – 1990

| 176⁴/₈ | 26²/₈ | 25³/₈ | 22⁴/₈ | 26⁶/₈ | 4²/₈ | 4¹/₈ | 5 | 6 | | 1158 | 53 |

■ Refugio Co. – William M. Murphy IV – William M. Murphy IV – 1997

| 176²/₈ | 24⁷/₈ | 26¹/₈ | 21 | 23 | 4¹/₈ | 4 | 6 | 6 | | 1209 | 57 |

■ Karnes Co. – Gideon Pace – Steve Mansfield – PR 1905

| 176¹/₈ | 24²/₈ | 23²/₈ | 17¹/₈ | 18⁶/₈ | 4⁷/₈ | 4⁷/₈ | 6 | 7 | 1²/₈ | 1243 | 58 |

■ Webb Co. – Robert L. Hixson, Jr. – Robert L. Hixson, Jr. – 1997

| 176¹/₈ | 28²/₈ | 27⁷/₈ | 20⁶/₈ | 22⁶/₈ | 4²/₈ | 4¹/₈ | 6 | 6 | 1⁷/₈ | 1243 | 58 |

■ Maverick Co. – Steve E. Holloway – Steve E. Holloway – 1997

| 175⁷/₈ | 23³/₈ | 24³/₈ | 20⁵/₈ | 23⁷/₈ | 4³/₈ | 4⁴/₈ | 5 | 6 | 1⁴/₈ | 1287 | 60 |

■ Kinney Co. – Walter Griener – John L. Stein – 1935

| 175⁶/₈ | 25⁶/₈ | 26 | 20²/₈ | 21⁶/₈ | 4 | 4 | 6 | 6 | | 1310 | 61 |

■ Webb Co. – William Bretthauer, Sr. – George H. Glass – 1915

Score	Length of Main Beam Right Left	Inside Spread	Greatest Spread	Circumference at Smallest Place Between Burr and First Point Right Left	Number of Points Right Left	Lengths Abnormal Points	All-Time Rank	State Rank
	■ *Location of Kill – Hunter – Owner – Date Killed*							
175⁶/₈	27²/₈ 26⁷/₈	22⁶/₈	24⁷/₈	5⁴/₈ 5	7 6	3⁴/₈	1310	61
	■ *Webb Co. – Norman Frede – John L. Stein – 1978*							
175⁶/₈	25⁴/₈ 26⁴/₈	20	22	5³/₈ 5²/₈	6 6		1310	61
	■ *Dimmit Co. – George E. Light III – George E. Light III – 1979*							
175³/₈	25 25	18¹/₈	20	4²/₈ 4¹/₈	6 6		1377	64
	■ *Dimmit Co. – Betsy Campbell – Betsy Campbell – 1978*							
175³/₈	25⁶/₈ 26¹/₈	22³/₈	24²/₈	4⁷/₈ 5¹/₈	6 7	4	1377	64
	■ *Collingsworth Co. – Eugene Hanna – John L. Stein – 1988*							
175²/₈	22⁷/₈ 22⁷/₈	19	22	4⁴/₈ 4⁵/₈	6 6		1403	66
	■ *Encinal – W.S. Benson, Sr. – W.S. Benson III – 1928*							
175²/₈	26²/₈ 26²/₈	21	22⁶/₈	4⁴/₈ 4³/₈	6 6		1403	66
	■ *Texas – Elmo Wilson – Joe B. Wilson – PR 1975*							
175²/₈	25⁶/₈ 26⁷/₈	15²/₈	17¹/₈	4⁴/₈ 4⁴/₈	6 6		1403	66
	■ *Frio Co. – India N. Shackelford – India N. Shackelford – 1992*							
175¹/₈	22⁷/₈ 23⁶/₈	19⁷/₈	22	4⁷/₈ 4⁷/₈	7 6	2⁶/₈	1440	69
	■ *Dimmit Co. – Ray Perry – Ray Perry – 1976*							
175	26²/₈ 26	18⁴/₈	20³/₈	4⁵/₈ 4⁴/₈	6 6		1472	70
	■ *Webb Co. – Leslie G. Fisher – Leslie G. Fisher, Jr. – 1935*							
175	24³/₈ 22⁷/₈	18⁶/₈	21	4⁷/₈ 4⁷/₈	7 7		1472	70
	■ *La Salle Co. – Leonard W. Bouldin – Leonard W. Bouldin – 1972*							
175	28⁴/₈ 28³/₈	18²/₈	20⁶/₈	4⁴/₈ 4⁴/₈	6 7	3	1472	70
	■ *La Salle Co. – Phil Lyne – Phil Lyne – 1972*							
175	26 27⁴/₈	21	23	5¹/₈ 5¹/₈	5 6		1472	70
	■ *Jim Hogg Co. – Carl D. Ellis – Lee H. Lytton, Jr. – 1984*							
175	24⁶/₈ 25¹/₈	19⁶/₈	22⁷/₈	4⁴/₈ 4³/₈	6 8	6	1472	70
	■ *Maverick Co. – William M. Wheless III – William M. Wheless III – 1992*							
175	25³/₈ 25⁴/₈	17⁴/₈	22⁴/₈	4 4¹/₈	6 6		1472	70
	■ *Maverick Co. – Gary L. Braun – Gary L. Braun – 1993*							
175	28⁷/₈ 28³/₈	21⁶/₈	25	5²/₈ 5³/₈	5 5		1472	70
	■ *Maverick Co. – John A. Cardwell – John A. Cardwell – 1999*							
174⁷/₈	25¹/₈ 25¹/₈	20⁶/₈	24	4¹/₈ 4³/₈	8 7	10⁵/₈	1513	77
	■ *Polk Co. – Charlie L. Albertson – Charlie L. Albertson – 1984*							
174⁵/₈	24 24⁷/₈	19³/₈	22²/₈	4⁴/₈ 4⁴/₈	5 6	1²/₈	1561†	78†
	■ *Webb Co. – Alan W. Saralecos – Alan W. Saralecos – 2000*							
174⁵/₈	25 25²/₈	24³/₈	26⁵/₈	4³/₈ 4²/₈	7 7	2²/₈	1561	78
	■ *Kleberg Co. – C.T. Burris – Darrel Pitts – 1959*							
174⁵/₈	27²/₈ 26⁵/₈	20³/₈	22¹/₈	4⁴/₈ 4⁴/₈	8 7	5⁶/₈	1561	78
	■ *Webb Co. – Edward O. Radke – Edward O. Radke – 1992*							
174⁴/₈	24⁷/₈ 24⁶/₈	20⁶/₈	22⁵/₈	4⁵/₈ 4⁵/₈	5 5		1592	81
	■ *La Salle Co. – H.C. Eppright – H.C. Sims – 1982*							
174³/₈	27¹/₈ 27²/₈	15⁵/₈	18²/₈	4⁴/₈ 4³/₈	7 7	7⁴/₈	1619	82
	■ *Texas – Unknown – Buckhorn Mus. & Saloon, Ltd. – PR 1956*							

Score	Length of Main Beam Right / Left	Inside Spread	Greatest Spread	Circumference at Smallest Place Between Burr and First Point Right / Left	Number of Points Right / Left	Lengths Abnormal Points	All-Time Rank	State Rank
	■ *Location of Kill – Hunter – Owner – Date Killed*							
174³/₈	28³/₈ 26²/₈	23¹/₈	26	4³/₈ 4⁴/₈	7 7		1619	82
	■ *Dimmit Co. – Steven W. Vaughn – Steven W. Vaughn – 1987*							
174²/₈	25⁴/₈ 26	20	21⁶/₈	4⁴/₈ 4⁴/₈	6 8	4²/₈	1652	84
	■ *Zavala Co. – Ernest Holdsworth – E.M. Holdsworth – 1908*							
174²/₈	24⁶/₈ 24²/₈	22	24	4⁶/₈ 4⁶/₈	6 5		1652	84
	■ *Dimmit Co. – Red Tollet – McLean Bowman – 1958*							
174²/₈	21⁴/₈ 22	17	18⁶/₈	4⁶/₈ 4⁵/₈	6 6		1652	84
	■ *Cass Co. – R.J. Perkins – John D. Small – 1963*							
174²/₈	23³/₈ 23⁶/₈	15⁶/₈	18	4⁴/₈ 4⁵/₈	10 9	4	1652	84
	■ *La Salle Co. – Walter L. Taylor – Walter L. Taylor – 1979*							
174²/₈	27⁵/₈ 27¹/₈	23⁴/₈	25⁷/₈	4⁶/₈ 4⁶/₈	5 5		1652	84
	■ *Dimmit Co. – Picked Up – John I. Kunert – PR 1991*							
174¹/₈	24⁷/₈ 24⁷/₈	17¹/₈	19⁴/₈	4 3⁷/₈	6 6		1678	89
	■ *Archer Co. – Wade G. Schreiber – Wade G. Schreiber – 1994*							
174	28 27⁶/₈	24⁷/₈	26⁶/₈	5¹/₈ 5	6 6	2⁷/₈	1717	90
	■ *La Salle Co. – Unknown – Lawson W. Walden – 1949*							
173⁷/₈	25⁴/₈ 26	19³/₈	21⁴/₈	5 5	6 6		1743	91
	■ *Starr Co. – Leonard A. Schwarz – Leonard A. Schwarz – 1965*							
173⁷/₈	27⁶/₈ 26⁶/₈	18⁴/₈	20⁷/₈	5⁶/₈ 5⁶/₈	4 6	1⁵/₈	1743	91
	■ *Wilbarger Co. – John T. Wright – John T. Wright – 1998*							
173⁶/₈	23²/₈ 24	19⁶/₈	22⁴/₈	4⁶/₈ 4⁶/₈	6 6		1766	93
	■ *Dimmit Co. – Booth W. Petry – Booth W. Petry – 1970*							
173⁶/₈	26⁴/₈ 25⁴/₈	18⁶/₈	21²/₈	4²/₈ 4²/₈	7 6	7⁴/₈	1766	93
	■ *Stephens Co. – Robert L. Murphy – Robert L. Murphy – 1986*							
173⁶/₈	24²/₈ 25³/₈	19⁵/₈	21⁴/₈	4⁴/₈ 4⁴/₈	8 8	2⁷/₈	1766	93
	■ *Webb Co. – Hunter McGrath – Hunter McGrath – 1995*							
173⁵/₈	26¹/₈ 26	20¹/₈	22	4⁵/₈ 4⁶/₈	7 6		1819	96
	■ *La Salle Co. – Jeff S. Golbow – Jeff S. Golbow – 1997*							
173⁴/₈	26⁶/₈ 27¹/₈	16	18⁴/₈	4⁷/₈ 4⁷/₈	5 5		1847	97
	■ *Zavala Co. – Roger Morris – Alvin Morris – 1931*							
173⁴/₈	24⁷/₈ 25⁶/₈	22⁴/₈	23⁷/₈	4⁷/₈ 4⁷/₈	5 5		1847	97
	■ *Maverick Co. – Clifton F. Douglass III – Clifton F. Douglass III – 1991*							
173⁴/₈	25⁷/₈ 25⁶/₈	19²/₈	21⁶/₈	4¹/₈ 4⁴/₈	5 5		1847	97
	■ *La Salle Co. – James K. Haney – James K. Haney – 1997*							
173²/₈	25⁵/₈ 25⁷/₈	19	20⁷/₈	4²/₈ 4¹/₈	6 6		1914	100
	■ *Texas – Unknown – Marvin Schwarz – PR 1940*							
173²/₈	25³/₈ 25⁴/₈	21²/₈	23³/₈	5³/₈ 5²/₈	6 8	3²/₈	1914	100
	■ *Webb Co. – Frank J. Sitterle – Frank J. Sitterle – 1987*							
173²/₈	27²/₈ 25⁵/₈	22	24²/₈	4⁶/₈ 4⁵/₈	5 5		1914	100
	■ *La Salle Co. – Wayne W. Webb – Wayne W. Webb – 1992*							
173	27³/₈ 27	21³/₈	23⁴/₈	4⁵/₈ 4³/₈	5 7	1¹/₈	1991†	103†
	■ *Jim Hogg Co. – Eliverto Cantu – Eddie M. Garza – 1985*							

Score	Length of Main Beam Right	Left	Inside Spread	Greatest Spread	Circumference at Smallest Place Between Burr and First Point Right	Left	Number of Points Right	Left	Lengths Abnormal Points	All-Time Rank	State Rank
173	$28^4/_8$	$28^2/_8$	25	$28^4/_8$	$4^2/_8$	$4^2/_8$	7	7	$9^4/_8$	1991	103

■ *Dimmit Co. – George Light IV – George Light IV – 1979*

| 173 | $25^2/_8$ | $24^2/_8$ | $21^7/_8$ | 24 | $4^5/_8$ | $4^6/_8$ | 9 | 6 | $5^3/_8$ | 1991 | 103 |

■ *Hidalgo Co. – William L. Turk – William L. Turk – 1979*

| 173 | $24^4/_8$ | $25^5/_8$ | $16^7/_8$ | $19^5/_8$ | $3^7/_8$ | $3^6/_8$ | 6 | 7 | $1^1/_8$ | 1991 | 103 |

■ *Trinity Co. – Don Knight – Don Knight – 1983*

| $172^7/_8$ | $25^1/_8$ | $23^3/_8$ | $16^5/_8$ | $19^1/_8$ | $4^6/_8$ | $4^5/_8$ | 6 | 6 | | 2038 | 107 |

■ *McMullen Co. – Steve Best – Steve Best – 1991*

| $172^7/_8$ | $28^3/_8$ | $27^6/_8$ | 29 | $31^1/_8$ | 5 | $5^2/_8$ | 6 | 5 | $2^4/_8$ | 2038 | 107 |

■ *Donley Co. – Barrett W. Thorne – Barrett W. Thorne – 1999*

| $172^6/_8$ | $25^6/_8$ | $24^7/_8$ | $23^4/_8$ | $25^1/_8$ | $4^2/_8$ | $4^2/_8$ | 5 | 5 | | 2065 | 109 |

■ *Texas – Unknown – Thomas P. Kosub – PR 1945*

| $172^6/_8$ | $28^6/_8$ | 29 | $22^4/_8$ | $24^4/_8$ | $4^4/_8$ | $4^4/_8$ | 5 | 6 | | 2065 | 109 |

■ *Webb Co. – B.A. Vineyard – B.A. Vineyard – 1964*

| $172^6/_8$ | $26^1/_8$ | $26^5/_8$ | $21^2/_8$ | $23^6/_8$ | 5 | 5 | 6 | 6 | | 2065 | 109 |

■ *Dimmit Co. – David R. Park – David R. Park, Jr. – 1978*

| $172^6/_8$ | $25^5/_8$ | 26 | $18^7/_8$ | $21^6/_8$ | $4^7/_8$ | $4^4/_8$ | 6 | 5 | $2^1/_8$ | 2065 | 109 |

■ *Bee Co. – John W. Galloway – John W. Galloway – 1990*

| $172^5/_8$ | $24^2/_8$ | $24^4/_8$ | $21^1/_8$ | 23 | $5^2/_8$ | 5 | 6 | 6 | | 2113 | 113 |

■ *Frio Co. – Unknown – Roy Hindes – PR 1940*

| $172^5/_8$ | 24 | $24^3/_8$ | $23^5/_8$ | $25^1/_8$ | $4^3/_8$ | $4^3/_8$ | 7 | 7 | $2^4/_8$ | 2113 | 113 |

■ *San Patricio Co. – Mary L. Edwards – Mary L. Edwards – 1967*

| $172^5/_8$ | $26^2/_8$ | $25^7/_8$ | $17^7/_8$ | 20 | $4^5/_8$ | $4^4/_8$ | 5 | 5 | | 2113 | 113 |

■ *Eastland Co. – Kevin L. Reed – Kevin L. Reed – 1995*

| $172^4/_8$ | $26^5/_8$ | $25^6/_8$ | $20^6/_8$ | $23^3/_8$ | $4^4/_8$ | $4^6/_8$ | 9 | 8 | $12^4/_8$ | 2156 | 116 |

■ *Mason Co. – Earl E. Allen – Allen Family – PR 1926*

| $172^4/_8$ | $25^6/_8$ | 27 | $20^2/_8$ | $21^5/_8$ | $5^2/_8$ | 5 | 6 | 6 | | 2156 | 116 |

■ *Cotulla – George E. Light III – George E. Light III – 1959*

| $172^4/_8$ | $24^4/_8$ | $24^4/_8$ | $18^4/_8$ | $20^6/_8$ | $4^4/_8$ | $4^4/_8$ | 6 | 7 | | 2156 | 116 |

■ *Webb Co. – A.M. Russell – A.M. Russell – 1961*

| $172^4/_8$ | $27^3/_8$ | $26^6/_8$ | $21^2/_8$ | $23^1/_8$ | 4 | 4 | 5 | 5 | | 2156 | 116 |

■ *Zavala Co. – Gaston F. Maurin – Clint Arnold – 1964*

| $172^2/_8$ | $28^3/_8$ | $28^2/_8$ | $19^6/_8$ | $21^7/_8$ | $4^4/_8$ | $4^4/_8$ | 4 | 4 | | 2237 | 120 |

■ *Frio Co. – Thomas W. Burell – Thomas W. Burell – 1999*

| $172^1/_8$ | $24^4/_8$ | $23^7/_8$ | $18^5/_8$ | $20^6/_8$ | $4^5/_8$ | $4^6/_8$ | 6 | 6 | | 2286 | 121 |

■ *Kenedy Co. – Lee M. Bass – Lee M. Bass – 1996*

| 172 | $26^3/_8$ | $26^5/_8$ | $20^7/_8$ | $24^1/_8$ | $5^2/_8$ | $5^4/_8$ | 7 | 6 | $5^1/_8$ | 2330 | 122 |

■ *Kenedy Co. – Lee M. Bass – Lee M. Bass – 1997*

| $171^7/_8$ | $24^6/_8$ | 26 | $17^2/_8$ | $18^6/_8$ | $4^2/_8$ | $4^1/_8$ | 7 | 7 | $7^3/_8$ | 2382 | 123 |

■ *Duval Co. – Dan Harrison – Mike Pillow – 1969*

| $171^7/_8$ | $24^4/_8$ | $24^4/_8$ | $17^5/_8$ | $19^4/_8$ | $4^4/_8$ | $4^4/_8$ | 5 | 6 | | 2382 | 123 |

■ *Maverick Co. – William H. Whitley – William H. Whitley – 1997*

Score	Length of Main Beam Right	Left	Inside Spread	Greatest Spread	Circumference at Smallest Place Between Burr and First Point Right	Left	Number of Points Right	Left	Lengths Abnormal Points	All-Time Rank	State Rank
171 6/8	24 2/8	24 2/8	19 4/8	21 2/8	4 2/8	4 2/8	6	5		2418†	125†
■ *Throckmorton Co. – D. David Teague – D. David Teague – 2000*											
171 6/8	25	24 6/8	22	23 2/8	4 6/8	4 6/8	7	6		2418	125
■ *Maverick Co. – Harry Garner – Harry Garner – 1962*											
171 6/8	26 5/8	25 3/8	21 6/8	24	5 1/8	5 1/8	6	6		2418	125
■ *Webb Co. – David W. Bivins – David W. Bivins – 1992*											
171 5/8	26 5/8	24 4/8	21 4/8	25 7/8	4 5/8	4 4/8	7	7	7 5/8	2470†	128†
■ *Webb Co. – Xavier Villasenor, Jr. – Xavier Villasenor, Jr. – 2001*											
171 5/8	23 6/8	24 1/8	19 7/8	21 6/8	4 7/8	4 6/8	6	6		2470	128
■ *La Salle Co. – Harvey N. Bouldin, Jr. – Harvey N. Bouldin, Jr. – 1992*											
171 4/8	25 2/8	24 7/8	22	23 5/8	4 5/8	4 5/8	5	5		2513†	130†
■ *Webb Co. – Willie H. Esse, Jr. – Willie H. Esse, Jr. – 2000*											
171 4/8	28 1/8	28 5/8	20 6/8	23 1/8	4 4/8	4 3/8	5	5		2513	130
■ *Dimmit Co. – Kenneth P. Crawford – Kenneth P. Crawford – 1997*											
171 3/8	31 1/8	29	16	19 2/8	5	5	7	9	11 3/8	2564	132
■ *Frio Co. – Leonard Van Horn – Leonard Van Horn – 1962*											
171 3/8	24 3/8	24 3/8	18 5/8	20 2/8	4 3/8	4 3/8	6	6		2564	132
■ *Parker Co. – Velton L. Ford – Velton L. Ford – 1963*											
171 3/8	26	24 4/8	15 1/8	16 7/8	4 3/8	4	5	6	1 4/8	2564	132
■ *La Salle Co. – Charles D. Johnson – Charles D. Johnson – 1964*											
171 3/8	20 4/8	22	19 1/8	22	4 7/8	5 1/8	6	6		2564	132
■ *Webb Co. – Robert K. Deligans – Robert K. Deligans – 1986*											
171 3/8	23 3/8	23 6/8	18 3/8	20 5/8	4 5/8	4 5/8	5	5		2564	132
■ *Stonewall Co. – Jay W. Knorr – Jay W. Knorr – 1987*											
171 3/8	24 6/8	24 7/8	17 1/8	19 1/8	4 5/8	4 6/8	6	6		2564	132
■ *Dimmit Co. – Robert E. Zaiglin – Robert E. Zaiglin – 1993*											
171 2/8	25 4/8	25 3/8	19 4/8	21 6/8	4 6/8	5	5	6		2621	138
■ *Webb Co. – Ernie Pavlas – Ernie Pavlas – 1970*											
171 1/8	26 4/8	25 3/8	17 4/8	20 2/8	4 2/8	4 2/8	6	6	2 1/8	2665	139
■ *La Salle Co. – Unknown – F. Gus Reinarz – PR 1980*											
171	27 1/8	27	19 2/8	21	4 5/8	4 5/8	6	6	7 4/8	2707†	140†
■ *Maverick Co. – William A. Jordan III – William A. Jordan III – 2001*											
171	24 7/8	24 7/8	21 1/8	22 7/8	4 4/8	4 7/8	7	7	2 7/8	2707	140
■ *Kleberg Co. – Darwin D. Baucum – Darwin D. Baucum – 1994*											
170 7/8	26 4/8	25 7/8	17 6/8	19 6/8	5	5	7	6	1 3/8	2769	142
■ *Frio Co. – Lex Stewart – Lex Stewart – 1930*											
170 7/8	25 5/8	26 7/8	22 4/8	24 4/8	4 3/8	4 1/8	7	7	3 7/8	2769	142
■ *Texas – Unknown – Larry Bollier – PR 1970*											
170 6/8	28 4/8	28 1/8	24 6/8	27 7/8	4 2/8	4 1/8	6	8	12	2828	144
■ *Zapata Co. – G.O. Elliff – Michael Elliff – 1926*											
170 6/8	25 6/8	26	21	23 2/8	5 4/8	5 2/8	5	5		2828	144
■ *Dimmit Co. – J.H. Hixon – J.H. Hixon – 1958*											

■ Location of Kill – Hunter – Owner – Date Killed

Score	Length of Main Beam Right Left	Inside Spread	Greatest Spread	Circumference at Smallest Place Between Burr and First Point Right Left	Number of Points Right Left	Lengths Abnormal Points	All-Time Rank	State Rank
170⁶/8	25⁷/8 24⁶/8	24⁴/8	26	4⁶/8 4⁶/8	5 5		2828	144
■ Kenedy Co. – John A. Cardwell – John A. Cardwell – 1996
170⁵/8	23⁶/8 25⁷/8	17⁵/8	19¹/8	4⁴/8 4⁴/8	6 6		2876	147
■ Kinney Co. – Don T. Barksdale – Marshall E. Kuykendall – 1925
170⁴/8	24²/8 25²/8	19	20⁶/8	4²/8 4⁴/8	6 6		2933	148
■ La Salle Co. – Jerome Knebel – Jerome Knebel – 1974
170⁴/8	27 27⁴/8	23⁴/8	27	4²/8 4²/8	5 6		2933	148
■ Webb Co. – R.W. Mann – R.W. Mann – 1979
170⁴/8	25⁴/8 26	19²/8	21²/8	4¹/8 4²/8	6 5		2933	148
■ Atascosa Co. – James C. Coffman – James C. Coffman – 1994
170⁴/8	28²/8 28⁴/8	22⁶/8	24⁵/8	4⁴/8 4⁴/8	6 6		2933	148
■ Dimmit Co. – Joe E. Coleman – Joe E. Coleman – 1998
170³/8	25²/8 25⁶/8	18¹/8	20	4⁴/8 4³/8	66 0		2992†	152†
■ Dimmit Co. – Robert E. Zaiglin – Robert E. Zaiglin – 2001
170³/8	25⁶/8 25¹/8	22²/8	22⁷/8	3⁷/8 3⁷/8	6 6	6⁷/8	2992	152
■ Travis Co. – W.A. Brown – W.A. Brown – 1922
170³/8	26²/8 25	21⁴/8	23	4⁷/8 4⁷/8	5 8	4¹/8	2992	152
■ Webb Co. – Clarence Zieschang – Clarence Zieschang – 1966
170³/8	24⁴/8 23⁴/8	22	24	5²/8 5	8 7	12⁵/8	2992	152
■ Duval Co. – R.L. Kruger – R.L. Kruger – 1968
170³/8	29⁵/8 29³/8	26	28	5³/8 5¹/8	4 5	2¹/8	2992	152
■ Dimmit Co. – McLean Bowman – McLean Bowman – 1981
170³/8	23⁶/8 24	17⁷/8	19⁴/8	4 4¹/8	6 6		2992	152
■ Maverick Co. – Jay C. Harmon – Jay C. Harmon – 1994
170³/8	24⁷/8 24⁶/8	17⁵/8	20⁷/8	4²/8 4¹/8	5 5		2992	152
■ Throckmorton Co. – Ken W. Youngblood – Ken W. Youngblood – 1997
170²/8	21²/8 21²/8	15	17	4⁴/8 4³/8	7 8	2⁴/8	3063†	159†
■ Maverick Co. – Steve E. Holloway – Steve E. Holloway – 2001
170²/8	27 27¹/8	19²/8	22³/8	4³/8 4⁴/8	5 7	3⁴/8	3063	159
■ Webb Co. – Roy C. Rice – Roy C. Rice – 1948
170²/8	24⁴/8 24	19⁴/8	21	4⁶/8 4⁶/8	6 5		3063	159
■ McMullen Co. – Earl Welch – Earl Welch – 1964
170²/8	24⁶/8 24³/8	19⁵/8	21⁶/8	4⁵/8 4⁵/8	8 7	3³/8	3063	159
■ Jim Hogg Co. – Tom P. Hayes – Tom P. Hayes – 1968
170²/8	25⁷/8 26	18⁶/8	20¹/8	4³/8 4³/8	6 6		3063	159
■ Dimmit Co. – Glenn H. Lau – Glenn H. Lau – 1992
170¹/8	25 25⁶/8	22¹/8	24¹/8	4²/8 4²/8	7 7		3143†	164†
■ La Salle Co. – Weldon L. Nichols – Weldon L. Nichols – 2001
170¹/8	25⁶/8 25¹/8	17⁵/8	19⁶/8	5⁵/8 5⁵/8	5 5	1⁴/8	3143	164
■ Comal Co. – Lyman Skolaut – Lyman Skolaut – 1987
170¹/8	23⁶/8 23¹/8	15³/8	17³/8	4⁵/8 4⁶/8	6 7	1	3143	164
■ Webb Co. – Gerald W. Rentz, Jr. – Gerald W. Rentz, Jr. – 1990

■ Location of Kill – Hunter – Owner – Date Killed

Score	Length of Main Beam Right	Left	Inside Spread	Greatest Spread	Circumference at Smallest Place Between Burr and First Point Right	Left	Number of Points Right	Left	Lengths Abnormal Points	All-Time Rank	State Rank
	■ Location of Kill – Hunter – Owner – Date Killed										
170 1/8	26 3/8	26 1/8	20 3/8	22 5/8	5	4 7/8	6	6	5 6/8	3143	164
	■ Webb Co. – Picked Up – William O. Carter – 1993										
170 1/8	25 3/8	24 3/8	21 5/8	23 4/8	5 1/8	5 2/8	5	5		3143	164
	■ Jim Hogg Co. – Frances Weil – Frances Weil – 1993										
170 1/8	22 7/8	22 7/8	17 5/8	19 7/8	4 1/8	4 1/8	5	5		3143	164
	■ Maverick Co. – Donald Gann – Donald Gann – 1997										
170 1/8	27 2/8	26 5/8	19 2/8	21 4/8	4 2/8	4 1/8	7	7	4 3/8	3143	164
	■ Kleberg Co. – Robert Nichols III – Robert Nichols III – 1997										
170 1/8	24 6/8	23 6/8	18 1/8	20	4 5/8	4 5/8	6	6		3143	164
	■ Kenedy Co. – Jarred W. Peeples – Jarred W. Peeples – 1998										
170	24 2/8	24 2/8	18 4/8	19 6/8	4 1/8	4 1/8	6	7		3224	172
	■ Oiltown – L.D. Roberts – L.D. Roberts – 1941										
170	27	28	22 4/8	25	4 4/8	4 4/8	6	5	1 4/8	3224	172
	■ Webb Co. – Herbert Zieschang – Herbert Zieschang – 1957										
170	27 5/8	26 5/8	24 1/8	25 4/8	4 1/8	4	6	8	7 5/8	3224	172
	■ Atascosa Co. – Ben H. Moore, Jr. – Ben H. Moore, Jr. – 1961										
169 3/8	29 7/8	28 3/8	17 3/8	19 4/8	4 3/8	4 3/8	6	6		3324	175
	■ McMullen Co. – Alfred A. Fischer – Susan E. Stewart – 1964										
169 3/8	26 3/8	25 5/8	20 6/8	22 6/8	4 2/8	4 2/8	6	5	1 3/8	3324	175
	■ Coleman Co. – Steven C. Fails – Steven C. Fails – 1986										
169 3/8	24 1/8	23 3/8	16 1/8	17 6/8	4 4/8	4 4/8	6	6		3324	175
	■ Atascosa Co. – Gary F. Keller – Gary F. Keller – 1996										
168 7/8	24 3/8	25 1/8	20 5/8	22 3/8	4 5/8	4 4/8	7	6	1	3361	178
	■ Dimmit Co. – David M. Shashy – David M. Shashy – 1997										
168 4/8	20 2/8	20 7/8	20 2/8	23	4 6/8	4 4/8	6	6		3385	179
	■ Dimmit Co. – Roy Hindes – Roy Hindes – 1960										
168 3/8	25	24 1/8	23 7/8	25 4/8	4 4/8	4 4/8	6	6		3399	180
	■ Dimmit Co. – Kelly K. Vesper – Kelly K. Vesper – 1992										
167 6/8	24	23 1/8	17 2/8	18	4 5/8	4 4/8	5	6		3461	181
	■ Webb Co. – David A. Soward – David A. Soward – 1990										
167 4/8	26	26 2/8	23	25 3/8	4 3/8	4 2/8	5	5		3485	182
	■ Webb Co. – Drouth Hancock – Ralph L. Hancock – 1932										
167 1/8	23 4/8	25 2/8	16 3/8	18	4 4/8	4 3/8	6	6	3	3539	183
	■ Maverick Co. – Frank W. McBee, Jr. – Frank W. McBee, Jr. – 1989										
167	25 4/8	26 2/8	22 1/8	24 2/8	4 5/8	4 3/8	6	5	2 3/8	3552†	184†
	■ Armstrong Co. – Lawrence W. Cieslewicz – Lawrence W. Cieslewicz – 2001										
167	24 6/8	24 1/8	23 2/8	25 1/8	4 3/8	4 3/8	6	6		3552	184
	■ La Salle Co. – Ford G. Martin – Ford G. Martin – 1953										
166 6/8	27 2/8	27 2/8	22	24 4/8	4 7/8	4 5/8	6	6		3582†	186†
	■ Jim Hogg Co. – Mark D. Cooper – Mark D. Cooper – 2002										
165 5/8	25 3/8	25 3/8	22 5/8	24 3/8	4 3/8	4 4/8	5	7	2 4/8	3598	187
	■ Dimmit Co. – Robert E. Zaiglin – Robert E. Zaiglin – 1987										

Score	Length of Main Beam Right	Length of Main Beam Left	Inside Spread	Greatest Spread	Circumference at Smallest Place Between Burr and First Point Right	Left	Number of Points Right	Left	Lengths Abnormal Points	All-Time Rank	State Rank
166 4/8	25 6/8	26 4/8	21 1/8	23 7/8	4 6/8	4 5/8	5	6	3 3/8	3609	188
■ La Salle Co. – Thomas E. Baine – Thomas E. Baine – 1999											
166 3/8	25 2/8	25 5/8	25 1/8	27	4 7/8	5	6	5	1	3620	189
■ Dimmit Co. – Stuart W. Stedman – Stuart W. Stedman – 1991											
166 2/8	24 4/8	23 4/8	18 4/8	20 3/8	3 7/8	4 1/8	6	6		3632	190
■ McMullen Co. – Jim Arnold – Jim Arnold – 1997											
166 1/8	24 4/8	24 5/8	19	22 6/8	4 3/8	4 2/8	7	6	1 5/8	3643†	191†
■ Duval Co. – Gary M. Burch – Gary M. Burch – 2000											
165 6/8	26 4/8	26 2/8	20 2/8	23 2/8	4 5/8	4 3/8	5	5		3680	192
■ Jim Hogg Co. – Byron Kibby – Byron Kibby – 1974											
165 4/8	24 6/8	24 2/8	21 4/8	23 2/8	4 3/8	4 3/8	9	8	5 6/8	3714	193
■ Maverick Co. – Robert L. Parker, Jr. – Robert L. Parker, Jr. – 1982											
165 3/8	25 3/8	24 4/8	18 5/8	21	5 4/8	5 2/8	5	5		3731	194
■ Frio Co. – Paul M. Rothermel, Jr. – Paul M. Rothermel, Jr. – 1940											
164 7/8	23	26 2/8	18 4/8	21 6/8	5	4 7/8	5	8	1 5/8	3792	195
■ Wilbarger Co. – Scott Taylor – Scott Taylor – 1992											
164 6/8	24	24	19 7/8	20 4/8	4 4/8	4 7/8	5	5	2 7/8	3809†	196†
■ Mason Co. – J. David Monaghan – J. David Monaghan – 2001											
164 6/8	22 4/8	23	18 7/8	20 5/8	4 4/8	4 4/8	7	7	9 1/8	3809	196
■ Dimmit Co. – Stuart W. Stedman – Stuart W. Stedman – 1997											
164 5/8	25 7/8	25 6/8	19 7/8	21 4/8	4 4/8	4 3/8	5	5		3835	198
■ Zavala Co. – Kielly Yates – Kielly Yates – 1987											
164 3/8	23 2/8	23 7/8	18	19 6/8	4 3/8	4 2/8	7	6	3 7/8	3864	199
■ Brown Co. – A.C. Ebensberger – A.C. Ebensberger – 1990											
164 1/8	27 3/8	27	19 2/8	23 2/8	4 2/8	4 1/8	6	8	3 7/8	3886	200
■ Houston Co. – Brian L. Frashier – Brian L. Frashier – 1990											
164	25	22 7/8	22 4/8	24	4 7/8	4 7/8	6	5		3908†	201†
■ Kleberg Co. – Johnnie R. Walters – Johnnie R. Walters – 2000											
164	25 6/8	24 2/8	19 7/8	23 4/8	4 5/8	4 4/8	9	8	7 5/8	3908	201
■ Brooks Co. – Si Weeks, Jr. – Si Weeks, Jr. – 1981											
164	25 1/8	24 6/8	23	25 2/8	4 6/8	4 7/8	6	5		3908	201
■ Webb Co. – William W. Lloyd – William W. Lloyd – 1999											
163 7/8	24	24 2/8	18 7/8	20 5/8	4 1/8	3 7/8	7	6	2 4/8	3928	204
■ Brooks Co. – Timothy C. Brady – Timothy C. Brady – 1997											
163 5/8	26 5/8	26 1/8	23 7/8	25 3/8	4 5/8	4 4/8	7	6	6 4/8	3961†	205†
■ Grayson Co. – Mark A. Wade – Mark A. Wade – 2000											
163 5/8	24 4/8	24 1/8	23 7/8	27 2/8	4 4/8	4 4/8	5	5		3961	205
■ Young Co. – Jeffery D. Hill – Jeffery D. Hill – 1997											
163 3/8	22 4/8	21 7/8	21 5/8	22 7/8	5 2/8	5 2/8	7	7	2	4002	207
■ Kenedy Co. – Crystal Ostos – Crystal Ostos – 1997											
163 2/8	22 4/8	22 3/8	13 4/8	15 2/8	4 2/8	4 2/8	7	7	4	4017†	208†
■ Walker Co. – Ryan M. Lampson – Ryan M. Lampson – 2000											

■ Location of Kill – Hunter – Owner – Date Killed

Score	Length of Main Beam		Inside Spread	Greatest Spread	Circumference at Smallest Place Between Burr and First Point		Number of Points		Lengths Abnormal Points	All-Time Rank	State Rank
	Right	Left			Right	Left	Right	Left			
163 2/8	26 7/8	25 7/8	19 6/8	22	4 6/8	4 6/8	6	6		4017	208
■ Dimmit Co. – Phil Barnes – Phil Barnes – 1997											
162 7/8	26 7/8	28	22 5/8	25	4 5/8	4 4/8	6	7	9	4067	210
■ Dimmit Co. – J. Burton Barnes – J. Burton Barnes – 1967											
162 5/8	23 2/8	23 4/8	17 2/8	21 2/8	4 2/8	4 2/8	6	7	1 7/8	4109†	211†
■ Atascosa Co. – James N. Meissner – James N. Meissner – 2000											
162 3/8	27 3/8	27 4/8	19 4/8	21	3 7/8	4	5	6	1 1/8	4140	212
■ Victoria Co. – Patrick S. Edwards – Patrick S. Edwards – 1990											
162 2/8	23	23 1/8	18 4/8	20 2/8	4 6/8	4 6/8	5	5		4153	213
■ Sutton Co. – Linda J. Corley – Linda J. Corley – 1983											
162 1/8	26 3/8	26	27 7/8	30 5/8	4 6/8	4 4/8	5	4		4174	214
■ Webb Co. – Lefty Stackhouse – F. Gus Reinarz – 1949											
162	23	22 1/8	19 6/8		3 7/8	3 6/8	6	6		4184	215
■ Zavala Co. – Rogers Bracy – Rogers Bracy – 1990											
162	23	24	19 4/8	22	4 4/8	4 4/8	6	7		4184	215
■ Webb Co. – William M. Wheless IV – William M. Wheless IV – 1996											
161 7/8	25 7/8	25 7/8	28 1/8	29 1/8	4 3/8	4 2/8	6	5		4212	217
■ Webb Co. – Unknown – Lawson W. Walden – 1949											
161 7/8	24	23 6/8	18 5/8	20 4/8	3 7/8	4	6	5		4212	217
■ Terrell Co. – S. Randall Hearne – S. Randall Hearne – 1997											
161 6/8	25 2/8	24 6/8	17 3/8	19 2/8	4 4/8	4 4/8	5	6	2 5/8	4223	219
■ Dimmit Co. – Robert E. Zaiglin – Robert E. Zaiglin – 1988											
161 6/8	24	23 7/8	16	18	4 3/8	4 4/8	7	6	1 4/8	4223	219
■ King Co. – Mike Stewart – Mike Stewart – 1999											
161 2/8	24 1/8	23 2/8	17 7/8	19 7/8	4 6/8	4 6/8	6	6	4 3/8	4310	221
■ Kleberg Co. – Janell Kleberg – Janell Kleberg – 1991											
161 2/8	23 5/8	23 6/8	22 6/8	24 7/8	4 5/8	4 5/8	5	5		4310	221
■ Dimmit Co. – John B. Brent – John B. Brent – 1993											
161 1/8	27 1/8	26 3/8	26 3/8	27 7/8	4 3/8	4 4/8	6	4	1 4/8	4332	223
■ Maverick Co. – D.L. Doyle – Pat Doyle – 1952											
161 1/8	26 3/8	26 6/8	18 5/8	20 2/8	4 4/8	4 1/8	6	6	4	4332	223
■ Parker Co. – Donald C. Stanley – Donald C. Stanley – 1999											
160 5/8	24	24 2/8	18 7/8	21 1/8	4 7/8	4 7/8	7	5	2	4423	225
■ Texas – Unknown – Buckhorn Mus. & Saloon, Ltd. – PR 1956											
160 5/8	21 2/8	21 4/8	14 7/8	17 2/8	4	3 7/8	6	6		4423	225
■ Kenedy Co. – Cal Adger – Cal Adger – 1987											
160 4/8	25 6/8	26 3/8	25	27 6/8	5	4 6/8	8	5	9 4/8	4443	227
■ Webb Co. – Melvin Huth – F. Gus Reinarz – PR 1959											
160 4/8	24 4/8	25	20 2/8	22 1/8	4 4/8	4 4/8	5	5		4443	227
■ Dimmit Co. – Stuart W. Stedman – Stuart W. Stedman – 1998											
160 2/8	24 4/8	23 7/8	19 6/8	21 3/8	5 1/8	4 6/8	5	5		4495	229
■ Webb Co. – Drew Nicholas – Drew Nicholas – 1977											

■ Location of Kill – Hunter – Owner – Date Killed

Score	Length of Main Beam		Inside Spread	Greatest Spread	Circumference at Smallest Place Between Burr and First Point		Number of Points		Lengths Abnormal Points	All-Time Rank	State Rank
	Right	Left			Right	Left	Right	Left			
	■ Location of Kill – Hunter – Owner – Date Killed										
160²/8	24⁶/8	24³/8	19⁴/8	21⁴/8	4³/8	4²/8	6	5		4495	229
	■ Dimmit Co. – John B. Brent – John B. Brent – 1991										
160	25⁷/8	24	20⁵/8	22⁵/8	3⁷/8	4¹/8	6	6	2¹/8	4565	231
	■ Goliad Co. – Michael V. Stewart – Michael V. Stewart – 1964										

† The scores and ranking for trophies from the 25th Awards Entry Period are not final until the banquet is held on June 19, 2004.

TEXAS

NON-TYPICAL WHITETAIL DEER

Score	Length of Main Beam Right Left ■ Location of Kill – Hunter – Owner – Date Killed	Inside Spread	Greatest Spread	Circumference at Smallest Place Between Burr and First Point Right Left		Number of Points Right Left		Lengths Abnormal Points	All-Time Rank	State Rank
284³/8	21⁴/8 19⁶/8	16²/8	26²/8	4⁴/8	4⁴/8	21	26	134³/8	5	1
	■ McCulloch Co. – Unknown – Buckhorn Mus. & Saloon, Ltd. – 1892									
272	23⁷/8 25	17⁵/8	22⁷/8	6²/8	5⁶/8	23	16	104⁷/8	13	2
	■ Junction – Picked Up – Fred Mudge – 1925									
259	16²/8 15³/8	15⁶/8	24	5⁴/8	5³/8	16	11	53⁶/8	25	3
	■ Frio Co. – William B. Brown – Bettie B. Brown – PR 1967									
247⁷/8	26¹/8 26	19⁵/8	25⁴/8	5⁵/8	5⁴/8	13	17	64⁴/8	74	4
	■ Frio Co. – Raul Rodriquez II – Raul Rodriquez II – 1966									
244²/8	20⁷/8 20	16¹/8	27	4⁷/8	4²/8	18	14	97³/8	89	5
	■ Zavala Co. – John R. Campbell – John L. Stein – 1947									
240²/8	20¹/8 20	22¹/8	24⁵/8	4⁵/8	4⁶/8	17	12	85³/8	117	6
	■ Hunt Co. – Tom Cole – John L. Stein – 1997									
240	26⁴/8 26	21⁵/8	26⁶/8	5⁴/8	5⁴/8	15	11	52³/8	119	7
	■ Kerr Co. – Walter R. Schreiner – Charles Schreiner III – 1905									
239⁴/8	26⁶/8 25¹/8	19⁴/8	24⁷/8	5¹/8	5	13	13	56²/8	121	8
	■ Kleberg Co. – Adan Alvarez – Adan Alvarez – 1998									
235¹/8	24 23⁷/8	21²/8	27	5	4⁷/8	14	15	64⁵/8	169	9
	■ Frio Co. – C.J. Stolle – John F. Stolle – 1919									
227⁴/8	22⁶/8 23⁶/8	24	27³/8	4⁷/8	4⁷/8	17	12	76²/8	270†	10†
	■ Fannin Co. – Joe P. Moore, Jr. – Joe P. Moore, Jr. – 2001									
227¹/8	24 23⁶/8	21⁴/8	25	4⁴/8	4⁴/8	8	9	32⁵/8	275	11
	■ Dimmit Co. – Stuart W. Stedman – Stuart W. Stedman – 1990									
226⁷/8	30²/8 28¹/8	20²/8	25	5	5	13	10	34⁷/8	284	12
	■ Dimmit Co. – Lake Webb – Warren N. Webb – 1937									
226⁴/8	26 26⁴/8	24⁷/8	26⁴/8	4⁷/8	4⁵/8	11	12	31¹/8	292	13
	■ La Salle Co. – A.L. Lipscomb, Sr. – John L. Stein – 1909									
226¹/8	25³/8 24⁷/8	22³/8	26⁵/8	5¹/8	5	12	14	67	301	14
	■ Kimble Co. – Coke R. Stevenson – Marguerite K. Stevenson – 1934									
225⁷/8	22⁵/8 19⁴/8	17⁴/8	25⁶/8	4⁷/8	4⁷/8	13	13	93¹/8	304†	15†
	■ Grayson Co. – Jeffery L. Duncan – Jeffery L. Duncan – 2001									
225¹/8	22⁴/8 22⁶/8	17¹/8	27³/8	4⁷/8	5	10	13	80	314	16
	■ Burnet Co. – Mr. Stevens – Mclean Bowman – 1938									
224⁷/8	20²/8 24²/8	17	22⁵/8	8	5⁵/8	19	11	62⁷/8	321	17
	■ Kinney Co. – Unknown – Joe L. Collins – 1900									
224⁶/8	22⁵/8 24²/8	15¹/8	24⁴/8	5⁴/8	5²/8	16	15	61¹/8	322	18
	■ La Salle Co. – Minnie D.B. Haynes – Minnie D.B. Haynes – 1992									
223²/8	24³/8 27³/8	25	31⁶/8	4⁴/8	4⁵/8	12	12	70⁴/8	359	19
	■ Madison Co. – B.C. Bienek – B.C. Bienek – 1967									

Score	Length of Main Beam		Inside Spread	Greatest Spread	Circumference at Smallest Place Between Burr and First Point		Number of Points		Lengths Abnormal Points	All-Time Rank	State Rank
	Right	Left			Right	Left	Right	Left			
	■ Location of Kill – Hunter – Owner – Date Killed										
222 1/8	22 2/8	24 2/8	14 3/8	19 7/8	4 2/8	4 4/8	11	13	99 2/8	392†	20†
■ Ellis Co. – David Krajca – David Krajca – 2001											
221 7/8	28 2/8	28	25 7/8	28	4 3/8	4 3/8	9	13	27 4/8	396	21
■ Texas – Unknown – Lawson W. Walden – PR 1988											
220 2/8	28 2/8	28 4/8	21	27 5/8	5	5	9	8	43 6/8	434	22
■ Zavala Co. – Jerry D. Jarratt – Jerry D. Jarratt – 1930											
219 3/8	27 4/8	27 4/8	20	24	5 2/8	5 2/8	11	10	27 3/8	455	23
■ Webb Co. – Richard O. Rivera – John L. Stein – 1972											
217 7/8	23 4/8	23 4/8	19 4/8	21 3/8	4 5/8	4 5/8	11	10	38 3/8	499	24
■ Dimmit Co. – Unknown – McLean Bowman – 1920											
216 1/8	25 2/8	23 4/8	19 6/8	25 4/8	4 4/8	4 3/8	13	12	51 3/8	561	25
■ Gillespie Co. – J.C. Park – John L. Stein – 1932											
215 3/8	21	23 4/8	15	20	7 2/8	6 6/8	12	15	57 5/8	587	26
■ Trinity Co. – Earl Smith – Lawson W. Walden – 1965											
215 2/8	21	19	24	27 6/8	4	4	9	16	84	589	27
■ Parker Co. – Pleasant Mitchell – Pleasant Mitchell – 1982											
213 6/8	23 7/8	24 4/8	18 6/8	20 6/8	4 6/8	5	10	11	27 6/8	644	28
■ Webb Co. – Unknown – John B. Collier, IV – 1961											
213 5/8	22 7/8	22 6/8	13 5/8		3 6/8	3 7/8	9	18	61 6/8	649	29
■ Webb Co. – Unknown – McLean Bowman – PR 1950											
213 5/8	18 5/8	18 1/8	17 5/8	22 1/8	4 1/8	4	14	15	95 2/8	649	29
■ Washington Co. – Thomas N. Holle – Thomas N. Holle – 1987											
213 4/8	22 1/8	23 1/8	19 2/8	24 4/8	5	5	15	15	62 4/8	657	31
■ Texas – Unknown – Buckhorn Mus. & Saloon, Ltd. – PR 1950											
213 1/8	30 1/8	28	23 5/8	26	4 6/8	4 6/8	10	7	33	664	32
■ Kimble Co. – Henry B. Allsup – Frederica Wyatt – 1941											
213	24 4/8	24	17 5/8	19	4 7/8	4 5/8	10	10	39 5/8	671	33
■ Kinney Co. – Rankin F. O'Neill – John L. Stein – 1960											
212 5/8	21 3/8	20 1/8	16 5/8	28 3/8	4	4	14	16	73	683	34
■ Brooks Co. – Ken Smith – Lawson W. Walden – 1975											
212 2/8	25	25 4/8	19 4/8	21	5 2/8	5 2/8	11	13	32 2/8	701	35
■ Webb Co. – Claude W. King – Claude W. King – 1949											
211 5/8	23 2/8	23 2/8	16	18 5/8	4 7/8	4 5/8	13	14	72 1/8	734	36
■ Rains Co. – Tommy Couch – Lawson W. Walden – PR 1988											
211 3/8	27 3/8	24 4/8	20 3/8	24 3/8	4 7/8	4 5/8	12	12	47 6/8	745	37
■ Dimmit Co. – L.C. Wright – H.R. Wright – 1927											
211	23 6/8	23 4/8	16 3/8	21 4/8	6	6	12	13	48 7/8	764	38
■ Dimmit Co. – D.V. Day – McLean Bowman – 1948											
209 4/8	23 3/8	23 1/8	22 5/8	25 7/8	4 4/8	4 5/8	10	14	53 3/8	848	39
■ Webb Co. – A. Holden – McLean Bowman – 1940											
209 4/8	25	24 2/8	19 2/8	20 4/8	4 2/8	4 1/8	8	9	33 2/8	848	39
■ Sterling Co. – Sam E. Kapavik – Sam E. Kapavik – 1973											

Score	Length of Main Beam Right Left	Inside Spread	Greatest Spread	Circumference at Smallest Place Between Burr and First Point Right Left	Number of Points Right Left	Lengths Abnormal Points	All-Time Rank	State Rank
	■ Location of Kill – Hunter – Owner – Date Killed							
209 3/8	26 1/8 26 1/8	21	26 2/8	5 1/8 5 1/8	13 9	23 1/8	852	41
■ La Salle Co. – Unknown – E.T. Reilly – 1931								
209 1/8	23 4/8 24 4/8	16 6/8	24 5/8	4 3/8 4 2/8	12 14	45 7/8	863	42
■ Kenedy Co. – Dick Roberts – Dick Roberts – 1988								
208 4/8	22 21 4/8	17 4/8	25 4/8	5 5	12 13	36 4/8	894	43
■ Webb Co. – Travis D. Kelly – Travis D. Kelly – 1978								
208 2/8	27 26 2/8	18 2/8	20 2/8	5 4/8 5 6/8	10 7	26 4/8	910	44
■ Frio Co. – Unknown – Roy Hindes – PR 1950								
207 7/8	24 6/8 25 5/8	15 5/8	21 4/8	4 2/8 4 2/8	7 9	23 4/8	938	45
■ McMullen Co. – Robert L. Hodges – William D. Connally – 1924								
207 6/8	22 2/8 20 1/8	15 4/8	23 3/8	5 5	14 16	55 6/8	951	46
■ Kleberg Co. – Unknown – King Ranch – 1940								
207 3/8	24 3/8 25 3/8	21 3/8	23 5/8	5 5 2/8	9 15	32	977	47
■ Throckmorton Co. – Jack Carlile – Watt R. Matthews – 1960								
207 3/8	25 7/8 25 4/8	20 2/8	25	4 4/8 4 4/8	10 8	26 3/8	977	47
■ Zapata Co. – Romeo H. Garcia – Romeo H. Garcia – 1977								
206 4/8	22 1/8 22 2/8	19 4/8	23 7/8	5 5	10 13	33 4/8	1043	49
■ Brooks Co. – John E. Wilson – James M. Hancock, Jr. – 1947								
206 3/8	22 7/8 23 2/8	19		4 7/8 4 5/8	11 11	40 5/8	1051	50
■ Webb Co. – Willard V. Brenizer – Gerry Elliff – 1942								
206 2/8	25 4/8 25	16 6/8	18 6/8	5 5	7 9	35 4/8	1059	51
■ Cotulla – George E. Light III – George E. Light III – 1950								
206	26 4/8 24 6/8	16 6/8	23 6/8	5 3/8 5 3/8	8 8	36	1075	52
■ McMullen Co. – Robert L. Hodges – Robert L. Connally – 1925								
205 7/8	25 6/8 25 4/8	20 6/8	28	4 4/8 4 3/8	10 10	36 5/8	1080	53
■ Houston Co. – Gary Rogers – Gary Rogers – 1969								
205 3/8	26 3/8 24 6/8	16 4/8	20 7/8	4 5/8 4 5/8	10 11	25 5/8	1116	54
■ Duval Co. – Daniel A. Pedrotti – Daniel A. Pedrotti – 1995								
204 5/8	23 4/8 23	22 4/8	26 5/8	4 4/8 4 4/8	12 12	53 1/8	1176	55
■ Bandera Co. – August Dienger – Larry L. Stahl – 1906								
204 4/8	25 3/8 25 1/8	20 1/8	26 5/8	5 5/8 5 5/8	12 10	31 3/8	1182	56
■ Fisher Co. – Keith H. Prince – Keith H. Prince – 1997								
204	27 6/8 27 3/8	21 1/8	24	4 7/8 5 1/8	9 14	50 3/8	1220	57
■ Sutton Co. – L.H. McMillan – L.H. McMillan – 1961								
203 7/8	27 4/8 27 4/8	17 4/8	22 2/8	4 6/8 4 6/8	11 8	21 5/8	1231	58
■ Eastland Co. – Picked Up – William B. Wright, Jr. – 1920								
203 7/8	25 25 4/8	18	18 4/8	4 7/8 4 6/8	8 11	26 5/8	1231	58
■ McMullen Co. – Bruce Phillips – Jeffery C. Phillips – 1941								
203 6/8	24 2/8 25 3/8	16 5/8	22	4 3 7/8	8 8	16 3/8	1237	60
■ Maverick Co. – Picked Up – Richard H. Bennett – 1941								
203 5/8	24 23 3/8	15 7/8	22 1/8	4 5/8 4 7/8	13 9	27 4/8	1248	61
■ Sabine Co. – Marvin E. Dickerson – Joe R. Dickerson – 1981								

Score	Length of Main Beam Right	Left	Inside Spread	Greatest Spread	Circumference at Smallest Place Between Burr and First Point Right	Left	Number of Points Right	Left	Lengths Abnormal Points	All-Time Rank	State Rank
	■ Location of Kill – Hunter – Owner – Date Killed										
204⁴/8	25	25¹/8	22	29³/8	4⁶/8	4⁵/8	13	12	36²/8	1259	62
	■ Live Oak Co. – Alec Coker – Henderson Coquat – 1916										
202⁶/8	24⁷/8	22⁶/8	15⁵/8	22⁴/8	4⁴/8	4⁴/8	12	10	47¹/8	1339	63
	■ Kenedy Co. – Alex Hixson – Alex Hixon – 1993										
202⁵/8	26⁷/8	26⁷/8	23¹/8	28	4⁵/8	4⁵/8	9	10	38²/8	1346	64
	■ Kleberg Co. – Richard J. Mills – Richard J. Mills – 1926										
202⁴/8	24⁷/8	24⁶/8	23⁶/8	24	4⁷/8	5	10	11	36	1355	65
	■ Texas – Unknown – Buckhorn Mus. & Saloon, Ltd. – PR 1920										
202³/8	24	25⁷/8	18³/8	20¹/8	4⁴/8	4⁴/8	9	8	16⁴/8	1362	66
	■ Houston Co. – Clint M. Croft – Clint M. Croft – 1999										
202	26¹/8	25⁷/8	17⁷/8	21⁴/8	4²/8	4³/8	11	9	28⁵/8	1395†	67†
	■ Falls Co. – Rudy Garcia – Rudy Garcia – 2000										
201⁶/8	24¹/8	24⁶/8	19³/8	23⁶/8	4²/8	4¹/8	12	12	23¹/8	1421	68
	■ Texas – Unknown – Buckhorn Mus. & Saloon, Ltd. – PR 1920										
201³/8	24⁴/8	25³/8	20²/8	24²/8	5	5²/8	14	12	42³/8	1461	69
	■ Grayson Co. – Donnie M. Brewer – Donnie M. Brewer – 1995										
201²/8	23⁴/8	25²/8	22⁴/8	26²/8	4²/8	4²/8	13	9	49⁶/8	1478	70
	■ San Saba Co. – Ted J. Bode – Ted J. Bode – 1965										
201	25⁷/8	26⁴/8	22¹/8	26²/8	4⁵/8	4⁴/8	11	13	33¹/8	1500	71
	■ Cooke Co. – Michael W. Lang – Michael W. Lang – 1997										
200⁷/8	23⁴/8	24³/8	21	27	4⁴/8	4⁵/8	11	10	40⁵/8	1512	72
	■ Kleberg Co. – Picked Up – John A. Larkin – 1982										
200⁵/8	23⁴/8	24¹/8	18⁴/8	23⁶/8	4⁵/8	4⁶/8	8	11	33⁷/8	1532	73
	■ Grayson Co. – Forrest L. Robertson – Forrest L. Robertson – 1995										
200⁴/8	23⁵/8	21⁴/8	21¹/8	26²/8	4⁵/8	4⁴/8	8	9	34³/8	1545	74
	■ Uvalde Co. – W.S. Gordon – 1st State Bank of Uvalde – 1923										
200⁴/8	26²/8	27¹/8	19⁶/8	22	4¹/8	4²/8	8	8	26⁴/8	1545	74
	■ Kleberg Co. – Charles Hoge – Charles Hoge – 1976										
200²/8	26⁴/8	26²/8	25	26⁶/8	4⁵/8	4⁴/8	9	9	26⁶/8	1569	76
	■ Live Oak Co. – E.W. Douglass – E.W. Douglass – 1993										
199⁵/8	24⁶/8	27⁶/8	19⁴/8	24⁵/8	4¹/8	4³/8	10	8	34⁵/8	1621	77
	■ Dimmit Co. – John T. Brannan III – John T. Brannan III – 1992										
198⁶/8	23³/8	23¹/8	17³/8	21²/8	4	4	11	12	39¹/8	1697†	78†
	■ Cherokee Co. – Randall L. Chandler – Randall L. Chandler – 1994										
198⁶/8	20	20⁶/8	17⁴/8	24⁶/8	4³/8	4³/8	9	19	48⁶/8	1697	78
	■ Angelina Co. – B. Tyler Fenley – Daniel Fenley – 1999 ■ See photo on page 55										
198⁵/8	26¹/8	25⁷/8	22⁴/8	24³/8	5	4⁷/8	8	7	21³/8	1716	80
	■ Webb Co. – Larry Bickham – Larry Bickham – 1962										
198⁵/8	24⁶/8	24¹/8	15⁶/8	17⁶/8	3⁷/8	3⁷/8	8	9	26⁷/8	1716	80
	■ Clay Co. – Glenn M. Lucas – Glenn M. Lucas – 1997										
198⁴/8	25	26²/8	23⁶/8	25⁶/8	4⁶/8	4⁶/8	7	8	23²/8	1736	82
	■ Webb Co. – Alvin C. Santleben, Jr. – Alvin C. Santleben, Jr. – 1983										

Score	Length of Main Beam Right	Left	Inside Spread	Greatest Spread	Circumference at Smallest Place Between Burr and First Point Right	Left	Number of Points Right	Left	Lengths Abnormal Points	All-Time Rank	State Rank

Location of Kill – Hunter – Owner – Date Killed

Score	R	L	IS	GS	CR	CL	PR	PL	Abn	Rank	State
198 4/8	22 3/8	17 4/8	13 6/8	20 6/8	5 2/8	5 1/8	15	14	62	1736	82

■ *Hamilton Co. – Randy L. Wright – Randy L. Wright – 1992*

| 198 4/8 | 25 3/8 | 24 6/8 | 17 4/8 | 25 4/8 | 4 2/8 | 4 4/8 | 14 | 9 | 30 2/8 | 1736 | 82 |

■ *Kleberg Co. – Glenn Thurman – Glenn Thurman – 1994* ■ *See photo on page 461*

| 198 3/8 | 25 7/8 | 27 | 20 3/8 | 25 4/8 | 5 | 5 1/8 | 9 | 8 | 27 | 1762 | 85 |

■ *Uvalde Co. – George Judson, Jr. – George Judson, Jr. – 1958*

| 197 7/8 | 24 1/8 | 23 2/8 | 17 6/8 | 20 2/8 | 4 5/8 | 4 6/8 | 6 | 7 | 15 1/8 | 1816† | 86† |

■ *Willacy Co. – Clifton L. Smith – Garcia Estate – 2000*

| 197 7/8 | 23 7/8 | 22 5/8 | 18 | 25 6/8 | 4 2/8 | 4 3/8 | 8 | 13 | 54 3/8 | 1816 | 86 |

■ *Hunt Co. – Wade Grimes – Wade Grimes – 1994*

| 197 6/8 | 26 2/8 | 25 2/8 | 19 4/8 | 23 4/8 | 4 2/8 | 4 4/8 | 8 | 9 | 13 2/8 | 1833 | 88 |

■ *Dimmit Co. – Michael H. Oldfather – Michael H. Oldfather – 1992*

| 197 2/8 | 23 7/8 | 23 5/8 | 15 5/8 | 22 4/8 | 4 7/8 | 4 6/8 | 15 | 14 | 39 3/8 | 1901 | 89 |

■ *Starr Co. – Matthew J. Arnold – Matthew J. Arnold – 1997*

| 197 1/8 | 20 6/8 | 20 5/8 | 18 4/8 | 22 5/8 | 4 5/8 | 4 6/8 | 13 | 17 | 39 7/8 | 1923 | 90 |

■ *Kenedy Co. – Manuel Amaya – Arturo R. Amaya – 1969*

| 197 1/8 | 27 4/8 | 27 3/8 | 18 3/8 | 26 | 4 5/8 | 4 5/8 | 9 | 9 | 18 4/8 | 1923 | 90 |

■ *Clay Co. – Dale L. Coleman – Dale L. Coleman – 1988*

| 196 6/8 | 19 4/8 | 21 5/8 | 19 | 23 4/8 | 4 2/8 | 4 2/8 | 16 | 14 | 53 | 1968 | 92 |

■ *Stephens Co. – Thomas N. Clark – Lawson W. Walden – 1995*

| 196 3/8 | 23 6/8 | 24 4/8 | 20 2/8 | 24 | 4 4/8 | 4 7/8 | 8 | 7 | 20 1/8 | 2010 | 93 |

■ *Texas – Unknown – Roy Hindes – PR 1950*

| 196 3/8 | 25 1/8 | 25 2/8 | 17 6/8 | 19 6/8 | 4 5/8 | 4 6/8 | 9 | 6 | 35 5/8 | 2010 | 93 |

■ *Webb Co. – R. Blair James – R. Blair James – 1954*

| 196 1/8 | 26 4/8 | 26 2/8 | 18 6/8 | 20 7/8 | 4 6/8 | 4 6/8 | 7 | 8 | 24 5/8 | 2045 | 95 |

■ *Frio Co. – Orville W. Simmang, Sr. – Orville W. Simmang, Sr. – 1999*

| 195 7/8 | 26 4/8 | 27 | 19 2/8 | 21 2/8 | 4 7/8 | 4 7/8 | 9 | 6 | 18 3/8 | 2076† | 96† |

■ *Webb Co. – Jimmie L. Speake – Jimmie L. Speake – 2000*

| 195 7/8 | 24 6/8 | 25 | 23 6/8 | | 3 9/8 | 3 9/8 | 8 | 6 | 16 5/8 | 2076 | 96 |

■ *Webb Co. – Charles J. Schelper, Sr. – Vernon L. Watson – 1930*

| 195 7/8 | 21 4/8 | 21 6/8 | 20 6/8 | 25 | 4 4/8 | 4 5/8 | 9 | 10 | 43 7/8 | 2076 | 96 |

■ *La Salle Co. – Steve A. Meyer – Steve A. Meyer – 1968*

| 195 7/8 | 26 6/8 | 26 4/8 | 23 6/8 | 24 7/8 | 5 1/8 | 5 2/8 | 8 | 6 | 26 3/8 | 2076 | 96 |

■ *Webb Co. – Marko T. Barrett – Marko T. Barrett – 1993*

| 195 7/8 | 24 3/8 | 24 4/8 | 18 5/8 | 21 4/8 | 4 2/8 | 4 3/8 | 9 | 8 | 19 | 2076 | 96 |

■ *Kenedy Co. – Michael D. Fain – Michael D. Fain – 1993*

| 195 5/8 | 21 4/8 | 22 4/8 | 16 7/8 | 25 | 4 4/8 | 4 4/8 | 11 | 14 | 52 2/8 | 2116 | 101 |

■ *Menard Co. – Don N. Jones, Jr. – Lawson W. Walden – 1987*

| 195 4/8 | 28 | 27 7/8 | 24 3/8 | 28 4/8 | 4 4/8 | 4 4/8 | 9 | 11 | 21 7/8 | 2134 | 102 |

■ *La Salle Co. – Unknown – John C. Korbell – 1952*

| 195 4/8 | 24 5/8 | 24 1/8 | 17 6/8 | 21 6/8 | 4 4/8 | 4 2/8 | 9 | 9 | 34 4/8 | 2134 | 102 |

■ *Maverick Co. – Ronald K. Hudson – Ronald K. Hudson – 1971*

Score	Length of Main Beam Right	Left	Inside Spread	Greatest Spread	Circumference at Smallest Place Between Burr and First Point Right	Left	Number of Points Right	Left	Lengths Abnormal Points	All-Time Rank	State Rank
	■ Location of Kill – Hunter – Owner – Date Killed										
$195^4/_8$	$23^5/_8$	$24^5/_8$	$20^7/_8$	$22^3/_8$	$4^5/_8$	$4^7/_8$	9	10	$31^1/_8$	2134	102
	■ Uvalde Co. – Gary G. Patterson – Gary G. Patterson – 1996										
$195^3/_8$	$25^4/_8$	$25^4/_8$	$22^4/_8$	25	5	$4^6/_8$	9	12	$22^7/_8$	2163	105
	■ Webb Co. – Sidney A. Lindsay, Jr. – Sidney A. Lindsay, Jr. – 1983										
$195^2/_8$	$23^3/_8$	$23^5/_8$	$21^2/_8$	$23^6/_8$	5	5	8	8	$27^6/_8$	2186†	106†
	■ Dimmit Co. – Guinn D. Crousen – Guinn D. Crousen – 2001										
$195^2/_8$	$24^4/_8$	22	$17^3/_8$	$19^1/_8$	$4^3/_8$	$4^2/_8$	12	10	$21^1/_8$	2186	106
	■ Kenedy Co. – Don E. Harrison – Don E. Harrison – 1975										
$195^2/_8$	$11^2/_8$	$12^4/_8$	$16^7/_8$	$21^7/_8$	$4^1/_8$	4	21	16	$89^6/_8$	2186	106
	■ Grimes Co. – Walter Schroeder, Jr. – Walter Schroeder, Jr. – 1990										
$195^1/_8$	26	$25^7/_8$	21	$23^7/_8$	$4^4/_8$	$4^6/_8$	9	9	$17^7/_8$	2208	109
	■ Zapata Co. – Corando Mirelez – Corando Mirelez – 1966										
195	$23^1/_8$	$21^4/_8$	$17^1/_8$	23	$4^4/_8$	$4^4/_8$	9	10	$34^1/_8$	2233	110
	■ Kenedy Co. – Phil Lyne – Phil Lyne – 1986										
195	$25^5/_8$	$27^2/_8$	$23^1/_8$	25	$4^3/_8$	$4^5/_8$	7	10	$31^1/_8$	2233	110
	■ Dimmit Co. – J. Marvin Smith IV – J. Marvin Smith IV – 1998										
$193^3/_8$	22	$23^4/_8$	$14^2/_8$	$15^5/_8$	7	$6^5/_8$	10	15	$64^3/_8$	2293	112
	■ Trinity Co. – Earl Smith – Syble Smith – 1960										
$192^2/_8$	$26^1/_8$	25	$16^6/_8$	$18^4/_8$	$4^4/_8$	$4^4/_8$	6	6	12	2335	113
	■ Kleberg Co. – Cissy H. Taub – Cissy H. Taub – 1983										
$191^4/_8$	$25^1/_8$	$26^2/_8$	$22^3/_8$	$25^6/_8$	$4^2/_8$	$4^3/_8$	9	8	$32^7/_8$	2357	114
	■ Young Co. – Picked Up – Lawson W. Walden – 1990										
$191^3/_8$	22	$22^7/_8$	$14^3/_8$	$17^6/_8$	$4^6/_8$	$4^7/_8$	10	10	$22^6/_8$	2364	115
	■ Webb Co. – Ken A. Harding – Ken A. Harding – 1999										
$190^4/_8$	$25^2/_8$	$25^4/_8$	$17^3/_8$	$19^2/_8$	5	4	8	6	$24^7/_8$	2401	116
	■ La Salle Co. – Leo W. Mack, Jr. – Leo W. Mack, Jr. – 1992										
$190^3/_8$	$25^6/_8$	$27^1/_8$	$17^6/_8$	20	$4^5/_8$	$4^6/_8$	8	8	$17^3/_8$	2408	117
	■ La Salle Co. – Raymond M. Otto – Raymond M. Otto – 1997										
190	$24^6/_8$	$23^5/_8$	$18^6/_8$	$22^3/_8$	$5^2/_8$	$4^7/_8$	11	6	17	2418	118
	■ Dimmit Co. – Stuart W. Stedman – Stuart W. Stedman – 1987										
$189^3/_8$	$20^6/_8$	$21^1/_8$	$15^1/_8$	21	$4^5/_8$	$4^2/_8$	17	6	$37^6/_8$	2443†	119†
	■ Montague Co. – Chris R. Burns – Chris R. Burns – 2001										
$189^3/_8$	$24^1/_8$	$24^5/_8$	23	$24^4/_8$	$4^5/_8$	$4^3/_8$	8	8	$17^7/_8$	2443	119
	■ McMullen Co. – Roy Hindes – Roy Hindes – 1948										
$188^7/_8$	$22^6/_8$	$24^1/_8$	$17^4/_8$	$20^1/_8$	$4^3/_8$	$4^4/_8$	9	10	$14^5/_8$	2462	121
	■ Medina Co. – David T. Wallace – J. Claude Wallace – PR 1917										
$188^7/_8$	$23^5/_8$	$23^2/_8$	$17^2/_8$	21	$4^6/_8$	$4^5/_8$	10	6	$26^1/_8$	2462	121
	■ La Salle Co. – Jane W. Hightower – Jane W. Hightower – 1992										
$188^3/_8$	$23^4/_8$	$23^6/_8$	$18^4/_8$	$22^6/_8$	4	4	8	10	$25^7/_8$	2478	123
	■ Maverick Co. – Robert L. Golding – Robert L. Golding – 1996										
$187^2/_8$	$27^3/_8$	$27^3/_8$	$23^5/_8$	26	$4^3/_8$	$4^3/_8$	8	7	$17^7/_8$	2534	124
	■ Brooks Co. – Richard Pilgrim – Richard Pilgrim – 1980										

Score	Length of Main Beam Right	Length of Main Beam Left	Inside Spread	Greatest Spread	Circumference at Smallest Place Between Burr and First Point Right	Circumference at Smallest Place Between Burr and First Point Left	Number of Points Right	Number of Points Left	Lengths Abnormal Points	All-Time Rank	State Rank
					■ *Location of Kill – Hunter – Owner – Date Killed*						
186⁶/8	22⁴/8	22⁴/8	14¹/8	18¹/8	4²/8	4²/8	9	9	26⁷/8	2559	125
	■ *Palo Pinto Co. – M. Scott Layne – M. Scott Layne – 1994*										
185⁴/8	24⁵/8	25¹/8	18²/8	21⁴/8	3⁶/8	3⁷/8	12	8	13	2616	126
	■ *Kinney Co. – Ruby Yoas – Donald Yoas – 1962*										
185³/8	20⁶/8	22⁴/8	21⁶/8	24²/8	4²/8	4²/8	10	9	37¹/8	2622	127
	■ *Maverick Co. – John N. Garner – Richard H. Bennett – 1954*										
185²/8	21⁵/8	21²/8	19²/8	23	4²/8	4⁵/8	8	9	18²/8	2632†	128†
	■ *Palo Pinto Co. – Michael L. Baze – Michael L. Baze – 2001*										

† The scores and ranking for trophies from the 25th Awards Entry Period are not final until the banquet is held on June 19, 2004.

TROPHIES IN THE FIELD

HUNTER: Glenn Thurman
SCORE: 198-4/8
CATEGORY: non-typical whitetail deer
LOCATION: Kleberg County, Texas
DATE: 1994

VERMONT
RECORD WHITETAILS

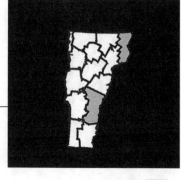

3 Typical whitetail deer entries
0 Non-typical whitetail deer entries
7,265 Total whitetail deer entries

0 Entries
1-2 Entries
3-5 Entries
6-10 Entries
11+ Entries

VERMONT STATE RECORD
Typical Whitetail Deer
Score: 171
Location: Windsor Co.
Hunter: Picked Up
Owner: Alfred A. Durkee
Date: 1935

VERMONT

TYPICAL WHITETAIL DEER

Score	Length of Main Beam Right Left	Inside Spread	Greatest Spread	Circumference at Smallest Place Between Burr and First Point Right Left		Number of Points Right Left		Lengths Abnormal Points	All-Time Rank	State Rank
	Location of Kill – Hunter – Owner – Date Killed									
171	28⁶/8 28⁵/8	20	22¹/8	5	5	4	5	1	2707	1
	▪ *Windsor Co. – Picked Up – Alfred A. Durkee – 1935*									
170¹/8	27¹/8 27²/8	20³/8	22	5⁶/8	5⁶/8	5	5		3143	2
	▪ *Essex Co. – Kevin A. Brockney – Kevin A. Brockney – 1986*									
166	24⁴/8 26	19⁴/8	24²/8	4³/8	4²/8	7	6	7	3657	3
	▪ *Essex Co. – Jack T. Szymanowski – Jack T. Szymanowski – 1991*									

VIRGINIA
RECORD WHITETAILS

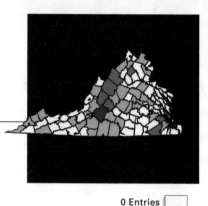

58 Typical whitetail deer entries
27 Non-typical whitetail deer entries
7,265 Total whitetail deer entries

0 Entries
1-2 Entries
3-5 Entries
6-10 Entries
11+ Entries

NEW
STATE
RECORD

VIRGINIA
STATE RECORD
Typical Whitetail Deer
Score: 189²/₈
Location: Buchanan Co.
Hunter and Owner: Jerry
    L. James
Date: 1999

VIRGINIA
STATE RECORD
Non-Typical Whitetail Deer
Score: 257⁴/₈
Location: Warren Co.
Hunter and Owner: James W. Smith
Date: 1992

VIRGINIA

TYPICAL WHITETAIL DEER

Score	Length of Main Beam		Inside Spread	Greatest Spread	Circumference at Smallest Place Between Burr and First Point		Number of Points		Lengths Abnormal Points	All-Time Rank	State Rank
	Right	Left			Right	Left	Right	Left			
	■ Location of Kill – Hunter – Owner – Date Killed										
189²/8	28⁵/8	27¹/8	18⁴/8	21	4³/8	4³/8	5	5		125	1
	■ Buchanan Co. – Jerry L. James – Jerry L. James – 1999										
188⁶/8	25³/8	25³/8	16²/8	18⁵/8	5²/8	5³/8	6	6		136	2
	■ Shenandoah Co. – Gene W. Wilson – Gene W. Wilson – 1985										
182⁶/8	26⁷/8	26¹/8	19	21⁷/8	4⁶/8	4⁶/8	5	5		409	3
	■ Roanoke Co. – Dwayne E. Webster – Dwayne E. Webster – 1999										
179²/8	27⁶/8	27⁷/8	21	23²/8	4⁵/8	5¹/8	6	6		763	4
	■ Henry Co. – Tony E. Meade – Tony E. Meade – 1995										
178³/8	27²/8	26⁴/8	18⁵/8	22⁴/8	4⁶/8	4⁶/8	6	6	4⁶/8	868	5
	■ Goochland Co. – Edward W. Fielder – Edward W. Fielder – 1981										
178²/8	25	25	22¹/8	24¹/8	4³/8	4⁴/8	5	6	1¹/8	891†	6†
	■ Greene Co. – Clyde E. Eppard, Sr. – Clyde E. Eppard, Sr. – 2000 ■ See photo on page 4										
177²/8	28¹/8	28	20⁶/8	22⁴/8	4⁶/8	4⁶/8	5	5		1025	7
	■ Augusta Co. – Donald W. Houser – Donald W. Houser – 1963										
176⁷/8	25⁵/8	27⁴/8	22⁴/8	25⁵/8	5	5¹/8	9	6	8³/8	1086	8
	■ Prince George Co. – Fred W. Collins – Fred W. Collins – 1949										
176²/8	25⁶/8	25⁷/8	20³/8	23³/8	5⁴/8	5⁴/8	7	6	5³/8	1209	9
	■ Rappahannock Co. – George W. Beahm – George W. Beahm – 1959										
176¹/8	25⁴/8	27	19¹/8	21²/8	4⁷/8	4⁶/8	5	5		1243	10
	■ Southampton Co. – Samuel B. Drewry, Jr. – Samuel B. Drewry, Jr. – 1997										
174⁴/8	26³/8	26²/8	19¹/8	21⁵/8	5²/8	5⁶/8	5	7	1⁵/8	1592	11
	■ Charlotte Co. – Jerry C. Claybrook – Jerry C. Claybrook – 1977										
173⁷/8	28⁷/8	28³/8	17³/8	19²/8	4⁵/8	4⁷/8	6	7	6²/8	1743†	12†
	■ Pittsylvania Co. – Picked Up – David Baker – 2001										
173⁴/8	26⁴/8	27	20⁶/8	24⁷/8	4⁴/8	4⁶/8	7	8	5²/8	1847	13
	■ Augusta Co. – David H. Wolfe – David H. Wolfe – 1957										
172⁶/8	24⁵/8	25¹/8	22	24	5³/8	5⁵/8	6	6		2065	14
	■ Surry Co. – Edward B. Jones – Edward B. Jones – 1984										
172⁵/8	25¹/8	27	20¹/8	22¹/8	5⁶/8	5²/8	6	5	7	2113	15
	■ Surry Co. – Picked Up – Virginia L. Logan – 1987										
172³/8	28³/8	27⁵/8	21¹/8	23⁶/8	4⁴/8	4³/8	5	6	1⁴/8	2200	16
	■ Bedford Co. – Robert A. McGann – Robert A. McGann – 1993										
171⁴/8	26	26⁶/8	22⁶/8	24²/8	4⁶/8	4⁷/8	5	6		2513	17
	■ Southampton Co. – Sam J. Pope, Jr. – Davis-Ridley Hunt Club – 1978										
171	26⁴/8	26⁴/8	20	22¹/8	4⁶/8	4⁶/8	7	6	5⁶/8	2707†	18†
	■ Albermarle Co. – Eddie W. Snow – Eddie W. Snow – 2001										
170⁷/8	26²/8	25⁷/8	19¹/8	20⁷/8	4⁶/8	4⁷/8	5	5		2769	19
	■ Bath Co. – Maurice Smith – Maurice Smith – 1953										

Score	Length of Main Beam Right	Left	Inside Spread	Greatest Spread	Circumference at Smallest Place Between Burr and First Point Right	Left	Number of Points Right	Left	Lengths Abnormal Points	All-Time Rank	State Rank
	■ Location of Kill – Hunter – Owner – Date Killed										
170⁶/8	23	22⁴/8	17⁶/8	19⁶/8	6¹/8	5⁵/8	5	5		2828	20
	■ Isle of Wight Co. – Picked Up – David A. Reese – 1999										
170⁴/8	27²/8	28⁵/8	21²/8	23⁶/8	5¹/8	5²/8	5	5		2933	21
	■ Bedford Co. – W. Bane Bowyer – W. Bane Bowyer – 1972										
170¹/8	26⁵/8	27	19³/8	21⁴/8	5⁷/8	5⁷/8	8	9	8⁶/8	3143	22
	■ Massanutton Mt. – Lloyd Lam – Lloyd Lam – 1955										
169	30²/8	28²/8	19⁴/8	21⁵/8	4⁷/8	5	6	8	6	3348	23
	■ Rockbridge Co. – Richard J. Lowe, Jr. – Richard J. Lowe, Jr. – 1999										
168⁵/8	24⁶/8	24⁶/8	21⁶/8	23²/8	4⁷/8	4⁷/8	6	5	2¹/8	3376	24
	■ Pittsylvania Co. – Jack B. Singletary – Jack B. Singletary – 1990										
168⁵/8	27	27³/8	18⁷/8	21²/8	5	4⁷/8	5	7	2⁴/8	3376	24
	■ Amherst Co. – Ronald P. Leary – Ronald P. Leary – 1997										
168⁴/8	28³/8	27¹/8	20⁵/8	23	5	5	5	7	3¹/8	3385	26
	■ Halifax Co. – Michael L. Phelps – Michael L. Phelps – 1994										
168⁴/8	27	26⁶/8	17⁶/8	20¹/8	4²/8	4¹/8	5	6		3385	26
	■ Rockbridge Co. – Richard C. Garrett III – Richard C. Garrett III – 1995										
168⁴/8	26⁶/8	26⁵/8	21	23³/8	4⁷/8	4⁷/8	7	8	4	3385	26
	■ Bedford Co. – Picked Up – Ronnie Goff – 1995										
167⁶/8	28¹/8	27¹/8	18⁴/8	20⁴/8	4⁴/8	4⁵/8	5	5		3461†	29†
	■ Albermarle Co. – James F. Shifflett – James F. Shifflett – 2001										
167⁴/8	27³/8	26²/8	19⁷/8	22⁶/8	4³/8	4⁴/8	6	5	2⁵/8	3485	30
	■ Augusta Co. – Terry L. Hammer – Terry L. Hammer – 1982										
167²/8	25²/8	26³/8	17³/8	19⁷/8	4⁶/8	4⁷/8	5	6	3⁷/8	3519	31
	■ Washington Co. – Dallas F. Hayden – Dallas F. Hayden – 1967										
167²/8	27²/8	25⁴/8	17⁶/8	20	5¹/8	5¹/8	5	5		3519	31
	■ Rappahannock Co. – Edwin Lillis – Edwin Lillis – 1998										
167¹/8	25³/8	24⁶/8	18⁵/8	20⁷/8	4¹/8	4¹/8	5	5		3539	33
	■ Franklin Co. – Timothy E. Burton – Timothy E. Burton – 1996										
166⁶/8	27²/8	27	18⁴/8	21²/8	4⁵/8	4⁶/8	8	6	7⁴/8	3582	34
	■ Albemarle Co. – Bobby K. Stanley, Jr. – Bobby K. Stanley, Jr. – 1995										
166⁴/8	27	25⁶/8	21⁴/8	23⁴/8	5⁴/8	5⁴/8	6	5	4⁶/8	3609	35
	■ Southampton Co. – Jack W. Lowe – Jack W. Lowe – 1991										
166³/8	24²/8	24⁵/8	19³/8	24⁶/8	5⁵/8	5⁴/8	6	8	6	3620	36
	■ Amherst Co. – Charles A. Poole – Charles A. Poole – 1991										
166	28⁴/8	27⁵/8	25²/8	27⁶/8	4⁴/8	4⁴/8	5	4		3657	37
	■ Campbell Co. – Bryan H. Mitchell – Bryan H. Mitchell – 1988										
165⁶/8	25³/8	26¹/8	19⁴/8	21³/8	4⁴/8	4³/8	6	6		3680	38
	■ Nelson Co. – Larry W. Toms – Larry W. Toms – 1986										
165⁴/8	30⁵/8	29⁶/8	18⁶/8	21¹/8	4⁶/8	4⁷/8	6	6	2⁴/8	3714	39
	■ Bedford Co. – T.A. Phillips – Loretta P. Harrison – 1976										
165⁴/8	25⁷/8	25⁴/8	23⁴/8	25³/8	4⁵/8	4⁵/8	5	5		3714	39
	■ Halifax Co. – Howard S. Elliott – Howard S. Elliott – 1997										

Score	Length of Main Beam		Inside Spread	Greatest Spread	Circumference at Smallest Place Between Burr and First Point		Number of Points		Lengths Abnormal Points	All-Time Rank	State Rank
	Right	Left			Right	Left	Right	Left			
	■ Location of Kill – Hunter – Owner – Date Killed										
165³/₈	25²/₈	27⁴/₈	21¹/₈	22⁷/₈	5²/₈	5³/₈	5	5		3731†	41†
■ Giles Co. – Jackie W. Vest – Jackie W. Vest – 2000											
165²/₈	25¹/₈	25⁶/₈	28⁶/₈	29⁵/₈	5¹/₈	5	5	5		3748	42
■ Accomack Co. – John W. Smith, Jr. – John W. Smith, Jr. – 1986											
164⁷/₈	25⁶/₈	25	17¹/₈	20¹/₈	4¹/₈	4¹/₈	6	8	2⁴/₈	3792†	43†
■ Rappahannock Co. – Larry W. Brown – Larry W. Brown – 2000											
164⁶/₈	25⁷/₈	25⁷/₈	23	26⁶/₈	4³/₈	4²/₈	5	5		3809	44
■ Prince William Co. – Edgar K. Armentrout – Edgar K. Armentrout – 1992											
163	22⁵/₈	21⁵/₈	18⁴/₈	20⁴/₈	4⁴/₈	4⁶/₈	5	6	1	4051	45
■ Spotsylvania Co. – Ricky Hairfield – Ricky Hairfield – 1997											
162⁷/₈	24	24⁴/₈	15⁶/₈	18⁵/₈	4⁴/₈	4³/₈	6	6	2⁵/₈	4067†	46†
■ Halifax Co. – David M. King – David M. King – 1999											
162⁴/₈	25⁵/₈	25⁴/₈	22	25	4⁷/₈	4⁷/₈	5	5		4129	47
■ Rockingham Co. – Ronald S. Rhodes – Ronald S. Rhodes – 1996											
162	28¹/₈	28³/₈	18	20³/₈	4³/₈	4⁶/₈	7	7	3⁴/₈	4184	48
■ Amherst Co. – David Deavers – Cornelius C. Smith – 1989											
161⁶/₈	25²/₈	25²/₈	17⁶/₈	19⁴/₈	4³/₈	4²/₈	5	5		4223	49
■ Loudoun Co. – Gary C. Smith – Gary C. Smith – 1986											
161³/₈	25⁴/₈	25⁴/₈	17¹/₈	19²/₈	5	4⁶/₈	5	5		4285	50
■ Lee Co. – Jimmy Mullins – Jimmy Mullins – 1988											
161³/₈	26⁵/₈	26	21³/₈	23	4	4	5	5		4285	50
■ Campbell Co. – Julian A. McFaden III – Cynthia McFaden – 1992											
161²/₈	27⁴/₈	25⁵/₈	22²/₈	24¹/₈	6¹/₈	6²/₈	6	6	2⁶/₈	4310	52
■ Bedford Co. – Kenneth M. Friess – Kenneth M. Friess – 1989											
161	27⁵/₈	26⁵/₈	22⁵/₈	24⁷/₈	4⁷/₈	5¹/₈	4	5	1⁷/₈	4356	53
■ Hanover Co. – Ernest E. Carneal, Jr. – Ernest E. Carneal, Jr. – 1995											
160⁷/₈	25	24⁶/₈	17⁷/₈	20¹/₈	4⁵/₈	4⁵/₈	5	5		4380	54
■ Augusta Co. – Gary D. Ritchey – Gary D. Ritchey – 1990											
160⁶/₈	24⁴/₈	25⁴/₈	16⁷/₈	19⁴/₈	5¹/₈	5¹/₈	5	7	4⁷/₈	4402	55
■ Rappahannock Co. – E.A. Martin – Robert A. Keller II – 1961											
160²/₈	24²/₈	23⁴/₈	15⁶/₈	18²/₈	4³/₈	4³/₈	5	5		4495†	56†
■ Loudoun Co. – Richard C. Vance – Richard C. Vance – 2000											
160¹/₈	25⁵/₈	26²/₈	16⁵/₈	19	4⁴/₈	4⁴/₈	7	6	1	4534†	57†
■ Franklin Co. – James D. Baker – James D. Baker – 2000											
160	24³/₈	25²/₈	18⁴/₈	20⁶/₈	5¹/₈	5	6	5		4565†	58†
■ Loudoun Co. – Stephen Marshall – Stephen Marshall – 2001											

† The scores and ranking for trophies from the 25th Awards Entry Period are not final until the banquet is held on June 19, 2004.

OLD-TIME TROPHY PHOTOS

1947

...ds of North American
Big Game

A PUBLICATION OF
BOONE AND CROCKETT CLUB
IN CARE OF
...ICAN MUSEUM OF NATURAL HISTORY
...OLUMBUS AVENUE AND 77TH STREET
NEW YORK, N. Y.

UNDER THE AUSPICES
OF
THE NATIONAL MUSEUM
OF HEADS AND HORNS
OF THE
NEW YORK ZOOLOGICAL
SOCIETY

D E E R

SPECIES _White Tailed Deer_

MEASUREMENTS	RIGHT	LEFT
Length on outside curve **A**	25	26¼
Circumference of main beam **B**	4½	4½
Circumference of burr **C**	6	6¼
Number of points on antler	6	4

Greatest spread: **D** _Twenty six 9¾, 26¾_

Exact locality where killed _Town of Edmeston, Otsego County, N.Y._

Date killed _December 2, 1938_

By whom killed _Warren R. Parker_

Owner _Warren R. Parker_

Address _Edmeston, N.Y._

Remarks: _about ½ inch broken off_
from tip of right horn 2 point on right horn

Photographs: Front view____✓____Profile_____
(Please place ✓ mark to indicate photographs furnished.)

We hereby certify that we have measured the above described trophy
on _August, 12_ 193 _9_, and that these measurements are
correct and made in accordance with the directions overleaf.

Warren R. Parker

By _Donald J. Schwoorm_

Parker 12.23.38 (auth. 9/5/39)

When the Boone and Crockett Club's original scoring system was developed in the 1930s, only the four measurements and the number of points were recorded for each deer. The system was refined in 1950 to the system that is used today. Several trophies from the earlier time period were remeasured and can be found in this book, as well as the all-time records book. Those entries that were not remeasured or did not make the minimum score are still maintained in the records archives as historical records.

VIRGINIA

NON-TYPICAL WHITETAIL DEER

Score	Length of Main Beam Right	Left	Inside Spread	Greatest Spread	Circumference at Smallest Place Between Burr and First Point Right	Left	Number of Points Right	Left	Lengths Abnormal Points	All-Time Rank	State Rank
	Location of Kill – Hunter – Owner – Date Killed										
257⁴/₈	29¹/₈	28²/₈	21	30	5⁵/₈	5³/₈	15	15	69⁶/₈	34	1
■ Warren Co. – James W. Smith – James W. Smith – 1992											
249³/₈	26³/₈	26³/₈	25³/₈	29⁴/₈	5¹/₈	5	14	14	71	62	2
■ Rockingham Co. – Jeffery W. Hensley – Jeffery W. Hensley – 1990											
242⁶/₈	24	24⁴/₈	18⁶/₈	26	6²/₈	6	22	18	86⁶/₈	99	3
■ Bedford Co. – Walter Hatcher – Walter Hatcher – 1993											
232⁴/₈	29²/₈	28⁶/₈	18⁷/₈	22¹/₈	5⁴/₈	5	14	18	52³/₈	203	4
■ Buckingham Co. – James R. Shumaker – James R. Shumaker – 1986											
226²/₈	27²/₈	28³/₈	22⁷/₈	25⁶/₈	5⁴/₈	5⁶/₈	11	10	43⁷/₈	298	5
■ Amherst Co. – Picked Up – Brent W. Campbell – 1994											
223⁴/₈	25⁵/₈	26³/₈	20²/₈	24⁵/₈	5⁵/₈	6	16	16	65⁶/₈	350	6
■ Dickenson Co. – Picked Up – James A. Cox – 1998											
221³/₈	26³/₈	25	19²/₈	27³/₈	6³/₈	7⁷/₈	11	13	67⁷/₈	407	7
■ Louisa Co. – Picked Up – James T. Rapalee – 1981											
217	23	25⁴/₈	25⁷/₈	30¹/₈	5⁷/₈	5⁶/₈	11	11	39⁶/₈	529	8
■ Isle of Wight Co. – Peter F. Crocker, Jr. – Peter F. Crocker, Jr. – 1963											
216⁴/₈	25²/₈	27³/₈	23	26³/₈	5	5	12	10	40	546	9
■ Surry Co. – Stanley M. Hall – Stanley M. Hall – 1986											
216³/₈	26⁶/₈	26³/₈	20³/₈	34²/₈	4⁷/₈	5	9	10	45⁶/₈	549	10
■ Powhatan Co. – William E. Schaefer – William E. Schaefer – 1970											
216²/₈	28⁷/₈	26⁷/₈	23³/₈	28	4⁷/₈	5¹/₈	10	9	34¹/₈	555	11
■ Floyd Co. – Ronnie T. Perdue – Ronnie T. Perdue – 1996											
215⁵/₈	28²/₈	29²/₈	18⁶/₈	20⁷/₈	4⁶/₈	4⁵/₈	9	11	20³/₈	578	12
■ Wise Co. – Edison Holcomb – Edison Holcomb – 1987											
213⁷/₈	22⁵/₈	25²/₈	18²/₈	23⁶/₈	5²/₈	5²/₈	10	10	50⁷/₈	635	13
■ Botetourt Co. – Craig A. Brogan – Craig A. Brogan – 1989											
213³/₈	31¹/₈	27⁶/₈	18⁶/₈	27	5⁵/₈	6⁶/₈	11	13	46¹/₈	660	14
■ Cumberland Co. – Jimmy E. Dedmond – Jimmy E. Dedmond – 1995											
211⁷/₈	25	25⁴/₈	20²/₈	23²/₈	4⁶/₈	4⁶/₈	10	12	35⁵/₈	724	15
■ Rockingham Co. – Dorsey O. Breeden – Dorsey O. Breeden – 1966											
209⁵/₈	25⁴/₈	25³/₈	21⁵/₈	26⁴/₈	5²/₈	5³/₈	10	8	31	840	16
■ Franklin Co. – Timothy J. Wright – Timothy J. Wright – 1989											
204	28²/₈	28⁵/₈	23³/₈	28⁴/₈	5¹/₈	5¹/₈	8	8	26⁷/₈	1220	17
■ Rockbridge Co. – Michael J. Shifflett – Michael J. Shifflett – 1993											
201⁵/₈	26¹/₈	25³/₈	21¹/₈	23⁴/₈	5²/₈	5¹/₈	6	10	39⁴/₈	1427	18
■ Roanoke Co. – James D. Scott – James D. Scott – 1994											
198⁶/₈	25⁴/₈	24⁷/₈	19²/₈	23	6²/₈	6	11	13	24⁶/₈	1697	19
■ Rappahannock Co. – Chris K. Foster – Chris K. Foster – 1989											

Score	Length of Main Beam Right	Left	Inside Spread	Greatest Spread	Circumference at Smallest Place Between Burr and First Point Right	Left	Number of Points Right	Left	Lengths Abnormal Points	All-Time Rank	State Rank
	■ Location of Kill – Hunter – Owner – Date Killed										
198³/₈	25⁷/₈	26⁶/₈	19⁵/₈	25²/₈	4⁶/₈	5	9	9	34⁴/₈	1762	20
	■ Rappahannock Co. – Collis W. Dodson, Jr. – Collis W. Dodson, Jr. – 1966										
197	25³/₈	29³/₈	21⁶/₈	23⁴/₈	5²/₈	4⁴/₈	13	14	62	1939	21
	■ Bedford Co. – John P. Kirby, Sr. – John P. Kirby, Sr. – 1981										
196⁴/₈	25¹/₈	24²/₈	20⁷/₈	27⁴/₈	4⁷/₈	4⁶/₈	15	17	41⁵/₈	1999	22
	■ Charlotte Co. – Paul S. Wray – Paul S. Wray – 1997										
195¹/₈	26¹/₈	25³/₈	20	23⁶/₈	4⁵/₈	4³/₈	7	10	26⁷/₈	2208	23
	■ Bath Co. – Joe W. Bond – Joe W. Bond – 1996										
194²/₈	24³/₈	23⁶/₈	14¹/₈	19²/₈	4⁶/₈	4⁷/₈	12	10	42⁵/₈	2267	24
	■ Pulaski Co. – Roger N. White – Roger N. White – 1996										
192⁷/₈	22⁵/₈	22⁶/₈	17²/₈	20⁷/₈	5⁵/₈	6¹/₈	10	11	42¹/₈	2312	25
	■ Bedford Co. – Claude J. Wilson – Claude J. Wilson – 1998										
190⁵/₈	29⁴/₈	26	19⁶/₈	22⁵/₈	5⁷/₈	6	12	12	23⁷/₈	2393	26
	■ Bedford Co. – J.B. Karnes – Mrs. J.B. Karnes – 1974										
188²/₈	23³/₈	24⁴/₈	19⁷/₈	22²/₈	4⁴/₈	4⁶/₈	13	9	32³/₈	2489	27
	■ Surry Co. – George M. Summerfield – George M. Summerfield – 1989										

† The scores and ranking for trophies from the 25th Awards Entry Period are not final until the banquet is held on June 19, 2004.

WASHINGTON
RECORD WHITETAILS

18 Typical whitetail deer entries
31 Non-typical whitetail deer entries
7,265 Total whitetail deer entries

0 Entries
1-2 Entries
3-5 Entries
6-10 Entries
11+ Entries

WASHINGTON
STATE RECORD
Typical Whitetail Deer
Score: 181$^7/_8$
Location: Whitman Co.
Hunter and Owner: George A. Cook III
Date: 1985

Photograph by Keith Balfourd

WASHINGTON
NEW STATE RECORD
Non-Typical Whitetail Deer
Score: 236$^5/_8$
Location: Pend Oreille Co.
Hunter: George Gretener
Owner: John E. Gretener
Date: Prior to 1931

Photograph courtesy of Northwest Big Game, Inc.

WASHINGTON

TYPICAL WHITETAIL DEER

Score	Length of Main Beam Right	Left	Inside Spread	Greatest Spread	Circumference at Smallest Place Between Burr and First Point Right	Left	Number of Points Right	Left	Lengths Abnormal Points	All-Time Rank	State Rank
	■ Location of Kill – Hunter – Owner – Date Killed										
181⁷/₈	27⁴/₈	27⁵/₈	20⁵/₈	23²/₈	4⁴/₈	4⁴/₈	5	6		478	1
	■ Whitman Co. – George A. Cook III – George A. Cook III – 1985										
180⁴/₈	30	29¹/₈	24⁵/₈	26⁵/₈	4⁷/₈	4⁷/₈	8	8	9⁷/₈	613	2
	■ Okanogan Co. – Joe Peone – Joe Peone – 1983										
179⁴/₈	24¹/₈	24²/₈	19²/₈	21⁶/₈	5²/₈	5¹/₈	7	6	2⁴/₈	733	3
	■ Spokane Co. – Bert E. Smith – Bert E. Smith – 1972										
178⁴/₈	28²/₈	28	22⁶/₈	25⁴/₈	4²/₈	4²/₈	5	5		850	4
	■ Lincoln Co. – Melvin Scheuss – Gary H. Wilcox – 1951										
178⁴/₈	23⁷/₈	24⁶/₈	21³/₈	23¹/₈	4³/₈	4³/₈	7	7	4¹/₈	850	4
	■ Addy – Irving Naff – Irving Naff – 1957										
176⁵/₈	24¹/₈	24²/₈	17⁶/₈	21³/₈	5	5¹/₈	8	8	8¹/₈	1134	6
	■ Washington – Unknown – Jonas Bros. of Seattle – PR 1953										
175¹/₈	25⁷/₈	27¹/₈	19⁵/₈	25	4²/₈	4¹/₈	6	7	2⁶/₈	1440	7
	■ Spokane Co. – Michael G. McBride – Michael G. McBride – 1999										
174⁷/₈	26¹/₈	26¹/₈	18⁴/₈	23⁷/₈	5¹/₈	5¹/₈	7	6	4¹/₈	1513	8
	■ Stevens Co. – Clifton W. Hamilton – Clifton W. Hamilton – 1990										
173³/₈	27³/₈	26⁵/₈	19³/₈	22⁴/₈	4⁶/₈	4⁶/₈	6	5	4⁴/₈	1883	9
	■ Pend Oreille Co. – Thomas R. Lentz – Thomas R. Lentz – 1987										
172⁶/₈	25⁴/₈	25⁵/₈	22⁴/₈	25⁵/₈	4⁵/₈	4⁴/₈	5	6		2065	10
	■ Spokane Co. – Maurice Robinette – Maurice Robinette – 1968										
172⁴/₈	25⁴/₈	25²/₈	17	20⁵/₈	4⁵/₈	4⁶/₈	6	6		2156†	11†
	■ Stevens Co. – Don Ledbeter – Don Ledbeter – 1990										
171³/₈	22³/₈	23¹/₈	14⁵/₈	16⁶/₈	5	5	7	6	1⁶/₈	2564	12
	■ Metaline Falls – Scott Hicks – Scott Hicks – 1970										
170⁵/₈	26⁴/₈	27²/₈	17³/₈	19⁵/₈	5⁴/₈	5²/₈	7	6	8⁴/₈	2876	13
	■ Spokane Co. – Laura M. Kaiser – Laura M. Kaiser – 1994										
170⁴/₈	25⁷/₈	25⁷/₈	18⁶/₈	20⁶/₈	4⁶/₈	4⁵/₈	5	6	2	2933	14
	■ Pend Oreille Co. – Picked Up – Eugene M. Bailey – 1944										
170²/₈	23²/₈	24²/₈	15	16⁶/₈	4⁴/₈	4⁴/₈	8	7	1	3063	15
	■ Spokane Co. – Edward A. Floch, Jr. – Edward A. Floch, Jr. – 1970										
170²/₈	24²/₈	25⁵/₈	18	20¹/₈	5	4⁷/₈	7	8	10⁴/₈	3063	15
	■ Pend Oreille Co. – George T. Law – George T. Law – 1988										
170	22⁷/₈	22⁴/₈	18⁴/₈	20⁵/₈	4⁶/₈	4⁷/₈	5	6		3224	17
	■ Stevens Co. – Clair Kelso – Clair Kelso – 1966										
160⁴/₈	24⁵/₈	24³/₈	18⁴/₈	20⁶/₈	4³/₈	4³/₈	5	5		4443	18
	■ Okanogan Co. – Michael D. Treadwell – Michael D. Treadwell – 1996										

† The scores and ranking for trophies from the 25th Awards Entry Period are not final until the banquet is held on June 19, 2004.

WASHINGTON

NON-TYPICAL WHITETAIL DEER

Score	Length of Main Beam Right Left	Inside Spread	Greatest Spread	Circumference at Smallest Place Between Burr and First Point Right Left	Number of Points Right Left	Lengths Abnormal Points	All-Time Rank	State Rank
236$\frac{5}{8}$	27$\frac{7}{8}$ 26	21$\frac{3}{8}$	26$\frac{3}{8}$	5$\frac{6}{8}$ 5$\frac{2}{8}$	14 17	58$\frac{4}{8}$	157	1
■ Pend Oreille Co. – George Gretener – John E. Gretener – PR 1931							
234$\frac{4}{8}$	29 28$\frac{2}{8}$	20$\frac{7}{8}$	24$\frac{6}{8}$	5$\frac{3}{8}$ 5$\frac{6}{8}$	14 16	42$\frac{7}{8}$	175	2
■ Stevens Co. – Larry G. Gardner – Legendary Whitetails – 1953							
233$\frac{6}{8}$	26$\frac{2}{8}$ 26	22	31	4$\frac{7}{8}$ 4$\frac{6}{8}$	14 13	67$\frac{6}{8}$	187	3
■ Thompson Creek – George Sly, Jr. – D.J. Hollinger & B. Howard – 1964							
231	26 25$\frac{7}{8}$	18	22$\frac{6}{8}$	5 5	12 12	43$\frac{6}{8}$	227	4
■ Stevens Co. – Joe Bussano – Joe Bussano – 1946							
227$\frac{4}{8}$	27$\frac{1}{8}$ 26$\frac{2}{8}$	20$\frac{2}{8}$	28	5$\frac{2}{8}$ 5$\frac{2}{8}$	12 9	44	270	5
■ Pullman – Glenn C. Paulson – Glenn C. Paulson – 1965							
223$\frac{5}{8}$	23$\frac{5}{8}$ 24$\frac{5}{8}$	17	21$\frac{6}{8}$	5$\frac{5}{8}$ 5$\frac{4}{8}$	10 12	40$\frac{1}{8}$	345	6
■ Stevens Co. – Mike W. Naff – Mike W. Naff – 1992							
215	25$\frac{4}{8}$ 25$\frac{6}{8}$	21$\frac{6}{8}$	26	5 5	11 12	44$\frac{6}{8}$	598	7
■ Stevens Co. – Unknown – Dick Rossum – PR 1989							
211$\frac{2}{8}$	24$\frac{2}{8}$ 23$\frac{4}{8}$	19$\frac{5}{8}$	21$\frac{4}{8}$	5$\frac{4}{8}$ 5$\frac{6}{8}$	9 8	35$\frac{7}{8}$	750	8
■ Spokane Co. – Cary C. Janson – Cary C. Janson – 1992							
210$\frac{7}{8}$	24$\frac{2}{8}$ 24$\frac{1}{8}$	18$\frac{1}{8}$	21$\frac{6}{8}$	5$\frac{2}{8}$ 5$\frac{2}{8}$	11 9	32$\frac{4}{8}$	773	9
■ Stevens Co. – Charles Tucker – Charles Tucker – 1966							
208$\frac{3}{8}$	26$\frac{2}{8}$ 28$\frac{6}{8}$	19$\frac{3}{8}$	27$\frac{1}{8}$	4$\frac{4}{8}$ 4$\frac{4}{8}$	10 6	27$\frac{6}{8}$	905†	10†
■ Okanogan Co. – Kenneth Anderson – Thomas S. Anderson – 1959							
208	25$\frac{4}{8}$ 25	19$\frac{6}{8}$	22	4$\frac{5}{8}$ 4$\frac{5}{8}$	9 10	16$\frac{4}{8}$	929	11
■ Chesaw – Charles Eder – Charles Eder – 1967							
207$\frac{2}{8}$	24$\frac{4}{8}$ 19$\frac{5}{8}$	11$\frac{7}{8}$	25$\frac{6}{8}$	5$\frac{6}{8}$ 5$\frac{5}{8}$	11 17	84$\frac{3}{8}$	985	12
■ Oroville – Victor E. Moss – Victor E. Moss – 1967							
206$\frac{5}{8}$	22 22$\frac{3}{8}$	18$\frac{1}{8}$	23$\frac{1}{8}$	4$\frac{4}{8}$ 4$\frac{5}{8}$	10 12	63$\frac{4}{8}$	1036	13
■ Stevens Co. – Dick E. Jones – Dick E. Jones – 1998							
206$\frac{1}{8}$	22 20$\frac{6}{8}$	20$\frac{7}{8}$	27$\frac{2}{8}$	4$\frac{5}{8}$ 4$\frac{6}{8}$	10 10	39$\frac{6}{8}$	1068	14
■ Loon Lake – Bill Quirt – Bill Quirt – 1955							
204$\frac{5}{8}$	27$\frac{2}{8}$ 27$\frac{3}{8}$	20$\frac{4}{8}$	26	5 5	9 12	24$\frac{7}{8}$	1176	15
■ Okanogan Co. – Matthew B. King – Matthew B. King – 1992							
204$\frac{3}{8}$	26 24$\frac{4}{8}$	18$\frac{3}{8}$	23$\frac{4}{8}$	4$\frac{7}{8}$ 5$\frac{2}{8}$	11 12	35$\frac{6}{8}$	1186	16
■ Newport – David R. Buchite – David R. Buchite – 1960							
203$\frac{5}{8}$	26$\frac{6}{8}$ 26$\frac{4}{8}$	20$\frac{4}{8}$	23$\frac{5}{8}$	6$\frac{4}{8}$ 6$\frac{1}{8}$	9 10	33$\frac{1}{8}$	1248†	17†
■ Spokane Co. – Jeff Whitman – Jeff Whitman – 1992							
203$\frac{3}{8}$	25$\frac{2}{8}$ 25$\frac{2}{8}$	21$\frac{5}{8}$	23$\frac{6}{8}$	5 5	10 8	28	1272	18
■ Okanogan Co. – Michael A. Anderson – Michael A. Anderson – 1961							
202$\frac{4}{8}$	26$\frac{2}{8}$ 25$\frac{3}{8}$	22$\frac{1}{8}$	25$\frac{1}{8}$	5$\frac{1}{8}$ 5$\frac{2}{8}$	9 8	30$\frac{3}{8}$	1355	19
■ Spokane Co. – Unknown – Dick Rossum – PR 1989							

■ Location of Kill – Hunter – Owner – Date Killed

Score	Length of Main Beam Right	Left	Inside Spread	Greatest Spread	Circumference at Smallest Place Between Burr and First Point Right	Left	Number of Points Right	Left	Lengths Abnormal Points	All-Time Rank	State Rank
201 4/8	25 2/8	23 1/8	16 5/8	18 4/8	4 5/8	5 2/8	14	13	69 3/8	1443	20
■ Stevens Co. – Robert W. Newell – Robert W. Newell – 1963											
200 6/8	25 6/8	24 4/8	18	23 1/8	4 7/8	4 6/8	16	12	43 6/8	1524	21
■ Okanogan Co. – Fred R. Miller – Fred R. Miller – 1993											
200	22 5/8	18 7/8	20 1/8	23 6/8	5 5/8	5 5/8	12	6	40 3/8	1591	22
■ Stevens Co. – Ronald F. Barber – Ronald F. Barber – 1991											
199 5/8	25 6/8	25 1/8	24 6/8	28 4/8	4 5/8	5 1/8	8	12	28 1/8	1621	23
■ Pend Oreille Co. – John C. Kroker – John C. Kroker – 1989											
197 6/8	23 5/8	26 2/8	20 2/8	26	5 2/8	5	10	8	35 2/8	1833	24
■ Hunters – Rachel Mally – Rachel Mally – 1961											
197 3/8	25	26	17 4/8	24 7/8	5 5/8	5 5/8	9	10	19 1/8	1884	25
■ Stevens Co. – Coulston W. Drummond – Coulston W. Drummond – 1948											
196 3/8	26 3/8	26 6/8	20 7/8	31 1/8	4 4/8	4 3/8	7	9	21 6/8	2010†	26†
■ Spokane Co. – Eric Friesen – Eric Friesen – 1986											
195 2/8	25 3/8	25 5/8	22 2/8	24	5 3/8	5 3/8	12	13	31 4/8	2186	27
■ Stevens Co. – Floyd E. Newell – Floyd E. Newell – 1981											
195 1/8	24 2/8	23 4/8	23 2/8	25 6/8	5 2/8	5 2/8	10	9	19 3/8	2208	28
■ Whitman Co. – R. & R. Boyer – R. & R. Boyer – 1975											
189 5/8	24 5/8	22 1/8	18 6/8	26 2/8	5 2/8	5 7/8	8	10	29 1/8	2429	29
■ Lincoln Co. – Darci D. Teel – Darci D. Teel – 1992											
187 4/8	21 2/8	15 2/8	20 5/8	25 7/8	4 7/8	4 6/8	10	13	46 7/8	2522	30
■ Pend Oreille Co. – Picked Up – Eugene M. Bailey – 1946											
185 5/8	27	27 2/8	17 4/8	23	4 5/8	4 5/8	6	9	13 1/8	2610†	31†
■ Stevens Co. – Robert E. Dudding – Robert E. Dudding – 1991											

† The scores and ranking for trophies from the 25th Awards Entry Period are not final until the banquet is held on June 19, 2004.

TROPHIES IN THE FIELD

HUNTER: Kevin W. Bouers
SCORE: 211-6/8
CATEGORY: non-typical whitetail deer
LOCATION: Green County, Wisconsin
DATE: 1999

WEST VIRGINIA
RECORD WHITETAILS

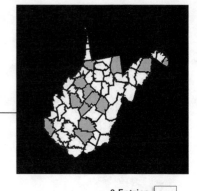

12 Typical whitetail deer entries
6 Non-typical whitetail deer entries
7,265 Total whitetail deer entries

0 Entries
1-2 Entries
3-5 Entries
6-10 Entries
11+ Entries

WEST VIRGINIA STATE RECORD
Typical Whitetail Deer
Score: 182³/₈
Location: Braxton Co.
Hunter and Owner:
    William D. Given
Date: 1976

WEST VIRGINIA
STATE RECORD
Non-Typical Whitetail Deer
Score: $231^5/_8$
Location: Wayne Co.
Hunter: Charles I. McLaughlin
Owner: D.J. Hollinger & B. Howard
Date: 1997

WEST VIRGINIA

TYPICAL WHITETAIL DEER

Score	Length of Main Beam Right	Left	Inside Spread	Greatest Spread	Circumference at Smallest Place Between Burr and First Point Right	Left	Number of Points Right	Left	Lengths Abnormal Points	All-Time Rank	State Rank
182³/₈	28¹/₈	27¹/₈	21⁵/₈	23⁶/₈	4⁴/₈	4⁵/₈	6	6		438	1
■ Braxton Co. – William D. Given – William D. Given – 1976											
180⁵/₈	25	23⁶/₈	23³/₈	24⁶/₈	5³/₈	5³/₈	7	6	10⁴/₈	599	2
■ Cheat Mt. – Joseph V. Volitis – Bass Pro Shops – 1969											
175¹/₈	27³/₈	27¹/₈	21²/₈	23⁶/₈	5⁷/₈	6	6	5	1¹/₈	1440	3
■ Wetzel Co. – Matthew Scheibelhood – Matthew Scheibelhood – 1984											
173³/₈	27⁵/₈	27²/₈	20⁷/₈	23¹/₈	5⁵/₈	5³/₈	8	6	2	1883	4
■ Fayette Co. – Richard L. Schoolcraft – Richard L. Schoolcraft – 1995											
171⁴/₈	26²/₈	27⁵/₈	22²/₈	24¹/₈	4⁶/₈	4³/₈	5	5		2513	5
■ Raleigh Co. – Omar O. Burns – Omar O. Burns – 1999											
171	27¹/₈	26³/₈	19⁴/₈	21⁶/₈	4⁴/₈	4⁴/₈	5	5		2707	6
■ Hampshire Co. – Conda L. Shanholtz – Conda L. Shanholtz – 1958											
166	27⁷/₈	28²/₈	20²/₈	23³/₈	5	5	5	6	1⁴/₈	3657	7
■ Webster Co. – Patrick A. DelVecchio – Patrick A. DelVecchio – 1995											
165⁶/₈	23³/₈	23⁵/₈	19⁴/₈	22¹/₈	4⁵/₈	4⁶/₈	6	6	5⁶/₈	3680	8
■ Clay Co. – Brian A. Rickmers – Brian A. Rickmers – 1997											
165²/₈	25¹/₈	24⁵/₈	18	20²/₈	4¹/₈	4²/₈	5	5		3748	9
■ Roane Co. – Robert L. Fitzwater – Robert L. Fitzwater – 1998											
165	24⁶/₈	24⁷/₈	17	18⁷/₈	4¹/₈	3⁶/₈	5	6		3782†	10†
■ Jefferson Co. – Karl O. Hamilton – Karl O. Hamilton – 2000											
164⁵/₈	25	25	16⁷/₈	18³/₈	4²/₈	4²/₈	6	6		3835†	11†
■ Kanawaha Co. – William S. Aldridge – William S. Aldridge – 2001											
161	25⁶/₈	25²/₈	17⁶/₈	19⁵/₈	4³/₈	4³/₈	6	6		4356†	12†
■ Preston Co. – Ronald B. Kopanko – Ronald B. Kopanko – 2000											

† The scores and ranking for trophies from the 25th Awards Entry Period are not final until the banquet is held on June 19, 2004.

WEST VIRGINIA

NON-TYPICAL WHITETAIL DEER

Score	Length of Main Beam Right Left	Inside Spread	Greatest Spread	Circumference at Smallest Place Between Burr and First Point Right Left		Number of Points Right Left		Lengths Abnormal Points	All-Time Rank	State Rank
	Location of Kill – Hunter – Owner – Date Killed									
$231^{5}/_{8}$	$26^{1}/_{8}$ 26	$20^{3}/_{8}$	$24^{2}/_{8}$	$5^{4}/_{8}$	$5^{2}/_{8}$	16	11	$55^{2}/_{8}$	214	1
	▪ *Wayne Co. – Charles I. McLaughlin – D.J. Hollinger & B. Howard – 1997*									
$205^{6}/_{8}$	$24^{3}/_{8}$ 24	21	23	5	$5^{2}/_{8}$	9	9	27	1094	2
	▪ *Ritchie Co. – Charles E. Bailey, Jr. – Charles E. Bailey, Jr. – 1979*									
$204^{6}/_{8}$	$28^{4}/_{8}$ $26^{5}/_{8}$	$21^{7}/_{8}$	$25^{1}/_{8}$	$5^{7}/_{8}$	$5^{7}/_{8}$	10	12	$22^{3}/_{8}$	1165	3
	▪ *Gilmer Co. – Brooks Reed – Brooks Reed – 1960*									
$203^{2}/_{8}$	28 $27^{7}/_{8}$	21	$30^{1}/_{8}$	$4^{7}/_{8}$	$4^{5}/_{8}$	9	10	$35^{2}/_{8}$	1287	4
	▪ *Preston Co. – Unknown – L. Keith Casteel – 1952*									
$203^{1}/_{8}$	$23^{7}/_{8}$ $24^{4}/_{8}$	$19^{6}/_{8}$	$24^{4}/_{8}$	$5^{4}/_{8}$	$5^{7}/_{8}$	10	12	$26^{1}/_{8}$	1305	5
	▪ *Wetzel Co. – Tom Kirkhart – Tom Kirkhart – 1981*									
$187^{5}/_{8}$	$27^{1}/_{8}$ $27^{3}/_{8}$	$18^{7}/_{8}$	$21^{1}/_{8}$	$4^{4}/_{8}$	$4^{5}/_{8}$	6	8	$15^{4}/_{8}$	2518	6
	▪ *Hancock Co. – Shawn J. Sargent – Shawn J. Sargent – 1990*									

WISCONSIN
RECORD WHITETAILS

469 Typical whitetail deer entries
213 Non-typical whitetail deer entries
7,265 Total whitetail deer entries

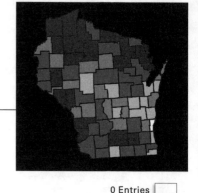

0 Entries	
1-2 Entries	
3-5 Entries	
6-10 Entries	
11+ Entries	

WISCONSIN
STATE RECORD
Typical Whitetail Deer
Score: 206$^1/8$
Location: Burnett Co.
Hunter: James Jordan
Owner: Bass Pro Shops
Date: 1914

Photograph courtesy of
Charles T. Arnold

WISCONSIN
NEW STATE RECORD
Non-Typical Whitetail Deer
Score: 247³/8
Location: Vernon Co.
Hunter and Owner: Arnold N. Stalsberg
Date: 1998

WISCONSIN

TYPICAL WHITETAIL DEER

Score	Length of Main Beam		Inside Spread	Greatest Spread	Circumference at Smallest Place Between Burr and First Point		Number of Points		Lengths Abnormal Points	All-Time Rank	State Rank
	Right	Left			Right	Left	Right	Left			
206¹/₈	30	30	20¹/₈	23⁶/₈	6²/₈	6¹/₈	5	5		2	1
■ Burnett Co. – James Jordan – Bass Pro Shops – 1914											
197⁶/₈	30	26⁷/₈	18⁷/₈	21³/₈	5⁷/₈	6	7	10	9⁵/₈	23	2
■ Kenosha Co. – Keith S. Brossard – Keith S. Brossard – 1999											
197⁵/₈	27²/₈	27⁵/₈	21⁶/₈	24¹/₈	5²/₈	5⁴/₈	7	8	2⁷/₈	25	3
■ Wood Co. – Joe Haske – Goldie Haske – 1945											
191³/₈	31⁶/₈	31¹/₈	27⁵/₈	30²/₈	6¹/₈	6¹/₈	5	6		85	4
■ Vilas Co. – Robert Hunter – May Docken – 1910											
189⁷/₈	29⁴/₈	29⁶/₈	19⁵/₈	21³/₈	5	4⁷/₈	9	6	6⁶/₈	113	5
■ Trempealeau Co. – Emil Stelmach – Emil Stelmach – 1959											
189¹/₈	26	26⁵/₈	17³/₈	19³/₈	5⁶/₈	5⁶/₈	8	9	16⁶/₈	127	6
■ Douglas Co. – Bryan Lawler – Bass Pro Shops – 1946											
188⁶/₈	29	29²/₈	22²/₈	24⁴/₈	4⁶/₈	4⁶/₈	5	6	2⁶/₈	136	7
■ Crawford Co. – Eli D. Randall – Eli D. Randall – 1995											
188⁴/₈	22²/₈	24²/₈	17	21⁴/₈	4⁶/₈	4⁵/₈	8	6	3	141	8
■ Crawford Co. – Roger W. Salmon – Roger W. Salmon – 1986											
187⁷/₈	28	28³/₈	21²/₈	24⁴/₈	5	5	7	8	2¹/₈	156	9
■ Bayfield Co. – Simon Jacobs – Jon Jacobs – 1951											
187⁷/₈	27⁴/₈	28⁷/₈	19⁵/₈	21⁴/₈	5	5	6	5		156	9
■ Langlade Co. – Kory J. Schumacher – Kory J. Schumacher – 1994											
186⁵/₈	24⁴/₈	24⁷/₈	16⁷/₈	20²/₈	4⁷/₈	4⁷/₈	7	10	3²/₈	202	11
■ Langlade Co. – Fred J. Hofmann – Fred J. Hofmann – 1994											
186⁵/₈	27¹/₈	26⁴/₈	21⁴/₈	23⁶/₈	4⁴/₈	4³/₈	7	8	5³/₈	202	11
■ Buffalo Co. – Kenneth H. Shane – Kenneth H. Shane – 2000											
186²/₈	25⁷/₈	27⁴/₈	20³/₈	22⁵/₈	4⁶/₈	5	7	7	2¹/₈	220	13
■ Bayfield Co. – Ken T. Johnson – Ken T. Johnson – 1994											
186¹/₈	28	26²/₈	21⁴/₈	25²/₈	6¹/₈	6	8	5	2⁵/₈	228	14
■ Waupaca Co. – Fred Penny – Dale Trinrud – 1963											
185	29¹/₈	28⁵/₈	18⁶/₈	20⁷/₈	4⁴/₈	4³/₈	5	5		272	15
■ Vernon Co. – Harold Christianson – Harold Christianson – 1968											
184⁶/₈	27	26	19⁴/₈	21⁶/₈	5⁵/₈	5⁴/₈	5	5		285	16
■ Sauk Co. – Jeffrey J. Wilson – Jeffrey J. Wilson – 1995											
184	24⁵/₈	24⁴/₈	18⁵/₈	22	5¹/₈	5²/₈	7	6	1¹/₈	334	17
■ Menominee Co. – Keith Miller – Charles Loberg – 1969											
184	27⁶/₈	25⁶/₈	24⁶/₈	26⁵/₈	4⁶/₈	4⁶/₈	6	6		334	17
■ Douglas Co. – David H. Johnson – David H. Johnson – 1998											
183⁷/₈	28	27¹/₈	19⁶/₈	22	5	4⁷/₈	7	5	2⁷/₈	343	19
■ Forest Co. – James M. Thayer – James M. Thayer – 1980											

Score	Length of Main Beam Right Left	Inside Spread	Greatest Spread	Circumference at Smallest Place Between Burr and First Point Right Left	Number of Points Right Left	Lengths Abnormal Points	All-Time Rank	State Rank
	▪ Location of Kill – Hunter – Owner – Date Killed							
183 6/8	26 7/8 25 1/8	18 6/8	21	5 4/8 5 4/8	7 7	1 2/8	350	20
▪ Pepin Co. – LaVerne Anibas – LaVerne Anibas – 1965								
183 5/8	27 1/8 26	23 2/8	25	4 6/8 4 6/8	7 6	4 5/8	357	21
▪ Buffalo Co. – Lee F. Spittler – Mrs. Lee F. Spittler – 1953								
183 4/8	26 4/8 27 1/8	24	26 6/8	4 6/8 4 7/8	7 7	2 6/8	361	22
▪ Douglas Co. – Michael Head – Michael Head – 1999								
183 2/8	26 7/8 26 7/8	16	20	5 5	7 7	5 4/8	378	23
▪ Ashland Co. – Unknown – Martin Bonack – 1900								
183 1/8	27 1/8 27 2/8	19 3/8	21 7/8	4 6/8 4 5/8	6 6		385	24
▪ Crawford Co. – Ray Volkert – Cabela's, Inc. – 1990								
182 6/8	28 2/8 28	22 6/8	25 2/8	4 6/8 4 6/8	6 5		409	25
▪ Vilas Co. – George Sparks – Mac's Taxidermy – 1942								
182 3/8	28 3/8 27 3/8	19 1/8	22 4/8	4 3/8 4 4/8	5 6		438	26
▪ Buffalo Co. – Anthony F. Wolfe – Anthony F. Wolfe – 1984								
182 2/8	29 3/8 29	19 4/8	22 3/8	5 7/8 6	5 6	1 2/8	450	27
▪ Forest Co. – Richard J. Moore – Richard J. Moore – 1987								
182	23 25	19	22 4/8	5 3/8 5 3/8	6 6		469	28
▪ Crawford Co. – Andrew D. Marg – Andrew D. Marg – 1995								
181 5/8	25 4/8 25 2/8	16 6/8	17 3/8	5 5/8 5 4/8	6 6	1 1/8	500†	29†
▪ Sawyer Co. – Picked Up – Teresa Kleutsch – 1996								
181 5/8	28 2/8 27 2/8	19 7/8	22 1/8	3 7/8 4 1/8	6 6		500	29
▪ Pierce Co. – Raymond G. Miller, Sr. – Raymond G. Miller, Sr. – 1960								
181 5/8	24 7/8 25 6/8	24 1/8	25 4/8	5 1/8 5 3/8	6 5		500	29
▪ Racine Co. – Andrae D'Acquisto – Andrae D'Acquisto – 1996								
181 4/8	26 1/8 26 6/8	18	22 1/8	5 3/8 5 3/8	6 7	6	516†	32†
▪ Vernon Co. – Timothy T. Nordengren – Timothy T. Nordengren – 2001								
181 4/8	26 1/8 27 2/8	20 2/8	22 3/8	4 5/8 4 6/8	6 6		516	32
▪ Trempealeau Co. – Randy A. Hoff – Randy A. Hoff – 1987								
181 4/8	29 1/8 29	21	24 4/8	5 5 1/8	7 7	7 6/8	516	32
▪ Grant Co. – Charles P. Fralick – Charles P. Fralick – 1996								
181 2/8	25 25 2/8	21	23 2/8	4 3/8 4 3/8	6 6		540	35
▪ Lafayette Co. – Michael H. Morrissey – Michael H. Morrissey – 1982								
181 1/8	30 1/8 29 1/8	22 3/8	24 4/8	5 1/8 5 3/8	8 6	5	551†	36†
▪ Waushara Co. – Kenneth G. Wilson – Kenneth G. Wilson – 2001								
181 1/8	25 5/8 25 6/8	20	22 1/8	5 1/8 5	7 7	9 5/8	551	36
▪ Crawford Co. – Randall E. Kreuscher – Randall E. Kreuscher – 1992								
181 1/8	25 7/8 25 6/8	20 1/8	22 5/8	5 5/8 5 4/8	8 6	2 6/8	551	36
▪ Manitowoc Co. – Ronald R. Rieth – Ronald R. Rieth – 1999								
181	25 6/8 26 5/8	19	21	5 6/8 5	5 5		563	39
▪ Langlade Co. – Elroy W. Timm – Elroy W. Timm – 1959								
181	28 3/8 28 4/8	20	22	4 4/8 4 4/8	5 5		563	39
▪ Wood Co. – James D. Wyman – James D. Wyman – 1977								

Score	Length of Main Beam Right	Left	Inside Spread	Greatest Spread	Circumference at Smallest Place Between Burr and First Point Right	Left	Number of Points Right	Left	Lengths Abnormal Points	All-Time Rank	State Rank
	■ Location of Kill – Hunter – Owner – Date Killed										
180⁷/₈	26⁵/₈	28	17³/₈	19¹/₈	4⁴/₈	4⁴/₈	5	5		573	41
■ Marinette Co. – Albert Giese – Kenneth J. Giese – 1938											
180⁴/₈	26⁴/₈	27	19²/₈	21⁴/₈	5⁴/₈	5³/₈	5	5		613	42
■ Washburn Co. – Timothy J. Clare – Timothy J. Clare – 1998											
180³/₈	28³/₈	28²/₈	22⁵/₈	24⁷/₈	5	4⁷/₈	5	5		630†	43†
■ Dodge Co. – Herman Pautsch – Brian E. Neitzel – 1965											
180³/₈	26⁴/₈	27	20²/₈	22⁴/₈	4³/₈	4⁶/₈	7	8	3³/₈	630	43
■ Sheboygan Co. – Unknown – James K. Lawton – 1955											
180²/₈	26³/₈	26³/₈	18²/₈	20⁴/₈	4⁵/₈	4⁵/₈	6	6		651	45
■ Eau Claire Co. – Dennis B. Bryan – Dennis B. Bryan – 1979											
180²/₈	30	28³/₈	23⁴/₈	25⁶/₈	5	5	6	6	5⁶/₈	651	45
■ Pepin Co. – William J. Bates – William J. Bates – 1991											
180²/₈	25³/₈	25⁶/₈	20¹/₈	22	4⁷/₈	4⁶/₈	8	7	4⁵/₈	651	45
■ Jefferson Co. – Randy Latsch – Randy Latsch – 1995											
180¹/₈	25⁴/₈	26⁶/₈	17³/₈	20⁴/₈	4⁷/₈	4⁶/₈	7	6	5⁴/₈	669	48
■ Ashland Co. – Audrey Kundinger – Audrey Kundinger – 1961											
180¹/₈	30²/₈	29¹/₈	23⁵/₈	25⁶/₈	5⁴/₈	5²/₈	8	9	6⁶/₈	669	48
■ Waukesha Co. – Kevin A. McNeven – Kevin A. McNeven – 2000											
180	27⁵/₈	27⁶/₈	20	22	4⁷/₈	5	5	6	4²/₈	688	50
■ Oneida Co. – Milo K. Fields – Milo K. Fields – 1938											
180	26⁷/₈	28	19⁴/₈	22³/₈	4⁴/₈	4⁵/₈	6	6		688	50
■ Florence Co. – Dale E. Samsa – Dale E. Samsa – 1988											
179⁴/₈	26³/₈	26⁵/₈	22³/₈	25	4²/₈	4³/₈	5	6	1¹/₈	733	52
■ Grant Co. – Rick L. Parker – Rick L. Parker – 1982											
179³/₈	26¹/₈	26²/₈	17⁷/₈	22⁶/₈	4⁷/₈	4⁶/₈	6	6		749	53
■ Vernon Co. – Alois V. Schendel – Alois V. Schendel – 1966											
179²/₈	26⁷/₈	28	16	18²/₈	4⁴/₈	4³/₈	6	5		763	54
■ Ashland Co. – Jack D. Hultman – Jack D. Hultman – 1981											
179²/₈	23⁶/₈	25¹/₈	19²/₈	21²/₈	5⁵/₈	5⁵/₈	7	7	1	763	54
■ Buffalo Co. – Jerome Kulig – Jerome Kulig – 1984											
179	25	23⁷/₈	18²/₈	21²/₈	5²/₈	5³/₈	5	6		786	56
■ Chippewa Co. – John F. Kukuska – John F. Kukuska – 1931											
179	26³/₈	26³/₈	18²/₈	21¹/₈	5²/₈	5³/₈	5	5		786	56
■ St. Croix Co. – Kelly A. Geraghty – Kelly A. Geraghty – 1999											
178⁶/₈	26	25⁷/₈	16	17⁷/₈	4⁶/₈	4⁵/₈	6	7	1	808	58
■ Shawano Co. – Gregory L. Teske – Gregory L. Teske – 1991											
178⁵/₈	27³/₈	27¹/₈	24¹/₈	26²/₈	5	5²/₈	6	5	4⁶/₈	819	59
■ Crawford Co. – Dale Check, Jr. – Dale Check, Jr. – 1985											
178⁵/₈	24⁷/₈	25¹/₈	18¹/₈	20³/₈	5	4⁷/₈	6	6		819	59
■ Grant Co. – I. James Meng – I. James Meng – 1985											
178⁴/₈	25²/₈	25²/₈	19¹/₈	21⁵/₈	4⁴/₈	4⁶/₈	6	8	9³/₈	850†	61†
■ Buffalo Co. – Edward P. Brannen – Edward P. Brannen – 2001											

Score	Length of Main Beam Right Left	Inside Spread	Greatest Spread	Circumference at Smallest Place Between Burr and First Point Right Left	Number of Points Right Left	Lengths Abnormal Points	All-Time Rank	State Rank
	■ Location of Kill – Hunter – Owner – Date Killed							
178²/8	25⁴/8 26¹/8	18⁴/8	20⁴/8	4⁷/8 4⁷/8	5 5		891	62
	■ Shawano Co. – Picked Up – Ray T. Charles – 1953							
178²/8	27⁶/8 28³/8	19⁴/8	21⁶/8	4⁴/8 4⁴/8	6 5		891	62
	■ Crawford Co. – Lance Bangen – Brant J. Mueller – PR 1980							
178¹/8	27⁵/8 27⁴/8	17⁴/8	20¹/8	4⁷/8 4⁷/8	8 7	7³/8	905	64
	■ Iron Co. – DuWayne A. Weichel – Robert G. Steidtmann – 1957							
178¹/8	27⁴/8 27⁴/8	21¹/8	23³/8	5⁵/8 5⁴/8	5 5		905	64
	■ Price Co. – Terry Staroba – Terry Staroba – 1983							
178	27 27²/8	17⁴/8	19⁶/8	4⁶/8 5	7 6	3⁴/8	922	66
	■ Price Co. – Emery Swan – Emery Swan – 1949							
178	27⁵/8 27²/8	20	22	5¹/8 5²/8	7 7	4²/8	922	66
	■ Price Co. – John E. Martinson – John E. Martinson – 1981							
178	28²/8 26⁵/8	18²/8	20⁶/8	4⁵/8 5	5 5		922	66
	■ Crawford Co. – Picked Up – Cabela's, Inc. – 1992							
177⁷/8	29²/8 29⁵/8	18²/8	21³/8	5³/8 5⁵/8	7 7	3⁷/8	936	69
	■ Burnett Co. – John Backlund – Lester Thor – 1916							
177⁷/8	25 25⁴/8	17	20	5 5¹/8	6 7	1⁷/8	936	69
	■ Vilas Co. – Dean A. Casper – Dean A. Casper – 1990							
177⁵/8	25⁵/8 25⁵/8	19⁵/8	21³/8	5³/8 5³/8	5 5		972	71
	■ Washburn Co. – Patrick Henk – Patrick Henk – 1984							
177⁵/8	26²/8 25⁴/8	20¹/8	22¹/8	4³/8 4³/8	5 5		972	71
	■ Buffalo Co. – Mark T. Gleiter – Mark T. Gleiter – 1998							
177⁴/8	26 26⁴/8	21⁵/8	24	4⁵/8 4⁴/8	8 6	1³/8	993	73
	■ Oneida Co. – Elmer Ahlborn – Gene Ahlborn – 1926							
177⁴/8	27²/8 27⁷/8	20	22⁴/8	4⁶/8 4⁵/8	7 5	2⁶/8	993	73
	■ Marinette Co. – Henry L. Hoffman – Henry L. Hoffman – 1942							
177⁴/8	25⁷/8 26²/8	16⁴/8	18⁶/8	4⁷/8 4⁵/8	6 7	2⁴/8	993	73
	■ Wisconsin – Unknown – Brant J. Mueller – PR 1975							
177³/8	27 26²/8	23¹/8	26²/8	5 5¹/8	5 5		1011	76
	■ Menominee Co. – William Matchopatow, Sr. – William Matchopatow, Sr. – 1981							
177³/8	26 26	20²/8	22⁶/8	5³/8 5²/8	6 5	1⁵/8	1011	76
	■ Rusk Co. – David A. Reichel – David A. Reichel – 1981							
177³/8	29¹/8 30¹/8	24⁷/8	27²/8	6⁴/8 6²/8	9 9	8⁴/8	1011	76
	■ Menominee Co. – Jeff N. Dixon – Jeff N. Dixon – 1987							
177³/8	26¹/8 25	20	22⁴/8	5¹/8 5²/8	7 6	4-9/8	1011	76
	■ Jefferson Co. – John L. Hausz – John L. Hausz – 1996							
177²/8	30 29⁴/8	20⁶/8	22⁶/8	5 5¹/8	5 6	1	1025†	80†
	■ Monroe Co. – Mark A. Schmitz – Mark A. Schmitz – 2000							
177²/8	29¹/8 29²/8	21	23³/8	4⁶/8 4⁵/8	5 5		1025	80
	■ Buffalo Co. – George W. Kees – George W. Kees – 1957							
177²/8	25⁵/8 25⁷/8	18²/8	20⁵/8	4⁶/8 4⁶/8	6 6		1025	80
	■ Richland Co. – Dewitt S. Pulham – Dewitt S. Pulham – 1982							

Score	Length of Main Beam Right	Length of Main Beam Left	Inside Spread	Greatest Spread	Circumference at Smallest Place Between Burr and First Point Right	Circumference at Smallest Place Between Burr and First Point Left	Number of Points Right	Number of Points Left	Lengths Abnormal Points	All-Time Rank	State Rank
\multicolumn{12}{l}{■ Location of Kill – Hunter – Owner – Date Killed}
177²/₈	24²/₈	23⁴/₈	20²/₈	22³/₈	5	5	6	6		1025	80
\multicolumn{12}{l}{■ Sawyer Co. – William H. Laney – William H. Laney – 1991}
177¹/₈	27²/₈	27	21⁷/₈	24⁵/₈	4⁴/₈	4⁴/₈	5	5		1048	84
\multicolumn{12}{l}{■ Walworth Co. – Daniel J. Brede – Daniel J. Brede – 1984}
177¹/₈	25⁷/₈	25³/₈	18⁵/₈	20⁵/₈	4⁵/₈	4⁴/₈	8	6	2²/₈	1048	84
\multicolumn{12}{l}{■ Forest Co. – Carl S. Ernst – Carl S. Ernst – 1990}
177¹/₈	27¹/₈	28⁶/₈	21²/₈	23²/₈	4⁶/₈	4⁶/₈	7	5	1¹/₈	1048	84
\multicolumn{12}{l}{■ St. Croix Co. – Phillip R. Hovde – Phillip R. Hovde – 1990}
177	28¹/₈	28	17²/₈	20	4⁶/₈	4⁶/₈	6	7	4⁶/₈	1066	87
\multicolumn{12}{l}{■ Bayfield Co. – Elof E. Sjostrom – Mrs. Elof E. Sjostrom – 1932}
176⁷/₈	27²/₈	28⁴/₈	24²/₈	26⁴/₈	4⁴/₈	4⁴/₈	5	6	2¹/₈	1086	88
\multicolumn{12}{l}{■ Lincoln Co. – Edmond H. Pay – Edmond H. Pay – 1959}
176⁷/₈	27³/₈	27²/₈	20³/₈	22⁴/₈	4⁵/₈	4⁵/₈	5	5		1086	88
\multicolumn{12}{l}{■ Pierce Co. – John M. Oelke – John M. Oelke – 1984}
176⁶/₈	27¹/₈	26	20⁷/₈	23	5²/₈	5²/₈	5	6	2⁵/₈	1103	90
\multicolumn{12}{l}{■ Vilas Co. – Porter Dean – Safari North Tax. – 1938}
176⁶/₈	26³/₈	25	19	21⁷/₈	5³/₈	5⁴/₈	5	6		1103	90
\multicolumn{12}{l}{■ Langlade Co. – Jack Ryan – Ray T. Charles – 1950}
176⁶/₈	27	27⁷/₈	22²/₈	24⁴/₈	5⁵/₈	5⁷/₈	5	5		1103	90
\multicolumn{12}{l}{■ Buffalo Co. – Dean Broberg – Dean Broberg – 1985}
176⁶/₈	26¹/₈	25	20⁵/₈	22¹/₈	6²/₈	5⁷/₈	6	6	1¹/₈	1103	90
\multicolumn{12}{l}{■ Adams Co. – Mark R. Faber – Mark R. Faber – 1987}
176⁶/₈	26⁵/₈	27	18³/₈	20⁵/₈	4²/₈	4²/₈	7	6	4³/₈	1103	90
\multicolumn{12}{l}{■ Rusk Co. – Kent E. Lund – Kent E. Lund – 1992}
176⁵/₈	23¹/₈	22⁷/₈	17¹/₈	19⁶/₈	4⁵/₈	4⁵/₈	6	8	2⁴/₈	1134†	95†
\multicolumn{12}{l}{■ Buffalo Co. – Michael A. Ward – Michael A. Ward – 2001}
176⁵/₈	23²/₈	26¹/₈	21¹/₈	23⁷/₈	5¹/₈	5	7	7	7⁴/₈	1134	95
\multicolumn{12}{l}{■ Rusk Co. – Ercel Dustin – Ercel Dustin – 1966}
176⁴/₈	25	25	19⁴/₈	23	4⁴/₈	4³/₈	7	6	2²/₈	1158	97
\multicolumn{12}{l}{■ Crawford Co. – Louis Franks – Louis Franks – 1969}
176⁴/₈	28⁵/₈	28⁵/₈	22⁴/₈	25¹/₈	5¹/₈	5²/₈	6	5		1158	97
\multicolumn{12}{l}{■ Ashland Co. – Thomas J. Warren – Thomas J. Warren – 1999}
176³/₈	24³/₈	24⁵/₈	16¹/₈	18⁵/₈	5	5	6	6		1182	99
\multicolumn{12}{l}{■ Juneau Co. – Paul F. Beall – Paul F. Beall – 1997}
176²/₈	23⁶/₈	23³/₈	19⁴/₈	24³/₈	5³/₈	5²/₈	8	7	1²/₈	1209	100
\multicolumn{12}{l}{■ Walworth Co. – Thomas G. Senft – Thomas G. Senft – 1993}
176¹/₈	28	27⁴/₈	21²/₈	23⁵/₈	5⁴/₈	5⁴/₈	6	5	1³/₈	1243	101
\multicolumn{12}{l}{■ Florence Co. – Theron A. Meyer, Sr. – Theron A. Meyer, Sr. – 1943}
176¹/₈	25⁶/₈	26¹/₈	20⁵/₈	22⁶/₈	5⁶/₈	5⁷/₈	5	5		1243	101
\multicolumn{12}{l}{■ Door Co. – Unknown – Steve Pluff – PR 1973}
176	28⁵/₈	29⁶/₈	17⁵/₈	20⁶/₈	5³/₈	5³/₈	8	7	10³/₈	1266	103
\multicolumn{12}{l}{■ Florence Co. – John G. Kozicki – Vernon J. Kozicki – 1936}

Score	Length of Main Beam Right Left	Inside Spread	Greatest Spread	Circumference at Smallest Place Between Burr and First Point Right Left		Number of Points Right Left		Lengths Abnormal Points	All-Time Rank	State Rank
■ *Location of Kill – Hunter – Owner – Date Killed*										
176	26 26	18⁴/8	21³/8	5⁷/8	6²/8	5	6	1	1266	103
■ *Racine Co. – Daniel P. Cramer – Daniel P. Cramer – 1985*										
176	26⁶/8 26⁶/8	18⁷/8	20¹/8	4²/8	4²/8	7	6	1⁵/8	1266	103
■ *Buffalo Co. – Guy A. Hansen – Guy A. Hansen – 1995*										
176	26⁴/8 26	23	25	4²/8	4³/8	5	5		1266	103
■ *Green Lake Co. – Timothy S. Judas – Timothy S. Judas – 1997*										
175⁷/8	28³/8 27⁷/8	22⁵/8	24⁷/8	5	4⁶/8	6	6		1287	107
■ *Washburn Co. – Terry A. Severson – Terry A. Severson – 1991*										
175⁷/8	24³/8 27	18	20	4⁵/8	4⁵/8	5	6	1³/8	1287	107
■ *Buffalo Co. – Larry L. Bloom – Larry L. Bloom – 1995*										
175⁶/8	26³/8 25	21⁴/8	24²/8	5⁴/8	5⁵/8	6	6		1310	109
■ *Crawford Co. – David R. Kluesner – David R. Kluesner – 1985*										
175⁵/8	26⁵/8 26⁷/8	18⁵/8	21	4⁵/8	4⁶/8	5	5		1333	110
■ *Rock Co. – Neil Laube – Neil Laube – 1965*										
175⁵/8	28⁴/8 25⁷/8	20⁵/8	23⁴/8	5⁵/8	5⁴/8	8	8	10²/8	1333	110
■ *Bayfield Co. – Lorry A. Hagstrom – Lorry A. Hagstrom – 1994*										
175⁴/8	26⁶/8 26¹/8	17⁷/8	20¹/8	5¹/8	5¹/8	6	5	1³/8	1352†	112†
■ *Grant Co. – Picked Up – Andrew J. Nelson – 2000*										
175⁴/8	25⁶/8 27	21²/8	24⁶/8	5¹/8	5¹/8	6	5		1352	112
■ *Pepin Co. – Carl E. Frick – Carl E. Frick – 1954*										
175⁴/8	25⁵/8 25⁵/8	20¹/8	22²/8	4⁷/8	4⁷/8	6	5	1¹/8	1352	112
■ *Buffalo Co. – Picked Up – Charles G. Dienger – 1983*										
175³/8	27 27	18⁶/8	22⁴/8	6²/8	5⁶/8	8	7	6¹/8	1377†	115†
■ *Richland Co. – Vince L. Fairchild – Vince L. Fairchild – 2000*										
175²/8	25⁵/8 25⁵/8	19⁴/8	23¹/8	4⁵/8	4⁶/8	5	5		1403	116
■ *Bayfield Co. – Bill Holiday – Douglas R. Plourde – PR 1920*										
175¹/8	26⁷/8 25⁷/8	17⁴/8	21²/8	5¹/8	5¹/8	5	6	1³/8	1440	117
■ *Taylor Co. – Jack L. Dittrich – Jack L. Dittrich – 1945*										
175¹/8	25⁶/8 27	20²/8	22⁶/8	5	5	8	7	3⁷/8	1440	117
■ *Menominee Co. – Gerald Ponfil – Gerald Ponfil – 1968*										
175¹/8	22¹/8 22⁷/8	20⁵/8	22⁵/8	5	5²/8	6	6		1440	117
■ *Marinette Co. – John Nielson – John Nielson – 1983*										
174⁷/8	28¹/8 27⁵/8	23⁵/8	27⁵/8	4⁴/8	4⁴/8	5	5		1513†	120†
■ *Door Co. – Keith N. Bink – Keith N. Bink – 2001*										
174⁷/8	24¹/8 24¹/8	18¹/8	19⁷/8	5	4⁷/8	7	6	2⁶/8	1513†	120†
■ *Barron Co. – Wayne Phillips – Wayne Phillips – 2001*										
174⁷/8	28¹/8 28¹/8	21³/8	23⁷/8	5	5	4	4		1513	120
■ *Burnett Co. – Myles T. Keller – Myles T. Keller – 1977*										
174⁶/8	23³/8 23⁵/8	15⁴/8	19	4⁴/8	4³/8	6	6		1534†	123†
■ *Jefferson Co. – Ronald Jongetjez – Ronald Jongetjez – 2000*										
174⁶/8	26⁴/8 26⁴/8	19⁶/8	22	4⁴/8	4³/8	6	6		1534†	123†
■ *Oneida Co. – Michael J. Krueger – Michael J. Krueger – 2000*										

Score	Length of Main Beam Right Left		Inside Spread	Greatest Spread	Circumference at Smallest Place Between Burr and First Point Right Left		Number of Points Right Left		Lengths Abnormal Points	All-Time Rank	State Rank
	■ *Location of Kill – Hunter – Owner – Date Killed*										
174⁶/8	26²/8	27⁴/8	21	25⁵/8	5⁶/8	5⁶/8	8	6	10²/8	1534	123
	■ *Hayward – Bill Metcalf – John Metcalf – 1924*										
174⁵/8	27⁵/8	27⁵/8	18³/8	20³/8	5²/8	5²/8	6	7	3⁴/8	1561	126
	■ *Door Co. – Patrick D. Madden – Patrick D. Madden – 1984*										
174⁵/8	26²/8	25³/8	18⁷/8	20⁷/8	5⁴/8	5²/8	6	6		1561	126
	■ *Buffalo Co. – Daniel L. Scharmer – Daniel L. Scharmer – 1990*										
174⁴/8	26⁴/8	25²/8	19⁴/8	23⁴/8	5⁷/8	6	5	5		1592	128
	■ *Buffalo Co. – Unknown – Douglas R. Plourde – 1961*										
174³/8	24	24	17⁴/8	19⁵/8	5⁴/8	5⁴/8	8	7	4⁵/8	1619	129
	■ *Sawyer Co. – Patrick E. Jasper – Patrick E. Jasper – 1985*										
174³/8	28	28⁴/8	21²/8	23⁴/8	4⁶/8	4⁷/8	5	6	1³/8	1619	129
	■ *La Crosse Co. – Kevin M. Kastenschmidt – Kevin M. Kastenschmidt – 1986*										
174³/8	26⁴/8	26⁴/8	23²/8	25⁵/8	5²/8	5²/8	6	7	1⁷/8	1619	129
	■ *Trempealeau Co. – Laverne Killian, Jr. – Laverne Killian, Jr. – 1986*										
174³/8	26¹/8	25⁶/8	15⁶/8	17⁶/8	5	4⁷/8	6	5	1⁵/8	1619	129
	■ *Bayfield Co. – Steven W. Schilthelm – Steven W. Schilthelm – 1994*										
174³/8	25²/8	25³/8	16¹/8	18	4¹/8	4²/8	6	6		1619	129
	■ *Outagamie Co. – Alan B. Conger – Alan B. Conger – 1998*										
174²/8	26³/8	26³/8	22²/8	25⁶/8	4⁴/8	4³/8	5	5		1652†	134†
	■ *Richland Co. – Mitch Shewchuk – Mitch Shewchuk – 2000*										
174²/8	27²/8	28¹/8	20²/8	23	5⁴/8	5³/8	5	5		1652	134
	■ *Langlade Co. – Lyman Aderman – David C. Aderman – PR 1963*										
174²/8	27⁷/8	27	21²/8	23⁴/8	5²/8	5¹/8	5	5		1652	134
	■ *Ashland Co. – Kelly J. McClaire – Kelly J. McClaire – 1986*										
174¹/8	27	26⁵/8	18⁴/8	21¹/8	4⁵/8	4⁶/8	5	6	5⁷/8	1678	137
	■ *Buffalo Co. – Apolinary Sonsalla – Apolinary Sonsalla – 1959*										
174	26⁴/8	26	17⁵/8	20	4⁴/8	4⁵/8	7	5	3¹/8	1717	138
	■ *Jefferson Co. – Gary A. Coates – Gary A. Coates – 1970*										
173⁶/8	25⁵/8	26	21	23⁶/8	5⁶/8	5⁶/8	5	5		1766†	139†
	■ *Menominee Co. – Picked Up – Ray T. Charles – 1994*										
173⁶/8	27¹/8	26¹/8	19⁴/8	21⁶/8	5²/8	5³/8	6	7	1⁴/8	1766	139
	■ *Florence Co. – Walter Knutson – Mark Shaw – 1902*										
173⁶/8	28¹/8	28¹/8	20⁶/8	23⁵/8	5¹/8	5²/8	6	6	3⁴/8	1766	139
	■ *Bayfield Co. – Henry Pajtash – Henry Pajtash – 1978*										
173⁶/8	28⁴/8	28	25	28	5²/8	5¹/8	6	6	2⁴/8	1766	139
	■ *Green Lake Co. – Steven J. Coda – Steven J. Coda – 1997*										
173⁵/8	26⁶/8	26⁶/8	17⁵/8	19⁶/8	4⁴/8	4⁴/8	5	5		1819	143
	■ *Sawyer Co. – Maurice Peterson – Mac's Taxidermy – 1940*										
173⁵/8	25³/8	25¹/8	19⁴/8	23⁴/8	4¹/8	4²/8	8	7	8⁵/8	1819	143
	■ *Buffalo Co. – James R. Gabrick – James R. Gabrick – 1996*										
173⁴/8	25⁴/8	25⁴/8	19⁴/8	21⁵/8	4⁷/8	4⁶/8	5	7	3	1847†	145†
	■ *Trempealeau Co. – Ross P. Lambert – Ross P. Lambert – 2001*										

Score	Length of Main Beam Right Left	Inside Spread	Greatest Spread	Circumference at Smallest Place Between Burr and First Point Right Left	Number of Points Right Left	Lengths Abnormal Points	All-Time Rank	State Rank
	■ *Location of Kill – Hunter – Owner – Date Killed*							
173⁴/₈	26 26	21	23	5³/₈ 5¹/₈	5 5		1847	145
	■ *Vilas Co. – Unknown – Donald Krueger – 1967*							
173⁴/₈	26 26¹/₈	18⁴/₈	20³/₈	4³/₈ 4³/₈	5 5		1847	145
	■ *Rusk Co. – Jody Lebal – Jody Lebal – 1998*							
173²/₈	25⁶/₈ 24²/₈	25²/₈	26⁴/₈	5⁴/₈ 5¹/₈	7 6	1⁴/₈	1914	148
	■ *Price Co. – Clarence Parmelee – J.D. Andrews – 1959*							
173¹/₈	27³/₈ 26⁶/₈	18¹/₈	20³/₈	5¹/₈ 5¹/₈	5 5		1950†	149†
	■ *Jackson Co. – David R. Stalheim – David R. Stalheim – 1999*							
173¹/₈	28 28²/₈	21⁵/₈	24	4⁶/₈ 4⁶/₈	7 7	2⁴/₈	1950	149
	■ *Dunn Co. – Jack K. Dodge – Jack K. Dodge – 1987*							
173¹/₈	27³/₈ 27³/₈	21⁴/₈	23³/₈	4⁴/₈ 4⁴/₈	5 7	1⁷/₈	1950	149
	■ *Buffalo Co. – Dale M. Komro – Dale M. Komro – 1992*							
173¹/₈	25⁵/₈ 24²/₈	23³/₈	25³/₈	4³/₈ 4³/₈	5 5		1950	149
	■ *Buffalo Co. – Thomas J. Johnson – Thomas J. Johnson – 1997*							
173	24⁴/₈ 24⁷/₈	18³/₈	20²/₈	4⁵/₈ 4⁵/₈	7 7	2⁷/₈	1991†	153†
	■ *Douglas Co. – Raymond J. Dolsen – Raymond J. Dolsen – 2000*							
173	29¹/₈ 28⁷/₈	21	24²/₈	4⁷/₈ 4⁶/₈	8 6	7	1991	153
	■ *Bayfield Co. – Unknown – Eagle Knob Lodge – PR 1930*							
173	28²/₈ 27	21²/₈	23⁵/₈	5⁶/₈ 5⁵/₈	6 7	5	1991	153
	■ *Oconto Co. – Donald P. Wimmer – Donald P. Wimmer – 1969*							
173	25⁴/₈ 26²/₈	21⁶/₈	23⁷/₈	4⁷/₈ 4⁶/₈	6 5		1991	153
	■ *Pepin Co. – William A. Gray – William A. Gray – 1990*							
173	24³/₈ 24⁷/₈	20	22⁴/₈	5⁵/₈ 5³/₈	5 5		1991	153
	■ *St. Croix Co. – James A. O'Keefe – James A. O'Keefe – 1994*							
172⁷/₈	24⁶/₈ 24³/₈	20¹/₈	23⁴/₈	5⁴/₈ 5³/₈	5 5		2038	158
	■ *Ashland Co. – Einar Sein – Rick Iacono – 1965*							
172⁷/₈	25²/₈ 24²/₈	19¹/₈	21	4⁵/₈ 4⁶/₈	5 5		2038	158
	■ *Jackson Co. – Donald R. Anderson – Donald R. Anderson – 1999*							
172⁷/₈	29¹/₈ 29¹/₈	19⁷/₈	21⁷/₈	5⁴/₈ 6	5 7	3²/₈	2038	158
	■ *Buffalo Co. – Robert H. Becker – Robert H. Becker – 2000*							
172⁶/₈	25¹/₈ 25¹/₈	18⁶/₈	21	4⁵/₈ 4⁵/₈	5 6	1²/₈	2065	161
	■ *Woodruff – Unknown – Mac's Taxidermy – 1918*							
172⁶/₈	25⁶/₈ 23²/₈	21⁴/₈	24¹/₈	4⁶/₈ 4⁶/₈	5 6		2065	161
	■ *Trempealeau Co. – Henry M. Hoff – Henry M. Hoff – 1956*							
172⁶/₈	27 26	15⁴/₈	18²/₈	5⁵/₈ 5⁶/₈	5 5		2065	161
	■ *Vilas Co. – James Homan – Cabela's, Inc. – 1967*							
172⁶/₈	27⁶/₈ 27⁶/₈	18	20²/₈	5¹/₈ 5	5 5		2065	161
	■ *Ashland Co. – Picked Up – David Sanborn – PR 1987*							
172⁶/₈	26⁵/₈ 26⁴/₈	18⁶/₈	20⁵/₈	4⁵/₈ 4⁵/₈	5 5		2065	161
	■ *Manitowoc Co. – Stephen J. Kortens – Stephen J. Kortens – 1992*							
172⁶/₈	27 26⁴/₈	21⁵/₈	23⁶/₈	5³/₈ 5⁶/₈	5 9	5¹/₈	2065	161
	■ *Menominee Co. – Marvin R. Ninham – Marvin R. Ninham – 1995*							

Score	Length of Main Beam Right Left	Inside Spread	Greatest Spread	Circumference at Smallest Place Between Burr and First Point Right Left	Number of Points Right Left	Lengths Abnormal Points	All-Time Rank	State Rank
172^5/$_8$	25^3/$_8$ 25^6/$_8$	18^3/$_8$	20^6/$_8$	5 5^2/$_8$	5 6		2113	167
■ Sauk Co. – Terry A. Diske – Terry A. Diske – 1987								
172^5/$_8$	24^5/$_8$ 25^1/$_8$	25^1/$_8$	27^2/$_8$	4^5/$_8$ 4^5/$_8$	5 5		2113	167
■ Adams Co. – Vernon J. Williams, Jr. – Vernon J. Williams, Jr. – 1998								
172^4/$_8$	29^4/$_8$ 28^6/$_8$	20	22^6/$_8$	5^3/$_8$ 5^2/$_8$	5 5	1	2156	169
■ Iron Co. – Dale D. Tuszke – Dale D. Tuszke – 1987								
172^3/$_8$	26 24^6/$_8$	24^5/$_8$	25	5^4/$_8$ 5^5/$_8$	5 5		2200†	170†
■ Walworth Co. – Daniel Miller – Daniel Miller – 2000								
172^3/$_8$	26^6/$_8$ 26^7/$_8$	19^2/$_8$	21^4/$_8$	4^6/$_8$ 5	7 7	4^1/$_8$	2200	170
■ Taylor Co. – Karl Raatz – Kathleen Powell – 1939								
172^3/$_8$	24^5/$_8$ 24^3/$_8$	18	21^3/$_8$	4^6/$_8$ 4^7/$_8$	8 7	7^5/$_8$	2200	170
■ Rusk Co. – Randy A. Jochem – Randy A. Jochem – 1984								
172^3/$_8$	27^6/$_8$ 26^5/$_8$	16	18^3/$_8$	4^6/$_8$ 4^6/$_8$	5 6	3^1/$_8$	2200	170
■ Dane Co. – Randy L. Letlebo – Randy L. Letlebo – 1987								
172^3/$_8$	28 27^5/$_8$	18^3/$_8$	20^5/$_8$	4^2/$_8$ 4^3/$_8$	5 5		2200	170
■ Jackson Co. – J. Esanbock & M. Finch – J. Esanbock & M. Finch – 1994								
172^3/$_8$	28 27^5/$_8$	22^2/$_8$	25	5 4^7/$_8$	5 6	1^5/$_8$	2200	170
■ Iowa Co. – Bruce E. Schuelke – Bruce E. Schuelke – 1997								
172^2/$_8$	27^7/$_8$ 28	20	22^2/$_8$	4^6/$_8$ 4^5/$_8$	5 6		2237	176
■ Lincoln Co. – Alfred Theilig – Ronald F. Lax – 1928								
172^2/$_8$	24^6/$_8$ 24^3/$_8$	18	20^2/$_8$	4^4/$_8$ 4^5/$_8$	6 6		2237	176
■ Vilas Co. – Ray Hermanson – J. James Froelich – 1936								
172^2/$_8$	23 23	19	22^4/$_8$	5 5^1/$_8$	6 7	5^4/$_8$	2237	176
■ Adams Co. – W.R. Ingraham – W.R. Ingraham – 1965								
172^2/$_8$	27^6/$_8$ 26^5/$_8$	20^2/$_8$	22^3/$_8$	4^4/$_8$ 4^4/$_8$	6 5	2^6/$_8$	2237	176
■ Ashland Co. – Arnold D. Miller – Arnold D. Miller – 1997								
172^2/$_8$	26^5/$_8$ 26^1/$_8$	19^6/$_8$	22^4/$_8$	5^1/$_8$ 4^7/$_8$	5 5		2237	176
■ Vernon Co. – Ronald J. Stilwell – Ronald J. Stilwell – 1999								
172^1/$_8$	24^5/$_8$ 24^4/$_8$	18^5/$_8$	21^4/$_8$	4^4/$_8$ 4^5/$_8$	5 5		2286†	181†
■ Buffalo Co. – David G. Lyga – David G. Lyga – 2000								
172^1/$_8$	25^6/$_8$ 25^5/$_8$	19^3/$_8$	22	5^4/$_8$ 5^2/$_8$	5 5		2286	181
■ Juneau Co. – Unknown – Clark G. Gallup – 1949								
172^1/$_8$	27^1/$_8$ 25^7/$_8$	20^3/$_8$	23	4^2/$_8$ 4^3/$_8$	5 5		2286	181
■ Buffalo Co. – Aaron Comero – Aaron Comero – 1986								
172^1/$_8$	29^3/$_8$ 30^2/$_8$	21	23^6/$_8$	5 4^4/$_8$	7 8	11^1/$_8$	2286	181
■ Rock Co. – Steven W. Kravick – Steven W. Kravick – 1996								
172	26^4/$_8$ 25^2/$_8$	19^1/$_8$	21^4/$_8$	5^2/$_8$ 5^3/$_8$	5 6	3^7/$_8$	2330	185
■ Oconto Co. – Henry J. Bredael – Henry J. Bredael – 1939								
172	25^4/$_8$ 26^3/$_8$	19^6/$_8$	22^7/$_8$	4^7/$_8$ 4^6/$_8$	5 5		2330	185
■ Sauk Co. – Rudy Lehnherr – Philip J. Rouse III – 1946								
172	26^2/$_8$ 23	21^4/$_8$	24	4^6/$_8$ 4^6/$_8$	5 6		2330	185
■ Buffalo Co. – Ralph Duellman – Ralph Duellman – 1960								

Score	Length of Main Beam Right Left	Inside Spread	Greatest Spread	Circumference at Smallest Place Between Burr and First Point Right Left	Number of Points Right Left	Lengths Abnormal Points	All-Time Rank	State Rank
	■ Location of Kill – Hunter – Owner – Date Killed							
172	25⁷/8 25²/8	19	21³/8	4⁵/8 4⁵/8	5 5		2330	185
	■ Waukesha Co. – Donald R. Friedlein – Donald R. Friedlein – 1983							
172	26¹/8 26³/8	17⁴/8	19⁶/8	5 4⁶/8	5 6		2330	185
	■ Dodge Co. – Dennis E. Schulteis – Dennis E. Schulteis – 1985							
172	26 26³/8	19⁵/8	22¹/8	5⁷/8 5⁴/8	5 6	3³/8	2330	185
	■ Buffalo Co. – James L. Sturz – James L. Sturz – 1994							
171⁷/8	25⁷/8 26¹/8	19⁴/8	21⁷/8	4⁵/8 4⁴/8	6 5	1¹/8	2382	191
	■ Portage Co. – Lawrence P. Wierzba – Lawrence P. Wierzba – 1994							
171⁶/8	27¹/8 27	21⁴/8	24⁴/8	5 5	5 5		2418†	192†
	■ Waukesha Co. – Ryan Bischop – Ryan Bischop – 2002							
171⁶/8	26⁵/8 26⁴/8	18	20	4⁶/8 4⁶/8	5 5		2418	192
	■ Niagara – Francis H. Van Ginkel – David Watson – 1945							
171⁶/8	28⁴/8 27²/8	19³/8	22	5³/8 5³/8	4 6	1¹/8	2418	192
	■ Buffalo Co. – Richard Schultz – Richard Schultz – 1973							
171⁶/8	24⁶/8 23⁴/8	20⁶/8	23	4⁶/8 4⁶/8	5 5		2418	192
	■ Dunn Co. – James W. Belmore – James W. Belmore – 1991							
171⁶/8	27³/8 27⁵/8	18⁵/8	22¹/8	4³/8 4³/8	7 7	5⁵/8	2418	192
	■ Juneau Co. – Thomas J. Brien – Thomas J. Brien – 1994							
171⁶/8	25⁶/8 25¹/8	16²/8	18²/8	4⁷/8 4⁶/8	5 5		2418	192
	■ Dunn Co. – David J. Tuschl, Sr. – David J. Tuschl, Sr. – 1998							
171⁵/8	27³/8 27⁷/8	17³/8	19²/8	4²/8 4²/8	5 5		2470	198
	■ Trempealeau Co. – Scott D. Schank – Scott D. Schank – 1993							
171⁴/8	27⁴/8 27²/8	19	21⁴/8	4⁷/8 4⁵/8	7 5	1²/8	2513†	199†
	■ St. Croix Co. – Picked Up – Mike Kessler – 2000							
171⁴/8	25⁵/8 24	17⁴/8	20¹/8	5²/8 5²/8	7 7	2⁶/8	2513	199
	■ Wood Co. – Unknown – Joe Hutwagner – 1918							
171⁴/8	25 24⁴/8	20⁴/8	22⁴/8	4³/8 4⁴/8	6 6		2513	199
	■ Rusk Co. – Luke Dernovsek III – Luke Dernovsek III – 1983							
171⁴/8	25¹/8 26	18⁵/8	20²/8	4⁶/8 4⁴/8	6 5	1⁵/8	2513	199
	■ Jefferson Co. – Bradley J. Hering – Bradley J. Hering – 1996							
171³/8	26⁵/8 26⁶/8	21⁵/8	24	4⁴/8 4⁴/8	9 7	7⁶/8	2564	203
	■ Juneau Co. – Fay Hammersley – Fay Hammersley – 1938							
171³/8	25³/8 26⁶/8	18⁵/8	21	5³/8 5²/8	5 5		2564	203
	■ Forest Co. – Chester Cox, Jr. – Chester Cox, Jr. – 1969							
171³/8	26¹/8 26²/8	23²/8	25³/8	5⁴/8 5⁵/8	5 6	1¹/8	2564	203
	■ Buffalo Co. – Donald C. Neitzel – Donald C. Neitzel – 1981							
171³/8	26⁵/8 25⁵/8	19⁶/8	22⁵/8	5 5	6 5	3⁷/8	2564	203
	■ Washington Co. – Joseph E. Kohler – Joseph E. Kohler – 1989							
171³/8	26¹/8 27	20⁷/8	23²/8	5⁶/8 6	6 7	1⁴/8	2564	203
	■ Washburn Co. – Dale M. Swan – Dale M. Swan – 1992							
171³/8	27 27⁶/8	21³/8	24	5 5	6 6		2564	203
	■ Washington Co. – Daniel J. Hanrahan – Daniel J. Hanrahan – 1995							

Score	Length of Main Beam Right	Left	Inside Spread	Greatest Spread	Circumference at Smallest Place Between Burr and First Point Right	Left	Number of Points Right	Left	Lengths Abnormal Points	All-Time Rank	State Rank
	■ Location of Kill – Hunter – Owner – Date Killed										
171 3/8	26 3/8	25 5/8	18 3/8	21	4 4/8	4 4/8	5	5		2564	203
	■ Buffalo Co. – Dave K. Kitzman – Dave K. Kitzman – 1996										
171 3/8	26 6/8	27 3/8	19 7/8	24 6/8	5	5	9	5	6 4/8	2564	203
	■ Trempealeau Co. – Heidi A. Daffinson – Heidi A. Daffinson – 1997										
171 2/8	25 6/8	25 7/8	19 4/8	21 2/8	5	5	5	6		2621	211
	■ Bayfield Co. – Lawrence Stumo – Lawrence Stumo – 1956										
171 2/8	27 6/8	27 5/8	20	22 1/8	5 1/8	5	6	5	1	2621	211
	■ Racine Co. – Charles Michna – Charles Michna – 1993										
171 2/8	25 5/8	26	17 2/8	20	4 5/8	4 5/8	5	5		2621	211
	■ Pepin Co. – Sharon M. Bauer – Sharon M. Bauer – 1995										
171 2/8	26 1/8	26 5/8	21	24 3/8	5 5/8	5 7/8	6	6		2621	211
	■ Green Lake Co. – Richard Waters – Richard Waters – 1999										
171 1/8	26 6/8	28	21 3/8	23 4/8	4 5/8	4 5/8	5	5		2665†	215†
	■ Menominee Co. – Robert L. Boyd – Robert L. Boyd – 2000										
171 1/8	25 2/8	24 7/8	19 1/8	22 1/8	4 3/8	4 3/8	6	5	1 6/8	2665†	215†
	■ Polk Co. – Jack G. Fleming – Jack G. Fleming – 2000										
171 1/8	24 6/8	25 1/8	18 7/8	21 7/8	5	5 1/8	5	5		2665†	215†
	■ Shawano Co. – Leo M. McDonald – Leo M. McDonald – 2000										
171 1/8	27	27	20 3/8	23	4 7/8	4 6/8	6	6	3 2/8	2665	215
	■ Polk Co. – Harold Dau – Harold Dau – 1966										
171 1/8	25 5/8	26 7/8	16 1/8	18	4 3/8	4 4/8	7	7	2 2/8	2665	215
	■ Menominee Co. – Vyron N. Dixon, Sr. – Vyron N. Dixon, Sr. – 1968										
171 1/8	23 4/8	23 4/8	18 3/8	20	7 2/8	6 3/8	5	5		2665	215
	■ Bayfield Co. – James A. Peters – James A. Peters – 1979										
171 1/8	25 3/8	24 7/8	16 2/8	18 4/8	4 5/8	4 7/8	7	6	1 5/8	2665	215
	■ Dunn Co. – Jamie W. Mittlestadt – Jamie W. Mittlestadt – 1993										
171 1/8	27 4/8	25 6/8	22 3/8	24 4/8	5 5/8	5 5/8	5	5		2665	215
	■ Buffalo Co. – George Clausen – George Clausen – 1995										
171 1/8	26 5/8	27 1/8	17 3/8	19 6/8	5 6/8	5 4/8	5	5		2665	215
	■ Dane Co. – Miles Weaver – Miles Weaver – 1996										
171 1/8	25 2/8	24 6/8	18 4/8	22 2/8	5	5 4/8	8	7	8 3/8	2665	215
	■ Sauk Co. – David K. Zimmerman – David K. Zimmerman – 1999										
171	26 2/8	25 6/8	20 5/8	22 4/8	4 1/8	4 1/8	6	6	1 5/8	2707	225
	■ Buffalo Co. – Clarence H. Castleberg, Jr. – Clarence H. Castleberg, Jr. – 1964										
171	26 1/8	26 1/8	17 2/8	20	5 2/8	5 3/8	6	5		2707	225
	■ Pierce Co. – Picked Up – Roger Hines – 1975										
171	25	25 4/8	20 2/8	22 2/8	4 2/8	4 2/8	5	6	1 2/8	2707	225
	■ Marinette Co. – Roger W. Gusick – Roger W. Gusick – 1993										
171	26 1/8	25 4/8	17 2/8	19	4 4/8	4 5/8	5	5		2707	225
	■ Vernon Co. – Larry C. Hooverson – Larry C. Hooverson – 1993										
170 7/8	29	29	20 1/8	22	4 4/8	4 6/8	8	8	6	2769	229
	■ Marinette Co. – Charles Rader – Thomas W. Goddard – 1909										

Score	Length of Main Beam Right	Left	Inside Spread	Greatest Spread	Circumference at Smallest Place Between Burr and First Point Right	Left	Number of Points Right	Left	Lengths Abnormal Points	All-Time Rank	State Rank
170 7/8	27 1/8	26 3/8	20 3/8	22 6/8	4 1/8	4	5	5		2769	229
■ Bayfield Co. – John Kavajecz – John Kavajecz – 1964											
170 7/8	23 4/8	23 5/8	18 7/8	20 7/8	4 6/8	4 6/8	6	7		2769	229
■ Polk Co. – Timothy J. Droher – Timothy J. Droher – 1988											
170 7/8	25 2/8	26 3/8	17 3/8	20 2/8	4 3/8	4 3/8	6	6		2769	229
■ Crawford Co. – Dale M. Hanson – Dale M. Hanson – 1988											
170 7/8	26	25 5/8	21 1/8	23 5/8	4 2/8	4 2/8	6	6		2769	229
■ Eau Claire Co. – John F. Prissel – John F. Prissel – 1988											
170 7/8	28 1/8	27	21 5/8	23 6/8	4 6/8	4 7/8	5	5		2769	229
■ Polk Co. – Dennis R. Measner – Dennis R. Measner – 1991											
170 7/8	25 4/8	25 4/8	23 5/8	25 3/8	4 5/8	4 4/8	5	5		2769	229
■ Price Co. – David A. Pritzl – David A. Pritzl – 1994											
170 7/8	27 5/8	28 1/8	21 3/8	23 3/8	5	4 7/8	6	6	1 4/8	2769	229
■ Dane Co. – Alison J. Baake – Alison J. Baake – 1997											
170 6/8	27	26 2/8	18	20 4/8	4 4/8	4 3/8	5	5		2828	237
■ Eau Claire Co. – Kenneth W. Kling – Mrs. Kenneth W. Kling – 1938											
170 6/8	25 6/8	26 7/8	19 1/8	22 6/8	4 6/8	4 5/8	6	5	1 7/8	2828	237
■ Bayfield Co. – Sigurd A. Sandstrom – Sigurd A. Sandstrom – 1955											
170 6/8	30	29	25 6/8	27 7/8	5	5 2/8	4	4		2828	237
■ Grant Co. – Randall J. Ertz – Randall J. Ertz – 1997											
170 6/8	27	25 3/8	20 4/8	22 4/8	5 2/8	5 1/8	5	6	1 4/8	2828	237
■ Rock Co. – Dan Davis – Dan Davis – 1998											
170 6/8	26 5/8	26 6/8	18	20 4/8	5	4 6/8	7	6	8	2828	237
■ Waukesha Co. – Jonathan A. Denk – Jonathan A. Denk – 1998											
170 6/8	25 3/8	24 2/8	19 6/8	22	5 3/8	5 6/8	5	6		2828	237
■ Columbia Co. – Robert J. Kau – Robert J. Kau – 1999											
170 5/8	27 3/8	27 7/8	18 1/8	20 1/8	5 2/8	5	5	5		2876†	243†
■ Fond du Lac Co. – Victor J. Ketchpaw – Victor J. Ketchpaw – 2000											
170 5/8	27 2/8	27 3/8	20 4/8	22 4/8	5 3/8	5 2/8	8	8	10 5/8	2876	243
■ Sawyer Co. – Virgil A. Scanlon – Virgil A. Scanlon – 1959											
170 5/8	27 5/8	26 5/8	19 3/8	22	4 6/8	4 6/8	7	7	1 2/8	2876	243
■ Douglas Co. – George Pettingill – George Pettingill – 1963											
170 5/8	26 6/8	27 2/8	18 3/8	23	5 4/8	5 4/8	6	8	6 6/8	2876	243
■ Price Co. – Nyle H. Rodman – Nyle H. Rodman – 1970											
170 5/8	27 6/8	29 4/8	23 3/8	25 4/8	5 4/8	5 3/8	7	8	8 2/8	2876	243
■ Sawyer Co. – Thorvald Skar – James M. Skar – PR 1990											
170 5/8	25 7/8	26	19 5/8	21 7/8	5 2/8	5 2/8	5	5		2876	243
■ Kenosha Co. – Gary Schaetten – Gary Schaetten – 1999											
170 4/8	25 2/8	24 2/8	16 4/8	19 1/8	5	5	7	7	3	2933	249
■ Oneida Co. – Leonard E. Westberg – Leonard E. Westberg – 1981											
170 4/8	27 2/8	26 5/8	20 2/8	22 5/8	4 2/8	4 3/8	5	5		2933	249
■ Buffalo Co. – Stephen F. Lang – Stephen F. Lang – 1987											

Score	Length of Main Beam Right	Left	Inside Spread	Greatest Spread	Circumference at Smallest Place Between Burr and First Point Right	Left	Number of Points Right	Left	Lengths Abnormal Points	All-Time Rank	State Rank
	Location of Kill – Hunter – Owner – Date Killed										
170⁴/8	25³/8	24⁷/8	20	22¹/8	5²/8	5³/8	6	6	3²/8	2933	249
	■ *Vilas Co. – Rick R. Lax – Rick R. Lax – 1990*										
170⁴/8	28¹/8	26⁴/8	19²/8	22¹/8	5²/8	5³/8	5	6		2933	249
	■ *Dunn Co. – Richard H. Damro – Richard H. Damro – 1999*										
170⁴/8	26⁶/8	27¹/8	21⁷/8	23⁷/8	5²/8	5	6	6	2³/8	2933	249
	■ *Marinette Co. – Randy J. Willms – Randy J. Willms – 1999*										
170³/8	25⁵/8	25¹/8	16⁴/8	18⁴/8	4⁷/8	5	9	9	11⁷/8	2992	254
	■ *Price Co. – N.J. Groelle – Melvin Guenther – 1905*										
170³/8	26¹/8	26¹/8	21¹/8	22⁶/8	4⁷/8	4⁷/8	7	7	4²/8	2992	254
	■ *Buffalo Co. – Lee E. Lang – Lee E. Lang – 1969*										
170³/8	24²/8	24²/8	19⁷/8	22	5	5	5	5		2992	254
	■ *Buffalo Co. – Ralph Pella – Cabela's, Inc. – 1970*										
170³/8	24⁶/8	24⁴/8	16⁷/8	21²/8	5	4⁷/8	6	6	3⁴/8	2992	254
	■ *Juneau Co. – Gaylord J. Downing – Gaylord J. Downing – 1996*										
170³/8	25⁴/8	25³/8	19³/8	21⁴/8	4²/8	4²/8	6	5	1	2992	254
	■ *St. Croix Co. – Earl L. Neumann – Earl L. Neumann – 1996*										
170²/8	26⁷/8	26⁴/8	20¹/8	22³/8	5¹/8	5¹/8	6	5	1⁷/8	3063	259
	■ *Shawano Co. – Jule Vandergate – Don E. Smith – 1932*										
170²/8	27¹/8	26⁷/8	18⁶/8	21¹/8	5¹/8	5²/8	6	6		3063	259
	■ *Florence Co. – Unknown – Cabela's, Inc. – 1940*										
170²/8	24²/8	25⁵/8	17²/8	19³/8	4⁴/8	4³/8	6	7	1²/8	3063	259
	■ *Marinette Co. – Phillip Marquis – Phillip Marquis – 1944*										
170²/8	24⁶/8	23⁶/8	18	20¹/8	4³/8	4³/8	6	8	3⁴/8	3063	259
	■ *Polk Co. – Robert G. Overman – Robert G. Overman – 1945*										
170²/8	26²/8	25⁵/8	22⁶/8	24⁷/8	4⁷/8	4⁶/8	5	5		3063	259
	■ *Lafayette Co. – Everett E. Mau – Everett E. Mau – 1990*										
170²/8	27	27⁴/8	19⁷/8	22²/8	5⁵/8	5⁶/8	5	7	7¹/8	3063	259
	■ *Rusk Co. – Fredrick J. Marcon – Fredrick J. Marcon – 1997*										
170²/8	27⁷/8	27¹/8	19²/8	21³/8	4⁶/8	4⁵/8	4	5		3063	259
	■ *Walworth Co. – Dale Wilson – Dale Wilson – 1998*										
170²/8	24⁶/8	25⁴/8	18⁴/8	21¹/8	4³/8	4⁶/8	6	6		3063	259
	■ *Langlade Co. – Jay P. Konetzke – Jay P. Konetzke – 1999*										
170¹/8	25⁴/8	26	19⁷/8	22³/8	4⁶/8	5	5	6		3143†	267†
	■ *Buffalo Co. – Dan Folkedahl – Dan Folkedahl – 2000*										
170¹/8	26⁷/8	26³/8	22³/8	25²/8	5²/8	5¹/8	5	5		3143†	267†
	■ *Iron Co. – Randy D. Szukalski – Randy D. Szukalski – 2001*										
170¹/8	30	27⁵/8	23¹/8	25²/8	4²/8	4²/8	6	7	8⁶/8	3143	267
	■ *Bayfield Co. – Roy Jacobson – David R. Jacobson – 1960*										
170¹/8	23⁶/8	25⁶/8	20⁵/8	23⁴/8	4²/8	4³/8	6	6		3143	267
	■ *Marinette Co. – Leonard Schartner – Leonard Schartner – 1968*										
170¹/8	23³/8	27⁴/8	20⁵/8	23⁴/8	4⁶/8	4⁷/8	5	5		3143	267
	■ *Racine Co. – Michael H. Poeschel – Michael H. Poeschel – 1989*										

Score	Length of Main Beam		Inside Spread	Greatest Spread	Circumference at Smallest Place Between Burr and First Point		Number of Points		Lengths Abnormal Points	All-Time Rank	State Rank
	Right	Left			Right	Left	Right	Left			
	■ Location of Kill – Hunter – Owner – Date Killed										
170¹/8	26⁶/8	26⁴/8	24²/8	27⁶/8	5	5¹/8	6	6	3⁷/8	3143	267
	■ La Crosse Co. – Scott R. Wavra – Scott R. Wavra – 1991										
170¹/8	26⁷/8	26⁷/8	22⁷/8	25³/8	5	5¹/8	5	5		3143	267
	■ Douglas Co. – Duane Christiansen – Duane Christiansen – 1995										
170¹/8	25³/8	27²/8	17	19	5²/8	5²/8	5	6	4³/8	3143	267
	■ Dunn Co. – Clarence P. Janota – Clarence P. Janota – 1995										
170	24⁷/8	26⁵/8	21⁶/8	24	4³/8	4⁴/8	5	5		3224†	275†
	■ Oneida Co. – Felix Holewinski, Sr. – Ray T. Charles – 1928										
170	26³/8	25⁷/8	15⁴/8	18	4⁷/8	5	5	5		3224†	275†
	■ Crawford Co. – Joel B. Oppriecht – Joel B. Oppriecht – 2000										
170	28⁷/8	27⁵/8	20	22⁴/8	5¹/8	5¹/8	5	5		3224	275
	■ Chippewa Co. – John J. Scheidler – Jim Falls Lions Club – 1959										
170	26	26	21	23	4⁴/8	4³/8	7	6	2⁶/8	3224	275
	■ Dunn Co. – James W. Seehaver – James W. Seehaver – 1976										
170	27⁵/8	27⁵/8	21⁶/8	23⁶/8	5⁵/8	5²/8	5	5		3224	275
	■ Jefferson Co. – Robert L. Becker – Robert L. Becker – 1987										
170	28	28¹/8	18⁵/8	20⁵/8	4⁴/8	4⁴/8	8	7	8³/8	3224	275
	■ Dane Co. – Patrick D. Anderson – Patrick D. Anderson – 1989										
170	25⁶/8	24⁵/8	20⁶/8	22⁴/8	5⁷/8	6	5	7	3⁶/8	3224	275
	■ Buffalo Co. – Gary G. Ruff – Gary G. Ruff – 1992										
170	26⁴/8	25⁴/8	22²/8	24²/8	4⁶/8	4⁶/8	5	5		3224	275
	■ Washington Co. – Alan R. Gehl – Alan R. Gehl – 1997										
169⁷/8	24⁴/8	24⁴/8	22³/8	25¹/8	4⁶/8	4⁶/8	5	5		3302	283
	■ Walworth Co. – James W. May – James W. May – 1995										
169⁶/8	25⁵/8	26⁴/8	22³/8	24⁵/8	5¹/8	5²/8	6	6	3³/8	3306	284
	■ Monroe Co. – Timothy E. Slonka – Timothy E. Slonka – 1994										
169³/8	27⁷/8	28⁴/8	19⁵/8	22⁵/8	5¹/8	5²/8	5	7	6	3324	285
	■ Jefferson Co. – Mark S. Chesney – Mark S. Chesney – 1994										
169¹/8	24⁶/8	23³/8	18⁶/8	21	6	6¹/8	9	9	10¹/8	3342	286
	■ Trempealeau Co. – Thomas E. Halderson – Thomas E. Halderson – 1990										
169¹/8	26¹/8	26⁵/8	17³/8	19⁶/8	5⁴/8	5⁶/8	5	5		3342	286
	■ Door Co. – Timothy M. Buhr – Timothy M. Buhr – 1997										
169	26²/8	25¹/8	19⁶/8	22	4⁵/8	4²/8	6	5		3348	288
	■ Polk Co. – Ronald L. Mork – Ronald L. Mork – 1993										
168⁶/8	25⁴/8	25⁴/8	22	24	5⁴/8	5⁵/8	5	5		3367	289
	■ Marathon Co. – Anthony Locascio – Anthony Locascio – 1997										
168⁴/8	28⁴/8	28⁵/8	22⁵/8	25	5	4⁷/8	7	5	3³/8	3385	290
	■ Oneida Co. – Raymond M. Lorbetske, Jr. – Raymond M. Lorbetske, Jr. – 1985										
168³/8	27⁶/8	25⁷/8	18⁵/8	20⁷/8	4¹/8	4¹/8	5	5		3399	291
	■ Barron Co. – Edwin I. Rurup – Edwin I. Rurup – 1992										
168³/8	24⁶/8	25²/8	21³/8	23⁴/8	4¹/8	4	6	7		3399	291
	■ Oconto Co. – Peter M. Meeuwsen – Peter M. Meeuwsen – 1993										

Score	Length of Main Beam Right	Left	Inside Spread	Greatest Spread	Circ. Right	Left	No. Points Right	Left	Lengths Abnormal Points	All-Time Rank	State Rank
$168^3/8$	$25^2/8$	$25^3/8$	$19^7/8$	23	$4^4/8$	$4^5/8$	6	5		3399	291

■ Richland Co. – Douglas E. Duhr – Douglas E. Duhr – 1994

| $168^3/8$ | $27^2/8$ | $27^5/8$ | $21^1/8$ | $26^1/8$ | 5 | 5 | 6 | 6 | 4 | 3399 | 291 |

■ Outagamie Co. – Rodney R. Schutt – Rodney R. Schutt – 1998

| $168^2/8$ | $22^4/8$ | $22^1/8$ | $15^6/8$ | $18^4/8$ | $5^2/8$ | $5^2/8$ | 6 | 8 | $4^4/8$ | 3414 | 295 |

■ Marathon Co. – Paul Leitza – Paul Leitza – 1995

| $168^2/8$ | $25^2/8$ | $24^2/8$ | 18 | 22 | $5^4/8$ | $5^1/8$ | 5 | 5 | | 3414 | 295 |

■ Iowa Co. – Craig A. Christians – Craig A. Christians – 1999

| $168^2/8$ | $25^2/8$ | $24^5/8$ | $19^2/8$ | $22^6/8$ | $4^3/8$ | $4^2/8$ | 5 | 5 | | 3414 | 295 |

■ Richland Co. – Bud G. Williams – Bud G. Williams – 1999

| $168^1/8$ | $22^4/8$ | 23 | $16^1/8$ | $18^4/8$ | $4^4/8$ | $4^5/8$ | 5 | 5 | | 3426† | 298† |

■ Trempealeau Co. – Thomas A. Clopper – Thomas A. Clopper – 2001

| 168 | $24^5/8$ | $26^2/8$ | $17^4/8$ | $19^6/8$ | $4^3/8$ | $4^4/8$ | 6 | 6 | | 3443 | 299 |

■ Grant Co. – Timothy G. Ginter – Timothy G. Ginter – 1988

| $167^7/8$ | 27 | $26^6/8$ | $22^4/8$ | $25^2/8$ | $5^2/8$ | $5^2/8$ | 8 | 7 | $10^7/8$ | 3451 | 300 |

■ Bayfield Co. – Charles L. Weiss – Charles L. Weiss – 1996

| $167^6/8$ | $26^3/8$ | $26^6/8$ | $17^4/8$ | 20 | $5^2/8$ | 5 | 4 | 5 | | 3461† | 301† |

■ Waupaca Co. – Robert L. Felkner – Robert L. Felkner – 2000

| $167^6/8$ | $25^3/8$ | $25^7/8$ | $20^4/8$ | $22^5/8$ | $4^6/8$ | $4^6/8$ | 5 | 5 | | 3461 | 301 |

■ Menominee Co. – Robert L. Boyd I – Robert L. Boyd I – 1971

| $167^6/8$ | $24^7/8$ | 25 | $16^4/8$ | $18^6/8$ | $4^4/8$ | $4^4/8$ | 7 | 6 | $8^4/8$ | 3461 | 301 |

■ Washburn Co. – Norem L. Cain – Norem L. Cain – 1990

| $167^5/8$ | $25^4/8$ | $24^7/8$ | $18^2/8$ | $20^4/8$ | $5^1/8$ | $5^2/8$ | 5 | 7 | $7^7/8$ | 3476† | 304† |

■ Oconto Co. – Scott E. Samp – Scott E. Samp – 2001

| $167^5/8$ | $27^1/8$ | $25^7/8$ | $21^3/8$ | $23^1/8$ | $4^4/8$ | $4^4/8$ | 5 | 5 | | 3476 | 304 |

■ Oconto Co. – Myron R. Hellmann – Myron R. Hellmann – 1994

| $167^4/8$ | $27^2/8$ | $26^1/8$ | $19^6/8$ | $21^6/8$ | $5^4/8$ | $5^3/8$ | 5 | 6 | | 3485 | 306 |

■ Polk Co. – Joel T. Berg – Joel T. Berg – 1995

| $167^4/8$ | $27^1/8$ | 27 | $22^2/8$ | $24^5/8$ | $5^1/8$ | $5^3/8$ | 6 | 6 | $2^2/8$ | 3485 | 306 |

■ Waupaca Co. – Daniel P. Hauk – Daniel P. Hauk – 1998

| $167^4/8$ | $27^5/8$ | $26^6/8$ | $21^2/8$ | $23^7/8$ | 5 | $4^6/8$ | 5 | 5 | | 3485 | 306 |

■ Buffalo Co. – Jay J. Snopek – Jay J. Snopek – 2000

| $167^3/8$ | $26^1/8$ | $25^6/8$ | $19^5/8$ | $21^7/8$ | $4^4/8$ | $4^4/8$ | 5 | 5 | | 3500† | 309† |

■ Buffalo Co. – Rocky H. Cornelius – Rocky H. Cornelius – 2000

| $167^3/8$ | $27^2/8$ | $27^1/8$ | $21^3/8$ | $23^7/8$ | 5 | $4^7/8$ | 8 | 7 | $11^2/8$ | 3500† | 309† |

■ Waukesha Co. – Picked Up – Scott A. Davis – 2001

| $167^3/8$ | $27^3/8$ | $26^3/8$ | $21^1/8$ | 23 | $4^7/8$ | 5 | 5 | 5 | | 3500 | 309 |

■ Buffalo Co. – Michael J. Barstad – Michael J. Barstad – 1995

| $167^2/8$ | $25^6/8$ | $25^4/8$ | $20^1/8$ | $22^2/8$ | $4^1/8$ | $4^1/8$ | 6 | 6 | $1^3/8$ | 3519 | 312 |

■ Dodge Co. – Wesley F. Braunschweig – Wesley F. Braunschweig – 1969

| $167^2/8$ | $25^3/8$ | $24^6/8$ | $16^6/8$ | $18^6/8$ | $4^7/8$ | 5 | 5 | 5 | | 3519 | 312 |

■ Douglas Co. – Mark E. Henck – Mark E. Henck – 1998

Score	Length of Main Beam Right	Left	Inside Spread	Greatest Spread	Circumference at Smallest Place Between Burr and First Point Right	Left	Number of Points Right	Left	Lengths Abnormal Points	All-Time Rank	State Rank
	■ Location of Kill – Hunter – Owner – Date Killed										
167	25⁵/8	25⁴/8	18²/8	20³/8	5²/8	5¹/8	6	5	2⁴/8	3552†	314†
	■ Eau Claire Co. – Brett D. Grill – Brett D. Grill – 2001										
167	26	24	18⁴/8	20⁷/8	4⁷/8	5²/8	6	6		3552†	314†
	■ Buffalo Co. – Edward J. Schlosser – Edward J. Schlosser – 1998										
167	25²/8	26²/8	17²/8	19⁶/8	4⁶/8	4⁷/8	6	7	1²/8	3552	314
	■ Washburn Co. – William Dahl – Morton Dahl – 1940										
167	24⁶/8	25³/8	19⁴/8	21³/8	4²/8	4²/8	6	5		3552	314
	■ Winnebago Co. – Richard C. Hanson – Richard C. Hanson – 1994										
166⁷/8	27⁴/8	27¹/8	20⁵/8	22⁶/8	4⁶/8	4⁶/8	4	4		3568	318
	■ Douglas Co. – James N. Johnson – James N. Johnson – 1992										
166⁷/8	28	27¹/8	19¹/8	21³/8	4⁵/8	4⁵/8	5	6	1²/8	3568	318
	■ Douglas Co. – Randy Stank – Randy Stank – 1995										
166⁶/8	25¹/8	26¹/8	18⁷/8	21⁴/8	6	6	8	6	7⁵/8	3582†	320†
	■ Forest Co. – Robert A. Karl – Robert A. Karl – 2001										
166⁵/8	28⁶/8	27⁶/8	18⁵/8	20⁵/8	5¹/8	5³/8	6	8	5	3598	321
	■ Douglas Co. – Robert W. Strauch – Robert W. Strauch – 1998										
166⁴/8	24¹/8	24³/8	16⁴/8	18⁶/8	4²/8	4³/8	5	5		3609	322
	■ Trempealeau Co. – John J. Kokett – John J. Kokett – 1963										
166⁴/8	24⁶/8	25	21²/8	22⁷/8	5	5	5	5		3609	322
	■ Washburn Co. – John D. Rindfleisch – John D. Rindfleisch – 1989										
166⁴/8	26	26⁶/8	19	21¹/8	5	4⁶/8	5	4		3609	322
	■ Pierce Co. – Garrett L. Fleishauer – Garrett L. Fleishauer – 1991										
166⁴/8	24⁵/8	26	19	21²/8	4⁵/8	4³/8	6	6		3609	322
	■ Washburn Co. – Thomas W. Johnson – Thomas W. Johnson – 1993										
166³/8	28¹/8	28⁵/8	18⁵/8	20³/8	4²/8	4³/8	6	8	5²/8	3620	326
	■ Buffalo Co. – Michael R. Wineski – Michael R. Wineski – 1988										
166³/8	26⁴/8	28²/8	17¹/8	20	5²/8	5	6	7	2-8/8	3620	326
	■ St. Croix Co. – John J. Wilson – John J. Wilson – 1998										
166²/8	27	26¹/8	20⁴/8	22⁵/8	5¹/8	5²/8	5	5		3632	328
	■ Marinette Co. – Wayne M. Blickhahn – Wayne M. Blickhahn – 1962										
166¹/8	26¹/8	26⁷/8	19¹/8	21²/8	4	4¹/8	5	5		3643†	329†
	■ Buffalo Co. – Philip L. Raikowski – Philip L. Raikowski – 2001										
166¹/8	26⁷/8	27⁵/8	18⁵/8	20⁶/8	4⁶/8	4⁷/8	5	5		3643	329
	■ Buffalo Co. – Michael Fleming – Michael Fleming – 1992										
166	25²/8	25⁷/8	18²/8	20	4²/8	4³/8	6	6		3657	331
	■ Douglas Co. – James Blosmore – James Blosmore – 1970										
165⁷/8	27⁵/8	28¹/8	21¹/8	23²/8	5⁴/8	5⁵/8	4	5		3672†	332†
	■ Green Co. – Thomas R. Krause – Thomas R. Krause – 2000										
165⁷/8	25⁶/8	26	18⁴/8	21²/8	5¹/8	5¹/8	5	6	2¹/8	3672	332
	■ Douglas Co. – George H. Norton – Gerald Hall – 1917										
165⁷/8	26³/8	26⁷/8	22¹/8	25³/8	4⁶/8	4⁵/8	5	5		3672	332
	■ Pepin Co. – Reuben E. Bignell – Reuben E. Bignell – 1966										

Score	Length of Main Beam Right Left	Inside Spread	Greatest Spread	Circumference at Smallest Place Between Burr and First Point Right Left	Number of Points Right Left	Lengths Abnormal Points	All-Time Rank	State Rank
	■ Location of Kill – Hunter – Owner – Date Killed							
165 7/8	23 1/8 24 1/8	18 1/8	20 4/8	4 7/8 4 6/8	5 5		3672	332
	■ Rusk Co. – Fredric P. Burak – Fredric P. Burak – 1976							
165 6/8	25 26 2/8	17 7/8	20	4 2/8 4 2/8	6 5	1 1/8	3680†	336†
	■ Juneau Co. – Kevin R. Dawson – Kevin R. Dawson – 1996							
165 6/8	25 6/8 25	21 1/8	23	5 6/8 5 6/8	6 6	3 7/8	3680†	336†
	■ Chippewa Co. – Rodney C. Lazarz – Rodney C. Lazarz – 2000							
165 5/8	26 2/8 26 3/8	18 1/8	20 4/8	4 6/8 4 5/8	5 5		3696†	338†
	■ Trempealeau Co. – Ramon E. Kohnert – Ramon E. Kohnert – 2000							
165 5/8	25 6/8 26 4/8	18 1/8	20 4/8	5 1/8 5 3/8	6 7	5 6/8	3696	338
	■ Walworth Co. – Greg A. Vegter – Greg A. Vegter – 1991							
165 5/8	24 3/8 24 1/8	17 7/8	20 6/8	5 5/8 5 5/8	4 4		3696	338
	■ Langlade Co. – Richard H. Frakes – Richard H. Frakes – 1994							
165 4/8	25 1/8 24 1/8	22 4/8	24 5/8	5 5	5 6		3714†	341†
	■ Trempealeau Co. – Ronald A. Williamson – Ronald A. Williamson – 1999							
165 4/8	29 1/8 28 3/8	18 1/8	21 4/8	4 6/8 5	7 8	7 5/8	3714	341
	■ Buffalo Co. – Patrick M. Ryan – Patrick M. Ryan – 1985							
165 4/8	25 5/8 25 5/8	19 4/8	21 4/8	4 6/8 4 6/8	5 5		3714	341
	■ Forest Co. – Todd Webb – Todd Webb – 1986							
165 3/8	26 5/8 26 3/8	17 7/8	20 7/8	5 4/8 5	8 6	4 2/8	3731	344
	■ Forest Co. – Virgil J. Gueths – Virgil J. Gueths – 1987							
165 3/8	25 24 4/8	17 3/8	19	4 6/8 4 5/8	6 6		3731	344
	■ Ashland Co. – Darren Carlson – Darren Carlson – 1991							
165 2/8	25 24 7/8	18 6/8	20 7/8	5 5	7 7	9 4/8	3748	346
	■ Dunn Co. – Lamoine E. Roatch – Lamoine E. Roatch – 1989							
165 2/8	27 2/8 24 2/8	23	25	4 4/8 4 3/8	6 5		3748	346
	■ St. Croix Co. – Ron W. Nelson – Ron W. Nelson – 1995							
165 1/8	25 4/8 26 1/8	17 3/8	21	5 5/8 5 7/8	5 5		3767	348
	■ Sawyer Co. – Shawn A. Campbell – Shawn A. Campbell – 1998							
165 1/8	23 2/8 21 5/8	19 7/8	23 1/8	4 5/8 4 6/8	6 6		3767	348
	■ Oconto Co. – Thomas M. Wagner – Thomas M. Wagner – 1998							
165 1/8	27 6/8 28	20 5/8	22 2/8	4 5/8 4 5/8	5 5		3767	348
	■ Buffalo Co. – Gary L. Fleishauer – Gary L. Fleishauer – 2000							
165	26 2/8 25	18 3/8	20 2/8	4 4/8 4	7 5	4 5/8	3782	351
	■ Waushara Co. – Glenn E. Mentink – Glenn E. Mentink – 1988							
165	25 5/8 25 4/8	18 7/8	21 4/8	5 4/8 5 3/8	5 6	1 3/8	3782	351
	■ Oconto Co. – Brian R. Belongea – Brian R. Belongea – 1999							
164 7/8	22 6/8 22 6/8	17 7/8	19 7/8	4 7/8 4 5/8	5 5		3792	353
	■ Marathon Co. – Eugene E. Zdanovec – Eugene E. Zdanovec – 1988							
164 7/8	27 3/8 27 6/8	22	23 7/8	5 2/8 5 2/8	7 7	10 3/8	3792	353
	■ Bayfield Co. – Frances M. Steen – Frances M. Steen – 1990							
164 7/8	24 6/8 23 5/8	15 3/8	18	4 4/8 4 5/8	5 6	2	3792	353
	■ Kewaunee Co. – William J. Derenne – William J. Derenne – 1998							

Score	Length of Main Beam Right	Left	Inside Spread	Greatest Spread	Circumference at Smallest Place Between Burr and First Point Right	Left	Number of Points Right	Left	Lengths Abnormal Points	All-Time Rank	State Rank
164⁶/8	25¹/8	24⁶/8	21⁴/8	23⁴/8	4⁴/8	4⁴/8	5	5		3809	356
■ Washburn Co. – Lawrence A. Radzak – Lawrence A. Radzak – 1989											
164⁶/8	27	25²/8	17⁶/8	21⁵/8	4⁵/8	4⁴/8	7	6	2⁴/8	3809	356
■ Vernon Co. – Michael J. Funk – Michael J. Funk – 1992											
164⁶/8	25²/8	25²/8	18⁴/8	20⁶/8	6¹/8	5⁵/8	6	6	1⁴/8	3809	356
■ Walworth Co. – Steven Markham – Steven Markham – 1995											
164⁶/8	26²/8	25⁵/8	20⁶/8	23⁷/8	5²/8	5⁴/8	6	5	5²/8	3809	356
■ Brown Co. – Cecil J. Skenandore – Cecil J. Skenandore – 1998											
164⁶/8	26⁷/8	26⁷/8	22	23⁷/8	4⁴/8	4³/8	6	5	1⁴/8	3809	356
■ Racine Co. – Thomas A. Wendt – Thomas A. Wendt – 1998											
164⁵/8	27⁶/8	25⁷/8	21³/8	23³/8	5	5¹/8	5	6	1	3835†	361†
■ Rusk Co. – Doug S. Nitek – Doug S. Nitek – 2000											
164⁵/8	25¹/8	25⁴/8	20⁷/8	22⁵/8	5	5	5	5		3835	361
■ Jefferson Co. – Jerald Behling – Jerald Behling – 1975											
164⁵/8	22⁶/8	22⁶/8	17²/8	19²/8	4⁶/8	4³/8	6	5	1³/8	3835	361
■ Rock Co. – David R. Dummer, Jr. – David R. Dummer, Jr. – 1995											
164⁵/8	23³/8	24²/8	21¹/8	23	5¹/8	5²/8	5	6	2⁴/8	3835	361
■ Pepin Co. – Oliver J. Grotthus – Oliver J. Grotthus – 1999											
164⁴/8	24¹/8	24	19	20⁶/8	5⁴/8	5²/8	6	6	2⁶/8	3855	365
■ La Crosse Co. – Donald K. Earley – Donald K. Earley – 1999											
164³/8	24⁷/8	25²/8	16⁴/8	18⁵/8	5	5	6	6	4⁵/8	3864	366
■ Iron Co. – Thomas D. Brye – Thomas D. Brye – 1992											
164²/8	26³/8	25⁶/8	17⁶/8	19⁷/8	5	5	5	6	1⁴/8	3876	367
■ Shawano Co. – Keith Wilcox – Keith Wilcox – 1999											
164¹/8	25⁴/8	25⁵/8	18⁷/8	21	4⁶/8	5	5	5		3886†	368†
■ Outagamie Co. – Craig C. Koch – Craig C. Koch – 2001											
164¹/8	26⁶/8	26⁶/8	20⁵/8	23²/8	4	4	5	5		3886†	368†
■ Jackson Co. – Carl Randall – Jeannine Lamb – 1948											
164¹/8	24⁵/8	25⁴/8	17¹/8	19³/8	4⁴/8	4⁴/8	5	6		3886	368
■ Monroe Co. – Gary A. Wright – Gary A. Wright – 1994											
164¹/8	26⁴/8	27²/8	20³/8	22⁵/8	5²/8	5¹/8	6	5	1	3886	368
■ Calumet Co. – Scott D. Bonlander – Scott D. Bonlander – 1998											
164¹/8	26¹/8	25⁴/8	21²/8	23³/8	5	4⁷/8	6	6	2⁷/8	3886	368
■ Vernon Co. – Todd M. Anderson – Todd M. Anderson – 1999											
164¹/8	25⁴/8	25¹/8	18³/8	21²/8	4⁷/8	4⁵/8	6	5	1⁴/8	3886	368
■ Vernon Co. – Troy D. Oldenburg – Troy D. Oldenburg – 1999											
164	25⁶/8	26²/8	18⁶/8	20⁴/8	5¹/8	5¹/8	5	6	2⁴/8	3908†	374†
■ Green Co. – James Newman – James Newman – 1994											
164	22	22²/8	17⁵/8	21⁵/8	4³/8	4⁴/8	5	6	5³/8	3908	374
■ Shawano Co. – Roy J. Habeck – Roy J. Habeck – 1958											
164	25⁶/8	23⁶/8	19²/8	21⁴/8	4⁵/8	4⁴/8	5	5		3908	374
■ Dane Co. – Bradley Behnke – Bradley Behnke – 1988											

Score	Length of Main Beam Right	Left	Inside Spread	Greatest Spread	Circumference at Smallest Place Between Burr and First Point Right	Left	Number of Points Right	Left	Lengths Abnormal Points	All-Time Rank	State Rank
	■ Location of Kill – Hunter – Owner – Date Killed										
163⁷/8	24²/8	23⁵/8	17	19	4¹/8	4²/8	7	6	1¹/8	3928	377
	■ Sauk Co. – Matthew G. Healy – Matthew G. Healy – 1996										
163⁶/8	25⁵/8	25⁵/8	17⁶/8	19⁵/8	4⁶/8	4⁶/8	5	5		3946	378
	■ Price Co. – Andrew P. Pohlod – Andrew P. Pohlod – 1965										
163⁶/8	25	25	17³/8	19⁴/8	5²/8	5	6	5	1³/8	3946	378
	■ Chippewa Co. – Rodney M. Gulich – Rodney M. Gulich – 1988										
163⁶/8	25⁶/8	25²/8	16⁴/8	19²/8	4⁵/8	4⁵/8	6	5	6	3946	378
	■ Pierce Co. – Larry J. Wiskerchen – Larry J. Wiskerchen – 1995										
163⁶/8	24¹/8	24⁴/8	21	24⁵/8	4⁶/8	4⁶/8	5	5		3946	378
	■ Shawano Co. – Donald A. Juers – Donald A. Juers – 1999										
163⁵/8	25⁴/8	25¹/8	19¹/8	21	4⁴/8	4⁷/8	5	5		3961†	382†
	■ Adams Co. – Bruce Sonnenberg – Bruce Sonnenberg – 2000										
163⁵/8	25³/8	24³/8	19⁵/8	22¹/8	4³/8	4⁵/8	6	7	5⁶/8	3961	382
	■ Pierce Co. – Jeffrey W. Gilles – Jeffrey W. Gilles – 1988										
163⁵/8	26⁶/8	26⁴/8	20¹/8	22⁷/8	5⁴/8	5³/8	6	5	4	3961	382
	■ Ashland Co. – Justin L. Dodge – Justin L. Dodge – 1996										
163⁵/8	25	24⁴/8	20	22⁷/8	4⁷/8	4⁶/8	7	7	3⁷/8	3961	382
	■ Iowa Co. – Ryan F. Lipska – Ryan F. Lipska – 1997										
163⁴/8	24⁷/8	23⁶/8	21⁶/8	23⁵/8	5¹/8	5²/8	8	6	9⁴/8	3984	386
	■ Racine Co. – Greg A. Hanson – Greg A. Hanson – 1991										
163⁴/8	27⁶/8	27¹/8	19¹/8	21¹/8	5³/8	5³/8	6	6	2⁵/8	3984	386
	■ Sawyer Co. – Lawrence J. Burger – Lawrence J. Burger – 1998										
163⁴/8	27³/8	29	19⁵/8	21⁶/8	4²/8	4²/8	6	6	1⁷/8	3984	386
	■ Jefferson Co. – Nathan J. Hrobsky – Nathan J. Hrobsky – 1999										
163³/8	26⁴/8	26³/8	25¹/8	27¹/8	4⁶/8	4⁵/8	6	6	4	4002	389
	■ Jackson Co. – Mark Rumler – Mark Rumler – 1993										
163	25¹/8	24⁷/8	22³/8	24⁴/8	4³/8	4³/8	6	5	3¹/8	4051†	390†
	■ Burnett Co. – Picked Up – Richard M. Shutt, Jr. – 2001										
163	25⁶/8	25⁶/8	22	26⁴/8	4⁵/8	4⁷/8	5	5		4051	390
	■ Bayfield Co. – Michael S. Statz – Michael S. Statz – 1990										
163	26³/8	27	22⁵/8	25	5¹/8	4⁶/8	6	8	10¹/8	4051	390
	■ Buffalo Co. – Laine W. Lahndt – Laine W. Lahndt – 1994										
162⁷/8	25¹/8	25²/8	18⁷/8	18⁷/8	4⁴/8	4⁴/8	5	5		4067†	393†
	■ Kewaunee Co. – Michael J. Witcpalck – Michael J. Witcpalck – 1994										
162⁶/8	29⁷/8	29⁷/8	24⁵/8	26⁴/8	4⁴/8	4⁵/8	5	8	8³/8	4089†	394†
	■ Dodge Co. – Duane A. McClyman – Duane A. McClyman – 2000										
162⁶/8	26²/8	25⁴/8	23³/8	25¹/8	4⁴/8	4⁵/8	6	5	1¹/8	4089†	394†
	■ Chippewa Co. – Marlene E. Olson – Marlene E. Olson – 2001										
162⁶/8	24³/8	25²/8	21	25³/8	4²/8	4³/8	6	5	1⁴/8	4089	394
	■ St. Croix Co. – Mark W. Raught – Mark W. Raught – 1993										
162⁶/8	27	26¹/8	21	23²/8	4⁴/8	4⁵/8	5	5		4089	394
	■ Iowa Co. – Talbert L. Connell – Talbert L. Connell – 1995										

Score	Length of Main Beam Right	Left	Inside Spread	Greatest Spread	Circumference at Smallest Place Between Burr and First Point Right	Left	Number of Points Right	Left	Lengths Abnormal Points	All-Time Rank	State Rank
	■ Location of Kill – Hunter – Owner – Date Killed										
162 6/8	26 2/8	25 4/8	21	23 3/8	5 2/8	5 3/8	5	6	4 6/8	4089	394
	■ Crawford Co. – Wayne C. Martin – Wayne C. Martin – 1999										
162 5/8	25 2/8	26 5/8	17 1/8	18 6/8	4 5/8	4 7/8	5	5		4109	399
	■ Iron Co. – James H. Wiedmeyer – James H. Wiedmeyer – 1994										
163 3/8	24 4/8	24 3/8	15 5/8	17 7/8	4 4/8	4 5/8	6	6		4140	400
	■ Wood Co. – Aldro M. Johnson – Jim Johnson – 1945										
163 3/8	25 6/8	25 6/8	16 7/8	19 2/8	5 5/8	5 4/8	5	5		4140	400
	■ Oconto Co. – Roland H. Ziesmer – Roland H. Ziesmer – 1948										
163 3/8	25 2/8	25 5/8	21 1/8	23 2/8	4 2/8	4 3/8	5	5		4140	400
	■ Dunn Co. – LaVerne Jones – LaVerne Jones – 1960										
163 3/8	25 1/8	24 7/8	20 5/8	22 5/8	5 2/8	5 2/8	8	6	8	4140	400
	■ Buffalo Co. – Michael J. Lurndal – Michael J. Lurndal – 1987										
163 3/8	25 5/8	24 3/8	19 3/8	21 3/8	5	4 6/8	6	6	5	4140	400
	■ Dane Co. – Ronald E. Goodrich – Ronald E. Goodrich – 1997										
162 2/8	24 4/8	26 1/8	16 6/8	19 1/8	4 7/8	4 7/8	5	5		4153†	405†
	■ Ashland Co. – Mark K. Hultman – Mark K. Hultman – 2001										
162 2/8	24 1/8	25 3/8	19 4/8	22	4 4/8	4 4/8	6	6		4153†	405†
	■ Waupaca Co. – Duane E. Koeller – Duane E. Koeller – 2001										
162 2/8	26 5/8	25 4/8	19 6/8	21 4/8	4	4	6	6		4153	405
	■ Jackson Co. – Wallace Crober – John E. Hendrickson – 1955										
162 2/8	25 3/8	25 6/8	18 5/8	21 1/8	5 2/8	5 1/8	6	5	4 1/8	4153	405
	■ Grant Co. – David A. Berther – David A. Berther – 1998										
162 1/8	24 4/8	24 3/8	17 5/8	20 2/8	4 7/8	4 6/8	5	5		4174	409
	■ Rusk Co. – Richard T. Cowan – Richard T. Cowan – 1997										
162 1/8	25 1/8	25	19 2/8	21 5/8	4 3/8	4 3/8	5	6	1 1/8	4174	409
	■ Bayfield Co. – Kevin S. Mytko – Kevin S. Mytko – 1998										
162	26	26 2/8	19 2/8	22 1/8	4 5/8	4 4/8	5	7	5 6/8	4184	411
	■ Chippewa Co. – Karl P. Blank, Sr. – Karl P. Blank, Sr. – 1952										
162	24 7/8	24 7/8	17	19 3/8	4 6/8	4 6/8	5	5		4184	411
	■ Marathon Co. – Greg A. Danke – Greg A. Danke – 1996										
161 6/8	28 2/8	27 3/8	18 4/8	21	4 1/8	4 2/8	5	5		4223	413
	■ Shawano Co. – Todd W. Davis – Todd W. Davis – 1999 ■ See photo on page 507										
161 5/8	24 2/8	25 1/8	18 1/8	20 3/8	5 3/8	5 2/8	7	6	6 6/8	4234†	414†
	■ Oconto Co. – Michael E. O'Connell – Michael E. O'Connell – 2000										
161 5/8	25 1/8	25 6/8	18 3/8	20 4/8	5 1/8	5 2/8	5	4		4234	414
	■ Sawyer Co. – Forrest Kunes – Claire Kunes – 1932										
161 5/8	24 4/8	24 1/8	17 1/8	19 2/8	4 4/8	4 3/8	5	6		4234	414
	■ Forest Co. – Daniel G. Van Hoosen – Daniel G. Van Hoosen – 1990										
161 5/8	25 4/8	25 3/8	18 7/8	21	4 3/8	4 5/8	5	6	1 2/8	4234	414
	■ Bayfield Co. – Donald R. Lahti – Donald R. Lahti – 1998										
161 4/8	28 3/8	27 4/8	20 1/8	24 5/8	4 3/8	4 3/8	5	5	1 1/8	4258†	418†
	■ Green Co. – Robert Taylor – Ann M. Brown – 1974										

Score	Length of Main Beam Right Left	Inside Spread	Greatest Spread	Circumference at Smallest Place Between Burr and First Point Right Left	Number of Points Right Left	Lengths Abnormal Points	All-Time Rank	State Rank
	■ Location of Kill – Hunter – Owner – Date Killed							
161⁴/₈	26¹/₈ 25⁴/₈	17⁴/₈	19⁶/₈	5 5	5 5		4258	418
	■ Price Co. – Fred J. Wisnewski – Fred J. Wisnewski – 1955							
161⁴/₈	26¹/₈ 26⁶/₈	16⁷/₈	19	5 4⁶/₈	5 6	1¹/₈	4258	418
	■ Oconto Co. – Jeffrey J. Brabant – Jeffrey J. Brabant – 1989							
161⁴/₈	24⁴/₈ 26	17⁶/₈	19¹/₈	4⁵/₈ 4⁴/₈	7 6	4	4258	418
	■ Waupaca Co. – Anthony J. Burton – Anthony J. Burton – 1998							
161⁴/₈	26⁵/₈ 27	17³/₈	21⁶/₈	4⁶/₈ 4⁶/₈	10 6	10³/₈	4258	418
	■ Oconto Co. – Richard L. Rosio – Richard L. Rosio – 1998							
161³/₈	25⁶/₈ 27¹/₈	24⁵/₈	25⁷/₈	4²/₈ 4²/₈	6 6	1²/₈	4285	423
	■ Ashland Co. – Burlin L. Jones – Burlin L. Jones – 1940							
161³/₈	23⁷/₈ 18¹/₈	17³/₈	20	4⁵/₈ 4⁶/₈	5 5		4285	423
	■ Buffalo Co. – David Fernholz – David Fernholz – 1982							
161³/₈	25²/₈ 25⁷/₈	18⁷/₈	20⁷/₈	4¹/₈ 4²/₈	5 5		4285	423
	■ Buffalo Co. – Glen A. Averbeck – Glen A. Averbeck – 1993							
161³/₈	27¹/₈ 24	16⁴/₈	18⁴/₈	5³/₈ 6²/₈	7 6	4⁵/₈	4285	423
	■ Jackson Co. – Randy R. Hughes – Randy R. Hughes – 1993							
161²/₈	25¹/₈ 26	19²/₈	21³/₈	5²/₈ 5⁴/₈	7 5		4310	427
	■ Buffalo Co. – Donald D. Ash – Donald D. Ash – 1959							
161²/₈	22³/₈ 21	18²/₈	20⁴/₈	4⁵/₈ 4⁷/₈	7 7	4⁴/₈	4310	427
	■ Langlade Co. – Timothy A. Zahurones – Timothy A. Zahurones – 1999							
161¹/₈	25⁴/₈ 25³/₈	18⁷/₈	21	4⁷/₈ 4⁴/₈	5 5		4332†	429†
	■ Douglas Co. – John Wohlwend – John Wohlwend – 1998							
161¹/₈	25⁵/₈ 25⁵/₈	21	23⁴/₈	4⁵/₈ 4⁴/₈	7 5	1¹/₈	4332	429
	■ Barron Co. – Marshall A. Johnson – Marshall A. Johnson – 1987							
161¹/₈	23⁶/₈ 24⁶/₈	18¹/₈	20⁴/₈	5⁴/₈ 5¹/₈	5 5		4332	429
	■ Buffalo Co. – Ronald T. Speltz – Ronald T. Speltz – 1994							
161¹/₈	26⁴/₈ 26⁵/₈	20	22⁴/₈	5²/₈ 5⁴/₈	9 6	8⁵/₈	4332	429
	■ Iron Co. – Bryan L. Bellows – Bryan L. Bellows – 1995							
161¹/₈	25²/₈ 25¹/₈	17⁵/₈	20¹/₈	5³/₈ 5²/₈	6 5	4⁶/₈	4332	429
	■ Iowa Co. – Terry L. Michaelis – Terry L. Michaelis – 1995							
161	25⁴/₈ 26¹/₈	15⁴/₈	17⁵/₈	4⁷/₈ 4⁷/₈	6 6		4356†	434†
	■ Dunn Co. – Joseph G. Treiber – Joseph G. Treiber – 2000							
161	26⁷/₈ 26³/₈	17⁴/₈	19⁷/₈	4⁶/₈ 4⁵/₈	5 5		4356	434
	■ St. Croix Co. – Mark H. Johnson – Mark H. Johnson – 1998							
160⁷/₈	26²/₈ 25⁵/₈	17⁵/₈	19⁶/₈	5 5²/₈	5 5		4380†	436†
	■ Marathon Co. – Frank Hojnacki – Frank Hojnacki – 2000							
160⁷/₈	25⁵/₈ 26⁵/₈	17⁶/₈	21	4⁶/₈ 4⁷/₈	7 6	4¹/₈	4380	436
	■ Trempealeau Co. – Glen A. Gibbons – Glen A. Gibbons – 1993							
160⁷/₈	25⁴/₈ 25²/₈	16⁵/₈	18⁴/₈	4⁶/₈ 4⁵/₈	5 6		4380	436
	■ La Crosse Co. – Picked Up – David J. Padesky – 1994							
160⁶/₈	23⁵/₈ 23⁶/₈	16⁷/₈	19²/₈	5⁴/₈ 5⁴/₈	5 6	2⁵/₈	4402†	439†
	■ Adams Co. – Todd W. Hajos – Todd W. Hajos – 2000							

Score	Length of Main Beam Right Left	Inside Spread	Greatest Spread	Circumference at Smallest Place Between Burr and First Point Right Left	Number of Points Right Left	Lengths Abnormal Points	All-Time Rank	State Rank
						■ *Location of Kill – Hunter – Owner – Date Killed*		
160 6/8	24 6/8 24 7/8	19 4/8	21 6/8	4 4/8 4 5/8	5 5		4402	439
	■ *Marinette Co. – Roland G. Ropson – Roland G. Ropson – 1953*							
160 6/8	25 6/8 26 1/8	18 5/8	22 2/8	5 2/8 5	6 8	6 3/8	4402	439
	■ *Bayfield Co. – Lawrence J. Kania – Lawrence J. Kania – 1977*							
160 6/8	23 7/8 23	17 1/8	20 1/8	5 3/8 5 3/8	7 5	2 1/8	4402	439
	■ *Oneida Co. – Robert L. Van Order – Robert L. Van Order – 1990*							
160 6/8	25 3/8 25 4/8	19 2/8	21 6/8	4 4	6 6		4402	439
	■ *Chippewa Co. – Richard Hunziker – Richard Hunziker – 1998*							
160 4/8	28 2/8 27 6/8	20 6/8	22 4/8	4 5/8 4 7/8	5 5		4443	444
	■ *Jackson Co. – Clarence R. Rezin – Vivian Rezin – 1945*							
160 4/8	24 6/8 24 6/8	18 4/8	20 6/8	4 4/8 4 5/8	5 5		4443	444
	■ *Jefferson Co. – Nancy L. Schmidt – Nancy L. Schmidt – 1987*							
160 4/8	26 6/8 25 3/8	19 4/8	21 5/8	4 1/8 4 1/8	6 5	1 2/8	4443	444
	■ *Chippewa Co. – Cleo L. Hoel – Cleo L. Hoel – 1989*							
160 4/8	26 1/8 25 7/8	20 3/8	22 4/8	4 5/8 4 5/8	5 7	1 1/8	4443	444
	■ *Pepin Co. – Robert R. Williams – Robert R. Williams – 1990*							
160 4/8	26 26 3/8	19	20 6/8	5 2/8 5 1/8	5 7	7 2/8	4443	444
	■ *Jackson Co. – James Rindahl – James Rindahl – 1991*							
160 4/8	23 4/8 23 4/8	18 1/8	20 1/8	5 5	5 6	1 5/8	4443	444
	■ *Polk Co. – Peter J. King – Peter J. King – 1992*							
160 4/8	25 1/8 24 5/8	18 3/8	21 1/8	5 6/8 5 7/8	7 6	8 1/8	4443	444
	■ *Douglas Co. – Mark J. Radzak – Mark J. Radzak – 1994*							
160 3/8	25 4/8 25	21 4/8	24	4 7/8 4 7/8	8 7	10 3/8	4470†	451†
	■ *La Crosse Co. – Greg D. Kastenschmidt – Greg D. Kastenschmidt – 2001*							
160 3/8	25 4/8 26 1/8	17 7/8	20 2/8	4 4/8 4 4/8	6 7	1 2/8	4470	451
	■ *Dane Co. – James H. Hageman – James H. Hageman – 1995*							
160 3/8	23 4/8 23	15 5/8	18 1/8	4 2/8 4 1/8	5 5		4470	451
	■ *Manitowoc Co. – Wayne J. Blaha – Wayne J. Blaha – 1997*							
160 3/8	25 7/8 21 1/8	18 5/8	20 7/8	4 7/8 5	6 5	1 6/8	4470	451
	■ *Washburn Co. – Larry R. Melton – Larry R. Melton – 1999*							
160 2/8	26 5/8 27 3/8	24 4/8	26 3/8	4 6/8 4 6/8	5 5		4495†	455†
	■ *Pepin Co. – Michael J. Anderson – Michael J. Anderson – 2000*							
160 2/8	24 6/8 25 2/8	18 5/8	20 7/8	5 4 7/8	8 5	3 1/8	4495	455
	■ *Langlade Co. – Peter G. Clabots – Peter G. Clabots – 1990*							
160 2/8	27 4/8 27 3/8	19	21 6/8	4 7/8 5	5 5		4495	455
	■ *Monroe Co. – Steven J. Boris – Steven J. Boris – 1992*							
160 2/8	27 7/8 26 2/8	18 6/8	20 2/8	5 6/8 6 1/8	9 7	10	4495	455
	■ *Langlade Co. – James A. Ausloos – James A. Ausloos – 1993*							
160 2/8	22 6/8 23	16 6/8	18 5/8	4 3/8 4 3/8	6 6		4495	455
	■ *St. Croix Co. – Thomas E. Dulon – Thomas E. Dulon – 1993*							
160 2/8	24 6/8 26	17 6/8	21	4 7/8 4 6/8	5 5		4495	455
	■ *Outagamie Co. – Matthew R. Heimann – Matthew R. Heimann – 1998*							

Score	Length of Main Beam Right	Left	Inside Spread	Greatest Spread	Circumference at Smallest Place Between Burr and First Point Right	Left	Number of Points Right	Left	Lengths Abnormal Points	All-Time Rank	State Rank
	■ Location of Kill – Hunter – Owner – Date Killed										
160²/₈	25⁴/₈	27	19¹/₈	22	4⁴/₈	4⁴/₈	7	6	6⁵/₈	4495	455
	■ Outagamie Co. – Jason Mathis – Jason Mathis – 1999										
160²/₈	27	24⁴/₈	18⁴/₈	20⁴/₈	3⁵/₈	4	5	5		4495	455
	■ Polk Co. – Jack B. Wilson – Jack B. Wilson – 1999										
160¹/₈	26⁶/₈	26⁶/₈	17⁷/₈	20²/₈	4⁷/₈	5	4	4		4534†	463†
	■ Sawyer Co. – Christopher M. Schloesser – Christopher M. Schloesser – 2001										
160¹/₈	24⁶/₈	23⁶/₈	17⁴/₈	20	4⁷/₈	4⁵/₈	5	6	1³/₈	4534	463
	■ Sawyer Co. – Wayne L. Beckwith – Wayne L. Beckwith – 1990										
160¹/₈	27	26⁵/₈	21⁵/₈	23¹/₈	4⁶/₈	4⁶/₈	5	5		4534	463
	■ Calumet Co. – David E. Schaefer – David E. Schaefer – 1999										
160	23¹/₈	23¹/₈	17⁴/₈	19⁶/₈	4⁷/₈	5	5	7	2²/₈	4565†	466†
	■ Clark Co. – Mark R. Lamers – Mark R. Lamers – 2000										
160	23⁷/₈	23⁴/₈	16	18³/₈	4	4²/₈	5	5		4565	466
	■ Juneau Co. – Gordon Moll – Gordon Moll – 1991										
160	24²/₈	23⁷/₈	19⁵/₈	22	5	4⁴/₈	8	6	6⁷/₈	4565	466
	■ Outagamie Co. – Kevin L. Lohrenz – Kevin L. Lohrenz – 1998										
160	28	27²/₈	20³/₈	22⁶/₈	4²/₈	4²/₈	6	7	8¹/₈	4565	466
	■ Lafayette Co. – Eric J. Straehl – Eric J. Straehl – 1998										

† The scores and ranking for trophies from the 25th Awards Entry Period are not final until the banquet is held on June 19, 2004.

TROPHIES IN THE FIELD

HUNTER: Todd W. Davis
SCORE: 161-6/8
CATEGORY: typical whitetail deer
LOCATION: Shawano County, Wisconsin
DATE: 1999

WISCONSIN

NON-TYPICAL WHITETAIL DEER

Score	Length of Main Beam Right	Left	Inside Spread	Greatest Spread	Circumference at Smallest Place Between Burr and First Point Right	Left	Number of Points Right	Left	Lengths Abnormal Points	All-Time Rank	State Rank

■ Location of Kill – Hunter – Owner – Date Killed

Score	Length of Main Beam Right	Left	Inside Spread	Greatest Spread	Circum. Right	Left	Points Right	Left	Lengths Abnormal Points	All-Time Rank	State Rank
247³/₈	23⁵/₈	24⁷/₈	24⁶/₈	28⁴/₈	5³/₈	5¹/₈	12	13	54³/₈	75	1

■ Vernon Co. – Arnold N. Stalsberg – Arnold N. Stalsberg – 1998 ■ See photo on page 519

245	27⁴/₈	27	20⁶/₈	27⁵/₈	5³/₈	5⁴/₈	15	15	57⁴/₈	86	2

■ Buffalo Co. – Elmer F. Gotz – Elmer F. Gotz – 1973

241³/₈	29²/₈	25⁷/₈	19³/₈	22⁵/₈	5²/₈	5	9	11	43⁶/₈	107	3

■ Wisconsin – Unknown – Robert Kietzman – 1940

236³/₈	25⁶/₈	25⁶/₈	18⁴/₈	25⁵/₈	5⁶/₈	5⁶/₈	9	13	49¹/₈	161	4

■ Bayfield Co. – Unknown – Jean B. Schultz – 1998

233⁷/₈	27	26⁷/₈	21⁴/₈	30¹/₈	5⁵/₈	5³/₈	16	15	47¹/₈	183	5

■ Loraine – Homer Pearson – Bass Pro Shops – 1937

233⁵/₈	27⁴/₈	28¹/₈	19³/₈	24⁵/₈	4⁷/₈	4⁶/₈	11	17	48²/₈	190†	6†

■ Chippewa Co. – Russell W. Jones – Russell W. Jones – 2000

232	25⁶/₈	25	17	21⁴/₈	6	6	18	11	47	209	7

■ Waukesha Co. – John Herr, Sr. – Mac's Taxidermy – 1955

232	30¹/₈	30⁷/₈	18⁷/₈	22³/₈	5⁴/₈	5³/₈	11	8	28¹/₈	209	7

■ Barron Co. – Wayne F. Lindemans – Cabela's, Inc. – 1988

231⁵/₈	28¹/₈	26⁵/₈	19²/₈	26	5¹/₈	5¹/₈	11	11	39⁵/₈	214	9

■ Dane Co. – Dennis D. Shanks – Dennis D. Shanks – 1979

231²/₈	25⁶/₈	26³/₈	18⁴/₈	24⁴/₈	5	4⁷/₈	17	13	65⁶/₈	221	10

■ Forest Co. – Robert Jacobson – Robert Jacobson – 1958

230²/₈	30	30	23⁷/₈	28⁴/₈	5⁵/₈	5⁶/₈	9	13	37⁷/₈	235	11

■ Walworth Co. – F. Dan Dinelli – F. Dan Dinelli – 1992

230	25¹/₈	25²/₈	23⁷/₈	28⁶/₈	5⁵/₈	5⁴/₈	14	16	53⁷/₈	240	12

■ Bayfield Co. – Picked Up – Cabela's, Inc. – 1958

228²/₈	26⁶/₈	29²/₈	21	34²/₈	5²/₈	5²/₈	13	10	45²/₈	263	13

■ Cable – Charles Berg – Eva M. Fisher – 1910

227⁴/₈	25³/₈	25²/₈	18⁴/₈	25⁴/₈	6⁴/₈	6⁴/₈	16	17	65²/₈	270	14

■ Bayfield Co. – Earl Holt – Mrs. Earl Holt – 1934

227¹/₈	26	27³/₈	16³/₈	20⁴/₈	4⁶/₈	4⁶/₈	8	10	31	275	15

■ Clark Co. – Edward W. Schoen – Edward W. Schoen – 1955

227¹/₈	22	23⁴/₈	19	24⁷/₈	6	5¹/₈	15	13	59¹/₈	275	15

■ Dunn Co. – David D. Dewey – David D. Dewey – 1999

226⁶/₈	25⁵/₈	27⁴/₈	15⁵/₈	20⁴/₈	4⁷/₈	5²/₈	22	25	64³/₈	285	17

■ Rusk Co. – Joe Michalets – John R. Michalets – 1911

224⁴/₈	26	26³/₈	25⁶/₈	29⁶/₈	5⁶/₈	5⁶/₈	11	14	40	327	18

■ Rock Co. – Joseph T. Fisher – Joseph T. Fisher – 1988

223³/₈	30¹/₈	29²/₈	24	26¹/₈	5⁵/₈	5⁵/₈	12	12	40⁵/₈	354	19

■ Iron Co. – Parker E. Milewski – Parker E. Milewski – 1994

Score	Length of Main Beam Right Left	Inside Spread	Greatest Spread	Circumference at Smallest Place Between Burr and First Point Right Left	Number of Points Right Left	Lengths Abnormal Points	All-Time Rank	State Rank
	■ Location of Kill – Hunter – Owner – Date Killed							
222^6/8	24^4/8 23^4/8	17^7/8	22	5^4/8 5^6/8	8 8	25^1/8	371	20
■ Rusk Co. – Raymond Charlevois – Philip Schlegel – 1936								
224^4/8	25^4/8 23^6/8	21^1/8	27^2/8	5^3/8 5^2/8	14 11	55^1/8	378	21
■ Richland Co. – Janice K. Beranek – Janice K. Beranek – 1983								
220^7/8	27^6/8 27^7/8	22^6/8	27^5/8	5^6/8 5^7/8	9 11	52^7/8	417	22
■ Sauk Co. – Bryan J. McGann – Bryan J. McGann – 1986								
219^2/8	26 30^5/8	19^2/8	22^4/8	6^2/8 6^2/8	13 11	32	460	23
■ Buffalo Co. – Glenn Lehman – Glenn Lehman – 1958								
218^7/8	28^1/8 27^7/8	20	22^1/8	5^2/8 4^7/8	12 11	43^3/8	472	24
■ Florence Co. – W.C. Gotstein – Bass Pro Shops – 1914								
218^4/8	27 26^3/8	18^7/8	24	5^2/8 5^3/8	12 12	27^7/8	487	25
■ Sawyer Co. – Walter Kittleson – Walter Kittleson – 1920								
218^3/8	27 24^3/8	17	20	5^7/8 5^5/8	9 11	36^3/8	490	26
■ La Crosse Co. – Daniel P. Cavadini – D.J. Hollinger & B. Howard – 1951								
218^2/8	27 26^7/8	18^6/8	22^3/8	5^4/8 5^6/8	8 7	25	495	27
■ Waukesha Co. – Picked Up – WI Dept. of Natl. Resc. – 1986								
217^3/8	28^1/8 25^2/8	21^2/8	24^2/8	5^7/8 6^4/8	11 8	47^5/8	514†	28†
■ Douglas Co. – Unknown – Ross A. Manthey – 1939								
215^7/8	26^2/8 26^7/8	21^4/8	23^3/8	6 5^5/8	10 10	35^5/8	569	29
■ Eau Claire Co. – Dale G. Planert – Dale G. Planert – 1997								
215^3/8	29^4/8 28^6/8	23^7/8	28	5^6/8 5^6/8	8 8	37	587	30
■ Lafayette Co. – Roger Vickers – Roger Vickers – 1969								
215^2/8	25^6/8 25^1/8	16^6/8	21^6/8	5^6/8 5^5/8	11 14	25	589†	31†
■ La Crosse Co. – Mark R. Thorn – Mark R. Thorn – 2000								
215^1/8	24^4/8 26^2/8	19^3/8	27	6^7/8 7^2/8	13 11	38^2/8	593†	32†
■ Racine Co. – Mike T. Thelen – Mike T. Thelen – 2001								
214^3/8	25 25^1/8	15^3/8	17^4/8	5^2/8 5^3/8	11 10	21^2/8	620	33
■ Price Co. – Henry J. Copt – James A. Copt – 1926								
214^3/8	27^3/8 26	17^5/8	25^5/8	5 5	11 11	50^4/8	620	33
■ Bayfield Co. – Clarence Lauer – Mrs. Clarence Lauer – 1963								
213^7/8	25 25^3/8	18	24	5^5/8 5^7/8	17 12	52^7/8	635	35
■ Sawyer Co. – Charles Ross – Charles Ross – 1949								
213^5/8	23 23^7/8	16^2/8	27^6/8	6 6^1/8	10 12	67^5/8	649	36
■ Buffalo Co. – Norman C. Ratz – Ed Klink – 1968								
213^1/8	27^3/8 28^4/8	21^2/8	23^5/8	6^3/8 6	8 9	26^1/8	664†	37†
■ Buffalo Co. – Picked Up – Byron H. Hoch – 2000								
213^1/8	24^4/8 25	20^6/8	26^3/8	5^6/8 6^2/8	9 11	42^3/8	664	37
■ Milwaukee Co. – Picked Up – WI Dept. of Natl. Resc. – 1988								
212^7/8	30 23^3/8	21^1/8	26^4/8	5^2/8 5	7 12	30	674	39
■ Waukesha Co. – Max Mollgaard – Max Mollgaard – 1976								
211^7/8	27^6/8 27	18^6/8	25^5/8	5^5/8 5^6/8	12 8	28^7/8	724	40
■ Waukesha Co. – Patrick F. Cherone III – Patrick F. Cherone III – 1989								

Score	Length of Main Beam Right Left ■ Location of Kill – Hunter – Owner – Date Killed		Inside Spread	Greatest Spread	Circumference at Smallest Place Between Burr and First Point Right Left		Number of Points Right Left		Lengths Abnormal Points	All-Time Rank	State Rank
211⁶/8	26⁴/8	26⁵/8	18³/8	21⁵/8	5	5	10	8	29⁵/8	729	41
	■ Green Co. – Kevin W. Bouers – Kevin W. Bouers – 1999 ■ See photo on page 477										
211⁴/8	23²/8	23²/8	13⁶/8	21⁵/8	6²/8	5⁶/8	12	10	47⁶/8	739	42
	■ Dodge Co. – Michael A. Koehler – Michael A. Koehler – 1984										
211⁴/8	24⁵/8	24⁴/8	18³/8	22	5⁵/8	6²/8	10	12	38⁵/8	739	42
	■ Washington Co. – LeRoy Neu – LeRoy Neu – 1999										
211	27³/8	28⁴/8	22²/8	26²/8	6⁴/8	6³/8	10	11	29⁶/8	764	44
	■ Rock Co. – Kevin C. Viken – Kevin C. Viken – 1990										
210⁵/8	25⁷/8	27¹/8	20³/8	23	6	5⁴/8	7	7	24⁴/8	783	45
	■ Waukesha Co. – Gerald J. Roethle, Jr. – Gerald J. Roethle, Jr. – 1991										
210⁴/8	26⁷/8	25⁶/8	20	23	5¹/8	5¹/8	12	11	29⁴/8	791	46
	■ Dane Co. – LaVerne W. Marten – LaVerne W. Marten – 1970										
210³/8	28⁴/8	27⁴/8	21⁴/8	24¹/8	5	5¹/8	9	10	18¹/8	796	47
	■ Marinette Co. – George E. Bierstaker – Mrs. G.E. Bierstaker – 1947										
210²/8	28³/8	28³/8	23⁶/8	26⁶/8	5⁶/8	5⁵/8	12	7	33⁶/8	803	48
	■ Washburn Co. – Dennis Loreth – William H. Lilienthal – 1982										
210	26⁵/8	27²/8	17⁵/8	21⁷/8	5⁶/8	5⁶/8	13	9	21⁵/8	816	49
	■ Vilas Co. – Elmer T. Reise – John A. Kellett – 1940										
209⁷/8	24⁶/8	24²/8	18²/8	22⁴/8	4⁶/8	4⁴/8	11	13	49³/8	825	50
	■ Waupaca Co. – Ryan A. Thiel – Ryan A. Thiel – 1999										
209³/8	23⁵/8	21⁶/8	16⁶/8	21¹/8	4³/8	4⁴/8	11	10	39¹/8	852	51
	■ Grant Co. – Tim Yanna – Tim Yanna – 1982										
209³/8	24⁶/8	26⁶/8	20¹/8	25²/8	5¹/8	5	10	9	41²/8	852	51
	■ Racine Co. – Lon M. Swatek – Lon M. Swatek – 1994										
209¹/8	24¹/8	24	17³/8	21¹/8	5⁴/8	6	9	17	39⁴/8	863	53
	■ Waupaca Co. – Vince Burns II – Vince Burns II – 1999										
208⁵/8	27⁴/8	28	22	31	6	5⁷/8	10	8	34⁵/8	888	54
	■ Taylor Co. – Unknown – Mac's Taxidermy – PR 1945										
208⁵/8	27	26¹/8	20⁴/8	22⁶/8	5¹/8	5¹/8	8	8	18⁵/8	888	54
	■ Dunn Co. – Milburn Fleege – Brant J. Mueller – 1986										
208²/8	28⁶/8	24⁶/8	21⁴/8	26	5	5⁴/8	9	13	42⁴/8	910	56
	■ Price Co. – Robin J. Manning – Robin J. Manning – 1993										
207⁷/8	24⁴/8	23⁶/8	20³/8	24	5¹/8	5³/8	10	12	41⁴/8	938	57
	■ Fond du Lac Co. – Henry Theisen – Henry Theisen – 1956										
207⁵/8	29³/8	28⁶/8	19³/8	28²/8	5¹/8	4⁷/8	10	11	26⁴/8	957	58
	■ Ashland Co. – Carl W. Moebius, Sr. – Eric Moebius – 1934										
207⁵/8	24	23⁶/8	23⁶/8	25⁴/8	6³/8	6²/8	10	8	34³/8	957	58
	■ Buffalo Co. – Dennis M. Eberhart – Dennis M. Eberhart – 1984										
207⁵/8	26⁷/8	27⁶/8	21	24⁴/8	5²/8	5⁶/8	6	9	21¹/8	957	58
	■ Dane Co. – William L. Myhre, Jr. – William L. Myhre, Jr. – 1997										
207⁴/8	28⁷/8	27⁶/8	19⁵/8	21⁶/8	4⁷/8	4⁴/8	10	9	26³/8	969	61
	■ Barron Co. – Charles Slayton – Gordon Lee – PR 1920										

Score	Length of Main Beam Right	Left	Inside Spread	Greatest Spread	Circumference at Smallest Place Between Burr and First Point Right	Left	Number of Points Right	Left	Lengths Abnormal Points	All-Time Rank	State Rank
$207^4/_8$	$25^2/_8$	$24^6/_8$	$16^2/_8$	$20^4/_8$	$5^2/_8$	$5^2/_8$	12	11	54	969	61
■ Burnett Co. – Harold Miller – Mac's Taxidermy – 1938											
$207^3/_8$	$25^4/_8$	$25^6/_8$	$20^4/_8$	$22^2/_8$	$4^1/_8$	$4^3/_8$	8	12	$18^5/_8$	977	63
■ Langlade Co. – Henry L. Schewe – John R. Konkel – 1907											
$207^3/_8$	$25^7/_8$	$26^3/_8$	$17^4/_8$	$22^7/_8$	$6^2/_8$	$6^1/_8$	12	9	$35^3/_8$	977	63
■ Dane Co. – Todd J. DeForest – Todd J. DeForest – 1989											
$207^2/_8$	$26^3/_8$	$24^6/_8$	$19^5/_8$	$28^2/_8$	$5^2/_8$	$5^4/_8$	7	13	$40^3/_8$	985	65
■ Crawford Co. – Brent Swiggum – Brent Swiggum – 1991											
207	$23^4/_8$	$23^1/_8$	$18^4/_8$	26	$5^6/_8$	$6^4/_8$	16	13	69	1005	66
■ Bayfield Co. – Francis F. Zifko – Francis F. Zifko – 1954											
207	$26^3/_8$	$23^6/_8$	$18^4/_8$	$25^1/_8$	5	5	10	9	$25^6/_8$	1005	66
■ Walworth Co. – Kurt Mohrbacher – Kurt Mohrbacher – 1997											
$206^7/_8$	$26^7/_8$	$26^5/_8$	$18^6/_8$	$22^2/_8$	$5^1/_8$	$5^1/_8$	7	13	$34^7/_8$	1011†	68†
■ Crawford Co. – Thomas Oppriecht – Thomas Oppriecht – 2001											
$206^7/_8$	$24^3/_8$	25	$16^5/_8$	$22^4/_8$	$5^5/_8$	$5^3/_8$	14	9	$32^4/_8$	1011	68
■ Oneida Co. – Clarence Staudenmayer – Clarence Staudenmayer – 1942											
$206^7/_8$	$23^4/_8$	$25^5/_8$	$18^4/_8$	$24^6/_8$	$5^1/_8$	$4^7/_8$	14	12	$61^5/_8$	1011	68
■ Horicon Marsh – Picked Up – Ronald A. Lillge – 1966											
$206^7/_8$	$28^1/_8$	$27^1/_8$	$21^4/_8$	$26^1/_8$	$5^4/_8$	5	12	14	$47^1/_8$	1011	68
■ Dodge Co. – Steven J. Schultz – Steven J. Schultz – 1989											
$206^7/_8$	$23^7/_8$	25	$19^6/_8$	23	$5^4/_8$	$5^3/_8$	10	9	$34^3/_8$	1011	68
■ Douglas Co. – Neil R. Hagen – Neil R. Hagen – 1996											
$206^6/_8$	$26^7/_8$	27	$20^1/_8$	$23^2/_8$	5	5	7	10	$23^3/_8$	1028	73
■ Buffalo Co. – Monte R. Nichols – Monte R. Nichols – 1996											
$206^4/_8$	$24^6/_8$	$23^7/_8$	$18^1/_8$	$21^5/_8$	$5^3/_8$	$5^3/_8$	9	13	$46^7/_8$	1043†	74†
■ Chippewa Co. – Richard C. Bennesch – Richard C. Bennesch – 2000											
$206^1/_8$	$23^2/_8$	$22^5/_8$	22	$29^1/_8$	$5^4/_8$	$5^4/_8$	10	9	$43^5/_8$	1068	75
■ Lincoln Co. – Picked Up – Louis Pond – PR 1974											
$205^4/_8$	$26^6/_8$	$26^4/_8$	$19^6/_8$	$23^4/_8$	$6^3/_8$	$6^2/_8$	11	8	$17^2/_8$	1107	76
■ Dodge Co. – John Steckling – John Steckling – 1998											
$205^3/_8$	$25^3/_8$	$27^1/_8$	$22^2/_8$	$23^6/_8$	$4^1/_8$	$4^1/_8$	10	9	$28^1/_8$	1116	77
■ Trempealeau Co. – Dennis L. Ulberg – Dennis L. Ulberg – 1968											
205	$25^4/_8$	$25^4/_8$	$18^7/_8$	$26^1/_8$	4	$3^7/_8$	12	10	$40^5/_8$	1144	78
■ Marathon Co. – Joshua J. Erdman – Joshua J. Erdman – 1994											
$204^7/_8$	$26^3/_8$	$26^4/_8$	$21^4/_8$	$26^6/_8$	$4^5/_8$	$4^6/_8$	6	8	$18^5/_8$	1156	79
■ Trempealeau Co. – Ralph Klimek – Ralph Klimek – 1960											
$204^3/_8$	$23^4/_8$	24	$20^4/_8$	$28^7/_8$	$5^5/_8$	$5^6/_8$	10	12	$44^1/_8$	1186	80
■ Waukesha Co. – Unknown – Mac's Taxidermy – PR 1975											
$204^3/_8$	$23^5/_8$	$23^6/_8$	$18^5/_8$	22	$5^4/_8$	$6^2/_8$	8	10	53	1186	80
■ Waushara Co. – Debra A. Schmalzer – Debra A. Schmalzer – 1998											
$204^2/_8$	$28^3/_8$	$28^1/_8$	$18^4/_8$	$21^4/_8$	$4^7/_8$	5	11	11	$29^4/_8$	1199†	82†
■ Grant Co. – Michael M. White – Michael M. White – 2001											

Score	Length of Main Beam Right	Left	Inside Spread	Greatest Spread	Circumference at Smallest Place Between Burr and First Point Right	Left	Number of Points Right	Left	Lengths Abnormal Points	All-Time Rank	State Rank
$204\frac{1}{8}$	$25\frac{6}{8}$	$25\frac{7}{8}$	$18\frac{6}{8}$	$24\frac{7}{8}$	$3\frac{4}{8}$	$3\frac{5}{8}$	9	8	$37\frac{3}{8}$	1210	83

■ Dodge Co. – Wesley F. Braunschweig – Wesley F. Braunschweig – 1976

$204\frac{1}{8}$	$27\frac{1}{8}$	$26\frac{6}{8}$	21	$24\frac{1}{8}$	$6\frac{2}{8}$	$5\frac{6}{8}$	7	9	$31\frac{7}{8}$	1210	83

■ Crawford Co. – Francis J. Manning – Francis J. Manning – 1994

$203\frac{5}{8}$	$25\frac{5}{8}$	$24\frac{4}{8}$	$24\frac{1}{8}$	$26\frac{2}{8}$	$5\frac{6}{8}$	$5\frac{6}{8}$	9	9	$26\frac{4}{8}$	1248	85

■ Buffalo Co. – Ronald J. Jilot – Ronald J. Jilot – 1997 ■ See photo on page 59

$203\frac{3}{8}$	$22\frac{3}{8}$	$24\frac{1}{8}$	$17\frac{5}{8}$	$22\frac{5}{8}$	$4\frac{3}{8}$	$4\frac{4}{8}$	11	10	$34\frac{4}{8}$	1272†	86†

■ Monroe Co. – Darrell G. Schultz – Darrell G. Schultz – 2001

$203\frac{3}{8}$	25	$24\frac{2}{8}$	19	$25\frac{1}{8}$	$5\frac{1}{8}$	$4\frac{7}{8}$	10	13	$43\frac{1}{8}$	1272	86

■ Marquette Co. – Joseph E. Bell – Jeffrey L. Morgan – 1969

$203\frac{3}{8}$	23	$24\frac{1}{8}$	$20\frac{2}{8}$	$22\frac{5}{8}$	$6\frac{4}{8}$	$6\frac{2}{8}$	10	13	$33\frac{1}{8}$	1272	86

■ Dunn Co. – Terry J. Evenson – Terry J. Evenson – 1987

$203\frac{2}{8}$	$27\frac{1}{8}$	$26\frac{6}{8}$	$16\frac{6}{8}$	$19\frac{4}{8}$	$5\frac{6}{8}$	$5\frac{6}{8}$	10	10	$23\frac{6}{8}$	1287	89

■ Marinette Co. – Marvin E. Holmgren – Marvin E. Holmgren – 1986

$203\frac{1}{8}$	$26\frac{2}{8}$	26	$19\frac{4}{8}$	$21\frac{5}{8}$	5	$5\frac{1}{8}$	8	10	$29\frac{1}{8}$	1305	90

■ Lafayette Co. – Vernus Larson – Bass Pro Shops – 1995

$202\frac{7}{8}$	$25\frac{1}{8}$	$24\frac{2}{8}$	$23\frac{7}{8}$	$26\frac{4}{8}$	5	5	7	10	38	1327	91

■ Marinette Co. – Theodore Maes – Theodore Maes – 1932

$202\frac{5}{8}$	29	$29\frac{3}{8}$	$20\frac{6}{8}$	$22\frac{7}{8}$	$4\frac{7}{8}$	$4\frac{7}{8}$	10	9	$16\frac{1}{8}$	1346	92

■ Dane Co. – Ray S. Outhouse – Ray S. Outhouse – 1964

$202\frac{5}{8}$	$26\frac{2}{8}$	$26\frac{2}{8}$	19	$21\frac{5}{8}$	$4\frac{6}{8}$	$4\frac{6}{8}$	8	11	$25\frac{7}{8}$	1346	92

■ Columbia Co. – William M. Bletsch – William M. Bletsch – 1992

$202\frac{4}{8}$	$26\frac{5}{8}$	$27\frac{1}{8}$	$20\frac{6}{8}$	$24\frac{7}{8}$	6	$6\frac{1}{8}$	8	9	14	1355†	94†

■ Fond du Lac Co. – Warren Miller – Warren Miller – 2000

202	$26\frac{3}{8}$	27	$22\frac{5}{8}$	25	$6\frac{1}{8}$	$6\frac{1}{8}$	6	9	$21\frac{3}{8}$	1395	95

■ Bayfield Co. – Native American – Bass Pro Shops – 1960

$201\frac{5}{8}$	$25\frac{6}{8}$	$26\frac{2}{8}$	$19\frac{7}{8}$	$25\frac{6}{8}$	$5\frac{1}{8}$	$5\frac{1}{8}$	13	8	$38\frac{2}{8}$	1427	96

■ Sheboygan Co. – Darren T. Winter – Darren T. Winter – 1995

$201\frac{4}{8}$	$28\frac{4}{8}$	29	$21\frac{1}{8}$	23	6	$5\frac{7}{8}$	8	9	$14\frac{5}{8}$	1443	97

■ Dane Co. – Picked Up – Susan Clack – 1995

201	$26\frac{1}{8}$	25	$22\frac{5}{8}$	$25\frac{1}{8}$	$4\frac{6}{8}$	$4\frac{6}{8}$	10	7	$18\frac{5}{8}$	1500	98

■ Crawford Co. – Lloyd C. Rickleff – Lloyd C. Rickleff – 1989

$200\frac{7}{8}$	23	$23\frac{7}{8}$	19	26	$4\frac{7}{8}$	$4\frac{6}{8}$	11	9	$33\frac{1}{8}$	1512	99

■ Rusk Co. – Gerald Cleven – Gerald Cleven – 1963

$200\frac{7}{8}$	$23\frac{1}{8}$	$23\frac{7}{8}$	$19\frac{6}{8}$	$24\frac{1}{8}$	$4\frac{4}{8}$	$4\frac{2}{8}$	11	9	$27\frac{3}{8}$	1512	99

■ Langlade Co. – Jordan Halverson – Jordan Halverson – 1998

$200\frac{6}{8}$	$24\frac{1}{8}$	$24\frac{3}{8}$	$17\frac{6}{8}$	$21\frac{1}{8}$	5	5	11	9	45	1524	101

■ Juneau Co. – Anker Nelson – Bass Pro Shops – 1946

$200\frac{4}{8}$	26	28	16	$22\frac{2}{8}$	$5\frac{1}{8}$	$5\frac{5}{8}$	13	11	$31\frac{2}{8}$	1545†	102†

■ Menominee Co. – Michael G. Firgens – Michael G. Firgens – 2001

$200\frac{4}{8}$	$27\frac{4}{8}$	28	$21\frac{1}{8}$	27	$5\frac{4}{8}$	$5\frac{5}{8}$	9	6	$16\frac{1}{8}$	1545†	102†

■ Sawyer Co. – Gary A. Haus – Gary A. Haus – 2000

Score	Length of Main Beam Right	Length of Main Beam Left	Inside Spread	Greatest Spread	Circumference at Smallest Place Between Burr and First Point Right	Circumference at Smallest Place Between Burr and First Point Left	Number of Points Right	Number of Points Left	Lengths Abnormal Points	All-Time Rank	State Rank
200	$22\frac{7}{8}$	$21\frac{6}{8}$	$18\frac{4}{8}$	$23\frac{2}{8}$	5	$4\frac{7}{8}$	10	12	$48\frac{2}{8}$	1591†	104†
	■ Buffalo Co. – John E. Blanchar – John E. Blanchar – 2000										
$199\frac{7}{8}$	$24\frac{5}{8}$	24	$16\frac{6}{8}$	$20\frac{4}{8}$	$5\frac{2}{8}$	$5\frac{4}{8}$	10	12	$35\frac{5}{8}$	1607†	105†
	■ Vernon Co. – D. & K.D. McClurg – D. & K.D. McClurg – 2001										
$199\frac{6}{8}$	$24\frac{2}{8}$	$26\frac{2}{8}$	$20\frac{2}{8}$	26	$4\frac{5}{8}$	$4\frac{6}{8}$	11	9	$28\frac{4}{8}$	1613	106
	■ Crawford Co. – John M. Kane – John M. Kane – 1996										
$199\frac{5}{8}$	29	$27\frac{7}{8}$	$19\frac{4}{8}$	22	$6\frac{3}{8}$	$6\frac{1}{8}$	8	6	$15\frac{7}{8}$	1621	107
	■ Jefferson Co. – Jerome Stockheimer – Jerome Stockheimer – 1968										
$199\frac{4}{8}$	$25\frac{3}{8}$	$25\frac{4}{8}$	$21\frac{2}{8}$	25	$5\frac{1}{8}$	5	9	7	$19\frac{4}{8}$	1631†	108†
	■ Columbia Co. – Cameron L. Gramse – Cameron L. Gramse – 2001										
199	$22\frac{7}{8}$	21	$17\frac{7}{8}$	22	$5\frac{3}{8}$	5	13	7	$64\frac{7}{8}$	1668	109
	■ Clark Co. – George Mashin – Douglas Wampole – 1946										
199	$23\frac{7}{8}$	$23\frac{7}{8}$	18	$20\frac{2}{8}$	$4\frac{4}{8}$	$4\frac{3}{8}$	8	9	$39\frac{4}{8}$	1668	109
	■ Crawford Co. – Jeff Sheckler – Jeff Sheckler – 1989										
199	$26\frac{1}{8}$	$25\frac{7}{8}$	$19\frac{7}{8}$	$23\frac{1}{8}$	$4\frac{5}{8}$	$4\frac{4}{8}$	6	8	$25\frac{1}{8}$	1668	109
	■ Vernon Co. – Manuel M. Bahr – Manuel M. Bahr – 1995										
$198\frac{6}{8}$	$25\frac{1}{8}$	$27\frac{4}{8}$	$15\frac{4}{8}$	$18\frac{1}{8}$	5	5	10	8	$24\frac{2}{8}$	1697	112
	■ Buffalo Co. – Rod Buck – Rod Buck – 1984										
$198\frac{6}{8}$	$25\frac{5}{8}$	$24\frac{7}{8}$	$19\frac{3}{8}$	$21\frac{6}{8}$	$4\frac{7}{8}$	$4\frac{7}{8}$	10	8	$19\frac{1}{8}$	1697	112
	■ Jefferson Co. – Picked Up – Wayne Perry – 1989										
$198\frac{6}{8}$	$26\frac{5}{8}$	$26\frac{3}{8}$	20	$23\frac{6}{8}$	$5\frac{6}{8}$	$5\frac{4}{8}$	9	9	$24\frac{6}{8}$	1697	112
	■ Buffalo Co. – Brady Weiss – Brady Weiss – 1993										
$198\frac{6}{8}$	$28\frac{3}{8}$	$27\frac{4}{8}$	$23\frac{4}{8}$	$25\frac{4}{8}$	$6\frac{1}{8}$	$6\frac{2}{8}$	7	7	21	1697	112
	■ Rock Co. – Robert D. Adamson – Robert D. Adamson – 1995										
$198\frac{5}{8}$	$24\frac{2}{8}$	$24\frac{2}{8}$	$17\frac{7}{8}$	$20\frac{4}{8}$	$5\frac{4}{8}$	$6\frac{4}{8}$	9	15	27	1716	116
	■ Hayward – Unknown – Harold Burrows – PR 1920										
$198\frac{5}{8}$	$25\frac{3}{8}$	$25\frac{2}{8}$	$23\frac{2}{8}$	$25\frac{4}{8}$	5	5	10	10	$33\frac{7}{8}$	1716	116
	■ Oconto Co. – Paul M. Krueger – Paul M. Krueger – 1977										
$198\frac{4}{8}$	26	$26\frac{4}{8}$	21	$27\frac{1}{8}$	$4\frac{4}{8}$	$4\frac{6}{8}$	13	9	$24\frac{2}{8}$	1736	118
	■ Forest Co. – John Lehner – Eric Lehner – 1946										
$198\frac{2}{8}$	$25\frac{5}{8}$	$24\frac{7}{8}$	$16\frac{6}{8}$	$21\frac{2}{8}$	$5\frac{2}{8}$	$5\frac{3}{8}$	11	10	$29\frac{4}{8}$	1772†	119†
	■ Marinette Co. – Stephen R. Couveau – Stephen R. Couveau – 2001										
$198\frac{1}{8}$	$27\frac{5}{8}$	$26\frac{5}{8}$	21	24	$6\frac{1}{8}$	6	7	9	$21\frac{1}{8}$	1785†	120†
	■ Jefferson Co. – Charles E. Emery – Charles E. Emery – 2001										
$198\frac{1}{8}$	$26\frac{3}{8}$	$26\frac{6}{8}$	$22\frac{6}{8}$	$25\frac{3}{8}$	$5\frac{3}{8}$	$5\frac{4}{8}$	12	10	$29\frac{1}{8}$	1785	120
	■ Iron Co. – Ben Benzine – Timothy C. Ashley – 1968										
$197\frac{5}{8}$	$22\frac{7}{8}$	$25\frac{4}{8}$	$17\frac{7}{8}$	$23\frac{7}{8}$	$4\frac{6}{8}$	$4\frac{6}{8}$	11	8	$46\frac{4}{8}$	1847	122
	■ Sawyer Co. – Unknown – Brant J. Mueller – 1940										
$197\frac{5}{8}$	$24\frac{4}{8}$	$24\frac{1}{8}$	$20\frac{3}{8}$	24	$6\frac{2}{8}$	$5\frac{1}{8}$	7	11	41	1847	122
	■ Sawyer Co. – James P. Borman – James P. Borman – 1945										
$197\frac{5}{8}$	$23\frac{3}{8}$	$23\frac{4}{8}$	$15\frac{6}{8}$	19	$5\frac{7}{8}$	$5\frac{6}{8}$	10	9	$23\frac{5}{8}$	1847	122
	■ Marathon Co. – Boots Greiner – Todd Rheinschmidt – 1951										

Score	Length of Main Beam Right / Left	Inside Spread	Greatest Spread	Circumference at Smallest Place Between Burr and First Point Right / Left	Number of Points Right / Left	Lengths Abnormal Points	All-Time Rank	State Rank
197 5/8	26 5/8 27	20 5/8	23	5 2/8 5 2/8	10 8	14 4/8	1847	122
Pierce Co. – Charles L. Wilkinson – Marilyn Wilkinson – 1993								
197 4/8	26 5/8 25	19 6/8	25	5 5/8 6 3/8	8 9	17 2/8	1866	126
Buffalo Co. – Dennis L. Mackeben – Dennis L. Mackeben – 1995								
197 3/8	24 4/8 22 4/8	18 6/8	21 2/8	6 2/8 5 7/8	9 12	29 5/8	1884	127
Buffalo Co. – Walter Mengelt – Timothy W. Trones – 1957								
197 3/8	26 3/8 26 7/8	17 3/8	20 2/8	5 1/8 5 2/8	10 12	19	1884	127
Douglas Co. – Unknown – Wayne G. Nevar – PR 1988								
197 3/8	23 5/8 24 2/8	18 2/8	24 7/8	5 5/8 5 5/8	10 12	26 3/8	1884	127
Iowa Co. – Luke J. Leiterman – Luke J. Leiterman – 1998								
197 2/8	23 5/8 23 7/8	23 1/8	26 4/8	5 5	14 9	39 1/8	1901†	130†
Vilas Co. – Unknown – Ross A. Manthey – 1943								
197 2/8	26 2/8 26 6/8	20	23 6/8	5 2/8 5 1/8	10 7	21 6/8	1901	130
Iron Co. – Unknown – Henry C. Gilbertson – PR 1940								
197	28 2/8 28 2/8	19 5/8	21 4/8	5 6/8 5 4/8	7 7	15 7/8	1939	132
Bayfield Co. – Larry M. Nyhus – Larry M. Nyhus – 1997								
196 7/8	26 5/8 26 5/8	19 2/8	21 6/8	5 1/8 5 3/8	7 8	17 7/8	1950	133
Pepin Co. – Jerry R. Breitung – Jerry R. Breitung – 1985								
196 7/8	27 5/8 28 4/8	24 1/8	28 3/8	5 2/8 5 7/8	8 8	16 6/8	1950	133
Shawano Co. – Robert D. Little – Robert D. Little – 1998								
196 6/8	22 2/8 22 5/8	17 5/8	21 6/8	5 5	8 8	18 1/8	1968	135
Vilas Co. – Joe Wilfer – Rick Iacono – 1934								
196 5/8	26 5/8 25 7/8	23 6/8		5 5/8 5 7/8	10 10	29 7/8	1985	136
Buffalo Co. – Bill Black, Sr. – Tom Black – 1956								
196 5/8	30 2/8 30 3/8	20 5/8	23	5 6/8 5 6/8	9 7	14 2/8	1985	136
Langlade Co. – Thomas G. Jahnke – Thomas G. Jahnke – 1990								
196 4/8	28 1/8 27	19 7/8	22 3/8	4 2/8 4 2/8	6 8	18 3/8	1999	138
Buffalo Co. – Scott T. Beach – Scott T. Beach – 1996								
196 3/8	22 4/8 23	23 6/8	26 4/8	6 3/8 6	10 11	42 7/8	2010	139
Dunn Co. – Unknown – Cabela's, Inc. – PR 1940								
196 3/8	26 2/8 25 7/8	18 3/8	20 6/8	4 4/8 4 5/8	11 8	24 2/8	2010	139
Price Co. – John R. Lemke – John R. Lemke – 1986								
196 2/8	23 4/8 24 3/8	16 4/8	20 3/8	6 1/8 5 6/8	7 9	19 4/8	2028†	141†
Pierce Co. – Mark P. Dolan – Mark P. Dolan – 2001								
196	25 24 2/8	20	22 3/8	4 6/8 4 6/8	8 8	13 6/8	2059	142
Forest Co. – Aaron E. Huettl – Aaron E. Huettl – 1939								
196	27 7/8 26 2/8	15 4/8	21 3/8	5 2/8 5 2/8	12 15	44	2059	142
Marinette Co. – Joseph Braun – Brant J. Mueller – 1940								
196	26 4/8 25 6/8	18 7/8	21 2/8	5 5 2/8	6 7	22 3/8	2059	142
Buffalo Co. – William A. Gatzlaff – William A. Gatzlaff – 1970								
196	24 24 4/8	18 5/8	25	4 6/8 4 5/8	10 7	28 5/8	2059	142
Richland Co. – Picked Up – Jeff DuCharme – 1992								

Location of Kill – Hunter – Owner – Date Killed

Score	Length of Main Beam		Inside Spread	Greatest Spread	Circumference at Smallest Place Between Burr and First Point		Number of Points		Lengths Abnormal Points	All-Time Rank	State Rank
	Right	Left			Right	Left	Right	Left			
	■ Location of Kill – Hunter – Owner – Date Killed										
195 7/8	26	27	20 4/8	22 4/8	5 2/8	5 2/8	10	8	15 5/8	2076†	146†
	■ Florence Co. – E.J. Nichols – Barbara R. Bowman – PR 1940										
195 7/8	27 1/8	25 2/8	20 2/8	23 2/8	5 2/8	5 2/8	11	10	18 7/8	2076	146
	■ Grant Co. – Roger Derrickson – Roger Derrickson – 1973										
195 6/8	28 2/8	29 5/8	16 4/8	26	5 4/8	5 6/8	7	8	41	2094	148
	■ Douglas Co. – Unknown – Buckhorn of Gordon, Inc. – PR 1970										
195 6/8	23 6/8	25	18 2/8	24 4/8	5 4/8	5 4/8	12	8	34 6/8	2094	148
	■ Vernon Co. – William T. Newman – William T. Newman – 1997										
195 6/8	29 1/8	29	21 3/8	24 7/8	5 1/8	4 7/8	7	8	22 7/8	2094	148
	■ Pierce Co. – Jody M. Anderson – Jody M. Anderson – 1998										
195 5/8	23 2/8	22 2/8	19 2/8	21 5/8	4 4/8	4 4/8	12	10	23 5/8	2116	151
	■ Florence Co. – Joseph R. Szczepanski, Jr. – Terry J. Baranczyk – PR 1945										
195 4/8	24 2/8	24 1/8	18 4/8	22	4 6/8	4 6/8	10	9	25 2/8	2134†	152†
	■ Door Co. – Robert F. Meingast – Robert F. Meingast – 2002										
195 4/8	24	23 5/8	21 2/8	25 2/8	4 7/8	5 1/8	14	9	39 2/8	2134	152
	■ Wisconsin – Unknown – Brant J. Mueller – PR 1942										
195 4/8	24 7/8	25 1/8	20	22 7/8	5 1/8	4 7/8	10	10	38 4/8	2134	152
	■ Eau Claire Co. – Sylvester Champa – Sylvester Champa – 1959										
195 3/8	26 1/8	24 2/8	18	21	5 1/8	5 1/8	7	11	26 7/8	2163†	155†
	■ Outagamie Co. – Michael S. Schernick – Michael S. Schernick – 2000										
195 3/8	27 4/8	26 7/8	22 3/8	24 4/8	5 1/8	5	7	6	14 4/8	2163	155
	■ Dane Co. – Gaylord N. Denner – Gaylord N. Denner – 1995										
195 3/8	25 2/8	25 2/8	20 5/8	26	4 6/8	4 5/8	7	7	17 6/8	2163	155
	■ Rock Co. – Dennis A. Losey – Dennis A. Losey – 1995										
195 3/8	28 2/8	27 2/8	22 1/8	25 2/8	5 4/8	5 3/8	8	8	12 4/8	2163	155
	■ Pierce Co. – Jesse W. Sullivan – Jesse W. Sullivan – 1999										
195 2/8	26	24 6/8	19 2/8	21 4/8	6 2/8	6 3/8	9	9	19 4/8	2186	159
	■ Rusk Co. – Alexander King – Roger King – 1890										
195 2/8	28 4/8	27 2/8	20 5/8	24 4/8	4 7/8	4 6/8	11	8	15 3/8	2186	159
	■ Du Charme Coulee – Eugene E. Morovitz – Eugene E. Morovitz – 1959										
195 2/8	23 7/8	24 4/8	16 3/8	21 4/8	5	5	17	13	45 1/8	2186	159
	■ Dodge Co. – Michael Peirick – Michael Peirick – 1999										
195 1/8	27 2/8	27 6/8	20 7/8	28	5 5/8	5 2/8	7	7	23 2/8	2208	162
	■ Buffalo Co. – Maynard Trones – Maynard Trones – 1958										
195 1/8	26	27	21 5/8	26	4 5/8	4 6/8	8	7	17 4/8	2208	162
	■ Polk Co. – Michael J. Wilson – Michael J. Wilson – 1992										
195 1/8	27	26 5/8	17 3/8	24 2/8	5 4/8	5 6/8	7	8	23 2/8	2208	162
	■ Ashland Co. – Jerry M. Anderson – Jerry M. Anderson – 1995										
195 1/8	23 3/8	25 3/8	22 2/8	26	6 2/8	6	14	7	37 7/8	2208	162
	■ Buffalo Co. – Michael J. Barstad – Michael J. Barstad – 1999										
195	24	24	20 2/8	22 4/8	4 7/8	4 6/8	9	8	26 6/8	2233	166
	■ Rusk Co. – Jon R. Lane – Jon R. Lane – 1993										

Score	Length of Main Beam		Inside Spread	Greatest Spread	Circumference at Smallest Place Between Burr and First Point		Number of Points		Lengths Abnormal Points	All-Time Rank	State Rank
	Right	Left			Right	Left	Right	Left			
	■ Location of Kill – Hunter – Owner – Date Killed										
195	24¹/₈	23⁵/₈	15⁷/₈	20³/₈	5	5²/₈	7	9	36³/₈	2233	166
	■ Bayfield Co. – Bradley A. Kuhnert – Bradley A. Kuhnert – 1994										
195	24⁷/₈	24⁴/₈	19⁵/₈	22²/₈	5⁵/₈	5¹/₈	9	8	21⁷/₈	2233	166
	■ Marquette Co. – Donald E. Voskuil – Donald E. Voskuil – 1994										
194⁶/₈	27⁶/₈	27²/₈	19⁵/₈	22²/₈	5	5³/₈	8	7	15⁵/₈	2262†	169†
	■ Iowa Co. – Mark A. Klosterman – Mark A. Klosterman – 2000										
194⁵/₈	27⁶/₈	28³/₈	20¹/₈	22⁶/₈	5⁶/₈	5⁵/₈	7	10	27	2263†	170†
	■ Walworth Co. – Michael R. Senft – Michael R. Senft – 2000										
194¹/₈	24⁴/₈	24²/₈	19⁵/₈	22⁵/₈	4⁷/₈	5	8	7	17⁴/₈	2271	171
	■ Portage Co. – Wendell A. Krogwold – Wendell A. Krogwold – 1950										
193⁵/₈	24⁶/₈	24⁷/₈	21⁶/₈	24³/₈	5⁴/₈	5⁵/₈	7	8	19⁷/₈	2281	172
	■ Vilas Co. – Unknown – Charles Glut – PR 1900										
193⁵/₈	27⁵/₈	28³/₈	25²/₈	27³/₈	4⁵/₈	4⁷/₈	6	9	21⁷/₈	2281	172
	■ Bayfield Co. – Mark Kinney – Mark Kinney – 1999										
193⁴/₈	26	26⁶/₈	17⁶/₈	23²/₈	5⁵/₈	5⁷/₈	9	10	34⁶/₈	2288†	174†
	■ Dane Co. – Aaron G. Tachon – Aaron G. Tachon – 2000										
193⁴/₈	26⁵/₈	25¹/₈	16¹/₈	22	5¹/₈	4⁷/₈	9	13	27¹/₈	2288	174
	■ Juneau Co. – Maurice Sterba – Maurice Sterba – 1955										
193	24¹/₈	22⁷/₈	20	22²/₈	6⁵/₈	7²/₈	6	7	19⁶/₈	2310†	176†
	■ Outagamie Co. – James C. Snortum – James C. Snortum – 2001										
192⁶/₈	24¹/₈	24¹/₈	20⁵/₈	23	5⁷/₈	5⁷/₈	7	9	26⁷/₈	2317	177
	■ Waukesha Co. – Curt Samanske – Curt Samanske – 1998										
192⁵/₈	24⁵/₈	25⁷/₈	17	22⁷/₈	5⁴/₈	5²/₈	10	8	15⁷/₈	2322	178
	■ Bayfield Co. – Donald R. Lahti – Donald R. Lahti – 1994										
192⁴/₈	25⁴/₈	26¹/₈	19¹/₈	21¹/₈	4⁶/₈	4⁷/₈	7	7	15³/₈	2325†	179†
	■ Buffalo Co. – Dale G. Hoch – Dale G. Hoch – 2000										
192³/₈	25¹/₈	24⁷/₈	17⁶/₈	20¹/₈	5	4⁷/₈	10	7	39¹/₈	2331	180
	■ Lafayette Co. – Thomas W. Waldman – Thomas W. Waldman – 1991										
191⁷/₈	25⁷/₈	25⁴/₈	16²/₈	18³/₈	4⁶/₈	4⁶/₈	11	9	17⁵/₈	2351	181
	■ Florence Co. – Lloyd Conger – Lloyd Conger – 1959										
191¹/₈	21⁶/₈	23⁵/₈	16²/₈	22⁴/₈	4⁴/₈	4²/₈	10	10	44⁷/₈	2374	182
	■ Fond du Lac Co. – Alan H. Woods – Alan H. Woods – 1999										
191	26⁵/₈	26	22	24⁷/₈	5	5³/₈	5	10	15⁶/₈	2380	183
	■ Bayfield Co. – William M. Larson – William M. Larson – 1977										
190⁶/₈	24⁷/₈	23⁵/₈	18²/₈	20³/₈	4³/₈	4¹/₈	7	11	17⁴/₈	2390	184
	■ Marathon Co. – August F. Bisping – Brian R. Bisping – 1945										
190⁶/₈	25⁶/₈	25²/₈	20³/₈	22⁶/₈	5	5²/₈	11	8	23⁵/₈	2390	184
	■ Crawford Co. – James A. Moore – James A. Moore – 1997										
190⁵/₈	23¹/₈	22	17²/₈	21⁷/₈	4⁴/₈	4³/₈	12	11	34⁵/₈	2393	186
	■ Outagamie Co. – Gerald J. Schmidt – Gerald J. Schmidt – 1996										
190⁴/₈	25⁵/₈	25⁶/₈	20²/₈	22⁷/₈	4⁵/₈	4⁵/₈	9	9	17²/₈	2401	187
	■ Dane Co. – Dean E. Goecks – Dean E. Goecks – 1995										

Score	Length of Main Beam Right	Left	Inside Spread	Greatest Spread	Circumference at Smallest Place Between Burr and First Point Right	Left	Number of Points Right	Left	Lengths Abnormal Points	All-Time Rank	State Rank
	■ Location of Kill – Hunter – Owner – Date Killed										
190 3/8	22 7/8	22 7/8	16 4/8	19 2/8	4 3/8	4 3/8	7	8	28 1/8	2408	188
	■ Shawano Co. – Scott W. Pludeman – Scott W. Pludeman – 1996										
189 5/8	27 3/8	28 2/8	22 1/8	25 6/8	4 7/8	4 7/8	8	8	13 4/8	2429	189
	■ Buffalo Co. – Cyril Mathis – Cyril Mathis – 1986										
189 4/8	27 5/8	27 5/8	20	22	5 6/8	5 7/8	7	11	19 2/8	2435	190
	■ Iron Co. – Bryan L. Bellows – Bryan L. Bellows – 1994										
189	24 4/8	24 5/8	21 1/8	22 7/8	4 6/8	4 4/8	7	9	19 5/8	2456	191
	■ Polk Co. – James T. Polski – James T. Polski – 1995										
189	25 3/8	24 6/8	17 4/8	20 4/8	5 4/8	5 1/8	9	8	26 2/8	2456	191
	■ Waushara Co. – Anthony E. O'Kon – Anthony E. O'Kon – 1999										
188 4/8	25 3/8	29 3/8	19	22 5/8	5 1/8	5	11	7	25	2475	193
	■ Bayfield Co. – Henry Schmidt – Jeffery Schmidt – 1939										
188 3/8	23 4/8	21 6/8	17 2/8	19 5/8	4 3/8	5	8	10	44 7/8	2478†	194†
	■ Sawyer Co. – James H. Tiffany – James H. Tiffany – 2000										
187 6/8	24 7/8	26 2/8	18 6/8	21 1/8	5 1/8	4 7/8	6	9	14	2512	195
	■ Vernon Co. – George E. Briggs – George E. Briggs – 1993										
187 3/8	23 2/8	23 1/8	17 1/8	20 4/8	4 5/8	4 3/8	11	10	31 2/8	2528	196
	■ Vernon Co. – Darrell A. Bendel – Darrell A. Bendel – 1986										
187 2/8	25 3/8	25 5/8	22 5/8	25 4/8	5 3/8	5 2/8	9	9	14 1/8	2534	197
	■ Langlade Co. – Carl J. McIlquham – Carl J. McIlquham – 1988										
187 1/8	26 4/8	28 2/8	19 6/8	24	5 2/8	5 3/8	8	9	21 5/8	2540	198
	■ Oneida Co. – Dean F. Look – Dean F. Look – 1989										
187	26 3/8	26 7/8	17 6/8	20 1/8	5 3/8	5 3/8	9	9	18 4/8	2545†	199†
	■ Jackson Co. – Jamie E. Peterson – Jamie E. Peterson – 2000										
186 7/8	24 5/8	25	16 1/8	18 4/8	4 6/8	4 5/8	11	9	21 2/8	2550	200
	■ Douglas Co. – Neil Lagro – Neil Lagro – 1982										
186 7/8	26 4/8	24 4/8	20	22 4/8	5 5/8	5 3/8	5	9	14 7/8	2550	200
	■ Waupaca Co. – Patrick M. Bailey – Patrick M. Bailey – 1995										
186 5/8	25 6/8	22 4/8	19	24	6 7/8	7 5/8	12	10	58 1/8	2565	202
	■ Outagamie Co. – Picked Up – Chad Schroeder – 1998										
186 2/8	25 2/8	24 2/8	18 3/8	20	5	4 7/8	10	6	24 1/8	2575†	203†
	■ Shawano Co. – Nathan Morris – Nathan Morris – 2000										
186 2/8	25 7/8	25 4/8	17 7/8	20 5/8	5 5/8	5 4/8	7	7	20 5/8	2575	203
	■ Washington Co. – Ronald L. Schneider – Ronald L. Schneider – 1996										
186	21 5/8	23 4/8	16 3/8	23	5 4/8	5 4/8	13	12	46 5/8	2586	205
	■ Marinette Co. – James Sanborn – Michael Brissette – PR 1945										
185 5/8	25 6/8	26	20	22	4 4/8	4 4/8	7	9	11 7/8	2610	206
	■ Lincoln Co. – Fred H. Storm – Fred H. Storm – 1977										
185 5/8	21 7/8	19 7/8	19	22	5 7/8	5 6/8	7	10	45 7/8	2610	206
	■ Forest Co. – Earl V. Conradt – Earl V. Conradt – 1988										
185 2/8	25	25	17 3/8	24 3/8	5 5/8	5 2/8	8	9	21 1/8	2632	208
	■ Buffalo Co. – Gale E. Zich – Gale E. Zich – 1995										

Score	Length of Main Beam Right Left	Inside Spread	Greatest Spread	Circumference at Smallest Place Between Burr and First Point Right Left		Number of Points Right Left		Lengths Abnormal Points	All-Time Rank	State Rank
	■ *Location of Kill – Hunter – Owner – Date Killed*									
185 1/8	24 26 5/8	16 5/8	19	5 1/8	5 4/8	11	9	14	2641	209
	■ *Bayfield Co. – Charles Hermansen – Donald D. Ash – 1914*									
185 1/8	26 4/8 24 1/8	23 3/8	24 3/8	4 7/8	4 7/8	7	8	15 4/8	2641	209
	■ *Columbia Co. – Wilfred Alt – Wilfred Alt – 1997*									
185 1/8	26 3/8 27 2/8	21	25 6/8	5 2/8	5 1/8	7	8	20 5/8	2641	209
	■ *Rock Co. – Lawrence O. Stomprude – Lawrence O. Stomprude – 1998*									
185	24 3/8 23 2/8	20 1/8	24	4 4/8	4 4/8	7	10	23 3/8	2653†	212†
	■ *Lincoln Co. – Ryan K. Stebnitz – Ryan K. Stebnitz – 2001*									
185	28 7/8 28 6/8	18 5/8	21	5 6/8	5 6/8	6	6	10 5/8	2653	212
	■ *Buffalo Co. – Chad R. Cook – Chad R. Cook – 1994*									

† The scores and ranking for trophies from the 25th Awards Entry Period are not final until the banquet is held on June 19, 2004.

518   **RECORDS OF NORTH AMERICAN WHITETAIL DEER ■ FOURTH EDITION**

TROPHIES IN THE FIELD

HUNTER: Arnold N. Stalsberg
SCORE: 247-3/8
CATEGORY: non-typical whitetail deer
LOCATION: Vernon County, Wisconsin
DATE: 1998

WYOMING
RECORD WHITETAILS

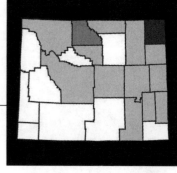

10 Typical whitetail deer entries
22 Non-typical whitetail deer entries
7,265 Total whitetail deer entries

0 Entries
1-2 Entries
3-5 Entries
6-10 Entries
11+ Entries

WYOMING
STATE RECORD
Typical Whitetail Deer
Score: 191$^5/_8$
Location: Albany Co.
Hunter and Owner: Robert D. Ross
Date: 1986

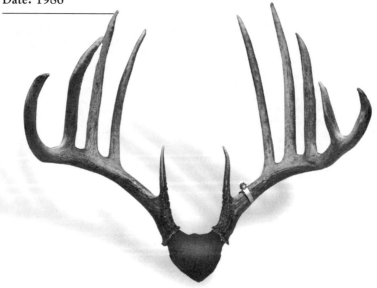

WYOMING
STATE RECORD
Non-Typical Whitetail Deer
Score: 238$^7/_8$
Location: Crook Co.
Hunter: Picked Up
Owner: J.D. Andrews
Date: 1962

WYOMING

TYPICAL WHITETAIL DEER

Score	Length of Main Beam Right Left	Inside Spread	Greatest Spread	Circumference at Smallest Place Between Burr and First Point Right Left		Number of Points Right Left		Lengths Abnormal Points	All-Time Rank	State Rank
	■ *Location of Kill – Hunter – Owner – Date Killed*									
191⁵/₈	25⁵/₈ 25	22⁷/₈	25⁶/₈	4³/₈	4⁴/₈	5	6		78	1
	■ *Albany Co. – Robert D. Ross – Robert D. Ross – 1986*									
177¹/₈	25⁵/₈ 26¹/₈	19	21⁵/₈	5¹/₈	5²/₈	7	10	9¹/₈	1048	2
	■ *Newcastle – H.W. Julien – H.W. Julien – 1954*									
176²/₈	24⁵/₈ 23¹/₈	15⁶/₈	18²/₈	6	6²/₈	7	7		1209	3
	■ *Converse Co. – Basil C. Bradbury – Basil C. Bradbury – 1990*									
174³/₈	25²/₈ 25³/₈	20¹/₈	23¹/₈	4⁵/₈	4⁶/₈	5	5		1619	4
	■ *Goshen Co. – Casey L. Hunter – Casey L. Hunter – 1984*									
173	27 26	20¹/₈	22²/₈	4¹/₈	4²/₈	6	7	6³/₈	1991	5
	■ *Big Horn Co. – Daniel D. Wood – Daniel D. Wood – 1989*									
173	24 25²/₈	18⁶/₈	21	4⁶/₈	4⁵/₈	5	6	2	1991	5
	■ *Sheridan Co. – Robert G. Green – Robert G. Green – 1991*									
171⁶/₈	23⁶/₈ 24	20	22³/₈	5⁴/₈	5⁴/₈	5	5		2418	7
	■ *Big Horn Co. – Thomas D. Dixon – Thomas D. Dixon – 1998*									
170⁵/₈	24²/₈ 23⁶/₈	23³/₈	25⁴/₈	3⁷/₈	3⁷/₈	6	5		2876	8
	■ *Crook Co. – Rick Shannon – Rick Shannon – 1991*									
170³/₈	23¹/₈ 23²/₈	19⁵/₈	21²/₈	4⁶/₈	4⁵/₈	6	6		2992	9
	■ *Niobrara Co. – Joseph A. Perry III – Joseph A. Perry III – 1985*									
170²/₈	25 24³/₈	18²/₈	20⁶/₈	5	5	5	5		3063	10
	■ *Platte Co. – Johnny Wehrmann – Johnny Wehrmann – 1992*									

WYOMING

NON-TYPICAL WHITETAIL DEER

Score	Length of Main Beam Right	Left	Inside Spread	Greatest Spread	Circumference at Smallest Place Between Burr and First Point Right	Left	Number of Points Right	Left	Lengths Abnormal Points	All-Time Rank	State Rank
$238\frac{7}{8}$	$22\frac{4}{8}$	$21\frac{6}{8}$	$18\frac{1}{8}$	$21\frac{4}{8}$	5	$5\frac{2}{8}$	17	15	68	129	1
■ Crook Co. – Picked Up – J.D. Andrews – 1962											
$224\frac{1}{8}$	25	$24\frac{7}{8}$	$19\frac{6}{8}$	$28\frac{2}{8}$	$4\frac{5}{8}$	$4\frac{3}{8}$	12	13	$37\frac{5}{8}$	334	2
■ Crook Co. – John S. Mahoney – John S. Mahoney – 1947											
$217\frac{7}{8}$	24	$22\frac{4}{8}$	$21\frac{1}{8}$	$23\frac{4}{8}$	$5\frac{3}{8}$	$7\frac{6}{8}$	8	20	$55\frac{6}{8}$	499	3
■ Washakie Co. – Kenneth A. Fossum – Kenneth A. Fossum – 1991											
$217\frac{3}{8}$	$22\frac{7}{8}$	$23\frac{6}{8}$	13	21	$4\frac{6}{8}$	$4\frac{6}{8}$	10	11	$54\frac{5}{8}$	514	4
■ Weston Co. – Harry Phillips – Harry Phillips – 1957											
$214\frac{7}{8}$	$21\frac{3}{8}$	$23\frac{1}{8}$	$12\frac{4}{8}$	$16\frac{7}{8}$	$5\frac{6}{8}$	$4\frac{6}{8}$	12	12	$76\frac{3}{8}$	605	5
■ Big Horn Co. – Michael K. Smith – Michael K. Smith – 1987											
$214\frac{2}{8}$	$24\frac{6}{8}$	$25\frac{3}{8}$	$20\frac{4}{8}$	$22\frac{7}{8}$	$6\frac{4}{8}$	$6\frac{2}{8}$	8	8	$33\frac{6}{8}$	625	6
■ Crook Co. – Clinton Berry – Clinton Berry – 1953											
$211\frac{7}{8}$	22	$23\frac{2}{8}$	$21\frac{4}{8}$	$24\frac{6}{8}$	$4\frac{4}{8}$	$4\frac{4}{8}$	15	15	$45\frac{1}{8}$	724	7
■ Crook Co. – Curtis U. Nelson – Curtis U. Nelson – 1971											
$209\frac{3}{8}$	$24\frac{2}{8}$	$24\frac{2}{8}$	$17\frac{1}{8}$	$19\frac{3}{8}$	$4\frac{4}{8}$	$4\frac{4}{8}$	13	10	$39\frac{4}{8}$	852	8
■ Crook Co. – Roy H. Lubbert – Murphy's Tavern – 1967											
$208\frac{6}{8}$	$27\frac{1}{8}$	$26\frac{6}{8}$	$20\frac{4}{8}$	23	$5\frac{3}{8}$	$5\frac{1}{8}$	7	10	$26\frac{2}{8}$	883	9
■ Crook Co. – Joe Engelhaupt – Joe Engelhaupt – 1956											
$204\frac{2}{8}$	23	23	$17\frac{2}{8}$	$23\frac{4}{8}$	$4\frac{6}{8}$	$4\frac{4}{8}$	11	15	44	1199	10
■ Crook Co. – David Sipe – David Sipe – 1956											
$203\frac{1}{8}$	$22\frac{4}{8}$	$19\frac{1}{8}$	$14\frac{3}{8}$	$20\frac{4}{8}$	$4\frac{4}{8}$	$4\frac{4}{8}$	10	13	$57\frac{6}{8}$	1305	11
■ Campbell Co. – Picked Up – John P. Riley – 1992											
$202\frac{3}{8}$	$23\frac{5}{8}$	$25\frac{3}{8}$	$16\frac{5}{8}$	$19\frac{2}{8}$	$4\frac{5}{8}$	$4\frac{5}{8}$	11	6	19	1362	12
■ Crook Co. – Marshall Miller – Marshall Miller – 1968											
$200\frac{3}{8}$	$24\frac{6}{8}$	$22\frac{4}{8}$	18	$20\frac{3}{8}$	$4\frac{3}{8}$	$4\frac{4}{8}$	8	10	$24\frac{3}{8}$	1556	13
■ Crook Co. – Paul L. Wolz – Paul L. Wolz – 1967											
$200\frac{3}{8}$	$25\frac{2}{8}$	$22\frac{1}{8}$	$21\frac{4}{8}$	$22\frac{4}{8}$	$5\frac{1}{8}$	$5\frac{2}{8}$	9	11	$27\frac{1}{8}$	1556	13
■ Fremont Co. – Wallace M. Oldman – Wallace M. Oldman – 1989											
200	$19\frac{5}{8}$	$18\frac{1}{8}$	$17\frac{1}{8}$	$19\frac{2}{8}$	$4\frac{7}{8}$	$5\frac{1}{8}$	6	11	$66\frac{5}{8}$	1591	15
■ Crook Co. – Ralph R. Van Beck – Ralph R. Van Beck – 1989											
$198\frac{7}{8}$	25	$23\frac{2}{8}$	$16\frac{5}{8}$	$23\frac{6}{8}$	$5\frac{1}{8}$	$5\frac{1}{8}$	11	11	$42\frac{2}{8}$	1686	16
■ Weston Co. – G. Huls & B.L. Arfmann – Chester S. Jones – 1973											
$198\frac{4}{8}$	$24\frac{2}{8}$	$23\frac{1}{8}$	18	$20\frac{1}{8}$	$5\frac{2}{8}$	$5\frac{4}{8}$	13	12	$31\frac{6}{8}$	1736	17
■ Cow Creek – Thelma Martens – Thelma Martens – 1951 ■ See photo on page 403											
$196\frac{2}{8}$	24	$24\frac{5}{8}$	$18\frac{5}{8}$	$22\frac{1}{8}$	$5\frac{3}{8}$	$5\frac{5}{8}$	11	10	$24\frac{1}{8}$	2028	18
■ Crook Co. – Donald W. Clements – Colleen B. Clements – 1958											
$195\frac{4}{8}$	$25\frac{1}{8}$	$25\frac{1}{8}$	$15\frac{3}{8}$	$22\frac{3}{8}$	$5\frac{2}{8}$	$4\frac{6}{8}$	17	11	$36\frac{5}{8}$	2134	19
■ Natrona Co. – Picked Up – Ann Ginder – 1998											

Location of Kill – Hunter – Owner – Date Killed

Score	Length of Main Beam Right	Left	Inside Spread	Greatest Spread	Circumference at Smallest Place Between Burr and First Point Right	Left	Number of Points Right	Left	Lengths Abnormal Points	All-Time Rank	State Rank
	■ *Location of Kill – Hunter – Owner – Date Killed*										
195 1/8	23 4/8	23 4/8	16 6/8	20 6/8	5	4 6/8	8	8	32 1/8	2208	20
	■ *Crook Co. – John P. Barrows – John P. Barrows – 1998*										
187 7/8	22 2/8	23	16 2/8	19 2/8	4 7/8	4 4/8	12	11	27 7/8	2506†	21†
	■ *Carbon Co. – John C. Heinrich, Jr. – John C. Heinrich, Jr. – 2001*										
261 5/8	25 6/8	23	21 5/8	29 1/8	5 7/8	6	16	15	97 4/8	*	*
	■ *Park Co. – Bobby L. Beeman – Bobby L. Beeman – 1998* ■ *See photo on page 525*										

† The scores and ranking for trophies from the 25th Awards Entry Period are not final until the banquet is held on June 19, 2004.
* Final score is subject to revision by additional verifying measurements.

TROPHIES IN THE FIELD

HUNTER: Bobby L. Beeman
SCORE: 261-5/8
CATEOGORY: non-typical whitetail deer
LOCATION: Park County, Wyoming
DATE: 1998

North American Whitetail Deer Provincial Listing

EDITOR'S NOTE: Geographical distribution analysis of records book whitetail entries was calculated by U.S. counties. A breakdown by county is not available for Canadian provinces and Mexico, therefore these two popular whitetail regions could not be included in this analysis.

ALBERTA
RECORD WHITETAILS

191 Typical whitetail deer entries
117 Non-typical whitetail deer entries
7,265 Total whitetail deer entries

ALBERTA
PROVINCIAL RECORD
Typical Whitetail Deer
Score: $204^2/8$
Location: Beaverdam Creek
Hunter and Owner: Stephen Jansen
Date: 1967

Photograph by Helen S. Sabin

ALBERTA
PROVINCIAL RECORD
Non-Typical Whitetail Deer
Score: $279^6/8$
Location: Whitemud Creek
Hunter: Neil J. Morin
Owner: Brad Gsell
Date: 1991

Photograph from B&C Archives

ALBERTA

TYPICAL WHITETAIL DEER

Score	Length of Main Beam Right	Left	Inside Spread	Greatest Spread	Circumference at Smallest Place Between Burr and First Point Right	Left	Number of Points Right	Left	Lengths Abnormal Points	All-Time Rank	State Rank
	■ Location of Kill – Hunter – Owner – Date Killed										
204²/8	26⁴/8	22⁶/8	25¹/8	26⁶/8	5¹/8	5¹/8	7	10	6⁷/8	5	1
	■ Beaverdam Creek – Stephen Jansen – Stephen Jansen – 1967										
199⁵/8	30¹/8	28	29¹/8	31⁵/8	5³/8	5³/8	6	6		13	2
	■ Edmonton – Don McGarvey – Don McGarvey – 1991										
197³/8	29¹/8	29⁷/8	21	23⁷/8	5¹/8	5²/8	9	7	14³/8	26	3
	■ Mann Lakes – Lawrence J. Youngman – Lawrence J. Youngman – 1992										
192⁷/8	26⁶/8	25⁶/8	18⁴/8	21	5¹/8	5¹/8	7	6	1¹/8	58	4
	■ Wabatansik Creek – Norman Trudeau – Norman Trudeau – 1992										
190⁷/8	29⁵/8	29⁴/8	24³/8	26³/8	4⁶/8	4⁴/8	6	6		89	5
	■ Leduc – Robert J. Kowalyshyn – Robert J. Kowalyshyn – 1997										
190⁵/8	22⁴/8	23⁵/8	19⁵/8	22⁴/8	4⁴/8	4⁴/8	7	6		95	6
	■ Buffalo Lake – Eugene L. Boll – Eugene L. Boll – 1969										
188⁴/8	27²/8	24⁵/8	22²/8	25²/8	5⁶/8	5⁵/8	5	5		141	7
	■ Metiskow – Norman T. Salminen – Norman T. Salminen – 1977										
188³/8	28⁴/8	28²/8	17²/8	21⁶/8	5³/8	5⁴/8	10	10	18¹/8	147	8
	■ Red Deer – Edwin Koberstein – Edwin Koberstein – 1991										
188	26²/8	27²/8	19¹/8	22⁶/8	5⁷/8	5⁶/8	8	7	8⁷/8	152	9
	■ N. Saskatchewan River – Darrel J. Patera – Darrel J. Patera – 1999										
187⁷/8	27¹/8	26⁴/8	24²/8	26¹/8	5²/8	5³/8	6	8	6²/8	180	10
	■ Wandering River – Jason L. Hayes – Jason L. Hayes – 1999										
186³/8	25	25³/8	21⁷/8	24³/8	5⁴/8	5⁴/8	6	5	1	210	11
	■ Rocky Mt. House – Wyndell A. Wroten – Wyndell A. Wroten – 1992										
186¹/8	29¹/8	27¹/8	19⁴/8	22¹/8	5³/8	5²/8	5	7	1¹/8	228	12
	■ Camrose – Dale A. Broker – Dale A. Broker – 1992										
185¹/8	26³/8	25⁶/8	24⁷/8	28	5⁷/8	5⁷/8	6	7	4⁶/8	266	13
	■ Bonnyville – Richard A. Rhoden – Richard A. Rhoden – 1996										
184⁷/8	28	28	23⁴/8	26³/8	6	6	9	8	16⁷/8	279	14
	■ Vermilion – C. Letawsky & B. Myshak – C. Letawsky & B. Myshak – 1986										
184⁵/8	27¹/8	27¹/8	21²/8	24⁶/8	5⁴/8	5³/8	8	6	11³/8	294	15
	■ Paddle River – Gregory D. Graff – Gregory D. Graff – 1988										
184⁴/8	26⁴/8	26	19	21	5¹/8	5²/8	7	6	1²/8	303	16
	■ Smoky Lake – Brendon Rezewski – Brendon Rezewski – 1995										
184²/8	25¹/8	28⁴/8	23¹/8	24⁴/8	5	5	5	6	3¹/8	319	17
	■ Dillberry Lake – Scott M. Rowein – Scott M. Rowein – 1992										
184²/8	28⁴/8	29⁴/8	21²/8	23⁶/8	5	5	5	5		319	17
	■ McLeod River – Clifford L. Haddock – Clifford L. Haddock – 1998										
183⁶/8	27⁶/8	27⁵/8	19	21⁴/8	5¹/8	5¹/8	5	5		350†	19†
	■ Soundng Lake – David W. Higman – David W. Higman – 2001										

Score	Length of Main Beam Right	Left	Inside Spread	Greatest Spread	Circumference at Smallest Place Between Burr and First Point Right	Left	Number of Points Right	Left	Lengths Abnormal Points	All-Time Rank	State Rank
	■ Location of Kill – Hunter – Owner – Date Killed										
183	25⁶/8	26	21	23	4⁶/8	4⁵/8	5	5		392	20
	■ Red Deer River – Picked Up – Ovar Uggen – 1966										
182⁶/8	24⁵/8	24³/8	20⁶/8	23⁶/8	5²/8	5¹/8	8	7	2⁶/8	409	21
	■ Pembina River – Curtis R. Siegfried – Curtis R. Siegfried – 1991										
182⁵/8	29⁴/8	30⁴/8	27¹/8	29³/8	5³/8	5³/8	4	5		420†	22†
	■ Viking – Charles D. Dobbs – Charles D. Dobbs – 2001										
182³/8	26⁴/8	25⁵/8	22	25	5⁶/8	6	7	7	6⁵/8	438	23
	■ Derwent – Michael A. Miller – Michael A. Miller – 1994										
182²/8	29	25⁷/8	18⁷/8	21²/8	5²/8	5¹/8	6	7	8³/8	450	24
	■ Bonnyville – Jim Baik – Jim Baik – 1998										
182¹/8	28	27⁴/8	25⁴/8	28	6	6²/8	7	6	1¹/8	460	25
	■ MacCafferty Lake – Alan S. Bell – Alan S. Bell – 1990										
181⁷/8	26⁴/8	26²/8	21³/8	24¹/8	4⁶/8	4⁶/8	5	5		478	26
	■ Hotchkiss – Andy G. Petkus – Andy G. Petkus – 1984										
181⁷/8	24⁶/8	25²/8	17¹/8	21²/8	5⁴/8	5⁴/8	6	7	1	478	26
	■ Lesser Slave Lake – Picked Up – Jerry Napier – 1985										
181⁷/8	25⁴/8	26³/8	21¹/8	24	5²/8	5²/8	5	5		478	26
	■ Alice Lake – Dave S. Seitz – Dave S. Seitz – 1989										
181⁷/8	25¹/8	27²/8	23⁶/8	26²/8	4⁷/8	5	8	9	7¹/8	478	26
	■ Ghost River – Dean Lee – Dean Lee – 1995										
181⁴/8	25⁶/8	25⁴/8	20	25²/8	5⁴/8	5⁴/8	5	6		516†	30†
	■ Valley Lake – Terrance O. Hobbs – Terrance O. Hobbs – 2000										
181⁴/8	25⁴/8	27	22⁶/8	25¹/8	5⁶/8	5⁶/8	6	7	3⁶/8	516	30
	■ Pine Lake – Robert Crosby – Robert Crosby – 1977										
181²/8	28³/8	26⁵/8	19⁷/8	22⁴/8	5⁵/8	6¹/8	8	8	8¹/8	540	32
	■ Fawcett Lake – Robert Neimor – Robert Neimor – 1998										
181	27	26⁵/8	20	22⁶/8	5⁷/8	5⁷/8	5	6	1⁴/8	563	33
	■ Stettler – Archie Smith – Archie Smith – 1962										
180⁷/8	25⁷/8	25³/8	17⁷/8	21	5¹/8	5¹/8	6	7	9	573	34
	■ Castor – Norman D. Stienwand – Norman D. Stienwand – 1981										
180⁶/8	27⁶/8	27⁶/8	26	27⁷/8	5¹/8	5¹/8	5	5		587	35
	■ Sounding Lake – Morris Thompson – Morris Thompson – 1993										
180⁶/8	23⁴/8	25²/8	24⁶/8	23⁴/8	5⁴/8	5⁶/8	6	6		587	35
	■ Drayton Valley – Peter Underwood – Peter Underwood – 1999										
180³/8	27⁵/8	26	21⁵/8	24⁴/8	4⁵/8	4⁵/8	5	5		630	37
	■ Antler Lake – German Wagenseil – German Wagenseil – 1964										
180³/8	25⁴/8	23⁶/8	21¹/8	23⁴/8	5⁵/8	5⁵/8	6	5	3	630	37
	■ Wapiti River – Terry D. Hagman – Terry D. Hagman – 1997										
180¹/8	24	24⁴/8	19¹/8	21⁶/8	4⁷/8	5	7	6	1²/8	669	39
	■ Vermilion – Ralph M. McDonald – Ralph M. McDonald – 1975										
180¹/8	25¹/8	24⁴/8	26⁷/8	28⁷/8	5⁶/8	5⁴/8	6	7	2⁶/8	669	39
	■ Hardisty – George R. Walker – George R. Walker – 1977										

Score	Length of Main Beam Right	Left	Inside Spread	Greatest Spread	Circumference at Smallest Place Between Burr and First Point Right	Left	Number of Points Right	Left	Lengths Abnormal Points	All-Time Rank	State Rank
	■ Location of Kill – Hunter – Owner – Date Killed										
180	26⁷/₈	26¹/₈	20⁴/₈	23	5⁷/₈	5⁷/₈	5	7	1²/₈	688	41
	■ Castor – Kenneth Larson – Kenneth Larson – 1969										
180	25⁴/₈	25⁶/₈	19⁴/₈	23⁶/₈	5¹/₈	5¹/₈	10	7	8	688	41
	■ Pembina River – Joe Jandl – Joe Jandl – 1989										
179⁶/₈	29¹/₈	28	21	23⁵/₈	5⁶/₈	5⁵/₈	7	6	10⁶/₈	712	43
	■ Longview – Eldred Umbach – Eldred Umbach – 1977										
179⁶/₈	25¹/₈	24⁷/₈	20	22⁶/₈	4⁶/₈	4⁶/₈	6	5	1²/₈	712	43
	■ Valhalla Centre – Terry D. Hagman – Terry D. Hagman – 1995										
179⁶/₈	25²/₈	25³/₈	22³/₈	26⁴/₈	5⁵/₈	5⁴/₈	7	5	5³/₈	712	43
	■ Plamondon – Edmond Bourassa – Edmond Bourassa – 1998										
179⁵/₈	25⁴/₈	25⁷/₈	19⁵/₈	23	6	6	5	6	1⁴/₈	729	46
	■ Rumsey – Arley Harder – Arley Harder – 1969										
179⁵/₈	25⁵/₈	25³/₈	20⁶/₈	24¹/₈	4³/₈	4³/₈	5	6	1¹/₈	729	46
	■ Handhill Lakes – D. Troutman & G. Amendt – Dave Troutman – 1996										
179⁴/₈	23⁴/₈	23⁵/₈	19²/₈	22	4⁶/₈	4⁵/₈	6	6		733	48
	■ Coronation – Harold McKnight – Harold McKnight – 1969										
179⁴/₈	27³/₈	27²/₈	20²/₈	22²/₈	4⁷/₈	5	6	5		733	48
	■ Cremona – E. Roger Jackson – E. Roger Jackson – 1985										
179³/₈	26¹/₈	26	22⁵/₈	24⁶/₈	4⁵/₈	4⁶/₈	7	7	4	749	50
	■ Pelican Mt. – Harold B. Biggs – Harold B. Biggs – 1993										
179³/₈	25	25⁴/₈	19⁵/₈	22¹/₈	4⁴/₈	4⁶/₈	8	7	7⁶/₈	749	50
	■ Priddis – Jeffrey C. Dunn – Jeffrey C. Dunn – 1996										
179³/₈	24⁶/₈	24⁶/₈	20³/₈	22⁵/₈	5⁷/₈	6	6	7	1	749	50
	■ High Prairie – Walter J. Malysh – Walter J. Malysh – 1997										
179²/₈	25⁷/₈	24²/₈	19⁴/₈	23³/₈	4⁷/₈	4⁷/₈	6	7	1	763	53
	■ Vernon Lake – Del Kirchmayer – Del Kirchmayer – 1997										
178⁶/₈	27	24⁴/₈	22¹/₈	24⁴/₈	5⁷/₈	5⁷/₈	7	7	4⁷/₈	808	54
	■ Breton – George Clark – George Clark – 1981										
178⁶/₈	25⁷/₈	26⁴/₈	22²/₈	26⁴/₈	4⁶/₈	4⁷/₈	6	6		808	54
	■ Vilna – M.M. Berrien, Jr. – M.M. Berrien, Jr. – 1990										
178⁵/₈	24¹/₈	24⁷/₈	20⁴/₈	23⁷/₈	4⁷/₈	5¹/₈	6	7	6⁵/₈	819	56
	■ Pincher Creek – Unknown – H. Bruce Freeman – 1973										
178⁵/₈	25²/₈	24⁷/₈	21³/₈	23⁴/₈	5	5	5	6		819	56
	■ Flat Lake – Paul Franchuk – Paul Franchuk – 1987										
178⁵/₈	25⁴/₈	25	17⁵/₈	20	4⁴/₈	4⁵/₈	6	6		819	56
	■ Blueberry Creek – Mark E. Wolney – Dennis Wolney – 1997										
177³/₈	27³/₈	27¹/₈	18⁶/₈	21⁵/₈	5⁴/₈	5⁵/₈	9	7	9⁵/₈	1011	59
	■ Weasel Creek – Ray M. Fels – Ray M. Fels – 1991										
177³/₈	26	25⁷/₈	20³/₈	22⁵/₈	4⁵/₈	4⁶/₈	6	6		1011	59
	■ Vermilion River – Larry Flaata – Larry Flaata – 1995										
177¹/₈	25⁵/₈	25⁵/₈	22³/₈	26	4⁵/₈	4⁶/₈	6	5		1048	61
	■ Thorsby – Adam Tomaszewski – Adam Tomaszewski – 1985										

Score	Length of Main Beam Right Left	Inside Spread	Greatest Spread	Circumference at Smallest Place Between Burr and First Point Right Left	Number of Points Right Left	Lengths Abnormal Points	All-Time Rank	State Rank
	■ Location of Kill – Hunter – Owner – Date Killed							
177¹/8	27⁷/8 26³/8	18⁴/8	22	5⁵/8 5⁶/8	6 7	7³/8	1048	61
	■ Wolf Lake – Keith W. Hamilton – Keith W. Hamilton – 1992							
177	28¹/8 26¹/8	20⁷/8	23⁷/8	5⁴/8 5⁶/8	7 6	5¹/8	1066	63
	■ Innisfree – Donald M. Baranec – Donald M. Baranec – 1984							
176⁶/8	25⁴/8 24⁷/8	20⁴/8	22⁶/8	5⁷/8 6¹/8	5 5		1103†	64†
	■ Athabasca – Nikki G. Wescott Haley – Nikki G. Wescott Haley – 2000							
176⁶/8	27⁴/8 26²/8	23	25⁶/8	5 4⁷/8	6 6		1103	64
	■ Sturgeon River – Michael G. Schmermund – Michael G. Schmermund – 1990							
176⁵/8	26¹/8 25⁷/8	21¹/8	25²/8	6¹/8 6¹/8	6 5	3	1134	66
	■ Buffalo – Bob Fraleigh – Bob Fraleigh – 1978							
176⁵/8	24⁶/8 25	19⁶/8	22	5⁷/8 5⁷/8	7 7	7⁵/8	1134	66
	■ Pigeon Lake – Milton Fawcett – Milton Fawcett – 1991							
176⁴/8	27⁵/8 28⁶/8	21³/8	25	5⁵/8 5⁴/8	8 7	9⁵/8	1158	68
	■ Chisholm – Paul Murray – Paul Murray – 1994							
176⁴/8	22⁵/8 24³/8	19²/8	21⁴/8	5³/8 5³/8	7 7		1158	68
	■ Oldman Lake – John Proud – John Proud – 1997 ■ See photo on page 57							
176²/8	25⁵/8 25⁵/8	20⁶/8	23	4⁶/8 4⁶/8	5 6	1⁶/8	1209	70
	■ Vermilion River – Edwin J. Bowman – Edwin J. Bowman – 1997							
176	24¹/8 23⁷/8	16	18⁵/8	4³/8 4⁴/8	5 5		1266	71
	■ Ghost Lake – Viktor Nill – Viktor Nill – 1989							
176	26⁷/8 28⁴/8	20⁶/8	23	4⁷/8 4⁷/8	7 6	4⁴/8	1266	71
	■ Redwater – Tim T. Bourne – Tim T. Bourne – 1993							
175⁷/8	27 26⁶/8	22⁵/8	24⁷/8	4⁴/8 4⁴/8	5 5		1287	73
	■ Sundre – Russell D. Holmes – Russell D. Holmes – 1984							
175⁷/8	25²/8 25¹/8	16³/8	19¹/8	5 5²/8	5 5		1287	73
	■ Barrhead – Hugh L. Schmaus – Hugh L. Schmaus – 1990							
175²/8	23²/8 24¹/8	19⁶/8	22⁴/8	4⁷/8 4⁵/8	5 5		1403	75
	■ Mayerthorpe – Gregory Graff – Gregory Graff – 1987							
175²/8	24²/8 23⁵/8	18¹/8	20⁶/8	5³/8 5⁴/8	7 8	9⁵/8	1403	75
	■ Pembina River – Curtis R. Siegfried – Curtis R. Siegfried – 1992							
175¹/8	23⁵/8 22⁷/8	22³/8	26	5⁶/8 5⁵/8	5 5		1440	77
	■ Chedderville – Larry Trimble – Larry Trimble – 1963							
175	26²/8 25³/8	19	21²/8	5²/8 5¹/8	7 6	1²/8	1472†	78†
	■ Lac La Biche – Tony J. Mitchell – Tony J. Mitchell – 2000							
175	26⁵/8 27	19²/8	21³/8	5³/8 5³/8	7 6	10	1472	78
	■ Rochester – Terry Hill – Terry Hill – 1991							
175	27³/8 27¹/8	22⁴/8	24⁷/8	4⁷/8 5²/8	6 6	3²/8	1472	78
	■ Lac La Biche – Ronald N. Carpenter – Ronald N. Carpenter – 1998							
	■ See photo on page 57							
174⁷/8	25⁷/8 25²/8	17⁴/8	19⁵/8	4⁷/8 5	6 6	1³/8	1513†	81†
	■ Elbow River – James W. Taylor – James W. Taylor – 2000							
174⁶/8	25³/8 25⁷/8	21²/8	23⁴/8	4⁵/8 4⁵/8	6 6	2	1534	82
	■ Franchere – Franklin B. Janz – Franklin B. Janz – 1997							

Score	Length of Main Beam Right	Left	Inside Spread	Greatest Spread	Circumference at Smallest Place Between Burr and First Point Right	Left	Number of Points Right	Left	Lengths Abnormal Points	All-Time Rank	State Rank
	■ Location of Kill – Hunter – Owner – Date Killed										
174⁵/₈	26⁵/₈	25⁶/₈	17⁵/₈	21³/₈	5³/₈	5⁵/₈	7	8	10⁶/₈	1561	83
	■ Lodgepole – Frank Spilak – Frank Spilak – 1995										
174⁴/₈	26¹/₈	25⁴/₈	18⁶/₈	21	4⁶/₈	4⁶/₈	5	5		1592†	84†
	■ Gull Lake – Robert Meredith – Robert Meredith – 2001										
174⁴/₈	24²/₈	24⁶/₈	20²/₈	22³/₈	5⁵/₈	5⁵/₈	5	5		1592	84
	■ Jensen Reservoir – Gary Stanford – Gary Stanford – 1976										
174³/₈	26²/₈	25	17³/₈	19⁷/₈	5²/₈	5⁷/₈	6	5	4⁶/₈	1619	86
	■ N. Saskatchewan River – James S. Romanchuk – James S. Romanchuk – 1988										
174³/₈	24⁴/₈	24	22⁷/₈	24¹/₈	4⁶/₈	4⁵/₈	6	7		1619	86
	■ Cynthia – Camillo J. Baratto – Camillo J. Baratto – 1998										
174¹/₈	24⁵/₈	23⁵/₈	19⁵/₈	22⁵/₈	5⁴/₈	5⁴/₈	5	5		1678	88
	■ Blackfoot – Thomas J. Slager – Thomas J. Slager – 1969										
174	24¹/₈	25	23⁵/₈	25⁶/₈	4³/₈	4⁴/₈	6	6	5⁵/₈	1717	89
	■ Battle River – Jeff White – Jeff White – 1998										
173⁷/₈	26¹/₈	26	19	21²/₈	4⁶/₈	5	6	8	4¹/₈	1743	90
	■ Barrhead – C.J. Fuller – C.J. Fuller – 1992										
173⁷/₈	27	26⁷/₈	16⁴/₈	18⁷/₈	5	5	6	5	2⁷/₈	1743	90
	■ Rocky Mt. House – Daniel F. Breton – Daniel F. Breton – 1994										
173⁶/₈	24¹/₈	26⁶/₈	25³/₈	27²/₈	5⁵/₈	5⁵/₈	9	7	11¹/₈	1766†	92†
	■ Ribstone Creek – Morgan J. Williams – Morgan J. Williams – 2000										
173⁶/₈	26⁶/₈	26⁶/₈	19¹/₈	21⁴/₈	4⁷/₈	4⁷/₈	5	7	3⁵/₈	1766	92
	■ Minburn – Joseph R. McGillis – Joseph R. McGillis – 1981										
173⁶/₈	27¹/₈	27³/₈	23³/₈	25⁶/₈	4⁵/₈	4⁵/₈	7	7	4⁵/₈	1766	92
	■ Dolcy Lake – Joseph P. Baker – Joseph P. Baker – 1993										
173⁶/₈	28⁶/₈	26	23⁶/₈	25⁴/₈	4⁶/₈	4⁷/₈	6	6		1766	92
	■ St. Lina – Don Felts – Don Felts – 1993										
173⁵/₈	26²/₈	26⁴/₈	22⁵/₈	24⁶/₈	5²/₈	5²/₈	6	7	2²/₈	1819	96
	■ Alberta – Frank Lind – Frank Lind – 1952										
173³/₈	24⁶/₈	25¹/₈	21¹/₈	24¹/₈	4⁶/₈	4⁷/₈	5	5		1883	97
	■ Pembina River – Adrian Marr – Adrian Marr – 1993										
173²/₈	25⁵/₈	25³/₈	19	21²/₈	4⁶/₈	4⁶/₈	5	5		1914	98
	■ Battle River – Steven M. Cooper – Steven M. Cooper – 1984										
173¹/₈	26⁶/₈	26⁷/₈	19⁶/₈	22	5³/₈	5³/₈	6	6	1⁵/₈	1950	99
	■ Gibbons – Thomas Kampjes – Thomas Kampjes – 1994										
173	23²/₈	25⁵/₈	19⁵/₈	22²/₈	4⁶/₈	4⁶/₈	7	8	6³/₈	1991	100
	■ Bunder Lake – Steve Swinhoe – Steve Swinhoe – 1983										
173	24⁵/₈	24⁷/₈	16⁴/₈	19³/₈	5³/₈	5²/₈	5	5		1991	100
	■ Bonnyville – Lionel P. Tercier – Lionel P. Tercier – 1983										
173	23⁶/₈	24	19	22³/₈	4⁶/₈	4⁷/₈	6	5		1991	100
	■ Westlock – Billy W. Kothmann – Billy W. Kothmann – 1992										
172⁶/₈	24³/₈	23⁴/₈	16⁵/₈	19¹/₈	5	5	7	6	9⁷/₈	2065	103
	■ Edgerton – Richard T. Abbott – Richard T. Abbott – 1980										

Score	Length of Main Beam Right / Left	Inside Spread	Greatest Spread	Circumference at Smallest Place Between Burr and First Point Right / Left	Number of Points Right / Left	Lengths Abnormal Points	All-Time Rank	State Rank
172⁵/₈	27¹/₈ 27⁷/₈	22⁵/₈	25¹/₈	5 4⁷/₈	6 5	4	2113†	104†
■ Long Island Lake – David G. McGraw – David G. McGraw – 2000								
172⁵/₈	26¹/₈ 26⁴/₈	19⁶/₈	21⁶/₈	4⁶/₈ 4⁶/₈	7 7	4⁷/₈	2113	104
■ Long Lake – Gerald Bodner – Gerald Bodner – 1995								
172⁴/₈	25⁴/₈ 25⁶/₈	18⁶/₈	21⁴/₈	4⁷/₈ 5	5 5		2156†	106†
■ Anselmo – Robert J. Wegner – Robert J. Wegner – 2001								
172⁴/₈	24⁴/₈ 24³/₈	20	22⁴/₈	5 5	6 6		2156	106
■ Chauvin – Ron D. Jakimchuk – Ron D. Jakimchuk – 1971								
172⁴/₈	22 25⁵/₈	23⁷/₈	25⁵/₈	4⁷/₈ 4⁶/₈	7 7	4⁵/₈	2156	106
■ Smoky River – Bevar C. Rose – Bevar C. Rose – 1988								
172⁴/₈	25⁴/₈ 25⁴/₈	18²/₈	20¹/₈	5⁶/₈ 5⁴/₈	5 5		2156	106
■ McLennan – Gordon Ristow – Gordon Ristow – 1995								
172⁴/₈	22⁴/₈ 23²/₈	16⁶/₈	20⁷/₈	5¹/₈ 5¹/₈	7 6	1²/₈	2156	106
■ Athabasca – Christopher Sawchyn – Christopher Sawchyn – 1997								
172⁴/₈	26⁶/₈ 25⁷/₈	18⁴/₈	20	4⁷/₈ 5	6 6		2156	106
■ Evansburg – Dana Baksa – Dana Baksa – 1998								
172³/₈	24 24¹/₈	17³/₈	19¹/₈	4⁵/₈ 4⁶/₈	6 6		2200	112
■ Sounding Lake – Neil Scammell – Neil Scammell – 1995								
172¹/₈	25 25⁵/₈	18³/₈	20⁶/₈	5⁴/₈ 5⁵/₈	5 6	2	2286	113
■ Lac Emilien – Dennis Ewanec – Dennis Ewanec – 1987								
172¹/₈	27⁷/₈ 22⁶/₈	17⁵/₈	19³/₈	5⁴/₈ 5⁵/₈	6 6		2286	113
■ Smoky River – Lawrence Zawacki – Lawrence Zawacki – 1990								
171⁶/₈	25⁵/₈ 25⁶/₈	16	19²/₈	5³/₈ 5³/₈	5 5		2418	115
■ Peace River – Austin V. Cowan, Jr. – Austin V. Cowan, Jr. – 1988								
171⁶/₈	28¹/₈ 29	19	21¹/₈	5 5²/₈	7 6	5⁴/₈	2418	115
■ Campbell Creek – K. Ryan & B. Winters – Ken Ryan – 1992								
171⁶/₈	23⁴/₈ 22⁶/₈	16²/₈	19¹/₈	5²/₈ 5⁶/₈	6 6		2418	115
■ Grande Prairie – Theodore H. Stegman – Theodore H. Stegman – 1995								
171⁶/₈	23⁵/₈ 24⁴/₈	16⁷/₈	19²/₈	4⁵/₈ 4⁵/₈	7 6	6¹/₈	2418	115
■ Chinook – Ian Proudfoot – Ian Proudfoot – 1996								
171⁵/₈	28³/₈ 27²/₈	19⁵/₈	26	5⁴/₈ 5⁴/₈	7 6	5⁴/₈	2470	119
■ Paradise Valley – Dale Luedtke – Dale Luedtke – 1999								
171⁴/₈	24⁶/₈ 26¹/₈	19²/₈	21⁵/₈	5²/₈ 5¹/₈	5 5		2513	120
■ Hayter – H.D.L. Loucks – H.D.L. Loucks – 1953								
171⁴/₈	24⁵/₈ 21⁷/₈	21³/₈	24⁷/₈	5 4⁷/₈	8 6	2⁵/₈	2513	120
■ Crooked Lake – Bruce J. Ferguson – Bruce J. Ferguson – 1984								
171⁴/₈	26¹/₈ 26	20¹/₈	22	4⁴/₈ 4⁵/₈	8 8	6³/₈	2513	120
■ Rocky Mt. House – Lloyd Cadrain – Lloyd Cadrain – 1987								
171⁴/₈	26 25¹/₈	21	23¹/₈	5²/₈ 5¹/₈	5 5		2513	120
■ Edson – Ted E. Mortimer – Ted E. Mortimer – 1998								
171³/₈	24⁴/₈ 23⁶/₈	21⁵/₈	24¹/₈	4⁴/₈ 4⁴/₈	5 5		2564	124
■ Athabasca River – Ron J. Holm – Ron J. Holm – 1977								

Score	Length of Main Beam Right	Left	Inside Spread	Greatest Spread	Circumference at Smallest Place Between Burr and First Point Right	Left	Number of Points Right	Left	Lengths Abnormal Points	All-Time Rank	State Rank
	■ Location of Kill – Hunter – Owner – Date Killed										
171³/8	23⁷/8	24⁵/8	18⁷/8	21³/8	5	5²/8	5	6	1²/8	2564	124
	■ Wabamun – Greg Crain – Greg Crain – 1992										
171³/8	21⁵/8	22⁶/8	17²/8	22³/8	5	5	10	6	11¹/8	2564	124
	■ N. Saskatchewan River – Picked Up – Dale Loosemore – 1995										
171²/8	26³/8	24⁴/8	18⁶/8	21²/8	4⁴/8	4⁴/8	5	5		2621	127
	■ Oyen – Daryl Peers – Daryl Peers – 1986										
171¹/8	22⁶/8	21	18⁵/8	20³/8	5¹/8	5²/8	6	6		2665	128
	■ Medicine Hat – Frank Chevalier – Marcel Houle – 1958										
171	24⁵/8	23⁶/8	21	24⁶/8	5	5	5	5		2707	129
	■ Seven Persons – Haven Lane – Haven Lane – 1968										
171	24	24¹/8	23²/8	25¹/8	4⁶/8	4⁶/8	5	5		2707	129
	■ Lac La Biche – Ken Harris – Ken Harris – 1994										
170⁷/8	23⁴/8	21⁶/8	16³/8	19⁶/8	5²/8	5³/8	6	8	4	2769†	131†
	■ Timeu Creek – Tom A. Wong – Tom A. Wong – 2000										
170⁷/8	26⁴/8	27⁴/8	21¹/8	23⁷/8	5⁶/8	5²/8	5	5		2769	131
	■ Kingman – Robert D. Kozack – Robert D. Kozack – 1971										
170⁷/8	26²/8	25⁷/8	18⁶/8	21²/8	5²/8	5	5	6	1¹/8	2769	131
	■ Lamont – Allen C. Johnston – Allen C. Johnston – 1989										
170⁶/8	27³/8	29³/8	28⁷/8	32⁵/8	5¹/8	5	6	8	6¹/8	2828	134
	■ Calling Lake – Fred J. Rein – Fred J. Rein – 1993										
170⁶/8	25⁴/8	24⁷/8	18⁶/8	22⁶/8	5	4⁶/8	7	6	10⁴/8	2828	134
	■ Derwent – Vincent D. Charchun – Vincent D. Charchun – 1996										
170⁵/8	24²/8	24³/8	17⁴/8	21²/8	5⁴/8	5⁴/8	6	6	2³/8	2876	136
	■ Rocky Mt. House – Robin L. McDonald – Robin L. McDonald – 1991										
170⁵/8	25⁵/8	25¹/8	17⁶/8	21⁶/8	5⁶/8	5⁵/8	7	7	7¹/8	2876	136
	■ St. Anne Lake – Allen T. Carstairs – Allen T. Carstairs – 1995										
170⁵/8	26²/8	27⁶/8	23⁶/8	29²/8	5²/8	5¹/8	8	6	8⁵/8	2876	136
	■ Paddle River – Dwayne C. Moore – Dwayne C. Moore – 1997										
170⁴/8	25⁴/8	25³/8	18²/8	21²/8	5	5¹/8	7	5	3⁴/8	2933	139
	■ Lesser Slave Lake – Adriaan Mik – Adriaan Mik – 1986										
170³/8	25²/8	24	16⁴/8	18⁷/8	4⁴/8	4⁵/8	8	9	8³/8	2992	140
	■ Cow Lake – Edward J. Burns – Edward J. Burns – 1986										
170²/8	25¹/8	26	20⁴/8	22⁵/8	6⁷/8	6⁷/8	5	5		3063	141
	■ Ribstone Creek – David H. Crum – David H. Crum – 1984										
170²/8	26⁶/8	28	21³/8	24	5⁵/8	5⁶/8	6	6	5¹/8	3063	141
	■ Hardisty – David W. Higman – David W. Higman – 1995										
170²/8	28¹/8	27⁶/8	20⁴/8	22⁷/8	5⁷/8	5⁶/8	6	5	2²/8	3063	141
	■ Battle River – Jeff Golka – Jeff Golka – 1999										
170²/8	26³/8	26²/8	24	25⁶/8	4³/8	4²/8	5	5		3063	141
	■ George Lake – Susan G. Isaacs – Susan G. Isaacs – 1999										
170¹/8	24³/8	24²/8	18¹/8	20³/8	4⁴/8	4²/8	5	5		3143	145
	■ Pincher Creek – Dave Simpson – Dave Simpson – 1971										

Score	Length of Main Beam Right Left	Inside Spread	Greatest Spread	Circumference at Smallest Place Between Burr and First Point Right Left	Number of Points Right Left	Lengths Abnormal Points	All-Time Rank	State Rank
	■ Location of Kill – Hunter – Owner – Date Killed							
170¹/8	20⁶/8 21⁴/8	16⁷/8	19⁵/8	4⁵/8 4⁵/8	6 5		3143	145
	■ Smoky River – Bernie Reiswig – Bernie Reiswig – 1980							
170¹/8	26⁴/8 27	20³/8	25	4⁶/8 4⁷/8	7 7	6	3143	145
	■ Vermilion River – Vince V. Philipps – Vince V. Philipps – 1986							
170¹/8	26⁵/8 25⁵/8	23⁶/8	25¹/8	5²/8 5²/8	8 6	3¹/8	3143	145
	■ Pine Creek – Daniel W. LaPierre – Daniel W. LaPierre – 1994							
170¹/8	24⁴/8 24⁴/8	17⁷/8	20⁶/8	5²/8 5	8 8	4²/8	3143	145
	■ Athabasca River – Patrick S. Casey – Patrick S. Casey – 1995							
170¹/8	27 25⁵/8	22⁷/8	25	4⁷/8 5	5 5		3143	145
	■ Alberta Beach – Rodney M. Janz – Rodney M. Janz – 1996							
170	29³/8 27⁵/8	21	23⁵/8	4⁵/8 4⁶/8	5 7	4	3224	151
	■ Sounding Lake – Bill Kostenuk – Bill Kostenuk – 1990							
170	27¹/8 26⁵/8	23	25¹/8	5¹/8 5²/8	5 5		3224	151
	■ Wabamun Lake – John Nagtegaal – John Nagtegaal – 1990							
169¹/8	23 25⁴/8	20³/8	22⁶/8	5 4⁶/8	6 5		3342	153
	■ Beaver River – Patrick W. Filewich – Patrick W. Filewich – 1993							
168¹/8	25⁴/8 25	19⁷/8	22	5²/8 5²/8	7 7	4⁶/8	3426†	154†
	■ Calling Lake – David A. Schmidt – David A. Schmidt – 2000							
167⁶/8	25⁷/8 25	18⁶/8	21²/8	6²/8 6	5 5		3461	155
	■ Athabasca River – David L. Bathke – David L. Bathke – 1992							
167³/8	21⁶/8 26⁴/8	23¹/8	26⁷/8	5¹/8 5	5 5		3500	156
	■ Thunder Lake – Darcy J. Zadunayski – Darcy J. Zadunayski – 1993							
167²/8	23⁶/8 24⁴/8	15⁶/8	18²/8	4²/8 4²/8	12 7	11²/8	3519	157
	■ Acadia Valley – Joseph H. Niwa – Joseph H. Niwa – 1979							
167²/8	24 24¹/8	21³/8	24²/8	4⁷/8 4⁵/8	5 7	5⁵/8	3519	157
	■ Sounding Lake – David W. Schmidt – David W. Schmidt – 1994							
164⁴/8	26⁶/8 26³/8	22³/8	24⁵/8	5⁵/8 5⁵/8	5 6	2¹/8	3609	159
	■ Valleyview – Wayne Yowell – Wayne Yowell – 1988							
166³/8	27²/8 27	19⁶/8	23⁶/8	5¹/8 5²/8	8 7	10⁵/8	3620	160
	■ Lesliville – R. Terrel Ross – R. Terrel Ross – 1989							
166	26¹/8 26²/8	15⁴/8	18	4³/8 4³/8	5 6	1⁶/8	3657†	161†
	■ Isle Lake – Gary H. Appleton – Gary H. Appleton – 2000							
165⁷/8	25⁴/8 25⁴/8	23⁵/8	27⁵/8	5⁶/8 5⁴/8	6 5	3	3672	162
	■ Bridge Lakes – Tom W. Franzen – Tom W. Franzen – 1992							
165⁵/8	26³/8 25³/8	17⁴/8	20⁷/8	5³/8 5⁶/8	7 8	3³/8	3696	163
	■ Flatbush – Grant Horosko – Grant Horosko – 1997							
165⁴/8	23³/8 23³/8	17²/8	19²/8	5³/8 5²/8	6 6		3714	164
	■ Cochrane – Robert P. Valnoski – Robert P. Valnoski – 1996							
165	23⁷/8 24	23¹/8	26²/8	5³/8 5¹/8	7 7	2¹/8	3782	165
	■ Battle River – William W. MacDonald – William W. MacDonald – 1989							
165	24⁵/8 25¹/8	21⁶/8	23	4⁶/8 4⁶/8	5 5		3782	165
	■ Iron River – Jimmy G. Oliver – Jimmy G. Oliver – 1993							

ALBERTA TYPICAL WHITETAIL DEER

Score	Length of Main Beam Right	Left	Inside Spread	Greatest Spread	Circumference at Smallest Place Between Burr and First Point Right	Left	Number of Points Right	Left	Lengths Abnormal Points	All-Time Rank	State Rank
164⁶/₈	25	24¹/₈	18¹/₈	20¹/₈	4⁴/₈	4⁵/₈	5	6	2³/₈	3809†	167†

■ *Stony Plain Indian Resv. – Michael G. Adams – Michael G. Adams – 1998*

| 164⁵/₈ | 25¹/₈ | 25²/₈ | 19⁷/₈ | 24²/₈ | 4⁷/₈ | 5 | 7 | 6 | 7²/₈ | 3835 | 168 |

■ *White Mud Hills – Peter J. Friesen – Peter J. Friesen – 1994*

| 164⁴/₈ | 26⁵/₈ | 25⁶/₈ | 21¹/₈ | 24⁷/₈ | 4³/₈ | 4³/₈ | 5 | 7 | 2¹/₈ | 3855 | 169 |

■ *Wandering River – Ed Kubash – Ed Kubash – 1976*

| 164³/₈ | 25⁶/₈ | 24⁶/₈ | 22 | 23⁷/₈ | 5 | 4⁷/₈ | 6 | 5 | 1⁵/₈ | 3864 | 170 |

■ *Sturgeon – Neal Heaton – Neal Heaton – 1992*

| 164³/₈ | 22 | 22⁵/₈ | 21⁷/₈ | 23²/₈ | 4⁷/₈ | 4⁵/₈ | 6 | 5 | 1²/₈ | 3864 | 170 |

■ *Madden – Albert R. Rakowski – Albert R. Rakowski – 1992*

| 164²/₈ | 26¹/₈ | 26⁷/₈ | 22²/₈ | 25⁴/₈ | 5²/₈ | 5³/₈ | 6 | 5 | 3 | 3876 | 172 |

■ *Peers – Anthony Burke – Anthony Burke – 1990*

| 164²/₈ | 25⁴/₈ | 26¹/₈ | 21 | 24¹/₈ | 5¹/₈ | 5³/₈ | 5 | 5 | | 3876 | 172 |

■ *Peace River – Greg L. Caldwell – Greg L. Caldwell – 1995*

| 164 | 23²/₈ | 23³/₈ | 20³/₈ | 23⁵/₈ | 4⁶/₈ | 4⁶/₈ | 6 | 6 | 1⁷/₈ | 3908 | 174 |

■ *Peace River – Jack Ondrack – Jack Ondrack – 1989*

| 163⁴/₈ | 25⁷/₈ | 25⁶/₈ | 23²/₈ | 25⁶/₈ | 5²/₈ | 5¹/₈ | 5 | 5 | | 3984 | 175 |

■ *Freeman River – Clyde L. Vongrad – Clyde L. Vongrad – 1991*

| 163⁴/₈ | 25⁶/₈ | 24⁶/₈ | 19¹/₈ | 23³/₈ | 4⁷/₈ | 4⁷/₈ | 6 | 5 | 3¹/₈ | 3984 | 175 |

■ *Swan Hills – Sandro Trulli – Sandro Trulli – 1997*

| 163²/₈ | 25 | 24⁴/₈ | 16⁴/₈ | 19 | 4¹/₈ | 4²/₈ | 5 | 5 | | 4017 | 177 |

■ *Driedmeat Lake – Everitt N. Davis – Everitt N. Davis – 1984*

| 162⁵/₈ | 25⁶/₈ | 25 | 20⁵/₈ | 22²/₈ | 5 | 5 | 6 | 6 | 6⁴/₈ | 4109† | 178† |

■ *Marwayne – Michael D. Wade – Michael D. Wade – 2000*

| 162⁵/₈ | 23⁴/₈ | 23³/₈ | 16³/₈ | 19 | 4⁶/₈ | 4⁶/₈ | 6 | 5 | | 4109 | 178 |

■ *Cadogan – Darcy Lakevold – Darcy Lakevold – 1992*

| 162⁴/₈ | 25³/₈ | 25¹/₈ | 17⁴/₈ | 21²/₈ | 4²/₈ | 4²/₈ | 6 | 5 | | 4129 | 180 |

■ *Wainwright – Everitt N. Davis – Everitt N. Davis – 1992*

| 162³/₈ | 27¹/₈ | 26¹/₈ | 21 | 24 | 5²/₈ | 5³/₈ | 4 | 5 | 1⁵/₈ | 4140 | 181 |

■ *George Lake – Shannon D. Kuzik – Shannon D. Kuzik – 1998*

| 162²/₈ | 23²/₈ | 22⁴/₈ | 18⁴/₈ | 21⁵/₈ | 4⁵/₈ | 4⁶/₈ | 6 | 6 | | 4153 | 182 |

■ *Peace River – Thomas E. Baine – Thomas E. Baine – 1998*

| 162¹/₈ | 27 | 25 | 22⁴/₈ | 24⁴/₈ | 4⁷/₈ | 5 | 5 | 5 | 2⁷/₈ | 4174 | 183 |

■ *Newbrook – James Helling – James Helling – 1994*

| 161⁶/₈ | 24³/₈ | 24⁴/₈ | 18³/₈ | 21²/₈ | 4³/₈ | 4⁴/₈ | 6 | 5 | 6³/₈ | 4223 | 184 |

■ *Crowsnest River – Gary Kuta – Gary Kuta – 1994*

| 161⁴/₈ | 24⁵/₈ | 25²/₈ | 19⁴/₈ | 20⁴/₈ | 5⁴/₈ | 5⁶/₈ | 5 | 5 | | 4258 | 185 |

■ *Driedmeat Lake – Curtis R. Siegfried – Curtis R. Siegfried – 1977*

| 160⁷/₈ | 25 | 24²/₈ | 20²/₈ | 23²/₈ | 4⁶/₈ | 4⁵/₈ | 5 | 6 | 1¹/₈ | 4380† | 186† |

■ *Amisk Creek – Brian S. Setree – Brian S. Setree – 2000*

| 160⁷/₈ | 22⁴/₈ | 23⁴/₈ | 19¹/₈ | 21⁶/₈ | 4⁴/₈ | 4⁵/₈ | 5 | 5 | | 4380 | 186 |

■ *Vilna – Marty Krohn – Marty Krohn – 1991*

Score	Length of Main Beam		Inside Spread	Greatest Spread	Circumference at Smallest Place Between Burr and First Point		Number of Points		Lengths Abnormal Points	All-Time Rank	State Rank
	Right	Left			Right	Left	Right	Left			
	■ Location of Kill – Hunter – Owner – Date Killed										
160⁵/₈	22⁴/₈	23	21³/₈	24²/₈	6	6⁴/₈	4	5		4423†	188†
	■ Logan River – Walter L. Goas III – Walter L. Goas III – 2000										
160⁵/₈	26⁵/₈	26⁶/₈	19	21	4⁵/₈	4⁶/₈	5	6	1⁷/₈	4423	188
	■ Beaver River – Robert F. Jordan – Robert F. Jordan – 1994										
160²/₈	24¹/₈	24⁴/₈	21	23²/₈	5⁶/₈	5⁷/₈	5	5		4495	190
	■ Valleyview – Carl L. Yowell – Carl L. Yowell – 1988										
160¹/₈	23	23¹/₈	19⁵/₈	22⁷/₈	5	5	5	6	5	4534	191
	■ Esson – Peter M. Konopacky – Peter M. Konopacky – 1998										

† The scores and ranking for trophies from the 25th Awards Entry Period are not final until the banquet is held on June 19, 2004.

ALBERTA

NON-TYPICAL WHITETAIL DEER

Score	Length of Main Beam Right Left	Inside Spread	Greatest Spread	Circumference at Smallest Place Between Burr and First Point Right Left	Number of Points Right Left	Lengths Abnormal Points	All-Time Rank	State Rank
	■ Location of Kill – Hunter – Owner – Date Killed							
279 6/8	27 6/8 26	21 6/8	27 2/8	6 6	13 14	98 2/8	9	1
	■ Whitemud Creek – Neil J. Morin – Brad Gsell – 1991							
277 5/8	27 5/8 28 4/8	24 6/8	30	6 6 1/8	17 16	93 1/8	10	2
	■ Hardisty – Doug Klinger – Doug Klinger – 1976							
267 7/8	25 24 4/8	22 6/8	29 2/8	6 1/8 6 2/8	20 18	95 3/8	16	3
	■ Shoal Lake – Jerry Froma – Jerry Froma – 1984							
255 4/8	23 2/8 22 7/8	18 1/8	27 2/8	5 6/8 5 5/8	18 15	61 7/8	42	4
	■ Pigeon Lake – Leo Eklund – Leo Eklund – 1973							
248 4/8	26 5/8 26 1/8	18 1/8	28 5/8	6 1/8 5 7/8	16 19	81 3/8	68	5
	■ Millet – Donald Mayer – D.J. Hollinger & B. Howard – 1995							
241 1/8	26 4/8 26 1/8	18 1/8	25 4/8	6 1/8 6	19 18	74	108	6
	■ Bighill Creek – Donald D. Dwernychuk – Donald D. Dwernychuk – 1984							
240 3/8	28 7/8 28 2/8	20 4/8	28 5/8	5 5	13 13	49 5/8	115	7
	■ Pine Lake – Edwin R. Pick – Edwin R. Pick – 1997							
233 7/8	27 6/8 30 1/8	21 4/8	26 1/8	5 6/8 5 6/8	10 13	38 5/8	183	8
	■ Blueberry Mt. – William Shumaker – William Shumaker – 1994							
233 2/8	26 7/8 26 2/8	24 6/8	28	4 3/8 4 5/8	9 9	39 4/8	193	9
	■ Acadia Valley – James J. Niwa – James J. Niwa – 1973							
232 5/8	23 2/8 23 7/8	18 2/8	25	7 6 5/8	15 11	57 5/8	200	10
	■ Winfield – Harry O. Hueppelshevser – Harry O. Hueppelshevser – 1986							
232 3/8	25 2/8 24 2/8	19 6/8	22 4/8	5 3/8 5 4/8	12 9	45 1/8	204	11
	■ Glendon – John Diedrich – John Diedrich – 1995							
232 2/8	23 3/8 22 7/8	17 2/8	21 7/8	5 6/8 5 4/8	12 18	68	207	12
	■ Thorsby – Robert G. MacRae – Robert G. MacRae – 1987							
231 6/8	26 1/8 25 3/8	23 2/8	26 1/8	6 6 1/8	11 13	44	213	13
	■ Peace River – Terry Doll – Terry Doll – 1978							
230 7/8	25 4/8 25 2/8	21 5/8	29 2/8	5 1/8 5 1/8	12 14	59	229	14
	■ Provost – Richard C. Nelson – Richard C. Nelson – 1990							
230 6/8	27 5/8 27 2/8	19 3/8	29	5 7/8 6	14 16	52 5/8	231	15
	■ Red Deer – Delmer E. Johnson – Bass Pro Shops – 1973							
227 2/8	26 4/8 26 5/8	29	31 1/8	6 6 1/8	11 8	56 1/8	274	16
	■ Pembina River – Joe Oleksiw – Joe Oleksiw – 1992							
227 1/8	24 7/8 26 6/8	18 6/8	25	5 1/8 4 7/8	11 14	47 7/8	275	17
	■ Sang Lake – V. Lynn Steeves – V. Lynn Steeves – 1992							
222 5/8	24 6/8 23 7/8	18 5/8	24 4/8	5 1/8 5 5/8	9 9	26 2/8	373	18
	■ Edgerton – Nick Leskow – Russell Thornberry – 1964							
221 6/8	23 2/8 25 7/8	21 5/8	25 6/8	5 5/8 5 6/8	13 10	55 3/8	400	19
	■ Snipe Lake – Robert Dickson, Sr. – Robert Dickson, Sr. – 1984							

Score	Length of Main Beam Right	Left	Inside Spread	Greatest Spread	Circumference at Smallest Place Between Burr and First Point Right	Left	Number of Points Right	Left	Lengths Abnormal Points	All-Time Rank	State Rank
219²/₈	23⁶/₈	23⁵/₈	23²/₈	25⁵/₈	4⁴/₈	4⁵/₈	12	12	44	460	20
■ Mud Creek – Hank Stainbrook – Caroline Supplies Ltd. – 1971											
217⁵/₈	26	23²/₈	18⁵/₈	21⁷/₈	5¹/₈	5⁵/₈	9	16	45⁶/₈	506	21
■ Flagstaff – Craig A. Miller – Craig A. Miller – 1990											
215⁶/₈	28¹/₈	28¹/₈	26²/₈	28³/₈	6⁶/₈	6¹/₈	10	9	26⁶/₈	575	22
■ Mayerthorpe – Gary F. Jamieson – Gary F. Jamieson – 1998											
215⁵/₈	21⁶/₈	22	15		5⁷/₈	6²/₈	14	15	52³/₈	578	23
■ Medicine Hat – Dave Moore – Dave Moore – 1998											
213⁷/₈	23³/₈	28⁴/₈	20⁷/₈	26⁶/₈	6³/₈	6⁶/₈	15	11	66²/₈	635	24
■ Athabasca River – Todd Armstrong – Todd Armstrong – 1990											
213⁴/₈	26³/₈	23²/₈	18⁶/₈	22⁵/₈	6¹/₈	6⁴/₈	12	11	42	657	25
■ Rochester – Lamar A. Windberg – Lamar A. Windberg – 1973											
213²/₈	26⁴/₈	26²/₈	20²/₈	25⁴/₈	5²/₈	5³/₈	10	13	34	662	26
■ Cold Lake – John F. Koreman – John F. Koreman – 1991											
213¹/₈	24⁶/₈	24⁵/₈	20⁷/₈	24⁵/₈	5³/₈	5³/₈	10	10	49²/₈	664†	27†
■ Leech Lake – Greg J. Gilbertson – Greg J. Gilbertson – 2001											
212⁶/₈	25³/₈	26³/₈	24¹/₈	28	5⁴/₈	5³/₈	7	8	19³/₈	677	28
■ Long Lake – Philip H. Preisel – Philip H. Preisel – 1995											
212⁵/₈	23⁷/₈	23⁵/₈	18³/₈	26²/₈	6¹/₈	6³/₈	12	12	54⁴/₈	683	29
■ Alberta – Picked Up – D.J. Hollinger & B. Howard – 1980											
212⁵/₈	25²/₈	26⁴/₈	21³/₈	24²/₈	5⁴/₈	5⁴/₈	11	9	44⁶/₈	683	29
■ Pelican River – John Kozyra – John Kozyra – 1993											
212²/₈	26¹/₈	26³/₈	25⁷/₈	28⁷/₈	5⁷/₈	5⁷/₈	9	10	29⁷/₈	701	31
■ Two Hills – Wesley I. Nikiforuk – Wesley I. Nikiforuk – 1999											
212	29⁴/₈	26³/₈	19¹/₈	23⁵/₈	5¹/₈	5¹/₈	10	10	36³/₈	717	32
■ Vermilion – Derry Heathcote – Derry Heathcote – 1995											
211²/₈	23²/₈	24⁴/₈	16⁶/₈	28⁷/₈	5⁷/₈	5⁷/₈	10	9	44²/₈	750	33
■ Hughenden – Morris Sather – Morris Sather – 1966											
211²/₈	29²/₈	29	24	28¹/₈	5¹/₈	5³/₈	7	7	20²/₈	750	33
■ Athabasca – Tim M. Shmigelsky – Tim M. Shmigelsky – 1995											
211²/₈	24⁶/₈	26²/₈	18⁶/₈	21⁵/₈	4⁷/₈	4⁷/₈	9	7	27⁶/₈	750	33
■ Pigeon Lake – Jeff Strandquist – Jeff Strandquist – 1997											
211¹/₈	26⁵/₈	26¹/₈	21³/₈	28	5⁴/₈	5⁴/₈	9	11	24⁴/₈	758	36
■ Rich Lake – Sammy J. Schrimsher – Sammy J. Schrimsher – 1994											
210⁷/₈	26⁷/₈	26	19⁵/₈	24³/₈	6³/₈	6²/₈	9	10	38²/₈	773	37
■ Lac La Biche – Render L. Crowder, Sr. – Render L. Crowder, Sr. – 1998											
210¹/₈	24¹/₈	24⁷/₈	21⁵/₈	25⁷/₈	4⁶/₈	5	14	12	54⁶/₈	808	38
■ Chain Lakes – Jim Chapman – Jim Chapman – 1989											
210¹/₈	24⁶/₈	25¹/₈	19	22	5⁵/₈	6¹/₈	8	12	52¹/₈	808	38
■ Lac La Biche – Otis W. Cowles – Otis W. Cowles – 1998											
210¹/₈	22⁶/₈	23	19²/₈	21⁶/₈	5¹/₈	5¹/₈	9	7	27³/₈	808	38
■ St. Paul – Richard C. Nelson – Richard C. Nelson – 1999											

Score	Length of Main Beam Right	Left	Inside Spread	Greatest Spread	Circumference at Smallest Place Between Burr and First Point Right	Left	Number of Points Right	Left	Lengths Abnormal Points	All-Time Rank	State Rank
	■ Location of Kill – Hunter – Owner – Date Killed										
208²/8	26⁵/8	24	19³/8	24¹/8	5³/8	7³/8	10	10	41¹/8	910	41
	■ Chauvin – Picked Up – Shane Hansen – 1981										
208¹/8	25²/8	26¹/8	19⁶/8	23⁷/8	4⁷/8	4⁷/8	9	9	27⁷/8	920	42
	■ Beaverhill Lake – Dean Hrehirchuk – Dean Hrehirchuk – 1989										
207⁷/8	26⁵/8	26	24²/8	26⁶/8	5³/8	5²/8	7	9	26¹/8	938	43
	■ Monitor – Raymond Worobo – Raymond Worobo – 1979										
207⁷/8	30³/8	31²/8	23⁷/8	27	6²/8	6¹/8	9	9	21	938	43
	■ Ribstone Creek – Trevor C. Thorpe – Trevor C. Thorpe – 1992										
207⁵/8	25⁴/8	25⁴/8	21²/8	25⁷/8	6	6	11	7	16⁵/8	957	45
	■ Keephills – Unknown – William J. Greenhough – PR 1970										
207²/8	27¹/8	26⁵/8	18³/8	20⁶/8	5²/8	5¹/8	7	10	23⁵/8	985	46
	■ Drayton Valley – Hassib Halabi – Hassib Halabi – 1977										
207¹/8	25⁷/8	24³/8	20⁶/8	23⁴/8	5¹/8	5²/8	9	10	40³/8	995	47
	■ Provost – Michael D. Kerley – Michael D. Kerley – 1977										
206⁷/8	25⁴/8	25⁶/8	21⁶/8	25	5⁶/8	5⁶/8	10	9	25³/8	1011	48
	■ Pine Lake – Richard D. Doan – Leila R. Doan – 1979										
206⁷/8	24⁷/8	24⁶/8	20	23³/8	5³/8	5²/8	13	12	27⁷/8	1011	48
	■ Baxter Lake – Terry F. Ermel – Terry F. Ermel – 1988										
206⁷/8	25	22⁵/8	18⁶/8	21³/8	5⁶/8	4⁷/8	9	11	45³/8	1011	48
	■ Deserters Creek – Duane Paisley – Duane Paisley – 1992										
206⁵/8	24⁵/8	24³/8	19⁶/8	23⁴/8	6	6¹/8	8	11	28³/8	1036	51
	■ Kevisville – Brian R. McKain – Brian R. McKain – 1990										
206²/8	26⁵/8	26⁴/8	19⁷/8	22³/8	5⁴/8	5¹/8	9	8	35¹/8	1059	52
	■ McLennan – Gordon E. Ristow – Gordon E. Ristow – 1993										
205⁷/8	24⁷/8	23⁵/8	20	24⁵/8	6	6	14	11	49⁵/8	1080	53
	■ Battle River – Bryan Champagne – Bryan Champagne – 1987										
205⁴/8	25⁴/8	26¹/8	23³/8	28³/8	4⁶/8	4⁶/8	10	6	16¹/8	1107	54
	■ Ram River – William Howard – William Howard – 1988										
205³/8	20⁴/8	23¹/8	20⁶/8	25⁴/8	5⁴/8	5³/8	9	9	31³/8	1116	55
	■ St. Anne Lake – Allen H. Wilkie – Allen H. Wilkie – 1995										
204⁷/8	25⁴/8	26³/8	21²/8	27⁴/8	5⁵/8	5⁴/8	13	9	42⁵/8	1156	56
	■ Bentley – Stanley A. Anderson – Stanley A. Anderson – 1968										
204⁶/8	26⁷/8	25⁷/8	21¹/8	24²/8	5¹/8	5	6	8	31³/8	1165	57
	■ Innisfree – Donald Baranec – Donald Baranec – 1977										
204⁶/8	24¹/8	25⁴/8	19¹/8	25⁴/8	6	6¹/8	10	10	25⁵/8	1165	57
	■ St. Anne Lake – Todd K. Kirk – Todd K. Kirk – 1996										
204³/8	24⁵/8	25⁶/8	19³/8	24	5³/8	5³/8	10	8	28	1186	59
	■ Nanton – Barry Flipping – Barry Flipping – 1986										
204²/8	25⁵/8	23¹/8	17¹/8	23¹/8	5¹/8	5⁴/8	7	15	76³/8	1199	60
	■ Silver Lake – Edwin Nelson – Gary Padleski – 1980										
204	27²/8	25²/8	21⁷/8	24³/8	5²/8	5³/8	7	12	55¹/8	1220	61
	■ Sheep River – Walter L. Brown – Walter L. Brown – 1966										

Score	Length of Main Beam Right	Left	Inside Spread	Greatest Spread	Circumference at Smallest Place Between Burr and First Point Right	Left	Number of Points Right	Left	Lengths Abnormal Points	All-Time Rank	State Rank

203²/₈ 23²/₈ 23⁵/₈ 22 26 5²/₈ 5³/₈ 10 9 50 1287 62
■ Open Creek – David Serhan – David Serhan – 1995

202¹/₈ 26 26³/₈ 20 25³/₈ 5³/₈ 5⁴/₈ 12 10 24³/₈ 1386 63
■ Whitefish Lake – Bill Yaceyko – Bill Yaceyko – 1997

201⁷/₈ 24²/₈ 23³/₈ 23⁴/₈ 26²/₈ 5⁴/₈ 5⁴/₈ 9 7 23³/₈ 1410 64
■ Burmis – Joe Tapay – Joe Tapay – 1964

201⁷/₈ 25⁵/₈ 26³/₈ 16 22⁶/₈ 6¹/₈ 6¹/₈ 9 9 27³/₈ 1410 64
■ Pembina River – Gordon Modanese – Gordon Modanese – 1995

201⁶/₈ 29 25⁶/₈ 25 28 5⁵/₈ 5⁷/₈ 8 11 32⁶/₈ 1421 66
■ Plamondon – Steve K. Swinhoe – Steve K. Swinhoe – 1996

201⁵/₈ 25 24⁷/₈ 17¹/₈ 21²/₈ 5²/₈ 5¹/₈ 10 8 28 1427 67
■ Ohaton – Curtis R. Siegfried – Curtis R. Siegfried – 1976

201⁴/₈ 22⁶/₈ 23³/₈ 21¹/₈ 24⁶/₈ 5²/₈ 5²/₈ 14 9 34³/₈ 1443 68
■ Athabasca – Aldo B. Zanon – Aldo B. Zanon – 1995

201²/₈ 21¹/₈ 20⁷/₈ 16²/₈ 23 5⁵/₈ 5³/₈ 12 9 29²/₈ 1478 69
■ McLeod River – Roy Schueler – Roy Schueler – 1992

201²/₈ 24⁷/₈ 26⁴/₈ 19⁵/₈ 23⁵/₈ 5⁴/₈ 5⁴/₈ 10 9 26³/₈ 1478 69
■ High Prairie – Leo Morawski – Leo Morawski – 1997

201 25⁷/₈ 26⁴/₈ 20³/₈ 24³/₈ 4⁴/₈ 4⁵/₈ 9 13 23⁷/₈ 1500 71
■ Cessford – Russell C. Chapman – Russell C. Chapman – 1966

201 28 27 21³/₈ 24⁴/₈ 4⁷/₈ 5 11 8 23³/₈ 1500 71
■ Empress – David Booker – David Booker – 1979

200⁷/₈ 28 29⁷/₈ 19 23¹/₈ 5 4⁷/₈ 11 9 21⁵/₈ 1512† 73†
■ Cochrane – Terry L. Raymond – Terry L. Raymond – 2001

200⁴/₈ 25¹/₈ 22⁴/₈ 19⁶/₈ 25³/₈ 6¹/₈ 6 10 10 29 1545 74
■ Wainwright – Paul Pryor – Paul Pryor – 1968

200¹/₈ 27¹/₈ 27⁴/₈ 23 26⁵/₈ 6²/₈ 6⁴/₈ 7 11 21⁷/₈ 1577 75
■ Smoky Lake – Brent Weber – Brent Weber – 1991

200 25⁶/₈ 26⁴/₈ 22³/₈ 24⁶/₈ 5²/₈ 5²/₈ 6 8 14¹/₈ 1591† 76†
■ Athabasca – John M. Gibbs – John M. Gibbs – 2000

199⁶/₈ 23²/₈ 24 17⁴/₈ 20⁴/₈ 5¹/₈ 5³/₈ 8 9 30²/₈ 1613 77
■ Rochester – James Weismantel – James Weismantel – 1979

199¹/₈ 23³/₈ 23²/₈ 22⁵/₈ 25⁶/₈ 5⁵/₈ 5⁶/₈ 9 8 25 1660 78
■ Smoky Lake – Helmuth Ritter – Helmuth Ritter – 1992

199 25¹/₈ 26 19²/₈ 22³/₈ 5⁵/₈ 5⁶/₈ 9 6 23⁶/₈ 1668 79
■ Grattan Creek – Torleif A. Larson – Torleif A. Larson – 1968

199 24⁷/₈ 27²/₈ 19⁷/₈ 25 5 5 8 7 23¹/₈ 1668 79
■ Westaskiwin – John Miller – John Miller – 1984

198⁷/₈ 24 25²/₈ 22³/₈ 24⁴/₈ 5⁴/₈ 5⁶/₈ 9 7 28²/₈ 1686 81
■ Morse River – Leo M. Schmaus – Leo M. Schmaus – 1985

198⁷/₈ 24²/₈ 24³/₈ 18²/₈ 20 6²/₈ 6²/₈ 7 7 24⁷/₈ 1686 81
■ Pembina River – Thomas Free – Thomas Free – 1992

Score	Length of Main Beam Right	Left	Inside Spread	Greatest Spread	Circumference at Smallest Place Between Burr and First Point Right	Left	Number of Points Right	Left	Lengths Abnormal Points	All-Time Rank	State Rank
	■ Location of Kill – Hunter – Owner – Date Killed										
198 6/8	26 2/8	25 2/8	17 3/8	20 3/8	6 1/8	5 3/8	10	8	25 3/8	1697	83
	■ James River – Hans Van Vlaanderen – Hans Van Vlaanderen – 1986										
198 4/8	25 1/8	22 5/8	19 1/8	22 5/8	5 6/8	5 7/8	10	5	26 3/8	1736†	84†
	■ Smoky River – Jim Boland – Jim Boland – 2000										
198 2/8	22 5/8	21 7/8	16 6/8	22 3/8	4 5/8	4 5/8	9	9	45 2/8	1772†	85†
	■ Dogpound Creek – Steve K. Thompson – Steve K. Thompson – 2001										
198 2/8	25 4/8	24 7/8	20 6/8	23	4 6/8	5	9	8	40 2/8	1772	85
	■ Rochester – Vern E. Alton – Vern E. Alton – 1995										
197 4/8	25 5/8	26 4/8	25 5/8	31	5	5	11	7	41 3/8	1866	87
	■ Wainwright – George Bauman – George Bauman – 1967										
197 3/8	21 4/8	20 5/8	18 5/8	21 1/8	4 7/8	5 3/8	12	11	49 6/8	1884	88
	■ Athabasca – Clinton Peredery – Clinton Peredery – 1999										
197 1/8	27 5/8	27 7/8	18 3/8	21 1/8	5 3/8	5 6/8	9	10	29	1923	89
	■ Rocky Mountain House – Robin L. McDonald – Robin L. McDonald – 1998										
196 7/8	26 3/8	27 3/8	21 7/8	26 4/8	5 4/8	5 3/8	10	5	16 6/8	1950	90
	■ Chipman – Don F. MacLean – Don F. MacLean – 1997										
196 6/8	24 5/8	22 7/8	20 3/8	23 3/8	5 4/8	5 3/8	7	9	29 5/8	1968	91
	■ Athabasca – Robert Camarillo – Robert Camarillo – 1994										
196 1/8	27 3/8	27 2/8	21 3/8	23 7/8	5 6/8	7 2/8	10	10	22 6/8	2045	92
	■ Leduc – Gordon Gulick – Gordon Gulick – 1993										
196 1/8	22 6/8	24 5/8	19 4/8	21 6/8	5 3/8	5 4/8	14	8	34 7/8	2045	92
	■ Rumsey – Greg Smith – Greg Smith – 1996										
195 6/8	24 2/8	24 6/8	18 3/8	20 5/8	5 1/8	5	7	7	18 1/8	2094	94
	■ Wetaskiwin – Lewis D. Callies – Lewis D. Callies – 1972										
195 5/8	25 4/8	25 6/8	19 1/8	21 2/8	5	5 2/8	8	8	21	2116	95
	■ Duffield – Robert A. Schaefer – Robert A. Schaefer – 1980										
195 3/8	24 5/8	25 2/8	18 3/8	22 6/8	5 2/8	5 1/8	14	6	40 4/8	2163†	96†
	■ Vermilion River – Greg O'Hare – Greg O'Hare – 2001										
195 3/8	25 2/8	26 3/8	20 1/8	25 3/8	5 3/8	5 2/8	11	8	26	2163	96
	■ Grassland – Frederick Neumann – Frederick Neumann – 1980										
195 3/8	24 2/8	23	18 2/8	23 7/8	5 1/8	5 2/8	9	11	22 7/8	2163	96
	■ N. Saskatchewan River – Thomas J. Procinsky – Thomas J. Procinsky – 1990										
195 2/8	26	26	22 7/8	25 2/8	5	5	8	8	23 7/8	2186	99
	■ Lily Lake – Richard J. Leclercq – Richard J. Leclercq – 1993										
195	25	25 4/8	18 7/8	22 5/8	5	5 1/8	8	9	20 1/8	2233	100
	■ Mitchell Creek – Gord Moreau – Gord Moreau – 1998										
193 5/8	26 3/8	27 3/8	20 1/8	26 5/8	5 2/8	5 3/8	9	10	27 2/8	2281	101
	■ High Level – Richard Provencher – Richard Provencher – 1998										
192 3/8	24 7/8	25 7/8	22	23 5/8	5 1/8	4 7/8	9	9	22 7/8	2331	102
	■ Peace River – Donald Neudorf – Donald Neudorf – 1992										
190	21 7/8	21 3/8	17 4/8	20	4 4/8	4 3/8	10	9	38 6/8	2418†	103†
	■ Glendon – Philip Kozak III – Philip Kozak III – 2001										

Score	Length of Main Beam		Inside Spread	Greatest Spread	Circumference at Smallest Place Between Burr and First Point		Number of Points		Lengths Abnormal Points	All-Time Rank	State Rank
	Right	Left			Right	Left	Right	Left			
	Location of Kill – Hunter – Owner – Date Killed										
189 6/8	24 3/8	24 6/8	19 7/8	23 1/8	7 2/8	7 3/8	12	8	20 1/8	2425	104
	Peace River – Alvin Johnson – Alvin Johnson – 1994										
189 5/8	26 6/8	27 1/8	19 5/8	20 1/8	5 2/8	5	7	7	15 2/8	2429	105
	Slave Lake – Steven W. Sasnett – Steven W. Sasnett – 1995										
189 4/8	22 7/8	23 4/8	15 4/8	17 7/8	6 2/8	6 4/8	9	7	30 2/8	2435	106
	Chipman – Kenneth H. Jackson – Kenneth H. Jackson – 1998										
189 1/8	24 3/8	23 7/8	22 1/8	24 1/8	5	5	7	7	13 6/8	2450	107
	Ross Lake – Lawrence Cahoon – Lawrence Cahoon – 1967										
189 1/8	24 5/8	26 1/8	18 7/8	21 4/8	5	5 2/8	9	10	14 4/8	2450	107
	Chisholm – Prosper L. Boisvert – Prosper L. Boisvert – 1990										
188 2/8	22 1/8	23	19 7/8	23 7/8	4 2/8	4 2/8	13	9	39 5/8	2489	109
	Whitecourt – Eric M. Mickailyk – Eric M. Mickailyk – 1992										
188 1/8	25 7/8	26 7/8	20 2/8	23 3/8	5 6/8	6	7	7	16 3/8	2497	110
	Carrot Creek – Gerald Bodner – Gerald Bodner – 1994										
188	24 6/8	23 3/8	16 4/8	19 7/8	5	5	9	7	14 4/8	2504	111
	N. Saskatchewan River – William N. Toth – William N. Toth – 1988										
186 2/8	24 2/8	24 2/8	17 3/8	21 7/8	5	4 7/8	7	10	21 5/8	2575	112
	Red Deer River – Lorne Proudfoot – Lorne Proudfoot – 1990										
185 6/8	23 6/8	19 6/8	18 4/8	21	5 4/8	5 2/8	8	8	9 4/8	2605†	113†
	Newton Lake – John J. McKeown – John J. McKeown – 2001										
185 5/8	22 4/8	22 6/8	18 7/8	20 5/8	5	4 7/8	9	7	14	2610	114
	St. Ann Lake – Brian Lehenki – Brian Lehenki – 1997										
185 3/8	24 4/8	25 3/8	21 2/8	23 7/8	5 2/8	5 4/8	8	9	31 7/8	2622†	115†
	Oldman Lake – Allen T. Carstairs – Allen T. Carstairs – 2000										
185	22 4/8	22 1/8	25	25 6/8	5 2/8	5	11	8	41 4/8	2653†	116†
	Long Lake – Bryan D. Hill – Bryan D. Hill – 2000										
252 6/8	27 1/8	24 5/8	17 1/8	26 3/8	5 7/8	5 5/8	9	15	71 7/8	*	*
	Sandy Lake – Donald Brenneman – Donald Brenneman – 1998										

† The scores and ranking for trophies from the 25th Awards Entry Period are not final until the banquet is held on June 19, 2004.

* Final score is subject to revision by additional verifying measurements.

BRITISH COLUMBIA
RECORD WHITETAILS

21 Typical whitetail deer entries
17 Non-typical whitetail deer entries
7,265 Total whitetail deer entries

NEW
PROVINCIAL
RECORD

**BRITISH COLUMBIA
NEW PROVINCIAL
RECORD**
Typical Whitetail Deer
Score: 185^4/8
Location: Brisco
Hunter: Baptiste Paul
Owner: Winston Wolfenden
Date: 1914

BRITISH COLUMBIA PROVINCIAL RECORD
Non-Typical Whitetail Deer
Score: 245⁷/₈
Location: Elk River
Hunter and Owner: James I. Brewster
Date: 1905

Photograph from B&C Archives

BRITISH COLUMBIA

TYPICAL WHITETAIL DEER

Score	Length of Main Beam Right	Left	Inside Spread	Greatest Spread	Circumference at Smallest Place Between Burr and First Point Right	Left	Number of Points Right	Left	Lengths Abnormal Points	All-Time Rank	State Rank
	■ Location of Kill – Hunter – Owner – Date Killed										
185⁴/₈	27¹/₈	27²/₈	22²/₈	26²/₈	4⁷/₈	5	6	8	1	251	1
	■ Brisco – Baptiste Paul – Winston Wolfenden – 1914										
184⁷/₈	24⁴/₈	23⁵/₈	17³/₈	21³/₈	5⁶/₈	5⁵/₈	6	7	2	279	2
	■ Aitken Creek – Guyle G. Cox – Guyle G. Cox – 1990										
183⁴/₈	29⁷/₈	29³/₈	23⁷/₈	27	5⁴/₈	5⁶/₈	8	8	16¹/₈	361	3
	■ Holmes River – Randy Lloyd – Randy Lloyd – 1991										
180	25⁶/₈	25⁴/₈	20	22⁵/₈	5⁴/₈	5⁶/₈	5	5		688	4
	■ Dawson Creek – H. Peter Bruhs – H. Peter Bruhs – 1989 ■ See photo on page 551										
177⁷/₈	24²/₈	23⁷/₈	19³/₈	22¹/₈	4⁶/₈	4⁴/₈	7	7		936	5
	■ Ymir – Frank Gowing – Frank Gowing – 1961										
175⁷/₈	27⁵/₈	27¹/₈	22⁵/₈	29⁴/₈	6⁵/₈	6²/₈	9	7	14²/₈	1287	6
	■ Pouce Coupe River – Dale Callahan – Dale Callahan – 1986										
175³/₈	27⁷/₈	25⁷/₈	19⁵/₈	22	5³/₈	5²/₈	6	6		1377	7
	■ Satellite Hill – Bill Shunter – Bill Shunter – 1990										
175	28²/₈	28⁷/₈	20²/₈	22⁴/₈	5⁶/₈	5⁶/₈	7	6	9⁶/₈	1472	8
	■ Peace River – Unknown – Shane Pallister – PR 1980										
174⁵/₈	26	26²/₈	21¹/₈	23³/₈	5³/₈	5³/₈	5	6	2	1561	9
	■ Baldonnel – D. Ian Williams – D. Ian Williams – 1978										
174⁴/₈	22⁵/₈	24¹/₈	16⁶/₈	19¹/₈	4⁵/₈	4⁶/₈	5	5		1592	10
	■ Fort Steele – John Lum – John Lum – 1958										
174¹/₈	26⁴/₈	26³/₈	20	23⁶/₈	5¹/₈	5	6	6	2⁷/₈	1678	11
	■ Anarchist Mt. – George Urban – George Urban – 1980										
173⁶/₈	24⁵/₈	24⁴/₈	23⁴/₈	27²/₈	5²/₈	5⁴/₈	5	5		1766	12
	■ Hart Creek – Greg Lamontange – Greg Lamontange – 1984										
172⁵/₈	23⁴/₈	23¹/₈	20¹/₈	22³/₈	5	5²/₈	6	7	1⁴/₈	2113	13
	■ Dawson Creek – J. Grant Bowie – J. Grant Bowie – 1992										
171⁶/₈	24⁴/₈	23²/₈	19⁴/₈	21⁵/₈	4⁵/₈	4⁵/₈	10	8	8⁴/₈	2418	14
	■ Gray Creek – Ross Oliver – Ross Oliver – 1982										
171³/₈	25³/₈	25³/₈	26³/₈	28³/₈	5¹/₈	5²/₈	5	6		2564	15
	■ Whatshan Lake – Ernest Roberts – Ernest Roberts – 1957										
171	25²/₈	25⁴/₈	19²/₈	22⁴/₈	4⁷/₈	4⁷/₈	5	6	1⁶/₈	2707	16
	■ Okanagan Range – Picked Up – Dennis A. Dorholt – 1984										
167²/₈	25⁶/₈	26³/₈	22	25¹/₈	5¹/₈	5¹/₈	6	6	3	3519	17
	■ Butler Ridge – Rodney A. Allen – Rodney A. Allen – 1994										
162⁶/₈	24³/₈	24²/₈	19	20⁶/₈	4⁶/₈	4⁵/₈	5	5		4089	18
	■ Woods Lake – Bill G. Schneider – Bill G. Schneider – 1994										
162⁵/₈	25⁵/₈	23⁵/₈	23¹/₈	27¹/₈	4³/₈	4⁴/₈	5	8	5²/₈	4109	19
	■ Kiskatinaw River – Dan Hachey – Dan Hachey – 1999										

Score	Length of Main Beam Right Left	Inside Spread	Greatest Spread	Circumference at Smallest Place Between Burr and First Point Right Left	Number of Points Right Left	Lengths Abnormal Points	All-Time Rank	State Rank
	■ Location of Kill – Hunter – Owner – Date Killed							
160⁴/8	23⁵/8 23³/8	18	20²/8	5 5	5 5		4443	20
	■ Dawson Creek – Craig Bahm – Craig Bahm – 1999							
160	26³/8 25	19²/8	22	4⁵/8 4⁵/8	5 5		4565	21
	■ Groundbirch – Peter H. Bruhs – Peter H. Bruhs – 1994							

BRITISH COLUMBIA

NON-TYPICAL WHITETAIL DEER

Score	Length of Main Beam Right	Left	Inside Spread	Greatest Spread	Circumference at Smallest Place Between Burr and First Point Right	Left	Number of Points Right	Left	Lengths Abnormal Points	All-Time Rank	State Rank
245 7/8	31 2/8	27 6/8	25 3/8	35 6/8	5 5/8	5 6/8	11	14	54 2/8	78	1
Elk River – James I. Brewster – James I. Brewster – 1905											
230 7/8	26 2/8	28 4/8	19 7/8	25 3/8	5 2/8	5	12	13	51	229	2
West Kootenay – Karl H. Kast – Karl H. Kast – 1940											
224 1/8	19 7/8	21 7/8	18 3/8	18 3/8	6 4/8	6	13	10	62 2/8	334†	3†
Rose Prairie – Rob White – Rob White – 2000											
220 5/8	22 1/8	23 6/8	16 6/8	24 6/8	4 3/8	4 3/8	10	15	75 5/8	424	4
Halfway River – Bill Miller – Deb Fleet – PR 1934											
219 2/8	26 2/8	26 6/8	22 3/8	24 5/8	4 7/8	5	11	12	43 7/8	460	5
Midway – Gordon Kamigochi – Gordon Kamigochi – 1980											
218 5/8	23 5/8	24 6/8	17 1/8	22	4 7/8	4 5/8	7	10	52 4/8	480	6
Dawson Creek – John D. Todd – John D. Todd – 1992											
205 5/8	24 6/8	25	21 4/8	26 5/8	5 1/8	5	14	12	46 7/8	1102	7
Fellers Heights – Billy L. Franks – Billy L. Franks – 1995											
204 5/8	26 5/8	26 6/8	19 7/8	22	4 7/8	4 7/8	8	10	27 4/8	1176	8
Bull River – Gary Nonis – Gary Nonis – 1994											
203 4/8	27	27 2/8	19 6/8	22 5/8	4 6/8	4 7/8	8	11	22 4/8	1259	9
Upper Cutbank – William E. Eckert – William E. Eckert – 1990											
202 2/8	25 1/8	24 7/8	19 2/8	24 2/8	4 6/8	4 7/8	9	9	25 2/8	1377	10
East Kooteney – Andrew W. Rosicky – Andrew W. Rosicky – 1956											
201 1/8	26 7/8	26 2/8	16 5/8	19 7/8	4 2/8	4 2/8	11	9	31	1489	11
King Edward Lake – Reiny Lippert – Reiny Lippert – 1994											
198 5/8	22	22	20 4/8	23 3/8	4 6/8	4 5/8	9	9	40 3/8	1716	12
Dawson Creek – Philip D. Springer – Philip D. Springer – 1990											
198 1/8	21 7/8	21 2/8	17	21	4 7/8	5	13	12	43 3/8	1785	13
Nelway – Edward John – Edward John – 1935											
195 7/8	26 7/8	27 5/8	18 3/8	22 4/8	5	4 7/8	11	11	22 4/8	2076†	14†
Blueberry River – Ernie Kuehne – Ernie Kuehne – 2000											
195	24 6/8	24 4/8	18 3/8	25 3/8	5 6/8	5 5/8	6	13	40 5/8	2233	15
Dome Creek – John Hale – John Charters – PR 1960											
190 4/8	22 1/8	22 6/8	18 2/8	19 6/8	4 4/8	4 5/8	9	12	37 6/8	2401	16
Belogo Dam – Darrell Orlesky – Darrell Orlesky – 1992											
185 4/8	24 5/8	24 3/8	19 7/8		4 6/8	4 7/8	8	9	17 5/8	2616	17
Dawson Creek – Doug Field – Doug Field – 1993											

■ *Location of Kill – Hunter – Owner – Date Killed*

† The scores and ranking for trophies from the 25th Awards Entry Period are not final until the banquet is held on June 19, 2004.

TROPHIES IN THE FIELD

HUNTER: H. Peter Bruhs
SCORE: 180
CATEGORY: typical whitetail deer
LOCATION: Dawson Creek, British Columbia
DATE: 1989

MANITOBA
RECORD WHITETAILS

75 Typical whitetail deer entries
36 Non-typical whitetail deer entries
7,265 Total whitetail deer entries

MANITOBA
PROVINCIAL RECORD
Typical Whitetail Deer
Score: 197$^7/_8$
Location: Assiniboine River
Hunter: Larry H. MacDonald
Owner: Bass Pro Shops
Date: 1980

MANITOBA
NEW PROVINCIAL RECORD
Non-Typical Whitetail Deer
Score: 265⁷/₈
Location: Souris River
Hunter and Owner: Howard G. Pauls
Date: 2001

New provincial record pending approval from the 25th Awards Program Judges Panel.

MANITOBA

TYPICAL WHITETAIL DEER

Score	Length of Main Beam Right	Length of Main Beam Left	Inside Spread	Greatest Spread	Circumference at Smallest Place Between Burr and First Point Right	Left	Number of Points Right	Left	Lengths Abnormal Points	All-Time Rank	State Rank
197⁷/₈	27⁴/₈	27²/₈	19⁴/₈	22⁴/₈	4⁶/₈	4⁶/₈	8	9	6⁵/₈	22	1

■ *Assiniboine River – Larry H. MacDonald – Bass Pro Shops – 1980*

| 189 | 25⁴/₈ | 25⁴/₈ | 23²/₈ | 26²/₈ | 5¹/₈ | 5¹/₈ | 8 | 8 | 8 | 131 | 2 |

■ *Red Deer Lake – Will Bigelow – Will Bigelow – 1986*

| 188⁴/₈ | 27¹/₈ | 27²/₈ | 20⁶/₈ | 23³/₈ | 6⁶/₈ | 6⁴/₈ | 5 | 5 | | 141 | 3 |

■ *Souris River – Wes Todoruk – Wes Todoruk – 1986*

| 188³/₈ | 24²/₈ | 26⁴/₈ | 18⁶/₈ | 20⁶/₈ | 5⁵/₈ | 5⁵/₈ | 8 | 7 | 14⁵/₈ | 147 | 4 |

■ *Sanford – Picked Up – MB Wildl. Branch – 1982*

| 187⁶/₈ | 25⁵/₈ | 23²/₈ | 17⁴/₈ | 19⁷/₈ | 6 | 5⁶/₈ | 6 | 8 | | 160 | 5 |

■ *Mantagao Lake – Picked Up – Mel Podaima – 1988*

| 187³/₈ | 26⁷/₈ | 26⁴/₈ | 19⁷/₈ | 23³/₈ | 5³/₈ | 5⁴/₈ | 6 | 7 | | 178† | 6† |

■ *Pine Creek – C. Anne Reddon – C. Anne Reddon – 2001*

| 187¹/₈ | 26³/₈ | 26¹/₈ | 24¹/₈ | 26³/₈ | 5²/₈ | 5²/₈ | 5 | 5 | | 185 | 7 |

■ *Rossburn – G. Wayne Preston – G. Wayne Preston – 1994*

| 185³/₈ | 27⁷/₈ | 27⁷/₈ | 23³/₈ | 27 | 5 | 5¹/₈ | 5 | 6 | 1²/₈ | 256 | 8 |

■ *Woodlands – Picked Up – Cabela's, Inc. – 1994*

| 183 | 26¹/₈ | 26¹/₈ | 19³/₈ | 21 | 5 | 5 | 6 | 8 | 1³/₈ | 392 | 9 |

■ *Lorne – Alain G. Comte – Alain G. Comte – 1987*

| 182⁵/₈ | 27⁶/₈ | 28⁴/₈ | 21⁵/₈ | | 5⁶/₈ | 5⁵/₈ | 7 | 8 | | 420 | 10 |

■ *Virden – Darryl Gray – Darryl Gray – 1957*

| 182⁵/₈ | 24⁴/₈ | 23⁵/₈ | 20⁵/₈ | 22⁷/₈ | 4⁶/₈ | 4⁶/₈ | 6 | 7 | 1²/₈ | 420 | 10 |

■ *Mantagao Lake – Stephen A. Obelnicki – Stephen A. Obelnicki – 1993*

| 180⁵/₈ | 23 | 23⁷/₈ | 19³/₈ | 21²/₈ | 4¹/₈ | 4¹/₈ | 7 | 7 | | 599 | 12 |

■ *Waterhen – Craig R. Zmijewski – Craig R. Zmijewski – 1996*

| 179⁷/₈ | 27⁶/₈ | 26⁶/₈ | 19⁷/₈ | 22²/₈ | 5⁴/₈ | 5⁴/₈ | 5 | 5 | | 705 | 13 |

■ *Hamiota – Alan J. Sheridan – Alan J. Sheridan – 1984*

| 179⁴/₈ | 26⁵/₈ | 26⁶/₈ | 20 | 22³/₈ | 5³/₈ | 5²/₈ | 5 | 5 | | 733 | 14 |

■ *Sandridge – Robert Anderson – Robert Anderson – 1971*

| 179⁴/₈ | 26²/₈ | 26²/₈ | 19⁵/₈ | 22 | 5⁶/₈ | 5³/₈ | 6 | 5 | 1³/₈ | 733 | 14 |

■ *Whitemud River – L. Greg Fehr – L. Greg Fehr – 1985*

| 179³/₈ | 26 | 26²/₈ | 17³/₈ | 22 | 6 | 5⁵/₈ | 6 | 6 | 7 | 749 | 16 |

■ *Oberon – Arnold W. Poole – Arnold W. Poole – 1968*

| 179 | 26 | 26⁶/₈ | 16 | 19⁷/₈ | 5⁵/₈ | 5⁶/₈ | 6 | 7 | 2²/₈ | 786† | 17† |

■ *Dauphin Lake – Maurice Theoret – Maurice Theoret – 2001*

| 179 | 25⁶/₈ | 25⁶/₈ | 19³/₈ | 21⁶/₈ | 5 | 5¹/₈ | 5 | 6 | 2¹/₈ | 786 | 17 |

■ *Waldersee – W. Wutke – W. Wutke – 1959*

| 178⁶/₈ | 26 | 25 | 22⁷/₈ | 25¹/₈ | 5²/₈ | 5¹/₈ | 6 | 6 | 2³/₈ | 808 | 19 |

■ *Elkhorn – Jerry May – Jerry May – 1959*

Score	Length of Main Beam Right	Left	Inside Spread	Greatest Spread	Circumference at Smallest Place Between Burr and First Point Right	Left	Number of Points Right	Left	Lengths Abnormal Points	All-Time Rank	State Rank
	■ Location of Kill – Hunter – Owner – Date Killed										
178 4/8	25 1/8	25 4/8	19 4/8	22 7/8	5 3/8	5 3/8	5	5		850	20
	■ Firdale – Randall J. Bean – Randall J. Bean – 1988										
177 7/8	27	27 7/8	19 5/8	22 3/8	5 5/8	5 4/8	5	6		936	21
	■ Rosieisle – Richard A. Fay – Richard A. Fay – 1995										
177 4/8	26 3/8	26 2/8	20 4/8	23 5/8	5	5	6	5	1 2/8	993	22
	■ Swan River – Myles T. Keller – Myles T. Keller – 1994										
177	24 7/8	25	16 2/8	22 4/8	5 1/8	5 1/8	8	9	12 6/8	1066	23
	■ Daly – Bruce A. Crofton – Bruce A. Crofton – 1984										
177	23 7/8	25 1/8	14 3/8	17 5/8	5 2/8	5 1/8	11	7	6 1/8	1066	23
	■ Lundar – Fred Thorkelson – Fred Thorkelson – 1986										
176 7/8	25 4/8	26	19 7/8		5 5/8	5 4/8	5	5		1086	25
	■ Pierson – Bud Smith – Bud Smith – 1960										
176 4/8	22 6/8	22 5/8	17 6/8	19 1/8	5 3/8	5 2/8	6	6		1158	26
	■ Turtle Mt. – David Murray – David Murray – 1992										
176 4/8	26	26 4/8	18 4/8	20 6/8	5 3/8	5 3/8	5	6		1158	26
	■ Duck Mt. – Kevin E. Scott – Kevin E. Scott – 1996										
176 3/8	25	25 1/8	17 5/8	21	4 5/8	5 1/8	6	5		1182	28
	■ Stockton – Robert R. Blain – Robert R. Blain – 1977										
176 2/8	27	27	21 4/8	23 3/8	4 6/8	4 6/8	5	5		1209	29
	■ Dauphin – Unknown – Wayne Selby – PR 1990										
176 1/8	25 1/8	23 7/8	24 1/8	25 6/8	5 5/8	5 5/8	5	6		1243	30
	■ Assiniboine River – G.G. Graham – G.G. Graham – 1984										
176 1/8	25 7/8	25 5/8	19 1/8	22 2/8	4 4/8	4 4/8	5	6		1243	30
	■ Grunthal – Edwin Froese – Edwin Froese – 1986										
175 6/8	26 5/8	27 2/8	19 6/8	22	4 6/8	4 7/8	6	7	5 2/8	1310	32
	■ Cypress River – Murray Jones – Murray Jones – 1973										
175 3/8	26	25 5/8	18 7/8	21 2/8	5 6/8	5 7/8	5	5		1377	33
	■ Carberry – H.E. & B. Calvert – H.E. & B. Calvert – 1987										
175 2/8	25	24 4/8	17	19 4/8	4 7/8	5	6	6	4	1403	34
	■ Russell – Emile DeCorby – Emile DeCorby – 1986										
175	27	27	21	23 4/8	5 2/8	5 2/8	5	5		1472	35
	■ Riverdale – David Hofer, Jr. – David Hofer, Jr. – 1989										
174 7/8	26 5/8	25	22 6/8	25 3/8	5 3/8	5 4/8	6	9	9 3/8	1513	36
	■ Rivers – N. Manchur – N. Manchur – 1954										
174 6/8	25 5/8	24	18	20 2/8	4 7/8	5	6	6		1534	37
	■ Fisher Branch – Paul Sanduliak – Paul Sanduliak – 1985										
174 5/8	24 2/8	24 3/8	19 6/8		5 5/8	5 4/8	7	6		1561	38
	■ Manitoba – C.S. Browning – C.S. Browning – 1960										
174 2/8	25 5/8	26	21 6/8	24 4/8	5 3/8	5 2/8	5	5		1652	39
	■ Lake of the Prairies – Stephen Davies – Stephen Davies – 1999										
174 1/8	25 3/8	25 5/8	19 2/8	21 3/8	5 4/8	5 4/8	6	6	8 3/8	1678	40
	■ Pierson – Art Minshull – Brad Minshull – PR 1950										

MANITOBA TYPICAL WHITETAIL DEER

Score	Length of Main Beam Right	Left	Inside Spread	Greatest Spread	Circumference at Smallest Place Between Burr and First Point Right	Left	Number of Points Right	Left	Lengths Abnormal Points	All-Time Rank	State Rank
174	26 5/8	26 5/8	18 3/8	22	5 4/8	5 4/8	6	6	5 7/8	1717	41
	■ Swan River – Picked Up – Clint Martin – 1991										
173 6/8	25	25 3/8	22 4/8	25	5 1/8	5	5	5		1766	42
	■ McAuley – Alex D. Vallance – Alex D. Vallance – 1967										
173 4/8	24 7/8	23 6/8	17	19 4/8	5 6/8	5 7/8	7	6	5 2/8	1847	43
	■ Clover Leaf – Walter Lucko – Walter Lucko – 1962										
172 5/8	25 1/8	24 5/8	19 1/8	22 1/8	5 7/8	5 6/8	7	5	6 2/8	2113	44
	■ Shoal Lake – Gary Phillips – Gary Phillips – 1967										
172 2/8	27 6/8	30	20 4/8	23 6/8	5 4/8	5 4/8	8	7	10	2237	45
	■ Minnedosa River – Eric W.C. Abel – Eric W.C. Abel – 1986										
172 2/8	25 5/8	25 2/8	18	19 7/8	5	4 7/8	7	5	2 6/8	2237	45
	■ Brandon – Robert W. Jonasson – Robert W. Jonasson – 1996										
172	24 4/8	23 6/8	17	20 2/8	5 2/8	5 4/8	5	5		2330	47
	■ Neepawa – Jim Sinclair – Jim Sinclair – 1947										
171 7/8	25 4/8	27	16 4/8		5 7/8	5 7/8	8	6		2382	48
	■ Scotch Bay – W.J. Harker – W.J. Harker – 1951										
171 6/8	24 6/8	24 6/8	19	21 4/8	5 2/8	5 1/8	5	5		2418	49
	■ Turtle Mt. – Roy Hainsworth – Roy Hainsworth – 1963										
171 6/8	26 2/8	24 4/8	23	24 7/8	4 6/8	4 6/8	5	7	1	2418	49
	■ Tamarack Lake – John L. Duncan – John L. Duncan – 1998										
171 5/8	26 5/8	26 6/8	17 4/8	19 6/8	5 2/8	5 2/8	6	5	3 7/8	2470	51
	■ Swan Lake – John Gidney – John Gidney – 1999										
171 4/8	26	26 3/8	21 6/8	23 7/8	5	4 7/8	11	6	16 2/8	2513	52
	■ Woodlands Dist. – Bill Rutherford – Bill Rutherford – 1961										
171 4/8	26 5/8	26 7/8	21 7/8	23 4/8	4 7/8	4 6/8	6	5	3 1/8	2513	52
	■ Treesbank – Tom J. Gross – Tom J. Gross – 1995										
171 2/8	23 3/8	24 6/8	18 6/8	21 7/8	5 2/8	5	5	5		2621	54
	■ Cowan – Scott P. Nigbor – Scott P. Nigbor – 1998										
171	25	25 2/8	18 4/8	18 1/8	5 7/8	5 5/8	5	5		2707	55
	■ Fisher Branch – Garth J. Lagimodiere – Garth J. Lagimodiere – 1993										
170 7/8	24 4/8	24 5/8	21 1/8	23 2/8	5	5	5	5		2769	56
	■ Ostenfeld – Karl E. Mistelbacher – Karl E. Mistelbacher – 1995										
170 6/8	24	24	21 2/8	24	5	5 1/8	6	6		2828	57
	■ Arnes – T. Litwin – T. Litwin – 1963										
170 3/8	26 3/8	26	20 3/8	23 3/8	5 2/8	5	5	5		2992	58
	■ Portage La Prairie – Robert Boyachek – Robert Boyachek – 1967										
170 2/8	24 6/8	26 1/8	18	20 6/8	5	5	5	5		3063	59
	■ Pembina River – Bernie Thiessen – Bernie Thiessen – 1987										
170	26 4/8	27	23	25 4/8	6 4/8	6 4/8	5	5		3224	60
	■ Virden – Jessie Byer – Jessie Byer – 1951										
169 6/8	25	24	17 4/8	19 2/8	5 2/8	5	5	6		3306	61
	■ Morton – Steve A. Smith – Steve A. Smith – 1996										

Score	Length of Main Beam Right	Left	Inside Spread	Greatest Spread	Circumference at Smallest Place Between Burr and First Point Right	Left	Number of Points Right	Left	Lengths Abnormal Points	All-Time Rank	State Rank
169 3/8	26 1/8	25 7/8	17 3/8	19 4/8	5 4/8	5 4/8	6	6	2 6/8	3324†	62†
■ Peonan Point – Robert J. Sztorc – Robert J. Sztorc – 1998											
166 3/8	26 1/8	24 6/8	20 1/8	22 1/8	5 4/8	5 1/8	5	6	1 4/8	3620	63
■ Portage Bay – Dan Hill – Dan Hill – 1986											
165 5/8	25 4/8	24 5/8	20 1/8	22 6/8	5	5	7	7	4	3696	64
■ Duck Mt. – Louis P. Fratta – Louis P. Fratta – 1994											
165 1/8	27 4/8	26 7/8	22 3/8	26 2/8	5	4 6/8	5	4		3767†	65†
■ Duck Mt. – Henry Sevcenko – Henry Sevcenko – 2000											
164 1/8	25 2/8	22 5/8	17 5/8	19 4/8	5	5	6	5		3886	66
■ Durban – Ike Rainey – Ike Rainey – 1992											
164 1/8	25 4/8	25 4/8	16 7/8	18 7/8	4 2/8	4 2/8	8	6	4 2/8	3886	66
■ Eriksdale – Alan D. Long – Alan D. Long – 1998											
163 2/8	25 5/8	25 2/8	25 4/8	27 4/8	4 2/8	4 2/8	5	6		4017	68
■ Brandon – Conrad McClure – Conrad McClure – 1982											
162 6/8	25 5/8	25 6/8	17 6/8	21 7/8	4 6/8	4 6/8	5	5		4089	69
■ Lake Winnipeg – Rodney M. Wozniak – Rodney M. Wozniak – 1993											
161 3/8	25	23 3/8	20 5/8	23 2/8	4 7/8	4 7/8	5	5		4285	70
■ Pipestone – Homer Perreault – Homer Perreault – 1985											
161 2/8	24 5/8	24 7/8	16 3/8	18 6/8	4 4/8	4 5/8	7	7	2 7/8	4310	71
■ Arborg – George W. Wescott – George W. Wescott – 1994											
161 1/8	27 4/8	27 1/8	20 3/8	22 6/8	4 6/8	4 6/8	6	7	4 2/8	4332	72
■ Carroll – Wayne Rudneski – Wayne Rudneski – 1984											
160 2/8	22 5/8	22 5/8	16 6/8	18 6/8	4 7/8	4 7/8	5	5		4495	73
■ Swan River – Ronald D. McMahan – Ronald D. McMahan – 1999											
160 1/8	24 1/8	24 2/8	18 5/8	21	4 6/8	4 6/8	7	5	1	4534	74
■ Sidney – Tony Kranjc – Tony Kranjc – 1987											
160	26 1/8	25 5/8	20 2/8	22 2/8	4 5/8	4 5/8	5	4	1 4/8	4565	75
■ Virden – Dan Olafson – Dan Olafson – 1986											

† The scores and ranking for trophies from the 25th Awards Entry Period are not final until the banquet is held on June 19, 2004.

MANITOBA

NON-TYPICAL WHITETAIL DEER

Score	Length of Main Beam Right	Left	Inside Spread	Greatest Spread	Circumference at Smallest Place Between Burr and First Point Right	Left	Number of Points Right	Left	Lengths Abnormal Points	All-Time Rank	State Rank
265⁷/₈	24²/₈	23³/₈	22⁶/₈	24²/₈	5⁴/₈	6	12	15	86⁵/₈	20†	1†
■ Souris River – Howard G. Pauls – Howard G. Pauls – 2001											
258⁴/₈	27³/₈	29	19⁵/₈	25⁶/₈	5⁷/₈	6	16	19	53⁷/₈	29	2
■ Steep Rock – John DeLorme – Bass Pro Shops – 1973											
257³/₈	25⁵/₈	23⁵/₈	16²/₈	27⁴/₈	4⁶/₈	4⁴/₈	21	17	73⁷/₈	35	3
■ Elkhorn – Harvey Olsen – Harvey Olsen – 1973											
248⁴/₈	26¹/₈	26³/₈	22³/₈	31⁴/₈	5⁵/₈	6	12	14	67⁷/₈	68	4
■ Wellwood – Paul A. Adriaansen – Paul A. Adriaansen – 1999											
245⁶/₈	24¹/₈	24³/₈	18⁷/₈	24⁷/₈	5⁵/₈	5⁶/₈	13	13	69⁷/₈	79†	5†
■ Souris River – Richard D. Pauls – Richard D. Pauls – 2000											
241⁵/₈	25	24⁴/₈	21³/₈	26³/₈	6²/₈	6²/₈	19	18	63²/₈	106	6
■ Manitoba – Unknown – Jack G. Brittingham – 1984											
238³/₈	28	26⁶/₈	22⁷/₈	25⁴/₈	6	5²/₈	12	10	35²/₈	134	7
■ Assiniboine River – Doug Hawkins – Doug Hawkins – 1981											
237³/₈	24²/₈	23⁷/₈	20²/₈	25⁵/₈	5⁴/₈	5⁴/₈	12	16	59¹/₈	146	8
■ Whiteshell – Angus McVicar – Angus McVicar – 1925											
231³/₈	28	28⁴/₈	26¹/₈	29⁷/₈	6⁶/₈	6³/₈	9	9	47⁴/₈	219	9
■ Holland – W. Ireland – Wayne Williamson – 1968											
223⁵/₈	25⁵/₈	24⁴/₈	19⁵/₈	28	5⁶/₈	5⁶/₈	13	16	52²/₈	345	10
■ Manitoba – Unknown – Wayne Selby – PR 1987											
216	24¹/₈	24¹/₈	19³/₈	21⁵/₈	5¹/₈	4⁶/₈	14	9	35¹/₈	565	11
■ Manitoba – Unknown – Robert J. Winnekens – 1990											
214⁷/₈	25²/₈	24⁴/₈	24³/₈	29²/₈	4⁶/₈	4⁶/₈	9	12	35²/₈	605	12
■ Aweme – Criddle Bros. – Criddle Bros. – 1954											
214⁶/₈	27	26³/₈	17²/₈	21¹/₈	5⁵/₈	5⁶/₈	10	8	35⁴/₈	610	13
■ Roseau River – Darcy J. Stewart – Darcy J. Stewart – 1990											
212⁴/₈	23¹/₈	23⁴/₈	19⁶/₈	26²/₈	4⁷/₈	4⁶/₈	10	8	29⁶/₈	695	14
■ Swan Lake – William A. Riel – William A. Riel – 1997											
212¹/₈	23³/₈	23	20³/₈	23¹/₈	5	5²/₈	8	7	46⁴/₈	709	15
■ Minnedosa – Albert Pfau – Albert Pfau – 1966											
210⁵/₈	25⁴/₈	25⁵/₈	21⁶/₈	30	6²/₈	6⁴/₈	8	12	43⁷/₈	783†	16†
■ Fork River – Jimmy D. Blaine – Jimmy D. Blaine – 2000											
209⁶/₈	25⁵/₈	25²/₈	16	20	5⁶/₈	5⁶/₈	10	9	38²/₈	831	17
■ Oak Lake – Michael W. Leochko – Michael W. Leochko – 1985											
209⁶/₈	23⁴/₈	19⁷/₈	15⁵/₈	18⁴/₈	5⁶/₈	5⁶/₈	9	14	45³/₈	831	17
■ Morton – Charles C. Dixon – Charles C. Dixon – 1996											
208¹/₈	25⁷/₈	24⁵/₈	19⁶/₈	21⁷/₈	4⁶/₈	4⁴/₈	8	8	46³/₈	920	19
■ Griswold – J.V. Parker – J.V. Parker – 1946											

Score	Length of Main Beam Right Left	Inside Spread	Greatest Spread	Circumference at Smallest Place Between Burr and First Point Right Left	Number of Points Right Left	Lengths Abnormal Points	All-Time Rank	State Rank
208	27 5/8 27 5/8	21 3/8	29	5 5/8 5 4/8	9 11	26 1/8	929†	20†
■ Pinehurst Lake – Steve Onciul – Steve Onciul – 2001							
207 7/8	23 4/8 23 6/8	23 4/8	30 2/8	5 6/8 5 4/8	11 10	49 7/8	938	21
■ Assiniboine River – Terry L. Simcox – Terry L. Simcox – 1987							
206 7/8	20 4/8 21 3/8	14 5/8	19	5 1/8 5	11 9	41 6/8	1011	22
■ Whitemouth River – Tom Clark, Jr. – Tom Clark, Jr. – 1987							
205 1/8	26 6/8 25 4/8	20 3/8	24 2/8	5 4/8 5 4/8	11 9	24 2/8	1138	23
■ Rat River – Ken L. Maxymowich – Ken L. Maxymowich – 1987							
204 6/8	23 1/8 24 2/8	19 7/8	22 4/8	5 6/8 5 6/8	8 12	41 7/8	1165	24
■ Saskatchewan River – Dieter Boehner – Dieter Boehner – 1973							
200 5/8	24 5/8 23 5/8	19 5/8	23 6/8	5 4/8 5 3/8	8 9	26 6/8	1532	25
■ Pembina Valley – Claude R.J. Chappellaz – Claude R.J. Chappellaz – 1992							
199 6/8	23 3/8 22 4/8	15 5/8	28 2/8	6 3/8 6	13 12	53 5/8	1613	26
■ Duck Mt. – Picked Up – Jim Whitt – PR 1986							
198 5/8	23 7/8 24 1/8	22 1/8	24 2/8	5 5	9 7	16	1716	27
■ Turtle Mt. – Charles C. Dixon – Charles C. Dixon – 1999							
198	25 7/8 23 4/8	17 5/8	21 6/8	5 5	8 8	29 7/8	1801	28
■ Assiniboine River – James A. Roberts – James A. Roberts – 1980							
197	23 4/8 24 2/8	19 4/8	24	5 5	11 9	44 4/8	1939	29
■ Oak River – Sam Henry – J.J. Henry – 1946 ■ See photo on page 413							
197	24 3/8 24 1/8	18	22	5 5	7 8	18 4/8	1939	29
■ Souris River – Picked Up – T. Allan Good – 1986							
196 5/8	29 2/8 28 5/8	19 1/8	23 6/8	6 2/8 5 6/8	7 9	26 2/8	1985†	31†
■ Winnipeg River – Mark S. Ilijanic – Mark S. Ilijanic – 2000							
195	26 25 4/8	19 3/8	21 6/8	4 5/8 4 5/8	9 7	17 3/8	2233†	32†
■ Shell River – Wayne Todoschuk – Wayne Todoschuk – 2000							
195	27 7/8 28 1/8	22 5/8	25 5/8	5 6/8 5 6/8	7 9	14 5/8	2233	32
■ Lac du Bonnet – Brad Ehinger – Brad Ehinger – 1993							
188 3/8	26 2/8 27 2/8	19 4/8	23 6/8	4 4/8 4 5/8	5 10	16 3/8	2478	34
■ Minnedosa River – Mark Usick – Mark Usick – 1986							
188 1/8	24 1/8 23 3/8	16 6/8	19 4/8	5 6/8 5 7/8	6 11	22 7/8	2497	35
■ Hamiota – Cecil Epp – Cecil Epp – 1985							
263 6/8	23 7/8 25	26 6/8	29 1/8	5 4/8 5 3/8	14 15	91	*	*
■ Ashern – Graeme E. McGinnis – Graeme E. McGinnis – 1994							

Location of Kill – Hunter – Owner – Date Killed

† The scores and ranking for trophies from the 25th Awards Entry Period are not final until the banquet is held on June 19, 2004.

NEW BRUNSWICK
RECORD WHITETAILS

18 Typical whitetail deer entries
13 Non-typical whitetail deer entries
7,265 Total whitetail deer entries

NEW BRUNSWICK
PROVINCIAL RECORD
Typical Whitetail Deer
Score: 182$^{7}/_{8}$
Location: Oromocto River
Hunter and Owner: Bruce MacGougan
Date: 1984

NEW BRUNSWICK
PROVINCIAL RECORD
Non-Typical Whitetail Deer
Score: 249$^7/_8$
Location: Kings Co.
Hunter: Ronald Martin
Owner: Bass Pro Shops
Date: 1946

NEW BRUNSWICK

TYPICAL WHITETAIL DEER

Score	Length of Main Beam Right	Left	Inside Spread	Greatest Spread	Circumference at Smallest Place Between Burr and First Point Right	Left	Number of Points Right	Left	Lengths Abnormal Points	All-Time Rank	State Rank
	■ Location of Kill – Hunter – Owner – Date Killed										
182 7/8	29 1/8	28 3/8	20 1/8	22 3/8	5 2/8	5 3/8	7	6	2 2/8	401	1
	■ Oromocto River – Bruce MacGougan – Bruce MacGougan – 1984										
180 6/8	31 6/8	31 2/8	19 4/8	23 2/8	6	5 5/8	6	8	15 6/8	587	2
	■ New Brunswick – Unknown – Acad. Nat. Sci., Phil. – 1937										
178 3/8	27	27 3/8	17 5/8	20 2/8	4 3/8	4 4/8	5	7	1 2/8	868	3
	■ Queens Co. – Bert Bourque – Bert Bourque – 1970										
176 6/8	26 5/8	26 2/8	19 4/8	22 2/8	5 2/8	5 2/8	5	5		1103	4
	■ River Glade – Dennis Halliday – Dennis Halliday – 1998										
176 4/8	24 6/8	24 5/8	19 4/8	21 2/8	4 5/8	4 5/8	6	7	2 6/8	1158	5
	■ Charlotte Co. – Albert E. Dewar – Albert E. Dewar – 1960										
175 6/8	26 4/8	27 6/8	20 2/8	22 5/8	5 2/8	5 2/8	5	5		1310	6
	■ Nine Mile Brook – Leopold Leblanc – Jim Oickle – 1973										
175 4/8	26 2/8	26 3/8	16 5/8	19	5 3/8	5 4/8	7	8	8 1/8	1352	7
	■ Canaan – Marcel Poirier – Marcel Poirier – 1985										
175 1/8	23 7/8	24 4/8	17 3/8	19 3/8	4 5/8	4 4/8	6	6		1440	8
	■ Kings Co. – Wayne F. Anderson – Wayne F. Anderson – 1987										
173 3/8	26 4/8	26 6/8	20 1/8	22 5/8	5	4 7/8	6	5	3 6/8	1883	9
	■ St. George – Gilbert L. Leavitt – Gilbert L. Leavitt – 1962										
172 3/8	29 5/8	29 1/8	20 3/8	23	4 2/8	4 4/8	5	6		2200	10
	■ Snider Mt. – Jack W. Brown – Jack W. Brown – 1975										
172	27 3/8	28 3/8	18 2/8	20 1/8	5	5 1/8	5	5		2330	11
	■ Westmoreland Co. – Edgar Cormier – Edgar Cormier – 1983										
171 5/8	25 4/8	26 5/8	19 3/8	21 5/8	5 5/8	5 6/8	7	7		2470	12
	■ Bonnell Brook – Steve R. McCutcheon – Steve R. McCutcheon – 1984										
171 1/8	25 5/8	25 2/8	19 5/8	22 1/8	5 4/8	5 5/8	5	6	1 6/8	2665	13
	■ Howard Brook – Ralph L. Orser – Ralph L. Orser – 1986										
171	26 4/8	27 2/8	20 2/8	22 5/8	4 4/8	4 4/8	5	5		2707	14
	■ Marshall Hill – Michael J. Maxwell – Michael J. Maxwell – 1992										
170 5/8	24 1/8	24 6/8	16 7/8	18 7/8	4 6/8	4 5/8	5	5		2876	15
	■ Kings Co. – Allen A. MacDonald – Allen A. MacDonald – 1986										
170 4/8	26 3/8	26	22 4/8	24 3/8	5 3/8	5 3/8	5	5		2933	16
	■ Oak Mts. – Michael E. Mertz – Michael E. Mertz – 1986										
165 5/8	25 5/8	25 2/8	19 1/8	22 6/8	5 4/8	5 4/8	5	5		3696	17
	■ Gaspereau River – Jacques Fugere – Jacques Fugere – 1992										
162 3/8	26 5/8	28 1/8	21 3/8	24 1/8	5	5	5	5		4140	18
	■ Tobique River – David A. DuFresne – David A. DuFresne – 1990										

NEW BRUNSWICK

NON-TYPICAL WHITETAIL DEER

Score	Length of Main Beam Right	Left	Inside Spread	Greatest Spread	Circumference at Smallest Place Between Burr and First Point Right	Left	Number of Points Right	Left	Lengths Abnormal Points	All-Time Rank	State Rank
\(\blacksquare\) Location of Kill – Hunter – Owner – Date Killed											
249⁷/₈	26⁵/₈	25⁶/₈	23²/₈	37	4¹/₈	4²/₈	12	22	79⁵/₈	61	1
■ Kings Co. – Ronald Martin – Bass Pro Shops – 1946											
243⁷/₈	26⁷/₈	26³/₈	16²/₈	27⁷/₈	8²/₈	8²/₈	18	15	67⁷/₈	94	2
■ Wirral – H. Glenn Johnston – Arnold Alward – 1962											
242²/₈	24³/₈	21⁵/₈	20⁵/₈	28⁴/₈	6¹/₈	6⁵/₈	18	14	83⁵/₈	102	3
■ Auburnville – John L. MacKenzie – Arnold Alward – 1958											
224²/₈	26⁴/₈	27⁶/₈	20⁵/₈	27⁷/₈	5	5¹/₈	11	11	40¹/₈	332	4
■ Salmon River – Ford Fulton – Legendary Whitetails – 1966											
215¹/₈	29²/₈	28¹/₈	21⁷/₈	25⁴/₈	5⁴/₈	5⁴/₈	11	10	45⁴/₈	593	5
■ Rusagonis River – Art Appleby – Art Appleby – 1998											
214⁷/₈	24⁶/₈	26⁶/₈	17	20⁵/₈	5²/₈	5¹/₈	15	10	41⁵/₈	605	6
■ St. John Co. – T. Emery – New Brunswick Museum – 1968											
205⁴/₈	25⁴/₈	25⁴/₈	17⁷/₈	23⁷/₈	4⁷/₈	5¹/₈	9	12	53⁵/₈	1107	7
■ Charlotte Co. – Clayton Tatton – J.D. Andrews – 1959											
204¹/₈	28⁵/₈	25⁷/₈	22²/₈	31⁴/₈	5⁷/₈	6¹/₈	12	9	32⁵/₈	1210	8
■ Charlotte Co. – Gary L. Lister – Gary L. Lister – 1984											
203⁶/₈	28	27³/₈	20	29⁴/₈	5¹/₈	5³/₈	7	10	21⁶/₈	1237	9
■ George Lake – Henry Kirk – Ronald Kirk – 1903											
199⁷/₈	24¹/₈	23²/₈	19	23⁷/₈	4⁶/₈	4⁶/₈	6	10	46³/₈	1607	10
■ Queens Lake – George Lacey – Wendell Lacey – 1915											
198³/₈	27	25⁶/₈	21⁶/₈	28¹/₈	5	4⁷/₈	10	9	23⁷/₈	1762	11
■ Clark's Brook – Bernard V. Sharp – Bernard V. Sharp – 1985											
197⁷/₈	25	25⁵/₈	25¹/₈	29⁴/₈	5³/₈	5⁴/₈	12	11	46²/₈	1816	12
■ St. John River – James A. Perruso – James A. Perruso – 1988											
196³/₈	25⁴/₈	26⁵/₈	20¹/₈	24¹/₈	6	6¹/₈	12	11	30²/₈	2010	13
■ Magaguadowic Lake – Albert Fawcett – Albert Fawcett – 1988											

NOVA SCOTIA
RECORD WHITETAILS

6 Typical whitetail deer entries
12 Non-typical whitetail deer entries
7,265 Total whitetail deer entries

NOVA SCOTIA
PROVINCIAL RECORD
Typical Whitetail Deer
Score: 193^6/$_8$
Location: Antigonish Co.
Hunter: Kevin Boyle
Owner: Bass Pro Shops
Date: 1987

Photograph courtesy of Gale Sup

NOVA SCOTIA
PROVINCIAL RECORD
Non-Typical Whitetail Deer
Score: 273$^6/_8$
Location: West Afton River
Hunter: Alexander C. MacDonald
Owner: Bass Pro Shops
Date: 1960

Photograph courtesy of Gale Sup

NOVA SCOTIA

TYPICAL WHITETAIL DEER

Score	Length of Main Beam Right	Left	Inside Spread	Greatest Spread	Circumference at Smallest Place Between Burr and First Point Right	Left	Number of Points Right	Left	Lengths Abnormal Points	All-Time Rank	State Rank
	■ Location of Kill – Hunter – Owner – Date Killed										
193⁶/8	29⁵/8	30	23¹/8	27²/8	5⁴/8	5⁴/8	6	6	3¹/8	49	1
	■ Antigonish Co. – Kevin Boyle – Bass Pro Shops – 1987										
179	27²/8	26⁴/8	19¹/8	21⁴/8	5¹/8	5⁴/8	5	6	2⁵/8	786	2
	■ Pictou Co. – Earl Perry – Earl Perry – 1990										
174⁶/8	27⁴/8	28	19⁴/8	22⁴/8	5²/8	5³/8	6	5		1534	3
	■ Lake William – Neil G. Oickle – Neil G. Oickle – 1985										
174²/8	25³/8	25³/8	21	23	4⁶/8	4⁶/8	5	5		1652	4
	■ Mt. Pleasant – Garth Hirtle – Garth Hirtle – 1993										
170⁷/8	25²/8	25⁴/8	17⁵/8	19⁶/8	5	5	5	5		2769	5
	■ McDonald Lake – Frederick Zwarum – Frederick Zwarum – 1976										
170⁶/8	24⁶/8	25⁶/8	19	21¹/8	4⁷/8	4⁵/8	5	5		2828	6
	■ Guysborough Co. – Roy B. Simpson – Roy B. Simpson – 1968										

NON-TYPICAL WHITETAIL DEER

Score	Length of Main Beam		Inside Spread	Greatest Spread	Circumference at Smallest Place Between Burr and First Point		Number of Points		Lengths Abnormal Points	All-Time Rank	State Rank
	Right	Left			Right	Left	Right	Left			
	■ Location of Kill – Hunter – Owner – Date Killed										
273⁶/₈	27³/₈	27⁵/₈	20⁶/₈	27	6	6	19	16	85	12	1
■ West Afton River – Alexander C. MacDonald – Bass Pro Shops – 1960											
253	28	28	21⁴/₈	27⁴/₈	5⁵/₈	5⁶/₈	14	26	69⁴/₈	45	2
■ Goldenville – Neil MacDonald – Bass Pro Shops – 1945											
233¹/₈	29²/₈	29	20⁴/₈	29³/₈	5⁶/₈	5⁶/₈	14	9	30¹/₈	195	3
■ Condon Lakes – Don McDonnell – Don McDonnell – 1987											
222⁴/₈	24²/₈	25⁶/₈	20⁶/₈	32⁷/₈	5⁶/₈	5³/₈	16	10	49⁶/₈	378	4
■ Ostrea Lake – Verden M. Baker – John L. Stein – 1949											
218⁷/₈	22⁶/₈	23³/₈	15⁴/₈	23³/₈	7³/₈	7¹/₈	16	11	81⁵/₈	472	5
■ Bay of Fundy – Basil S. Lewis – Basil S. Lewis – 1983											
217³/₈	27⁵/₈	29²/₈	18⁷/₈	26⁵/₈	4²/₈	4³/₈	9	11	49	514	6
■ Dewer River – Alan Fahey – Alan Fahey – 1989											
214⁶/₈	24⁷/₈	26⁷/₈	23¹/₈	28	4³/₈	4³/₈	13	9	50⁵/₈	610	7
■ Quinlan Creek – Fred Doucette – Fred Doucette – 1962											
200¹/₈	26	24²/₈	23	25²/₈	6	6	11	12	56³/₈	1577	8
■ Parrsboro – Allison Smith – Edward B. Shaw – 1960											
199⁶/₈	25²/₈	24⁷/₈	27	30⁶/₈	5³/₈	5²/₈	11	9	23⁶/₈	1613	9
■ Musquodoboit River – David W. Brown – David W. Brown – 1993											
197²/₈	27⁴/₈	26³/₈	20	29⁵/₈	5	5	12	11	55⁴/₈	1901	10
■ Tiudish River – Clayton Ward – Clayton Ward – 1982											
196	28⁷/₈	30⁴/₈	25¹/₈	28³/₈	5⁴/₈	5²/₈	12	10	29⁵/₈	2059	11
■ Annapolis Valley – David Cabral – David Cabral – 1984											
187²/₈	19²/₈	20⁶/₈	30⁵/₈	32²/₈	4⁷/₈	4⁶/₈	10	8	41⁶/₈	2534	12
■ Cape Brenton – Bernard T. Langlais – Bernard T. Langlais – 1989											

ONTARIO
RECORD WHITETAILS

29 Typical whitetail deer entries
8 Non-typical whitetail deer entries
7,265 Total whitetail deer entries

NEW
PROVINCIAL
RECORD

ONTARIO
PROVINCIAL RECORD
Typical Whitetail Deer
Score: $177^7/8$
Location: Sioux Narrows
Hunter and Owner: Michael Christopher
Date: 1999

ONTARIO
PROVINCIAL RECORD
Non-Typical Whitetail Deer
Score: $250^{1}/_{8}$
Location: Rainy Lake
Hunter and Owner: Grant Gustafson
Date: 1995

ONTARIO

TYPICAL WHITETAIL DEER

Score	Length of Main Beam Right	Left	Inside Spread	Greatest Spread	Circumference at Smallest Place Between Burr and First Point Right	Left	Number of Points Right	Left	Lengths Abnormal Points	All-Time Rank	State Rank
177⁷/₈	24²/₈	24⁷/₈	19⁷/₈	22¹/₈	4⁵/₈	4⁴/₈	5	6		936	1
■ Sioux Narrows – Michael Christopher – Michael Christopher – 1999											
177²/₈	27⁴/₈	27¹/₈	21²/₈	23	5¹/₈	5	5	5		1025	2
■ Rainy River – Lynn Wilson – Lynn Wilson – 1972											
177¹/₈	26⁶/₈	26⁶/₈	25¹/₈	27²/₈	5³/₈	5³/₈	8	7	4⁶/₈	1048†	3†
■ Golden City Lake – Beverly E. Bennett – Beverly E. Bennett – 2001											
177	25¹/₈	25³/₈	17²/₈	21¹/₈	5	5¹/₈	7	7		1066	4
■ Rainey River – Robert K. Hayes – Robert K. Hayes – 1949											
176⁴/₈	30¹/₈	31³/₈	25²/₈	27⁶/₈	5⁴/₈	5⁵/₈	5	6		1158	5
■ Long Sault – Robert Archambault, Jr. – Robert Archambault, Jr. – 1998											
176²/₈	29⁴/₈	29	15⁵/₈	17⁴/₈	5⁶/₈	5⁵/₈	5	6	1⁷/₈	1209	6
■ Aitkokan – Robert G. Schlingmann – Robert G. Schlingmann – 1998											
175⁷/₈	24⁷/₈	25²/₈	19²/₈	22	5⁴/₈	5²/₈	9	6	1¹/₈	1287	7
■ Bennett Lake – Randy M. Love – Randy M. Love – 1994											
174¹/₈	26³/₈	26⁴/₈	20⁷/₈	23⁵/₈	4⁷/₈	4⁷/₈	5	5		1678	8
■ Amherstview – Tony H. Stranak – Tony H. Stranak – 1987											
172⁶/₈	25⁴/₈	25²/₈	18¹/₈	20³/₈	5⁷/₈	5⁵/₈	7	9	6⁵/₈	2065	9
■ Lost Bay – Peter Marcinuk – Peter Marcinuk – 1999											
172³/₈	26⁴/₈	26⁶/₈	17¹/₈	19⁴/₈	5	5²/₈	7	6	1	2200†	10†
■ Credit River – Eugene Bulizo – Eugene Bulizo – 2001											
172³/₈	27	28	23⁶/₈	25⁴/₈	4⁶/₈	4⁶/₈	7	8	6¹/₈	2200	10
■ Rainy Lake – Floyd Kielczewski – Floyd Kielczewski – 1953											
172²/₈	22⁷/₈	27¹/₈	16³/₈	19³/₈	5³/₈	5⁴/₈	8	7	5⁷/₈	2237	12
■ Rainy Lake – Andrew Brigham – Andrew Brigham – 1989											
172¹/₈	28³/₈	28¹/₈	25⁵/₈	30	5	5²/₈	5	5	2	2286	13
■ Morson – Almer Godin – Almer Godin – 1957											
171⁷/₈	28¹/₈	28	17⁷/₈	20²/₈	5²/₈	5³/₈	5	6	1²/₈	2382	14
■ Almonte – Scott K. Camp – Scott K. Camp – 1995											
171³/₈	24⁴/₈	24²/₈	17⁴/₈	19⁶/₈	5	5¹/₈	7	8	4³/₈	2564	15
■ Hamilton Twp. – Peter Francis – Peter Francis – 1998											
171²/₈	27¹/₈	27⁶/₈	20⁶/₈	24	5	5¹/₈	6	8	2⁶/₈	2621†	16†
■ Rainy Lake – John N. Nelson – John N. Nelson – 2000											
171²/₈	26²/₈	25	22⁴/₈	25³/₈	5⁶/₈	5⁶/₈	5	5		2621	16
■ Macintosh – Richard Kouhi – Richard Kouhi – 1967											
171¹/₈	28¹/₈	27¹/₈	24⁶/₈	27	6⁵/₈	6²/₈	5	7	3¹/₈	2665	18
■ Perth – Robert J. Moir – Robert J. Moir – 1992											
170⁷/₈	26⁷/₈	26³/₈	19⁷/₈	22⁴/₈	4⁷/₈	4⁷/₈	5	5		2769	19
■ Parry Sound – Gary Jackson – Gary Jackson – 1998											

Score	Length of Main Beam Right	Left	Inside Spread	Greatest Spread	Circumference at Smallest Place Between Burr and First Point Right	Left	Number of Points Right	Left	Lengths Abnormal Points	All-Time Rank	State Rank
170 6/8	26 3/8	27 2/8	19 4/8	22	4 4/8	4 5/8	6	6		2828	20
■ Kasshabog Lake – Clarence Holdcroft – Jim Holdcroft – PR 1948											
170 3/8	27	26 4/8	19 7/8	22 2/8	4 2/8	4 3/8	5	5		2992	21
■ Bruton – Mark Vesters – Mark Vesters – 1989											
170 3/8	26	25 6/8	18 7/8	21 4/8	4 6/8	5	5	5		2992	21
■ Lake Rosseau – Picked Up – Philip Giroday – PR 1994											
170 2/8	28 2/8	29 4/8	23 7/8	26 2/8	5 6/8	5 6/8	5	5	4 3/8	3063†	23†
■ Clythe Creek – Bill T. Henshall – Bill T. Henshall – 2000											
170	27	26 7/8	19 2/8	22	4 7/8	5	7	5	4	3224	24
■ Emo – Jack Booth – Jack Booth – 1986											
166 7/8	24 6/8	25	20 1/8	22 4/8	4 6/8	4 6/8	5	5		3568	25
■ Bunting Creek – Boyd Wade – Boyd Wade – 1994											
163 7/8	28 2/8	25 6/8	20 1/8	23	5	4 7/8	5	5		3928	26
■ Dry Lake – Clarence C. Kauffeldt – Wallace C. Kauffeldt – 1988											
163	26 6/8	25 6/8	20 3/8	22 4/8	4 6/8	4 5/8	7	6	1 1/8	4051†	27†
■ Rushing River – Michael J. Eugair – Michael J. Eugair – 2000											
162 2/8	25 4/8	25 4/8	16 6/8	20	4 2/8	4 2/8	7	9	11	4153†	28†
■ Ogema Bay – Daniel C. Johnson – Daniel C. Johnson – 2000											
162	25 1/8	25 4/8	19 4/8	21 5/8	4 4/8	4 4/8	5	6		4184	29
■ Rainy Lake – Rick Johnson – Rick Johnson – 1990											

† The scores and ranking for trophies from the 25th Awards Entry Period are not final until the banquet is held on June 19, 2004.

ONTARIO

NON-TYPICAL WHITETAIL DEER

Score	Length of Main Beam Right	Length of Main Beam Left	Inside Spread	Greatest Spread	Circumference at Smallest Place Between Burr and First Point Right	Circumference at Smallest Place Between Burr and First Point Left	Number of Points Right	Number of Points Left	Lengths Abnormal Points	All-Time Rank	State Rank

Location of Kill – Hunter – Owner – Date Killed

250$^{1}/_{8}$	27$^{3}/_{8}$	27$^{3}/_{8}$	19	23$^{2}/_{8}$	5$^{7}/_{8}$	6$^{1}/_{8}$	16	17	70$^{7}/_{8}$	59	1

■ *Rainy Lake – Grant Gustafson – Grant Gustafson – 1995*

234$^{5}/_{8}$	28$^{6}/_{8}$	23$^{3}/_{8}$	17$^{1}/_{8}$	27$^{3}/_{8}$	4$^{7}/_{8}$	6$^{4}/_{8}$	9	15	81	172	2

■ *Round Lake – Picked Up – Harry Jones – 1990*

219$^{5}/_{8}$	22$^{7}/_{8}$	24$^{2}/_{8}$	16$^{5}/_{8}$	22$^{2}/_{8}$	4$^{5}/_{8}$	4$^{4}/_{8}$	13	10	58$^{6}/_{8}$	451	3

■ *Black Hawk – Picked Up – Marc M. Jackson – 1990*

208$^{7}/_{8}$	27$^{1}/_{8}$	27	23$^{5}/_{8}$	29$^{3}/_{8}$	6$^{3}/_{8}$	6	11	13	45$^{4}/_{8}$	877	4

■ *Rideau River – Harry Rathwell – Harry Rathwell – 1988*

208	27	26	21$^{5}/_{8}$	27	4$^{5}/_{8}$	4$^{7}/_{8}$	9	10	31$^{7}/_{8}$	929	5

■ *Rainy River – Leroy Berglund – Marc M. Jackson – PR 1930*

204$^{2}/_{8}$	23$^{2}/_{8}$	23$^{7}/_{8}$	17$^{2}/_{8}$	19$^{2}/_{8}$	5$^{6}/_{8}$	5$^{3}/_{8}$	12	12	35$^{4}/_{8}$	1199	6

■ *Rainy Lake – Rod Hebert – Rod Hebert – 1969*

196$^{6}/_{8}$	24$^{2}/_{8}$	24	25$^{6}/_{8}$	27	4$^{7}/_{8}$	4$^{7}/_{8}$	9	10	35$^{2}/_{8}$	1968	7

■ *Whitefish Bay – Matthew R. Rydberg – Matthew R. Rydberg – 1998*

196$^{5}/_{8}$	27$^{7}/_{8}$	27$^{5}/_{8}$	20$^{6}/_{8}$	23$^{3}/_{8}$	6$^{3}/_{8}$	6$^{3}/_{8}$	9	9	25$^{1}/_{8}$	1985†	8†

■ *Nottawasaga River – James P. Baird – James P. Baird – 2000*

† The scores and ranking for trophies from the 25th Awards Entry Period are not final until the banquet is held on June 19, 2004.

TROPHIES IN THE FIELD

HUNTER: Karen R. Seginak
SCORE: 204-3/8
CATEGORY: non-typical whitetail deer
LOCATION: Assiniboine River, Saskatchewan
DATE: 2000

QUEBEC
RECORD WHITETAILS

3 Typical whitetail deer entries
2 Non-typical whitetail deer entries
7,265 Total whitetail deer entries

QUEBEC
NEW PROVINCIAL RECORD
Typical Whitetail Deer
Score: 173
Location: St. Marie Lake
Hunter and Owner: Philippe Gratton
Date: 1998

QUEBEC
PROVINCIAL RECORD
Non-Typical Whitetail Deer
Score: 207⁵/₈
Location: Argenteuil Co.
Hunters: R. Desjardins & A. Dobie
Owner: R. Desjardins & R. Morrison
Date: 1959

QUEBEC

TYPICAL WHITETAIL DEER

Score	Length of Main Beam		Inside Spread	Greatest Spread	Circumference at Smallest Place Between Burr and First Point		Number of Points		Lengths Abnormal Points	All-Time Rank	State Rank
	Right	Left			Right	Left	Right	Left			
	■ *Location of Kill – Hunter – Owner – Date Killed*										
173	24³/8	24⁵/8	18	20²/8	4²/8	4²/8	6	6		1991	1
	■ *St. Marie Lake – Philippe Gratton – Philippe Gratton – 1998*										
172⁵/8	26²/8	25	24¹/8	26⁵/8	5¹/8	5²/8	5	5		2113	2
	■ *Acton-Vale – Guy Cusson – Guy Cusson – 1996*										
161	25⁶/8	27¹/8	21⁴/8	24²/8	5²/8	5²/8	5	5		4356	3
	■ *Dominion Lake – Francois Brunet – Francois Brunet – 1987*										

QUEBEC

NON-TYPICAL WHITETAIL DEER

Score	Length of Main Beam Right / Left	Inside Spread	Greatest Spread	Circumference at Smallest Place Between Burr and First Point Right / Left	Number of Points Right / Left	Lengths Abnormal Points	All-Time Rank	State Rank
	■ Location of Kill – Hunter – Owner – Date Killed							
207⁵/₈	25⁴/₈ 25⁴/₈	15⁴/₈	23²/₈	4⁷/₈ 5	11 7	27⁵/₈	957	1
	■ Argenteuil Co. – R. Desjardins & A. Dobie – R. Desjardins & R. Morrison – 1959							
198⁴/₈	29 29⁴/₈	23⁴/₈	27²/₈	5 5¹/₈	9 5	24	1736†	2†
	■ Missisquoi – Mario L. Quintin – Mario L. Quintin – 1990							

† The scores and ranking for trophies from the 25th Awards Entry Period are not final until the banquet is held on June 19, 2004.

SASKATCHEWAN
RECORD WHITETAILS

314 Typical whitetail deer entries
156 Non-typical whitetail deer entries
7,265 Total whitetail deer entries

**SASKATCHEWAN
PROVINCIAL RECORD
WORLD'S RECORD**
Typical Whitetail Deer
Score: 213$^5/_8$
Location: Biggar
Hunter and Owner:
  Milo N. Hanson
Date: 1993

Photograph from B&C Archives

SASKATCHEWAN PROVINCIAL RECORD
Non-Typical Whitetail Deer
Score: 265³/₈
Location: White Fox
Hunter: Elburn Kohler
Owner: Bass Pro Shops
Date: 1957

Photograph courtesy of Larry L. Huffman, Legendary Whitetails

SASKATCHEWAN

TYPICAL WHITETAIL DEER

Score	Length of Main Beam Right	Length of Main Beam Left	Inside Spread	Greatest Spread	Circumference at Smallest Place Between Burr and First Point Right	Left	Number of Points Right	Left	Lengths Abnormal Points	All-Time Rank	State Rank
					■ Location of Kill – Hunter – Owner – Date Killed						
213⁵/8	28⁴/8	28⁴/8	27²/8	29	4⁶/8	5	8	6	3¹/8	1	1
	■ Biggar – Milo N. Hanson – Milo N. Hanson – 1993										
202⁶/8	28	27¹/8	21²/8	25⁵/8	5³/8	5³/8	9	8	6⁴/8	7	2
	■ Barrier Valley – Bruce Ewen – Bruce Ewen – 1992										
200²/8	26³/8	27¹/8	24	26⁵/8	5	4⁷/8	6	7	2²/8	11	3
	■ Whitkow – Peter J. Swistun – Peter J. Swistun – 1983										
195⁴/8	25³/8	25⁷/8	19	23⁵/8	4⁷/8	4⁷/8	9	7	6²/8	37	4
	■ Porcupine Plain – Philip Philipowich – Philip Philipowich – 1985										
195¹/8	25⁶/8	28¹/8	19⁶/8	22⁶/8	5²/8	5²/8	8	5	6⁵/8	39	5
	■ Brightsand Lake – Larry Pellerin – D.J. Hollinger & B. Howard – 1993										
194⁴/8	26²/8	26	18⁷/8	21⁶/8	5⁶/8	5⁴/8	8	9	15¹/8	42	6
	■ Nipawin – Gerald Whitehead – Gerald Whitehead – 1990										
193⁶/8	24⁵/8	24⁴/8	18¹/8	20³/8	5	5	7	7	4¹/8	49	7
	■ Christopher Lake – Jerry Thorson – Jerry Thorson – 1959										
193³/8	25⁶/8	24⁵/8	19¹/8	22⁴/8	5⁶/8	5⁵/8	8	8	5	52	8
	■ Witchekan Lake – Marcel Tetreault – Marcel Tetreault – 1998										
193²/8	29⁴/8	29¹/8	24⁶/8	27⁵/8	5²/8	5²/8	7	5	1⁴/8	53	9
	■ Chitek Lake – David L. Wilson – David L. Wilson – 1992										
192⁷/8	25⁶/8	25⁷/8	18⁵/8	22¹/8	5⁴/8	5³/8	6	9	4⁴/8	58	10
	■ Makwa Lake – Ken Brown – Ken Brown – 1993										
191⁶/8	27	26	19⁶/8	21⁷/8	4⁵/8	4⁶/8	5	6		76	11
	■ Hudson Bay – George Chalus – Bass Pro Shops – 1973										
190⁶/8	27⁷/8	27⁵/8	22⁴/8	25²/8	5³/8	5⁶/8	5	5		93	12
	■ Pelly – James R. Strelioff – James R. Strelioff – 1980										
189⁵/8	28	28³/8	21⁶/8	24⁶/8	4⁵/8	4⁷/8	6	7	2¹/8	116	13
	■ Ministikwan Lake – James L. Cohick – James L. Cohick – 1992										
188⁴/8	25	26³/8	22⁵/8	24⁶/8	4⁷/8	4⁶/8	5	6	1¹/8	141	14
	■ Burstall – W.P. Rolick – W.P. Rolick – 1957										
187⁴/8	26⁶/8	26⁷/8	21³/8	24	5	5	7	6	1⁷/8	172	15
	■ Plunkett – Myles Mann – Myles Mann – 1996										
186⁵/8	27	26⁵/8	22¹/8	25	5²/8	5²/8	5	5		202	16
	■ Kelvington – David Martin – David Martin – 1999										
185³/8	27⁶/8	28	20⁵/8	22⁶/8	4⁷/8	4⁷/8	5	5		256	17
	■ Canwood – Clark Heimbechner – Clark Heimbechner – 1984										
185³/8	27⁷/8	27⁷/8	21⁵/8	24⁵/8	5¹/8	5¹/8	5	5		256	17
	■ Helene Lake – Wayne A. Foster – Wayne A. Foster – 1991										
184⁶/8	24¹/8	26¹/8	21²/8	24¹/8	5³/8	5⁴/8	6	6		285	19
	■ Dore Lake – Garvis C. Coker – Garvis C. Coker – 1971										

Score	Length of Main Beam Right Left	Inside Spread	Greatest Spread	Circumference at Smallest Place Between Burr and First Point Right Left	Number of Points Right Left	Lengths Abnormal Points	All-Time Rank	State Rank
	■ Location of Kill – Hunter – Owner – Date Killed							
184⁶/8	26⁶/8 27⁷/8	27⁶/8	30¹/8	4⁷/8 5	6 8	5⁶/8	285	19
	■ St. Brieux – Ted Gaillard – Ted Gaillard – 1996							
184⁵/8	26⁷/8 26⁵/8	23¹/8	25⁴/8	5²/8 5²/8	6 5		294†	21†
	■ Birch Lake – Michael G. Taylor – Michael G. Taylor – 2000							
184⁵/8	24⁷/8 24⁴/8	19³/8	21⁵/8	5³/8 5²/8	5 5		294	21
	■ Hudson Bay – Picked Up – Wade Hersikorn – 1986							
184⁴/8	27³/8 26⁴/8	20	22	4⁶/8 4⁷/8	6 6		303	23
	■ Echo Lake – Dale McKay – Dale McKay – 1997							
184⁴/8	27⁷/8 26⁷/8	19²/8	21⁶/8	5³/8 5³/8	5 6	1⁴/8	303	23
	■ Eagle Creek – Preston Haanen – Preston Haanen – 1999							
184³/8	26³/8 27¹/8	23⁷/8	26⁴/8	5²/8 5¹/8	6 6	2⁴/8	313	25
	■ Porcupine Plain – Lee Krantz – Lee Krantz – 1998							
184²/8	24⁷/8 24⁶/8	18⁴/8	21⁴/8	5⁶/8 5⁷/8	7 7	6⁶/8	319	26
	■ Meeting Lake – Dennis Woloshyn – Dennis Woloshyn – 1996							
183⁵/8	28²/8 28⁶/8	21⁵/8	24²/8	4⁵/8 4⁴/8	7 7	9²/8	357†	27†
	■ Qu' Appelle River – Anthony Roberts – Anthony Roberts – 2000							
183²/8	24⁴/8 22⁶/8	18⁷/8	22⁴/8	5⁵/8 5⁶/8	7 7	2³/8	378	28
	■ Invermay – Trevor Jennings – Trevor Jennings – 1996							
182⁶/8	26 26	18⁴/8	21²/8	4⁴/8 4⁵/8	6 5		409	29
	■ Kelvington – Roger D. Bibee – Roger D. Bibee – 1999							
182⁵/8	24 23⁴/8	21⁶/8	24	6⁶/8 6⁵/8	8 7	6⁷/8	420	30
	■ Crawford Creek – Dale C. Conacher – Dale C. Conacher – 1991							
182⁴/8	28⁵/8 29	23⁶/8	23⁶/8	5³/8 5¹/8	7 5		431	31
	■ Carrot River – Lori Lonson – J.D. Andrews – 1960							
182³/8	25⁵/8 26	19⁷/8	21⁶/8	4²/8 4³/8	6 6	4⁴/8	438	32
	■ S. Saskatchewan River – Jim Clary – Jim Clary – 1996							
182¹/8	25⁶/8 25²/8	22⁷/8	25³/8	5⁶/8 5⁵/8	5 5		460	33
	■ Round Lake – Jesse Bates – Jesse Bates – 1984							
181⁶/8	28⁷/8 30⁴/8	24	26⁶/8	5⁶/8 5⁶/8	7 5	9	492	34
	■ Cando – Karl Oliver – Karl Oliver – 1998 ■ See photo on page 55							
181⁵/8	27²/8 27³/8	22¹/8	24⁵/8	6⁷/8 6⁷/8	5 6	1⁶/8	500	35
	■ Porcupine Hills – Brian R. Anderson – Brian R. Anderson – 1993							
181⁵/8	26⁵/8 25⁷/8	24¹/8	26³/8	4⁵/8 4⁵/8	7 6	3	500	35
	■ Nipawin – Steve Clifford – Steve Clifford – 1996							
181³/8	25²/8 24³/8	21²/8	23³/8	5⁶/8 5⁶/8	7 6	1¹/8	528	37
	■ Southey – A.K. Flaman – Sam Peterson – 1955							
181³/8	26³/8 27	19⁷/8	22¹/8	5¹/8 5²/8	7 8	4⁶/8	528	37
	■ Meadow Lake – Freeman R. Bell – Freeman R. Bell – 1997 ■ See photo on page 57							
181²/8	25⁶/8 27	19⁵/8	22⁵/8	5 5	6 6	2⁷/8	540	39
	■ McBride Lake – Bryan Rothenburger – Bryan Rothenburger – 1993							
181¹/8	27³/8 27⁶/8	20⁷/8	23⁷/8	6²/8 5⁶/8	10 7	12²/8	551	40
	■ Empress – Don Leach – Don Leach – 1960							

Score	Length of Main Beam Right	Left	Inside Spread	Greatest Spread	Circumference at Smallest Place Between Burr and First Point Right	Left	Number of Points Right	Left	Lengths Abnormal Points	All-Time Rank	State Rank
181¹/8	24⁵/8	25¹/8	20⁵/8	22⁵/8	5³/8	5²/8	7	7	10²/8	551	40
■ Wood River – Jeremy Egan – Jeremy Egan – 1990											
181	26⁴/8	27⁶/8	20²/8	22²/8	4⁷/8	5	7	7	5²/8	563†	42†
■ Saskatchewan – Unknown – Tom Eustace – 1999											
181	27¹/8	27²/8	20⁷/8	23⁴/8	5²/8	5²/8	7	8	9³/8	563	42
■ Foam Lake – Ray Howe – Ray Howe – 1991											
180⁷/8	26⁶/8	25⁷/8	19	22⁴/8	5⁴/8	5²/8	8	8	5³/8	573	44
■ Dafoe – Jamin Bolt – Jamin Bolt – 1996											
180⁶/8	27²/8	28³/8	22	24⁶/8	4⁷/8	5	6	7	3⁴/8	587	45
■ Pike Lake – Roger Ireland – Roger Ireland – 1990											
180⁶/8	29⁶/8	27¹/8	22⁵/8	25¹/8	4⁶/8	4⁵/8	6	5	5¹/8	587	45
■ Horse Lake – Cheryl Kaban – Cheryl Kaban – 1999											
180⁵/8	27⁶/8	27²/8	23³/8	26¹/8	5⁴/8	5⁴/8	6	8	9⁶/8	599	47
■ Good Spirit Lake – Grant Landstad – Grant Landstad – 1993											
180³/8	25⁷/8	24⁵/8	17¹/8	20¹/8	4⁶/8	4⁶/8	8	7	4⁶/8	630†	48†
■ Mountain Lake – James Sinclair – James Sinclair – 2001											
180³/8	25⁶/8	26³/8	21⁵/8	24⁵/8	5	5¹/8	7	6	1	630	48
■ Stoughton – Joe Zbeetnoff – Joe Zbeetnoff – 1961											
180³/8	26⁵/8	27³/8	21¹/8	23¹/8	5¹/8	5²/8	5	5		630	48
■ Crane Lake – Darron J. Corfield – Darron J. Corfield – 1994											
180²/8	26⁴/8	25	22⁵/8	24⁴/8	5⁴/8	5²/8	7	7	2⁷/8	651	51
■ Lumsden – Mike Lukas – E.M. Gazda – 1959											
180¹/8	23³/8	23⁵/8	17⁵/8	20	5²/8	5²/8	5	5		669	52
■ Maryfield – Donald Cook – Richard J. Christoforo – 1956											
180¹/8	25⁶/8	25⁴/8	22¹/8	24²/8	4³/8	4²/8	6	6		669	52
■ Parry – Doug Hennie – Doug Hennie – 1993											
180	23⁵/8	25²/8	19⁵/8	22	5²/8	5³/8	7	7	5⁵/8	688	54
■ Torch River – David Matchett – David Matchett – 1991											
180	24⁵/8	24⁵/8	22⁶/8	24⁶/8	5	5	5	5		688	54
■ Helene Lake – Kevin R. Garner – Kevin R. Garner – 1993											
180	23³/8	22⁷/8	17⁴/8	19⁷/8	6	6	5	7		688	54
■ Moose Mt. Prov. Park – Robin Hilts – Robin Hilts – 1997											
180	26	26	19	21²/8	5¹/8	5	5	5		688	54
■ Redberry Lake – Steven Hupaelo – Steven Hupaelo – 1998											
179⁷/8	25⁴/8	27⁵/8	21²/8	23⁵/8	5⁵/8	5⁶/8	7	9	8⁵/8	705	58
■ Pasquia Hills – Jeffrey S. Metzler – Jeffrey S. Metzler – 1998											
179⁶/8	26⁴/8	26⁴/8	22¹/8	23⁵/8	5⁵/8	5⁶/8	6	6	2⁷/8	712†	59†
■ Cutarm Creek – Rick Schuster – Rick Schuster – 2001											
179⁴/8	24⁶/8	24¹/8	22	24	5⁴/8	5³/8	6	5	4⁴/8	733	60
■ Yankee Lake – Leo Stieb – Leo Stieb – 1990											
179³/8	28⁵/8	28	20⁷/8	23²/8	5⁶/8	5⁶/8	5	5		749	61
■ Parkman – Harold Larsen – Sam Peterson – 1958											

Score	Length of Main Beam Right Left ■ Location of Kill – Hunter – Owner – Date Killed	Inside Spread	Greatest Spread	Circumference at Smallest Place Between Burr and First Point Right Left		Number of Points Right Left		Lengths Abnormal Points	All-Time Rank	State Rank
179²/8	27⁶/8 27	20	25¹/8	5⁴/8	5⁶/8	9	9	14	763	62
	■ Cypress Hills – Raymond McCrea – Raymond McCrea – 1964									
178⁷/8	28³/8 28³/8	19¹/8	21³/8	4⁶/8	5	5	5		801	63
	■ Pierce Lake – Edwin Johnson – Edwin Johnson – 1984									
178⁶/8	27⁶/8 27⁶/8	25⁴/8	27⁶/8	5³/8	5⁴/8	6	5		808	64
	■ Windthorst – Clarence E. Genest – Clarence E. Genest – 1965									
178⁵/8	28⁷/8 27	24	26⁵/8	5¹/8	5¹/8	7	7	2⁷/8	819	65
	■ Beechy – Archie D. McRae – Archie D. McRae – 1957									
178⁵/8	27⁷/8 29²/8	26³/8	28⁵/8	5²/8	5²/8	6	7	3²/8	819	65
	■ Debden – Henry Rydde – Henry Rydde – 1966									
178⁵/8	28³/8 28¹/8	18⁶/8	21¹/8	4⁵/8	4⁴/8	6	6	3⁷/8	819	65
	■ Saskatoon – Patrick D. Shendruk – Patrick D. Shendruk – 1992									
178⁴/8	26³/8 25⁴/8	23	24⁷/8	4⁶/8	4⁶/8	6	6		850	68
	■ Jack Fish Lake – Michael J. Frawley – Michael J. Frawley – 1997									
178²/8	28⁷/8 28⁷/8	21⁶/8	24	4⁷/8	5	4	4		891	69
	■ Yorkton – Wayde Morley – Wayde Morley – 1999									
178¹/8	26⁵/8 26⁵/8	20⁴/8	23²/8	4²/8	4³/8	5	6	1¹/8	905	70
	■ Vonda – Orest Hilkewich – Orest Hilkewich – 1980									
178¹/8	26⁵/8 26²/8	20⁷/8	23	5¹/8	5¹/8	5	5		905	70
	■ Coteau Hills – Trevor A. Broom – Trevor A. Broom – 1997									
178	28²/8 27⁵/8	19³/8	21⁷/8	5¹/8	5²/8	7	6	10⁵/8	922	72
	■ Shell Lake – Brent Brewer – Brent Brewer – 1994									
178	28 28⁶/8	19²/8	23³/8	4⁴/8	4⁴/8	5	7	4⁴/8	922	72
	■ Sweet Grass – Leo J. Lefevre – Leo J. Lefevre – 1999									
177⁶/8	26⁴/8 26⁴/8	18²/8	22⁶/8	5	5¹/8	9	7	11²/8	956	74
	■ Shaunavon – Stan J. Crawford – Stan J. Crawford – 1979									
177⁶/8	26²/8 27²/8	18²/8	20³/8	5⁴/8	5⁴/8	6	6		956	74
	■ Antler River – Larry Sterling – Larry Sterling – 1989									
177⁵/8	25⁵/8 26²/8	19¹/8	23²/8	5⁴/8	5³/8	5	5		972	76
	■ Endeavour – Terry L. Halgrimson – Terry L. Halgrimson – 1971									
177⁴/8	28⁶/8 27²/8	20	23³/8	5²/8	5³/8	7	5	5⁴/8	993†	77†
	■ Meeting Lake – Carl C. Sankey – Carl C. Sankey – 2001									
177⁴/8	25 24⁴/8	21¹/8	23²/8	5²/8	5⁴/8	5	6	1¹/8	993	77
	■ Dundurn – L.B. Galbraith – L.B. Galbraith – 1956									
177⁴/8	26 28	21⁶/8	24³/8	5⁶/8	5³/8	7	6	6⁶/8	993	77
	■ Krydor – Julian Shewchuk – Julian Shewchuk – 1985									
177⁴/8	26³/8 25⁶/8	17	19²/8	4⁶/8	4⁶/8	6	6		993	77
	■ Torquay – Wayne Daae – Wayne Daae – 1996									
177⁴/8	27⁶/8 26⁵/8	18⁶/8	21³/8	4⁴/8	4⁴/8	9	6	7⁶/8	993	77
	■ Arborfield – Tyler Johnson – Terry L. Amos – 1998									
176⁷/8	28¹/8 28⁶/8	19¹/8	22³/8	4⁷/8	4⁷/8	6	5	4⁴/8	1086	82
	■ Qu'Appelle River – W. Leo Bumphrey – W. Leo Bumphrey – 1992									

Score	Length of Main Beam Right	Left	Inside Spread	Greatest Spread	Circumference at Smallest Place Between Burr and First Point Right	Left	Number of Points Right	Left	Lengths Abnormal Points	All-Time Rank	State Rank
176 6/8	25 1/8	23 6/8	19 2/8	24 5/8	5 4/8	5 2/8	8	9	8	1103	83
■ Saskatchewan – Unknown – D. Ross Sayrs – 1986											
176 6/8	24 6/8	23 7/8	17 6/8	23 7/8	4 5/8	4 4/8	7	9	7 2/8	1103	83
■ Moose Mt. – Dwight C. Tonn – Dwight C. Tonn – 1991											
176 6/8	27	26	22 2/8	24 5/8	5 3/8	5 3/8	6	5	1 2/8	1103	83
■ Mozart – Frank Prisciak – Frank Prisciak – 1997											
176 6/8	26 2/8	25 6/8	19 6/8	25	5	4 7/8	7	5	7	1103	83
■ Little Quill Lake – Jonathan Rorquist – Jonathan Rorquist – 1999											
176 5/8	25 1/8	25	15 4/8	17 6/8	5 5/8	5 4/8	5	5	1 3/8	1134†	87†
■ Carrot River – Larry K. Trout – Larry K. Trout – 2001											
176 4/8	23 3/8	23 4/8	22	23 7/8	5 3/8	5 5/8	6	5	1 2/8	1158	88
■ Esterhazy – Albert Kristoff – Albert Kristoff – 1960											
176 3/8	25 7/8	25 5/8	18 1/8	21	4 5/8	4 3/8	7	9	4	1182†	89†
■ Lanigan – Derek Fisher – Derek Fisher – 2000											
176 3/8	25 4/8	26 1/8	17 4/8	20	5 6/8	5 6/8	6	6	4 7/8	1182†	89†
■ S. Saskatchewan River – Cory M. Schommer – Cory M. Schommer – 2000											
176 3/8	24 5/8	24 3/8	17 1/8	19 4/8	4 7/8	4 7/8	7	6	2 4/8	1182	89
■ Round Lake – Randy Tulloch – Randy Tulloch – 1989											
176 3/8	27 3/8	28 4/8	23 3/8	25 7/8	5 2/8	5 2/8	10	10	11 4/8	1182	89
■ Cypress Hills – Dwight W. Dobson – Dwight W. Dobson – 1990											
176 3/8	25 4/8	25 5/8	18 1/8	21 1/8	5 1/8	5	6	6		1182	89
■ Fremont – Earl M. Gilles – Earl M. Gilles – 1992											
176 3/8	25 6/8	24 2/8	18 1/8	20 4/8	5 3/8	5 2/8	8	6	3 4/8	1182	89
■ Craven – Steven G. Ries – Steven G. Ries – 1993											
176 2/8	23	25 5/8	18 6/8	21	5	4 7/8	5	5		1209	95
■ Swanson – L.S. Wood – L.S. Wood – 1959											
176 2/8	26 6/8	26 3/8	20 3/8	23	5 5/8	5 5/8	8	6	8 3/8	1209	95
■ Moose Creek – Joseph Romer – Joseph Romer – 1993											
176 2/8	25 5/8	26 4/8	18 7/8	21 3/8	4 5/8	4 6/8	6	6	3 3/8	1209	95
■ Meyers Lake – Trent Derkatz – Trent Derkatz – 1999											
176 2/8	27 2/8	27 1/8	19 1/8	22 6/8	4 6/8	4 7/8	7	5	8 3/8	1209	95
■ Foam Lake – Stanley Kaban – Stanley Kaban – 1999											
176 1/8	25 4/8	24 4/8	21 5/8	23 3/8	4 6/8	5 1/8	6	6		1243†	99†
■ Solberg Lake – Dale W. Brinkman – Dale W. Brinkman – 2001											
176 1/8	23 4/8	25 4/8	21 1/8	24 6/8	5 2/8	5 3/8	9	8	5 4/8	1243	99
■ Pierce Lake – Edwin Johnson – Edwin Johnson – 1989											
176 1/8	25 7/8	26 4/8	24 2/8	26 5/8	5	5	7	8	7 7/8	1243	99
■ Lenore Lake – Emile Creurer – Emile Creurer – 1998											
176	27 3/8	27 3/8	24 5/8	27 3/8	5 4/8	5 3/8	7	5	4 5/8	1266	102
■ Duck Lake – Larry Attig – Larry Attig – 1993											
175 7/8	23	23 1/8	16 7/8	19 2/8	5 1/8	5 1/8	5	5		1287	103
■ Hanley – G. Koyl & W. King – Gavin Koyl – 1964											

■ Location of Kill – Hunter – Owner – Date Killed

Score	Length of Main Beam Right / Left	Inside Spread	Greatest Spread	Circumference at Smallest Place Between Burr and First Point Right / Left	Number of Points Right / Left	Lengths Abnormal Points	All-Time Rank	State Rank
175 7/8	25 7/8 25 6/8	20	21 7/8	5 4/8 5 4/8	6 5	1 5/8	1287	103
	■ Shipman – William L. Cox – William L. Cox – 1998							
175 6/8	25 3/8 26 1/8	19 6/8	22 5/8	5 3/8 5 3/8	5 5		1310	105
	■ Southey – J.A. Maier – J.A. Maier – 1958							
175 5/8	26 3/8 25 6/8	18 5/8	21 2/8	5 4 7/8	6 7	1 6/8	1333	106
	■ Leoville – Frank J. Tucek, Jr. – Frank J. Tucek, Jr. – 1998							
175 4/8	24 6/8 24 3/8	20 2/8	23 1/8	5 5/8 5 6/8	5 7	4 2/8	1352	107
	■ Meyers Lake – Picked Up – Chad Nickeson – 1997							
175 4/8	26 2/8 25	15 2/8	17 1/8	4 7/8 4 7/8	5 5		1352	107
	■ Kaposvar Creek – Scott W. Soyka – Scott W. Soyka – 1999							
175 3/8	26 5/8 26 5/8	19 3/8	21 1/8	4 5/8 4 6/8	6 6		1377	109
	■ Endeavour – Alfred Norman – Terry L. Amos – 1954							
175 3/8	26 1/8 25 4/8	23 3/8	26 1/8	5 1/8 5 2/8	5 5		1377	109
	■ Bridgeford – Elgin T. Gates – Elgin T. Gates – 1958							
175 3/8	25 4/8 25 5/8	20 1/8	23 1/8	5 5 1/8	5 5		1377	109
	■ Basin Lake – Kurt R. Moorman – Kurt R. Moorman – 1996							
175 2/8	24 23 6/8	19 6/8	23 2/8	5 4/8 5 5/8	6 5	2 2/8	1403	112
	■ Qu'Appelle – Douglas Garden – Douglas Garden – 1965							
175 2/8	28 1/8 28 6/8	17 6/8	20 7/8	5 2/8 5 2/8	5 6	1	1403	112
	■ Val Marie – Leon Perrault – Leon Perrault – 1977							
175 2/8	25 3/8 26 3/8	23 4/8	25 3/8	5 5/8 5 7/8	6 6		1403	112
	■ Krydor – Lorne M. Shewchuk – Lorne M. Shewchuk – 1986							
175 2/8	26 3/8 25 4/8	19 5/8	21 6/8	5 1/8 5 3/8	8 7	8 3/8	1403	112
	■ Meadow Lake – Joseph V. Caccamo, Jr. – Joseph V. Caccamo, Jr. – 1995							
175 1/8	25 5/8 25 5/8	22 1/8	25 3/8	4 5/8 4 5/8	5 5		1440	116
	■ Gerald – Ken Cherewka – Ken Cherewka – 1964							
175 1/8	25 4/8 24 5/8	19 7/8	22 4/8	5 2/8 5 1/8	6 5		1440	116
	■ Shaunavon – Richard Klink – Richard Klink – 1981							
175 1/8	24 5/8 25 4/8	17 5/8	21 4/8	5 4/8 5 4/8	5 5		1440	116
	■ Witchekan Lake – Brent A. Smith – Brent A. Smith – 1987							
175 1/8	23 23 7/8	17 1/8	21	5 1/8 5	9 9	10 2/8	1440	116
	■ Loon Lake – Thomas P. Shields – Thomas P. Shields – 1992							
175 1/8	26 4/8 25 5/8	17 3/8	19 3/8	5 1/8 5	6 5	2	1440	116
	■ Jackfish Lake – Dan Fitch – Dan Fitch – 1996							
175	26 2/8 28 2/8	22	24 4/8	5 5	5 5		1472	121
	■ Bjork Lake – Don C. Wright – James E. Nelson – 1992							
175	27 26 4/8	21 4/8	23 7/8	5 3/8 5 1/8	6 5	1 2/8	1472	121
	■ Echo Lake – Kelvin E. Karpinski – Kelvin E. Karpinski – 1998							
174 7/8	23 24 1/8	17 7/8	20	4 6/8 4 7/8	6 6		1513†	123†
	■ Pipestone River – Brent M. Urschel – Brent M. Urschel – 2000							
174 7/8	22 22 3/8	18 5/8	21 1/8	5 3/8 5 4/8	6 6		1513	123
	■ Langbank – Allan Brehaut – Allan Brehaut – 1996							

SASKATCHEWAN TYPICAL WHITETAIL DEER

Score	Length of Main Beam Right Left	Inside Spread	Greatest Spread	Circumference at Smallest Place Between Burr and First Point Right Left	Number of Points Right Left	Lengths Abnormal Points	All-Time Rank	State Rank
	■ Location of Kill – Hunter – Owner – Date Killed							
174⁵/₈	25⁶/₈ 25²/₈	20³/₈	22⁴/₈	4⁶/₈ 4⁵/₈	5 5		1561	125
■ Saskatoon – Kelly D. Day – Kelly D. Day – 1996								
174⁵/₈	25⁶/₈ 26²/₈	20⁷/₈	22⁶/₈	4⁵/₈ 4⁶/₈	5 5		1561	125
■ Jumping Deer Creek – Doug Blaha – Doug Blaha – 1998								
174⁴/₈	24²/₈ 24²/₈	23⁴/₈	24⁶/₈	5¹/₈ 5²/₈	5 8	3²/₈	1592	127
■ Glaslyn – Roger D. Matheny – Roger D. Matheny – 1993								
174³/₈	24⁴/₈ 24²/₈	17¹/₈	19⁶/₈	4⁷/₈ 5¹/₈	7 7		1619	128
■ Roddick Lake – Peter J. Laroque – Peter J. Laroque – 1993								
174²/₈	25³/₈ 25	22²/₈	24	4 4¹/₈	7 6	3²/₈	1652	129
■ Leask – Brian Brad – Brian Brad – 1994								
174²/₈	24¹/₈ 24	16⁴/₈	18⁴/₈	4⁶/₈ 4⁶/₈	6 6		1652	129
■ Moosomin – Jim Toth – Jim Toth – 1999								
174¹/₈	26 24⁴/₈	18⁷/₈	24	5¹/₈ 5¹/₈	6 5		1678	131
■ Stockholm – Rienhold S. Kulcsar – Rienhold S. Kulcsar – 1991								
174	26¹/₈ 26²/₈	20⁴/₈	24	5 4⁶/₈	7 7	10	1717	132
■ Bulyea – W.H. Dodsworth – Edward B. Shaw – 1961								
174	27 25⁷/₈	16⁶/₈	19	4⁶/₈ 4⁶/₈	6 6		1717	132
■ Lake of the Prairies – Brian Wonitowy – Brian Wonitowy – 1994								
174	23⁶/₈ 21⁷/₈	16	18⁷/₈	4⁴/₈ 4³/₈	7 8	2⁴/₈	1717	132
■ Pierce Lake – James W. Beresford – James W. Beresford – 1999								
173⁷/₈	24⁵/₈ 23⁷/₈	23³/₈	25²/₈	5¹/₈ 4⁷/₈	8 7	8	1743	135
■ Dundurn – Herb Wilson – Herb Wilson – 1960								
173⁷/₈	24³/₈ 23¹/₈	18²/₈	20⁶/₈	4⁷/₈ 5	5 7	1⁵/₈	1743	135
■ Esterhazy – Garry Hawcutt – Garry Hawcutt – 1992								
173⁶/₈	24¹/₈ 24¹/₈	17⁶/₈	21¹/₈	4⁶/₈ 4⁶/₈	6 6		1766	137
■ Regina – Don Wolk – Don Wolk – 1982								
173⁶/₈	26⁵/₈ 26⁵/₈	19	21⁴/₈	4⁶/₈ 5	7 6	8	1766	137
■ Meadow Lake – Ike Rainey – Ike Rainey – 1993								
173⁶/₈	24 24³/₈	21	23²/₈	5²/₈ 5³/₈	5 5		1766	137
■ Good Spirit Lake – Blair Sawka – Blair Sawka – 1998								
173⁵/₈	26⁶/₈ 26⁶/₈	19¹/₈	22¹/₈	4⁶/₈ 5	6 8	8	1819	140
■ Webb – Roger R. Zimmer – Roger R. Zimmer – PR 1976								
173⁵/₈	25²/₈ 25¹/₈	19⁷/₈	23⁵/₈	4⁶/₈ 4⁵/₈	8 7	6²/₈	1819	140
■ Duck Creek – Barry Marquette – Barry Marquette – 1991								
173⁵/₈	25³/₈ 25¹/₈	19¹/₈	23⁵/₈	4⁷/₈ 4⁷/₈	6 7	10⁶/₈	1819	140
■ Atwater – Gary Griffith – Gary Griffith – 1996								
173⁴/₈	26⁴/₈ 27³/₈	18⁴/₈	20⁷/₈	5⁵/₈ 5⁵/₈	7 6	6²/₈	1847†	143†
■ Meadow Lake – David A. Holmes – David A. Holmes – 2000								
173⁴/₈	24³/₈ 25	20¹/₈	22⁶/₈	5²/₈ 5³/₈	5 6	2⁵/₈	1847	143
■ Tuffnell – Ed Mattson – Ed Mattson – 1964								
173⁴/₈	25¹/₈ 25²/₈	18⁶/₈	21¹/₈	4⁵/₈ 4⁵/₈	6 6	1⁴/₈	1847	143
■ Porcupine Plain – Picked Up – Terry L. Amos – PR 1997								

Score	Length of Main Beam Right Left	Inside Spread	Greatest Spread	Circumference at Smallest Place Between Burr and First Point Right Left		Number of Points Right Left		Lengths Abnormal Points	All-Time Rank	State Rank
	■ *Location of Kill – Hunter – Owner – Date Killed*									
173⁴/₈	24⁶/₈ 25	17¹/₈	21⁶/₈	6	6	5	6	3¹/₈	1847	143
	■ *Sweet Grass – Steven Riley – Steven Riley – 1998*									
173²/₈	24³/₈ 25³/₈	20⁶/₈	23²/₈	4⁵/₈	4⁶/₈	5	5		1914	147
	■ *Bemersyde – R.L. McCullough – R.L. McCullough – 1959*									
173²/₈	25⁵/₈ 25⁶/₈	21	24	6	5⁶/₈	8	5	4⁶/₈	1914	147
	■ *Whitewood – L. Reichel – L. Reichel – 1964*									
173²/₈	26⁷/₈ 24³/₈	20⁶/₈	22⁷/₈	5²/₈	5	5	5		1914	147
	■ *Antler – Elmer Lowry – Elmer Lowry – 1966*									
173²/₈	24⁴/₈ 22⁵/₈	19⁴/₈	22²/₈	5	5⁵/₈	6	8	6⁴/₈	1914	147
	■ *Eagle Creek – Perry Haanen – Perry Haanen – 1984*									
173²/₈	22²/₈ 21⁵/₈	17²/₈	19¹/₈	5	5	6	5		1914	147
	■ *Loon Lake – J. Ronnie Ray – J. Ronnie Ray – 1993*									
173¹/₈	23⁶/₈ 24¹/₈	20³/₈	24²/₈	5	5	6	5	4	1950	152
	■ *Marie – King Trew – King Trew – 1957*									
173¹/₈	25⁵/₈ 24⁷/₈	19²/₈	22⁶/₈	5	5	7	7	8⁵/₈	1950	152
	■ *Estuary – Melvin J. Anderson – Melvin J. Anderson – 1962*									
173¹/₈	24⁴/₈ 25³/₈	16³/₈	19⁷/₈	4³/₈	4³/₈	5	5		1950	152
	■ *Big Muddy Valley – Lyndon T. Ross – Lyndon T. Ross – 1984*									
173¹/₈	23⁵/₈ 24¹/₈	13⁷/₈	15⁶/₈	4⁶/₈	4⁴/₈	6	6		1950	152
	■ *Torch River – Debbie Karle – Debbie Karle – 1999*									
173	23⁵/₈ 23⁷/₈	19²/₈	23	5⁶/₈	5⁷/₈	7	7	4⁴/₈	1991	156
	■ *Whitewood Lake – Geordie D. McKay – Geordie D. McKay – 1995*									
172⁷/₈	25⁶/₈ 25⁵/₈	22⁵/₈	25⁶/₈	4⁷/₈	5	6	6	3⁴/₈	2038	157
	■ *Windthorst – Jack Glover – Jack Glover – 1951*									
172⁷/₈	25 26	18³/₈	20³/₈	4⁵/₈	4⁵/₈	6	5		2038	157
	■ *Estevan – Brent Barreth – Brent Barreth – 1998*									
172⁶/₈	24⁴/₈ 21	18⁶/₈	22⁶/₈	5	5	5	5		2065	159
	■ *Biggar – Roy Polsfut – Roy Polsfut – 1989*									
172⁶/₈	26⁴/₈ 27³/₈	20	22	4⁶/₈	4⁶/₈	6	5		2065	159
	■ *Crawford Creek – Scott Macnab – Scott Macnab – 1990*									
172⁶/₈	26⁵/₈ 25²/₈	20⁴/₈	23⁵/₈	4⁶/₈	4⁴/₈	5	5		2065	159
	■ *Horsehide Creek – Gene Markowsky – Gene Markowsky – 1992*									
172⁵/₈	26⁶/₈ 28⁵/₈	19¹/₈	21⁴/₈	5¹/₈	5²/₈	5	5		2113†	162†
	■ *Porcupine Plain – Ron Daunheimer – Ron Daunheimer – 2001*									
172⁵/₈	25⁴/₈ 26	22⁶/₈	25	4³/₈	4⁴/₈	6	5	1¹/₈	2113	162
	■ *Esterhazy – J. Weise – J. Weise – 1960*									
172⁵/₈	22⁵/₈ 23³/₈	19⁷/₈	21⁵/₈	4⁵/₈	4⁴/₈	6	6		2113	162
	■ *Short Creek – Neil Fornwald – Neil Fornwald – 1989*									
172⁵/₈	26⁵/₈ 24⁵/₈	18⁶/₈	21²/₈	5⁴/₈	5⁴/₈	5	5	1⁵/₈	2113	162
	■ *Buffalo Lake – Garth Sander – Garth Sander – 1992*									
172⁵/₈	25⁵/₈ 24⁷/₈	18²/₈	20⁵/₈	5³/₈	5¹/₈	5	7	2⁵/₈	2113	162
	■ *N. Saskatchewan River – Blaine LaRose – Blaine LaRose – 1995*									

Score	Length of Main Beam Right	Left	Inside Spread	Greatest Spread	Circumference at Smallest Place Between Burr and First Point Right	Left	Number of Points Right	Left	Lengths Abnormal Points	All-Time Rank	State Rank
■ Location of Kill – Hunter – Owner – Date Killed											
172⁵/₈	25⁵/₈	27	21⁷/₈	24	4⁶/₈	4⁵/₈	6	5		2113	162
■ Kipling – Tim Davies – Tim Davies – 1999											
172⁴/₈	26⁶/₈	26⁴/₈	21⁶/₈	27	5⁷/₈	5⁷/₈	5	5		2156†	168†
■ Mozart – Wesley M. Spuzak – Wesley M. Spuzak – 2001											
172⁴/₈	27³/₈	26⁷/₈	22⁵/₈	25¹/₈	4⁶/₈	5¹/₈	5	4	2⁷/₈	2156	168
■ Laird – A.E. Nikkel – A.E. Nikkel – 1963											
172⁴/₈	24	23⁶/₈	20⁴/₈	22⁵/₈	5³/₈	5⁴/₈	6	7		2156	168
■ Battle River – Ronald Bexfield – Ronald Bexfield – 1991											
172⁴/₈	25⁶/₈	25¹/₈	20	22⁷/₈	5	4⁷/₈	6	5		2156	168
■ Fir River – Andrew Dyess – Andrew Dyess – 1998											
172³/₈	30¹/₈	30³/₈	22³/₈	26⁴/₈	5⁴/₈	5⁴/₈	9	9	13⁴/₈	2200	172
■ Porcupine Plain – Kim Mikkonen – Kim Mikkonen – 1985											
172²/₈	26⁴/₈	25⁶/₈	20	27⁵/₈	6	5⁶/₈	7	7	9⁴/₈	2237	173
■ Weyburn – Wilfred LaValley – Wilfred LaValley – 1958											
172²/₈	27⁴/₈	26⁴/₈	19⁴/₈	24³/₈	4⁵/₈	4⁶/₈	6	8	15²/₈	2237	173
■ Manor – Albert McConnell – Albert McConnell – 1962											
172¹/₈	27³/₈	27³/₈	22³/₈	24⁵/₈	5⁵/₈	5³/₈	4	4		2286	175
■ Goose Lake – Joe W. Schmidt – Joe W. Schmidt – 1991											
172¹/₈	25⁴/₈	25⁷/₈	24	26¹/₈	4⁵/₈	4⁵/₈	6	6	1⁵/₈	2286	175
■ Pipestone Creek – Clayton Roberts – Clayton Roberts – 1997											
172¹/₈	28⁴/₈	25⁷/₈	17⁵/₈	20⁴/₈	4⁵/₈	4⁶/₈	4	5		2286	175
■ Crooked Lake – Gil Mountney – Gil Mountney – 1999											
172	25⁷/₈	26	18⁴/₈	20⁶/₈	5	5	5	5		2330†	178†
■ Govan – James J. King – James J. King – 2000											
172	26²/₈	27²/₈	18⁵/₈	23³/₈	5⁵/₈	5⁵/₈	9	8	10¹/₈	2330	178
■ Wadena – Edgar Smale – Edgar Smale – 1959											
172	24³/₈	24	17⁷/₈	19⁶/₈	5²/₈	5²/₈	5	6	1⁵/₈	2330	178
■ N. Battleford – Dick Napastuk – Dick Napastuk – 1962											
172	25	26⁴/₈	21⁴/₈	23⁴/₈	5¹/₈	5²/₈	5	5		2330	178
■ Parkman – A.T. Mair – A.T. Mair – 1963											
172	26³/₈	24⁶/₈	19¹/₈	25⁴/₈	5¹/₈	5¹/₈	5	9	6⁵/₈	2330	178
■ Battle River – Robert J. Bullock – Robert J. Bullock – 1992											
172	22²/₈	22	16²/₈	18³/₈	5	5	7	8	9⁶/₈	2330	178
■ Ebel Creek – Cory Zastrizny – Cory Zastrizny – 1992											
172	23³/₈	23³/₈	19⁴/₈	22¹/₈	5⁶/₈	5⁵/₈	5	5		2330	178
■ Little Red River – Peter LoPiccolo – Peter LoPiccolo – 1998											
172	27⁵/₈	29⁶/₈	21²/₈	24²/₈	4⁷/₈	5¹/₈	6	6	6⁶/₈	2330	178
■ Pasquia Hills – Easton C. Kapeller – Easton C. Kapeller – 1999											
171⁷/₈	25⁵/₈	25²/₈	18³/₈	20⁶/₈	5	5	5	5		2382	186
■ Romance – Cameron Kirzinger – Cameron Kirzinger – 1999											
171⁶/₈	27¹/₈	26⁵/₈	21⁵/₈	25⁴/₈	4⁶/₈	5²/₈	6	9	15¹/₈	2418	187
■ Asquith – M.S. Vanin – M.S. Vanin – 1963											

Score	Length of Main Beam Right	Length of Main Beam Left	Inside Spread	Greatest Spread	Circumference at Smallest Place Between Burr and First Point Right	Circumference at Smallest Place Between Burr and First Point Left	Number of Points Right	Number of Points Left	Lengths Abnormal Points	All-Time Rank	State Rank
171 6/8	25 6/8	25 6/8	18 2/8	20 3/8	4 4/8	4 5/8	5	5		2418	187
	■ Maple Creek – G.J. Burch – G.J. Burch – 1967										
171 6/8	28	25 4/8	19 1/8	21 6/8	5	5 3/8	7	9	6 7/8	2418	187
	■ Endeavour – Jeffery A. Duckworth – Jeffery A. Duckworth – 1993										
171 6/8	26 3/8	26 1/8	19 6/8	22 2/8	4 6/8	4 6/8	5	5		2418	187
	■ Lone Rock – Keith R. Fournier – Keith R. Fournier – 1994										
171 6/8	28 6/8	28 3/8	20 4/8	23 2/8	4 3/8	4 3/8	8	5	9	2418	187
	■ S. Saskatchewan River – Garry Kennon – Garry Kennon – 1997										
171 6/8	25 3/8	25 7/8	18 5/8	20 7/8	5 1/8	5 2/8	5	6	1 7/8	2418	187
	■ Cookson – Bry Loyd – Bry Loyd – 1999										
171 5/8	25 6/8	26 4/8	20 6/8	23 4/8	5 1/8	5 1/8	7	6	1 3/8	2470	193
	■ Hanley – L.R. Libke – L.R. Libke – 1961										
171 5/8	26	25 3/8	24 4/8	25 6/8	4 6/8	4 7/8	7	8	16 5/8	2470	193
	■ Langbank – Thomas K. Grimm – Thomas K. Grimm – 1968										
171 5/8	27 2/8	27	17 6/8	20 1/8	4 4/8	4 6/8	5	6	7 3/8	2470	193
	■ Willowbrook – William Hrebenik – William Hrebenik – 1976										
171 5/8	26	27 1/8	21 6/8	27	4 4/8	4 7/8	6	6	9 1/8	2470	193
	■ Turtle Lake – Andrew M. Milanowski – Andrew M. Milanowski – 1996										
171 5/8	23 3/8	23 6/8	15 4/8	17 6/8	5 2/8	5 4/8	6	6	1 5/8	2470	193
	■ Strasbourg – Donald A. Williamson – Donald A. Williamson – 1998										
171 4/8	25 2/8	26 2/8	25 4/8	27 1/8	4 4/8	4 6/8	6	6		2513†	198†
	■ Thickwood Hills – Brian C. Sankey – Brian C. Sankey – 1996										
171 4/8	24	23 7/8	17	19 5/8	4 7/8	4 7/8	5	5		2513	198
	■ Thunder Hill – James R. Riddick – James R. Riddick – 1994										
171 4/8	28	28 1/8	21 1/8	24 5/8	4 1/8	4 2/8	9	9	12 1/8	2513	198
	■ Buffalo Pound Lake – Troy E. Riche – Troy E. Riche – 1995										
171 4/8	24 5/8	27 1/8	16 4/8	18 7/8	4 6/8	4 6/8	6	5		2513	198
	■ Pierceland – Stacer Helton – Stacer Helton – 1997										
171 3/8	22 5/8	22 4/8	18	21 1/8	5 3/8	5 3/8	7	6	1 3/8	2564	202
	■ Grenfell – George DeMontigny – George DeMontigny – 1965										
171 3/8	27 2/8	27 2/8	19 5/8	22	5 6/8	6	7	7	15 2/8	2564	202
	■ Crooked Lake – John Duryba – John Duryba – 1994										
171 3/8	27 3/8	26 5/8	19 5/8	23	4 7/8	4 7/8	7	8	10 4/8	2564	202
	■ Biggar – Milo N. Hanson – Milo N. Hanson – 1994										
171 3/8	27 4/8	26 2/8	20 5/8	23 7/8	5	4 7/8	5	6		2564	202
	■ Bayne – William Matsalla – William Matsalla – 1995										
171 3/8	27 4/8	25 5/8	19 6/8	23 6/8	5 5/8	5 3/8	6	9	11 7/8	2564	202
	■ Glaslyn – Brian Huscroft – Brian Huscroft – 1996										
171 3/8	27 2/8	28 5/8	22 7/8	26 5/8	4 7/8	4 7/8	5	6	2 6/8	2564	202
	■ Little Manitou Lake – Bruce Soderberg – Bruce Soderberg – 1998										
171 2/8	26	25 7/8	18 1/8	22 4/8	5	5 1/8	6	7	3 3/8	2621	208
	■ Duck Lake – Colin P. Laroque – Colin P. Laroque – 1992										

Score	Length of Main Beam Right Left	Inside Spread	Greatest Spread	Circumference at Smallest Place Between Burr and First Point Right Left		Number of Points Right Left		Lengths Abnormal Points	All-Time Rank	State Rank
	■ Location of Kill – Hunter – Owner – Date Killed									
171²/8	26³/8 25⁵/8	19⁵/8	22⁵/8	6 5⁷/8		6 6		3¹/8	2621	208
	■ S. Saskatchewan River – Cheri Boeschen – Cheri Boeschen – 1997									
171¹/8	23²/8 23¹/8	20⁶/8	23⁴/8	5 5²/8		5 6		1¹/8	2665	210
	■ Whitewood – W. Cook – W. Cook – 1966									
171¹/8	25²/8 24⁵/8	18⁴/8	21⁷/8	4⁶/8 4⁶/8		6 7		1¹/8	2665	210
	■ Huard Lake – Garner H. Travelpiece – Garner H. Travelpiece – 1994									
171	25²/8 25³/8	17²/8	20²/8	5 5²/8		6 8		10²/8	2707†	212†
	■ Bulyea – Tracy K. Hubick – Tracy K. Hubick – 2000									
171	23⁵/8 26	19²/8	21⁵/8	5¹/8 5¹/8		5 6			2707	212
	■ Windthorst – Thomas Dovell – Thomas Dovell – 1961									
171	28¹/8 26⁷/8	21	23⁴/8	4⁶/8 4⁶/8		5 5			2707	212
	■ Speers – Charles E. Strautman – Charles E. Strautman – 1969									
171	26²/8 25⁴/8	21⁴/8	23⁴/8	5⁴/8 5⁴/8		5 5			2707	212
	■ Okemasis Lake – Rick Galloway – Rick Galloway – 1989									
171	24²/8 23⁷/8	17⁶/8	19⁶/8	4 4¹/8		6 7		1	2707	212
	■ Gooseberry Lake – Terry R. McGillicky – Terry R. McGillicky – 1999									
170⁷/8	25 25⁵/8	18⁶/8	22	5⁶/8 5⁵/8		6 5		1¹/8	2769†	217†
	■ Porcupine Plain – Edward H. Marinelli – Edward H. Marinelli – 2000									
170⁷/8	24⁵/8 24⁴/8	22	24³/8	5¹/8 5		7 6		4³/8	2769†	217†
	■ Qu' Appelle River – Mel Tuck – Mel Tuck – 2000									
170⁷/8	24 23⁶/8	17⁷/8	20⁴/8	5³/8 5²/8		5 5			2769	217
	■ Jones Creek – Andre Verville – Andre Verville – 1992									
170⁷/8	25³/8 25⁴/8	19⁴/8	21⁵/8	4⁶/8 4⁶/8		5 6		1⁷/8	2769	217
	■ Loon Lake – James D. Schatz – James D. Schatz – 1998									
170⁶/8	24⁴/8 23⁴/8	18	20²/8	4⁵/8 4⁷/8		5 5			2828†	221†
	■ Torch River – William H. Worley – William H. Worley – 2000									
170⁶/8	25²/8 24⁴/8	24²/8	26	4⁵/8 4⁶/8		6 5		1	2828	221
	■ Elbow – W.H. Crossman – W.H. Crossman – 1959									
170⁶/8	25³/8 25¹/8	19⁴/8	22³/8	5³/8 5³/8		7 6		6⁶/8	2828	221
	■ Gerald – Jerry Norek – Jerry Norek – 1959									
170⁶/8	23³/8 23³/8	19⁵/8	22⁷/8	4⁶/8 4⁵/8		5 6		2¹/8	2828	221
	■ Great Sand Hills – Ralph L. Cervo – Ralph L. Cervo – 1984									
170⁶/8	28²/8 26³/8	19²/8	22	5⁵/8 5⁵/8		5 5			2828	221
	■ Saskatchewan – Unknown – James B. Sisco III – PR 1995									
170⁶/8	22⁷/8 21⁷/8	17	19⁶/8	4⁴/8 4⁴/8		6 7		1⁴/8	2828	221
	■ Waskesiu Lake – Edwin W. Ehler – Edwin W. Ehler – 1999									
170⁵/8	25²/8 25	20⁷/8	22⁶/8	5²/8 5³/8		6 5			2876†	227†
	■ S. Saskatchewan River – Jack Clary – Jack Clary – 2001									
170⁵/8	22⁷/8 26⁴/8	18²/8	21	4⁶/8 4⁶/8		6 9		6¹/8	2876†	227†
	■ Meadow Lake – John W. Stoothoff, Jr. – John W. Stoothoff, Jr. – 2000									
170⁵/8	25²/8 26¹/8	18⁵/8	21²/8	5 5¹/8		5 5			2876	227
	■ Wawota – Benjamin F. Kregel – Benjamin F. Kregel – 1965									

Score	Length of Main Beam Right	Left	Inside Spread	Greatest Spread	Circumference at Smallest Place Between Burr and First Point Right	Left	Number of Points Right	Left	Lengths Abnormal Points	All-Time Rank	State Rank
	■ Location of Kill – Hunter – Owner – Date Killed										
$170^5/8$	$26^2/8$	$26^5/8$	18	$21^1/8$	$4^6/8$	$4^7/8$	5	8	$4^5/8$	2876	227
	■ Mervin – Terry Brett – Terry Brett – 1991										
$170^5/8$	$27^4/8$	$27^7/8$	22	$24^1/8$	$5^2/8$	$5^1/8$	8	7	$10^5/8$	2876	227
	■ Eagle Creek – Perry Haanen – Perry Haanen – 1995										
$170^5/8$	$25^1/8$	$25^7/8$	$21^2/8$	$23^5/8$	$5^5/8$	$5^5/8$	5	7	$3^7/8$	2876	227
	■ Melfort – Dave Parfitt – Dave Parfitt – 1995										
$170^5/8$	$26^4/8$	$25^3/8$	$18^2/8$	$21^1/8$	6	$5^6/8$	6	6	$4^5/8$	2876	227
	■ Spruce Lake – Shawn Bleakney – Shawn Bleakney – 1996										
$170^4/8$	$23^2/8$	$23^5/8$	19	$22^4/8$	5	$5^1/8$	5	5		2933†	234†
	■ Etomami River – Kenyon Batty – Kenyon Batty – 2001										
$170^4/8$	$25^4/8$	$24^5/8$	$19^1/8$	$21^4/8$	$4^7/8$	$4^5/8$	8	7	$10^7/8$	2933	234
	■ Craven – Ted Paterson – Ted Paterson – 1960										
$170^4/8$	21	$22^6/8$	$17^3/8$	$19^6/8$	$5^2/8$	$5^3/8$	7	6	$1^5/8$	2933	234
	■ Great Sand Hills – Picked Up – Frank Yeast – PR 1960										
$170^4/8$	$24^2/8$	24	$20^6/8$	$23^3/8$	$5^5/8$	$5^6/8$	5	5		2933	234
	■ Preeceville – Vernon Hoffman – Vernon Hoffman – 1965										
$170^4/8$	$23^7/8$	26	$19^6/8$	$21^5/8$	$5^5/8$	$5^2/8$	5	5		2933	234
	■ Chitek Lake – Timothy E. Baxley – Timothy E. Baxley – 1992										
$170^4/8$	$24^2/8$	$23^3/8$	21	$23^6/8$	$5^6/8$	$5^6/8$	8	8	$8^6/8$	2933	234
	■ Swan Plain – Chris Halsey – Chris Halsey – 1997										
$170^3/8$	$25^3/8$	$24^6/8$	$18^7/8$	21	$5^3/8$	$5^2/8$	6	7	2	2992†	240†
	■ Quill Lake – Eddy Korolchuk – Eddy Korolchuk – 2000										
$170^3/8$	$27^3/8$	$26^2/8$	$25^6/8$	$27^6/8$	$5^4/8$	$5^5/8$	5	5	$4^3/8$	2992	240
	■ Fort Qu'Appelle – L.A. Magnuson – L.A. Magnuson – 1962										
$170^3/8$	25	$25^1/8$	$18^3/8$	$21^1/8$	$5^2/8$	5	6	6	$7^6/8$	2992	240
	■ Griffin – Leonard Mitchall – Leonard Mitchall – 1989										
$170^3/8$	$23^2/8$	$23^4/8$	$21^5/8$	$25^2/8$	$4^7/8$	$4^7/8$	7	6	1	2992	240
	■ Smeaton – Samuel D. Singer – Samuel D. Singer – 1997										
$170^3/8$	$23^7/8$	$23^3/8$	$21^3/8$	24	$5^6/8$	$5^7/8$	5	5		2992	240
	■ Turtle Ford – Gordon E. Janz – Gordon E. Janz – 1999										
$170^2/8$	$27^6/8$	$28^5/8$	$20^6/8$	$24^4/8$	$4^4/8$	$4^3/8$	6	4	2	3063†	245†
	■ Crane Lake – Jeff M. Slabik – Jeff M. Slabik – 2000										
$170^2/8$	$27^2/8$	$26^6/8$	20	$22^3/8$	5	$5^1/8$	5	5		3063	245
	■ Dafoe – A. Linder – A. Linder – 1959										
$170^2/8$	$26^2/8$	$25^7/8$	22	26	$5^1/8$	$5^2/8$	7	6	$11^6/8$	3063	245
	■ Lestock – Zoltan Blaskovich – Zoltan Blaskovich – 1965										
$170^2/8$	$24^3/8$	$24^7/8$	$21^6/8$	24	$4^3/8$	$4^3/8$	6	6		3063	245
	■ Avonlea – Doug English – Doug English – 1965										
$170^2/8$	$24^7/8$	25	20	$22^5/8$	$4^7/8$	$4^7/8$	5	6	$1^4/8$	3063	245
	■ Esterhazy – Sidney W. Golling – Sidney W. Golling – 1998										
$170^2/8$	$27^3/8$	$27^6/8$	20		$4^6/8$	$4^7/8$	5	5		3063	245
	■ Tobin Lake – Trevor Rehaluk – Trevor Rehaluk – 1998										

Score	Length of Main Beam Right	Left	Inside Spread	Greatest Spread	Circumference at Smallest Place Between Burr and First Point Right	Left	Number of Points Right	Left	Lengths Abnormal Points	All-Time Rank	State Rank
	■ Location of Kill – Hunter – Owner – Date Killed										
170¹/8	25⁴/8	25³/8	21²/8	23⁴/8	5⁶/8	6	7	6	9⁵/8	3143†	251†
	■ Little Quill Lake – Bennie Buttram – Bennie Buttram – 2000										
170¹/8	23⁷/8	22⁷/8	16¹/8	18⁴/8	5⁵/8	5⁵/8	7	6	1⁴/8	3143	251
	■ Swift Current – Brian Baumann – Brian Baumann – 1966										
170¹/8	25³/8	25⁷/8	18⁴/8	20⁴/8	4⁵/8	4⁵/8	6	5	1³/8	3143	251
	■ Hubbard – Lionel Rokosh – Lionel Rokosh – 1995										
170¹/8	23⁴/8	23²/8	17⁷/8	20⁴/8	5	5³/8	7	6	2	3143	251
	■ Cochin – John M. Hanger II – John M. Hanger II – 1997										
170	24⁷/8	24⁴/8	18²/8	20²/8	5	4⁷/8	5	5		3224	255
	■ Porcupine Forest – Jeff B. Brigham – Jeff B. Brigham – 1993										
170	24⁴/8	25	17⁶/8	19⁴/8	4³/8	4²/8	6	5		3224	255
	■ Porcupine Plain – Picked Up – Terry L. Amos – 1996										
170	25⁶/8	24⁵/8	20²/8	22⁶/8	4⁵/8	4⁵/8	5	5		3224	255
	■ Wakaw Lake – Nolan Balone – Nolan Balone – 1999										
169⁶/8	24³/8	24⁴/8	18¹/8	20⁴/8	5⁴/8	5²/8	8	8	7³/8	3306†	258†
	■ Saskatchewan River – Trevor Folden – Trevor Folden – 2000										
169⁵/8	27⁴/8	25⁷/8	21	22⁷/8	5	5	8	8	8¹/8	3314†	259†
	■ Arcola – Jeff Hesketh – Jeff Hesketh – 2000										
169⁴/8	25³/8	25⁷/8	20³/8	22²/8	4⁷/8	4⁶/8	6	6	2¹/8	3316	260
	■ Wishart – Kelly Bzdel – Kelly Bzdel – 1996										
169⁴/8	24⁴/8	25	20⁶/8	24¹/8	4¹/8	4¹/8	5	5		3316	260
	■ Sheho – Trevor Walchuk – Trevor Walchuk – 1999										
169¹/8	25⁷/8	25⁶/8	18³/8	20⁴/8	5¹/8	5²/8	5	5		3342†	262†
	■ Leoville – John B. Triplett – John B. Triplett – 2002										
169	22⁶/8	19⁶/8	15⁶/8	17⁶/8	4⁴/8	4⁴/8	6	6		3348	263
	■ Meadow Lake – Eugene M. Callaway, Jr. – Eugene M. Callaway, Jr. – 1993										
168⁴/8	24⁶/8	26¹/8	18⁴/8	21¹/8	4⁴/8	4⁴/8	6	5	3⁴/8	3385	264
	■ Keeley Lake – Vincent C. Buono – Vincent C. Buono – 1994										
168²/8	24³/8	24⁵/8	16	18²/8	4⁴/8	4⁵/8	6	8	3⁴/8	3414	265
	■ Moose Mt. – Barry Adair – Barry Adair – 1997										
168	25⁶/8	26²/8	19²/8	21³/8	5¹/8	5¹/8	5	5		3443	266
	■ Leoville – James Bierstine – James Bierstine – 1994										
167⁶/8	28⁵/8	28⁷/8	22³/8	25⁷/8	5¹/8	5	5	7	6³/8	3461	267
	■ Biggar – Nibal Achkar – Nibal Achkar – 1992										
167⁶/8	24⁵/8	25⁴/8	21	24¹/8	5	5	4	4		3461	267
	■ Bannoc – Joe Dillon – Joe Dillon – 1998										
167⁴/8	26¹/8	26	19⁶/8	21⁷/8	4³/8	4⁴/8	5	6		3485	269
	■ Preeceville – Gerald Swiderski – Gerald Swiderski – 1999										
167	24¹/8	24⁶/8	18⁴/8	21	4⁴/8	4⁴/8	5	6	1⁶/8	3552†	270†
	■ Loon Lake – Robert J. Breheney – Robert J. Breheney – 2001										
167	26³/8	25²/8	18¹/8	20⁶/8	4⁴/8	4³/8	6	6	3⁷/8	3552	270
	■ Crooked Creek – Robert J. Hurry – Robert J. Hurry – 1984										

Score	Length of Main Beam Right Left	Inside Spread	Greatest Spread	Circumference at Smallest Place Between Burr and First Point Right Left		Number of Points Right Left		Lengths Abnormal Points	All-Time Rank	State Rank
	▪ Location of Kill – Hunter – Owner – Date Killed									
166⁷/₈	25⁷/₈ 25²/₈	16⁴/₈	19	4⁷/₈	5¹/₈	6	6	1³/₈	3568†	272†
	▪ Big River – Bret D. Hamm – Bret D. Hamm – 2000									
166⁵/₈	23³/₈ 24³/₈	21³/₈	23⁵/₈	4⁴/₈	4⁴/₈	5	5		3598	273
	▪ Eagle Creek – Percy A. Summach – Percy A. Summach – 1959									
166⁵/₈	25⁶/₈ 25⁵/₈	19	21⁴/₈	5⁵/₈	5⁴/₈	8	7	7⁵/₈	3598	273
	▪ Beaver River – Graham Dalziel – Graham Dalziel – 1989									
166¹/₈	25 24	19²/₈	21³/₈	4⁴/₈	4⁴/₈	6	5	1⁵/₈	3643†	275†
	▪ N. Saskatchewan River – John P. McMillan – John P. McMillan – 2000									
166	23⁴/₈ 24²/₈	18⁴/₈	21⁶/₈	5³/₈	5⁴/₈	8	8	11⁶/₈	3657	276
	▪ Swan River – Phil Ryan – Phil Ryan – 1993									
166	26⁵/₈ 25⁴/₈	19	21⁴/₈	5⁷/₈	5⁵/₈	4	4		3657	276
	▪ The Dirt Hills – Gordon Popescul – Gordon Popescul – 1998									
165⁷/₈	26 25⁵/₈	19³/₈	21³/₈	4⁶/₈	4⁷/₈	5	5		3672	278
	▪ Cochin – J. Mark Hanger – J. Mark Hanger – 1995									
165⁶/₈	24⁶/₈ 24	17³/₈	19⁷/₈	4⁶/₈	5	6	5	1⁵/₈	3680	279
	▪ Onion Lake – Ronald K. Lamb – Ronald K. Lamb – 1996									
165³/₈	25¹/₈ 26³/₈	19⁷/₈	21⁶/₈	4⁵/₈	4⁴/₈	5	5		3731†	280†
	▪ Poundmaker Creek – Jeffrey Johnston – Jeffrey Johnston – 2000									
165²/₈	26²/₈ 26²/₈	17⁶/₈	19⁵/₈	4⁵/₈	4⁴/₈	5	5		3748	281
	▪ Jedburgh – Lawrence Grodecki – Lawrence Grodecki – 1996									
165¹/₈	26³/₈ 24⁷/₈	17⁵/₈	20²/₈	5	5³/₈	6	7	2⁴/₈	3767	282
	▪ Lashburn River – Rick Woods – Rick Woods – 1992									
165¹/₈	25⁶/₈ 26	19⁷/₈	22³/₈	5³/₈	5⁵/₈	6	6	5²/₈	3767	282
	▪ Fort-a-la-Corne – Steve Clifford – Steve Clifford – 2000									
164⁶/₈	24⁴/₈ 24³/₈	21³/₈	23⁵/₈	5¹/₈	5	6	6	5³/₈	3809†	284†
	▪ Little Nut Lake – Floyd C. Lowry – Floyd C. Lowry – 2001									
164⁵/₈	26⁵/₈ 26	18⁶/₈	21⁶/₈	5	5⁵/₈	6	6	4⁷/₈	3835†	285†
	▪ Pierce Lake – Mark V. Mauro – Mark V. Mauro – 2001									
164⁵/₈	25⁶/₈ 25²/₈	19²/₈	22⁴/₈	5	5	6	7	8⁷/₈	3835	285
	▪ Loon Lake – John Clark, Jr. – John Clark, Jr. – 1985									
164⁴/₈	25⁶/₈ 25⁵/₈	20	22⁴/₈	5¹/₈	5¹/₈	6	6	2²/₈	3855	287
	▪ Ruby Lake – George M. O'Brien – George M. O'Brien – 1999									
164³/₈	24²/₈ 25²/₈	15¹/₈	17	4⁵/₈	4⁴/₈	7	7	2²/₈	3864	288
	▪ Big River – David F. Doebler – David F. Doebler – 1991									
164²/₈	24 23⁷/₈	23²/₈	25³/₈	4⁵/₈	4⁶/₈	9	5	6⁴/₈	3876	289
	▪ Central Butte – Mark Hicks – Mark Hicks – 1993									
163⁷/₈	23⁴/₈ 23	20¹/₈	22³/₈	5	5	5	6		3928†	290†
	▪ Swan River – Milo J. Conklin – Milo J. Conklin – 2000									
163⁷/₈	23⁵/₈ 23⁵/₈	21³/₈	24³/₈	5³/₈	5³/₈	5	5		3928	290
	▪ Spiritwood – Richard P. Smith – Richard P. Smith – 1999									
163⁶/₈	22⁵/₈ 22³/₈	17	19¹/₈	5³/₈	5³/₈	5	5		3946	292
	▪ Great Sand Hills – Jack Clary – Jack Clary – 1990									

Score	Length of Main Beam Right Left	Inside Spread	Greatest Spread	Circumference at Smallest Place Between Burr and First Point Right Left	Number of Points Right Left	Lengths Abnormal Points	All-Time Rank	State Rank
	■ Location of Kill – Hunter – Owner – Date Killed							
163⁵/₈	25⁶/₈ 26³/₈	19²/₈	22²/₈	4⁶/₈ 4⁶/₈	6 6	2⁷/₈	3961	293
	■ Meadow Lake – Lewis E. Hartenstine – Lewis E. Hartenstine – 1998							
163²/₈	24³/₈ 23⁷/₈	17	19⁴/₈	5 5	5 5		4017	294
	■ Turtle Lake – William G. Johnson III – William G. Johnson III – 1993							
163²/₈	22⁶/₈ 23	19²/₈	21²/₈	4⁵/₈ 4⁴/₈	6 6		4017	294
	■ Candle Lake – Chester Beatty – Chester Beatty – 1994							
163¹/₈	23⁴/₈ 24⁴/₈	16⁴/₈	18³/₈	4³/₈ 4³/₈	6 7	1¹/₈	4035	296
	■ Cold Lake – John S. Fenner – John S. Fenner – 1993							
162⁷/₈	26⁴/₈ 25	23³/₈	25³/₈	4²/₈ 4¹/₈	5 5		4067	297
	■ Chitek Lake – William J. Schlich – William J. Schlich – 1994							
162	25²/₈ 24¹/₈	21⁶/₈	24²/₈	5⁵/₈ 5⁵/₈	5 5		4184	298
	■ Cochin – Chris Gooch – Chris Gooch – 1995							
162	24⁵/₈ 24²/₈	19⁵/₈	22	5⁴/₈ 5⁴/₈	6 5	1⁷/₈	4184	298
	■ Pierceland – Frank J. Fatti, Sr. – Frank J. Fatti, Sr. – 1998							
161⁷/₈	23⁷/₈ 23²/₈	16²/₈	18²/₈	5⁶/₈ 5⁷/₈	7 6	4³/₈	4212†	300†
	■ Hudson Bay – Scott Griswold – Scott Griswold – 2001							
161⁷/₈	24²/₈ 24³/₈	19³/₈	22	4²/₈ 4²/₈	6 7	1²/₈	4212	300
	■ Candle Lake – William A. Brooks, Sr. – William A. Brooks, Sr. – 1991							
161⁴/₈	23¹/₈ 23	18²/₈	21⁴/₈	5⁴/₈ 5⁵/₈	5 6	1⁴/₈	4258	302
	■ Pierce Lake – Kenneth Rhinesmith – Kenneth Rhinesmith – 1988							
161⁴/₈	22⁷/₈ 23⁴/₈	15⁵/₈	17⁶/₈	4³/₈ 4³/₈	5 6	1⁵/₈	4258	302
	■ Leoville – Frank V. Incorvaia – Frank V. Incorvaia – 1994							
161²/₈	22 23	18	20²/₈	4⁵/₈ 4⁵/₈	6 5		4310	304
	■ Prince Albert – Picked Up – C.J. Fuller – PR 1990							
161¹/₈	24⁴/₈ 23⁵/₈	18¹/₈	20³/₈	5¹/₈ 5¹/₈	6 6	3²/₈	4332	305
	■ McBride Lake – John LaCroix – John LaCroix – 1995							
160⁷/₈	22⁵/₈ 23²/₈	19¹/₈	21¹/₈	5³/₈ 5	8 6	10⁶/₈	4380	306
	■ Moose Creek – Angelo DeFeo – Angelo DeFeo – 1993							
160⁵/₈	24⁷/₈ 24⁷/₈	17¹/₈	19⁴/₈	4⁷/₈ 5	5 5		4423	307
	■ Torch River – Wes Shahan – Wes Shahan – 1998							
160³/₈	26⁵/₈ 26⁵/₈	22⁷/₈	25²/₈	5²/₈ 5³/₈	6 5		4470	308
	■ Montreal Lake – Dick A. Jacobs – Dick A. Jacobs – 1989							
160²/₈	25³/₈ 24¹/₈	18¹/₈	20⁶/₈	5³/₈ 5³/₈	6 6	4⁷/₈	4495	309
	■ Dorintosh – Uwe K. Terner – Uwe K. Terner – 1989							
160²/₈	22³/₈ 22¹/₈	18⁶/₈	20³/₈	4³/₈ 4³/₈	6 6		4495	309
	■ Cabri – Ken Currie – Ken Currie – 1997							
160¹/₈	23⁷/₈ 25⁷/₈	20¹/₈	21⁶/₈	4⁴/₈ 4³/₈	6 5	4²/₈	4534	311
	■ Huard Lake – Garner H. Travelpiece – Garner H. Travelpiece – 1993							
160	24⁴/₈ 22⁶/₈	19	21	4²/₈ 4³/₈	7 5	1	4565	312
	■ Meadow Lake – Robin J. Margolis – Robin J. Margolis – 1994							
198⁷/₈	24⁶/₈ 25³/₈	18¹/₈	22⁷/₈	5 5	6 6		*	*
	■ Moose Mountain Lake – Mark Hordeski – Mark Hordeski – 1999							

Score	Length of Main Beam		Inside Spread	Greatest Spread	Circumference at Smallest Place Between Burr and First Point		Number of Points		Lengths Abnormal Points	All-Time Rank	State Rank
	Right	Left			Right	Left	Right	Left			
	■ *Location of Kill – Hunter – Owner – Date Killed*										
195⁶/₈	26²/₈	26⁴/₈	20	23³/₈	5	4⁶/₈	6	6		*	*
	■ *Good Spirit Lake – Carl L. Sawchuk, Sr. – Carl A. Sawchuk, Jr. – 1954*										

† The scores and ranking for trophies from the 25th Awards Entry Period are not final until the banquet is held on June 19, 2004.

* Final score is subject to revision by additional verifying measurements.

SASKATCHEWAN

NON-TYPICAL WHITETAIL DEER

Score	Length of Main Beam Right	Left	Inside Spread	Greatest Spread	Circumference at Smallest Place Between Burr and First Point Right	Left	Number of Points Right	Left	Lengths Abnormal Points	All-Time Rank	State Rank
$265\frac{3}{8}$	$25\frac{7}{8}$	26	$18\frac{3}{8}$	$28\frac{4}{8}$	$6\frac{6}{8}$	$6\frac{5}{8}$	16	17	$67\frac{4}{8}$	21	1
	■ White Fox – Elburn Kohler – Bass Pro Shops – 1957										
$251\frac{4}{8}$	$26\frac{5}{8}$	$26\frac{6}{8}$	$22\frac{6}{8}$	$26\frac{1}{8}$	6	$5\frac{6}{8}$	13	10	60	50	2
	■ Meeting Lake – Greg Brataschuk – Brad Gsell – 1987										
$248\frac{4}{8}$	$22\frac{6}{8}$	$24\frac{3}{8}$	22	$30\frac{2}{8}$	$5\frac{7}{8}$	$5\frac{7}{8}$	13	11	$87\frac{4}{8}$	68	3
	■ Moose Mt. Park – Walter Bartko – George Hooey – 1964										
$245\frac{4}{8}$	$24\frac{6}{8}$	$21\frac{5}{8}$	$16\frac{5}{8}$	$21\frac{2}{8}$	$5\frac{3}{8}$	5	18	12	$71\frac{1}{8}$	82	4
	■ Carrot River – Picked Up – Ken Halloway – 1962										
$243\frac{5}{8}$	$24\frac{1}{8}$	$24\frac{1}{8}$	$22\frac{2}{8}$	26	$5\frac{1}{8}$	5	11	15	$35\frac{3}{8}$	96	5
	■ Govan – A.W. Davis – Bass Pro Shops – 1951										
$242\frac{4}{8}$	$26\frac{4}{8}$	27	$20\frac{6}{8}$	$29\frac{2}{8}$	$5\frac{1}{8}$	$5\frac{1}{8}$	10	12	$55\frac{4}{8}$	101	6
	■ S. Saskatchewan River – Earl W. Green – Bass Pro Shops – 1993										
$240\frac{4}{8}$	$24\frac{4}{8}$	$24\frac{5}{8}$	$18\frac{7}{8}$	$26\frac{4}{8}$	$6\frac{3}{8}$	$6\frac{3}{8}$	12	18	$54\frac{3}{8}$	113	7
	■ Tisdale – John Law – John Law – 1988										
$239\frac{4}{8}$	$26\frac{1}{8}$	$25\frac{7}{8}$	$19\frac{6}{8}$	$25\frac{6}{8}$	$6\frac{5}{8}$	$6\frac{5}{8}$	13	12	$56\frac{6}{8}$	121	8
	■ Glasyn – Mark Schumlick – Wayne Williamson – 1997										
$238\frac{1}{8}$	$24\frac{2}{8}$	$21\frac{7}{8}$	22	$25\frac{6}{8}$	$5\frac{2}{8}$	$5\frac{2}{8}$	13	15	$86\frac{1}{8}$	139	9
	■ Whitewood – Jack Davidge – Jack Davidge – 1967										
$237\frac{6}{8}$	$27\frac{2}{8}$	$27\frac{6}{8}$	$19\frac{5}{8}$	$23\frac{2}{8}$	$5\frac{4}{8}$	$5\frac{4}{8}$	14	17	$41\frac{3}{8}$	143	10
	■ Meadow Lake – Picked Up – Darrell Roney – 1996										
$236\frac{4}{8}$	$24\frac{6}{8}$	25	$20\frac{5}{8}$	$27\frac{5}{8}$	$5\frac{4}{8}$	5	17	12	$77\frac{5}{8}$	160	11
	■ Reserve – Harry Nightingale – Legendary Whitetails – 1959										
$235\frac{4}{8}$	$25\frac{4}{8}$	$24\frac{5}{8}$	$19\frac{6}{8}$	$26\frac{6}{8}$	$5\frac{4}{8}$	$5\frac{7}{8}$	9	20	$60\frac{2}{8}$	166	12
	■ Pipestone Valley – E.J. Marshall – E.J. Marshall – 1958										
$233\frac{7}{8}$	$23\frac{6}{8}$	$22\frac{4}{8}$	$16\frac{5}{8}$	24	6	$5\frac{7}{8}$	9	14	$62\frac{6}{8}$	183	13
	■ Tompkins – Don Stueck – McLean Bowman – 1961										
233	$20\frac{2}{8}$	$23\frac{4}{8}$	$19\frac{6}{8}$	23	$6\frac{4}{8}$	$5\frac{2}{8}$	12	7	$64\frac{6}{8}$	196	14
	■ Punnichy – Steve Kapay – Gale Sup – 1968										
$232\frac{3}{8}$	28	$27\frac{1}{8}$	17	$20\frac{2}{8}$	$5\frac{4}{8}$	$5\frac{5}{8}$	10	11	$36\frac{7}{8}$	204†	15†
	■ Glass Lake – Karpo R. Stokalko – Karpo R. Stokalko – 2001										
$231\frac{7}{8}$	24	$22\frac{2}{8}$	18	$25\frac{3}{8}$	$5\frac{5}{8}$	$5\frac{4}{8}$	10	20	$70\frac{3}{8}$	212	16
	■ Harris – Herman Cox – R.M. Burnett – 1954										
$231\frac{5}{8}$	$26\frac{6}{8}$	$27\frac{5}{8}$	23	$25\frac{6}{8}$	$6\frac{1}{8}$	$6\frac{1}{8}$	10	9	$42\frac{3}{8}$	214	17
	■ Battle River – Kevin Rowswell – Kevin Rowswell – 1998										
$226\frac{6}{8}$	$28\frac{4}{8}$	$28\frac{2}{8}$	$22\frac{1}{8}$	$25\frac{6}{8}$	$5\frac{4}{8}$	$5\frac{5}{8}$	10	12	$23\frac{3}{8}$	285	18
	■ Manor – Stan Balkwill – Cabela's Inc. – 1960										
$226\frac{5}{8}$	$26\frac{5}{8}$	26	$18\frac{7}{8}$	$22\frac{3}{8}$	$6\frac{1}{8}$	6	15	12	$26\frac{6}{8}$	289	19
	■ Shell Lake – Marcel Proulx – D.J. Hollinger & B. Howard – 1984										

Note: ■ *Location of Kill – Hunter – Owner – Date Killed*

Score	Length of Main Beam Right	Length of Main Beam Left	Inside Spread	Greatest Spread	Circumference at Smallest Place Between Burr and First Point Right	Left	Number of Points Right	Left	Lengths Abnormal Points	All-Time Rank	State Rank
225	$25^6/8$	$24^5/8$	23	25	5	$4^7/8$	12	14	$45^6/8$	318	20
■ Alameda Dam – Duane Gervais – Duane Gervais – 1992											
224	$24^4/8$	$24^2/8$	$16^6/8$	$22^1/8$	6	$6^1/8$	13	10	$34^6/8$	337	21
■ Torch River – Gus Fomradas – Helmut Fomradas – 1993											
$223^4/8$	$26^3/8$	$27^4/8$	$23^2/8$	$27^1/8$	$6^4/8$	$6^4/8$	8	13	$31^2/8$	350	22
■ Turtle Lake – Blaine LaRose – Blaine LaRose – 1996											
$223^3/8$	$20^7/8$	$24^5/8$	19	$26^3/8$	$5^5/8$	$5^3/8$	19	12	$99^5/8$	354	23
■ Cochin – Vic Pearsall – D.J. Hollinger & B. Howard – 1960											
$222^5/8$	27	$25^5/8$	$19^2/8$		$5^3/8$	$5^7/8$	9	12	$35^3/8$	373	24
■ Mair – R.A. McGill – Mr. & Mrs. M. Melom – 1952											
$220^4/8$	$27^4/8$	$26^3/8$	$20^3/8$	$25^4/8$	$4^5/8$	$4^6/8$	14	14	$52^7/8$	427	25
■ Chitek Lake – Douglas Falone – Douglas Falone – 1998											
$220^1/8$	$27^4/8$	$27^5/8$	$24^3/8$	$27^2/8$	$4^7/8$	$4^6/8$	12	9	$41^4/8$	439	26
■ Redvers – Ira E. Sampson – Ira E. Sampson – 1969											
$219^7/8$	$23^4/8$	$26^1/8$	$23^2/8$	26	$5^2/8$	$5^5/8$	11	8	$36^1/8$	444	27
■ Saskatchewan River – Don Thorimbert – Don Thorimbert – 1996											
$219^6/8$	25	$27^7/8$	$21^1/8$	$25^4/8$	$5^4/8$	$5^5/8$	10	15	$43^7/8$	447	28
■ N. Saskatchewan River – Terry D. Redpath – Terry D. Redpath – 1993											
$219^1/8$	$24^6/8$	$24^6/8$	$17^4/8$	24	$4^5/8$	$4^6/8$	10	9	$45^3/8$	465	29
■ S. Saskatchewan River – Picked Up – Thad W. Karwandy – 2000											
$218^3/8$	$20^7/8$	$24^3/8$	$19^3/8$	$28^2/8$	$4^6/8$	5	13	15	$80^6/8$	490	30
■ South Goodeve – Fred Bohay – Fred Bohay – 1958											
$217^5/8$	$24^4/8$	$24^3/8$	$17^3/8$	$24^2/8$	$4^5/8$	$4^4/8$	11	16	$48^4/8$	506	31
■ Tobin Lake – Picked Up – SK Parks & Renew. Resc. – 1991											
$217^4/8$	$27^4/8$	$27^6/8$	$23^5/8$	$25^7/8$	$5^3/8$	$5^3/8$	8	8	$33^7/8$	510	32
■ Bethune – Ronald N. Riche – Ronald N. Riche – 1998 ■ See photo on page 58											
$217^2/8$	$23^3/8$	$23^1/8$	19	26	$5^3/8$	$5^2/8$	11	11	$45^4/8$	519	33
■ Sprucehome – Tom Pillar – Tom Pillar – 1957											
$217^2/8$	$23^6/8$	$24^2/8$	19	$23^2/8$	$5^4/8$	$5^4/8$	13	10	$50^2/8$	519	33
■ Hudson Bay – Ron Kenyon – Ron Kenyon – 1987											
$217^1/8$	$25^2/8$	$27^6/8$	$20^6/8$	$23^7/8$	6	$5^7/8$	12	8	$34^3/8$	527	35
■ Sturgeon River – Francis Rask – Francis Rask – 1995											
$216^2/8$	$23^5/8$	24	$18^4/8$	$23^4/8$	$4^4/8$	$4^4/8$	10	8	$41^4/8$	555	36
■ Buchanan – Mike Spezrivka – Linda Christoforo – 1961											
215	$25^1/8$	$24^5/8$	$18^1/8$	$23^6/8$	$4^4/8$	$4^5/8$	11	15	$40^1/8$	598	37
■ Wood River – Scott Cowie – Scott Cowie – 1997											
$214^5/8$	$24^6/8$	$24^5/8$	18	$23^2/8$	$6^1/8$	$5^7/8$	13	12	$40^5/8$	614	38
■ Turtle Lake – Scott Macnab – Scott Macnab – 1993											
$213^7/8$	$24^5/8$	$25^2/8$	$18^5/8$		$5^7/8$	$5^6/8$	10	8	$29^2/8$	635†	39†
■ S. Saskatchewan River – Keith A. Graves – Keith A. Graves – 2000											
$213^7/8$	$27^3/8$	$25^3/8$	$16^5/8$	21	$5^3/8$	$5^3/8$	12	8	27	635	39
■ Bresaylor – Barry Braun – Barry Braun – 1966											

Score	Length of Main Beam Right	Left	Inside Spread	Greatest Spread	Circumference at Smallest Place Between Burr and First Point Right	Left	Number of Points Right	Left	Lengths Abnormal Points	All-Time Rank	State Rank
213 3/8	25 4/8	24 5/8	18 5/8	28 2/8	4 7/8	4 7/8	9	10	41 6/8	660	41
■ Midale – Picked Up – Dick Rossum – 1969											
213	25 7/8	24 1/8	20 6/8		5 4/8	5 6/8	5	15	56	671	42
■ Rush Lake – Jim Runzer – Murray Bromley – 1966											
212 6/8	25 4/8	25 4/8	22 7/8	24 7/8	4 7/8	5 1/8	10	9	32 7/8	677	43
■ Shell Lake – Robert Barlow – Robert Barlow – 1996											
212 5/8	24 6/8	25 2/8	17 6/8	20 4/8	5	5	11	13	32 3/8	683	44
■ Glentworth – Garnet Fortnum – Garnet Fortnum – 1984											
212 2/8	25 3/8	27 1/8	22 5/8	25 2/8	5 5/8	5 5/8	9	9	31 5/8	701	45
■ Langenburg – Hartley Biley – Hartley Biley – 1996											
211 7/8	25 6/8	26 3/8	24 1/8	29 1/8	6	5 7/8	14	11	39 4/8	724	46
■ Raymore – Adolf Wulff – Adolf Wulff – 1951											
211 5/8	28 2/8	28 4/8	23	29 4/8	5 7/8	6	11	11	40 3/8	734	47
■ Glaslyn – Carl R. Frohaug – Carl R. Frohaug – 1981											
211 3/8	24 7/8	25 2/8	16 6/8	21 5/8	5 6/8	5 6/8	11	10	24 7/8	745	48
■ Borden – Leonard Verishine – Leonard Verishine – 1972											
210 7/8	23 1/8	22 6/8	21 1/8	26 3/8	4 6/8	4 6/8	11	11	52	773	49
■ Patience Lake – Rick Schindel – Rick Schindel – 1990											
210 6/8	25 2/8	26 2/8	23 6/8	27 3/8	5 3/8	5 4/8	14	11	51	779	50
■ N. Saskatchewan River – Brent La Clare – Brent La Clare – 1998											
210 5/8	25 2/8	22 5/8	20 4/8	26 2/8	5 3/8	5 1/8	10	10	34 7/8	783†	51†
■ Qu' Appelle Valley – Bryce Burns – Bryce Burns – 2000											
210 1/8	23 4/8	24	18 5/8	23 3/8	5 1/8	5	9	7	40	808	52
■ Harris – Kenneth M. Lepp – Kenneth M. Lepp – 1985											
210 1/8	24	26	20 2/8	22 3/8	6 1/8	5 4/8	8	9	32 3/8	808	52
■ Leoville – Ray J. Guarisco – Ray J. Guarisco – 1994											
210	26	26 1/8	18	22 4/8	5 5/8	5 4/8	10	9	23	816	54
■ Glenewen – H. Frew – H. Frew – 1955											
209 7/8	25 2/8	24 1/8	22 4/8	25	4 4/8	4 5/8	9	9	39 1/8	825	55
■ Maryfield – W.W. Nichol – W.W. Nichol – 1967											
209 4/8	26 3/8	25 4/8	17 7/8	21 5/8	5 1/8	5	10	12	37 3/8	848†	56†
■ Manitou Lake – Dustin Elchyson – Dustin Elchyson – 2001											
209 1/8	26	27 7/8	28 5/8	32 5/8	5 4/8	5 5/8	8	6	34 2/8	863	57
■ N. Saskatchewan River – Gerald Hamel – Gerald Hamel – 1986											
209	24 6/8	24 4/8	17	19 3/8	6 1/8	6	12	6	32 4/8	872	58
■ Saskatchewan – Unknown – Aly M. Bruner – PR 1996											
208 4/8	28 3/8	29 2/8	22 5/8	27 1/8	5 4/8	5 4/8	10	9	43 5/8	894	59
■ Grenfell – Clayton Roberts – Clayton Roberts – 1998											
208 1/8	25 1/8	25 5/8	19 4/8	23 7/8	4 6/8	4 6/8	11	8	31 1/8	920	60
■ Peterson – Albert Huber – Albert Huber – 1993											
207 6/8	22 4/8	24 6/8	24 3/8	24 7/8	5	5 2/8	9	9	19 7/8	951	61
■ MacNutt – Delwin Andres – Delwin Andres – 1993											

Location of Kill – Hunter – Owner – Date Killed

Score	Length of Main Beam Right	Left	Inside Spread	Greatest Spread	Circumference at Smallest Place Between Burr and First Point Right	Left	Number of Points Right	Left	Lengths Abnormal Points	All-Time Rank	State Rank
	■ Location of Kill – Hunter – Owner – Date Killed										
207⁶/8	24⁶/8	25¹/8	22⁶/8	26⁴/8	6⁶/8	6⁶/8	10	9	32	951	61
	■ Edgeley – Ian G. Gilchrist – Ian G. Gilchrist – 1995										
207⁵/8	24²/8	23⁶/8	17⁵/8	23³/8	5⁶/8	5⁴/8	7	8	30⁶/8	957	63
	■ Moosomin – Leslie Hanson – Sam Peterson – 1961										
207²/8	23⁴/8	23⁷/8	20²/8	26²/8	6¹/8	6³/8	15	10	35²/8	985	64
	■ Swan Plain – Gary A. Markofer – Gary A. Markofer – 1991										
207	23³/8	23⁶/8	20	23	5⁵/8	5⁶/8	7	10	22⁶/8	1005	65
	■ Eagle Creek – Perry Haanen – Perry Haanen – 1993										
206⁷/8	25⁵/8	27¹/8	22⁴/8	26²/8	4⁵/8	4⁶/8	11	9	24⁷/8	1011	66
	■ Maple Creek – Theodore Reierson – Theodore Reierson – 1984										
206⁶/8	25⁴/8	25⁴/8	24	27	5⁴/8	5⁴/8	7	11	29	1028	67
	■ Beechy – Harold Penner – Spanky Greenville – 1959										
206⁶/8	27⁵/8	24¹/8	16⁶/8	21⁵/8	6⁴/8	6	6	14	50²/8	1028	67
	■ N. Saskatchewan River – David C. Pezderic – David C. Pezderic – 1997										
206⁵/8	26⁵/8	25²/8	19⁷/8	22¹/8	5¹/8	5	11	9	20²/8	1036	69
	■ Outlook – Unknown – Dick Rossum – 1971										
206³/8	25	24⁷/8	18⁶/8	21¹/8	6	5⁷/8	9	11	23³/8	1051	70
	■ Kuroki – Picked Up – K. Ian Cooper – 1995										
206¹/8	22²/8	22⁵/8	18⁴/8	21	5⁴/8	5¹/8	15	10	44⁷/8	1068	71
	■ Kisbey – J. Harrison – J. Harrison – 1956										
205⁴/8	23⁵/8	22⁷/8	19	24⁷/8	4¹/8	4¹/8	9	11	30	1107	72
	■ Armit River – Marvin B. Borsa – Marvin B. Borsa – 1995										
205³/8	23³/8	21⁷/8	18⁷/8	27¹/8	4⁷/8	5	6	12	71	1116	73
	■ Kelvington – D. Minor – D. Minor – 1954										
205²/8	24	23⁵/8	27	29⁵/8	5⁴/8	5⁴/8	11	8	50⁶/8	1131	74
	■ Hungry Hollow – K.W. Henderson – K.W. Henderson – 1954										
205²/8	25	25²/8	16³/8	20³/8	5¹/8	5³/8	14	11	45⁵/8	1131	74
	■ Willow Brook – Alvie Warcomika – Alvie Warcomika – 1993										
205¹/8	25⁷/8	25⁷/8	25³/8	28¹/8	4⁶/8	4⁶/8	8	9	31⁴/8	1138†	76†
	■ Moose Mountain Creek – Darrell Arndt – Darrell Arndt – 1999										
205¹/8	26⁴/8	24⁴/8	20³/8	28¹/8	4⁷/8	5	10	9	42⁴/8	1138	76
	■ Leross – R. Weger – R. Weger – 1961										
205¹/8	24⁵/8	24⁴/8	20²/8	25¹/8	5	4⁷/8	13	11	32⁷/8	1138	76
	■ Antler – Regina K.V. Ross – Regina K.V. Ross – 1987										
205	24²/8	22¹/8	18	25²/8	6²/8	5⁷/8	8	9	30⁶/8	1144	79
	■ White Fox – Richard N. Kimball – Richard N. Kimball – 1997 ■ See photo on page 61										
204⁷/8	27²/8	25⁵/8	18⁴/8	24³/8	5¹/8	5¹/8	7	8	23¹/8	1156	80
	■ Battle River – Corey M. Young – Corey M. Young – 1992										
204⁶/8	23⁴/8	23⁴/8	15²/8	26⁶/8	5⁴/8	6⁶/8	9	10	32	1165	81
	■ Moose Jaw – Earl Sears – Earl Sears – 1958										
204³/8	24³/8	25	19⁶/8	24⁵/8	4¹/8	4¹/8	10	10	30³/8	1186†	82†
	■ Assiniboine River – Karen R. Seginak – Karen R. Seginak – 2000 ■ See photo on page 573										

Score	Length of Main Beam Right Left	Inside Spread	Greatest Spread	Circumference at Smallest Place Between Burr and First Point Right Left	Number of Points Right Left	Lengths Abnormal Points	All-Time Rank	State Rank
	■ Location of Kill – Hunter – Owner – Date Killed							
$204^3/8$	$26^1/8$ $26^3/8$	$17^2/8$	$20^1/8$	$5^6/8$ $5^6/8$	9 9	$21^3/8$	1186	82
	■ Montgomery Creek – Don L. Davey – Don L. Davey – 1997							
204	$23^5/8$ $23^6/8$	$18^3/8$	21	$5^7/8$ $5^6/8$	13 14	$39^7/8$	1220	84
	■ Holbein – Jesse Bates – Jesse Bates – 1981							
204	25 $26^6/8$	$22^6/8$	$24^4/8$	$4^6/8$ 5	9 11	$37^2/8$	1220	84
	■ Buffalo Pound Lake – Jim Weatherall – Jim Weatherall – 1997							
$203^3/8$	$22^4/8$ $23^3/8$	$20^4/8$	25	$4^4/8$ $4^4/8$	10 9	$27^5/8$	1272†	86†
	■ Candle Lake – Joseph R. Conard – Joseph R. Conard – 2001							
$203^3/8$	$22^4/8$ $23^2/8$	$19^2/8$	$22^6/8$	6 $6^1/8$	8 8	$25^1/8$	1272	86
	■ Piapot – Frank Kelly – John R. Steffes, Sr. – 1966							
$203^3/8$	26 $23^2/8$	$17^1/8$	$21^5/8$	$5^4/8$ $5^6/8$	12 11	$65^6/8$	1272	86
	■ Red Pheasant Indian Res. – Douglas A. Salomon – Douglas A. Salomon – 1998							
$203^2/8$	$23^7/8$ $23^3/8$	$17^2/8$	$20^1/8$	$5^1/8$ $5^3/8$	13 13	$27^2/8$	1287	89
	■ Esterhazy – Walter Tucker – Walter Tucker – 1966							
$203^2/8$	$23^4/8$ $23^6/8$	$15^5/8$	20	$5^3/8$ $5^3/8$	11 12	$45^7/8$	1287	89
	■ Churchbridge – Kevin W. Prince – Kevin W. Prince – 1991							
$203^1/8$	$29^2/8$ $28^2/8$	$19^3/8$	22	$5^3/8$ $5^3/8$	11 8	16	1305	91
	■ Swan River – Edwin E. Orr – Edwin E. Orr – 1993							
$203^1/8$	$25^7/8$ $26^1/8$	$24^5/8$	27	$5^2/8$ $6^1/8$	8 8	$30^4/8$	1305	91
	■ N. Saskatchewan River – Barrie Taylor – Barrie Taylor – 1997							
203	$29^1/8$ $27^6/8$	$22^2/8$	$24^5/8$	6 6	10 12	$42^6/8$	1317†	93†
	■ Lake of the Prairies – Eldon Conrad – Eldon Conrad – 2000							
$202^7/8$	$27^6/8$ $27^6/8$	$20^6/8$	$24^2/8$	$5^2/8$ $5^1/8$	8 7	$23^3/8$	1327†	94†
	■ Cutarm River – Charles Bassingthwaite – Charles Bassingthwaite – 2001							
$202^1/8$	$25^1/8$ $25^2/8$	$22^6/8$	$28^3/8$	$4^7/8$ 5	9 9	$29^3/8$	1386	95
	■ Zehner – Lee Danison – Lee Danison – 1958							
202	$23^6/8$ $24^1/8$	$23^5/8$	$25^5/8$	$5^1/8$ $5^2/8$	9 12	$29^5/8$	1395	96
	■ Manito Lake – Barry Manchester – Barry Manchester – 1992							
$201^5/8$	$23^5/8$ $22^7/8$	$20^2/8$	$23^1/8$	$4^6/8$ $4^6/8$	11 11	$45^3/8$	1427	97
	■ Candle Lake – Brian F. Prior – Brian F. Prior – 1993							
$201^4/8$	$25^4/8$ $25^5/8$	$19^3/8$	$22^3/8$	$4^7/8$ 5	9 9	$35^3/8$	1443	98
	■ Ebel Creek – Barry D. Koshman – Barry D. Koshman – 1992							
$201^3/8$	$25^5/8$ $27^7/8$	$20^4/8$	23	$4^5/8$ $4^6/8$	9 10	$20^7/8$	1461	99
	■ Donovan – Glen E. Kristoff – Glen E. Kristoff – 1992							
$200^6/8$	$25^1/8$ 26	$13^7/8$	$17^4/8$	$6^5/8$ $6^5/8$	8 10	$34^1/8$	1524	100
	■ Saskatchewan – Picked Up – Ron Lavoie – 1989							
$200^1/8$	$25^4/8$ $26^3/8$	$20^3/8$	23	$5^2/8$ 5	8 9	$24^2/8$	1577	101
	■ Indian Lake – Glen Lantz – Glen Lantz – 1992							
200	$25^1/8$ $25^4/8$	$18^4/8$	$23^4/8$	$4^7/8$ $4^5/8$	11 10	$22^2/8$	1591	102
	■ Outlook – Earl B. Schmitt – Earl B. Schmitt – 1966							
200	$24^1/8$ $23^3/8$	$23^1/8$	$24^7/8$	5 5	8 9	$27^1/8$	1591	102
	■ Lake of the Prairies – Phil Olshewski – Phil Olshewski – 1999							

Score	Length of Main Beam Right	Left	Inside Spread	Greatest Spread	Circumference at Smallest Place Between Burr and First Point Right	Left	Number of Points Right	Left	Lengths Abnormal Points	All-Time Rank	State Rank
					■ Location of Kill – Hunter – Owner – Date Killed						
1997/8	281/8	285/8	191/8	215/8	6	6	8	8	176/8	1607	104
	■ Peesane – Pete Prosofsky – Pete Prosofsky – 1982										
1993/8	26	241/8	281/8	315/8	51/8	52/8	8	9	373/8	1639	105
	■ Charette Lake – Chris J. Weinkauf – Chris J. Weinkauf – 1998										
1992/8	214/8	215/8	206/8	227/8	56/8	56/8	8	8	216/8	1649	106
	■ Jasmin – Richard Gill – Richard Gill – 1958										
199	255/8	242/8	171/8	196/8	51/8	47/8	8	8	17-9/8	1668	107
	■ Qu'Appelle River – Gilbert Brule – Gilbert Brule – 1998										
1986/8	25	222/8	146/8	203/8	46/8	46/8	11	12	52	1697†	108†
	■ Greenwater Lake – Picked Up – Don Kjelshus – 2000										
1985/8	254/8	235/8	182/8	231/8	63/8	62/8	7	9	133/8	1716	109
	■ Pleasantdale – Picked Up – Don Kjelshus – PR 1992										
1985/8	22	231/8	204/8	243/8	56/8	51/8	8	8	161/8	1716	109
	■ N. Saskatchewan River – Robin McLean – Robin McLean – 1998										
1984/8	263/8	266/8	197/8	24	46/8	44/8	10	9	231/8	1736	111
	■ Arborfield – Terry G. Haugo – Terry G. Haugo – 1989										
1984/8	265/8	264/8	205/8	254/8	55/8	54/8	7	10	141/8	1736	111
	■ Meacham – Darren B. Maroniuk – Darren B. Maroniuk – 1993										
1983/8	253/8	244/8	181/8	226/8	52/8	5	7	10	26	1762	113
	■ Pike Lake – Robert J. MacDonald – Robert J. MacDonald – 1992										
1983/8	232/8	232/8	175/8	192/8	41/8	42/8	6	8	172/8	1762	113
	■ Pasqua Lake – Trent Mattick – Trent Mattick – 1998										
1982/8	273/8	274/8	222/8	246/8	61/8	63/8	5	8	194/8	1772	115
	■ Raymore – William Kobzey – Cabela's Inc. – PR 1958										
1981/8	256/8	262/8	202/8	274/8	46/8	46/8	10	8	253/8	1785	116
	■ Carrot River – Wayne W. Karlin – Wayne W. Karlin – 1989										
198	254/8	223/8	205/8	224/8	5	51/8	9	12	367/8	1801	117
	■ Kipling – Robert Lyons – Robert Lyons – 1993										
1977/8	265/8	255/8	232/8	264/8	56/8	6	7	9	257/8	1816	118
	■ Eagle Creek – Preston Haanen – Preston Haanen – 1992										
1977/8	246/8	251/8	162/8	186/8	47/8	5	11	11	315/8	1816	118
	■ Great Sand Hills – Craig Schwengler – Craig Schwengler – 1996										
1977/8	262/8	263/8	177/8	225/8	56/8	55/8	7	6	16	1816	118
	■ Fishing Lake – Nicole Hrycak – Nicole Hrycak – 1999										
1976/8	24	244/8	184/8	206/8	51/8	54/8	10	7	236/8	1833	121
	■ Langham – Leonard Waldner – Leonard Waldner – 1967										
1976/8	26	261/8	193/8	23	42/8	42/8	7	5	175/8	1833	121
	■ Box Elder Creek – David A. Thomson – David A. Thomson – 1991										
1976/8	236/8	235/8	206/8	23	53/8	55/8	9	10	316/8	1833	121
	■ Spy Hill – William Gilchuk – William Gilchuk – 1996										
1976/8	274/8	271/8	211/8	261/8	47/8	5	9	9	171/8	1833	121
	■ Foam Lake – Tom Taylor – Tom Taylor – 1999										

Score	Length of Main Beam		Inside Spread	Greatest Spread	Circumference at Smallest Place Between Burr and First Point		Number of Points		Lengths Abnormal Points	All-Time Rank	State Rank
	Right	Left			Right	Left	Right	Left			
	■ Location of Kill – Hunter – Owner – Date Killed										
197⁴/₈	27³/₈	25	17⁵/₈	23³/₈	4³/₈	4⁴/₈	10	9	19¹/₈	1866	125
	■ Willow Creek – Arie Vandertweel – Arie Vandertweel – 1997										
197⁴/₈	25⁶/₈	27³/₈	20⁵/₈	24⁵/₈	5³/₈	5⁴/₈	8	12	18³/₈	1866	125
	■ Dore Lake – Erwin W. Brown – Erwin W. Brown – 1998										
197³/₈	24⁶/₈	24³/₈	16²/₈	19	4³/₈	4⁴/₈	9	9	23¹/₈	1884	127
	■ Cold Lake – Anthony Clemenza, Jr. – Anthony Clemenza, Jr. – 1994										
197²/₈	24⁵/₈	24³/₈	18⁵/₈	25⁴/₈	4⁴/₈	4³/₈	9	14	39¹/₈	1901	128
	■ Redvers – Eugene M. Gazda – Eugene M. Gazda – 1984										
197¹/₈	26²/₈	25	18³/₈	22	5³/₈	5³/₈	6	7	23	1923	129
	■ Preeceville – Dale Prestie – Dale Prestie – 1996										
197¹/₈	24	23³/₈	17³/₈	20⁵/₈	5⁵/₈	5⁴/₈	8	7	32²/₈	1923	129
	■ S. Saskatchewan River – Barry D. Miller – Barry D. Miller – 1999										
196⁶/₈	24¹/₈	24²/₈	20	23³/₈	5³/₈	5³/₈	10	12	31²/₈	1968	131
	■ Birch Lake – Brent V. Trumbo – Brent V. Trumbo – 1994										
196⁶/₈	23⁷/₈	26⁴/₈	22⁴/₈	25⁶/₈	5²/₈	5²/₈	12	13	30⁴/₈	1968	131
	■ Porcupine Plain – Picked Up – Terry L. Amos – PR 1997										
196⁵/₈	23¹/₈	23²/₈	19³/₈	25	4⁷/₈	4⁵/₈	9	11	25⁶/₈	1985†	133†
	■ Rabbit Lake – Jim Clary – Jim Clary – 2000										
196⁵/₈	26⁷/₈	26⁵/₈	20²/₈	21⁴/₈	5	4⁷/₈	9	9	21⁷/₈	1985†	133†
	■ Kayosuar Creek – Kelly Schuster – Kelly Schuster – 2000										
196⁴/₈	24⁴/₈	24²/₈	18⁶/₈	21³/₈	6	6²/₈	8	10	22²/₈	1999†	135†
	■ Crystal Lakes – Andrew Gazdewich – Andrew Gazdewich – 2001										
196³/₈	25⁶/₈	24⁴/₈	22⁷/₈	28⁴/₈	5	5²/₈	7	9	26⁴/₈	2010	136
	■ Prairie River – Herb Kopperud – Herb Kopperud – 1959										
196³/₈	23²/₈	23⁵/₈	23⁵/₈	24	5¹/₈	5¹/₈	8	7	25²/₈	2010	136
	■ Pierceland – Robert B. Rhyne – Robert B. Rhyne – 1994										
196¹/₈	25²/₈	25¹/₈	20²/₈	27¹/₈	5¹/₈	5²/₈	7	7	19⁷/₈	2045	138
	■ Ketchen – Vernon C. Hoffman – Vernon C. Hoffman – 1993										
195⁶/₈	25⁵/₈	25⁷/₈	18	23⁶/₈	5¹/₈	5¹/₈	10	9	27⁶/₈	2094†	139†
	■ Little Moose Lake – Carl Grundman – Carl Grundman – 2001										
195⁶/₈	26⁴/₈	27⁴/₈	19⁶/₈	22¹/₈	5³/₈	5³/₈	11	10	39²/₈	2094	139
	■ Moosomin – Tom Ryan – Tom Ryan – 1961										
195⁶/₈	21⁷/₈	25⁷/₈	27⁶/₈	31	6³/₈	5²/₈	14	8	27¹/₈	2094	139
	■ Greenwater Creek – Picked Up – Edward R. Mielke – 1988										
195⁵/₈	25⁴/₈	25⁶/₈	19	26	6	6¹/₈	10	10	27⁷/₈	2116	142
	■ Parkman – H.E. Kennett – H.E. Kennett – 1949										
195⁴/₈	24	23⁷/₈	20	22²/₈	5	5	9	8	25⁴/₈	2134	143
	■ Red Deer River – Glen Gulka – Glen Gulka – 1993										
195⁴/₈	25³/₈	26²/₈	18⁵/₈	21⁴/₈	5¹/₈	5³/₈	9	8	17³/₈	2134	143
	■ Grenfell – Anthony Roberts – Anthony Roberts – 1998										
195³/₈	25¹/₈	25²/₈	17	23⁴/₈	5¹/₈	5¹/₈	9	10	28⁵/₈	2163	145
	■ Souris River – Corinne Biette – Corinne Biette – 1998										

Score	Length of Main Beam Right	Left	Inside Spread	Greatest Spread	Circumference at Smallest Place Between Burr and First Point Right	Left	Number of Points Right	Left	Lengths Abnormal Points	All-Time Rank	State Rank
	■ Location of Kill – Hunter – Owner – Date Killed										
195 2/8	24	24 4/8	20	24 4/8	5 1/8	5	8	8	25 4/8	2186	146
	■ Chitek Lake – Charles E. Gambino – Charles E. Gambino – 1990										
195 2/8	23 2/8	24 6/8	17 5/8	22 5/8	4 5/8	4 5/8	8	8	24 5/8	2186	146
	■ Witchekan Lake – Kim Tiringer – Kim Tiringer – 1990										
194	24 5/8	24 3/8	16 5/8	8 3/8	4 7/8	4 7/8	9	7	21 5/8	2275	148
	■ Porcupine Plain – Jeff Unteriner – Terry L. Amos – 1998										
193 7/8	22 1/8	22 2/8	16 2/8	23 7/8	5 3/8	5 2/8	12	11	36 3/8	2277	149
	■ McBride Lake – Patrick G. Stoia – Patrick G. Stoia – 1999										
193 5/8	27 7/8	27 2/8	19 5/8	22 7/8	5	5	9	7	19 2/8	2281†	150†
	■ Meadow Lake – Keith A. Field – Keith A. Field – 2000										
193 3/8	24 4/8	25 4/8	19 7/8	24	4 5/8	4 5/8	8	11	31 2/8	2293	151
	■ Turtleford – Michael J. Berardis – Michael J. Berardis – 1993										
190 7/8	24 7/8	23 5/8	18 7/8	22 5/8	6 1/8	5 6/8	7	8	19 2/8	2385	152
	■ Swan Plain – John S. Smith – John S. Smith – 1993										
190	25 6/8	26 3/8	19 1/8	22 4/8	5	5	9	10	21 1/8	2418	153
	■ Hunting Lake – Walter J. Benton – Walter J. Benton – 1997										
189 7/8	22 7/8	23 2/8	17 2/8	21 3/8	5 4/8	5 6/8	12	10	38 3/8	2424	154
	■ Saskatchewan – Unknown – D. Ross Sayrs – PR 1986										
185 2/8	25 5/8	25 6/8	17 1/8	19 3/8	4 6/8	4 6/8	6	6	9 3/8	2632	155
	■ Turtle Lake – William F. Gogol – William F. Gogol – 1992										
254 2/8	26 3/8	25 1/8	19 1/8	28 4/8	5 6/8	5 6/8	13	11	78 5/8	*	*
	■ Frenchman Butte – Dwayne Erb – Dwayne Erb – 1999										

† The scores and ranking for trophies from the 25th Awards Entry Period are not final until the banquet is held on June 19, 2004.

* Final score is subject to revision by additional verifying measurements.

North American Whitetail Deer Listing from Mexico

MEXICO
RECORD WHITETAILS

26 Typical whitetail deer entries
8 Non-typical whitetail deer entries
7,265 Total whitetail deer entries

MEXICO
RECORD
Typical Whitetail Deer
Score: 184^5/$_8$
Location: Nuevo Leon
Hunter and Owner: Charles H. Priess
Date: 1985

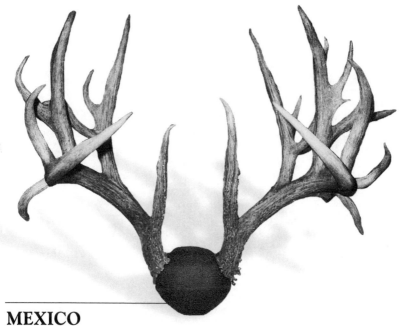

MEXICO
RECORD
Non-Typical Whitetail Deer
Score: 223^{6}/$_{8}$
Location: Nuevo Leon
Hunter and Owner: Ron Kolpin
Date: 1983

MEXICO

TYPICAL WHITETAIL DEER

Score	Length of Main Beam Right	Left	Inside Spread	Greatest Spread	Circumference at Smallest Place Between Burr and First Point Right	Left	Number of Points Right	Left	Lengths Abnormal Points	All-Time Rank	State Rank
	■ Location of Kill – Hunter – Owner – Date Killed										
184⁵/₈	28²/₈	29	23²/₈	25⁴/₈	5¹/₈	5²/₈	5	4	1³/₈	294	1
	■ Nuevo Leon – Charles H. Priess – Charles H. Priess – 1985										
183¹/₈	25³/₈	26¹/₈	21⁵/₈	23⁶/₈	5	5⁴/₈	7	8	5⁴/₈	385	2
	■ Nuevo Leon – Thomas D. Brittingham – Thomas D. Brittingham – 1990										
182⁶/₈	25³/₈	25¹/₈	22	24²/₈	4³/₈	4³/₈	6	6	1⁴/₈	409	3
	■ Coahuila – Manuel A. Flores Rojas – Manuel A. Flores Rojas – 1990										
181⁷/₈	28⁵/₈	27⁴/₈	22¹/₈	24⁴/₈	4⁶/₈	4⁶/₈	5	5		478	4
	■ Coahuila – German L. Flores – German L. Flores – 1986										
181⁶/₈	26⁶/₈	25⁵/₈	24	26²/₈	4⁶/₈	4⁶/₈	6	7		492	5
	■ Nuevo Leon – J.P. Davis – J.P. Davis – 1985										
180³/₈	22⁷/₈	23⁶/₈	19⁷/₈	21⁴/₈	5	4⁷/₈	7	6	1⁶/₈	630	6
	■ Nuevo Leon – Melbourn Shillings – Melbourn Shillings – 1992										
178⁷/₈	26⁴/₈	26⁴/₈	22⁷/₈	25	4⁵/₈	4⁵/₈	5	5		801	7
	■ Coahuila – Donald R. Summers – Donald R. Summers – 1990										
176²/₈	27⁴/₈	27²/₈	21²/₈	23	4⁴/₈	4⁴/₈	6	7		1209	8
	■ Nueva Leon – Al Mendoza – Al Mendoza – 2000										
174⁶/₈	23³/₈	23⁷/₈	16	18³/₈	4⁷/₈	4⁷/₈	6	6		1534	9
	■ Coahuila – Gustavo Garza – Gustavo Garza – 1994										
174²/₈	28²/₈	27³/₈	25²/₈	27³/₈	5²/₈	5⁴/₈	4	4		1652	10
	■ Cerralvo – Unknown – Antonio G. Gonzalez – 1900										
174¹/₈	27¹/₈	27⁴/₈	20¹/₈	22²/₈	4⁵/₈	4⁴/₈	5	5		1678	11
	■ Coahuila – Wayne Glover – Wayne Glover – 1999										
173⁴/₈	24²/₈	24²/₈	20²/₈	22¹/₈	4⁷/₈	4⁷/₈	7	7	2⁶/₈	1847	12
	■ Tamaulipas – John F. Sontag, Jr. – John F. Sontag, Jr. – 1987										
173⁴/₈	25⁶/₈	25	16³/₈	18⁴/₈	4⁴/₈	4³/₈	7	6	1⁷/₈	1847	12
	■ Coahuila – Fernando G. Fuentes – Fernando G. Fuentes – 1994										
172²/₈	26³/₈	25	21²/₈	23¹/₈	5	4⁶/₈	6	5		2237	14
	■ Coahuila – G. Rone Allen – G. Rone Allen – 1992										
172	25⁴/₈	25⁴/₈	17⁴/₈	19⁴/₈	4⁶/₈	4⁴/₈	6	6		2330	15
	■ Coahuila – Picked Up – Carl Kallina – 1986										
171¹/₈	26	25⁷/₈	19²/₈	18⁴/₈	4⁷/₈	4⁷/₈	6	5	2¹/₈	2665†	16†
	■ Nuevo Leon – Jose L. Flores – Jose L. Flores – 1986										
171	26	26²/₈	21²/₈	23⁵/₈	5¹/₈	5³/₈	5	6		2707	17
	■ Nuevo Leon – Farryl Holub – Farryl Holub – 1991										
170¹/₈	27³/₈	26	22¹/₈	24⁵/₈	4⁷/₈	4⁷/₈	5	5		3143	18
	■ Coahuila – Rodolfo F. Barrera – Rodolfo F. Barrera – 1988										
170¹/₈	26⁵/₈	27⁶/₈	21¹/₈	23⁴/₈	4⁷/₈	4⁵/₈	5	5		3143	18
	■ Nuevo Laredo – John F. Taylor – John F. Taylor – 1996										

Score	Length of Main Beam Right Left	Inside Spread	Greatest Spread	Circumference at Smallest Place Between Burr and First Point Right Left		Number of Points Right Left		Lengths Abnormal Points	All-Time Rank	State Rank
	■ *Location of Kill – Hunter – Owner – Date Killed*									
169	24⁴/8 24⁵/8	22⁴/8	24¹/8	4¹/8	4³/8	5	5		3348	20
	■ *Hidalgo – Ray J. Guarisco – Ray J. Guarisco – 1995*									
167⁴/8	23 24⁵/8	21³/8	25³/8	4⁵/8	4⁷/8	6	6	8⁵/8	3485†	21†
	■ *Coahuila – Thomas W. Powell – Thomas W. Powell – 2000*									
163⁵/8	26⁵/8 25⁶/8	19⁶/8	21⁴/8	4⁵/8	4⁵/8	6	6	4¹/8	3961	22
	■ *Coahuila – Michael L. Olson – Michael L. Olson – 1991*									
163⁴/8	25⁷/8 26⁵/8	19⁴/8	21⁷/8	4⁴/8	4⁵/8	5	5		3984	23
	■ *Coahuila – Ronald B. Wardell, Jr. – Ronald B. Wardell, Jr. – 1993*									
163⁴/8	24⁴/8 24²/8	18⁴/8	23²/8	4²/8	4²/8	6	6		3984	23
	■ *Coahuila – Thomas F. Priestly – Thomas F. Priestly – 1997*									
163⁴/8	23⁴/8 23²/8	16	18	4	4¹/8	6	6		3984	23
	■ *Coahuila – Myron Cole – Myron Cole – 1998*									
160²/8	23⁶/8 23⁶/8	20⁶/8	26	4¹/8	4¹/8	5	5		4495	26
	■ *Coahuila – Jesus H.Garza-Villarreal – Jesus H.Garza-Villarreal – 1988*									

† The scores and ranking for trophies from the 25th Awards Entry Period are not final until the banquet is held on June 19, 2004.

MEXICO

NON-TYPICAL WHITETAIL DEER

Score	Length of Main Beam Right	Left	Inside Spread	Greatest Spread	Circumference at Smallest Place Between Burr and First Point Right	Left	Number of Points Right	Left	Lengths Abnormal Points	All-Time Rank	State Rank
Location of Kill – Hunter – Owner – Date Killed											
223⁶/8	25¹/8	24²/8	16³/8	25⁴/8	4³/8	4³/8	10	13	53¹/8	342	1
▪ *Nuevo Leon – Ron Kolpin – Ron Kolpin – 1983*											
210⁶/8	23⁶/8	25⁴/8	22	24	5	5	11	8	44⁴/8	779	2
▪ *Coahuila – Picked Up – John L. Stein – 1981*											
208¹/8	25⁶/8	24²/8	18²/8	23³/8	4⁷/8	5	12	12	38¹/8	920	3
▪ *Mexico – Unknown – William M. Day – 1959*											
200⁶/8	27¹/8	26²/8	17⁷/8	23³/8	4⁴/8	4³/8	11	9	28³/8	1524	4
▪ *Coahuila – Biff MacCollum – Biff MacCollum – 1992* ▪ *See photo on page 611*											
196³/8	22⁵/8	26²/8	17³/8	20²/8	5¹/8	4⁴/8	10	6	29⁶/8	2010	5
▪ *Coahuila – Jeanie D. Willard – Jeanie D. Willard – 1993*											
193²/8	24⁴/8	23²/8	16⁶/8	21²/8	5⁴/8	5²/8	10	7	23	2300	6
▪ *Coahuila – H. Kent Hill – H. Kent Hill – 1985*											
190³/8	24¹/8	22⁵/8	23⁶/8	26⁶/8	5	5	11	10	29⁷/8	2408	7
▪ *Coahuila – Picked Up – Javier de los Santos – 1983*											
189³/8	26³/8	25³/8	20	23¹/8	4⁷/8	4⁷/8	6	7	11¹/8	2443	8
▪ *Tamaulipas – Thomas A. Moy, Jr. – Thomas A. Moy, Jr. – 1997*											

TROPHIES IN THE FIELD

HUNTER: Biff MacCollum
SCORE: 200-6/8
CATEGORY: non-typical whitetail deer
LOCATION: Coahuila, Mexico
DATE: 1992

North American Coues' Whitetail Deer Listing

TOP TEN COUES' WHITETAIL DEER

TYPICAL COUES' WHITEAIL DEER

RANK	SCORE	LOCATION – HUNTER – DATE KILLED — PAGE NUMBER
1	144$\frac{1}{8}$	Arizona – Ed Stockwell – 1953 – 618
2	143	Arizona – Larry Johnson – 1995 – 618
3	134$\frac{4}{8}$	New Mexico – Victor P. Giacoletti, Jr. – 1981 – 636
4	133	Arizona – Michael E. Duperret – 1990 – 618
5†	132$\frac{7}{8}$	Arizona – Sergio Orozco – 2001 – 618
6	131$\frac{7}{8}$	Arizona – George W. Kouts – 1935 – 618
7	130$\frac{5}{8}$	Mexico – Wayne Kleinman – 1958 – 642
8	130$\frac{4}{8}$	Arizona – Kim J. Poulin – 1981 – 618
9†	128$\frac{1}{8}$	Arizona – Bradley Johns – 2000 – 618
10	128	New Mexico – Ramon C. Borrego – 1988 – 636

NON-TYPICAL COUES' WHITEAIL DEER

RANK	SCORE	LOCATION – HUNTER – DATE KILLED — PAGE NUMBER
1	186$\frac{1}{8}$	New Mexico – Peter M. Chase – 1941 – 638
2	158$\frac{4}{8}$	Arizona – Picked Up – 1988 – 630
3	155	Arizona – Charles E. Erickson, Jr. – 1988 – 630
4†	154$\frac{1}{8}$	Mexico – Picked Up – 2001 – 646
5†	152	Arizona – Picked Up – 1971 – 630
6	151$\frac{3}{8}$	Arizona – Picked Up – 1997 – 630
7	150$\frac{5}{8}$	Arizona – Charles C. Mabry – 1929 – 630
7	150$\frac{5}{8}$	Arizona – Robert Rabb – 1954 – 630
9	150$\frac{3}{8}$	Arizona – Jeffrey K. Volk – 1992 – 630
10	149$\frac{7}{8}$	Arizona – Marvin R. Hardin – 1950 – 630

TABULATIONS OF RECORDED COUES' WHITETAIL

By Jack Reneau

The trophy data shown on the following pages are taken from score charts in the Records Archives of the Boone and Crockett Club from 1950 through December 31, 2002, the second year of the 25th Awards Program Entry Period. Trophies accepted in the 25th Awards Program are indicated with a cross symbol (†). The score and rank of trophies so designated will not be final until after the 25th Awards Program banquet that takes place on June 19, 2004. The scores of a few of the higher scoring 25th Awards Program entries need to be verified by the 25th Awards Program Judges Panel that will convene in late April 2004.

A comparison of the all-time rankings of this book with those of the current all-time records book (**Records of North American Big Game**, 11th Edition, 1999) will show some significant differences due to the addition of trophies accepted during the 24th Awards Program (1998-2000) and the first two years of the 25th Awards Program (2001-2002). The rankings in this book supercede those in the 11th Edition.

The Coues' subspecies of the common whitetail deer is found in arid portions of the southwest where conditions are apparently too harsh for its larger cousin. Acceptable areas for entry are currently defined as central and southern Arizona and the Mexican states of Sonora and Chihuahua. In New Mexico the Coues' whitetail deer boundary is defined as the Arizona border to the west, the New Mexico border to the south, the Rio Grande River to the east, and I-40 to the north.

The scores and ranks of trophies shown with an asterisk (*) at the end of a state/provincial listing are not final. The asterisk identifies entry scores subject to verification by an Awards Program Judges Panel. The asterisk can be removed (except in the case of a potential new World's Record) by the submission of two additional, independent scorings by B&C Official Measurers. The Club's Records Committee will then review the three scorings available and determine which, if any, will be accepted in lieu of the Judges Panel measurement. When the score of an asterisked trophy has been accepted as final, the asterisk will be removed and that trophy will take its rightful place in the listings of future editions of the Club's records books. If an asterisk is not removed as outlined above, that trophy will be listed in one Awards book and one All-time book before it is dropped from the trophy listings.

In the case of a potential new World's Record, the trophy must come before an Awards Program Judges Panel or a Special Judges Panel, which may convene during an Awards Program to certify the status and score of a potential World's Record. A potential World's Record will be asterisked if its score is not verified by a Judges Panel since only a Boone and Crockett Club Judges Panel can certify a new World's Record.

Dates of kill for years preceded with the abbreviation "PR" in the following trophy listings means the exact date that trophy was taken, found, acquired, etc., is unknown, but that it was known to exist "Prior to" the year listed. Unless stated otherwise, photographs are courtesy of the trophy owners.

ARIZONA
RECORD COUES' WHITETAILS

245 Typical whitetail deer entries
70 Non-typical whitetail deer entries
437 Total whitetail deer entries

ARIZONA
STATE RECORD
WORLD'S RECORD
Typical Coues' Whitetail Deer
Score: $144^{1}/_{8}$
Location: Pima Co.
Hunter: Ed Stockwell
Owner: Barbara Stockwell
Date: 1953

Photograph by Eldon L. "Buck" Buckner

ARIZONA
STATE RECORD
Non-Typical Coues' Whitetail Deer
Score: 158⁴/₈
Location: Santa Cruz Co.
Hunter: Picked Up
Owner: B&C National Collection
Date: 1988

Photograph from B&C Archives

ARIZONA

TYPICAL COUES' WHITETAIL DEER

Score	Length of Main Beam Right	Left	Inside Spread	Greatest Spread	Circumference at Smallest Place Between Burr and First Point Right	Left	Number of Points Right	Left	Lengths Abnormal Points	All-Time Rank	State Rank
	■ Location of Kill – Hunter – Owner – Date Killed										
144¹/8	20²/8	20⁵/8	15³/8	176/8	54/8	56/8	5	5		1	1
	■ Pima Co. – Ed Stockwell – Barbara Stockwell – 1953										
143	197/8	20³/8	13²/8	154/8	46/8	46/8	5	5		2	2
	■ Navajo Co. – Larry Johnson – Alan C. Ellsworth – 1995										
133	206/8	197/8	18	19⁵/8	37/8	37/8	6	6		4	3
	■ Pima Co. – Michael E. Duperret – M.E. Duperret & J.K. Volk – 1990										
132⁷/8	20⁵/8	207/8	15³/8	18	4	4	5	6	5	5†	4†
	■ Santa Cruz Co. – Sergio Orozco – Sergio Orozco – 2001										
131⁷/8	196/8	192/8	16¹/8	196/8	4²/8	4²/8	5	5		6	5
	■ Cochise Co. – George W. Kouts – George W. Kouts – 1935										
130⁴/8	206/8	206/8	156/8	194/8	46/8	4⁵/8	8	6	4	8	6
	■ Pima Co. – Kim J. Poulin – Kim J. Poulin – 1981										
128¹/8	19³/8	19³/8	154/8	184/8	4²/8	4⁵/8	7	6	5⁵/8	9†	7†
	■ Graham Co. – Bradley Johns – Bradley Johns – 2000										
126/8	20	187/8	176/8	194/8	47/8	5¹/8	5	5		11	8
	■ Yavapai Co. – Picked Up – Joshua E. Epperson – 1999										
126⁵/8	216/8	196/8	14	17	4	4²/8	6	5	1³/8	13	9
	■ Cochise Co. – Mike Kasun – Mike Kasun, Jr. – 1959										
126⁵/8	194/8	186/8	11¹/8	14	4⁵/8	4³/8	5	6	14/8	13	9
	■ Pima Co. – DeWayne M. Hanna – DeWayne M. Hanna – 1977										
126¹/8	19⁵/8	197/8	16²/8	20	37/8	4	6	6	4⁵/8	15	11
	■ Pima Co. – Robert G. McDonald – Robert G. McDonald – 1986										
125⁴/8	186/8	19	16²/8	18²/8	37/8	36/8	5	5		16	12
	■ Arivaca – Gerald Harris – Gerald Harris – 1953										
125	196/8	197/8	154/8	17²/8	4¹/8	4¹/8	5	5		17	13
	■ Ft. Apache Res. – Picked Up – Jerry S. Pippen – PR 1969										
124⁷/8	206/8	20⁵/8	14³/8	157/8	4³/8	4³/8	5	4		19†	14†
	■ Santa Cruz Co. – Kirk Kelso – Kirk Kelso – 2001 ■ See photo on page 53										
124⁶/8	167/8	17¹/8	15¹/8	17	37/8	4¹/8	7	6	1³/8	21	15
	■ Gila Co. – Tommy T. Zienka – Tommy T. Zienka – 1998										
124⁵/8	196/8	19	14¹/8	157/8	4	4¹/8	6	6		22	16
	■ Rincon Mts. – James Pfersdorf – Mrs. J.E. Pfersdorf, Sr. – 1936										
124	19¹/8	19¹/8	166/8	18³/8	37/8	37/8	5	5		24	17
	■ Greenlee Co. – Ronald H. Gerdes – Ronald H. Gerdes – 1993										
123⁷/8	17²/8	17³/8	137/8	16¹/8	4³/8	4³/8	6	6		26	18
	■ Gila Co. – Stephen P. Hayes – Stephen P. Hayes – 1965										
123⁷/8	21³/8	19⁵/8	15³/8	17³/8	4²/8	4¹/8	5	4		26	18
	■ Pima Co. – Kenneth R. Murray – Kenneth R. Murray – 1996										

Score	Length of Main Beam Right	Left	Inside Spread	Greatest Spread	Circumference at Smallest Place Between Burr and First Point Right	Left	Number of Points Right	Left	Lengths Abnormal Points	All-Time Rank	State Rank
123⁶/8	18²/8	17⁷/8	14²/8	16³/8	4⁴/8	4⁴/8	6	6	2⁶/8	28	20

■ Cochise Co. – Larry Vance, Jr. – Larry Vance, Jr. – 1985

| 122⁷/8 | 18⁷/8 | 18²/8 | 14¹/8 | 18 | 4¹/8 | 4 | 5 | 6 | | 30 | 21 |

■ Chiricahua Mts. – Roger Becksted – Roger Becksted – 1960

| 121⁵/8 | 20¹/8 | 19³/8 | 15⁵/8 | 17³/8 | 4²/8 | 4 | 4 | 4 | | 34 | 22 |

■ Pima Co. – Joe Fanning – Joe Fanning – 1964

| 121⁴/8 | 19 | 17⁶/8 | 14¹/8 | 15⁷/8 | 4 | 3⁶/8 | 6 | 6 | 5¹/8 | 35 | 23 |

■ Santa Rita Mts. – Max E. Wilson – Max E. Wilson – 1965

| 121³/8 | 16¹/8 | 17 | 10⁷/8 | 13¹/8 | 3⁴/8 | 3⁴/8 | 6 | 6 | | 36 | 24 |

■ Santa Rita Mts. – George Shaar – George Shaar – 1964

| 121¹/8 | 19⁵/8 | 19²/8 | 15⁷/8 | 17⁵/8 | 3⁷/8 | 3⁷/8 | 5 | 5 | | 37 | 25 |

■ Pima Co. – T. Reed Scott – T. Reed Scott – 1975

| 120⁷/8 | 20⁷/8 | 19⁴/8 | 16³/8 | 19 | 4³/8 | 4¹/8 | 5 | 6 | | 39 | 26 |

■ Santa Rita Mts. – Harold Lyons – Harold Lyons – 1956

| 120⁵/8 | 20¹/8 | 19²/8 | 16³/8 | 17⁷/8 | 3⁵/8 | 3⁶/8 | 4 | 4 | | 41 | 27 |

■ Cochise Co. – Becki D. Goffrier – Becki D. Goffrier – 1984

| 120¹/8 | 18 | 18⁵/8 | 13⁵/8 | 15⁶/8 | 4 | 4 | 5 | 6 | 1²/8 | 44 | 28 |

■ Baboquivari Mts. – Homer R. Edds – Homer R. Edds – 1961

| 119⁷/8 | 20⁷/8 | 21²/8 | 17⁵/8 | 19⁶/8 | 4¹/8 | 3⁷/8 | 4 | 4 | | 46 | 29 |

■ Gila Co. – Tom Connolly – Tom Connolly – 1960

| 119⁶/8 | 20¹/8 | 19 | 12²/8 | 14¹/8 | 4 | 4¹/8 | 5 | 4 | | 48 | 30 |

■ Canelo Hills – George W. Parker – George W. Parker – 1960

| 119⁴/8 | 19⁷/8 | 19⁷/8 | 15⁴/8 | 17⁴/8 | 4³/8 | 4 | 5 | 4 | 1⁴/8 | 50 | 31 |

■ Cochise Co. – James A. Hall – James A. Hall – 1991

| 119⁴/8 | 18⁴/8 | 18²/8 | 16⁴/8 | 18⁴/8 | 4²/8 | 4¹/8 | 4 | 4 | | 50 | 31 |

■ Gila Co. – Allen J. Anspach – Allen J. Anspach – 1992

| 119³/8 | 19⁶/8 | 20¹/8 | 12 | 14³/8 | 3⁷/8 | 3⁷/8 | 6 | 6 | 3¹/8 | 52 | 33 |

■ Canelo Hills – A.R. Anglen – A.R. Anglen – 1967

| 119²/8 | 16⁷/8 | 18⁶/8 | 15 | 17 | 3⁷/8 | 4 | 7 | 6 | | 53 | 34 |

■ Gila Co. – Bert M. Pringle – Mrs. Bert M. Pringle – 1952

| 119¹/8 | 18 | 19²/8 | 10⁵/8 | 12⁵/8 | 5 | 5³/8 | 6 | 4 | | 55 | 35 |

■ Santa Rita Mts. – Monte L. Colvin – Monte L. Colvin – 1965

| 119¹/8 | 19⁶/8 | 19 | 14³/8 | 16 | 3⁵/8 | 3³/8 | 4 | 4 | | 55 | 35 |

■ Cochise Co. – James A. Leiendecker – James A. Leiendecker – 1986

| 119¹/8 | 18²/8 | 18 | 15³/8 | 17 | 3⁷/8 | 3⁷/8 | 4 | 4 | | 55 | 35 |

■ Pima Co. – Scott Davis – Scott Davis – 1995

| 118⁵/8 | 19⁵/8 | 19⁷/8 | 14⁵/8 | 16⁴/8 | 4⁴/8 | 4³/8 | 4 | 4 | | 60 | 38 |

■ Chiricahua Mts. – Ward Becksted – Ward Becksted – 1958

| 118¹/8 | 17¹/8 | 17³/8 | 15¹/8 | 16⁶/8 | 3⁷/8 | 3⁷/8 | 5 | 5 | | 62 | 39 |

■ Santa Cruz Co. – David W. Ahnell – David W. Ahnell – 1977

| 118 | 16⁶/8 | 16⁵/8 | 14¹/8 | 16 | 4¹/8 | 4²/8 | 8 | 7 | 3⁵/8 | 63 | 40 |

■ Washington Mts. – Ralph Vaga – Ralph Vaga – 1962

Score	Length of Main Beam Right	Left	Inside Spread	Greatest Spread	Circumference at Smallest Place Between Burr and First Point Right	Left	Number of Points Right	Left	Lengths Abnormal Points	All-Time Rank	State Rank
	■ Location of Kill – Hunter – Owner – Date Killed										
118	18²/₈	19²/₈	12⁶/₈	14⁴/₈	3⁵/₈	3⁷/₈	4	4		63	40
	■ Santa Cruz Co. – Michael L. Valenzuela – Michael L. Valenzuela – 1982										
118	17⁷/₈	18¹/₈	13	15³/₈	4¹/₈	4	7	7		63	40
	■ Pima Co. – Larry C. Dixon – Larry C. Dixon – 1995										
117⁷/₈	19	18¹/₈	16⁵/₈	18⁴/₈	4	4	4	4		66	43
	■ Rincon Mts. – Picked Up – H.L. Russell – 1963										
117⁷/₈	19⁵/₈	19⁴/₈	12³/₈	14¹/₈	4¹/₈	3⁷/₈	6	5	1⁴/₈	66	43
	■ Santa Rita Mts. – George Shaar – George Shaar – 1965										
117⁶/₈	18⁶/₈	17⁷/₈	14	15⁵/₈	3⁵/₈	3⁵/₈	4	5		68	45
	■ Canelo Hills – Raymond J. Kassler – Raymond J. Kassler – 1958										
117⁴/₈	17⁷/₈	17¹/₈	14⁴/₈	16	4⁶/₈	4⁵/₈	4	4		70	46
	■ Graham Co. – Steven J. Stayner – Steven J. Stayner – 1993										
117⁴/₈	18¹/₈	18	15⁶/₈	17¹/₈	4³/₈	4¹/₈	4	4		70	46
	■ Apache Co. – Harry Neff – Harry Neff – 1995										
117³/₈	17⁴/₈	17¹/₈	14³/₈	17	4³/₈	4³/₈	4	4		72	48
	■ Atasco Mts. – F.O. Haskell – F.O. Haskell – 1939										
117³/₈	17²/₈	17²/₈	12⁵/₈	15⁵/₈	3⁶/₈	3⁶/₈	5	6	1⁶/₈	72	48
	■ Sicritta Mts. – George S. Tsaguris – George S. Tsaguris – 1958										
117²/₈	19	19³/₈	11⁶/₈	15	4⁷/₈	4⁴/₈	8	6	9	75	50
	■ Santa Rita Mts. – George L. Garlits – George L. Garlits – 1957										
117²/₈	17⁶/₈	18²/₈	17⁵/₈	19²/₈	4⁴/₈	4²/₈	4	5	1³/₈	75	50
	■ Chiricahua Mts. – Picked Up – Warren A. Cartier – 1963										
117²/₈	18	18	12	14²/₈	3⁵/₈	3⁴/₈	5	5		75	50
	■ Tumacacori Mts. – Charles H. Pennington – Charles H. Pennington – 1968										
117	18³/₈	18²/₈	14²/₈	16	4¹/₈	4²/₈	4	4		78	53
	■ Cochise Co. – W.R. Tanner – Fred Tanner – 1941										
117	18⁷/₈	19¹/₈	16	18⁷/₈	3⁶/₈	3⁶/₈	7	6	3⁶/₈	78	53
	■ Pima Co. – Arthur L. Butler – Arthur L. Butler – 1974										
116⁷/₈	18¹/₈	17³/₈	13¹/₈	15⁵/₈	3⁶/₈	3⁶/₈	5	5		80	55
	■ Santa Cruz Co. – Seymour H. Levy – Seymour H. Levy – 1967										
116⁷/₈	19	19⁶/₈	16³/₈	18⁴/₈	4	3⁶/₈	5	5		80	55
	■ Pima Co. – Arcenio G. Valdez – Arcenio G. Valdez – 1971										
116⁶/₈	17⁷/₈	18³/₈	14	15⁴/₈	4⁷/₈	5	4	4		82	57
	■ Coconino Co. – Clay McDonald – Clay McDonald – 1985										
116⁶/₈	18²/₈	18¹/₈	15⁴/₈	17³/₈	4⁵/₈	4³/₈	5	5		82	57
	■ Yavapai Co. – Kevin S. Stimple – Kevin S. Stimple – 1992										
116⁵/₈	17⁵/₈	19	14³/₈	16	4	4	5	5		84	59
	■ Santa Rita Mts. – Mike Holloran – Mike Holloran – 1962										
116⁵/₈	17²/₈	17³/₈	14⁷/₈	15⁶/₈	4⁶/₈	4⁵/₈	4	4		84	59
	■ Gila Co. – Richard A. Thom – Richard A. Thom – 1978										
116⁵/₈	20⁷/₈	19⁶/₈	17⁷/₈	19⁶/₈	4³/₈	4³/₈	6	4	1⁴/₈	84	59
	■ Greenlee Co. – John R. Primasing, Jr. – John R. Primasing, Jr. – 1997										

Score	Length of Main Beam		Inside Spread	Greatest Spread	Circumference at Smallest Place Between Burr and First Point		Number of Points		Lengths Abnormal Points	All-Time Rank	State Rank
	Right	Left			Right	Left	Right	Left			
■ Location of Kill – Hunter – Owner – Date Killed											
116 4/8	19 5/8	20 2/8	14 5/8	16 4/8	3 7/8	3 6/8	5	6	1 1/8	87	62
■ Gila Co. – Nathan Ellison – Nathan Ellison – 1950											
116 3/8	19 2/8	19	14 7/8	16 4/8	4 1/8	4 2/8	5	5		88	63
■ Blue River – Earl H. Harris – Earl H. Harris – 1965											
116 2/8	15 2/8	16 4/8	13 4/8	17 7/8	4 3/8	4 3/8	6	6	1 4/8	89	64
■ Chiricahua Mts. – Freeman Neal – R.M. Woods – 1947											
116 2/8	16 2/8	16 5/8	14	15 5/8	4	4	5	5		89	64
■ Graham Co. – Dale J. Holladay – Dale J. Holladay – 1984											
116 1/8	19 4/8	19 5/8	12 7/8	15 4/8	3 6/8	3 6/8	4	5	1 4/8	91	66
■ Greenlee Co. – Richard A. Benson – Richard A. Benson – 1991											
116	17 4/8	17 3/8	13 2/8	15	4 6/8	4 7/8	4	4		92	67
■ Santa Cruz Co. – Ben Richardson – Ben Richardson – 1978											
116	19	18 7/8	14	16 1/8	3 5/8	3 5/8	4	4		92	67
■ Santa Cruz Co. – Jeffrey C. Lichtenwalter – Jeffrey C. Lichtenwalter – 1982											
115 7/8	19 2/8	18 6/8	14 1/8	15 5/8	4	4	5	5		94	69
■ Yavapai Co. – Robert W. Gaylor – Robert W. Gaylor – 1987											
115 5/8	18 5/8	18 4/8	14 3/8	16 2/8	3 6/8	3 7/8	4	5	1	96	70
■ Breadpan Mt. – Mitchell R. Holder – Mitchell R. Holder – 1966											
115 4/8	15 6/8	16 6/8	13	14 6/8	4	4 2/8	4	4		97	71
■ Santa Rita Mts. – Picked Up – James Bramhall – PR 1963											
115 4/8	18 6/8	18 2/8	15	17	4	4	5	4		97	71
■ Cochise Co. – Bill F. Byrd – Bill F. Byrd – 1983											
115 4/8	18	17 1/8	15 4/8	17 5/8	4 2/8	4 2/8	5	4		97	71
■ Gila Co. – Doug J. Althoff – Doug J. Althoff – 1985											
115 3/8	19 1/8	19 5/8	19 5/8	21 3/8	3 7/8	3 6/8	4	4		100	74
■ Pima Co. – William H. Taylor – William H. Taylor – 1986											
115 2/8	17 2/8	17	13 4/8	15	5	4 7/8	5	4		101	75
■ Santa Rita Mts. – Denis Wolstenholme – Denis Wolstenholme – 1958											
115 2/8	18	20 1/8	15		4	4	5	4		101	75
■ Cerro Colo. Mts. – Manuel V. Guillen – Manuel V. Guillen – 1962											
115 2/8	20 4/8	19 4/8	12 6/8	14 7/8	4 2/8	4 3/8	5	5		101	75
■ Santa Rita Mts. – Bill J. Ford – Bill J. Ford – 1965											
115 2/8	20 1/8	19	16 4/8	19 6/8	4 2/8	4 3/8	5	5	2 6/8	101	75
■ Catalina Mts. – Jim Stough – Jim Stough – 1972											
115 1/8	18 3/8	18 1/8	13 1/8	14 6/8	4	4	5	5		105	79
■ Pima Co. – Robert A. Finelli – Robert A. Finelli – 1997											
115	19 5/8	19 5/8	17 6/8	19 5/8	4 2/8	4 1/8	4	4		106	80
■ Baboquivari Mts. – Karl G. Ronstadt – Karl G. Ronstadt – 1967											
115	19 6/8	20 1/8	18 2/8	19 5/8	4	4	4	4		106	80
■ Coconino Co. – Picked Up – Jerry C. Walters – PR 1970											
115	18 4/8	18 1/8	16 6/8	22	4	4	5	5	4 2/8	106	80
■ Pima Co. – Glen A. Elmer – Glen A. Elmer – 1980											

COUES' WHITETAIL DEER LISTING

Score	Length of Main Beam Right	Left	Inside Spread	Greatest Spread	Circumference at Smallest Place Between Burr and First Point Right	Left	Number of Points Right	Left	Lengths Abnormal Points	All-Time Rank	State Rank
									■ *Location of Kill – Hunter – Owner – Date Killed*		
115	18⁶/₈	18	17²/₈	18⁷/₈	4	4²/₈	5	5		106	80
			■ *Pinal Co. – George Martin – George Martin – 1983*								
114⁷/₈	18²/₈	18⁶/₈	12³/₈	14⁶/₈	4⁷/₈	4⁷/₈	4	4		110	84
			■ *Ruby – Richard McDaniel – Richard McDaniel – 1963*								
114⁷/₈	20	19⁴/₈	16¹/₈	18	3⁶/₈	3⁶/₈	5	4		110	84
			■ *Santa Rita Mts. – John H. Lake – John H. Lake – 1965*								
114⁶/₈	19⁵/₈	19³/₈	14⁵/₈	16⁶/₈	4⁴/₈	4⁵/₈	6	8	11⁷/₈	113	86
			■ *Chiricahua Mts. – John Miller – John Miller – 1949*								
114⁶/₈	17⁴/₈	16	15²/₈	18	4⁵/₈	4⁴/₈	4	5		113	86
			■ *Santa Rita Mts. – Art Pollard – Art Pollard – 1951*								
114⁶/₈	17²/₈	17⁴/₈	16²/₈	18⁴/₈	4²/₈	4	4	4		113	86
			■ *Cochise Co. – Rudy Alvarez – Rudy Alvarez – 1960*								
114⁶/₈	18³/₈	18	15¹/₈	16	4	3⁷/₈	6	5	6¹/₈	113	86
			■ *Canelo Hills – Guy Perry – Guy Perry – 1960*								
114⁶/₈	16⁶/₈	16⁴/₈	11	13¹/₈	4²/₈	4³/₈	5	7	1⁴/₈	113	86
			■ *Santa Rita Mts. – John Bessett – John Bessett – 1965*								
114⁶/₈	17⁵/₈	17⁵/₈	14⁴/₈	17¹/₈	4	4¹/₈	5	5		113	86
			■ *Nogales – Arthur N. Lindsey – Arthur N. Lindsey – 1967*								
114⁵/₈	18⁶/₈	18²/₈	15⁵/₈	18⁴/₈	3⁵/₈	3⁶/₈	4	4		120	92
			■ *Pima Co. – James A. Reynolds – James A. Reynolds – 1984*								
114⁵/₈	15²/₈	14⁷/₈	14³/₈	17¹/₈	3⁴/₈	3⁵/₈	5	5		120	92
			■ *Gila Co. – J. Bradley Johns – J. Bradley Johns – 1992*								
114⁴/₈	19³/₈	20⁴/₈	15	17¹/₈	4²/₈	4⁴/₈	4	4		122	94
			■ *Graham Mts. – Robert R. Stonoff – Robert R. Stonoff – 1962*								
114⁴/₈	15⁶/₈	16¹/₈	12⁴/₈	15³/₈	3⁷/₈	4¹/₈	6	4		122	94
			■ *Patagonia Mts. – Verna Conlisk – Verna Conlisk – 1964*								
114⁴/₈	17⁵/₈	17¹/₈	13⁷/₈	16²/₈	3⁵/₈	3⁵/₈	6	5	3¹/₈	122	94
			■ *Cherry Creek – Alan G. Adams – Alan G. Adams – 1968*								
114⁴/₈	19⁶/₈	18³/₈	14⁴/₈	16²/₈	3⁶/₈	3⁶/₈	4	4		122	94
			■ *Pima Co. – James M. Machac – James M. Machac – 1985*								
114⁴/₈	18	17⁵/₈	15	16⁵/₈	4²/₈	4¹/₈	4	4		122	94
			■ *Gila Co. – Dallas J. Duhamell, Jr. – Dallas J. Duhamell, Jr. – 1990*								
114³/₈	18	18³/₈	12⁵/₈	14²/₈	4	3⁷/₈	4	4		129	99
			■ *Atasco Mts. – Antonio Lopez – Antonio Lopez – 1961*								
114³/₈	17²/₈	18⁵/₈	13³/₈	15	3⁷/₈	4	5	4		129	99
			■ *Pima Co. – James A. Reynolds – James A. Reynolds – 1980*								
114²/₈	18⁴/₈	15⁷/₈	15²/₈	18	4³/₈	4²/₈	5	6		131	101
			■ *Catalina Mts. – Wayne L. Heckler – Wayne L. Heckler – 1958*								
114²/₈	16²/₈	17¹/₈	11⁵/₈	15³/₈	4	4²/₈	5	6	5³/₈	131	101
			■ *Canelo – Earl Stillson – Earl Stillson – 1967*								
114²/₈	19⁶/₈	18⁵/₈	13⁶/₈	15⁵/₈	4¹/₈	4²/₈	5	4		131	101
			■ *Pima Co. – Steven E. Shooks – Steven E. Shooks – 1998*								

Score	Length of Main Beam Right	Left	Inside Spread	Greatest Spread	Circumference at Smallest Place Between Burr and First Point Right	Left	Number of Points Right	Left	Lengths Abnormal Points	All-Time Rank	State Rank
									■ Location of Kill – Hunter – Owner – Date Killed		
114 1/8	17 2/8	17 2/8	16 7/8	17 6/8	3 4/8	3 4/8	5	5		135	104
	■ Yavapai Co. – Jim D. Snodgrass – Jim D. Snodgrass – 1983										
114	18 5/8	18 3/8	13	15	3 5/8	3 4/8	4	5		137†	105†
	■ Pima Co. – M.E. Duperret & J.K. Volk – Michael E. Duperret – 2001										
	■ See photo on page 54										
113 7/8	18 4/8	17 6/8	14 2/8	15 5/8	3 5/8	3 4/8	4	5	1 5/8	139	106
	■ Galiuro Mts. – Clifford Kouts – Clifford Kouts – 1964										
113 7/8	20 1/8	19 7/8	12	14 6/8	4 5/8	4 5/8	5	5	3 3/8	139	106
	■ Santa Rita Mts. – Joe M. Moore, Jr. – Joe M. Moore, Jr. – 1968										
113 7/8	19	18 7/8	14 3/8	16 5/8	4 2/8	4 2/8	4	5	1 2/8	139	106
	■ Pima Co. – James A. Reynolds – James A. Reynolds – 1985										
113 7/8	17 3/8	18 1/8	15 5/8	17 4/8	3 7/8	3 6/8	4	4		139	106
	■ Pinal Co. – James L. Boyd – James L. Boyd – 1997										
113 7/8	19 6/8	20 4/8	14 3/8	16 6/8	3 6/8	3 7/8	5	6	1 4/8	139	106
	■ Santa Cruz Co. – Picked Up – James A. Reynolds – 1999										
113 6/8	15 4/8	16	13 6/8	16	4	4	5	5		146	111
	■ Mt. Graham – Bill Sizer – Bill Sizer – 1963										
113 6/8	17 3/8	16	13 5/8	19 6/8	4 2/8	4 5/8	7	6	6 3/8	146	111
	■ Galiuro Mts. – Doran V. Porter – Doran V. Porter – 1966										
113 6/8	18	17 7/8	14 6/8	16 6/8	4	4	4	4		146	111
	■ Pima Co. – Richard N. Huber – Richard N. Huber – 1979										
113 6/8	18 4/8	18	13 2/8	14 6/8	3 6/8	4	5	5		146	111
	■ Pima Co. – Andy A. Ramirez – Andy A. Ramirez – 1979										
113 5/8	19	17 6/8	16 5/8	18 3/8	4 1/8	4	4	5		151	115
	■ Graham Mts. – J.H. Hunt – J.H. Hunt – 1962										
113 5/8	19	18 6/8	17 1/8	19 2/8	4 1/8	3 7/8	4	4		151	115
	■ Pinal Co. – Randall E. Martin – Randall E. Martin – 1992										
113 4/8	16 7/8	16 2/8	12 4/8	13 6/8	3 7/8	3 7/8	6	6	2 2/8	154	117
	■ Santa Rita Mts. – Jack Englet – Jack Englet – 1962										
113 4/8	19 6/8	19	14 2/8	15 6/8	4 4/8	4 5/8	4	6	3	154	117
	■ Santa Rita Mts. – George W. Parker – George W. Parker – 1962										
113 4/8	17 4/8	17 1/8	12 2/8	15	4 1/8	4	4	5		154	117
	■ Santa Cruz Co. – Robert A. Smith – Robert A. Smith – 1985										
113 3/8	16	16 3/8	12 5/8	14 3/8	4 5/8	4 4/8	5	5		158	120
	■ Santa Teresa Mts. – D.B. Sanford – D.B. Sanford – 1950										
113 3/8	17 3/8	16 7/8	13 3/8	14 7/8	4	4 2/8	4	4		158	120
	■ Tumacacori Mts. – Tom W. Caid – Tom W. Caid – 1958										
113 3/8	18	17	14 3/8	19	4	4	4	4		158	120
	■ Four Peaks Mt. – Carl J. Slagel – Carl J. Slagel – 1963										
113 3/8	16 5/8	16 4/8	12 4/8	15	4 4/8	4 4/8	5	6	1 7/8	158	120
	■ Pima Co. – Sam E. Harrison, Jr. – Sam E. Harrison, Jr. – 1969										
113 3/8	17 2/8	18 2/8	15 3/8	18	4 1/8	4 1/8	4	4		158	120
	■ Navajo Co. – Picked Up – Harry Neff – 1997										

Score	Length of Main Beam Right	Left	Inside Spread	Greatest Spread	Circumference at Smallest Place Between Burr and First Point Right	Left	Number of Points Right	Left	Lengths Abnormal Points	All-Time Rank	State Rank
	■ Location of Kill – Hunter – Owner – Date Killed										
113²/8	16⁷/8	17⁶/8	15⁴/8	17	3⁶/8	3⁶/8	5	5		163	125
	■ Santa Rita Mts. – Donna Greene – Donna Greene – 1958										
113²/8	18⁷/8	17⁵/8	14⁴/8	16¹/8	4	4	5	5		163	125
	■ Tumacacori Mts. – Carlos G. Touche – Carlos G. Touche – 1961										
113²/8	18	17	14²/8	16¹/8	4¹/8	4¹/8	4	5		163	125
	■ Santa Cruz Co. – Hector Guglielmo – Hector Guglielmo – 1984										
113²/8	19³/8	18⁵/8	16	17⁷/8	4³/8	4⁴/8	4	4		163	125
	■ Gila Co. – David W. Miller, Jr. – David W. Miller, Jr. – 1984										
113²/8	18³/8	18¹/8	14²/8	16⁷/8	4	4	5	4	2²/8	163	125
	■ Pima Co. – James A. Reynolds – James A. Reynolds – 1995										
113¹/8	20¹/8	19⁶/8	19	20⁶/8	4	4¹/8	5	6	7⁷/8	170	130
	■ Chiricahua Mts. – Ralph Hopkins – Fred Tanner – 1928										
113	18²/8	18³/8	11⁴/8	13⁴/8	4³/8	4³/8	4	5		172†	131†
	■ Pima Co. – Frank C. Benvenuto – Frank C. Benvenuto – 1967										
113	18¹/8	18	15⁴/8	18⁴/8	4²/8	4²/8	4	4		172	131
	■ Canelo Hills – Carlos Ochoa – Carlos Ochoa – 1955										
113	19	18⁷/8	12²/8	15¹/8	3⁶/8	3⁶/8	5	5		172	131
	■ Tumacacori Mts. – Basil C. Bradbury – Unknown – 1968										
113	18¹/8	18⁴/8	15⁴/8	17³/8	3⁷/8	3⁷/8	5	5		172	131
	■ Pima Co. – Jeffrey K. Volk – M.E. Duperret & J.K. Volk – 1998										
112⁷/8	17	17¹/8	14⁵/8	17⁴/8	4²/8	4²/8	4	4		176	135
	■ Ruby – Roger Scott – Roger Scott – 1962										
112⁷/8	17⁵/8	18²/8	13¹/8	15	3⁶/8	4¹/8	6	6	2⁶/8	176	135
	■ Gila Co. – James J. Zanzot – James J. Zanzot – 1995										
112⁶/8	17⁵/8	18⁴/8	14⁴/8	16⁷/8	5¹/8	4⁶/8	5	6	3²/8	179	137
	■ Baboquivari Mts. – Charles R. Whitfield – Charles R. Whitfield – 1969										
112⁶/8	17⁴/8	18⁶/8	15⁷/8	17⁶/8	4⁷/8	4⁶/8	6	6	4³/8	179	137
	■ Cochise Co. – Mike York – Mike York – 1973										
112⁵/8	17⁶/8	17⁴/8	15³/8	18¹/8	5	4⁷/8	4	4		182	139
	■ Greenlee Co. – John W. Barber – John W. Barber – 1985										
112⁴/8	17³/8	17³/8	15	17⁴/8	4²/8	4³/8	5	4	2	186	140
	■ Gila Co. – R.T. Beach & L.A. Mossinger – Ronald T. Beach – 1974										
112⁴/8	14⁶/8	15⁶/8	13	16	3⁵/8	3⁴/8	6	5	2⁴/8	186	140
	■ Pima Co. – Gary D. Ramirez – Gary D. Ramirez – 1993										
112⁴/8	19⁶/8	19¹/8	12⁶/8	14³/8	4	4	4	4		186	140
	■ Pima Co. – Donald H. McBride – Donald H. McBride – 1999										
112³/8	17³/8	17	15⁵/8	17²/8	4¹/8	4²/8	4	5		190	143
	■ White Mts. – Dennis E. Nolen – Dennis E. Nolen – 1961										
112³/8	19	19⁵/8	13³/8	15³/8	4²/8	4⁴/8	5	4		190	143
	■ Santa Cruz Co. – W.C. Grant – W.C. Grant – 1973										
112³/8	17²/8	17³/8	15⁷/8	17³/8	3⁴/8	3³/8	4	4		190	143
	■ Pima Co. – Robert H. Conway – Robert H. Conway – 1998										

Score	Length of Main Beam Right Left	Inside Spread	Greatest Spread	Circumference at Smallest Place Between Burr and First Point Right Left	Number of Points Right Left	Lengths Abnormal Points	All-Time Rank	State Rank
	■ Location of Kill – Hunter – Owner – Date Killed							
112²/8	18 17⁶/8	17	18⁵/8	4 3⁷/8	5 5		194	146
	■ Maricopa Co. – Gary D. Nichols – Gary D. Nichols – 1980							
112²/8	16²/8 16	13²/8	14⁶/8	4⁶/8 4⁶/8	4 5		194	146
	■ Pima Co. – William W. Sharp – William W. Sharp – 1981							
112²/8	18²/8 17⁵/8	15	16⁶/8	4⁴/8 4²/8	4 4		194	146
	■ Pima Co. – Angel J. Yslas – Angel J. Yslas – 1994							
112¹/8	17³/8 18⁶/8	14⁴/8	16³/8	3⁷/8 3⁷/8	7 6	5¹/8	198	149
	■ Cochise Co. – Edwin L. Hawkins – Edwin L. Hawkins – 1977							
112¹/8	18²/8 17¹/8	10⁷/8	13³/8	3⁷/8 3⁷/8	4 5	1²/8	198	149
	■ Pima Co. – David J. Vancas – David J. Vancas – 1985							
112¹/8	17²/8 18²/8	17¹/8	18⁷/8	4⁴/8 4³/8	5 4	1⁶/8	198	149
	■ Pima Co. – Travis D. Robbins – Travis D. Robbins – 1992							
112	18³/8 18⁷/8	14²/8	16⁴/8	3⁶/8 3⁶/8	5 5		202	152
	■ Bartlett Mts. – Keith Robbins – Keith Robbins – 1957							
112	17²/8 18	13⁶/8		4 4	5 5		202	152
	■ Baboquivari Mts. – Jesse Genin – Jesse Genin – 1961							
112	15⁴/8 15⁶/8	12⁴/8	14²/8	3⁶/8 3⁷/8	5 5		202	152
	■ Greenlee Co. – Jerald S. Wager – Jerald S. Wager – 1982							
111⁷/8	18⁶/8 17⁶/8	13⁷/8	15⁵/8	4 4	4 4		207	155
	■ Canelo Hills – Walter G. Sheets – Walter G. Sheets – 1959							
111⁷/8	20⁵/8 20⁵/8	15³/8	17²/8	4 4	4 6	1⁶/8	207	155
	■ Greenlee Co. – Ronald H. Gerdes – Ronald H. Gerdes – 1992							
111⁶/8	17¹/8 16⁴/8	13²/8	16	3²/8 3²/8	5 5		209	157
	■ Gila Co. – Karl J. Payne – Karl J. Payne – 1955							
111⁶/8	18⁶/8 19⁵/8	14¹/8	16²/8	4⁵/8 3⁷/8	6 5	3³/8	209	157
	■ Patagonia Mts. – Norval L. Wesson – Norval L. Wesson – 1967							
111⁶/8	18²/8 18⁵/8	14⁴/8	16⁷/8	3⁵/8 3⁴/8	5 5		209	157
	■ Baboquivari Mts. – Stanley W. Gaines – Stanley W. Gaines – 1971							
111⁶/8	17¹/8 16⁵/8	14	16²/8	3⁷/8 3⁷/8	4 4		209	157
	■ Pima Co. – George V. Borquez – George V. Borquez – 1979							
111⁶/8	16⁵/8 16⁶/8	12³/8	15¹/8	4⁴/8 4⁴/8	5 8	2⁵/8	209	157
	■ Cochise Co. – Gregory F. Lucero – Gregory F. Lucero – 1991							
111⁵/8	18⁷/8 19	14⁶/8	17⁴/8	4³/8 4³/8	5 6	3³/8	216	162
	■ Santa Rita Mts. – Rick Detwiler – Rick Detwiler – 1968							
111⁵/8	17²/8 18²/8	13⁷/8	15⁵/8	3⁷/8 3⁶/8	4 5		216	162
	■ Pima Co. – Kevin T. Murray – Kevin T. Murray – 1996							
111⁴/8	17⁴/8 18	15	17³/8	3⁶/8 4	4 4		218	164
	■ Santa Rita Mts. – Tom L. Swanson – Tom L. Swanson – 1965							
111⁴/8	17⁶/8 17⁷/8	15⁴/8	18	4⁶/8 4⁴/8	5 4	2	218	164
	■ Coconino Co. – Picked Up – Dennis L. Campbell – 1987							
111⁴/8	18²/8 17⁷/8	17⁶/8	19³/8	4²/8 4¹/8	5 4		218	164
	■ Graham Co. – Robert L. Osborn – Robert L. Osborn – 1993							

Score	Length of Main Beam Right	Left	Inside Spread	Greatest Spread	Circumference at Smallest Place Between Burr and First Point Right	Left	Number of Points Right	Left	Lengths Abnormal Points	All-Time Rank	State Rank
111 3/8	18 6/8	18 2/8	12 5/8	14 4/8	3 6/8	3 6/8	5	5		222	167
■ Pima Co. – Unknown – Ruel Holt – PR 1974											
111 3/8	17 6/8	18 5/8	16 5/8	18 2/8	4 1/8	4 1/8	4	4		222	167
■ Santa Cruz Co. – Frank Yubeta III – Frank Yubeta III – 1983											
111 2/8	17 6/8	17	15 2/8	17	4	4	4	4		226	169
■ Graham Co. – C.R. Hale – C.R. Hale – 1958											
111 2/8	19 2/8	19 4/8	16 6/8	18 6/8	4	4	5	6	1 4/8	226	169
■ Graham Mts. – Bill Barney – Bill Barney – 1962											
111 2/8	19 1/8	19	15 6/8	17 7/8	4 2/8	4 3/8	4	4		226	169
■ Atascosa Mt. – Henry B. Carrillo – Henry B. Carrillo – 1964											
111 2/8	17 5/8	17 3/8	11 2/8	15 1/8	4	3 6/8	6	6	3 6/8	226	169
■ Santa Rita Mts. – Lon E. Bothwell – Lon E. Bothwell – 1969											
111 2/8	16 4/8	16 4/8	15 2/8	17 3/8	3 4/8	3 4/8	5	5		226	169
■ Santa Cruz Co. – Robert L. Rabb – Robert L. Rabb – 1977											
111 1/8	17 5/8	17 4/8	14 5/8	16	4 1/8	4 1/8	5	5		233	174
■ Cochise Co. – Harvey G. Ward, Jr. – Harvey G. Ward, Jr. – 1988											
111 1/8	18	17	14 5/8	16 2/8	4	3 7/8	5	5		233	174
■ Pinal Co. – John P. Garcia – John P. Garcia – 1991											
111	17 6/8	17 6/8	17 6/8	19 4/8	3 7/8	3 7/8	4	4		237	176
■ Pima Co. – William G. Roberts – William G. Roberts – 1992											
111	18 6/8	17 2/8	15	17 3/8	4	4	4	4		237	176
■ Pima Co. – Michael W. Lynch – Michael W. Lynch – 1996											
111	17 6/8	17	14 6/8	17 6/8	4 1/8	4 2/8	5	4	1 4/8	237	176
■ Santa Cruz Co. – David M. Yearin – David M. Yearin – 1999											
110 7/8	19 2/8	19 4/8	13 1/8	14 4/8	3 6/8	3 6/8	4	4		241	179
■ Chiricahua Mts. – Wayne A. Dirst – Wayne A. Dirst – 1954											
110 7/8	17 2/8	18 6/8	11 2/8	14 5/8	4	4 1/8	5	7	3 5/8	241	179
■ Canelo Hills – Bill Fidelo – Bill Fidelo – 1958											
110 7/8	19 3/8	19	15 7/8	17 5/8	3 6/8	3 5/8	5	4		241	179
■ Rincon Mts. – Ollie O. Barney, Jr. – Ollie O. Barney, Jr. – 1961											
110 7/8	16 6/8	16 5/8	13 1/8	16 6/8	4	4	6	4	3 4/8	241	179
■ Pima Co. – William W. Sharp – William W. Sharp – 1974											
110 7/8	18 6/8	19 2/8	15 6/8	17 6/8	4 2/8	4 3/8	5	5	3 7/8	241	179
■ Gila Co. – Kristin M. Currie – Kristin M. Currie – 1994											
110 6/8	17	17	12 6/8	14 4/8	3 3/8	3 3/8	5	5		246†	184†
■ Santa Cruz Co. – Andrew M. Lopez – Andrew M. Lopez – 2000											
110 6/8	18	18 2/8	13 4/8	15 4/8	3 6/8	3 6/8	4	5		246	184
■ Catalina Mts. – H.C. Ruff – H.C. Ruff – 1959											
110 6/8	18 5/8	18 2/8	15 6/8	17 4/8	4	4	4	4		246	184
■ Santa Rita Mts. – John S. McFarling – John S. McFarling – 1965											
110 6/8	17 2/8	16 2/8	14 2/8	16 1/8	4 4/8	4 1/8	4	4		246	184
■ Pima Co. – Rudolph B. Aguilar – Rudolph B. Aguilar – 1998											

■ Location of Kill – Hunter – Owner – Date Killed

Score	Length of Main Beam Right	Left	Inside Spread	Greatest Spread	Circumference at Smallest Place Between Burr and First Point Right	Left	Number of Points Right	Left	Lengths Abnormal Points	All-Time Rank	State Rank
110 6/8	17 4/8	17 5/8	13 1/8	15 4/8	4 2/8	4	5	4	3 3/8	246	184
■ Santa Cruz Co. – Julie L. Hopkins – Julie L. Hopkins – 1998											
110 5/8	19 5/8	19 2/8	16 1/8	17 5/8	3 7/8	4	4	4		252†	189†
■ Pinal Co. – Chuck Adams – Chuck Adams – 1989 ■ See photo on page 59											
110 5/8	18 5/8	18 4/8	15	18 7/8	3 2/8	3 5/8	5	4	3 5/8	252	189
■ Pima Co. – David E. Furnas – David E. Furnas – 1990											
110 5/8	17 5/8	17 2/8	18	19 4/8	3 5/8	3 5/8	4	4		252	189
■ Pima Co. – James E. Hatcher – James E. Hatcher – 1993											
110 4/8	16 7/8	17 6/8	14 2/8	15 7/8	4 4/8	4 4/8	4	4		255	192
■ Canelo Hills – Otto L. Fritz – Otto L. Fritz – 1947											
110 4/8	16 7/8	16 6/8	14 2/8	16 1/8	4 1/8	4	5	5		255	192
■ Tumacacori Mts. – John N. Doyle – John N. Doyle – 1966											
110 4/8	18 6/8	18 3/8	14 6/8	16 3/8	4 2/8	4 2/8	4	5		255	192
■ Pima Co. – William T. Crutchley – William T. Crutchley – 1992											
110 3/8	18 4/8	18 7/8	13 5/8	15 6/8	3 3/8	3 4/8	4	4		260†	195†
■ Santa Cruz Co. – Benjamin H. Richardson – Benjamin H. Richardson – 2000											
110 3/8	17 7/8	17 7/8	13 7/8	15 6/8	4 1/8	4	4	4		260	195
■ Santa Rita Mts. – Edward L. Blixt – Edward L. Blixt – 1946											
110 3/8	18 7/8	18 4/8	12 6/8	14 1/8	3 7/8	3 4/8	4	4	3 3/8	260	195
■ Santa Rita Mts. – Lyle K. Sowls – Lyle K. Sowls – 1956											
110 2/8	15	16 7/8	13 6/8	15 3/8	4	4	5	5		265†	198†
■ Pima Co. – Kurt J. Kreutz – Kurt J. Kreutz – 2000											
110 2/8	17	16 3/8	14	16 1/8	4 6/8	4 6/8	5	5		265	198
■ Gila Co. – William P. Hampton, Jr. – William P. Hampton, Jr. – 1976											
110 2/8	18 6/8	18	16	18 2/8	4 1/8	4	4	5		265	198
■ Pima Co. – David G. Mattausch – David G. Mattausch – 1984											
110 2/8	19 1/8	17 5/8	16	18	3 7/8	3 6/8	5	4		265	198
■ Yavapai Co. – Fred J. Nobbe, Jr. – Fred J. Nobbe, Jr. – 1994											
110 1/8	16 7/8	16 3/8	15 7/8	17 1/8	4 4/8	4 6/8	4	4		270	202
■ Payson – Picked Up – Richard Noonan – PR 1963											
110 1/8	16 4/8	17	12 3/8	14 2/8	4 7/8	4 4/8	4	4		270	202
■ Pima Co. – Andy C. Strebe – Andy C. Strebe – 1981											
110 1/8	18 2/8	17 6/8	16 4/8	17 6/8	4 5/8	4 6/8	5	5	3 1/8	270	202
■ Cochise Co. – Richard T. Ziehmer – Richard T. Ziehmer – 1995											
110	18 1/8	17 6/8	14 5/8	18 3/8	4 6/8	5	4	6	1 5/8	274	205
■ Cochise Co. – Bill Saathoff – Bill Saathoff – 1987											
110	18 1/8	18 2/8	18 1/8	19 4/8	3 6/8	4	5	4	3 1/8	274	205
■ Pima Co. – David E. Furnas – David E. Furnas – 1991											
110	15 5/8	15 7/8	13	14 6/8	4 3/8	4 2/8	5	6	3 2/8	274	205
■ Maricopa Co. – Picked Up – L. Pangerl & B. Johnson – 1998											
109 4/8	18 3/8	18 4/8	12 4/8	15	4 1/8	4 1/8	4	5	1 4/8	278	208
■ Pima Co. – William W. Sharp – William W. Sharp – 1982											

■ Location of Kill – Hunter – Owner – Date Killed

Score	Length of Main Beam Right	Left	Inside Spread	Greatest Spread	Circumference at Smallest Place Between Burr and First Point Right	Left	Number of Points Right	Left	Lengths Abnormal Points	All-Time Rank	State Rank
	▪ Location of Kill – Hunter – Owner – Date Killed										
109 3/8	18 2/8	18	13 3/8	15 3/8	3 7/8	3 7/8	5	5		279	209
▪ Pima Co. – Gary D. Gorsuch – Gary D. Gorsuch – 1973											
108 5/8	17 5/8	17 5/8	14 7/8	16 6/8	3 7/8	3 7/8	4	4		284	210
▪ Navajo Co. – Richard Velasquez – Connie Pierce – 1992											
108 1/8	15 6/8	15 5/8	14 1/8	15 6/8	4 2/8	4 1/8	5	5		286	211
▪ Gila Co. – Frank J. Cecelic – Frank J. Cecelic – 1989											
108 1/8	15 6/8	16 1/8	15 5/8	17 6/8	4	3 7/8	5	5	2	286	211
▪ Pima Co. – Tim S. Murray – Tim S. Murray – 1995											
108	18 2/8	18 3/8	12 4/8	14 4/8	4 2/8	4 3/8	4	4		288	213
▪ Greenlee Co. – Jeff S. Loree – Jeff S. Loree – 1994											
107 4/8	16 4/8	16 5/8	10 6/8	12 4/8	3 6/8	3 6/8	5	5		291	214
▪ Santa Cruz Co. – William W. Sharp – William W. Sharp – 1986											
107 2/8	17 4/8	17 2/8	16 5/8	19 3/8	4 1/8	4 1/8	5	5	3 1/8	295	215
▪ Pima Co. – William W. Sharp – William W. Sharp – 1961											
107 1/8	17 3/8	16	12 1/8	13 6/8	4	3 6/8	5	6	2	296	216
▪ Santa Cruz Co. – Richard G. Acedo, Jr. – Richard G. Acedo, Jr. – 1984											
107 1/8	17 3/8	17 7/8	16 1/8	17 4/8	4 4/8	4 3/8	4	5	1 6/8	296	216
▪ Greenlee Co. – Joseph C. McGill – Joseph C. McGill – 1993											
106 4/8	17 4/8	17 4/8	16	18	3 4/8	3 6/8	4	4		298	218
▪ Maricopa Co. – Jerry E. Mason – Jerry E. Mason – 1983											
106 2/8	16 6/8	16 4/8	15	16 5/8	4 3/8	4 3/8	4	4		301	219
▪ Santa Cruz Co. – Jack K. Rouge – Jack K. Rouge – 1984											
106 2/8	21 2/8	19 6/8	15 6/8	17 4/8	3 3/8	3 4/8	4	4		301	219
▪ Greenlee Co. – Ronald H. Gerdes – Ronald H. Gerdes – 1991											
105 5/8	17 4/8	17 4/8	16 1/8	17 5/8	4 1/8	4 2/8	4	4		306†	221†
▪ Pima Co. – Frank C. Benvenuto – Frank C. Benvenuto – 1971											
105 5/8	16 4/8	16 4/8	14 7/8	16 6/8	4	4 2/8	5	5		306†	221†
▪ Gila Co. – Jack R. Cook – Jack R. Cook – 1993											
105 3/8	16 4/8	15 6/8	13 7/8	17 5/8	3 4/8	3 5/8	4	4		309	223
▪ Pima Co. – James J. McBride – James J. McBride – 1973											
104 7/8	16 2/8	16	13	15 2/8	3 6/8	3 7/8	5	6	3 1/8	311	224
▪ Pima Co. – William W. Sharp – William W. Sharp – 1985											
104 4/8	15 6/8	16	13 4/8	15 1/8	4 1/8	4 2/8	4	4		313	225
▪ Cochise Co. – Bruce Asbury – Bruce Asbury – 1966											
104 3/8	17 6/8	16 6/8	12 4/8	14 2/8	4 2/8	4 3/8	4	5	1 3/8	315	226
▪ Pima Co. – George R. Skaggs – George R. Skaggs – 1994											
104 1/8	17 6/8	17 6/8	13 4/8	15 4/8	4 1/8	3 7/8	4	6	2 7/8	317	227
▪ Santa Cruz Co. – Warren A. Cartier – Warren A. Cartier – 1984											
104 1/8	16	15	12 3/8	15 4/8	4	4 4/8	4	5	2 6/8	317	227
▪ Pima Co. – John B. Kerfoot – John B. Kerfoot – 1993											
103 6/8	18 4/8	18	14 6/8	16 3/8	3 5/8	3 4/8	5	4	1	321	229
▪ Cochise Co. – Robert J. Gribble – Robert J. Gribble – 1996											

Score	Length of Main Beam Right Left ■ Location of Kill – Hunter – Owner – Date Killed		Inside Spread	Greatest Spread	Circumference at Smallest Place Between Burr and First Point Right Left		Number of Points Right Left		Lengths Abnormal Points	All-Time Rank	State Rank
103²/8	17⁴/8	17⁷/8	15⁶/8	17⁴/8	3⁴/8	3⁵/8	5	4	1⁴/8	323†	230†
	■ Pima Co. – Kirk Kelso – Kirk Kelso – 1997										
102⁷/8	17⁷/8	17⁷/8	13⁷/8	15⁴/8	3⁶/8	3⁶/8	4	4		324†	231†
	■ Pima Co. – Kirk Kelso – Kirk Kelso – 1994										
104⁴/8	17³/8	16⁶/8	13⁴/8	15¹/8	4³/8	4⁴/8	4	5	3⁶/8	325	232
	■ Pima Co. – Jared L. Baker – Jared L. Baker – 1998										
102²/8	18⁶/8	19¹/8	15²/8	17	3⁶/8	3⁵/8	4	4		327	233
	■ Cochise Co. – Kenneth D. Rupkalvis – Kenneth D. Rupkalvis – 1985										
102	16⁶/8	17¹/8	16²/8	19	3⁷/8	3⁷/8	4	4		329	234
	■ Gila Co. – Richard L. Wolfel – Richard L. Wolfel – 1994										
101⁷/8	17²/8	16⁵/8	14⁵/8	16³/8	4¹/8	4²/8	4	5		330†	235†
	■ Pima Co. – Kirk Kelso – Kirk Kelso – 1992										
101⁷/8	16⁷/8	17	14⁵/8	15⁶/8	4	4	4	4		330	235
	■ Pima Co. – Picked Up – Jonny House – 1997										
101⁶/8	17¹/8	17	15⁶/8	17³/8	4¹/8	4¹/8	4	4		333	237
	■ Graham Co. – Picked Up – Edward N. Dixon – PR 1994										
101⁴/8	19¹/8	17⁴/8	13	15¹/8	4²/8	4	4	4		334†	238†
	■ Gila Co. – Jack R. Cook – Jack R. Cook – 1994										
101⁴/8	15¹/8	14⁶/8	12²/8	14⁶/8	4	4	5	5		334	238
	■ Graham Co. – Patrick J. Bernard – Patrick J. Bernard – 1995										
101²/8	15⁷/8	16⁴/8	14⁴/8	16¹/8	4	4	4	4		336	240
	■ Pima Co. – Kimball B. Taylor – Kimball B. Taylor – 1992										
101	17⁷/8	17⁷/8	13²/8	17¹/8	3⁶/8	3⁷/8	4	5	2	337	241
	■ Pima Co. – Keith L. Miller – Keith L. Miller – 1984										
100⁷/8	18⁴/8	18	12¹/8	13⁷/8	3⁶/8	3⁵/8	5	4	2⁶/8	338	242
	■ Santa Cruz Co. – Carlos E. Menendez – Carlos E. Menendez – 1993										
100³/8	15⁶/8	16⁴/8	15³/8	16⁷/8	4³/8	4³/8	6	6	4⁴/8	343	243
	■ Maricopa Co. – Gregory M. Moore – Gregory M. Moore – 1994										
100¹/8	17²/8	18	13⁷/8	15⁵/8	4	4	4	4		345†	244†
	■ Pima Co. – Frank C. Benvenuto – Frank C. Benvenuto – 1959										
121³/8	20	19⁵/8	13⁴/8	15	4⁴/8	4⁴/8	7	5	4⁵/8	*	*
	■ Pima Co. – William A. Ball – William A. Ball – 1999										

† The scores and ranking for trophies from the 25th Awards Entry Period are not final until the banquet is held on June 19, 2004.

* Final score is subject to revision by additional verifying measurements.

ARIZONA

NON-TYPICAL COUES' WHITETAIL DEER

Score	Length of Main Beam Right Left	Inside Spread	Greatest Spread	Circumference at Smallest Place Between Burr and First Point Right Left		Number of Points Right Left		Lengths Abnormal Points	All-Time Rank	State Rank
	■ Location of Kill – Hunter – Owner – Date Killed									
158⁴/8	17¹/8 16⁷/8	12⁶/8	18¹/8	3⁷/8	4¹/8	11	11	42²/8	2	1
	■ Santa Cruz Co. – Picked Up – B&C National Collection – 1988									
155	19 20	16⁶/8	20	4⁷/8	4⁵/8	9	8	24⁴/8	3	2
	■ Gila Co. – Charles E. Erickson, Jr. – Charles E. Erickson, Jr. – 1988									
152	20²/8 20	17⁴/8	19³/8	4⁴/8	4⁴/8	8	8	15⁴/8	5†	3†
	■ Graham Co. – Picked Up – Mike Sullivan – 1971									
151³/8	19⁶/8 19⁷/8	15³/8	18²/8	4³/8	4⁴/8	7	8	18	6	4
	■ Pima Co. – Picked Up – Patrick H. Taylor – 1997									
150⁵/8	18⁴/8 18⁵/8	15⁶/8	18⁶/8	5⁴/8	5⁴/8	9	8	8³/8	7	5
	■ Cochise Co. – Charles C. Mabry – Cabela's, Inc. – 1929									
150⁵/8	18⁴/8 19	12⁵/8	14⁶/8	4³/8	4⁴/8	8	8	30²/8	7	5
	■ Sasabe – Robert Rabb – Robert Rabb – 1954									
150³/8	18³/8 18	15²/8	20⁶/8	4³/8	4³/8	7	7	16⁷/8	9	7
	■ Pima Co. – Jeffrey K. Volk – M.E. Duperret & J.K. Volk – 1992									
149⁷/8	17²/8 18⁵/8	13³/8	16⁶/8	4⁶/8	4²/8	10	8	23⁴/8	10	8
	■ Chiricahua Mts. – Marvin R. Hardin – Marvin R. Hardin – 1950									
148⁶/8	16³/8 15⁷/8	18⁴/8	21⁶/8	4⁶/8	4⁴/8	12	8	28⁷/8	11	9
	■ Gila Co. – Clay E. Goldman – Clay E. Goldman – 1993									
147	18⁶/8 19⁶/8	16⁶/8	19	5	4⁵/8	10	7	30⁶/8	12	10
	■ Pima Co. – James A. Reynolds – James A. Reynolds – 1991									
143⁶/8	17³/8 16⁵/8	14⁵/8	19⁴/8	4²/8	5	6	9	33³/8	13	11
	■ Pima Co. – Oscar C. Truex – Oscar C. Truex – 1983									
142⁷/8	20⁴/8 18⁷/8	13³/8	20	4⁴/8	4⁵/8	9	7	15²/8	14	12
	■ Apache Indian Res. – Native American – AZ Game & Fish Dept. – 1950									
142⁶/8	17⁶/8 17¹/8	14²/8	20³/8	4⁶/8	4⁵/8	8	8	22⁶/8	15	13
	■ Pinal Mts. – Phil Rothengatter – Phil Rothengatter – 1967									
140⁷/8	17 18	14	17²/8	4⁴/8	4²/8	10	7	28³/8	17	14
	■ Santa Cruz Co. – Randal W. Reaves – Randal W. Reaves – 1998									
139⁷/8	18³/8 18³/8	15	17³/8	4⁷/8	4⁷/8	8	6	8³/8	18	15
	■ Patagonia Mts. – Howard W. Drake – Howard W. Drake – 1968									
137⁶/8	19⁴/8 19²/8	14⁵/8	19⁴/8	4⁴/8	4⁴/8	6	7	9⁷/8	20	16
	■ Patagonia Mts. – Ivan J. Buttram – Ivan J. Buttram – 1969									
137³/8	16⁶/8 16⁷/8	13⁶/8	16⁵/8	4⁵/8	4⁵/8	8	8	21¹/8	21	17
	■ Gila Co. – Cal W. Bryant – Cal W. Bryant – 1991									
134³/8	21³/8 21	16⁶/8	19⁷/8	4⁵/8	4⁴/8	8	5	14³/8	22	18
	■ Cochise Co. – Brian Childers – Brian Childers – 1990									
134²/8	20⁶/8 20⁴/8	13⁵/8	18⁶/8	4²/8	4³/8	7	8	15⁵/8	23	19
	■ Yavapai Co. – William B. Bullock – William B. Bullock – 1986									

Score	Length of Main Beam		Inside Spread	Greatest Spread	Circumference at Smallest Place Between Burr and First Point		Number of Points		Lengths Abnormal Points	All-Time Rank	State Rank
	Right	Left			Right	Left	Right	Left			
	■ Location of Kill – Hunter – Owner – Date Killed										
132 3/8	17 4/8	17 1/8	13 7/8	16 7/8	5	5	6	8	13 2/8	25	20
	■ Gila Co. – Dale J. Little – Dale J. Little – 1989										
131 5/8	18 2/8	18 2/8	13	15 1/8	4 6/8	4 6/8	8	5	9 3/8	27	21
	■ Cochise Co. – Phil M. Krentz – Phil M. Krentz – 1991										
131 3/8	19 1/8	18 1/8	14 7/8	18 1/8	3 7/8	4 1/8	6	6	16 4/8	28	22
	■ Cochise Co. – Erik M. Thorsrud – Erik M. Thorsrud – 1986										
131 2/8	16 1/8	18	13 5/8	15 6/8	6 6/8	5	9	8	24 1/8	29	23
	■ Gila Co. – Nathan E. Ellison – Nathan E. Ellison – 1958										
131	18 7/8	19 2/8	18 2/8	23	4 4/8	4	9	7	22 4/8	30	24
	■ Greenlee Co. – Linda A. Reese – Dee Charles – 1993										
130 3/8	17 2/8	17 5/8	13 2/8	18 3/8	4 1/8	4 2/8	7	9	21 1/8	31	25
	■ Santa Cruz Co. – Jack Everhart – Fred Baker – 1946										
130 2/8	14 5/8	15 7/8	10 1/8	15 1/8	5	3 7/8	10	8	37 5/8	32	26
	■ Rincon Mts. – Velton Clark – Velton Clark – 1962										
130 1/8	17	18 3/8	14 5/8	21 3/8	4 3/8	4 5/8	8	4	10 4/8	33	27
	■ Yavapai Co. – David K. Moore – David K. Moore – 1988										
130	17 3/8	16 2/8	13 7/8	18 7/8	4 3/8	5 2/8	6	11	16 7/8	34	28
	■ Whetstone Range – Unknown – Roger Clyne – PR 1967										
129 7/8	20 6/8	20 5/8	17 3/8	20	4	4	5	7	10 2/8	35†	29†
	■ Apache Co. – Picked Up – Donald H. McBride – 1999										
129 5/8	19 6/8	19 7/8	16 6/8	18	3 4/8	3 5/8	7	8	9 3/8	36	30
	■ Cochise Co. – James C. Cornelius – James C. Cornelius – 1994										
128 3/8	17 4/8	17 6/8	15 1/8	17 1/8	4 2/8	4 1/8	5	7	10 2/8	37	31
	■ Pima Co. – Gary D. Gorsuch – Gary D. Gorsuch – 1992										
128	18 6/8	19 1/8	16 2/8	19 5/8	5 2/8	4 3/8	5	8	17 2/8	39	32
	■ Santa Cruz Co. – Carlos G. Touche – Carlos G. Touche – 1968										
127 5/8	20	18 2/8	18	20	4 7/8	4 7/8	6	5	10 5/8	41	33
	■ Pima Co. – Robert E. Pierce – R.E. Pierce & D. May – 1993										
126 5/8	17 6/8	17 5/8	13 3/8	19 3/8	4	4	9	6	27 2/8	43	34
	■ Gila Co. – Paul A. Stewart – Paul A. Stewart – 1992										
126 2/8	17	16 3/8	15 6/8	18	4 2/8	5	6	8	20 6/8	44†	35†
	■ Graham Co. – Steve T. Letcher – Steve T. Letcher – 2001										
126 1/8	14 7/8	15 2/8	11 2/8	15	4 5/8	4 6/8	8	6	15 7/8	45	36
	■ Pima Co. – William F. Crull – William F. Crull – 1979										
125 7/8	16 7/8	16 2/8	13 4/8	17 3/8	4 4/8	4 2/8	6	8	8 1/8	46	37
	■ Pima Co. – Fred W. Havens – Fred W. Havens – 1966										
125 7/8	18 7/8	17 7/8	12 1/8	15 2/8	4	4	6	8	12 4/8	46	37
	■ Arizona – Picked Up – Michael J. Tamboli – PR 1976										
125 1/8	16 3/8	16 4/8	12	17	3 4/8	3 6/8	8	8	11 1/8	49	39
	■ Santa Cruz Co. – Lee E. Sullivan – Lee E. Sullivan – 1996										
124 7/8	15 3/8	17 1/8	11 3/8	14 4/8	4 6/8	4 7/8	8	5	20 6/8	50	40
	■ Las Guijas Mts. – Aubrey F. Powell – Aubrey F. Powell – 1966										

Score	Length of Main Beam Right	Left	Inside Spread	Greatest Spread	Circumference at Smallest Place Between Burr and First Point Right	Left	Number of Points Right	Left	Lengths Abnormal Points	All-Time Rank	State Rank
124 5/8	20	18 4/8	17 7/8	19 6/8	3 7/8	4	6	6	13 1/8	51	41
■ Pinal Co. – C.J. Adair – C.J. Adair – 1966											
124 4/8	17 4/8	19	15	17	4 3/8	4 4/8	6	6	11 6/8	52	42
■ Yavapai Co. – James W.P. Roe – James W.P. Roe – 1971											
124 3/8	19 4/8	19 5/8	16 2/8	20 2/8	4 3/8	4 1/8	5	8	19 7/8	53	43
■ Arizona – C. Touche – Alan C. Ellsworth – 1977											
124	17 6/8	16 4/8	12 7/8	14 6/8	4	4 2/8	7	6	6 5/8	54	44
■ Arizona – Unknown – George L. Cooper – 1977											
123 5/8	19 5/8	17 6/8	15 4/8	17	4 4/8	4 4/8	4	7	7 5/8	55	45
■ Cochise Co. – William H. Nollsch – William H. Nollsch – 1994											
123 1/8	16 6/8	18 5/8	14 3/8	19 3/8	4	4	7	6	9 4/8	56†	46†
■ Pima Co. – Doug Field – Doug Field – 2001											
122 4/8	15 7/8	16 7/8	12	15 1/8	4 1/8	4	9	7	13 4/8	59	47
■ Cochise Co. – Randy D. Goll – Randy D. Goll – 1984											
122 2/8	17 2/8	16 5/8	13 4/8	15 4/8	4 4/8	4 4/8	4	7	9	61	48
■ Santa Cruz Co. – Clifton E. Cox – Clifton E. Cox – 1980											
121 7/8	18 5/8	18 5/8	13 6/8	16 1/8	4 5/8	4 6/8	5	6	4 7/8	62	49
■ Gila Co. – Ken Ashley – Ken Ashley – 1988											
121 6/8	12 5/8	18 5/8	14 2/8	18 2/8	4 2/8	4 3/8	7	9	17 2/8	63	50
■ Pima Co. – Rene E. Rodriguez – Rene E. Rodriguez – 1998											
121 5/8	15 7/8	17 1/8	14 1/8	16 6/8	4	4	7	6	8 6/8	64	51
■ Pima Co. – James A. Reynolds – James A. Reynolds – 1979											
121 2/8	17 2/8	17 2/8	15 3/8	16 7/8	4 2/8	4 4/8	6	7	6 7/8	65	52
■ Apache Co. – Picked Up – Harry Neff – 1998											
121	16 6/8	16 5/8	14	19	3 6/8	3 5/8	8	6	10 6/8	66	53
■ Gila Co. – James E. Stinson – James E. Stinson – 1983											
120 7/8	16 7/8	17	13 3/8	16 5/8	4 6/8	4 4/8	6	6	10 2/8	67	54
■ Pima Co. – Carl E. Fasel – Carl E. Fasel – 1981											
120 7/8	17 2/8	17 6/8	15 2/8	17	5 1/8	4 7/8	6	6	9 5/8	67	54
■ Gila Co. – David M. Conrad – David M. Conrad – 1982											
120 5/8	20 7/8	20	13 4/8	15 4/8	3 7/8	4	6	4	4 5/8	69	56
■ Santa Cruz Co. – Jerry M. Myers – Jerry M. Myers – 1970											
120 2/8	14 4/8	17 5/8	11 5/8	15 6/8	4 3/8	4 3/8	8	8	34 3/8	70	57
■ Pima Co. – Unknown – Mike Yeager – PR 1966											
120 1/8	18 5/8	19	13 6/8	18 5/8	4 1/8	4	8	6	9 3/8	71	58
■ Santa Cruz Co. – Gerald M. Kluzik – Gerald M. Kluzik – 1981											
120 1/8	16 5/8	17 6/8	15	18 6/8	3 4/8	3 6/8	7	8	12 5/8	71	58
■ Pima Co. – Eugene S. Robinson – Eugene S. Robinson – 1985											
120	19 3/8	18 4/8	13 6/8	15	4 2/8	4 2/8	5	5	6 6/8	73	60
■ Apache Co. – Picked Up – Harry Neff – 1998											
117	17 1/8	17	13 1/8	14 4/8	4 1/8	4 1/8	9	7	11 3/8	76	61
■ Pima Co. – William W. Sharp – William W. Sharp – 1976											

Score	Length of Main Beam		Inside Spread	Greatest Spread	Circumference at Smallest Place Between Burr and First Point		Number of Points		Lengths Abnormal Points	All-Time Rank	State Rank
	Right	Left			Right	Left	Right	Left			
	■ Location of Kill – Hunter – Owner – Date Killed										
114 1/8	17 5/8	18 4/8	14 1/8	16	6	4 2/8	6	4	21 6/8	79	62
■ Greenlee Co. – Randall C. Barnes – Randall C. Barnes – 1996											
113 6/8	17 2/8	18 6/8	13 7/8	15 6/8	3 4/8	4	6	5	6 5/8	80	63
■ Cochise Co. – Robert D. Kelley – Robert D. Kelley – 1997											
112 5/8	16 4/8	16 2/8	12 1/8	14 3/8	4 2/8	4 3/8	4	7	7 6/8	81	64
■ Santa Cruz Co. – John DePonte III – John DePonte III – 1995											
111 6/8	16 5/8	16 2/8	17 4/8	17 4/8	3 7/8	3 7/8	6	5	5 7/8	82	65
■ Cochise Co. – Frank E. Safford – Frank E. Safford – 1982											
109 2/8	16 2/8	17	14 7/8	16 3/8	4 2/8	4	5	6	5 1/8	84	66
■ Cochise Co. – Warren A. Adams – Warren A. Adams – 1995											
107 5/8	15	15 2/8	12 6/8	16 1/8	4	4	5	5	2 7/8	86	67
■ Graham Co. – Noel S. Allen – Noel S. Allen – 1989											
105 3/8	15 2/8	15 2/8	14 2/8	16	3 6/8	3 6/8	4	5	3 3/8	89	68
■ Pima Co. – Kirk Kelso – Kirk Kelso – 1993											
159	18 4/8	18 1/8	15 5/8	18 7/8	5	7 6/8	7	7	28 3/8	*	*
■ Pima Co. – Daniel D. King – SCI International Wildlife Museum – 1991											
129 2/8	18 6/8	18 7/8	16 4/8	18 6/8	4 7/8	4 5/8	4	8	17 6/8	*	*
■ Pima Co. – Daniel D. King – Daniel D. King – 1993											

† The scores and ranking for trophies from the 25th Awards Entry Period are not final until the banquet is held on June 19, 2004.

* Final score is subject to revision by additional verifying measurements.

NEW MEXICO
RECORD COUES' WHITETAILS

23 Typical whitetail deer entries
3 Non-typical whitetail deer entries
437 Total whitetail deer entries

NEW MEXICO
STATE RECORD
Typical Coues' Whitetail Deer
Score: 134^4/8
Location: Grant Co.
Hunter and Owner: Victor P. Giacoletti, Jr.
Date: 1981

NEW MEXICO
STATE RECORD
WORLD'S RECORD
Non-Typical Coues' Whitetail Deer
Score: 186$^1/_8$
Location: Hidalgo Co.
Hunter: Peter M. Chase
Owner: W.B. Darnell
Date: 1941

Photograph from B&C Archives

NEW MEXICO

TYPICAL COUES' WHITETAIL DEER

Score	Length of Main Beam Right Left	Inside Spread	Greatest Spread	Circumference at Smallest Place Between Burr and First Point Right Left	Number of Points Right Left	Lengths Abnormal Points	All-Time Rank	State Rank
	■ Location of Kill – Hunter – Owner – Date Killed							
134 4/8	20 5/8 21 1/8	16	18 2/8	4 5/8 4 3/8	5 5		3	1
	■ Grant Co. – Victor P. Giacoletti, Jr. – Victor P. Giacoletti, Jr. – 1981							
128	21 1/8 20	19 2/8	21 1/8	4 6/8 4 4/8	4 4		10	2
	■ Grant Co. – Ramon C. Borrego – Ramon C. Borrego – 1988							
124 7/8	18 4/8 18 5/8	12 6/8	16 3/8	4 4/8 4 5/8	6 4	1 7/8	19	3
	■ Hidalgo Co. – Martha M. Montes – Martha M. Montes – 1994							
119 6/8	19 3/8 19 4/8	13 2/8	15 5/8	3 7/8 3 6/8	5 5		48	4
	■ Hidalgo Co. – Frank L. Riley – Frank L. Riley – 1990							
119	17 5/8 17 4/8	13 6/8	16 6/8	3 4/8 3 5/8	7 6	5 2/8	58	5
	■ Hidalgo Co. – Jesse E. Williams – Jesse E. Williams – 1971							
118 3/8	18 1/8 18 7/8	13 7/8	16 1/8	3 4/8 3 6/8	4 4		61	6
	■ Hidalgo Co. – Michael E. Duperret – M.E. Duperret & J.K. Volk – 1993							
114 4/8	17 5/8 18 3/8	14 4/8	16 4/8	4 1/8 4	4 5	1 6/8	122	7
	■ Hidalgo Co. – Travis Darnell – W.B. Darnell – 1986							
114 2/8	20 7/8 17 4/8	17	18 4/8	4 2/8 4 2/8	5 5		131	8
	■ Grant Co. – Picked Up – Victor P. Giacoletti, Jr. – 1985							
114	18 4/8 18 1/8	10 4/8	12	3 6/8 3 6/8	4 4		137	9
	■ Animas Mts. – Frank C. Hibben – Frank C. Hibben – 1955							
113 5/8	19 19	14 7/8	16 2/8	3 5/8 3 6/8	4 4		151†	10†
	■ Socorro Co. – Gerad Montoya – Gerad Montoya – 1999							
113 1/8	15 6/8 16 2/8	13 7/8	15 7/8	4 4/8 4 5/8	5 5		170	11
	■ Grant Co. – Andrew A. Musacchio – Andrew A. Musacchio – 1985							
112 7/8	18 3/8 17 6/8	14 5/8	16 7/8	3 4/8 3 4/8	4 4		176	12
	■ Catron Co. – Picked Up – Mark Barboa – 1994							
112	19 1/8 19 3/8	16 5/8	18 4/8	4 1/8 4	5 6	2 1/8	202†	13†
	■ Grant Co. – Charles Arendt – Bud Arendt – 1924							
111 6/8	17 17 1/8	11 6/8	6 5/8	3 5/8 3 5/8	5 5		209	14
	■ Catron Co. – Charles Tapia – Charles Tapia – 1959							
111 2/8	16 2/8 15 6/8	12 3/8	15	4 3 6/8	5 6	1 5/8	226	15
	■ Hidalgo Co. – Jess T. Jones – Jess T. Jones – 1993							
110 3/8	17 6/8 18 6/8	15 7/8	17 4/8	3 6/8 3 4/8	4 5		260	16
	■ Hidalgo Co. – Ronald M. Gerdes – Ronald M. Gerdes – 1979							
110 2/8	16 15 4/8	15 4/8	18 1/8	3 6/8 4	5 4		265	17
	■ Hidalgo Co. – Jay M. Gates III – Jay M. Gates III – 1981							
110 1/8	16 1/8 16 3/8	11 5/8	13 6/8	4 4/8 4 3/8	4 4		270	18
	■ Hidalgo Co. – Neuman Sanford – Neuman Sanford – 1981							
109 3/8	18 1/8 17 1/8	14 3/8	16 4/8	3 7/8 4	5 4		279	19
	■ Grant Co. – Henry G. Cole – Henry G. Cole – 1981							

Score	Length of Main Beam		Inside Spread	Greatest Spread	Circumference at Smallest Place Between Burr and First Point		Number of Points		Lengths Abnormal Points	All-Time Rank	State Rank
	Right	Left			Right	Left	Right	Left			
	■ *Location of Kill – Hunter – Owner – Date Killed*										
109¹/8	18⁵/8	17⁴/8	15⁴/8	17⁶/8	4²/8	4¹/8	4	5	1³/8	282	20
	■ *Sierra Co. – Brad R. Barker – Brad R. Barker – 1993*										
107⁵/8	17	17³/8	14⁷/8	16	3⁷/8	4	4	4		290	21
	■ *Sierra Co. – Lonnie Seipp – Lonnie Seipp – 1999*										
107⁴/8	16⁷/8	15¹/8	12	13⁷/8	4²/8	4⁴/8	4	4		291	22
	■ *Hidalgo Co. – Clyde G. Kain – Clyde G. Kain – 1990*										
106¹/8	18	18⁴/8	12⁷/8	14⁵/8	3³/8	3⁴/8	4	5	1⁴/8	303	23
	■ *Hidalgo Co. – John B. Wasson, Jr. – John B. Wasson, Jr. – 1993*										

† The scores and ranking for trophies from the 25th Awards Entry Period are not final until the banquet is held on June 19, 2004.

NEW MEXICO

NON-TYPICAL COUES' WHITETAIL DEER

Score	Length of Main Beam		Inside Spread	Greatest Spread	Circumference at Smallest Place Between Burr and First Point		Number of Points		Lengths Abnormal Points	All-Time Rank	State Rank
	Right	Left			Right	Left	Right	Left			
	■ *Location of Kill – Hunter – Owner – Date Killed*										
186^1/8	17^6/8	16^5/8	18^2/8	20^3/8	4^5/8	4^6/8	8	8	51^5/8	1	1
	■ *Hidalgo Co. – Peter M. Chase – W.B. Darnell – 1941*										
127^6/8	17^2/8	17^3/8	13^4/8	16^4/8	4^1/8	4^2/8	6	6	9	40	2
	■ *Hidalgo Co. – Michael C. Finley – Michael C. Finley – 1983*										
122^6/8	16^7/8	16^6/8	12^4/8	15^2/8	4^2/8	4^2/8	6	6	6^2/8	58	3
	■ *Hidalgo Co. – Jack Samson – Jack Samson – 1984*										

TROPHIES IN THE FIELD

HUNTER: William A. Keebler
SCORE: 120
CATEGORY: non-typical Coues' whitetail deer
LOCATION: Sonora, Mexico
DATE: 2001

MEXICO
RECORD COUES' WHITETAILS

78 Typical whitetail deer entries
18 Non-typical whitetail deer entries
437 Total whitetail deer entries

MEXICO
RECORD
Typical Coues' Whitetail Deer
Score: $130^5/8$
Location: Chihuahua
Hunter and Owner: Wayne Kleinman
Date: 1958

MEXICO
RECORD
Non-Typical Coues' Whitetail Deer
Score: 154¹/₈
Location: Sonora
Hunter: Picked Up
Owner: Jorge Camou
Date: 2001

MEXICO

TYPICAL COUES' WHITETAIL DEER

Score	Length of Main Beam Right Left	Inside Spread	Greatest Spread	Circumference at Smallest Place Between Burr and First Point Right Left	Number of Points Right Left	Lengths Abnormal Points	All-Time Rank	State Rank
	■ Location of Kill – Hunter – Owner – Date Killed							
130⁵/₈	20⁵/₈ 19³/₈	14⁵/₈	16²/₈	3²/₈ 3²/₈	5 5		7	1
	■ Chihuahua – Wayne Kleinman – Wayne Kleinman – 1958							
126⁶/₈	19⁷/₈ 20	15⁴/₈	16⁷/₈	3²/₈ 3⁴/₈	5 7	1²/₈	11†	2†
	■ Sonora – Picked Up – Kirk Kelso – 2002							
125	21 20⁶/₈	16²/₈	18	4³/₈ 4⁴/₈	4 5		17	3
	■ Sonora – Enrique Barrett – Enrique Barrett – 1995							
124⁵/₈	18²/₈ 18⁷/₈	13⁵/₈	16¹/₈	3⁶/₈ 3⁶/₈	5 5		22	4
	■ Sonora – Enrique Lares – Enrique Lares – 1959							
124	18⁷/₈ 18⁶/₈	15	16²/₈	3⁴/₈ 3⁴/₈	6 5		24	5
	■ Sonora – Joseph P. Kalt – Joseph P. Kalt – 1998							
123⁶/₈	19⁷/₈ 19⁶/₈	14⁴/₈	16⁷/₈	3⁷/₈ 3⁷/₈	5 4	1²/₈	28†	6†
	■ Sonora – William J. Mills – William J. Mills – 2002							
122⁵/₈	20⁵/₈ 20⁶/₈	15	16⁵/₈	4⁴/₈ 4⁴/₈	5 4	3⁵/₈	31	7
	■ Chihuahua – Kirk Kelso – Kirk Kelso – 1997							
122⁴/₈	22 20⁴/₈	15²/₈	16²/₈	3¹/₈ 3²/₈	5 5		32	8
	■ Sonora – Lloyd L. Ward, Jr. – Lloyd L. Ward, Jr. – 1945							
122¹/₈	19⁶/₈ 20⁶/₈	16⁷/₈	19²/₈	4²/₈ 4	4 4		33	9
	■ Sonora – J. Marvin Smith III – J. Marvin Smith III – 1990							
121	20³/₈ 19⁵/₈	13	14⁵/₈	3⁷/₈ 3⁷/₈	5 5		38	10
	■ Sierra Madre Mts. – Herb Klein – Herb Klein – 1965							
120⁶/₈	19⁴/₈ 18²/₈	14⁴/₈	17³/₈	4 4	5 5		40	11
	■ Sonora – Manuel A. Caravantez – Manuel A. Caravantez – 1960							
120⁵/₈	19 19²/₈	12¹/₈	14	4²/₈ 4⁴/₈	4 5	1⁴/₈	41	12
	■ Sonora – George W. Parker – George W. Parker – 1969							
120⁴/₈	17⁶/₈ 18³/₈	13	15	4²/₈ 4	4 4		43	13
	■ Sonora – Diego G. Sada – Diego G. Sada – 1969							
120	18⁵/₈ 17⁷/₈	14²/₈	15³/₈	4 4	4 4		45†	14†
	■ Sonora – Picked Up – Kirk Kelso – 2000							
119⁷/₈	20²/₈ 20⁴/₈	15¹/₈	16⁵/₈	4⁴/₈ 4⁶/₈	4 5		46	15
	■ Sonora – Picked Up – George W. Parker – 1960							
119²/₈	18 19²/₈	15⁴/₈	17⁶/₈	4¹/₈ 3⁷/₈	4 4		53	16
	■ Sonora – Michael Lonuzzi – Michael Lonuzzi – 1996							
118⁶/₈	18 17⁷/₈	16⁴/₈	18⁵/₈	3⁷/₈ 4	5 5		59	17
	■ Chihuahua – Alberto Trouselle – Alberto Trouselle – 1996							
117⁵/₈	20³/₈ 20	18⁵/₈	20⁴/₈	4²/₈ 4	4 4		69	18
	■ Libertad – Abe R. Hughes – Abe R. Hughes – 1967							
117³/₈	19²/₈ 19³/₈	16³/₈	18³/₈	3⁶/₈ 3⁶/₈	4 4		72	19
	■ Sonora – Charles B. Leonard – Charles B. Leonard – 1974							

Score	Length of Main Beam		Inside Spread	Greatest Spread	Circumference at Smallest Place Between Burr and First Point		Number of Points		Lengths Abnormal Points	All-Time Rank	State Rank
	Right	Left			Right	Left	Right	Left			
	Location of Kill – Hunter – Owner – Date Killed										
115⁷/₈	18⁶/₈	16⁷/₈	14³/₈	19	4⁶/₈	4⁶/₈	5	7	5²/₈	94	20
	Sonora – Berry B. Brooks – Berry B. Brooks – 1954										
114⁷/₈	18	19	13¹/₈	15	4³/₈	4²/₈	5	4		110	21
	Sonora – Carlos G. Hermosillo – Carlos G. Hermosillo – 1995										
114⁶/₈	16⁶/₈	16⁶/₈	13⁶/₈	16³/₈	4¹/₈	4¹/₈	5	5		113	22
	Chihuahua – Tom Jones – George B. Johnson – 1932										
114⁴/₈	15⁶/₈	15⁴/₈	14²/₈	15¹/₈	3⁵/₈	3⁵/₈	5	5		122	23
	Chiricahua Mts. – Elgin T. Gates – Elgin T. Gates – 1968										
114¹/₈	18⁷/₈	16³/₈	14¹/₈	15⁶/₈	4⁴/₈	4²/₈	4	4		135	24
	Sonora – Unknown – Bill Quimby – PR 1965										
113⁷/₈	18¹/₈	17⁷/₈	12¹/₈	14¹/₈	4²/₈	4²/₈	6	5	2²/₈	139†	25†
	Sonora – Craig T. Boddington – Craig T. Boddington – 2000										
113⁷/₈	17	16¹/₈	14⁵/₈	16⁷/₈	3⁴/₈	3³/₈	5	5		139	25
	Sonora – James W. Hutcheson – James W. Hutcheson – 1996										
113⁶/₈	18²/₈	18⁴/₈	13⁴/₈	19¹/₈	3⁶/₈	3⁶/₈	8	8	4⁴/₈	146	27
	Chihuahua – Herb Klein – Herb Klein – 1957										
113⁴/₈	19²/₈	19²/₈	15	16⁷/₈	3⁶/₈	3⁷/₈	4	4		154	28
	Sonora – George W. Parker – George W. Parker – 1947										
113²/₈	17⁴/₈	17⁵/₈	12²/₈	15⁵/₈	3⁷/₈	3⁶/₈	5	5		163†	29†
	Sonora – Betsy S. Grainger – Betsy S. Grainger – 2001										
113²/₈	19⁵/₈	19³/₈	14⁶/₈	16¹/₈	3⁷/₈	3⁷/₈	4	4		163†	29†
	Sonora – Brian K. Murray – Brian K. Murray – 2001										
112⁶/₈	16³/₈	17	10⁶/₈	12⁶/₈	3⁷/₈	3⁶/₈	4	4		179	31
	Sonora – Lee Christmas – Lee Christmas – 1999										
112⁵/₈	17⁷/₈	18²/₈	10³/₈	11⁵/₈	4¹/₈	4¹/₈	4	5		182†	32†
	Sonora – Michael C. Cupell – Michael C. Cupell – 2000										
112⁵/₈	18¹/₈	17²/₈	14¹/₈	17	4	3⁷/₈	4	4		182	32
	Sonora – Henry Lares – Henry Lares – 1959										
112⁵/₈	18⁶/₈	19¹/₈	13¹/₈	16⁶/₈	3⁴/₈	3⁵/₈	5	6	3²/₈	182	32
	Sonora – William W. Sharp – William W. Sharp – 1968										
112⁴/₈	17²/₈	16⁷/₈	13⁶/₈	15⁴/₈	4¹/₈	4¹/₈	4	5		186†	35†
	Sonora – Kirk Kelso – Kirk Kelso – 2001										
112³/₈	17³/₈	16³/₈	12³/₈	13⁶/₈	3⁴/₈	3⁶/₈	5	5		190†	36†
	Sonora – Michael M. Golightly – Michael M. Golightly – 2001										
112²/₈	19⁶/₈	19¹/₈	11⁶/₈		3⁴/₈	3⁵/₈	5	4		194	37
	Sonora – George W. Parker – George W. Parker – 1960										
112¹/₈	18⁶/₈	19	13⁶/₈	15²/₈	3⁶/₈	3⁶/₈	4	5	1⁵/₈	198†	38†
	Sonora – Kerry L. Mailloux – Kerry L. Mailloux – 1996										
112	18	18	12⁴/₈	14²/₈	3⁴/₈	3⁴/₈	5	5		202	39
	Sonora – Mark G. Mills – Mark G. Mills – 1998										
111⁶/₈	19²/₈	19⁶/₈	11⁴/₈	12⁷/₈	3⁷/₈	3⁷/₈	4	5	1⁴/₈	209†	40†
	Sonora – Lynn H. Stinson – Lynn H. Stinson – 2000										

MEXICO TYPICAL COUES' WHITETAIL DEER

Score	Length of Main Beam Right	Left	Inside Spread	Greatest Spread	Circumference at Smallest Place Between Burr and First Point Right	Left	Number of Points Right	Left	Lengths Abnormal Points	All-Time Rank	State Rank
111 4/8	20 1/8	19 5/8	14 2/8	17 6/8	4	3 7/8	5	5	2 6/8	218	41
■ Sonora – George W. Parker – George W. Parker – 1926											
111 3/8	20 6/8	21 2/8	12 3/8	14 2/8	3 6/8	3 4/8	4	4		222	42
■ Sierra Madre Mts. – Herb Klein – Herb Klein – 1965											
111 3/8	17 4/8	17 4/8	14 1/8	16 2/8	3 7/8	4	4	4		222	42
■ Sonora – Larry J. Kruse – Larry J. Kruse – 1999											
111 2/8	18 7/8	19 5/8	11 6/8	13 7/8	3 4/8	3 4/8	4	5		226	44
■ Sonora – George W. Parker – George W. Parker – 1960											
111 1/8	18 5/8	18 4/8	14 2/8	16 2/8	4	4	5	4	3 1/8	233†	45†
■ Sonora – David J. Lechel – David J. Lechel – 2001 ■ See photo on page 63											
111 1/8	17 5/8	17 6/8	16	17 3/8	4	3 7/8	5	6	1 3/8	233	45
■ Sonora – Joe Daneker, Jr. – Joe Daneker, Jr. – 1973											
111	19 5/8	18 6/8	11 3/8	13 2/8	4 1/8	4 2/8	5	4	2 5/8	237	47
■ Sonora – Jack Atcheson, Jr. – Jack Atcheson, Jr. – 1998											
110 6/8	17 2/8	17 2/8	13 4/8	15	4	4 1/8	4	4		246†	48†
■ Sonora – Travis J. Adams – Travis J. Adams – 2001											
110 4/8	17 2/8	17 2/8	13 6/8	15 2/8	3 5/8	3 6/8	4	4		255†	49†
■ Sonora – Lynn H. Stinson – Lynn H. Stinson – 2001											
110 4/8	18	18 4/8	14 2/8	16 1/8	3 3/8	3 2/8	4	4		255	49
■ Sonora – Ricardo A. Andrade – Ricardo A. Andrade – 1988											
110 3/8	18 2/8	18 2/8	13 5/8	15 4/8	3 7/8	4	4	4		260	51
■ Sonora – Michael G. Adams – Michael G. Adams – 1998											
110	19 4/8	18 6/8	14 2/8	16	4 2/8	4 3/8	5	5	3	274	52
■ Sonora – Enrique C. Cicero – Enrique C. Cicero – 1966											
109 3/8	19 5/8	19 3/8	14 5/8	16 2/8	3 4/8	3 4/8	5	4		279	53
■ Sonora – Mitchell A. Thorson – Mitchell A. Thorson – 1988											
108 6/8	20	19 1/8	16 4/8	18	3 6/8	3 7/8	4	4		283	54
■ Sonora – Lee M. Wahlund – Lee M. Wahlund – 1999											
108 4/8	17 4/8	16 3/8	13 4/8	15 4/8	4 1/8	4	4	4		285†	55†
■ Sonora – Picked Up – Kirk Kelso – 1999											
108	16 6/8	16 4/8	14 2/8	15 5/8	3 7/8	3 5/8	5	4	1	288	56
■ Sonora – Robert A. Carlson – Robert A. Carlson – 1997											
107 4/8	16 2/8	15 6/8	14 6/8	16 2/8	3 4/8	3 3/8	5	5		291†	57†
■ Sonora – Peter W. Spear – Peter W. Spear – 2000											
107 4/8	18 4/8	18 5/8	13 3/8	16 4/8	3 6/8	3 6/8	4	6	1 5/8	291	57
■ Sonora – Timothy M. Gomez – Timothy M. Gomez – 1996											
106 4/8	16 2/8	16 5/8	12	14 4/8	3 7/8	3 7/8	4	5	1 2/8	298†	59†
■ Chihuahua – Richard M. Young – Richard M. Young – 2001											
106 3/8	16 1/8	15 4/8	13 1/8	15 7/8	3 7/8	3 6/8	5	5		300†	60†
■ Sonora – Michael J. Hoppis – Michael J. Hoppis – 2002											
106	17 3/8	17 1/8	13 2/8	15	3 6/8	3 5/8	5	4		304	61
■ Sonora – David V. Collis – David V. Collis – 1985											

Location of Kill – Hunter – Owner – Date Killed

Score	Length of Main Beam Right	Left	Inside Spread	Greatest Spread	Circumference at Smallest Place Between Burr and First Point Right	Left	Number of Points Right	Left	Lengths Abnormal Points	All-Time Rank	State Rank
105 6/8	18 5/8	18 4/8	14 2/8	16 4/8	3 5/8	3 5/8	4	4		305	62

■ *Sonora – David E. Evanow – David E. Evanow – 1999*

| 105 4/8 | 17 5/8 | 17 4/8 | 13 5/8 | 15 4/8 | 3 6/8 | 3 7/8 | 5 | 5 | 3 3/8 | 308 | 63 |

■ *Sonora – Kevin L. Reid – Kevin L. Reid – 1994*

| 105 | 17 5/8 | 17 5/8 | 12 6/8 | 15 2/8 | 3 7/8 | 3 7/8 | 5 | 4 | | 310 | 64 |

■ *Sonora – Peter W. Spear – Peter W. Spear – 1997*

| 104 5/8 | 17 2/8 | 17 5/8 | 12 3/8 | 14 1/8 | 3 6/8 | 3 6/8 | 4 | 4 | | 312† | 65† |

■ *Chihuahua – Louie I. Venturacci – Louie I. Venturacci – 2000*

| 104 4/8 | 17 7/8 | 17 1/8 | 13 2/8 | 15 5/8 | 3 4/8 | 3 4/8 | 4 | 4 | | 313 | 66 |

■ *Sonora – Greg C. Bond – Greg C. Bond – 1994*

| 104 2/8 | 15 4/8 | 17 | 11 6/8 | 13 | 3 4/8 | 3 4/8 | 5 | 5 | | 316 | 67 |

■ *Sonora – Peeler G. Lacey – Peeler G. Lacey – 1998* ■ *See photo on page 647*

| 104 1/8 | 19 6/8 | 19 6/8 | 14 1/8 | 15 5/8 | 3 3/8 | 3 2/8 | 4 | 4 | | 317 | 68 |

■ *Sonora – William D. Gentner – William D. Gentner – 1995*

| 104 | 17 3/8 | 17 2/8 | 16 4/8 | 17 7/8 | 3 6/8 | 4 | 4 | 4 | | 320† | 69† |

■ *Sonora – Jon R. Reardon – Jon R. Reardon – 2002*

| 103 6/8 | 15 2/8 | 15 7/8 | 13 6/8 | 17 | 3 3/8 | 3 1/8 | 5 | 5 | | 321 | 70 |

■ *Sonora – Norbert D. Bremer – Norbert D. Bremer – 1991*

| 102 3/8 | 16 6/8 | 16 6/8 | 12 7/8 | 14 2/8 | 3 4/8 | 4 | 5 | 4 | | 326 | 71 |

■ *Sonora – Arthur E. Ashcraft – Arthur E. Ashcraft – 1997*

| 102 1/8 | 16 4/8 | 17 3/8 | 14 1/8 | 16 4/8 | 4 4/8 | 4 4/8 | 5 | 4 | 2 6/8 | 328† | 72† |

■ *Sonora – Kirk Kelso – Kirk Kelso – 2002*

| 101 7/8 | 16 6/8 | 17 | 12 3/8 | 13 6/8 | 3 6/8 | 3 4/8 | 4 | 5 | | 330† | 73† |

■ *Sonora – Kirk Kelso – Kirk Kelso – 2000*

| 100 5/8 | 17 | 17 4/8 | 15 3/8 | 17 2/8 | 3 7/8 | 4 | 3 | 4 | | 339† | 74† |

■ *Sonora – Gary L. Barneson – Gary L. Barneson – 2001*

| 100 5/8 | 17 6/8 | 17 1/8 | 16 1/8 | 18 2/8 | 3 2/8 | 3 1/8 | 4 | 4 | | 339† | 74† |

■ *Sonora – George F. Daum – George F. Daum – 2000*

| 100 4/8 | 19 | 17 7/8 | 16 | 18 3/8 | 3 4/8 | 3 4/8 | 5 | 5 | 1 | 341† | 76† |

■ *Chihuahua – T.R. White – T.R. White – 2002*

| 100 4/8 | 14 5/8 | 13 6/8 | 10 2/8 | 13 1/8 | 3 6/8 | 3 7/8 | 5 | 6 | 2 | 341 | 76 |

■ *Sonora – William G. Farley – William G. Farley – 1996*

| 100 3/8 | 17 6/8 | 17 7/8 | 12 3/8 | 14 | 3 5/8 | 3 4/8 | 4 | 4 | | 343† | 78† |

■ *Sonora – Kirk Kelso – Kirk Kelso – 1998*

† The scores and ranking for trophies from the 25th Awards Entry Period are not final until the banquet is held on June 19, 2004.

MEXICO

NON-TYPICAL COUES' WHITETAIL DEER

Score	Length of Main Beam Right Left	Inside Spread	Greatest Spread	Circumference at Smallest Place Between Burr and First Point Right Left	Number of Points Right Left	Lengths Abnormal Points	All-Time Rank	State Rank
	■ Location of Kill – Hunter – Owner – Date Killed							
154 1/8	15 6/8 15 6/8	15 6/8	22 6/8	4 1/8 4 2/8	7 7	26 5/8	4†	1†
	■ Sonora – Picked Up – Jorge Camou – 2001							
141	21 6/8 22	15 3/8	17 4/8	4 6/8 4 5/8	5 6	7 5/8	16†	2†
	■ Sonora – Picked Up – Jorge Camou – 2001							
138 5/8	16 6/8 16 6/8	11 5/8	17	4 3/8 4 3/8	9 6	19	19†	3†
	■ Sonora – Glenn Hall – Glenn Hall – 2000							
134 2/8	17 7/8 16 5/8	13 1/8	14 6/8	4 5/8 4 5/8	6 7	18 1/8	23	4
	■ Sonora – Unknown – Ronald D. Hyatt – PR 1986							
132	20 19 7/8	14 5/8	16 5/8	3 6/8 3 6/8	5 5	6 7/8	26	5
	■ Sonora – Picked Up – Harry P. Samarin – PR 1988							
128 2/8	19 1/8 19 3/8	13 4/8	20	3 5/8 3 5/8	7 8	11 6/8	38†	6†
	■ Sonora – Michael L. Braegelmann – Michael L. Braegelmann – 2000							
127 1/8	19 4/8 19 5/8	13 3/8	16	4 2/8 4 2/8	7 8	8 6/8	42	7
	■ Sonora – Picked Up – D.J. Hollinger & B. Howard – 1993							
125 3/8	15 3/8 16 4/8	13 6/8	17 3/8	4 2/8 4 3/8	9 6	20 3/8	48	8
	■ Sonora – Enrique C. Cicero – Enrique C. Cicero – 1967							
122 7/8	16 2/8 15 1/8	11 5/8	15	4 4	6 5	18 2/8	57	9
	■ Sonora – Edwin L. Robinson – Edwin L. Robinson – 1992							
122 4/8	19 2/8 20	15 5/8	20 5/8	4 1/8 4 1/8	8 4	5 7/8	59	10
	■ Sonora – Robert P. Ellingson III – Robert P. Ellingson III – 1997							
120	17 2/8 17 4/8	13 7/8	15 6/8	3 5/8 3 5/8	6 5	15 1/8	73†	11†
	■ Sonora – William A. Keebler – William A. Keebler – 2001 ■ See photo on page 639							
117 4/8	17 4/8 18 5/8	15 4/8	19 3/8	4 3/8 4 3/8	6 6	9 4/8	75†	12†
	■ Chihuahua – William G. Farley – William G. Farley – 2002							
115 5/8	18 4/8 18 1/8	13 1/8	15	4 3 6/8	5 6	5 2/8	77	13
	■ Sonora – Thomas Bowman – Thomas Bowman – 2000							
115 1/8	15 3/8 14 5/8	14 2/8	18 3/8	3 7/8 5	5 8	23 3/8	78	14
	■ Sonora – Harold K. Han, Jr. – Harold K. Han, Jr. – 1999							
111 4/8	17 2/8 16 6/8	13 6/8	20 4/8	3 6/8 3 7/8	7 6	11 2/8	83	15
	■ Sonora – H.E. Smith – William E. Smith – 1935							
108 1/8	18 1/8 18 3/8	13	14 5/8	3 5/8 3 6/8	5 6	7 7/8	85	16
	■ Sonora – Robert A. Dodson – Robert A. Dodson – 1997							
106 6/8	16 5/8 16 4/8	12	14 4/8	3 3/8 3 4/8	5 8	8 4/8	87	17
	■ Sonora – Lonnie L. Ritchey – Lonnie L. Ritchey – 1988							
106 2/8	18 5/8 17 3/8	15 3/8	16 6/8	4 4	7 6	6 7/8	88	18
	■ Sonora – David F. Myrup – David F. Myrup – 1999							

† The scores and ranking for trophies from the 25th Awards Entry Period are not final until the banquet is held on June 19, 2004.

TROPHIES IN THE FIELD

HUNTER: Peeler G. Lacey
SCORE: 104-2/8
CATEGORY: typical Coues' whitetail deer
LOCATION: Sonora, Mexico
DATE: 1998

Typical and Non-Typical Whitetail Deer Score Charts

Records of
North American
Big Game

250 Station Drive
Missoula, MT 59801
(406) 542-1888

BOONE AND CROCKETT CLUB®
OFFICIAL SCORING SYSTEM FOR NORTH AMERICAN BIG GAME TROPHIES

MINIMUM SCORES
AWARDS ALL-TIME
whitetail 160 170
Coues' 100 110

TYPICAL
WHITETAIL AND COUES' DEER

KIND OF DEER (check one)
☒ whitetail
☐ Coues'

Detail of Point
Measurement

Abnormal Points	
Right Antler	Left Antler
1 2/8	
1 7/8	
SUBTOTALS	3 1/8	
TOTAL TO E	3 1/8	

SEE OTHER SIDE FOR INSTRUCTIONS

		COLUMN 1 Spread Credit	COLUMN 2 Right Antler	COLUMN 3 Left Antler	COLUMN 4 Difference
A. No. Points on Right Antler	8	No. Points on Left Antler	6			
B. Tip to Tip Spread	24 3/8	C. Greatest Spread	29			
D. Inside Spread of Main Beams	27 2/8	SPREAD CREDIT MAY EQUAL BUT NOT EXCEED LONGER MAIN BEAM	27 2/8		
E. Total of Lengths of Abnormal Points					3 1/8
F. Length of Main Beam			28 4/8	28 4/8	
G-1. Length of First Point			6 5/8	6	5/8
G-2. Length of Second Point			12 4/8	13 1/8	5/8
G-3. Length of Third Point			13 6/8	14	2/8
G-4. Length of Fourth Point, If Present			11 4/8	11 5/8	1/8
G-5. Length of Fifth Point, If Present			5	7	2
G-6. Length of Sixth Point, If Present					
G-7. Length of Seventh Point, If Present					
H-1. Circumference at Smallest Place Between Burr and First Point			4 6/8	5	2/8
H-2. Circumference at Smallest Place Between First and Second Points			4 2/8	4 2/8	
H-3. Circumference at Smallest Place Between Second and Third Points			4 3/8	4 2/8	1/8
H-4. Circumference at Smallest Place Between Third and Fourth Points			4 2/8	4 2/8	
TOTALS		27 2/8	95 4/8	98	7 1/8

ADD	Column 1	27 2/8	Exact Locality Where Killed: Biggar, Saskatchewan
	Column 2	95 4/8	Date Killed: November 23, 1993 Hunter: Milo N. Hanson
	Column 3	98	Owner: Milo N. Hanson Telephone #:
	Subtotal	220 6/8	Owner's Address:
SUBTRACT Column 4		7 1/8	Guide's Name and Address:
FINAL SCORE		213 5/8	Remarks: (Mention Any Abnormalities or Unique Qualities)

COPYRIGHT © 2000 BY BOONE AND CROCKETT CLUB®

I, ___William L. Cooper_____, certify that I have measured this trophy on ____5/02/1995____
       PRINT NAME   MM/DD/YYYYY

at __Dallas Museum of Natural History_____   Dallas   Texas
   STREET ADDRESS   CITY   STATE/PROVINCE

and that these measurements and data are, to the best of my knowledge and belief, made in accordance with the instructions given.

Witness: Gerard Beaulieu & Ron Boucher   Signature:_____   I.D. Number ☐☐☐☐
                                                   B&C OFFICIAL MEASURER

INSTRUCTIONS FOR MEASURING TYPICAL WHITETAIL AND COUES' DEER

All measurements must be made with a 1/4-inch wide flexible steel tape to the nearest one-eighth of an inch. (Note: A flexible steel cable can be used to measure points and main beams only.) Enter fractional figures in eighths, without reduction. Official measurements cannot be taken until the antlers have air dried for at least 60 days after the animal was killed.

  A. Number of Points on Each Antler: To be counted a point, the projection must be at least one inch long, with the length exceeding width at one inch or more of length. All points are measured from tip of point to nearest edge of beam as illustrated. Beam tip is counted as a point but not measured as a point.

  B. Tip to Tip Spread is measured between tips of main beams.

  C. Greatest Spread is measured between perpendiculars at a right angle to the center line of the skull at widest part, whether across main beams or points.

  D. Inside Spread of Main Beams is measured at a right angle to the center line of the skull at widest point between main beams. Enter this measurement again as the Spread Credit if it is less than or equal to the length of the longer main beam; if greater, enter longer main beam length for Spread Credit.

  E. Total of Lengths of all Abnormal Points: Abnormal Points are those non-typical in location (such as points originating from a point or from bottom or sides of main beam) or extra points beyond the normal pattern of points. Measure in usual manner and enter in appropriate blanks.

  F. Length of Main Beam is measured from the center of the lowest outside edge of burr over the outer side to the most distant point of the main beam. The point of beginning is that point on the burr where the center line along the outer side of the beam intersects the burr, then following generally the line of the illustration.

  G-1-2-3-4-5-6-7. Length of Normal Points: Normal points project from the top of the main beam. They are measured from nearest edge of main beam over outer curve to tip. Lay the tape along the outer curve of the beam so that the top edge of the tape coincides with the top edge of the beam on both sides of the point to determine the baseline for point measurements. Record point lengths in appropriate blanks.

  H-1-2-3-4. Circumferences are taken as detailed in illustration for each measurement. If brow point is missing, take H-1 and H-2 at smallest place between burr and G-2. If G-4 is missing, take H-4 halfway between G-3 and tip of main beam.

ENTRY AFFIDAVIT FOR ALL HUNTER-TAKEN TROPHIES

For the purpose of entry into the Boone and Crockett Club's® records, North American big game harvested by the use of the following methods or under the following conditions are ineligible:

    I.   Spotting or herding game from the air, followed by landing in its vicinity for the purpose of pursuit and shooting;
    II. Herding or chasing with the aid of any motorized equipment;
    III. Use of electronic communication devices, artificial lighting, or electronic light intensifying devices;
    IV. Confined by artificial barriers, including escape-proof fenced enclosures;
    V. Transplanted for the purpose of commercial shooting;
    VI. By the use of traps or pharmaceuticals;
    VII. While swimming, helpless in deep snow, or helpless in any other natural or artificial medium;
    VIII. On another hunter's license;
    IX. Not in full compliance with the game laws or regulations of the federal government or of any state, province, territory, or tribal council on reservations or tribal lands;

I certify that the trophy scored on this chart was not taken in violation of the conditions listed above. In signing this statement, I understand that if the information provided on this entry is found to be misrepresented or fraudulent in any respect, it will not be accepted into the Awards Program and 1) all of my prior entries are subject to deletion from future editions of **Records of North American Big Game** 2) future entries may not be accepted.

FAIR CHASE, as defined by the Boone and Crockett Club®, is the ethical, sportsmanlike and lawful pursuit and taking of any free-ranging wild, native North American big game animal in a manner that does not give the hunter an improper advantage over such game animals.

The Boone and Crockett Club® may exclude the entry of any animal that it deems to have been taken in an unethical manner or under conditions deemed inappropriate by the Club.

Date:_____ Signature of Hunter:_____
                                (SIGNATURE MUST BE WITNESSED BY AN OFFICIAL MEASURER OR A NOTARY PUBLIC.)

Date:_____ Signature of Notary or Official Measurer:_____

Records of
North American
Big Game

250 Station Drive
Missoula, MT 59801
(406) 542-1888

BOONE AND CROCKETT CLUB®
OFFICIAL SCORING SYSTEM FOR NORTH AMERICAN BIG GAME TROPHIES

**NON-TYPICAL
WHITETAIL AND COUES' DEER**

MINIMUM SCORES		
	AWARDS	ALL-TIME
whitetail	185	195
Coues'	105	120

KIND OF DEER (check one)
☐ whitetail
☒ Coues'

Abnormal Points	
Right Antler	Left Antler
4 7/8	5 1/8
3 4/8	7 4/8
7 3/8	3 4/8
9 6/8	10
SUBTOTALS	
25 4/8	26 1/8

Detail of Point Measurement

E. TOTAL	
51 5/8	

SEE OTHER SIDE FOR INSTRUCTIONS			COLUMN 1	COLUMN 2	COLUMN 3	COLUMN 4
A. No. Points on Right Antler	8	No. Points on Left Antler	8	Spread Credit	Right Antler	Left Antler	Difference
B. Tip to Tip Spread	18 1/8	C. Greatest Spread	20 3/8				
D. Inside Spread of Main Beams	18 2/8	SPREAD CREDIT MAY EQUAL BUT NOT EXCEED LONGER MAIN BEAM	17 6/8				
F. Length of Main Beam					17 6/8	16 5/8	1 1/8
G-1. Length of First Point					4 4/8	4 3/8	1/8
G-2. Length of Second Point					13 2/8	13 6/8	4/8
G-3. Length of Third Point					11	8	3
G-4. Length of Fourth Point, If Present							
G-5. Length of Fifth Point, If Present							
G-6. Length of Sixth Point, If Present							
G-7. Length of Seventh Point, If Present							
H-1. Circumference at Smallest Place Between Burr and First Point					4 5/8	4 6/8	1/8
H-2. Circumference at Smallest Place Between First and Second Points					4 1/8	4 3/8	2/8
H-3. Circumference at Smallest Place Between Second and Third Points					4 6/8	4 5/8	1/8
H-4. Circumference at Smallest Place Between Third and Fourth Points					2 6/8	3 1/8	3/8
			TOTALS	17 6/8	62 6/8	59 5/8	5 5/8

ADD	Column 1	17 6/8	Exact Locality Where Killed: Hidalgo County, New Mexico
	Column 2	62 6/8	Date Killed: November 1941 Hunter: Peter M. Chase
	Column 3	59 5/8	Owner: W.B. Darnell Telephone #:
	Subtotal	140 1/8	Owner's Address:
SUBTRACT Column 4		5 5/8	Guide's Name and Address:
	Subtotal	134 4/8	Remarks: (Mention Any Abnormalities or Unique Qualities)
ADD Line E Total		51 5/8	
FINAL SCORE		186 1/8	

COPYRIGHT © 2000 BY BOONE AND CROCKETT CLUB®

I, __L. Victor Clark_____, certify that I have measured this trophy on ___5/02/2001___
    PRINT NAME   MM/DD/YYYYY

at __Bass Pro Shops_____   Springfield   Missouri
    STREET ADDRESS   CITY   STATE/PROVINCE

and that these measurements and data are, to the best of my knowledge and belief, made in accordance with the instructions given.

Witness: __Jack Graham_____   Signature:_____   I.D. Number□□□□
                                                     B&C OFFICIAL MEASURER

INSTRUCTIONS FOR MEASURING NON-TYPICAL WHITETAIL AND COUES' DEER

All measurements must be made with a 1/4-inch wide flexible steel tape to the nearest one-eighth of an inch. (Note: A flexible steel cable can be used to measure points and main beams only.) Enter fractional figures in eighths, without reduction. Official measurements cannot be taken until the antlers have air dried for at least 60 days after the animal was killed.

A. Number of Points on Each Antler: To be counted a point, the projection must be at least one inch long, with the length exceeding width at one inch or more of length. All points are measured from tip of point to nearest edge of beam as illustrated. Beam tip is counted as a point but not measured as a point.

B. Tip to Tip Spread is measured between tips of main beams.

C. Greatest Spread is measured between perpendiculars at a right angle to the center line of the skull at widest part, whether across main beams or points.

D. Inside Spread of Main Beams is measured at a right angle to the center line of the skull at widest point between main beams. Enter this measurement again as the Spread Credit If it is less than or equal to the length of the longer main beam; if greater, enter longer main beam length for Spread Credit.

E. Total of Lengths of all Abnormal Points: Abnormal Points are those non-typical in location (such as points originating from a point or from bottom or sides of main beam) or extra points beyond the normal pattern of points. Measure in usual manner and enter in appropriate blanks.

F. Length of Main Beam is measured from the center of the lowest outside edge of burr over the outer side to the most distant point of the main beam. The point of beginning is that point on the burr where the center line along the outer side of the beam intersects the burr, then following generally the line of the illustration.

G-1-2-3-4-5-6-7. Length of Normal Points: Normal points project from the top of the main beam. They are measured from nearest edge of main beam over outer curve to tip. Lay the tape along the outer curve of the beam so that the top edge of the tape coincides with the top edge of the beam on both sides of the point to determine the baseline for point measurement. Record point lengths in appropriate blanks.

H-1-2-3-4. Circumferences are taken as detailed in illustration for each measurement. If brow point is missing, take H-1 and H-2 at smallest place between burr and G-2. If G-4 is missing, take H-4 halfway between G-3 and tip of main beam.

ENTRY AFFIDAVIT FOR ALL HUNTER-TAKEN TROPHIES

For the purpose of entry into the Boone and Crockett Club's® records, North American big game harvested by the use of the following methods or under the following conditions are ineligible:

    I.   Spotting or herding game from the air, followed by landing in its vicinity for the purpose of pursuit and shooting;
    II.   Herding or chasing with the aid of any motorized equipment;
    III. Use of electronic communication devices, artificial lighting, or electronic light intensifying devices;
    IV. Confined by artificial barriers, including escape-proof fenced enclosures;
    V.   Transplanted for the purpose of commercial shooting;
    VI. By the use of traps or pharmaceuticals;
   VII. While swimming, helpless in deep snow, or helpless in any other natural or artificial medium;
  VIII. On another hunter's license;
    IX. Not in full compliance with the game laws or regulations of the federal government or of any state, province, territory, or tribal council on reservations or tribal lands;

I certify that the trophy scored on this chart was not taken in violation of the conditions illustrated above. In signing this statement, I understand that if the information provided on this entry is found to be misrepresented or fraudulent in any respect, it will not be accepted into the Awards Program and 1) all of my prior entries are subject to deletion from future editions of **Records of North American Big Game** 2) future entries may not be accepted.

FAIR CHASE, as defined by the Boone and Crockett Club®, is the ethical, sportsmanlike and lawful pursuit and taking of any free-ranging wild, native North American big game animal in a manner that does not give the hunter an proper advantage over such game animals.

The Boone and Crockett Club® may exclude the entry of any animal that it deems to have been taken in an unethical manner or under conditions deemed inappropriate by the Club.

Date:_____ Signature of Hunter:_____
                                    (SIGNATURE MUST BE WITNESSED BY AN OFFICIAL MEASURER OR A NOTARY PUBLIC.)

Date:_____ Signature of Notary or Official Measurer:_____

ACKNOWLEDGMENTS

RECORDS OF NORTH AMERICAN WHITETAIL DEER, FOURTH EDITION

Compiled with the Able Assistance of:
Eldon L. "Buck" Buckner
Jack Reneau
Sandy Poston
Julie T. Houk
Keith Balfourd
George A. Bettas
Joanna Giffin
Emily McKeever
Amy Nelson
Wendy Nichols

Photograph Coordination:
Jack Reneau
Keith Balfourd
Julie T. Houk

Cover and Book Design by:
Julie T. Houk

Cover Photograph by:
Mike and Christie Duplan

Copy Editing by:
Keith Balfourd
Jack Reneau
Mary L. Webster

Maps Generated by:
Joel W. Helmer

Printed and bound by:
Phoenix Color
Hagerstown, Maryland